April 17–19, 2012
Beijing, China

**Association for
Computing Machinery**

Advancing Computing as a Science & Profession

HSCC'12

Proceedings of the 15th ACM International Conference on

Hybrid Systems: Computation and Control

Sponsored by:
ACM SIGBED

Supported by:
NEC and CNRS

**Association for
Computing Machinery**

Advancing Computing as a Science & Profession

The Association for Computing Machinery
2 Penn Plaza, Suite 701
New York, New York 10121-0701

ISBN: 978-1-4503-1220-2

Additional copies may be ordered prepaid from:

ACM Order Department
PO Box 30777
New York, NY 10087-0777, USA

Phone: 1-800-342-6626 (USA and Canada)
+1-212-626-0500 (Global)
Fax: +1-212-944-1318
E-mail: acmhelp@acm.org
Hours of Operation: 8:30 am – 4:30 pm ET

ACM Order Number: 100121

Printed in the USA

HSCC 2012 Chairs' Welcome

It is our great pleasure to welcome you to the 15th ACM International Conference on Hybrid Systems: Computation and Control (HSCC 2012), held in Beijing, April 17–19, 2012. This year's conference continues its tradition of being the premier forum for presentation of theoretical, computational, and practical research results on leading edge issues involving the interplay between discrete and continuous dynamic behaviors in embedded, reactive, and cyber-physical systems.

The mission of the conference is to share information on the latest advancements in the design, analysis, control, verification, optimization, implementation and applications of hybrid systems. Previous editions of HSCC were held in Berkeley (1998), Nijmegen (1999), Pittsburgh (2000), Rome (2001), Palo Alto (2002), Prague (2003), Philadelphia (2004), Zurich (2005), Santa Barbara (2006), Pisa (2007), St. Louis (2008), San Francisco (2009), Stockholm (2010), and Chicago (2011).

HSCC 2012 takes place under the umbrella of the 5th Cyber-Physical Systems Week (CPSWeek), which is a collocated cluster of five conferences: HSCC, the International Conference on Cyber-Physical Systems (ICCPS), the International Conference on Information Processing in Sensor Networks (IPSN), the Real-Time and Embedded Technology and Application Symposium (RTAS), and the brand new International Conference on High Confidence Networked Systems (HiCoNS). Through CPSWeek, the five conferences will share three joint plenary speakers (including long-time HSCC contributor Claire Tomlin from UC Berkeley), a poster and demo session, several pre-conference workshops and tutorials, and joint social events.

The HSCC call for papers attracted submissions—46 regular papers and 3 tool papers—from North and South America, Asia, and Europe. Each paper received 3–6 reviews from PC members and external reviewers. New this year was an author response period: the reviews (including scores and comments) were sent to the authors by email, and the authors were given nine days to respond to questions or factual errors in the reviews in 1000 words or less of plain text. After taking these responses into account during an in-depth PC discussion, 28 regular papers and 2 tool papers were selected for the final program. Based on a survey of authors and PC members conducted after decisions were announced, the author response period was a successful experiment and we hope to see it repeated in future years.

As we write this welcome message, a select group of submissions has been nominated for a new HSCC best paper award and honorable mentions, all to be announced at the conference. Also new this year is an HSCC invited talk (in addition to the CPSWeek plenaries). We are delighted to have Calin Belta from Boston University giving the first in what we hope is an annual lecture series.

Putting together HSCC 2012 was a team effort. We thank the authors for providing us an outstanding collection of research from which to choose. We thank the Program Committee members and the additional reviewers for their help in composing a strong program. We thank the Steering Committee and HSCC 2011 PC chairs Emilio Frazzoli and Radu Grosu for their help organizing the conference and their support of the new author response period, best paper award, and invited talk. We thank the CPSWeek organizing body—in particular the finance chair Chris Gill—for all of the financial and local arrangements that made the conference possible. We thank EasyChair for hosting the submission and review process, and Lisa Tolles at Sheridan Printing

Company and Adrienne Griscti at ACM for managing the production of this proceedings. We are grateful for the continued sponsorship of ACM SIGBED, and for financial support of the invited speaker and student participation from NEC Laboratories America and from the Centre National de la Recherche Scientifique (CNRS) in France.

We hope that by adding these small innovations to the traditionally strong collection of HSCC submissions, we have produced a program that you will find interesting and thought-provoking. We look forward to opportunities at the conference and continuing afterward to share ideas with researchers and practitioners from around the work who share our interest in hybrid systems.

Thao Dang
Program Committee Co-Chair
CNRS / VERIMAG
Grenoble, France

Ian M. Mitchell
Program Committee Co-Chair
University of British Columbia
Vancouver, Canada

Table of Contents

Session: Verification (3) – Abstraction & Randomized Search

Session: Applications and Modelling

Session: Stability and Switched Systems

Session: Stochastic Systems (1)

Session: Quantized and Symbolic Control Systems

Session: Stochastic Systems (2)

Tool Papers

Author Index

HSCC 2012 Conference Organization

Program Chairs: Thao Dang *(CNRS/VERIMAG, France)*
Ian M. Mitchell *(University of British Columbia, Canada)*

Publicity Chairs: Sriram Sankaranarayanan *(University of Colorado at Boulder, USA)*
Georgios E. Fainekos *(Arizona State University, USA)*

Steering Committee Chair: Werner Damn *(OFFIS, Germany)*

Steering Committee: Rajeev Alur *(University of Pennsylvania, USA)*
Bruce Krogh *(Carnegie Mellon University, USA)*
Oded Maler *(VERIMAG, France)*
Manfred Morari *(ETH, Switzerland)*
George Pappas *(University of Pennsylvania, USA)*

Program Committee: Alessandro Abate *(TU Delft, The Netherlands)*
Erika Abraham *(RWTH Aachen, Germany)*
Aaron Ames *(Texas A&M University, USA)*
Patrick Cousot *(New York University, USA)*
Stefano Di Cairano *(Mitsubishi Electric Research Laboratories, MA, USA)*
Alexandre Bayen *(University of California at Berkeley, USA)*
Calin Belta *(Boston University, USA)*
Emilio Frazzoli *(Massachusetts Institute of Technology, USA)*
Goran Frehse *(VERIMAG, France)*
Antoine Girard *(Joseph Fourier University, Grenoble, France)*
Radu Grosu *(SUNY Stony Brook, USA)*
Klaus Havelund *(NASA Jet Propulsion Laboratory, USA)*
Holger Hermanns *(Saarland University, Germany)*
Jianghai Hu *(Purdue University, USA)*
Jun-Ichi Imura *(Tokyo Institute of Technology, Japan)*
Franjo Ivancic *(NEC, USA)*
T. John Koo *(Chinese Academy of Sciences, China)*
Kim Larsen *(Aalborg University, Denmark)*
Mircea Lazar *(TU Eindhoven, The Netherlands)*
Hai Lin *(National University of Singapore, Singapore)*
Jan Lunze *(Ruhr-University Bochum, Germany)*
Rupak Majumdar *(Max Planck Institute for Software Systems, Germany)*
Sayan Mitra *(University of Illinois at Urbana-Champaign, USA)*
Dragan Nesic *(University of Melbourne, Australia)*
Songhwai Oh *(Seoul National University, Korea)*
Paritosh Pandya *(Tata Institute of Fundamental Research, India)*
Andre Platzer *(Carnegie Mellon University, USA)*

Program Committee (continued): Stefan Ratschan *(Academy of Sciences of Czech Republic, Czech Republic)*
Ricardo Sanfelice *(University of Arizona, USA)*
Sriram Sankaranarayanan *(University of Colorado at Boulder, USA)*
Thomas Stauner *(BMW, Munich, Germany)*
Paulo Tabuada *(University of California at Los Angeles, USA)*
Ashish Tiwari *(SRI, USA)*
Pascal Traverse *(Airbus, France)*
Shaofa Yang *(Chinese Academy of Sciences, China)*
Qianchuan Zhao *(Tsinghua University, China)*

Additional reviewers:

Dieky Adzkiya
Nikolaos Athanasopoulos
Shun-Ichi Azuma
Laurent Bako
Maximilian Balandat
Davide Barcelli
Ezio Bartocci
Dario Bauso
Alessandro Borri
Juan Pablo Carbajal
Antoine Chaillet
Xin Chen
Eugenio Cinquemani
Alessandro Colombo
David Copp
Florian Corzilius
Sergey Dashkovskiy
Richard Defrancisco
Benoit Delahaye
Xu Chu Ding
Alexandre Donzé
Laurent Doyen
Parasara S. Duggirala
Jérôme Feret
Thomas Martin Gawlitza
Khalil Ghorbal
Rob Gielen
Hernan Baro Graf
Ernst Moritz Hahn
Arnd Hartmanns
Erik Henriksson
Kenji Hirata
Ping Hou
Takayuki Ishizaki

Md Ariful Islam
Nils Jansen
Bertrand Jeannet
Shu Jiang
Taylor Johnson
Line Juhl
Johannes Kloos
Koichi Kobayashi
Morteza Lahijanian
Colas Le Guernic
Michael Lemmon
Zhiyun Lin
Jiang Liu
Sarah Loos
Ulrich Loup
João G. Martins
Pieter Mosterman
Abhishek Murthy
Johanna Nellen
Ulrik Nyman
Meeko Oishi
Reza Olfati-Saber
Simone Paoletti
Traverse Pascal
Murali Pasupuleti
Mikkel L. Pedersen
Andreas Podelski
Riccardo Porreca
Ioannis Poulakakis
Matthew Powell
Anders Ravn
David Renshaw
Laurie Ricker
Indranil Saha

Additional reviewers (continued):

Peter Schrammel
Wendelin Serwe
Ryan Sinnet
Christoffer Sloth
Sadegh Esmaeil Zadeh Soudjani
Veaceslav Spinu
Jonathan Sprinkle
Ilya Tkachev
Roland Toth

Jana Tumova
Baobing Wang
Shuling Wang
Verena Wolf
Shishir Nadubettu Yadukumar
Rongjie Yan
Boyan Yordanov
Majid Zamani
Erik Zawadzki

Sponsor:

Supporters:

Verification and Control of Hybrid Systems using Reachability Analysis with Machine Learning

Anil Aswani
UC Berkeley
aaswani@eecs.berkeley.edu

Jerry Ding
UC Berkeley
jding@eecs.berkeley.edu

Haomiao Huang
Stanford University
haomiao@stanford.edu

Michael Vitus
Stanford University
vitus@stanford.edu

Jeremy Gillula
Stanford University
jgillula@stanford.edu

Patrick Bouffard
UC Berkeley
bouffard@eecs.berkeley.edu

Claire J. Tomlin
UC Berkeley
tomlin@eecs.berkeley.edu

ABSTRACT

This talk will present reachability analysis as a tool for model checking and controller synthesis for dynamic systems. We will consider the problem of guaranteeing reachability to a given desired subset of the state space while satisfying a safety property defined in terms of state constraints. We allow for nonlinear and hybrid dynamics, and possibly non-convex state constraints. We use these results to synthesize controllers that ensure safety and reachability properties under bounded model disturbances that vary continuously.

The resulting control policy is a set-valued feedback map involving both a selection of continuous inputs and discrete switching commands as a function of system state. We show that new control policies based on machine learning are included in this map, resulting in high performance with guarantees of safety. We discuss real-time implementations of this, and present several examples from multiple aerial vehicle control, human-robot interaction, and multiple player games.

Categories and Subject Descriptors

G.0 [**Mathematics of Computing**]: General

General Terms

Algorithms, Verification

Keywords

Hybrid systems, Reachability

1. Biography

Claire Tomlin is a Professor of Electrical Engineering and Computer Sciences at the University of California at Berkeley, where she holds the Charles A. Desoer Chair in Engineering. She held the positions of Assistant, Associate, and Full Professor at Stanford from 1998-2007, and in 2005 joined Berkeley. She received the Erlander Professorship of the Swedish Research Council in 2009, a MacArthur Fellowship in 2006, and the Eckman Award of the American Automatic Control Council in 2003. She works in hybrid systems and control, with applications to air traffic systems, robotics, and biology.

Formal Methods for Dynamical Systems

Calin Belta
Mechanical Engineering
Boston University
Boston, MA

cbelta@bu.edu

ABSTRACT

In control theory, "complex" models of physical processes, such as systems of differential equations, are usually checked against "simple" specifications, such as stability and set invariance. In formal methods, "rich" specifications, such as languages and formulae of temporal logics, are checked against "simple" models of software programs and digital circuits, such as finite transition graphs. With the development and integration of cyber physical and safety critical systems, there is an increasing need for computational tools for verification and control of complex systems from rich, temporal logic specifications.

The formal verification and synthesis problems have been shown to be undecidable even for very simple classes of infinite-space continuous and hybrid systems. However, provably correct but conservative approaches, in which the satisfaction of a property by a dynamical system is implied by the satisfaction of the property by a finite over-approximation (abstraction) of the system, have received a lot of attention in recent years.

Some classes of systems allowing for computationally efficient verification and control from temporal logic specifications are reviewed. For continuous and discrete-time linear systems and continuous-time multi-linear systems, it is shown that finite abstractions can be constructed through polyhedral operations only. By using techniques from model checking and automata games, this allows for verification and control from specifications given as Linear Temporal Logic (LTL) formulae over linear predicates in the state variables.

The usefulness of these computational tools is illustrated with various examples such as verification and synthesis of biological circuits in synthetic biology and motion planning and control in robotics.

Categories and Subject Descriptors

I.2.8 [**Artificial Intelligence**]: Problem Solving, Control Methods, and Search – *Control Theory.* D.2.4 [**Software Engineering**]: Software/Program Verification – *Formal Methods*

General Terms

Algorithms, Design, Languages, Theory, Verification.

Keywords

Linear Systems, Temporal Logics

BIO

Calin Belta is an Associate Professor in the Department of Mechanical Engineering and the Division of Systems Engineering at Boston University, where he is also affiliated with the Center for Information and Systems Engineering (CISE), the Bioinformatics Program, and the Center for Biodynamics (CBD). His research focuses on dynamics and control theory, with particular emphasis on hybrid and cyber-physical systems, formal synthesis and verification, and applications in robotics and systems biology. Calin Belta is a Senior Member of the IEEE and an Associate Editor for the SIAM Journal on Control and Optimization (SICON). He received the Air Force Office of Scientific Research Young Investigator Award and the National Science Foundation CAREER Award.

HSCC'12, April 17–19, 2012, Beijing, China.
ACM 978-1-4503-1220-2/12/04.

Low Complexity Resilient Consensus in Networked Multi-Agent Systems with Adversaries

Heath J. LeBlanc
heath.j.leblanc@vanderbilt.edu

Xenofon Koutsoukos
xenofon.koutsoukos@vanderbilt.edu

Institute for Software Integrated Systems
Department of Electrical Engineering and Computer Science
Vanderbilt University
Nashville, TN, USA

ABSTRACT

Recently, many applications have arisen in distributed control that require consensus protocols. Concurrently, we have seen a proliferation of malicious attacks on large-scale distributed systems. Hence, there is a need for (i) consensus problems that take into consideration the presence of adversaries and specify correct behavior through appropriate conditions on agreement and safety, and (ii) algorithms for distributed control applications that solve such consensus problems resiliently despite breaches in security. This paper addresses these issues by (i) defining the adversarial asymptotic agreement problem, which requires that the uncompromised agents asymptotically align their states while satisfying an invariant condition in the presence of adversaries, and (ii) by designing a low complexity consensus protocol, the Adversarial Robust Consensus Protocol (ARC-P), which combines ideas from distributed computing and cooperative control. Two types of omniscient adversaries are considered: (i) Byzantine agents can convey different state trajectories to different neighbors in the network, and (ii) malicious agents must convey the same information to each neighbor. For each type of adversary, sufficient conditions are provided that ensure ARC-P guarantees the agreement and safety conditions in static and switching network topologies, whenever the number of adversaries in the network is bounded by a constant. The conservativeness of the conditions is examined, and the conditions are compared to results in the literature.

Categories and Subject Descriptors

C.2.4 [**Computer-Communication Networks**]: Distributed Systems; H.1.1 [**Models and Principles**]: Systems and Information Theory—*General Systems Theory*

General Terms

Algorithms, Security, Theory

Keywords

Consensus, Multi-agent network, Resilience, Adversary, Byzantine

1. INTRODUCTION

Due to recent improvements in computation and communication, control system design has made a shift in many applications from centralized to decentralized and distributed approaches. This trend has been fueled by the need for increased flexibility, reliability, and performance in applications such as coordination of vehicle formations [3], flocking [6], and belief propagation in Bayesian networks [15]. For these applications and many others, reaching some form of consensus is fundamental to coordination [11, 14]. However, large-scale distributed systems have many entry points for malicious attacks and intrusions. If a security breach occurs, traditional consensus algorithms will fail to produce desirable results, and therefore lack robustness [5]. Hence, there is a need for resilient consensus algorithms that guarantee correct behavior even after sustaining security breaches.

Of course, there is a long history in distributed computing of studying consensus problems in the presence of faults and adversarial processors [11, 20]. The most potentially harmful form of adversary is the Byzantine processor, which may behave arbitrarily within the limitations set by the model of computation [7]. Therefore, worst case executions must be considered. Typically, the number of processors that may be Byzantine are bounded and fundamental tight bounds have been established on the ratio of Byzantine to normal processors [1, 7], as well as on the connectivity of the graph representing the communication network [1].

From a control theoretic viewpoint, consensus in the presence of adversaries has only been considered recently, and has focused on detection and identification of misbehaving nodes in linear consensus networks [16–19, 24, 25]. While detection is clearly an important problem, these techniques require each node to have information of the network topology beyond its local neighborhood. This requirement of *nonlocal information* renders these techniques inapplicable to general time-varying networks. Further, the detection algorithms are computationally expensive and do not consider safety constraints on the states of the agents. Using these approaches, it is possible that the adversaries may drive the states of the agents outside of a predetermined safe set during the detection phase, which may not be suitable for certain safety critical applications.

In our work, we study a consensus protocol, or algorithm, that is low complexity and uses *only local information* to achieve resilience against a bounded number of adversaries in the network. In order to codify a notion of correct behavior of the uncompromised, or cooperative, agents in the presence of adversaries, we define a consensus problem that specifies formal agreement and safety conditions. The agreement condition requires that all cooperative agents asymptotically align their states. The safety condition requires that the state trajectories of the cooperative agents remain inside the minimal hypercube formed by the initial states of the cooperative agents. This safety constraint is applicable to cases where the unsafe regions are unknown, but the minimal hypercube containing the initial states is known to be safe. Together, these conditions form the *adversarial asymptotic agreement problem*, which is a continuous-time consensus problem analogous to the Byzantine approximate agreement problem [2, 11].

For this problem, we model the networked system in continuous-time and study both static and dynamic (or switching) network topologies with directed information flow. The agents have continuous dynamics and convey state information to each other over a network that switches between a finite number of discrete topologies. In this paper, we define two types of omniscient adversaries: malicious and Byzantine. Malicious agents share the same information with each neighbor in the network and are analogous to the discrete-time malicious agents studied in [16–19, 24]. Byzantine agents are capable of conveying different information to different neighbors in the network, and are therefore more deceitful than malicious agents.

The proposed consensus protocol is the Adversarial Robust Consensus Protocol (ARC-P), which borrows ideas from computer science and cooperative control. It combines the elimination of extremal values used in Byzantine resilient consensus algorithms in distributed computing [2, 11], with the standard consensus technique in cooperative control of summing the neighboring relative states as input to an integrator agent [14].

We introduced ARC-P in [8], where we studied resilience to malicious agents in complete networks. Here we extend the study of ARC-P to more general network topologies. We present sufficient conditions on the set of possible network topologies that allow us to prove agreement for both fixed and switching topologies using a common Lyapunov function. For safety, we use an invariant set argument similar to the argument made in [8]. We also provide a necessary condition on consensus using ARC-P. Then, we relate the sufficient conditions to known necessary and sufficient conditions set forth in the literature–which have addressed different consensus problems under different models of computation. Although the sufficient conditions are conservative, we provide pathological examples in which the conditions are relaxed minimally and consensus is precluded. Finally, we illustrate the theoretical results through a simulation example.

The rest of the paper is organized as follows. Section 2 covers some preliminaries including the terminology, system model, and problem statement. ARC-P is then described in Section 3. Section 4 studies the convergence properties of ARC-P in a class of directed networks. Section 5 examines more closely the sufficient conditions given in Section 4, and illustrates the results through simulation. Section 6 gives an account of related works, and Section 7 provides conclusions and directions for future work.

2. PRELIMINARIES

2.1 Review of Graph Theory

In this section we review some fundamentals of graph theory pertinent to this paper. As is common when dealing with multi-agent networks, we model the networked multi-agent system with a (finite, simple, labelled) *digraph*, $\mathcal{D} = (\mathcal{V}, \mathcal{E})$ [12]. The *node set* $\mathcal{V} = \{1, \ldots, n\}$ abstracts the n dynamic agents as *nodes*, and the *directed edge set* $\mathcal{E} \subset \mathcal{V} \times \mathcal{V}$ models the information flow between the agents, which is realized either through communication or sensing. For each ordered pair $(i, j) \in \mathcal{E}$, state information flows from node i to node j. We also consider the *underlying graph* $\mathcal{G}(\mathcal{D})$,

which is defined by replacing directed edges of $\mathcal{D}$ by undirected ones, resulting in the edge set $\mathcal{E}_\mathcal{G}$.

For local information flow, we consider the set of *in-neighbors* of node j, defined by $\mathcal{N}_j^{\text{in}} = \{i \in \mathcal{V} | (i, j) \in \mathcal{E}\}$, and the set of *inclusive in-neighbors* of node j, defined by $\mathcal{J}_j^{\text{in}} = \mathcal{N}_j^{\text{in}} \cup \{j\}$. The *in-degree* of j is denoted $d_j^{\text{in}} \triangleq |\mathcal{N}_j^{\text{in}}|$, and the *minimum in-degree* of $\mathcal{D}$ is denoted $\delta^{\text{in}}(\mathcal{D})$. Likewise, the *maximum in-degree* of $\mathcal{D}$ is denoted $\Delta^{\text{in}}(\mathcal{D})$. There are, of course, analogous definitions for *out-neighbors*, e.g., the *out-degree* of j is $d_j^{\text{out}} \triangleq |\mathcal{N}_j^{\text{out}}|$ and the *minimum out-degree* of $\mathcal{D}$ is $\delta^{\text{out}}(\mathcal{D})$.

In order to describe information flow across the network, we consider the following definitions. A *path* is a sequence of distinct vertices $i_0, i_1, \ldots, i_k$ such that $(i_j, i_{j+1}) \in \mathcal{E}$, $j = 0, 1, \ldots, k - 1$. We use the notion of path to define different forms of connectedness. We say that $\mathcal{D}$ is *strongly connected* if for every $i, j \in \mathcal{V}$, there exists a path starting at i and ending at j. If the underlying graph is connected, then $\mathcal{D}$ is *weakly connected*. Alternatively, if the underlying graph is disconnected, then $\mathcal{D}$ is *disconnected*.

To measure the robustness and redundancy of information flow, we define a *vertex cut* as a set of vertices $\mathcal{K}$ such that the removal of $\mathcal{K}$ results in either a disconnected digraph or the trivial digraph consisting of a single node. The *connectivity* $\kappa(\mathcal{D})$ is the size of a minimal vertex cut. A digraph is said to be *k-connected* if $\kappa(\mathcal{D}) \geq k$. A simple consequence of defining connectivity in this manner is $\kappa(\mathcal{D}) = \kappa(\mathcal{G}(\mathcal{D}))$ [4].[1]

2.2 System Model

This section details the system model, with the assumptions on the cooperative agents and adversaries. To allow for time-varying, or switching, network topologies, we consider the finite set of all digraphs on n vertices, $\Gamma_n = \{\mathcal{D}_1, \ldots, \mathcal{D}_d\}$. Each digraph $\mathcal{D}_k \in \Gamma_n$ has the same vertex set $\mathcal{V}$, whereas the directed edge sets $\mathcal{E}_1, \ldots, \mathcal{E}_d$ are all distinct. Without loss of generality, $\mathcal{V}$ is partitioned into a set of p *cooperative agents* $\mathcal{V}_c = \{1, \ldots, p\}$ and a set of q *adversaries* $\mathcal{V}_a = \{p + 1, \ldots, n\}$, with $q = n - p$. A *switching signal* $\sigma: \mathbb{R}_{\geq 0} \to \{1, \ldots, d\}$ determines which digraph $\mathcal{D}_{\sigma(t)} \in \Gamma_n$ describes the network at time $t \in \mathbb{R}_{\geq 0}$. We assume a finite number of switches on any finite time interval.

For simplicity of notation, we assume each agent's state is scalar. Collectively, $x_c(t) = [x_1(t), \ldots, x_p(t)]^\top \in \mathbb{R}^p$ is the state of the cooperative agents. Likewise, the collective state of the adversaries conveyed to agent $j \in \mathcal{V}_c$ is $x_{a_j}(t) = [x_{p+1,j}(t), \ldots, x_{n,j}(t)]^\top \in \mathbb{R}^q$. If $k \notin \mathcal{J}_j^{\text{in}}(t)$, then adversary k does not directly influence agent j at time t, in which case agent j does not receive $x_{k,j}(t)$. While this notation may seem overly cumbersome, it simplifies dealing with Byzantine agents. One may take the viewpoint that $x_{k,j}(t)$ is the trajectory Byzantine agent k would like to convey to agent j, but the topological constraints on the network prevent it from doing so. With this justification, we denote $x: \mathbb{R} \times \mathcal{V}_c \to \mathbb{R}^n$ by $x(t, j) = [x_c^\top(t), x_{a_j}^\top(t)]^\top \in \mathbb{R}^n$. Whenever the context is understood, we will drop the arguments and write x_c, x_{a_j}, and x. Finally, we denote by x_a the set of all x_{a_j}, $j \in \mathcal{V}_c$.

2.2.1 Cooperative Agents

Each cooperative agent $i \in \mathcal{V}_c$ has dynamics given by $\dot{x}_i = u_i$, where $u_i = f_{i, \sigma(t)}(x_c, x_{a_i})$ is a control input. The states of the neighboring adversaries, within x_{a_i}, are analyzed as uncertain inputs; however, because there is no prior knowledge about which agents are adversaries, the control input must treat the state infor-

---

[1] In [4], this form of connectivity is defined as $\kappa_1(\mathcal{D})$ and other forms of connectivity in digraphs are studied (most notably strong connectivity). For our purposes, the definition given here suffices.

mation from neighboring agents in the same manner. The dynamics of the system of cooperative agents are then defined for $t \geq 0$ by

$$\dot{x}_c = f_{c,\sigma(t)}(x_c, x_a), \quad x_c(0) \in \mathbb{R}^p, \mathcal{D}_{\sigma(t)} \in \Gamma_n, \quad (1)$$

where $f_{c,\sigma(t)}(x_c, x_a) = [f_{1,\sigma(t)}(x_c, x_{a_1}), \ldots, f_{p,\sigma(t)}(x_c, x_{a_p})]^\mathsf{T}$. The dynamics of (1) define a switched system without impulse effects, so the trajectory of any solution is absolutely continuous [10].

2.2.2 Adversaries

The q adversaries are assumed to be designed for the purpose of disrupting the objective of the cooperative agents. It is assumed that the number of adversaries in the network is bounded above by a constant $F \in \mathbb{Z}_{\geq 0}$, so that $q \leq F$. We consider two different adversary models, defined as follows.

DEFINITION 1. *The q adversaries have continuous state trajectories; i.e., x_{a_j} is continuous for $j \in \mathcal{V}_c$. An adversary is*

(i) **Byzantine** *if it can convey different state trajectories to different neighbors; i.e., we may have $x_{a_i} \neq x_{a_j}$, or $x_{k,i} \neq x_{k,j}$, whenever $k \in \mathcal{V}_a \cap \mathcal{J}_i^{in}(t) \cap \mathcal{J}_j^{in}(t)$ for $i, j \in \mathcal{V}_c$;*

(ii) **Malicious** *if it must convey the same state trajectory to each neighbor; i.e., $x_{a_i} \equiv x_{a_j}$ for all $i, j \in \mathcal{V}_c$.*

Both classes of adversaries are assumed to be omniscient and behave in a worst case manner. Hence, the adversaries are able to carefully select their continuous state trajectories to cause maximal disruption to the consensus objective of the cooperative agents.

2.3 Problem Statement

The *adversarial asymptotic agreement problem* is defined by two conditions, agreement and safety, along with the type of adversary considered. The *agreement condition* requires that the state of the cooperative agents, x_c, converges to the agreement space, $\mathcal{A} = \mathrm{span}\{1_p\} \subset \mathbb{R}^p$, despite the influence of the adversaries. That is, given $q \leq F$ adversaries and $x_c(0) \in \mathbb{R}^p$, then

$$x_c(t) \to \mathcal{A} \text{ as } t \to \infty. \quad (2)$$

The *safety condition* requires that the state trajectory of each cooperative agent is contained in the interval formed by the initial states of cooperative agents and that the limit exists, despite the influence of the adversaries. That is, if we define the interval

$$\mathcal{I}_0 = [\min_{i \in \mathcal{V}_c} x_i(0), \max_{j \in \mathcal{V}_c} x_j(0)],$$

then the safety condition requires that given $q \leq F$ adversaries,

$$x_j(t) \in \mathcal{I}_0, \forall t \in \mathbb{R}_{\geq 0} \text{ and } \lim_{t \to \infty} x_j(t) \in \mathcal{I}_0 \text{ exists}, \forall j \in \mathcal{V}_c. \quad (3)$$

Equivalently, the safety condition can be stated in terms of x_c. Let $\mathcal{H}_0 = \mathcal{I}_0^p \subset \mathbb{R}^p$ denote the hypercube formed by the Cartesian product of p copies of $\mathcal{I}_0$. Then the safety condition requires $x_c(t) \in \mathcal{H}_0$ for all $t \geq 0$ and $\lim_{t \to \infty} x_c(t) \in \mathcal{H}_0$, despite the influence of the adversaries. It is important to explicitly require that the limit exists because convergence to a single point is desired.

The safety condition in (3) is similar to the validity condition defined in [8], which in turn was motivated by the validity condition of the Byzantine approximate agreement problem [2, 11]. The definition ensures that the value chosen by each normal node lies within the range of good values. This is important in applications where the values are measurements and only measurements within the range obtained by the normal nodes are considered valid. The safety condition entails this notion along with an invariant condition, which is important for safety critical applications.

3. CONSENSUS PROTOCOL

Here, we describe the Adversarial Robust Consensus Protocol (ARC-P) with respect to parameter $F \in \mathbb{Z}_{\geq 0}$. The main idea of the protocol is for each cooperative agent $i \in \mathcal{V}_c$ to sort the relative states of its inclusive in-neighbors and then remove the F largest and F smallest ones. This results in $m_i(t) = d_i^{in}(t) + 1 - 2F$ relative states if $d_i^{in}(t) \geq 2F$, which are summed to determine the first order dynamics of the agent. To make the protocol well-defined for all network topologies, i.e., whenever $d_i^{in}(t) < 2F$, in this case the agent removes all neighboring values from consideration and the input is zero. This approach adheres to the philosophy that whenever there is insufficient information to act in a way that is resilient to adversarial influence, it is best to do nothing.

In order to formally express ARC-P with parameter F, let $\xi_i(t)$ denote the vector of sorted values of the states in the inclusive in-neighborhood of node i at time $t \in \mathbb{R}_{\geq 0}$. The elements of ξ_i are denoted by $\xi_i^1, \ldots, \xi_i^{d_i^{in}(t)+1}$ and satisfy

$$\xi_i^1 \leq \xi_i^2 \leq \cdots \leq \xi_i^{d_i^{in}(t)+1}. \quad (4)$$

Then, cooperative agent $i \in \mathcal{V}_c$ calculates $u_i = f_{i,\sigma(t)}(x_c, x_{a_i})$ at time $t \in \mathbb{R}_{\geq 0}$ by

$$f_{i,\sigma(t)}(x_c, x_{a_i}) = \begin{cases} \sum_{l=F+1}^{d_i^{in}(t)+1-F} \left(\xi_i^l(t) - x_i(t) \right) & d_i^{in}(t) \geq 2F; \\ 0 & d_i^{in}(t) < 2F. \end{cases} \quad (5)$$

If each cooperative agent uses ARC-P, then existence and uniqueness of solutions to (1) is guaranteed $\forall t \geq 0$ since $\sigma(t)$ is piecewise constant, x_{a_i} is continuous and effectively restricted to a compact set with respect to (5) (see the discussion after Lemma 2), and $f_{i,\sigma(t)}(x_c, x_{a_i})$ is globally Lipschitz in x_c and x_{a_i} $\forall i \in \mathcal{V}_c$ [8].

Figure 1 illustrates the computation that occurs at time t for cooperative agent i whenever $d_i^{in}(t) \geq 2F$. In the figure, the state, $x_i(t)$, of the agent, whose dynamics are $\dot{x}_i(t) = u_i(t)$, is subtracted from each of the other states in its inclusive neighborhood, with each of the in-neighbors denoted $x_i^j, j = 1, 2, \ldots, d_i^{in}(t)$. The resulting relative state values are sorted and then reduced by eliminating the largest and smallest F elements. Finally, the remaining elements are summed to produce the control input $u_i(t)$ to the integrator agent. The only difference if $d_i^{in}(t) < 2F$ is that the output of the Reduce block is 0.

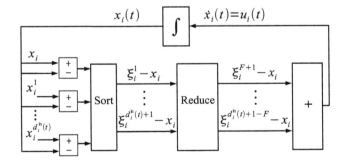

Figure 1: Synchronous data flow model of ARC-P for agent i.

From a complexity standpoint, ARC-P consists of low complexity operations in both time and space, including sort, reduce, and sum methods (see Figure 1). The worst performing subroutine of ARC-P is the sort method. But, if quicksort is used, it is worst-case quadratic in time and linear in space, with respect to the size of the inclusive in-neighborhood. Therefore, ARC-P is also worst-case quadratic in time and linear in space, and hence low complexity.

4. ANALYSIS

This section details the analysis of ARC-P with parameter F. We begin by introducing a function that characterizes the maximum disagreement amongst the cooperative agents' states. Define $\Psi : \mathbb{R}^p \to \mathbb{R}$ by

$$\Psi(x_c) = \max_{k \in \mathcal{V}_c}\{x_k\} - \min_{k \in \mathcal{V}_c}\{x_k\}. \tag{6}$$

The function Ψ has several attractive properties: (i) it is nonnegative with $\Psi(x_c) = 0$ for all $x_c \in \mathcal{A}$ and $\Psi(x_c) > 0$ $\forall x_c \notin \mathcal{A}$, (ii) it is Lipschitz, (iii) it is increasing away from $\mathcal{A}$ in the sense that $\Psi(y_1) > \Psi(y_2)$ $\forall y_1, y_2 \in \mathbb{R}^p$ satisfying $\text{dist}(y_1, \mathcal{A}) > \text{dist}(y_2, \mathcal{A})$, and (iv) it is radially unbounded away from $\mathcal{A}$ in the sense that $\Psi(y) \to \infty$ as $\text{dist}(y, \mathcal{A}) \to \infty$. These properties make Ψ an excellent Lyapunov candidate for proving global convergence to $\mathcal{A}$. Ψ has been used to prove convergence of asynchronous consensus algorithms whenever all nodes are cooperative [26].

But, one issue with Ψ is that it is not everywhere differentiable. Therefore, to study the monotonicity of $\psi(t) = \Psi(x_c(t))$, we consider the *upper-right Dini derivative* $D^+\psi(t)$ of ψ at t, defined by

$$D^+\psi(t) = \limsup_{h \to 0^+} \frac{\psi(t+h) - \psi(t)}{h},$$

and the *upper-directional derivative* of Ψ with respect to (1):

$$D^+\Psi(x_c, x_a) = \limsup_{h \to 0^+} \frac{\Psi(x_c + h f_{c,\sigma(t)}(x_c, x_a)) - \Psi(x_c)}{h}.$$

The motivation for considering the upper directional derivative of Ψ is that $D^+\psi(t) = D^+\Psi(x_c(t), x_a(t))$ for almost all t along solutions of (1) since Ψ is locally Lipschitz [21]. In this case,

$$D^+\Psi(x_c, x_a) = \limsup_{h \to 0^+} \frac{N_1(h)}{h} + \limsup_{h \to 0^+} \frac{N_2(h)}{h}, \tag{7}$$

with $\quad N_1(h) = \max_{i \in \mathcal{V}_c}\{x_i + h f_{i,\sigma(t)}(x_c, x_{a_i})\} - \max_{i \in \mathcal{V}_c}\{x_i\},$
$\qquad N_2(h) = \min_{i \in \mathcal{V}_c}\{x_i\} - \min_{i \in \mathcal{V}_c}\{x_i + h f_{i,\sigma(t)}(x_c, x_{a_i})\}.$

4.1 Preliminary Results

At this point, we derive some preliminary results that hold for all network topologies. We begin with a fundamental result for ARC-P that bounds $\dot{x}_c$ to a time-dependent compact convex set, which includes the origin.

LEMMA 1. *Consider the cooperative agent $i \in \mathcal{V}_c$ executing ARC-P with parameter $F \in \mathbb{Z}_{\geq 0}$ and at most $F < n$ malicious or Byzantine agents. Then, for $t \in \mathbb{R}_{\geq 0}$ and $\mathcal{D}_{\sigma(t)} \in \Gamma_n$*

$$m_i(t)(x_{i,\mathrm{lmin}} - x_i) \leq f_{i,\sigma(t)}(x_c, x_{a_i}) \leq m_i(t)(x_{i,\mathrm{lmax}} - x_i),$$

where $x_{i,\mathrm{lmin}}(t) = \min\{x_j | j \in \mathcal{J}_i^{in}(t) \cap \mathcal{V}_c\}$ and $x_{i,\mathrm{lmax}}(t) = \max\{x_j | j \in \mathcal{J}_i^{in}(t) \cap \mathcal{V}_c\}$ are defined for $t \in \mathbb{R}_{\geq 0}$, and

$$m_i(t) = \begin{cases} d_i^{in}(t) + 1 - 2F & \text{if } d_i^{in}(t) \geq 2F; \\ 1 & \text{otherwise}. \end{cases}$$

PROOF. If $d_i^{\mathrm{in}}(t) < 2F$, $f_{i,\sigma(t)}(x_c, x_{a_i}) = 0$ and the result follows. Therefore, assume $d_i^{\mathrm{in}}(t) \geq 2F$. Since there are at most F adversaries, we know $x_{i,\mathrm{lmin}} \leq \xi_i^{F+1}$ and $\xi_i^{d_i^{\mathrm{in}}(t)+1-F} \leq x_{i,\mathrm{lmax}}$. Hence, (4) implies

$$m_i(x_{i,\mathrm{lmin}} - x_i) \leq \sum_{l=F+1}^{d_i^{\mathrm{in}}(t)+1-F} (\xi_i^l - x_i) \leq m_i(x_{i,\mathrm{lmax}} - x_i).$$

$\square$

While Lemma 1 restricts the behavior of $\dot{x}_c$ almost everywhere, the next result restricts the feasible trajectories of $x_c(t)$. It shows that the minimal hypercube $\mathcal{H}_0$ formed by the initial values of the cooperative agents is *robustly positively invariant*.

DEFINITION 2. *The set $\mathcal{S} \subset \mathbb{R}^p$ is **robustly positively invariant** for the system given by (1) if for all $x_c(0) \in \mathcal{S}$, $x_{a_i}(t) \in \mathbb{R}^q$ $i \in \mathcal{V}_c$, and $t \geq 0$, the solution satisfies $x_c(t) \in \mathcal{S}$.*

LEMMA 2. *Suppose the cooperative agents in $\mathcal{V}_c$ execute ARC-P with parameter $F \in \mathbb{Z}_{\geq 0}$ and at most $F < n$ malicious or Byzantine agents. Then, for every $\mathcal{D}_{\sigma(t)} \in \Gamma_n$ the hypercube*

$$\mathcal{H}_0 = \{y \in \mathbb{R}^p | x_{0,min} \leq y_i \leq x_{0,max}, \; i = 1, 2, \ldots, p\},$$

where $x_{0,min} = \min_{i \in \mathcal{V}_c}\{x_i(0)\}$ and $x_{0,max} = \max_{i \in \mathcal{V}_c}\{x_i(0)\}$, is robustly positively invariant for the system (1).

PROOF. Since $\mathcal{H}_0$ is compact and any solution of (1) using (5) is continuous with $x_c(0) \in \mathcal{H}_0$, we must show that $f_{c,\sigma(t)}(x_c, x_a)$ is not directed outside of $\mathcal{H}_0$, whenever $x_c(t) \in \partial\mathcal{H}_0$, for all $\mathcal{D}_{\sigma(t)} \in \Gamma_n$ and $x_{a_i}(t) \in \mathbb{R}^q$ for $i \in \mathcal{V}_c$. The boundary $\partial\mathcal{H}_0$ is given by

$$\partial\mathcal{H}_0 = \{y \in \mathcal{H}_0 | \exists i \in \{1, 2, \ldots, p\} \text{ s.t. } y_i \in \{x_{0,\min}, x_{0,\max}\}\}.$$

Fix $x_c(t) \in \partial\mathcal{H}_0$. Let e_j denote the j-th canonical basis vector and denote $\mathcal{I}_{x_c,\min}, \mathcal{I}_{x_c,\max} \subseteq \{1, 2, \ldots, p\}$ as the sets defined by

$$j \in \mathcal{I}_{x_c,\min} \Leftrightarrow x_j = x_{0,\min} \text{ and } k \in \mathcal{I}_{x_c,\max} \Leftrightarrow x_k = x_{0,\max}.$$

Then, from the geometry of the hypercube, we require

$$e_j^{\mathsf{T}} f_{c,\sigma(t)}(x_c, x_a) \geq 0 \quad \forall j \in \mathcal{I}_{x_c,\min},$$
$$e_k^{\mathsf{T}} f_{c,\sigma(t)}(x_c, x_a) \leq 0 \quad \forall k \in \mathcal{I}_{x_c,\max}.$$

These conditions are true for all $\mathcal{D}_{\sigma(t)} \in \Gamma_n$ and $x_{a_i}(t) \in \mathbb{R}^q$ with $i \in \mathcal{V}_c$ by Lemma 1, in which the lower bound is used for $j \in \mathcal{I}_{x_c,\min}$ since $x_j = x_{j,\mathrm{lmin}} = x_{0,\min}$, and the upper bound is used for $k \in \mathcal{I}_{y,\max}$ since $x_k = x_{k,\mathrm{lmax}} = x_{0,\max}$. $\square$

The argument made in Lemma 1 implies that any time an adversary is outside of $\mathcal{I}_t = [\min_{i \in \mathcal{V}_c}\{x_i(t)\}, \max_{i \in \mathcal{V}_c}\{x_i(t)\}]$, its influence is guaranteed to be removed by its cooperative neighbors, and therefore has the same effect as if it were on the boundary of $\mathcal{I}_t$. Using Lemma 2 we conclude $\mathcal{I}_t \subseteq \mathcal{I}_0$, $\forall t \geq 0$. Hence, each adversary is effectively restricted to the compact set $\mathcal{I}_0$, with respect to (1). This fact enables us to allow adversary states in $\mathbb{R}^q$ rather than explicitly restricting them to a compact set, while still ensuring existence and uniqueness of solutions. Next, we derive an explicit equation for $D^+\Psi(x_c, x_a)$, valid at a fixed time $t \geq 0$.

LEMMA 3. *Fix $t \geq 0$ and $x_c(t) \in \mathbb{R}^p$. Suppose each cooperative agent in $\mathcal{V}_c$ executes ARC-P with parameter $F \in \mathbb{Z}_{\geq 0}$ and at most $F < n$ Byzantine or malicious agents. Let $\mathcal{D}_{\sigma(t)} \in \Gamma_n$ and define $\mathcal{S}_{min}(t), \mathcal{S}_{max}(t): \mathbb{R} \to \{1, \ldots, p\}$ by*

$$j \in \mathcal{S}_{min}(t) \Leftrightarrow x_j(t) = \min_{i \in \mathcal{V}_c}\{x_i(t)\},$$
$$k \in \mathcal{S}_{max}(t) \Leftrightarrow x_k(t) = \max_{i \in \mathcal{V}_c}\{x_i(t)\}.$$

Fix $j_t \in \mathcal{S}_{min}(t)$ such that

$$f_{j_t,\sigma(t)}(x_c, x_{a_{j_t}}) \leq f_{j,\sigma(t)}(x_c, x_{a_j}), \quad \forall j \in \mathcal{S}_{min}(t).$$

Likewise, fix $k_t \in \mathcal{S}_{max}(t)$ such that

$$f_{k_t,\sigma(t)}(x_c, x_{a_{k_t}}) \geq f_{k,\sigma(t)}(x_c, x_{a_k}), \quad \forall k \in \mathcal{S}_{max}(t).$$

Then, at time t, we have

$$D^+\Psi(x_c(t), x_a(t)) = f_{k_t,\sigma(t)}(x_c, x_{a_{k_t}}) - f_{j_t,\sigma(t)}(x_c, x_{a_{j_t}}), \tag{8}$$

and $D^+\Psi(x_c, x_a) \leq 0$ for all $t \geq 0$.

PROOF. Let $m_{t,\max} = \max_{i \in \mathcal{V}_c}\{m_i(t)\}$, where $m_i(t)$ is defined in Lemma 1. Lemma 1 implies that

$$-m_{t,\max}\Psi(x_c) \leq f_{i,\sigma(t)}(x_c, x_{a_i}) \leq m_{t,\max}\Psi(x_c)$$

holds $\forall i \in \mathcal{V}_c$. If $x_c(t) \notin \mathcal{A}$, then there exists $\epsilon_{\min} > 0$ such that $x_i - x_j \geq \epsilon_{\min} > 0$ for all $j \in \mathcal{S}_{\min}(t)$ and $i \in \mathcal{V}_c \setminus \mathcal{S}_{\min}(t)$. Similarly, there exists $\epsilon_{\max} > 0$ such that $x_k - x_i \geq \epsilon_{\max}$ for all $k \in \mathcal{S}_{\max}(t)$ and $i \in \mathcal{V}_c \setminus \mathcal{S}_{\max}(t)$. Then, by letting $\epsilon = \min\{\epsilon_{\min}, \epsilon_{\max}\}$ and taking $h \leq \epsilon/(2m_{t,\max}\Psi(x_c(t)))$, we may write

$$\begin{aligned}
x_i + h f_{i,\sigma(t)}(x_c, x_{a_i}) &\geq x_i - h m_{t,\max}\Psi(x_c(t)) \\
&\geq x_i - \epsilon/2 \\
&\geq x_j + \epsilon/2 \\
&\geq x_j + h m_{t,\max}\Psi(x_c(t)) \\
&\geq x_j + h f_{j,\sigma(t)}(x_c, x_{a_j}) \\
&\geq x_{j_t} + h f_{j_t,\sigma(t)}(x_c, x_{a_{j_t}})
\end{aligned}$$

for all $i \in \mathcal{V}_c \setminus \mathcal{S}_{\min}(t)$, $j \in \mathcal{S}_{\min}(t)$. Therefore, at time t

$$\min_{i \in \mathcal{V}_c}\{x_i + h f_{i,\sigma(t)}(x_c, x_{a_i})\} = x_{j_t} + h f_{j_t,\sigma(t)}(x_c, x_{a_{j_t}}).$$

Following a similar argument, we deduce

$$\max_{i \in \mathcal{V}_c}\{x_i + h f_{i,\sigma(t)}(x_c, x_{a_i})\} = x_{k_t} + h f_{k_t,\sigma(t)}(x_c, x_{a_{k_t}}).$$

Combining this with (7), gives (8). On the other hand, if $x_c(t) \in \mathcal{A}$ then both $\Psi(x_c)$ and $D^+\Psi(x_c, x_a)$ are zero. Finally, applying Lemma 1 with $x_{j_t,\mathrm{lmin}} = x_{j_t}$ and $x_{k_t,\mathrm{lmax}} = x_{k_t}$ shows that $D^+\Psi(x_c, x_a) \leq 0$. □

Notice in (8) that the agents acting as k_t and j_t may change with time. It will be important to show in the convergence argument that bounds on $D^+\Psi(x_c, x_a)$ hold for all $t \in \mathbb{R}_{\geq 0}$, regardless of which cooperative agents fill the roles of k_t and j_t. Next, we show that $\Psi(x_c)$ is bounded by scaled versions of $\mathrm{dist}(x_c, \mathcal{A}) = \inf_{y \in \mathcal{A}}\|x_c - y\|_2$. For this argument, we use the following properties of the min and max functions. If $\alpha \in \mathbb{R}$, then

$$\begin{aligned}
\min_{i \in \mathcal{V}_c}\{x_i + \alpha\} &= \min_{i \in \mathcal{V}_c}\{x_i\} + \alpha \\
\max_{i \in \mathcal{V}_c}\{x_i + \alpha\} &= \max_{i \in \mathcal{V}_c}\{x_i\} + \alpha.
\end{aligned} \quad (9)$$

LEMMA 4. *Given $x_c \in \mathbb{R}^p$, $\Psi(x_c)$ is bounded by*

$$\frac{1}{\sqrt{p}}\mathrm{dist}(x_c, \mathcal{A}) \leq \Psi(x_c) \leq 2\,\mathrm{dist}(x_c, \mathcal{A}), \quad (10)$$

PROOF. Consider the decomposition of x_c: $x_c = v_{\mathcal{A}} + v_{\mathcal{A}\perp}$, in which $v_{\mathcal{A}} \in \mathcal{A}$ and $v_{\mathcal{A}\perp} \in \mathcal{A}^\perp$. Given this decomposition, we conclude $\|v_{\mathcal{A}\perp}\|_2 = \mathrm{dist}(x_c, \mathcal{A})$ and $\exists \gamma \in \mathbb{R}$ such that $v_{\mathcal{A}} = \gamma 1_p$. Because of this, we can use (9) to write

$$\Psi(x_c) = \max_{i \in \mathcal{V}_c}\{(v_{\mathcal{A}\perp})_i\} - \min_{i \in \mathcal{V}_c}\{(v_{\mathcal{A}\perp})_i\}, \quad (11)$$

in which $(v_{\mathcal{A}\perp})_i$ is the i-th element of $v_{\mathcal{A}\perp}$. From this, we obtain the upper bound

$$\Psi(x_c) \leq \max_{i \in \mathcal{V}_c}\{(v_{\mathcal{A}\perp})_i\} + |\min_{i \in \mathcal{V}_c}\{(v_{\mathcal{A}\perp})_i\}| \leq 2\|v_{\mathcal{A}\perp}\|_2.$$

On the other hand, since $v_{\mathcal{A}\perp} \in \mathcal{A}^\perp$, $\sum_{i=1}^p (v_{\mathcal{A}\perp})_i = 0$, so that $\max_{i \in \mathcal{V}_c}\{(v_{\mathcal{A}\perp})_i\} \geq 0$ and $\min_{i \in \mathcal{V}_c}\{(v_{\mathcal{A}\perp})_i\} \leq 0$. From this and (11) we conclude $\Psi(x_c) \geq |(v_{\mathcal{A}\perp})_j|$ for all $j \in \mathcal{V}_c$. Thus, we obtain the lower bound

$$\frac{1}{\sqrt{p}}\|v_{\mathcal{A}\perp}\|_2 \leq \frac{1}{\sqrt{p}}\sqrt{p\Psi^2(x_c)} = \Psi(x_c). \quad □$$

In the sequel, we first consider fixed network topology, and prove exponential convergence of $x_c(t)$ to $\mathcal{A}$ for a subset of network topologies by using properties of $\Psi(x_c)$ and $D^+\Psi(x_c, x_a)$. We then combine the agreement result with an invariant set argument to prove safety. Afterwards, we prove a necessary condition, and then generalize the results to the case of switching topology by using Ψ as a common Lyapunov function.

4.2 Fixed Topology

In this section, we assume that $\sigma(t) \equiv s$ and $\mathcal{D}_s$ belongs to $\Gamma_{M,F} \subset \Gamma_n$ or $\Gamma_{B,F} \subset \Gamma_n$ whenever the adversaries are, respectively, malicious or Byzantine. When dealing with malicious agents, we consider the following class of digraphs with restricted in-degrees or out-degrees, defined by

$$\Gamma_{M,F} = \{\mathcal{D}_k \in \Gamma_n \mid \text{at least one of } M1_F \text{ and } M2_F \text{ holds}\}, \quad (12)$$

where

$M1_F$: $\delta^{\mathrm{in}}(\mathcal{D}_k) \geq \lfloor n/2 \rfloor + F$;

$M2_F$: $\exists \mathcal{S} \subseteq \mathcal{V}(\mathcal{D}_k), |\mathcal{S}| \geq 2F+1$, such that $d_i^{\mathrm{out}} = n-1, \forall i \in \mathcal{S}$.

When dealing with Byzantine agents, we require stronger assumptions on the in-degrees and out-degrees. In this case, we define

$$\Gamma_{B,F} = \{\mathcal{D}_k \in \Gamma_n \mid \text{at least one of } B1_F \text{ and } B2_F \text{ holds}\}, \quad (13)$$

where

$B1_F$: $\delta^{\mathrm{in}}(\mathcal{D}_k) \geq \begin{cases} n/2 + \lfloor 3F/2 \rfloor & \text{if } n \text{ is even and } F \text{ is odd;} \\ \lfloor n/2 \rfloor + \lceil 3F/2 \rceil & \text{otherwise.} \end{cases}$

$B2_F$: $\exists \mathcal{S} \subseteq \mathcal{V}(\mathcal{D}_k), |\mathcal{S}| \geq 3F+1$, such that $d_i^{\mathrm{out}} = n-1, \forall i \in \mathcal{S}$.

It follows from these definitions that $\Gamma_{B,F} \subseteq \Gamma_{M,F}$. Additionally, the conditions in (12) and (13) implicitly bound the maximum number of adversaries F by a function of the total number of agents n. Specifically, property $M1_F$ implies

$$n - 1 \geq \delta^{\mathrm{in}}(\mathcal{D}_s) \geq \lfloor n/2 \rfloor + F \implies F \leq \lceil n/2 \rceil - 1.$$

Similarly, property $M2_F$ implies

$$n \geq |\mathcal{S}| \geq 2F + 1 \implies 2F \leq n - 1.$$

In either case, $n > 2F$. Analogously, the properties $B1_F$ and $B2_F$ imply $n > 3F$. Therefore, it follows that $F \leq \lceil n/2 \rceil - 1$ (or $F \leq \lceil n/3 \rceil - 1$) whenever $\mathcal{D}_s \in \Gamma_{M,F}$ (or $\mathcal{D}_s \in \Gamma_{B,F}$). A consequence of this is that $\delta^{\mathrm{in}}(\mathcal{D}_s) \geq 2F$ for all $\mathcal{D}_s \in \Gamma_{M,F}$ (or $\mathcal{D}_s \in \Gamma_{B,F}$). Hence, in this case, (8) may be rewritten using (5) as

$$D^+\Psi(x_c, x_a) = \sum_{m=F+1}^{d_{k_t}^{\mathrm{in}}(t)+1-F} (\xi_{k_t}^m - x_{k_t}) - \sum_{l=F+1}^{d_{j_t}^{\mathrm{in}}(t)+1-F} \left(\xi_{j_t}^l - x_{j_t}\right). \quad (14)$$

This equation is the basis of the agreement argument below.

4.2.1 Agreement

Here we combine Lemmas 3 and 4 with the assumption $\mathcal{D}_s \in \Gamma_{M,F}$ or $\mathcal{D}_s \in \Gamma_{B,F}$ for malicious or Byzantine adversaries, respectively, in order to show global exponential convergence of x_c to $\mathcal{A}$.

THEOREM 1. *Suppose each cooperative agent in $\mathcal{V}_c$ executes ARC-P with parameter $F \in \mathbb{Z}_{\geq 0}$ and at most (i) F malicious agents with $\mathcal{D}_s \in \Gamma_{M,F}$, or (ii) F Byzantine agents with $\mathcal{D}_s \in \Gamma_{B,F}$. Then x_c globally exponentially converges to the agreement space $\mathcal{A}$, and therefore the agreement condition (2) is satisfied. Moreover, the convergence to the agreement space is bounded by*

$$\mathrm{dist}(x_c(t), \mathcal{A}) \leq 2\sqrt{p}\,\mathrm{dist}(x_c(0), \mathcal{A})e^{-t}. \quad (15)$$

PROOF. (i) Fix $t \geq 0$ and consider (14). Since there are at most F adversaries, each term in the first sum is nonpositive and each term in the second sum is nonnegative. If at least one of the sorted values in the second sum is greater than or equal to any of the values in the first, say $\xi_{k_t}^{m'} \leq \xi_{j_t}^{l'}$, then

$$D^+ \Psi(x_c, x_a) \leq -\Psi(x_c), \qquad (16)$$

since, in this case,

$$D^+ \Psi(x_c, x_a) = \sum_{\substack{m=F+1 \\ m \neq m'}}^{d_{k_t}^{\text{in}}(t)+1-F} (\xi_{k_t}^m - x_{k_t}) - \sum_{\substack{l=F+1 \\ l \neq l'}}^{d_{j_t}^{\text{in}}(t)+1-F} (\xi_{j_t}^l - x_{j_t})$$
$$+ \left(\xi_{k_t}^{m'} - \xi_{j_t}^{l'} \right) - \Psi(x_c) \leq -\Psi(x_c).$$

A sufficient condition for this to hold, given that *all* agents convey the same values to all neighbors, is to ensure there is a common value in the two sums, e.g., $\xi_{k_t}^{m'} = \xi_{j_t}^{l'}$. This is guaranteed if $|\mathcal{J}_{j_t}^{\text{in}} \cap \mathcal{J}_{k_t}^{\text{in}}| > 2F$, which is obviously true if property $M2_F$ holds. If only property $M1_F$ holds, it must also be the case, since otherwise, we reach the contradiction

$$n \geq |\mathcal{J}_{j_t}^{\text{in}} \cup \mathcal{J}_{k_t}^{\text{in}}| = |\mathcal{J}_{j_t}^{\text{in}}| + |\mathcal{J}_{k_t}^{\text{in}}| - |\mathcal{J}_{j_t}^{\text{in}} \cap \mathcal{J}_{k_t}^{\text{in}}|$$
$$\geq 2(\lfloor \tfrac{n}{2} \rfloor + F + 1) - 2F \geq n+1.$$

Therefore, (16) holds for all $t \geq 0$, and hence it can be shown that

$$\Psi(x_c(t)) \leq \Psi(x_c(0))e^{-t}.$$

Finally, using (10), we conclude (15). Thus, we have shown global exponential convergence of x_c to $\mathcal{A}$.

(ii) The argument is identical to (i), except here to ensure there exists m' and l' such that $\xi_{k_t}^{m'} = \xi_{j_t}^{l'}$ and thereby guarantee (16), we need $|\mathcal{J}_{j_t}^{\text{in}} \cap \mathcal{J}_{k_t}^{\text{in}}| > 3F$. This is required if there are F Byzantine agents in the intersection because of the following argument. Suppose F of the cooperative agents' states are strictly greater than F other cooperative agents in the intersection. Then there are $3F$ agents in the intersection, and the adversaries may create $2F$ different values all strictly between these two sets of cooperative agent states. Thus, at least one more cooperative agent in the intersection is necessary to ensure a common value. Analogously to (i), property $B2_F$ guarantees $|\mathcal{J}_{j_t}^{\text{in}} \cap \mathcal{J}_{k_t}^{\text{in}}| > 3F$ by construction, and so does property $B1_F$. Otherwise, we reach the contradiction

$$n \geq \begin{cases} 2(\tfrac{n}{2} + \lfloor \tfrac{3F}{2} \rfloor + 1) - 3F \geq n+1 & n \text{ even \& } F \text{ odd;} \\ 2(\lfloor \tfrac{n}{2} \rfloor + \lceil \tfrac{3F}{2} \rceil + 1) - 3F \geq n+1 & \text{otherwise.} \end{cases} \qquad \square$$

Notice in the proof of Theorem 1 that it is not necessary that there exists a common in-neighbor in the reduced set of in-neighbors of j_t and k_t to show (16), and therefore (15). All that is required is that there exist $\xi_{k_t}^{m'}$ and $\xi_{j_t}^{l'}$ such that $\xi_{k_t}^{m'} \leq \xi_{j_t}^{l'}$. However, because this must hold globally (i.e., for all $x_c(0) \in \mathbb{R}^p$ and $x_{a_i}(t) \in \mathbb{R}^p$ for $i \in \mathcal{V}_c$) and for all $t \geq 0$, it is untenable to depend on the values in those neighborhoods without insisting that there is a cooperative agent as a common in-neighbor.

4.2.2 Safety

In this section, we verify that the safety condition (3) holds by using an invariant set argument.

THEOREM 2. *Suppose each cooperative agent in $\mathcal{V}_c$ executes ARC-P with parameter $F \in \mathbb{Z}_{\geq 0}$ and at most (i) F malicious agents with $\mathcal{D}_s \in \Gamma_{M,F}$, or (ii) F Byzantine agents with $\mathcal{D}_s \in \Gamma_{B,F}$. Then the safety condition (3) is satisfied.*

PROOF. Lemma 1 implies that for each $i \in \mathcal{V}_c$

$$-(n-2F)\Psi(x_c) \leq f_{i,\sigma(t)}(x_c, x_{a_i}) \leq (n-2F)\Psi(x_c). \quad (17)$$

It was shown in the proof of Theorem 1 that under either (i) or (ii), $\lim_{t \to \infty} \Psi(x_c(t)) = 0$. Hence, (17) implies

$$\lim_{t \to \infty} f_{i,\sigma(t)}(x_c, x_a) = 0,$$

and thus $\lim_{t \to \infty} x_i(t)$ exists. Since $\mathcal{H}_0$ is compact, Lemma 2 implies the result. $\square$

4.3 Necessary Condition

Next, we consider the following necessary condition for ARC-P to achieve agreement in networks with fixed topology.

THEOREM 3. *Consider a networked multi-agent system that executes ARC-P with parameter $F \in \mathbb{Z}_{\geq 0}$ and at most $F < n$ malicious or Byzantine agents. If the agreement condition is satisfied, then $\delta^{\text{in}}(\mathcal{D}_s) \geq 2F$.*

PROOF. The case $F = 0$ is vacuously true, so assume $F \geq 1$. Suppose $\exists i \in \mathcal{V}_c$ with $d_i^{\text{in}} < 2F$ and $\exists \epsilon > 0$ such that $x_j(0) - x_i(0) > \epsilon \ \forall j \in \mathcal{V}_c \setminus \{i\}$. If $d_i^{\text{in}} \geq F-1$, let $F-1$ of i's in-neighbors be adversaries with values smaller than $x_i(0)$. Then, $\dot{x}_i \equiv 0$ since both the cooperative and adversary values are removed. On the other hand, using Lemma 2 while treating i as an adversary, ensures $x_j(t) - x_i(t) > \epsilon \ \forall j \in \mathcal{V}_c \setminus \{i\}$ and $t \geq 0$. $\square$

Recall that the sufficient conditions imply the necessary condition, $\delta^{\text{in}}(\mathcal{D}_s) \geq 2F$. However, the converse is clearly not true. The question then arises, are the sufficient conditions also necessary? The answer is no, but we delay further discussion of the conservativeness of the sufficient conditions until Section 5. Next, we study the sufficient conditions under switching network topologies.

4.4 Switching Topology

Switching network topologies can arise from a number of factors: temporary removal of edges due to lossy communication channels, the addition or loss of edges caused by mobile agents, and so on. The results of the previous sections may be extended to switching topologies in a straightforward manner by assuming $\mathcal{D}_{\sigma(t)} \in \Gamma_{M,F}$ or $\mathcal{D}_{\sigma(t)} \in \Gamma_{B,F}$ for $t \geq 0$ whenever the adversaries are malicious or Byzantine, respectively. It is shown in Theorem 1 that Ψ is a Lyapunov function for each possible digraph $\mathcal{D}_s \in \Gamma_{M,F}$ or $\mathcal{D}_s \in \Gamma_{B,F}$. Further, the upper bound on convergence of x_c to $\mathcal{A}$ (15) holds globally and for each digraph $\mathcal{D}_s \in \Gamma_{M,F}$ or $\mathcal{D}_s \in \Gamma_{B,F}$. Therefore, Ψ is a common Lyapunov function, thus proving global exponential convergence of x_c to $\mathcal{A}$ for the switched system (1). On the other hand, Lemma 2 and (17) hold for all network topologies. Therefore, the same argument used in the proof of Theorem 2 may be used for the case of switching topologies. Hence, we have the following result.

COROLLARY 1. *Suppose each cooperative agent in $\mathcal{V}_c$ executes ARC-P with parameter $F \in \mathbb{Z}_{\geq 0}$ and at most (i) F malicious agents with $\mathcal{D}_{\sigma(t)} \in \Gamma_{M,F}$ for all $t \in \mathbb{R}_{\geq 0}$, or (ii) F Byzantine agents with $\mathcal{D}_{\sigma(t)} \in \Gamma_{B,F}$ for all $t \in \mathbb{R}_{\geq 0}$. Then the agreement condition (2) is satisfied with the convergence to the agreement space bounded by (15), and the safety condition (3) is satisfied. Therefore, under these conditions, ARC-P **solves** the adversarial asymptotic agreement problem in the presence of (i) malicious and (ii) Byzantine agents.*

So far we have studied explicit switching in the network topology when the range of the switching signal is appropriately restricted

10

(i.e., $\mathcal{D}_{\sigma(t)} \in \Gamma_{M,F}$ or $\mathcal{D}_{\sigma(t)} \in \Gamma_{B,F}$ for all $t \in \mathbb{R}_{\geq 0}$). But, even in fixed network topology, the algorithm ARC-P may be viewed as the linear consensus protocol of [14] with state-dependent switching. In ARC-P, the sort and reduce functions effectively remove the influence of a subset of neighbors based on the state values of those neighbors. The remaining relative states are summed as input to the integrator in the same manner as all of the neighbors are in the linear consensus protocol of [14], which justifies the analogy. Hence, the results of Section 4.2 provide new insight into the convergence of the protocol of [14] with state-dependent switching.

5. EXAMINATION OF CONDITIONS

In this section, we examine the conditions $M1_F$ and $M2_F$ that define $\Gamma_{M,F}$ and $B1_F$ and $B2_F$ that define $\Gamma_{B,F}$. Important questions arise with regard to these properties: (i) How do these conditions relate to known conditions on the maximum number of Byzantine processors in the network [1,7]; (ii) How do they relate to conditions on the connectivity of the network when reaching agreement with Byzantine processors [1], or detecting and isolating malicious agents [18,24]; (iii) How conservative are the conditions with respect to achieving the adversarial agreement problem using ARC-P; and (iv) How applicable are the conditions to networks of interest? The first question has been answered in Section 4.2, where we showed that $B1_F$ and $B2_F$ imply $n > 3F$, which is a necessary condition when dealing with Byzantine behavior of finite automata in synchronous networks [1,7]. The rest of this section is devoted to addressing the remaining questions.

To address (ii), we show that $M1_F$ and $M2_F$–and therefore also $B1_F$ and $B2_F$–imply $\kappa(\mathcal{D}) \geq 2F + 1$, which is a necessary and sufficient condition for the existence of an algorithm that can (a) ensure agreement of the nonfaulty nodes in the presence of at most F Byzantine nodes in synchronous networks [1], or (b) detect and isolate up to F malicious nodes in linear consensus networks [18, 24].

THEOREM 4. *If $F \in \{0, 1, \ldots, \lfloor n/2 \rfloor - 1\}$ and the digraph satisfies (i) $M1_F$ or (ii) $M2_F$, then $\mathcal{D}$ is $2F + 1$-connected.*

PROOF. (i) Fix $F \in \{0, 1, \ldots, \lfloor n/2 \rfloor - 1\}$ and consider the underlying graph $\mathcal{G}$, which must satisfy $\delta(\mathcal{G}) \geq \lfloor n/2 \rfloor + F$. By Menger's Theorem, $\kappa(\mathcal{G}) \geq 2F + 1$ is equivalent to $\mathcal{G}$ having at least $2F + 1$ vertex-disjoint paths between any distinct vertices $i, j \in \mathcal{V}$. Indeed, this is the case if $|\mathcal{J}_i \cap \mathcal{J}_j| \geq 2F + 2$ for all $i, j \in \mathcal{V}$. On the other hand, we know that $|\mathcal{J}_i \cap \mathcal{J}_j| \geq 2F + 1$ (c.f. the proof of Theorem 1). From this we conclude that if $(i, j) \notin \mathcal{E}_\mathcal{G}$ then there are at least $2F + 1$ vertex-disjoint paths between i and j. Therefore, assume there exists $i, j \in \mathcal{V}$ such that $(i, j) \in \mathcal{E}_\mathcal{G}$ and $|\mathcal{J}_i \cap \mathcal{J}_j| = 2F + 1$. In this case, there are $2F$ vertex-disjoint paths accounted for with vertices in $\mathcal{J}_i \cap \mathcal{J}_j$. But, because $F \leq \lfloor n/2 \rfloor - 1$, we know

$$|\mathcal{J}_i|, |\mathcal{J}_j| \geq \lfloor n/2 \rfloor + F + 1 \geq 2F + 2,$$

which means there exists $i' \in \mathcal{J}_i \setminus \mathcal{J}_i \cap \mathcal{J}_j$ and $j' \in \mathcal{J}_j \setminus \mathcal{J}_i \cap \mathcal{J}_j$. If $(i', j') \in \mathcal{E}_\mathcal{G}$, then i, i', j', j is the last vertex-disjoint path necessary to conclude $2F + 1$-connectivity. If $(i', j') \notin \mathcal{E}_\mathcal{G}$, then we know that $|\mathcal{J}_{i'} \cap \mathcal{J}_{j'}| \geq 2F + 1$, and there are at most $2F - 1$ vertices in $(\mathcal{J}_{i'} \cap \mathcal{J}_{j'}) \cap (\mathcal{J}_i \cap \mathcal{J}_j)$ because i and j cannot be in $\mathcal{J}_{i'} \cap \mathcal{J}_{j'}$. Hence, there exists $m \in \mathcal{J}_{i'} \cap \mathcal{J}_{j'} \setminus \mathcal{J}_i \cap \mathcal{J}_j$, so that i, i', m, j', j is the last vertex-disjoint path necessary to conclude $2F + 1$-connectivity.

(ii) Any vertex cut must contain at least $2F + 1$ vertices, because otherwise a vertex remains in $\mathcal{S}$ adjacent to all other vertices. $\quad\square$

To address the conservativeness of the conditions with respect to convergence of ARC-P, we show that we can do no better using

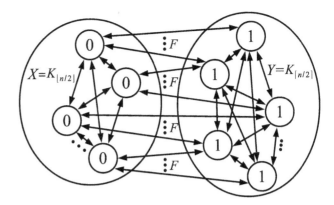

Figure 2: Relax $M1_F$ with $\delta^{\mathrm{in}}(\mathcal{D}) = \lfloor n/2 \rfloor + F - 1$.

traditional metrics such as in-degree, out-degree, or connectivity. We do this by demonstrating that minimally relaxing these conditions leads to pathological examples with high connectivity in which ARC-P does not achieve agreement.

Example 1 [Relax $M1_F$ with $\delta^{\mathrm{in}}(\mathcal{D}) = \lfloor n/2 \rfloor + F - 1$]. Consider the network topology in Figure 2, in which $K_{\lceil n/2 \rceil}$ is the complete digraph on $\lceil n/2 \rceil$ vertices, and each vertex in X has exactly F neighbors in Y and each vertex in Y has either $F - 1$ or F neighbors in X. Now, assume there are no adversaries and let all states in X have value 0 and all states in Y have value 1. Then, by (5), all agents in X will remove the influence of their neighbor in Y and vice versa. Hence, no consensus is reached, and no agent even changes its state. Furthermore, this graph is $(\lfloor n/2 \rfloor + F - 1)$-connected, which for large n may be much larger than $\kappa(\mathcal{D}) \geq 2F + 1$.

From this example, we see that reducing the minimum in-degree by just one from $M1_F$ is not sufficient for global convergence of x_c to $\mathcal{A}$. Additionally, in this example, the connectivity is very high. This suggests that the minimum in-degree and connectivity are not appropriate metrics to use in characterizing the network topologies in which ARC-P achieves agreement. The following example demonstrates that the minimum out-degree is also inadequate and further emphasizes the inadequacy of connectivity. Here, the number of nodes in $\mathcal{S}$ from $M2_F$ is reduced by one.

Example 2 [Relax $M2_F$ with $|\mathcal{S}| = 2F$ and $d_i^{\mathrm{out}} = n - 2, \forall i \in \mathcal{V} \setminus \mathcal{S}$, so that $\delta^{\mathrm{out}}(\mathcal{D}) = n - 2$]. Consider the example of Figure 3, which has $|\mathcal{S}| = 2F$, with $\mathcal{S} = \mathcal{S}' \cup \{j\}$ and $d_i^{\mathrm{in}} = n - 2, \forall i \in \mathcal{V} \setminus \mathcal{S}$, so that $\delta^{\mathrm{out}}(\mathcal{D}) = n - 2$. Since $d_j^{\mathrm{in}} = 2F - 1$, this example does not satisfy the necessary condition of Theorem 3. The argument in the proof shows that the agreement condition is not satisfied. Since the underlying graph is complete, this digraph is $(n - 1)$-connected, which emphasizes the inadequacy of connectivity in characterizing the convergence properties of ARC-P.

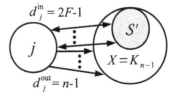

Figure 3: Relax $M2_F$ with $|\mathcal{S}| = 2F$ and $\delta^{\mathrm{out}}(\mathcal{D}) = n - 2$.

Example 3 [Relax $B1_F$ with $\delta^{\mathrm{in}}(\mathcal{D}) = n/2 + \lfloor 3F/2 \rfloor - 1$ if n is even and F is odd, and $\delta^{\mathrm{in}}(\mathcal{D}) = \lfloor n/2 \rfloor + \lceil 3F/2 \rceil - 1$ otherwise]. Consider the digraph shown in Figure 4. In the figure, the digraph is partitioned into 3 cliques (i.e., complete subdigraphs), $\mathcal{D} = X_1 \cup X_2 \cup X_3$, and each clique has $\lfloor n/2 \rfloor - \lfloor F/2 \rfloor$, F, and $\lceil n/2 \rceil - \lceil F/2 \rceil$ nodes, respectively. For clarity, we do not show edges internal to the cliques. We only show one representative node from the sets X_1 and X_3, but all nodes in each of these sets have F in-neighbors in each of the other two sets–which is possible since $n > 3F$. This leads to an in-degree of $d_i^{in} = \lfloor n/2 \rfloor + \lceil 3F/2 \rceil - 1$ for each $i \in X_1$, and an in-degree of $d_j^{in} = \lceil n/2 \rceil + \lfloor 3F/2 \rfloor - 1$ for each $j \in X_3$. On the other hand, the nodes in X_2 exchange information bidirectionally with all other nodes, so that $d_k^{in} = d_k^{out} = n - 1$ for all $k \in X_2$. Therefore, the minimum in-degree depends on the parity of n and F. If they have the same parity, $|X_1| = |X_3|$, and $\delta^{in}(\mathcal{D}) = \lfloor n/2 \rfloor + \lceil 3F/2 \rceil - 1$. If n is odd and F is even, $|X_3| = |X_1| + 1$, and $\delta^{in}(\mathcal{D}) = \lfloor n/2 \rfloor + \lceil 3F/2 \rceil - 1$. But, if n is even and F is odd, $|X_3| = |X_1| - 1$, and $\delta^{in}(\mathcal{D}) = n/2 + \lfloor 3F/2 \rfloor - 1$, which means, in any case, $B1_F$ is minimally relaxed.

To show that ARC-P may not achieve agreement in this digraph, let each node in X_1 and X_3 have initial value 1 and 3, respectively. Suppose all nodes in X_2 are Byzantine, and they transmit a constant trajectory of 1 to nodes in X_1 and 3 to nodes in X_3. Then nodes in X_1 remove the influence from their F neighbors in X_3 and vice versa, so that agreement fails.

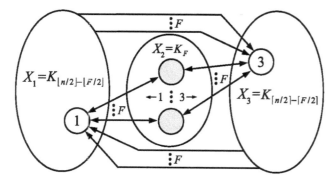

Figure 4: Relax $B1_F$ with $\delta^{in}(\mathcal{D}) = n/2 + \lfloor 3F/2 \rfloor - 1$ **if n is even and F is odd, and** $\delta^{in}(\mathcal{D}) = \lfloor n/2 \rfloor + \lceil 3F/2 \rceil - 1$ **otherwise.**

Example 4 [Relax $B2_F$ with $|\mathcal{S}| = 3F$ and $\mathcal{S} = S_1 \cup S_2 \cup S_3$]. Consider the digraph in Figure 5. In this example, $\mathcal{S} = S_1 \cup S_2 \cup S_3$, with $|S_i| = F$ for $i = 1, 2, 3$. The remaining nodes in $\mathcal{V} \setminus \mathcal{S}$ form a clique, K_{n-3F}. Nodes in S_1 and S_3 have value 1 and 3, respectively, and nodes in $\mathcal{V} \setminus \mathcal{S}$ have value 2. Nodes in S_2 are Byzantine and send values 1, 2, and 3, respectively, to nodes in S_1, $\mathcal{V} \setminus \mathcal{S}$, and S_3. Clearly, as in the previous examples, the cooperative nodes do not reach agreement, but remain fixed at their initial values.

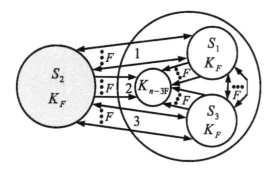

Figure 5: Relax $B2_F$ with $|\mathcal{S}| = 3F$ and $\mathcal{S} = S_1 \cup S_2 \cup S_3$.

Although this section is replete with pathological examples in which ARC-P fails to achieve agreement–even when the networks

have high minimum degrees and high connectivity–the news is not all bad. First, we now know that the sufficient conditions studied in Section 4.2 are the best we can have using minimum degrees and connectivity. Second, we can discern a pattern in the various examples. A common property is that there are pairs of subsets with high connectivity within the subsets, but nodes in each subset have relatively few in-neighbors outside of their subsets. Therefore, new toplogical conditions for digraphs that deal with (a) pairs of subsets of nodes and (b) the number of nodes with "enough" in-neighbors outside of their respective subset will be crucial to better understanding the convergence properties of ARC-P. Finally, we end the section by demonstrating the results with the following example.

Example 5: [Morale dynamics on fixed topology with single Byzantine agent] Consider a variation of the Byzantine generals problem in which the loyal generals attempt to improve the morale of their troops and reach consensus on the level of morale despite the influence of a subset of Byzantine generals. In addition, the troops have no knowledge of the goal of the generals. For the purposes of this example, the state value represents the level of morale. The sign of the value indicates either good (positive) or bad (negative) morale and the magnitude signifies the relative levels of morale. Here, we assume that the morale dynamics of each node behave as an integrator with the input (influence) either given by ARC-P, as in (5), or simply by the sum of relative morale values:

$$\dot{x}_i(t) = \sum_{j \in \mathcal{N}_i} (x_j(t) - x_i(t)), \; x_i(0) = x_{0_i}, \quad (18)$$

where $x_i(t)$ is the morale value of node i and x_{0_i} is the initial morale value of node i. We refer to the influence rule of (18) as the linear consensus protocol (LCP), which is a special case of the weighted sum of relative states studied extensively in the literature [14], and has been compared with ARC-P in the special case of complete networks in [8].

Each general is able to continuously influence all of the troops and the other generals, and the generals can provide different influence to different individuals. The influence network is shown in Figure 6, in which nodes 17 through 20 form a clique and are the generals (shown as squares). The other nodes are the troops (shown as circles). Troop i has initial morale $-i$, for $i = 1, \ldots, 16$, and the generals have initial morale of 1, 2, 3, and 4, respectively, for nodes 17, 18, 19, and 20.

The central question of this example is whether either LCP or ARC-P can ensure that the troops reach asymptotic consensus on a positive morale given that it is possible that one of the generals is Byzantine (i.e., $F = 1$). Observe that the network of Figure 6 satisfies $B2_F$ whenever $F = 1$, with $\mathcal{S} = \{17, 18, 19, 20\}$, and can therefore sustain the compromise of a single node as Byzantine whenever the troops and loyal generals use ARC-P. In this case, we choose node 20 to be the Byzantine general. In order to elude detection, the Byzantine general conveys a morale trajectory that satisfies the preassigned strategy–either ARC-P or LCP–to the other generals. But, to the troops, the Byzantine general conveys a highly negative morale of -87.5. The results for LCP and ARC-P are shown in Figure 7. The Byzantine morale trajectory shown in the figures is the one conveyed to the other generals. Using LCP, the troops reach consensus at a negative morale of -20 and the generals reach consensus at 2.5, whereas with ARC-P the troops reach consensus at the same value of the other generals at 2.5.

This example illustrates an important property of ARC-P: *It only requires local information for resilience against adversaries.* In contrast, without nonlocal information, the detection and identification techniques of [16–19, 22–25] would not successfully detect the Byzantine general. This is because from the perspective of the

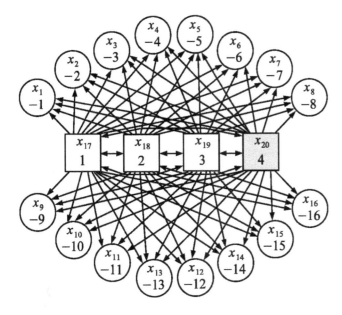

Figure 6: Influence network in which square nodes are generals and circular nodes are troops. Node 20 is Byzantine.

loyal generals, the Byzantine general behaves as it should and they receive no feedback from the troops. From the perspective of the troops, the Byzantine general appears to be influenced by no other node. Hence, without prior knowledge of at least some nonlocal aspects of the network topology, the Byzantine general remains undetected.

6. RELATED WORK

The research most closely related to this work is [16–19, 22–25]. In [16], the issue of detecting and identifying a single misbehaving agent using a linear iterative strategy in discrete-time synchronous networks is introduced. Then, Sundaram and Hadjicostis show in [22] that $\kappa(G) \geq 2F + 1$ is a necessary condition for detecting and identifying up to F malicious agents using linear iterations in synchronous networks. In the companion paper [23], $\kappa(G) \geq 2F + 1$ is shown to be sufficient for the problem. In this case, the linearity of the protocol is exploited so that every node is able to calculate the initial values exactly, and thus any function of the initial states, in at most n steps. The results of [22, 23] are generalized in [24] to characterize under which conditions any subset of nodes can obtain all of the initial values.

The authors of [16], later extend the analysis done in [22, 23] by characterizing the type of behavior of the malicious agents that is most troublesome to the linear network and by characterizing the network connectivity required to tolerate both malicious agents and non-colluding agents in [17]. A computationally expensive but exact algorithm is presented in [17] to detect and identify up to F malicious agents in networks with connectivity at least $2F + 1$. This exact algorithm requires each node to know the topology of the entire network. In [19], two approaches are considered to reduce the computational complexity and require only partial network information. The first assumes the network is comprised of weakly interconnected subcomponents and restricts the behavior of the misbehaving nodes. The second imposes a hierarchical structure to detect and isolate the malicious agents. These results are combined and extended in [18].

In [25], the authors study detection and identification of cyber attacks on networked control systems modeled as continuous-time

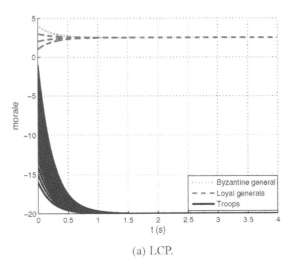

(a) LCP.

(b) ARC-P.

Figure 7: Byzantine general attempts to reduce morale of the troops. Byzantine morale shown is the one conveyed to other generals. Byzantine morale conveyed to troops is -87.5. ARC-P succeeds in the goal of improving the morale while reaching consensus, but LCP fails.

linear systems. Attacks on nodes and on their outgoing communication channels are both studied, and it is shown that from the perspective of other nodes, the two cases are indistinguishable. As in [18], unknown input observers are used for the FDI scheme. The approach is demonstrated on a network of nodes using the linear consensus protocol of (18) augmented with the FDI scheme, and on the swing equation of a power network.

There are several differences between the related works and this paper. First, the aforementioned works require nonlocal information on the network topology to ensure consensus. ARC-P requires *only local information*. Second, the computational burden of the FDI algorithms is greater than ARC-P, which is low complexity. Third, we study directed information flow in both fixed and switching topologies. The FDI schemes would not be able to handle this case because of the nonlocal information required on the network topology. Fourth, the other works do not consider safety conditions and are therefore not suitable for safety critical applications. Lastly, we study both malicious and Byzantine agents, whereas the aforementioned works do not consider Byzantine agents.

Finally, the reader may wonder how this paper relates to robust consensus algorithms designed to withstand outliers [9, 13]. The problem of robust consensus to outliers does not assume a threat model, such as malicious or Byzantine nodes. Instead, some measurements may be statistical outliers caused by noisy measurements and the goal is to reach consensus on the measurements in a manner that reduces the error introduced by the outliers. In these works the nodes with outlier measurements are cooperative in the consensus process. Therefore, such techniques are not designed to work in the presence of adversaries.

7. CONCLUSIONS

In this paper, we have studied a low complexity protocol (algorithm), ARC-P, for reaching consensus in networked multi-agent systems with adversaries. We formulated a consensus problem, the adversarial asymptotic agreement problem, appropriate for distributed control applications. We defined two different models for adversaries depending on how information is conveyed. Malicious agents must convey the same information to each neighbor, whereas Byzantine agents may convey different information to each neighbor. We analyzed the convergence properties of ARC-P in directed networks with fixed and switching topologies in the presence of malicious and Byzantine agents, while restricting the range of the switching signal so that each topology satisfies sufficient conditions on the in-degrees and out-degrees of nodes in the network. Finally, we examined the conservativeness of the conditions.

Based on the examples in Section 5, it is clear that traditional graph theoretic metrics like minimum degree and connectivity are not suitable for characterizing under which conditions ARC-P ensures agreement. Therefore, to ascertain conditions which are both necessary and sufficient, new graph theoretic metrics are needed.

8. ACKNOWLEDGMENTS

The authors would like to thank Shreyas Sundaram for suggesting the example of Figure 2. This work is supported in part by the National Science Foundation (CNS-1035655, CCF-0820088), the U.S. Army Research Office (ARO W911NF-10-1-0005), and Lockheed Martin.

9. REFERENCES

[1] D. Dolev. The Byzantine generals strike again. *Journal of Algorithms*. 3(1):14 – 30, 1982.

[2] D. Dolev, N. A. Lynch, S. S. Pinter, E. W. Stark, and W. E. Weihl. Reaching approximate agreement in the presence of faults. *Journal of the ACM*, 33(3):499 – 516, 1986.

[3] J. A. Fax and R. M. Murray. Information flow and cooperative control of vehicle formations. *IEEE Trans. on Aut. Control*, 49(9):1465 – 1476, 2004.

[4] D. Geller and F. Harary. Connectivity in digraphs. In *Recent Trends in Graph Theory*, volume 186 of *Lect. Notes in Math.*, pages 105–115. Springer Berlin / Heidelberg, 1971.

[5] V. Gupta, C. Langbort, and R. Murray. On the robustness of distributed algorithms. In *IEEE Conf. on Decision and Control*, Dec. 2006.

[6] T. T. Johnson and S. Mitra. Safe flocking in spite of actuator faults using directional failure detectors. *Journal of Nonlinear Sys. and App.*, 2(1-2):73–95, 2011.

[7] L. Lamport, R. Shostak, and M. Pease. The Byzantine generals problem. *ACM Trans. Program. Lang. Syst.*, 4(3):382–401, 1982.

[8] H. J. LeBlanc and X. D. Koutsoukos. Consensus in networked multi-agent systems with adversaries. In *Proc. of the 14th Int. Conf. on Hybrid systems: Computation and Control*, (HSCC '11), pages 281–290, Chicago, IL, 2011.

[9] J. Li, E. Elhamifar, I.-J. Wang, and R. Vidal. Consensus with robustness to outliers via distributed optimization. In *IEEE Conf. on Decision and Control*, pages 2111–2117, Dec. 2010.

[10] D. Liberzon. *Switching in Systems and Control*. Birkhauser, Boston, MA, USA, 2003.

[11] N. A. Lynch. *Distributed Algorithms*. Morgan Kaufmann Publishers Inc., San Francisco, California, 1997.

[12] M. Mesbahi and M. Egerstedt. *Graph Theoretic Methods in Multiagent Networks*. Princeton University Press, Princeton, New Jersey, 2010.

[13] E. Montijano, S. Martínez, and S. Sagués. De-RANSAC: robust distributed consensus in sensor networks. *IEEE Transactions on Systems, Man, and Cybernetics: part B*. Submitted, May 2010.

[14] R. Olfati-Saber, J. A. Fax, and R. M. Murray. Consensus and cooperation in networked multi-agent systems. *Proceedings of the IEEE*, 95(1):215–233, 2007.

[15] R. Olfati-Saber, E. Franco, E. Frazzoli, and J. Shamma. Belief consensus and distributed hypothesis testing in sensor networks. In *Networked Embedded Sensing and Control*, volume 331 of *Lecture Notes in Control and Information Sciences*, pages 169–182. Springer Berlin / Heidelberg, 2006.

[16] F. Pasqualetti, A. Bicchi, and F. Bullo. Distributed intrusion detection for secure consensus computations. In *IEEE Conf. on Decision and Control*, pages 5594 –5599, Dec. 2007.

[17] F. Pasqualetti, A. Bicchi, and F. Bullo. On the security of linear consensus networks. In *IEEE Conf. on Decision and Control*, pages 4894 – 4901, Dec. 2009.

[18] F. Pasqualetti, A. Bicchi, and F. Bullo. Consensus computation in unreliable networks: A system theoretic approach. *IEEE Trans. on Aut. Control*, 57(1):90–104, Jan. 2012.

[19] F. Pasqualetti, R. Carli, A. Bicchi, and F. Bullo. Identifying cyber attacks under local model information. In *IEEE Conf. on Decision and Control*, pages 5961–5966, Dec. 2010.

[20] M. Pease, R. Shostak, and L. Lamport. Reaching agreement in the presence of faults. *J. ACM*, 27(2):228–234, 1980.

[21] N. Rouche, P. Habets, and M. Laloy. *Stability Theory by Liapunov's Direct Method*, volume 22 of *Applied Mathematical Sciences*. Springer-Verlag, New York, 1977.

[22] S. Sundaram and C. Hadjicostis. Distributed function calculation via linear iterations in the presence of malicious agents; part I: Attacking the network. In *American Control Conf.*, pages 1350 –1355, June 2008.

[23] S. Sundaram and C. Hadjicostis. Distributed function calculation via linear iterations in the presence of malicious agents; part II: Overcoming malicious behavior. In *American Control Conf.*, pages 1356 –1361, June 2008.

[24] S. Sundaram and C. Hadjicostis. Distributed function calculation via linear iterative strategies in the presence of malicious agents. *IEEE Trans. on Aut. Control*, 56(7):1495 –1508, July 2011.

[25] A. Teixeira, H. Sandberg, and K.H. Johansson. Networked control systems under cyber attacks with applications to power networks. In *American Control Conf.*, pages 3690–3696, July 2010.

[26] J. N. Tsitsiklis. *Problems in Decentralized Decision Making and Computation*. PhD thesis, Dept of EECS, MIT, 1984.

Compositional Safety Analysis using Barrier Certificates *

Christoffer Sloth
Department of Computer
Science
Aalborg University
9220 Aalborg East, Denmark
csloth@cs.aau.dk

George J. Pappas
Department of Electrical and
Systems Engineering
University of Pennsylvania
Philadelphia, PA 19104 USA
pappasg@seas.upenn.edu

Rafael Wisniewski
Section for Automation &
Control
Aalborg University
9220 Aalborg East, Denmark
raf@es.aau.dk

ABSTRACT

This paper proposes a compositional method for verifying the safety of a dynamical system, given as an interconnection of subsystems. The safety verification is conducted by the use of the barrier certificate method; hence, the contribution of this paper is to show how to obtain compositional conditions for safety verification.

We show how to formulate the verification problem, as a composition of coupled subproblems, each given for one subsystem. Furthermore, we show how to find the compositional barrier certificates via linear and sum of squares programming problems.

The proposed method makes it possible to verify the safety of higher dimensional systems, than the method for centrally computed barrier certificates. This is demonstrated by verifying the safety of an emergency shutdown of a wind turbine.

Categories and Subject Descriptors

I.6.4 [**Simulation and Modeling**]: Model Validation and Analysis

General Terms

Verification,Theory

Keywords

Compositionality, Safety analysis, Dynamical systems, Reachable sets, Sum of squares

1. INTRODUCTION

Safety verification is an important part of developing a control system. Safety verification ensures that a control system does not violate any state constraints. Numerous methods have been developed for verifying the safety of a

*This work was supported by MT-LAB, a VKR Centre of Excellence for the Modeling of Information Technology.

system; see [5] for a review. These methods range over analytical methods, numerical simulation-based methods, and discrete abstraction methods.

The safety verification determines if the reachable states of a system intersect a set of unsafe states. Computing the reachable states of a dynamical system is in general very difficult, as seen in [9]; hence, it may only be possible for systems of low dimension. Therefore, several methods have been developed to approximate the reachable set of a dynamical system. In [4], the reachable states are approximated based on simulated trajectories, by exploiting that trajectories initialized close to each other stay in the proximity of each other.

Another class of methods, e.g., [1] verifies the safety of a system, by using the vector field to find invariant sets that do not include the unsafe states. Similarly, the papers [13, 12], provide a method for calculating barrier certificates for safety analysis of continuous, stochastic, and hybrid systems. The idea of these works is to find a barrier function that is decreasing along system trajectories, and has a zero level set (a so called barrier), which no solution trajectory crosses. If the set of initial states is a subset of the zero sublevel set of the barrier function, and the set of unsafe states is in its complement, then the system is safe.

Common to the previously mentioned methods is that they verify the safety of a system, by studying a system directly. However, it may be beneficial to study a system as an interconnection of subsystems, and decompose the verification problem into smaller subproblems. This is suggested for compositional stability analysis in [16].

In this paper, we show how the barrier certificates in [13, 12] can be generated for a system, given as an interconnection of subsystems. Compositional conditions are given for finding barrier certificates. Additionally, linear matrix inequalities (LMIs) and sum of squares (SOS) are used to generate the barrier certificates, which are solved numerically, by use of SOSTOOLS for MATLAB [14].

The paper is organized as follows. Section 2 explains the verification problem in terms of barrier certificates, and Section 3 explains how to reformulate the verification problem by a composition of certificates generated individually for each subsystem. Section 4 shows how to compute the barrier certificates, both via LMIs and polynomial inequalities. Section 5 demonstrates the use of the method, by proving safety of a shutdown procedure for a wind turbine, and Section 6 comprises conclusions.

2. SAFETY VERIFICATION USING BARRIER CERTIFICATES

In this section, we present the barrier certificate method, which can be used to verify the safety of a dynamical system.

We consider a continuous system given as a system of ordinary differential equations

$$\dot{x} = f(x, d), \tag{1}$$

where $x \in \mathbb{R}^n$ is the state and $d \in D \subseteq \mathbb{R}^m$ is the disturbance input.

For some measurable and essentially bounded disturbance function $\bar{d} : \mathbb{R}_{\geq 0} \to D$, i.e., $\bar{d} \in \mathcal{L}_\infty(\mathbb{R}_{\geq 0}, D)$, we denote the solution of the Cauchy problem (1) with $x(0) = x_0$ on an interval $[0, T]$ by $\phi_{x_0}^{\bar{d}}$, i.e.,

$$\frac{d\phi_{x_0}^{\bar{d}}(t)}{dt} = f\left(\phi_{x_0}^{\bar{d}}(t), \bar{d}(t)\right) \tag{2}$$

for almost all $t \in [0, T]$.

We consider a system given by $\Gamma = (f, X, X_0, X_u, D)$, where $f : \mathbb{R}^{n+m} \to \mathbb{R}^n$ is continuous, $X \subseteq \mathbb{R}^n$, $X_0 \subseteq X$, $X_u \subseteq X$, and $D \subseteq \mathbb{R}^m$. In the safety verification, we only consider trajectories initialized in X_0 that are contained in the set X. We verify if there exists a trajectory that can reach an unsafe set X_u.

For a map $f : A \to B$ and subset $C \subset A$, we write $f(C) \equiv \{f(x)| x \in C\}$. Thus, the safety of a system Γ is defined as follows.

DEFINITION 1 (SAFETY). *Let $\Gamma = (f, X, X_0, X_u, D)$ be given. A trajectory $\phi_{X_0}^{\bar{d}} : [0, T] \to \mathbb{R}^n$ is unsafe if there exists a time $t \in [0, T]$ and a disturbance $\bar{d} \in \mathcal{L}_\infty(\mathbb{R}_{\geq 0}, D)$, such that $\phi_{X_0}^{\bar{d}}([0, t]) \cap X_u \neq \emptyset$ and $\phi_{X_0}^{\bar{d}}([0, t]) \subseteq X$.*

We say that a system Γ is safe if there are no unsafe trajectories.

For a function $f : \mathbb{R}^n \to \mathbb{R}$, $\mathcal{Z}(f)$ denotes the set

$$\mathcal{Z}(f) = \{x \in \mathbb{R}^n | f(x) = 0\}. \tag{3}$$

The safety property can be verified using the following.

PROPOSITION 1 (STRICT BARRIER CERTIFICATE [13]). *Let $\Gamma = (f, X, X_0, X_u, D)$ be given. If there exists a differentiable function $B : X \to \mathbb{R}$ satisfying*

$$B(x) \leq 0 \quad \forall x \in X_0, \tag{4a}$$
$$B(x) > 0 \quad \forall x \in X_u, \text{ and} \tag{4b}$$
$$\frac{\partial B}{\partial x}(x)f(x, d) < 0 \quad \forall(x, d) \in \mathcal{Z}(B) \times D. \tag{4c}$$

Then the system Γ is safe.

Proposition 1 states that a trajectory initialized within the zero sublevel set of a function B, cannot cross the zero level set $\mathcal{Z}(B)$, if B is decreasing (along system trajectories) on the zero level set. This is illustrated in Figure 1.

The set of barrier certificates satisfying Proposition 1 is nonconvex, due to (4c). However, the following more conservative proposition has a convex set of feasible barrier certificates. The convexity property becomes apparent in the computation of the barrier certificates in Section 4.

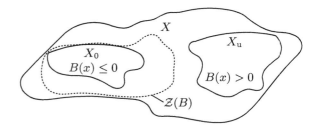

Figure 1: Illustration of a set X, which contains the initial set X_0 and the unsafe set X_u. The dashed line illustrates the zero level set of B.

COROLLARY 1 (WEAK BARRIER CERTIFICATE [13, 12]). *Let $\Gamma = (f, X, X_0, X_u, D)$ be given. If there exists a differentiable function $B : X \to \mathbb{R}$ satisfying*

$$B(x) \leq 0 \quad \forall x \in X_0, \tag{5a}$$
$$B(x) > 0 \quad \forall x \in X_u, \text{ and} \tag{5b}$$
$$\frac{\partial B}{\partial x}(x)f(x, d) \leq 0 \quad \forall(x, d) \in X \times D. \tag{5c}$$

Then the system Γ is safe.

Corollary 1 states that a trajectory of a system initialized in a state within the zero sublevel set of a nonincreasing function (along system trajectories), cannot reach the complement of the zero sublevel set.

The difference between Proposition 1 and Corollary 1 is that (5c), in contrast to (4c), must hold for all states and all disturbances. Additionally, the inequality constraint (4c) is strict weathers it is weak in (5c).

3. COMPOSITIONAL BARRIER CERTIFICATES

In this section, we assume that a dynamical system is given as an interconnection of subsystems. This allows the safety verification to be split up into smaller subproblems in addition to some coupling constraints.

To provide an overview of the proposed compositional setup, we initially consider an example from [16], consisting of three interconnected subsystems. The interconnection of the three subsystems is shown in Figure 2. Properties of the interconnected system are to be analyzed by studying its components as isolated systems, in conjunction with their coupling.

Let each subsystem be described by a system of continuous ordinary differential equations and an output map

$$\Sigma_1 : \begin{cases} \dot{x}_1 = f_1(x_1, d_1, u_1) \\ y_1 = h_1(x_1) \end{cases} \tag{6a}$$

$$\Sigma_2 : \begin{cases} \dot{x}_2 = f_2(x_2, d_2, u_2) \\ y_2 = h_2(x_2) \end{cases} \tag{6b}$$

$$\Sigma_3 : \begin{cases} \dot{x}_3 = f_3(x_3, d_3, u_3) \\ y_3 = h_3(x_3), \end{cases} \tag{6c}$$

where $x_i \in X_i \subseteq \mathbb{R}^{n_i}$ is the state, $d_i \in D_i \subseteq \mathbb{R}^{m_i}$ is the disturbance, and $u_i \in \mathbb{R}^{q_i}$ is an interconnection input, given by $u_i = g_i(x_1, \ldots, \hat{x}_i, \ldots, x_k)$. Here, $\hat{x}_i$ indicates that x_i is removed. Additionally, $y_i \in \mathbb{R}^{r_i}$ is an interconnection

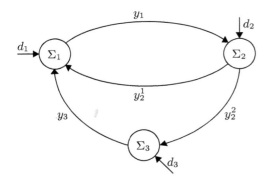

Figure 2: **Interconnection of three subsystems** $\Sigma_1, \Sigma_2, \Sigma_3$.

output, given by the map $h_i : \mathbb{R}^{n_i} \to \mathbb{R}^{r_i}$. Note that the interconnection of the subsystems gives a relation between u_i and y_i. In Figure 2, $y_2 = (y_2^1, y_2^2)$, $u_1 = (y_2^1, y_3)$, $u_2 = y_1$, and $u_3 = y_2^2$.

The output y_i belongs to the set

$$Y_i \equiv h_i(X_i) \subseteq \mathbb{R}^{r_i}. \tag{7a}$$

Similarly, u_i belongs to the set

$$U_i \equiv g_i(X_1, \ldots, \hat{X}_i, \ldots, X_k) \subseteq \mathbb{R}^{q_i}. \tag{7b}$$

In the remainder of the paper, we present a method for generating barrier certificates for some general topology of the interconnection of subsystems.

Let $k \in \mathbb{N}$ be the number of subsystems. For $i = 1, \ldots, k$ we consider a system $\Gamma = (\{f_i\}, \{X_i\}, \{X_{0,i}\}, \{X_{u,i}\}, \{D_i\})$, where $\{f_i\}$ is a collection of continuous vector fields with $f_i : \mathbb{R}^{n_i + m_i + q_i} \to \mathbb{R}^{n_i}$, $X_i \subseteq \mathbb{R}^{n_i}$, $X_{0,i}, X_{u,i} \subseteq X_i$, and $D_i \subseteq \mathbb{R}^{m_i}$. Let

$$X = X_1 \times \cdots \times X_k \subseteq \mathbb{R}^n, \tag{8a}$$
$$X_0 = X_{0,1} \times \cdots \times X_{0,k} \subseteq X, \tag{8b}$$
$$X_u = X_{u,1} \times \cdots \times X_{u,k} \subseteq X, \tag{8c}$$
$$D = D_1 \times \cdots \times D_k \subseteq \mathbb{R}^m, \tag{8d}$$
$$U = U_1 \times \cdots \times U_k \subseteq \mathbb{R}^q, \text{and} \tag{8e}$$
$$Y = Y_1 \times \cdots \times Y_k \subseteq \mathbb{R}^r. \tag{8f}$$

REMARK 1. *The assumption that the sets X and D are given as cartesian products of X_i and D_i in (8), limits the sets that can be directly expressed; however, by using multiple sets, the original set can, in principle, be approximated. Therefore, the previous restriction does not theoretically restrict the method, but it may complicate the computations involved in the safety verification.*

In the following, we present two lemmas that show how to compose the inequality constraints on the barrier function and its derivative in Proposition 1 into separate constraints for the subsystems and coupling constraints. We omit the proofs of both lemmas, as they are straightforward.

In Lemma 1, we let the vector field be given as an interconnection of subsystems, and show that (4c) can be composed into an inequality constraint for each subsystem, and a coupling constraint.

LEMMA 1. *Let $k \in \mathbb{N}$. Let $x = (x_1, \ldots, x_k) \in X$, $d = (d_1, \ldots, d_k) \in D$, $u = (u_1, \ldots, u_k) \in U$, $y = (y_1, \ldots, y_k) \in$*

Y, *where X, D, U, Y are given as shown in (8). For $i = 1, \ldots, k$ let*

$$\begin{bmatrix} \dot{x}_1 \\ \vdots \\ \dot{x}_k \end{bmatrix} = \begin{bmatrix} f_1(x_1, d_1, u_1) \\ \vdots \\ f_k(x_k, d_k, u_k) \end{bmatrix} = f(x, d), \tag{9a}$$

$$u_i = g_i(x_1, \ldots, \hat{x}_i, \ldots, x_k), \tag{9b}$$

$$y_i = h_i(x_i). \tag{9c}$$

Suppose that there is a bijective map $\Upsilon : U \to Y$.

Then there exists a continuous function $\varphi : \mathbb{R}^n \to \mathbb{R}$ such that

$$\varphi(x)f(x, d) < 0 \quad \forall (x, d) \in X \times D \tag{10}$$

if for $i = 1, \ldots, k$ there exist continuous functions $\varphi_i : \mathbb{R}^{n_i} \to \mathbb{R}$ and $\gamma_i : \mathbb{R}^{q_i + r_i} \to \mathbb{R}$ such that for all $(x_i, d_i, u_i) \in X_i \times D_i \times U_i$

$$\varphi_i(x_i)f_i(x_i, d_i, u_i) < \gamma_i(u_i, h(x_i)) \quad and \tag{11a}$$

$$\sum_i \gamma_i(u_i, h(x_i)) \leq 0. \tag{11b}$$

Lemma 1 can be used to decompose (4c) into an inequality constraint for each subsystem in addition to a coupling constraint.

LEMMA 2. *Let $k \in \mathbb{N}$. For $i = 1, \ldots, k$ let $f_i : \mathbb{R}^{n_i} \to \mathbb{R}$ be a continuous function, and $X_i \subseteq \mathbb{R}^{n_i}$ be compact. There exists a constant $c_i \in \mathbb{R}$ for all i such that*

$$f_i(x_i) - c_i \leq 0 \quad \forall x_i \in X_i \quad and \tag{12a}$$

$$\sum_i c_i \leq 0 \quad \forall x_i \in X_i \tag{12b}$$

if and only if

$$\sum_i f_i(x_i) \leq 0 \quad \forall x_i \in X_i. \tag{13}$$

Using Lemma 1 and Lemma 2, we rewrite Proposition 1 as follows.

PROPOSITION 2. *Let $k \in \mathbb{N}$ and let the dynamical system $\Gamma = (\{f_i\}, \{X_i\}, \{X_{0,i}\}, \{X_{u,i}\}, \{D_i\})$ be given. If there exist differentiable functions $B_i : X_i \to \mathbb{R}$, constants $\alpha_i, \beta_i \in \mathbb{R}$, and functions $\gamma_i : \mathbb{R}^{q_i + r_i} \to \mathbb{R}$ for $i = 1, \ldots, k$ such that*

$$B_i(x_i) + \alpha_i \leq 0 \quad \forall x_i \in X_{0,i}, \tag{14a}$$

$$B_i(x_i) - \beta_i > 0 \quad \forall x_i \in X_{u,i}, \tag{14b}$$

$$\frac{\partial B_i}{\partial x_i}(x_i)f_i(x_i, d_i, u_i) < \gamma_i(u_i, h_i(x_i)) \tag{14c}$$
$$\text{for all } u_i \in U_i, x_i \in \mathcal{Z}(B_i), d_i \in D_i,$$

and for all $u_i \in U_i$, $x_i \in \mathcal{Z}(B_i)$

$$\sum_i \alpha_i \geq 0, \ \sum_i \beta_i \geq 0, \ \sum_i \gamma_i(u_i, h_i(x_i)) \leq 0. \tag{14d}$$

Then the system Γ is safe.

PROOF. We show that Proposition 2 ensures that the conditions in Proposition 1 are satisfied. Let $x \equiv (x_1, \ldots, x_k)^{\mathrm{T}}$ and $B : \mathbb{R}^{n_1 + \cdots + n_k} \to \mathbb{R}$ be defined as $B(x) = \sum_i B_i(x_i)$.

By Lemma 2, (14a) and (14b) are by the satisfaction of (14d) equivalent to

$$B(x) \leq 0 \quad \forall x \in X_0, \tag{15a}$$

$$B(x) > 0 \quad \forall x \in X_{\mathrm{u}}. \tag{15b}$$

Finally, by (14c) and (14d)

$$\sum_i \frac{\partial B_i}{\partial x_i}(x_i) f(x_i, d_i, u_i) < \sum_i \gamma_i(u_i, h_i(x_i)) \leq 0 \tag{15c}$$

$$for \ all \ u_i \in U_i, \ x_i \in \mathcal{Z}(B_i), \ d_i \in D_i.$$

This is by Lemma 1 equivalent to (4c). Hereby, the system Γ is safe. $\square$

The inequality constraints (14a)-(14c) must be satisfied for each subsystem, and (14d) couples the subproblems. Notice that the function B is decreasing along the solution, but each function B_i is not necessarily decreasing along the solution.

In the following, we rewrite Corollary 1 using the same technique.

COROLLARY 2. *Let $k \in \mathbb{N}$ and let the dynamical system $\Gamma = (\{f_i\}, \{X_i\}, \{X_{0,i}\}, \{X_{\mathrm{u},i}\}, \{D_i\})$ be given. If there exist differentiable functions $B_i : X_i \to \mathbb{R}$, constants $\alpha_i, \beta_i \in \mathbb{R}$, and functions $\gamma_i : \mathbb{R}^{q_i + r_i} \to \mathbb{R}$ for $i = 1, \ldots, k$ such that*

$$B_i(x_i) + \alpha_i \leq 0 \quad \forall x_i \in X_{0,i}, \tag{16a}$$

$$B_i(x_i) - \beta_i > 0 \quad \forall x_i \in X_{\mathrm{u},i}, \tag{16b}$$

$$\frac{\partial B_i}{\partial x_i}(x_i) f_i(x_i, d_i, u_i) \leq \gamma_i(u_i, h_i(x_i)) \tag{16c}$$

$$for \ all \ u_i \in U_i, \ x_i \in X_i, \ d_i \in D_i,$$

and for all $u_i \in U_i$, $x_i \in X_i$

$$\sum_i \alpha_i \geq 0, \ \sum_i \beta_i \geq 0, \ \sum_i \gamma_i(u_i, h_i(x_i)) \leq 0. \tag{16d}$$

Then the system Γ is safe.

Proposition 2 and Corollary 2 provide compositional conditions for the safety verification. In the next section, we show how to compute the barrier certificates.

4. COMPUTATION OF BARRIER CERTIFICATES

In this section, we show how to compute barrier certificates from the conditions set up in Section 2 and Section 3.

Remark that any desired computational method may be applied to find the barrier certificates, and that different methods can be applied on different subproblems for the compositional conditions in Section 3. This is beneficial if some subsystems are linear and others are polynomial.

To demonstrate the computation of barrier certificates, we show how to compute the barrier certificates using sum of squares programming and linear programming. The primary focus is on sum of squares programming, as it is a generalization of linear programming. Therefore, we only explicitly formulate LMI conditions for the solution of Corollary 2.

To do the computations in a tool such as MATLAB, we restrict the vector fields to be linear (for linear programs) and polynomial (for sum of squares programs). Furthermore, we parameterize the barrier certificates as polynomials, respectively quadratic forms, and require the invariant, initial,

unsafe, and disturbance sets to be given by linear and polynomial equality or inequality constraints.

First, we set up some notation about polynomials.

DEFINITION 2 (POLYNOMIAL [10]). *A polynomial p in n variables $x_1, \ldots, x_n$ is a finite linear combination of monomials*

$$p(x) = \sum_{\alpha} c_{\alpha} x^{\alpha} = \sum_{\alpha} c_{\alpha} x_1^{\alpha_1} \cdot \ldots \cdot x_n^{\alpha_n}, \tag{17}$$

where $c_{\alpha} \in \mathbb{R}$ and the sum is over a finite number of n-tuples $\alpha = [\alpha_1, \ldots, \alpha_n]$ with $\alpha_i \geq 0$.

The total degree of a monomial x^{α} is $\alpha_1 + \cdots + \alpha_n$. Additionally, the total degree of a polynomial is equal to the highest degree of its component monomials. The degree of a polynomial p is denoted by $\deg(p)$.

We only consider polynomials with real valued variables, and denote the set of polynomials in n variables by $\mathcal{P}_n$. Recall that a map $f : \mathbb{R}^n \to \mathbb{R}^m$ is said to be polynomial if its coordinate functions are polynomials, i.e., $f_i \in \mathcal{P}_n$ for $i = 1, \ldots, m$; hence, $f \in \mathcal{P}_n^m$.

Sum of squares polynomials are used in the generation of safety certificates and are explained in the following, based on [10].

DEFINITION 3. *A polynomial $p \in \mathcal{P}_n$ is called sum of squares (SOS) if*

$$p = \sum_{i=1}^{k} p_i^2 \tag{18}$$

for some polynomials $p_i \in \mathcal{P}_n$ with $i = 1, \ldots, k$.

We denote the set of sum of squares polynomials in n variables by Σ_n.

The set of sum of squares polynomials is a subset of non-negative polynomials [10], which can be treated using semidefinite programming, as described below.

The existence of a sum of squares decomposition of a polynomial $p \in \mathcal{P}_n$, with $d = \deg(p)$, can be expressed as a semidefinite programming feasibility problem. Therefore, the formulation of a problem as sum of squares makes the problem computationally tractable; however, the number of decision variables in the program is

$$N = \binom{n + 2d}{2d} = \frac{(n+2d)!}{2d! n!}. \tag{19}$$

In the search for sum of squares polynomials, it is exploited that the existence of a SOS decomposition of a polynomial p is equivalent to the existence of a positive semidefinite matrix $Q = Q^{\mathrm{T}} \geq 0$ such that

$$p = Z^{\mathrm{T}} Q Z, \tag{20}$$

where Z is a vector of monomials of degree less than or equal to half the degree of p.

Let $k, l \in \mathbb{N}$, let $\alpha_{i,j} \in \mathcal{P}_n$ for $(i, j) \in \{1, \ldots, l\} \times \{1, \ldots, k\}$, and $w_j \in \mathbb{R}$. An SOS programming problem is

$$\underset{(c_1, \ldots, c_k) \in \mathbb{R}^k}{\text{minimize}} \sum_{j=1}^{k} w_j c_j \text{ subject to} \tag{21a}$$

$$\alpha_{i,0} + \sum_{j=1}^{k} \alpha_{i,j} c_j \text{ is SOS } \forall i = 1, \ldots, l. \tag{21b}$$

It is seen that an SOS programming problem is a minimization of a linear cost, subject to SOS feasibility constraints.

4.1 Computation of Barrier Certificates

To compute barrier certificates using sum of squares programming, we restrict the vector fields to be polynomial. Furthermore, the invariant, initial, unsafe, and disturbance sets must be semialgebraic sets, i.e., be given by polynomial inequalities, as follows.

Let $g_X : \mathbb{R}^n \to \mathbb{R}^{k_X}$, $g_{X_0} : \mathbb{R}^n \to \mathbb{R}^{k_{X_0}}$, $g_{X_u} : \mathbb{R}^n \to \mathbb{R}^{k_{X_u}}$, and $g_D : \mathbb{R}^m \to \mathbb{R}^{k_D}$ for some $k_X, k_{X_0}, k_{X_u}, k_D \in \mathbb{N}$ be given as vectors of polynomials $g_i \in \mathcal{P}_n$, i.e., for example $g_X \in \mathcal{P}_n^{k_X}$ and $g_X = [g_1, \ldots, g_{k_X}]^{\mathrm{T}}$. Then

$$X \equiv \{x \in \mathbb{R}^n | g_X(x) \geq 0\}, \tag{22a}$$

$$X_0 \equiv \{x \in \mathbb{R}^n | g_{X_0}(x) \geq 0\}, \tag{22b}$$

$$X_u \equiv \{x \in \mathbb{R}^n | g_{X_u}(x) \geq 0\}, \tag{22c}$$

$$D \equiv \{d \in \mathbb{R}^m | g_D(d) \geq 0\}, \tag{22d}$$

where the inequalities in (22) are satisfied *entry-wise*.

EXAMPLE 1. *We show how* (22) *can be used to form a cylindrical set. Let* $x \in \mathbb{R}^3$, $x_{1,\min}, x_{1,\max}, x_{2,c}, x_{3,c}, r \in \mathbb{R}$ *and* g_X *be*

$$g_X(x) = \begin{bmatrix} (x_1 - x_{1,\min})(x_{1,\max} - x_1) \\ r^2 - (x_2 - x_{2,c})^2 - (x_3 - x_{3,c})^2 \end{bmatrix}. \tag{23}$$

It is seen that $g_X(x) \geq 0$, *when* $x_1 \in [x_{1,\min}, x_{1,\max}]$ *and* (x_2, x_3) *is in the disk centered at* $(x_{2,c}, x_{3,c})$ *with radius* r. *This implies that the set* X *given by* (22a) *and* (23) *is a cylinder.*

In the computation of barrier certificates, we use a generalization of the $\mathcal{S}$-procedure [2], which is shown in Lemma 3.

LEMMA 3. *Let* V *be a subset of* $X \subseteq \mathbb{R}^n$. *Let* $f \in \mathcal{P}_n$ *and* $g \in \mathcal{P}_n^k$. *Suppose* $g(x) \geq 0$ *(element-wise) for any* $x \in V$. *If*

1. $\lambda \in \Sigma_n^k$ *and*

2. $f - \lambda^{\mathrm{T}} g \in \Sigma_n$.

Then $f(x) \geq 0$ *for all* $x \in V$.

Now we can compute barrier certificates that satisfy Proposition 1 using sum of squares.

PROPOSITION 3. *Let the system* $\Gamma = (f, X, X_0, X_u, D)$ *and polynomials* g_* *shown in* (22) *be given, and let* $\epsilon_1, \epsilon_2 > 0$. *If there exist* $B \in \mathcal{P}_n$, $\lambda_{X_0} \in \Sigma_n^{k_{X_0}}$, $\lambda_{X_u} \in \Sigma_n^{k_{X_u}}$, $\lambda_B \in \mathcal{P}_{n+m}$, *and* $\lambda_D \in \Sigma_{n+m}^{k_D}$ *such that*

$$-B - \lambda_{X_0}^{\mathrm{T}} g_{X_0}, \tag{24a}$$

$$B - \epsilon_1 - \lambda_{X_u}^{\mathrm{T}} g_{X_u}, \; and \tag{24b}$$

$$-\frac{\partial B}{\partial x} f - \epsilon_2 - \lambda_D^{\mathrm{T}} g_D - \lambda_B^{\mathrm{T}} B \tag{24c}$$

are sum of squares. Then the system Γ *is safe.*

As Proposition 3 follows directly from Proposition 20 in [13], no proof is provided. However, all conditions follow directly from Lemma 3. Consider (24a), where $B \in \mathcal{P}_n$, $g_{X_0} \in \mathcal{P}_n^{k_{X_0}}$, $\lambda_{X_0} \in \Sigma_n^{k_{X_0}}$, (24a)$\in \Sigma_n$, and $g_{X_0}(x) \geq 0$ for any $x \in X_0$. Then $B(x) \leq 0$ for all $x \in X_0$.

Note that (24c) contains a scalar product between λ_B and B, which are both unknown. This is the reason why the conditions in Proposition 3 cannot be found directly by an SOS programming problem, neither by a linear program for

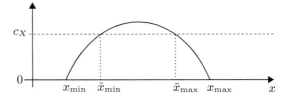

Figure 3: Illustration of g_X and the sets $X = [x_{\min}, x_{\max}]$ and $\tilde{X} = [\tilde{x}_{\min}, \tilde{x}_{\max}]$, given by g_X and $\tilde{g}_X$.

quadratic B. Therefore, we generate an iterative algorithm for solving the problem. This algorithm is similar to iterative algorithms used for solving bilinear matrix inequalities via LMIs, see [6].

In the following iterative algorithm, it is necessary to get a feasible solution in each step. Therefore, the barrier certificate is initially found for only a subset of the disturbances $\tilde{D} \subseteq D$, initial conditions $\tilde{X}_0 \subseteq X_0$, etc., to ease the feasibility. Let $c_X \in \mathbb{R}^{k_X}_{\geq 0}$ be a vector of nonnegative numbers. Let $\tilde{g}_X = g_X - c_X$ and define

$$\tilde{X} \equiv \{x \in \mathbb{R}^n | \tilde{g}_X(x) \geq 0\} \subseteq X. \tag{25}$$

By decreasing each entry of c_X, the set $\tilde{X}$ is enlarged, and if $c_X = 0$ then $\tilde{X} = X$. This is illustrated in Figure 3 for a set given by $g_X(x) = (x - x_{\min})(x_{\max} - x)$.

It is seen that the map g_X generates the set $X = [x_{\min}, x_{\max}]$ and $\tilde{X} = [\tilde{x}_{\min}, \tilde{x}_{\max}]$. If c_X is greater than the maximum value of g_X, then $\tilde{X} = \emptyset$.

ALGORITHM 1. *Let the system* $\Gamma = (f, X, X_0, X_u, D)$ *and polynomials* g_* *shown in* (22) *be given.*

0. **Initialization:** *Choose vectors* $c_{X_0} \in \mathbb{R}^{k_{X_0}}_{\geq 0}, c_{X_u} \in \mathbb{R}^{k_{X_u}}_{\geq 0}, c_D \in \mathbb{R}^{k_D}_{\geq 0}$ *such that each entry* $c_{i,*}$ *is sufficiently large and define polynomials* $\tilde{g}_* \equiv g_* - c_*$. *Choose* $\epsilon_1, \epsilon_2 > 0$ *and specify a polynomial* $\lambda_B \in \mathcal{P}_{n+m}$, *e.g., by choosing* $\lambda_B = 0$ *or* 1. *Find* $B \in \mathcal{P}_n$, $\lambda_{X_0} \in \Sigma_n^{k_{X_0}}$, $\lambda_{X_u} \in \Sigma_n^{k_{X_u}}$, *and* $\lambda_D \in \Sigma_{n+m}^{k_D}$ *such that*

$$-B - \lambda_{X_0}^{\mathrm{T}} \tilde{g}_{X_0}, \tag{26a}$$

$$B - \epsilon_1 - \lambda_{X_u}^{\mathrm{T}} \tilde{g}_{X_u}, \; and \tag{26b}$$

$$-\frac{\partial B}{\partial x} f - \epsilon_2 - \lambda_D^{\mathrm{T}} \tilde{g}_D - \lambda_B^{\mathrm{T}} B \tag{26c}$$

are sum of squares.

1. **Fix the barrier certificate:** *Fix* B *obtained from the previous step. Choose vectors* $\Delta c_* \geq 0$ *and update* c_*, *such that* $c_* := c_* - \Delta c_*$ *and redefine the polynomials* $\tilde{g}_* \equiv g_* - c_*$. *Find* $\lambda_{X_0} \in \Sigma_n^{k_{X_0}}$, $\lambda_{X_u} \in \Sigma_n^{k_{X_u}}$, $\lambda_B \in \mathcal{P}_{n+m}$, *and* $\lambda_D \in \Sigma_{n+m}^{k_D}$ *such that* (26) *are sum of squares.*

2. **Fix multiplier:** *Fix* λ_B *obtained in the previous step. Choose vectors* $\Delta c_* \geq 0$ *and update* c_*, *such that* $c_* := c_* - \Delta c_*$ *and redefine the polynomials* $\tilde{g}_* \equiv g_* - c_*$. *Find* $B \in \mathcal{P}_n$, $\lambda_{X_0} \in \Sigma_n^{k_{X_0}}$, $\lambda_{X_u} \in \Sigma_n^{k_{X_u}}$, *and* $\lambda_D \in \Sigma_{n+m}^{k_D}$ *such that* (26) *are sum of squares.*

If all entries of the vector c_* *are zero, then terminate the algorithm; otherwise, go to step 1.*

If Algorithm 1 terminates, then Γ is safe.

Algorithm 1 alternates between freezing the coefficients of λ_B and B, to remove the product between the two unknown polynomials in (26c). Furthermore, the set of disturbances and the sets for which B should be positive or negative are initially smaller than D, X_0 and X_u and are gradually enlarged until they are equal to X_0 and X_u. In the enlargement of the sets, it is important that a feasible solution is found in each step of the algorithm. Notice that Algorithm 1 is not guaranteed to terminate or converge to the global optimum; however, this is a general problem with non-convex optimization problems, see e.g. [7].

Corollary 1 can be solved directly, via the following SOS programming problem.

COROLLARY 3. *Let the system* $\Gamma = (f, X, X_0, X_u, D)$ *and polynomials* g_* *shown in (22) be given, and let* $\epsilon_1 > 0$. *If there exist* $B \in \mathcal{P}_n$, $\lambda_{X_0} \in \Sigma_n^{k_{X_0}}$, $\lambda_{X_u} \in \Sigma_n^{k_{X_u}}$, $\lambda_X \in \Sigma_{n+m}^{k_X}$, *and* $\lambda_D \in \Sigma_{n+m}^{k_D}$ *such that*

$$-B - \lambda_{X_0}^{\mathrm{T}} g_{X_0}, \tag{27a}$$

$$B - \epsilon_1 - \lambda_{X_u}^{\mathrm{T}} g_{X_u}, \text{ and} \tag{27b}$$

$$-\frac{\partial B}{\partial x} f - \lambda_X^{\mathrm{T}} g_X - \lambda_D^{\mathrm{T}} g_D \tag{27c}$$

are sum of squares. Then the system Γ *is safe.*

4.2 Computation of Compositional Barrier Certificates

In this subsection, we show how barrier certificates can be expressed in a compositional manner, using SOS optimization for Proposition 2 and Corollary 2, and using LMIs for Corollary 2. The interconnected system can be formulated as one system, but this would increase the number of decision variables involved in the safety verification, compared to the proposed compositional approach. This is an important issue when working with SOS optimization, and is apparent from (19).

Let $k \in \mathbb{N}$ be the number of subsystems, and define $g_* \in \mathcal{P}^{k_*}$. In the decomposition, the considered sets are restricted, as shown in (8), where

$$X_i \equiv \{x_i \in \mathbb{R}^{n_i} | g_{X_i}(x_i) \geq 0\}, \tag{28a}$$

$$X_{0,i} \equiv \{x_i \in \mathbb{R}^{n_i} | g_{X_{0,i}}(x_i) \geq 0\}, \tag{28b}$$

$$X_{u,i} \equiv \{x_i \in \mathbb{R}^{n_i} | g_{X_{u,i}}(x_i) \geq 0\}, \tag{28c}$$

$$D_i \equiv \{d_i \in \mathbb{R}^{m_i} | g_{D_i}(d_i) \geq 0\}, \tag{28d}$$

$$U_i \equiv \{u_i \in \mathbb{R}^{q_i} | g_{U_i}(u_i) \geq 0\}. \tag{28e}$$

Proposition 2 is written in terms of SOS in the following.

PROPOSITION 4. *Let* $k \in \mathbb{N}$, *the polynomials* g_* *shown in (28) and the system* $\Gamma = (\{f_i\}, \{X_i\}, \{X_{0,i}\}, \{X_{u,i}\}, \{D_i\})$ *be given, and let* $\epsilon_1, \epsilon_2 > 0$. *If there exist* $B_i \in \mathcal{P}_{n_i}$, $\alpha_i \in \mathbb{R}$, $\beta_i \in \mathbb{R}$, $\gamma_i \in \mathcal{P}_{q_i+r_i}$, $\lambda_{X_{0,i}} \in \Sigma_{n_i}^{k_{X_{0,i}}}$, $\lambda_{X_{u,i}} \in \Sigma_{n_i}^{k_{X_{u,i}}}$, $\lambda_{B_i} \in \mathcal{P}_{n_i+m_i+q_i}$, $\lambda_{D_i} \in \Sigma_{n_i+m_i+q_i}^{k_{D_i}}$, *and* $\lambda_{U_i} \in \Sigma_{n_i+m_i+q_i}^{k_{U_i}}$ *such that*

$$-B_i - \lambda_{X_{0,i}}^{\mathrm{T}} g_{X_{0,i}} - \alpha_i, \tag{29a}$$

$$B_i - \epsilon_1 - \lambda_{X_{u,i}}^{\mathrm{T}} g_{X_{u,i}} - \beta_i, \text{ and} \tag{29b}$$

$$-\frac{\partial B_i}{\partial x_i} f_i - \epsilon_2 + \gamma_i - \lambda_{D_i}^{\mathrm{T}} g_{D_i} - \lambda_{B_i}^{\mathrm{T}} B_i - \lambda_{U_i}^{\mathrm{T}} g_{U_i} \tag{29c}$$

are sum of squares and

$$\sum_i \alpha_i, \sum_i \beta_i, \text{ and } -\sum_i \gamma_i \tag{29d}$$

are sum of squares. Then the system Γ *is safe.*

Proposition 4 has a product between $\lambda_{B_i}^{\mathrm{T}}$ and B_i, which implies that Algorithm 1 must be used to solve it. Additionally, dual decomposition should be used to decompose the conditions; however, this is only demonstrated for the following SOS program for solving Corollary 2.

COROLLARY 4. *Let* $k \in \mathbb{N}$, *the polynomials* g_* *shown in (28) and the system* $\Gamma = (\{f_i\}, \{X_i\}, \{X_{0,i}\}, \{X_{u,i}\}, \{D_i\})$ *be given, and let* $\epsilon_1 > 0$. *If there exist* $B \in \mathcal{P}_{n_i}$, $\alpha_i \in \mathbb{R}$, $\beta_i \in \mathbb{R}$, $\gamma_i \in \mathcal{P}_{q_i+r_i}$, $\lambda_{X_{0,i}} \in \Sigma_{n_i}^{k_{X_{0,i}}}$, $\lambda_{X_{u,i}} \in \Sigma_{n_i}^{k_{X_{u,i}}}$, $\lambda_{X_i} \in \Sigma_{n_i+m_i+q_i}^{k_{X_i}}$, $\lambda_{D_i} \in \Sigma_{n_i+m_i+q_i}^{k_{D_i}}$, *and* $\lambda_{U_i} \in \Sigma_{n_i+m_i+q_i}^{k_{U_i}}$ *such that*

$$-B_i - \lambda_{X_{0,i}}^{\mathrm{T}} g_{X_{0,i}} - \alpha_i, \tag{30a}$$

$$B_i - \epsilon_1 - \lambda_{X_{u,i}}^{\mathrm{T}} g_{X_{u,i}} - \beta_i, \text{ and} \tag{30b}$$

$$-\frac{\partial B_i}{\partial x_i} f_i + \gamma_i - \lambda_{X_i}^{\mathrm{T}} g_{X_i} - \lambda_{D_i}^{\mathrm{T}} g_{D_i} - \lambda_{U_i}^{\mathrm{T}} g_{U_i} \tag{30c}$$

are sum of squares and

$$\sum_i \alpha_i, \sum_i \beta_i, \text{ and } -\sum_i \gamma_i. \tag{30d}$$

are sum of squares. Then the system Γ *is safe.*

In the following, we show how to prove safety using LMIs based on Corollary 2. The vector field f_i is given by

$$\dot{x} = A_i x_i + B_{1,i} d_i + B_{2,i} u_i \tag{31a}$$

$$y_i = C_i x_i, \tag{31b}$$

where A_i is an $n_i \times n_i$ matrix, $B_{1,i}$ is an $n_i \times m_i$ matrix, $B_{2,i}$ is an $n_i \times m_i$ matrix, and C_i is an $q_i \times n_i$ matrix. We say that $B_i(x_i) = x_i^{\mathrm{T}} P_i x_i$, $g_*(x_i) = x_i^{\mathrm{T}} G_* x_i$ where P_i and G_* are symmetric matrices, and $\alpha_i, \beta_i \in \mathbb{R}$. Furthermore, we define γ_i as

$$\gamma_i = \begin{bmatrix} u_i \\ x_i \end{bmatrix}^{\mathrm{T}} \begin{bmatrix} \Gamma_{u,i} & 0 \\ 0 & \Gamma_{x,i} \end{bmatrix} \begin{bmatrix} u_i \\ x_i \end{bmatrix}, \tag{32}$$

where $\Gamma_{u,i}$ and $\Gamma_{x,i}$ are diagonal matrices.

COROLLARY 5. *Let* $k \in \mathbb{N}$, *the polynomials* g_* *shown in (28) and the system* $\Gamma = (\{f_i\}, \{X_i\}, \{X_{0,i}\}, \{X_{u,i}\}, \{D_i\})$ *be given, where* $\{f_i\}$ *is a collection of linear vector fields, and* G_* *is symmetric. If there exist* $P_i = P_i^{\mathrm{T}}$, $\alpha_i, \beta_i \in \mathbb{R}$, *and matrices* $\Gamma_{u,i}, \Gamma_{x,i}$ *given in (32),* $\lambda_{X_{0,i}} \in \mathbb{R}_{\geq 0}$, $\lambda_{X_i} \in \mathbb{R}_{\geq 0}$, $\lambda_{D_i} \in \mathbb{R}_{\geq 0}$, *and* $\lambda_{U_i} \in \mathbb{R}_{\geq 0}$ *such that*

$$-P_i - \lambda_{X_{0,i}} G_{X_{0,i}} - \alpha_i I \geq 0 \tag{33a}$$

$$P_i - \lambda_{X_i} G_{X_i} - \beta_i I > 0, \text{ and} \tag{33b}$$

$$\begin{bmatrix} A_i^{\mathrm{T}} P_i + P_i A_i + \lambda_{X_i} G_{X_i} & P_i B_{1,i} & P_i B_{2,i} & C^{\mathrm{T}} \\ B_{1,i}^{\mathrm{T}} P_i & \lambda_{D_i} G_{D_i} & 0 & 0 \\ B_{2,i}^{\mathrm{T}} P_i & 0 & \lambda_{U_i} G_{U_i} - \Gamma_{u,i} & 0 \\ C & 0 & 0 & -\Gamma_{x,i} \end{bmatrix} < 0, \tag{33c}$$

20

and

$$\sum_i \alpha_i \geq 0, \ \sum_i \beta_i \geq 0, \ \sum_i \gamma_i \leq 0. \qquad (33\text{d})$$

Then the system Γ is safe.

To practically solve the safety problem in Corollary 4, we set up an optimization problem by use of dual decomposition [3]. Dual decomposition can be used to solve different types of optimization problems. We consider only the following type of optimization problem.

$$\text{minimize } f(x) = f_1(x_1, y) + f_2(x_2, y) \text{ subject to}$$
$$x_1 \in C_1, \ x_2 \in C_2, \ h_1(x_1, y) + h_2(x_2, y) \leq 0. \qquad (34)$$

We decompose (34) into two separate optimization problems, which are coupled through some additional decision variables as follows

$$\text{minimize } f(x) = f_1(x_1, y_1) + f_2(x_2, y_2) \text{ subject to}$$
$$x_1 \in C_1, \ x_2 \in C_2, \ y_1 = y_2, \ h_1(x_1, y_1) + h_2(x_2, y_2) \leq 0.$$

The dual problem can be set up, as f_1 and f_2 have no shared variables. The Lagrangian for the problem is

$$L(x_1, y_1, x_2, y_2, \lambda_1, \lambda_2) = f_1(x_1, y_1) + f_2(x_2, y_2)$$
$$+ \lambda_1^{\text{T}}(y_1 - y_2) + \lambda_2 \left(h_1(x_1, y_1) + h_2(x_2, y_2) \right). \qquad (35)$$

Let $\lambda = (\lambda_1, \lambda_2)$. The dual function becomes

$$\varphi(\lambda_1, \lambda_2) = \varphi_1(\lambda_1, \lambda_2) + \varphi_2(\lambda_1, \lambda_2), \qquad (36)$$

where

$$\varphi_1(\lambda) = \inf_{x_1, y_1} \left(f_1(x_1, y_1) + \lambda_1^{\text{T}} y_1 + \lambda_2 h_1(x_1, y_1) \right), \qquad (37\text{a})$$

$$\varphi_2(\lambda) = \inf_{x_2, y_2} \left(f_2(x_2, y_2) - \lambda_1^{\text{T}} y_2 + \lambda_2 h_2(x_2, y_2) \right). \qquad (37\text{b})$$

The optimization problems for φ_1 and φ_2 can be solved independently, given values for λ_1 and λ_2. Finally, the master problem is

$$\text{maximize } \varphi_1(\lambda_1, \lambda_2) + \varphi_2(\lambda_1, \lambda_2), \qquad (38)$$

with variables λ_1 and λ_2.

To solve the master problem, we utilize the subgradient algorithm given in [15]. Note that all functions in this paper are polynomial, thus differentiable; hence, other gradient methods can be used instead of the subgradient method.

Let $f : \mathbb{R}^n \to \mathbb{R}$ be a convex function, and let $x, y \in \mathbb{R}^n$. Then any vector $g \in \mathbb{R}^n$ that satisfies

$$f(y) \geq f(x) + g^{\text{T}}(y - x) \qquad (39)$$

is called a subgradient at x.

Let $f : \mathbb{R}^n \to \mathbb{R}$ be a convex function. Then the subgradient algorithm gives a sequence of points $\{x^{(k)}\}_{k=0}^{\infty}$ according to

$$x^{(k+1)} = x^{(k)} - \Delta_k g^{(k)}, \qquad (40)$$

where $x^{(k)}$ is the kth iterate, $x^{(0)}$ is the initial point, $g^{(k)}$ is a subgradient of f at $x^{(k)}$, and Δ_k is the step size. When the function f to be minimized is differentiable, then $g^{(k)}$ is the unique gradient of f at point $x^{(k)}$.

For diminishing step size, the algorithm is guaranteed to converge to the optimal value, see [11]. Therefore, we use the following diminishing step size

$$\Delta_k = \frac{a}{b+k}, \qquad (41)$$

where $a > 0$ and $b \geq 0$.

The following algorithm is used to solve the dual decomposition for the problem shown in (34). Note that we denote by $\bar{x}_1^{(k)}$ and $\bar{y}_1^{(k)}$ the optimal values of x_1 and y_1 for problem (37a) at iteration k, given some λ_1, λ_2.

ALGORITHM 2. *Given an optimization problem, as shown in* (34).

0. **Initialization:** *Let $k = 0$, define the step size Δ_k, and choose some $\lambda_1^{(0)}, \lambda_2^{(0)}, \epsilon > 0$.*

1. **Solve subproblems:**
   Solve (37a) *to find $\bar{x}_1^{(k)}$ and $\bar{y}_1^{(k)}$,
   solve* (37b) *to find $\bar{x}_2^{(k)}$ and $\bar{y}_2^{(k)}$.*

2. **Update dual variables:**
   $\lambda_1^{(k+1)} := \lambda_1^{(k)} - \Delta_k (\bar{y}_2^{(k)} - \bar{y}_1^{(k)})$,
   $\lambda_2^{(k+1)} := \lambda_2^{(k)} + \Delta_k (h_1(\bar{x}_1^{(k)}, \bar{y}_1^{(k)}) + h_2(\bar{x}_2^{(k)}, \bar{y}_2^{(k)}))$,
   $k := k + 1$.
   If $|\lambda_1^{(k+1)} - \lambda_1^{(k)}| > \epsilon$, then go to step 1. Otherwise, terminate the algorithm.

Note that step 2 in Algorithm 2 tries to maximize (38).

The first observation in the considered problem is that γ_i has to be a diagonal matrix; otherwise, the cost of the optimization problem is not linear. For convenience, we let $\bar{\gamma}_i$ be a vector containing the diagonal elements of γ_i. Let $\lambda \equiv (\lambda_1, \lambda_2, \lambda_3)$ the dual function is

$$\varphi(\lambda) = \sum_i \varphi_i(\lambda), \qquad (42)$$

where

$$\varphi_i(\lambda) \equiv \inf_{\alpha_i, \beta_i, \bar{\gamma}_i} -\lambda_1 \alpha_i - \lambda_2 \beta_i + \lambda_3^{\text{T}} \bar{\gamma}_i \qquad (43)$$

subject to

$$- B_i - \lambda_{X_{0,i}}^{\text{T}} g_{X_{0,i}} - \alpha_i, \qquad (44\text{a})$$

$$B_i - \epsilon_1 - \lambda_{X_{\text{u},i}}^{\text{T}} g_{X_{\text{u},i}} - \beta_i, \text{ and} \qquad (44\text{b})$$

$$- \frac{\partial B_i}{\partial x_i} f_i + \gamma_i - \lambda_{D_i}^{\text{T}} g_{D_i} \qquad (44\text{c})$$

are sum of squares.

Remark that λ_3 is a vector. The dual problem becomes

$$\sup_{\lambda \geq 0} \sum_i \varphi_i(\lambda). \qquad (45)$$

In the following, we explain how the subgradient algorithm can be used to solve the previous optimization problem. Let $\alpha_i^*(\lambda)$ be the optimal value of α_i for a given λ. Then the gradients of $\varphi_1(\lambda), \ldots, \varphi_k(\lambda)$ are

$$g_i(\lambda) = \begin{bmatrix} \alpha_i^*(\lambda) & \beta_i^*(\lambda) & \gamma_i^*(\lambda) \end{bmatrix}. \qquad (46)$$

From (39) and (46), we get for all $\mu \equiv (\mu_1, \mu_2, \mu_3)$ and $i = 1, \ldots, k$

$$\varphi_i(\mu) \geq \varphi_i(\lambda) + g_i(\mu - \lambda). \qquad (47)$$

The function to be maximized is $\varphi(\lambda) = \sum_i \varphi_i(\lambda)$, which has a gradient $g(\lambda^{(k)}) = \sum_i g_i(\lambda^{(k)})$. The vector of multipliers is updated according to (40), and is

$$\lambda^{(k+1)} = \lambda^{(k)} - \Delta_k g^{\text{T}}\left(\lambda^{(k)}\right). \qquad (48)$$

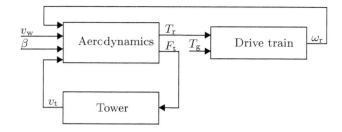

Figure 4: Wind turbine modeled as an interconnection of three subsystems.

It is seen that if $\sum_i \alpha_i \geq 0$ is violated, then $\lambda_1^{(k+1)} > \lambda_1^{(k)}$, as the first element of $g(\lambda^{(k)})$ is negative. This puts a larger penalty on the violation of the constraint through the dual variable λ_1.

5. EXAMPLE

In this section, we demonstrate the applicability of the compositional safety analysis, by analyzing the safety of an emergency shutdown of a wind turbine. The emergency shutdown procedure is simplified for presentation, and the wind turbine model is a slight modification of the CART3 wind turbine model [8].

The wind turbine is modeled as an interconnection of three subsystems: aerodynamics (subsystem 1), tower (subsystem 2), and drive train (subsystem 3). A block diagram of the wind turbine is shown in Figure 4.

The wind turbine is driven by an exogenous input - the wind v_w. Via the aerodynamics, the wind exerts a torque T_r on the rotor shaft, and a force F_t on the top of the tower. This bends the tower and makes the rotor shaft rotate. The rotor shaft is connected to a generator through a gear and a generator shaft. A converter applies a torque T_g to the generator shaft.

The magnitude of the torque T_r and the force F_t depends on the pitch angle β, the rotor speed ω_r, and the wind speed at the rotor $v_w - v_t$, given by the speed of the wind v_w and the velocity of the tower v_t. These relations are usually described by lookup tables (C_p and C_t tables); however, we approximate them by polynomials.

In case of severe faults, a wind turbine is shut down by pitching the blades to an angle of $\beta = 90°$, while applying a constant generator torque $T_g = 3,580$ Nm, until the rotor speed is below a threshold of 0.77 rad/s, from which it is not possible to apply a torque from the generator; hence, the wind turbine is left uncontrolled. At a pitch angle of $90°$, the aerodynamic thrust is acting in the opposite direction of the nominal rotation; hence, it decelerates. Additionally, by applying a relatively high generator torque, the rotor shaft is decelerated even faster. This may cause the tower to sway too much or twist the rotor shaft beyond the limit accepted by the turbine structure. Therefore, we verify that this does not happen. The subsystems of the wind turbine

are modeled as shown in (49), and will be left without further explanation.

$$\begin{bmatrix} \dot{v}_r \\ \dot{\omega}_{r,f} \end{bmatrix} = \begin{bmatrix} -c_{v_r} v_r + (v_w - v_t) \\ -c_{\omega_{r,f}} \omega_{r,f} + \omega_r \end{bmatrix}$$
$$h_1 = \begin{bmatrix} p_1 \\ p_2 \end{bmatrix}, \tag{49a}$$

$$\begin{bmatrix} \dot{v}_t \\ \dot{x}_t \end{bmatrix} = \begin{bmatrix} \frac{1}{M_t}(F_t - B_t v_t - k_t x_t) \\ v_t \end{bmatrix}$$
$$h_2 = v_t \tag{49b}$$

$$\begin{bmatrix} \dot{\omega}_r \\ \dot{\theta}_\Delta \\ \dot{\omega}_g \end{bmatrix} = \begin{bmatrix} \frac{1}{J_r}(T_r - k_r \theta_\Delta - B_r(\omega_r - \frac{1}{N_g}\omega_g)) \\ \omega_r - \frac{1}{N_g}\omega_g \\ \frac{1}{J_g}\left(\frac{1}{N_g}(k_r\theta_\Delta + B_r(\omega_r - \frac{1}{N_g}\omega_g)) - T_g\right) \end{bmatrix}$$
$$h_3 = \omega_r \tag{49c}$$

where

$$p_1 = \left(c_{11} + c_{12}\omega_{r,f} + c_{13}v_r + c_{14}\omega_{r,f}^2 + c_{15}v_r^2 + c_{16}\omega_{r,f}v_r\right)v_r^3$$

$$p_2 = \left(c_{21} + c_{22}\omega_{r,f} + c_{23}v_r + c_{24}v_r^2 + c_{25}\omega_{r,f}v_r\right)v_r^2 + c_{26} + c_{27}\omega_{r,f}^2$$

The parameters of the wind turbine are the following: $M_t = 7.76 \cdot 10^3$ kg, $B_t = 18.6$ kN/(m/s), $k_t = 2.7$ MN/m, $N_g = 43$, $J_r = 611.1 \cdot 10^3$ kgm^2, $B_r = 24$ kNm/(rad/s), $k_r = 24.7 \cdot 10^6$ Nm/rad, $c_{v_r} = 11.65$, $c_{\omega_{r,f}} = 21$, $c_{11} = -32.42 \cdot 10^6$, $c_{12} = -746.0 \cdot 10^6$, $c_{13} = 53.03 \cdot 10^6$, $c_{14} = -1.128 \cdot 10^9$, $c_{15} = -18.63 \cdot 10^6$, $c_{16} = 384.6 \cdot 10^6$, $c_{21} = 8492.6$, $c_{22} = 300.88 \cdot 10^3$, $c_{23} = -11.85 \cdot 10^3$, $c_{24} = 3584.0$, $c_{25} = -90.32 \cdot 10^3$, $c_{26} = 318.3$, and $c_{27} = 1.692 \cdot 10^6$. We have omitted the units on the constants c_*, as they have no physical interpretation.

The considered region of the state space is

$$X_1 = [2, 28] \times [0.77, 4], \tag{50a}$$
$$X_2 = [-0.01, 0.07] \times [-0.05, 0.05], \tag{50b}$$
$$X_3 = [0.77, 4] \times [-25, 25] \cdot 10^{-3} \times [33.2, 172.7]. \tag{50c}$$

Furthermore, the inputs to the subsystems take values in the following sets

$$D_1 = [5, 25], \tag{51a}$$
$$U_1 = [0.77, 4] \times [-0.5, 0.5], \tag{51b}$$
$$U_2 = [1.3554, 94.413] \cdot 10^3, \tag{51c}$$
$$U_3 = [-141.86, -0.126] \cdot 10^6. \tag{51d}$$

It is chosen to initialize the system in the so called full load region, corresponding to a wind speed between 11.7 m/s and 25 m/s, where the wind turbine is operated at a constant rotor speed of 3.88 rad/s; hence, the set of initial states is

$$X_{0,1} = [11.7, 25] \times [3.8, 3.95], \tag{52a}$$
$$X_{0,2} = [-0.005, 0.005] \times [0.01, 0.02], \tag{52b}$$
$$X_{0,3} = [3.8, 3.95] \times [6.25, 6.27] \cdot 10^{-3} \times [164, 171]. \tag{52c}$$

We should verify that the following unsafe sets cannot be

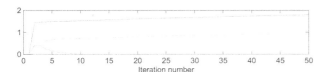

Figure 5: Values of the multipliers λ as a function of the number of iterations.

reached

$$X_{u,1} = [2,\, 3] \cup [27,\, 28] \times [0.77,\, 4], \tag{53a}$$

$$X_{u,2} = [-0.01,\, 0] \cup [0.06,\, 0.07]$$
$$\times [-0.04,\, -0.03] \cup [0.03,\, 0.04], \tag{53b}$$

$$X_{u,3} = [0.77,\, 4] \times [-25,\, -10] \cdot 10^{-3} \cup [10,\, 25] \cdot 10^{-3}$$
$$\times [33.2,\, 172.7]. \tag{53c}$$

Now the verification problem has been set up, and we do the verification using Corollary 4. To allow the verification, we need to characterize X_i, $X_{0,i}$, $X_{u,i}$, and U_i by polynomials. This is accomplished as by specifying a maximum value x_{max} and minimum value x_{min} of some variable x, and then defining

$$g \equiv -(x - x_{min})(x - x_{max}). \tag{54}$$

The polynomial g is nonnegative for $x \in [x_{min},\, x_{max}]$ and otherwise negative.

To give an impression of the convergence of the algorithm, the values of the multipliers $\lambda_1, \ldots, \lambda_6$ are shown in Figure 5. The safety of the system is verified by Corollary 4, and the barrier function is

$$\begin{aligned}
B(x) &= 0.0388\omega_r^2\theta_\Delta^2 + 0.0350\omega_r^2\theta_\Delta + 0.748\omega_r^2 \\
&\quad - 0.00869\omega_r\omega_g + 0.569\omega_g^2 - 0.00332\omega_g\theta_\Delta \\
&\quad + 1.223\theta_\Delta^2 - 97.0 \cdot 10^{-6}v_t^2 x_t - 0.256v_t^2 \\
&\quad + 0.00173v_t x_t^2 - 2.15v_t x_t + 0.0658v_t - 0.755x_t^2 \\
&\quad + 0.0785x_t + 0.00387v_r^2 - 0.00943v_r\omega_{r,f} \\
&\quad - 0.107v_r + 0.0207\omega_{r,f}^2 + 0.103\omega_{r,f} + 1.609.
\end{aligned} \tag{55}$$

6. CONCLUSION

We have presented a method for verifying the safety of an interconnection of subsystems. The method is based on the identification of barrier certificates, where the certificates are found for each subsystem, but are coupled through some additional constraints.

The presented method allows the safety verification of higher dimensional systems, as the verification is decomposed into smaller coupled subproblems, and allows subsystems to be analyzed with different computational methods.

The method has been used to verify the safety of an emergency shutdown procedure for a wind turbine.

7. REFERENCES

[1] A. Abate, A. Tiwari, and S. Sastry. Box invariance in biologically-inspired dynamical systems. *Automatica*, 45(7):1601–1610, 2009.

[2] S. Boyd, L. E. Ghaoui, E. Feron, and V. Balakrishnan. *Linear Matrix Inequalities in System and Control Theory*, volume 15 of *SIAM studies in applied mathematics*. SIAM, 1994.

[3] S. Boyd, L. Xiao, A. Mutapcic, and J. Mattingley. Notes on decomposition methods, 2008.

[4] A. Girard and G. Pappas. Verification using simulation. In J. Hespanha and A. Tiwari, editors, *Hybrid Systems: Computation and Control*, volume 3927 of *Lecture Notes in Computer Science*, pages 272–286. Springer Berlin / Heidelberg, 2006.

[5] H. Guéguen, M.-A. Lefebvre, J. Zaytoon, and O. Nasri. Safety verification and reachability analysis for hybrid systems. *Annual Reviews in Control*, 33(1):25–36, 2009.

[6] J. Helton and O. Merino. Coordinate optimization for bi-convex matrix inequalities. In *Proceedings of the 36th IEEE Conference on Decision and Control*, pages 3609–3613, December 1997.

[7] T. Iwasaki. The dual iteration for fixed-order control. *IEEE Transactions on Automatic Control*, 44(4):783–788, April 1999.

[8] J. Laks, L. Pao, and A. Wright. Control of wind turbines: Past, present, and future. In *American Control Conference*, pages 2096–2103, June 2009.

[9] I. Mitchell, A. Bayen, and C. Tomlin. A time-dependent Hamilton-Jacobi formulation of reachable sets for continuous dynamic games. *IEEE Transactions on Automatic Control*, 50(7):947–957, 2005.

[10] P. A. Parrilo. Semidefinite programming relaxations for semialgebraic problems. *Mathematical Programming*, 96(2):293–320, 2003.

[11] B. T. Polyak. Subgradient methods: A survey of Soviet research. In *Proceedings of a IIASA Workshop*, volume 3 of *Nonsmooth Optimization*, pages 5–29, 1977.

[12] S. Prajna and A. Jadbabaie. Safety verification of hybrid systems using barrier certificates. In *Hybrid Systems: Computation and Control*, volume 2993 of *Lecture Notes in Computer Science*, pages 271–274. Springer Berlin / Heidelberg, 2004.

[13] S. Prajna, A. Jadbabaie, and G. J. Pappas. A framework for worst-case and stochastic safety verification using barrier certificates. *IEEE Transactions on Automatic Control*, 52(8):1415–1428, August 2007.

[14] S. Prajna, A. Papachristodoulou, P. Seiler, and P. A. Parrilo. SOSTOOLS and its control applications. In *Positive Polynomials in Control*, volume 312 of *Lecture Notes in Control and Information Sciences*, pages 273–292. Springer Berlin / Heidelberg, 2005.

[15] N. Z. Shor, K. C. Kiwiel, and A. Ruszcayński. *Minimization methods for non-differentiable functions*. Springer-Verlag New York, Inc., New York, NY, USA, 1985.

[16] U. Topcu, A. Packard, and R. Murray. Compositional stability analysis based on dual decomposition. In *Proceedings of the 48th IEEE Conference on Decision and Control*, pages 1175–1180, December 2009.

Transcendental Inductive Invariants Generation for Non-linear Differential and Hybrid Systems

Rachid Rebiha[*]
Univ. Campinas, Brazil.
Univ. Lugano, Switzerland.
rachid.rebiha@usi.ch

Nadir Matringe
LMA - Univ. Poitiers, France.
Univ. Paris 7, France.
matringe@math.univ-poitiers.fr

Arnaldo V. Moura[†]
Univ. Campinas, Brazil.
arnaldo@ic.unicamp.br

ABSTRACT

We present the first verification methods that automatically generate bases of invariants expressed by *multivariate formal power series* and *transcendental functions*. We discuss the convergence of solutions generated over hybrid systems that exhibit non-linear models augmented with parameters. We reduce the invariant generation problem to linear algebraic matrix systems, from which one can provide effective methods for solving the original problem. We obtain very general sufficient conditions for the existence and the computation of formal power series invariants over multivariate polynomial continuous differential systems. The formal power series invariants generated are often composed by the expansion of some well-known transcendental functions like *log* or *exp* and have an analysable closed-form. This facilitates their use to verify safety properties. Moreover, we generate *inequality* and *equality* invariants. Our examples, dealing with non-linear continuous evolution similar to those present today in many critical hybrid embedded systems, show the strength of our results and prove that some of them are beyond the limits of other recent approaches.

Categories and Subject Descriptors

F.3.1 [**Logics and Meanings of Programs**]: Specifying and Verifying and Reasoning about Programs

Keywords

Invariants Generation, Hybrid Systems

1. INTRODUCTION

Hybrid systems [11, 2] exhibit discrete and continuous behaviors, as one often finds when modeling digital system

---

*Supported by FAPESP grant 2011/08947-1.

†Supported by grants CNPq-473867/2010-9 and FAPESP-2007/56052-8.

embedded in analog environments. Moreover, most safety-critical systems, *e.g.* aircraft, automobiles, chemical plants and biological systems, operate as non-linear hybrid systems and can only be adequately modeled by means of non-linear arithmetic over the real numbers and involving multivariate polynomial, fractional or transcendental functions.

In this work, we will use hybrid automata as computational models for hybrid systems. A hybrid automaton can describe interactions between discrete transitions and continuous dynamics, the latter being governed by local differential equations. We look for invariants that strengthen what we wish to prove, and so allow us to establish the desired property. Also, they can provide precise over approximations of the set of reachable states in the continuous state space. Given that, they can be used to determine which discrete transitions are possible and can also be used to verify if a given property is fulfilled or not.

Some known verification approaches are based on inductive invariant generation [12] and abstract interpretation [7, 8], which can be extended to hybrid systems to verify safety-critical properties. Other recent approaches to invariant generation are constraint based [24, 21, 19]. In these cases, a template form, described by a polynomial with fixed degree and unknown parametric coefficients, is proposed as the target invariant to be generated. The conditions for invariance are then encoded, resulting in constraints over the unknown coefficients whose solutions yield the desired invariants. But they still require several computations of Gröbner bases [6], first-order quantifier elimination [27] or abstraction operations at several steps, and known algorithms for those problems are, at least, of double exponential time complexity. SAT modulo theory decision procedures and polynomial systems [10, 21, 4] also could eventually lead to decision procedures for treating linear theories and decidable systems. Such works strive to generate linear or polynomial invariants over hybrid systems that exhibit affine or polynomial systems as continuous evolution modes.

Despite tremendous progress over the past years [24, 26, 20, 21, 1, 18, 3, 25, 23, 22, 9], generating invariants for hybrid systems remains very challenging for non-linear discrete systems, as well as for non-linear differential systems with non-trivial local and initial conditions. In this work, we present new methods for the automatic generation of invariants in the form of assertions where continuous functions are expressed by multivariate formal power series. Such methods can then be applied to systems with continuous evolution modes described by multivariate polynomials or fractional differential rules. As far as we know, there are no other methods that deal with this type of systems or that can generate this type of invariants.

We develop the new methods by first extending our previous work on non-linear invariant generation for discrete models with nested loops and conditional statements that describe multivariate polynomial or fractional systems [13]. Then, we generalize our previous work on non-linear invariant generation for hybrid systems [17, 16, 15].

We summarize our contributions as follows:
• To the best of our knowledge, we present the first methods which generate bases of *formal power series and transcendental invariants*, while dealing with non-linear continuous models present in many critical hybrid and embedded systems. The problem of synthesizing power series invariants and the results are clearly novel. We consider very general forms of continuous modes, *i.e.*, they are non-linear and augmented with parameters. Moreover, we generate both *inequality* and *equality* invariants.
• We introduce a more general approximation of consecution, dealing with assertions expressed by multivariate formal power series. We show that the preconditions for discrete transitions and the Lie-derivatives for continuous evolution can be viewed as morphisms and suitably represented by matrices. In this way, we reduce the invariant generation problem to linear algebraic matrix manipulations. We present an analysis of these matrices.
• We also provide resolution and convergence analysis for techniques that generate non trivial bases of provable multivariate formal power series and generate transcendental invariants for each local continuous evolution rules.
• Mathematically, we develop very general sufficient conditions allowing the existence and computation of solutions defined by formal power series for multivariate polynomial differential systems. In order to achieve this goal we develop new methods, in the spirit of Boularas [5].
• The contribution is significant as it provides invariants that can be used to prove safety properties which also exhibit formal power series expressions or transcendental functions. To reason symbolically about formal power series and transcendental functions, it is necessary to be able to generate formal power series invariants, since they provide a more precise reachability analysis. The formal power series invariants generated are often composed by expansions involving transcendental functions like *log* or *exp*, which have analyzable closed forms, and thus facilitates the use of these invariants to verify properties.

EXAMPLE 1. (Motivational Example) *Consider the following non-linear continuous system with 2 variables $x(t), y(t)$ and 2 parameters a, b:*

$$(S_3) = \begin{cases} \dot{x}(t) = ax(t) \\ \dot{y}(t) = ay(t) + bx(t)y(t). \end{cases}$$

Note that for this kind of systems, one could prove that no invariant can be obtained via the standard constraint-based approaches based on constant, polynomial or fractional scaling methods. Our method exhibits the following basis for the vector space of invariants $\{x, e^{-bx/a}y\}$. Almost all elements in this space would provide transcendental invariants. More precisely, by considering $F^1(x,y) = x$ and $F^2(x,y) = e^{-bx/a}y$ we will be able to generate strong invariants expressed in a very simple form (e.g. $x = 0$) and others ex-

pressed by multivariate formal power series and transcendental functions (e.g. $e^{-bx/a}y = 0$).

For instance, given any initial condition $x(0) = x_0$, $y(0) = y_0$, the following assertion

$$x(e^{-bx_0/a})y_0 - x_0(e^{-bx/a})y = 0$$

is an inductive invariant whatever the initial conditions are. It depends smoothly on the initial value and it is convergent everywhere. We are also able to generate inequality invariants, e.g., if we initially have $a \leq 0$ and $F^2(x_0, y_0) \leq 0$ then we have the inequality invariant $e^{-bx_0/a}y_0 \leq e^{-bx/a}y \leq 0$. Such invariants are beyond the reach of current invariant generation techniques, even these in a simple forms. □

This article is organized as follows. In Section 2 we first recall the notion of algebraic hybrid systems, we introduce our notations and representations for multivariate formal series. In Section 3 we present new forms for approximating consecution with multivariate formal power series and we reduce the problem to triangular linear algebraic matrix systems. In Section 4 we provide very general sufficient conditions for the existence of invariants and, further, we show how to automatically compute such invariants. In Section 5 we show how we treat general triangularizable systems. In Section 6 we present a running example and a convergence analysis. We show the efficiency of our methods in Section 7 by generating closed-form invariants for systems that are intractable by other state-of-the-art formal methods and static analysis approaches. In Section 8 we show how we handle algebraic discrete transitions. Section 9 offers our conclusions.

2. HYBRID SYSTEMS, INDUCTIVE ASSERTIONS AND FORMAL POWER SERIES

We present our approaches within a framework for hybrid systems. Let $\mathbb{K}[X_1, .., X_n]$ be the ring of multivariate polynomials over the set of variables $\{X_1, .., X_n\}$. An ideal is any set $I \subseteq \mathbb{K}[X_1, .., X_n]$ which contains the null polynomial and is closed under addition and multiplication by any element in $\mathbb{K}[X_1, .., X_n]$. Let $E \subseteq \mathbb{K}[X_1, .., X_n]$ be a set of polynomials. The ideal generated by E is the set of finite sums $(E) = \{\sum_{i=1}^{k} P_i Q_i \mid P_i \in \mathbb{K}[X_1, \ldots, X_n], Q_i \in E, k \geq 1\}$. A set of polynomials E is said to be a *basis* of an ideal I if $I = (E)$. By the Hilbert basis theorem, we know that all ideals have a *finite basis*. Notationally, as is standard in static program analysis, a primed symbol x' refers to next state value of x after a transition is taken. We may also write $\dot{x}$ for the derivative $\frac{dx}{dt}$. We denote by $\mathbb{R}_d[X_1, .., X_n]$ the ring of multivariate polynomials of degree at most d over the set of real variables $\{X_1, .., X_n\}$.

We use the notion of hybrid automata as the computational models for hybrid systems.

DEFINITION 1. *A hybrid system is described by a tuple $\langle V, V_t, L, \mathcal{T}, \mathcal{C}, \mathcal{S}, l_0, \Theta \rangle$, where $V = \{a_1, .., a_m\}$ is a set of parameters, $V_t = \{X_1(t), .., X_n(t)\}$ where $X_i(t)$ is a function of t, L is a set of locations and l_0 is the initial location. A transition $\tau \in \mathcal{T}$ is given by $\langle l_{pre}, l_{post}, \rho_\tau \rangle$, where l_{pre} and l_{post} name the pre- and post- locations of τ, and the transition relation ρ_τ is a first-order assertion over $V \cup V_t \cup V' \cup V'_t$. Also, Θ is the initial condition, given as a first-order assertion over $V \cup V_t$. And $\mathcal{C}$ maps each location $l \in L$ to a local condition $\mathcal{C}(l)$ denoting an assertion over $V \cup V_t$. Finally, $\mathcal{S}$ associates each location $l \in L$ to a differential rule*

$\mathcal{S}(l)$ corresponding to an assertion over $V \cup \{dX_i/dt | X_i \in V_t\}$. A state is any pair from $L \times \mathbb{R}^{|V \cup V_t|}$, that is a location and interpretation of the variables. $\square$

The evolution of variables and functions in an interval must satisfy the local conditions and differential rules.

DEFINITION 2. A run of a hybrid automaton is an infinite sequence $(l_0, \kappa_0) \to \cdots \to (l_i, \kappa_i) \to \cdots$ of states where l_0 is the initial location and $\kappa_0 \models \Theta$. For any two consecutive states $(l_i, \kappa_i) \to (l_{i+1}, \kappa_{i+1})$ in such a run, the condition describes a discrete consecution if there exists a transition $\langle q, p, \rho_i \rangle \in \mathcal{T}$ such that $q = l_i$, $p = l_{i+1}$ and $\langle \kappa_i, \kappa_{i+1} \rangle \models \rho_i$ where the primed symbols refer to κ_{i+1}. Otherwise, it is a continuous consecution condition and there is some $\varepsilon \in \mathbb{R}$, $\varepsilon > 0$, and a differentiable function $\phi : [0, \varepsilon) \to \mathbb{R}^{|V \cup V_t|}$ such that the following conditions hold: (i) $l_i = l_{i+1} = q$; (ii) $\phi(0) = \kappa_i$, $\phi(\varepsilon) = \kappa_{i+1}$; (iii) During the time interval $[0, \varepsilon)$, ϕ satisfies the local condition $\mathcal{C}(q)$ and the local differential rule $\mathcal{S}(q)$ such that for all $t \in [0, \varepsilon)$ we must have $\phi(t) \models \mathcal{C}(q)$ and $\langle \phi(t), d\phi(t)/dt \rangle \models \mathcal{S}(q)$. A state (ℓ, κ) is reachable if there is a run and some $i \geq 0$ such that $(\ell, \kappa) = (l_i, \kappa_i)$. $\square$

DEFINITION 3. Let W be a hybrid system. An assertion φ over $V \cup V_t$ is an invariant at $l \in L$ if $\kappa \models \varphi$ whenever (l, κ) is a reachable state of W. $\square$

DEFINITION 4. Let W be a hybrid system and let $\mathbb{D}$ be an assertion domain. An assertion map for W is a map $\gamma : L \to \mathbb{D}$. We say that γ is inductive if and only if the following conditions hold:
1. **Initiation**: $\Theta \models \gamma(l_0)$;
2. **Discrete Consecution**: for all $\langle l_i, l_j, \rho_\tau \rangle \in \mathcal{T}$ we have $\gamma(l_i) \wedge \rho_\tau \models \gamma(l_j)'$;
3. **Continuous Consecution**: for all $l \in L$, and two consecutive states (l, κ_i) and (l, κ_{i+1}) in a possible run of W such that κ_{i+1} is obtained from κ_i according to the local differential rule $\mathcal{S}(l)$, if $\kappa_i \models \gamma(l)$ then $\kappa_{i+1} \models \gamma(l)$. . $\square$

Hence, if γ is an inductive assertion map then $\gamma(l)$ is an invariant at l for W. Note that, in a continuous consecution, if $\gamma(l) \equiv (P(X_1(t), .., X_n(t)) = 0)$, for all $t \in [0, \varepsilon)$, where P is a multivariate polynomial in $\mathbb{R}[X_1, .., X_n]$ such that it has null values on the trajectory $(X_1(t), .., X_n(t))$ during the time interval $[0, \varepsilon)$, which is not to say that P is the null polynomial, then $\mathcal{C}(l) \wedge (P(X_1(t), .., X_n(t)) = 0) \models (\frac{d(P(X_1(t), ..., X_n(t))}{dt} = 0)$ during the local time interval.

DEFINITION 5. A formal power series in the indeterminates $x_1, \ldots, x_n$ is an expression of the following form:

$$\sum_{(i_1, \ldots, i_n) \in \mathbb{N}^n} f_{i_1, \ldots, i_n} x^{i_1} \ldots x^{i_n},$$

where the coefficients $f_{i_1, \ldots, i_n}$ belong to $\mathbb{R}$. $\square$

DEFINITION 6. Whenever $i = (i_1, ..., i_n) \in \mathbb{N}^n$, we denote the sum $i_1 + \cdots + i_n$ by $|i|$. We say that an order $<$ is a lexicographical total ordering in $\mathbb{N}^n$ if for any two elements $i = (i_1, ..., i_n)$ and $j = (j_1, ..., j_n)$ in $\mathbb{N}^n$ we have that $(j_1, ..., j_n) < (i_1, ..., i_n)$ holds if and only if one of the following condition holds: (i) $|j| < |i|$; or (ii) $|j| = |i|$, and the first non null component of $i - j$ is positive. $\square$

With $|i| = k$, where $i = (i_1, .., i_n)$, the monomials $x_1^{i_1} \cdots x_n^{i_n}$, form an ordered basis for the vector space of homogeneous polynomials of total degree k. This means that any homogeneous polynomial of total degree k can be written in the following ordered form: $\sum_{|i|=k} f_{i_1, ..., i_n} x_1^{i_1} \ldots x_n^{i_n}$. As a consequence, since a formal power series $F(x_1, .., x_n)$ is the direct sum of its homogeneous components, it can be written in the following ordered form:

$$F(x_1, .., x_n) = \sum_{k \geq 1} \sum_{|i|=k} f_{i_1, ..., i_n} x_1^{i_1} \ldots x_n^{i_n}.$$

We will denote the coefficients of homogeneous polynomials of degree k by [5]

$$F_k = \begin{bmatrix} f_{k,0,0,...,0} & f_{k-1,1,0,...,0} & f_{k-1,0,1,...,0} & \cdots & f_{0,0,0,...,k} \end{bmatrix}^\top$$

and the basis of homogeneous monomials of degree k will be denoted by the following vector

$$X^k = \begin{bmatrix} x_1^k & x_1^{k-1} x_2 & x_1^{k-1} x_3 & \cdots & x_n^k \end{bmatrix}^\top,$$

with the coordinates ordered with respect to the lexicographical total ordering given in Definition 6. We may now write the formal power series $F(x_1, .., x_n)$ as

$$\sum_{k \geq 1} F_k \cdot X^k = F_1 \cdot X^1 + ... + F_k \cdot X^k + ...,$$

where $F_k \cdot X^k$ denotes the scalar product $\langle F_k, X^k \rangle$. The polynomial $P_i(x_1, \ldots, x_n)$ can thus be written in the form $P_i(x_1, \ldots, x_n) = P_1^i \cdot X^1 + ... + P_m^i \cdot X^m$, where m is the maximal degree among all polynomials P_i, and the P_j^i are the coefficient vectors of P_i. Denote by $x(t)$ the vector $(x_1(t), ..., x_n(t))^\top$. Then S can be written as

$$\dot{x} = A_1 \cdot X^1(t) + ... + A_m \cdot X^m(t),$$

where $A_j = \begin{bmatrix} P_j^1 & \cdots & P_j^n \end{bmatrix}^\top$. In particular, A_1 is the $n \times n$ matrix equal to the Jacobian matrix of the polynomial system given by the P_i's at zero.

From now on, let us describe the continuous evolution rules by a polynomial differential system S of the form:

$$S = \begin{bmatrix} \dot{x}_1(t) = P_1(x_1(t), ..., x_n(t)) \\ \dot{x}_2(t) = P_2(x_1(t), ..., x_n(t)) \\ \cdots \\ \dot{x}_n(t) = P_n(x_1(t), ..., x_n(t)) \end{bmatrix} \quad (1)$$

3. REDUCTION TO LINEAR ALGEBRA

Now, we encode differential continuous consecution conditions. Let S be a polynomial differential system as in Eq.(1).

DEFINITION 7. A function F from $\mathbb{R}^n$ to $\mathbb{R}$ is said to be a λ-invariant for a system S if $\frac{d}{dt} F(x_1(t), .., x_n(t)) = \lambda F(x_1(t), .., x_n(t))$, for any solution $x(t) = (x_1(t), .., x_n(t))$ of S. $\square$

In Definiton 7, the numerical value of the Lie derivative of F is given by λ times its numerical value throughout the time interval $[0, \varepsilon)$. Without loss of generality we will assume that λ is a constant. It is worth noticing, however, that our methods will also work when λ is a multivariate fractional or multivariate polynomial, as is the case for multivariate polynomial invariants generation [16, 15]. Next, we establish sufficient conditions over S for it to admit λ-invariants which are formal power series. Note that a formal power series $F(x) = F_1 \cdot X^1 + ... + F_k \cdot X^k + ...$ is a λ-invariant if

the following conditions holds: $\sum_{i=0}^{n} \frac{\partial F(x)}{\partial x_i} P_i(x) = \lambda F(x)$.
Using our notation, we obtain:

$$\sum_{i=0}^{n} \frac{\partial(F_1 \cdot X^1 + ... + F_k \cdot X^k + ...)}{\partial x_i}(P_1^i \cdot X^1 + ... + P_m^i \cdot X^m)$$
$$-\lambda(F_1 \cdot X^1 + ... + F_k \cdot X^k + ...) = 0.$$

By directly expanding the left side of the equation described just above and collecting terms corresponding to increasing degrees, we have:

$(1):$ $\sum_{j=1}^{n} \frac{\partial(F_1 X^1)}{\partial x_j} P_1^j X^1 - \lambda F_1 X^1 = 0$

$(2):$ $\sum_{j=1}^{n}[\frac{\partial(F_1 X^1)}{\partial x_j} P_2^j X^2 + \frac{\partial(F_2 X^2)}{\partial x_j} P_1^j X^1] - \lambda F_2 X^2 = 0$

$(3):$ $\sum_{j=1}^{n}[\frac{\partial(F_1 X^1)}{\partial x_j} P_3^j X^3 + \frac{\partial(F_2 X^2)}{\partial x_j} P_2^j X^2 + \frac{\partial(F_3 X^3)}{\partial x_j} P_1^j X^1]$
$-\lambda F_3 X^3 = 0$

$\cdots$

$(m):$ $\sum_{j=1}^{n}[\frac{\partial(F_1 X^1)}{\partial x_j} P_m^j X^m + \frac{\partial(F_2 X^2)}{\partial x_j} P_{m-1}^j X^{m-1} +$
$+ \cdots + \frac{\partial(F_m X^m)}{\partial x_j} P_1^j X^1] - \lambda F_m X^m = 0$

$(m+1):$ $\sum_{j=1}^{n}[\frac{\partial(F_2 X^2)}{\partial x_j} P_m^j X^m + \frac{\partial(F_3 X^3)}{\partial x_j} P_{m-1}^j X^{m-1} +$
$+ \cdots + \frac{\partial(F_{m+1} X^{m+1})}{\partial x_j} P_1^j X^1] - \lambda F_{m+1} X^{m+1} = 0$

$\cdots$ $\cdots$

The equation corresponding to degree k is:

$$\sum_{j=1}^{n}[\ \frac{\partial(F_{k-min(k,m)+1} X^{k-min(k,m)+1})}{\partial x_j} P_{min(k,m)}^j X^{min(k,m)}$$
$$+ \frac{\partial(F_{k-min(k,m)+2} X^{k-min(k,m)+2})}{\partial x_j} P_{min(k,m)-1}^j X^{min(k,m)-1}$$
$$+ \cdots + \frac{\partial(F_k X^k)}{\partial x_j} P_1^j X^1\ ] - \lambda F_k X^k = 0.$$

With a different notion of consecution, we can treat more general systems than those that appeared in the determinant analysis of integrability of differential systems in Boularas [5]. Take the linear morphism $D_{p-k,p}$ from $\mathbb{R}_{p-k}[x_1, \ldots, x_n]$ to $\mathbb{R}_p[x_1, \ldots, x_n]$, given by

$$\mathbb{R}_{p-k}[x_1, \ldots, x_n] \mapsto \mathbb{R}_p[x_1, \ldots, x_n]$$
$$P(X = x_1, \ldots, x_n) \mapsto \sum_{j=1,\ldots,n} (\partial_j P(X)) P_{k+1}^j \cdot X^{k+1}.$$

which is the matrix $M_{p-k,p}$ in the ordered canonical basis of $\mathbb{R}_{p-k}[x_1, \ldots, x_n]$ and $\mathbb{R}_p[x_1, \ldots, x_n]$, respectively. Its l-th column represents the decomposition of the polynomial $\sum_{j=1,\ldots,n}(\partial_j P(X)) P_{k+1}^j \cdot X^{k+1}$, where $P(X)$ is the l-th monomial in the ordered basis $\{x_1^p, x_1^{p-1}x_2, x_1^{p-1}x_3, \ldots, x_n^p\}$. We can reduce the infinite system, described just above, to the following linear algebraic system:

$$\begin{cases} (M_{1,1} - \lambda I_2)F_1 = 0 \\ M_{1,2}F_1 + (M_{2,2} - \lambda I_2)F_2 = 0 \\ M_{1,3}F_1 + M_{2,3}F_2 + (M_{3,3} - \lambda I_4)F_3 = 0 \\ \cdots \\ M_{k-min(k,m)+1,k}F_{k-min(k,m)+1} + \\ + M_{k-min(k,m)+2,k}F_{k-min(k,m)+2} + \\ + \cdots + (M_{k,k} - \lambda I_{k+1})F_k = 0 \\ \cdots \end{cases}$$

By using the definitions of $D_{p-k,p}$ and $D_{p,p}$, we will see that we can symbolically compute all the matrices that will appear during the resolution of the mentioned linear algebraic system. We will use the following result.

Lemma 3.1. *Assume that matrix* $A = M_{1,1}$ *is triangular, i.e.* $A = \begin{bmatrix} \lambda_1 & & & & \\ \star & \lambda_2 & & & \\ \star & \star & \ddots & & \\ \star & \star & \star & \lambda_{n-1} & \\ \star & \star & \star & \star & \lambda_n \end{bmatrix}$. *Then* $M_{p,p}$ *is also triangular with diagonal terms* $i_1\lambda_1 + \cdots + i_n\lambda_n$, *where* $i_1 + \cdots + i_n = p$. $\square$

Proof. We get $P_1^j.X^1 = \lambda_j x_j + a_{j,j+1}x_{j+1} + \cdots + a_{j,n}x_n$. Now consider the monomial basis $P(X) = x_1^{i_1} \ldots x_n^{i_n}$, where $i_1 + \cdots + i_n = p$. One has

$$D_{p,p}(X) = i_1 x_1^{i_1-1} \ldots x_n^{i_n}(\lambda_1 x_1 + a_{1,2}x_2 + \cdots + a_{1,n}x_n)$$
$$+ i_2 x_1^{i_1} x_2^{i_2-1} \ldots x_n^{i_n}(\lambda_2 x_2 + a_{2,3}x_3 + \cdots + a_{2,n}x_n)$$
$$+ \cdots + i_n x_1^{i_1} \ldots x_n^{i_n-1}(\lambda_n x_n)$$
$$= (i_1\lambda_1 + \cdots + i_n\lambda_n)x_1^{i_1} \ldots x_n^{i_n} + \Omega,$$

where Ω is a sum of higher term monomials that come after $x_1^{i_1} \ldots x_n^{i_n}$ in the ordered basis of $R_p[x_1, \ldots, x_n]$.

Then, the matrix $M_{p,p}$ corresponding to $D_{p,p}$ in the canonical ordered basis of $\mathbb{R}_p[x_1, \ldots, x_n]$, is:

$$\begin{bmatrix} p\lambda_1 & & & & & & \\ \star & (p-1)\lambda_1 + \lambda_2 & & & & & \\ \star & \star & \ddots & & & & \\ \star & \star & \star & \sum_{k=1}^{n} i_k\lambda_k & & & \\ \star & \star & \star & \star & \ddots & & \\ \star & \star & \star & \star & \star & \lambda_{n-1} + (p-1)\lambda_n & \\ \star & \star & \star & \star & \star & \star & p\lambda_n \end{bmatrix}$$

Thus, it is also triangular with diagonal $i_1\lambda_1 + \cdots + i_n\lambda_n$, where $i_1 + \cdots + i_n = p$. $\square$

4. SUFFICIENT EXISTENCE CONDITIONS

First, we show what happens when a λ-invariant converges. Next, we examine the computation of λ-invariants.

Theorem 1. (Soundness) *Let* F *be a* λ-invariant *for a system* S. *Let* U *be an open subset of* $\mathbb{R}^n$, *where* F *is defined by a normally convergent power series. If there is an initial condition* $x_1(0), ..., x_n(0)$ *in* U *such that* $F(x_1(0), ..., x_n(0)) = 0$, *then* $F(x_1(t), ..., x_n(t)) = 0$ *for all* t *such that* $x_1(t), ..., x_n(t)$ *remain in* U, *i.e.,* F *is an invariant of* S *for the initial condition* $(x_1(0), ..., x_n(0))$. $\square$

Proof. As the power series defining F converges normally on U, so does any of its derivatives. Thus,

$$\begin{aligned} \dot{F}(x_1(t), ..., x_n(t)) &= \sum_{i=1}^{n} \partial_i F(x_1(t), ..., x_n(t))\dot{x}_i(t) \\ &= \lambda F(x_1(t), ..., x_n(t)) \end{aligned},$$

given the λ-invariant property. So, $F(x_1(t), ..., x_n(t))$ must be equal to $t \mapsto ke^{\lambda t}$ for some constant k. Thus k is zero since $F(x_1(0), ..., x_n(0)) = 0$. Hence, so is $F(x_1(t), ..., x_n(t))$, for any t such that $(x_1(t), \ldots, x_n(t)) \in U$. $\square$

Now we can state the following results, which allow for the computation of invariants which are inequality assertions.

Corollary 4.1. (Inequality invariants) *Given the system* S *and an* λ-invariant F *for* S. *Let* U *be an open subset of* $\mathbb{R}^n$ *on which* F *is defined by a normally convergent power series. For any initial value* $x_1(0), ..., x_n(0)$ *in* U *denote* $F(x_1(0), .., x_n(0))$ *by* $F(x(0))$ *and denote* $F(x_1(t), ..., x_n(t))$ *by* $F(x(t))$. *The following holds:*

(i) If $\lambda \geq 0$ and $F(x(0)) \geq 0$, then for all $t \geq 0$ we have the invariant $F(x(t)) \geq F(x(0))$;

(ii) If $\lambda \geq 0$ and $F(x(0)) \leq 0$, then for all $t \geq 0$ we have the inequality invariant $F(x(t)) \leq F(x(0))$;

(iii) If $\lambda < 0$ and $F(x(0)) \geq 0$, then for all $t \geq 0$ we have the invariant $0 \leq F(x(t)) \leq F(x(0))$;

(iv) If $\lambda < 0$ and $F(x(0)) \leq 0$, then for all $t \geq 0$ we have the invariant $F(x(0)) \leq F(x(t)) \leq 0$. $\square$

PROOF. Let F be a λ-invariant system S. By definition, we have $\frac{d}{dt}F(x(t)) = \lambda F(x(t))$ for solutions $(x_1(t),..,x_n(t))$ of S. So, $F(x(t))$ must be equal to $t \mapsto ce^{\lambda t}$ with $c = F(x_1(0),..,x_n(0))$. (i)For all $t \geq 0$ we know that $e^{\lambda t} \geq 1$ (as the function exp increases). So, we have $F(x(t)) = F(x(0))e^{\lambda t} \geq F(x(0))$ for all $t \geq 0$. (ii) We still have $e^{\lambda t} \geq 1$ but $F(x(t)) = F(x(0))e^{\lambda t} \leq F(x(0))$. (iii) We have $0 < e^{\lambda t} \leq 1$ and $0 \leq F(x(t)) = F(x(0))e^{\lambda t} \leq F(x(0))$ for all $t \geq 0$. (iv) We still have $0 < e^{\lambda t} \leq 1$ but $0 \geq F(x(t)) = F(x(0))e^{\lambda t} \geq F(x(0))$ for all $t \geq 0$. $\square$

4.1 Sufficient general existence conditions

We have the following main results on the existence of formal power series invariants for systems described by Eq. (1).

THEOREM 2. *Let A be the Jacobian matrix at zero for the polynomial $P = (P_1,...,P_n)$ defining system S. Its expression is: $(\partial_i P_j(0,...,0), i, j \in [1, n]^2)$. Let $P_k(0,..,0) = 0$. If A is triangularizable with eigenvalues $\lambda_1 \leq ... \leq \lambda_n$, then there exists a λ-invariant formal power series for S when all eigenvalues are positive, or are all negative, with $\lambda = \lambda_1$.* $\square$

PROOF. Up to a linear change of variables, we can assume that matrix A is triangular with diagonal terms $\lambda_1 \leq ... \leq \lambda_n$. We know that matrix $M_{k,k}$ has the form described in Lemma 3.1 and its proof. As A is triangular, so is $M_{k,k}$, and its diagonal terms are the real numbers $i_1\lambda_1 + \cdots + i_n\lambda_n$, where $i_1 + \cdots + i_n = k$. Hence, the diagonal terms of $M_{k,k} - \lambda I_{k+1}$ are $0 \leq \lambda_2 - \lambda... \leq \lambda_n - \lambda$ when $k = 1$. Also, it has a nontrivial kernel, and so we can chose a nonzero F_1 such that $(M_{1,1} - \lambda I_2)F_1 = 0$. For $k \geq 2$ and $i_1 + \cdots + i_n = k$, the diagonal terms $i_1\lambda_1 + \cdots + i_n\lambda_n - \lambda$ of the triangular matrix $M_{k,k} - \lambda I_{k+1}$ are greater than $i_1\lambda_1 + \cdots + i_n\lambda_n - \lambda = k\lambda - \lambda > \lambda > 0$. So, $M_{k,k} - \lambda I_{k+1}$ is invertible.

Hence, we can choose:

- $F_2 = -(M_{2,2} - \lambda I_3)^{-1}M_{1,2}F_1$,
- $F_3 = -(M_{3,3} - \lambda I_4)^{-1}(M_{1,3}F_1 + M_{2,3}F_2)$,
- ...
- $F_k = -(M_{k,k} - \lambda I_{k+1})^{-1}(M_{\ell,k}F_{\ell,k} + \cdots + M_{k-1,k}F_{k-1})$,

where $\ell = k - \min\{k, m\} + 1$. Then, $(F_1, F_2, \ldots, F_k, \ldots)$ is a nonzero solution of the system and the formal power series $\sum_i F_i X^i$ is a λ-invariant. $\square$

The proof also describes a method for the resolution of the triangular matrix system. We can, then, generate nonzero formal power series $\sum_i F_i X^i$ which are λ-invariants associated to the nonzero solution $(F_1, F_2, \ldots)$. In the examples that follow, we used Maple to compute the matrix products necessary to obtain F_k in its symbolic form. We treat the case when all eigenvalues are negative in a similar way. That is, with $\lambda = \lambda_n$, λ will be the eigenvalue with the minimum absolute value. Also, we recall that triangularizable matrices of $M_n(\mathbb{R})$ with eigenvalues of the same sign form a positive measure in the set of all matrices.

4.2 Inductive invariants and initial conditions

We state the following important result.

THEOREM 3. *Let A be the Jacobian matrix at zero of the polynomial $P = (P_1,...,P_n)$ defining a system S, as in Eq. (1), and whose expression is $(\partial_i P_j(0,...,0), i, j \in [1, n]^2)$. Assume, further, that $P_k(0,..,0) = 0$. Suppose that A is triangularizable with eigenvalues $\lambda_1 \leq ... \leq \lambda_n$. Denote λ_1 by λ and assume that the eigenspace associated with λ is of dimension at least 2. Let F_1 and F_2 be two independent λ-invariants. Then, for any initial value $(x_{1,0}, \ldots, x_{n,0})$, the power series $F_2(x_{1,0}, \ldots, x_{n,0})F_1 - F_1(x_{1,0}, \ldots, x_{n,0})F_2$ defines an inductive invariant on U for the solution of S with initial conditions $x_1(0) = x_{1,0}, \ldots, x_n(0) = x_{n,0}$.* $\square$

PROOF. We can see that both F_1 and F_2 converge to a solution $(x_1(t),...,x_n(t))$ with initial values $(x_{1,0},...,x_{n,0})$. Moreover, since F_1 and F_2 are independent,

$$F = F_2(x_{1,0}, \ldots, x_{n,0})F_1 - F_1(x_{1,0}, \ldots, x_{n,0})F_2$$

is a nonzero λ-invariant which vanishes at $(x_{1,0},..,x_{n,0})$. So, according to Theorem 1, F is an inductive invariant. $\square$

5. TRIANGULARIZABLE SYSTEMS

Now we show how to treat the following general system with parameters a, b, c, $a_{1,1}$, $a_{1,2}$, $a_{2,2}$, $b_{1,1}$, $b_{1,2}$, $b_{2,2}$ in V, and variables x, y in V_t:

$$\dot{x}(t) = ax(t) + by(t) + a_{1,1}x^2(t) + a_{1,2}x(t)y(t) + a_{2,2}y^2(t)$$

$$\dot{y}(t) = cy(t) + b_{1,1}x^2(t) + b_{1,2}x(t)y(t) + b_{2,2}y^2(t).$$

The Jacobian matrix at zero of the polynomials defining the system is $\begin{pmatrix} a & 0 \\ b & c \end{pmatrix}$. From Theorem 2, we already know how to find a formal power series F which is an a-invariant. Looking more closely at the coefficients of such a series we will show that it must converge in some appropriate neighborhood of 0. In this section it is not necessary to assume that $a > c$ or $a < c$, since we will choose $\lambda = min\{a, c\}$.

In subsection 5.1 we compute symbolically the matrices $M_{p-k,p}$ as they naturally appear in the resolution of the linear system. In subsection 5.2 we show how to reduce and solve the latter in order to generate λ-invariants by applying Theorem 2. In subsection 5.3 we present our convergence analysis methods for the discovered λ-invariants. We take $a = c$ only from subsection 5.4 onwards, in which case Theorem 3 applies and we obtain inductive invariants that hold for any initial conditions.

5.1 The matrices $M_{p-k,p}$

Using our notation, we have $P_i^1 = 0$ and $P_i^2 = 0$ for all $i > 2$. Then $M_{p-k,p}$ is the matrix whose l-th column is the vector corresponding to the decomposition of the polynomial

$$\partial_1[(0,...,0,\underbrace{1}_{l-th\ position},0,...,0)X^{p-k}]P_{k+1}^1 X^{k+1}$$
$$+\partial_2[(0,...,0,\underbrace{1}_{l-th\ position},0,...,0)X^{p-k}]P_{k+1}^2 X^{k+1}$$

in the ordered canonical basis of $\mathbb{R}_p[x, y]$. Here, the polynomial $(0,..,0,\underbrace{1}_{l-th\ position},0,..,0)X^{p-k}$ is the l-th monomial of the canonical basis of $\mathbb{R}_{p-k}[x, y]$. Therefore, the matrices $M_{p-k,p}$ are zero unless $k = 0$ or $k = 1$. When $k = 0$, the general form of $M_{p,p}$ is given in Section 3 and, in our particular case, it is

$$\begin{pmatrix} pa & & & & & \\ p.b & (p-1)a+c & & & & \\ & (p-1)b & (p-2)a+2c & & & \\ & & \ddots & & \ddots & \\ & & & 2b & a+(p-1)c & \\ & & & & b & pc \end{pmatrix}.$$

Note that $p+1$ is actually the dimension of $\mathbb{R}_p[x,y]$ and so $M_{p-1,p}$ is rectangular with $p+1$ rows and p columns. Here, the l-th monomial in the basis of $\mathbb{R}_{p-1}[x,y]$ is $x^{p-l-1}y^l$. Also, the polynomial $P_2^1 X^2$ is $a_{1,1}x^2 + a_{1,2}xy + a_{2,2}y^2$ and the polynomial $P_2^2 X^2$ is $b_{1,1}x^2 + b_{1,2}xy + b_{2,2}y^2$. Hence, matrix $M_{p-1,p}$ can be written as depicted in Figure (1):

5.2 Resolution of the infinite system

We are looking for λ-scale invariants and we know that we can choose $\lambda = min\{a,c\}$. Then, the system to solve is

$$(M_{1,1} - \lambda I_2)F_1 = 0$$
$$M_{1,2}F_1 + (M_{2,2} - \lambda I_3)F_2 = 0$$
$$M_{2,3}F_2 + (M_{3,3} - \lambda I_4)F_3 = 0$$
$$\cdots$$
$$M_{k-1,k}F_{k-1} + (M_{k,k} - \lambda I_{k+1})F_k = 0$$
$$\cdots .$$

This linear algebraic system can be written as:
$$(M_{1,1} - \lambda I_2)F_1 = 0$$
$$F_2 = -(M_{2,2} - \lambda I_3)^{-1}M_{1,2}F_1$$
$$F_3 = -(M_{3,3} - \lambda I_4)^{-1}M_{2,3}F_2$$
$$\cdots$$
$$F_k = -(M_{k,k} - \lambda I_{k+1})^{-1}M_{k-1,k}F_{k-1}$$
$$\cdots .$$

One can choose any F_1, and then let $F_k = (-1)^{k+1}U_k(F_1)$, where U_k is the matrix with $k+1$ rows and 2 columns:

$[\,(M_{k,k} - \lambda I_{k+1})^{-1}M_{k-1,k}]\cdot[(M_{k-1,k-1} - \lambda I_k)^{-1}M_{k-2,k-1}]\cdot$
$\cdots\cdot[(M_{3,3} - \lambda I_4)^{-1}M_{2,3}]\cdot[(M_{2,2} - \lambda I_3)^{-1}M_{1,2}\,].$

We know that matrix $M_{k,k}$ has the form described in Section 3, Lemma 3.1 and its proof. Then, $M_{k,k} - \lambda I_{k+1}$ is

$$\begin{pmatrix} ka-\lambda & & & & & \\ k.b & (k-1)a+c-\lambda & & & & \\ & (k-1)b & (k-2)a+2c-\lambda & & & \\ & & \ddots & & \ddots & \\ & & & 2b & a+(k-1)c-\lambda & \\ & & & & b & kc-\lambda \end{pmatrix}$$

which can be decomposed as the product DT:

$$\begin{pmatrix} d_1 & & & & & \\ & d_2 & & & & \\ & & d_3 & & & \\ & & & \ddots & & \\ & & & & d_k & \\ & & & & & d_{k+1} \end{pmatrix} \begin{pmatrix} 1 & & & & & \\ t_2 & 1 & & & & \\ & t_3 & 1 & & & \\ & & \ddots & \ddots & & \\ & & & t_k & 1 & \\ & & & & t_{k+1} & 1 \end{pmatrix},$$

where $d_i = (k+1-i)a + (i-1)c - \lambda$ and $t_j = (k+2-j)b/d_j$. So, $(M_{k,k} - \lambda I_{k+1})^{-1} = T^{-1}D^{-1}$, where D^{-1} has the obvious form and T^{-1} is

$$\begin{pmatrix} 1 & & & & & \\ -t_2 & 1 & & & & \\ t_2 t_3 & -t_3 & 1 & & & \\ -t_2 t_3 t_4 & t_3 t_4 & -t_4 & 1 & & \\ \star & \star & \star & \star & \star & \\ (-1)^k t_2 \ldots t_{k+1} & (-1)^{k-1}t_3 \ldots t_{k+1} & \ldots & t_k t_{k+1} & -t_{k+1} & 1 \end{pmatrix}.$$

We also know that $M_{k-j,k}$ has the form described in Section 5.1. Finally, all the matrices appearing in the product U_k are defined and F_k can be symbolically computed.

5.3 Convergence of the λ-invariant

We want to show that if $\lambda > 2b$, the coefficients of the F_i vectors decrease quickly enough so that the invariant F converges in a neighborhood of zero. Let us first recall some basic properties of norms in finite dimension real vector spaces, as well as the associated matrix norms. If v, with coordinates v_i, belongs to $\mathbb{R}^n$, we denote by $|v|_\infty$ the value $max_{i=1,\ldots,n}|v_i|$. If A is a matrix with m rows and n columns, representing a morphism from $(\mathbb{R}^n, |.|_\infty)$ to $(\mathbb{R}^m, |.|_\infty)$ in the canonical basis, it is well-known that associated with the norm $|.|_\infty$ is the matricial norm $||.||$ on $M_{m,n}(\mathbb{R})$, where $||A|| = max_{i=1,\ldots,m}(\sum_{j=1}^n |A_{i,j}|)$. Moreover, using this norm, if $v \in \mathbb{R}^n$ then one has $|Av|_\infty \leq ||A||.|v|_\infty$. This implies that if A and B are two matrices belonging, respectively, to $M_{m,n}(\mathbb{R})$ and $M_{n,p}(\mathbb{R})$, then we get $||AB|| \leq ||A|| \cdot ||B||$. In particular,

$$||U_k|| \leq ||M_{k,k} - \lambda I_{k+1}|| \cdot |||M_{k-1,k}|| \ldots ||M_{2,2} - aI_3|| \cdot ||M_{1,2}||.$$

But, from the expressions for the $M_{k-1,k}$ matrices, we have that $||M_{k-1,k}|| \leq f(k-1)$, where $f = 4 \cdot max(|a_{i,j}|, |b_{i',j'}|)$. From the preceding paragraph again, we deduce that

$$||(M_{k,k} - \lambda I_{k+1})^{-1}|| \leq ||D^{-1}|| \cdot ||T^{-1}||.$$

But $||D^{-1}|| = max_i(d_i^{-1}) \leq [(k-1)\lambda]^{-1}$, because $\lambda = min(a,c)$, and so $||T^{-1}|| = max_i(1 + t_i + t_{i-1}t_i + \cdots + t_2 t_3 \ldots t_{i-1}t_i)$. But each t_j is less than $(k+2-j)b/d_j \leq kb/[(k-1)\lambda] \leq 2b/\lambda$. Suppose that $\lambda > 2b$. Then $||T^{-1}|| \leq 1 + 2b/\lambda + \cdots + (2b/\lambda)^k \leq 1/(1 - 2b/\lambda)$. By letting e be the constant $1/(1 - 2b/\lambda)$, we can write $||(M_{k,k} - \lambda I_{k+1})^{-1}|| \leq e/(k-1)\lambda$. Finally, $||U_k||$ is less than $(ef/\lambda)^{k-2} = r^{k-2}$. Eventually, $|F_k|_\infty = |U_k(F_1)|_\infty \leq ||U_k||.|F_1|_\infty \leq r^{k-2}|F_1|_\infty$.

Let t be $max\{|x|, |y|\}$. Then,

$$|F(x,y)| \leq |F_1 X^1| + |F_2 X^2| \cdots + |F_k X^k| + \ldots$$
$$\leq 2|F_1|_\infty t + 3|F_2|_\infty t^2 + \cdots + (k+1)|F_k|_\infty t^k + \ldots .$$

The right part of the inequality is itself inferior to

$$1/r^2 |F_1|_\infty [2(rt) + 3(rt)^2 + \cdots + (k+1)(rt)^k + \ldots],$$

which, from the classical theory of one variable power series, is convergent in the open disk centered at zero and of radius $1/r$. Hence, we have proved the following.

PROPOSITION 5.1. *Consider the system described at the beginning of Section 5 with a and c positive and greater than 2b. Let λ be the minimum between a and c. Then there exists a λ-invariant, obtained as described in Theorem 2, and which always converges in a neighborhood of zero.* $\square$

5.4 The case of eigenspaces with dimension 2

Now, suppose that the eigenspace corresponding to λ has multiplicity 2, i.e. $a = c = \lambda > 0$ and $b = 0$. We know, from the previous subsection, that any λ-invariant will converge in a ball of radius $1/r$ and centered at zero. Moreover, according to Theorem 3, this will give an inductive invariant for the system for any initial solutions within this ball. More precisely, by letting $F_1^1 = (1,0)^\top$ and $F_1^2 = (0,1)^\top$, we get a basis $F^1(x,y)$ and $F^2(x,y)$ of λ-invariants that converge in the open $|.|_\infty$-disk of radius $1/r$ and centered at zero.

$$\begin{pmatrix} (p-1)a_{1,1} & b_{1,1} & & & & & \\ (p-1)a_{1,2} & (p-2)a_{1,1}+b_{1,2} & 2b_{1,1} & & & & \\ (p-1)a_{2,2} & (p-2)a_{1,2}+b_{2,2} & (p-3)a_{1,1}+2b_{1,2} & 3b_{1,1} & & & \\ & \ddots & \ddots & \ddots & \ddots & & \\ & & 3a_{2,2} & 2a_{1,2}+(p-3)b_{1,2} & a_{1,1}+(p-2)b_{1,2} & (p-1)b_{1,1} \\ & & & 2a_{2,2} & a_{1,2}+(p-2)b_{2,2} & (p-1)b_{1,2} \\ & & & & a_{2,2} & (p-1)b_{2,2} \end{pmatrix}.$$

Figure 1: The matrix $M_{p-1,p}$

Note that the monomial of degree one in the Taylor series of F^1 is x, and it is y in the Taylor series of F^2. In other words, if we take the first coefficient of F as $(1,0)^\top$, we obtain a λ-invariant $F = F^1(x,y)$ and, similarly, if we take the second coefficient of F as $(0,1)^\top$, we obtain another λ-invariant $F = F^2(x,y)$.

Moreover, these two invariants form a basis for invariants that converge in the open $|.|_\infty$-disk of radius $1/r$ and centered at zero. Assume now that we are given initial values, $x(0) = x_0$ and $y(0) = y_0$, as solutions in this open disk. Then, there will always exist two real numbers, λ and μ, such that $\lambda(x_0,y_0)F^1(x_0,y_0) + \mu(x_0,y_0)F^2(x_0,y_0) = 0$, where $\lambda(x_0,y_0) = F^2(x_0,y_0)$ and $\mu(x_0,y_0) = -F^1(x_0,y_0)$. Then,

$$(\lambda(x_0,y_0)F^1 + \mu(x_0,y_0)F^2 = 0)$$

is an inductive invariant for the solution corresponding to the initial condition (x_0,y_0). So, given (x_0,y_0) in the $|.|_\infty$-disk of radius $1/r$ and centered at zero, the invariant depends smoothly on the initial condition.

6. A RUNNING EXAMPLE

In this section, we discuss a running example and explain how the sufficient conditions for invariance are used, and how a basis for invariant ideals is automatically obtained. We treat sub-classes of non linear differential rules that we often find in local continuous modes in hybrid systems. More specifically, we show how our method applies to systems:

$$\dot{x}(t) = ax(t) + bx(t)y(t)$$
$$\dot{y}(t) = ay(t) + dx(t)y(t).$$

Next, we show how to generate invariant ideals. The Jacobian matrix at zero is $\begin{pmatrix} a & 0 \\ 0 & a \end{pmatrix}$. From Theorem 2, we can find a formal power series F which is an a-invariant. We will show that it must converge in some neighborhood of 0.

Step 1: Computation of the matrices $M_{p-k,p}$.

The coefficient vectors P_i are zero, for $i \geq 2$. So, $M_{p-k,p}$ is the matrix whose l-th column is the vector corresponding to the decomposition of the polynomial

$$\partial_1[(0,\ldots,0,\underbrace{1}_{l-th \ position},0,\ldots,0)X^{p-k}]P^1_{k+1}X^{k+1}$$
$$+\partial_2[(0,\ldots,0,\underbrace{1}_{l-th \ position},0,\ldots,0)X^{p-k}]P^2_{k+1}X^{k+1}$$

in the ordered canonical basis of $\mathbb{R}_p[x,y]$. Hence, in this case, the matrices $M_{p-k,p}$ are zero unless $k = 0$ or $k = 1$. When $k = 0$, the general form of $M_{p,p}$, as detailed in Section 3, is given by paI_{p+1}. But $p+1$ is actually the dimension of $\mathbb{R}_p[x,y]$ and so $M_{p-1,p}$ is rectangular with $p+1$ rows, and p columns. Then the l-th monomial of the basis of $\mathbb{R}_{p-1}[x,y]$ is $x^{p-l-1}y^l$. Then, the polynomial

$P^1_2 X^2$ is bxy, and the polynomial $P^2_2 X^2$ is dxy. Hence,

$$\partial_1[(0,..,0,\underbrace{1}_{l-th \ position},0,..,0)X^{p-1}]P^1_2X^2+$$
$$\partial_2[(0,..,0,\underbrace{1}_{l-th \ position},0,..,0)X^{p-1}]P^2_2X^2$$

reduces to $b(p-l-1)x^{p-l-1}y^{l+1} + dlx^{p-l}y^l$. Eventually, it can be seen that the matrix can be written as:

$$M_{p-1,p} = \begin{pmatrix} 0 & & & \\ (p-1)b & d & & \\ & (p-2)b & 2d & \\ & & \ddots & \ddots \\ & & & 2b & (p-2)d \\ & & & & b & (p-1)d \\ & & & & & 0 \end{pmatrix}.$$

Step 2: Resolution of the linear system.

When looking for λ-scale invariants, we already know that we must choose $\lambda = a$. Then, we need to solve

$$(M_{1,1} - aI_2)F_1 = 0$$
$$M_{1,2}F_1 + (M_{2,2} - aI_2)F_2 = 0$$
$$M_{2,3}F_2 + (M_{3,3} - aI_3)F_3 = 0$$
$$\cdots$$
$$M_{k-1,k}F_{k-1} + (M_{k,k} - aI_k)F_k = 0$$
$$\cdots$$

Since $M_{k,k}$ is equal to kaI_{k+1}, the system becomes:

$$0 \cdot F_1 = 0$$
$$F_2 = -a^{-1}M_{1,2}F_1$$
$$F_3 = -(2a)^{-1}M_{2,3}F_2$$
$$\cdots$$
$$F_k = -[(k-1)a]^{-1}M_{k-1,k}F_{k-1}$$
$$\cdots$$

This means that one can choose any F_1, and then choose F_k as $(-1)^{k+1}a^{-k+1}U_k(F_1)$, where U_k is the matrix with $k+1$ rows and 2 columns given by the product

$$[1/(k-1)M_{k-1,k}] \cdot [1/(k-2)M_{k-2,k-1}] \ldots [1/2M_{2,3}]M_{1,2}.$$

Step 3: Convergence of the invariant.

Now we show that the invariant F converges in a neighborhood of zero. In particular, the norm $||U_k||$ is less than or equal to the product $\frac{1}{(k-1)!}||M_{k-1,k}|| \ldots ||M_{1,2}||$. Then from $M_{k-1,k}$ we get $||M_{k-1,k}|| \leq ck$, where $c = \max\{|b|,|d|\}$. Hence, $||U_k|| \leq ck!/(k-1)! = ck$. Eventually, we get

$$|F(x,y)| \leq |F_1X^1| + |F_2X^2| \cdots + |F_kX^k| + \cdots$$
$$\leq 2|F_1|_\infty t + 3|F_2|_\infty t^2 + \cdots + (k+1)|F_k|_\infty t^k + \cdots$$

The right side of the inequality is inferior to

$$ac|F_1|_\infty[2(\frac{t}{a}) + 3.2(\frac{t}{a})^2 + \cdots + (k+1)k(\frac{t}{a})^k + \cdots].$$

From the theory of one variable power series, it must converge in the open disk of radius a and centered at zero.

More precisely, taking F^1 and F^2, respectively, as $(1,0)^\top$ and $(0,1)^\top$, we get a basis $F^1(x,y)$ and $F^2(x,y)$ for a-invariants which converge in the open $|.|_\infty$-disk of radius a and centered at zero. Assume now that we are given initial values with parameters $x_0 = x(0)$ and $y_0 = y(0)$ for solutions of the system within this open disk. Then,

$$F^2(x_0, y_0)F^1(x,y) - F^1(x_0, y_0)F^2(x,y) = 0$$

is an inductive invariant. Again, for (x_0, y_0) in the $|.|_\infty$-disk of radius a and centered at zero it depends smoothly on the initial condition.

7. EXPERIMENTAL RESULTS

We give some examples in dimension 2 where x, y are variables in V_t and a, b are parameters in V. All the following systems will have a Jacobian matrix $\begin{pmatrix} a & 0 \\ 0 & a \end{pmatrix}$. We will see that we already get interesting invariants which are polynomial in the first case, rational in the second case, transcendental in the last case.

First, as we already saw in the previous sections, for all $k \geq 1$, only $M_{k,k}$ and $M_{k-1,k}$ are nonzero. Moreover $M_{k,k}$ is equal to $Diag(ka, \ldots, ka)$ in $\mathcal{M}_{k+1,k+1}(\mathbb{R})$. And we saw in Section 5.2 that $F(X) = \sum_i F_i X^i$ is an a-invariant if and only if $F_k = (-1)^{k-1}U_k(F_1)$ with $k \geq 2$ and where $U_k = [(M_{k,k} - aI_{k+1})^{-1}M_{k-1,k}]\ldots\ldots[(M_{2,2} - aI_3)^{-1}M_{1,2}]$ is in $\mathcal{M}_{k+1,2}(\mathbb{R})$. Because of the form of $M_{k,k}$, we get

$$U_k = \frac{1}{a^{k-1}(k-1)!}.M_{k-1,k}.\ldots.M_{1,2}.$$

From the results of Section 5, in all these cases the vector space of a-invariants will be of dimension 2 and we can find precise invariants convergent near zero . Also, the transcendental invariants obtained in the forthcoming Example (4) converge everywhere for any initial conditions.

EXAMPLE 2. *Consider S_1 as*

$$\dot{x}(t) = ax(t)$$
$$\dot{y}(t) = ay(t) + bx^2(t).$$

Here $P_1(x,y) = ax$ and $P_2(x,y) = ay + bx^2$ and we have

$$M_{k-1,k} = \begin{pmatrix} 0 & b & & & \\ 0 & 0 & 2b & & \\ & \ddots & \ddots & \ddots & \\ & & 0 & 0 & (k-1)b \\ & & & 0 & 0 \\ & & & & 0 \end{pmatrix} \in \mathcal{M}_{k+1,k}(\mathbb{R}). \text{ Thus}$$

$$U_2 = \begin{pmatrix} 0 & b/a \\ 0 & 0 \\ 0 & 0 \end{pmatrix} \in \mathcal{M}_{3,2}(\mathbb{R}), \text{ and } U_k \text{ is zero for } k \geq 3.$$

Taking first $F_1 = (1,0)^\top$, one has $F_k = (0,0,\ldots,0)^\top$ for $k \geq 2$ and then we get $F^1(x,y) = x$ as the first basis-vector of the space of a-invariants.

Now, with $F_1 = (0,1)^\top$, one has $F_2 = (-b/a)(1,0,\ldots,0)^\top$, and F_k is zero for $k \geq 3$. So, we get $F^2(x,y) = y - bx^2/a$ as the second basis-vector of the space of a-invariants. Hence, $F^1(x,y) = x$ and $F^2(x,y) = y - bx^2/a$ form a basis of the vector space of a-invariants:

```
Lambda=a
U[2]=[[0,0,0],[-b/a,0,0]]
```

```
F[1]=[[1,0]]; F[k]=[[0,..,0]]
F[1]=[[0,1]]; F[k]=[[-b/a,0,..,0]]
Basis of Vector Space Lambda Invariants:
{x, y- b*x^2/a}
```

Finally for an initial condition (x_0, y_0),

$$F(x,y) = x_0(y - bx_0^2/a) - x(y_0 - bx^2/a) = 0$$

is an inductive polynomial invariant whatever are the initial conditions, i.e. for all x_0 and y_0. Applying Corollary 4.1, we can observe several box or inequality invariants. If $a > 0$ and $F^2(x_0, y_0) \geq 0$ then we have the following inequality invariants, that hold for any solution $x(t), y(t)$ of S_1 with initial conditions (x_0, y_0):

$$y - bx^2/a \geq y_0 - bx_0^2/a \geq 0.$$

If we still have $a > 0$ and $F^1(x_0, y_0) \geq 0$ then we have the following inequality invariants $x \geq x_0 \geq 0$. Also, if $a < 0$ and $F^2(x_0, y_0) \geq 0$ then we have the following (box) inequality invariants: $0 \leq y - bx^2/a \leq y_0 - bx_0^2/a$. □

EXAMPLE 3. *Let S_2 be*

$$\dot{x}(t) = ax(t) + bx^2(t)$$
$$\dot{y}(t) = ay(t).$$

Here $P_1(x,y) = ax + bx^2$ and $P_2(x,y) = ay$ and

$$M_{k-1,k} = \begin{pmatrix} (k-1)b & 0 & & & \\ 0 & (k-2) & 0 & & \\ & \ddots & \ddots & \ddots & \\ & & 0 & b & 0 \\ & & & 0 & 0 \\ & & & & 0 \end{pmatrix} \in \mathcal{M}_{k+1,k}(\mathbb{R}).$$

Thus $U_k = \begin{pmatrix} (-b/a)^{k-1} & 0 \\ 0 & 0 \\ \vdots & \vdots \\ 0 & 0 \end{pmatrix} \in \mathcal{M}_{k+1,2}(\mathbb{R}).$

Taking $F_1 = (1,0)^\top$, one has $F_k = (-b/a)^{k-1}(1,0,\ldots,0)^\top$. Then, we obtain the rational function

$$F^1(x,y) = \sum_{k \geq 1}(-b/a)^{k-1}x^k = x/(1 + bx/a)$$

as the first basis-vector of the space of a-invariants, which is convergent for $|x| < |a/b|$.

Now, if we take $F_1 = (0,1)^\top$, one has $F_k = (0,0,\ldots,0)^\top$ for $k \geq 2$, and we get $F^2(x,y) = y$ as the second basis-vector of the space of a-invariants:

```
Lambda=a
U[k]=[[(-b/a)^(k-1),0,..,0],[0,..,0]]
F[1]=[[1,0]]; F[k]=[[(-b/a)^(k-1),..,0]]
F[1]=[[0,1]]; F[k]=[[0,..,0]]
Basis of Vector Space Lambda Invariants:
{x/(1+b*x/a), y}
```

For an initial condition (x_0, y_0) with $|x_0| < |a/b|$, we obtain, for instance, the following inductive rational invariants:

$$F(x,y) = x_0y/(1 + bx_0/a) - xy_0/(1 + bx/a) = 0.$$

Using Corollary 4.1, we can also identify several inequality invariants. For instance, if we initially have $a > 0$ and $F^1(x_0, y_0) \geq 0$ then we get the inequality invariant $x/(1 + bx/a) \geq x_0/(1 + bx_0/a) \geq 0$. Also, if we initially have $a < 0$ and $F^1(x_0, y_0) \leq 0$ the have the inequality invariant $x_0/(1 + bx_0/a) \leq x/(1 + bx/a) \leq 0$. □

32

EXAMPLE 4. *Here is an example where our method exhibits a transcendental invariant. Most importantly, note that this kind of results can not be obtained via the classical constant, polynomial or fractional scale methods. Moreover, the invariant obtained converge everywhere.*

The formal power series invariant generated are often composed by expansion of some well-known transcendental function and hence has an analyzable closed form. Being able to compute closed forms for the invariants allows us to reason symbolically about formal power series. This facilitates the use of the invariants to verify properties. Consider the system S_3 given by

$$\dot{x}(t) = ax(t)$$

$$\dot{y}(t) = ay(t) + bx(t)y(t).$$

Here $P_1(x, y) = ax$ and $P_2(x, y) = ay + bxy$ and we get

$$M_{k-1,k} = \begin{pmatrix} 0 & 0 & & & \\ 0 & b & 0 & & \\ & \ddots & \ddots & \ddots & \\ & & 0 & (k-2)b & 0 \\ & & & 0 & (k-1)b \\ & & & & 0 \end{pmatrix} \in \mathcal{M}_{k+1,k}(\mathbb{R}),$$

thus U_k is equal to $\frac{(-b)^{k-1}}{a^{k-1}(k-1)!} \begin{pmatrix} 0 & 1 \\ 0 & 0 \\ \vdots & \vdots \\ 0 & 0 \end{pmatrix} \in \mathcal{M}_{k+1,2}(\mathbb{R}).$

Taking $F_1 = (1,0)^\top$, one has $F_k = (0,0,\ldots,0)^\top$ for $k \geq 2$, so that we get $F^1(x, y) = x$ as the first basis-vector of the space of a-invariants.

With $F_1 = (0,1)^\top$, one has $F_k = (0, \frac{(-b)^{k-1}}{a^{k-1}(k-1)!}, \ldots, 0)^\top$ for $k \geq 2$. Then we obtain the transcendental function $F^2(x, y) = \sum_{k \geq 1} \frac{(-bx)^{k-1}y}{a^{k-1}(k-1)!} = e^{-bx/a}y$ as the second basis-vector of the space of a-invariants.

```
Lambda=a
U[k]=[[0,..,0],[((-b)^(k-1))/(a^(k-1)*(k-1)!),0,..0]]
F[1]=[[1,0]]; F[k]=[[0,..,0]]
F[1]=[[0,1]]; F[k]=[[0,((-b)^(k-1))/(a^(k-1)*(k-1)!),0,..,0]]
Basis of Vector Space Lambda Invariants:
{x, exp(-b*x/a)*y}
```

Finally, for any given initial condition (x_0, y_0), the following assertion

$$F(x, y) = x(e^{-bx_0/a})y_0 - x_0(e^{-bx/a})y = 0$$

is an inductive invariant whatever are the initial conditions, i.e. for all x_0 and y_0. Clearly it depends smoothly on the initial value and is convergent everywhere. By applying Corollary 4.1, we can also identify several inequality invariants. For instance, if we initially have $a > 0$ and $F^1(x_0, y_0) \leq 0$ then we get the inequality invariant $e^{-bx/a}y \leq e^{-bx_0/a}y_0$. Also, if we initially have $a \leq 0$ and $F^1(x_0, y_0) \leq 0$ we get the inequality invariant $e^{-bx_0/a}y_0 \leq e^{-bx/a}y \leq 0$. $\square$

In Table 1 we summarizes some experimental results. The second column gives the closed-form type of the basis generators. We emphasize the fact that the issue of finding invariants absolutely does not reduce only to the computation of such a radius. The main issue is the computations of the coefficients U_k, which is equivalent to the knowledge of the invariant. As a consequence, the fact that we are able to find closed forms is a nice observation, but should not be considered as the most important one. The invariant is really given by its coefficients.

Table 1: Examples and experimental results: generation of basis of transcendental invariants.

Diff. Syst.	Closed-form	Time/s
Ex.(2)	Polynomial	6.1
Ex.(3)	Rational	7.6
Ex.(4)	Transcendental	18.9
$\dot{x} = 7x,$ $\dot{y} = 1/2x^2 + 7y.$	Polynomial	.7
$\dot{x} = 3x,$ $\dot{y} = 9x * y + 3y.$	Transcendental	1.1
$\dot{x} = 8x^2 + 5x,$ $\dot{y} = 5y.$	Rational	.8
$\dot{x} = b * x,$ $\dot{y} = b * y * (1 + x).$	Transcendental	11.3
$\dot{x} = b * x * (1 + x),$ $\dot{y} = b * y.$	Rational	6.5
$\dot{x} = b * x,$ $\dot{y} = b * (x^2 + y).$	Polynomial	4.5
$\dot{x} = x - x * y,$ $\dot{y} = y - x * y.$	Transcendental	2.1
$\dot{x} = x * y,$ $\dot{y} = x * y.$	Transcendental	1.6
$\dot{x} = x + a * x^2,$ $\dot{y} = y.$	Rational	4.1
[17] Ex.(2)	Transcendental	1.8
[14] Eq.(3)	Transcendental	1.4
[14] Eq.(4)	Transcendental	.4
[15]	Polynomial	2.4

8. HANDLING DISCRETE TRANSITIONS

The methods presented so far automatically generate bases of non trivial multivariate formal power series invariants for each differential rule associated to locations in the hybrid automaton. The basis of vector space invariants provided by our techniques, generate very precise invariants that could be used as a primitive in any static reachability analysis and verification framework for hybrid systems with non-linear continuous modes.

In order to handle the discrete transition relations, we can adapt and extend the methods proposed in our previous works on static analysis of hybrid systems [17, 16, 15] and discrete programs [17, 13]. Such techniques are completely orthogonal and different from those presented here. Those provide methods to handle discrete algebraic transitions that can be integrated in order to develop a full technique for hybrid systems. In fact, many other methods from different approaches could be seen as complementary techniques.

9. CONCLUSIONS

Invariant generation problems for continuous time evolution is the most challenging step in static analysis and verification of hybrid systems. Computationally, hybrid systems were an inspiration and motivation for this research. Once these invariants are generated, we are able to use and compose several techniques from static analysis for discrete state jumps. In order to verify safety properties expressed with transcendental functions and to reason symbolically about formal power series, it is necessary to be able to generate formal power series invariants. We presented methods which generate bases of *multivariate formal power series and transcendental invariants* for hybrid systems with non-linear behavior. Also, our methods generate *inequality* and *equality* invariants.

The problem of generating power series invariants and the results are clearly novel. Importantly, there is no other known methods that generate this type of invariants. We can prove that some of the examples that were dealt with do not have"finite" polynomial invariants. Hence, they are beyond the limits of other recent approaches. As for efficiency, we used linear algebra methods which do not require several Gröebner basis computations or quantifier eliminations. We also provide very general sufficient conditions allowing for the existence and computation of invariants defined by convergent formal power series for multivariate polynomial differential systems. Those conditions could also be used directly as primitives in any static analysis and verification framework for hybrid systems.

10. REFERENCES

[1] B. Akbarpour and L. C. Paulson. Applications of metitarski in the verification of control and hybrid systems. In *HSCC '09: Proc. of the 12th Inter. Conf. on Hybrid Systems: Computation and Control*, 2009.

[2] R. Alur, C. Courcoubetis, N. Halbwachs, T. A. Henzinger, P. h. Ho, X. Nicollin, A. Olivero, J. Sifakis, and S. Yovine. The algorithmic analysis of hybrid systems. *Theoretical Computer Science*, 138:3–34, 1995.

[3] E. Asarin, T. Dang, and A. Girard. Hybridization methods for the analysis of nonlinear systems. *Acta Inf.*, 43(7):451–476, 2007.

[4] C. Borralleras, S. Lucas, R. Navarro-Marset, E. Rodriguez-Carbonell, and A. Rubio. Solving non-linear polynomial arithmetic via sat modulo linear arithmetic. *CADE*, pages 294–305, 2009.

[5] D. Boularas and A. Chouikrat. Equations d'amorcage d'integrales premieres formelles. In *Linear and Multilinear Algebra*, volume 54, pages 219–233, 2006.

[6] B. Buchberger. Symbolic computation: Computer algebra and logic. In *Frontiers of Combining Systems: Proc. of the 1st Int. Workshop*, pages 193–220, 1996.

[7] P. Cousot and R. Cousot. Abstract interpretation: a unified lattice model for static analysis of programs by construction or approximation of fixpoints. In *Conf. Record of the 4th Annual ACM SIGPLAN-SIGACT Symposium on Principles of Programming Languages*, pages 238–252, Los Angeles, California, 1977. ACM Press, NY.

[8] P. Cousot and R. Cousot. Abstract interpretation and application to logic programs. *Journal of Logic Programming*, 13(2–3):103–179, 1992.

[9] T. Dang and D. Salinas. Image computation for polynomial dynamical systems using the bernstein expansion. In *CAV*, pages 219–232, 2009.

[10] M. Franzle, C. Herde, T. Teige, S. Ratschan, and T. Schubert. Efficient solving of large non-linear arithmetic constraint systems with complex boolean structure. *JSAT*, 1(3-4):209–236, 2007.

[11] T. Henzinger. The theory of hybrid automata. In *Proc. of the 11th Annual IEEE Symposium on Logic in Computer Science (LICS '96)*, pages 278–292, 1996.

[12] Z. Manna. *Mathematical Theory of Computation*. McGrw-Hill, 1974.

[13] N. Matringe, A. V. Moura, and R. Rebiha. Endomorphisms for non-trivial non-linear loop invariant generation. In *5th Int. Conf. Theoretical Aspects of Computing*, pages 425–439. LNCS, 2008.

[14] N. Matringe, A. V. Moura, and R. Rebiha. Morphisms for non-trivial non-linear invariant generation for algebraic hybrid systems. Technical Report TR-IC-08-32, Institute of Computing, University of Campinas, November 2008.

[15] N. Matringe, A. V. Moura, and R. Rebiha. Morphisms for analysis of hybrid systems. In *ACM/IEEE Cyber-Physical Systems CPSWeek'09, 2nd Inter. Conf. on Numerical Software Verification.(NSV2009) Verification of Cyber-Physical Software Systems*, 2009.

[16] N. Matringe, A. V. Moura, and R. Rebiha. Morphisms for non-trivial non-linear invariant generation for algebraic hybrid systems. In *12th Int. Conf. Hybrid Systems: Computation and Control (HSCC2009)*. LNCS, 2009.

[17] N. Matringe, A. V. Moura, and R. Rebiha. Generatin invariants for non-linear hybrid systems by linear algebraic methods. In *17th Int. Static Analysis Symposium, SAS2010*. LNCS, 2010.

[18] A. Platzer and E. M. Clarke. Computing differential invariants of hybrid systems as fixedpoints. In *Computer-Aided Verification, CAV'08*, LNCS, 2008.

[19] S. Prajna and A. Jadbabaie. Safety verification of hybrid systems using barrier certificates, 2004.

[20] E. Rodriguez-Carbonell and A. Tiwari. Generating polynomial invariants for hybrid systems. In *Hybrid Systems: Computation and Control, HSCC 2005*, volume 3414 of *LNCS*, pages 590–605, 2005.

[21] S. Gulwani and A. Tiwari. Constraint-based approach for analysis of hybrid systems. In *Proc. of the 14th Int. Conf. on Computer Aided Verification CAV*, 2008.

[22] S. Sankaranarayanan. Automatic invariant generation for hybrid systems using ideal fixed points. In *Proc. of the 13th ACM Inter. Conf. on Hybrid systems: computation and control*, HSCC '10, 2010.

[23] S. Sankaranarayanan. Automatic abstraction of non-linear systems using change of variables transformations. In *Inter. Conf. on Hybrid Systems: Computation and Control (HSCC)*, 2011.

[24] S. Sankaranarayanan, H. Sipma, and Z. Manna. Constructing invariants for hybrid system. In *Hybrid Systems: Computation and Control HSCC*, volume 2993 of *LNCS*, pages 539–554, 2004.

[25] T. Sturm and A. Tiwari. Verification and synthesis using real quantifier elimination. In *Proceedings of the 36th international symposium on Symbolic and algebraic computation*, ISSAC '11, pages 329–336, New York, NY, USA, 2011. ACM.

[26] A. Tiwari and G. Khanna. Nonlinear systems: Approximating reach sets. In *Hybrid Systems: Computation and Control HSCC*, volume 2993 of *LNCS*, pages 600–614, 2004.

[27] V. Weispfenning. Quantifier elimination for real algebra - the quadratic case and beyond. *Applicable Algebra in Engineering, Communication and Computing*, 8(2):85–101, 1997.

Heterogeneous Verification of Cyber-Physical Systems using Behavior Relations

Akshay Rajhans
arajhans@ece.cmu.edu

Bruce H. Krogh
krogh@ece.cmu.edu

Department of Electrical and Computer Engineering
Carnegie Mellon University
Pittsburgh, PA 15213

ABSTRACT

Today's complex cyber-physical systems are being built increasingly using model-based development (MBD), where mathematical models for the system behavior are checked against design specifications using analysis tools. Different types of models and analysis tools are used to address different aspects of the system. While the use of heterogeneous formalisms supports a divide-and-conquer approach to complexity and allows engineers with different types of expertise to work on various aspects of the design, system integration problems can arise due to the lack of an underlying unifying formalism. In this paper, we introduce the notion of behavior relations to address the problem of heterogeneity and propose constraints over parameters as a mechanism to manage inter-model dependencies and ensure consistency. In addition, we present structured constructs of nested conjunctive and disjunctive analyses to enable multi-model heterogeneous verification. The theoretical concepts are illustrated using an example of a cooperative intersection collision avoidance system (CICAS).

Categories and Subject Descriptors

G.4 [**Mathematical Software**]: Verification; I.6.4 [**Simulation and Modeling**]: Model Validation and Analysis

Keywords

Heterogeneous Verification, Cyber-Physical Systems, Behavior Relations

1. INTRODUCTION

Model-based development (MBD) refers to the creation of mathematical models of systems under design and checking those models against design specifications using suitable analysis tools. The MBD approach has the ability to catch errors early in the system design before the system or

prototypes are built, thereby avoiding costly re-design/re-development cycles. For all but the most trivial systems, many types of models need to be created and analyzed. This introduces the problem of heterogeneity: without a single comprehensive modeling formalism, how can it be guaranteed that the heterogeneous models are consistent with each other, and how can verification results from the different formalisms be combined to infer system-level properties? In this paper, we propose a general framework based on *behavior relations* and *constraints over parameters* as a formal basis for the design and verification of complex systems using multiple heterogeneous models.

Heterogeneity is inherent in cyber-physical systems (CPS) due to the tight coupling between computation elements, physical dynamics and communication networks. Typical heterogeneous aspects of a CPS are its physical dynamics, control logic, software implementation, real-time execution, communication networking and so on. For example, consider the cooperative intersection collision avoidance system for stop-sign assist (CICAS-SSA) [1] illustrated in Fig. 1. The figure depicts a vehicle called the *subject vehicle* (SV) waiting on a minor road to cross through major-road traffic at a stop-sign-controlled intersection. The system aims to augment human judgment about safe gaps in oncoming traffic by *sensing* the speeds and positions of the oncoming vehicles using cameras, magnetic induction loops or other sensors, *communicating* these values to a decision system via wired or wireless networks and *computing* safe gaps based on the *physical dynamics* of the vehicles and speed limits, implemented either on a dedicated road-side computer or onboard a smart vehicle. There is no good unified formalism for modeling all aspects of this complex heterogeneous system. And even if there were, verifying the correctness of the system design using a single model would be an intractable problem.

MBD of CPS involves creating a collection of different models using a variety of formalisms that are best suited for the different aspects of the overall design problem. Common formalisms used for design and analysis of a CPS include: acausal equation-based models in tools such as MapleSim and Modelica, suited for modeling the underlying physics of a system, e.g., the plant dynamics; signal-flow models in tools such as Simulink, suitable for control design and simulation; finite state machines and labeled transition systems in tools such as LTSA, best suited for modeling decision logic and communication protocols; hybrid-dynamic models such as hybrid automata in tools such as SpaceEx, useful for

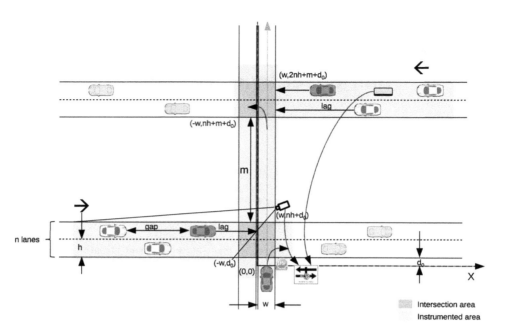

Figure 1: **A pictorial sketch of CICAS-SSA. Parameters** w, n, h, m, d_0 **depend on the intersection geometry.**

analyzing abstract unified behaviors of continuous dynamics and discrete mode switches; network simulation models in tools such as OMNET++, useful for analyzing communication network properties such as packet loss, communication delay and so on; and software models in tools such as Spin, useful for analyzing whether the decision logic is correctly implemented.

These heterogeneous models are usually created and analyzed by different engineers due to the wide range of expertise necessary for designing complex systems. In current practice, methods for maintaining consistency between the models and composing verification results from the various models to infer system-level properties are ad hoc at best. This paper presents a formal basis for addressing these problems.

The rest of the paper is organized as follows. We begin with a review of the relevant literature in Sec. 2. In Sec. 3, a general framework is developed for verification using heterogeneous models. Sec. 4 provides conjunctive and disjunctive constructs to enable heterogeneous verification. Sec. 5 illustrates the concepts using the CICAS-SSA example. Sec. 6 introduces the notion of semantic consistency using constraints over parameters and these concepts are illustrated in Sec. 7. The paper concludes with a discussion and future work in Sec. 8.

2. RELATED WORK

The idea of using an abstraction in a simpler modeling formalism in order to verify safety properties of a more complex model in the original formalism has been frequently used in the literature. Hybrid abstractions of nonlinear systems [15, 12], LHA abstractions of linear hybrid systems [13], discrete abstractions of hybrid systems [4, 11, 3] and continuous abstractions of hybrid systems [2] are some of the examples where simpler abstractions are successfully created and used. These approaches use specific pairs of formalisms. Our ob-

jective is to create a general framework for abstraction that can support any set of heterogeneous formalisms.

Towards the aim of heterogeneous multi-model development, several research efforts have focused on supporting simulation of heterogeneous elements in a common framework. Ptolemy II, for example, supports hierarchical integration of multiple "models of computation" into a single simulation model based on an actor-oriented formalism [8]. MILAN [18] is an integrated simulation framework that allows different components of a system to be built using different tools. The Metropolis toolchain [5] supports multiple analysis tools for design and simulation. However, the focus of these efforts has been simulation and not verification.

Inference-based approaches that use ontologies have been proposed for static analysis and type checking [20]. In a similar spirit, the work in [17] focuses on integrating the results of disparate verification efforts and analysis techniques using static and epistemic ontologies. Rather than using an ontology-based approach, we use a behavioral approach to compare and relate behaviors of different types.

The work by Julius [16] uses a behavioral approach in the spirit of Willems' work [22] and creates a framework for comparing and interconnecting behaviors based on the different time axis structures for discrete, continuous and hybrid behaviors. For embedded software applications, the Behavior-Interaction-Priority (BIP) framework [9] leverages the component structure of a system and supports behavioral annotation of the components in the form of state diagrams [6] to support system analysis. In contrast to Julius's approach of incorporating behaviors in the definition of models, we see behaviors as the semantic interpretation of systems, which allows us to observe behaviors in different domains. This idea is similar to the one proposed in [14], where timed and time-abstract traces serve as different semantics for the same hybrid automaton. The notion of tagged signal semantics has been proposed to compare [19] and compose

[7] heterogeneous reactive systems. Unlike [9, 7], the focus of this work is not to compose heterogeneous components into one big system, but rather to use heterogeneous models independently towards a common system-verification goal.

The TLA+ proof system deploys a proof manager that breaks down a complex verification task logically into proof obligations that are proved using theorem provers and SMT solvers [10]. We use a similar approach for logically composing the results of verification activities, but their framework based on temporal logic of actions (TLA) is primarily aimed towards software systems, whereas our framework supports more general (e.g. continuous, hybrid) dynamics and non-deductive analysis methods.

3. HETEROGENEOUS VERIFICATION

Our objective is to use models and their specifications to reason about the underlying system. The first step in analyzing heterogeneous models and specifications together in a common framework is to create a mechanism to compare their associated sets of behaviors. In our previous work, we dealt with heterogeneity based on the assumption that one can create semantic mappings from each model and specification onto one common behavioral domain [21]. Here create we a framework using behavior relations to support true semantic heterogeneity by allowing the use of several different types of behavior formalisms for different models and specifications.

A *behavior formalism* B is the set of all possible behaviors of a particular type. There is no restriction on the type of behaviors: they could be event traces, continuous trajectories, hybrid traces, input-output maps or something else.

Definition 1 (Behavior Relation) *Given behavior formalisms B_1 and B_2, a behavior relation is a set $R \subseteq B_1 \times B_2$ that associates pairs of behaviors from the two sets B_1 and B_2.*

For a subset of behaviors $B_1' \subseteq B_1$, let $R(B_1')$ denote the set of behaviors in B_2 associated with behaviors in B_1', i.e., $R(B_1') = \{b_2 \mid \exists b_1 \in B_1' \text{ s.t. } (b_1, b_2) \in R\}$. Similarly, for $B_2' \subseteq B_2$, let $R^{-1}(B_2')$ represent the set of behaviors in B_1 associated with behaviors in B_2', i.e., $R^{-1}(B_2') = \{b_1 \mid \exists b_2 \in B_2' \text{ s.t. } (b_1, b_2) \in R\}$.

A *specification* S is a a logical assertion written in a specification formalism $\mathcal{S}$. There is no restriction on what specification formalism can be used. Specifications could be written in, for example, various temporal logics, Kripke structures, automata, sets of unsafe states to be avoided, or even in English language, so long as their semantic interpretation is clear in terms of the associated behavioral formalism. The *semantic interpretation* of S in a behavior formalism B, denoted by $[\![S]\!]^B$, is defined as the set of all behaviors in B for which, the specification is satisfied.

When semantically interpreted over the same set of behaviors B, a (stronger) specification S_2 is said to imply a (weaker) specification S_1, written $S_2 \Rightarrow^B S_1$ if $[\![S_2]\!]^B \subseteq [\![S_1]\!]^B$. The following definition extends this notion to heterogeneous behavior spaces using behavior relations.

Definition 2 (Heterogeneous Implication) *Given behavior formalisms B_1, B_2 and a behavior relation $R \subseteq B_1 \times B_2$, we say that specification S_2 implies specification S_1 via R, written $S_2 \Rightarrow^R S_1$, if*

$$R^{-1}([\![S_2]\!]^{B_2}) \subseteq [\![S_1]\!]^{B_1}.$$

This definition requires that if a behavior $b_1 \in B_1$ is associated through R with a behavior in $b_2 \in B_2$ that satisfies S_2, then b_1 satisfies S_1.

A *modeling formalism* $\mathcal{M}$ is a set of models of a particular type. Transition systems, hybrid automata, signal-flow models, acausal equation-based models, and network models are some of the modeling formalisms used in CPS; however the discussion is valid for any modeling formalism. A *model* M is an element of some formalism $\mathcal{M}$. Given a behavior formalism B, the *semantic interpretation* of a model M is the set of behaviors $[\![M]\!]^B \subseteq B$ that it allows.

When interpreted over the same behavioral formalism B, a model M_2 is an *abstraction* of a model M_1, written $M_1 \sqsubseteq^B M_2$, if $[\![M_1]\!]^B \subseteq [\![M_2]\!]^B$. This is the standard definition of abstraction common among the literature, using, for example, language or trace inclusion.

Definition 3 (Heterogeneous Abstraction) *Given behavior formalisms B_1, B_2 and a behavior relation $R \subseteq B_1 \times B_2$, a model M_2 is an abstraction of a model M_1 through R, written $M_1 \sqsubseteq^R M_2$, if*

$$[\![M_1]\!]^{B_1} \subseteq R^{-1}([\![M_2]\!]^{B_2}).$$

This definition asserts that for every behavior in B_1 of model M_1, the behavior relation R associates at least one corresponding behavior in B_2 of model M_2.

In a given behavior formalism B, a model M *entails* a specification S, written $M \models^B S$, if $[\![M]\!]^B \subseteq [\![S]\!]^B$. When true, this simply asserts that the set of behaviors of the model M do not violate the set of safe behaviors allowed by the specification S. To establish this type of entailment, formal approaches such as reachability analysis and theorem proving, or semi-formal approaches like systematic state-space exploration, need to be used whenever possible. We do not restrict what method the system designer chooses to use to establish entailment.

Proposition 1 *Given behavior formalisms B_1 and B_2, models M_1 and M_2, specifications S_1 and S_2, and a behavior relation $R \subseteq B_1 \times B_2$, if $M_1 \sqsubseteq^R M_2$, $M_2 \models^{B_2} S_2$ and $S_2 \Rightarrow^R S_1$, then $M_1 \models^{B_1} S_1$.*

PROOF. From $M_1 \sqsubseteq^R M_2$, we have

$$[\![M_1]\!]^{B_1} \subseteq R^{-1}([\![M_2]\!]^{B_2})$$
$$(\text{From } M_2 \models^{B_2} S_2) \subseteq R^{-1}([\![S_2]\!]^{B_2})$$
$$(\text{From } S_2 \Rightarrow^R S_1) \subseteq [\![S_1]\!]^{B_1}.$$

Therefore, $M_1 \models^{B_1} S_1$.

This proposition gives us the conditions under which a heterogeneous abstraction of a complex model can be used to verify a property of the underlying system. In the following section, we further develop this idea to use *several* abstractions to verify properties of a given system.

4. MULTI-MODEL HETEROGENEITY

There are two natural ways of using multiple models and specifications. In one, models individually are abstractions of the underlying system and the conjunction of their associated specifications needs to imply the system specification. Alternatively, each model may represent only a subset of the behaviors of the underlying system, and the collection of models provides an abstraction of the complete system.

In this second case, the specification for each model needs to imply the specification of interest for the underlying system for the set of behaviors covered by the model. The following develops these two notions in the context of heterogeneous verification.

We first consider the case where each model is a heterogeneous abstraction of the underlying system. In this case, we need to ensure that the specifications checked against each model together imply the specification of the underlying system. The following definition makes this notion formal.

Definition 4 (Conjunctive Heterogeneous Implication)
Given a system behavior formalism B_0, behavior formalisms B_i and behavior relations $R_i \subseteq B_0 \times B_i$, $i = 1, \ldots, n$, specifications $S_i, i = 1, \ldots, n$ conjunctively imply the system specification S_0 if

$$\bigcap_i R_i^{-1}(\llbracket S_i \rrbracket^{B_i}) \subseteq \llbracket S_0 \rrbracket^{B_0}.$$

This definition allows the individual specifications S_i to not imply S_0, but their conjunction (intersection of the allowed behaviors) is required to be stronger than S_0.

Proposition 2 (Heterogeneous Conjunctive Analysis)
For a system model M_0 with a behavioral formalism B_0 and specification S_0, given models M_i with the corresponding behavior formalisms B_i, specifications S_i and behavior relations $R_i \subseteq B_0 \times B_i$, if $M_0 \sqsubseteq^{R_i} M_i$, specifications S_i conjunctively imply S_0, and $M_i \models^{B_i} S_i$ for each $i = 1, \ldots, n$, then $M_0 \models^{B_0} S_0$.

PROOF. From $M_0 \sqsubseteq^{R_i} M_i$ for each i, we have

$$\llbracket M_0 \rrbracket^{B_0} \subseteq \bigcap_i R_i^{-1}(\llbracket M_i \rrbracket^{B_i})$$

$$\text{(since } M_i \models^{B_i} S_i) \subseteq \bigcap_i R_i^{-1}(\llbracket S_i \rrbracket^{B_i})$$

$$\text{(Conj. Het. Implication)} \subseteq \llbracket S_0 \rrbracket^{B_0}.$$

Therefore, $M_0 \models^{B_0} S_0$.

Now we consider the case where different models are built to represent different subsets of behaviors of a system. This is typically useful when there are different behaviors in different operating regimes best modeled by different models, where neither one fully represents the whole set of behaviors of the system, but their union does. This notion is made formal by the following definition.

Definition 5 (Model Coverage) *For a system model M_0 with a behavioral formalism B_0, given a set of models M_i with corresponding behavior formalisms B_i and behavior relations $R_i \subseteq B_0 \times B_i$, models M_i, $i = 1, \ldots, n$ cover M_0 if there exists a partition $\{B_0^1, B_0^2, \ldots, B_0^n\}$ of $\llbracket M_0 \rrbracket^{B_0}$ s.t. $\forall i = 1, 2, \ldots, n$*

$$B_0^i \subseteq R_i^{-1}(\llbracket M_i \rrbracket^{B_i}).$$

This definition requires that every behavior of the underlying system M_0 to be accounted for by at least one model.

Lemma 1 *If models M_i cover M_0 through R_i, $i = 1, \ldots, n$, we have*

$$\llbracket M_0 \rrbracket^{B_0} \subseteq \bigcup_{i=1}^{n} R_i^{-1}(\llbracket M_i \rrbracket^{B_i}).$$

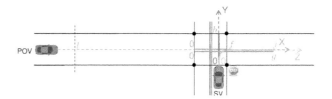

Figure 2: A simple variant of the CICAS-SSA with one near-side oncoming lane with one POV. Road coordinates X, Y and Z are along the POV path, SV path going straight and SV turning right respectively. Conflict areas along the paths shown using bold line segments.

PROOF. From the definition of partition, we have

$$\llbracket M_0 \rrbracket^{B_0} = \bigcup_{i=1}^{n} B_0^i$$

$$\text{(Def. 5)} \subseteq \bigcup_{i=1}^{n} R_i^{-1}(\llbracket M_i \rrbracket^{B_i}).$$

In this case, since each model is not an abstraction of the underlying system, to imply a specification for the underlying system it is necessary that we verify specifications that are at least as strong as the system specification, as stated in the following proposition.

Proposition 3 (Heterogeneous Disjunctive Analysis)
For a system model M_0 with a behavioral formalism B_0 and specification S_0, given models M_i with the corresponding behavior formalisms B_i, specifications S_i and behavior relations $R_i \subseteq B_0 \times B_i$, if each specification S_i heterogeneously implies S_0, models M_i cover M_0, and $M_i \models^{B_i} S_i$ for each $i = 1, \ldots, n$, then $M_0 \models^{B_0} S_0$.

PROOF. From the definition of model coverage, we have

$$\llbracket M_0 \rrbracket^{B_0} \subseteq \bigcup_i R_i^{-1}(\llbracket M_i \rrbracket^{B_i})$$

$$\text{(since } M_i \models^{B_i} S_i) \subseteq \bigcup_i R_i^{-1}(\llbracket S_i \rrbracket^{B_i})$$

$$\text{(Het. Implication)} \subseteq \llbracket S_0 \rrbracket^{B_0}.$$

Therefore, $M_0 \models^{B_0} S_0$.

Finally, we note that the conjunctive and disjunctive analysis constructs can be nested arbitrarily. For example, the jth conjunctive verification subtask $M_j \models^{B_j} S_j$ can be broken down disjunctively into its subtasks $M_{ji} \models^{B_{ji}} S_{ji}$ by creating new models that cover M_j and specifications that imply S_j. Thus, using the nesting of conjunctive and disjunctive constructs, any arbitrary logical breakdown of a system verification task can be achieved. This is illustrated in an example in the following section.

5. EXAMPLE

Consider a simple variant of the CICAS-SSA as shown in Fig. 2, with a single major-road lane and one oncoming principal other vehicle (POV). The subject vehicle (SV) can either go straight or turn right to merge into POV's path. The SV is able to sense the position of the POV, and the decision of whether to start driving or not is made on-board

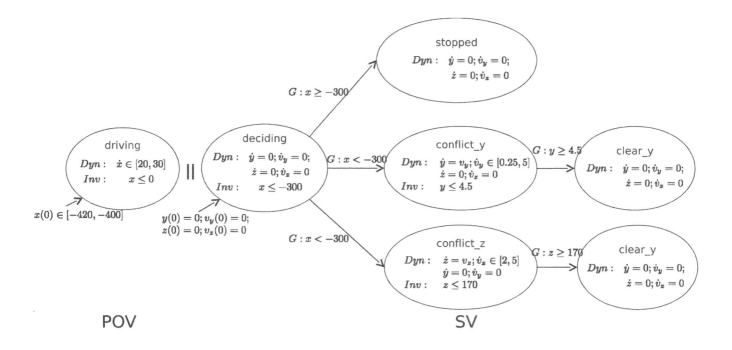

Figure 3: A single universal model M_0 for the simple SSA system.

the SV using this sensed position of the POV. The road coordinates along the path of the POV and along the straight and right-turn paths of the SV are assumed to be along dimensions X, Y and Z respectively. The conflict areas where crashes can occur (depending on the intersection geometry) are either $x \in [0, f = 3]$ and $y \in (0, h = 4.5)$ or $x \in [0, g]$ and $z \in (0, j)$, where f and h depend on the intersection geometry, and g and j are chosen large enough (here, 170m) such that the SV has a chance to accelerate to the highway speed so that after the turn there is no (intersection-related) collision.

Fig. 3 shows a model of the system made up of two hybrid automata components SV and POV. The decision strategy implemented on-board the SV is that if the POV hasn't crossed an imaginary marker at position $l = -300$ along the X axis, the SV is permitted to start driving, but it doesn't have to. When POV crosses l, the SV has to stay stopped, forced by the invariant in `deciding`. Whenever permitted, whether the SV decides to go straight or turn right is represented as a nondeterministic choice; however once it has committed to one, it isn't allowed to change its mind. The evolution stops when the SV clears the conflict regions or when the POV enters the intersection. By the time the POV enters the intersection, if the SV is still in the conflict zone, there is a safety violation (a potential collision). Alternatively, if the SV has cleared the conflict zone or hasn't entered it, there is no safety violation. The objective is to guarantee collision freedom for this particular strategy. The collision-freedom specification S_0 can be defined by the temporal logic formula $S_0 : \Box \neg ((x == 0 \land 0 < y < 4.5) \lor (x == 0 \land 0 < z < 170))$.

5.1 Disjunctive analysis

We first disjunctively break down the problem into two subproblems. We create two models, one for the case where

SV is only allowed to go straight and the other where the SV is only allowed to go right, as shown in Fig. 4 and 5. The behavior domain of M_0 (i.e., B_0) is the set of all five dimensional hybrid traces, while B_1 and B_2 are each sets of all three dimensional hybrid traces. The behavior relations for this breakdown are as follows:

- $R_1 : \{(b_0, b_1) | b_0 \downarrow_{z, v_z} == \bar{0} \text{ and } b_0 \downarrow_{x, y, v_y} == b_1\}$
- $R_2 : \{(b_0, b_2) | b_0 \downarrow_{y, v_y} == \bar{0} \text{ and } b_0 \downarrow_{x, z, v_z} == b_2\}$

where $\bar{0}$ represents a 2-d trace of zeros over all time and $\downarrow_{()}$ represents the projection on $()$.

The specifications to be checked for the two models are

- $S_1 : \Box \neg (x == 0 \land 0 < y < 4.5)$ and
- $S_2 : \Box \neg (x == 0 \land 0 < z < 170)$.

We have heterogeneous implication $S_1 \Rightarrow^{R_1} S_0$ because $R_1^{-1}(\llbracket S_1 \rrbracket^{B_1})$ forces that y be conflict-free and z be 0, which implies that y is conflict-free and z is conflict-free. Similarly, we have $S_2 \Rightarrow^{R_2} S_0$. Further, we note that in every behavior of M_0, either $\{y, v_y\}$ or $\{z, v_z\}$ are zero and both the possibilities are covered by either model. Therefore, from Prop. 3, if $M_1 \models^{B_1} S_1$ and $M_2 \models^{B_2} S_2$, we can conclude $M_0 \models^{B_0} S_0$. Out of these two verification sub-tasks, we show how $M_1 \models^{B_1} S_1$ can be proved using conjunctive analysis in the next subsection. $M_2 \models^{B_2} S_2$ can be shown in a similar manner.

5.2 Conjunctive analysis

Consider the subtask of showing $M_1 \models^{B_1} S_1$. We break down this task conjunctively by creating three models M_{1i} and constructing corresponding specifications S_{1i}, $i = 1, 2, 3$, as shown in Fig. 5. M_{11} models the behaviors of the POV, and is exactly the same as the POV automaton in M_1. M_{12}

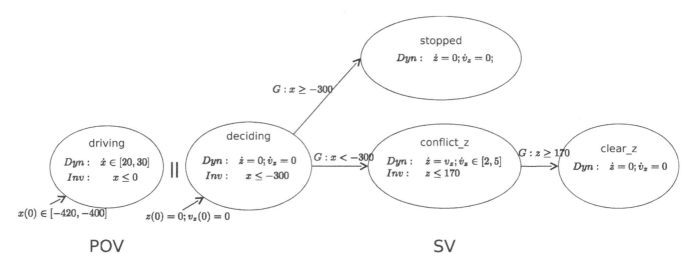

POV ‖ SV

$x(0) \in [-420, -400]$ $z(0) = 0; v_z(0) = 0$

Figure 4: A model M_2 for SV only going right.

models the behavior of the SV only while it is in the conflict zone and has the same dynamics as that of the `conflict_y` location of M_1. M_{13} is a discrete model consisting of two elements. The component POV is a created by partitioning the component POV of M_1 into discrete states `far`,`close`, and `inInt` using predicates $x \leq -300$, $-300 \leq x \leq 0$, and $0 \leq x$. The second component SV is merely a discrete control graph of the hybrid automaton model for SV in M_1. The only synchronized pair of transitions is $(\texttt{far} \xrightarrow{\sigma_1} \texttt{close})$ and $(\texttt{deciding} \xrightarrow{\sigma_1} \texttt{stopped})$. Non-blocking self loops have been dropped from the pictorial representation for simplicity.

The behavior relations are

- $R_{11} : \{(b_1, t_{11}) | b_{11} == b_1 \downarrow_x \}$,

- $R_{12} : \{(b_1, b_{12}) | b_{12} == s_1 \downarrow_{y, v_y}$ where s_1 is b_1 restricted to the discrete location $(\texttt{driving}, \texttt{conflict\_y})\}$ and

- $R_{13} : \{(b_1, b_{13}) | b_1$ is a hybrid trajectory that visits the discrete locations corresponding to ones in b_{13} in that order $\}$.

For these behavior relations, we first note that $M_1 \sqsubseteq^{R_{1i}} M_{1i}$ because neither of the models M_{1i} is more restrictive than M_1. The specifications for the three models are

- $S_{11} : \Box (x == -300 \Rightarrow \Box_9 \ x < 0)$,

- $S_{12} : \Box (\Diamond_8 \ y \geq h)$ and

- $S_{13} : \Box ((\phi_1 \wedge \neg \phi_2) \rightarrow \neg(\Diamond \phi_2))$, where ϕ_1 is the predicate "POV is close" satisfied in states $(\texttt{close}, \cdot)$ and $(\texttt{inInt}, \cdot)$; and ϕ_2 is the predicate "SV is driving" satisfied in states $(\cdot, \texttt{con\_y})$.

The behaviors effectively allowed in B_1 by the specifications S_{1i} are as follows:

- $R_{11}^{-1}(\llbracket S_{11} \rrbracket)$: system behaviors where POV takes at least 9 seconds to get from $l = -300$ to the intersection.

- $R_{12}^{-1}(\llbracket S_{12} \rrbracket)$: system behaviors where SV clears the intersection within 8 seconds of starting to drive.

- $R_{13}^{-1}(\llbracket S_{13} \rrbracket)$: system behaviors where SV does not start driving after POV crosses l.

There can only be two cases:

1. The SV has already started driving before the POV crosses l and is in the intersection: in this case, from $R_{11}^{-1}(\llbracket S_{11} \rrbracket)$ and $R_{12}^{-1}(\llbracket S_{12} \rrbracket)$ together, it will clear the intersection in at most 8 seconds and the POV won't get to the intersection in at least 9 seconds, OR

2. The SV hasn't started driving when the POV crosses l: in this case, from $R_{13}^{-1}(\llbracket S_{13} \rrbracket)$, the SV cannot start driving anymore.

Therefore, from all the specifications put together, the two cars can't be in the intersection at the same time, which implies S_1, i.e., we have conjunctive heterogeneous implication.

$M_{11} \models^{B_{11}} S_{11}$ can be shown by algebraic computations: for the fastest velocity (30m/s) it takes 10s to travel 300m. $M_{12} \models^{B_{12}} S_{12}$ can be shown by Newton's laws of motion: the longest time needed to cross 4.5m with initial velocity 0 and minimum acceleration 0.25m/s^2 is $\sqrt{\frac{2*4.5}{0.25}} = 6$ seconds. $M_{13} \models^{B_{13}} S_{13}$ can be shown by using Labeled Transition System Analyzer (LTSA). Under these conditions, using Prop. 2, we can infer that $M_1 \models^{B_1} S_1$.

6. HETEROGENEOUS CONSISTENCY

The framework developed in Sec. 4 treats the model abstraction and model coverage in terms of the entire sets of behaviors. At that level, the interdependencies between individual behaviors of the models are lost. In our earlier work [21], we introduced the use of constraints over parameters as a mechanism to capture interdependencies between models and to ensure consistency. Here, we redevelop a consistency framework based on constraints over parameters for our new approach using behavior relations introduced in Sec. 3 and 4 and extend the idea to also capture interdependencies between specifications.

A *parameter* p of a system is a real-valued static variable that affects the system behavior. The *valuation* of a set of

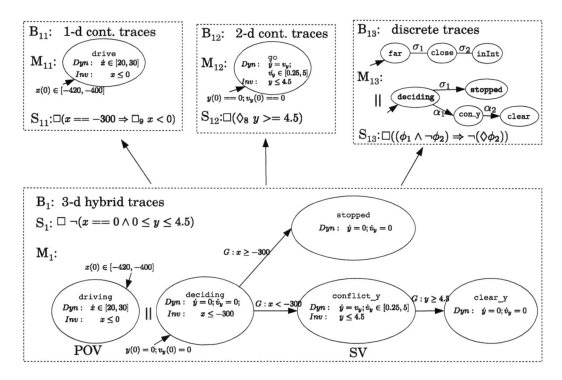

Figure 5: Heterogeneous conjunctive analysis of a model M_1 for SV going only straight.

parameters P is a function $v : P \to \mathbb{R}$ that associates each parameter with a value. $V(P)$ denotes the set of all possible valuations of the parameters in P.

A *constraint* $C(P)$ over a set of parameters P is an expression written in a constraint formalism $\mathcal{C}$, such as first-order logic of real arithmetic. For a given $v \in V(P)$, $[\![C(P)]\!]_v \in \{\top, \bot\}$ denotes the evaluation of the constraint $C(P)$ at v, and $[\![C(P)]\!]$ denotes the set of all valuations v of P for which $[\![C(P)]\!]_v = \top$.

Conjunction of constraints $C_1(P)$ and $C_2(P)$, written $C_1(P) \wedge C_2(P)$, is also a constraint whose corresponding parameter valuations are the intersection of the parameter valuations of the original constraints, i.e., $[\![C_1(P) \wedge C_2(P)]\!] = [\![C_1(P)]\!] \cap [\![C_2(P)]\!]$. Similarly, disjunction of constraints is a constraint whose corresponding parameter valuations are the union of the parameter valuations of the original constraints. We write $C'(P) \Rightarrow C(P)$ when $[\![C'(P)]\!] \subseteq [\![C(P)]\!]$.

Given two sets of parameters P and P', the *projection* of a constraint $C(P)$ onto P', written as $C(P) \downarrow_{P'}$, is the constraint over P' defined by existential quantification of the parameters in $P \setminus P'$. Its valuations $[\![C(P) \downarrow_{P'}]\!]$ are

$$\{v' \in V(P') \mid \exists v \in [\![C(P)]\!] : v'(p') = v(p') \; \forall p' \in P' \cap P\}.$$

We now consider that a set of parameters P_i is introduced for every i^{th} analysis task. Parameters $P_i^M \subseteq P_i$ are associated with the models M_i and parameters $P_i^S \subseteq P_i$ are associated with the specifications S_i. Constraints C_i^M and C_i^S determine the values of the parameters in P_i^M and P_i^S for models M_i and specifications S_i, respectively. The *semantic interpretation* of a parameterized model M_i with a constraint C_i^M, written $[\![C_i^M, M_i]\!]^{B_i}$, is the set of all possible behaviors in B_i associated with the model M_i for all parameter valuations in $[\![C_i^M(P_i^M)]\!]$. Similarly, the semantic

interpretation of a parameterized specification $[\![C_i^S, S_i]\!]^{B_i}$ is the set of all behaviors in B_i that are permitted by S_i for the values of parameters P_i^S determined by the constraint C_i^S. The *parametric entailment* $C_i^M, M_i \models^{B_i} C_i^S, S_i$ needs to establish that $[\![C_i^M, M_i]\!]^{B_i} \subseteq [\![C_i^S, S_i]\!]^{B_i}$.

We observe that the set of possible behaviors of a given model grows or shrinks monotonically with increasing or decreasing sets of parameter valuations, i.e., if $C' \Rightarrow C$, then $[\![C', M]\!]^B \subseteq [\![C, M]\!]^B$ for any model M. We assume that the specifications are parameterized such that increasing sets of parameter valuations allow increasing sets of behaviors, i.e., if $C' \Rightarrow C$, then $[\![C', S]\!]^B \subseteq [\![C, S]\!]^B$ for any specification S.

We let the constraint $C_{aux}(P)$ denote the auxiliary constraints that capture the dependencies across the set of all parameters $P = \bigcup_{j=0}^n P_j$, which is the set of all parameters being used, including the original system-level parameters P_0. Without loss of generality we assume the sets P_j, $j = 0, 1, \ldots, n$ are disjoint.

Definition 6 *We say that an auxiliary constraint C_{aux} is non-conflicting for a given system-level constraint C_0 if*

$$(C_0 \wedge C_{aux}) \downarrow_{P_0} = C_0.$$

Definition 7 (Parametric Abstraction) *Given a parameterized model M_0 with a behavioral domain B_0, a parameterized model M_i with a corresponding behavior formalism B_i and a behavior relation $R_i \subseteq B_0 \times B_i$, M_i is said to be a parametric abstraction of M_0 under an auxiliary constraint C_{aux} if for any constraint C_0^M such that C_{aux} is non-conflicting for C_0^M, we have*

$$[\![C_0^M, M_0]\!]^{B_0} \subseteq R_i^{-1}([\![(C_{aux} \wedge C_0^M) \downarrow_{P_i^M}, M_i]\!]^{B_i}).$$

The following definition creates a notion of coverage for parameterized models given their parameter dependencies.

Definition 8 (Parametric Coverage) *For a parameterized system model M_0 with a corresponding behavior formalism B_0, a given set of parameterized models M_i with corresponding behavior formalisms B_i and behavior relations $R_i \subseteq B_0 \times B_i$, $i = 1, \ldots, n$ form a* parametric cover *for M_0 under an auxiliary constraint C_{aux} if for any constraint C_0^M such that C_{aux} is non-conflicting for C_0^M, there exists a partition $\{B_0^1, B_0^2, \ldots, B_0^n\}$ of $[\![C_0^M, M_0]\!]^{B_0}$ s.t. $\forall i = 1, 2, \ldots, n$*

$$B_0^i \subseteq R_i^{-1}([\![(C_{aux} \wedge C_0^M) \downarrow_{P_i^M}, M_i]\!]^{B_i}).$$

Now we develop analogous definitions for parameterized specifications.

Definition 9 (Parametric Implication) *For a parameterized system specification S_0 with a corresponding behavioral formalism B_0, a parameterized specification S_i with a corresponding behavior formalism B_i and a behavior relation $R_i \subseteq B_0 \times B_i$ is said to* parametrically imply *S_0 under an auxiliary constraint C_{aux} if for any constraint C_0^S such that C_{aux} is non-conflicting for C_0^S, we have*

$$R_i^{-1}([\![(C_{aux} \wedge C_0^S) \downarrow_{P_i^S}, S_i]\!]^{B_i}) \subseteq [\![C_0^S, S_0]\!]^{B_0}.$$

Definition 10 (Conjunctive Parametric Implication) *For a parameterized system specification S_0 with a corresponding behavioral formalism B_0, a given set of parameterized specifications S_i with corresponding behavior formalisms B_i and behavior relations $R_i \subseteq B_0 \times B_i$, S_i, $i = 1, \ldots, n$* conjunctively parametrically imply *S_0 under an auxiliary constraint C_{aux} if for any constraint C_0^S such that C_{aux} is non-conflicting for C_0^S, we have*

$$\bigcap_i R_i^{-1}([\![(C_{aux} \wedge C_0^S) \downarrow_{P_i^S}, S_i]\!]^{B_i}) \subseteq [\![C_0^S, S_0]\!]^{B_0}.$$

Definition 11 *The pair of constraints (C_i^M, C_i^S) for i^{th} analysis task is said to be* original-constraint consistent *if*

$$(C_0^M \wedge C_{aux}) \downarrow_{P_i^M} \Rightarrow C_i^M \text{ and } C_i^S \Rightarrow (C_0^S \wedge C_{aux}) \downarrow_{P_i^S}.$$

Given these definitions, the following two propositions give sufficient conditions for parametric conjunctive and disjunctive analysis.

Proposition 4 *Given parameterized system model M_0 and specification S_0 with corresponding behavior formalism B_0 and the pair of constraints (C_0^M, C_0^S) over the system-level parameters P_0^M and P_0^S, a set of parameterized models M_i and specifications S_i with corresponding behavior formalisms B_i, behavior relations $R_i \subseteq B_0 \times B_i$ and pairs of constraints (C_i^M, C_i^S) over parameters P_i^M and P_i^S for $i = 1, \ldots, n$, if*

i. *constraints (C_i^M, C_i^S) are original-constraint consistent,*

ii. *each model M_i is a parametric abstraction of M_0,*

iii. *specifications S_i conjunctively parametrically imply S_0, and*

iv. *$C_i^M, M_i \models^{B_i} C_i^S, S_i$*

then $C_0^M, M_0 \models^{B_0} C_0^S, S_0$.

PROOF. From the definition of parametric abstraction, we have

$$\begin{aligned}
[\![C_0^M, M_0]\!]^{B_0} &= \bigcap_i R_i^{-1}([\![(C_{aux} \wedge C_0^M) \downarrow_{P_i^M}, M_i]\!]^{B_i}) \\
(\text{Def. 11}) &\subseteq \bigcap_i R_i^{-1}([\![C_i^M, M_i]\!]^{B_i}) \\
(C_i^M, M_i \models^{B_i} C_i^S, S_i) &\subseteq \bigcap_i R_i^{-1}([\![C_i^S, S_i]\!]^{B_i}) \\
(\text{Def. 11}) &\subseteq \bigcap_i R_i^{-1}([\![(C_{aux} \wedge C_0^S) \downarrow_{P_i^S}, S_i]\!]^{B_i}) \\
(\text{Def. 10}) &\subseteq [\![C_0^S, S_0]\!]^{B_0}
\end{aligned}$$

Therefore, $C_0^M, M_0 \models^{B_0} C_0^S, S_0$.

Proposition 5 *Given parameterized system model M_0 and specification S_0 with a behavior formalism B_0 and the pair of constraints (C_0^M, C_0^S) over the system-level parameters P_0^M and P_0^S, a set of parameterized models M_i and specifications S_i with corresponding behavior formalisms B_i, behavior relations $R_i \subseteq B_0 \times B_i$ and pairs of constraints (C_i^M, C_i^S) over parameters P_i^M and P_i^S for $i = 1, \ldots, n$, if*

i. *constraints (C_i^M, C_i^S) are original-constraint consistent,*

ii. *models M_i form a parametric cover for M_0,*

iii. *specifications S_i each parametrically imply S_0 and*

iv. *$C_i, M_i \models^{B_i} C_i^S, S_i$*

then $C_0^M, M_0 \models^{B_0} C_0^S, S_0$.

PROOF. From the definition of parametric coverage, there exists a partition $\{B_0^1, \ldots, B_0^n\}$ of $[\![C_0^M, M_0]\!]^{B_0}$ s.t.

$$\begin{aligned}
[\![C_0^M, M_0]\!]^{B_0} &\subseteq \bigcup_i R_i^{-1}([\![(C_{aux} \wedge C_0^M) \downarrow_{P_i^M}, M_i]\!]^{B_i}) \\
(\text{Def. 11}) &\subseteq \bigcup_i R_i^{-1}([\![C_i^M, M_i]\!]^{B_i}) \\
(C_i^M, M_i \models^{B_i} C_i^S, S_i) &\subseteq \bigcup_i R_i^{-1}([\![C_i^S, S_i]\!]^{B_i}) \\
(\text{Def. 11}) &\subseteq \bigcup_i R_i^{-1}([\![(C_{aux} \wedge C_0^S) \downarrow_{P_i^S}, S_i]\!]^{B_i}) \\
(\text{Def. 9}) &\subseteq [\![C_0^S, S_0]\!]^{B_0}
\end{aligned}$$

Therefore, $C_0^M, M_0 \models^{B_0} C_0^S, S_0$.

7. EXAMPLE WITH PARAMETERS

To illustrate the use of parametrized models and specifications, we return to the conjunctive analysis example from Sec. 5. The bounds on the POV velocity, the bounds on the SV acceleration, the position of the marker l and the lane width of the major road h are represented as parameters as shown in Fig. 6. These parameters embedded in the unparameterized models are now explicitly identified as follows.

- $P_1^M : \{M_1.\underline{v}_x, M_1.\overline{v}_x, M_1.l, M_1.h, M_1.\underline{a}_y, M_1.\overline{a}_y\}$,

- $P_1^S : \{M_1.h\}$,

- $P_{11}^M : \{M_{11}.\underline{v}_x, M_{11}.\overline{v}_x, M_{11}.l\}$,

- $P_{11}^S : \{M_{11}.l, M_{11}.t_x\}$,

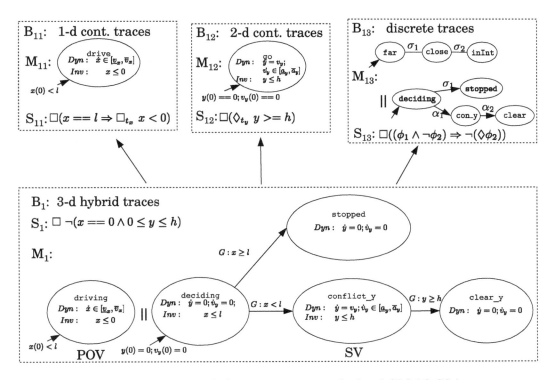

Figure 6: Parametric heterogeneous analysis of CICAS-SSA.

- $P_{12}^M : \{M_{12}.h, M_{12}.\underline{a}_y, M_{12}.\overline{a}_y\}$,

- $P_{12}^S : \{M_{12}.h, M_{12}.t_y\}$,

- $P_{13}^M : \{\}$,

- $P_{13}^S : \{\}$.

The following constraints identify the ranges of these parameters.

- $C_1^M : 20 \leq M_1.\underline{v}_x \leq M_1.\overline{v}_x \leq 30 \wedge M_1.l == -300 \wedge M_1.h == 4.5 \wedge 0.25 \leq M_{12}.\underline{a}_y \leq M_{12}.\overline{a}_y \leq 5$

- $C_1^S : M_1.h == 4.5$

- $C_{11}^M : 18 \leq M_{11}.\underline{v}_x \leq M_{11}.\overline{v}_x \leq 32 \wedge M_{11}.l == -300$

- $C_{11}^S : M_{11}.l == -300 \wedge 9 \leq M_{11}.t_x \leq 10$

- $C_{12}^M : M_{12}.h == 4.5 \wedge 0.2 \leq M_{12}.\underline{a}_y \leq M_{12}.\overline{a}_y \leq 5.2$

- $C_{12}^S : M_{12}.h == 4.5 \wedge 7 \leq M_{12}.t_y \leq 8$

Now, we know that the time needed for the POV to get from l to 0 needs to be bigger than the time needed for the SV to start accelerating from a stationary position and clear the intersection (i.e., $t_y < t_x$). From Newton's laws of motion, we note that $\sqrt{\frac{2h}{\underline{a}_y}} \leq t_y$ and $t_x \leq \frac{-l}{\overline{v}_x}$. We add this to C_{aux} along with the equality constraints between the parameters that are identical between M_{1i}s and M_1:

$$C_{\text{aux}} : \quad (M_1.\underline{v}_x == M_{11}.\underline{v}_x) \wedge \ldots \wedge (M_1.\overline{a}_y == M_{12}.\overline{a}_y) \wedge$$
$$(\sqrt{\frac{2h}{\underline{a}_y}} \leq t_y < t_x \leq \frac{-l}{\overline{v}_x})$$

We have a parametric abstraction for each model because due to the equality constraints in C_{aux}, we get equal parameter valuations for the corresponding models, and under the same parameter valuations, M_{1i} are not more restrictive

than M_1. Note that we have parametric conjunctive specification implication so long as $t_y < t_x$ holds, and here it does.

$C_{11}^M, M_{11} \models^{B_{11}} C_{11}^S, S_{11}$ and $C_{12}^M, M_{12} \models^{B_{12}} C_{12}^M, S_{12}$ can be shown using Newton's laws so long as $\sqrt{\frac{2h}{\underline{a}_y}} \leq t_y$ and $t_x \leq \frac{-l}{\overline{v}_x}$ hold, which they do. $C_{13}^M, M_{13} \models^{B_{13}} C_{13}^M, S_{13}$ still holds since it hasn't changed.

Finally, we get the following projections of C_1^M and C_1^S on P_{1i}^M and P_{1i}^S through C_{aux}:

- $(C_1^M \wedge C_{\text{aux}}) \downarrow_{P_{11}^M}: 20 \leq M_{11}.\underline{v}_x \leq M_{11}.\overline{v}_x \leq 30 \wedge M_{11}.l == -300 \wedge M_{11}.\overline{v}_x < 33.33$

- $(C_1^S \wedge C_{\text{aux}}) \downarrow_{P_{11}^S}: \top$

- $(C_1^M \wedge C_{\text{aux}}) \downarrow_{P_{12}^M}: 0.25 \leq M_{12}.\underline{a}_y \leq M_{12}.\overline{a}_y \leq 5 \wedge M_{12}.h == 4.5 \wedge M_{12}.\underline{a}_y > 0.19$

- $(C_1^S \wedge C_{\text{aux}}) \downarrow_{P_{12}^S}: M_{12}.h == 4.5$

We have $(C_1^M \wedge C_{\text{aux}}) \downarrow_{P_{11}^M} \Rightarrow C_{11}^M, C_{11}^S \Rightarrow (C_1^S \wedge C_{\text{aux}}) \downarrow_{P_{11}^S}$; and $(C_1^M \wedge C_{\text{aux}}) \downarrow_{P_{12}^M} \Rightarrow C_{12}^M, C_{12}^S \Rightarrow (C_1^S \wedge C_{\text{aux}}) \downarrow_{P_{12}^S}$. Now we can use Prop. 4 to turn this into a parametric conjunctive analysis and conclude that $C_1^M, M_1 \models^{B_1} C_1^S, S_1$.

In this parameterized example, because we are able to capture the parameter dependencies, we now know how fast the SV needs to accelerate given ranges of $\overline{v}_x$, h and l. Alternatively, if the system is implemented as a road-side infrastructure-based solution, where $\underline{a}_y$ cannot be chosen but is known empirically from driver behavior data, we know how l should be chosen. While the heterogeneous verification of the unparameterized example succeeds, there is no support for capturing these interdependencies. Therefore, there is value added in exposing parameters and identifying interdependencies.

8. DISCUSSION

This paper addresses the use of heterogeneous models for verifying system-level properties of cyber-physical systems. Behavior relations are introduced to relate the different semantic frameworks used to model different aspects of the system. Structured nesting of verification activities using Boolean combinations of conjunctive and disjunctive constructs is introduced to make it possible to infer system-level properties from the properties of heterogeneous models. The notion of semantic consistency critical for inferring system-level properties from model-level analyses is also introduced based on constraints over parameters.

The application of the proposed approach to real-scale problems will require tool support for managing various behavior relations, parameters, constraints and sufficient conditions for conjunctive and disjunctive analysis constructs. We are currently working on creating this verification management tool support. Future work will focus on integrating structural connectivity information available from architectural modeling of CPS with the semantic information regarding behavior relations and parameter constraints. Another direction is to support dynamic interdependencies between models by using temporal or dynamic logic constraints.

Acknowledgments

The authors gratefully acknowledge helpful discussions of the CICAS application with Prashant Ramachandra and Ken Butts of the Toyota Technical Center, Ann Arbor, MI, and support from NSF Grants CNS 1035800-NSF and CCF-0926181.

9. REFERENCES

[1] Cooperative intersection collision avoidance systems (CICAS). http://www.its.dot.gov/cicas/.

[2] M. Althoff, A. Rajhans, B. H. Krogh, S. Yaldiz, X. Li, and L. Pileggi. Formal verification of phase-locked loops using reachability analysis and continuization. In *Proceedings of the IEEE/ACM 2011 International Conference on Computer-Aided Design (ICCAD)*, San Jose, Nov 2011.

[3] R. Alur, T. Dang, and F. Ivancic. Predicate abstraction for reachability analysis of hybrid systems. *ACM Transactions on Embedded Computing Systems*, 5(1):152–199, 2006.

[4] R. Alur, T. A. Henzinger, G. Laffarriere, and G. J. Pappas. Discrete abstractions of hybrid systems. *Proceedings of the IEEE*, 88:971–984, 2000.

[5] F. Balarin, Y. Watanabe, H. Hsieh, L. Lavagno, C. Passerone, and A. Sangiovanni-Vincentelli. Metropolis: an integrated electronic system design environment. *Computer*, 36(4):45–52, april 2003.

[6] A. Basu, S. Bensalem, M. Bozga, J. Combaz, M. Jaber, T.-H. Nguyen, and J. Sifakis. Rigorous component-based system design using the BIP framework. *IEEE Software*, 28(3):41–48, 2011.

[7] A. Benveniste, L. P. Carloni, P. Caspi, and A. L. Sangiovanni-Vincentelli. Composing heterogeneous reactive systems. *ACM Transactions on Embedded Computing Systems*, 7(4), July 2008.

[8] S. S. Bhattacharyya, E. Cheong, and I. Davis. Ptolemy II heterogeneous concurrent modeling and design in java. Technical report, University of California, Berkeley, 2003.

[9] S. Bliudze and J. Sifakis. The algebra of connectors - structuring interaction in BIP. *IEEE Trans. Computers*, 57(10):1315–1330, 2008.

[10] K. Chaudhari, D. Doligez, L. Lamport, and S. Merz. The TLA+ proof system: building a heterogeneous verification platform. In *International Colloquium on Theoretical Aspects of Computing (ICTAC-7)*, volume LNCS 6256, page 44, Natal, Brazil, 2010.

[11] A. Chutinan and B. H. Krogh. Verification of infinite-state dynamic systms using approximate quotient transition systems. *IEEE Transactions on Automatic Control*, 46:1401–1410, 2001.

[12] T. Dang, O. Maler, and R. Testylier. Accurate hybridization of nonlinear systems. In *Proceedings of the International Conference on Hybrid Systems: Computation and Control (HSCC)*, 2010.

[13] G. Frehse. PHAVer: Algorithmic verification of hybrid systems past HyTech. *International Journal on Software Tools for Technology Transfer (STTT)*, 10(3), 2008.

[14] T. A. Henzinger. The theory of hybrid automata. *Verification of Digital and Hybrid Systems*, 170:296–292, 2000.

[15] T. A. Henzinger, P.-H. Ho, and H. Wong-Toi. Algorithmic analysis of nonlinear hybrid systems. *IEEE Transactions on Automatic Control*, 43:225–238, 1998.

[16] A. A. Julius. *On interconnection and equivalence of continuous and discrete systems: a behavioral perspective*. PhD thesis, University of Twente, 2005.

[17] R. Kumar, B. H. Krogh, and P. Feiler. An ontology-based approach to heterogeneous verification of embedded control systems. In *Hybrid Systems: Computation and Control*. Springer, 2005.

[18] A. Ledeczi, J. Davis, S. Neema, and A. Agrawal. Modeling methodology for integrated simulation of embedded systems. *ACM Trans. Model. Comput. Simul.*, 13:82–103, January 2003.

[19] E. A. Lee and A. Sangiovanni-Vincentelli. A framework for comparing models of computations. *IEEE Transactions on Computer-Aided Design of Integrated Circuits and Systems*, 17(12):1217–1229, Dec 1998.

[20] J. Leung, T. Mandl, E. Lee, E. Latronico, C. Shelton, S. Tripakis, and B. Lickly. Scalable semantic annotation using lattice-based ontologies. In *12th International Conference on Model Driven Engineering Languages and Systems*, pages 393–407. ACM/IEEE, October 2009.

[21] A. Rajhans, A. Bhave, S. Loos, B. H. Krogh, A. Platzer, and D. Garlan. Using parameters in architectural views to support heterogeneous design and verification. In *50th IEEE Conference on Decision and Control*, Orlando, Dec 2011.

[22] J. Willems. The behavioral approach to open and interconnected systems. *IEEE Control Systems Magazine*, (6):46–99, 2007.

Avoiding Geometric Intersection Operations in Reachability Analysis of Hybrid Systems

Matthias Althoff
malthoff@ece.cmu.edu

Bruce H. Krogh
krogh@ece.cmu.edu

Department of Electrical and Computer Engineering
Carnegie Mellon University
Pittsburgh, PA 15213

ABSTRACT

Although a growing number of dynamical systems studied in various fields are hybrid in nature, the verification of properties, such as stability, safety, etc., is still a challenging problem. Reachability analysis is one of the promising methods for hybrid system verification, which together with all other verification techniques faces the challenge of making the analysis scale with respect to the number of continuous state variables. The bottleneck of many reachability analysis techniques for hybrid systems is the geometrically computed intersection with guard sets. In this work, we replace the intersection operation by a nonlinear mapping onto the guard, which is not only numerically stable, but also scalable, making it possible to verify systems which were previously out of reach. The approach can be applied to the fairly common class of hybrid systems with piecewise continuous solutions, guard sets modeled as halfspaces, and urgent semantics, i.e. discrete transitions are immediately taken when enabled by guard sets. We demonstrate the usefulness of the new approach by a mechanical system with backlash which has 101 continuous state variables.

Categories and Subject Descriptors

G.1.0 [**Numerical Analysis**]: General; I.6.4 [**Simulation and Modeling**]: Model Validation and Analysis

General Terms

Algorithms, Theory, Verification

Keywords

Reachability Analysis, Hybrid Systems, Guard Intersection, Zonotopes, Safety

1. INTRODUCTION

Reachability analysis essentially provides the set of states that a hybrid system can reach in finite or infinite time. In contrast to numerical simulation, reachable set algorithms compute the reachable states starting from sets with infinitely many initial states and in many cases also sets of infinitely many inputs/disturbances and parameters. When the reachable set is obtained in an overapproximative way (all reachable states are enclosed), reachability analysis serves as a formal method for safety verification and other control problems: invariant computation [27], abstraction to discrete systems [9], guaranteed state observation [29], and the like.

Typically, the main difficulty for the hybrid (combined discrete and continuous) reachability problem lies in the continuous part, requiring set operations in continuous space. Over the years, many representations for continuous reachable sets have been introduced, each of them having advantages for specific types of system dynamics: ellipsoids [20], polytopes [8], oriented rectangular hulls [30], zonotopes [12], zonotope bundles [2], support functions [13], level sets [23], and others. For reachability problems with large discrete state spaces, specialized representations are also used for sets of discrete states, see e.g. [10].

Zonotopes [4, 15] and support functions [13] have shown great performance and scalability for purely continuous systems, but are challenging for intersections with guard sets. In this paper, we consider guard sets modeled as polyhedra, which is the most commonly used modeling formalism. Even reachable sets represented by polytopes (bounded polyhedra), which are closed under intersection with polyhedra, are not computationally efficient for guard intersection since partial intersections have to be unified by a convex hull to avoid a combinatorial explosion in the representation size and time required to compute the reachable set. Since the computation of the convex hull is itself costly and in many cases numerically unstable [5], alternative approaches have been proposed for unifying reachable sets with simpler representations, such as two-dimensional projections of zonotopes [14], bundles of parallelotopes (a special case of zonotopes) [2], and template polyhedra [11].

When the guard sets are modeled more generally as level sets, a representation of the intersection of the reachable set with the guard set can be computed by determining the time interval in which an intersection takes place, and using the complete reachable set of this time interval as an overapproximation of the intersection. This approach is often used in so-called *guaranteed integration* methods for hybrid systems, typically enclosing a single trajectory rather than a set of trajectories [24]. To compute tight overapproximations of the reachable set using this method, the set of initial states has to be partitioned and the reachable states are computed from each set in the partition, resulting in a possibly large computational load [28].

A completely different approach for reachability analysis of hybrid systems is suggested in [16]. There, only the reachable set propagating from guard intersection to guard intersection is computed by solving linear matrix inequalities (LMIs) embedded in a convex optimization routine, where guards are modeled as hyperplanes. A disadvantage of this approach is that it does not consider uncertain inputs and it is semi-formal, since the LMIs have to be fulfilled for time intervals, whereas only a finite number of points in time can be checked. In this work, we propose an approach which also computes guard set intersections without explicitly computing set intersections. We use hyperplanes to define guard sets, but in contrast to [16], we (i) compute the reachable set for all times in between guard intersections, (ii) present a formal approach, and (iii) use operations that break down to simple operations (addition, multiplication, and division) on reals, instead of solving LMIs. Our algorithm has a complexity of $\mathcal{O}(n^6)$ with respect to the number of continuous state variables n, which can be reduced to $\mathcal{O}(n^3)$ for "simple" dynamics and/or "small" sets of states. Due to the simple operations involved, the algorithm is numerically stable. A requirement for the proposed approach, which is shared with the approach in [16], is that the time interval of a guard intersection for all trajectories within the reachable tube has to be bounded. If the reachable tube only partially intersects a guard set, a case which can be automatically detected, one has to use the classical geometric intersection technique.

2. PROBLEM FORMULATION

We present a technique to compute the reachable set of a hybrid automaton with urgent transition semantics, i.e., a transition is taken as soon as a guard is hit [17]. Due to the urgent transitions, guard sets modeled as hyperplanes or halfspaces enforce the same behavior, but halfspaces are used in order to remove ambiguity when a reachable set hits several guard sets (see Sec. 5.5).

DEFINITION 1 (HYBRID AUTOMATON). *The hybrid automaton used in this work is defined as a tuple* HA = ($\mathcal{V}$, $\mathcal{X}$, $\mathcal{U}$, T, g, h, f) *with:*

- *the discrete state space* $\mathcal{V} = \{v_1, \ldots, v_\xi\}$. *Elements of* $\mathcal{V}$ *are referred to as locations.*
- *the continuous state space* $\mathcal{X} \subseteq \mathbb{R}^n$ *and input space* $\mathcal{U} \subset \mathbb{R}^m$.
- *the set of discrete transitions* T $\subseteq \mathcal{V} \times \mathcal{V}$. *A transition from* v_i *to* v_j *is denoted by* (v_i, v_j).
- *the guard function* g : T $\to 2^{\mathcal{X}}$ *($2^{\mathcal{X}}$ denotes the powerset of* $\mathcal{X}$*), which associates a guard set* g$((v_i, v_j))$ *with each transition* (v_i, v_j).
- *the jump function* h : T $\times \mathcal{X} \to \mathcal{X}$, *which returns the next continuous state when a transition is taken.*
- *the flow function* f : $\mathcal{V} \times \mathcal{X} \times \mathcal{U} \to \mathbb{R}^n$, *which defines a vector field for the time derivative of* x: $\dot{x} = $ f(v, x, u).

The guard sets g *are modeled as halfspaces* $\mathcal{H} = \{x | n^T x \leq d; x, n \in \mathbb{R}^n; d \in \mathbb{R}\}$. *The jump function is restricted to an affine map* $x' = K_{(v_i,v_j)} x + l_{(v_i,v_j)}$, *where* x' *denotes the state after the transition is taken and* $K_{(v_i,v_j)} \in \mathbb{R}^{n \times n}$, $l_{(v_i,v_j)} \in \mathbb{R}^n$ *are given for each transition* (v_i, v_j).

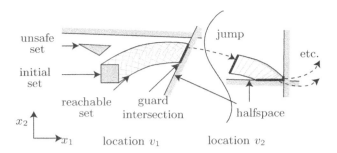

Figure 1: Illustration of the evolution of a reachable set of a hybrid automaton.

In contrast to other definitions of hybrid automata, we do not include invariants since a discrete transition is already forced by the guard itself. Assuming that the hybrid automaton has no Zeno behavior, the combined discrete and continuous state $(v(t), x(t))$ starts from (v^0, x^0) and $x(t)$ changes according to the flow function, while $v(t)$ remains constant. If the continuous state hits a guard set, the corresponding transition is taken immediately. In the event of hitting more than one guard set at the same time, the transition is chosen non-deterministically. After the transition from the previous location v_i to the next location v_j is taken (in zero time), the continuous state is updated according to the jump function and the continuous evolution is continued in the next location. This procedure is also illustrated in Fig. 1. Given the behavior of the hybrid automaton, we are interested in the reachable continuous states:

DEFINITION 2 (EXACT REACHABLE SET). *Given an initial location* v^0 *and a set of initial continuous states* $\mathcal{X}^0$, *the continuous reachable set* $\mathcal{R}^e_{v_i}(r)$ *of a hybrid automaton as specified in Def. 1 at time* r *in location* v_i *is:*

$$\mathcal{R}^e_{v_i}(r) = \left\{ \tilde{x} \middle| \exists \text{ some trajectory } (v(t), x(t)) \text{ of HA with} \right.$$

$$\left. v(0) = v^0, x(0) \in \mathcal{X}^0 \subset \mathcal{X}, \text{ such that } v(r) = v_i, x(r) = \tilde{x} \right\}.$$

The exact reachable set can be computed for only a limited class of hybrid automata [21]. Therefore, we compute over-approximations $\mathcal{R}_{v_i}(t) \supseteq \mathcal{R}^e_{v_i}(t)$. In order to compute for all times, we compute reachable sets for consecutive time intervals $[t_{k-1}, t_k]$, where $t_k = k\,r$, $r \in \mathbb{R}^+$ is the time increment, and $k \in \mathbb{N}$. Next, we explain the basic procedure of computing reachable sets $\mathcal{R}_{v_i}([t_{k-1}, t_k])$ for consecutive time intervals in a single location plus the subsequent computation for determining the initial set of the next location. Since this process is executed repeatedly, it is sufficient to focus on one location, so we drop the location index for $\mathcal{R}(t)$ from now on for simplicity of notation.

3. BASIC PROCEDURE

We begin with the reachable set computation for the continuous evolution and briefly describe the extension to hybrid systems with the classical and the new approach.

3.1 Continuous Dynamics

We first explain the reachable set computation for linear dynamics ($\dot{x} = Ax(t) + u(t)$, $A \in \mathbb{R}^{n \times n}$, $x, u \in \mathbb{R}^n$) and later discuss the extension to nonlinear dynamics. For linear systems, the reachable set of the first time interval $[t_0, t_1]$ is computed as shown in Fig. 2:

1. Compute the reachable set at $t = t_1$, neglecting uncertain inputs (the homogeneous solution, $\mathcal{R}^h(t_1)$);

2. Generate the convex hull of the solution at $t = t_1$ and the initial set; and

3. Enlarge the convex hull to ensure enclosure of all trajectories for the time interval $t \in [t_0, t_1]$, including the effects of uncertain inputs.

The computation of further time intervals is performed as in [15], which is similar to the computation of the first time interval, but no further convex hull computations are required and further computations are carried out without the wrapping effect, i.e. without accumulating overapproximation errors.

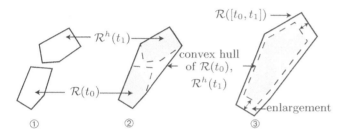

Figure 2: Steps for the computation of an overapproximation of the reachable set.

For hybrid systems, it is necessary to also consider discrete transitions activated by guards. Once these sets are determined, the mapping due to possible jumps is performed and the continuous reachable set computation can be continued. Two methods for guard intersection are presented: geometric guard intersection and the new technique mapping reachable sets onto guard sets.

3.2 Geometric Guard Intersection

The classical approach to computing reachable sets across discrete transitions in hybrid systems considers all possible states hitting a guard by computing the intersection of the reachable set with the guard set, see e.g. [7, 8, 11, 14, 18]. This is done by first intersecting all reachable sets of individual time intervals $[t_{k-1}, t_k]$ with the guard set in an exact or overapproximative way. In a second step, the individual intersections are unified into one or a few sets in order to bound the number of initial sets for continuing the reachability computations in the newly reached location, see [11]. This procedure is illustrated in Fig. 3(a) for polyhedral sets, where $\mathcal{R}_g$ is the intersection with the guard set and the displayed vertices indicate individual intersections.

When using representations other than general polyhedra, such as ellipsoids [7], multidimensional intervals [18], zonotopes [14], or template polyhedra [11], the intersection with polyhedral guard sets (which is the most common type) might result in large overapproximations. This problem is avoided by general polyhedra [8], but there are two problems with polyhedral computations: (i) the result is not numerically stable unless infinite precision arithmetic is used [6], and (ii) the unification of individual intersections by a convex hull is computationally expensive [5].

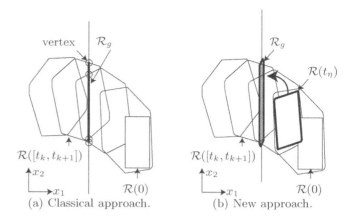

(a) Classical approach.   (b) New approach.

Figure 3: Guard intersection using the classical and the new approach.

3.3 Mapping onto Guard Sets

In the following, we propose a new technique to avoid geometric operations and directly map reachable sets to sets enclosing guard intersections. We compute this mapping from the last reachable set at a point in time t_η that does not intersect the guard. This point in time is determined by the first reachable set of the time interval $[t_\eta, t_{\eta+1}]$ which intersects the guard set. It is obvious that although for $[t_\eta, t_{\eta+1}]$ there is an intersection, there is no intersection for t_η since there was no intersection for $[t_{\eta-1}, t_\eta]$. In Fig. 3(b), the mapping from $\mathcal{R}(t_\eta)$ (bold border) to the overapproximative guard intersection $\mathcal{R}_g$ is indicated by a curved arrow.

We motivate our new technique by a simple example, where the flow is constant $\dot{z} = b$; $z(0) = z^0$; $z, b, z^0 \in \mathbb{R}^n$, such that the solution is $z(t) = z^0 + b\,t$. We use z to denote the state of the constant-flow system to distinguish it from the continuous state x for general continuous dynamics (such as linear systems). Given a halfspace $\mathcal{H} = \{z | n^T z \leq d\}$, the time t_h for hitting the halfspace for the constant flow is computed by solving $n^T(z^0 + b\,t_h) = d$, which implies $t_h = -\frac{n^T}{n^T b} z^0 + \frac{d}{n^T b}$. Inserting t_h into the solution $z(t)$ results in a map from z^0 to the state z_h on the bordering hyperplane:

$$z_h = \underbrace{\left(I - \frac{bn^T}{n^T b}\right)}_{=:C} z^0 + \underbrace{\frac{bd}{n^T b}}_{=:w},$$

where I is the identity matrix and $z_h = Cz^0 + w$ is an affine map. For any initial state $z^0 \in \mathcal{R}(0)$, this mapping can be easily performed for most set representations (ellipsoids, zonotopes, polytopes, support functions, etc.).

A possible extension from constant flow to linear dynamics ($\dot{x} = Ax(t) + u(t)$, $x(0) = x^0$, $A \in \mathbb{R}^{n \times n}$, $x, u \in \mathbb{R}^n$) is to first assume constant flow, e.g. $\dot{z} = b = Ax^0 + u(0)$. We can then add a set that bounds the error between the constant flow and the trajectories of the linear dynamic system. This error $\mathcal{E} = \{e(t) = x(t) - z(t) | t \in [0, t_{h,\max}]\}$ is added via Minkowski addition ($\mathcal{A} \oplus \mathcal{B} := \{a + b | a \in \mathcal{A}, b \in \mathcal{B}\}$) to $z(t)$, which assures $x(t) \in z(t) \oplus \mathcal{E}$ for $t \in [0, t_{h,\max}]$, where $t_{h,\max}$ is the time until all initial states have hit the guard set. Thus, $t_h \in -\frac{n^T}{n^T b}(x^0 \oplus \mathcal{E}) \oplus \frac{d}{n^T b}$, which after insertion into $x(t) \in z(t) \oplus \mathcal{E}$ yields

$$x_h \in \left(\left(I - \frac{bn^T}{n^T b} \right) x^0 + \frac{bd}{n^T b} \right) \oplus \left(-\frac{bn^T}{n^T b} \otimes \mathcal{E} \right) \oplus \mathcal{E}, \quad (1)$$

where x_h denotes a state of the linear dynamic system when a trajectory has hit the guard set and $\mathcal{A} \otimes \mathcal{B} := \{ab | a \in \mathcal{A}, b \in \mathcal{B}\}$ is referred to as set-based multiplication. In the following, the operator $\otimes$ is sometimes omitted for simplicity.

We have used the constant flow to motivate the approach described in the next section using a more general class of dynamics we call *state-dependent constant flow*, which gives a much tighter approximation than (1) to the guard set intersection for linear dynamics. If the dynamics is nonlinear, we propose to first abstract to linear dynamics as shown in [4], where also a set of errors is computed in order to preserve the overapproximation of the result. Since an abstraction to linear dynamics already exists, we focus on the abstraction of linear dynamics to state-dependent constants flows.

4. STATE-DEPENDENT CONSTANT FLOW

We define state-dependent constant flow using the system matrix $A \in \mathbb{R}^{n \times n}$, the initial state $y^0 = y(0) \in \mathbb{R}^n$, and a given vector b as

$$\dot{y} = Ay^0 + b. \quad (2)$$

For a given y^0, this is simply a constant-flow system. The difference is that by including the initial state explicitly, we will be able to compute the mapping as a function of the initial state. The solution of (2) is

$$y(t) = y^0 + (Ay^0 + b)t. \quad (3)$$

A nice property of state-dependent constant flow is that the hitting time of a hyperplane has a closed-form solution as derived in the previous section.

We compute the error made when abstracting a linear system to state-dependent constant flow, where the linear system has constant input u_c:

$$\dot{x}(t) = Ax(t) + u_c. \quad (4)$$

The solution of the linear system for $x(0) = x^0$ is

$$x(t) = e^{At} x^0 + \underbrace{\int_0^t e^{A(t-\tau)} \mathrm{d}\tau}_{=:\Gamma(t)} u_c. \quad (5)$$

When A is invertible, the matrix $\Gamma(t)$ can be computed as $\Gamma(t) = A^{-1}(e^{At} - I)$, where I is the identity matrix. However, $\Gamma(t)$ is not always invertible, so we compute $\Gamma(t)$ by integrating the Taylor series of e^{At} with remainder term

$$e^{At} = \sum_{i=0}^{\infty} \frac{(At)^i}{i!} \in \sum_{i=0}^{\eta} \frac{(At)^i}{i!} \oplus \hat{\mathcal{E}}(t). \quad (6)$$

The error term for the finite Taylor series is modeled as an interval matrix $\hat{\mathcal{E}}(t) = [-W(t), W(t)]$, where

$$W(t) = \left| \sum_{i=\eta+1}^{\infty} \frac{A^i}{i!} t^i \right| \le \sum_{i=\eta+1}^{\infty} \frac{|A|^i t^i}{i!} = e^{|A|t} - \sum_{i=0}^{\eta} \frac{|A|^i t^i}{i!}.$$

Integration yields

$$\Gamma(t) = \sum_{i=0}^{\infty} \frac{A^i t^{i+1}}{(i+1)!} \in \sum_{i=0}^{\eta} \frac{A^i t^{i+1}}{(i+1)!} \oplus \tilde{\mathcal{E}}(t), \quad (7)$$

where one can choose $\tilde{\mathcal{E}}(t) = \hat{\mathcal{E}}(t)t$, see [3]. The approximation error made for computing the hitting state based on state-dependent constant flow can be made arbitrarily small for a single initial state:

PROPOSITION 1 (MINIMIZING THE STATE DIFFERENCE). *The error* $e(\tilde{t}_h) = x(\tilde{t}_h) - y(\tilde{t}_h)$, *where* $\tilde{t}_h$ *is the hitting time of the linear dynamics and* $x(0) = y(0) = x^0$, *is minimized by choosing*

$$b = \Theta(\tilde{t}_h) x^0 + \Gamma^*(\tilde{t}_h) u_c$$

$$\Theta(t) = \sum_{i=2}^{\eta} \frac{A^i t^{i-1}}{i!}, \quad \Gamma^*(t) = \sum_{i=0}^{\eta} \frac{A^i t^i}{(i+1)!}$$

such that $\lim_{\eta \to \infty} e(\tilde{t}_h) = \mathbf{0}$ *and* $\mathbf{0}$ *is a vector of zeros of proper dimension.*

PROOF. We compute the error under the assumption that $x(0) = y(0) = x^0$, and $\xi \ne x^0$ is used for obtaining b according to the proposition. Using (5) and (3) we have for the proposed choice of b

$$e(t) = x(t) - y(t)$$

$$= \left(\sum_{i=0}^{\eta} \frac{A^i t^i}{i!} \oplus \hat{\mathcal{E}}(t) \right) x^0 \oplus \left(\sum_{i=0}^{\eta} \frac{A^i t^{i+1}}{(i+1)!} \oplus \tilde{\mathcal{E}}(t) \right) u_c$$

$$- \left(x^0 + Ax^0 t + \left(\sum_{i=2}^{\eta} \frac{A^i \tilde{t}_h^{i-1}}{i!} \xi + \sum_{i=0}^{\eta} \frac{A^i \tilde{t}_h^i}{(i+1)!} u_c \right) t \right) \quad (8)$$

$$= t \left(\sum_{i=2}^{\eta} \frac{A^i}{i!} (t^{i-1} x^0 - \tilde{t}_h^{i-1} \xi) \oplus \sum_{i=0}^{\eta} \frac{A^i (t^i - \tilde{t}_h^i)}{(i+1)!} u_c \right)$$

$$\oplus \hat{\mathcal{E}}(t) x^0 \oplus \hat{\mathcal{E}}(t) \, t \, u_c.$$

Since $x^0 + Ax^0 t$ cancels out, the error of the initial state x^0 is only $\mathcal{O}(t^2)$, whereas it would be $\mathcal{O}(t)$ when one chooses constant flow. For $x^0 = \xi$ and $t = \tilde{t}_h$, the error reduces to $e(\tilde{t}_h) = \hat{\mathcal{E}}(\tilde{t}_h) x^0 \oplus \hat{\mathcal{E}}(\tilde{t}_h) \tilde{t}_h u_c$, so that $\lim_{\eta \to \infty} e(\tilde{t}_h) = \mathbf{0}$. $\square$

When $x(0), y(0) \in \mathcal{R}(0)$, the heuristics of computing b as presented above with x^0 as the center of $\mathcal{R}(0)$ has proven successful in our numerical experiments. Thus far, we have approximated the intersection of reachable states with the guard set for a given initial state. The following section extends this approximation to a set of initial states.

5. SET-BASED COMPUTATIONS

In this section, we compute (i) the set of states y_h and (ii) the error $e(t)$ when the initial state is within a set of states $x(0) = y(0) \in \mathcal{R}(0)$. Thereto, we first introduce matrix zonotopes, which are used for intermediate results, and vector zonotopes, which are used for the representation of the reachable set.

DEFINITION 3 (MATRIX ZONOTOPE). *Given a matrix center* $C \in \mathbb{R}^{n \times n}$ *and matrix generators* $G^{(i)} \in \mathbb{R}^{n \times n}$, *a matrix zonotope is defined as*

$$\mathcal{Z} = \left\{ C + \sum_{i=1}^{p} \beta_i G^{(i)} \Big| \beta_i \in [-1, 1]; C, G^{(i)} \in \mathbb{R}^{n \times n} \right\} \quad (9)$$

We write in short $\mathcal{Z} = (C, G^{(1)}, \ldots, G^{(p)})$ and define the *order* as $\rho = \frac{p}{n}$, where p is the number of generators. By replacing the matrix center with a vector center $c \in \mathbb{R}^n$ and the matrix generators with vector generators $g^{(i)} \in \mathbb{R}^n$, one obtains the standard vector zonotope, which is simply called a *zonotope*. Zonotopes are a compact way of representing sets in high dimensions, which, as is shown in the following, scale well for the operations required in our procedure.

5.1 Operations on Zonotopes

We start with the addition of two zonotopes $\mathcal{Z}_1 = (c, g^{(1)}, \ldots, g^{p_1})$ and $\mathcal{Z}_2 = (d, h^{(1)}, \ldots, h^{(p_2)})$, and the multiplication with a matrix $L \in \mathbb{R}^{o \times n}$, where both operations are a direct consequence of the zonotope definition (see [19]):

$$\mathcal{Z}_1 \oplus \mathcal{Z}_2 = (c + d, g^{(1)}, \ldots, g^{(p_1)}, h^{(1)}, \ldots, h^{(p_2)})$$
$$L \otimes \mathcal{Z}_1 = (L\,c, L\,g^{(1)}, \ldots, L\,g^{(p_1)}) \tag{10}$$

Additionally, we require the scalar interval multiplication

$$[-1, 1] \otimes \mathcal{Z}_1 \subseteq (\mathbf{0}, c, g^{(1)}, \ldots, g^{(p_1)}), \tag{11}$$

where $\mathbf{0}$ is a vector of zeros of proper dimension. We also require the quadratic map of a zonotope, which is newly derived.

LEMMA 1 (QUADRATIC MAP). *Given a zonotope* $\mathcal{Z} = (c, g^{(1)}, \ldots, g^{(p)})$ *and a discrete set of matrices* $Q^{(i)} \in \mathbb{R}^{n \times n}$, $i = 1 \ldots n$, *the set*

$$\mathcal{Z}_Q = \{\lambda | \lambda_i = x^T Q^{(i)} x, \, x \in \mathcal{Z}\}$$

is overapproximated by a zonotope $(d, h^{(1)}, \ldots, h^{(\sigma)})$, *where* $\sigma = \binom{p+2}{2} - 1$. *The center is computed as*

$$d_i = c^T Q^{(i)} c + 0.5 \sum_{s=1}^{p} g^{(s)T} Q^{(i)} g^{(s)},$$

and the generators are computed as

$$j = 1 \ldots p : \qquad h_i^{(j)} = c^T Q^{(i)} g^{(j)} + g^{(j)T} Q^{(i)} c$$
$$j = 1 \ldots p : \qquad h_i^{(p+j)} = 0.5 g^{(j)T} Q^{(i)} g^{(j)}$$
$$l = \sum_{j=1}^{p-1} \sum_{k=j+1}^{p} 1 : \quad h_i^{(2p+l)} = g^{(j)T} Q^{(i)} g^{(k)} + g^{(k)T} Q^{(i)} g^{(j)}$$

The complexity of constructing this zonotope overapproximation with respect to the dimension n *is* $\mathcal{O}(n^5)$.

PROOF. Inserting the definition of a zonotope into the set $\mathcal{Z}_Q = \{\lambda | \lambda_i = x^T Q^{(i)} x, \, x \in \mathcal{Z}\}$ yields

$$\left\{ \lambda \Big| \lambda_i = (c + \sum_{j=1}^{p} \beta_j g^{(j)})^T Q^{(i)} (c + \sum_{j=1}^{p} \beta_j g^{(j)}), \, \beta_j \in [-1, 1] \right\},$$

which can be rearranged to

$$\mathcal{Z}_Q = \Big\{ \lambda \Big| \lambda_i = \underbrace{c^T Q^{(i)} c + \sum_{j=1}^{p} 0.5 g^{(j)T} Q^{(i)} g^{(j)}}_{d_i}$$
$$+ \sum_{j=1}^{p} \beta_j \underbrace{(c^T Q^{(i)} g^{(j)} + g^{(j)T} Q^{(i)} c)}_{h_i^{(j)}}$$
$$+ \sum_{j=1}^{p} (2\beta_j^2 - 1) \underbrace{0.5 g^{(j)T} Q^{(i)} g^{(j)}}_{h_i^{(p+j)}}$$

$$+ \sum_{j=1}^{p-1} \sum_{k=j+1}^{p} \beta_j \beta_k \underbrace{(g^{(j)T} Q^{(i)} g^{(k)} + g^{(k)T} Q^{(i)} g^{(j)})}_{h_i^{(2p+l)}},$$
$$\beta_i \in [-1, 1] \Big\}$$
$$\subseteq \Big(d, h^{(1)}, \ldots, h^{(\sigma)} \Big).$$

The obtained zonotope is an overapproximation since $\beta_j \in [-1, 1]$, $(2\beta_j^2 - 1) \in [-1, 1]$, and $\beta_j \beta_k \in [-1, 1]$ for $j \neq k$. The number of new generators is obtained from the fact that the new generators $h^{(j)}$ are computed by picking two elements from the set containing all generators and the center, where replacement is allowed and order does not matter. By subtracting the possibility that one can choose two centers, one obtains $\sigma = \binom{p+2}{2} - 1$ generators.

It remains to derive the complexity. Quadratic operations such as $g^{(j)T} Q^{(i)} g^{(k)}$ have complexity $\mathcal{O}(n^2)$. The number p of generators of $\mathcal{Z}$ can be expressed by its order as $\rho\,n$, such that the resulting zonotope has $\binom{(\rho n)+2}{2} - 1$ generators, a number which can be bounded by $\mathcal{O}(n^2)$, so we have $\mathcal{O}(n^4)$ for all generator computations for each dimension and $\mathcal{O}(n^5)$ for all dimensions. $\square$

The quadratic map can be generalized to the case when all $Q^{(i)}$ are elements of a matrix zonotope:

THEOREM 1 (MATRIX ZONOTOPE MAP). *We have* $\mathcal{Z} = (c, g^{(1)}, \ldots, g^{(p)})$ *and the matrices* $Q^{(i)} \in \mathcal{Q}^{(i)} = (D^{(i)}, K^{(i,1)}, \ldots, K^{(i,\nu)})$. *The zonotope enclosing the set* $\{\lambda | \lambda_i = x^T Q^{(i)} x, \, x \in \mathcal{Z}, Q^{(i)} \in \mathcal{Q}^{(i)}\}$ *can be overapproximated by*

$$\mathcal{Z}_D \oplus ([-1, 1] \otimes \mathcal{Z}_{K^{(1)}}) \oplus \ldots \oplus ([-1, 1] \otimes \mathcal{Z}_{K^{(\nu)}}),$$

where the addition and interval multiplication is performed as in (10) and (11), and the partial solutions are computed as in Lemma 1, where

$$\mathcal{Z}_D \supseteq \{\lambda | \lambda_i = x^T D^{(i)} x, \, x \in \mathcal{Z}\}$$
$$\mathcal{Z}_{K^{(j)}} \supseteq \{\lambda | \lambda_i = x^T K^{(i,j)} x, \, x \in \mathcal{Z}\}$$

The complexity with respect to the dimension n *is* $\mathcal{O}(n^6)$.

PROOF. After inserting the definition of the matrix zonotope into $\lambda_i = x^T Q^{(i)} x$, one obtains

$$\lambda_i = x^T (D^{(i)} + \sum_{j=1}^{\nu} \beta_j K^{(i,j)}) x$$
$$= \underbrace{x^T D^{(i)} x}_{\in I_i \otimes \mathcal{Z}_D} + \beta_1 \underbrace{x^T K^{(i,1)} x}_{\in I_i \otimes \mathcal{Z}_{K^{(1)}}} + \ldots + \beta_\nu \underbrace{x^T K^{(i,\nu)} x}_{\in I_i \otimes \mathcal{Z}_{K^{(\nu)}}}, \tag{12}$$

where I_i is the ith row of the identity matrix. Since each β_j is within $[-1, 1]$, we obtain $\mathcal{Z}_D \oplus ([-1, 1] \otimes \mathcal{Z}_{K^{(1)}}) \oplus \ldots \oplus ([-1, 1] \otimes \mathcal{Z}_{K^{(\nu)}})$.

Given that the complexity for each partial zonotope $\mathcal{Z}_{K^{(j)}}$ is $\mathcal{O}(n^5)$ from the previous lemma, and that $\tilde{\rho}$ is the order of the matrix zonotopes $\mathcal{Q}^{(i)}$, we have $\tilde{\rho}\,n + 1$ partial zonotopes, giving an overall complexity of $\mathcal{O}(n^6)$. $\square$

5.2 Hitting Times

Before we compute the mapping onto guard sets, we have to find a bound on the times when the guard set is hit. Determining when a zonotope $\mathcal{Z}$ intersects a halfspace $\mathcal{H} = \{x | n^T x \leq d\}$ is computationally efficient since it only evolves checking if $(n^T \otimes \mathcal{Z}) \oplus (-d) \leq 0$. By interpreting d as a zonotope with no generators, this expression can be evaluated by (10), resulting in a zonotope of dimension 1, which we express as $\omega_c \oplus ([-1,1] \otimes \omega^{(1)}) \oplus \ldots \oplus ([-1,1] \otimes \omega^{(p)})$; $\omega_c, \omega^{(i)} \in \mathbb{R}$. The interval $[\underline{\omega}, \overline{\omega}]$ of zonotope values is obtained by

$$\underline{\omega} = \omega_c - \sum_{i=1}^{p} |\omega^{(i)}|, \quad \overline{\omega} = \omega_c + \sum_{i=1}^{p} |\omega^{(i)}|.$$

If $\underline{\omega} \geq 0$, no intersection occurs and if $\overline{\omega} \leq 0$, the reachable set is completely in the guard set. The union of all consecutive time intervals $[t_k, t_{k+1}]$, for which $\overline{\omega} \geq 0$ and $\underline{\omega} \leq 0$, forms the interval of hitting times. This interval is used below to bound the error of the state-dependent constant flow assumption. Note that in the event that no guard set is hit, only the continuous evolution has to be considered.

5.3 Set of Abstraction Errors

For a given initial state, the error between the state-dependent constant flow solution $y(t)$ and the linear system solution $x(t)$ has already been presented in (8). Now, we consider a set of initial states $\mathcal{R}(0) = \xi \oplus \mathcal{Y}$, where $\mathcal{Y}$ is the deviation from ξ, and for simplicity we reset the time such that the interval of hitting times is $\mathcal{T} = [0, t_{\max}]$. The set of errors based on (8) is

$$\mathcal{E} = \{e(t) = x(t) - y(t) | t \in \mathcal{T}; x^0, y^0 \in (\xi \oplus \mathcal{Y})\}$$

$$= \mathcal{T} \left(\underbrace{\bigoplus_{i=2}^{\eta} \frac{A^i}{i!} \left(\mathcal{T}^{i-1}(\xi \oplus \mathcal{Y}) \oplus (-\tilde{t}_h^{i-1}\xi) \right)}_{= \sum_{i=2}^{\eta} \frac{A^i}{i!} \left(\mathcal{T}^{i-1}\mathcal{Y} \oplus (\mathcal{T}^{i-1} \oplus (-\tilde{t}_h^{i-1}))\xi \right)} \right.$$

$$\left. \oplus \bigoplus_{i=0}^{\eta} \frac{A^i(\mathcal{T}^i \oplus (-\tilde{t}_h^i))}{(i+1)!} u_c \right) \oplus \hat{\mathcal{E}}(t_{\max})x^0 \oplus \hat{\mathcal{E}}(t_{\max})t_{\max}u_c,$$

$$\tag{13}$$

which is computed with complexity $\mathcal{O}(n^3)$. Note that due to the monotonic growth of $\hat{\mathcal{E}}(t)$, it is sufficient to use the latest time $t_{\max}$ for $\hat{\mathcal{E}}(t)$. Since all values of $\mathcal{T}$ are positive, we have $\mathcal{T}^i = [0, t_{\max}^i]$ such that we can bound $\mathcal{T}^i$ by a zonotope (T, T), where $T = 0.5t_{\max}^i$. The multiplication $\mathcal{T}^i \otimes \mathcal{Y}$ in (13) is performed similar to Theorem 1 as $\mathcal{T}^i \otimes \mathcal{Y} \supseteq T\mathcal{Y} \oplus ([-1,1] \otimes T\mathcal{Y})$. Other operations in (13) are performed similarly, by e.g. considering ξ as a zonotope with no generators.

5.4 Set of State-Dependent Constant Flow Solutions

Using the previously introduced operations on zonotopes and matrix zonotopes, we compute the set of states x_h hitting the halfspace $\mathcal{H} = \{x | n^T x \leq d\}$ by bounding $x(t)$ with constant individual flow and the error set $\mathcal{E}$:

$$x(t) \in x^0 + (Ax^0 + b)t \oplus \mathcal{E} \text{ for } t \in [0, t_{\max}], \tag{14}$$

By replacing b with $(Ax^0 + b)$ in (1), one obtains the set of states $\mathcal{R}_h(x^0)$ enclosing x_h:

$$\mathcal{R}_h(x^0) := x^0 + (Ax^0 + b)\frac{d - n^T(x^0 \oplus \mathcal{E})}{n^T(Ax^0 + b)} \oplus \mathcal{E}, \tag{15}$$

which is split into the hitting state $y_h(x^0)$ of $y(t)$ and $\mathcal{R}_{h,\mathcal{E}}(x^0)$,

such that $\mathcal{R}_h(x^0) = y_h(x^0) \oplus \mathcal{R}_{h,\mathcal{E}}(x^0)$ and

$$y_h(x^0) = x^0 + (Ax^0 + b)\frac{d - n^T x^0}{n^T(Ax^0 + b)},$$

$$\mathcal{R}_{h,\mathcal{E}}(x^0) = (Ax^0 + b)\frac{-n^T\mathcal{E}}{n^T(Ax^0 + b)} \oplus \mathcal{E}.$$

We will first focus on $y_h(x^0)$. The set of states $y_h(x^0)$ for $x^0 \in \mathcal{R}(0)$ is

$$\left\{ x^0 + (Ax^0 + b)\frac{d - n^T x^0}{n^T(Ax^0 + b)} \Big| x^0 \in \mathcal{R}(0) \right\},$$

which requires to divide by $n^T(Ax^0 + b)$ with $x^0 \in \mathcal{R}(0)$. This could be resolved by first computing the interval

$$\mathcal{I} = \{n^T(Ax^0 + b) | x^0 \in \mathcal{R}(0)\}, \tag{16}$$

and then computing the set of y_h as $\{x^0 + (Ax^0 + b)(d - n^T x^0)/a | x^0 \in \mathcal{R}(0), a \in \mathcal{I}\}$. However, this approach neglects the dependency of x^0 and thus is too conservative. We capture the dependency in a much better way by applying a Taylor series to the expression for y_h, for which we first need the partial derivatives.

PROPOSITION 2 (PARTIAL DERIVATIVES OF y_h). We use

$$\Lambda(y) := n^T(Ay + b), \qquad \Upsilon := n^T A,$$

$$\Theta(y) := -n\Lambda(y) - (d - n^T y)\Upsilon^T, \quad \Omega := -n\Upsilon + \Upsilon^T n^T.$$

for a concise notation of the partial derivatives with respect to x^0 in index notation:

$$L_{il}(x^0) := \frac{\partial y_{h,i}}{\partial x_l^0} = I_{il} + \frac{A_{il}}{\Lambda(x^0)}(d - \sum_{j=1}^{n} n_j x_j^0)$$

$$+ (\sum_{j=1}^{n} A_{ij}x_j^0 + b_i)\frac{\Theta_l(x^0)}{\Lambda(x^0)^2},$$

$$\tilde{Q}_{lm}^{(i)}(x^0) := \frac{\partial^2 y_{h,i}}{\partial x_l^0 \partial x_m^0} = \frac{1}{\Lambda(x^0)^2}Q_{lm}^{(i)}(x^0), \text{ where}$$

$$Q_{lm}^{(i)}(x^0) = A_{il}\Theta_m(x^0) + A_{im}\Theta_l(x^0)$$

$$+ (\Omega_{lm} - \frac{\Theta_l(x^0)}{\Lambda(x^0)}2\Upsilon_m)(\sum_{j=1}^{n} A_{ij}x_j^0 + b_i).$$

The derivatives are obtained via standard derivation.

PROPOSITION 3 (TAYLOR SERIES OF y_h). The first-order Taylor series with Lagrange remainder of the state y_h is

$$y_{h,i}(x^0) \in \left(y_{h,i}(\xi) + L_i(\xi)\nu \right) \oplus \left(\frac{1}{2}\nu^T \tilde{\mathcal{Q}}^{(i)}\nu \right), \tag{17}$$

where $\nu = x^0 - \xi$, L_i is the ith row of the matrix L, $\tilde{\mathcal{Q}}^{(i)} = [\underline{\varphi}, \overline{\varphi}] \otimes \mathcal{Q}^{(i)}$, $[\underline{\varphi}, \overline{\varphi}]$ is the interval of $\{1/\Lambda(x^0)^2 | x^0 \in \mathcal{R}(0)\}$,

$$\mathcal{Q}^{(i)} = \{Q^{(i)}(x^0) | x^0 \in \mathcal{R}(0)\} \subseteq (\tilde{C}^{(i)}, \tilde{G}^{(i,1)}, \ldots, \tilde{G}^{(i,1+2p)}),$$

where

$$\tilde{C}_{lm}^{(i)} = A_{il}\Theta_{c,m} + A_{im}\Theta_{c,l}$$

$$+ (\Omega_{lm} - \psi_{c,l}2\Upsilon_m)(\sum_{j=1}^{n} A_{ij}c_{x,j} + b_i),$$

$$\tilde{G}_{lm}^{(i,1)} = -\psi_{g,l}2\Upsilon_m(\sum_{j=1}^{n} A_{ij}c_{x,j} + b_i),$$

$$\tilde{G}_{lm}^{(i,1+\alpha)} = A_{il}\Theta_{g,m}^{(\alpha)} + A_{im}\Theta_{g,l}^{(\alpha)}$$

$$+ (\Omega_{lm} - \psi_{c,l}2\Upsilon_m)\sum_{j=1}^{n} A_{ij}g_{x,j}^{(\alpha)},$$

$$\tilde{G}_{lm}^{(i,1+p+\alpha)} = -\psi_{g,l}2\Upsilon_m\sum_{j=1}^{n} A_{ij}g_{x,j}^{(\alpha)}.$$

PROOF. The Lagrange remainder in (17) encloses all higher order terms if $\{\tilde{Q}^{(i)}(x^0)|x^0 \in \mathcal{R}(0)\} \subseteq \tilde{\mathcal{Q}}^{(i)}$. Based on the computation of $\tilde{Q}^{(i)}(x^0)$ in Proposition 2, we first compute the interval of $\{1/\Lambda(x^0)^2|x^0 \in \mathcal{R}(0)\}$ and then $\{Q_{lm}^{(i)}(x^0)|x^0 \in \mathcal{R}(0)\}$, which we enclose by the proposed matrix zonotope. Since the initial set is a zonotope, we have that $x^0 = c_x + \sum_{\alpha=1}^{p} \beta_\alpha g_x^{(\alpha)}$, and $\Theta_l(x^0) = \Theta_{c,l} + \sum_{\alpha=1}^{p} \beta_\alpha \Theta_{g,l}^{(\alpha)}$, where

$$\begin{aligned} \Theta_{c,l} &= -n(n^T(Ac_x + b)) - (d - n^Tc_x)\Upsilon^T, \\ \Theta_{g,l}^{(\alpha)} &= -n(n^TAg_x^{(\alpha)}) + n^Tg_x^{(\alpha)}\Upsilon^T. \end{aligned} \tag{18}$$

Next, we obtain the overapproximation

$$\{\Theta_l(x^0)/\Lambda(x^0)|x^0 \in \mathcal{R}(0)\} \subseteq \psi_{c,l} \oplus [-1,1]\psi_{g,l} \tag{19}$$

using interval arithmetic. The center and the generators of the matrix zonotope $(\tilde{C}^{(i)}, \tilde{G}^{(i,1)}, \ldots, \tilde{G}^{(i,1+2p)})$ result from inserting (18), (19), and x^0 in zonotope form into $Q^{(i)}(x^0)$ in Proposition 2. $\square$

It remains to compute $\mathcal{R}_{h,\mathcal{E}}(\mathcal{R}(0))$, which is much smaller compared to the set of y_h. Thus, it is sufficient to use (16) and compute $\mathcal{R}_{h,\mathcal{E}}(\mathcal{R}(0)) = (A\mathcal{R}(0) \oplus b)(-n^T\mathcal{E})(1/\mathcal{I}) \oplus \mathcal{E}$.

Using Proposition 3, the zonotope $\mathcal{R}_g$ enclosing the guard intersection is computed as

$$\mathcal{R}_g = y_h(\xi) \oplus L \otimes (\mathcal{R}(0) \oplus (-\xi)) \oplus \frac{1}{2}[\underline{\varphi}, \overline{\varphi}] \otimes \mathcal{R}_{\text{quad}} \oplus \mathcal{R}_{h,\mathcal{E}}(\mathcal{R}(0)),$$

where $[\underline{\varphi}, \overline{\varphi}] \otimes \mathcal{R}_{\text{quad}} \subseteq 0.5(\underline{\varphi}+\overline{\varphi})\mathcal{R}_{\text{quad}} \oplus 0.5(\overline{\varphi}-\underline{\varphi}) \otimes [-1,1] \otimes \mathcal{R}_{\text{quad}}$ is computed using (10), (11), and $\mathcal{R}_{\text{quad}} \supseteq \{\lambda | \lambda_i = x^TQ^{(i)}x, x \in (\mathcal{R}(0) \oplus (-\xi)), Q^{(i)} \in \mathcal{Q}^{(i)}\}$ is computed as in Theorem 1. The overall complexity of computing $\mathcal{R}_g$ is determined by the computation of $\mathcal{R}_{\text{quad}}$, such that it is $\mathcal{O}(n^6)$. When the constant flow approximation is sufficient, the complexity reduces to $\mathcal{O}(n^3)$.

Note that in case of uncertain inputs $u(t) \in \mathcal{U}$, one needs an additional Minkowski addition to $\mathcal{R}_g$ due to uncertain inputs as described in [3].

5.5 Hitting Several Guard Sets

A problem, which is not addressed in [16], is how to deal with reachable sets that hit several guard sets. A straightforward way would be to separately compute the intersection for each guard using the presented approach, as illustrated by $\tilde{\mathcal{R}}_{g,1}, \tilde{\mathcal{R}}_{g,2}$ in Fig. 4. Without further intersection of other overlapping guard sets, one could continue the computation with $\tilde{\mathcal{R}}_{g,1}, \tilde{\mathcal{R}}_{g,2}$ as new initial sets. However, this often leads to a substantial overapproximation. In this case we suggest to intersect the mapped guard set with all other guards that have been hit, resulting in $\mathcal{R}_{g,1} = \tilde{\mathcal{R}}_{g,1} \cap \mathcal{H}_2$, $\mathcal{R}_{g,2} = \tilde{\mathcal{R}}_{g,2} \cap \mathcal{H}_1$ for the example in Fig. 4.

As mentioned earlier, zonotopes are not closed under intersection, but intersection can be tightly overapproximated using zonotopes or zonotope bundles [2]. Although hitting several guard sets requires a classical intersection operation, one has the huge advantage that the guard intersection for all times is represented by a single set $\mathcal{R}_g$, while for the classical approach, one first has to enclose partial intersections by a single set, which can be a costly or even unstable operation.

6. NUMERICAL EXAMPLE

We present the usefulness and scalability of the presented approach on instances of a mechanical system with backlash.

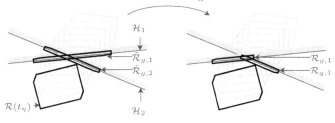

Figure 4: Procedure for hitting several halfspaces.

Methods for analyzing such systems is of great interest since backlash drastically reduces control performance [25]. The considered system in Fig. 5 is taken from an automotive drivetrain problem [22] and enhanced by additional rotating masses. Similar versions of this problem can be found in robotics, automation, and production machines. We first derive the differential equations of the system and then present the results in comparison with other approaches.

6.1 System Equations

The indices m and l refer to the motor and the load, numbered indices refer to the numbering of additional rotating masses, which are sometimes generalized by i. Moments of inertia are denoted by J [kg m^2], viscous friction constants by b [Nm s/rad], shaft stiffness by k [Nm/rad], angular positions by Θ [rad], and torque by T [Nm] (see Fig. 5).

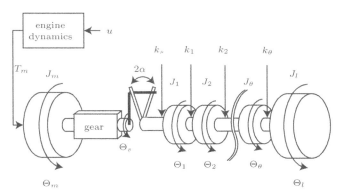

Figure 5: Powertrain model.

The differential equations of the rotating masses are

$$\begin{aligned} J_m\ddot{\Theta}_m + b_m\dot{\Theta}_m &= T_m - T_g \\ J_1\ddot{\Theta}_1 + b_1\dot{\Theta}_1 &= T_s - T_1 \\ &\cdots \\ J_n\ddot{\Theta}_\theta + b_\theta\dot{\Theta}_\theta &= T_{\theta-1} - T_\theta \\ J_l\ddot{\Theta}_l + b_l\dot{\Theta}_l &= T_\theta \end{aligned}$$

The dead-zone nonlinearity of the backlash is

$$T_s = k_s \begin{cases} \Theta_s - \Theta_1 - \alpha \text{ if } \Theta_s - \Theta_1 \geq \alpha \\ 0 \text{ if } |\Theta_s - \Theta_1| < \alpha \\ \Theta_s - \Theta_1 + \alpha \text{ if } \Theta_s - \Theta_1 \leq -\alpha \end{cases}$$

and the engine dynamics is modeled as $\dot{T}_m = (v - T_m)/\tau_{eng}$, where v [Nm] is the requested engine torque and τ_{eng} is the time constant. The remaining torques T_i with indices $i =$

$1 \dots (\theta - 1)$ and index θ are computed as $T_i = k_i(\Theta_i - \Theta_{i+1})$ using the shaft stiffness, and the last torque is $T_\theta = k_\theta(\Theta_\theta - \Theta_l)$. The gearbox ratio $\gamma = 12$ constrains the torques and angles to $T_g = T_s/\gamma$, $\Theta_s = \Theta_m/\gamma$ and a PID controller is used to control the motor velocity, such that

$$v = k_P(\dot\Theta_{ref} - \dot\Theta_m) + k_I(\Theta_{ref} - \Theta_m) + k_D(\ddot\Theta_{ref} - \ddot\Theta_m).$$

In order to write the equations in state space form, we introduce the state variables $x_1 = \Theta_s - \Theta_1 = \Theta_m/i - \Theta_1$, $x_2 = T_m$, $x_3 = \Theta_{ref}$, $x_4 = \dot\Theta_{ref}$, $x_5 = \Theta_l$, $x_6 = \dot\Theta_l$, $x_7 = \dot\Theta_m$, $x_8 = \Theta_1$, $x_9 = \dot\Theta_1$, $\dots$, $x_{2\theta+6} = \Theta_\theta$, $x_{2\theta+7} = \dot\Theta_\theta$. We also define the input $u = \ddot\Theta_{ref}$, which is the acceleration of the reference angle. For $x_1 \geq \alpha$, which we refer to as location 1, the system dynamics in state space form results from the previous equations as

$$\dot x_1 = \frac{1}{\gamma}x_7 - x_9$$

$$\dot x_2 = \frac{1}{\tau_{eng}}\Big((k_P(\gamma x_4 - x_7) + k_I(\gamma x_3 - \gamma(x_1 + x_8))$$
$$+ k_D\big(\gamma v - \frac{1}{J_m}(x_2 - \frac{1}{\gamma}k_s(x_1 - \alpha) - b_m x_7)\big) - x_2\Big)$$

$$\dot x_3 = x_4$$

$$\dot x_4 = u$$

$$\dot x_5 = x_6$$

$$\dot x_6 = \frac{1}{J_l}(k_\theta(x_{2\theta+6} - x_5) - b_l x_6)$$

$$\dot x_7 = \frac{1}{J_m}(x_2 - \frac{1}{\gamma}k_s(x_1 - \alpha) - b_m x_7)$$

$$\dot x_8 = x_9$$

$$\dot x_9 = \frac{1}{J_1}(k_s(x_1 - \alpha) - k_1(x_8 - x_{10}) - b_1 x_9)$$

$$\dots$$

$$\dot x_{2\theta+6} = x_{2\theta+7}$$

$$\dot x_{2\theta+7} = \frac{1}{J_n}(k_{\theta-1}(x_{2\theta+4} - x_{2\theta+6}) - k_\theta(x_{2\theta+6} - x_5) - b_\theta x_{2\theta+7}).$$

The above dynamics can be written in linear form as $\dot x = A_1 x(t) + b_1 u(t) + c_1$, where the index refers to the location and $A_1 \in \mathbb{R}^{n \times n}$; $b_1, c_1 \in \mathbb{R}^n$, where $n = 2\theta + 7$. By setting $k_s = 0$ in the system equations, one obtains the dynamics of location 2 when the system is in the dead-zone, and by changing the sign of α, one obtains the dynamics of location 3 when the system is on the other side of the contact zone than location 1.

The parameters of the system taken from [22] are listed in Table 1. Parameters from the additional masses, which can be interpreted as rotating elements in a gearbox and further drivetrain elements, are taken from [26]. The PID parameters tuned by the authors are $k_P = 0.5$, $k_I = 0.5$, $k_D = 0.5$.

Table 1: Powertrain parameters in SI units.

α	τ_{eng}	b_l	b_m	b_i	k_s	k_i	J_l	J_m	J_i
0.03	0.1	5.6	0	1	10^4	10^5	140	0.3	0.01

6.2 Reachable Set Computation

Many engineering questions of the considered powertrain can be solved by computing the reachable set, such as guaranteeing upper bounds on the torques for a set of initial states in order to ensure that no shaft will brake. Other problems could be the verification of a maximum settling time, or showing that the system does not reach the dead-zone for certain maneuvers.

In this work, we choose a benchmark maneuver from an assumed maximum negative acceleration of $\ddot\Theta_{ref} = -5$ [rad/s^2] to maximum positive acceleration of 5 [rad/s^2], where the first acceleration command lasts 0.2 s and the second one 1.8 s. We consider a wide range of possible initial angular velocities in the interval [20, 40] [rad/s], which would correspond to a range of [2292, 4584] RPM of the motor for the given gear ratio. Based on the range of initial angular velocities, the other initial states are chosen as the steady state solution for an external load of 300 [Nm], resulting in a zonotope with center $c = [-0.0432, -11, 0, 30, 0, 30, 360, -0.0013, 30, \dots, -0.0013, 30]^T$ and generator $g = [0.0056, 4.67, 0, 10, 0, 10, 120, 0.0006, 10, \dots, 0.0006, 10]^T$. The time step size is chosen as $r = 5 \cdot 10^{-4}$ s, and the maximum zonotope order for quadratic evaluations is limited to $\rho = 1.2$ using the reduction technique in [12].

We computed the reachable sets for different problem instances ($\theta = \{0, 1, \dots, 47\}$), resulting in up to 101 continuous state variables. The overall computational time, as well as the individual intersection times with guard sets (there are 2 intersections) are listed in Tab. 2. Computations were done in MATLAB on an i7 Processor and 6GB memory. Different projections of reachable sets for the instance with 101 continuous state variables are shown in Fig. 6, which also displays simulations from sampled initial states. Since the continuous dynamics can be computed wrapping-free [15], the overapproximation is small for all times, which can be seen by comparison with sample trajectories.

Table 2: Computational times in seconds ($n = 2\theta + 7$).

dim. n	11	21	31	41	51	101
CPU time	8.122	14.31	23.72	31.83	53.74	1550
1st guard	0.087	0.413	2.620	4.858	11.40	663.7
2nd guard	0.094	0.467	2.704	4.774	11.71	522.4

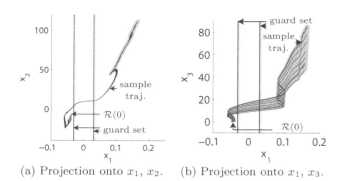

(a) Projection onto x_1, x_2.   (b) Projection onto x_1, x_3.

Figure 6: Reachable set of the powertrain for $n = 101$ ($\theta = 47$). Black lines show sampled trajectories and the gray region shows the reachable set.

For problem instances with $\theta = \{0, 1\}$ we compare the results with a classical geometrical approach [1, Chap. 3.5] in which different enclosure techniques are discussed; in this paper, we use the one based on principal component analysis (see also [30]). Simpler techniques, such as a box enclosure result in unacceptably large overapproximations. The approximation in [30] is accurate, but computed based on vertices, which is not feasible for larger instances of the powertrain problem. The comparison of reachable sets at both guard sets for $\theta = 1$ is shown in Fig. 7. One can see that both approaches have small overapproximation error, with an even smaller error for the classical geometric approach, but the new approach scales much more favorably. For both guards and $\theta = 0$, the classical approach consumes 12.56 s (new approach: 0.133 s), and 286.7 s (new approach: 0.154 s) for $\theta = 1$, while the classical approach is infeasible for $\theta = 2$.

Additionally, we compared the results to the reachability tool *SpaceEx* [11]. There, the geometric intersection is computed using linear programming, by which one can solve higher-dimensional problems compared to vertex-based geometrical approaches, but one needs good normal vectors for bounding halfspaces, while their absence might result in substantial overapproximations. For the powertrain example the overapproximation is substantial so that we could only compute rather tight results for $\theta = 0$ and an initial set $\mathcal{R}^{0.05}(0)$, which is 5% of the original set in each direction. We used the following SpaceEx parameters: 0.01 flowpipe tolerance, 100% clustering, and the template directions are chosen octogonal plus 500 random directions. The results are shown together with the mapping approach in Fig. 8. Due to the large number of required directions, the computational time of SpaceEx is 10023 s compared to 0.133 s for the mapping approach. However, we emphasize that SpaceEx is a general-purpose tool, while our approach requires that all trajectories in a location actually hit the guard set.

One reason why the mapping approach outperforms the classical geometric approach is that the guard intersection of the presented example is bounded by a zonotope with 2020 generators for 101 continuous state variables, which is a compact representation of a polyhedral set bounded by $2\binom{2020}{100} = 3.04 \cdot 10^{171}$ halfspaces, a number that is out of reach for classical approaches. However, classical approaches are still required when guard sets are hit by only some of the trajectories.

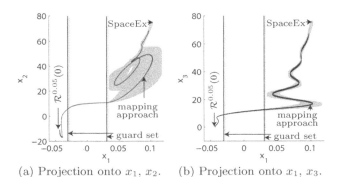

(a) Projection onto x_1, x_2.   (b) Projection onto x_1, x_3.

Figure 8: Guard intersection for $n = 7$ ($\Theta = 0$) using SpaceEx and the mapping approach. The gray and black areas show the reachable set obtained from SpaceEx and the mapping approach.

7. CONCLUSIONS

We present a new approach for avoiding geometric intersection operations in reachability analysis of hybrid systems by overapproximating the intersection with a nonlinear map for guard sets modeled as halfspaces. The approach scales well with the system dimension, making it possible to verify systems which were previously out of reach. An important factor for the accuracy of the presented approach is the time interval of possible guard intersection times. When this time interval is too large, it might be necessary to split the reachable set used as the initial set for the mapping onto the guard, in order to refine the computation. As mentioned in the introduction, if the time interval is unbounded, a classical geometrical approach has to be applied.

Intermediate results of the presented approach can be used for other reachability problems. For example, the linearization error of nonlinear reachability problems based on the Lagrangian remainder (see [4]) can be drastically tightened when computed as in Theorem 1. Also, the linear part of the Taylor series in Proposition 3 can be used to map normal vectors of polyhedral reachable sets to distinctive normal vectors of the guard intersection, which is useful for the classical geometric approach when bounding the intersection using linear programming.

Acknowledgments

This research was supported in part by U.S. National Science Foundation grant number CCF-0926181 and the U.S. Air Force Office of Scientific Research grant number FA9550-06-1-0312.

8. REFERENCES

[1] M. Althoff. *Reachability Analysis and its Application to the Safety Assessment of Autonomous Cars.* Dissertation, Technische Universität München, 2010. http://nbn-resolving.de/urn/resolver.pl?urn:nbn:de:bvb:91-diss-20100715-963752-1-4.

[2] M. Althoff and B. H. Krogh. Zonotope bundles for the efficient computation of reachable sets. In *Proc. of the 50th IEEE Conference on Decision and Control*, pages 6814–6821, 2011.

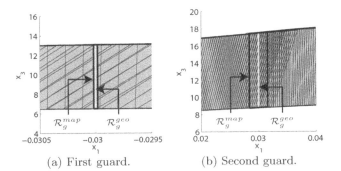

(a) First guard.   (b) Second guard.

Figure 7: Guard intersection using the geometrical (geo) and the mapping (map) approach for $n = 9$ ($\theta = 1$). The gray area shows the reachable set using the geometrical approach, black lines indicate the bounds of the reachable set of the mapping approach.

[3] M. Althoff, C. Le Guernic, and B. H. Krogh. Reachable set computation for uncertain time-varying linear systems. In *Hybrid Systems: Computation and Control*, pages 93–102, 2011.

[4] M. Althoff, O. Stursberg, and M. Buss. Reachability analysis of nonlinear systems with uncertain parameters using conservative linearization. In *Proc. of the 47th IEEE Conference on Decision and Control*, pages 4042–4048, 2008.

[5] D. Avis, D. Bremner, and R. Seidel. How good are convex hull algorithms? *Computational Geometry: Theory and Applications*, 7:265–301, 1997.

[6] R. Bagnara, P. M. Hill, and E. Zaffanella. The Parma Polyhedra Library: Toward a complete set of numerical abstractions for the analysis and verification of hardware and software systems. *Science of Computer Programming*, 72:3–21, 2008.

[7] O. Botchkarev and S. Tripakis. Verification of hybrid systems with linear differential inclusions using ellipsoidal approximations. In *Hybrid Systems: Computation and Control*, LNCS 1790, pages 73–88. Springer, 2000.

[8] A. Chutinan and B. H. Krogh. Computational techniques for hybrid system verification. *IEEE Transactions on Automatic Control*, 48(1):64–75, 2003.

[9] E. Clarke, A. Fehnker, Z. Han, B. Krogh, O. Stursberg, and M. Theobald. *Tools and Algorithms for the Construction and Analysis of Systems*, chapter Verification of Hybrid Systems based on Counterexample-Guided Abstraction Refinement, pages 192–207. LNCS 2619. Springer, 2003.

[10] W. Damm, S. Disch, H. Hungar, S. Jacobs, J. Pang, F. Pigorsch, C. Scholl, U. Waldmann, and B. Wirtz. Exact state set representations in the verification of linear hybrid systems with large discrete state space. In *Proc. of the 5th Int. Symposium on Automated Technology for Verification and Analysis*, pages 425–440, 2007.

[11] G. Frehse, C. Le Guernic, A. Donzé, S. Cotton, R. Ray, O. Lebeltel, R. Ripado, A. Girard, T. Dang, and O. Maler. SpaceEx: Scalable verification of hybrid systems. In *Proc. of the 23rd International Conference on Computer Aided Verification*, LNCS 6806, pages 379–395. Springer, 2011.

[12] A. Girard. Reachability of uncertain linear systems using zonotopes. In *Hybrid Systems: Computation and Control*, LNCS 3414, pages 291–305. Springer, 2005.

[13] A. Girard and C. Le Guernic. Efficient reachability analysis for linear systems using support functions. In *Proc. of the 17th IFAC World Congress*, pages 8966–8971, 2008.

[14] A. Girard and C. Le Guernic. Zonotope/hyperplane intersection for hybrid systems reachability analysis. In *Proc. of Hybrid Systems: Computation and Control*, LNCS 4981, pages 215–228. Springer, 2008.

[15] A. Girard, C. Le Guernic, and O. Maler. Efficient computation of reachable sets of linear time-invariant systems with inputs. In *Hybrid Systems: Computation and Control*, LNCS 3927, pages 257–271. Springer, 2006.

[16] A. Hamadeh and J. Goncalves. Reachability analysis of continuous-time piecewise affine systems. *Automatica*, 44(12):189–3194, 2008.

[17] T. A. Henzinger and P.-H. Ho. HyTech: The Cornell Hybrid Technology Tool. In *Hybrid Systems II*, LNCS 999, pages 265–294. Springer, 1995.

[18] T. A. Henzinger, B. Horowitz, R. Majumdar, and H. Wong-Toi. Beyond HyTech: Hybrid systems analysis using interval numerical methods. In *Hybrid Systems: Computation and Control*, LNCS 1790, pages 130–144. Springer, 2000.

[19] W. Kühn. Rigorously computed orbits of dynamical systems without the wrapping effect. *Computing*, 61:47–67, 1998.

[20] A. A. Kurzhanskiy and P. Varaiya. Ellipsoidal techniques for reachability analysis of discrete-time linear systems. *IEEE Transactions on Automatic Control*, 52(1):26–38, 2007.

[21] G. Lafferriere, G. J. Pappas, and S. Yovine. A new class of decidable hybrid systems. In *Hybrid Systems: Computation and Control*, LNCS 1569, pages 137–151. Springer, 1999.

[22] A. Lagerberg. A benchmark on hybrid control of an automotive powertrain with backlash. Technical Report R005/2007, Signals and Systems, Chalmers University of Technology, 2007.

[23] I. M. Mitchell, A. M. Bayen, and C. J. Tomlin. A time-dependent Hamilton–Jacobi formulation of reachable sets for continuous dynamic games. *IEEE Transactions on Automatic Control*, 50:947–957, 2005.

[24] N. S. Nedialkov and M. von Mohrenschildt. Rigorous simulation of hybrid dynamic systems with symbolic and interval methods. In *Proc. of the American Control Conference*, pages 140–147, 2002.

[25] M. Nordin and P.-O. Gutman. Controlling mechanical systems with backlash – a survey. *Automatica*, 38:1633–1649, 2002.

[26] E.-A. M. A. Rabeih. *Torsional Vibration Analysis of Automotive Drivelines*. PhD thesis, University of Leeds, 1997.

[27] S. V. Raković, P. Grieder, M. Kvasnica, D. Q. Mayne, and M. Morari. Computation of invariant sets for piecewise affine discrete time systems subject to bounded disturbances. In *Proc. of the 43rd IEEE Conference on Decision and Control*, pages 1418–1423, 2004.

[28] N. Ramdani and N. S. Nedialkov. Computing reachable sets for uncertain nonlinear hybrid systems using interval constraint-propagation techniques. *Nonlinear Analysis: Hybrid Systems*, 5(2):149–162, 2010.

[29] F. M. Schlaepfer and F. C. Schweppe. Continuous-time state estimation under disturbances bounded by convex sets. *IEEE Transactions on Automatic Control*, 17(2):197–205, 1972.

[30] O. Stursberg and B. H. Krogh. Efficient representation and computation of reachable sets for hybrid systems. In *Hybrid Systems: Computation and Control*, LNCS 2623, pages 482–497. Springer, 2003.

Computing the Viability Kernel Using Maximal Reachable Sets[*]

Shahab Kaynama
Department of Electrical and
Computer Engineering
University of British Columbia
Vancouver, BC, Canada
kaynama@ece.ubc.ca

John Maidens
Department of Electrical and
Computer Engineering
University of British Columbia
Vancouver, BC, Canada
jmaidens@ece.ubc.ca

Meeko Oishi
Department of Electrical and
Computer Engineering
University of New Mexico
Albuquerque, NM, USA
oishi@unm.edu

Ian M. Mitchell
Department of Computer
Science
University of British Columbia
Vancouver, BC, Canada
mitchell@cs.ubc.ca

Guy A. Dumont
Department of Electrical and
Computer Engineering
University of British Columbia
Vancouver, BC, Canada
guyd@ece.ubc.ca

ABSTRACT

We present a connection between the viability kernel and maximal reachable sets. Current numerical schemes that compute the viability kernel suffer from a complexity that is exponential in the dimension of the state space. In contrast, extremely efficient and scalable techniques are available that compute maximal reachable sets. We show that under certain conditions these techniques can be used to conservatively approximate the viability kernel for possibly high-dimensional systems. We demonstrate the results on two practical examples, one of which is a seven-dimensional problem of safety in anesthesia.

Categories and Subject Descriptors

J.2 [**Physical Sciences & Engineering**]: Engineering; I.6.4 [**Simulation & Modeling**]: Model Validation & Analysis

Keywords

reachability, viability, controlled-invariance, set-theoretic methods, scalability, safety-critical systems

1. INTRODUCTION

Reachability analysis and viability theory provide solid frameworks for control synthesis and trajectory analysis of constrained dynamical systems in a set-valued fashion (cf. [1, 18, 3]) and have

[*]Research supported by NSERC Discovery Grants #327387 and #298211, NSERC Collaborative Health Research Project #CHRPJ-350866-08, NSERC Canada Graduate Scholarship, and the Institute for Computing, Information and Cognitive Systems (ICICS) at UBC.

been utilized in diverse applications such as aircraft collision avoidance and air traffic management [2, 27, 32], stabilization of underwater vehicles [35], and control of uncertain oscillatory systems [7], among others.

Reachability analysis identifies the set of states backward (forward) reachable by a constrained dynamical system from a given target (initial) set of states. The notions of *maximal* and *minimal* reachability analysis were introduced in [29]. Their corresponding constructs differ in how the time variable and the bounded input are quantified. In formation of the maximal reachability construct, the input tries to steer as many states as possible to the target set. In formation of the minimal reachability construct, the trajectories reach the target set regardless of the input applied. Based on these differences, the maximal and minimal *reachable sets* and *tubes* (the set of states traversed by the trajectories over the time horizon [29, 19]) are formed.

Viability theory can provide insight into the behavior of the trajectories inside a given constraint set. The *viability kernel* is the set of initial states for which there exists an input (drawing from a specified set) such that the system respects the state constraint for all time. Another closely related construct is the *invariance kernel* which contains the set of states that remain in the constraint set for all possible inputs for all time.

It is shown in [29] and [1] that the minimal reachable tube and the viability kernel are the only constructs that can be used to prove safety/viability of the system and to synthesize inputs (controllers) that preserve this safety. Since the viability kernel and the minimal reachable tube are duals of one another, they need not be treated separately. In this paper we only focus on the former.

In [17], we formally examined the existing connections between various backward constructs generated by reachability and viability frameworks. Here, we will draw a new connection between the viability kernel and the maximal reachable sets of a constrained dynamical system.

Backward constructs are computed using two separate categories of algorithms [29]: The *Eulerian methods* (e.g. [32, 36, 6, 9]) are capable of computing the viability kernel (and by duality, the minimal reachable tubes). Although versatile in terms of ability to handle complex dynamics and constraints, these algorithms rely on gridding the state space and therefore their computational complexity increases exponentially with the dimension of the state, rendering them impractical for systems of dimensionality higher than three or four. The second category of algorithms are *Lagrangian methods* (e.g. [19, 22, 12, 11, 13]) that follow the trajectories and compute the maximal reachable sets and tube in a scalable and efficient manner. Their computational complexity is usually polynomial in time and space, making them suitable for application to high-dimensional systems.

Our main contribution in this paper is as follows: By bridging the gap between the viability kernel and the maximal reachable sets we pave the way for more efficient computation of the viability kernel through the use of Lagrangian algorithms. Significant reduction in the computational costs can be achieved since instead of a single calculation with exponential complexity one can perform a series of calculations with polynomial complexity.

Complexity reduction for the computation of the viability kernel and the minimal reachable tube has previously been addressed using Hamilton-Jacobi projections [33] and structure decomposition [38, 16, 15, 31].

In Section 2 we formally define the viability kernel and the maximal reachable set and formulate our problem. Section 3 presents our main results: the connection between these constructs in continuous time and discrete time. Computational algorithms are provided in Section 4, and the results are demonstrated on two practical examples in Section 5. Conclusions are provided in Section 6.

1.1 Basic Notations

For any two subsets $\mathcal{A}$ and $\mathcal{S}$ of the Euclidean space $\mathbb{R}^n$, the *erosion* of $\mathcal{A}$ by $\mathcal{S}$ is defined as $\mathcal{A} \ominus \mathcal{S} := \{x \in \mathbb{R}^n \mid \mathcal{S}_x \subseteq \mathcal{A}\}$ where $\mathcal{S}_x := \{y + x \mid y \in \mathcal{S}\}, \forall x \in \mathbb{R}^n$. We denote by $\overset{\circ}{\mathcal{S}}$ the interior of $\mathcal{S}$ and use $\mathcal{B}(\gamma)$ to denote a norm-ball of radius $\gamma \in \mathbb{R}^+$ centered at the origin in $\mathbb{R}^n$.

2. PROBLEM FORMULATION

Consider a continuously valued dynamical system

$$\mathcal{L}(x(t)) = f(x(t), u(t)), \quad x(0) = x_0 \qquad (1)$$

with state space $\mathcal{X} := \mathbb{R}^n$, state vector $x(t) \in \mathcal{X}$, and input $u(t) \in \mathcal{U}$ where $\mathcal{U}$ is a compact and convex subset of $\mathbb{R}^m$. Depending on whether the system evolves in continuous time ($t \in \mathbb{R}^+$) or discrete time ($t \in \mathbb{Z}^+$), $\mathcal{L}(\cdot)$ denotes the derivative operator or the unit forward shift operator, respectively. In the continuous-time case, we assume that the vector field $f : \mathcal{X} \times \mathcal{U} \to \mathcal{X}$ is Lipschitz in x and continuous in u. Let $\mathscr{U}_{[0,t]} := \{u : [0,t] \to \mathbb{R}^m$ measurable, $u(t) \in \mathcal{U}$ a.e.$\}$. With an arbitrary, finite time horizon $\tau > 0$, for every $t \in [0, \tau]$, $x_0 \in \mathcal{X}$, and $u(\cdot) \in \mathscr{U}_{[0,t]}$, there exists a unique trajectory $x_{x_0}^u : [0, t] \to \mathcal{X}$ that satisfies the initial condition $x_{x_0}^u(0) = x_0$ and the differential/difference equation (1) almost everywhere. When clear from the context, we shall drop the subscript and superscript from the trajectory notation.

Take a state constraint ("safe") set $\mathcal{K}$ with a nonempty interior. We examine the following *backward* constructs:

Definition 1. (**Viability Kernel**) The (finite horizon) viability kernel of $\mathcal{K}$ is the set of all initial states in $\mathcal{K}$ for which there exists an input such that the trajectories emanating from those states remain within $\mathcal{K}$ for all time $t \in [0, \tau]$:

$$\begin{aligned} Viab_{[0,\tau]}(\mathcal{K}) := \{x_0 \in \mathcal{X} \mid \exists u(\cdot) \in \mathscr{U}_{[0,\tau]}, \forall t \in [0, \tau], \\ x_{x_0}^u(t) \in \mathcal{K}\}. \end{aligned} \qquad (2)$$

Definition 2. (**Maximal Reachable Set**) The maximal reachable set at time t is the set of initial states for which there exists an input such that the trajectories emanating from those states reach $\mathcal{K}$ exactly at time t:

$$Reach_t^\sharp(\mathcal{K}) := \{x_0 \in \mathcal{X} \mid \exists u(\cdot) \in \mathscr{U}_{[0,t]}, x_{x_0}^u(t) \in \mathcal{K}\}. \qquad (3)$$

Problem 1. Express the viability kernel $Viab_{[0,\tau]}(\mathcal{K})$ in terms of the maximal reachable sets $Reach_t^\sharp(\mathcal{K})$, $t \in [0, \tau]$.

The viability kernel has traditionally been computed using Eulerian methods [6, 32, 26]. By addressing Problem 1, we enable the use of efficient Lagrangian methods for the computation of the viability kernel for possibly high-dimensional systems.

3. MAIN RESULTS

3.1 Continuous-Time Systems

Consider the case in which (1) is the continuous-time system

$$\dot{x}(t) = f(x(t), u(t)), \quad x(0) = x_0, \quad t \in \mathbb{R}^+. \qquad (4)$$

We will show that we can approximate $Viab_{[0,\tau]}(\mathcal{K})$ by considering a nested sequence of sets that are reachable in small sub-time intervals of $[0, \tau]$.

Definition 3. We say that a vector field $f : \mathcal{X} \times \mathcal{U} \to \mathcal{X}$ is bounded on $\mathcal{K}$ if there exists a norm $\|\cdot\| : \mathcal{X} \to \mathbb{R}^+$ and a real number $M > 0$ such that for all $x \in \mathcal{K}$ and $u \in \mathcal{U}$ we have $\|f(x, u)\| \le M$.

Definition 4. A partition $P = \{t_0, t_1, \ldots, t_n\}$ of $[0, \tau]$ is a set of distinct points $t_0, t_1, \ldots, t_n \in [0, \tau]$ with $t_0 = 0$, $t_n = \tau$ and $t_0 < t_1 < \cdots < t_n$. Further, we denote

- the number n of intervals $[t_{k-1}, t_k]$ in P by $|P|$,
- the size of the largest interval by $\|P\| := \max_{k=1}^{|P|}\{t_{k+1} - t_k\}$, and
- the set of all partitions of $[0, \tau]$ by $\mathscr{P}([0, \tau])$.

Definition 5. For a signal $u : [0, \tau] \to \mathcal{U}$ and a partition $P = \{t_0, \ldots, t_n\}$ of $[0, \tau]$, define the tokenization $\{u_k\}_k$ of u corresponding to P as the set of functions $u_k : [0, t_k - t_{k-1}] \to \mathcal{U}$ such that

$$u_k(t) = u(t + t_{k-1}). \qquad (5)$$

Conversely, for a set of functions $u_k : [0, t_k - t_{k-1}] \to \mathcal{U}$, define their concatenation $u : [0, \tau] \to \mathcal{U}$ as

$$u(t) = u_k(t - t_{k-1}) \quad \text{if} \quad t \ne 0, \qquad (6a)$$

$$u(0) = u_1(0) \qquad (6b)$$

where k is the unique integer such that $t \in (t_{k-1}, t_k]$.

Definition 6. The $\|\cdot\|$-distance of a point $x \in \mathcal{X}$ from a nonempty set $\mathcal{S} \subset \mathcal{X}$ is defined as

$$\text{dist}(x, \mathcal{S}) := \inf_{s \in \mathcal{S}} \|x - s\|. \qquad (7)$$

For a fixed set $\mathcal{S}$, the map $x \mapsto \text{dist}(x, \mathcal{S})$ is continuous.

3.1.1 Computing an Under-Approximation of the Viability Kernel

Assume that the vector field f is bounded by M in the norm $\|\cdot\|$. We begin by defining an under-approximation of the state constraint set (Figure 1(a)):

$$\mathcal{K}_\downarrow(P) := \{x \in \mathcal{K} \mid \text{dist}(x, \mathcal{K}^c) \ge M\|P\|\}. \qquad (8)$$

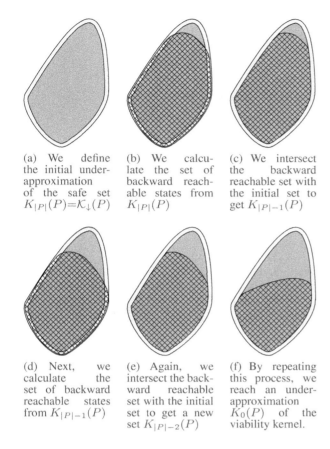

(a) We define the initial under-approximation of the safe set $K_{|P|}(P) = \mathcal{K}_\downarrow(P)$

(b) We calculate the set of backward reachable states from $K_{|P|}(P)$

(c) We intersect the backward reachable set with the initial set to get $K_{|P|-1}(P)$

(d) Next, we calculate the set of backward reachable states from $K_{|P|-1}(P)$

(e) Again, we intersect the backward reachable set with the initial set to get a new set $K_{|P|-2}(P)$

(f) By repeating this process, we reach an under-approximation $K_0(P)$ of the viability kernel.

Figure 1: Iteratively constructing an under-approximation of $Viab_{[0,\tau]}(\mathcal{K})$.

We under-approximate $\mathcal{K}$ by a distance $M\|P\|$ because we are only considering the system's state at discrete times $t_0, t_1, \dots, t_n$. At a time t in the interval $[t_i, t_{i+1}]$, a trajectory $x(\cdot)$ can travel a distance of at most

$$\|x(t) - x(t_i)\| \leq \int_{t_i}^{t} \|\dot{x}(\tau)\| d\tau \leq M(t - t_i) \leq M\|P\| \quad (9)$$

from its initial location $x(t_i)$. As we shall see, formulating the subset (8) will ensure that the state does not leave $\mathcal{K}$ at any time during $[0, \tau]$.

This set defines the first step of our recursion. We then define a sequence of $|P|$ sets recursively:

$$K_{|P|}(P) = \mathcal{K}_\downarrow(P), \quad (10a)$$

$$K_{k-1}(P) = \mathcal{K}_\downarrow(P) \cap Reach_{t_k - t_{k-1}}^{\sharp}(K_k(P))$$

$$\text{for } k \in \{1, \dots, |P|\}. \quad (10b)$$

At each time step, we calculate the set of states from which you can reach $K_k(P)$, then intersect this set with the set of safe states (see Figure 1). The final set $K_0(P)$ is an approximation of $Viab_{[0,\tau]}(\mathcal{K})$.

Note that the resulting set depends on our choice of a partition P of the time interval $[0, \tau]$. We claim that for any partition P, $K_0(P)$ is an under-approximation.

PROPOSITION 1. *Suppose that the vector field $f : \mathcal{X} \times \mathcal{U} \to \mathcal{X}$ is bounded on a set $\mathcal{K} \subseteq \mathcal{X}$. Then for any partition P of $[0, \tau]$ the final set $K_0(P)$ defined by the recurrence relation (10) satisfies*

$$K_0(P) \subseteq Viab_{[0,\tau]}(\mathcal{K}). \quad (11)$$

PROOF. Since f is bounded on $\mathcal{K}$, there exists a norm $\|\cdot\|$ and a real number $M > 0$ with $\|f(x, u)\| \leq M$ for all $x \in \mathcal{K}$. Now, fix a partition P of $[0, \tau]$ and take a point $x_0 \in K_0(P)$. By the construction of $K_0(P)$, this means that for each $k = 1, \dots, |P|$ there is some point $x_k \in K_k(P)$ and an input $u_k : [0, t_k - t_{k-1}] \to \mathcal{U}$ such that x_k can be reached from x_{k-1} at time $t_k - t_{k-1}$ using input u_k. Thus, taking the concatenation of the inputs u_k, we get an input $u : [0, \tau] \to \mathcal{U}$ such that the solution $x : [0, \tau] \to \mathcal{X}$ to the initial value problem $\dot{x} = f(x, u)$, $x(0) = x_0$, satisfies $x(t_k) = x_k \in K_k(P) \subseteq \{x \in \mathcal{K} \mid \text{dist}(x, \mathcal{K}^c) \geq M\|P\|\}$. We claim that this guarantees that $x(t) \in \mathcal{K}$ for all $t \in [0, \tau]$. Indeed, any $t \in [0, \tau)$ lies is some interval $[t_k, t_{k+1}]$. Since f is bounded by M, we have

$$\|x(t) - x(t_k)\| \leq M(t - t_k) < M(t_{k+1} - t_k) \leq M\|P\|. \quad (12)$$

Further, $x(t_k) \in K_k(P)$ implies that $\text{dist}(x(t_k), \mathcal{K}^c) \geq M\|P\|$. Combining these, we see that

$$\text{dist}(x(t), \mathcal{K}^c) \geq \text{dist}(x(t_k), \mathcal{K}^c) - \|x(t) - x(t_k)\|$$
$$> M\|P\| - M\|P\| = 0 \quad (13)$$

and hence $x(t) \in \mathcal{K}$. Thus, $x_0 \in Viab_{[0,\tau]}(\mathcal{K})$. $\square$

3.1.2 Precision of the Approximation

The approximation can be made to be arbitrarily precise by choosing a sufficiently fine partition. This is true in the sense that the union of the approximating sets $K_0(P)$ taken over all possible partitions P of $[0, \tau]$ is bounded between the viability kernels of $\mathcal{K}$ and its interior $\overset{\circ}{\mathcal{K}}$.

PROPOSITION 2. *Suppose that the vector field $f : \mathcal{X} \times \mathcal{U} \to \mathcal{X}$ is bounded on a set $\mathcal{K} \subseteq \mathcal{X}$. Then we have*

$$Viab_{[0,\tau]}(\overset{\circ}{\mathcal{K}}) \subseteq \bigcup_{P \in \mathscr{P}([0,\tau])} K_0(P) \subseteq Viab_{[0,\tau]}(\mathcal{K}). \quad (14)$$

In particular, when $\mathcal{K}$ is open,

$$\bigcup_{P \in \mathscr{P}([0,\tau])} K_0(P) = Viab_{[0,\tau]}(\mathcal{K}). \quad (15)$$

PROOF. The second inclusion in (14) follows directly from Proposition 1. To prove the first inclusion, take a state $x_0 \in Viab_{[0,\tau]}(\overset{\circ}{\mathcal{K}})$. There exists an input $u : [0, \tau] \to \mathcal{U}$ such that the solution $x(\cdot)$ to the initial value problem $\dot{x} = f(x, u)$, $x(0) = x_0$, satisfies $x(t) \in \overset{\circ}{\mathcal{K}}$ for all $t \in [0, \tau]$. Since $\overset{\circ}{\mathcal{K}}$ is open, for any $x \in \overset{\circ}{\mathcal{K}}$ we have $\text{dist}(x, \mathcal{K}^c) > 0$. Further, $x : [0, \tau] \to \mathcal{X}$ is continuous so the function $t \mapsto \text{dist}(x(t), \mathcal{K}^c)$ is continuous on the compact set $[0, \tau]$. Thus, we can define $d > 0$ to be its minimum value. Now take a partition P of $[0, \tau]$ such that $M\|P\| < d$. We need to show that $x_0 \in K_0(P)$.

First note that our partition P is chosen such that $\text{dist}(x(t), \mathcal{K}^c) > M\|P\|$ for all $t \in [0, \tau]$. Hence $x(t_k) \in K_{|P|}(P)$ for all $k = 0, \dots, |P|$. To show that $x(t_{k-1}) \in Reach_{t_k - t_{k-1}}^{\sharp}(K_k(P))$ for all $k = 1, \dots, |P|$, consider the tokenization $\{u_k\}_k$ of the input u corresponding to P. It is easy to verify that for all k, we can reach $x(t_k)$ from $x(t_{k-1})$ at time $t_k - t_{k-1}$ using input u_k. Thus, in particular, we have $x_0 = x(t_0) \in Reach_{t_1 - t_0}^{\sharp}(K_1(P))$. So $x_0 \in K_0(P)$. Hence $Viab_{[0,\tau]}(\overset{\circ}{\mathcal{K}}) \subseteq \bigcup_{P \in \mathscr{P}([0,\tau])} K_0(P)$. $\square$

3.2 Discrete-Time Systems

Consider the case in which (1) is the discrete-time system

$$x(t + 1) = f(x(t), u(t)), \quad x(0) = x_0, \quad t \in \mathbb{Z}^+. \quad (16)$$

Computing $Viab_{[0,\tau]}(\mathcal{K})$ under this system is a particular case of the results presented in Section 3.1. Define a sequence of sets recursively as

$$K_n = \mathcal{K}, \tag{17a}$$

$$K_{k-1} = \mathcal{K} \cap Reach_1^\sharp(K_k), \quad k \in \{1, \dots, n\} \tag{17b}$$

where $\tau = n$ and $Reach_1^\sharp(\cdot)$ is the unit time-step maximal reachable set.

PROPOSITION 3. *Let K_0 be the final set obtained from the recurrence relation* (17). *Then,*

$$Viab_{[0,\tau]}(\mathcal{K}) = K_0. \tag{18}$$

PROOF. Notice that the time variable t is integer valued. As a result, the tokenization of the input signal u is a discrete sequence $\{u_k\}_k$ with $u_k := u(t)$ with $t = k - 1$ for $k = 1, \dots, n$.

To show $K_0 \subseteq Viab_{[0,\tau]}(\mathcal{K})$, via recursion (17) we have that at each step k there exists u_k such that $x_{k-1} \in K_{k-1}$ reaches $x_k \in K_k$. Thus, $x_0 \in K_0$ implies there exists a concatenation $u(\cdot) = \{u_k\}_k \in \mathcal{U}_{[0,\tau]}$ such that $x(t) \in \mathcal{K}$ for all $t \in [0, \tau]$. Therefore, $x_0 \in Viab_{[0,\tau]}(\mathcal{K})$.

To show $Viab_{[0,\tau]}(\mathcal{K}) \subseteq K_0$, take $x_0 \in Viab_{[0,\tau]}(\mathcal{K})$. There exists $u(\cdot) = \{u_k\}_k$ such that $x(t) \in \mathcal{K}$ for every t. Using the tokenization of $\{u_k\}_k$ we can verify that for some u_k we can reach $x_k := x(t+1)$ from $x_{k-1} := x(t)$. Hence, $x_{k-1} \in Reach_1^\sharp(K_k)$ for all $k \in \{1, \dots, n\}$. In particular, for $k = 1$ we have $x_0 := x(0) \in Reach_1^\sharp(K_1)$. Thus, $x_0 \in \mathcal{K} \cap Reach_1^\sharp(K_1) = K_0$. $\square$

Remark 1. Note that the above iterative scheme is closely related to the set-valued description of the discrete viability kernel presented in [36, 6] and the recursive construction of the controlled-invariant set for discrete-time systems presented in [3].

4. COMPUTATIONAL ALGORITHMS

Thanks to the results in the previous section, any technique that is capable of computing the maximal reachable set can be used to compute the viability kernel. Most currently available Lagrangian methods yield an (under- and/or over-) approximation of the maximal reachable set. The viability kernel should not be over-approximated since an over-approximation would contain initial states for which the viability of the system is inevitably at stake. Thus, to correctly compute $Viab_{[0,\tau]}(\mathcal{K})$ all approximations must be in the form of under-approximations.

Every step of the recursions (10) and (17) involves a reachability computation and an intersection operation. Ideally, the sets that are being intersected should be drawn from classes of shapes that are closed under such an operation, e.g. polytopes. However, the currently available reachability techniques that are based on polytopes (e.g. [24]) do not, in general, scale well with the dimension of the state. Moreover, the scalable reachability techniques, such as the methods of zonotopes [12], ellipsoids [19, 23], and support functions [11], generate sets that may prove to be difficult to transform into a polytope. For instance, one may compute a polytopic under-approximation of the reachable sets using their support functions based on the approach presented in [25]. However, that approach requires calculation of the facet representation of the resulting polytopes from their vertices before each intersection operation, which is known to be computationally demanding in higher dimensions.

4.1 A Piecewise Ellipsoidal Approach

Here we showcase our results using an efficient algorithm, based on ellipsoidal techniques [19] implemented in the Ellipsoidal Toolbox (ET) [22], that sacrifices accuracy in exchange for scalability.

We consider the case in which (1) is a linear time-invariant (**LTI**) system

$$\mathcal{L}(x(t)) = Ax(t) + Bu(t) \tag{19}$$

with $A \in \mathbb{R}^{n \times n}$ and $B \in \mathbb{R}^{n \times m}$.

An *ellipsoid* in $\mathbb{R}^n$ is defined as

$$\mathcal{E}(q, Q) := \left\{ x \in \mathbb{R}^n \mid \langle (x - q), Q^{-1}(x - q) \rangle \leq 1 \right\} \tag{20}$$

with center $q \in \mathbb{R}^n$ and shape matrix $\mathbb{R}^{n \times n} \ni Q = Q^T \succ 0$. A *piecewise ellipsoidal* set is the union of a finite number of ellipsoids.

Among many advantages, ellipsoidal techniques [19, 22] allow for an efficient computation of *under-approximations* of the maximal reachable sets, making them a particularly attractive choice for the reachability computations involved in our formulation of the viability kernel.

Suppose $\mathcal{K}$ and $\mathcal{U}$ are (or can be closely under-approximated as) compact ellipsoids with nonempty interior. Consider the continuous-time case and the recursion (10). (The arguments in the discrete-time case are similar.) Given a partition P and some $k \in \{1, \dots, |P|\}$, let $K_k(P) = \mathcal{E}(x_\delta, X_\delta) \subset \mathcal{X}$. As in [20], with $\mathcal{N} := \{v \in \mathbb{R}^n \mid \langle v, v \rangle = 1\}$ and $\delta := t_k - t_{k-1}$ we have

$$Reach_{\delta-t}^\sharp(K_k(P)) = \bigcup_{\ell_\delta \in \mathcal{N}} \mathcal{E}(x^*(t), X_\ell^-(t)), \quad \forall t \in [0, \delta], \tag{21}$$

where $x^*(t)$ and $X_\ell^-(t)$ are the center and the shape matrix of the *internal approximating* ellipsoid at time t that is tangent to $Reach_{\delta-t}^\sharp(K_k(P))$ in the direction $\ell(t) \in \mathbb{R}^n$. For a fixed $\ell(\delta) = \ell_\delta \in \mathcal{N}$, the direction $\ell(t)$ is obtained from the adjoint equation $\dot{\ell}(t) = -A^T \ell(t)$. The center $x^*(t)$ (with $x^*(\delta) = x_\delta$) and the shape matrix $X_\ell^-(t)$ (with $X_\ell^-(\delta) = X_\delta$) are determined from differential equations described in [21]. (cf. [23] for their discrete-time counterparts.)

In practice, only a finite number of directions is used for the maximal reachable set computations. Let $\mathcal{M}$ be a finite subset of $\mathcal{N}$. Then,

$$Reach_{\delta-t}^\sharp(K_k(P)) \supseteq \bigcup_{\ell_\delta \in \mathcal{M}} \mathcal{E}(x^*(t), X_\ell^-(t)), \quad \forall t \in [0, \delta]. \tag{22}$$

Note that the under-approximation in (22) is in general an arbitrarily shaped, non-convex set. Performing our desired operations on this set while maintaining efficiency may be difficult, if not impossible.

Now, consider the final backward reachable set $Reach_\delta^\sharp(K_k(P))$ and let $Reach_\delta^{\sharp(\tilde{\ell}_\delta)}(K_k(P))$ denote the maximal reachable set corresponding to a single terminal direction $\tilde{\ell}_\delta := \tilde{\ell}(\delta) \in \mathcal{M}$. We have that

$$
\begin{aligned}
Reach_\delta^{\sharp(\tilde{\ell}_\delta)}(K_k(P)) &= \mathcal{E}(x^*(0), X_{\tilde{\ell}}^-(0)) \\
&\subseteq \bigcup_{\ell_\delta \in \mathcal{M}} \mathcal{E}(x^*(0), X_\ell^-(0)) \\
&\subseteq Reach_\delta^\sharp(K_k(P)).
\end{aligned} \tag{23}
$$

Therefore, the reachable set computed for a single direction is an *ellipsoidal subset* of the actual reachable set.

Let $\bigcirc(\cdot)$ be a function that maps a set to its maximum volume inscribed ellipsoid. Algorithms 1 and 2 compute a piecewise ellipsoidal under-approximation of $Viab_{[0,\tau]}(\mathcal{K})$ for continuous-time and discrete-time systems, respectively.

Algorithm 1 Piecewise ellipsoidal approximation of $Viab_{[0,\tau]}(\mathcal{K})$ (continuous-time)

1: Choose $P \in \mathscr{P}([0,\tau])$ ▷ Affects precision of approximation
2: $K_{|P|}(P) \leftarrow \mathcal{K} \ominus \mathcal{B}(M\|P\|)$
 ▷ Find $\{x \in \mathcal{K} \mid \text{dist}(x, \mathcal{K}^c) \geq M\|P\|\}$
3: $K_0^*(P) \leftarrow \emptyset$
4: **while** $\mathcal{M} \neq \emptyset$ **do**
5: $\quad l \leftarrow \ell_\tau \in \mathcal{M}$
6: $\quad k \leftarrow |P|$
7: $\quad$**while** $k \neq 0$ **do**
8: $\quad\quad$**if** $K_k(P) = \emptyset$ **then**
9: $\quad\quad\quad K_0(P) \leftarrow \emptyset$
10: $\quad\quad\quad$**break**
11: $\quad\quad$**end if**
12: $\quad\quad \mathcal{G} \leftarrow Reach_{t_k - t_{k-1}}^{\sharp(l)}(K_k(P))$
 ▷ Compute the maximal reach set along the direction l
13: $\quad\quad K_{k-1}(P) \leftarrow \bigcirc(K_{|P|}(P) \cap \mathcal{G})$
 ▷ Find the maximum volume inscribed ellipsoid in $K_{|P|}(P) \cap \mathcal{G}$
14: $\quad\quad k \leftarrow k - 1$
15: $\quad$**end while**
16: $\quad K_0^*(P) \leftarrow K_0^*(P) \cup K_0(P)$
17: $\quad \mathcal{M} \leftarrow \mathcal{M} \setminus \{l\}$
18: **end while**
19: **return** $(K_0^*(P))$

Algorithm 2 Piecewise ellipsoidal approximation of $Viab_{[0,\tau]}(\mathcal{K})$ (discrete-time)

1: $K_n \leftarrow \mathcal{K}$
2: $K_0^* \leftarrow \emptyset$
3: **while** $\mathcal{M} \neq \emptyset$ **do**
4: $\quad l \leftarrow \ell_\tau \in \mathcal{M}$
5: $\quad k \leftarrow n$
6: $\quad$**while** $k \neq 0$ **do**
7: $\quad\quad$**if** $K_k = \emptyset$ **then**
8: $\quad\quad\quad K_0 \leftarrow \emptyset$
9: $\quad\quad\quad$**break**
10: $\quad\quad$**end if**
11: $\quad\quad \mathcal{G} \leftarrow Reach_1^{\sharp(l)}(K_k)$
12: $\quad\quad K_{k-1} \leftarrow \bigcirc(K_n \cap \mathcal{G})$
13: $\quad\quad k \leftarrow k - 1$
14: $\quad$**end while**
15: $\quad K_0^* \leftarrow K_0^* \cup K_0$
16: $\quad \mathcal{M} \leftarrow \mathcal{M} \setminus \{l\}$
17: **end while**
18: **return** (K_0^*)

PROPOSITION 4. *For a given partition $P \in \mathscr{P}([0,\tau])$, let $K_0^*(P)$ be the set generated by Algorithm 1. Then,*

$$K_0^*(P) \subseteq Viab_{[0,\tau]}(\mathcal{K}). \tag{24}$$

PROOF. Let $\widetilde{K}_0(P)$ denote the final set constructed recursively by (10). Also, for a fixed direction l, let $K_0^{(l)}(P)$ denote the set produced at the end of each outer loop in Algorithm 1. Notice that via (23), for every $l \in \mathcal{M}$, $K_0^{(l)}(P) \subseteq \widetilde{K}_0(P)$. Therefore, $\bigcup_{l \in \mathcal{M}} K_0^{(l)}(P) \subseteq \widetilde{K}_0(P)$. Thus, $K_0^*(P) = \bigcup_{l \in \mathcal{M}} K_0^{(l)}(P) \subseteq Viab_{[0,\tau]}(\mathcal{K})$. □

Remark 2. A similar argument holds for the discrete-time case in Algorithm 2, i.e. $K_0^* \subseteq Viab_{[0,\tau]}(\mathcal{K})$.

4.1.1 $\bigcirc(\cdot)$: *Computing the Maximum Volume Inscribed Ellipsoid*

Notice that in the continuous-time case, the sets $\mathcal{Y} := K_{|P|}(P)$ and $\mathcal{G} := Reach_{t_k - t_{k-1}}^{\sharp(l)}(K_k(P))$ are compact ellipsoids for every $l \in \mathcal{M}$, $P \in \mathscr{P}([0,\tau])$, and $k \in \{1, \ldots, |P|\}$. Similarly in the discrete-time case, $\mathcal{Y} := K_n$ and $\mathcal{G} := Reach_1^{\sharp(l)}(K_k)$ are compact ellipsoids for every $l \in \mathcal{M}$ and $k \in \{1, \ldots, n\}$. Their intersection is, in general, not an ellipsoid but can be easily under-approximated by one. The operation $\bigcirc(\cdot)$ under-approximates this intersection by computing the maximum volume inscribed ellipsoid in $\mathcal{Y} \cap \mathcal{G}$. The result is an ellipsoid that, while aiming to minimize the accuracy loss, can be used directly as the target set for the reachability computation in the subsequent time step.

Let us re-write the general ellipsoid as $\mathcal{E}(q, Q) = \{Hx + q \mid \|x\|_2 \leq 1\}$ with $H = Q^{\frac{1}{2}}$. Assume $\mathcal{Y} \cap \mathcal{G} \neq \emptyset$ and suppose $\mathcal{Y} = \mathcal{E}(q_1, Q_1)$ and $\mathcal{G} = \mathcal{E}(q_2, Q_2)$. Following [4], the computation of the maximum volume inscribed ellipsoid in $\mathcal{Y} \cap \mathcal{G}$ (a readily-available feature in ET) can be cast as a convex semidefinite program (SDP):

$$\underset{H \in \mathbb{R}^{n \times n}, q \in \mathbb{R}^n, \lambda_i \in \mathbb{R}}{\text{minimize}} \quad \log \det H^{-1} \tag{25a}$$

$$\text{subject to} \quad \begin{bmatrix} 1 - \lambda_i & 0 & (q - q_i)^T \\ 0 & \lambda_i I & H \\ q - q_i & H & Q_i \end{bmatrix} \succeq 0 \tag{25b}$$

$$\lambda_i > 0, \quad i = 1, 2. \tag{25c}$$

Using the optimal values for H and q, we will have $\bigcirc(\mathcal{Y} \cap \mathcal{G}) = \mathcal{E}(q, H^T H)$.

4.1.2 Loss of Accuracy

A set generated by Algorithms 1 or 2 could be an inaccurate approximation of $Viab_{[0,\tau]}(\mathcal{K})$, especially for large time horizons. The loss of accuracy is mainly attributed to the function $\bigcirc(\cdot)$, the under-approximation of the intersection at every iteration with its maximum volume inscribed ellipsoid. This approximation error propagates through the algorithms making them subject to the "wrapping effect".

In the continuous-time case, the quality of approximation is also affected by the choice of time interval partition (Proposition 2). Choosing a finer partition increases the quality of approximation. However, doing so would also require a larger number of intersections to be performed in the intermediate steps of the recursion. As such, one would expect that the error generated by $\bigcirc(\cdot)$ would be amplified. Luckily, since with a finer partition the reachable sets change very little from one time step to the next, the intersection error at every iteration becomes smaller. The end result is a smaller accumulative error and therefore a better approximation.

We show this using a trivial example: Consider the double integrator

$$\dot{x}(t) = \begin{bmatrix} 0 & 1 \\ 0 & 0 \end{bmatrix} x(t) + \begin{bmatrix} 0 \\ 1 \end{bmatrix} u(t) \tag{26}$$

subject to ellipsoidal constraints $u(t) \in \mathcal{U} := [-0.25, 0.25]$ and $x(t) \in \mathcal{K} := \mathcal{E}(\mathbf{0}, \begin{bmatrix} 0.25 & 0 \\ 0 & 0.25 \end{bmatrix})$, $\forall t \in [0, 1]$. We employ eight different partitions P of the time interval such that we have $|P| = 13, 21, 34, 55, 89, 144, 233, 377$, all with equi-length sub-time intervals. The linear vector field is bounded on $\mathcal{K}$ in the infinity norm by $M = \|\begin{bmatrix} 0 & 1 \\ 0 & 0 \end{bmatrix}\| \sup_{x \in \mathcal{K}} \|x\| + \|\begin{bmatrix} 0 \\ 1 \end{bmatrix}\| \sup_{u \in \mathcal{U}} \|u\| = 0.75$. Thus, in Algorithm 1, $K_{|P|}(P) = \mathcal{K} \ominus \mathcal{B}(0.75 \times \|P\|)$. A piecewise ellipsoidal under-approximation of $Viab_{[0,1]}(\mathcal{K})$ for every partition P (with $|\mathcal{M}| = 10$ randomly chosen initial directions) is shown in Figure 2. Notice that as $|P|$ increases, the fidelity of approxi-

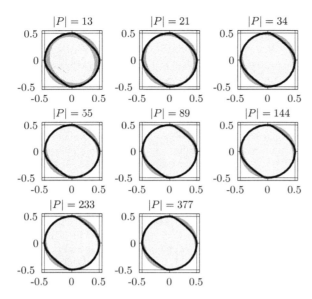

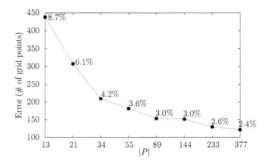

Figure 3: Convergence plot of the error as a function of $|P|$ for the double-integrator example. Error is quantified as the fraction of grid points (total of 71×71) contained in the set difference between the level-set approximation of the viability kernel and its piecewise ellipsoidal under-approximation.

Figure 2: For the set $\mathcal{K}$ (red), $K_0(P)$ (green) under-approximates $Viab_{[0,1]}(\mathcal{K})$ (outlined in thick black lines via [30]) using Algorithm 1 under the double integrator dynamics. A finer time interval partition results in better approximation.

mation improves. A plot of the error in the accuracy of the under-approximation as a function of $|P|$ is provided in Figure 3.

5. PRACTICAL EXAMPLES

All computations are performed on a dual core Intel-based computer with 2.8 GHz CPU, 6 MB of L2 cache and 3 GB of RAM running single-threaded 32-bit MATLAB 7.5.

5.1 Flight Envelope Protection (Continuous-Time)

Consider the longitudinal aircraft dynamics $\dot{x}(t) = Ax(t) + B\delta_e(t)$,

$$A = \begin{bmatrix} -0.003 & 0.039 & 0 & -0.322 \\ -0.065 & -0.319 & 7.740 & 0 \\ 0.020 & -0.101 & -0.429 & 0 \\ 0 & 0 & 1 & 0 \end{bmatrix}, B = \begin{bmatrix} 0.010 \\ -0.180 \\ -1.160 \\ 0 \end{bmatrix}$$

with state $x = [u, v, \dot{\theta}, \theta]^T \in \mathbb{R}^4$ comprised of deviations in aircraft velocity [ft/s] along and perpendicular to body axis, pitch-rate [crad/s], and pitch angle [crad] respectively[1], and with input $\delta_e \in [-13.3°, 13.3°] \subseteq \mathbb{R}$ the elevator deflection. These matrices represent stability derivatives of a Boeing 747 cruising at an altitude of 40 kft with speed 774 ft/s [5]. The state constraint set

$$\mathcal{K} = \mathcal{E}\left(\begin{bmatrix} 0 \\ 0 \\ 2.18 \\ 0 \end{bmatrix}, \begin{bmatrix} 1075.84 & 0 & 0 & 0 \\ 0 & 67.24 & 0 & 0 \\ 0 & 0 & 42.7716 & 0 \\ 0 & 0 & 0 & 76.0384 \end{bmatrix} \right)$$

represents the flight envelope. We require $x(t) \in \mathcal{K}, \forall t \in [0, 2]$.

A partition P is chosen such that $|P| = 400$ with equi-length sub-time intervals. Algorithm 1 (with $|\mathcal{M}| = 8$) computes via ET a piecewise ellipsoidal under-approximation of the viability kernel $Viab_{[0,2]}(\mathcal{K})$ as shown in Figures 4 and 5. Note that for any state belonging to this set, there exists an input that can protect the flight

[1]crad = 0.01 rad $\approx 0.57°$.

envelope over the specified time horizon. The overall computation time was roughly 10 mins. In comparison, the level-set approximation of the viability kernel (also shown in Figure 5) is computed in 5.4 hrs with significantly larger memory footprint over a grid with 45 nodes in each dimension using the Level-Set Toolbox [30]. Since the computed sets are 4D, we plot a series of 3D and 2D projections of these 4D objects.

5.2 Safety in Anesthesia Automation (Discrete-Time)

To improve patient recovery, lessen anesthetic drug usage, and reduce time spent at drug saturation levels, a variety of approaches to controlling depth of anesthesia have been proposed e.g. in [37, 14, 39, 8, 34, 28].

Over the past few years, an interdisciplinary team of researchers at the University of British Columbia has been developing an automated drug delivery system for anesthesia. As part of this effort, an open-loop bolus-based neuromuscular blockade system was developed and clinically validated in [10]. Discrete-time Laguerre-based LTI models of the dynamic response to rocuronium were identified using data collected from more than 80 patients via clinical trials. To obtain regulatory certificates to fully close the loop while employing an infusion-based administration of the drugs, mathematical guarantees of safety and performance of the system are likely to be required. The viability kernel and the continual reachability set [17], respectively, can provide such guarantees. (We note that while both this paper and [17] use maximal reachable sets for computation, the method in [17] computes the continual reachability set while here we compute the viability kernel.)

Consider the problem of computing the viability kernel for a constrained discrete-time LTI system (sampled every 20 s) that describes the pharmacological response of a patient under anesthesia. The therapeutic target is defined in the output space (as opposed to the state space) and the output signal should track a reference set-point. As in [17], to perform the desired analysis we reformulate the problem by projecting the output bounds onto the state space while making the control action regulatory. As such, the original dynamics are augmented and transformed into an appropriate coordinate system of dimension seven. In this new state space, the first state z_1 represents the drug pseudo-occupancy (a metric related to the patient's plasma concentration of the anesthetic [10]) minus its setpoint value of 0.9 units, the next five states are the second to sixth Laguerre states transformed from the original coordinates, and the last state z_7 is a constant corresponding to the pseudo-

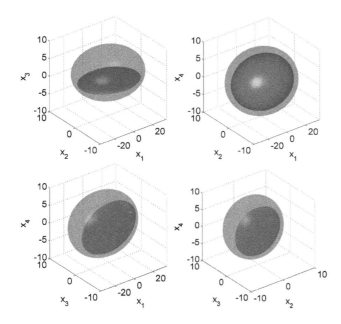

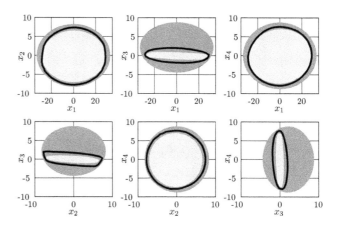

Figure 5: 2D projections of the under-approximation of $Viab_{[0,2]}(\mathcal{K})$ **for Example 5.1. The constraint set** $\mathcal{K}$ **(red) and a piecewise ellipsoidal under-approximation of the viability kernel (green) are shown. The level-set approximation of the viability kernel, computed via [30], is outlined in thick black lines.**

Figure 4: 3D projections of the under-approximation of $Viab_{[0,2]}(\mathcal{K})$ **for Example 5.1. The flight envelope** $\mathcal{K}$ **is the red transparent region. The green piecewise ellipsoidal sets under-approximate the viability kernel.**

occupancy setpoint. The states are assumed to be constrained by a slab in $\mathbb{R}^7$ that is only bounded in the z_1 direction. Note that with this formulation, the last state z_7 is allowed to take on values that are not needed; of actual interest is the behavior of the remaining states when z_7 equals the pseudo-occupancy setpoint. The input constraint, which represents the actuator's physical limitations (i.e. hard bounds on rocuronium infusion rate), is a closed and bounded interval in $\mathbb{R}$.

The input constraint set is a one-dimensional ellipsoid. To under-approximate the state constraint with a non-degenerate ellipsoid we use *a priori* knowledge about the typical values of the (Laguerre) states $z_2, \ldots, z_6$ and bound them by an ellipsoid with a large spectral radius of $\lambda_{\max} = 30$ in those directions. (This imposed constraint can be further relaxed if necessary.) Guaranteeing that this ellipsoidal target set $\mathcal{K}$, which is our desired clinical effect, is not violated during the surgery provides a certificate of safety of the closed-loop system. Therefore, for a 30 min long surgery for instance, we require $z(t) \in \mathcal{K}$, $\forall t \in [0, 90]$ despite bounded input authority. Using appropriately synthesized infusion policies, the states belonging to the viability kernel of $\mathcal{K}$ under the extended system will never leave the desired clinical effect for the duration of the surgery.

We under-approximate $Viab_{[0,90]}(\mathcal{K})$ in 986 s using Algorithm 2 with $|\mathcal{M}| = 30$. Of the 30 randomly chosen initial directions used in the ellipsoidal computations, 15 resulted in nonempty ellipsoids that make up the piecewise ellipsoidal under-approximation of the viability kernel (Figure 6). Note that no similar computations are currently possible in such high dimensions using Eulerian methods directly.

6. CONCLUSIONS AND FUTURE WORK

We presented a connection between the viability kernel (and by duality, the minimal reachable tube) and the maximal reachable sets of possibly nonlinear systems. Owing to this connection, the efficient and scalable Lagrangian techniques can be used to approximate the viability kernel. Motivated by a high-dimensional problem of guaranteed safety in control of anesthesia, we proposed a scalable algorithm that computes a piecewise ellipsoidal under-approximation of the viability kernel for LTI systems based on ellipsoidal techniques for reachability.

Empirically quantifying the computational complexity of the piecewise ellipsoidal algorithm is a work under way for which we expect a polynomial complexity in the order of $|\mathcal{M}||P| \, (\mathcal{O}(\mathfrak{R}_\delta) + \mathcal{O}(\mathfrak{S}))$ where $\mathcal{O}(\mathfrak{R}_\delta)$ is the complexity of computing the maximal reachable set along a given direction over the time interval δ and $\mathcal{O}(\mathfrak{S})$ is the complexity of solving the SDP (25).

While the presented algorithm has shown to be effective and efficient, it may be subject to excessive conservatism particularly for large time horizons. We are currently developing alternative approaches that yield a more accurate under-approximation of the viability kernel while still preserving the scalability property.

Finally, the presented connection between the viability kernel and the maximal reachable sets paves the way to synthesizing "safety-preserving" optimal control laws in a more efficient and scalable manner.

7. REFERENCES

[1] J.-P. Aubin. *Viability Theory*. Systems and Control: Foundations and Applications. Birkhäuser, Boston, MA, 1991.

[2] A. M. Bayen, I. M. Mitchell, M. Oishi, and C. J. Tomlin. Aircraft autolander safety analysis through optimal control-based reach set computation. *Journal of Guidance, Control, and Dynamics*, 30(1):68–77, 2007.

[3] F. Blanchini and S. Miani. *Set-Theoretic Methods in Control*. Springer, 2008.

[4] S. P. Boyd and L. Vandenberghe. *Convex optimization*. Cambridge University Press, 2004.

[5] A. E. Bryson. *Control of Spacecraft and Aircraft*. Princeton Univ. Press, 1994.

[6] P. Cardaliaguet, M. Quincampoix, and P. Saint-Pierre. Set-valued numerical analysis for optimal control and differential games. In M. Bardi, T. Raghavan, and

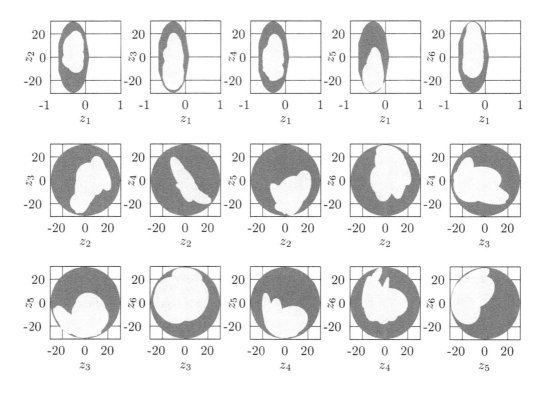

Figure 6: 2D projections of the under-approximation of $Viab_{[0,90]}(\mathcal{K})$ **for Example 5.2 for the first six states when** z_7 **equals the setpoint value. The constraint set** $\mathcal{K}$ **(blue) and a piecewise ellipsoidal under-approximation of the provably safe regions (green) are shown.**

T. Parthasarathy, editors, *Stochastic and Differential Games: Theory and Numerical Methods*, number 4 in Annals of the International Society of Dynamic Games, pages 177–247, Boston, MA, 1999. Birkhäuser.

[7] A. N. Daryin, A. B. Kurzhanski, and I. V. Vostrikov. Reachability approaches and ellipsoidal techniques for closed-loop control of oscillating systems under uncertainty. In *Proc. IEEE Conference on Decision and Control*, pages 6385–6390, San Diego, CA, 2006.

[8] G. Dumont, A. Martinez, and J. Ansermino. Robust control of depth of anesthesia. *International Journal of Adaptive Control and Signal Processing*, 23:435–454, 2009.

[9] Y. Gao, J. Lygeros, and M. Quincampoix. The reachability problem for uncertain hybrid systems revisited: a viability theory perspective. In J. Hespanha and A. Tiwari, editors, *Hybrid Systems: Computation and Control, LNCS 3927*, pages 242–256, Berlin Heidelberg, 2006. Springer-Verlag.

[10] T. Gilhuly. *Modeling and control of neuromuscular blockade*. PhD thesis, University of British Columbia, Vancouver, Canada, 2007.

[11] A. Girard and C. Le Guernic. Efficient reachability analysis for linear systems using support functions. In *IFAC World Congress*, Seoul, Korea, July 2008.

[12] A. Girard, C. Le Guernic, and O. Maler. Efficient computation of reachable sets of linear time-invariant systems with inputs. In J. Hespanha and A. Tiwari, editors, *Hybrid Systems: Computation and Control, LNCS 3927*, pages 257–271. Springer-Verlag, 2006.

[13] Z. Han and B. H. Krogh. Reachability analysis of nonlinear systems using trajectory piecewise linearized models. In *Proc. American Control Conference*, pages 1505–1510, Minneapolis, MN, 2006.

[14] C. Ionescu, R. De Keyser, B. Torrico, T. De Smet, M. Struys, and J. Normey-Rico. Robust predictive control strategy applied for propofol dosing using BIS as a controlled variable during anesthesia. *IEEE Transactions on Biomedical Engineering*, 55(9):2161–2170, 2008.

[15] S. Kaynama and M. Oishi. Complexity reduction through a Schur-based decomposition for reachability analysis of linear time-invariant systems. *International Journal of Control*, 84(1):165–179, 2011.

[16] S. Kaynama and M. Oishi. A modified Riccati transformation for complexity reduction in reachability analysis of linear time-invariant systems. *IEEE Transactions on Automatic Control*, 2011. (accepted; preprint available at www.ece.ubc.ca/~kaynama).

[17] S. Kaynama, M. Oishi, I. M. Mitchell, and G. A. Dumont. The continual reachability set and its computation using maximal reachability techniques. In *Proc. IEEE Conference on Decision and Control, and European Control Conference*, pages 6110–6115, Orlando, FL, 2011.

[18] A. B. Kurzhanski and I. Vályi. *Ellipsoidal Calculus for Estimation and Control*. Birkhäuser, Boston, MA, 1996.

[19] A. B. Kurzhanski and P. Varaiya. Ellipsoidal techniques for reachability analysis. In N. Lynch and B. Krogh, editors, *Hybrid Systems: Computation and Control, LNCS 1790*, pages 202–214, Berlin Heidelberg, 2000. Springer-Verlag.

[20] A. B. Kurzhanski and P. Varaiya. Ellipsoidal techniques for

reachability analysis: internal approximation. *Systems & Control Letters*, 41:201–211, 2000.

[21] A. B. Kurzhanski and P. Varaiya. On reachability under uncertainty. *SIAM Journal on Control and Optimization*, 41(1):181–216, 2002.

[22] A. A. Kurzhanskiy and P. Varaiya. Ellipsoidal Toolbox (ET). In *Proc. IEEE Conference on Decision and Control*, pages 1498–1503, San Diego, CA, Dec. 2006.

[23] A. A. Kurzhanskiy and P. Varaiya. Ellipsoidal techniques for reachability analysis of discrete-time linear systems. *IEEE Transactions on Automatic Control*, 52(1):26–38, 2007.

[24] M. Kvasnica, P. Grieder, M. Baotić, and M. Morari. Multi-Parametric Toolbox (MPT). In R. Alur and G. J. Pappas, editors, *Hybrid Systems: Computation and Control, LNCS 2993*, pages 448–462, Berlin, Germany, 2004. Springer.

[25] C. Le Guernic. *Reachability analysis of hybrid systems with linear continuous dynamics*. PhD thesis, Université Grenoble 1 – Joseph Fourier, 2009.

[26] J. Lygeros. On reachability and minimum cost optimal control. *Automatica*, 40(6):917–927, June 2004.

[27] K. Margellos and J. Lygeros. Air traffic management with target windows: An approach using reachability. In *Proc. IEEE Conference on Decision and Control*, pages 145–150, Shanghai, China, Dec 2009.

[28] T. Mendonca, J. Lemos, H. Magalhaes, P. Rocha, and S. Esteves. Drug delivery for neuromuscular blockade with supervised multimodel adaptive control. *IEEE Transactions on Control Systems Technology*, 17(6):1237–1244, November 2009.

[29] I. M. Mitchell. Comparing forward and backward reachability as tools for safety analysis. In A. Bemporad, A. Bicchi, and G. Buttazzo, editors, *Hybrid Systems: Computation and Control, LNCS 4416*, pages 428–443, Berlin Heidelberg, 2007. Springer-Verlag.

[30] I. M. Mitchell. A toolbox of level set methods. Technical report, UBC Department of Computer Science, TR-2007-11, June 2007.

[31] I. M. Mitchell. Scalable calculation of reach sets and tubes for nonlinear systems with terminal integrators: a mixed implicit explicit formulation. In *Proc. Hybrid Systems: Computation and Control*, pages 103–112, Chicago, IL, 2011. ACM.

[32] I. M. Mitchell, A. M. Bayen, and C. J. Tomlin. A time-dependent Hamilton-Jacobi formulation of reachable sets for continuous dynamic games. *IEEE Transactions on Automatic Control*, 50(7):947–957, July 2005.

[33] I. M. Mitchell and C. J. Tomlin. Overapproximating reachable sets by Hamilton-Jacobi projections. *Journal of Scientific Computing*, 19(1–3):323–346, 2003.

[34] P. Oliveira, J. P. Hespanha, J. M. Lemos, and T. Mendonça. Supervised multi-model adaptive control of neuromuscular blockade with off-set compensation. In *Proc. European Control Conference*, 2009.

[35] D. Panagou, K. Margellos, S. Summers, J. Lygeros, and K. J. Kyriakopoulos. A viability approach for the stabilization of an underactuated underwater vehicle in the presence of current disturbances. In *Proc. IEEE Conference on Decision and Control*, pages 8612–8617, Dec. 2009.

[36] P. Saint-Pierre. Approximation of the viability kernel. *Applied Mathematics and Optimization*, 29(2):187–209, Mar 1994.

[37] O. Simanski, A. Schubert, R. Kaehler, M. Janda, J. Bajorat, R. Hofmockel, and B. Lampe. Automatic drug delivery in anesthesia: From the beginning until now. In *Proc. Mediterranean Conf. Contr. Automation*, Athens, Greece, 2007.

[38] D. M. Stipanović, I. Hwang, and C. J. Tomlin. Computation of an over-approximation of the backward reachable set using subsystem level set functions. In *Proc. IEE European Control Conference*, Cambridge, UK, Sept. 2003.

[39] S. Syafiie, J. Niño, C. Ionescu, and R. De Keyser. NMPC for propofol drug dosing during anesthesia induction. In *Nonlinear Model Predictive Control*, volume 384, pages 501–509. Springer Berlin Heidelberg, 2009.

Reachability Games for Linear Hybrid Systems

Massimo Benerecetti
bene@na.infn.it

Marco Faella
mfaella@na.infn.it

Stefano Minopoli
minopoli@na.infn.it

Università di Napoli
"Federico II", Italy

ABSTRACT

We consider the problem of computing the controllable region of a Linear Hybrid Automaton with controllable and uncontrollable transitions, w.r.t. a reachability objective. We provide a semi-algorithm for the problem, by proposing the first algorithm in the literature for computing the set of states that must reach a given polyhedron while avoiding another one, subject to a polyhedral constraint on the slope of the trajectory. Experimental results are presented, based on an implementation of the proposed algorithm on top of the tool PHAVer.

Categories and Subject Descriptors

F.3.1 [**Logics and Meanings of Programs**]: Specifying and Verifying and Reasoning about Programs

Keywords

Hybrid Automata, Controller Synthesis, Formal Methods

1. INTRODUCTION

Hybrid systems are an established formalism for modeling physical systems which interact with a digital controller. From an abstract point of view, a hybrid system is a dynamic system whose state variables are partitioned into discrete and continuous ones.

Hybrid automata [12] are the most common syntactic variety of hybrid system: a finite set of locations, similar to the states of a finite automaton, represents the value of the discrete variables. The current location, together with the current value of the (continuous) variables, form the instantaneous description of the system. Change of location happens via discrete transitions, and the evolution of the variables is governed by differential equations attached to each location. In a Linear Hybrid Automaton (LHA), the allowed differential equations are in fact differential inclusions of the type $\dot{x} \in P$, where $\dot{x}$ is the vector of the first derivatives of all variables and $P \subseteq \mathbb{R}^n$ is a convex polyhedron. Notice

that differential inclusions are non-deterministic, allowing for infinitely many solutions.

We study LHAs whose discrete transitions are partitioned into controllable and uncontrollable ones, and we wish to compute the set of states from which the controller can ensure a given goal, regardless of the trajectory followed by the continuous variables and despite the occurrence of uncontrollable discrete transitions. Hence, the problem can be viewed as a *two player game* [19]: on one side the controller, who can only issue controllable transitions, on the other side the environment, who can choose the trajectory of the variables and can take uncontrollable transitions whenever they are enabled.

As control goal, we consider reachability, i.e., the objective of reaching a given set T of target states. The problem is known to be undecidable, being harder than the standard reachability verification (i.e., 1-player reachability) for triangular hybrid automata [14], a special case of LHAs. We present a sound and complete semi-algorithm for the problem[1], based on a novel algorithm for computing, within a given location, the set of states that must reach a given polyhedral region while avoiding another one.

We recently presented a semi-algorithm for the control problem of LHAs with *safety* objectives [6, 5]. Although the control goal we examine, as a language of infinite traces, is the dual of safety, the corresponding synthesis problems are not dual, because our game model is asymmetric (the continuous behavior is always uncontrollable). Hence, it is not possible to solve the control problem with reachability goal T by exchanging the roles of the two players and then solving the safety control problem with goal $\overline{T}$ (i.e., the complement of T). To the best of our knowledge, the reachability goal was never considered for LHAs.

We present an implementation of the proposed semi-algorithm in a tool called PHAVer+, and a set of preliminary experiments.

Related work. The idea of automatically synthesizing controllers for dynamic systems arose in connection with discrete systems [17]. Then, the same idea was applied to real-time systems modeled by timed automata [16], thus coming one step closer to the continuous systems that control theory usually deals with. Finally, it was the turn of hybrid systems [13, 10], and in particular of Linear Hybrid Automata [20], the very model that we analyze in this paper. Wong-Toi proposed a symbolic semi-algorithm to compute

---

[1]In other words, a procedure that may or may not terminate, and that provides the correct answer whenever it terminates.

the controllable region of a LHA w.r.t. a safety goal [20]. Our recent work [6] revisits the solution proposed by Wong-Toi, identifying some inaccuracies which prevent completeness of the procedure, and proposes a sound and complete semi-algorithm for the problem.

Tomlin et al. [19] and Balluchi et al. [4] analyze much more expressive models, with generality in mind rather than automatic synthesis.

Asarin et al. [3] investigate the synthesis problem for hybrid systems where all discrete transitions are controllable and the trajectories satisfy given linear differential equations of the type $\dot{\mathbf{x}} = A\mathbf{x}$. The expressive power of these constraints is incomparable with the one offered by LHAs. In particular, linear differential equations give rise to deterministic trajectories, while differential inclusions are non-deterministic. In control theory terms, differential inclusions can represent the presence of environmental *disturbances*. Bouyer et al. [8] propose a general abstraction technique for hybrid systems, and focus on decidable classes of o-minimal automata.

The rest of the paper is organized as follows. Section 2 introduces and motivates the model. The proposed semi-algorithm is presented as divided in two layers: Section 3 illustrates the outer layer, dealing with multiple locations and discrete transitions, while Section 4 focuses on the geometric problem arising from the analysis of a single location. Finally, Section 5 reports some experiments performed on our implementation of the procedure.

2. LINEAR HYBRID AUTOMATA

A *convex polyhedron* is a subset of $\mathbb{R}^n$ that is the intersection of a finite number of strict and non-strict affine half-spaces. A *polyhedron* is a subset of $\mathbb{R}^n$ that is the union of a finite number of convex polyhedra. For a general (i.e., not necessarily convex) polyhedron $G \subseteq \mathbb{R}^n$, we denote by $cl(G)$ its topological closure, and by $[\![G]\!] \subseteq 2^{\mathbb{R}^n}$ its representation as a finite set of convex polyhedra.

Given an ordered set $X = \{x_1, \ldots, x_n\}$ of variables, a *valuation* is a function $v : X \to \mathbb{R}$. Let $Val(X)$ denote the set of valuations over X. There is an obvious bijection between $Val(X)$ and $\mathbb{R}^n$, allowing us to extend the notion of (convex) polyhedron to sets of valuations. We denote by $CPoly(X)$ (resp., $Poly(X)$) the set of convex polyhedra (resp., polyhedra) on X. Let A be a set of valuations, states or points in $\mathbb{R}^n$, we denote by $\overline{A}$ its complement.

We use $\dot{X}$ to denote the set $\{\dot{x}_1, \ldots, \dot{x}_n\}$ of dotted variables, used to represent the first derivatives, and X' to denote the set $\{x'_1, \ldots, x'_n\}$ of primed variables, used to represent the new values of variables after a transition. Arithmetic operations on valuations are defined in the straightforward way. An *activity* over X is a differentiable function $f : \mathbb{R}^{\geq 0} \to Val(X)$. Let $Acts(X)$ denote the set of activities over X. The *derivative* $\dot{f}$ of an activity f is defined in the standard way and it is an activity over $\dot{X}$. A *Linear Hybrid Automaton* $H = \langle Loc, X, Edg_c, Edg_u, Flow, Inv, Init \rangle$ consists of the following:

- A finite set Loc of *locations*.

- A finite set $X = \{x_1, \ldots, x_n\}$ of continuous, real-valued *variables*. A *state* is a pair $\langle l, v \rangle$ of a location l and a valuation $v \in Val(X)$.

- Two sets Edg_c and Edg_u of *controllable* and *uncontrollable transitions*, respectively. They describe instantaneous changes of locations, in the course of which variables may change their value. Each transition $(l, \mu, l') \in Edg_c \cup Edg_u$ consists of a *source location* l, a *target location* l', and a *jump relation* $\mu \in Poly(X \cup X')$, that specifies how the variables may change their value during the transition. The projection of μ on X describes the valuations for which the transition is enabled; this is often referred to as a *guard*.

- A mapping $Flow : Loc \to CPoly(\dot{X})$ attributes to each location a set of valuations over the first derivatives of the variables, which determines how variables can change over time.

- A mapping $Inv : Loc \to Poly(X)$, called the *invariant*.

- A mapping $Init : Loc \to Poly(X)$, contained in the invariant, defining the *initial states* of the automaton.

We use the abbreviations $S = Loc \times Val(X)$ for the set of states and $Edg = Edg_c \cup Edg_u$ for the set of all transitions. Moreover, we let $InvS = \bigcup_{l \in Loc} \{l\} \times Inv(l)$ and $InitS = \bigcup_{l \in Loc} \{l\} \times Init(l)$. Notice that $InvS$ and $InitS$ are sets of states. Given a set of states A and a location l, we denote by $A|_l$ the projection of A on l, i.e. $\{v \in Val(X) \mid \langle l, v \rangle \in A\}$.

2.1 Semantics

The behavior of a LHA is based on two types of transitions: *discrete* transitions correspond to the Edg component, and produce an instantaneous change in both the location and the variable valuation; *timed* transitions describe the change of the variables over time in accordance with the $Flow$ component.

Given a state $s = \langle l, v \rangle$, we set $loc(s) = l$ and $val(s) = v$. An activity $f \in Acts(X)$ is called *admissible from* s if *(i)* $f(0) = v$ and *(ii)* for all $\delta \geq 0$ it holds $\dot{f}(\delta) \in Flow(l)$. We denote by $Adm(s)$ the set of activities that are admissible from s. Additionally, for $f \in Adm(s)$, the *span* of f in l, denoted by $span(f, l)$ is the set of all values $\delta \geq 0$ such that $\langle l, f(\delta') \rangle \in InvS$ for all $0 \leq \delta' \leq \delta$. Intuitively, δ is in the span of f iff f never leaves the invariant in the first δ time units. If all non-negative reals belong to $span(f, l)$, we write $\infty \in span(f, l)$.

Runs. Given two states s, s', and a transition $e \in Edg$, there is a *discrete step* $s \xrightarrow{e} s'$ with *source* s and *target* s' iff: *(i)* $s, s' \in InvS$, *(ii)* $e = (loc(s), \mu, loc(s'))$, and *(iii)* $(val(s), val(s')[X'/X]) \in \mu$, where $val(s')[X/X']$ is the valuation in $Val(X')$ obtained from s' by renaming the variables. Whenever there is a discrete step $s \xrightarrow{e} s'$, we say that e is *enabled in* s.

There is a *timed step* $s \xrightarrow{\delta, f} s'$ with *duration* $\delta \in \mathbb{R}^{\geq 0}$ and activity $f \in Adm(s)$ iff: *(i)* $s \in InvS$, *(ii)* $\delta \in span(f, loc(s))$, and *(iii)* $s' = \langle loc(s), f(\delta) \rangle$. For technical convenience, we admit timed steps of duration zero[2]. A special timed step is denoted $s \xrightarrow{\infty, f}$ and represents the case when the system follows an activity forever. This is only allowed if

---

[2] Timed steps of duration zero can be disabled by adding a clock variable t to the automaton and requesting that each discrete transition happens when $t > 0$ and resets t to 0 when taken.

$\infty \in span(f, loc(s))$. Finally, a *joint step* $s \xrightarrow{\delta, f, e} s'$ represents the timed step $s \xrightarrow{\delta, f} \langle loc(s), f(\delta) \rangle$ followed by the discrete step $\langle loc(s), f(\delta) \rangle \xrightarrow{e} s'$.

A *run* is a sequence

$$r = s_0 \xrightarrow{\delta_0, f_0} s_0' \xrightarrow{e_0} s_1 \xrightarrow{\delta_1, f_1} s_1' \xrightarrow{e_1} s_2 \cdots s_n \cdots \quad (1)$$

of alternating timed and discrete transitions, such that either the sequence is infinite, or it ends with a timed transition of the type $s_n \xrightarrow{\infty, f}$. If the run r is finite, we define $len(r) = n$ to be the length of the run, otherwise we set $len(r) = \infty$. The above run is *non-Zeno* if for all $\delta \geq 0$ there exists $i \geq 0$ such that $\sum_{j=0}^{i} \delta_j > \delta$. We denote by $States(r)$ the set of all states visited by r. Formally, $States(r)$ is the set of all states $\langle loc(s_i), f_i(\delta) \rangle$, for all $0 \leq i \leq len(r)$ and all $0 \leq \delta \leq \delta_i$. Notice that the states from which discrete transitions start (states s_i' in (1)) appear in $States(r)$. Moreover, if r contains a sequence of one or more zero-time timed transitions, all intervening states appear in $States(r)$.

Zenoness and well-formedness. A well-known problem of real-time and hybrid systems is that definitions like the above admit runs that take infinitely many discrete transitions in a finite amount of time (i.e., *Zeno* runs), even if such behaviors are physically meaningless. In this paper, we assume that the hybrid automaton under consideration generates no such runs. This is easily achieved by using an extra variable, representing a clock, to ensure that the delay between any two transitions is bounded from below by a constant. We leave it to future work to combine our results with the more sophisticated approaches to Zenoness known in the literature [4, 9].

Moreover, we assume that the hybrid automaton under consideration is *non-blocking*, i.e., before all system trajectories leave the invariant, there must be an uncontrollable transition enabled. Formally, for all states s in the invariant, if all activities $f \in Adm(s)$ eventually leave the invariant, there exists one such activity f and a time $\delta \in span(f, loc(s))$ such that $s' = \langle loc(s), f(\delta) \rangle$ is in the invariant and there is an uncontrollable transition $e \in Edg_u$ that is enabled in s'. If a hybrid automaton is non-Zeno and non-blocking, we say that it is *well-formed*. In the following, all hybrid automata are assumed to be well-formed.

EXAMPLE 1. *Consider the LHAs in Figure 1, in which locations contain the invariant (first line) and the flow constraint (second line). Solid (resp., dashed) edges represent controllable (resp., uncontrollable) transitions, and guards are* true. *The fragment in Figure 1(a) is well-formed, because the system may choose derivative $\dot{x} = 0$ and remain indefinitely in location l. The fragment in Figure 1(b) is also well-formed, because the system cannot remain in l forever, but an uncontrollable transition leading outside is always enabled. Finally, the fragment in Figure 1(c) is not well-formed, because the system cannot remain in l forever, and no uncontrollable transition is enabled.*

Strategies. We consider *non-deterministic* and *memoryless* (or *positional*) strategies. Let $\perp$ denotes the null action.

A *strategy* is a function $\sigma : S \to 2^{Edg_c \cup \{\perp\}} \setminus \emptyset$ such that:

(a) for all $s \in S$, if $e \in \sigma(s) \cap Edg_c$, then there exists $s' \in S$ such that $s \xrightarrow{e} s'$;

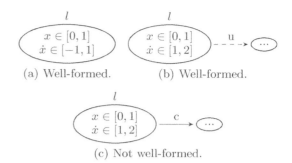

(a) Well-formed.   (b) Well-formed.

(c) Not well-formed.

Figure 1: Three LHA fragments.

(b) if $\perp \in \sigma(s)$, for all $f \in Adm(s)$ there exists $\delta > 0$ such that for all $0 < \delta' < \delta$ it holds $\delta' \notin span(f, loc(s))$ or $\perp \in \sigma(\langle loc(s), f(\delta') \rangle)$.

Condition (a) ensures that a strategy can only choose transitions allowed by the automaton. Condition (b) requires that if a strategy chooses the null action, then it must continue to do so for a positive amount of time along each activity that remains in the invariant. This ensures that the null action is enabled in right-open regions, so that there is an earliest instant in which a controllable transition becomes mandatory.

Notice that a strategy can always choose the null action. The well-formedness condition ensures that the system can always evolve in some way, be it a timed step or an uncontrollable transition. In particular, even if we are on the boundary of the invariant we allow the controller to choose the null action, because, in our interpretation, it is not the responsibility of the controller to ensure that the invariant is not violated.

We say that a run like (1) is *consistent* with a strategy σ if for all $0 \leq i < len(r)$ the following conditions hold:

• for all $\delta \geq 0$ such that $\sum_{j=0}^{i-1} \delta_j \leq \delta < \sum_{j=0}^{i} \delta_j$, we have $\perp \in \sigma(\langle loc(s_i), f_i(\delta - \sum_{j=0}^{i-1} \delta_j) \rangle)$;
• if $e_i \in Edg_c$ then $e_i \in \sigma(s_i')$.

We denote by $Runs(s, \sigma)$ the set of runs starting from the state s and consistent with the strategy σ.

Reachability control problem. Given a hybrid automaton and a set of states $T \subseteq InvS$, the *reachability control problem* asks whether there exists a strategy σ such that, for all initial states $s \in InitS$ and all runs $r \in Runs(s, \sigma)$ it holds $States(r) \cap T \neq \emptyset$. We call the above σ a *winning strategy*.

3. THE GLOBAL SEMI-ALGORITHM

The semi-algorithm for solving the reachability control problem is based on the so-called *controllable predecessor* operator $CPre^R(\cdot)$. For a set of states A, the operator $CPre^R(A)$ returns the set of states from which the controller can ensure that the system reaches A within the next joint step. Based on the activity chosen by the environment, this may happen for three reasons: (1) at some point during the activity a controllable transition is enabled that leads into A, and all uncontrollable transitions enabled in the meanwhile also lead to A; (2) the activity naturally enters A, and all uncontrollable transitions enabled in the meanwhile also lead to A; (3) the activity eventually leaves the invariant, and all uncontrollable transitions that are ever enabled along the activity lead to A. Notice that in case (3) the system is forced to reach A because, by well-formedness, an uncontrollable transition must be enabled before the activity leaves the invariant.

The three cases can be formalized as the following predicates Φ_i, on an activity f, location l, and target set A. For a set of states A and $x \in \{u, c\}$, let $Pre_x(A)$ be the set of states in $InvS$ where some discrete transition belonging to Edg_x is enabled, which leads to A.

$$\Phi_1(f, l, A) = \exists \delta \in span(f, l) : \langle l, f(\delta) \rangle \in Pre_c(A) \text{ and}$$
$$\forall 0 \leq \delta' \leq \delta : \langle l, f(\delta') \rangle \notin Pre_u(\overline{A})$$
$$\Phi_2(f, l, A) = \exists \delta \in span(f, l) : \langle l, f(\delta) \rangle \in A \text{ and}$$
$$\forall 0 \leq \delta' < \delta : \langle l, f(\delta') \rangle \notin Pre_u(\overline{A})$$
$$\Phi_3(f, l, A) = \infty \notin span(f, l) \text{ and}$$
$$\forall \delta \in span(f, l) : \langle l, f(\delta) \rangle \notin Pre_u(\overline{A})$$

We then have:

$$CPre^R(A) = \Big\{ \langle l, u \rangle \in InvS \, \Big| \, \forall f \in Adm(\langle l, u \rangle) :$$
$$\Phi_1(f, l, A) \text{ or } \Phi_2(f, l, A) \text{ or } \Phi_3(f, l, A) \Big\}.$$

In discrete games, the CPre operator used for solving reachability games is the same as the one used for the safety goal [15]. In both cases, when the operator is applied to a set of states T, it returns the set of states from which Player 1 can force the game into T in one step. In hybrid games, the situation is different: a joint step represents a possibly complex behavior, extending over a (possibly) non-zero time interval. While the CPre for reachability only requires T to be visited once during such interval, CPre for safety requires that the entire behavior constantly remains in T. Hence, in Section 3.1 we present a novel algorithm for computing $CPre^R$.

The following theorem states the general procedure for solving the reachability control problem. Due to space constraints, we only provide a proof sketch for one direction of the theorem.

THEOREM 1. *The answer to the reachability control problem for target set $T \subseteq InvS$ is positive if and only if*

$$InitS \subseteq \mu W . T \cup CPre^R(W), \qquad (2)$$

where μW denotes the least fixpoint.

PROOF SKETCH. [*if*] Assume equation 2 holds, we shall build a winning strategy in two steps. Let

- $W_0 = T$,

- $W_\alpha = T \cup CPre^R(W_{\alpha-1})$, for a successor ordinal α, and

- $W_\alpha = \bigcup_{\beta < \alpha} W_\beta$ for a limit ordinal α.

Moreover, let $W^* = \mu W . T \cup CPre^R(W)$. By Knaster-Tarski theorem and the well-ordering of ordinals, if $s \in W^*$ then there exists the smallest ordinal α such that $s \in W_\alpha$. If α is a limit ordinal, by definition of W_α there exists $\beta < \alpha$ such

that $s \in W_\beta$, which contradicts minimality of α. Hence α is either 0 or a successor ordinal.

Let σ be a strategy defined as follows, for all states s:

- $\perp \in \sigma(s)$ and

- for all $s \in W^* \setminus T$, let $\alpha = \beta + 1$ be the smallest ordinal such that $s \in W_\alpha$; for all $e \in Edg_c$, we have $e \in \sigma(s)$ if and only if $s \xrightarrow{e} s'$ and $s' \in W_\beta$.

While σ is clearly a strategy, it is not necessarily a winning strategy, as it may admit consistent runs which delay a controllable action either beyond the winning set W^* or beyond its availability. We can, however, recover a winning strategy by removing the null action $\perp$ from certain states. Let σ' be any strategy which coincides with σ on all the states, except for the states $s \in W^*$ with $\sigma(s) \cap Edg_c \neq \emptyset$, where it satisfies $\sigma'(s) \cap Edg_c = \sigma(s) \cap Edg_c$ and the following two conditions (a) and (b). For all $f \in Adm(s)$, let $D_{f,s} = \{\delta > 0 \mid \forall 0 \leq \delta' \leq \delta : \langle loc(s), f(\delta') \rangle \in W_\alpha$ and $\sigma(\langle loc(s), f(\delta') \rangle) \cap Edg_c \neq \emptyset\}$:

(a) If there is $f \in Adm(s)$ such that $D_{f,s} = \emptyset$ then $\perp \notin \sigma'(s)$;

(b) For all $f \in Adm(s)$, if $D_{f,s} \neq \emptyset$ then there exists $\delta \in D_{f,s}$ such that $\perp \notin \sigma'(\langle loc(s), f(\delta) \rangle)$ and $\perp \in \sigma'(\langle loc(s), f(\delta') \rangle)$ for all $0 \leq \delta' < \delta$.

Intuitively, the new strategy σ' ensures that following any activity from a state $s \in W^*$ in which some controllable action is enabled, such an action will always be taken before none of them is available and before leaving W^*. It can be proved that σ' is a winning strategy.

3.1 Computing the Predecessor Operator

In order to compute the predecessor operator, we introduce the *Must Reach While Avoiding* operator, denoted by RWA^M. Given a location l and two sets of variable valuations U and V, $RWA_l^M(U, V)$ contains the set of valuations from which all continuous trajectories of the system reach U while avoiding V [3]. Formally, we have:

$$RWA_l^M(U, V) = \Big\{ u \in Val(X) \, \Big| \, \forall f \in Adm(\langle l, u \rangle) \exists \delta \geq 0 :$$
$$f(\delta) \in U \text{ and } \forall 0 \leq \delta' \leq \delta : f(\delta') \notin V \Big\}. \quad (3)$$

By rephrasing the definition of $CPre^R$, we observe that $s = \langle l, u \rangle \in CPre^R(A)$ iff all activities f starting from u reach a set of "good" points while avoiding a set of "bad" points. Good points include $C_l = Pre_c(A)|_l$ according to $\Phi_1(f, l, A)$, $A|_l$ according to $\Phi_2(f, l, A)$, and $\overline{Inv(l)}$ according to $\Phi_3(f, l, A)$. As to the bad points, all predicates Φ_i require that the activity avoids $B_l = Pre_u(\overline{A})|_l$, with subtle distinctions at the instant when a good point is reached. According to Φ_1, B_l must be avoided also in that instant (when C_l is reached), while Φ_2 permits the activity f to reach B_l at the same time as $A|_l$. Since satisfaction of one Φ_i is enough for an activity to comply with the requirements of $CPre^R$, the least restrictive avoidance condition prevails, namely, $B_l \setminus A|_l$. The following lemma formalizes the above argument. We say that a set of states $A \subseteq S$ is *polyhedral* if for all $l \in Loc$, the projection $A|_l$ is a polyhedron.

---

[3] In ATL notation [2], we have $RWA^M(U, V) \equiv \langle\!\langle ctr \rangle\!\rangle \overline{V} \, \mathcal{U} \, (U \wedge \overline{V})$, where ctr is the player representing the controller.

LEMMA 1. *For all polyhedral sets of states $A \subseteq InvS$, we have*

$$CPre^{R}(A) = InvS \cap$$

$$\bigcup_{l \in Loc} \{l\} \times RWA_l^{M}\left(A|_l \cup C_l \cup \overline{Inv(l)}, B_l \setminus A|_l\right),$$

where $B_l = Pre_u(\overline{A})|_l$ and $C_l = Pre_c(A)|_l$.

PROOF. [$\subseteq$] Let $s = \langle l, u \rangle \in CPre^{R}(A)$ and let $f \in Adm(s)$. If $\Phi_1(f, l, A)$ holds, there is $\delta \in span(f, l)$ such that $f(\delta) \in C_l$ and for all $0 \le \delta' \le \delta$ it holds $f(\delta') \notin B_l$ and hence $f(\delta') \notin B_l \setminus A|_l$, satisfying the requirements of (3). If $\Phi_2(f, l, A)$ holds, there is $\delta \in span(f, l)$ such that $f(\delta) \in A|_l$ and for all $0 \le \delta' < \delta$ it holds $f(\delta') \notin B_l$. Since $f(\delta) \notin B_l \setminus A|_l$, the requirements of (3) are satisfied again. Finally, if $\Phi_3(f, l, A)$ holds, we have $\infty \notin span(f, l)$ and $\langle l, f(\delta) \rangle \notin B_l$ for all $\delta \in span(f, l)$. Pick a time δ^* when f has left $Inv(l)$ and it has never re-entered it. Formally, we have $\delta^* \notin span(f, l)$, $f(\delta^*) \notin Inv(l)$, and $f(\delta) \in span(f, l) \cup \overline{Inv(l)}$ for all $\delta \le \delta^*$. We obtain $f(\delta^*) \in \overline{Inv(l)}$ and $f(\delta) \notin B_l$ for all $0 \le \delta \le \delta^*$, satisfying (3) once again.

[$\supseteq$] Let $l \in Loc$ and $u \in RWA_l^{M}(A|_l \cup C_l \cup \overline{Inv(l)}, B_l \setminus A|_l)$. For all $f \in Adm(\langle l, u \rangle)$, let D_f be the set of all $\delta \ge 0$ such that $f(\delta) \in A|_l \cup C_l \cup \overline{Inv(l)}$ and for all $0 \le \delta' \le \delta$ it holds $f(\delta') \notin B_l \setminus A|_l$. By definition of RWA_l^{M}, we have $D_f \ne \emptyset$. Let $\delta^* = \inf D_f$ and assume for simplicity that $\delta^* \in D_f$, as the other case can be treated similarly.

For all $0 \le \delta' < \delta^*$ we have both $f(\delta') \in (\overline{A|_l} \cap \overline{C_l} \cap Inv(l))$ since $\delta' \notin D_f$, and $f(\delta') \in (\overline{B_l} \cup A|_l)$ since $\delta' < \delta^*$ and $\delta^* \in D_f$. Moreover, $(\overline{A|_l} \cap \overline{C_l} \cap Inv(l)) \cap (\overline{B_l} \cup A|_l) = \overline{B_l} \cap \overline{A|_l} \cap \overline{C_l} \cap Inv(l)$, and we can conclude that $f(\delta') \in \overline{B_l} \cap \overline{A|_l} \cap \overline{C_l} \cap Inv(l)$. If $f(\delta^*) \in A|_l$, we have $\delta^* \in span(f, l)$ and $\Phi_2(f, l, A)$. If $f(\delta^*) \in C_l$, we have $\delta^* \in span(f, l)$ again and $\Phi_1(f, l, A)$. Finally, if $f(\delta^*) \in \overline{Inv(l)}$ we have $\Phi_3(f, l, A)$. Therefore, it holds $\langle l, u \rangle \in CPre^{R}(A)$. ∎

4. THE LOCAL ALGORITHM

The previous section reduces the solution of the reachability control problem to the computation of the operator RWA^{M}. Let us start by examining the basic properties of RWA^{M}.

EXAMPLE 2. *As witnessed by Figure 2(a), the first argument of RWA^{M} does not distribute over union, in other words $RWA_l^{M}(U_1 \cup U_2, V) \ne RWA_l^{M}(U_1, V) \cup RWA_l^{M}(U_2, V)$. In particular, in Figure 2(a) we have $RWA_l^{M}(U_1, V) = U_1 \cup R_1$, $RWA_l^{M}(U_2, V) = U_2 \cup R_2$, and $RWA_l^{M}(U_1 \cup U_2, V) = U_1 \cup U_2 \cup R_1 \cup R_2 \cup R_3$. Hence, computing $RWA_l^{M}(U, V)$ for convex U (a relatively simple task) does not extend to general polyhedra.*

Additionally, it is not possible to restrict the analysis from arbitrary activities (i.e., any differentiable function which stays in the invariant and whose slope belongs to $Flow(l)$) to straight-line activities. In Figure 2(b), the dotted area contains the set of points that must reach $U_1 \cup U_2$ following straight-line activities. On the other hand, $RWA_l^{M}(U_1 \cup U_2, \emptyset) = U_1 \cup U_2$, because all other points (including those in the dotted area) can avoid $U_1 \cup U_2$ by passing through the gap between U_1 and U_2.

Here, we show how to compute RWA^{M} based on the operator which is used to solve *safety* control problems: the

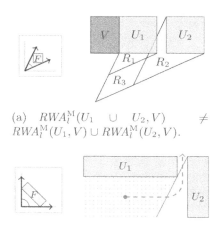

(a) $RWA_l^{M}(U_1 \cup U_2, V) \ne RWA_l^{M}(U_1, V) \cup RWA_l^{M}(U_2, V)$.

(b) Straight-line activities are not sufficient to avoid $U_1 \cup U_2$.

Figure 2: Basic properties of RWA^{M}. The boxes on the left represent the convex polyhedron $F = Flow(l)$ in the $(\dot{x}, \dot{y})$ plane. Thick arrows represent the *extremal directions* of flow.

May Reach While Avoiding operator $RWA_l^{m}(U, V)$, returning the set of states from which *there exists* a trajectory that reaches U while avoiding V. Formally,

$$RWA_l^{m}(U, V) = \Big\{ u \in Val(X) \ \Big|\ \exists f \in Adm(\langle l, u \rangle), \delta \ge 0 :$$

$$f(\delta) \in U \text{ and } \forall 0 \le \delta' < \delta : f(\delta') \in \overline{V} \cup U \Big\}.$$

In safety control problems, RWA^{m} is used to compute the states from which the environment may reach an unsafe state (in U) while avoiding the states from which the controller can take a transition to a safe state (in V). Notice that RWA^{m} is a classical operator, known under different names such as *Reach* [19], *Unavoid_Pre* [4], and *flow_avoid* [20]. We recently gave the first sound and complete algorithm for computing it on LHAs in [6, 5].

In this section, we consider a fixed location $l \in Loc$. exampleFor a polyhedron G and $p \in G$, we say that p is *l-bounded in G* (resp., *l-thin in G*) if all admissible activities starting from p eventually (resp., immediately) exit from G. Formally, p is *l-bounded* if for all $f \in Adm(\langle l, p \rangle)$ there exists $\delta \ge 0$ such that $f(\delta) \notin G$; p is *l-thin* if for all $f \in Adm(\langle l, p \rangle)$ and all $\delta > 0$, it holds $f(\delta) \notin G$. We denote by $bounded_l(G)$ the set of points of G that are *l-bounded* in it, and we say that G is *l-bounded* (resp., *l-thin*) if all points $p \in G$ are *l-bounded* (resp., *l-thin*) in G.

EXAMPLE 3. *Consider the L-shaped polyhedron G depicted in Figure 3, where the only flow direction is upwards. Point p_1 is not l-bounded in G, because G extends indefinitely upwards from p_1. Point p_2 is l-thin (and hence l-bounded) because it sits on the upper boundary of G, and finally p_3 is l-bounded (but not l-thin) in G, as the activity that starts from p_3 eventually (but not immediately) exits from G. The gray region of G is $bounded_l(G)$.*

The following result connects RWA^{M} to RWA^{m}, by exploiting the following idea. All points in $U \setminus V$ belong to $RWA_l^{M}(U, V)$ by definition. Accordingly, let us set $Under = U \setminus V$, for *under-approximation.*

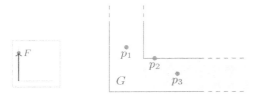

Figure 3: A non-convex polyhedron containing l-thin, l-bounded and non-l-bounded points.

Now, the content of $RWA_l^{\mathrm{M}}(U,V)$ can be partitioned into two regions: the first region is $Under$; the second region must be l-bounded, because each point in the second region must eventually reach $Under$. If we can find a polyhedron $Over$ that over-approximates $RWA_l^{\mathrm{M}}(U,V)$ and such that $Over \setminus Under$ is l-bounded, we can use RWA^{m} to refine it. Precisely, we can use RWA^{m} to identify and remove the points of $Over$ that may leave $Over$ without hitting U first.

If $Over \setminus Under$ was not l-bounded, the above technique would not work, because RWA^{m} cannot identify (and remove) the points that may remain forever in $Over$ without ever reaching $Under$.

THEOREM 2. *For all polyhedra U and V, let $Under = U \setminus V$ and let $Over$ be a polyhedron such that: (i) $RWA_l^{\mathrm{M}}(U,V) \subseteq Over \subseteq \overline{V}$ and (ii) $Over \setminus Under$ is l-bounded. Then,*

$$RWA_l^{\mathrm{M}}(U,V) = Over \setminus RWA_l^{\mathrm{m}}(\overline{Over}, U). \quad (4)$$

PROOF. $[\subseteq]$ Let $u \in RWA_l^{\mathrm{M}}(U,V)$. By assumption *(i)*, it holds $u \in Over$. We prove that $u \notin RWA_l^{\mathrm{m}}(\overline{Over}, U)$. Assume the contrary; according to the definition of RWA_l^{m}, there exist an activity $f \in Adm(\langle l, u \rangle)$ and a delay $\delta \geq 0$ such that $f(\delta) \in \overline{Over}$ and $f(\delta') \in U \cup \overline{Over}$ for all $0 \leq \delta' < \delta$. Since $\overline{Over} \subseteq \overline{RWA_l^{\mathrm{M}}(U,V)}$, the activity f leads from u to a point in $\overline{RWA_l^{\mathrm{M}}(U,V)}$, without passing through $Under$.

Let f' be an activity witnessing the fact that $f(\delta) \notin RWA_l^{\mathrm{M}}(U,V)$. If U is never reached by f before time δ, the activity obtained by starting with f and then switching to f' from time δ is a witness for $u \notin RWA_l^{\mathrm{M}}(U,V)$ (contradiction). If instead f reaches U at time $\delta' < \delta$, it also holds $f(\delta') \in V$. Then, let $D = \{\delta' \mid f(\delta') \in V\} \neq \emptyset$ and let $\delta^* = \inf D$. For all $\delta' < \delta^*$, it holds $f(\delta') \in \overline{U}$. If $\delta^* \in D$ then $f(\delta^*) \in V$, and f is a witness to the fact that $u \notin RWA_l^{\mathrm{M}}(U,V)$ (contradiction).

Finally, if $\delta^* \notin D$, let $\bar{\delta}$ be any time when f visits U. This time must be strictly greater than δ^*. By definition of δ^*, there exists another time between δ^* and $\bar{\delta}$ where f visits V, proving once again that $u \notin RWA_l^{\mathrm{M}}(U,V)$ (contradiction). We conclude that $u \notin RWA_l^{\mathrm{m}}(\overline{Over}, U)$, and the thesis.

$[\supseteq]$ Let $u \notin RWA_l^{\mathrm{M}}(U,V)$. It is immediate that $u \notin Under$. We prove that $u \notin Over \setminus RWA_l^{\mathrm{m}}(\overline{Over}, U)$. If $u \notin Over$, we are done. Hence, assume that $u \in Over$. Since $u \notin RWA_l^{\mathrm{M}}(U,V)$, there is an activity $f \in Adm(\langle l, u \rangle)$ such that for all $\delta \geq 0$ either *(a)* $f(\delta) \notin U$, or *(b)* there exists $\delta' \leq \delta$ such that $f(\delta') \in V$. We distinguish two cases:

- First, assume that the activity f never reaches U (and hence, $Under$). By assumption *(ii)*, there exists $\delta' \geq 0$ such that $f(\delta') \notin Over \setminus Under$. Since $f(\delta') \notin Under$, we conclude $f(\delta') \notin Over$. As a consequence, it holds $u \in RWA_l^{\mathrm{m}}(\overline{Over}, U)$, and we are done.

- Otherwise, let $D_U = \{\delta \geq 0 \mid f(\delta) \in U\} \neq \emptyset$ and $\delta_U = \inf D_U$. There can be two cases: first assume $\delta_U \in D_U$; by *(b)* there exists $\delta' \leq \delta_U$ with $f(\delta') \in V$. This implies that f reaches V (and hence $\overline{Over}$) at time δ' while remaining in $\overline{U}$ up until δ' (included). As a consequence, $u \in RWA_l^{\mathrm{m}}(\overline{Over}, U)$ and we are done.

  Next, assume $\delta_U \notin D_U$. Let $D_V = \{\delta \mid f(\delta) \in V\}$. We have $D_V \neq \emptyset$ due to $D_U \neq \emptyset$ and property *(b)* above. Let $\delta_V = \inf D_V$. If $\delta_V < \delta_U$, there exists a time between δ_V and δ_U when f reaches V (and hence $\overline{Over}$). Since f remains in $\overline{U}$ until δ_U, we can conclude that $u \in RWA_l^{\mathrm{m}}(\overline{Over}, U)$.

  Otherwise, $\delta_V \geq \delta_U$. For all δ' such that $f(\delta') \in U$, $\delta_V \leq \delta'$ by *(b)* and the fact that $\delta_V = \inf D_V$. As a consequence, since all possible intermediate points between δ_U and δ_V cannot belong to U, and $\delta_U = \inf D_U$, no such point exists, i.e., $\delta_V = \delta_U$.

  Now, if $\delta_V \in D_V$, then it immediately follows that $u \in RWA_l^{\mathrm{m}}(\overline{Over}, U)$. Otherwise, there are elements of D_V arbitrarily close to δ_V. Since V is a polyhedron and f is differentiable, there exists $\delta' > \delta_V$ such that $f(\delta) \in V \subseteq \overline{Over}$ for all $\delta_V < \delta \leq \delta'$. Therefore, at all times up to δ' (included), f remains in $\overline{U} \cup \overline{Over}$, once again we obtain that $u \in RWA_l^{\mathrm{m}}(\overline{Over}, U)$. ∎

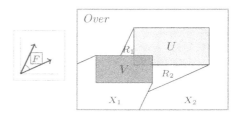

Figure 4: Relationship between RWA^{M} and RWA^{m}.

EXAMPLE 4. *An example of the application of Theorem 2 is depicted in Figure 4, where U and V are the gray boxes and $Over$ is the outer box, excluding V. The set $RWA_l^{\mathrm{m}}(\overline{Over}, U)$ can be divided in two areas: area X_1 contains the points that may reach V (which is a part of $\overline{Over}$) while avoiding U, and area X_2 contains the points that may exit $Over$ through its top and right sides. Following Equation 4, we remove X_1 and X_2 from $Over$, and we are left with the region $U \setminus V$ and the two regions R_1 and R_2, whose points are forced to enter U while avoiding V, as requested by $RWA_l^{\mathrm{M}}(U,V)$.*

4.1 Computing a Suitable Over-Approximation

Theorem 2 leaves us with one problem: We need to compute a polyhedron $Over$ satisfying the assumptions of the theorem. To this purpose, we introduce the following notions.

Given a polyhedron G and a convex polyhedron F, the *positive pre-flow* operator $G \swarrow_{>0} F$ is defined as follows:

$$G \swarrow_{>0} F = \{u - \delta c \mid u \in G, c \in F, \delta > 0\}.$$

Intuitively, $G \swarrow_{>0} F$ contains the points that may reach G via a straight trajectory of non-zero length whose slope is in F. We write $G \swarrow_{>0}$ as an abbreviation for $G \swarrow_{>0} Flow(l)$.

For a (not necessarily convex) polyhedron G and a convex polyhedron F, we say that G is *bounded w.r.t.* F if for all $p \in G$ and all $c \in F$ there exists a constant $\delta \geq 0$ such that $p + \delta c \notin G$. Intuitively, G is bounded w.r.t. F if all straight lines starting from G and whose slope belongs to F eventually exit from G. The relationship between this definition of boundedness and the notion of l-boundedness is explored in Section 4.2.

We define the operator RU (for *Remove Unbounded*) that, given a polyhedron G, removes some convex regions of G that are not l-bounded, in such a way that the resulting set is l-bounded, and every point that was l-bounded in G belongs to the resulting set. Let B be the subset of $[\![G]\!]$ containing the convex polyhedra that are bounded w.r.t. $cl(Flow(l))$. We set

$$\text{RU}(G) = \bigcup_{P \in B} P \cup \bigcup_{P \in [\![G]\!] \setminus B} (P \setminus P \swarrow_{>0}). \qquad (5)$$

The following result summarizes the main properties of the RU operator and it is proved in Section 4.2.

THEOREM 3. *For all polyhedra G, the following hold:* (i) $\text{RU}(G)$ *is l-bounded, and* (ii) $bounded_l(G) \subseteq \text{RU}(G)$.

Given two polyhedra U and V, define $Under = U \setminus V$ and

$$Over = Under \cup \text{RU}(\overline{U} \cap \overline{V}).$$

We prove that $Under$ and $Over$ satisfy the two assumptions of Theorem 2. Theorem 3 ensures that $Over \setminus Under$ is l-bounded. The following lemma proves the other assumption.

LEMMA 2. *It holds $RWA_l^M(U, V) \subseteq Over \subseteq \overline{V}$.*

PROOF. For the first inclusion, let $u \in RWA_l^M(U, V)$. If $u \in Under = U \setminus V$, we are done. Otherwise, $u \in \overline{U} \cup \overline{V}$. Moreover, by definition of RWA^M, $u \in \overline{V}$ (and hence $u \in \overline{U} \cap \overline{V}$) and for all activities $f \in Adm(\langle l, u \rangle)$ there exists $\delta \geq 0$ such that $f(\delta) \in U$. Hence, u is l-bounded in $\overline{U} \cap \overline{V}$. By property *(ii)* of Theorem 3, $u \in \text{RU}(\overline{U} \cap \overline{V}) \subseteq Over$.

For the second inclusion, let $u \in Over$. If $u \in Under = U \setminus V$, clearly $u \notin V$. Otherwise, $u \in \text{RU}(\overline{U} \cap \overline{V}) \subseteq \overline{U} \cap \overline{V} \subseteq \overline{V}$, and we are done. ∎

Section 4.3 shows how to effectively compute $\text{RU}(\cdot)$, and hence $Over$, using basic operations on polyhedra. Moreover, $RWA_l^m(\cdot, \cdot)$ is shown to be computable in [6, 5]. Therefore, we can compute $RWA_l^M(U, V)$ using equation (4). In turn, this allows us to compute $CPre^R(\cdot)$ using Lemma 1.

THEOREM 4. *For all polyhedral sets of states A, $CPre^R(A)$ is computable.*

Notice that the above result provides no guarantee of termination for the global fixpoint (2). In particular, it does not imply semi-decidability of the reachability control problem, as fixpoint (2) may not be reached within ω iterations of $CPre^R$.

4.2 On Bounded and Thin Polyhedra

The objective of this section is to prove the properties of the $\text{RU}(\cdot)$ operator pertaining l-boundedness, which are stated by Theorem 3. Since l-boundedness is hard to directly reason about, we relate it to *geometric* boundedness, i.e., boundedness w.r.t. straight-line activities.

Let us first recall the following lemma, which is an adaptation of Lemma 4.1 in [1], and states that any point reached by an admissible trajectory can be reached with a straight-line admissible trajectory as well.

LEMMA 3 ([1]). *For all points $p \in Inv(l)$, activities $f \in Adm(\langle l, p \rangle)$ and $\delta > 0$, there exists $c \in Flow(l)$ such that $f(\delta) = p + \delta c$.*

The following is a trivial observation.

PROPOSITION 1. *If F is a convex polyhedron containing the origin, then no polyhedron is bounded w.r.t. F.*

We say that a polyhedron G is *thin w.r.t.* F if for all $p \in G$, $c \in F$, and $\delta > 0$, it holds $p + \delta c \notin G$. Intuitively, G is bounded (resp., thin) w.r.t. F if all straight lines starting from G and whose slope belongs to F eventually (resp., immediately) exit from G. The relationships between the geometric concepts defined in this section and the notions of l-thin and l-bounded are summarized in Figure 5.

Obviously, being thin w.r.t. F implies being bounded w.r.t. F. Moreover, being l-thin implies being thin w.r.t. $Flow(l)$, since straight-line activities are a special case of general activities. The following lemma shows that the converse also holds.

LEMMA 4. *For all convex polyhedra P, if P is thin w.r.t. $Flow(l)$ then P is l-thin.*

PROOF. Assume that P is not l-thin. Then, there exists a point $p \in P$, an activity $f \in Adm(\langle l, p \rangle)$ and a time $\delta > 0$ such that $f(\delta) \in P$. By Lemma 3, there exists $c \in Flow(l)$ such that $f(\delta) = p + \delta c \in P$. Hence, P is not thin w.r.t. $Flow(l)$. ∎

We shall now show with the following lemma that all points of G that are removed by $\text{RU}(G)$ are not l-bounded in G (i.e., $\text{RU}(G)$ does not "remove too much").

LEMMA 5. *If a convex polyhedron P is not bounded w.r.t. $cl(Flow(l))$ then each point in $P \cap P \swarrow_{>0}$ is not l-bounded in P.*

Next, we show that the result of $\text{RU}(G)$ is l-bounded (i.e., $\text{RU}(G)$ does not "remove too little"). In order to obtain this result (stated as Lemma 8), we need a few preliminary lemmata.

First, we show that if the origin does not belong to the topological closure of the flow, then there is a flow direction u such that all possible flows advance in the direction u by at least $|u|$ for each time unit. We denote by $\mathbf{0}$ the origin, i.e., the point whose coordinates are 0.

LEMMA 6. *Assume $\mathbf{0} \notin cl(Flow(l))$. Then there exists $u \in cl(Flow(l))$ such that for all $v \in Flow(l)$ the scalar projection of v onto u is at least $|u|$ (i.e., $\frac{u \cdot v}{|u|} \geq |u|$, where $\cdot$ denotes the inner product).*

The following fact is obvious, since straight lines are a special case of activities.

PROPOSITION 2. *If a polyhedron is l-bounded, then it is bounded w.r.t. $Flow(l)$.*

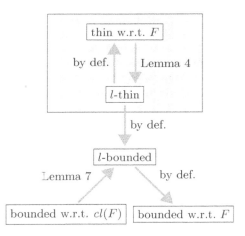

Figure 5: Relationships between properties of convex polyhedra. Arrows represent implications and $F = Flow(l)$.

Being bounded w.r.t. $Flow(l)$ is necessary but not sufficient for a polyhedron to be l-bounded, as shown by the following example.

EXAMPLE 5. *Consider the unbounded polyhedron P shown on the r.h.s. of Figure 6. The dashed contour of F (on the l.h.s. of the figure) indicates that F (i.e., $Flow(l)$) is topologically open, so that its extremal directions $(1,0)$ and $(0,1)$ are not proper (i.e., they do not belong to F). It turns out that P is bounded w.r.t. $Flow(l)$, because all straight lines whose slope belongs to F eventually exit from it, but it is not l-bounded. The figure shows an activity that remains forever in P. Its slope approaches asymptotically the extremal direction $(1,0)$.*

Lemma 7 presents a sufficient condition for being l-bounded.

Figure 6: On the right, a polyhedron which is bounded w.r.t. $Flow(l)$ but not l-bounded, and an activity that remains forever in it.

LEMMA 7. *If a polyhedron is bounded w.r.t. $cl(Flow(l))$ then it is l-bounded.*

PROOF. Let $F = cl(Flow(l))$. By Proposition 1, F does not contain the origin. By Lemma 6, there exists $u \in F$ such that for all $v \in Flow(l)$ it holds $u \cdot v \geq |u|^2$.

Let G be a polyhedron which is bounded w.r.t. F, and let $p \in G$ and $f \in Adm(\langle l, p \rangle)$. For all $\delta \geq 0$, it holds $\dot{f}(\delta) \in Flow(l)$. From the above argument, the vector projection of $\dot{f}(\delta)$ on the direction u has length at least $|u|$. Hence, for each time unit, the activity f advances in the direction u by at least $|u|$. Since G is bounded w.r.t. $\{u\}$, we obtain the thesis. ∎

The following lemma lifts l-boundedness from convex polyhedra to general polyhedra.

LEMMA 8. *Let G be a polyhedron such that each $P \in [\![G]\!]$ is l-bounded. Then, G is l-bounded.*

PROOF OF THEOREM 3. *(i)* RU(G) *is l-bounded.* For a convex polyhedron P, the set $P \setminus (P \diagup_{>0})$ is l-thin, as may be easily verified from the definitions. Hence, each convex polyhedron in $[\![\mathrm{RU}(G)]\!]$ is either bounded w.r.t. $cl(Flow(l))$ or l-thin. Since each l-thin polyhedron is l-bounded by definition, and by Lemma 7, we obtain that each convex polyhedron in $[\![\mathrm{RU}(G)]\!]$ is l-bounded. By Lemma 8, RU(G) is l-bounded.

(ii) $bounded_l(G) \subseteq \mathrm{RU}(G)$. Let $p \in bounded_l(G)$. Then there must be at least one convex polyhedron $P \in [\![G]\!]$ with $p \in P$. If P is bounded w.r.t. $cl(Flow(l))$ then, by equation (5), $p \in \mathrm{RU}(G)$. If, on the other hand, P is not bounded w.r.t. $cl(Flow(l))$, by Lemma 5 we have that $P \cap P \diagup_{>0}$ is not l-bounded in P and, *a fortiori*, not l-bounded in G. Therefore, $p \in P \setminus P \diagup_{>0}$ and, by equation (5), $p \in \mathrm{RU}(G)$. Hence the conclusion. ∎

4.3 Computing the RU Operator

As shown in the previous section, the operator RWA^{M} requires the computation of the operator RU (*Remove Unbounded*) defined by equation (5). In order to compute the operator RU, we must be able to *(i)* compute the positive-preflow $P \diagup_{>0} F$ of a convex polyhedron P w.r.t. another convex polyhedron F, and *(ii)* collect, for any polyhedron G, the convex polyhedra $P \in [\![G]\!]$ which are bounded w.r.t. the convex polyhedron F. In the remainder of the section we shall show how these two operations can be efficiently implemented employing a canonical representation of convex polyhedra.

Any convex polyhedron admits a finite representation, in terms of *generators*. The generator representation consists in three finite sets of *points*, *closure points*, and *rays*, that generate all points in the polyhedron by linear combination. More precisely, for each convex polyhedron $P \subseteq \mathbb{R}^n$ there exists a triple (V_P, C_P, R_P) such that V_P, C_P, and R_P are finite sets of vectors in $\mathbb{R}^n$, and $x \in P$ if and only if it can be written as

$$\sum_{v \in V_P} \alpha_v \cdot v + \sum_{c \in C_P} \beta_c \cdot c + \sum_{r \in R_P} \gamma_r \cdot r, \qquad (6)$$

where all coefficients α_v, β_c and γ_r are non-negative reals, $\sum_{v \in V_P} \alpha_v + \sum_{c \in C_P} \beta_c = 1$, and there exists $v \in V_P$ such that $\alpha_v > 0$. We call the triple (V_P, C_P, R_P) a *generator system* for P.

Intuitively, the elements of V_P are the proper vertices of the polyhedron P, the elements of C_P are vertices of the topological closure of P that do not belong to P, and each element of R_P represents a direction of unboundedness (or infinity) of P.

4.3.1 Computing the Pre-Flow operator

Notice first that the positive pre-flow of P w.r.t. F is equivalent to the *positive post-flow* of P w.r.t. $-F$:

$$P \diagup_{>0} F = P \diagup_{>0} -F = \{x + \delta \cdot y \mid x \in P, y \in -F, \delta > 0\}.$$

The following recent result shows how to efficiently compute the positive post-flow $P \diagup_{>0} F$ of a convex polyedron P w.r.t. another convex polyhedron F, using the generator representation. For two sets of points A and B, the *Minkowski sum* $A \oplus B$ is $\{a + b \mid a \in A, b \in B\}$.

THEOREM 5. *[7] Given two convex polyhedra P and F, let (V_P, C_P, R_P) (resp., (V_F, C_F, R_F)) be a generator system for P (resp., F). The triple $(V_P \oplus V_F, C_P \cup V_P, R_P \cup V_F \cup C_F \cup R_F)$ is a generator system for $P \nearrow_0 F$.*

4.3.2 Testing for boundedness w.r.t. the flow

For a convex polyhedron P, let $O_P = (\{\mathbf{0}\}, \emptyset, R_P)$ denote its *characteristic cone*, i.e., the closed polyhedron generated by the origin $\mathbf{0}$ and all the rays of P. The following theorem shows how we can effectively and efficiently test whether P is bounded w.r.t. F.

THEOREM 6. *For all convex polyhedra P and F, P is bounded w.r.t. F iff $O_P \cap F = \emptyset$.*

PROOF. $[\Rightarrow]$ By hypothesis, for all $p \in P$ and for all $c \in F$ there exists $\delta \geq 0$ such that $p + \delta \cdot c \notin P$. By Proposition 1 we have that $\mathbf{0} \notin F$. Let $c \in F$, we show that $c \notin O_P$. Assume by contradiction that $c \in O_P$, we can write $c = 1 \cdot \mathbf{0} + \sum_{r \in R_p} \beta_r r = \sum_{r \in R_p} \beta_r r$. Now, let $x \in V_p$ be a vertex of P, we show that for all $\gamma \geq 0$ the point $x' = x + \gamma c$ belongs to P. Indeed, we have

$$x' = x + \gamma c = 1 \cdot x + \gamma \sum_{r \in R_p} \beta_r r = 1 \cdot x + \sum_{r \in R_p} \gamma \beta_r r.$$

Therefore, $x' \in P$, i.e. P is not bounded w.r.t. F, contradicting the hypothesis.

$[\Leftarrow]$ Assume by contradiction that $c \in F \cap O_P$. By the decomposition theorem for convex polyhedra [18], since O_P is the characteristic cone of P, there exists a non-empty convex polyhedron P' such that $P = P' \oplus O_P$. Moreover, since $c \in O_P$, also $\delta c \in O_P$ for all $\delta \geq 0$. We can then conclude that for all $p' \in P'$, it holds $p' + \delta c \in P$ for all $\delta \geq 0$. Therefore, P is not bounded w.r.t. $\{c\}$ and *a fortiori* w.r.t. F. ∎

5. EXPERIMENTS WITH PHAVER+

We implemented the algorithms described in the previous sections on top of the open-source tool PHAVer[4] [11]. The following experiments were performed on an Intel Xeon (2.80GHz) PC.

The maze example. A vehicle navigates in an environment whose shape is depicted in Figure 8(a), by taking 90-degree left or right turns: the possible directions are thus North (N), South (S), West (W) and East (E). One time unit (say, second) must pass between two changes of direction, while the vehicle speed is 2 unit of length per second. The corridors of the maze are 1 unit wide, so that the vehicle can never u-turn without hitting a wall. The goal consists in reaching a target area positioned along the topmost corridor. We tested our implementation on progressively more complex mazes, by increasing downwards the number of corridors (the angle between consecutive corridors is 90-degrees). For instance, Figure 8(a) shows the shape of the maze with 5 corridors.

The LHA modeling the system with two corridors has one location for each direction, where the derivative of the position variables (x and y) are set according to the corresponding direction. Figure 7 shows the LHA fragment related to

[4]A binary pre-release of our implementation, called PHAVer+, can be downloaded at http://people.na.infn.it/mfaella/phaverplus.

the N location. The variable t represents a clock ($\dot{t} = 1$), used to enforce a one-time-unit delay between turns. Each change of direction is modeled by a controllable transition (solid arrows in Figure 7) enabled when $t \geq 1$. The maze walls are modeled by uncontrollable transitions (dashed arrows in Figure 7). They are enabled when the variables x and y identify an invalid position (i.e., when the vehicle hits a wall) and lead to the special *Abort* location.

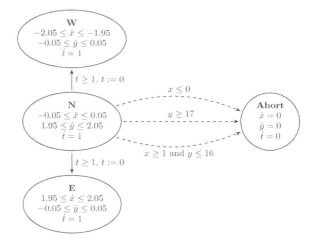

Figure 7: Fragment of the LHA modeling the maze with two corridors. The goal consists in reaching $\{2 \leq x \leq 2.5, y = 17\}$.

The maze example described above features a non-deterministic flow, allowing some uncertainty on the exact direction taken by the vehicle. A deterministic version has also been considered, where environmental disturbances are disallowed. This version can be obtained by, e.g., replacing the differential equations for x and y in location N with the differential constraints $\dot{x} = 0$ and $\dot{y} = 2$.

Figure 8(a) shows the cross-section of the solution for $t = 0$, in the case of a maze with two corridors and the vehicle initially going along the *North* direction: the gray areas A and B in the l.h.s. of the figure contain the points that can reach the target T in the case of deterministic flow. If the vehicle is located in A, it can reach the target by turning *East* and then *North* again. Notice that the area A covers only half the width of the vertical corridor. In fact, if the vehicle is located in the other half of the corridor, when turning *East* it will be too close to the target and it will not be able to take the second turn towards the target in time. The area A ends 2 units of length before the north wall, as beyond that the vehicle cannot avoid hitting the wall before being able to turn *East*. Finally, the points in the area B are trivially winning, as they can reach the target by proceeding *North*.

The solution in the corresponding non-deterministic case is shown in the r.h.s. of Figure 8(a). Notice that the winning region A' is contained in the region A and similarly B' is contained in B. Due to the uncertainty in the vehicle direction, both winning regions become gradually smaller as we move away from the target T.

We also experimented with a three-dimensional version of the maze. In addition to the vehicle directions of the 2D case, in the 3D version the vehicle can perform 90-degree turns upwards (U) and downwards (D). The resulting LHA includes two additional locations to move up or down, and one additional continuous variable z for the position of the vehicle along the third dimension, for a total of four variables. The flows associated to each location in the non-deterministic case are shown in Table 1.

N	W	E
$-0.05 \leq \dot{x} \leq 0.05$ $1.95 \leq \dot{y} \leq 2.05$ $\dot{z} = 0$	$-2.05 \leq \dot{x} \leq -1.95$ $-0.05 \leq \dot{y} \leq 0.05$ $\dot{z} = 0$	$1.95 \leq \dot{x} \leq 2.05$ $-0.05 \leq \dot{y} \leq 0.05$ $\dot{z} = 0$
S	**U**	**D**
$-0.05 \leq \dot{x} \leq 0.05$ $-2.05 \leq \dot{y} \leq -1.95$ $\dot{z} = 0$	$-0.05 \leq \dot{x} \leq 0.05$ $-0.05 \leq \dot{x} \leq 0.05$ $\dot{z} = 2$	$-0.05 \leq \dot{x} \leq 0.05$ $-0.05 \leq \dot{y} \leq 0.05$ $\dot{z} = -2$

Table 1: Flows associated to each location in the 3D version of maze. In all locations it holds $\dot{t} = 1$.

The table in Figure 8(b) shows the run time in seconds for the four different versions of the maze of increasing size, in terms of number of corridors. Although still limited in scope, the results show that the proposed approach is practical, at least for relatively small problems.

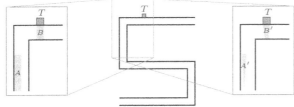

(a) Structure of the maze and controllable region for the deterministic (left) and non-deterministic (right) case.

# of corridors	2D	2D NDet	3D	3D NDet
2	0.4	1.1	1.3	4.2
3	0.8	9.6	2.1	25.4
4	1.3	15.5	3.6	47.7
5	3.4	149.5	8.9	337.0
6	5.1	216.2	13.1	394.9

(b) Performance in seconds.

Figure 8: The maze example.

6. REFERENCES

[1] R. Alur, T. Henzinger, and P.-H. Ho. Automatic symbolic verification of embedded systems. *IEEE Trans. Softw. Eng.*, 22:181–201, March 1996.

[2] R. Alur, T. Henzinger, and O. Kupferman. Alternating-time temporal logic. In *38th IEEE Symp. Found. of Comp. Sci.*, pages 100–109. IEEE Computer Society Press, 1997.

[3] E. Asarin, O. Bournez, T. Dang, O. Maler, and A. Pnueli. Effective synthesis of switching controllers for linear systems. *Proceedings of the IEEE*, 88(7):1011–1025, 2000.

[4] A. Balluchi, L. Benvenuti, T. Villa, H. Wong-Toi, and A. Sangiovanni-Vincentelli. Controller synthesis for hybrid systems with a lower bound on event separation. *Int. J. of Control*, 76(12):1171–1200, 2003.

[5] M. Benerecetti, M. Faella, and S. Minopoli. Automatic synthesis of switching controllers for linear hybrid automata. Technical report, Università di Napoli "Federico II", 2011. arXiv:1103.4584.

[6] M. Benerecetti, M. Faella, and S. Minopoli. Revisiting synthesis of switching controllers for linear hybrid systems. In *Proc. of the 50th IEEE Conf. on Decision and Control*. IEEE, 2011.

[7] M. Benerecetti, M. Faella, and S. Minopoli. Towards efficient exact synthesis for linear hybrid systems. In *GandALF 11: 2nd Int. Symp. on Games, Automata, Logics and Formal Verification*, volume 54 of *Elec. Proc. in Theor. Comp. Sci.*, 2011.

[8] P. Bouyer, T. Brihaye, and F. Chevalier. O-minimal hybrid reachability games. *Logical Methods in Computer Science*, 6, 2010.

[9] L. de Alfaro, M. Faella, T. Henzinger, R. Majumdar, and M. Stoelinga. The element of surprise in timed games. In *CONCUR 03: Concurrency Theory. 14th Int. Conf.*, volume 2761 of *Lect. Notes in Comp. Sci.*, pages 144–158. Springer, 2003.

[10] L. de Alfaro, T. Henzinger, and R. Majumdar. Symbolic algorithms for infinite-state games. In *CONCUR 01: Concurrency Theory. 12th Int. Conf.*, Lect. Notes in Comp. Sci. Springer, 2001.

[11] G. Frehse. PHAVer: Algorithmic verification of hybrid systems past hyTech. In *Proc. of Hybrid Systems: Computation and Control (HSCC), 8th International Workshop*, volume 3414 of *Lect. Notes in Comp. Sci.*, pages 258–273. Springer, 2005.

[12] T. Henzinger. The theory of hybrid automata. In *11th IEEE Symp. Logic in Comp. Sci.*, pages 278–292, 1996.

[13] T. Henzinger, B. Horowitz, and R. Majumdar. Rectangular hybrid games. In *CONCUR 99: Concurrency Theory. 10th Int. Conf.*, volume 1664 of *Lect. Notes in Comp. Sci.*, pages 320–335. Springer, 1999.

[14] T. Henzinger, P. Kopke, A. Puri, and P. Varaiya. What's decidable about hybrid automata? In *Proc. of the 27th annual ACM symposium on Theory of computing*, STOC '95, pages 373–382. ACM, 1995.

[15] O. Maler. Control from computer science. *Annual Reviews in Control*, 26(2):175–187, 2002.

[16] O. Maler, A. Pnueli, and J. Sifakis. On the synthesis of discrete controllers for timed systems. In *12th Annual Symp. on Theor. Asp. of Comp. Sci.*, volume 900 of *Lect. Notes in Comp. Sci.* Springer, 1995.

[17] P. Ramadge and W. Wonham. Supervisory control of a class of discrete-event processes. *SIAM Journal of Control and Optimization*, 25:206–230, 1987.

[18] A. Schrijver. *Theory of linear and integer programming*. John Wiley and Sons, 1986.

[19] C. Tomlin, J. Lygeros, and S. Shankar Sastry. A game theoretic approach to controller design for hybrid systems. *Proc. of the IEEE*, 88(7):949–970, 2000.

[20] H. Wong-Toi. The synthesis of controllers for linear hybrid automata. In *36th IEEE Conf. on Decision and Control*, pages 4607 – 4612, San Diego, CA, 1997. IEEE.

Optimal Scheduling for Constant-Rate Multi-Mode Systems

Rajeev Alur
University of Pennsylvania,
Philadelphia, USA
alur@cis.upenn.edu

Ashutosh Trivedi
University of Pennsylvania,
Philadelphia, USA
ashut@cis.upenn.edu

Dominik Wojtczak
University of Liverpool,
Liverpool, UK
d.wojtczak@liv.ac.uk

ABSTRACT

Constant-rate multi-mode systems are hybrid systems that can switch freely among a finite set of modes, and whose dynamics is specified by a finite number of real-valued variables with mode-dependent constant rates. The schedulability problem for such systems is to design a mode-switching policy that maintains the state within a specified safety set. The main result of the paper is that schedulability can be decided in polynomial time. We also generalize our result to optimal schedulability problems with average cost and reachability cost objectives. Polynomial-time scheduling algorithms make this class an appealing formal model for design of energy-optimal policies. The key to tractability is that the only constraints on when a scheduler can switch the mode are specified by global objectives. Adding local constraints by associating either invariants with modes, or guards with mode switches, lead to undecidability, and requiring the scheduler to make decisions only at multiples of a given sampling rate, leads to a PSPACE-complete schedulability problem.

Categories and Subject Descriptors

D.4.7 [**Organization and Design**]: Real-time systems and embedded systems; B.5.2 [**Design Aids**]: Optimization, Verification; I.2.8 [**Problem Solving, Control Methods, and Search**]: Scheduling

General Terms

Theory, Verification

Keywords

Switched Systems, Cyber-Physical Systems, Peak Minimization, Green Scheduling, Hybrid Automata

1. INTRODUCTION

Our study of optimal scheduling on constant-rate multi-mode systems is motivated largely by a series of work by

Nghiem et al. [18, 19] on energy peak demand reduction within a large organization by synchronizing switching decisions of various "heating, ventilation, and air conditioning" (HVAC) systems. The correlation between extreme weather and energy demand peaks is well documented [6, 21], and hence reducing the energy peak demand due to HVAC systems can potentially significantly reduce the total energy peak demand. In [18] Nghiem et al. considered a model of an organization where at any given time the HVAC system of a zone can be in either ON or OFF mode, and in each mode the temperature of the corresponding zone changes with a mode-dependent constant rate. In order to minimize peak energy-usage they studied the following schedulability problem: find a switching schedule of HVAC systems across different zones so as to maintain the temperature in each zone within a given interval, with the restriction that simultaneously at most a fix number of HVAC systems are switched ON. They showed that the schedulability problem can be reduced to testing an inequality involving the rates of temperature change. Our motivation is to explore that to what extent this result can be generalized, and to identify where this result fits into the existing literature on schedulability such as real-time scheduling theory [9] and hybrid automata based schedulability analysis [1, 2].

Real-time scheduling is a mature research area [9] with an excellent collection of well-studied algorithms for periodic scheduling, for instance the rate monotonic and the earliest deadline first algorithms. However, as noted by Nghiem et al. [19], generally these algorithms are restricted to tasks whose worst case execution times are fixed and known in advance, and hence they are not directly applicable to energy peak reduction problem as posed in [19, 18].

Another prominent approach [1, 2] to real-time schedulability analysis is via reduction to optimization problems on timed and hybrid automata. Timed automata [3] can model multi-mode systems with a finite set of continuous variables, called clocks, that grow with uniform rate. Clocks can be used to constrain mode-switches and to specify mode-dependent invariants. The decidability of a number of optimization problems [4, 7] on timed automata, and availability of efficient tool support, e.g. Kronos and UPPAAL [16, 20], make them an attractive choice for real-time scheduling. They are, however, not applicable in energy peak reduction problem as the temperature variables in our system grow with non-uniform rates. Hybrid automata generalize timed automata by allowing mode-dependent variable rates, however having two variables with different rates leads to undecidability [12] even for reachability problems. As we see later the key property of our systems that contributes to decidability (and even tractability) of schedulability problems is the absence of structure in the system, i.e. intuitively speaking as long as global safety set is not violated schedulers are allowed to switch among modes without any restriction.

Results. We define our model, a constant-rate multi-mode system (MMS), as a hybrid system with a finite set of modes where dynamics of each mode is specified by a finite set of continuous variables with mode-dependent constant-rates. Given a bounded convex set of safe states (variable valuations) and a starting state, the *safe schedulability problem* for an MMS is to find a non-Zeno schedule that visits only safe states. Another closely related problem is *safe reachability problem* that asks if there exists a schedule to steer the system from a given starting state to a given set of target states while only visiting states from a given safety set.

Our first result concerning safe schedulability problem is that for all the starting states in the interior of the safety set, a safe schedule exists iff there is an assignment of dwell times to modes that allows the system to return to the starting state. Due to constant-rate dynamics of the system this condition can easily be posed as a linear programming (LP) feasibility problem. The algorithm for finding safe schedule is more involved if the starting state is on the boundary of the safety set. A key contribution of the paper is a polynomial-time algorithm for computing a safe schedule for an arbitrary starting state when the safety set is given as a bounded convex polytope.

For safe reachability problem we show that if a state is reachable from a given starting state for some assignment of dwell times to modes, then it is safely reachable for any arbitrary bounded and convex safety set as long as both states lie in the interior of the safety set. We show via an example that this observation is not valid when one of the states lies on the boundary of the safety set. We present a polynomial-time algorithm to find safe schedules for reachability problems when both the starting and the target states lie in the interior of the safety set.

In Section 3 we extend these results to optimization problem with average-cost and reachability-cost objectives, and present polynomial-time algorithms to solve these problems. Furthermore, we prove that reachability-cost optimal and average-cost optimal strategies always exist, and have a particular simple periodic structure as long as both the target and the starting states are in the interior of the safety set. In Section 4 we show that requiring the scheduler to make decisions only at multiples of a given clock-rate makes the safe schedulability and safe reachability problems complete for PSPACE. We also show that the largest sampling rate for which safe schedulability problem yields a positive answer can be approximated in polynomial space.

Related Work. The work most closely related to our is of Nghiem et al. [18]. The energy peak reduction problem was first posed in [18] and safe schedulability checking for this problem was reduced to checking a simple formula on temperature rates. Authors also presented a lazy scheduling algorithm where scheduler is required to take decisions only at multiples of a given sampling rate. Although the practical motivation of our approach is the same as [18] we have different goals. The central focus of our research is to characterize the complexity of various schedulability problems in

this context. Safe schedulability problem for MMSs generalizes the energy peak reduction problem studied by Nghiem et al. in [18] since MMSs can model HVAC systems with more modes than simply ON and OFF. Moreover, MMSs allow safety set to be an arbitrary bounded convex set as opposed to hyperrectangular sets in [18]. Unlike [18] our algorithm can analyze the safe schedulability problem for starting states on the boundary of the safety set, assuming it is a polytope. Moreover, we also extend our results to safe reachability problem, and optimization problems for average-cost and reachability-cost objectives. We also establish PSPACE-completeness of finding the optimal sampling rate for safe schedulability of our more general systems.

In [19] Nghiem et al. generalized their work to multi-mode systems with linear dynamics. Using similar restrictions as [19] the ideas presented in this paper can be generalized to handle linear dynamics with some effort. Heymann et al. [13] study checking whether a given hybrid system, under several restrictions, is strongly Zeno and characterize LP feasibility test for this problem. Like Nghiem et al. [18], Heymann et al. only consider hyperrectangular safety states and starting states in the interior of the safety region.

The *practical stabilization* problem studied by Xu and Antsaklis [22] roughly corresponds in our model to an unconstrained reachability followed by a specifically constrained safe schedulability problem where the system cannot leave a ball of radius ε when starting from anywhere inside a ball with the same origin and radius δ. The existence and synthesis of a scheduler satisfying such constraints can be solved in polynomial time using our algorithms, while the running time of the method suggested in [22] is exponential in the number of modes. Moreover, the scheduler proposed in [22] is more complicated than ours and requires solving multiple linear programs as opposed to essentially one in our algorithm. Finally, the problem of computing a lower bound on the optimal sampling rate studied there was for systems with two variables, and the problem was left open for systems with more variables. We show that even approximation of the optimal sampling rate within a constant error is PSPACE-hard, which makes the existence of a tractable general procedure unlikely for that problem.

We also mention the work of Jha et al. [14, 15] where they synthesize guards for multi-mode systems so as to satisfy certain optimization criteria. Their model is more general than ours as it allows guards on mode-switches, and moreover variables are allowed to have more general dynamics, however authors did not present any complexity or decidability results. Henzinger and Kopke [11] studied the safe reachability problem for hybrid automata where the scheduler is allowed to make decisions at multiples of a given sampling rate, and showed the problem to be PSPACE-complete. Upper bound for the similar problem for MMSs directly follows from their work. Bouyer et al. [8] study the safe schedulability problem on *weighted timed automata* (timed automata extended with a cost variable having mode-dependent constant-rate) with global cost constraints. The safe schedulability problem is to find a schedule that keeps the value of the cost variable within a given interval. MMSs and weighted timed automata are incomparable models: the former disallow guards on mode-switches, while the latter disallow more than one variable with mode-dependent rate.

An extended version of this paper with complete proofs is available as a technical report [5].

2. SAFE SCHEDULABILITY

Before we formally introduce constant-rate multi-mode systems, we need to introduce the notation used throughout the rest of the paper. We write $\mathbb{N}$ for the set of natural numbers, $\mathbb{R}$ for the set of real numbers, and $\mathbb{Z}$ for the set of integers. Also, we write $\mathbb{R}_{\geq 0}$ for the set of non-negative reals and $\mathbb{N}_{>0}$ for the set of positive integers.

States of our system will be points in $\mathbb{R}^n$ which is equipped with the standard *Euclidean norm* $\|\cdot\|$. By $\overline{x}, \overline{y}$ we denote points in this state space, by $\vec{f}, \vec{v}$ vectors, while $\overline{x}(i)$ and $\vec{f}(i)$ will denote the i-th coordinate of point $\overline{x}$ and vector $\vec{f}$, respectively. We denote the distance between $\overline{x}$ and $\overline{y}$ by $\|\overline{x}, \overline{y}\| \stackrel{\text{def}}{=} \|\overline{x} - \overline{y}\|$. For two vectors $\vec{v}_1, \vec{v}_2 \in \mathbb{R}^n$, we write $\vec{v}_1 \circ \vec{v}_2$ to denote their dot product defined as $\sum_{i=1}^{n} \vec{v}_1(i)\vec{v}_2(i)$. We write $\vec{0}$ for any vector with all its coordinates equal to 0; its exact dimension will depend on the context.

We say that a point $\overline{x}$ is a convex combination of a set of points $X = \{\overline{x}_1, \overline{x}_2, \ldots, \overline{x}_k\}$ if there exist $\lambda_1, \lambda_2, \ldots, \lambda_k \in [0, 1]$ such that $\sum_{i=1}^{k} \lambda_i = 1$ and $\overline{x} = \sum_{i=1}^{k} \lambda_i \overline{x}_i$. We say that the set $S \subseteq \mathbb{R}^n$ is *convex* iff for all $\overline{x}, \overline{y} \in S$ and all $\lambda \in [0, 1]$ we have $\lambda \overline{x} + (1 - \lambda)\overline{y} \in S$ and moreover, S is a *convex polytope* if there exists $k \in \mathbb{N}$, a matrix A of size $k \times n$ and a vector $\vec{b} \in \mathbb{R}^k$ such that $\overline{x} \in S$ iff $A\overline{x} \leq \vec{b}$. Let $B_d(\overline{x}) = \{\overline{y} \in \mathbb{R}^n : \|\overline{x}, \overline{y}\| \leq d\}$ denote a *closed ball* of radius $d \in \mathbb{R}_{\geq 0}$ centered at $\overline{x}$. We say that a set $S \subseteq \mathbb{R}^n$ is *bounded* if there exists $d \in \mathbb{R}_{\geq 0}$ such that for all $\overline{x}, \overline{y} \in S$ we have $\|\overline{x}, \overline{y}\| \leq d$. The *interior* of a set S, $\text{int}(S)$, is the set of all points $\overline{x} \in S$ for which there exists $d > 0$ s.t. $B_d(\overline{x}) \subseteq S$.

2.1 Constant-Rate Multi-Mode Systems

A constant-rate multi-mode system consists of a finite number of modes and a finite number of real-valued variables whose dynamics is specified by mode-dependent constant rates. Formally,

DEFINITION 1. *A constant-rate multi-mode system (MMS) is a tuple* $\mathcal{H} = (M, n, R)$ *where* M *is a finite nonempty set of* modes, n *is the number of continuous variables in the system, and* $R : M \to \mathbb{R}^n$ *gives for each mode the* rate vector *whose i-th entry specifies the change in value of the i-th variable per time unit.*

For computation purposes, we assume that all real numbers are rational and represented in the standard way by writing down the numerator and denominator in binary.

A *schedule* of an MMS specifies a timed sequence of mode switches. Formally, a *schedule* is defined as a finite or infinite sequences of *timed actions*, where a timed action $(m, t) \in M \times \mathbb{R}_{\geq 0}$ is a tuple consisting of a mode and a time delay. We say that an infinite schedule $\langle (m_1, t_1), (m_2, t_2), \ldots \rangle$ is *periodic* if there exists $k \geq 1$ such that for all $i \geq 1$ we have $(m_i, t_i) = (m_{(i \bmod k)+1}, t_{(i \bmod k)+1})$, and it is *ultimately periodic* if it has a suffix that is periodic. We say that an infinite schedule $\langle (m_1, t_1), (m_2, t_2), \ldots \rangle$ is *Zeno* if $\sum_{i=1}^{\infty} t_i < \infty$. Zeno schedules require infinitely many mode-switches within a finite time, and hence, are physically unrealizable.

For a (finite or infinite) schedule $\sigma = \langle (m_1, t_1), (m_2, t_2), \ldots \rangle$, we write $T_k(\sigma) \stackrel{\text{def}}{=} \sum_{i=1}^{k} t_i$ for the total time elapsed up to step k of the schedule σ, and we write $T_k^m(\sigma) \stackrel{\text{def}}{=} \sum_{i \leq k : m_i = m} t_i$ for the total time spent in mode m up to step k. For any non-Zeno schedule σ we have that $\lim_{k \to \infty} T_k(\sigma) = \infty$.

A finite *run* of an MMS $\mathcal{H}$ is a finite sequence of states and timed actions $r = \langle \overline{x}_0, (m_1, t_1), \overline{x}_1, \ldots, (m_k, t_k), \overline{x}_k \rangle$ such that

for all $1 \leq i \leq k$ we have that $\overline{x}_i = \overline{x}_{i-1} + t_i \cdot R(m_i)$. For such a run r we say that $\overline{x}_0$ is the *starting state*, while $\overline{x}_k$ is its *terminal state*. Given a state $\overline{x}$ and a finite schedule $\sigma = \langle (m_1, t_1), (m_2, t_2), \ldots, (m_k, t_k) \rangle$, we write $Run(\overline{x}, \sigma)$ for the (unique) finite run $\langle \overline{x}_0, (m_1, t_1), \overline{x}_1, (m_2, t_2), \ldots, (m_k, t_k), \overline{x}_k \rangle$ such that $\overline{x}_0 = \overline{x}$. In this case, we also say that schedule σ leads the system $\mathcal{H}$ from state $\overline{x}_0$ to state $\overline{x}_k$. The concepts of an *infinite run* and an infinite run $Run(\overline{x}, \sigma)$ corresponding to an infinite schedule σ are defined in an analogous manner.

Given a set $S \subseteq \mathbb{R}^n$ of safe states, we say that an infinite run $\langle \overline{x}_0, (m_1, t_1), \overline{x}_1, (m_2, t_2), \ldots \rangle$ is S-safe if for all $i \geq 0$ we have that $\overline{x}_i \in S$ and $\overline{x}_i + \tau_{i+1} \cdot R(m_{i+1}) \in S$ for all $\tau_{i+1} \in [0, t_{i+1}]$. Notice that if S is a convex set then $\overline{x}_i \in S$ for all $i \geq 0$, implies that $\overline{x}_i + \tau_{i+1} \cdot R(m_{i+1}) \in S$ for all $i \geq 0$ and all $\tau_{i+1} \in [0, t_{i+1}]$. Given a set $S \subseteq \mathbb{R}^n$ of safe states and a starting state $\overline{x} \in \mathbb{R}^n$, we say that an infinite schedule $\sigma = \langle (m_1, t_1), (m_2, t_2), \ldots \rangle$ is S-safe at $\overline{x}$ if the corresponding run $Run(\overline{x}, \sigma)$ is S-safe. The concept of S-safety for finite runs and schedules is defined in a similar manner. Sometimes we simply call a schedule or a run safe when the safety set and the starting state is clear from the context.

We say that a state $\overline{x}'$ is "S-safe reachable" from a state $\overline{x}$ if there exists a finite schedule σ that is S-safe at $\overline{x}$ and leads the system from state $\overline{x}$ to state $\overline{x}'$. The following observations will be useful in some of the proofs later.

PROPOSITION 1. *For every MMS $\mathcal{H}$ and a convex safety set S we have that any convex combination $\overline{x}^* = \sum_{i=1}^{k} \lambda_i \overline{x}_i$ of S-safe reachable states $\overline{x}_1, \overline{x}_2, \ldots, \overline{x}_k$ from a given state $\overline{x}$ is also S-safe reachable from $\overline{x}$. Moreover, if mode m is safe for t amount of time at $\overline{x}_i \in S$, then it is safe for $\lambda_i t$ amount of time at $\overline{x}^*$.*

Two fundamental problems for MMS are the following *safe schedulability* and *safe reachability* problems.

DEFINITION 2 (SAFE SCHEDULABILITY). *Given an MMS $\mathcal{H}$, a bounded convex set $S \subseteq \mathbb{R}^n$, and a state $\overline{x} \in S$, decide if a non-Zeno infinite schedule exists that is S-safe at $\overline{x}$.*

DEFINITION 3 (SAFE REACHABILITY). *Given an MMS $\mathcal{H}$, a bounded convex set $S \subseteq \mathbb{R}^n$, and a pair of states $\overline{x}, \overline{x}' \in S$ decide if $\overline{x}'$ is S-safe reachable from $\overline{x}$.*

We present algorithms to solve safe schedulability and safe reachability problems in Section 2.3 and 2.4, respectively. We next present two examples of posing scheduling problems using constant-rate multi-mode systems.

2.2 Examples

The first example generalizes energy peak demand minimization problem as studied by Nghiem et al. [18].

EXAMPLE 1. *Consider an organization with two zones A and B. HVAC units in each zone can be in one of the three modes 0 (OFF), 1 (LOW), and 2 (HIGH). We write the mode of the combined system as $m_{i,j}$ to represent the fact that unit A is in mode i and unit B is in mode j. The rate of temperature change and the energy usage for each zone in each mode is summarized in the following table:*

Zones	HIGH	LOW	OFF
A (temp. change rate/ usage)	-2/3	-1/2	2/0.2
B (temp. change/ usage)	-2/3	-1/2	3/0.2

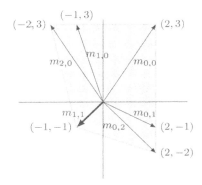

Figure 1: Rate vectors from Example 1.

For instance, if HVAC unit in zone A is in mode LOW then the temperature of the zone A drops 1 unit per second, while the HVAC unit consumes 2 energy units per second. To simplify energy pricing, we assume that the energy cost is equal to energy usage if peak energy usage (sum of the energy usage in all units) at every given point in time is less than or equal to 4 units, otherwise energy cost is 10 times of that standard rate. This assumption is in agreement with the bucket-based pricing [10] used by some energy providers.

It follows that to minimize energy cost, the peak usage, if possible, must not be higher than 4 units at any given time. Hence we model the system as an MMS with modes $m_{0,0}$, $m_{0,1}$, $m_{1,0}$, $m_{0,2}$, $m_{2,0}$, and $m_{1,1}$, because these are the only ones that have peak usage at most 4. The temperature of the zones are the variables of the MMS, while the safety set as the constraint that temperature of both zones should be between $65°F$ to $75°F$. The existence of a safe non-Zeno schedule implies the existence of a switching schedule with energy peak demand less than or equal to 4 units. The rates of the variables in different modes is shown in Figure 1.

Two tank system model, a popular [17, 13] example of hybrid systems, can be modeled as MMS as shown below.

EXAMPLE 2. *Consider a system consisting of two leaking tanks and a hose, such that each tank leaks water with some constant rate, and the hose can pump water in either of the tanks with a constant rate. The goal is to find a non-Zeno schedule to keep the water level of both tanks within a given range. It is straightforward to see that this problem can be modeled as a safe schedulability problem on MMS with two variables (water levels of tanks) and three modes that correspond to the positions of the water hose.*

2.3 Safe Schedulability Problem

There exists a simple characterization of safe schedulability if the starting state $\overline{x}$ is in the interior of set S. However, if the starting state $\overline{x}$ is on the boundary of safety set S, then the safe schedulability problem is more involved. We treat these two cases separately.

2.3.1 Starting state is in the interior of the safety set

For all starting states in the interior of the safety set a safe non-Zeno schedule exists iff the following constraints are feasible for some vector $(f^{(1)}, f^{(2)}, \ldots, f^{(|M|)}) \in \mathbb{R}_{\geq 0}^{|M|}$:

$$\sum_{i=1}^{|M|} R(i)(j) \cdot f^{(i)} = 0 \text{ for } 1 \leq j \leq n \text{ and } \sum_{i=1}^{|M|} f^{(i)} = 1. \quad (1)$$

The first constraint simply states that starting from an arbitrary state if the system spends $f^{(i)}$ fraction of total time in mode i then system comes back to the original state, while the second constraint is required to ensure non-Zenoness. The "if" part is straightforward as for any starting state $\overline{x}$ a satisfying assignment to $f^{(i)}$ can be used to characterize a non-Zeno periodic S-safe schedule that forces all intermediate states to stay within a closed ball of arbitrary non-zero radius centered at the starting state. The "only if" part follows from Farkas' lemma that states that constraints in (1) are feasible if and only if the following constraints are infeasible for all vectors $(v^{(1)}, v^{(2)}, \ldots, v^{(n)}) \in \mathbb{R}^n$:

$$(v^{(1)}, v^{(2)}, \ldots, v^{(n)}) \circ R(i) > 0 \text{ for all } 1 \leq i \leq |M| \quad (2)$$

Hence if constraints in (1) are infeasible, then constraints in (2) are feasible, i.e. there exists a vector $(v^{(1)}, v^{(2)}, \ldots, v^{(n)})$ such that no matter which mode system stays in, it makes a positive progress along that vector. Since we assume the safety set is bounded, it implies that no safe non-Zeno schedule can exists in this case. This observation also implies that if there exist a safe non-Zeno schedule then there exists one that is periodic.

We say that a mode m is S-safe at $\overline{x} \in S$ for $t > 0$ amount of time iff $\overline{x} + tR(m) \in S$, and we say that a mode m is S-safe at $\overline{x}$ if there exists such a $t > 0$. We show that the constraints in (1) give a necessary and sufficient condition for safe schedulability for all starting states where all modes are S-safe. Algorithm 1 returns an S-safe schedule from a given starting state $\overline{x}_0 \in S$ where all modes are S-safe, while Theorem 2 states the correctness and the complexity of the algorithm.

Algorithm 1: Returns an S-safe schedule, if it exists, from a given $\overline{x}_0$ where all modes are safe.

Input: MMS $\mathcal{H}$, staring state $\overline{x}_0$ and $t > 0$ such that all modes of $\mathcal{H}$ are safe at $\overline{x}_0$ for t amount of time.

Output: A periodic S-safe schedule from $\overline{x}$ or NO if no such a schedule exists.

1 Check whether the following linear program is feasible:

$$\sum_{m \in M} R(m) \cdot f^{(m)} = \vec{0}$$
$$\sum_{m \in M} f^{(m)} = 1 \quad (3)$$
$$f^{(m)} \geq 0 \text{ for all } m \in M.$$

    if *no satisfying assignment exists* **then**

2 | return NO

3 **else**

4 | Find a polynomial size assignment $\{f^{(m)}\}_{m \in M}$.

5 | **return** the following periodic schedule with period
    | $|M|$: $m_k = (k \bmod |M|) + 1$ and $t_k = f^{(m_k)} \cdot t$.

THEOREM 2. *Given an MMS $\mathcal{H}$, a bounded convex safety set S, a state $\overline{x}_0 \in S$ and $t > 0$ s.t. all modes are safe at $\overline{x}_0$ for at least t amount of time, Algorithm 1 returns an S-safe non-Zeno periodic schedule (if exists) in polynomial time.*

Notice that Algorithm 1 solves safe reachability problem for all starting states in the interior of the safety set, thanks to the following proposition.

PROPOSITION 3. *If $\overline{x} \in \text{int}(S)$ then there exists $t > 0$ such that all modes are safe at $\overline{x}$ for at least t amount of time.*

PROOF. Since $\overline{x} \in \text{int}(S)$, there exists $d > 0$ such that $B_d(\overline{x}) \subseteq S$. We can set t to be $\min_{m \in M} d/\|R(m)\| > 0$, as then for any $m \in M$ we have $\|tR(m)\| \leq t\|R(m)\| \leq d$ and so $\overline{x} + tR(m) \in B_d(\overline{x}) \subseteq S$. $\square$

The constraints (1) and (2) give us two ways to test safe schedulability of an MMS for staring states in the interior of the safety set. From (1) it follows that there exists a safe non-Zeno schedule if and only if the origin lies in the convex hull of the points corresponding to the rate vector of each mode. While from (2) it follows that there is no safe non-Zeno schedule if there exists a vector such that the angles between that vector and every other rate vector are all less than $90°$.

EXAMPLE 3. *Using Figure 1 one can easily check that for the MMS from Example 1 there exists a safe non-Zeno schedule for all starting states in the interior of the safety set, as the convex hull (the shaded area) of the points corresponding to the rate vectors includes the origin, and also there is no vector which makes an angle less than $90°$ with all the vectors. It can also be easily verified that if we remove mode $m_{1,1}$ then there is no safe non-Zeno schedule.*

2.3.2 Starting state is on the boundary of safety set

Feasibility of constraints (1) is not a sufficient condition for safe schedulability if the starting state lies on the boundary of the safe region as shown in the following example.

EXAMPLE 4. *In the following figure we revisit Example 1 and draw the safety set (shaded region) S and four states s_0, s_1, s_2 and s_3 inside the safety set. The state s_3 is in the interior of the set S, while other states are on the boundary of the set S.*

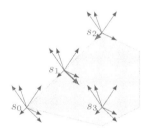

From Theorem 2 it follows that from the starting state s_3 there exists a safe non-Zeno schedule. Now let us consider the state s_0. It is clear that no mode is safe at s_0 as making any infinitesimally small progress along one of the rate vectors leads outside of the safety set S. Hence, for the starting state s_0 there is no safe non-Zeno schedule. On the other hand, from state s_1 choosing the vector $(2, -2)$ corresponding to mode $m_{0,2}$ leads into the interior of the safety region from where there exists a safe non-Zeno schedule. Similarly, from state s_2 first choosing the vector $(-1, -1)$ corresponding to mode $m_{1,1}$, and then choosing vector $(2, -2)$ corresponding to mode $m_{0,2}$ leads into the interior of the safe set.

The algorithm for the safe schedulability problem for boundary starting states follows from Theorem 7 presented in Section 3 and crucially depends on our results for the safe reachability problem presented next.

2.4 Safe Reachability Problem

Given an MMS $\mathcal{H} = (M, n, R)$, a bounded convex safety set S, and a starting state $\overline{x} \in S$, and a target state $\overline{x}' \in S$, the safe reachability problem is to decide whether $\overline{x}'$ is S-safe reachable from $\overline{x}$. When all modes of $\mathcal{H}$ are safe at $\overline{x}$ and $\overline{x}'$, a safe schedule from $\overline{x}$ to $\overline{x}'$ exists iff the following constraints are satisfied for some vector $\vec{t} = (t^{(1)}, t^{(2)}, \ldots, t^{(|M|)}) \in \mathbb{R}^{|M|}_{\geq 0}$:

$$\overline{x}(j) + \sum_{i=1}^{|M|} R(i)(j) \cdot t^{(i)} = \overline{x}'(j) \text{ for all } 1 \leq j \leq n \qquad (4)$$

This constraint expresses that using a combination of rate vectors it is possible to reach $\overline{x}'$ from $\overline{x}$. If the set of constraints in (4) is feasible and $\overline{x}, \overline{x}'$ are in the interior of the safe set—or more generally all modes are safe at $\overline{x}$ and $\overline{x}'$—then a satisfying assignment to $t^{(i)}$ can be used to make progress towards the vector $\overline{x}' - \overline{x}$ by scaling the $t^{(i)}$-s appropriately without leaving the safety set. Repeating this process, $\overline{x}'$ can be reached from $\overline{x}$ in finitely many steps.

Algorithm 2 returns an S-safe schedule, if exists, that leads the system from $\overline{x}$ to $\overline{x}'$ given all modes are safe at both states. Theorem 4 establishes the correctness and the computational complexity of the algorithm.

Algorithm 2: Returns an S-safe schedule, if exists, from states $\overline{x}$ and $\overline{x}'$ when all modes are safe at $\overline{x}$ and $\overline{x}'$.

Input: MMS $\mathcal{H}$, two points $\overline{x}, \overline{x}'$ and $t > 0$ such that all modes are safe at $\overline{x}$ and $\overline{x}'$ for time t.

Output: NO, if no S-safe schedule from $\overline{x}$ to $\overline{x}'$ exists, and a periodic such schedule, otherwise.

1 Check whether the following linear program is feasible:

$$\overline{x} + \sum_{m \in M} R(m)t^{(m)} = \overline{x}' \text{ and} \qquad (5)$$

$$t^{(m)} \geq 0 \text{ for all } m \in M.$$

2 **if** *no satisfying assignment exists* **then**
3   **return** NO
4 **else**
5   Find a polynomial size assignment $\{t^{(m)}\}_{m \in M}$.
6   Let l be the smallest natural number greater than $\sum_{m \in M} t^{(m)}/t$.
7   **return** the following schedule of length $l|M|$ with period $|M|$: $m_k = (k \mod |M|) + 1$ and $t_k = t^{(m_k)}/l$ for $k = 1, 2, \ldots, l|M|$.

THEOREM 4. *Given an MMS $\mathcal{H}$, a bounded convex set $S \subseteq \mathbb{R}^n$, a starting state $\overline{x} \in S$ and a target state $\overline{x}' \in S$, and a $t > 0$ such that all modes are safe at $\overline{x}$ and $\overline{x}'$ for at least t amount of time, Algorithm 2 returns an S-safe schedule (if exists) from $\overline{x}$ to $\overline{x}'$ in polynomial time.*

PROOF. Assume that the linear constraints are feasible, and consider the schedule constructed in Algorithm 2. Let us denote that schedule by σ and consider the run $r = Run(\overline{x}, \sigma)$ corresponding to this schedule from state $\overline{x}$. Let us denote the state visited after the k-th step of r by $\overline{x}_k$, and also look at the states when the schedule σ is extended by $|M|$ extra steps. Notice that because σ is periodic with period $|M|$, for any $i < l$ and $j \leq |M|$ the following holds:

$$\overline{x}_{i|M|+j} = (1 - i/l)\overline{x}_j + (i/l)\overline{x}_{l|M|+j}.$$

So it suffices to prove that the points $\overline{x}_j$ and $\overline{x}_{l|M|+j}$ are S-safe for $j \leq |M|$. Let us denote for $j = 0, \ldots, |M|$ by a_j the expression $1 - \sum_{m=1}^{j} t^{(m)} / (t \cdot l)$. Notice that

$$a_j \geq 1 - \sum_{m=1}^{j} t^{(m)} / \sum_{m \in M} t^{(m)} \geq 0,$$

because $t \cdot l \geq \sum_{m \in M} t^{(m)}$. On the other hand, $\overline{x}_j = \overline{x} + \sum_{m=1}^{j} R(m) t^{(m)} / l = a_j \overline{x} + \sum_{m=1}^{j} (t^{(m)} / (t \cdot l))(\overline{x} + t R(m))$. However, all modes were assumed to be safe at $\overline{x}$ for t amount of time and so $\overline{x}_j \in S$ for all $j \leq M$, because it is a convex combination of states from the convex set S. In exactly the same manner we show $\overline{x}_{l|M|+j} \in S$ for all $j \leq |M|$. This concludes the proof that the schedule returned by Algorithm 1 is S-safe. $\square$

The safe reachability problem can be solved in polynomial time, since the main computation of the algorithm involves solving a linear program, Moreover, although the schedule can be of exponential length, it can be represented compactly in polynomial space, because it has a period $|M|$. $\square$

2.4.1 General Case

Feasibility of the set of constraints in (5) does not guarantee safe reachability of state $\overline{x}'$ from state $\overline{x}$ if both states are on the boundary of the safety set. Moreover, in such a case the state $\overline{x}'$ may not be reachable in finitely many step as shown in the following example.

EXAMPLE 5. *In the following figure we present a MMS with two variables and two modes $(1, 1)$ and $(1, -1)$, and the starting state is s, while the target state is s'.*

The safety set is shown as the shaded area such that the angle at state s' is 30°. It is easy to see that the constraint in Equation 5 is feasible for this example, however, as we can see from the figure, the distance between states s_k and s' is equal to $\|s, s'\| \cdot (\frac{\sqrt{3}-1}{\sqrt{3}+1})^k$. Hence, although $\overline{x}'$ can be approached arbitrarily close using the two available modes, it is impossible to reach that state using a non-Zeno run.

3. OPTIMAL SCHEDULABILITY

In the previous section we presented algorithms to compute an arbitrary schedule out of all possible safe schedules. However, for most practical control problems when more than one safe schedule exists, it is often desirable to use a schedule that is optimal according to some quantitative objective. In this section we study a priced extension of MMS where every mode is associated with a cost incurred per time unit when the system is that mode, and the natural generalization of safe schedulability and safe reachability problems to optimal average-cost and optimal reachability-cost problems for such extension.

DEFINITION 4. *A priced constant-rate multi-mode system is a tuple $\mathcal{H} = (M, n, R, \pi)$ where (M, n, R) is a MMS and*

$\pi : M \to \mathbb{R}$ *is a price function such that $\pi(m)$ characterizes the price per time-unit of staying in mode m.*

The price function can be extended to define costs for finite and infinite schedules. The cost of a finite schedule $\sigma = \langle (m_1, t_1), (m_2, t_2), \ldots, (m_k, t_k) \rangle$ is defined as the sum of the costs of its timed actions, i.e., $Cost(\sigma) \stackrel{\text{def}}{=} \sum_{i=1}^{k} \pi(m_i) \cdot t_i$. The cost of an infinite schedule $\sigma = \langle (m_1, t_1), (m_2, t_2), \ldots \rangle$ is defined as the average-cost per time-unit, i.e.

$$AvgCost(\sigma) = \limsup_{k \to \infty} \frac{\sum_{i=1}^{k} \pi(m_i) \cdot t_i}{\sum_{i=1}^{n} t_i}.$$

Notice that we could define $AvgCost(\sigma)$ with lim inf instead of lim sup. However, because the aim is to find a schedule with the minimum average-cost, it makes more sense to pick lim sup in order to minimize the maximal recurring average-cost along a run. Also, as we will see later, this assumption is crucial in the proof of a key theorem of this paper.

Let $\Sigma(\overline{x}, \overline{x}', S)$ be the set of finite schedules that are S-safe at $\overline{x}$ and lead the system from $\overline{x}$ to $\overline{x}'$. The *optimal reachability-cost* $Cost^S_*(\overline{x}, \overline{x}')$ for a starting state $\overline{x}$, a target state $\overline{x}'$, and a safety set S is defined as:

$$Cost^S_*(\overline{x}, \overline{x}') = \inf \left\{ Cost(\sigma) : \sigma \in \Sigma(\overline{x}, \overline{x}', S) \right\}.$$

We say that a schedule σ is reachability-cost optimal for a starting state $\overline{x}$, a target state $\overline{x}'$ and a safety set S, if $\sigma \in \Sigma(\overline{x}, \overline{x}', S)$ and $Cost(\sigma) = Cost^S_*(\overline{x}, \overline{x}')$.

Let $\Sigma(\overline{x}, S)$ be the set of non-Zeno infinite schedules that are S-safe at $\overline{x}$. The optimal average-cost of a state $\overline{x}$ and a safety set S is defined as

$$AvgCost^S_*(\overline{x}) = \inf \left\{ AvgCost(\sigma) : \sigma \in \Sigma(\overline{x}, S) \right\}.$$

We say that a schedule σ is average-cost optimal for a starting state $\overline{x}$ and a safety set S if $\sigma \in \Sigma(\overline{x}, S)$ and $AvgCost(\sigma) = AvgCost^S_*(\overline{x})$.

Two fundamental problems for priced MMS are the following optimal reachability and optimal average schedulability problems.

DEFINITION 5 (OPTIMAL REACHABILITY). *Given a priced MMS $\mathcal{H}$, a bounded convex set $S \in \mathbb{R}^n$, a starting state $\overline{x} \in S$, and a target state $\overline{x}' \in S$, compute the optimal reachability-cost $Cost^S_*(\overline{x}, \overline{x}')$ and find, if exists, a reachability-cost optimal schedule.*

DEFINITION 6 (OPTIMAL AVERAGE SCHEDULABILITY). *Given a priced MMS $\mathcal{H}$, a bounded convex set $S \in \mathbb{R}^n$, and a state $\overline{x} \in S$ compute the optimal average-cost $AvgCost^S_*(\overline{x})$ and find, if exists, an average-cost optimal schedule.*

In Sections 3.1 and 3.2 we present algorithms to solve optimal reachability and optimal average schedulability problems, respectively.

3.1 Optimal Reachability Problem

Let us fix a priced MMS $\mathcal{H} = (M, n, R, \pi)$, a starting state $\overline{x}$, a target state $\overline{x}'$, and a bounded convex safety set S for this section. As we noticed in Example 5, if the points $\overline{x}$ and $\overline{x}'$ are on the boundary of the safe set, optimal schedules may not always exist. We now show that using Algorithm 3, we can solve in polynomial time the optimal reachability problem between any two points in the interior of S.

Algorithm 3: Given all modes are safe for time $t > 0$ at $\overline{x}, \overline{x}'$ and at least one S-safe schedule from $\overline{x}$ to $\overline{x}'$ exists, the algorithm returns a cost-optimal such schedule.

Input: MMS $\mathcal{H}$, two points $\overline{x}, \overline{x}'$ and $t > 0$ such that all modes of $\mathcal{H}$ are safe at $\overline{x}$ and $\overline{x}'$ for time t.
Output: NO, if no S-safe schedule from $\overline{x}$ to $\overline{x}'$ exists, and an optimal periodic such schedule, o/w.

1 Check whether the following linear programming problem with variables $\{t^{(m)}\}_{m \in M}$ has a solution.

$$\text{Minimize } \sum_{m \in M} \pi(m) t^{(m)} \text{ subject to:}$$

$$\overline{x} + \sum_{m \in M} R(m) t^{(m)} = \overline{x}' \text{ and}$$

$$t^{(m)} \geq 0 \text{ for all } m \in M.$$

2 **if** *no satisfying assignment exists* **then**
3 | **return** NO
4 **else**
5 | Find a polynomial size assignment $\{t^{(m)}\}_{m \in M}$.
6 | Let l be the smallest natural number greater or equal to $\sum_{m \in M} t^{(m)}/t$.
7 | **return** the following schedule of length $l|M|$ with period $|M|$: $m_k = (k \bmod |M|) + 1$ and $t_k = t^{(m_k)}/l$ for $k = 1, 2, \ldots, l|M|$.

THEOREM 5. *Given an MMS $\mathcal{H}$, a bounded convex set $S \subseteq \mathbb{R}^n$, states $\overline{x}, \overline{x}'$, and $t > 0$ such that all modes of $\mathcal{H}$ are safe at $\overline{x}$ and $\overline{x}'$ for at least t amount of time, Algorithm 3 returns a reachability-cost optimal schedule (if exists) in polynomial time.*

PROOF. It follows from the proof of Theorem 4 that the schedule, σ_*, returned by Algorithm 3 is S-safe. We now show σ_* is also reachability-cost optimal.

Assume that there is at least one S-safe schedule from $\overline{x}$ to $\overline{x}'$. Let σ be an arbitrary such schedule and let k be its length. Notice that of course we have

$$\overline{x}' = \overline{x} + \sum_{m \in M} R(m) T_k^m(\sigma),$$

and for all $m \in M$ we have that $T_k^m(\sigma) \geq 0$, since recall that $T_k^m(\sigma)$ is the total time spent in mode m up to step k. Therefore, by setting $t^{(m)} \mapsto T_k^m(\sigma)$ for all $m \in M$, the linear constraints in Algorithm 1 become satisfied. Furthermore, we have $Cost(\sigma) = \sum_{m \in M} \pi(m) \cdot T_k^m(\sigma)$, which is exactly the same as the value of the objective function for such an assignment. Hence, $Cost(\sigma) \geq Cost(\sigma_*)$ because σ_* has the minimal value of the objective function among all assignments that satisfy the linear constraints in Algorithm 1. However, we picked σ arbitrarily and so we have that $Cost(\sigma_*) = Cost_*^S(\overline{x}, \overline{x}')$. $\square$

3.2 Optimal Average Schedulability Problem

Let us fix a priced MMS $\mathcal{H} = (M, n, R, \pi)$ and a bounded convex set S. We first present an algorithm for computing the average-optimal schedule for the case when all the modes are safe at the starting state. From Proposition 3 such starting states include all states in the interior of the safe set S.

3.2.1 Starting state is in the interior of the safety set

We show that the optimal average-cost does not depend on the starting state as long as all modes are S-safe at that state. Moreover, there always exists a period schedule that has the optimal average-cost among all S-safe schedules.

THEOREM 6. *Given a MMS $\mathcal{H}$, a bounded convex set $S \subseteq \mathbb{R}^n$, $t > 0$, an initial state $\overline{x}_0 \in S$ such that all modes of $\mathcal{H}$ are S-safe at $\overline{x}_0$ for t amount of time, Algorithm 4 returns a periodic average-cost optimal schedule in polynomial time.*

PROOF. We first show that for any S-safe schedule, $\sigma = \langle (m_1, t_1), (m_2, t_2), \ldots \rangle$, from $\overline{x}_0$ we can construct a periodic schedule with period $|M|$ whose average-cost is not greater than that of σ.

Let $f_k^{(m)} = T_k^m(\sigma)/T_k(\sigma)$ represents the fraction of the time spent by σ in mode m up to step k; note that $f_k^{(m)} \in [0, 1]$, and $\sum_{m \in M} f_k^{(m)} = 1$ for all k. Also, from the definitions,

$$\overline{x}_k = \overline{x}_0 + \sum_{m \in M} R(m) T_k^m(r) = \overline{x}_0 + T_k(r) \sum_{m \in M} R(m) f_k^{(m)},$$

for any k, and $AvgCost(r) = \limsup_{k \to \infty} \sum_{m \in M} \pi(m) f_k^{(m)}$. The definition of $\limsup$ stipulates that we can pick a subsequence of the sequence $\langle \sum_{m \in M} \pi(m) f_k^{(m)} \rangle_{k=1}^{\infty}$ that converges to $AvgCost(r)$. In other words, there exists an increasing integer sequence $i_1, i_2, \ldots$ such that $AvgCost(r) = \lim_{k \to \infty} \sum_{m \in M} \pi(m) f_{i_k}^{(m)}$. Let us now look at the sequence of vectors $\langle \vec{f}_k \in [0, 1]^M \rangle_{k=1}^{\infty}$ where we set $\vec{f}_k(m) = f_{i_k}^{(m)}$. Since this sequence is bounded, by the Bolzano-Weierstrass theorem, there exists an increasing integer sequence $j_1, j_2, \ldots$ such that $\lim_{k \to \infty} \vec{f}_{j_k}$ exists and let us denote this limit by $\vec{f}$. We next prove by contradiction that

$$\sum_{m \in M} R(m) \vec{f}(m) = \vec{0}. \tag{6}$$

Assume that $\sum_{m \in M} R(m) \vec{f}(m) \neq \vec{0}$. Then for some variable $1 \leq v \leq n$ we have $c := \sum_{m \in M} R(m)(v) \vec{f}(m) \neq 0$ and wlog assume this value to be positive. From the definition of $\vec{f}$, for any $\varepsilon > 0$ we can pick N such that for all $k > N$ and $m \in M$ we have $|\vec{f}_{j_k}(m) - \vec{f}(m)| < \varepsilon$. Now, notice that

$$\overline{x}_{i_{j_k}}(v) - \overline{x}_0(v) = T_{i_{j_k}} \sum_{m \in M} R(m)(v) f_{i_{j_k}}^{(m)}$$

$$= T_{i_{j_k}} \sum_{m \in M} R(m)(v) \vec{f}_{j_k}(m)$$

$$= T_{i_{j_k}} \sum_{m \in M} R(m)(v) \cdot (\vec{f}(m) + (\vec{f}_{j_k}(m) - \vec{f}(m)))$$

$$\geq T_{i_{j_k}} \sum_{m \in M} (R(m)(v) \cdot \vec{f}(m) - R_{\max}\varepsilon)$$

$$= T_{i_{j_k}} (c - |M| R_{\max}\varepsilon)$$

where $R_{\max} := \max_{m \in M, w \in V} |R(m)(w)|$. If we now set ε to be $c/(2|M|R_{\max})$ for $R_{\max} \neq 0$ and $\varepsilon = 0$ otherwise, then $\overline{x}_{i_{j_k}}(v) - \overline{x}_0(v) \geq \frac{1}{2} T_{i_{j_k}} c$, where the right-hand side tends to ∞, because $\lim_{k \to \infty} i_{j_k} = \infty$ and $c > 0$. Therefore, we have $\lim_{k \to \infty} \|\overline{x}_{i_{j_k}}, \overline{x}_0\| = \infty$, which would imply that either S is not bounded or r is not S-safe; a contradiction.

Let the periodic schedule $\sigma' = \langle (m_1', t_1'), (m_2', t_2'), \ldots \rangle$ be s.t. $m_k' = (k \bmod |M|) + 1$ and $t_k' = \vec{f}(m_k) \cdot t$ for each $k \geq 1$. Also, let $r' = \langle \overline{x}_0, (m_1', t_1'), \overline{x}_1', \ldots \rangle$ be the corresponding run from $\overline{x}_0$. It is straightforward to see that σ' is non-Zeno. We show that σ' is S-safe at $\overline{x}_0$. Notice that from (6) it follows

$$\overline{x}'_{|M|} = \overline{x}_0 + \sum_{m \in M} R(m) t \vec{f}(m) = \overline{x}_0.$$

So it suffices to show that the finite prefix of length $|M|$ of r' is S-safe. However, this prefix is exactly the same schedule that we would construct in the proof of Proposition 1 for the convex combination of points $\{\overline{x}_0 + tR(m) | m \in M\}$, where $\vec{f}(m)$ is picked as the coefficient of the point $\overline{x}_0 + tR(m)$ in this combination. All these points are trivially reachable by a finite path from $\overline{x}_0$, because all modes were assumed to be safe for t amount of time at $\overline{x}_0$.

We now show that σ' has the average-cost not greater than the original schedule σ.

$$
\begin{aligned}
AvgCost(\sigma) &= \limsup_{k \to \infty} \sum_{m \in M} \pi(m) f_k^{(m)} \\
&\geq \limsup_{k \to \infty} \sum_{m \in M} \pi(m) f_{j_k}^{(m)} = \sum_{m \in M} \pi(m) \lim_{k \to \infty} f_{j_k}^{(m)} \\
&= \sum_{m \in M} \pi(m) \vec{f}(m) = AvgCost(\sigma').
\end{aligned}
$$

The first inequality follows from the fact that removing elements from a sequence can only lower its $\limsup$ value, while the second equality follows as the $\limsup$ of a sum of bounded converging sequences is equal to the sum of its limits. This proves that the optimal average-cost among all S-safe schedules is equal to the infimum of the average-cost over S-safe periodic runs with period $|M|$.

Notice that Algorithm 4 differs from Algorithm 1 only at line 1 where an objective function is added to the linear program (7). The linear constraints guarantee the periodic schedule constructed at the end of the algorithm to be S-safe, while the objective function guarantees its average-cost to be the lowest among all S-safe schedules. $\square$

3.2.2 General Case

In this section we show how to handle arbitrary starting states as long as the safety set is a convex polytope.

THEOREM 7. *Given any MMS $\mathcal{H}$, bounded convex polytope $S \subseteq \mathbb{R}^n$, and an initial state $\overline{x}_0 \in S$, Algorithm 5 returns in polynomial time an ultimately periodic S-safe schedule with the minimum average-cost.*

PROOF. The algorithm first computes an increasing sequence of sets of modes $M_1 \subset M_2 \subset \ldots$, where M_1 is the set of modes safe at $\overline{x}_0$, and for $i \geq 1$ the set M_{i+1} consists of all modes safe at states S-safe reachable from $\overline{x}_0$ using only modes in M_i. Let k be the smallest number such that $M_{k+1} = M_k$. Of course $k \leq |M|$, because M_{i+1} has to have at least one more mode than M_i and the total number of modes is $|M|$. We will show that no mode outside of M_k can ever become safe during a S-safe schedule starting at $\overline{x}_0$. First, we need the following lemma that can transform any S-safe schedule into a S-safe schedule with the set of safe modes never decreasing as the new schedule progresses.

LEMMA 8. *Any S-safe finite schedule σ from $\overline{x}_0 \in S$ can be modified to a S-safe finite schedule σ' of length polynomial in σ in a way that all modes that were safe at any state along σ will be safe at the terminal state of σ' and no safe mode along σ' can become unsafe as σ' progresses.*

Algorithm 4: Given all modes are safe for time $t > 0$ at $\overline{x}$ and an S-safe non-Zeno schedule exists from $\overline{x}$, the algorithm returns average-cost optimal such schedule.

Input: MMS $\mathcal{H}$, initial point $\overline{x} \in \text{int}(S)$, and $t > 0$ such that all modes of $\mathcal{H}$ are safe for time t.

Output: NO, if no S-safe non-Zeno schedule exists from $\overline{x}$, and a periodic such schedule with the minimum average-cost, otherwise.

1 Check whether the following linear programming problem with variables $\{f^{(m)}\}_{m \in M}$ has a solution.

$$
\begin{aligned}
&\text{Minimize} \sum_{m \in M} \pi(m) \cdot f^{(m)} \text{ subject to} \\
&\sum_{m \in M} R(m) \cdot f^{(m)} = \vec{0} \\
&\sum_{m \in M} f^{(m)} = 1 \quad\quad (7) \\
&f^{(m)} \geq 0 \text{ for all } m \in M.
\end{aligned}
$$

2 **if** *no satisfying assignment exists* **then**
3   **return** NO
4 **else**
5   Find a polynomial size assignment $\{f^{(m)}\}_{m \in M}$.
6   **return** the following periodic schedule with period $|M|$: $m_k = (k \bmod |M|) + 1$ and $t_k = f^{(m_k)} \cdot t$.

Now, let σ be an arbitrary S-safe schedule starting at $\overline{x}_0$. First, using Lemma 8, we construct a new schedule σ' based on σ with the property which implies the existence of a finite list of states, $\overline{x}_1, \overline{x}_2, \ldots$, along the run $Run(\overline{x}_0, \sigma')$, such that for any $i \geq 0$ the set of safe modes at $\overline{x}_{i+1}$ is strictly greater than at $\overline{x}_i$ and does not change at the states between $\overline{x}_i$ and $\overline{x}_{i+1}$ in $Run(\overline{x}_0, \sigma')$. Hence, for any $i \geq 0$ the point $\overline{x}_{i+1}$ has to be reachable from $\overline{x}_0$ using modes safe at $\overline{x}_i$ only. From the definition of the sets M_i and an easy induction on i, the set of modes safe at $\overline{x}_i$ has to be a subset of M_{i+1}. Therefore, the set of safe modes at the terminal state of σ' is also a subset of M_i for some i. However, the set of safe modes at the terminal state of σ' was supposed to contain all the modes safe along $Run(\overline{x}_0, \sigma)$ and so any mode safe along a S-safe schedule from $\overline{x}_0$ has to belong to M_k.

We now show that a very specific schedule always exists.

LEMMA 9. *There exist states $\overline{x}_1, \overline{x}_2, \ldots, \overline{x}_k \in S$ such that for all $1 \leq i \leq k$ we have that state $\overline{x}_i$ is S-safe reachable from $\overline{x}_{i-1}$ using only modes in M_i, and all modes in M_i are safe at $\overline{x}_{i-1}$.*

PROOF. Pick any mode $q \in M_k$ and let $I(q)$ be the lowest index such that $q \in M_{I(q)}$. Next, pick any finite S-safe schedule such that mode q is the first mode in $M_{I(q)} \setminus M_{I(q)-1}$ to become safe at a state along the run of this schedule from $\overline{x}_0$. Such a schedule has to exist from the definition of the sets M_i. Let σ^q be the result of the transformation of this schedule into a new one using Lemma 8. For $1 \leq i \leq I(q)-1$, denote by $\overline{x}_i^q$ the first state along the run $Run(\overline{x}_0, \sigma^q)$ when a mode from $M_{i+1} \setminus M_i$ becomes safe, some of these states may coincide, and for all $i \geq I(q)$ let the terminal state of $Run(\overline{x}_0, \sigma^q)$ be assigned to $\overline{x}_i^q$. Notice that mode q is already safe at state $\overline{x}_{i-1}^q$, because of the way we picked σ^q.

Let us define $\overline{x}_i := \frac{1}{|M_k|} \sum_{q \in M_k} \overline{x}_i^q$ for all i. From Proposition 1, we know that $\overline{x}_i^q \in S$ and any mode safe at $\overline{x}_i^q$ is safe at $\overline{x}_i$. But this means that all modes in M_i are safe at $\overline{x}_{i-1}$, because any mode $q \in M_i$ is safe at $\overline{x}_j^q$ for all $j \geq i-1$. Furthermore, we know that $\overline{x}_i^q$ is S-safe reachable from $\overline{x}_{i-1}^q$ in $Run(\overline{x}_0, \sigma^q)$ using only modes from M_i, because only these modes are safe before this run reaches $\overline{x}_i^q$. Therefore, it has to be $\overline{x}_i^q - \overline{x}_{i-1}^q = \sum_{m \in M_i} R(m) t_m^q$ for some $t_m^q \geq 0$. But this means that $\overline{x}_i - \overline{x}_{i-1} = \frac{1}{|M_k|} \sum_{q \in M_k} \overline{x}_i^q - \overline{x}_{i-1}^q = \sum_{m \in M_i} R(m)(\frac{1}{|M_k|} \sum_{q \in M_k} t_m^q)$. Moreover, all modes from M_i are safe both at $\overline{x}_i$ and $\overline{x}_{i-1}$. Hence, based on the S-safe reachability characterization given in Theorem 4, we get that $\overline{x}_i$ is reachable from $\overline{x}_{i-1}$ via a S-safe schedule. $\square$

Algorithm 5 computes the sets of modes M_i iteratively. Having computed M_i for all $i \leq j$, it checks for every mode $q \in M \setminus M_j$ whether there exists a sequence of states $\overline{x}_1, \ldots, \overline{x}_j$ with the properties as in Lemma 9 and mode q being safe at $\overline{x}_j$. Lemma 9 guarantees that all safe modes from M_{j+1} will be found this way. We can use Theorem 4 to characterize the S-safe reachability of $\overline{x}_i$ from $\overline{x}_{i-1}$ via a set of linear constraints. Combining all of these for $i = 1, 2, \ldots, j$, and some additional checks regarding the safety of the states and modes used, we obtain the same linear program as in step 6 of Algorithm 5. In the end, the algorithm finds a polynomial size solution to the whole system of constraints while maximizing t, the minimum amount of time for which each mode is safe. Algorithm 3 can then be used to find a polynomial length schedule from $\overline{x}_i$ to $\overline{x}_{i+1}$ for each i.

After that, Algorithm 5 calls Algorithm 4 to find the optimal average-cost S-safe schedule σ from $\overline{x}_{k-1}$ that uses only modes from M_k. If no such schedule exists, then there is no S-safe schedule from $\overline{x}_0$ either. We already know that only modes from M_k can be used along a S-safe schedules from $\overline{x}_0$ and a finite prefix of a schedule does not influence its average-cost. Therefore, the schedule consisting of the polynomial length S-safe schedules leading the system from $\overline{x}_0$ to $\overline{x}_{k-1}$ followed by σ is not only an ultimately periodic S-safe schedule from $\overline{x}_0$, but also has the minimum average-cost. Finally, Algorithm 5 runs in polynomial time, because at most $|M|$ iterations of the loop is needed to find the sets of modes $M_1, \ldots, M_k$ and it calls other algorithms that were already shown to run in polynomial time.

4. DISCRETE-TIME SCHEDULABILITY

In the previous section, we showed that there exist optimal schedules for the average-cost and reachability-cost criteria with time delays in each mode expressible as rational numbers of the size polynomial in the size of the MMS. Also, the optimal average-cost schedule can be made periodic with period $|M|$ and the time delays for the optimal cost one are also periodic with period $|M|$. It follows that such schedules are implementable by a discrete controller with the sampling rate Δ being the least common multiple of all these $|M|$ rational time delays. Such a number will also be a polynomial sized rational number, however it may be exponentially smaller than any of the time delays used. Such a sampling rate may not be acceptable in practice, e.g., the switching frequency is too high, or the dwell time for some modes is too low. In this section we discuss discrete-time schedulers that are allowed to switch modes only at times multiple of a given sampling rate. We present results on deciding

---

Algorithm 5: Finds a S-safe non-Zeno run from a given $\overline{x}_0 \in S$ with the minimal average-cost, where S is a bounded convex polytope.

Input: MMS $\mathcal{H}$, $l \times n$ matrix A and vector $\vec{b} \in \mathbb{R}^l$ that together define a bounded convex polytope S such that $\overline{x} \in S$ iff $A\overline{x} \leq \vec{b}$, and initial point $\overline{x}_0 \in S$.

Output: NO if no S-safe non-Zeno schedule exists from $\overline{x}_0$, and an average-cost optimal ultimately periodic such schedule, otherwise.

1 $M_0 := \emptyset; k := -1;$
2 **repeat**
3     $k := k + 1;$
4     $M_{k+1} := M_k;$
5   **foreach** *mode* $q \in M \setminus M_k$ **do**
6   **if** *the following set of linear constraints is satisfiable for some assignment to the variables* $t, \{t_1^{(m)}\}_{m \in M_1}, \{t_2^{(m)}\}_{m \in M_2}, \ldots, \{t_k^{(m)}\}_{m \in M_k}$

$$t > 0$$

For all $i = 1, \ldots, k$
$$t_i^{(m)} \geq 0 \text{ for all } m \in M_i$$
$$\overline{x}_i = \overline{x}_{i-1} + \sum_{m \in M_i} R(m) t_i^{(m)}$$
$$A\overline{x}_i \leq \vec{b}$$
$$A(\overline{x}_{i-1} + R(m)t) \leq \vec{b} \text{ for all } m \in M_i$$
$$A(\overline{x}_k + R(m)t) \leq \vec{b} \text{ for all } m \in M_k \cup \{q\} \quad (8)$$

       then
7          $M_{k+1} := M_{k+1} \cup \{q\};$

8 **until** $M_{k+1} = M_k$;
9 Compute a polynomial sized solution to the linear program in step 6 but with the constraints (8) removed and the objective function *Maximize* t.
10 Call Algorithm 4 with the set of modes M_k, starting point $\overline{x}_{k-1}$ and the safe time bound t.
11 **if** *the call returned NO* **then**
12   **return** NO
13 **else**
14   Let σ be the periodic schedule returned otherwise.
15   Repeatedly call Algorithm 3 to find S-safe schedules of polynomial length from $\overline{x}_0$ to $\overline{x}_1$ using only modes in M_1, from $\overline{x}_1$ to $\overline{x}_2$ using only modes in M_2, $\ldots$, from $\overline{x}_{k-2}$ to $\overline{x}_{k-1}$ using only modes in M_{k-1}.
16   **return** the ultimately periodic schedule created by composing the S-safe finite schedules from $\overline{x}_i$ to $\overline{x}_{i+1}$ for $i = 0, 1, \ldots, k-2$ with the average-cost optimal S-safe periodic schedule σ from $\overline{x}_{k-1}$.

---

whether a given Δ suffices for schedulability or optimality (Theorem 10), and how to find the maximum sampling rate among all feasible Δ values (Theorem 11).

Let $\mathcal{H} = (M, n, R)$ be an MMS and let Δ be a given sampling rate. We say that a schedule $\sigma = \langle (m_1, t_1), (m_2, t_2), \ldots \rangle$ is Δ-clocked if for all $i \geq 1$ there is $d_i \in \mathbb{N}_{>0}$ such that $t_i = d_i \cdot \Delta$. Given a bounded convex set S and states $\overline{x}, \overline{x}' \in \mathbb{R}^n$, the optimal average-cost $AvgCost_\Delta^S(\overline{x})$ and optimal reachability-cost $Cost_\Delta^S(\overline{x}, \overline{x}')$ over all Δ-clocked S-safe schedules starting from $\overline{x}$ are defined in a straightforward manner.

THEOREM 10. *Given a priced MMS $\mathcal{H} = (M, n, R, \pi)$, a bounded polytope S, a sampling rate Δ, and states $\overline{x}_0, \overline{x}_d \in \mathbb{R}^n$ the discrete average-cost and the discrete reachability-cost problems are PSPACE-complete.*

PSPACE-membership of both problems is shown via discretization of the state space of $\mathcal{H}$. Since the set S is given as a bounded polytope, the size of the discretization can be shown to be at most exponential in the size of $\mathcal{H}$ and Δ. We prove PSPACE-hardness by a reduction from the acceptance problem for the linear bounded automata (LBAs).

Lower bound on Δ can be computed using Theorems 6 and 7, while the upper bound can be obtained from the diameter of the safety set. Given a target average-cost, using a straightforward binary search algorithm we can approximate the maximum sampling rate for which the optimal average-cost does not exceed the target. Since the total number of iterations is polynomial and in each iteration the optimality can be checked in PSPACE, the following theorem follows.

THEOREM 11. *Given a MMS $\mathcal{H}$, a bounded polytope S, a starting state s, a budget B, and $\varepsilon > 0$, the maximum sampling rate for which the optimal average-cost is not greater than B can be approximated within ε in PSPACE.*

5. CONCLUSION

We have proposed a model for constant-rate multi-mode systems (MMSs) to analyze hybrid systems with variables having mode-dependent constant-rates and no constraints on mode-switching. For this model, we have developed polynomial time algorithms to solve safe schedulability and safe reachability problems, as well as their corresponding optimization problems. From a practical perspective, a number of quantitative analysis problems for hybrid systems, in particular, energy peak demand minimization problem proposed recently by Nghiem et al., can be formalized as optimal schedulability problems for MMSs. Our analysis algorithms reduce the problem to linear programming, and are tractable. As such, MMSs are a new promising, natural and expressive subclass of hybrid systems. There are, however, some natural optimization problems on MMSs where the linear programming formulation breaks down. For instance, if we allow different prices for mode-switches then the choice of the mode switching sequence plays a crucial role in the average-cost of a schedule, and the linear programming characterization presented in this paper does not work. For this setting, the exact complexity of optimal schedulability problem remains open.

Acknowledgments

We thank Madhur Behl, Rahul Mangharam, Truong Nghiem, and George Pappas for fruitful discussions on scheduling for energy optimization problems. This research was partially supported by NSF awards CNS 0931239, CNS 1035715, CCF 0915777, and EPSRC grant EP/G050112/2.

6. REFERENCES

[1] Y. Abdeddaïm, E. Asarin, and O. Maler. Scheduling with timed automata. *TCS*, 354:272–300, March 2006.

[2] Y. Abdeddaïm and O. Maler. Preemptive job-shop scheduling using stopwatch automata. In *TACAS*, volume 2280 of *LNCS*, pages 39–53. Springer, 2002.

[3] R. Alur and D. Dill. A theory of timed automata. *TCS*, 126(2):183–235, 1994.

[4] R. Alur, S. La Torre, and G. J. Pappas. Optimal paths in weighted timed automata. In *HSCC*, pages 49–62. Springer, 2001.

[5] R. Alur, A. Trivedi, and D. Wojtczak. Optimal scheduling for constant-rate mulit-mode systems. Technical Report MS-CIS-12-01, University of Pennsylvania, 2012.

[6] D. Belzer, M. Scott, and R. Sands. Climate change impacts on U.S. commercial building consumption: An analysis using sample survey data. *Energy Sources*, 18(2):77–201, 1996.

[7] P. Bouyer, E. Brinksma, and K. G. Larsen. Staying alive as cheaply as possible. In *HSCC*, volume 2993 of *LNCS*, pages 203–218. Springer, 2004.

[8] P. Bouyer, U. Fahrenberg, K. G. Larsen, N. Markey, and J. Srba. Infinite runs in weighted timed automata with energy constraints. In *FORMATS*, pages 33–47, 2008.

[9] G. C. Buttazzo. *Hard Real-time Computing Systems*. Springer-Verlag, 2004.

[10] The Reinvestment Fund (TRF) Energy Group. Understanding PECO's general service tariff. www.trfund.com/financing/energy/energy.html.

[11] T. A. Henzinger and P. W. Kopke. Discrete-time control for rectangular hybrid automata. *TCS*, 221(1-2):369–392, 1999.

[12] T. A. Henzinger, P. W. Kopke, A. Puri, and P. Varaiya. What's decidable about hybrid automata? *Journal of Comp. and Sys. Sciences*, 57:94–124, 1998.

[13] M. Heymann, L. Feng, G. Meyer, and S. Resmerita. Analysis of Zeno behaviors in a class of hybrid systems *IEEE Trans. on Automatic Control*, 50:376–383, 2005.

[14] S. Jha, S. Gulwani, S. A. Seshia, and A. Tiwari. Synthesizing switching logic for safety and dwell-time requirements. In *International Conference on Cyber-physical Systems*, pages 22–31, 2010.

[15] S. Jha, S. A. Seshia, and A. Tiwari. Synthesizing switching logic to minimize long-run cost. *CoRR*, abs/1103.0800, 2011.

[16] Kronos. www-verimag.imag.fr/TEMPORISE/kronos.

[17] J. Lygeros. *Lecture Notes on Hybrid Systems*. Cambridge, 2003.

[18] T. X. Nghiem, M. Behl, R. Mangharam, and G. J. Pappas. Green scheduling of control systems for peak demand reduction. In *IEEE CDC*, December 2011.

[19] T. X. Nghiem, M. Behl, G. J. Pappas, and R. Mangharam. Green scheduling: Scheduling of control systems for peak power reduction. *2nd International Green Computing Conference*, July 2011.

[20] UPPAAL. www.uppaal.com.

[21] E. Valor, V. Meneu, and V. Caselles. Daily air temperature and electricity load in Spain. *Journal of Applied Meteorology*, 40:1413–1421, 2001.

[22] X. Xu and P. J. Antsaklis. Practical stablization of integrator switched systems. In *American Control Conference*, pages 2767–2772, 2003.

On Synthesizing Robust Discrete Controllers under Modeling Uncertainty[*]

Ufuk Topcu, Necmiye Ozay, Jun Liu, and Richard M. Murray
California Institute of Technology, Pasadena, CA
{utopcu, necmiye, liu, murray}@cds.caltech.edu

ABSTRACT

We investigate the robustness of reactive control protocols synthesized to guarantee system's correctness with respect to given temporal logic specifications. We consider uncertainties in open finite transition systems due to unmodeled transitions. The resulting robust synthesis problem is formulated as a temporal logic game. In particular, if the specification is in the so-called generalized reactivity [1] fragment of linear temporal logic, so is the augmented specification in the resulting robust synthesis problem. Hence, the robust synthesis problem belongs to the same complexity class with the nominal synthesis problem, and is amenable to polynomial time solvers. Additionally, we discuss reasoning about the effects of different levels of uncertainties on robust synthesizability and demonstrate the results on a simple robot motion planning scenario.

Categories and Subject Descriptors

D.2.4 [**SOFTWARE ENGINEERING**]: Software/Program Verification

Keywords

Discrete controller synthesis; Robustness; Temporal logic

1. INTRODUCTION

Robustness—a system's ability to function correctly under uncertainties, for example, due to imperfections in the way the evolution of the system and its interactions with its environment are modeled—is a key attribute to predictable operation (and graceful failure). Though well-studied for physical engineering artifacts, it has been hardly explored for distributed embedded systems. Approaching this from a computer science perspective, a reason for the lack of suitable robustness notions is that computing systems are conveniently

*This work is supported by the Boeing Corporation, NSF grants CNS 0911041, the NSERC of Canada, the FCRP consortium through the Multiscale Systems Center (MuSyC).

modeled as discrete mathematical objects with no underlying (non-trivial) topology where uncertainties and their impact can be quantified [9]. Furthermore, even though controls have explicitly modeled such uncertainties and developed dedicated methods and tools, they have been limited to rather restrictive representations and cannot directly address the critical interplay between physical components and computing/communication. Consequently, there is a need for characterizations and computable metrics to support the analysis, design, and construction of robust embedded control systems.

As a step toward addressing this need, we consider robustness of discrete, reactive control protocols synthesized to guarantee system's correctness with respect to given temporal logic specifications. Such control protocols—in the context of embedded control systems, robot motion planning, and hybrid systems—have attracted considerable attention recently. The special case, where there is no uncontrolled, environment, has been studied, for example, in [2, 11]. These methods generally formulate a problem that is amenable to model checking [5]. More recently, the case with a priori unknown, dynamic environment has been investigated, for example, in [12, 22]. In this case, the problem is generally formulated as a temporal logic game [1].

We consider uncertainties in open finite transition systems, i.e., transition systems with uncontrolled inputs, due to unmodeled transitions. We reformulate the resulting robust synthesis problem as a temporal logic game. In particular, we utilize specifications that belong to the so-called generalized reactivity [1] (GR[1]) fragment of linear temporal logic for which there exist polynomial complexity solvers [19]. We show that if the specification is a GR[1] formula, so is the augmented specification in the resulting robust synthesis problem. Hence, robustification of protocol synthesis with the specific uncertainty model consider in this paper does not change its complexity class. Finally, we discuss reasoning about the effects of different levels of uncertainties on robust synthesizability. Specifically, we embed partial orders on the family of sets of unmodeled transitions, which reflect on designer's intent or prior knowledge, as a means to compare different uncertainty sets. For a class of partial orders that satisfy certain monotonicity conditions, we propose a bisection-type search to compute maximum level robustness a system possesses with respect to given specifications and a partially ordered family of uncertainty sets.

The work in [20] extends notions, such as input-output gains and small-gain theorems, well-known in controls to systems over finite alphabets. This study is limited to the verification of stability and amplification of a measure of energy from the input channels to the output channels. A recent collection of papers including [3, 13] consider the *sensitivity* of the outputs of discrete systems to the variations in the inputs. For example, [3] focuses on safety properties and uses the ratio of the "distance" between allowed and observed system behavior to that of the environment behavior as a measure for sensitivity. The recent work [?] considers fault tolerance in the context of discrete controller synthesis, where such tolerance is achieved by taking various fault conditions as adversarial inputs and modifying the state space according to each fault hypotheses against which fault-tolerance is desired. We emphasize, though, that what matters for satisfactory operation of engineering systems is *robustness* (i.e., how much the input specifications can be violated and still the output specifications hold), beyond mere *sensitivity* (i.e., how much the output specifications are violated due to the violations in the input specifications).

The organization of the paper is straightforward. We continue with some background material used in the rest of the paper. The problem formulation in section 4 is followed by the main results of the paper and a demonstration of these results on a simple robot motion planning problem. We conclude with a critique of the problems and progress reported in the paper focusing on the limitations and potential extensions.

2. BACKGROUND

We now present some of the definitions and background material used throughout the paper.

2.1 Finite transition system

We consider two types of finite transition system models. Roughly speaking, the first one does not interact with its external environment (after possibly being started by the environment). The other one explicitly accounts for the interactions with possibly adversarial environments and reacts to the changes in the environment.

Definition 1. A *finite transition system* is a tuple $TS = (Q, I, \mathcal{A}, R)$ where Q is the finite set of states, $I \subseteq Q$ is the set of initial states, $\mathcal{A}$ is the finite set of actions (i.e. controllable input variables) and $R \subseteq Q \times \mathcal{A} \times Q$ is a transition relation.

TS is called *action deterministic* if I is a singleton and for all $q \in Q$, for all $u \in \mathcal{A}$, there is at most one $q' \in Q$ such that $(q, u, q') \in R$. TS is called *non-blocking* if for all $q \in Q$, there exists a pair $(u, q') \in \mathcal{A} \times Q$ such that $(q, u, q') \in R$.

An *execution* of the transition system TS is a sequence $(q_0, u_0), (q_1, u_1), (q_2, u_2), \ldots$ such that $q_0 \in I$ and $(q_i, u_i, q_{i+1}) \in R$ for all $i \geq 0$. For simplicity, we assume TS is non-blocking and consider only infinite executions. This assumption introduces no loss of generality since one can add an auxiliary sink state with a self-transition and complete the finite executions to infinite ones.

We also consider a more general class of transition systems, so-called *open* systems, where part of the actions are uncontrollable (e.g., controlled by the environment).

Definition 2. An *open finite transition system* is defined as a tuple $TS = (Q, I, \mathcal{A}_{uc}, \mathcal{A}_c, R)$ where Q is the finite set of states, $I \subseteq Q$ is the set of initial states, $\mathcal{A}_{uc}$ is the finite set of uncontrollable actions (i.e. environment decisions), $\mathcal{A}_c$ is

the finite set of controllable actions (i.e. control inputs) and $R \subseteq Q \times \mathcal{A}_{uc} \times \mathcal{A}_c \times Q$ is a transition relation.

An open finite transition system TS is called *action deterministic* if I is a singleton and for any pair of transitions $(q_1, e_1, u_1, q_1') \in R$ and $(q_2, e_2, u_2, q_2') \in R$, if $q_1 = q_2$, $e_1 = e_2$ and $u_1 = u_2$, then $q_1' = q_2'$. TS is called *non-blocking* if for all $q \in Q$, there exists a triple $(e, u, q') \in \mathcal{A}_{uc} \times \mathcal{A}_c \times Q$ such that $(q, e, u, q') \in R$. An execution for an open transition system is defined similarly.

2.2 Linear temporal logic

We use linear temporal logic (LTL) [17, 14] as a formal language to specify correct behaviors of systems and admissible behaviors of their environments. LTL is a rich specification language that can express properties often used in control, robot motion planning, and embedded systems, including safety, reachability, invariance, response, and/or a combination of these [14] (see [21] for examples). Roughly speaking, LTL specifications impose constraints on the infinite sequences of the values a certain set of variables can take (e.g., the executions in finite transition systems).

LTL is an extension of propositional logic by including temporal operators. Apart from the logical connectives negation ($\neg$), disjunction ($\vee$), conjunction ($\wedge$) and implication ($\rightarrow$), it includes temporal operators next ($\bigcirc$), always ($\square$), eventually ($\Diamond$) and until ($\mathcal{U}$). By combining these operators, it is possible to specify a wide range of requirements on the desired behavior of a system.

An *atomic proposition* is a statement that has a unique truth value (*True* or *False*) at a given state[1]. Given a set Π of atomic propositions, an LTL formula is defined inductively as follows: (i) any atomic proposition $p \in \Pi$ is an LTL formula; and (ii) given LTL formulas φ and ψ, $\neg \varphi$, $\varphi \vee \psi$, $\bigcirc \varphi$ and $\varphi \, \mathcal{U} \, \psi$ are also LTL formulas. Formulas involving other operators can be derived from these basic ones.

Semantics of LTL: An LTL formula is interpreted over an infinite sequence of states. Given a sequence of states $\sigma = q_0 q_1 q_2 \ldots$ and an LTL formula φ, we say that φ *holds at position* $i \geq 0$ of σ, written $q_i \models \varphi$, if and only if (iff) φ holds for the remainder of the sequence σ starting at position i. The semantics of LTL is defined inductively as follows:

- For an atomic proposition p, $q_i \models p$ iff $q_i \Vdash p$;
- $q_i \models \neg \varphi$ iff $q_i \not\models \varphi$;
- $q_i \models \varphi \vee \psi$ iff $q_i \models \varphi$ or $q_i \models \psi$;
- $q_i \models \bigcirc \varphi$ iff $q_{i+1} \models \varphi$; and
- $q_i \models \varphi \, \mathcal{U} \, \psi$ iff there exists $j \geq i$ such that $q_j \models \psi$ and $\forall k \in [i, j), q_k \models \varphi$.

Based on this definition, $\bigcirc \varphi$ holds at position i of σ iff φ holds at the next state q_{i+1}, $\square \varphi$ holds at position i iff φ holds at every position in σ starting at position i, and $\Diamond \varphi$ holds at position i iff φ holds at some position $j \geq i$ in σ.

2.3 Control strategy

Given a transition system TS and an LTL specification of the admissible environment behaviors and requirements on

---

[1]Here, state refers to a valuation of the variables the atomic proposition involves or is evaluated over; e.g., some $(q, e, u) \in Q \times \mathcal{A}_{uc} \times \mathcal{A}_c$ if one wants to reason about an element in an execution.

the system behavior, we aim to synthesize control protocols that, when implemented on the system, guarantee that the executions of the system satisfy the specification.

A *control strategy* for an open transition system TS is a partial function

$$f : (q_0, e_0, u_0, \cdots, q_{i-1}, e_{i-1}, u_{i-1}, q_i, e_i) \mapsto u_i,$$

such that $(q_i, e_i, u_i, q_{i+1}) \in R$ for all $i \geq 0$. A control strategy is said to be *memoryless* if f is a partial function $f : (q_i, e_i) \mapsto u_i$, for all $i \geq 0$.

Similarly, if the transition system TS is closed in the sense that all actions are controllable (i.e., $\mathcal{A}_{uc}$ is empty), a control strategy is given by

$$f : (q_0, u_0, \cdots, q_{i-1}, u_{i-1}, q_i) \mapsto u_i,$$

such that $(q_i, u_i, q_{i+1}) \in R$ for all $i \geq 0$. A memoryless control strategy is given by $f : q_i \mapsto u_i$, for all $i \geq 0$.

A *controlled execution* of a transition system TS is an execution of TS, where for each $i \geq 0$, u_i is chosen according to the control strategy f. Note that, in each step of a controlled execution, an uncontrollable action is followed by a controlled action, i.e., the control decision is made after the uncontrolled action is observed.

Synthesis Problem: Given a transition system TS and a temporal logic formula φ, compute a strategy f of the form $u_i = f(e_0, u_0, \cdots, e_{i-1}, u_{i-1}, q_i, e_i)$ such that any controlled execution of TS satisfies φ. If such a strategy exists, we call the tuple (TS, φ) to be *synthesizable*.

We use a simple example to illustrate the meaning of a control strategy for transition systems.

Example 1. Consider a finite transition system TS with $I = \{q_0\}$, $Q = \{q_0, q_1, q_2\}$, $\mathcal{A} = \{a, b\}$. The transition relation R is shown in Figure 1. We consider two memoryless

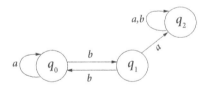

Figure 1: A finite transition system TS with three states $Q = \{q_0, q_1, q_2\}$ and two controllable actions $\mathcal{A} = \{a, b\}$.

control strategies. Let f_a be the memoryless control strategy that chooses action a for each $q \in Q$, and f_b be the memoryless control strategy that chooses action b for each $q \in Q$. We want the system state to always stay in $\{q_0\} \cup \{q_1\}$, i.e., satisfies the LTL specification $\varphi = \Box(q_0 \vee q_1)$. It is clear that, with either of the two strategies f_a or f_b, the controlled executions of TS satisfy φ.

More generally, if the transition system is an open system that has environment inputs, the corresponding control strategy provides a reactive control mechanism such that the controlled executions of the overall system satisfy certain assumption-guarantee type specification $\varphi_e \rightarrow \varphi_s$, as shown schematically in Figure 2 where φ_e and φ_s are LTL formulas. In other words, the control strategy should ensure correct behavior of the system (specified by φ_s) for all allowable behavior of the environment (specified by φ_e).

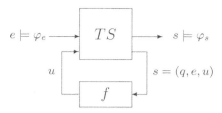

Figure 2: The interconnection of a finite transition system model TS and a control strategy f.

Before formulating the robust synthesis problem, we present a simple motivating example.

Example 2. With the transition system in Figure 1, we consider the case where such a model may not be an exact model of the plant to be controlled, e.g., there are possible unmodeled transitions. Let $\delta_1 = (q_0, a, q_1)$ be such an uncertain transition. With this uncertainty, the control strategy f_a can lead to executions that no longer satisfy the same specification $\varphi = \Box(q_0 \vee q_1)$, whereas the control strategy f_b still ensures the same specification is satisfied. As another case, adding the uncertain transition $\delta_2 = (q_1, b, q_2)$ will make the strategy f_b no longer ensure correct executions, whereas the strategy f_a still does so.

Example 2 shows that, due to different modeling uncertainties, we may prefer one control strategy over another. The goal of this paper is to synthesize robust control strategies that ensure correct behavior of the system under such modeling uncertainties. The problem will be formally stated in the next section.

3. PROBLEM FORMULATION

Most control design procedures are based on the use of a design model of the plant under control. Since no single fixed model can respond exactly like the true plant, one needs to account for the mismatch between the model and the plant in the design procedure. A common approach is to design controllers that are guaranteed to be correct when implemented not only on a design model but also on a family of models that contain the design model as the nominal representation of the plant behavior. We will call such controllers to be robust to modeling uncertainties.

The effectiveness of the design of robust controllers heavily relies on the extent as well as the representation of modeling uncertainties due to a number of factors including: (a) As the extent at which the modeling uncertainties are accounted for in the design procedure increases, the likelihood that the true plant behavior is covered increases. Hence, it is more likely that the resulting control protocol works when implemented on the true plant. On the other hand, increasing modeling uncertainty may increase the conservatism of the procedure. (b) The representation of uncertainties—coupled with that of the plant itself—will determine the technique which can be used for synthesis and its computational complexity. In general, synthesis of robust control protocols requires a computational cost higher than that for nominal control protocols and may even become intractable.

3.1 Robust synthesis problem

With the issues discussed earlier in this section, we now introduce the uncertainty model used in this paper. In the following, unless noted otherwise, we consider open transition systems and drop the adjective "open" for brevity. Consider an action-deterministic and non-blocking nominal transition system $TS = (Q, I, \mathcal{A}_{uc}, \mathcal{A}_c, R_{nom})$ and the set of transitions

$$\boldsymbol{\Delta} := \{(q, e, u, q') \in (Q \times \mathcal{A}_{uc} \times \mathcal{A}_c \times Q) \backslash R_{nom} :$$
$$\exists q'' \in Q \text{ s.t. } (q, e, u, q'') \in R_{nom}\}.$$

The set $\boldsymbol{\Delta}$, for each nominal transition (q, e, u, q') under the uncontrolled action e and controlled action u, includes all the possible transitions that can be taken from the state q excluding those already in R_{nom}.

Definition 3. Let an action-deterministic and non-blocking nominal transition system $TS = (Q, I, \mathcal{A}_{uc}, \mathcal{A}_c, R_{nom})$ and a subset Δ of $\boldsymbol{\Delta}$, associated with TS as defined above, be given. Then, an uncertain transition system (TS, Δ) is defined as

$$(TS, \Delta) := (Q, I, \mathcal{A}_{uc}, \mathcal{A}_c, R_{nom} \cup \Delta).$$

An execution of (TS, Δ) is a sequence

$$(q_0, e_0, u_0), (q_1, e_1, u_1), (q_2, e_2, u_2), \ldots$$

such that $q_0 \in I$ and $(q_i, e_i, u_i, q_{i+1}) \in R_{nom} \cup \Delta$ for all $i \geq 0$.

Then, the robust synthesis problem is as follows.

Robust Synthesis Problem: Given a nominal transition system TS, a set $\Delta \subseteq \boldsymbol{\Delta}$ of possible unmodeled transitions, and a temporal logic formula φ, compute a strategy f of the form $u_i = f(q_0, e_0, u_0, \cdots, q_{i-1}, e_{i-1}, u_{i-1}, q_i, e_i)$ such that any controlled execution of the uncertain transition system (TS, Δ) satisfies φ. If such a strategy exists, we call the tuple $((TS, \Delta), \varphi)$ to be *robustly synthesizable*.

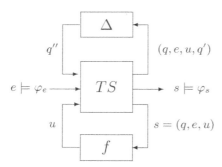

Figure 3: The interconnection of nominal plant model TS, the perturbations due to the unmodeled transitions in Δ, and the strategy f.

The resulting system structure is shown in Figure 3. The transition (q, e, u, q') to be taken by the system under the controlled action u and the uncontrolled, environment action e may be perturbed to a transition $(q, e, u, q'') \in \Delta$ (but not in R_{nom}). The robust strategy f picks the control action u so that the system interconnection between the nominal transition system TS perturbed by the possible unmodeled transitions, and the strategy satisfies an assumption-guarantee type specification $\varphi_e \to \varphi_s$. In each step of the controlled

execution of the uncertain transition system, an uncontrollable action is followed by a controlled action which, in turn, is followed by an "action" by Δ.

Remark 1. In this section and throughout the paper, the "action" due to the unmodeled transitions in Δ is not explicitly notated and it is implicitly accounted for as nondeterminism in the state space. On the other hand, if this action is denoted by δ, then each transition $(q, e, u, q') \in R_{nom} \cup \Delta$ can be considered as $(e, q) \xrightarrow{u} q'' \xrightarrow{\delta} q'$ for some $q'' \in Q$. As such the system in Figure 3 can be considered as a combination of the so-called Mealy $((e, q) \xrightarrow{u} q''$ part) and Moore $(q'' \xrightarrow{\delta} q'$ part) machines [6].

3.2 Assessing the level of robustness

In order to reason about the effects of different sets of unmodeled transitions, we consider a finite family $\mathcal{C}$ of subsets of $\boldsymbol{\Delta}$ and partial orders over $\mathcal{C}$ that formalize a notion for comparing the sets in $\mathcal{C}$.

Definition 4. Let P be a set. A partial order on P is a binary relation $\leq$ on P such that, for all $x, y, z \in P$, (i) $x \leq x$, (ii) $x \leq y$ and $y \leq x$ imply $x = y$, and (ii) $x \leq y$ and $y \leq z$ imply $x \leq z$. A set P equipped with a partial order relation $\leq$ is said to be a partially ordered set. We sometimes use the shorthand notation $(P, \leq)$ to denote that the set P is partially ordered with respect to the order relation $\leq$.

Now, assume that the partially ordered set $(\mathcal{C}, \leq)$ is equipped with a rank function $r : \mathcal{C} \to \mathbb{N}$ such that (a) $r(x) < r(y)$ whenever $x < y$, and (b) $r(y) = r(x) + 1$ whenever $y > x$ is an immediate neighbor of x. For $\alpha \in \mathbb{N}$, let $C_\alpha := \{\Delta \in \mathcal{C} : r(\Delta) = \alpha\}$.

A partial order on $\mathcal{C}$ may represent a qualitative preference over the sets of unmodeled transitions in $\mathcal{C}$. For example, in a robot motion planning problem, a designer may consider uncertainties in translation to be more critical than those in rotation and prefer those strategies that are robust to uncertainties in translation. Another natural choice as a partial order $\leq$ is defined through set inclusion $\subseteq$, that is, for $\Delta_1, \Delta_2 \in \mathcal{C}$, $\Delta_1 \leq \Delta_2$ if and only if $\Delta_1 \subseteq \Delta_2$. Partial orders induced by set inclusion will be of particular interest in the subsequent sections.

The representation of $\boldsymbol{\Delta}$ is explicitly parametrized in the state q and the actions e and u for simplicity. Under certain conditions, more compact representations of uncertainty may be available. Uncertain transitions may only depend on the controlled actions. For example, in a robot motion planning scenario, they may depend on which one of the translation and rotation motion primitives are applied rather than at what particular state they are applied. Furthermore, a partial order may be induced by a metric on the state space Q in cases where a notion of "closeness" in Q exists.

Example 3. Consider the example introduced in section 2 and the family $\mathcal{C}$ composed of the following sets of unmodeled transitions.

$$\Delta_0 = \{\}, \ \Delta_1 = \{(q_1, a, q_1)\}, \ \Delta_2 = \{(q_1, b, q_2)\},$$
$$\Delta_3 = \{(q_1, a, q_1), (q_1, b, q_2)\},$$
$$\Delta_4 = \{(q_1, a, q_1), (q_2, a, q_1)\}, \text{ and}$$
$$\Delta_5 = \{(q_2, a, q_1), (q_1, a, q_1), (q_1, b, q_2)\}.$$

A partial order $\leq$ on $\mathcal{C} = \{\Delta_0, \Delta_1, \ldots, \Delta_5\}$ induced by set inclusion is depicted in Figure 4. For example, $\Delta_3 \geq \Delta_2$

because $\Delta_2 \subseteq \Delta_3$. On the other hand, Δ_3 and Δ_4 cannot be distinguished by $\leq$.

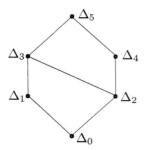

Figure 4: Graphical representation of $(\mathcal{C}, \leq)$ in Example 3.

Given a nominal plant model TS, a temporal logic specification φ, and a partially ordered set $(\mathcal{C}, \leq)$, define the maps $h : \mathcal{C} \to \{0, 1\}$ and $h_\forall : \mathbb{N} \to \{0, 1\}$ as

$$h(\Delta) := \begin{cases} 1, & \text{if } ((TS, \Delta), \varphi) \text{ is robustly synthesizable,} \\ 0, & \text{otherwise;} \end{cases}$$

$$h_\forall(\alpha) := \begin{cases} 1, & \text{if } h(\Delta) = 1 \text{ for all } \Delta \in C_\alpha, \\ 0, & \text{otherwise} \end{cases}$$

and consider the following optimization, which aims to assess the level (induced by the partial order $(\mathcal{C}, \leq)$) of robustness.

$$\text{maximize } \alpha \text{ subject to } h_\forall(\alpha) = 1 \qquad (1)$$

over $\alpha \in \mathbb{N}$. The problem in (1) computes the maximum α^* such that $((TS, \Delta), \varphi)$ is robustly synthesizable for all Δ with $r(\Delta) = \alpha^*$. This problem is relevant when the system operates under different modes associated with different types of uncertainties of varying levels and correct operation is desired in all these modes. Consider now a different scenario where the sets in $\mathcal{C}$ correspond to the unmodeled transitions in different modes of the system among which a selection is possible. For example, such modes may be due to the availability of a collection of different sensing or actuation equipment. In this case, the following optimization searches for a maximal uncertainty set Δ—and its rank in the partial order—for which $(TS, \Delta), \varphi$ is robustly synthesizable.

$$\text{maximize } \alpha \text{ subject to } h_\exists(\alpha) = 1 \qquad (2)$$

over $\alpha \in \mathbb{N}$. The problem in (2) computes the maximum rank α^* in the partial order such that $((TS, \Delta), \varphi)$ is robustly synthesizable for at least one Δ with $r(\Delta) = \alpha^*$.

Both problems (1) and (2) are optimizations over discrete sets and, as such, may require to check the robust synthesizability of $((TS, \Delta), \varphi)$ for all $\Delta \in \mathcal{C}$. Under certain conditions on the partial order, systematic search (which is faster than exhaustive search over $\mathcal{C}$) may be possible. We discuss one such case, where the partial order is induced from set inclusion, in section 4.3.

4. ROBUST DISCRETE SYNTHESIS

We now present the main results of the paper: reformulation of the robust synthesis problem as a temporal logic game, a polynomial complexity solution procedure for a fragment of LTL specifications, and methods for assessing the level of robustness as characterized by the optimizations in (1) and (2).

4.1 Game reformulation

One approach to the problem of synthesizing a control strategy for an open system is recasting the problem as an infinite horizon game (also known as infinite games [8, 15]). We first introduce the elements of such games and then apply to the robust synthesis problem.

In particular, we consider two-player turn-based games where, at each turn, a move by player 1 is followed by a move by player 2. Roughly speaking, we treat player 1 as an adversarial environment that tries to falsify the specification and player 2 as the system that tries to satisfy it. Formally, a game is defined as follows.

Definition 5. [4] A *game structure* is a tuple

$$G = \langle \mathcal{V}, \mathcal{X}, \mathcal{Y}, \theta_e, \theta_s, \rho_e, \rho_s, \phi \rangle,$$

where

- $\mathcal{V}$ is a finite set of *state variables*,

- $\mathcal{X} \subseteq \mathcal{V}$ is a set of *input variables*, i.e., variables controlled by player 1,

- $\mathcal{Y} = \mathcal{V} \setminus \mathcal{X}$ is the set of *output variables*, i.e., variables controlled by player 2,

- θ_e is an atomic proposition over $\mathcal{X}$ characterizing initial states of the input variables,

- θ_s is an atomic proposition over $\mathcal{Y}$ characterizing initial states of the output variables,

- $\rho_e(\mathcal{V}, \mathcal{X}')$ is the transition relation for player 1, which is an atomic proposition that relates a state and possible next input values (primed variables represent the value of a variable in the next step),

- $\rho_s(\mathcal{V}, \mathcal{X}', \mathcal{Y}')$ is the transition relation for player 2, which is an atomic proposition that relates a state and an input value to possible output values,

- ϕ is the winning condition given by an LTL formula over $\mathcal{V}$.

Valuations of the variables are denoted by lower case letters (e.g., $v \in dom(V)$ for $V \in \mathcal{V}$); and the valuations of the state variables $\mathcal{V}$ are called *states*. A *play* (i.e., a sequence of states) is said to be winning for player 2 if (i) either at a given state v in the sequence there is no $x' \in \mathcal{X}$ such that (v, x') satisfies ρ_e or (ii) the sequence is infinite and it satisfies ϕ. A *strategy* for player 2 is a partial function $f : (v_0, v_1, \ldots, v_{k-1}, x_k) \mapsto y_k$ which chooses a move of player 2 among its allowable moves based on the state sequence so far and the last move of player 1. Strategy f is said to be *winning* for player 2, if all plays starting from the initial states characterized by θ_e and θ_s, and compliant with f are winning. For LTL specifications, if there exists a winning strategy for player 2, it is known that there always exists a finite memory winning strategy [8].

Next, we discuss how synthesis problems and finding a winning strategy in a game are related. Consider an open nominal transition system $TS = (Q, I, \mathcal{A}_{uc}, \mathcal{A}_c, R_{nom})$ and an LTL specification φ. Define the game structure $G_o(TS)$

with the following elements:

$$\mathcal{X} = Q \times \mathcal{A}_{uc},$$
$$\mathcal{Y} = \mathcal{A}_c,$$
$$\theta_e = \{(q, e) \ : \ q \in I \text{ and } \exists u, q' \text{ s.t. } (q, e, u, q') \in R_{nom}\},$$
$$\theta_s = \{(q, e, u) \ : \ q \in I \text{ and } \exists q' \text{ s.t. } (q, e, u, q') \in R_{nom}\},$$
$$\rho_e = \{(q, e, u, q', e') \ : \ (q, e, u, q') \in R_{nom} \text{ and }$$
$$\exists u', q'' \text{ s.t. } (q', e', u', q'') \in R_{nom}\},$$
$$\rho_s = \{(q, e, u, q', e', u') \ : \ (q, e, u, q') \in R_{nom} \text{ and }$$
$$\exists q'' \text{ s.t. } (q', e', u', q'') \in R_{nom}\},$$
$$\phi = \varphi,$$

where, by slight abuse of notation, θ_α, ρ_α for $\alpha = \{e, s\}$ are given as sets but they should be understood as the indicator functions of the corresponding sets. Given an uncertainty set Δ, the game structure $G_o((TS, \Delta))$ is defined similarly by replacing R_{nom} with $R_{nom} \cup \Delta$ in the above formulation associating the elements of the game structure with those of the transition system.

Proposition 1. $((TS, \Delta), \varphi)$ is robustly synthesizable if and only if there exists a winning strategy for player 2 in game $G_o((TS, \Delta))$.

Note that, by construction, there is a one-to-one correspondence between the plays of the game $G_o((TS, \Delta))$ and the executions of the transition system (TS, Δ). Since we assume that TS is non-blocking, so is (TS, Δ). Hence all executions of (TS, Δ) and all plays of the game will be infinite sequences which implies a play winning for player 2 should satisfy ϕ (equivalently, φ). Therefore, Proposition 1 follows from the definitions of winning strategies for the games and synthesizability of control strategies for transition systems.

The relation between the game structures and synthesis problems is quite generally applicable (see [4] for more details). For example, the nominal synthesis problem for an open transition system can be solved through $G_o(TS)$. Furthermore, for a nominal closed transition system $TS = (Q, I, \mathcal{A}, R_{nom})$, a robust control strategy can be computed through a slight modification, namely by redefining

$$\mathcal{X} = Q, \ \mathcal{Y} = \mathcal{A}_c, \ \phi = \varphi, \ \theta_e = I,$$
$$\theta_s = \{(q, u) \ : \ q \in I \text{ and } \exists q' \text{ s.t. } (q, u, q') \in R_{nom} \cup \Delta\},$$
$$\rho_e = \{(q, u, q') \ : \ (q, u, q') \in R_{nom} \cup \Delta \text{ and }$$
$$\exists u', q'' \text{ s.t. } (q', u', q'') \in R_{nom} \cup \Delta\},$$
$$\rho_s = \{(q, u, q', u') \ : \ (q, u, q') \in R_{nom} \cup \Delta \text{ and }$$
$$\exists q'' \text{ s.t. } (q', u', q'') \in R_{nom} \cup \Delta\}.$$

In summary, the two-player temporal logic game formulation provides a flexible framework to solve the (robust and nominal) synthesis questions discussed in this paper.

Remark 2. The nominal synthesis problem for a closed transition system fits the temporal logic game framework. On the other hand, this problem can also be recast (and can be more efficiently solved) as a model checking question.

4.2 Polynomial-complexity solutions

Solving the two-player game discussed in section 4.1, i.e., checking which one of the system and environment wins and, if the system can win, extracting a control strategy, is known to have 2EXPTIME complexity for general LTL specifications φ [18]. On the other hand, recent advances mostly exploiting the observation, that "typical" specifications in practice have a structure that can be algorithmically exploited [7], have focused on relatively expressive fragments

of LTL. For example, if the winning condition is one of the LTL formulas $\Box p$, $\Diamond q$, $\Box \Diamond p$, or $\Diamond \Box q$, where p and q are atomic propositions, then the computational cost of solving the corresponding game is quadratic in the number possible valuations of the pairs $(x, y) \in \mathcal{X} \times \mathcal{Y}$.

A quite more expressive winning condition for which there are polynomial complexity algorithms is the so-called generalized reactivity [1] (GR[1]) specifications, i.e., formulas of the form [4]

$$\varphi_e \to \varphi_s,$$

where for $\beta \in \{e, s\}$,

$$\varphi_\beta = \bigwedge_{i \in I_\beta} \Box \sigma_i^\beta \wedge \bigwedge_{j \in J_\beta} \Box \Diamond \pi_j^\beta$$

with the finite set of indices I_e, J_e, I_s, and J_s and propositional logic formulas σ_i^e, π_j^e, σ_i^s, and σ_j^s. Here, σ_i^e and π_j^e describe the safety and liveness assumptions on the environment. Similarly, σ_i^s and σ_j^s describe the safety and liveness guarantees on the system behavior, respectively. The computational cost of solving GR[1] games is $O(N^3 |J_e||J_s|)$ where $|\cdot|$ indicates the cardinality of the respective sets and N is the number of possible valuations of the pair $(x, y) \in \mathcal{X} \times \mathcal{Y}$. Moreover, there exists computational tools that leverage this polynomial complexity bound, e.g., the digital design synthesis tool in the JTLV framework [19]. This tool has been used for applications including correct-by-construction synthesis of control protocols for autonomous navigation [21] and design of bus arbiter [10].

We now establish that robustification of the synthesis problem as discussed in the previous sections preserves the GR[1] property, i.e., if the nominal problem can be solved as a GR[1] game, then the robust synthesis problem can be solved as a GR[1] game as well. To this end, for a nominal transition system $TS = (Q, I, \mathcal{A}_{uc}, \mathcal{A}_c, R_{nom})$ and an uncertainty set Δ, define

$$B_{(q,e,u)}^\Delta := \{q' \in Q \ : \ (q, e, u, q') \in R_{nom} \cup \Delta\}.$$

Proposition 2. Let φ be a GR[1] specification. Then, the robust synthesizability of $((TS, \Delta), \varphi)$ can be solved as a GR[1] game.

Proof: Observe that the winning condition for the robust synthesis problem can be written as

$$\left\{ \bigwedge_{(\tilde{q}, \tilde{e}, \tilde{u})} \Box \left[(q = \tilde{q} \wedge e = \tilde{e} \wedge u = \tilde{u}) \to (q' \in B_{(\tilde{q}, \tilde{e}, \tilde{u})}^\Delta) \right] \right\} \to \varphi. \quad (3)$$

If φ is a GR[1] formula, then that in (3) is also a GR[1] formula and the result follows. $\square$

By Proposition 2 and the definition of the two-player game in section 4.1, the worst-case computational complexity of the robustified GR[1] synthesis problem is cubic in the number of possible valuations of $(x, y) \in \mathcal{X} \times \mathcal{Y}$; hence, its complexity class is the same as the nominal synthesis problem. Note that the numbers $|J_e|$ and $|J_s|$ are not affected by robustification.

4.3 Algorithms for assessing the level of robustness

We now revisit the optimization problems formulated in section 3.2. We discuss procedures for computing upper and lower bound on their optimal values and for systematic reduction of the gap between these bounds.

Note that both problems, in general, involve search over a finite, discrete $\mathcal{C}$. As such they can be solved with a worst-case computational cost that is linear in the cardinality of $\mathcal{C}$, i.e., evaluate $h(\Delta)$ for each $\Delta \in \mathcal{C}$. Yet, each evaluation of h requires solving a robust synthesis problem and is computationally demanding. Hence, it is desirable to limit the number of evaluations of h. To this end, we now discuss a bisection-type procedure for partially ordered sets $(\mathcal{C}, \leq)$ which satisfies the following monotonicity condition.

Monotonicity condition: For each $\Delta_1, \Delta_2 \in \mathcal{C}$ such that $\Delta_1 \geq \Delta_2$, it holds that $h(\Delta_1) \leq h(\Delta_2)$.

That is, for given nominal transition system TS and specification φ, if $((TS, \Delta_1), \varphi)$ is robustly synthesizable for some $\Delta_1 \in \mathcal{C}$ (i.e., $h(\Delta_1) = 1$), the $((TS, \Delta_2), \varphi)$ is robustly synthesizable for every $\Delta_2 \in \mathcal{C}$ such that $\Delta_2 \leq \Delta_1$.

Proposition 3. Let $\mathcal{C}$ be a finite family of subsets of $\boldsymbol{\Delta}$ and let $\leq$ be a partial order induced from set inclusion. Then, $(\mathcal{C}, \leq)$ satisfies the monotonicity condition.

Let $\Delta_1, \Delta_2 \in \mathcal{C}$ be such that $\Delta_1 \geq \Delta_2$. The proof of Proposition 3 relies on the fact that the robust synthesizability of $((TS, \Delta_1), \varphi)$ does not only imply robust synthesizability of $((TS, \Delta_2), \varphi)$, but also the control strategy of the former is a control strategy for the other.

For partially ordered set $(\mathcal{C}, \leq)$ that satisfies the monotonicity condition, the bisection-type algorithm in Figure 5 can be used to compute upper and lower bounds on the optimal value of the optimization in (1). In Figure 5 and hereafter, for a real number a, $\lfloor a \rfloor$ denotes the largest integer smaller than or equal to a. A number of remarks about this algorithm is in order. First, it exploits the monotonicity condition: If $h_\forall(\tilde{\alpha})$ is evaluated to be 1 for some $\tilde{\alpha}$, then it must be equal to 1 for all $\alpha \leq \tilde{\alpha}$ and, therefore, the sets in $\mathcal{C}$ with $r(\Delta) < \tilde{\alpha}$ can be disregarded in the search for a solution for the optimization in (1) and $\tilde{\alpha}$ is a lower bound. Similarly, if $h_\forall(\tilde{\alpha}) = 0$ for some $\tilde{\alpha}$, then $h_\forall(\Delta) = 0$ for all $\alpha \leq \tilde{\alpha}$ and, therefore, the sets in $\mathcal{C}$ with $r(\Delta) > \tilde{\alpha}$ can be disregarded and $\tilde{\alpha}$ is an upper bound on the optimal value. Second, assuming that the empty set is in $\mathcal{C}$ and (TS, φ) is nominally synthesizable, the algorithm maintains a lower bound b_l and an upper bound b_u at each iteration. Hence, at any iteration the algorithm is terminated, it returns a value of $\alpha = b_l$ such that $((TS, \Delta), \varphi)$ is robustly synthesizable for all $\Delta \in \mathcal{C}_\alpha$ and a measure of suboptimality, i.e., $b_u - b_l$. This measure of suboptimality is reduced, roughly, by half, in each iteration.

The algorithm in Figure 5 can be adapted for the optimization in (2) by replacing $h_\forall$ in line 5 to $h_\exists$. The main difference between the two algorithms is the potential number of evaluations of h in line 5. Each evaluation of $h_\forall(\alpha)$ to 1 requires solving as many robust synthesis problems as the cardinality of $\mathcal{C}_\alpha$ whereas it is enough to find a single $\Delta \in \mathcal{C}_\alpha$ to conclude that $h_\forall(\alpha) = 0$. On the other hand, finding a single $\Delta \in \mathcal{C}_\alpha$ to conclude that $h_\exists(\alpha) = 0$.

Remark 3. Note that while running the algorithm in Figure 5, the monotonicity condition provides a means to prune the search space which, in turn, potentially reduces the number of synthesizability checks required during the search. However, the worst-case complexity in general remains the same.

Given: nominal transition system TS, partially ordered set $(\mathcal{C}, \leq)$, upper and lower bounds b_l and b_u with $b_l < b_u$, tolerance TOL, and maximum number $N_{max} \geq 1$ of iterations.
Output: Upper and lower bounds b_l and b_u such that $b_u - b_l < TOL$ or their values at iteration N_{max}.

1. $N \leftarrow 1$
2. while $N \leq N_{max}$
3.   while $b_u - b_l \geq TOL$
4. $\alpha \leftarrow \lfloor (b_l + b_u)/2 \rfloor$
5.   if $h_\forall(\alpha) = 1$ then $b_l \leftarrow \alpha$
6.   else $b_u \leftarrow \alpha$
7. $N \leftarrow N + 1$

Figure 5: Bisection-type algorithm for the optimization in (1).

The problems in (1) and (2) provide means for quantifying the level of robust synthesizability of (TS, φ) with respect to the unmodeled transitions captured by $(\mathcal{C}, \leq)$. Another way of such quantification would be determining a "maximal uncertainty set" $\Delta \in \mathcal{C}$ such that $((TS, \Delta), \varphi)$ is robustly synthesizable. We now formalize this notion and discuss, through an example, why it may not be a suitable way of quantification in general.

Definition 6. Given a nominal transition system TS, an LTL specification φ, and a partially ordered set $(\mathcal{C}, \leq)$ of unmodeled transitions where $\leq$ is induced from set inclusion, a *maximal uncertainty set* Δ_{max} is one such that $((TS, \Delta_{max}), \varphi)$ is robustly synthesizable and $(TS, \Delta), \varphi)$ is not robustly synthesizable for any $\Delta \geq \Delta_{max}$.

Fact: Maximal uncertainty set Δ_{max} (as defined in Definition 6) may not be unique in general.

Indeed, consider the setup in Example 2. Note that both $((TS, \{\delta_1\}), \varphi)$ and $((TS, \{\delta_2\}), \varphi)$ robustly synthesizable. On the other hand, it can be shown that $((TS, \{\delta_1, \delta_2\}), \varphi)$ is not robustly synthesizable. Let now $\tilde{\Delta} \in \mathcal{C}$ be such that $\tilde{\Delta} \geq \{\delta_1\}$, $\tilde{\Delta} \geq \{\delta_2\}$, and $((TS, \tilde{\Delta}, \varphi)$ is robustly synthesizable. Then, the fact that $\tilde{\Delta} \geq \{\delta_1, \delta_2\}$ leads to a contradiction by Proposition 3. Therefore, such a set $\tilde{\Delta}$ cannot exist and $\{\delta_1\}$ and $\{\delta_2\}$ are either maximal uncertainty sets or contained in two different maximal uncertainty sets. Note that the counterexample, which demonstrated the non-uniqueness of maximal uncertainty sets, discussed here is a safety formula and that it is possible to construct counterexamples that include liveness formulas.

Finally, note that the maximal uncertainty set Δ—among all the maximal uncertainty sets—with the highest rank solves the optimization in (2).

5. EXAMPLE

We demonstrate the robust discrete synthesis framework presented in the previous sections on a simple robot motion planning scenario. Consider a mobile robot in a 2D plane.

Nominal transition system: We start with a nominal transition system TS with three different controlled actions, $\mathcal{A}_c = \{L, R, S\}$, which correspond to `turn_left`, `turn_right`, and `go_straight`, respectively. Let $q = (x, y, \theta)$ be a tuple, where x, y are the coordinates of the robot in an $N \times N$ grid of cells and θ is the heading angle. The nominal transitions of TS are given by the following equations.

- Action $= L$: $x' = x$, $y' = y$, $\theta' = \theta + \frac{\pi}{2}$,
- Action $= R$: $x' = x$, $y' = y$, $\theta' = \theta - \frac{\pi}{2}$,
- Action $= S$: $x' = x + \cos(\theta)$, $y' = y + \sin(\theta)$, $\theta' = \theta$,

where $q' = (x', y', \theta')$ is the valuation of (x, y, θ) at the next time step under a given transition. The transition system TS can be obtained by an abstraction of the underlying dynamics of the mobile robot. In the nominal case, we require that, following a turning action L or R, the robot completes a corresponding 90-degree turn and remains in the same cell, whereas the robot moves forward by 1 cell following an S action. Note that θ only takes value in integer multiples of $\pi/2$ modulo 2π, and (x, y) only nonnegative integers in $[0, N-1]$. We introduce an additional boolean state Out to indicate when the location of the robot (x, y) goes out the $N \times N$ grid.

Specifications: Depicted in Figure 6, the desired properties for the robot to satisfy are specified as follows:

(S1) Always remain inside of the $N \times N$ region.

(S2) Visit each of the red cells, labeled as P_1, P_2, and P_3, infinitely often.

(S3) Eventually go to the blue cell P_0 after a PARK signal is received.

Here, the PARK signal is an environment variable that constrains the behavior of the robot. The following assumption is made on the PARK signal.

(A1) Infinitely often, a PARK signal is not received.

We use the positive integer n to indicate the size of the target sets P_i, $i = 1, 2, 3, 4$.

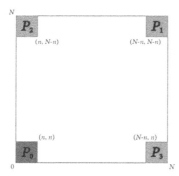

Figure 6: The robot should visit P_1, P_2, and P_3 infinitely often, and eventually go to P_0 after receiving a PARK signal.

Uncertain transition system: Furthermore, to demonstrate our robust discrete synthesis framework, we introduce unmodeled transitions following both the turning actions $\{L, R\}$ and the action $\{S\}$. These transitions are given by the following equations.

- Action $= L$:
$$\begin{bmatrix} x' \\ y' \\ \theta' \end{bmatrix} = \begin{bmatrix} x + \delta_x \sqrt{2}\cos(\theta + \pi/4) \\ y + \delta_y \sqrt{2}\sin(\theta + \pi/4) \\ \theta + \frac{\pi}{2} \end{bmatrix}, \; \delta_x, \delta_y \in [0, \delta_1].$$

- Action $= R$:
$$\begin{bmatrix} x' \\ y' \\ \theta' \end{bmatrix} = \begin{bmatrix} x + \delta_x \sqrt{2}\cos(\theta - \pi/4) \\ y + \delta_y \sqrt{2}\sin(\theta - \pi/4) \\ \theta - \frac{\pi}{2} \end{bmatrix}, \; \delta_x, \delta_y \in [0, \delta_1].$$

- Action $= S$:
$$\begin{bmatrix} x' \\ y' \\ \theta' \end{bmatrix} = \begin{bmatrix} x + (\delta_x + 1)\cos(\theta) \\ y + (\delta_y + 1)\sin(\theta) \\ \theta \end{bmatrix}, \; \delta_x, \delta_y \in [0, \delta_2].$$

Here, δ_1 and δ_2 are nonnegative integers used to indicate different levels of uncertainties, and hence demonstrate different levels of robustness of a control strategy. The nominal transitions are given by letting $\delta_1 = \delta_2 = 0$. Note that, again, θ only takes value in integer multiples of $\pi/2$, and (x, y) only nonnegative integers. We keep the same additional state Out to indicate when the location of the robot (x, y) goes out the $N \times N$ grid.

Assessing the level of robustness: Different values of δ_1 and δ_2 introduce different number of uncertain transitions, which can be used to demonstrate different levels of robustness of a control strategy. Let R_{nom} denote the set of nominal transitions. Define $\Delta_{i,j}$ to be the set of uncertain transitions introduced by choosing $\delta_1 = i$ and $\delta_2 = j$, where $0 \le i, j \le 10$, excluding the nominal transitions R_{nom}. Let $\mathcal{C} = \{\Delta_{i,j} : 0 \le i, j \le 10\} \subset \mathbf{\Delta}$. We choose the partial order to be the one induced by set inclusion and define a natural rank function $r : \mathcal{C} \to \mathbb{N}$ to be $r(\Delta_{i,j}) = i + j$. Figure 7 gives a graphical representation of $(\mathcal{C}, \le)$ and the rank function r, which shows a few sets of uncertainties at different levels.

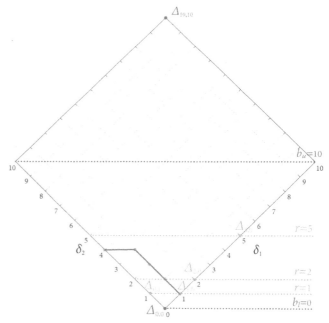

Figure 7: Graphical representation of $(\mathcal{C}, \le)$. The Δ_{ij}'s show the the uncertainty sets checked in a bisection-type algorithm to solve the optimization problem (1) with $n = 5$. The dashed lines show relevant levels of robustness assessed. The maximal uncertainty sets are connected by thick blue lines, which bound the region of robust synthesizability for $n = 5$.

Results: Following the results in Section 4, the robust synthesis problem can be reformulated as a temporal logic game with GR[1] specifications. We then apply the Temporal Logic Planning (TuLiP) Toolbox, a Python-based code suite for automatic synthesis of correct-by-construction embedded control software [23] to solve such games. TuLiP provides an interface to the JTLV framework.

For illustration, we choose $n = 5$ and consider the optimization problem given by (1). We use a bisection-type algorithm as introduced in Section 4.3 to solve the problem. Starting with $b_l = 0$ and $b_u = 10$, we check whether $h_\forall(\alpha) = 1$ for $\alpha = \lfloor (b_l + b_u)/2 \rfloor = 5$. It is found that $(TS, \Delta_{5,0})$ is not synthesizable. Therefore, $h_\forall(5) = 0$. We update $b_u = 5$. Next, we check if $h_\forall(\alpha) = 1$ holds for $\alpha = 2$. It is found that $(TS, \Delta_{2,0})$ is not synthesizable. We update $b_u = 2$. We then check if $h_\forall(1) = 1$ holds for $\alpha = 1$. It is found that both $(TS, \Delta_{1,0})$ and $(TS, \Delta_{0,1})$ are synthesizable. Therefore, $h_\forall(1) = 1$. The optimal solution for (1) is $\alpha^* = 1$. A similar bisection-type algorithm can be applied to solve the problem (2). In this case, $\alpha^* = 4$, with both $(TS, \Delta_{1,3})$ both $(TS, \Delta_{0,4})$ synthesizable. The procedure is illustrated in Figure 7. Moreover, by using a depth-first search on the graph representing the partial order on $\mathcal{C}$, we can plot all the maximal uncertainty sets for $n = 5$ (not unique as discussed earlier in Section 4.3) as shown in Figure 7.

Note that the solution for the optimization problem (1) is given by the maximum level α such that the level set $\mathcal{C}_\alpha$ is totally contained in the region of robust synthesizability, whereas the solution for the optimization problem (2) is given by the maximum level α such that the level set $\mathcal{C}_\alpha$ has nonempty intersection with this region.

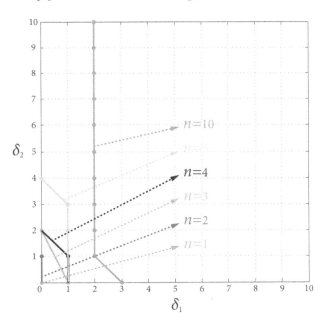

Figure 8: Robustness-performance tradeoff: the colored thick lines mark the exact regions of robust synthesizability for different n. As n increases (i.e., performance degrades), the region of robust synthesizability grows.

Robustness-performance tradeoff: By plotting the maximal uncertainty sets for different n, we can show certain tradeoffs between robustness and performance. As mentioned earlier, the size of the target sets can be seen as a performance indicator of the control strategy. With $n = 1$, only the nominal system is synthesizable. For r changing from 2 to 5, control strategies with increasing levels of robustness with respect to uncertainties can be synthesized. When $n = 10$, the specification reduces to a pure safety constraint $(S1)$. It is shown that for $\delta_1 \leq 2$, there exists a control strategy which only uses the turning actions to achieve safety. For $\delta_1 = 3$, such strategies no longer exist. A control strategy relying the action S can be found if the action S is deterministic. The results are depicted in Figure 8. As n increases (i.e., performance degrades), the exact region of robust synthesizability as bounded by the maximal uncertainty sets grows, which clearly shows a tradeoff between robustness and performance.

6. CRITIQUE

We now discuss some of the limitations and potential extensions of the preliminary results on robustness of discrete control protocols presented in this paper.

Uncertainty representation: The uncertainty representation as captured by the set Δ explicitly enumerates unmodeled transitions from each state for every controlled and uncontrolled action possible at that state. As mentioned before and used in the presentation of the example in section 5, unmodeled transitions can be represented more compactly. For example, they may only depend on the controlled actions in the case where the controlled actions are chosen from a finite family control/motion primitives. Moreover, if there exists a metric-type function defined over the state space Q, it may be possible to compactly characterize uncertainty sets as sublevel sets of these functions. More specifically, consider the set $B_{(q,e,u)}$ defined in the proof of Proposition 2 and let $d : Q \times Q \to \mathbb{R}$ be a metric. Then, a compact representation of $B^\Delta_{(q,e,u)}$ as defined in section 4.2 may be of the form $\{q' : d(d, q') \leq \gamma\}$ for some $\gamma \geq 0$. Reference [13] uses a metric-based representation of uncertainty. However, the question in [13] is one of sensitivity rather than robustness and no constructive procedure for the synthesis of reactive control protocols was presented.

We emphasize that it is not straightforward to exploit this compactness in representation toward computational complexity reduction in synthesis. For example, the augmented GR[1] specification in (3) is based on explicit listing of all unmodeled transitions. Therefore, uncertainty models that can be exploited in the symbolic manipulations and fixed point iterations [16] of the underlying game solver are needed.

Other uncertainty models: The uncertainty model used here captures the transitions not modeled in the nominal system. These uncertainties, for example, may be due to inaccuracies in actuation. An enabling factor that has been exploited in the paper is that even though these uncertainties introduce uncontrolled actions, the impact of these actions can be sensed after the action is taken and before the next environment observation is made. Further work is needed in order to relax this assumption and also to account for the effects of sensing inaccuracies on the synthesis of discrete control protocols.

Game formulation of robust synthesis: We modeled effects of unmodeled transitions as a new uncontrolled input (in addition to environment in the case of open transition systems) that acts after the environment is observed and controlled action is taken. This modeling choice enabled us to straightforwardly extend the two-player game approach in a way that the two types of uncontrolled actions, the environment and the unmodeled transitions, are treated identically. A deeper understanding of the differences between the two types of uncontrolled actions and exploitation toward reductions in computation complexity are needed.

Other robustness questions: We investigated the robustness of the reactive control protocols to the uncertainties to unmodeled transitions. Investigation of the robustness properties to other types of inaccuracies is subject to current research. For example, the resulting control protocol is guaranteed to be correct with respect to the specification $\varphi_e \to \varphi_s$ as long as the environment does not violate φ_e. Otherwise, no guarantees can be established (because $\varphi_e \to \varphi_s$ holds trivially). Design of controllers that not only react to the modeled behaviors of the environment but also tolerate those that violate the assumptions is desirable. More specifically. If $\varphi_e \to \varphi_s$ is realizable, what is the "least-restrictive" assumption φ_e' such that $\varphi_e' \to \varphi_s$ is realizable and $\varphi_e \to \varphi_e'$ holds?

Assessing the level of robustness: We introduced graded partial orders over the family of uncertainty sets as a means to capture the level of robustness a system possesses and also to encode the preference/intent of the designer. In particular, partial orders for which a monotonicity condition holds, we proposed a systematic search for the solutions of the problems in (1) and (2). Effects of different choices of partial orders on the search process and optimal solutions of (1) and (2) are of particular interest. Moreover, often the discrete control protocols are utilized in higher level of hierarchical control structures where the lower levels correspond to continuous evolution controlled by continuous controllers. Therefore, it may be possible to induce metrics from the underlying continuous state space.

In robust control theory, there are quantifiable notions to establish robustness and performance tradeoffs. The example in section 5 demonstrates a similar tradeoff in the context of discrete control protocols where the performance is interpreted as the level of "relaxation" in the liveness part of the specification (until practically reducing to a safety property). Further work is needed for systematically establishing robustness and performance tradeoff in this context.

7. CONCLUSIONS

We studied the robustness of reactive control protocols synthesized to guarantee system's correctness with respect to given temporal logic specifications. Specifically, we investigated the effects of unmodeled transitions on (open) finite transition systems. We formulated the robust synthesis problem as a temporal logic game and showed that robustification preserves attracting worst-case computational complexity bounds for a fragment of linear temporal logic specifications. Finally, we discussed preliminary results on the assessment of the effects of different levels of uncertainties on robust synthesizability.

8. REFERENCES

[1] R. Alur and S. La Torre. Deterministic generators and games for LTL fragments. *ACM Trans. Comput. Logic*, 5(1):1–25, 2004.

[2] C. Belta, A. Bicchi, M. Egerstedt, E. Frazzoli, E. Klavins, and G. J. Pappas. Symbolic planning and control of robot motion: State of the art and grand challenges. *Robotics and Automation Magazine*, 14(1):61–70, 2007.

[3] R. Bloem, K. Greimel, T. A. Henzinger, and B. Jobstmann. Synthesizing robust systems. In *Formal Methods in Computer Aided Design*, 2009.

[4] R. Bloem, B. Jobstmann, N. Piterman, A. Pnueli, and Y. Saar. Synthesis of reactive (1) designs. *Journal of Computer and System Sciences, to appear*, 2011.

[5] E. M. Clarke, O. Grumberg, and D. A. Peled. *Model Checking*. The MIT Press, 1999.

[6] D. I. A. Cohen. *Introduction to Computer Theory*. Wiley, 1997.

[7] R. Ehlers. Experimental aspects of synthesis. In *Proc. of Workshop on Interactions, Games and Protocols*, 2011. Available at http://arxiv.org/pdf/1102.4117.

[8] E. Grädel, W. Thomas, and T. Wilke, editors. *Automata, Logics, and Infinite Games: A Guide to Current Research*, volume 2500 of *Lecture Notes in Computer Science*. Springer, 2002.

[9] T. A. Henzinger. Two challenges in embedded systems design: predictability and robustness. *Philosophical Transactions of the Royal Society - Series A: Mathematical, Physical and Engineering Sciences*, 366(1881):3727–3736, 2008.

[10] B. Jobstmann, S. Galler, M. Weiglhofer, and R. Bloem. Anzu: A Tool for Property Synthesis. In *Computer Aided Verification*, pages 258–262, 2007.

[11] M. Kloetzer and C. Belta. A fully automated framework for control of linear systems from temporal logic specifications. *IEEE Trans. on Automatic Control*, 53(1):287–297, 2008.

[12] H. Kress-Gazit, T. Wongpiromsarn, and U. Topcu. Correct, reactive robot control from abstraction and temporal logic specifications. *Robotics and Automation Magazine*, 18(3):65–74, 2011.

[13] R. Majumdar, E. Render, and P. Tabuada. Robust discrete synthesis against unspecified disturbances. In *Proc. Hybrid Systems: Computation and Control*, pages 211–220, 2011.

[14] Z. Manna and A. Pnueli. *The temporal logic of reactive and concurrent systems*. Springer-Verlag, 1992.

[15] D. Perrin and J.-E. Pin. *Infinite Words: Automata, Semigroups, Logic and Games*, volume 141 of *Pure and Applied Mathematics*. Elsevier, 2004.

[16] N. Piterman, A. Pnueli, and Y. Sa'ar. Synthesis of reactive(1) designs. In *Verification, Model Checking and Abstract Interpretation*, volume 3855 of *Lecture Notes in Computer Science*, pages 364 – 380. Springer-Verlag, 2006.

[17] A. Pnueli. The temporal logic of programs. In *Proc. of the 18th Annual Symposium on the Foundations of Computer Science*, pages 46–57. IEEE, 1977.

[18] A. Pnueli and R. Rosner. On the Synthesis of an Asynchronous Reactive Module. In *Proc. of Colloquium on Automata, Languages and Programming*, pages 652–671. Springer-Verlag, 1989.

[19] A. Pnueli, Y. Sa'ar, and L. Zuck. JTLV: A framework for developing verification algorithms. In *Proc. of Conference on Computer Aided Verification*, volume 6174, pages 171–174, 2010.

[20] D. C. Tarraf, A. Megretski, and M. A. Dahleh. A framework for robust stability of systems over finite alphabets. *IEEE Transactions on Automatic Control*, 53:1133–1146, 2008.

[21] T. Wongpiromsarn, U. Topcu, and R. M. Murray. Receding horizon control for temporal logic specifications. In *Proc. of Conf. on Hybrid Systems: Computation and Control*, 2010.

[22] T. Wongpiromsarn, U. Topcu, and R. M. Murray. Formal synthesis of embedded control software for vehicle management systems. In *Proc. AIAA Infotech@Aerospace*, 2011.

[23] T. Wongpiromsarn, U. Topcu, N. Ozay, H. Xu, and R. Murray. TuLiP: a software toolbox for receding horizon temporal logic planning. In *Proc. of Conference on Hybrid Systems: Computation and Control*, pages 313–314, 2011.

Language-Guided Controller Synthesis
for Discrete-Time Linear Systems

Ebru Aydin Gol
Boston University
Boston, MA 02215, USA
ebru@bu.edu

Mircea Lazar
Eindhoven University of
Technology
Den Dolech 2, 5600MB,
Eindhoven, The Netherlands.
m.lazar@tue.nl

Calin Belta
Boston University
Boston, MA 02215, USA
cbelta@bu.edu

ABSTRACT

This paper considers the problem of controlling discrete-time linear systems from specifications given as formulas of syntactically co-safe linear temporal logic over linear predicates in the state variables of the system. A systematic procedure is developed for the automatic computation of sets of initial states and feedback controllers such that all the resulting trajectories of the corresponding closed-loop system satisfy the given specifications. The procedure is based on the iterative construction and refinement of an automaton that enforces the satisfaction of the formula. Interpolation and polyhedral Lyapunov function based approaches are proposed to compute the polytope-to-polytope controllers that label the transitions of the automaton. The algorithms developed in this paper were implemented as a software package that is available for download. Their application and effectiveness are demonstrated for two challenging case studies.

Categories and Subject Descriptors

I.2.8 [**Artificial Intelligence**]: Problem Solving, Control Methods, and Search—*Control theory*; D.2.4 [**Software Engineering**]: Software/Program Verification—*Formal methods*

Keywords

Linear temporal logic, Automata theory, Constrained control, Polytope-to-polytope control, Polyhedral Lyapunov functions

1. INTRODUCTION

Temporal logics, such as linear temporal logic (LTL) and computation tree logic (CTL), and model checking algorithms [1] have been primarily used for specifying and verifying the correctness of software and hardware systems. In recent years, due to their expressivity and resemblance to natural language, temporal logics have gained increasing popularity as specification languages in other areas such as dynamical systems [2–6], biology [7–9], and robotics [10–14]. These new application areas also have emphasized the need for formal synthesis, where the goal is to generate a

HSCC'12, April 17–19, 2012, Beijing, China.
Copyright 2012 ACM 978-1-4503-1220-2/12/04 ...$10.00.

control strategy for a dynamical system from a specification given as a temporal logic formula. Recent efforts resulted in control algorithms for continuous and discrete-time linear systems from specifications given as LTL formulas [3, 6], motion planning and control strategies for robotic systems from specifications given in μ-calculus [11], CTL [12], LTL [13], and fragments of LTL such as GR(1) [5, 10] and syntactically co-safe LTL [14].

In this paper, we consider the following problem: given a discrete-time linear system and a syntactically co-safe LTL formula [15] over linear predicates in the states of the system, find a set of initial states, if possible, the largest, for which there exists a control strategy such that all the trajectories of the closed-loop system satisfy the formula. The syntactically co-safe fragment of LTL is rich enough to express a wide spectrum of finite-time properties of dynamical systems, such as finite-time reachability of a target with obstacle avoidance ("go to A and avoid B and C for all times before reaching A"), enabling conditions ("do not go to D unless E was visited before"), and temporal logic combinations of the above. For example, the syntactically co-safe LTL formula "$(\neg O \; \mathcal{U} \; T) \wedge (\neg T \; \mathcal{U} \; (R_1 \vee R_2))$" requires convergence to target region T through regions R_1 or R_2 while avoiding obstacle O.

Central to our "language-guided" approach to the above problem is the construction and refinement of an automaton that restricts the search for initial states and control strategies in such a way that the satisfaction of the specifications is guaranteed at all times. The states of the automaton correspond to polytopic subsets of the state-space. Its transitions are labeled by state-feedback controllers that drive the states of the original system from one polytope to another. We propose techniques based on vertex interpolation and polyhedral Lyapunov functions (LFs) for the construction of these controllers. The refinement procedure iteratively partitions the state regions, modifies the automaton, and updates the set of initial satisfying states by performing a search and a backward reachability analysis on the graph of the automaton. The automaton obtained at the end of the iteration process provides a control strategy that solves the initial problem.

The contribution of this work is twofold. First, we provide a computational framework in which the exploration of the state-space is "guided" by the specification. This is in contrast with existing related works [6, 16], in which an abstraction is first constructed through the design of polytope-to-polytope feedback controllers, and then controlled by solving a temporal logic game on the abstraction. By combining the abstraction and the automaton control processes, the method proposed in this paper avoids regions of the state-space that do not contain satisfying initial states, and is, as a result, more efficient. In addition, it naturally induces an iterative refinement and enlargement of the set of initial conditions, which was not possible in [16] and was not formula-guided in [6].

Second, this paper provides an extension of previous results on obstacle avoidance [17–19] in certain directions. For example, it provides a systematic way to explore the feasible state-space from "rich" temporal logic specifications that are not limited to going to a target while avoiding a set of obstacles. Furthermore, it does not necessarily involve paths characterized by unions of overlapping polytopes and the existence of artificial closed-loop equilibria. Also, as a byproduct, the approach developed in this paper provides an upper bound for the time necessary to satisfy the temporal logic specifications by all the trajectories originating from the constructed set of initial states.

The remainder of the paper is organized as follows. We review some notions necessary throughout the paper in Sec. 2 before formulating the problem and outlining the approach in Sec. 3. The iterative construction of the abstraction is presented in Sec. 4. The LP-based algorithms for solving polytope-to-polytope control problems are described in Sec. 5. The main theorem is stated in Sec. 6, while illustrative examples are shown in Sec. 7. Conclusions are summarized in Sec. 8.

2. NOTATION AND PRELIMINARIES

In this section, we introduce the notation and provide some background on temporal logic and automata theory. For a set $\mathscr{S}$, $\mathrm{int}(\mathscr{S})$, $\mathrm{Co}(\mathscr{S})$, $\#\mathscr{S}$, and $2^{\mathscr{S}}$ stand for its interior, convex hull, cardinality, and power set, respectively. For $\lambda \in \mathbb{R}$ and $\mathscr{S} \subset \mathbb{R}^n$, let $\lambda\mathscr{S} := \{\lambda x | x \in \mathscr{S}\}$. We use $\mathbb{R}$, $\mathbb{R}_+$, $\mathbb{Z}$, and $\mathbb{Z}_+$ to denote the sets of real numbers, non-negative reals, integer numbers, and non-negative integers. For $m, n \in \mathbb{Z}_+$, we use $\mathbb{R}^n$ and $\mathbb{R}^{m \times n}$ to denote the set of column vectors and matrices with n and $m \times n$ real entries. $I_n \in \mathbb{R}^{n \times n}$ stands for the $n \times n$ identity matrix. For a matrix A, $A_{i\bullet}$ and $A_{\bullet j}$ denote its i-th row and j-th column, respectively. Given a vector $x \in \mathbb{R}^n$, $\|x\|$ denotes its p-norm (the value of p will be clear from the context).

A polyhedron (polyhedral set) in $\mathbb{R}^n$ is the intersection of a finite number of open and/or closed half-spaces. A polytope is a compact polyhedron. We use $\mathscr{V}(\mathscr{P})$ to denote the set of vertices of a polytope $\mathscr{P}$. Both the $\mathscr{V}$-representation ($\mathrm{Co}(\mathscr{V}(\mathscr{P}))$) and the $\mathscr{H}$-representation ($\{x \in \mathbb{R}^n \mid H_{\mathscr{P}} x \leq h_{\mathscr{P}}\}$, where matrix $H_{\mathscr{P}}$ and vector $h_{\mathscr{P}}$ have suitable dimensions) [20] of a polytope $\mathscr{P}$ will be used throughout the paper.

In this work, the control specifications are given as formulas of syntactically co-safe linear temporal logic (scLTL).

Definition 2.1 [21] A scLTL formula over a set of atomic propositions P is inductively defined as follows:

$$\Phi := p | \neg p | \Phi \vee \Phi | \Phi \wedge \Phi | \Phi \; \mathscr{U} \; \Phi | \bigcirc \Phi | \Diamond \Phi, \quad (1)$$

where p is an atomic proposition, $\neg$ (negation), $\vee$ (disjunction), $\wedge$ (conjunction) are Boolean operators, and $\bigcirc$ ("next"), $\mathscr{U}$ ("until"), and $\Diamond$ ("eventually") are temporal operators.

The semantics of scLTL formulas is defined over infinite words over 2^P as follows:

Definition 2.2 The satisfaction of a scLTL formula Φ at position $i \in \mathbb{Z}_+$ of a word w over 2^P, denoted by $w_i \models \Phi$, is recursively defined as follows: 1) $w_i \models p$ if $p \in w_i$, 2) $w_i \models \neg p$ if $p \notin w_i$, 3) $w_i \models \Phi_1 \vee \Phi_2$ if $w_i \models \Phi_1$ or $w_i \models \Phi_2$, 4) $w_i \models \bigcirc \Phi$ if $w_{i+1} \models \Phi$, 5) $w_i \models \Phi_1 \; \mathscr{U} \; \Phi_2$ if there exists $j \geq i$ such that $w_j \models \Phi_2$ and for all $i \leq k < j$ $w_k \models \Phi_1$, and 6) $w_i \models \Diamond \Phi$ if there exists $j \geq i$ such that $w_j \models \Phi$.

A word w satisfies a scLTL formula Φ, written as $w \models \Phi$, if $w_0 \models \Phi$.

An important property of scLTL formulas is that, even though they have infinite-time semantics, their satisfaction is guaranteed in finite time. Explicitly, for any scLTL formula Φ over P, any satisfying infinite word over 2^P contains a satisfying finite prefix. We use $\mathscr{L}_\Phi$ to denote the set of all (finite) prefixes of all satisfying infinite words.

Definition 2.3 A deterministic finite state automaton (FSA) is a tuple $\mathscr{A} = (Q, \Sigma, \rightarrow_{\mathscr{A}}, Q_0, F)$ where Q is a finite set of states, Σ is a set of symbols, $Q_0 \subseteq Q$ is a set of initial states, $F \subseteq Q$ is a set of final states and $\rightarrow_{\mathscr{A}} \subseteq Q \times \Sigma \times Q$ is a deterministic transition relation.

An accepting run $r_{\mathscr{A}}$ of an automaton $\mathscr{A}$ on a finite word $w = w_0 w_1 \ldots w_d$ over Σ is a sequence of states $r_{\mathscr{A}} = q_0 q_1 \ldots q_{d+1}$ such that $q_0 \in Q_0$, $q_{d+1} \in F$ and $(q_i, w_i, q_{i+1}) \in \rightarrow_{\mathscr{A}}$ for all $i = 0, \ldots, d$. The set of all words corresponding to all of the accepting runs of $\mathscr{A}$ is called the language accepted by $\mathscr{A}$ and is denoted as $\mathscr{L}_{\mathscr{A}}$.

For any scLTL Φ formula over P, there exists a FSA $\mathscr{A}$ with input alphabet 2^P that accepts the prefixes of all the satisfying words, i.e., $\mathscr{L}_\Phi$ [21]. There are algorithmic procedures and off-the-shelf tools, such as *scheck2* [22], for the construction of such an automaton.

Definition 2.4 A finite state generator automaton is a tuple $\mathscr{A} = (Q, \rightarrow_{\mathscr{A}}, \Gamma, \tau, Q_0, F)$ where Q is a finite set of states, $\rightarrow_{\mathscr{A}} \subseteq Q \times Q$ is a non-deterministic transition relation, Γ is a set of output symbols, $\tau : Q \rightarrow \Gamma$ is an output function, $Q_0 \subseteq Q$ is a set of initial states and $F \subseteq Q$ is a set of final states.

An accepting run $r_{\mathscr{A}}$ of a finite state generator automaton is a sequence of states $r_{\mathscr{A}} = q_0 q_1 \ldots q_d$ such that $q_0 \in Q_0$, $q_d \in F$ and $(q_i, q_{i+1}) \in \rightarrow_{\mathscr{A}}$ for all $i = 0, \ldots, d - 1$. An accepting run $r_{\mathscr{A}}$ produces a word $w = w_0 w_1 \ldots w_d$ over Γ such that $\tau(q_i) = w_i$, for all $i = 0, \ldots, d$. The output language $\mathscr{L}_{\mathscr{A}}$ of a finite state generator automaton $\mathscr{A}$ is the set of all words that are generated by accepting runs of $\mathscr{A}$.

3. PROBLEM FORMULATION

Consider a discrete-time linear control system of the form

$$x_{k+1} = A x_k + B u_k, \quad x_k \in \mathbb{X}, u_k \in \mathbb{U}, \quad (2)$$

where $A \in \mathbb{R}^{n \times n}$ and $B \in \mathbb{R}^{n \times m}$ describe the system dynamics and $x_k \in \mathbb{X} \subset \mathbb{R}^n$ and $u_k \in \mathbb{U} \subset \mathbb{R}^m$ are the state and applied control at time $k \in \mathbb{Z}_+$, respectively.

Let $P = \{p_i\}_{i=0,\ldots,l}$ for some $l \geq 1$ be a set of atomic propositions given as linear inequalities in $\mathbb{R}^n$. Each atomic proposition p_i induces a half-space

$$[p_i] := \{x \in \mathbb{R}^n \mid c_i^\top x + d_i \leq 0\}, \; c_i \in \mathbb{R}^n, d_i \in \mathbb{R}. \quad (3)$$

A trajectory $x_0 x_1 \ldots$ of system (2) produces a word $P_0 P_1 \ldots$ where $P_i \subseteq P$ is the set of atomic propositions satisfied by x_i, i.e., $P_i = \{p_j \mid \exists j \in \{0, \ldots, l\}, x_i \in [p_j]\}$. The specifications are given as scLTL formulas over the set of predicates P. A system trajectory satisfies a specification if the word produced by the trajectory satisfies the corresponding formula. The main problem considered in this paper can be formulated as follows:

Problem 3.1 Given a scLTL formula Φ over a set of linear predicates P and a dynamical system as defined in Eqn. (2), construct a set of initial states $\mathbb{X}_0$ and a feedback control strategy such that all the words produced by the closed-loop trajectories originating in $\mathbb{X}_0$ satisfy formula Φ.

We propose a solution to the above problem by relating the control synthesis problem with a finite state generator automaton (Def. (2.4)), whose states correspond to polyhedral subsets of the system state-space and whose transitions are mapped to state feedback controllers. This automaton will be constructed as the dual of the automaton that accepts the language satisfying formula Φ. Its states will be refined until feasible polytope-to-polytope control problems are obtained. This approach reduces the controller synthesis part of Prob. 3.1 to solving a finite number of polytope-to-polytope control problems.

The proposed solutions to polytope-to-polytope controller synthesis will supply a worst case time bound such that every trajectory originating from the source polytope reaches the target polytope within the provided time bound. These bounds can be further used to compute an upper time bound for a given initial state, such that the trajectory starting from this state satisfies the specification within the computed time bound.

4. AUTOMATON GENERATION AND REFINEMENT

In this section, we present algorithms for the construction and refinement of the dual automaton that corresponds to a desired set of LTL specifications.

4.1 FSA and dual automaton

All words that satisfy the specification formula Φ are accepted by a FSA $\mathscr{A} = (Q, 2^P, \rightarrow_{\mathscr{A}}, Q_0, F)$. The dual automaton $\mathscr{A}^D = (Q^D, \rightarrow^D, \Gamma^D, \tau^D, Q_0^D, F^D)$ is constructed as a finite state generator automaton by interchanging the states and the transitions of the automaton $\mathscr{A}$. As the transitions of $\mathscr{A}$ become states of $\mathscr{A}^D$, elements from 2^P label the states and define polyhedral sets within the state-space of system (2).

Definition 4.1 Given a FSA $\mathscr{A} = (Q, \Sigma, \rightarrow_{\mathscr{A}}, Q_0, F)$, its dual automaton is a tuple $\mathscr{A}^D = (Q^D, \rightarrow^D, \Gamma^D, \tau^D, Q_0^D, F^D)$ where

$$
\begin{aligned}
Q^D &= \{(q, \sigma, q') \mid (q, \sigma, q') \in \rightarrow_{\mathscr{A}}\}, \\
\rightarrow^D &= \{((q, \sigma, q'), (q', \sigma', q'')) \mid (q, \sigma, q'), (q', \sigma', q'') \in \rightarrow_{\mathscr{A}}\}, \\
\Gamma^D &= 2^P, \\
\tau^D &: Q^D \to \Gamma^D, \quad \tau^D((q, \sigma, q')) = \sigma, \\
Q_0^D &= \{(q_0, \sigma, q) \mid q_0 \in Q_0\}, \\
F^D &= \{(q, \sigma, q') \mid q' \in F\}.
\end{aligned}
$$

Informally, the states of the dual automaton $\mathscr{A}^D$ are the transitions of the automaton $\mathscr{A}$. A transition is defined between two states of $\mathscr{A}^D$ if the corresponding transitions are connected by a state in $\mathscr{A}$. The set of output symbols of $\mathscr{A}^D$ is the same as the set of symbols of $\mathscr{A}$. For a state of $\mathscr{A}^D$, the output function produces the symbol that enables the transition in $\mathscr{A}$. The set of initial states Q_0^D of $\mathscr{A}^D$ is the set of all transitions that leave an initial state in $\mathscr{A}$. Similarly, the set of final states F^D of $\mathscr{A}^D$ is the set of transitions that end in a final state of $\mathscr{A}$. The construction of $\mathscr{A}^D$ guarantees that any word produced by $\mathscr{A}^D$ is accepted by $\mathscr{A}$:

Proposition 4.2 The output language of the dual automaton $\mathscr{A}^D$ coincides with the language accepted by the automaton $\mathscr{A}$, i.e., $\mathscr{L}_{\mathscr{A}} = \mathscr{L}_{\mathscr{A}^D}$.

The proof of Prop. 4.2 follows directly from the definitions of the automata and is omitted for brevity.

4.1.1 Automaton Representation

A FSA $\mathscr{A}$ that accepts the language of a scLTL formula Φ over P is constructed with the tool *scheck2* [22]. This tool labels each transition of the produced FSA with a disjunctive normal form (DNF) $C_1 \vee C_2 \vee \ldots \vee C_d$, where each C_i is a conjunctive clause over P. This is a compact representation of the corresponding FSA in which each transition is labeled by a conjunctive clause.

In what follows, we use $\mathscr{P}_q \subseteq \mathbb{X}$ to denote the set of states of system (2) that satisfy the Boolean formula of a dual automaton state q. Given a DNF formula $D = C_1 \vee C_2 \vee \ldots \vee C_d$, $\mathscr{P}_{C_i} := [p_{i_1}] \cap \ldots \cap [p_{i_c}]$ denotes the set of states of system (2) that satisfy $C_i = p_{i_1} \wedge \ldots \wedge p_{i_c}$ where $i_j \in 0, \ldots, l, \forall j \in 1, \ldots, c$ and $\mathscr{P}_D := \cup_{i=1}^{d} \mathscr{P}_{C_i}$ denotes the set of states of system (2) that satisfy D.

While constructing the dual automaton, each of the conjunctive clauses is used as a separate transition, which ensures that all corresponding subsets of the state-space are polyhedra. Before constructing the dual automaton each DNF formula $C_1 \vee C_2 \vee \ldots \vee C_d$ is simplified by applying the following rules:

- *Empty set elimination:* C_i is eliminated if the corresponding region is empty, i.e., $\mathscr{P}_{C_i} = \emptyset$. The symbols that satisfy such clauses can not be generated by the system trajectories.
- *Subset elimination:* C_i is eliminated if its corresponding set is a subset of the set corresponding to C_j, $j \neq i$, i.e., $\mathscr{P}_{C_i} \subseteq \mathscr{P}_{C_j}$. The system states that satisfy C_i also satisfy C_j which enables the same transition.

Even though these simplifications change the language of the dual automaton, it can be easily seen that the set of corresponding satisfying trajectories of system (2) is preserved.

Example 4.3 A simple example is used to explain the construction routines. Consider the following scLTL formula:

$$\Phi_1 = (p_0 \wedge p_1 \wedge p_2) \ \mathscr{U} \ (p_1 \wedge p_2 \wedge p_3 \wedge p_4) \tag{4}$$

over $P = \{p_0, p_1, p_2, p_3, p_4\}$, where $c_0 = [-1, 1]^\top$, $d_0 = 0$, $c_1 = [1, 1]^\top$, $d_1 = 4$, $c_2 = [0, 1]^\top$, $d_2 = -0.1$, $c_3 = [-1, 0]^\top$, $d_3 = -3$, $c_4 = [1, 0]^\top$, $d_4 = 5$. The trajectories that satisfy Φ_1 evolve in the region $[p_0] \cap [p_1] \cap [p_2]$ until they reach the target region $[p_1] \cap [p_2] \cap [p_3] \cap [p_4]$. The regions defined by this set of predicates are given in Fig. 1. The compact representation of a FSA that accepts the language satisfying formula Φ_1 is shown in Fig. 2. For example, the transition from the state labeled with "0" to the state labeled with "1", which is labeled by $(p_4 \wedge p_3 \wedge p_2 \wedge p_1)$, corresponds to two transitions labeled by $\{p_0, p_1, p_2, p_3, p_4\}$ and $\{p_1, p_2, p_3, p_4\}$, respectively.

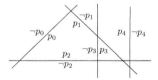

Figure 1: Half-spaces generated by the linear predicates in Eqn. (4).

The compact representations of dual automata constructed with and without simplifying the DNF formulas are shown in Fig. 3, where a state label corresponds to the subsets of 2^P which can be produced by τ^D in that state. The simplification deletes $(\neg p_4 \wedge p_2 \wedge p_1 \wedge p_0)$ from the self transition of the state labeled with "0" in Fig. 2, since the set of states that satisfies this clause is empty.

An accepting run $r_D = q_0 q_1 \ldots q_d$ of $\mathscr{A}^D$ defines a sequence of polyhedral sets $\mathscr{P}_{q_0} \mathscr{P}_{q_1} \ldots \mathscr{P}_{q_d}$. Any trajectory $x_0 x_1 \ldots x_d$ of the

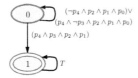

Figure 2: Compact representation of a FSA that accepts the language satisfying formula Φ_1 in Eqn. (4). The initial states are filled with grey and the final state is marked with a double circle.

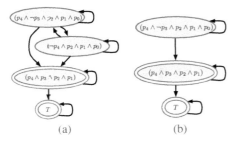

    (a)   (b)

Figure 3: Dual automata for the FSA from Fig. 2: (a) without Boolean simplification; (b) with Boolean simplification. T stands for the Boolean constant true.

original system (2) with $x_i \in \mathscr{P}_{q_i}$, $i = 0,\ldots,d$ satisfies the specification by Prop. 4.2.

We say that a transition (q,q') of $\mathscr{A}^D$ is *enabled* if there exists an admissible control law that achieves the transition for all $x \in \mathscr{P}_q$. Two conditions are introduced for constructing admissible controllers according to existence of a self transition of the source state q. When $(q,q) \in \to^D$, a controller *enables* a transition (q,q') if the corresponding closed-loop trajectories originating in $\mathscr{P}_q$ reach $\mathscr{P}_{q'}$ in finite time and remain within $\mathscr{P}_q$ until they reach $\mathscr{P}_{q'}$. When $(q,q) \notin \to^D$, a transition (q,q') is only enabled if there exists a controller such that the resulting closed-loop trajectory originating in $\mathscr{P}_q$ reaches $\mathscr{P}_{q'}$ at the next discrete-time instant. For every transition of $\mathscr{A}^D$, if a controller that enables the transition can be constructed, then every resulting closed-loop trajectory originating in $\cup_{q_0 \in Q_0^D} \mathscr{P}_{q_0}$ will satisfy the specifications by Prop. 4.2. However, existence of such controllers is not guaranteed for all the states of system (2) within $\mathbb{X}$.

Prob. 3.1 aims at finding a subset of $\mathbb{X}$ for which the polytope-to-polytope control problems induced by scLTL specifications are feasible. To this end, first, the dual automaton is pruned by checking the feasibility of transitions and states for the given system (2). Second, an iterative partitioning procedure based on a combination of backward and forward reachability will be applied to the automaton states, which correspond to polytopic subsets of $\mathbb{X}$.

4.1.2 Initial Pruning

The feasibility of the transitions of the dual automaton is first checked by considering the particular dynamics of system (2) and the set $\mathbb{U}$ where the control input takes values. $Post(\mathscr{P})$ denotes the set of states that can be reached from $\mathscr{P}$ in one discrete-time instant under the dynamics (2). For a transition (q,q'), if $Post(\mathscr{P}_q) \cap \mathscr{P}_{q'} = \emptyset$, then this transition is considered *infeasible*, since there is no admissible controller that enables this transition. As $\mathscr{P}$ and $\mathbb{U}$ are polytopes, $Post(\mathscr{P})$ can be computed as follows:

$$Post(\mathscr{P}) = Co(\{Ax + Bu \mid x \in \mathscr{V}(\mathscr{P}), u \in \mathscr{V}(\mathbb{U})\}). \quad (5)$$

Alg. 1 summarizes the pruning procedure. Once the infeasible transitions are removed as in line 1, the following feasibility tests

are performed. A state and all of its adjacent transitions are deleted either if it does not have an outgoing transition and it is not a final state or if it does not have an incoming transition and it is not an initial state (line 6). Removing such states and transitions does not reduce the solution space since such states cannot be part of any satisfying trajectory.

Algorithm 1 Initial Pruning of $\mathscr{A}^D$

1:   $\to^D := \to^D \setminus \{(q,q') \mid Post(\mathscr{P}_q) \cap \mathscr{P}_{q'} = \emptyset\}$
2:   $\bar{Q} := Q^D$
3:   **while** $\bar{Q} \neq \emptyset$ **do**
4:     **for all** $q \in \bar{Q}$ **do**
5:       $\bar{Q} := \bar{Q} \setminus \{q\}$
6:       **if** ($q \notin F^D$ AND $\{q' \mid (q,q') \in \to^D\} = \emptyset$) OR ($q \notin Q_0^D$ AND $\{q' \mid (q',q) \in \to^D\} = \emptyset$) **then**
7:         $Q^D := Q^D \setminus \{q\}$
8:         $\bar{Q} := \bar{Q} \cup (\{q' \mid (q,q') \in \to^D\} \cup \{q' \mid (q',q) \in \to^D\})$
9:         $\to^D := \to^D \setminus (\{(q,q') \mid (q,q') \in \to^D\} \cup \{(q',q) \mid (q',q) \in \to^D\})$
10:     **end if**
11:    **end for**
12: **end while**

4.2 Automaton Refinement

Alg. 1 guarantees that a non-empty polyhedral subset of a source polytope $\mathscr{P}_q$ is one-step controllable to the target polytope $\mathscr{P}_{q'}$ corresponding to the transition (q,q'). However, this does not imply the feasibility of the corresponding polytope-to-polytope control problem. An iterative algorithm is developed to refine the polytope $\mathscr{P}_q$ and hence, the corresponding state of the dual automaton, whenever the feasibility test fails. Alg. 2 refines the automaton at each iteration by partitioning the states for which there does not exist an admissible sequence of control actions with respect to reaching a final state. The algorithm does not affect the states of system (2) that can reach a final state region and as such, it results in a monotonically increasing, with respect to set inclusion, set of states of system (2) for which there exists an admissible control strategy.

For a transition $(q,q') \in \to^D$, the set of states in $\mathscr{P}_q$ that can reach $\mathscr{P}_{q'}$ in one step is called a *beacon*. We use $\mathscr{B}_{qq'}$ to denote the beacon corresponding to transition (q,q'), which can be obtained as $\mathscr{B}_{qq'} := \mathscr{P}_q \cap Pre(\mathscr{P}_{q'})$, where

$$Pre(\mathscr{P}) := \{x \in \mathbb{X} \mid \exists u \in \mathbb{U}, Ax + Bu \in \mathscr{P}\}, \quad \forall \mathscr{P} \subseteq \mathbb{R}^n. \quad (6)$$

If $\mathscr{P}$ and $\mathbb{U}$ are polytopes, then $Pre(\mathscr{P})$ can be computed via orthogonal projection. Given a controller that enables a transition (q,q'), the cost $J((q,q'))$ of transition (q,q') is defined as the worst-case time bound such that every trajectory originating in $\mathscr{P}_q$ reaches $\mathscr{P}_{q'}$. The cost $J^P(q)$ of a state q is defined as the shortest path cost from q to a final state on the graph of the automaton weighted with transition costs.

The refinement algorithm uses three subroutines: *ShortestPath*, *Partitioning* and *FeasibilityTest*(q,q'). The *ShortestPath* procedure computes a shortest path cost for every state of $\mathscr{A}^D$ using Dijkstra's algorithm [23]. The *Partitioning* procedure, which will be presented in detail in the next subsection, partitions a state region and modifies $\mathscr{A}^D$ accordingly.

The *FeasibilityTest*(q,q') procedure checks if there exists a controller that enables (q,q') and returns the cost $J((q,q'))$ of the transition. The computational aspects of this procedure are presented in Sec. 5. The cost is set to infinity when no feasible controller is found. When q has a self transition, the procedure checks if there exists a controller that steers all trajectories originating in $\mathscr{P}_q$ to the beacon of (q,q'), i.e., $\mathscr{B}_{qq'}$, in finite time without leaving the set $\mathscr{P}_q$. Notice that to solve the $\mathscr{P}_q$-to-$\mathscr{P}_{q'}$ problem it suffices to solve the $\mathscr{P}_q$-to-$\mathscr{B}_{qq'}$ problem, since a trajectory originating in $\mathscr{P}_q$ will reach $\mathscr{P}_{q'}$ without leaving $\mathscr{P}_q$ only through the beacon $\mathscr{B}_{qq'}$. By definition, there exists an admissible control action for all $x \in \mathscr{B}_{qq'}$ such that $\mathscr{P}_{q'}$ is reached in one step. If q does not have a self transition, the transition (q,q') is only enabled when $\mathscr{P}_q = \mathscr{B}_{qq'}$, since $\mathscr{B}_{qq'}$ is the largest set of states in $\mathscr{P}_q$ that can reach $\mathscr{P}_{q'}$ in one step.

Algorithm 2 Refinement of $\mathscr{A}^D$

1: **for all** $(q,q') \in \to_D$ **do**
2:    $J((q,q')) := FeasibilityTest(q,q')$
3: **end for**
4: $J^P := ShortestPath(J,F^D)$
5: $CandidateSet = \{(q_i,q_j) \mid (q_i,q_j) \in \to^D, J^P(q_i) = \infty, J^P(q_j) \neq \infty\}$
6: **while** $CandidateSet \neq \emptyset$ **do**
7:    $(q_s,q_d) := \min_{J^P(q_j)}\{(q_i,q_j) \mid (q_i,q_j) \in CandidateSet\}$
8:    $[\mathscr{A}^D,J] := Partitioning(\mathscr{A}^D,q_s,(q_s,q_d))$
9:    $J^P := ShortestPath(J,F^D)$
10:    $CandidateSet := \{(q_i,q_j) \mid (q_i,q_j) \in \to^D, J^P(q_i) = \infty, J^P(q_j) \neq \infty\}$
11: **end while**

At each iteration of the refinement algorithm, the transition costs and shortest path costs are updated, and the set of candidate states for partitioning is constructed as follows. A state q_i that has an infinite cost ($J^P(q_i) = \infty$) and a transition ($(q_i,q_j) \in \to^D$) to a state that has a finite cost ($J^P(q_j) < \infty$) is chosen as a candidate state for partitioning (lines 5 and 10). Then, a state q_s is selected from the set of candidate states for partitioning by considering the path costs in line 7. The algorithm stops when there are no transitions from infinite cost states to finite cost states, i.e., when the set of candidate states for partitioning is empty.

4.2.1 Partitioning

A state q is partitioned into a set of states $\{q_1, \ldots, q_d\}$ via a polytopic partition of $\mathscr{P}_q$. The transitions of the new states are inherited from the state q and new states are set as start states if $q \in Q_0^D$ to preserve the automaton language. The partitioning procedure is summarized in Alg. 3.

Algorithm 3 Partitioning of q in $\{q_1, \ldots, q_d\}$

1: $Q^D := (Q^D \setminus \{q\}) \cup \{q_1, \ldots, q_d\}$
2: **for all** $(q'.q) \in \to^D$ **do**
3:    $\to^D := \to^D \setminus \{(q',q)\}$
4:    **for** $i = 1 : d$ **do**
5:      **if** $Post(q') \cap \mathscr{P}_{q_i} \neq \emptyset$ **then**
6:        $\to^D := \to^D \cup \{(q',q_i)\}$
7:        $J((q',q_i)) := FeasibilityTest(q',q_i)$
8:      **end if**
9:    **end for**
10: **end for**
11: **for all** $(q,q') \in \to^D$ **do**
12:    $\to^D := \to^D \setminus \{(q,q')\}$
13:    **for** $i = 1 : d$ **do**
14:      **if** $Post(q_i) \cap \mathscr{P}_{q'} \neq \emptyset$ **then**
15:        $\to^D := \to^D \cup \{(q_i,q')\}$
16:        $J((q_i,q')) := FeasibilityTest(q_i,q')$
17:      **end if**
18:    **end for**
19: **end for**

A heuristic partitioning strategy guided by a transition (q,q') is used: the region is partitioned in two subregions using a hyperplane of the beacon $\mathscr{B}_{qq'}$. Notice that beacons will always be polytopes, as $Pre(\mathscr{P}_{q'})$ is a polytope for linear dynamics, $\mathbb{U}$ is a polytope and the intersection of two polytopes is a polytope. The hyperplane which maximizes the radius of the Chebyshev ball that can fit in

any of the resulting regions is chosen as the partitioning criterion. Choosing a hyperplane of the beacon ensures that only one of the resulting states can have a transition to q'. Even if a controller that enables the transition to q' does not exist for this state, after further partitioning the beacon becomes a state itself and the transition is enabled for it. The employed maximal radius criterion is likely to result in a less-complex partition, as opposed to iteratively computing one-step controllable sets to $\mathscr{B}_{qq'}$, and it is applicable to high dimensional state-spaces.

Let $\mathscr{A}^{D_i} = (Q^{D_i}, \to^{D_i}, \Gamma^{D_i}, \tau^{D_i}, Q_0^{D_i}, F^{D_i})$ denote the dual automaton after refinement iteration i, and let $\mathscr{A}^{D_0}$ denote the initial dual automaton. For a dual automaton $\mathscr{A}^{D_i}$, the set $\mathbb{X}_0^i \subseteq \mathbb{X}$ denotes the union of the regions corresponding to start states of automaton $\mathscr{A}^{D_i}$ with finite path costs, i.e.,

$$\mathbb{X}_0^i := \bigcup_{q \in \{q' \in Q_0^{D_i} \mid J^P(q') < \infty\}} \mathscr{P}_q \subseteq \mathbb{X}. \tag{7}$$

Example 4.4 Consider system (2) with $A = I_2$, $B = I_2$, $\mathbb{U} = \{u \in \mathbb{R}^2 \mid 0 \leq u_1 \leq 0.2, -0.1 \leq u_2 \leq 0.2\}$ and specification from[1] Ex. 4.3. $\mathscr{A}^{D_0}$ has two states $\{q_1, q_2\}$; both are initial states and q_2 is a final state. Since $J((q_1,q_2)) = \infty$, initially only q_2 has finite cost and q_1 is a candidate state for partitioning. Using a hyperplane of $\mathscr{B}_{q_1 q_2}$ generates the state regions and the automaton shown in Fig. 4c and Fig. 4d. As $Post(\mathscr{P}_{q_3}) \cap \mathscr{P}_{q_2} = \emptyset$, the transition (q_3,q_2) is removed. In the next iteration q_1 is partitioned using $\mathscr{B}_{q_1 q_2}$ and the algorithm terminates after this iteration, since there exists a finite cost automaton path from all states to the final state and the candidate set is empty. The control synthesis tools of Sec. 5 were used in this example to check the costs of the transitions.

Proposition 4.5 *Assume $\mathbb{X}_0^0$ is non-empty. Given an arbitrary iteration $i \geq 1$ of Alg. 2, the set $\mathbb{X}_0^i$ as defined in Eqn. (7) has the following properties:*

(i) There exists a sequence of admissible control actions such that every closed-loop trajectory of system (2) originating in $\mathbb{X}_0^i$ satisfies formula Φ, and
(ii) $\mathbb{X}_0^{i-1} \subseteq \mathbb{X}_0^i$.

PROOF. *(i)* A finite path cost for a state $q_0 \in Q_0^{D_i}$ implies that there exists an automaton run $q_0 q_1 \ldots q_d$ with $J((q_j,q_{j+1})) < \infty$ for all $j = 0, \ldots, d-1$ and $J^P(q_0) = \sum_{j=0}^{d-1} J((q_j,q_{j+1}))$. As a transition cost is assigned according to the existence of the controller that enables the transition, there exists a control sequence that ensures that every closed-loop trajectory originating in $\mathscr{P}_{q_0}$ reaches $\mathscr{P}_{q_d}$ by following the automaton path. Considering that removing states and transitions only reduces the language of the automaton, by Prop. 4.2 it follows that $\mathscr{L}_{\mathscr{A}^{D_0}} \subseteq \mathscr{L}_\Phi$. Since the proposed partitioning procedure preserves the language, we have $\mathscr{L}_{\mathscr{A}^{D_i}} \subseteq \mathscr{L}_{\mathscr{A}^{D_{i-1}}}$. Consequently, $\mathscr{L}_{\mathscr{A}^{D_i}} \subseteq \mathscr{L}_\Phi$ and the resulting trajectories satisfy the formula.

(ii) For any $x \in \mathbb{X}_0^{i-1}$, there exists an accepting automaton run $r_D = q_0 q_1 \ldots q_d$ with $x \in \mathscr{P}_{q_0}$ and $J^P(q_0) = \sum_{j=0}^{d-1} J((q_j,q_{j+1})) < \infty$. Let q_s be the state chosen for partitioning at iteration i. Then, $J^P((q_s)) = \infty$ and $q_s \neq q_j$ for all $j = 0, \ldots, d$ as $J^P(q_j) < \infty$ for all $j = 0, \ldots, d$. As only the transitions adjacent to q_s are affected by partitioning, $q_j \in Q_i^D$ for all $j = 0, \ldots, d$ and $(q_j,q_{j+1}) \in \to^{D_i}$ for all $j = 0, \ldots, d-1$. Therefore, $x \in \mathscr{P}_{q_0}$, $r_D = q_0 q_1 \ldots q_d$ is an accepting run of A^{D_i} with finite cost and thus, $x \in \mathbb{X}_0^i$. Observing that $x \in \mathbb{X}_0^{i-1}$ was chosen arbitrary completes the proof. $\square$

---

[1] Note that the automata in Fig. 2 and in Fig. 6a represent $\mathscr{A}^{D_0}$. For simplicity the final state labeled by T is not shown in Fig. 6a.

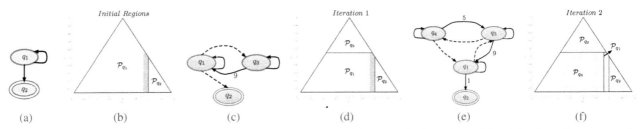

Figure 4: Automata and their corresponding polytopic state-space partitions for the iterations of Ex. 4.4. The polytopes are shown with black borders and $\mathbb{X}_0^i$ is shown in yellow. The beacon of transition (q_1, q_2) is shown in blue. A transition is shown with dashed line if a controller that enables the transition was not found, otherwise the transition is marked with a time bound.

The automaton refinement algorithms presented in this section generate a finite set of polytope-to-polytope control problems. Several tractable approaches for solving these problems are proposed in the next section.

5. POLYTOPE-TO-POLYTOPE CONTROL

Enabling a transition (q, q') requires an admissible control law that solves the $\mathscr{P}_q$-to-$\mathscr{P}_{q'}$ control problem. By the definition of $\mathscr{B}_{qq'}$, this problem can be decomposed in two subproblems. The first problem concerns the computation of a control law which generates a closed-loop trajectory, for all $x \in \mathscr{B}_{qq'}$, that reaches $\mathscr{P}_{q'}$ in one discrete-time instant. The second problem concerns the construction of a control law which generates a closed-loop trajectory, for all $x \in \mathscr{P}_q$, that reaches $\mathscr{B}_{qq'}$ in a finite number of discrete-time instants. These synthesis problems are formally stated next.

Problem 5.1 Let $\mathscr{B}, \mathscr{P} \in \mathscr{P}(\mathbb{R}^n)$ with $\mathscr{B} \subseteq Pre(\mathscr{P})$ and consider system (2). Construct a state-feedback control law $g : \mathbb{R}^n \to \mathbb{R}^m$ such that

$$Ax + Bg(x) \in \mathscr{P}, \ g(x) \in \mathbb{U}, \qquad \forall x \in \mathscr{B}.$$

Problem 5.2 Let $N \in \mathbb{Z}_{\geq 1}$, $\mathscr{B}, \mathscr{P} \in \mathscr{P}(\mathbb{R}^n)$ with $\mathscr{B} \subseteq \mathscr{P}$ and consider system (2). Construct a state-feedback control law $g : \mathbb{R}^n \to \mathbb{R}^m$ such that for all $x \in \mathscr{P}$ it holds that

$$\begin{aligned}
x_0 &:= x, \\
x_{k+1} &= Ax_k + Bg(x_k), \quad \forall k = 0, \ldots, N-1, \\
x_k &\in \mathscr{P}, \ g(x_k) \in \mathbb{U}, \quad \forall k = 0, \ldots, N-1, \\
x_N &\in \mathscr{B}.
\end{aligned}$$

Notice that while Prob. 5.1 is always feasible since $\mathscr{B} \subseteq Pre(\mathscr{P})$, Prob. 5.2 needs not be feasible for any set $\mathscr{P}$ and corresponding beacon $\mathscr{B}$. In what follows, sufficient conditions for feasibility of Prob. 5.2 will be indicated.

Firstly, let us present a vertex interpolation-based solution to Prob. 5.1. Let $\{v^i\}_{i=1,\ldots,\#\mathscr{V}(\mathscr{B})}$ denote the set of vertices of $\mathscr{B}$ and let $\{u^i\}_{i=1,\ldots,\#\mathscr{V}(\mathscr{B})}$ denote a corresponding set of control actions. Consider the following set of linear inequalities in the variables $\{u^i\}_{i=1,\ldots,\#\mathscr{V}(\mathscr{B})}$:

$$\begin{aligned}
H_{\mathscr{P}}(Av^i + Bu^i) &\leq h_{\mathscr{P}}, \\
H_{\mathbb{U}} u^i &\leq h_{\mathbb{U}}.
\end{aligned} \tag{8}$$

A solution to (8) can be obtained *off-line* by solving a feasibility LP. It is trivial to deduce that the control law

$$g(x) := \sum_{i=1}^{\#\mathscr{V}(\mathscr{B})} \lambda_i u^i, \tag{9}$$

where $\lambda_i \in \mathbb{R}$, $0 \leq \lambda_i \leq 1$, are such that $x = \sum_{i=1}^{\#\mathscr{V}(\mathscr{B})} \lambda_i v^i$, solves Prob. 5.1. The evaluation of the control law (9) requires *on-line* calculation of the coefficients $\{\lambda_i\}_{i=1,\ldots,\#\mathscr{V}(\mathscr{B})}$, which amounts to solving a system of linear equations and can also be formulated as a feasibility LP.

Alternatively, an explicit piecewise affine (PWA) form of $g(\cdot)$ can be obtained by a simplicial partition of $\mathscr{B}$. Then, the evaluation of g requires solving *on-line* a point location problem, which consists of checking a finite number of linear inequalities. Although efficient ways to solve point location problems exist, depending on the complexity of the partition (number of simplices), the point location problem may be more computationally expensive than calculating the coefficients $\{\lambda_i\}_{i=1,\ldots,\#\mathscr{V}(\mathscr{B})}$ *on-line*. Yet another explicit PWA solution to Prob. 5.1 can be obtaining via direct synthesis of a PWA control law defined over an arbitrary polytopic partition of $\mathscr{B}$, which can still be formulated as a LP. While this approach may lead to a less complex point location problem, however, feasibility is not necessarily guaranteed for an arbitrary partition.

Next, two approaches are proposed to solve Prob. 5.2, i.e., vertex interpolation and polyhedral LFs.

Vertex interpolation Let $\{v^i\}_{i=1,\ldots,\#\mathscr{V}(\mathscr{P})}$ be the vertices of $\mathscr{P}$ and let $\{\mathbf{u}^i\}_{i=1,\ldots,\#\mathscr{V}(\mathscr{P})}$ denote a corresponding set of finite sequences of control actions, where $\mathbf{u}^i := \{u_k^i\}_{k=0,\ldots,N-1}$ for all $i \in \mathbb{Z}_{i=1,\ldots,\#\mathscr{V}(\mathscr{P})}$ and $N \in \mathbb{Z}_{\geq 1}$. For each $v^i \in \mathscr{V}(\mathscr{P})$ define the following set of linear equality and inequality constraints in the variables $\{\mathbf{u}^i\}_{i \in \mathbb{Z}_{i=1,\ldots,\#\mathscr{V}(\mathscr{P})}}$:

$$\begin{aligned}
x_0^i &:= v^i, \\
x_{k+1}^i &= Ax_k^i + Bu_k^i, \quad \forall k = 0, \ldots, N-1, \\
H_{\mathscr{P}} x_k^i &\leq h_{\mathscr{P}}, \ H_{\mathbb{U}} u_k^i \leq h_{\mathbb{U}}, \quad \forall k = 0, \ldots, N-1, \\
H_{\mathscr{B}} x_N^i &\leq h_{\mathscr{B}}.
\end{aligned} \tag{10}$$

A solution to the set of problems (10) can be searched for *off-line* by solving repeatedly a corresponding set of feasibility LPs starting with $N = 1$, for all $i = 1, \ldots, \#\mathscr{V}(\mathscr{P})$, and increasing N until a feasible solution is obtained for all LPs and the same value of N. Let $N^* \geq 1$ denote the minimal N for which a feasible solution was found. Then, it is straightforward to establish that for any $x \in \mathscr{P}$, the control law

$$g(x_k) := \sum_{i=1}^{\#\mathscr{V}(\mathscr{P})} \lambda_i u_k^i, \quad k = 0, \ldots, N^* - 1, \tag{11}$$

where $x_0 = x$ and $\lambda_i \in \mathbb{R}$, $0 \leq \lambda_i \leq 1$, are such that $x = \sum_{i=1}^{\#\mathscr{V}(\mathscr{P})} \lambda_i v^i$, solves Prob. 5.2 and yields closed-loop trajectories that reach $\mathscr{B}$ in at most N^* discrete-time instants.

Evaluation of the control law g of (11) at time $k = 0$ requires *on-line* calculation of the coefficients $\{\lambda_i\}_{i=1,\ldots,\#\mathscr{V}(\mathscr{P})}$, which is a LP, while at every $k = 1, \ldots, N^* - 1$ the analytic expression of g is implemented. However, a faster convergence to $\mathscr{B}$ can be obtained by taking $\lambda_i \in \mathbb{R}$, $0 \leq \lambda_i \leq 1$, such that $x = \sum_{i=1}^{\#\mathscr{V}(\mathscr{P})} \lambda_i x_{j^*}^i$, where

$$j^* := \arg\max\{j \in \{0,\ldots,N^*\} \mid x \in \text{Co}(\{x_j^i\}_{i=1,\ldots,\#\mathscr{V}(\mathscr{P})})\}.$$

Then, the resulting closed-loop trajectories will reach $\mathscr{B}$ in at most $N^* - j^*$ discrete-time instants.

Similarly as in the case of the control law (9), simplicial decompositions of $\mathscr{P}$ can be employed to obtain an explicit PWA form of the control law $g(x_k)$, $k = 0,\ldots,N^*-1$, both for its standard and faster variants presented above.

Remark 5.3 In general, existence of a finite, common N such that all LPs (10) are feasible is not guaranteed. If a certain upper bound on N is reached, the *off-line* synthesis procedure is stopped and Alg. 3 is employed to further partition the set $\mathscr{P}$. In the "worst" case, the partitioning converges to the maximal controllable subset of $\mathscr{P}$ with respect to $\mathscr{B}$, which ultimately recovers the "one-step controllable sets" partition of the state-space. However, if a solution is found for a finite N, there is no need to further partition $\mathscr{P}$, which can result in a significant complexity reduction, as it is illustrated for the case studies presented in Sec. 7.

Sufficient conditions for feasibility of the LPs (10) can be obtained as follows. Consider the set

$$\mathscr{E}_{\mathscr{B}} := \{x^s \in \text{int}(\mathscr{B}) \mid \exists u^s \in \mathbb{U} : x^s = Ax^s + Bu^s\}.$$

If $\mathscr{E}_{\mathscr{B}} \neq \emptyset$ and the Minkowski function of the polytope $\mathscr{P}$ is a local control Lyapunov function [24] for system (2), there always exists a $N_i \geq 1$ such that the LPs (10) are feasible for all $i = 1,\ldots,\#\mathscr{V}(\mathscr{P})$. Then interpolation becomes feasible as control sequences of equal length can be obtained via augmentation with a suitable control action $u^{s,i}$, which corresponds to some $x^{s,i} \in \mathscr{E}_{\mathscr{B}}$. Notice that the same assumptions were employed in [19], where only obstacle avoidance specifications were considered and polyhedral LFs were employed.

In this respect, the proposed vertex interpolation solution for solving Prob. 5.2 can be regarded as a relaxation of standard interpolation synthesis methods, where existence of a closed-loop equilibrium is assumed.

Polyhedral LFs However, if $\mathscr{E}_{\mathscr{B}} \neq \emptyset$, a simpler explicit PWA solution to Prob. 5.2 can be obtained via polyhedral LFs, see, e.g., [19, 25], as follows. Let $\mathscr{M}(x) := \max_{i=1,\ldots,w} W_{i\bullet}(x - x^s)$, where $w \geq n+1$ is the number of lines of the matrix $H_{\mathscr{P}}$ and $x^s \in \mathscr{E}_{\mathscr{B}}$, denote the Minkowski function of the polytope $\mathscr{P}$. Next, consider the conic polytopic partition $\{\mathscr{C}_i\}_{i=1,\ldots,w}$ of $\mathscr{P}$ induced by x^s, which is constructed as follows:

$$\mathscr{C}_i := \{x \in \mathscr{P} \mid (W_{i\bullet} - W_{j\bullet})(x - x^s) \geq 0, j = 1,\ldots,w\} \cup \{x^s\}.$$

Notice that $\cup_{i=0,\ldots,w} \mathscr{C}_i = \mathscr{P}$ and $\text{int}(\mathscr{C}_i) \cap \text{int}(\mathscr{C}_j) = \emptyset$ for all $i \neq j$. Let $\rho \in \mathbb{R}$ with $0 \leq \rho < 1$ denote a desired convergence rate. Consider the PWA control law

$$g(x) := K_i x + a_i \quad \text{if} \quad x \in \mathscr{C}_i \tag{12}$$

and the following feasibility LP in the variables $\{K_i, a_i\}_{i=1,\ldots,w}$, to be solved *off-line*:

$$\rho W_{i\bullet}(x - x^s) - W_{j\bullet}(Ax + Bg(x) - x^s) \geq 0,$$
$$\forall x \in \mathscr{V}(\mathscr{C}_i), \forall j = 1,\ldots,w,$$
$$K_i x + a_i \in \mathbb{U}, \quad \forall i = 1,\ldots,w,$$
$$(A + K_i)x^s + a_i = x^s, \quad \forall i = 1,\ldots,w. \tag{13}$$

Notice that ρ can be minimized to obtain an optimal convergence rate and a different ρ_i can be assigned to each cone $\mathscr{C}_i$, while (13) remains a LP.

Proposition 5.4 *Suppose that the LP (13) is feasible. Then the function $\mathscr{M}$ is a Lyapunov function and $\mathscr{P}$ is a ρ-contractive set for system (2) in closed-loop with the PWA control law (12), with respect to the equilibrium $x^s \in \text{int}(\mathscr{B})$.*

The proof of Prop. 5.4 is a straightforward application of Thm. III.6 from [25] and it is omitted for brevity.

Letting $k^* := \arg\min\{k \geq 1 \mid \rho^k \mathscr{P} \subseteq \mathscr{B}\}$, one obtains that all trajectories of system (2) in closed-loop with (12) that start in $\mathscr{P}$ reach $\mathscr{B}$ in at most k^* discrete-time instants. Thus, the PWA control law (12) solves Prob. 5.2. The *on-line* evaluation of (12) reduces to a point location problem that can be solved in logarithmic time due to the specific conic partition.

6. COMPLETE CONTROL STRATEGY

The proposed control strategy that solves Prob. 3.1 is composed of a finite state generator automaton $\mathscr{A}^C$ and a map M from transitions of $\mathscr{A}^C$ to state feedback controllers. The automaton $\mathscr{A}^C = (Q^C, \to^C, \Gamma^C, \tau^C, Q_0^C, F^C)$ is constructed from the dual automaton $\mathscr{A}^{D_R} = (Q^{D_R}, \to^{D_R}, \Gamma^{D_R}, \tau^{D_R}, Q_0^{D_R}, F^{D_R})$ and it results from Alg. 2 as follows:

$$\begin{aligned}
Q^C &= \{q \in Q^{D_R} \mid J^P(q) < \infty\}, \\
\to^C &= \{(q, q') \mid J((q, q')) < \infty, (q, q') \in \to^{D_R}\}, \\
\Gamma^C &= \Gamma^{D_R}, \\
\tau^C &: Q^C \to \Gamma^C, \quad \tau^C(q) = \{p \mid [p] \cap \mathscr{P}_q \neq \emptyset\}, \\
Q_0^C &= Q_0^D \cap Q^C, \\
F^C &= F^{D_R}.
\end{aligned} \tag{14}$$

The state feedback controllers assigned by M are constructed as described in Sec. 5. Existence of these controllers are guaranteed, since $\mathscr{A}^C$ has only finite cost transitions.

Given a state $x_0 \in \mathscr{P}_{q_0}$ of system (2) for some $q_0 \in Q_0^C$, there exists an accepting run $r_C = q_0 q_1 \ldots q_d$ of $\mathscr{A}^C$. The run corresponds to a control sequence $M_{r_C} = M((q_0, q_1)), \ldots, M((q_{d-1}, q_d))$. Starting from $x_0 \in \mathscr{P}_{q_0}$, the state feedback controller $M((q_0, q_1))$ is applied to system (2) until the trajectory reaches $\mathscr{P}_{q_1}$. Then, the applied feedback controller switches to $M((q_1, q_2))$. This process continues until the trajectory reaches $\mathscr{P}_{q_d}$ while $M((q_{d-1}, q_d))$ is applied.

The union of the regions corresponding to the initial states of automaton $\mathscr{A}^C$ defines the set of initial system states $\mathbb{X}_0$, such that closed-loop trajectories originating in $\mathbb{X}_0$ satisfy formula Φ:

$$\mathbb{X}_0 = \bigcup_{q \in Q_0^C} \mathscr{P}_q. \tag{15}$$

For a given accepting run $r_C = q_0 q_1 \ldots q_d$ of $\mathscr{A}^C$, the time required to satisfy the specification for trajectories originating in $\mathscr{P}_{q_0}$ is upper bounded by $\sum_{i=0}^{d-1} J((q_i, q_{i+1}))$ when $M_{r_C} = M((q_0, q_1)), \ldots, M((q_{d-1}, q_d))$ is applied. If the control sequences are chosen according to shortest paths for each $q_0 \in Q_0^C$, the time required to satisfy the specification starting from any state $x_0 \in \mathbb{X}_0$ of system (2) is upper bounded by $\max_{q_0 \in Q_0^C} J^P(q_0)$. Moreover, the control sequences can also be chosen to minimize the number of controller switches. In this case, the number of maximum controller switches for the trajectories originating in $\mathbb{X}_0$ is bounded by $\max_{q_0 \in Q_0^C} J^L(q_0)$, where $J^L(q_0)$ is the minimal length of an accepting run of $\mathscr{A}^C$ starting from q_0.

The following theorem states that when the refinement algorithm terminates, the proposed solution to Prob. 3.1 is correct and complete.

Theorem 6.1 *Suppose Alg. 2 terminates. Then any closed-loop trajectory that originates in $\mathbb{X}_0$ satisfies the formula Φ and any trajectory of system (2) that produces a word $w \in \mathscr{L}_\Phi$ originates in $\mathbb{X}_0$.*

PROOF. The proof that all the trajectories of the closed loop system satisfy the formula follows immediately from Prop. 4.5 since $\mathbb{X}_0 = \mathbb{X}_0^{D_R}$.

To show that any satisfying trajectory originates in $\mathbb{X}_0$, assume by contradiction that there exist $x_0 \notin \mathbb{X}_0$ such that $x_0 x_1 \ldots x_d$ is a satisfying trajectory of system (2), i.e., $P_0 P_1 \ldots P_d \in \mathscr{L}_\Phi$. Then by Prop. 4.2, there exists an accepting run $r_D = q_0 q_1 \ldots q_d$ of the initial dual automaton $\mathscr{A}^{D_0}$ such that $x_k \in \mathscr{P}_{q_k}, \forall k = 0, \ldots, d$. The run r_D induces a unique refined dual automaton run $r_{D^R} = q'_0 q'_1 \ldots q'_d$ where q'_k and q_k coincide or q'_k is obtained from q_k through partitioning and $x_k \in \mathscr{P}_{q'_k} \subseteq \mathscr{P}_{q_k}$ for all $k = 0, \ldots, d$.

Let $r'_{D^R} = q_{s_0} q_s \ldots q_{s_{d'}}$ be obtained by eliminating consecutive duplicates in r_{D^R}. Then, for each $i = 0, \ldots, d'-1$, $s_i < s_{i+1}$ and $x_k \in \mathscr{P}_{q_{s_i}}$ for all $k = s_i, s_i+1, \ldots, s_{i+1}-1$. Then, $x_0 \notin \mathbb{X}_0$ indicates that $J^P(q_{s_0}) = \infty$. Hence, either $Post(\mathscr{P}_{q_{s_i}}) \cap \mathscr{P}_{q_{s_{i+1}}} = \emptyset$ or $J((q_{s_i}, q_{s_{i+1}})) = \infty$ for some $i = 0, \ldots, d'$. Let s_i be the maximal index where $Post(\mathscr{P}_{q_{s_i}}) \cap \mathscr{P}_{q_{s_{i+1}}} = \emptyset$ or $J((q_{s_i}, q_{s_{i+1}})) = \infty$. Therefore, $J((q_{s_k}, q_{s_{k+1}})) < \infty, \forall k = i+1, \ldots, d'-1$ and $J^P(q_{s_k}) < \infty$, $\forall k = i+1, \ldots, d'$. As Alg. 2 terminates, it holds that

$$Post(\mathscr{P}_q) \bigcap \left\{ \bigcup_{J^P(q') < \infty, (q,q') \in \to^{D^R}} \mathscr{P}_{q'} \right\} = \emptyset \quad (16)$$

for all q with $J^P(q) = \infty$. Consequently, $Post(\mathscr{P}_{q_{s_i}}) \cap \mathscr{P}_{q_{s_{i+1}}} = \emptyset$. As $x_{s_{i+1}-1} \in \mathscr{P}_{q_{s_i}}$ and $x_{s_{i+1}} \in \mathscr{P}_{q_{s_{i+1}}}$, there is no control $u \in \mathbb{U}$ that satisfies $x_{s_{i+1}} = Ax_{s_{i+1}-1} + Bu$. Therefore $x_0 x_1 \ldots x_d$ is not a trajectory of system (2) and thus, we reached a contradiction. $\square$

Remark 6.2 As shown in Prop. 4.5, Alg. 2 establishes a set iteration which produces a monotonically increasing, with respect to set inclusion, sequence of sets described by unions of polytopes. Thm. 6.1 states that when this iteration converges in finite time then the maximal set of satisfying states has been obtained. This is possible whenever the maximal set is a polytope or a union of polytopes. As this is not necessarily the case for any specification, in practice, to guarantee finite time termination, an artificial stopping criterion can be used, such as, e.g., the size of the region of satisfying states of system (2).

Remark 6.3 The complexity of the proposed solution can be analyzed in two aspects: off-line and on-line parts. The complexity of the off-line part essentially depends on the number of iterations required to reach the stopping criterion of Alg. 2. At each iteration, Alg. 2 involves shortest path computation, basic polyhedral operations and linear programming. The on-line part deals with the generation of the control input for system (2) and involves linear programming.

7. IMPLEMENTATION AND CASE STUDIES

The proposed computational framework was implemented as a Matlab software package, which is freely downloadable from hyness.bu.edu/software. The toolbox takes as input a scLTL formula over a set of linear predicates, the matrices of a discrete-time linear system, and the control constraints set, and produces a solution to Prob. 3.1 in the form of a set of initial states and a state-feedback control strategy. The tool, which uses *scheck2* [22]

for the construction of the FSA and MPT [26] for polyhedral operations, also allows for displaying the set of initial states and simulating the trajectories of the closed-loop system for 2D or 3D state-spaces.

7.1 Case Study 1 : Double Integrator

Obstacle avoidance for double integrators is a particularly challenging problem [18]. The discrete-time double integrator dynamics with sampling time of 1 second are of the form given in Eqn. (2), where

$$A = \begin{bmatrix} 1 & 1 \\ 0 & 1 \end{bmatrix}, \quad B = \begin{bmatrix} 0.5 \\ 1 \end{bmatrix}. \quad (17)$$

We assume that the control constraint set is given by $\mathbb{U} = \{u \mid -2 \leq u \leq 2\}$. The control specification is to visit region $\mathbb{A}$ or region $\mathbb{B}$, and then the target region $\mathbb{T}$, while always avoiding obstacles $\mathbb{O}_1$ and $\mathbb{O}_2$, and staying inside a safe region given by $\mathbb{X} = \{x \mid -10 \leq x_1 \leq 1.85, -10 \leq x_2 \leq 2\}$. The sets $\mathbb{X}, \mathbb{U}$ and the obstacles $\mathbb{O}_1$ and $\mathbb{O}_2$ are the same as the ones used in [18]. All these polytopic regions, together with the linear predicates used in their definitions, are shown in Fig. 5 (a). Using these predicates, the specification can be written as the following scLTL formula:

$\Phi_2 = ((p_0 \land p_1 \land p_2 \land p_3 \land \neg(p_4 \land p_5) \land \neg(\neg p_5 \land \neg p_6 \land p_7)) \mathscr{U} (\neg p_8 \land p_9 \land \neg p_{10} \land p_{11}) \land (\neg(\neg p_8 \land p_9 \land \neg p_{10} \land p_{11}) \mathscr{U} ((p_5 \land \neg p_{12} \land \neg p_{13}) \lor (\neg p_5 \land \neg p_7 \land p_{14} \land p_{15})))$.

The FSA that accepts $\mathscr{L}_{\Phi_2}$ has 3 states and 6 transitions. The DNF simplification deletes 2425 conjunctive clauses with empty state regions. The initial dual automaton has 72 states and 2452 transitions; 3 of the states and 1921 of the transitions are removed via the pruning algorithm. After 183 iterations of the refinement algorithm, 228 of the dual automaton states have finite cost. The maximal set of initial states and a sample of satisfying trajectories of the closed loop system are shown in Fig. 6b. Every trajectory originating in $\mathbb{X}_0$ satisfies the specification within 20 discrete-time instants. The polytope-to-polytope controllers are synthesized using vertex interpolation. The computation took 10 minutes on a iMac with a Intel Core i5 processor at 2.8GHz with 8GB of memory.

As discussed in the paper, the upper time bound is affected by the choice of candidate polytopes for partitioning. In this example, a transition is selected from the candidate set according to the cost of the target state as described in Alg. 2. Our experiments showed that choosing the state with the highest Chebychev ball radius resulted in a faster coverage (117 iterations). However, it also produced a higher time bound of 28 steps.

For the double integrator dynamics (17), the control strategy developed in this paper was also tested for a classical control specification, i.e., computation of the maximal constrained control invariant set within $\mathbb{X}$. The method converged to the actual maximal set for the dynamics (17) and the given sets $\mathbb{X}$ and $\mathbb{U}$, which is an indication of the non-conservatism of the vertex interpolation method that solves Prob. 5.2.

7.2 Case Study 2 : Triple Integrator

Consider a triple integrator with sampling time of 1 second, whose dynamics are described by Eqn. (2) with

$$A = \begin{bmatrix} 1 & 1 & 0.5 \\ 0 & 1 & 1 \\ 0 & 0 & 1 \end{bmatrix}, B = \begin{bmatrix} 0.167 \\ 0.5 \\ 1 \end{bmatrix}, \quad (18)$$

and $\mathbb{U} = \{u \in \mathbb{R} \mid -2 \leq u \leq 2\}$. The specification is to reach a target region $\mathbb{T}$, while always staying inside a safe set $\mathbb{X}$ and avoiding

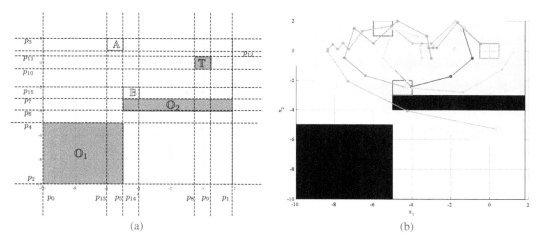

(a)   (b)

Figure 5: Case study 1: (a) The regions and the corresponding linear predicates. The predicates are shown in the half planes where they are satisfied; (b) The set of satisfying initial states $\mathbb{X}_0$ (yellow region) and some trajectories of the closed loop system (the initial states are marked by circles).

obstacles $\mathbb{O}_1$ and $\mathbb{O}_2$, where

$$\mathbb{T} = \{x \mid -0.5 \leq x_i \leq 0.5, i = 1, 2, 3\}$$
$$\mathbb{X} = \{x \mid -4 \leq x_i \leq 4, i = 1, 2, 3\}$$
$$\mathbb{O}_1 = \{x \mid 0.5 \leq x_1 \leq 4, -4 \leq x_2 \leq 4, -4 \leq x_3 \leq 0.5, \}$$
$$\mathbb{O}_2 = \{x \mid -4 \leq x_1 \leq -0.5, -4 \leq x_2 \leq 4, 2 \leq x_3 \leq 4\}.$$

These regions, which are all boxes (i.e., hyper-rectangular polytopes), are shown in Fig. 6 (b). Each box is represented using six predicates, one for each facet, where $[c_i^\top, c_{i+1}^\top, c_{i+2}^\top] = -I_3$, $i = 0, 6$; $[c_i^\top, c_{i+1}^\top, c_{i+2}^\top] = I_3$, $i = 3, 9$; $d_i = 4, i = 0, \ldots, 5$; $d_i = 0.5i = 6, \ldots, 11$ and $c_{12} = -e_3, d_{12} = 2$. The specification can be formally stated as the following scLTL formula:

$$\Phi_3 = (p_0 \wedge p_1 \wedge p_2 \wedge p_3 \wedge p_4 \wedge p_5 \wedge \neg(p_3 \wedge \neg p_9 \wedge p_1 \wedge p_4 \wedge p_2 \wedge p_{11}) \wedge \neg(p_0 \wedge \neg p_6 \wedge p_1 \wedge p_4 \wedge p_{12} \wedge p_5)) \, \mathcal{U} \, (p_6 \wedge p_7 \wedge p_8 \wedge p_9 \wedge p_{10} \wedge p_{11}).$$

The FSA that accepts $\mathscr{L}_{\Phi_3}$ has 2 states and 3 transitions. The DNF simplification deletes 21 conjunctive clauses with empty state regions. The initial dual automaton has 16 states and 225 transitions, and 101 of the transitions are removed via the pruning algorithm. The refinement algorithm terminates after 4790 iterations and the refined dual automaton has 3612 states with finite cost. $\mathbb{X}_0$ and a sample of satisfying trajectories are shown in Fig. 6. Note that $\mathbb{X}_0$ covers 37% of the obstacle free safe region and any trajectory originating in $\mathbb{X}_0$ satisfies the specification in less than 10 steps. This computation took approximatively 5 hours using the same computer as in the Case Study 1.

In this experiment, the candidate states for partitioning are chosen according to the Chebychev ball radius. This example presents a worst case scenario for the developed framework, since most of the encountered controller synthesis problems of the type Prob. 5.2 were infeasible, and the states were partitioned until most of them became a beacon for a transition. Only 162 out of 6578 transition controllers were not one-step controllers.

8. CONCLUSIONS

This paper considered the problem of controlling discrete-time linear systems from specifications given as formulas of syntactically co-safe linear temporal logic over linear predicates in the state variables of the system. A systematic procedure was developed for the automatic computation of sets of initial states and feedback con-

trollers such that all the resulting trajectories of the corresponding closed-loop system satisfy the given specifications. The developed procedure is based on the iterative construction and refinement of an automaton that enforces the satisfaction of the formula. Interpolation and polyhedral Lyapunov function based approaches were proposed to compute the polytope-to-polytope controllers for the transitions of the automaton. The algorithms developed in this paper were implemented as a software package that is available for download. Their application and effectiveness were demonstrated for two challenging case studies.

9. ACKNOWLEDGEMENTS

We would like to acknowledge the help of Dr. Amit Bhatia and Dr. Lydia E. Kavraki for sharing useful modifications of the scheck code. This work was partially supported at Boston University by the NSF under grants CNS-0834260 and CNS-1035588, by the ONR under grants 014-001-0303-5 and N00014-10-10952, and by the ARO under grant W911NF-09-1-0088.

The second author gratefully acknowledges the support of the Veni grant 10230 from the Dutch organizations NWO and STW.

10. REFERENCES

[1] E. M. M. Clarke, D. Peled, and O. Grumberg, *Model checking*. MIT Press, 1999.

[2] A. Girard, "Synthesis using approximately bisimilar abstractions: state-feedback controllers for safety specifications," in *Hybrid Systems: Computation and Control*. ACM, 2010, pp. 111–120.

[3] M. Kloetzer and C. Belta, "A fully automated framework for control of linear systems from temporal logic specifications," *IEEE Transactions on Automatic Control*, vol. 53, no. 1, pp. 287–297, 2008.

[4] G. E. Fainekos and A. Girard, "Hierarchical synthesis of hybrid controllers from temporal logic specifications," in *Hybrid Systems: Computation and Control*. Springer, 2007, pp. 203–216.

[5] T. Wongpiromsarn, U. Topcu, and R. M. Murray, "Receding horizon temporal logic planning for dynamical systems," in *IEEE Conf. on Decision and Control*, Shanghai, China, 2009, pp. 5997–6004.

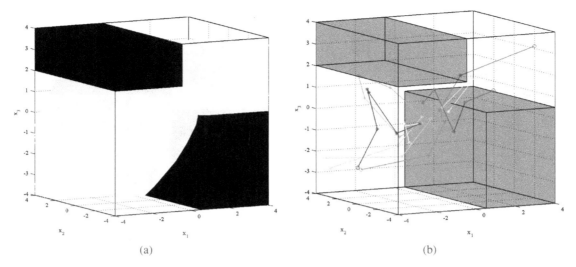

(a)   (b)

Figure 6: Case study 2: (a) The set of satisfying initial states is shown in yellow; (b) Some satisfying trajectories of the closed loop system (the initial states are marked by circles).

[6] P. Tabuada and G. Pappas, "Model checking LTL over controllable linear systems is decidable," ser. Lecture Notes in Computer Science, O. Maler and A. Pnueli, Eds. Springer-Verlag, 2003, vol. 2623.

[7] G. Batt, D. Ropers, H. de Jong, J. Geiselmann, R. Mateescu, M. Page, and D. Schneider, "Validation of qualitative models of genetic regulatory networks by model checking: analysis of the nutritional stress response in e.coli," in *Thirteen International Conference on Intelligent Systems for Molecular Biology*, 2005.

[8] M. Antoniotti, F. Park, A. Policriti, N. Ugel, and B. Mishra, "Foundations of a query and simulation system for the modeling of biochemical and biological processes," ser. Proceedings of the Pacific Symposium on Biocomputing, Lihue, Hawaii, 2003, pp. 116–127.

[9] G. Batt, C. Belta, and R. Weiss, "Temporal logic analysis of gene networks under parameter uncertainty," *IEEE Trans. on Circuits and Systems and IEEE Trans. on Automatic Control, joint special issue on Systems Biology*, vol. 53, pp. 215–229, 2008.

[10] H. K. Gazit, G. Fainekos, and G. J. Pappas, "Where's Waldo? Sensor-based temporal logic motion planning," in *IEEE Conference on Robotics and Automation*, Rome, Italy, 2007.

[11] S. Karaman and E. Frazzoli, "Sampling-based motion planning with deterministic μ-calculus specifications," in *IEEE Conf. on Decision and Control*, Shanghai, China, 2009, pp. 2222–2229.

[12] M. M. Quottrup, T. Bak, and R. Izadi-Zamanabadi, "Multi-robot motion planning: A timed automata approach," in *Proceedings of the 2004 IEEE International Conference on Robotics and Automation*, New Orleans, LA, April 2004, pp. 4417–4422.

[13] M. Kloetzer and C. Belta, "Automatic deployment of distributed teams of robots from temporal logic motion specifications," *IEEE Transactions on Robotics*, vol. 26, no. 1, pp. 48–61, 2010.

[14] A. Bhatia, L. E. Kavraki, and M. Y. Vardi, "Motion planning with hybrid dynamics and temporal goals," in *IEEE Conf. on Decision and Control*, Atlanta, GA, 2010, pp. 1108–1115.

[15] A. P. Sistla, "Safety, liveness and fairness in temporal logic," *Formal Aspects of Computing*, vol. 6, pp. 495–511, 1994.

[16] J. Tumova, B. Yordanov, C. Belta, I. Cerna, and J. Barnat, "A symbolic approach to controlling piecewise affine systems," in *IEEE Conf. on Decision and Control*, Atlanta, GA, 2010, pp. 4230–4235.

[17] S. V. Rakovic, F. Blanchini, E. Cruck, and M. Morari, "Robust obstacle avoidance for constrained linear discrete time systems: A set-theoretic approach," in *IEEE Conf. on Decision and Control*, 2007, pp. 188–193.

[18] S. V. Rakovic and D. Mayne, "Robust Model Predictive Control for Obstacle Avoidance: Discrete Time Case," *Lecture Notes in Control and Information Sciences (LNCIS)*, vol. 358, pp. 617–627, Sep. 2007.

[19] F. Blanchini, S. Miani, F. Pellegrino, and B. van Arkel, "Enhancing controller performance for robot positioning in a constrained environment," *Control Systems Technology, IEEE Transactions on*, vol. 16, no. 5, pp. 1066–1074, 2008.

[20] G. M. Ziegler, *Lectures on polytopes*. Springer, 2007.

[21] O. Kupferman and M. Y. Vardi, "Model checking of safety properties," *Formal Methods in System Design*, vol. 19, pp. 291–314, 2001.

[22] T. Latvala, "Efficient model checking of safety properties," in *In Model Checking Software. 10th International SPIN Workshop*. Springer, 2003, pp. 74–88.

[23] T. Cormen, *Introduction to Algorithms*. MIT press, 2001.

[24] V. Spinu, M. Lazar, and P. P. J. van den Bosch, "An explicit state-feedback solution to constrained stabilization of DC-DC power converters," in *IEEE Conference on Control Applications*, september 2011, pp. 520–525.

[25] M. Lazar, "On infinity norms as Lyapunov functions: Alternative necessary and sufficient conditions," in *IEEE Conf. on Decision and Control*, 2010, pp. 5936–5942.

[26] M. Kvasnica, P. Grieder, and M. Baotić, "Multi-Parametric Toolbox (MPT)," 2004. [Online]. Available: http://control.ee.ethz.ch/~mpt/

A Generic Ellipsoid Abstract Domain
for Linear Time Invariant Systems[*]

Pierre Roux
ONERA
Toulouse, FRANCE
pierre.roux@onera.fr

Romain Jobredeaux
Georgia Tech
Atlanta, Georgia, USA
rjobredeaux3@gatech.edu

Pierre-Loïc Garoche
ONERA
Toulouse, FRANCE
pierre-loic.garoche@onera.fr

Éric Féron
Georgia Tech
Atlanta, Georgia, USA
feron@gatech.edu

ABSTRACT

Embedded system control often relies on linear systems, which admit quadratic invariants. The parts of the code that host linear system implementations need dedicated analysis tools, since intervals or linear abstract domains will give imprecise results, if any at all, on these systems. Previous work by FERET proposes a specific abstraction for digital filters that addresses this issue on a specific class of controllers.

This paper aims at generalizing the idea. It works directly on system representation, relying on existing methods from control theory to automatically generate quadratic invariants for linear time invariant systems, whose stability is provable. This class encompasses n-th order digital filters and, in general, controllers embedded in critical systems.

While control theorists only focus on the existence of such invariants, this paper proposes a method to effectively compute tight ones. The method has been implemented and applied to some benchmark systems, giving good results. It also considers floating points issues and validates the soundness of the computed invariants.

Categories and Subject Descriptors

D.2.4 [**Software/Program Verification**]: Formal methods; F.3.1 [**Specifying and Verifying and Reasoning about Programs**]: Invariants; F.3.2 [**Semantics of Programming Languages**]: Program analysis

[*]This work has been partially supported by the FNRAE Project CAVALE.

Keywords

stable linear systems, ellipsoids, quadratic invariants, Lyapunov functions, semi-definite programming, floating point errors, abstract interpretation.

1. CONTROL-COMMAND BASED CRITICAL SYSTEMS

A wide range of today's real-time embedded systems, especially their most critical parts, rely on a control-command computation core. The control-command of an aircraft, a satellite or a car engine, is processed into a global loop repeated indefinitely during the activity of the controlled device. This loop models the acquisition of new input values via sensors, the update of internal state variables and the generation of new outputs. The acquisition is made either from environmental measurements (like wind speed, acceleration or engine RPM for instance) or from human input via the brakes, the accelerator, the stick or wheel control.

Control theorists are used to model both the environment and the system behavior. Then using their own set of tools, they add the necessary elements to obtain the target controlled system. After discretizing the system, they mathematically prove its stability and its performance by exhibiting a quadratic form, i.e. an ellipsoid, that overapproximates the system behavior with respect to a given input. All these steps are well known by control theory specialists. Reference [15] is a good introduction to these approaches. In this paper, we focus on a class of such systems where control is computed using stable linear systems, i.e. the controller is open-loop stable.

The system control law is then compiled from its description to executable code, like embedded C. This description is usually specified in Matlab Simulink, Scilab Scicos or in a dedicated synchronous language such as Lustre or Scade.

Fig. 1 sketches the loop body of a coupled mass controller, as generated by Matlab. It corresponds to a one step evaluation of the following linear system $x_{k+1} = Ax_k + Bu_k$, where $||u_k||_\infty \le 1$. Vector x_k represents the state of the system at a given time. Matrix A models the system update according to its previous state, while matrix B expresses the effect of the input values u_k.

```c
// DiscreteStateSpace_A : A
real_T A[16] =
    { 0.6227, 0.3871, -0.113, 0.0102,
    -0.3407, 0.9103, -0.3388, 0.0649,
    0.0918, -0.0265, -0.7319, 0.2669,
    0.2643, -0.1298, -0.9903, 0.3331 };

// DiscreteStateSpace_A : B
real_T B[8] =
    { 0.3064, 0.1826,
    -0.0054, 0.6731,
    -0.0494, 1.6138,
    -0.0531, 0.4012 };
```

system definition (A and B matrices)

loop body update

$x_{k+1} = A \times x_k + B \times u_k$

```c
static void MIMC_update(int_T tid) {
    static real_T xnew[4];
    xnew[0] = (A[0])*St[0] + (A[1])*St[1] + (A[2])*St[2]
        + (A[3])*St[3];
    xnew[0] += (B[0])*INPUT[0] + (B[1])*INPUT[1];
    xnew[1] = (A[4])*St[0] + (A[5])*St[1] + (A[6])*St[2]
        + (A[7])*St[3];
    xnew[1] += (B[2])*INPUT[0] + (B[3])*INPUT[1];
    xnew[2] = (A[8])*St[0] + (A[9])*St[1] + (A[10])*St[2]
        + (A[11])*St[3];
    xnew[2] += (B[4])*INPUT[0] + (B[5])*INPUT[1];
    xnew[3] = (A[12])* St[0] + (A[13])*St[1] +
        (A[14])*St[2] + (A[15])*St[3];
    xnew[3] += (B[6])*INPUT[0] + (B[7])*INPUT[1];
    (void) memcpy(St, xnew, sizeof(real_T)*4);
}
```

Figure 1: System update for a coupled mass system controller generated by Matlab.

Once such controller source code is generated, it is embedded in the controlled device, eg. an aircraft. Critical embedded systems are then a major target for static analysis in order to ensure their good behavior. The success story of Astrée [7] illustrates such needs: it targets the analysis of the control command of the Airbus A380, and was used to formally prove the absence of any runtime error on the 700kloc of the controller source code. It relies on the theory of abstract interpretation [5, 6] to compute a sound overapproximation of all possible values of the program variables in any reachable states. Then it is able to ensure that this over-approximation does not reach any possible bad state like overflows, division by zero, or invalid pointer dereferencing. In [7], the authors enumerate the different abstractions used to compute this over-approximation like intervals or octagons. Among them, we focus here on digital filters abstractions represented by ellipsoid abstract domains.

In [8], FERET proposes an analysis dedicated to stable linear filters in control command programs. These short pieces of code correspond to the kind of systems illustrated in Fig. 1, restricted to only one input argument and its past history, i.e. the matrix B is a column vector, and specific types of matrices A, i.e. companion matrices.

Most of the abstract domains available in actual tools only represent linear properties, leading on our target systems at best to rather costly analysis [11] or at worst to no result at all. For example, *no interval invariant exists* for the example of Fig. 1. Thus analyzing it with intervals will give the $(-\infty; +\infty)$ over-approximation, whereas quadratic invariants will bound all parameters in $[-5; 5]$.

In this paper, we propose to generalize the approach of [8] by considering any inherently stable linear system. In particular, we

- characterize quadratic forms, invariants of the linear system analyzed, with techniques inspired by the control theory community;
- propose an open implementation of the analysis that handles floating point rounding errors;
- validate the result using a sound external solver.

Unlike in [8], current work is supposed to take place during the development process and matrices A and B are assumed to be given.

The paper is structured as follow: Section 2 introduces the reader to the notion of stability based on Lyapunov invariants. Section 3 presents our global approach and the steps of our algorithm. Sections 4, 5 and 6 detail the main steps while Section 7 covers floating point issues and soundness. Finally concrete results and related work are presented in Sections 8 and 10.

2. INTRODUCTION TO LYAPUNOV STABILITY THEORY

One common way to establish stability of a discrete, time-invariant closed (i.e. with no inputs) system described in state space form, (i.e $x_{k+1} = f(x_k)$) is to use what is called a Lyapunov function. It is a function $V : \mathbb{R}^n \to \mathbb{R}$ which must satisfy the following properties

$$V(0) = 0 \wedge \forall x \in \mathbb{R}^n \backslash \{0\}, V(x) > 0 \wedge \lim_{||x|| \to \infty} V(x) = \infty \tag{1}$$

$$\forall x \in \mathbb{R}^n, V(f(x)) - V(x) \leq 0. \tag{2}$$

It is shown for example in [13] that exhibiting such a function proves the so-called Lyapunov stability of the system, meaning that its state variables will remain bounded through time. Equation (2) expresses the fact that the function $k \mapsto V(x_k)$ decreases, which, combined with (1), shows that the state variables remain in the bounded sublevel-set $\{x \in \mathbb{R}^n | V(x) \leq V(x_0)\}$ at all instants $k \in \mathbb{N}$.

In the case of Linear Time Invariant systems (of the form $x_{k+1} = Ax_k$, with $A \in \mathbb{R}^{n \times n}$), one can always look for V as a quadratic form in the state variables of the system: $V(x) = x^T P x$ with $P \in \mathbb{R}^{n \times n}$ a symmetric matrix such that

$$P \succ 0 \tag{3}$$

$$A^T P A - P \preceq 0 \tag{4}$$

where "$P \succ 0$" means that the matrix P is positive definite, i.e. for all non-zero vector $x, x^T P x > 0$.

Now, to account for the presence of an external input to the system (which is usually the case with controllers: they use data collected from sensors to generate their output), the model is usually extended into the form

$$x_{k+1} = Ax_k + Bu_k, ||u_k||_\infty \leq 1. \tag{5}$$

To study this equation as precisely as possible, another model, expressing the behavior of the controlled system (the plant), is usually introduced. The two systems taken together form a closed system with no inputs which can be analyzed by looking for a P matrix matching the criteria mentioned before. Such an analysis is refered to as 'closed loop stability analysis'. Here we seek not to model the plant, instead we only require for $||u||_\infty$ to remain bounded[1]. Then, through a slight reinforcement of Equation (4) into

$$A^T P A - P \prec 0 \tag{6}$$

[1]While we could consider different bounds for each component of the input u, we will only deal with $||u||_\infty \leq 1$ for simplicity of the exposition.

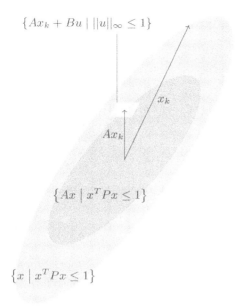

$\{Ax_k + Bu \mid ||u||_\infty \leq 1\}$

x_k

Ax_k

$\{Ax \mid x^T P x \leq 1\}$

$\{x \mid x^T P x \leq 1\}$

Figure 2: Illustration of the stability concepts: if x_k is in the light gray ellipse, then, after a time step, Ax_k is in the dark gray ellipse, which is exactly what is expressed by Equation (4). The white box represents the potential values of x_{k+1} after adding the effect of the bounded input u_k. We see here the necessity that the dark gray ellipse be strictly included in the light gray one, which is the stronger condition expressed by Equation (6).

we can still guarantee that the state variables of (9) will remain in a sublevel set $\{x \in \mathbb{R}^n \mid x^T P x \leq \lambda\}$ (for some $\lambda > 0$), which is an ellipsoid in this case. This approach only enables us to study control laws that are inherently stable, i.e stable when taken separately from the plant they control. Nevertheless a wide range of controllers remain that can be analyzed, and this encompasses in particular all those handled by Astrée. In addition, inherent stability is required in a context of critical applications.

These stability proofs have the very nice side effect that they provide a quadratic invariant on the state variables, which can be used at the code level to find bounds on the program variables. Furthermore, there are many P matrices that fulfill the equations described above. This gives some flexibility as to the choice of such a matrix: by adding relevant constraints on P, one can obtain increasingly better bounds.

3. OVERALL METHOD

3.1 Separate Shape and Ratio

We keep the same overall representation as FERET [8, 9], representing an ellipsoid by a pair (P, λ) where $P \in \mathbb{R}^{n \times n}$ is a symmetric positive definite matrix giving the *shape* of the ellipsoid and $\lambda \in \mathbb{R}$ a scalar giving its *ratio*. The represented ellipsoid is then the set of all $x \in \mathbb{R}^n$ such that $x^T P x \leq \lambda$, i.e. the concretization function γ is given by $\gamma : (P, \lambda) \mapsto \{x \in \mathbb{R}^n \mid x^T P x \leq \lambda\}$. To avoid having multi-

ple representations for the same ellipsoid[2] we can normalize P for instance by requiring its largest coefficient to be 1. The underlying lattice also remains the same. In particular the join of two abstract values (P, λ) and (P', λ') is $(P, \max(\lambda, \lambda'))$ if $P = P'$ and $\top$ otherwise.

This seemingly strange choice at first sight allows us to decompose the computation in two successive steps

1. first determine the shape of the ellipsoid by choosing a well suited matrix P;

2. then find the smallest possible ratio λ such that $x \in \gamma(P, \lambda)$ is an invariant.

Various methods for both steps are detailed and compared in Sections 4 and 5.

3.2 Instrumentation: Use of Semidefinite Programming

To perform the aforementioned computations we rely heavily on semidefinite programming [4, 10]. These tools allow us to compute in polynomial time a solution to a linear matrix inequality (LMI) while minimizing a linear objective function. A LMI is an inequality of the form

$$A_0 + \sum_{i=1}^{k} y_i A_i \succeq 0$$

where the A_i are known matrices, the y_i are the unknowns and "$P \succeq 0$" means that the matrix P is positive semidefinite, i.e. $x^T P x \geq 0$ for all vector x. Indeed we can easily have unknown matrices since a matrix $A \in \mathbb{R}^{n \times n}$ can be expressed as $\sum_{i=1, j=1}^{n,n} A_{i,j} E^{i,j}$, where $E^{i,j}$ is the matrix with zeros everywhere except a one at line i and column j. Likewise multiple LMIs can be grouped into one since $A \succeq 0 \wedge B \succeq 0$ is equivalent to $\begin{pmatrix} A & 0 \\ 0 & B \end{pmatrix} \succeq 0$.

We will also have to deal with some implications which will be achieved by transforming them into a LMI thanks to the following theorem.

THEOREM 1 (S-PROCEDURE). *For any $P, P' \in \mathbb{R}^{n \times n}$, $a, a' \in \mathbb{R}^n$ and $b, b' \in \mathbb{R}$, following conditions are equivalent*

1. $\forall x \in \mathbb{R}^n$,
   $x^T P x + 2a^T x + b \geq 0 \Rightarrow x^T P' x + 2a'^T x + b' \geq 0$

2. $\exists \tau \in \mathbb{R}, \quad \tau > 0 \quad \wedge \quad \begin{pmatrix} P' & a' \\ a'^T & b' \end{pmatrix} - \tau \begin{pmatrix} P & a \\ a^T & b \end{pmatrix} \succeq 0$

PROOF. Soundness ($2 \Rightarrow 1$) is obvious. A proof of completeness ($1 \Rightarrow 2$) can be found in [15]. $\square$

4. SHAPE OF THE ELLIPSOID

As was presented in Section 2, any positive definite matrix P satisfying the Lyapunov equation

$$A^T P A - P \prec 0 \tag{7}$$

will yield a proof of stability and provide *some* bound on the variables. However, additional constraints on P can be introduced that make it possible to obtain better results than others.

---

[2]For instance $(P, 2\lambda)$ and $\left(\frac{P}{2}, \lambda\right)$ represent exactly the same ellipsoid.

While in Control Theory the existence of such ellipsoids is sufficient to prove stability of the system, we are here interested in characterizing it concretely. Investigating heuristically multiple possible shapes allows us to find one which is more adequate, i.e. more precise, with respect to the analyzed system.

The following subsections describe three different types of additional constraints on P and their respective advantages.

4.1 Minimizing Condition Number

Graphically, the condition number of a positive definite matrix expresses a notion similar to that addressed by excentricity for ellipses in dimension 2. It measures how 'close' to a circle (or its higher dimension equivalent) the resulting ellipsoid will be. Multiples of the identity matrix, which all represent a circle, have a condition number of 1. Thus one idea of constraint we can impose on P is to have its condition number as close to 1 as possible. One reason is that 'flat' ellipsoids can yield a very bad bound on one of the variables. This is done [3] by minimizing a new variable, r, in the following matrix inequality

$$I \preceq P \preceq rI.$$

This constraint, along with the others (Lyapunov equation, positive definiteness, ...), can be expressed as an LMI, which is solved using the semi definite programming techniques mentioned in Section 2.

4.2 Preserving the Shape

Another approach [25] is to minimize $r \in (0, 1)$ in the following inequality

$$A^T P A - rP \preceq 0.$$

Intuitively, this corresponds to finding the shape of ellipsoid that gets 'preserved' the best when the update $x_{k+1} = Ax_k$ is applied. This is the choice implicitly made in [8] for a particular case of 2×2 matrices A. With this technique however, the presence of a quadratic term rP in the equation prevents the use of usual LMI solving tools 'as is'. To overcome this we chose an approach where we try a value for r and refine it by dichotomy. Only a few steps are required to obtain a good approximation of the optimal value.

4.3 All in One

The two previous methods were based only on A, completely abstracting B away, which could lead to rather coarse abstractions. We try here to take both A and B into account by finding the smallest possible ellipsoid P such that

$$\forall x, \forall u, ||u||_\infty \leq 1 \Rightarrow x^T P x \leq 1 \Rightarrow (Ax + Bu)^T P (Ax + Bu) \leq 1$$

which, using the S procedure, amounts to the existence of $\tau_i > 0$ such that

$$\begin{pmatrix} -A^T P A & -A^T P B e_i \\ -e_i^T B^T P A & 1 - e_i^T B^T P B e_i \end{pmatrix} - \tau_i \begin{pmatrix} -P & 0 \\ 0 & 1 \end{pmatrix} \succeq 0$$

for all the vertices e_i of the hypercube of dimension p, the number of inputs. The rationale behind this formula is explained in Section 5.2. This is not an LMI since τ and P are both variables but a reasonably good solution can be found by trying various values of τ between some $\tau_{min} \in (0, 1)$, which can be found by dichotomy, and 1.

4.4 Comparison and Combination

There is no proof that one method always performs better than the others, and, for each method, there exists examples where it performs better than the other two, see Section 8. It appears, however, that the third method, albeit a little more costly, yields the best bounds in general. In fact the cost is also debatable since, despite being costlier, it does not require the search for the ratio, a necessary step for the first two methods described in Sections 4.1 and 4.2.

In any case, the methods are not exclusive of each other and can be combined: the resulting (sound) value will be the intersection of the projection of each obtained ellipsoids. Having multiple, not-always-comparable values will only yield more precise results.

5. FINDING A STABLE RATIO

Now that we have chosen a matrix P, we need to find a ratio λ such that $x^T P x \leq \lambda$ is an invariant for the whole system $x_{k+1} = Ax_k + Bu_k$ with a bounded input u that satisfies $||u||_\infty \leq 1$. The existence of such a λ is guaranteed by the choice of P as a solution of the Lyapunov inequality (7). Those λ are exactly the fixpoints of the function mapping λ_k to the maximum of λ_k and the least λ_{k+1} such that

$$\forall x_k \in \mathbb{R}^n, u_k \in \mathbb{R}^p, ||u_k||_\infty \leq 1 \Rightarrow x_k^T P x_k \leq \lambda_k \Rightarrow \\ x_{k+1}^T P x_{k+1} \leq \lambda_{k+1} \quad (8)$$

where $x_{k+1} = Ax_k + Bu_k$. We are of course interested in the least fixpoint.

5.1 Initial Ratio λ_0

Since the system starts in state x_0, we initialize λ_0 as $x_0^T P x_0$. If instead of a simple point the initial conditions are only known to lie in a polyhedron, we just have to take the maximum of $x^T P x$ among all vertices x of the polyhedron.

5.2 One Iteration

Given some λ_k, we want to compute the least λ_{k+1} satisfying Equation (8). By a convexity argument[3], it is enough to have the following for every vertex $e_i, i \in [\![1, 2^p]\!]$ of the hypercube[4] $\{u_k \mid ||u_k||_\infty \leq 1\}$ of dimension p

$$\forall x_k \in \mathbb{R}^n, x_k^T P x_k \leq \lambda_k \Rightarrow \\ (Ax_k + Be_i)^T P (Ax_k + Be_i) \leq \lambda_{k+1}.$$

Using the S-procedure[5] we get the equivalent formulation

$$\forall i \in [\![1, 2^p]\!], \exists \tau_i, \tau_i \geq 0 \wedge \\ \begin{pmatrix} -A^T P A & -A^T P B e_i \\ -e_i^T B^T P A & \lambda_{k+1} - e_i^T B^T P B e_i \end{pmatrix} \\ - \tau_i \begin{pmatrix} -P & 0 \\ 0 & \lambda_k \end{pmatrix} \succeq 0$$

which is an LMI in λ_{k+1} and the τ_i which is solved by minimizing λ_{k+1}.

We can notice that, by a symmetry argument, we can forget about half of the e_i as depicted on Figure 3.

---

[3]See Figure 2 for a graphical illustration of this.
[4]A major drawback of the approach is that the number of vertices is exponential in the number of inputs p. We could design a cheaper abstraction but it would be coarser, in addition the number of inputs p often remains reasonable.
[5]See Theorem 1.

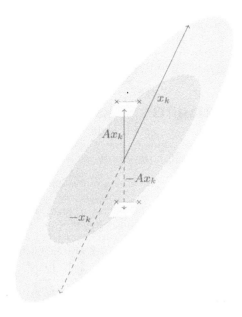

Figure 3: We can forget half of the vertices of the white box as they will be taken into account on the opposite side.

5.3 Iterating to Fixpoint and Widening

Now we can compute Kleene iterates but it will be slow to converge to a fixpoint. To accelerate, we can use a widening with thresholds, which allows us to find a value for λ up to some factor q of the least one by using a sequence of powers of q as thresholds.

5.4 An alternative to Classical Widening

When looking for a good postfixpoint we are indeed looking for a small λ satisfying the following equation

$$\forall i \in [\![1, 2^p]\!], \tau_i > 0 \wedge$$
$$\begin{pmatrix} -A^T P A & -A^T P B e_i \\ -e_i^T B^T P A & \lambda - e_i^T B^T P B e_i \end{pmatrix} \tag{9}$$
$$- \tau_i \begin{pmatrix} -P & 0 \\ 0 & \lambda \end{pmatrix} \succeq 0.$$

This is not an LMI because of the τ_i but if we used the method described in Section 4.2 for choosing the shape of P, we have obtained[6] a parameter $r \in (0,1)$ such that $\tau_i \in [r, 1]$. Computing the smallest λ satisfying the following LMI then directly gives a postfixpoint

$$\forall i \in [\![1, 2^p]\!], \begin{pmatrix} -A^T P A & -A^T P B e_i \\ -e_i^T B^T P A & \lambda - e_i^T B^T P B e_i \end{pmatrix}$$
$$- \frac{r+1}{2} \begin{pmatrix} -P & 0 \\ 0 & \lambda \end{pmatrix} \succeq 0.$$

5.5 Refining a Postfixpoint by Dichotomy

Once we have found a postfixpoint λ_{max} using widening with thresholds, we can refine it through decreasing iterations with narrowing but this usually does not lead quickly to anything close to the least fixpoint. However, an interesting property of this least fixpoint λ_{min} is that $\lambda_{k+1} \leq \lambda_k$

---
[6]Otherwise we can still recompute such a parameter r.

exactly when $\lambda_k \geq \lambda_{min}$, then enabling to efficiently and tightly overapproximate it by a dichotomy testing satisfiability of the LMI (9) for values of λ between zero[7] and λ_{max}.

6. BACK TO INTERVALS

While quadratic forms precisely over-approximate the set of reachable states of linear systems subject to bounded inputs, they are hardly usable as such in conjunction with other abstractions. We can solve LMIs to project the obtained ellipsoid and get bounds on the variables, $x_i \in [-a, a]$ with a the least value such that

$$\begin{pmatrix} 0 & -\frac{e_i}{2} \\ -\frac{e_i^T}{2} & a \end{pmatrix} - \tau \begin{pmatrix} -P & 0 \\ 0 & \lambda \end{pmatrix} \succeq 0$$

where e_i is the ith vector of the canonical base.

This is not limited to intervals, the same thing can be done for octagons [16] or more generally linear [23] or even quadratic [1, 10] templates.

7. FLOATING POINT ISSUES

Two fundamentally different issues with floating point numbers must be considered

the analyzed system contains floating point computations with rounding errors making it behave differently from the way it would if the same computations were done with real numbers, this is discussed in Section 7.1;

the implementation of the abstract domain is also carried out with floating point computations for the sake of efficiency, this usually works well in practice but can give erroneous results, hence the need for some a posteriori validation, see Section 7.2 for further details.

7.1 Taking Rounding Errors Into Account

The sum of two floating point values is, in all generality, not representable as a floating point value and must consequently be rounded. The accumulation of rounding errors can potentially lead to far different results from the ones expected with real numbers, thus floating point computations must be taken into account in our analysis [19].

The rounding errors can be of two different types :

- for normalized numbers represented with a fixed number of bits, we get a relative error: $\text{round}(a + b) \in [(1 - \epsilon)(a + b), (1 + \epsilon)(a + b)]$;

- for denormalized numbers (i.e ones very close to 0), we get an absolute error: $\text{round}(a+b) \in [a+b-\omega, a+b+\omega]$.

A common and easy solution to take both possible errors into account is to sum them which in practice leads only to a very slight overapproximation: $\text{round}(a + b) \in [(1 - \epsilon)(a + b) - \omega, (1 + \epsilon)(a + b) + \omega]$. Although only addition is illustrated here, the method works exactly the same way for any other floating point operation. The actual values of ϵ and ω depend on the characteristics of the considered floating point system. For instance we will take $\epsilon = 2^{-23}$ and $\omega = 2^{-149}$ for single precision[8].

---
[7]Or, better, the last prefixpoint encountered during the widening iterations.
[8]Type `float` in C.

Combining these elementary errors we get a simple post-processing for each iteration of Section 5.2 to soundly over-approximate rounding errors.

Definition 1. $\exists(e)$ represents floating point evaluation of expression e with any rounding mode and any order of evaluation[9] [22].

LEMMA 1. *Assuming $\epsilon \leq 2^{-23}$, $\omega \leq 2^{-149}$ and $n \leq 2^{11} = 2048$, we have*[10]

$$\text{fl}\left(\sum_{i=1}^{n} a_i x_i\right) \leq (1 + (n+1)\epsilon)\left(\sum_{i=1}^{n} a_i x_i\right) + n(n+1)\omega.$$

PROOF. By induction on n. $\square$

LEMMA 2. *For any $a \in \mathbb{R}$, $x, y \in \mathbb{R}^n$, $P \in \mathbb{R}^{n \times n}$ a symmetric positive definite matrix and $\lambda, \mu \in \mathbb{R}$, if we have $\|y\|_2 \leq \mu$ and $x^T P x \leq \lambda$ then*

$$(ax + y)^T P (ax + y) \leq a^2 \lambda + 2ab\sqrt{\lambda} + b^2$$

with $b = \sqrt{r}$ with r the least scalar such that there exists $\tau \in \mathbb{R}$ satisfying

$$\tau \geq 0 \wedge \begin{pmatrix} -P & 0 \\ 0 & r \end{pmatrix} - \tau \begin{pmatrix} -I & 0 \\ 0 & \mu \end{pmatrix} \succeq 0.$$

PROOF. Using Theorem 1 we have $y^T P y \leq r$ hence the result by expansion and Cauchy-Schwartz inequality. $\square$

THEOREM 2. *For any $x \in \mathbb{R}^n$, $u \in \mathbb{R}^p$, $A \in \mathbb{R}^{n \times n}$, $B \in \mathbb{R}^{n \times p}$, $P \in \mathbb{R}^{n \times n}$ a symmetric positive definite matrix and $\lambda \in \mathbb{R}$ if $n + p \leq 2048$ then*

$$(Ax + Bu)^T P (Ax + Bu) \leq \lambda \Rightarrow$$
$$(\text{fl}(Ax + Bu))^T P \text{fl}(Ax + Bu) \leq a^2 \lambda + 2ab\sqrt{\lambda} + b^2$$

with $a = 1 + (n + p + 1)\epsilon$ and b defined as in Lemma 2 for $\mu = \sqrt{n}(n + p)(n + p + 1)\omega$.

PROOF. By successive applications of Lemmas 1 and 2. $\square$

Thus, provided that the number of variables of the system plus its number of inputs is less than 2048, which is a reasonable assumption, we just have to compute a and b once as defined in Theorem 2 then apply to each step of Section 5.2 the postprocessing $\lambda \mapsto a^2 \lambda + 2ab\sqrt{\lambda} + b^2$ to take into account computation with floats, whatever the rounding mode and the order of evaluation.

Such use of abstract domains in the real field to soundly analyze floating point computations is not new [17] and some techniques even allow to finely track rounding errors and their origin in the analyzed program [12].

7.2 Checking Soundness of the Result

Because the LMI solver is implemented with floating point computations, we have no guarantee on the results it provides[11]. Hence the need to check them. This amounts to checking that a given matrix is actually positive definite.

---

[9]Order of evaluation matters since floating point addition is not associative.

[10]Those are the values for single precision but it would work just the same for any other precision with adequate values.

[11]There also exists guaranteed SDP solvers now [14] over and underapproximating the primal and the dual problem to guarantee an error bound on the result. However we only need to check the final result. Thanks to Éric GOUBAULT for pointing that to us.

This is done by carefully bounding the rounding error on a floating point Cholesky decomposition [22][12]. Proof of positive definiteness of an $n \times n$ matrix can then be achieved in time $O(n^3)$ which in practice induces only a very small overhead to the whole analysis.

8. EXPERIMENTAL RESULTS

All the elements presented in this paper have been implemented as an autonomous linear system analysis engine. The tool is composed of three parts:

- The core mathematical computations are done with Scilab [24], mainly with the LMI solver [20] from an OCaml front-end. This part is a set of functions that implement the algorithms presented in Sections 4, 5, 6 and 7.1, as well as projections of ellipsoids over intervals. Computation in Scilab are done using double precision floats.

- The front-end is an OCaml code using rational numbers (Num library). It loads the A and B matrices and interacts with Scilab to compute the different sequence of calls to Scilab functions.

- A last part, also in OCaml, interfaces the obtained quadratic form with a particular C implementation of a Cholesky decomposition [22] to ensure its stability as explained in Section 7.2.

The code is released under a GPLv2 license and is available at http://cavale.enseeiht.fr/.

Experiments were conducted on a set of stable linear systems. These systems were extracted from [9], [1] or from basic controllers found in the literature. Table 1 illustrates the value computed using the different techniques as well as the time spent at each step. Figure 4 compares some plots of the obtained quadratic forms depending on the approach used to find the ellipsoid.

9. DETAILED NUMERICAL EXAMPLE

We will describe here with all details and figures one of the examples from the previous section, namely Ex. 5 from Table 1 and Figure 4.

All the systems studied in this paper are of the form

$$x_{k+1} = Ax_k + Bu_k, \|u_k\|_\infty \leq 1$$

for all $k \in \mathbb{N}$ and start from some $x_0 \in \mathbb{R}^n$. In this example, matrices A and B take the following values

$$A = \begin{pmatrix} 0.6227 & 0.3871 & -0.113 & 0.0102 \\ -0.3407 & 0.9103 & -0.3388 & 0.0649 \\ 0.0918 & -0.0265 & -0.7319 & 0.2669 \\ 0.2643 & -0.1298 & -0.9903 & 0.3331 \end{pmatrix}$$

$$B = \begin{pmatrix} 0.3064 & 0.1826 \\ -0.0054 & 0.6731 \\ 0.0494 & 1.6138 \\ -0.0531 & 0.4012 \end{pmatrix}.$$

This would be implemented by the C code shown in Figure 1.

---

[12]Thanks to Timothy WANG for pointing this to us.

	Method	t_1		λ	$\lambda_\triangledown$	Bounds	t_2	Valid. t_3
Ex. 1 From [9, slides] n=2, 1 input	I	0.07	fp	131072	105341	[140.4; 189.9]	0.48	0.01
			τ	105351			0.40	0.01
	P	0.16	fp	128.0	96.0	[22.2; 26.5]	0.35	0.01
			τ	96.8			0.28	0.01
	U	0.23		$1+\epsilon$		[16.2; 17.6]	0.20	0.01
Ex. 2 From [9, slides] n=4, 1 input	I	0.09	fp	2048	1371	[18.1; 25.2; 24.3; 33.7]	0.48	0.02
			τ	1376			0.40	0.01
	P	0.27	fp	8.0	4.2	[6.3; 7.7; 2.2; 3.4]	0.35	0.01
			τ	6.4			0.27	0.02
	U	0.40		$1+\epsilon$		[1.7; 2.0; 2.2; 2.5]	0.21	0.01
Ex. 3 Discretized lead-lag controller n=2, 1 input	I	0.07	fp	262144	204241	[391.4; 21.6]	0.54	0.01
			τ	$\perp$			$\perp$	$\perp$
	P	0.17	fp	2048	1281	[36.2; 36.1]	0.44	0.02
			τ	1632			0.33	0.01
	U	0.20		$1+\epsilon$		[38.8; 20.3]	0.20	0.01
Ex. 4 Linear quadratic gaussian regulator n=3, 1 input	I	0.09	fp	16.0	10.3	[1.2; 0.9; 0.5]	0.38	0.02
			τ	10.9			0.32	0.02
	P	0.19	fp	1.0	0.7	[0.9; 0.9; 0.9]	0.31	0.02
			τ	1.1			0.26	0.01
	U	0.24		$1+\epsilon$		[0.7; 0.4; 0.3]	0.22	0.02
Ex. 5 Observer based controller for a coupled mass system n=4, 2 inputs	I	0.09	fp	512.0	304.6	[9.8; 8.9; 11.0; 16.8]	0.48	0.03
			τ	323.0			0.43	0.03
	P	0.24	fp	32.0	24.3	[5.7; 5.6; 6.4; 10.1]	0.42	0.03
			τ	28.6			0.33	0.03
	U	0.48		$1+\epsilon$		[5.0; 4.9; 4.8; 4.7]	0.22	0.03
Ex. 6 Butterworth low-pass filter n=5, 1 input	I	0.10	fp	128.0	102.4	[7.5; 8.7; 6.1; 7.0; 6.5]	0.44	0.02
			τ	113.1			0.38	0.03
	P	0.32	fp	8.0	7.1	[3.6; 5.0; 4.7; 8.1; 8.9]	0.37	0.02
			τ	7.7			0.29	0.02
	U	0.78		$1+\epsilon$		[2.3; 1.1; 1.9; 2.0; 2.9]	0.24	0.03
Ex. 7 Dampened oscillator from [1] n=2, no input	I	0.07	fp	353.6	353.6	[1.7; 2.1]	0.22	0.01
			τ	353.6			0.23	0.01
	P	0.15	fp	3.0	3.0	[2.0; 2.0]	0.22	0.01 ($\perp$)
			τ	3.0			0.20	0.01 ($\perp$)
	U	0.27		$1+\epsilon$		[1.5; 1.5]	0.16	0.01
Ex. 8 Harmonic oscillator from [1] n=2, no input	I	0.08	fp	22.9	22.9	[1.5; 1.5]	0.22	0.01
			τ	22.9			0.23	0.01
	P	0.24	fp	2.0	2.0	[1.5; 1.5]	0.24	0.01 ($\perp$)
			τ	2.0			0.20	0.01 ($\perp$)
	U	0.15		$1+\epsilon$		[1.5; 1.5]	0.16	0.01

Table 1: Result of the experiments: quadratic invariants computation. Times are expressed in seconds, t_1 is the time spent to compute the shape of the ellipsoid, t_2 is the time spend to find the appropriate ratio λ and project the resulting invariant on intervals and t_3 is the time needed to validate the stability of the resulting ellipsoid, as explained in Section 7.2. I, P and U are respectively the methods of Sections 4.1, 4.2 and 4.3. $\lambda_\triangledown$ denotes the refined value of λ by dichotomy.

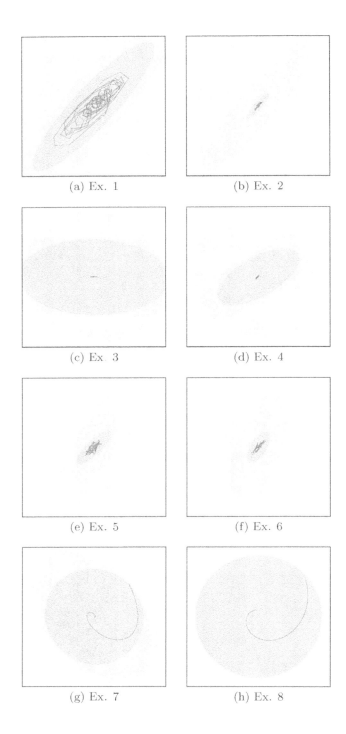

(a) Ex. 1   (b) Ex. 2

(c) Ex. 3   (d) Ex. 4

(e) Ex. 5   (f) Ex. 6

(g) Ex. 7   (h) Ex. 8

Figure 4: Comparison of obtained ellipsoids by methods of Sections 4.1, 4.2 and 4.3 from lighter to darker, plus a random simulation trace ((b), (d), (e) and (f), being of dimension greater than 2, are cuts along planes containing the origin and two vectors of the canonical base, to show how the three different templates compare together).

In the rest of this section we will first determine the *shape* on an ellipsoid $P \in \mathbb{R}^{4 \times 4}$, then look for a *ratio* λ such that any point x of the ellipsoid remains in it after an iteration of the system

$$||u||_\infty \le 1 \Rightarrow x^T P x \le \lambda \Rightarrow (Ax + Bu)^T P(Ax + Bu) \le \lambda.$$

This way, we will ensure that for all $k \in \mathbb{N}$

$$x_k \in \left\{ x \mid x^T P x \le \lambda \right\}$$

since we choose to start from $x_0 = 0$ for the sake of simplicity. We will eventually project this ellipsoid on each dimension to get the bounds on all of the four components of x shown in the column "Bounds" of Table 1.

9.1 Shape of the Ellipsoid

9.1.1 Minimizing Condition Number

Looking for a shape as close to a circle as possible for the ellipsoid, following Section 4.1, we have to find $P \in \mathbb{R}^{4 \times 4}$ minimizing a variable r such that

$$\begin{cases} P = P^T \\ A^T P A - P \prec 0 \\ I \preceq P \preceq rI. \end{cases}$$

Scilab[13] returns

$$P_I = \begin{pmatrix} 3.47677 & -1.12772 & -0.0378711 & 0.0598661 \\ -1.12772 & 4.46224 & -0.706604 & 0.0369274 \\ -0.0378711 & -0.706604 & 3.01613 & -0.659782 \\ 0.0598661 & 0.0369274 & -0.659782 & 1.22887 \end{pmatrix}.$$

9.1.2 Preserving the Shape

Looking for an ellipsoid as in Section 4.2, we have to find $P \in \mathbb{R}^{4 \times 4}$ minimizing a variable $r \in (0, 1)$ such that

$$\begin{cases} P = P^T \\ P \succ 0 \\ A^T P A - rP \preceq 0. \end{cases}$$

Trying values of r by dichotomy, Scilab returns

$$P_P = \begin{pmatrix} 0.923982 & -0.389107 & 0.0523332 & -0.0646109 \\ -0.389107 & 1 & -0.209378 & 0.0752329 \\ 0.0523332 & -0.209378 & 0.842523 & -0.266348 \\ -0.0646109 & 0.0752329 & -0.266348 & 0.328153 \end{pmatrix}.$$

for $r = \frac{1447}{2048}$ after 11 iterations.

9.1.3 All in One

Looking for an ellipsoid as described in Section 4.3, we have to find $P \in \mathbb{R}^{4 \times 4}$ maximizing a variable $r > 0$ such that

$$\begin{cases} P = P^T \\ P \succ 0 \\ \begin{pmatrix} -A^T P A & -A^T P B e_0 \\ -e_0^T B^T P A & 1 - e_0^T B^T P B e_0 \end{pmatrix} - \tau \begin{pmatrix} -P & 0 \\ 0 & 1 \end{pmatrix} \succeq 0 \\ \begin{pmatrix} -A^T P A & -A^T P B e_1 \\ -e_1^T B^T P A & 1 - e_1^T B^T P B e_1 \end{pmatrix} - \tau \begin{pmatrix} -P & 0 \\ 0 & 1 \end{pmatrix} \succeq 0 \\ P - rI \succ 0. \end{cases}$$

with $e_0 = (1\ 1)^T$ and $e_1 = (-1\ 1)^T$.

---

[13] Again, our code is available at http://cavale.enseeiht. fr/.

Trying 12 equally spaced values for τ in $[0.7109375, 1)$, we keep the one allowing for the biggest r (i.e. the ellipsoid P included in the smallest sphere) which yields

$$P_U = \begin{pmatrix} 0.048421 & -0.0204237 & 0.0107759 & -0.0148744 \\ -0.0204237 & 0.0593613 & -0.0380607 & 0.0357011 \\ 0.0107759 & -0.0380607 & 0.134433 & -0.110095 \\ -0.0148744 & 0.0357011 & -0.110095 & 0.138309 \end{pmatrix}.$$

9.2 Finding a Stable Ratio

Now that we have a template ellipsoid, we need to look for a proper *ratio*. We will only describe the process for the first template P_I since it works just the same for the two others.

9.2.1 Initial Ratio λ_0

Since the system starts from $x_0 = 0$, we just have to take $\lambda_0 = 0$.

9.2.2 One Iteration

Given λ_k, we compute λ_{k+1} as the smallest value such that there exist τ_0 and τ_1 non negatives satisfying

$$\begin{cases} \begin{pmatrix} -A^T P A & -A^T P B e_0 \\ -e_0^T B^T P A & \lambda_{k+1} - e_0^T B^T P B e_0 \end{pmatrix} - \tau_0 \begin{pmatrix} -P & 0 \\ 0 & \lambda_k \end{pmatrix} \succeq 0 \\ \begin{pmatrix} -A^T P A & -A^T P B e_1 \\ -e_1^T B^T P A & \lambda_{k+1} - e_1^T B^T P B e_1 \end{pmatrix} - \tau_0 \begin{pmatrix} -P & 0 \\ 0 & \lambda_k \end{pmatrix} \succeq 0 \end{cases}$$

with $e_0 = (1\ 1)^T$ and $e_1 = (-1\ 1)^T$.

To take into account rounding errors in a computation with single precision floating point values, we will actually take $\lambda'_{k+1} = a^2 \lambda_{k+1} + 2ab\sqrt{\lambda_{k+1}} + b^2$ with $a = 1.000000834465$ and $b = 2.539600776 \times 10^{-20}$ according to Section 7.1.

9.2.3 Iterating to Fixpoint and Widening

Trying powers of 2 and stopping at the first one such that $\lambda'_{k+1} \leq \lambda_k$ we get a value of 512.0 for λ.

9.2.4 An alternative to Classical Widening

Following method of Section 5.4, we get a better $\lambda = 323.0$.

9.3 Refining a Postfixpoint by Dichotomy

Following Section 5.5, those can be refined to $\lambda = 304.6$

Finally, projections to intervals give the bounds shown in Table 1 and soundness of the result is successfully checked.

10. RELATED WORK

Many work in abstract interpretation, and its use to analyze programs, focus on linear patterns to abstract properties. However few work address non linear invariant synthesis.

FERET's work [8, 9] on the one hand is a practical approach to the problem. Its goal is to address the need by Astrée to handle the linear filters present in Airbus' real time software. Previous work [18] by MONNIAUX also addressed the same class of systems at the same level as in this paper rather than on actual code. As mentioned earlier, this effort addresses a strict subset of the systems we consider. However, it is hard to compare both works in terms of precision on the set of systems they both handle due to the lack of publicly available implementation or figures. Although FERET's work is probably a bit more precise thanks to the

way it takes into account a limited number of previous inputs, performing a kind of unrolling, we use better ellipsoids of higher dimension and Figure 4 indicates that the resulting precision is often far from disastrous.

On the other hand, there are work that target similar properties but are more theory oriented and motivated. One can cite the Lagrangian Relaxation approach applied to program termination analysis as introduced by COUSOT in [4] and ROOZBEHANI, FÉRON and MEGRETSKI in [21], or the works of ADJÉ, GAUBERT and GOUBAULT [1] and GAWLITZA and SEIDL [10] on policy iterations and non linear forms. The latter two aim at replacing a Kleene based fixpoint computation by a symbolic reasoning based on semi-definite programming. They are more inspired by theoretical results leading to the analysis. [1, 2] even cites the existence of Lyapunov based invariant as a prerequisite for the method. *These works are more general than ours*: they address the analysis of non linear systems, even with non convex properties. However *none of them automatically finds the appropriate shape*: templates need to be given, e.g by providing a Lyapunov function, whereas we automatically compute an, in some sense "optimal", template[14]. *They also do not address the floating point issues.*

Our work should be considered as an in-between solution. It takes ideas from control theory results but targets the analysis of specific realistic systems. Furthermore it addresses floating point errors as well as the validity analysis of the obtained invariants.

11. CONCLUSION AND PERSPECTIVES

We have presented a set of analysis allowing us to characterize quadratic invariants, i.e. ellipsoids, for a subset of linear systems: inherently stable linear systems subject to bounded inputs.

Most of the critical embedded control command systems rely on such linear systems. But intervals and linear invariants in general will not allow to precisely describe their state space.

This analysis is based on ideas from control theory. They are used to prove the stability of the system by exhibiting a proof of existence of a so-called Lyapunov quadratic form.

This work addresses the explicit computation of such a form by exploring the instantiation of multiple generic templates to find the most appropriate ellipsoids to bound the analyzed system.

Our effort also considers floating point errors and addresses the validity of the computed solution. It has been implemented and applied on several examples. The reduced product between the different templates instantiated gives extremely precise results as illustrated by the experimentations.

The approach of this paper presents the major drawback of being unable to directly analyze actual systems at code level, in particular because such systems are usually equipped with saturations or resets. We believe this can be addressed by using policy iteration methods [1, 10]. The computation of templates does not play any role in soundness of the analysis and may be able to accommodate heuristics extracting

---

[14]It can be interesting to notice that in case of Ex. 7 of Table 1, such an automatically computed template allows to find more precise bounds than in [1, 10] with a manually chosen template.

potential A and B matrices from the code[15]. Methods used to address floating point issues should also be adaptable to policy iteration.

Acknowledgments.

We deeply thanks Éric GOUBAULT and Jérôme FERET for useful comments on this paper.

12. REFERENCES

[1] A. Adjé, S. Gaubert, and E. Goubault. Coupling policy iteration with semi-definite relaxation to compute accurate numerical invariants in static analysis. In *ESOP*, volume 6012 of *LNCS*. Springer, 2010.

[2] F. Alegre, E. Féron, and S. Pande. Using ellipsoidal domains to analyze control systems software. 2009. http://arxiv.org/abs/0909.1977.

[3] S. Boyd, L. El Ghaoui, E. Féron, and V. Balakrishnan. *Linear Matrix Inequalities in System and Control Theory*, volume 15 of *Studies in Applied Mathematics*. SIAM, Philadelphia, PA, June 1994.

[4] P. Cousot. Proving program invariance and termination by parametric abstraction, lagrangian relaxation and semidefinite programming. In *VMCAI*, volume 3385 of *Lecture Notes in Computer Science*. Springer, 2005.

[5] P. Cousot and R. Cousot. Abstract interpretation: A unified lattice model for static analysis of programs by construction or approximation of fixpoints. In *POPL*, 1977.

[6] P. Cousot and R. Cousot. Systematic design of program analysis frameworks. In *POPL*, 1979.

[7] P. Cousot, R. Cousot, J. Feret, L. Mauborgne, A. Miné, D. Monniaux, and X. Rival. Combination of abstractions in the ASTRÉE static analyzer. In *ASIAN*, Tokyo, Japan, LNCS 4435, 2006. Springer.

[8] J. Feret. Static analysis of digital filters. In *ESOP*, number 2986 in LNCS. Springer, 2004.

[9] J. Feret. Numerical abstract domains for digital filters. In *International workshop on Numerical and Symbolic Abstract Domains (NSAD)*, 2005.

[10] T. M. Gawlitza and H. Seidl. Computing relaxed abstract semantics w.r.t. quadratic zones precisely. In *SAS*, volume 6337 of *LNCS*. Springer, 2010.

[11] K. Ghorbal, E. Goubault, and S. Putot. The zonotope abstract domain taylor1+. In *CAV*, volume 5643 of *LNCS*. Springer, 2009.

[12] E. Goubault and S. Putot. Static analysis of finite precision computations. In *VMCAI*, volume 6538 of *LNCS*. Springer, 2011.

[13] W. M. Haddad and V. S. Chellaboina. *Nonlinear Dynamical Systems and Control: A Lyapunov-Based Approach*. Princeton University Press, 2008.

[14] C. Jansson, D. Chaykin, and C. Keil. Rigorous error bounds for the optimal value in semidefinite programming. *SIAM J. Numerical Analysis*, 46(1), 2007.

[15] U. T. Jönsson. A lecture on the S-Procedure, 2001.

[16] A. Miné. The octagon abstract domain. In *AST 2001 in WCRE 2001*, IEEE. IEEE CS Press, October 2001.

[17] A. Miné. Relational abstract domains for the detection of floating-point run-time errors. In *ESOP*, volume 2986 of *LNCS*. Springer, 2004.

[18] D. Monniaux. Compositional analysis of floating-point linear numerical filters. In *CAV*, volume 3576 of *LNCS*. Springer, 2005.

[19] D. Monniaux. The pitfalls of verifying floating-point computations. *ACM Trans. Program. Lang. Syst.*, 30(3), 2008.

[20] R. Nikoukhah, F. Delebecque, and L. El Ghaoui. LMITOOL: a Package for LMI Optimization in Scilab User's Guide. Research Report RT-0170, INRIA, Feb. 1995.

[21] M. Roozbehani, E. Féron, and A. Megretski. Modeling, optimization and computation for software verification. In *HSCC*, volume 3414 of *LNCS*. Springer, 2005.

[22] S. M. Rump. Verification of positive definiteness. *BIT Numerical Mathematics*, 46, 2006.

[23] S. Sankaranarayanan, M. Colón, H. B. Sipma, and Z. Manna. Efficient strongly relational polyhedral analysis. In *VMCAI*, volume 3855 of *LNCS*. Springer, 2006.

[24] Scilab Team. Scilab. http://www.scilab.org.

[25] Q. Yang. *Minimum Decay Rate of a Family of Dynamical Systems*. PhD thesis, Stanford, 1992.

---

[15]The only limitation being to avoid generating too much spurious templates which would lead to a too costly analysis.

Lyapunov Abstractions for Inevitability of Hybrid Systems[*]

Parasara Sridhar Duggirala
Department of Computer Science
University of Illinois at Urbana Champaign
Urbana, IL
duggira3@illinois.edu

Sayan Mitra
Coordinate Science Laboratory
University of Illinois at Urbana Champaign
Urbana, IL
mitras@illinois.edu

ABSTRACT
A set of states S is said to be inevitable for a hybrid automaton $\mathcal{A}$ if every behavior of $\mathcal{A}$ ultimately reaches S within bounded time. Inevitability captures various commonly occurring liveness properties. In this paper, we present an algorithm for verifying inevitability of Linear Hybrid Automata (LHA). The algorithm combines (a) Lyapunov function-based relational abstractions for the continuous dynamics with (b) automated construction of well-founded relations for the loops of the hybrid automaton. The algorithm is complete for automata that are symmetric with respect to the chosen Lyapunov functions. The algorithm is implemented in a prototype tool (*LySHA*) which is integrated with a Simulink/Stateflow frontend for modeling hybrid systems. The experimental results demonstrate the effectiveness of the methodology in verifying inevitability of hybrid automata with up to five continuous dimensions and forty locations.

Categories and Subject Descriptors
H.4 [**Verification**]: Hybrid Systems, Algorithms, Theory

Keywords
Hybrid Systems; Liveness; Stability; Switching Systems; Abstraction; Formal Methods; Verification; Theory;

1. INTRODUCTION
In this paper, we present a technique for verifying a type of liveness property called *inevitability* [21, 3] for systems involving both discrete and continuous dynamics. The hybrid system formalisms [1, 13] provide a convenient mathematical framework for modeling such systems. A behavior or an *execution* of a hybrid automaton is an alternating sequence of discrete state transitions and continuous trajectories, where the latter are often specified by differential and

---

[*]This research is supported by a research grant from the National Science Foundation (CNS-1016791).

Permission to make digital or hard copies of all or part of this work for personal or classroom use is granted without fee provided that copies are not made or distributed for profit or commercial advantage and that copies bear this notice and the full citation on the first page. To copy otherwise, to republish, to post on servers or to redistribute to lists, requires prior specific permission and/or a fee.
HSCC'12, April 17–19, 2012, Beijing, China.
Copyright 2012 ACM 978-1-4503-1220-2/12/04 ...$10.00.

algebraic equations. A set of states S is said to be *inevitable* for a hybrid automaton (HA) $\mathcal{A}$ if starting from arbitrary initial states, every execution of $\mathcal{A}$ reaches S within bounded time. Inevitability captures practical liveness requirements such as: a robot must arrive within a neighborhood of a waypoint, a traffic control algorithm must allow vehicles to make progress along all intersecting routes, and a routing protocol must arrive at a valid forwarding scheme after some nodes fail.

The *switched system* model (see, for example the books [15] and [25] and the references therein) can be viewed as an abstraction of hybrid automata. Here the guards and resets are abstracted by exogenous switching signals. Naturally, the problem of verifying inevitability for hybrid automata is connected to the problem of analyzing stability of switched systems. Research on the latter problem has focused on establishing necessary and sufficient conditions for stability. These conditions typically assume (a) existence of common or multiple Lyapunov functions and (b) timing-dependent restrictions on families of switching signals for guaranteeing stability [5, 12]. Although, there are some examples of verification algorithms which build upon these results (for example [19]), in general, a systematic framework for liveness verification of hybrid systems is still missing. In this paper, we propose such a framework which combines Lyapunov functions with program analysis techniques. We present an instance of this framework as an abstraction-refinement algorithm for inevitability verification of Linear Hybrid Automata. Our prototype implementation of the algorithm automatically verifies inevitability and suggests counterexamples for HA with upto five continuous variables and forty locations.

1.1 Overview
Throughout this paper we will assume that the system model $\mathcal{A}$ is nonblocking, that is, it allows time to diverge. For reactive systems which are expected to run for long periods of time this assumption is reasonable. Now, suppose we want to prove the inevitability of hybrid automaton $\mathcal{A}$ to the set S. Let $\mathcal{B}$ be the automaton obtained by removing the set S from $\mathcal{A}$. In [9], we observed that $\mathcal{A}$ inevitably reaches S if and only if the automaton $\mathcal{B}$ is blocked within finite time. In other words, time cannot diverge to infinity in $\mathcal{B}$ if and only if S is inevitable for $\mathcal{A}$. This suggests that inevitability can be verified by verifying the blocking property. This blocking property is related to termination of programs and we will leverage available and recently developed techniques for program termination verification.

The standard technique for proving program termination

involves finding a *well-founded relation* which subsumes the transitions of the program. A well-founded relation has no infinite chains, and hence, the program cannot have infinite executions. Unlike programs, however, HA have uncountable states which evolve both through discrete transitions and continuous trajectories. Furthermore, a single continuous trajectory can be decomposed into arbitrarily many small steps and seemingly violate the well-foundedness criteria. The first step in our approach is to define a new transition relation (called *hybrid step relation (HSR)*) which combines the continuous trajectories and the discrete transitions. Through the lens of program analysis, then, verifying inevitability of $\mathcal{A}$ becomes equivalent to proving well-foundedness of $\mathcal{B}$'s HSR.

The HSR captures detailed information about the state evolution. For linear dynamics it involves real arithmetic formulas with exponentials and trigonometric functions. Therefore, the above methodology faces computational barriers from two directions: first in computing HSRs and in computing the composition of these HSRs, second in checking the well-foundedness of HSRs. To address these issues, we abstract the HSR with a collection of Lyapunov-like functions for the individual locations. A wide variety of standard techniques based on semidefinite and convex optimization are available for finding Lyapunov functions [14, 4, 22]. For instance, for linear HA, the focus of this paper, Lyapunov functions for the individual modes are obtained by solving the (linear) Lyapunov equations. We abstract the state space of the system using Lyapunov-like functions and this defines a *Lyapunov Step Relation*(LSR) which overapproximates the HSR. We show how LSR can be computed effectively for time-triggered linear HA. We also identify a class of HA for which there is no loss of precision in abstracting the HSR with Lyapunov abstractions.

Even with the Lyapunov abstractions, proving well-foundedness of the LSR of complex hybrid systems can become intractable. Leveraging recent results in program termination analysis which have led to effective new tools for termination analysis of realistic software systems [8, 6], we show that it suffices to find well-founded relations for the LSRs corresponding to individual loops of the HA. Roughly, if all the loops of $\mathcal{B}$ are well-founded, then none of them can be sustained forever, and we can conclude that the $\mathcal{B}$ is blocking, and that $\mathcal{A}$ inevitably reaches S.

One final barrier to the above approach is that the number of loops of $\mathcal{B}$ can be infinite. To address this, we abstract the individual loop LSRs with finitely many transition predicates. This guarantees termination of our algorithm, even though it may sometimes fail to prove inevitability or the blocking property. Putting it all together, we obtain a new abstraction-refinement based framework for verifying inevitability of HA. Based on our experimental results with a prototype implementation of the algorithm for linear HA, the method appears to scale to system models with more than forty locations and five or so continuous states.

1.2 Related Work
Abstractions over the state space of dynamical systems have been used to prove safety properties in [24, 16]. Both, of these approaches, use timed automaton for abstracting the behavior of dynamical system. In [24], however, Lyapunov functions were used for creating the timers in the timed automaton abstraction. This paper shows how similar Lyapunov-based abstractions can be applied to linear HA for verifying inevitability.

In [23], transitional abstractions (relational abstractions) were used to prove safety properties of the systems. These transitional abstractions capture the relation among the state variables from the beginning to the end of a trajectory (i.e. continuous evolution of the system). These transitional abstractions are computed from the eigenstructure of the relevant matrices and by performing quantifier elimination. In contrast, our abstractions differ from this approach primarily in two ways, First, we require the transitional abstractions to also capture the discrete behavior of the system by defining the Hybrid Step Relation which captures both the continuous trajectories and the discrete transitions of the system. Secondly, we require explicit Laypunov functions for abstraction of the state space of the system. The techniques of [23] may provide effective means of computing abstractions of the type we need for inevitability. This direction will be explored in the future.

A different algorithm for stability of a linear HA which relies on finiteness of certain sequences called snapshot sequences has been presented in [21]. In [21], stability of a linear hybrid system is characterized as *finiteness* of certain sequences called *snapshot sequences* . Three types of snapshot sequences are identified and a new hybrid automaton representing the execution of these three snapshot sequences are created. Further, by analyzing the unary reachability of these automaton using reachability tools like PHAVer [10], finiteness of these sequences is determined and hence stability of the given automaton is verified. Our approach of first computing Lyapunov abstractions could be combined with this analysis of snapshot sequences.

2. PRELIMINARIES
We briefly introduce the basic concepts of the hybrid automaton framework and refer the reader to [1, 13, 18] for details. For a vector x in $\mathbb{R}^k$ then we denote its components by $x[1], x[2], \ldots, x[k]$. A relation $R \subseteq S \times S$ on a set S is *well-founded* if it does not contain any infinite sequence of pairwise related elements. A set of variables, say V, is used to define the state of a hybrid automaton. Each variable $v \in V$ is associated with a *type*, denoted by $type(v)$, which defines the set of values it can take. A valuation $\mathbf{v}$ for a set of variables V maps each $v \in V$ to an element in $type(v)$. We use the standard $\mathbf{v}.v$ notation to refer to the valuation of a variable $v \in V$ at $\mathbf{v}$. The set of all valuations of V is denoted by $val(V)$.

The state of a hybrid automaton, that is, the valuation of its variables can change through instantaneous *discrete transitions* and continuously over an interval of time by following a *trajectory*. A trajectory for a set of variables V is a function $\tau : [0, t] \rightarrow val(V)$, where either $t \in \mathbb{R}_{\geq 0}$ or ∞. The domain of τ is denoted by $\tau.dom$. The first state of τ, denoted by τ.fstate, is $\tau(0)$. A trajectory is closed if t is finite and in this case we define τ.ltime $\triangleq t$, τ.lstate $\triangleq \tau(t)$, and we write τ.fstate $\xrightarrow{\tau}$ τ.lstate.

Definition 1. *A Hybrid Automata (HA) $\mathcal{A}$ is a tuple $\langle V, Loc, A, \mathcal{D}, \mathcal{T} \rangle$ where*

(a) *$V = X \cup \{loc\}$ is a set of variables. Here loc is a discrete variable of finite type Loc. Elements of Loc are called locations. Each $x \in X$ is a continuous variable of type $\mathbb{R}$. Elements of $val(V)$ are called states.*

(b) A is a finite set of actions *or* transition labels.

(c) $\mathcal{D} \subseteq val(V) \times A \times val(V)$ *is the set of* discrete transitions. *A transition* $(\mathbf{v}, a, \mathbf{v}') \in \mathcal{D}$ *is written as* $\mathbf{v} \xrightarrow{a} \mathbf{v}'$. *The discrete transitions are specified by finitely many guards and reset maps involving* V.

(d) $\mathcal{T}$ *is a set of trajectories for* X *which is closed under suffix, prefix and concatenation (see [13, ?] for details). For each* $l \in Loc$, *a set of trajectories* $\mathcal{T}_l$ *for location* l *are specified by differential equations* E_l *and an invariant* $I_l \subseteq val(X)$. *Over any trajectory* $\tau \in \mathcal{T}_l$, loc *remains constant and the variables in* X *evolve according to* E_l *such that for all* $t \in \tau.dom, \tau(t) \in I_l$. $\mathcal{T} \triangleq \cup_{l \in Loc} \mathcal{T}_l$.

Later in this paper, we introduce a class of HA called *time-triggered* hybrid automaton which have a special timer variable *now* that tracks the time spent in each location.

2.1 Semantics of Hybrid Automata

An execution of a hybrid automaton $\mathcal{A}$ records all the information (about variables) over a particular run. Formally, an *execution* is an alternating sequence $\tau_0 a_1 \tau_1 ...$ where each τ_i (except possibly the last) is a closed trajectory and $\tau_i.\text{lstate} \xrightarrow{a_{i+1}} \tau_{i+1}.\text{fstate}$. Note that executions may start from any state of the automaton. The first state of α is denoted by $\alpha.\text{fstate} = \tau_0.\text{fstate}$. The duration of α is defined as $\alpha.\text{ltime} = \sum_i \tau_i.\text{ltime}$. The property of interest in this paper is inevitability: A set of states $S \subseteq val(V)$ is said to be *inevitable* for $\mathcal{A}$ if every execution of $\mathcal{A}$ reaches S in finite time.

An execution is *finite* if it is a finite sequence, otherwise it is *infinite*. An execution α is said to be *nonblocking* if its duration is infinite or if along all its infinite extensions time diverges to infinity; otherwise α is said to be *blocking*. A hybrid automata $\mathcal{A}$ is *blocking (nonblocking)* if all its executions are blocking (nonblocking, respectively). A hybrid automaton is said to be *Zeno* if there exists an execution of finite duration with infinitely many transitions.

The notion of a simulation relation will be used later in our development.

Definition 2. *A relation* $R \subseteq val(V) \times val(V)$ *is a* simulation relation *if for every* $\mathbf{v}_1, \mathbf{v}_2, \mathbf{v}_1' \in val(V)$ *and* $\mathbf{v}_1 R \mathbf{v}_2$, *(a) if* $\mathbf{v}_1 \xrightarrow{a} \mathbf{v}_1'$ *then there exists* $\mathbf{v}_2'$ *such that* $\mathbf{v}_1' R \mathbf{v}_2', \mathbf{v}_2 \xrightarrow{a} \mathbf{v}_2'$, *and (b) if* $\mathbf{v}_1 \xrightarrow{\tau} \mathbf{v}_1'$ *then there exists* $\mathbf{v}_2'$ *such that* $\mathbf{v}_1' R \mathbf{v}_2', \mathbf{v}_2 \xrightarrow{\tau} \mathbf{v}_2'$.

2.2 Three Assumptions

We assume that the hybrid automata to be verified is *nonblocking*. This is a natural assumption for systems which are expected to run for long time periods.

A hybrid automaton may be non-blocking because it stays in one location forever. In such cases, the verification problem reduces to the well-studied problem of analyzing the stability of the differential equations of that location with respect to the target set. Our goal is to study the hybrid aspect of inevitability verification, and therefore, we assume that the automaton is *locally blocking*. That is, time cannot diverge within a single location.

Finally, we will assume that the automaton does not have Zeno executions. Systems can be designed to be non-Zeno with built-in dwell times. Furthermore, several techniques have been developed for checking Zenoness and dwell time properties [2, 19].

3. VERIFYING INEVITABILITY

We begin this section by setting up inevitability verification as a problem of checking well-foundedness of a certain relation which we call the *Hybrid Step Relation (HSR)*. Next, we introduce Lyapunov function-based abstractions for over-approximating HSRs. We show that for a special class of HA which conform to the symmetries of the Lyapunov functions, Lyapunov abstractions provide a complete method for proving well-foundedness of HSR. Finally, we show how Lyapunov abstractions can be computed for time-triggered or periodically-controlled hybrid automata.

3.1 Inevitability to Well-Foundedness

Unlike programs which evolve in atomic discrete transitions, a trajectory can be split into infinitely many small trajectories. The relation relating all these intermediate states in a trajectory is not well-founded. The hybrid step relation combines a trajectory with a following transition, and thereby relates a state $\mathbf{v}$ with the maximal state $\mathbf{v}'$ that can follow a trajectory from $\mathbf{v}$.

Definition 3. *For HA* $\mathcal{A}$, *the* hybrid step relation (HSR) $\Gamma \subseteq val(V) \times val(V)$ *is defined as:* $(\mathbf{v}, \mathbf{v}') \in \Gamma$ *iff there exist* $\mathbf{v}'' \in val(V), a \in A, \tau \in \mathcal{T}$ *such that* $\mathbf{v} = \tau.\text{fstate}, \mathbf{v}'' = \tau.\text{lstate}$ *and* $\mathbf{v}'' \xrightarrow{a} \mathbf{v}'$.

In other words, from $\mathbf{v}$ there is a trajectory followed by a transition which takes it to $\mathbf{v}'$.

A key observation from [9] (restated as Theorem 1 below) relates inevitability to blocking: A set of states S is inevitable for HA $\mathcal{A}$ if an only if $\mathcal{A}_{S^c}$ is blocking, where $\mathcal{A}_{S^c}$ is obtained by (1) removing the states S from the state-space of $\mathcal{A}$ (2) removing the transitions into S from the transitions of $\mathcal{A}$ and (3) removing the non-trivial trajectories in S from the trajectories of $\mathcal{A}$.

Theorem 1. *(from [9]) A locally blocking, non-Zeno HA* $\mathcal{A}$ *is blocking iff* Γ *is well-founded.*

Proof. Suppose that $\mathcal{A}$ is not blocking, i.e. there exists an execution α in which time diverges. Since $\mathcal{A}$ is locally closed, the execution α is of the form $\tau_0, a_1, \dots$. Let $\beta = \mathbf{v}_0, \mathbf{v}_1, \dots$, where $\mathbf{v}_i = \tau_i.\text{fstate}$. Hence, we have that $\forall i, (\mathbf{v}_i, \mathbf{v}_{i+1}) \in \Gamma$. Thus β is an infinite sequence and Γ is not well-founded.

Suppose that the HSR Γ is not well-founded. Hence, we have an infinite sequence $\beta = \mathbf{v}_0, \mathbf{v}_1, \dots$, where $(\mathbf{v}_i, \mathbf{v}_{i+1}) \in \Gamma$. From β and Γ, we can construct a sequence $\beta' = \mathbf{v}_0$, $\mathbf{v}_0', \mathbf{v}_1, \mathbf{v}_1', \dots$ such that $\forall i, \exists \tau_i, a_i$ such that $\mathbf{v}_i = \tau_i.\text{fstate}, \mathbf{v}_i' = \tau_i.\text{lstate}$ and $\mathbf{v}_i' \xrightarrow{a_{i+1}} \mathbf{v}_{i+1}$. Thus we have that $\alpha = \tau_0, a_1, \tau_1, \dots$ is an admissible execution of the system. Since $\mathcal{A}$ is non-Zeno, it means that time diverges along execution α and thus $\mathcal{A}$ is not blocking. $\square$

For rectangular hybrid automata [11] the hybrid step relation can be computed exactly and a concrete algorithm is presented in our previous work in [9]. For general hybrid automata, computing the hybrid step relation is undecidable. For this purpose, we compute the abstractions of hybrid step relation with respect to an abstraction β over the state space of the system. The next theorem illustrates the utility of abstractions for proving well-foundedness.

Definition 4. *Given a HSR* Γ, *an abstract domain* D, *and a function* $\beta: val(V) \to D$, *we define* $\beta(\Gamma) \subseteq D \times D$ *as the relation* $(y, y') \in \beta(\Gamma)$ *iff* $\exists \mathbf{v}, \mathbf{v}' \in val(V)$, *such that* $(\mathbf{v}, \mathbf{v}') \in \Gamma$, $y = \beta(\mathbf{v})$ *and* $y' = \beta(\mathbf{v}')$.

Theorem 2 follows from Theorem 1 in [7]

Theorem 2. *If $\beta(\Gamma)$ is well-founded then Γ is also well-founded.*

Theorem 2 will be useful, for example, in the case of time-triggered linear hybrid automata, where computing the hybrid step relation involves real arithmetic with exponentials while computing the abstraction of the HSR will involve only linear real arithmetic.

3.2 Lyapunov Abstractions

We assume that all the locations of the hybrid automata are either asymptotically stable or asymptotically unstable. In the case of linear systems, this implies that we can effectively compute Lyapunov-like functions that exponentially decay or grow along the trajectories. Formally, for every location, $l \in Loc$, we have k such functions, denoted by $L_{l,1}, L_{l,2}, \ldots, L_{l,k}$. If the location l is stable, then for each $i \in \{1, \ldots, k\}, \exists \lambda_{l,i} < 0$ and $B_{l,i} > 0$, such that for every trajectory $\tau \in \mathcal{T}_l$, $L_{l,i}(\tau(t)) \leq B_{l,i} e^{\lambda_{l,i} t} L_{l,i}(\tau(0))$. If the location l is unstable, then $\exists \lambda_{l,i} > 0$ and $B_{l,i} > 0$, such that for every trajectory $\tau \in \mathcal{T}_l$, $L_{l,i}(\tau(t)) \leq B_{l,i} e^{\lambda_{l,i} t} L_{l,i}(\tau(0))$.

Definition 5 (Lyapunov Abstraction). *Let $\mathfrak{L} = \{L_{\ell,i}\}, \ell \in Loc, i \in \{1, \ldots, k\}$ be an ordered collection of $k|Loc|$ Lyapunov functions. The Lyapunov Abstraction is a function $\mathcal{L}: val(V) \rightarrow Loc \times \mathbb{R}^k$ defined as:*

$$\mathcal{L}(\mathbf{v}) = \langle \mathbf{v}.loc, L_{\mathbf{v}.loc,1}(\mathbf{v}.X), \ldots, L_{\mathbf{v}.loc,1}(\mathbf{v}.X) \rangle.$$

For convenience, we also define $\mathcal{L}(\mathbf{v}).loc = \mathbf{v}.loc$ and

$$\mathcal{L}(\mathbf{v}).X = (L_{\mathbf{v}.loc,1}(\mathbf{v}.X), \ldots, L_{\mathbf{v}.loc,k}(\mathbf{v}.X)).$$

$\mathcal{L}(\Gamma) \subseteq (Loc \times \mathbb{R}^k) \times (Loc \times \mathbb{R}^k)$ *is called the* Lyapunov Step Relation(LSR).

It follows from Theorem 2 that if a LSR $\mathcal{L}(\Gamma)$ is well-founded then the corresponding HSR Γ is also well-founded. For computing LSR, we need to construct Lyapunov-like functions for each location. For linear hybrid systems, for asymptotically stable modes, a quadratic Lyapunov function $x^T P x$ can be effectively computed by solving the Lyapunov equations in the matrix form: $AP + PA^T = -Q$, where Q is a positive semidefinite matrix. Similarly, for asymptotically unstable modes, a quadratic Lyapunov-like function $x^T P x$ can be obtained by solving the matrix equation $AP + PA^T = Q$, where Q is a positive semidefinite matrix.

Definition 6 (Symmetric States). *Given a HA $\mathcal{A}$ and a Lyapunov abstraction $\mathcal{L}$, we define the relation $\mathcal{S}_\mathcal{L}$ as $(\mathbf{v}, \mathbf{v}') \in \mathcal{S}_\mathcal{L}$ iff $\mathcal{L}(\mathbf{v}) = \mathcal{L}(\mathbf{v}')$. We say that two $\mathcal{S}_\mathcal{L}$-related states are symmetric with respect to $\mathcal{L}$.*

Definition 7 (Symmetric Hybrid Automata). *Given a HA $\mathcal{A}$ and a Lyapunov abstraction $\mathcal{L}$, $\mathcal{A}$ is said to be symmetric with respect to $\mathcal{L}$ iff $\mathcal{S}_\mathcal{L}$ is a simulation relation for $\mathcal{A}$.*

Informally, an automaton is symmetric with respect to a collection of Lyapunov functions if any two states with identical valuation of those Lyapunov functions behave indistinguishably. Since the transitions and the trajectories of the HA preserve any simulation relation between states, it follows that the hybrid step relation also preserves symmetry.

Proposition 3. *Given a HA $\mathcal{A}$ that is symmetric with respect to a Lyapunov abstraction $\mathcal{L}$, for any $\mathbf{v}_1, \mathbf{v}'_1, \mathbf{v}_2 \in val(V)$, if $(\mathbf{v}_1, \mathbf{v}'_1) \in \Gamma$ and $(\mathbf{v}_1, \mathbf{v}_2) \in \mathcal{S}_\mathcal{L}$ then there exists $\mathbf{v}'_2 \in val(V)$, and $(\mathbf{v}'_1, \mathbf{v}'_2) \in \mathcal{S}_\mathcal{L}$ such that $(\mathbf{v}_2, \mathbf{v}'_2) \in \Gamma$.*

Example 1 We illustrate the *Lyapunov step relation* using a simple example. Consider the HA in Figure 1. At location $i \in \{1, 2, 3\}$, the dynamics of the system is defined by $\dot{x} = A_i x$. Notice that all the invariants depend only on the timer *now*. Suppose

$$A_1 = \begin{pmatrix} -1 & 0 \\ 5 & -3 \end{pmatrix} A_2 = \begin{pmatrix} 2 & 1 \\ 0 & -1 \end{pmatrix} A_3 = \begin{pmatrix} -4 & -2 \\ 0 & -9 \end{pmatrix}.$$

Eigenvalues for A_1 and A_3 are negative and those of A_2 are positive, therefore, locations 1 and 3 are asymptotically stable while 2 is unstable. Consider an execution starting from

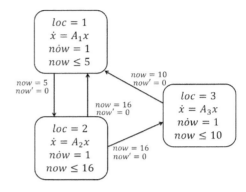

Figure 1: Linear hybrid automaton with 3 locations.

the state $\mathbf{v}$ where $\mathbf{v}.loc = 1, \mathbf{v}.x_1 = 2, \mathbf{v}.x_2 = 5$. Initially, the system will evolve according to the continuous dynamics $\dot{x} = A_1 x$. After 5 time units, the location changes to 2. By solving the differential equation for mode A_1, we obtain that $\mathbf{v} \xrightarrow{\tau} \mathbf{v}''$ where $\mathbf{v}''.loc = 1, \mathbf{v}''.x_1 = 0.0135$ and $\mathbf{v}''.x_2 = 0.0337$, and $\tau.\text{ltime} = 5$. Further, the system changes its location from 1 to 2, i.e. $\mathbf{v}'' \rightarrow \mathbf{v}'$, we have $\mathbf{v}'.loc = 2, \mathbf{v}'.x_1 = 0.0135$ and $\mathbf{v}'.x_2 = 0.0337$. Therefore, we get that $(\mathbf{v}, \mathbf{v}') \in \Gamma$.

The two Lyapunov functions for locations 1 and 2 are obtained as

$$
\begin{aligned}
L_{1,1} &= 0.5x_1^2 + 1.25x_1x_2 + 1.2083x_2^2 \\
L_{1,2} &= 0.5x_1^2 + 1.75x_1x_2 + 1.625x_2^2 \\
L_{2,1} &= x_1^2/3 - x_1x_2/3 + x_2^2/2, \text{ and} \\
L_{2,2} &= x_1^2/6 + x_1x_2/3 + x_2^2/2.
\end{aligned}
$$

Let $y = \mathcal{L}(\mathbf{v}) = \langle 1, L_{1,1}(\mathbf{v}), L_{1,2}(\mathbf{v}) \rangle = \langle 1, 44.7705, 60.1250 \rangle$. Let $y' = \mathcal{L}(\mathbf{v}') = \langle 2, L_{2,1}(\mathbf{v}'), L_{2,2}(\mathbf{v}) \rangle = \langle 2, 4.7691 \times 10^{-4}, 7.4991 \times 10^{-4} \rangle$. Hence, we have $(y, y') \in \mathcal{L}(\Gamma)$. $\square$

3.3 Refinement and Completeness

In general, the abstract relation $\mathcal{L}(\Gamma)$ may not be well-founded even if the HSR Γ is. In other words, $\mathcal{L}(\Gamma)$ may contain an infinite chain $\sigma = y_1, y_2, \ldots$ such that there is no concrete execution of $\mathcal{A}$ corresponding to the infinite sequence of concrete states $\mathcal{L}^{-1}(\sigma) \triangleq \mathcal{L}^{-1}(y_1), \mathcal{L}^{-1}(y_2), \ldots$. Such sequences are called *potential counterexamples*. If any one of these executions is indeed an execution of HA, then the system is not *blocking*. Otherwise, the counterexample is said to be *spurious*. In such cases, we would like to *refine* the abstraction to $\mathcal{L}'$, such that, the set of *potential counterexample* $\mathcal{L}'^{-1}(\sigma)$ decreases by some measure. Ideally, we would like this sequence of refinements to terminate. That is, proving the well-foundedness of some kLSR should suffice for proving well-foundedness of the concrete HSR. In this section, we present a technique for refining Lyapunov abstractions and identify a class of hybrid automata for which this procedure is guaranteed to terminate.

Definition 8 (Distinguishing Lyapunov function). *For a given set of k Lyapunov-like functions $L_1, \ldots, L_k$, a $(k+1)st$ function L_{k+1} is said to be* distinguishing *if $\forall x_1, x_2, \ldots, x_k \in \mathbb{R}_{\geq 0}$, if $\bigcap_{i=1}^{k} L_i^{-1}(x_i) \neq \emptyset$, then there exists $x_{k+1} \in \mathbb{R}_{\geq 0}$ such that*

$$\bigcap_{i=1}^{k+1} L_i^{-1}(x_i) \subsetneq \bigcap_{i=1}^{k} L_i^{-1}(x_i).$$

Informally, the $(k+1)^{st}$ function is able to distinguish points in any subspace defined by the intersection of level-sets of all the other k Lyapunov functions. We now prove that the number of *potential counterexamples* decrease when a distinguishing Lyapunov function is added to each location for the Lyapunov abstraction.

Proposition 4. *Given $\mathfrak{L} = \{L_{\ell,i}\}, \ell \in Loc, i \in \{1, \ldots, k\}$ define a Lyapunov abstraction $\mathcal{L}$, a refinement of this abstraction $\mathfrak{L}'$ can be obtained by adding a distinguishing Lyapunov function for each location.*

Proof. Suppose that $\sigma = y_1, y_2, \ldots$ be a counterexample for the abstraction $\mathcal{L}$ where $y_i \in Loc \times \mathbb{R}^k$ and let $\mathbf{v}_1, \mathbf{v}_2, \ldots$ be the set of *potential counterexamples* $\mathcal{L}^{-1}(\sigma)$. Now, consider the counterexample $\sigma' = (y_1, z_1), (y_2, z_2), \ldots$ of $\mathcal{L}'$ where $(y_i, z_i) \in Loc \times \mathbb{R}^{k+1}$ and $\mathbf{v}_1', \mathbf{v}_2', \ldots$ be the set of *potential counterexamples* $\mathcal{L}^{-1}(\sigma')$. Let $V_i = \{\mathbf{v}_i\}$ and $V_i' = \{\mathbf{v}_i'\}$ From Definitions 5 8, we have that whenever V_i is non-empty, we have that $V_i' \subsetneq V_i$, in which case, the number of potential counter examples decreases. If V_i is an empty set, then the sequence $y_1, y_2, \ldots$ is not an abstract counter example as (y_{i-1}, y_i) cannot be in $\mathcal{L}(\Gamma)$. $\square$

We observe that Lyapunov function $x^T P_{k+1} x$ is *distinguishing* from $x^T P_1 x, \ldots, x^T P_k x$ only when $P_1, \ldots, P_{k+1}$ are *linearly independent*. In practice, we follow this strategy to add *distinguishing* Lyapunov functions during refinement of Lyapunov abstractions.

Example 2 To illustrate the refinement process, we consider the hybrid automata in Example 1. Consider the execution of the system starting from $\mathbf{v}$ where $\mathbf{v}.loc = 1, \mathbf{v}.x_1 = 2, \mathbf{v}.x_2 = 5$. We have established in Example 1 that $\mathbf{v}$ will evolve according to continuous dynamics for 5 time units and reaches the state $\mathbf{v}''$ where $\mathbf{v}''.loc = 1, \mathbf{v}''.x_1 = 0.0135$ and $\mathbf{v}''.x_2 = 0.0337$ and then takes a discrete transition to $\mathbf{v}'$ where $\mathbf{v}'.loc = 2, \mathbf{v}'.x_1 = 0.0135$ and $\mathbf{v}'.x_2 = 0.0337$. Therefore, we get that $\mathbf{v}\Gamma\mathbf{v}'$.

Now consider the abstraction $\mathcal{L}$ of the system where we have one Lyapunov function associated with each location, i.e. $L_{1,1}$ for location 1 and $L_{2,1}$ for location 2. Now in this abstraction, the Lyapunov step relation would be $y = \langle 1, L_{1,1}(\mathbf{v})\rangle$ and $y' = \langle 2, L_{2,1}(\mathbf{v}')\rangle$. Thus we have that $y = \langle 1, 44.7705\rangle$ and $y' = \langle 2, 4.7691 \times 10^{-4}\rangle$. Hence $(y, y') \in \mathcal{L}(\Gamma)$. However, this approximation is too coarse because this abstract transition corresponds to all the states on the level set of $L_{1,1} = 44.7705$, related to all the states on the level set of $L_{2,1} = 4.7691 \times 10^{-4}$. To make the abstraction *finer* we add 2 more Lyapunov functions $L_{1,2}$ and $L_{2,2}$ to $\mathcal{L}$

and obtain $\mathcal{L}'$. The kLSR for $\mathcal{L}'$ corresponding to the *refined* Lyapunov abstraction is $(y, y') \in \mathcal{L}(\Gamma)$, where $y = \mathcal{L}'(\mathbf{v}) = \langle 1, L_{1,1}(\mathbf{v}), L_{1,2}(\mathbf{v})\rangle = \langle 1, 44.7705, 60.1250\rangle$, $y' = \mathcal{L}'(\mathbf{v}') = \langle 2, L_{2,1}(\mathbf{v}'), L_{2,2}(\mathbf{v}')\rangle = \langle 2, 4.7691 \times 10^{-4}, 7.4991 \times 10^{-4}\rangle$. It can be observed that by adding a new Lyapunov function for each location, one can eliminate a lot of spurious transitions. In this example, this corresponds to eliminating some of the transitions where the states in level set $L_{1,1} = 44.7705$ are not related to $L_{2,1} = 4.7691 \times 10^{-4}$. $\square$

Theorem 5. *For a symmetric hybrid automaton $\mathcal{A}$ w.r.t. a Lyapunov abstraction $\mathcal{L}$, we have that Γ is well-founded iff $\mathcal{L}(\Gamma)$ is well-founded.*

Proof. From Theorem 2 we have that whenever $\mathcal{L}(\Gamma)$ is well-founded, Γ is also well-founded. Now, we need to prove that when $\mathcal{L}(\Gamma)$ is not well-founded, Γ is also not well-founded. We prove this as follows: we consider an infinite chain $\mathcal{L}(\Gamma)$ and from this chain, we prove that there exists an infinite chain in Γ.

Let $y_1, y_2, \ldots$ be an infinite chain in $\mathcal{L}(\Gamma)$. Now, since $(y_1, y_2) \in \mathcal{L}(\Gamma)$, by Definition 5, we have that $\exists (\mathbf{v}_1, \mathbf{v}_2) \in \Gamma$ such that $\mathcal{L}(\mathbf{v}_1) = y_1, \mathcal{L}(\mathbf{v}_2) = y_2$. Now, since $(y_2, y_3) \in \mathcal{L}(\Gamma)$, we have that $\exists (\mathbf{v}_2', \mathbf{v}_3') \in \Gamma$ such that $\mathcal{L}(\mathbf{v}_2') = y_2$ and $\mathcal{L}(\mathbf{v}_3') = y_3$. Further since $\mathcal{L}(\mathbf{v}_2) = \mathcal{L}(\mathbf{v}_2')$, we have that $\mathbf{v}_2 \mathcal{S}_{\mathcal{L}} \mathbf{v}_2'$. From Theorem 3, we have that Γ is also symmetric and hence $\exists \mathbf{v}_3$ such that $\mathcal{L}(\mathbf{v}_3) = \mathcal{L}(\mathbf{v}_3') = y_3$ and $(\mathbf{v}_2, \mathbf{v}_3) \in \Gamma$. Similarly, we get $(\mathbf{v}_3, \mathbf{v}_4) \in \Gamma$. Hence, one can construct an infinite chain $\mathbf{v}_1, \mathbf{v}_2, \ldots$ such that $(\mathbf{v}_i, \mathbf{v}_{i+1}) \in \Gamma$ and thus Γ is not well-founded. $\square$

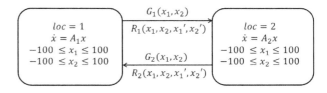

Figure 2: A Symmetric Linear hybrid automaton with 2 locations.

Next, we now look at examples of hybrid automata that are symmetric and asymmetric.

Example 3 Consider the automaton shown in Figure 2. It consists of two continuous variables variables x_1, x_2, where $A_1 = \begin{pmatrix} -2 & 0 \\ 1 & -3 \end{pmatrix}$ and $A_2 = \begin{pmatrix} -1 & 2 \\ 1 & -3 \end{pmatrix}$. Let $L_1(x_1, x_2) \triangleq 0.25x_1^2 + 0.1x_1x_2 + (0.55/3)x_2^2$ and $L_2(x_1, x_2) \triangleq 1.75x_1^2 + 1.25x_1x_2 + 0.375x_2^2$. The guards and reset maps are defined as $G_1(x_1, x_2) \triangleq L_1(x_1, x_2) = 6.25, R_1(x_1, x_2, x_1', x_2') \triangleq L_2(x_1', x_2') = 175, G_2(x_1, x_2) \triangleq L_2(x_1, x_2) = 25,$ $R_1(x_1, x_2, x_1', x_2') \triangleq L_1(x_1', x_2') = 2$. We can observe that L_1 is a Lyapunov function for location 1 and L_2 is a Lyapunov function for location 2. Hence for a Lyapunov abstraction $\mathcal{L}$ with the set of Lyapunov function $\mathfrak{L} = \{L_1, L_2\}$, we get that the system is symmetric. In Section 5, we observe how to prove inevitability for this system using $\mathcal{L}$. $\square$

Example 4 Now consider the trivial hybrid system shown in Figure 3. It consists of only one location and only one con-

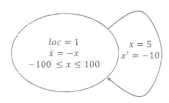

Figure 3: An asymmetric Linear hybrid automaton with 1 location.

tinuous variable. A quadratic Lyapunov function for the system is $L_{1,1} = x^2$. We can see that the system is not symmetric with respect to the Lyapunov abstraction because of the discrete transitions. We observe that the state where the value of $x = -5$ is symmetric with respect to $x = 5$. However, the state $x = 5$ can take a discrete transition and go to state $x = -10$ whereas $x = -5$ cannot have such a transition. Later, in Section 5, we observe that even though the given system satisfies inevitability, since the Lyapunov abstraction is not complete, we cannot prove it using Lyapunov abstractions. □

3.4 Time-Triggered Hybrid Automata

In this section, we will derive the *LSR* for Time-Triggered Hybrid Automata. In Time-Triggered Hybrid Automata, the transition guards are always predicated on the timer variable *now* and may also depend on other variables.

Definition 9. *A time-triggered hybrid automaton $\mathcal{A}$ is a HA with (a) a guard $G : A \to 2^{val(V)}$ which associates each action $a \in A$ with an enabling predicate, (b) a special clock variable called now, and (c) a constraint function $C : Loc \to \mathbb{R}_+$ which associates a timing constraint for each location. In addition, the following axioms are satisfied:*

(i) For a discrete transition $\mathbf{v} \xrightarrow{a} \mathbf{v}'$, $\mathbf{v} \in G(a)$ and $\mathbf{v}'.X = \mathbf{v}.X$. Further, if $\mathbf{v}.loc$ is stable, then $\mathbf{v}.now \geq C(\mathbf{v}.loc)$ and $\mathbf{v}'.now = 0$. If $\mathbf{v}.mode$ is unstable, then $\mathbf{v}.now \leq C(\mathbf{v}.loc)$ and $\mathbf{v}'.now = 0$.

(ii) For any trajectory τ in a stable location l, either $\tau.ltime \geq C(l)$ or there exists a τ' for which τ is a prefix and $\tau'.ltime \geq C(l)$.

(iii) For any trajectory τ in an unstable location l, $\tau.ltime \leq C(l)$.

A hybrid system is called *strictly time-triggered* when all the switching conditions involve only the clock variable *now*. An example of such a hybrid system is given in Figure 1. We assume that one can come up with $\{L_{l,i}\}, l \in Loc, i \leq i \leq k$ Lyapunov functions which decays (grows) exponentially for stable (unstable) locations.

Now, compute the *LSR* for time-triggered HA. Consider $(\mathbf{v}, \mathbf{v}') \in \Gamma$ where $\mathbf{v}.loc = l$ and $\mathbf{v}'.loc = m$. Let $\mu_{l,m}$ be a constant such that $\forall \mathbf{v} \xrightarrow{a} \mathbf{v}', \mathcal{L}(\mathbf{v}').X[i] \leq \mu_{l,m}\mathcal{L}(\mathbf{v}').X[i]$. Let $max_{G(a)}$ and $min_{G(a)}$ be arrays of real numbers such that $1 \leq i \leq k$, $min_{G(a)}[i]$ and $max_{G(a)}[i]$ are the least upper bound and greatest lower bound of the set $S_i = \{y | \exists \mathbf{v} \in G(a), y = \mathcal{L}(\mathbf{v}).X[i]\}$.

Theorem 6. *We say that $(y, y') \in \mathcal{L}(\Gamma)$ when $(min_{G(a)}[i] \leq B_{l,i}e^{\lambda_{l,i} \times C(l)}y.X[i]) \wedge (y'.X[i] \leq \mu_{l,m}B_{l,i}e^{\lambda_{l,i} \times C(l)}y.X[i])$ where $l = y.loc$*

Proof. Let $(\mathbf{v}, \mathbf{v}') \in \Gamma$, then $\exists \mathbf{v}''$ such that $\exists \tau \in \mathcal{T}_{\mathbf{v}.loc}$, $\tau.fstate = \mathbf{v}, \tau.lstate = \mathbf{v}''$ and $\exists a \in \mathcal{D}, (\mathbf{v}'', a, \mathbf{v}')$. Hence, we have that $\mathbf{v}''.X \in G(a)$ and since the reset map is identity, we have $\mathbf{v}'.X \in G(a)$. Now, let $y = \mathcal{L}(\mathbf{v}), y' = \mathcal{L}(\mathbf{v}'), y'' = \mathcal{L}(\mathbf{v}''), l = \mathbf{v}.loc, l' = \mathbf{v}.loc$. Since we have that the system should stay in location l for at least $C(l)$ time if l is stable, or else it should stay at most for $C(l)$ time in unstable modes, we have that $y.loc = l$, $y''.loc = l$ and $y'.loc = l'$. Further, we have,

$$y''.X[i] \leq B_{l,i}e^{\lambda_{l,i} \times C(l)}y.X[i] \tag{1}$$

Further, since $v'' \in G(a)$, we have

$$min_{G(a)}[i] \leq y''.X[i] \leq max_{G(a)}[i] \tag{2}$$

And by the value of μ_{ij}, we also have

$$y'.X[i] \leq \mu_{l,m}y''.X[i] \tag{3}$$

By combining equations 1, 2 and 3, we get that $(y, y') \in \mathcal{L}(\Gamma)$ when

$$(min_{G(a)}[i] \leq B_{l,i}e^{\lambda_{l,i} \times C(l)}y.X[i]) \wedge \tag{4}$$

$$(y'.X[i] \leq \mu_{l,m}B_{l,i}e^{\lambda_{l,i} \times C(l)}y.X[i]) \tag{5}$$

□

Equation (4) represents the LSR relation for time-triggered HA.

In this section we have seen how to obtain the Lyapunov step relation $\mathcal{L}(\Gamma)$ for time-triggered hybrid systems. To prove the blocking property, we need to prove the well-foundedness of $\mathcal{L}(\Gamma)$ which we discuss next.

4. ABSTRACTION REFINEMENT FOR WELL-FOUNDEDNESS

We have established that inevitability can be verified by finding a well-founded relation R that contains the HSR Γ or its Lyapunov abstraction $\mathcal{L}(\Gamma)$. In general, finding such a well-founded relation R is difficult as it must subsume the hybrid-steps along all possible paths or sequences of locations that can be visited by the hybrid automaton. Theorem 1 from [20] gives an alternative method for searching for such relations by allowing us to come up with a well-founded relation for each loop (sequence of locations starting and ending at the same location). Restated in our context, this theorem gives that Γ is well-founded iff its transitive closure Γ^+ is contained in the disjunctive union of a finite collection of well-founded relations. That is, $\Gamma^+ \subseteq \cup_{i=1}^{m} R_i$, where R_i is a well-founded relation and m is a natural number. An algorithm for verifying inevitability in rectangular hybrid systems based on this observation is presented in [9].

Applying the same algorithm for linear hybrid systems poses two challenges. First, the HSR in the case of linear hybrid systems involves exponentials. In order to overcome this challenge, we prove the well-foundedness of LSR for the loops. Second, the number of loops to be considered can be possibly infinite. To overcome this challenge, we perform standard predicate abstraction of the loop LSRs. Even if the number of loops and hence the number of loop LSRs is infinite, with respect to a finite collection of predicates, the set of abstract loop LSRs becomes finite.

Proposition 7. *The Lyapunov step relation $\mathcal{L}(\Gamma)$ is blocking if and only if its transitive closure of $(\mathcal{L}(\Gamma))^+$ is contained in the disjunctive union of finite well-founded relations. That is, there exists a collection $\{R_1, \ldots, R_m\}$ of well-founded relations such that $(\mathcal{L}(\Gamma))^+ \subseteq \cup_{i=1}^m R_i$.*

Proposition 7 follows from the application of Theorem 1 in [20] to Lyapunov Step Relation. For a given $(y, y') \in (\mathcal{L}(\Gamma))^+$, it corresponds to an execution fragment α of $\mathcal{A}$ starting from $\mathbf{v}$ and ending at $\mathbf{v}'$ such that $\mathcal{L}(\mathbf{v}) = y$ and $\mathcal{L}(\mathbf{v}') = y'$. If we can find a finite collection of well-founded relations containing the Lyapunov abstractions of the first and last states of every execution, then we are done. First, observe that α is such that $\mathbf{v}.loc = l_1$ and $\mathbf{v}'.loc = l_2$ and $l_1 \neq l_2$, then the trivial relation $\{(y, y') \mid y.loc = l_1 \wedge y'.loc = l_2\}$ proves the well-foundedness of the relation $\{(y, y')\}$. Since there are finitely many locations, there are finite number of relations of this type which cover all executions which do not start and end at the same location. Hence, it suffices to consider (y, y') pairs with $y.loc = y'.loc$.

Next, to restrict the set of loops to be checked, we perform predicate abstractions over LSR. An abstraction with respect to a collection of transition predicates $\mathcal{P}$ is a function that maps a relation ρ to another relation $abs_{\mathcal{P}}(\rho)$ where $\rho \subseteq abs_{\mathcal{P}}(\rho)$. For every relation $\rho \subseteq \mathbb{R}_{\geq 0}^k \times \mathbb{R}_{\geq 0}^k$, we define the abstraction of ρ with respect to the set of predicates $\mathcal{P}$ as the conjunction of all the predicates that are weaker than ρ. In other words, if $p_1, \ldots, p_n \in \mathcal{P}$ such that $\rho \subseteq p_i$, we have that $abs_{\mathcal{P}}(\rho) = p_1 \wedge \ldots \wedge p_n$. For a relation $\sigma = \rho_1 \circ \ldots \circ \rho_n$, obtained by composing several relations, we define $abs_{\mathcal{P}}(\sigma)$ inductively as follows

$$
\begin{aligned}
abs(\sigma) &= abs_{\mathcal{P}}(\rho_1 \circ abs_{\mathcal{P}}(\sigma_1)) \\
&\quad \text{where } \sigma_1 = \rho_2 \circ \ldots \circ \rho_n \\
abs_{\mathcal{P}}(\sigma_{n-1}) &= abs_{\mathcal{P}}(\rho_n)
\end{aligned}
$$

Now we present the algorithm for proving well-foundedness. The algorithm iteratively adds to a collection of predicates $\mathcal{P}$ and a collection of well-founded relations $\mathcal{R}$ as it checks each loop. For each loop of the hybrid automaton (say π), compute the LSR $\mathcal{L}(\Gamma)_\pi$ of the loop and its abstraction $abs_{\mathcal{P}}(\mathcal{L}(\Gamma)_\pi)$. If this abstract relation is subsumed by one of the well-founded relations in $\mathcal{R}$ then this loop cannot be sustained forever, and we move on to the next loop. Otherwise, there are three possibilities: (1) If provably well-founded by a new relation R (but not by any relation in $\mathcal{R}$), then add R to $\mathcal{R}$ increasing the arsenal of well-founded relations[1]. (2) Else if $\mathcal{L}(\Gamma)_\pi$ is well-founded (though its abstraction is not), then refine the abstraction by adding the path and loop predicated to $\mathcal{P}$. (3) If $\mathcal{L}(\Gamma)_\pi$ is not well-founded then the π loop could be sustained forever and it is suggested as a potential counter-example to the inevitability/blocking property. If the automaton is symmetric with respect to $\mathcal{L}$, then π will indeed correspond to an infinite execution that never satisfies the desired property. For general automata, as a practical measure, we resort to simulations for identifying real infinite executions corresponding to a suggested counter-example loop.

---

[1] The algorithm may fail if we are unable to infer well-founded ness of this relation.

```
R ← ∅; P ← ∅                                                              1
while
    if exists π = v₁ ... vₙ s.t. v₁.loc = vₙ.loc, ∀i < n, (vᵢ, vᵢ₊₁) ∈ Γ    3
    and absₚ(L(Γ)π) ⊈ R for any R ∈ R then
        if exists R ∈ R such that L(Γ)π ⊆ R then                           5
            Refine Abstraction
            P_path ← ⋃_{i∈0..n} Preds(L(vᵢ, vᵢ₊₁) ∘ ... ∘ L(vₙ₋₁, vₙ))     7
            P_loop ← Preds(R)∪
                ⋃_{i∈0..n} Preds(L(vᵢ, vᵢ₊₁) ∘ ... ∘ L(vₙ₋₁, vₙ) ∘ R)     9
            P ← P ∪ P_path ∪ P_loop
        else                                                               11
            if L(Γ)π is well-founded relation by a (new) ranking relation R then
                Weaken disjunctive well-founded relation                   13
                R ← R ∪ R
            else                                                           15
                return "Unable to infer the blocking property of A, v₁ ... vₙ"
    else                                                                   17
        return "A is blocking"
end                                                                        19
```

Figure 4: Algorithm 1. Abstraction refinement based verification algorithm for blocking properties of hybrid automata.

4.1 Abstraction Refinement for Time-Triggered Hybrid Automata

Checking well-foundedness of LSR for time-triggered LHA can be performed using real arithmetic. Observe that Theorem 6 gives the LSR for time-triggered HA as follows:

$$
min_{G_a}[i] \leq B_l e^{\lambda_{l,i} \times C(l)} y.X[i] \wedge
$$
$$
y'.X[i] \leq \mu_{l,m} B_l e^{\lambda_{l,i} \times C(l)} y.X[i]
$$

We observe that the values of $\lambda_{l,i}$ for linear system $\dot{x} = A_l x$ are dependent on the eigenvalues of A_l. Further, the values $\mu_{l,m}$, B_l and min_{G_a} can be calculated given the dynamics and guards of each of the modes. Note that computing these values is simple only because we are dealing with *polynomial functions*. Also, $C(l)$ is provided along with the description of hybrid automata. Hence, the above relation can be simplified to the form as shown:

$$
y'.X[i] \leq \frac{y.X[i]}{K_i} \wedge y.X[i] \geq c_i \text{ where } c_i \geq 0, K_i > 0 \quad (6)
$$

A useful property of the above structure in Equation (6) is that this structure is closed under composition. Hence, composition of several LSRs for each loop can be easily performed. Further, such a relation is well-founded iff $K > 1$. Also, we have that a relation $R_1 \triangleq \{y'.X[i] \leq \frac{y.X[i]}{K_1} \wedge y.X[i] \geq c_1 \text{ where } c_1 \geq 0, K_1 > 0\}$ is an abstraction of the relation $R_2 \triangleq \{y' \leq \frac{y.X[i]}{K_2} \wedge y.X[i] \geq c_2 \text{ where } c_2 \geq 0, K_2 > 0\}$ whenever $K_1 \geq K_2$ and $c_1 \leq c_2$.

Hence all the required operations— composition, checking well-foundedness, and abstraction with respect to a set of predicates can be computed effectively using real arithmetic for the relations described in Equation (6).

5. EXPERIMENTS

We have implemented a prototype tool LySHA in MATLAB for verifying *inevitability* of hybrid automata. LySHA is integrated with Mathworks' Simulink/Stateflow (SLSF) modeling environment through HyLink which translates SLSF models to hybrid automata [17].

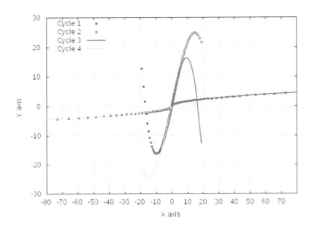

Figure 5: Non-inevitable behavior of the system described in Figure 1 discovered with LySHA . Four (of infinitely many) executions over the two locations and the corresponding values of x and y are shown.

Model $(n, |L|)$	Unstable modes	Time Taken (sec)	Is $\mathcal{B}_\epsilon$ inevitable
(2,5)	2	0.01	Yes
(2,20)	5	1.88	No
(2,50)	9	391.85	Yes
(3,20)	5	2.02	Yes
(3,40)	8	100.49	No
(4,20)	5	2.34	No
(4,40)	8	110.34	Yes
(5,20)	5	2.98	No
(5,40)	8	146.28	Yes

Figure 6: Experimental results: (Columns left to right) continuous dimensions (n), number of locations ($|L|$), number of unstable locations, execution time, and answer given by LySHA .

5.1 Case Studies

We have created a suite of linear time-triggered HA for evaluating LySHA. These automata are similar to the one shown in Figure 1. Each such HA consists of a set of locations Loc and a certain number (n) of continuous variables. When the system is in a location $l \in Loc$, the continuous variables evolve according to the linear dynamics $\dot{x} = A_l x$, where x is n-dimensional vector. As shown in Table 6, some of the locations are stable while others are unstable. The system switches from one location to another based on the timer variable *now* and state predicates. We verify the inevitability property of the system for the set of states $\mathcal{B}_\epsilon$—an ϵ ball around origin with $\epsilon = 0.001$. Given the description of the system in SLSF, HyLink generates the intermediate hybrid automaton representation, which is then used by LySHA .

LySHA computes the LSR for each loop and checks whether its abstraction is well-founded. If not, we refine the *Lyapunov abstraction* by adding a *linearly independent* Lyapunov function to each location and again compute LSR for the loop. After adding n such Lyapunov functions (where n is the dimension of the system), it terminates with a "failure to verify". In such cases, we simulate the loop and check whether the loop satisfies the inevitability property or not. For the hybrid automaton shown in Figure 1, LySHA was unable to infer inevitability for the loop $1 \to 2 \to 1$. Observe in Figure 5, that the loop $1 \to 2 \to 1$ does not satisfy the inevitability property. The figure represents the evolution of the two continuous variables x and y for four different executions of the loop $1 \to 2 \to 1$. Observe that when the system enters into location 2 (sharp change in execution near $(0,0)$), there is a very rapid growth in the values of x and y. Hence, for each loop, the state of the execution moves farther from origin. This is the reason for the non-inevitable behavior of the system. Further, LySHA confirmed that the loop $1 \to 2 \to 3 \to 1$ satisfies the inevitability property. The well-founded relation in this case is given by the relation:

$$y' \leq \frac{y}{2} \wedge y > 0.001 \qquad (7)$$

In general, the technique may produce spurious counter-examples. For example, upon verification of the in-evitability property for the HA in Figure 3, LySHA returns an abstract counter-example which does not correspond to any real counter-example. However, since the algorithm is complete for symmetric HA (HA of Figure 2), upon computing the Lyapunov step relation for the loop $1 \to 2 \to 1$, the tool computes the LSR as $(y, y') \in \mathcal{L}(\Gamma)$ iff $y.loc = y'.loc = 1$ and $y.X > 6.25 \wedge y'.X \leq 2$. This relation is well-founded and hence the system satisfies the inevitability property. Note that the algorithm presented for verifying inevitability is sound, i.e. whenever LySHA infers inevitability, it indeed holds.

We have tested LySHA for a variant of Navigation Benchmark with a different number of modes. The results are shown in Table 6. Model TTLHA_n_m denotes the time-triggered linear hybrid automaton of n dimensions (i.e. continuous variables) with m locations.

As expected, with a larger number of locations LySHA has to analyze larger number of loops, and the running time increases. Observe that LySHA could prove inevitability of systems even when some of the locations are unstable. Whenever the LySHA inferred that the system does not satisfy inevitability, we checked the behavior of the system through simulations and the results matched with LySHA . Typically, in these examples, the HA fails inevitability because of a loop with several unstable locations.

5.2 Generating Timing Constraints for Inevitability

LySHA can be used for designing *strictly time-triggered* systems, where the linear HA changes its location purely based on the time spent at each location. Consider the scenario where one desires to design a time-triggered LHA for which $\mathcal{B}_\epsilon$ is inevitable. LySHA can aid in computing these timing constraints. LySHA will produce a set of linear inequalities on the time constraints for each location derived the from well-foundedness of a LSR for a loop. If the system is designed in such a way that these timing constraints are satisfied, then the HA is guaranteed to satisfy the inevitability property.

Give the time-triggered system shown in Figure 1, LySHA displays the following set of constraints and the values of the dwell-times of each of these modes:

$$-C(1) + 2C(2) - 4C(3) < -3.991$$
$$-C(1) + 2C(2) < -3.2582$$

The two constraints specified in the above equation correspond to well-foundedness of loops $1 \rightarrow 2 \rightarrow 3 \rightarrow 1$ and $1 \rightarrow 2 \rightarrow 1$ respectively. We observe that $C(1) = 40$, $C(2) = 16$ and $C(3) = 10$ satisfies these constraints and we can check that the system satisfies the inevitability property. In general, the set of constraints produced by the LySHA can be fed into a linear programming solver to obtain (if feasible) the constraints for inevitability.

6. CONCLUSIONS & FUTURE WORK

Exploiting the relationship between inevitability, program termination and asymptotic stability, in this paper, we have presented a technique for automatic verification of the inevitability property of hybrid automata. We show how Lyapunov function-based abstractions and automated construction of well-founded relations for loops can be combined. The implementation of the resulting algorithm in a software tool (integrated with Simulink/Stateflow) shows promising results in analyzing time-triggered linear HA.

Instantiating the general verification for HA with nonlinear dynamics is an obvious direction for future exploration. For this, we have to use techniques for computing Lyapunov functions for such systems and develop algorithms for composing such Lyapunov relations.

7. REFERENCES

[1] R. Alur, C. Courcoubetis, N. Halbwachs, T. A. Henzinger, P.-H. Ho, X. Nicollin, A. Olivero, J. Sifakis, and S. Yovine. The algorithmic analysis of hybrid systems. *Theoretical Computer Science*, 138(1):3–34, 1995.

[2] A. D. Ames, P. Tabuada, and S. Sastry. On the stability of zeno equilibria. In *Hybrid Systems: Computation and Control (HSCC), volume LNCS 3927, pages 34 Ű 48*, page 3927. Springer-Verlag. 148, 2006.

[3] S. Bogomolov, C. Mitrohin, and A. Podelski. Composing reachability analyses of hybrid systems for safety and stability. ATVA'10, pages 67–81, Berlin, Heidelberg, 2010. Springer-Verlag.

[4] S. Boyd and C. Barratt. *Linear controller design: limits of performance*. Citeseer, 1991.

[5] M. Branicky. Multiple lyapunov functions and other analysis tools for switched and hybrid systems. *IEEE Transactions on Automatic Control*, 43:475–482, 1998.

[6] A. Chawdhary, B. Cook, S. Gulwani, M. Sagiv, and H. Yang. Ranking abstractions. In *ESOP'08/ETAPS'08*, pages 148–162, Berlin, Heidelberg, 2008. Springer-Verlag.

[7] E. M. Clarke, O. Grumberg, and D. E. Long. Model checking and abstraction. *ACM Trans. Program. Lang. Syst.*, 16:1512–1542, September 1994.

[8] B. Cook, A. Podelski, and A. Rybalchenko. Termination proofs for systems code. In *PLDI '06: Proceedings of the 2006 ACM SIGPLAN conference on Programming language design and implementation*, pages 415–426, New York, NY, USA, 2006. ACM.

[9] P. S. Duggirala and S. Mitra. Abstraction-refinement for stability. In *Proceedings of International Conference on Cyber-physical systems (ICCPS 2011)*, Chicago, IL, April 2011.

[10] G. Frehse. Phaver: Algorithmic verification of hybrid systems past hytech. In M. Morari and L. Thiele, editors, *HSCC*, volume 3414 of *LNCS*, pages 258–273. Springer, 2005.

[11] T. A. Henzinger, P. W. Kopke, A. Puri, and P. Varaiya. What's decidable about hybrid automata? In *ACM Symposium on Theory of Computing*, pages 373–382, 1995.

[12] J. Hespanha and A. Morse. Stability of switched systems with average dwell-time. In *Proceedings of 38th IEEE Conference on Decision and Control*, pages 2655–2660, 1999.

[13] D. K. Kaynar, N. Lynch, R. Segala, and F. Vaandrager. *The Theory of Timed I/O Automata*. Synthesis Lectures on Computer Science. Morgan Claypool, November 2005. Also available as Technical Report MIT-LCS-TR-917.

[14] H. K. Khalil. *Nonlinear Systems*. Prentice Hall, New Jersey, 3rd edition, 2002.

[15] D. Liberzon. *Switching in Systems and Control*. Systems and Control: Foundations and Applications. Birkhauser, Boston, June 2003.

[16] O. Maler and G. Batt. Approximating continuous systems by timed automata. In *Proceedings of the 1st international workshop on Formal Methods in Systems Biology*, FMSB '08, pages 77–89, Berlin, Heidelberg, 2008. Springer-Verlag.

[17] K. Manamcheri, S. Mitra, S. Bak, and M. Caccamo. A step towards verification and synthesis from simulink/stateflow models. In *Hybrid Systems: Computation and Control (HSCC 2011)*, 2011.

[18] S. Mitra. *A Verification Framework for Hybrid Systems*. PhD thesis, Massachusetts Institute of Technology, Cambridge, MA 02139, September 2007.

[19] S. Mitra, D. Liberzon, and N. Lynch. Verifying average dwell time of hybrid systems. *ACM Trans. Embed. Comput. Syst.*, 8(1):1–37, 2008.

[20] A. Podelski and A. Rybalchenko. Transition invariants. In *LICS '04: Proceedings of the 19th Annual IEEE Symposium on Logic in Computer Science*, pages 32–41, Washington, DC, USA, 2004. IEEE Computer Society.

[21] A. Podelski and S. Wagner. Model checking of hybrid systems: From reachability towards stability. In *HSCC*, pages 507–521, 2006.

[22] S. Prajna, A. Papachristodoulou, and P. A. Parrilo. Introducing SOSTOOLS: A general purpose sum of squares programming solver. In *In Proceedings of the 41st IEEE Conf. on Decision and Control*, pages 741–746, 2002.

[23] S. Sankaranarayanan and A. Tiwari. Relational abstractions for continuous and hybrid systems. In *CAV*, 2011.

[24] C. Sloth and R. Wisniewski. Abstraction of continuous dynamical systems utilizing lyapunov functions. In *Decision and Control (CDC), 2010 49th IEEE Conference on*, pages 3760 –3765, dec. 2010.

[25] A. van der Schaft and H. Schumacher. *An Introduction to Hybrid Dynamical Systems*. Springer, London, 2000.

Falsification of Temporal Properties of Hybrid Systems Using the Cross-Entropy Method

Sriram Sankaranarayanan
University of Colorado, Boulder, CO, USA.
srirams@colorado.edu

Georgios Fainekos
Arizona State University, Tempe, AZ, USA
fainekos@asu.edu

ABSTRACT

Randomized testing is a popular approach for checking properties of large embedded system designs. It is well known that a uniform random choice of test inputs is often sub-optimal. Ideally, the choice of inputs has to be guided by choosing the right input distributions in order to expose corner-case violations. However, this is also known to be a hard problem, in practice. In this paper, we present an application of the cross-entropy method for adaptively choosing input distributions for falsifying temporal logic properties of hybrid systems. We present various choices for representing input distribution families for the cross-entropy method, ranging from a complete partitioning of the input space into cells to a factored distribution of the input using graphical models.

Finally, we experimentally compare the falsification approach using the cross-entropy method to other stochastic and heuristic optimization techniques implemented inside the tool S-Taliro over a set of benchmark systems. The performance of the cross entropy method is quite promising. We find that sampling inputs using the cross-entropy method guided by trace robustness can discover violations faster, and more consistently than the other competing methods considered.

Categories and Subject Descriptors

G.3 [**Mathematics of Computing**]: Probability and Statistics—*Probabilistic algorithms (including Monte Carlo)*

General Terms

Verification

Keywords

Hybrid Systems, Testing, Robustness, Metric Temporal Logic, Monte-Carlo Simulation, Cross-Entropy Method.

1. INTRODUCTION

In this paper, we propose the use of the cross-entropy method [33, 32] for falsifying Metric Temporal Logic (MTL) properties on

complex hybrid systems. Testing through the random sampling of input vectors is a simple, yet popular approach for checking hybrid system models that are too complex to be verified using more rigorous formal verification techniques. However, the algorithm used for choosing input vectors is crucial for the success of randomized testing. Often, the choice of inputs needs to incorporate detailed knowledge about the system in the form of appropriate input distributions that are easy to sample from, while also providing a bias towards input choices exhibiting property violations. Such user guidance is often impractical, since it requires a detailed knowledge of the system's internals along with insights as to how this knowledge may be incorporated into an appropriate input distribution. Secondly, distributions that are ideal for exposing property violations tend to be quite hard to sample from, in practice.

In this paper, we employ a versatile approach to sampling known as the *Cross-Entropy Method* [6, 32, 33], guided by the notion of *robustness* of execution traces of continuous and hybrid systems w.r.t MTL properties [17, 18, 28], in order to solve the problem of generating test inputs that falsify a given set of MTL properties.

The robustness semantics of MTL associates a real value with each trajectory. Formally, this value denotes the radius of a cylinder around the trajectory (defined using an appropriate metric over states), such that all trajectories inside this cylinder have an identical outcome for the given property as the given reference trajectory (Cf. Figure 2). As a result, the robustness value of a trajectory provides a mathematically sound notion of distance that can be used to express how "far away" a given trace is from violating a property. The notion of robustness of MTL formulae can, in turn, be used to associate an ideal probability distribution that samples each input according to the robustness of the resulting trajectory. However, this distribution is often complex and not known in a closed form.

In this work, the *cross-entropy* (CE) method is used to sample from this complex distribution. The CE method is, fundamentally, a technique for sampling from a complex probability distribution that is not necessarily known in a closed form. The applications of this method include rare-event simulation, variance reduction for estimation problems and stochastic optimization [33]. The CE method seeks to approximate the target distribution by choosing amongst a family of distributions such as piecewise uniform distributions or Gaussian distributions, that are "easy" to sample from [32, 6]. The technique iteratively searches for a specific distribution from this family that is "as close as possible" to the intended distribution. Here closeness of distributions is measured using the standard *Kullback-Liebler* (KL) divergence (also known as the cross-entropy distance) between the distributions. At each step, cross-entropy method generates samples according to a current candidate distribution from the family. Next, it uses these samples to *tilt* the current candidate distribution towards a new candidate that minimizes the empirically estimated KL divergence over the current set of samples between the new candidate and the target distribution. As a result of this iteration, the candidate distribution is seen to get closer in the sense of KL divergence to the target distribution.

Applying the cross-entropy method requires choosing a family of distributions that is easy to sample from, while at the same time able to approximate the complex distribution induced by the trajectory robustness values. We find that a natural approach is to use piecewise uniform distributions, whenever the space of inputs is bounded. Such distributions are defined by subdividing the space of input vectors into finitely many cells and associating a fixed probability of choosing an input from a given cell. However, the number of cells grows exponentially in the number of components in the input vector. Therefore, we consider the application of cross-entropy method on factored input representations, wherein the distribution is factored into various marginal probability distributions that relate a small set of input variables. In this paper, we derive the necessary rules for tilting the cross entropy method for factorings based on graphical models.

Finally, we present a prototype implementation of our approach on the S-Taliro tool for testing Simulink/Stateflow models [3]. Our experimental evaluation compares the performance of the Cross-Entropy method against Monte-Carlo methods [28, 33] and simple uniform random sampling.

Summary of Contributions: (a) We present the use of the CE method for falsifying MTL properties using the robustness metrics over hybrid trajectories. (b) We consider the problem of specifying a family of input distributions that can approximate complex distributions with small KL divergences, while at the same time, be parameterized by a small number of parameters. We explore the use of factored input distributions using graphical models. (c) We present an experimental evaluation of our approach over a set of benchmarks, using a prototype implementation in our tool S-Taliro, along with a comparison with other optimization approaches supported inside S-Taliro that are also guided by MTL robustness.

Finally, proofs of key propositions have been omitted due to space considerations. These will be made available on-line or upon request. The techniques presented in this paper have been implemented as part of our tool S-Taliro. S-Taliro is available as an open source tool on-line at http://sites.google.com/a/asu.edu/s-taliro.

2. PRELIMINARIES

In this section, we present some background on system models, metric temporal logics (MTL) and roubstness of traces. More details on our approach are available from our previous work on using stochastic optimization techniques for temporal falsification [28].

2.1 Systems and Inputs

We assume a black-box model of deterministic systems including continuous, discrete, and hybrid systems that combine continuous-time dynamics with instantaneous discrete switches [1].

A system S maps the initial conditions $\vec{x}_0 \in \mathbb{R}^n$, and input signals $\vec{u} : [0, T] \mapsto \mathbb{R}^k$ to output values $\vec{y} : [0, T] \mapsto Y$, wherein $T > 0$ is assumed to be a large, but finite time limit[1]. We assume that the initial state $\vec{x}_0 \in X_0$ for some set $X_0 \subseteq \mathbb{R}^n$ and $\vec{u}(t) \in U \subseteq \mathbb{R}^k$ for all time $t \in [0, T]$. Furthermore, the sets X_0 and U are assumed to be *boxes*, which are Cartesian products of intervals of the form $[a_1, b_1] \times [a_2, b_2] \times \cdots \times [a_n, b_n]$, wherein

[1]Since the goal in this paper is that of testing hybrid systems, it is not strictly necessary to define input and output maps that extend for all time.

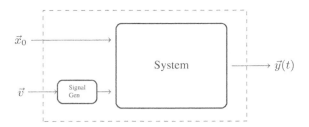

Figure 1: Block diagram of the system after parameterizing input signals.

$a_i, b_i \in \mathbb{R} \cup \pm\infty$. Since the system is assumed to be deterministic, its output $\vec{y} = S(\vec{x}_0, \vec{u})$ can be written as a function of its initial state $\vec{x}_0$ and inputs $\vec{u}$.

Parameterizing Input Signals: Let $\mathcal{U}$ denote the space of all measurable functions $\vec{u} : [0, T] \mapsto \mathbb{R}^k$. The overall goal of randomized testing is to explore many points in the space the space $X_0 \times \mathcal{U}$ of inputs. However, arbitrary (measurable) input signals from a function space $\mathcal{U}$ are often hard to represent. Therefore, we restrict our attention to a class of signals from $\mathcal{U}$ that can be succinctly described in a finite dimensional space by a finite set of real valued parameters. Common examples of such families include:

- Piecewise constant (or linear) signals that are described by the values $\vec{u}_0, \vec{u}_1, \ldots, \vec{u}_k$ at a fixed set of time points:

$$0 = T_0 < T_1 < T_2 < \cdots < T_k < T_{k+1} = T ,$$

  wherein $\vec{u}(t) = \vec{u}_j$ for all $t \in [T_j, T_{j+1})$ and $j = 0, \ldots, k$.

- Polynomial signals defined by parameters $\vec{a}_1, \ldots, \vec{a}_l$, wherein, $\vec{u}(t) = \vec{a}_0 + \vec{a}_1 t + \vec{a}_2 t^2 + \cdots + \vec{a}_l t^l$.

- Splines [15] can be specified piecewise by specifying a finite set of time points along with signal values and derivatives at these time points.

In practice, the family is chosen so that any signal of interest from $\mathcal{U}$ can be represented approximately with some small error. Thus, the chosen representation R for the signals ensures a finite set of parameters $\vec{v} \in V$ such that each $\vec{v}$ can be mapped onto a unique input $\mathbb{U}(\vec{v}) : [0, T] \to U$. The process of sampling described in this paper can therefore focus on sampling real numbers.

2.2 Metric Temporal Logic

Functional specifications for real-time embedded systems usually involve a number of critical properties such as timing requirements, stability and bounded response. Metric Temporal Logic (MTL) introduced by Koymans [24] is a popular formalism for expressing such properties. The problem of verifying MTL specifications is undecidable for hybrid systems. Consequently, the *bounded-time* verification or falsification of such properties has been studied [28, 17].

Table 1 summarizes the syntax of MTL formulae. Let φ be an MTL formula, $t_0 \geq 0$ be a time instant and $\vec{y} : [0, T] \mapsto Y$ be an output trajectory. To define the semantics, we first define observation maps that provide meaning to the atomic propositions.

DEFINITION 2.1 (OBSERVATION MAP). *An observation map* $\mathcal{O} : AP \to \mathcal{P}(Y)$ *maps each proposition* $p \in AP$ *to a set* $\mathcal{O}(p) \subseteq Y$. *For simplicity, we assume that* $\mathcal{O}(p) \subseteq Y$ *is closed and compact for each* $p \in AP$.

Table 1: Metric Temporal Logic (MTL) Operators and their formal semantics at time $t = t_0$.

$\top$	*true*	Tautology
$p \in \mathrm{AP}$	$\vec{y}(t_0) \in \mathcal{O}(p)$	Atomic Proposition holds
$\varphi_1 \wedge \varphi_2$	$(\vec{y}, t_0, \mathcal{O}) \models \varphi_1 \wedge (\vec{y}, t_0, \mathcal{O}) \models \varphi_2$	Conjunction
$\varphi_1 \vee \varphi_2$	$(\vec{y}, t_0, \mathcal{O}) \models \varphi_1 \vee (\vec{y}, t_0, \mathcal{O}) \models \varphi_2$	Disjunction
$\neg\, \varphi$	$(\vec{y}, t_0, \mathcal{O}) \not\models \varphi$	Negation
$\Box_{\mathcal{I}}\varphi$	$(\forall t \in \mathcal{I})((t_0 + t < T) \Rightarrow (\vec{y}, t_0 + t, \mathcal{O}) \models \varphi)$	φ is Invariant in $\mathcal{I}$
$\Diamond_{\mathcal{I}}\varphi$	$(\exists t \in \mathcal{I})((t_0 + t < T) \wedge (\vec{y}, t_0 + t, \mathcal{O}) \models \varphi)$	φ eventually holds in $\mathcal{I}$
$\varphi_1 \mathcal{U}_{\mathcal{I}}\varphi_2$	$(\exists t \in \mathcal{I})((t_0 + t < T) \wedge (\vec{y}, t_0 + t, \mathcal{O}) \models \varphi_2 \wedge (\forall t' \in [0, t))\, (\vec{y}, t_0 + t', \mathcal{O}) \models \varphi_1)$	φ_1 until φ_2

We denote the satisfaction of the formula φ by the trajectory $\vec{y}$ starting from time $t = t_0$ by $(\vec{y}, t_0, \mathcal{O}) \models \varphi$. The semantics of MTL in terms of the $\models$ relation is also provided in Table 1.

PROBLEM 2.1 (MTL FALSIFICATION). *For an MTL specification φ, the MTL falsification problem consists of finding valid initial state $\vec{x}_0$ and input signals $\vec{u} : [0, T] \to U$, such that the resulting output trajectory $\vec{y} : [0, T] \to Y$ falsifies the specification φ, i.e., $(\vec{y}, 0, \mathcal{O}) \not\models \varphi$.*

Robustness of Trajectories Our proposed solution for Problem 2.1 quantifies the *robustness of satisfaction* of an MTL formula over a system trajectory to guide the search for falsifications [18].

We briefly present the robust interpretation (semantics) of MTL formulas. Details are available from our previous work [18, 28].

We provide semantics that maps an MTL formula φ and a trajectory $\vec{y}(t)$ to a value drawn from the linearly ordered set $\overline{\mathbb{R}} = \mathbb{R} \cup \{\pm\infty\}$. The semantics for the atomic propositions evaluated for $\vec{y}(t)$ consists of the distance between $\vec{y}(t)$ and the set $\mathcal{O}(p)$ labeling the atomic proposition p. Intuitively, this distance represents how robustly the point $\vec{y}(t)$ lies within (or outside) the set $\mathcal{O}(p)$.

First, let d be a distance metric on Y. For each point $\vec{y} \in Y$, we define the open ball $B_d(\vec{y}, \epsilon) = \{\vec{z} \mid d(\vec{y}, \vec{z}) < \epsilon\}$.

DEFINITION 2.2 (SIGNED DISTANCE). *Let $y \in Y$ be a point, $S \subseteq Y$ be a set and d be a distance metric on Y. We define the signed distance from y to S to be*

$$\mathbf{Dist}_d(y, S) := \begin{cases} -\inf\{d(y, y') \mid y' \in S\} & \text{if } y \notin S \\ \inf\{d(y, y') \mid y' \in Y \backslash S\} & \text{if } y \in S \end{cases}$$

If this distance is zero, then the smallest perturbation of the point y can affect the outcome of $y \in \mathcal{O}(p)$. We denote the robust valuation of the formula φ over the signal $\vec{y}$ at time t by $[\![\varphi, \mathcal{O}]\!]_d(\vec{y}, t)$. Formally, $[\![\cdot, \cdot]\!]_d : (MTL \times \mathcal{P}(Y)^{AP}) \to (Y^{[0,T]} \times [0, T] \to \overline{\mathbb{R}})$.

DEFINITION 2.3 (ROBUST SEMANTICS). *Let $\vec{y} \in Y^{[0,T]}$, $c \in \overline{\mathbb{R}}$ and $\mathcal{O} \in \mathcal{P}(Y)^{AP}$, then the robust semantics of any formula $\varphi \in MTL$ with respect to $\vec{y}$ is recursively defined as follows for $t \in [0, T]$:*

$$
\begin{aligned}
[\![\top, \mathcal{O}]\!]_d(\vec{y}, t) &:= +\infty \\
[\![p, \mathcal{O}]\!]_d(\vec{y}, t) &:= \mathbf{Dist}_d(\vec{y}(t), \mathcal{O}(p)) \\
[\![\neg\varphi_1, \mathcal{O}]\!]_d(\vec{y}, t) &:= -[\![\varphi_1, \mathcal{O}]\!]_d(\vec{y}, t) \\
[\![\varphi_1 \vee \varphi_2, \mathcal{O}]\!]_d(\vec{y}, t) &:= \max([\![\varphi_1, \mathcal{O}]\!]_d(\vec{y}, t), [\![\varphi_2, \mathcal{O}]\!]_d(\vec{y}, t)) \\
[\![\varphi_1 \mathcal{U}_{\mathcal{I}}\varphi_2, \mathcal{O}]\!]_d(\vec{y}, t) &:=
\end{aligned}
$$

$$\sup_{t' \in (t +_{[0,T]} \mathcal{I})} \min\left([\![\varphi_2, \mathcal{O}]\!]_d(\vec{y}, t'), \inf_{t \le t'' < t'}[\![\varphi_1, \mathcal{O}]\!]_d(\vec{y}, t'')\right)$$

where $t +_{[0,T]} \mathcal{I} = \{\tau \mid \exists \tau' \in \mathcal{I} . \tau = t + \tau'\} \cap [0, T]$.

It is easy to show that if the trajectory satisfies the property, then its robustness is non-negative and, similarly, it the trajectory does

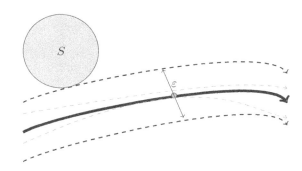

Figure 2: Illustration of robustness of trajectory shown in solid line. The property asserts the "unreachability" of the set S. The robustness value ε defines a cylinder around the trajectory, so that all trajectories that lie inside a cylinder of radius ε (dashed lines) also satisfy the property.

not satisfy the property, then its robustness is non-positive. The following result holds [18].

THEOREM 2.1. *Given a formula $\varphi \in MTL$, an observation map $\mathcal{O} \in \mathcal{P}(Y)^{AP}$ and a trajectory $\vec{y} \in Y^{[0,T]}$, the following hold:*

(1) If $(\vec{y}, t, \mathcal{O}) \models \varphi$, then $[\![\varphi, \mathcal{O}]\!]_d(\vec{y}, t) \ge 0$.

(2) Conversely, if $[\![\varphi, \mathcal{O}]\!]_d(\vec{y}, t) > 0$, then $(\vec{y}, t, \mathcal{O}) \models \varphi$.

(3) If for some $t \in \mathbb{R}^+$, $\varepsilon = [\![\varphi, \mathcal{O}]\!]_d(\vec{y}, t) \ne 0$, then for all $\vec{y}' \in B_d(\vec{y}, |\varepsilon|)$, we have $(\vec{y}, t, \mathcal{O}) \models \varphi$ if and only if $(\vec{y}', t, \mathcal{O}) \models \varphi$. I.e, ε defines a cylinder around the trajectory such that trajectories lying entirely inside this cylinder also satisfy φ.

In other words, if a trajectory $\vec{y}$ satisfies the formula φ at time instant $t \ge 0$ then its robustness value is non-negative.

Theorem 2.1 establishes the robust semantics of MTL as a natural measure of trajectory robustness. Namely, a trajectory is ε robust with respect to an MTL specification φ, if it can tolerate perturbations up to size ε and still maintain its current Boolean truth value. Alternatively, a trajectory with the opposite outcome for φ, if it exists, has a distance of at least ε away.

The efficient computation of MTL robustness over continuous and hybrid system trajectories has been investigated in [18, 17]. Implementations are available as part of the tool Taliro, which forms the core of our approach to temporal logic falsification [3].

2.3 Temporal Falsification as Optimization

Given a system $\mathcal{S} : X_0 \times V \mapsto Y$ (Cf. Figure 1), along with a MTL specification φ, we are interested in finding input signals $\vec{u}$

and initial conditions $\vec{x}_0$ such that the resulting output falsifies φ. More generally, we can search for inputs such that the robustness value of the resulting output trajectory w.r.t specification φ is the least possible. Let $R(\vec{x}_0, \vec{v}; \varphi, \mathcal{S})$ denote the robustness value w.r.t φ for the trajectory $\vec{y}$ resulting from inputs $\vec{x}_0, \vec{u}$ to system $\mathcal{S}$

$$R(\vec{x}_0, \vec{v}; \varphi, \mathcal{S}) = [\![\varphi, \mathcal{O}]\!]_d(\vec{y}, 0), \text{ wherein } \vec{y} = \mathcal{S}(\vec{x}_0, \vec{v}).$$

Consider the optimization problem of finding inputs that yield the minimal robustness value possible:

$$(\vec{x}_0, \vec{v}) = \operatorname*{argmin}_{\vec{x}_0 \in X_0, \vec{v} \in V} R(\vec{x}_0, \vec{v}; \mathcal{S}, \varphi).$$

If the minimal robustness value is negative then the corresponding inputs yield a falsifying test case. Solving for $\vec{x}_0, \vec{v}$ is hard, even for the simplest of systems. Our goal is therefore to search for trajectories $\vec{y}$ that have small robustness values by sampling from the space of initial conditions X_0 and input signals V. If we discover a violation in the process, we can report such a violation to the user. Failing this, our search simply presents the least robust trajectory discovered thus far.

The strategy used for finding a trajectory with as small a robustness value by sampling is to draw samples according to a probability distribution. Let p be a probability density function over a set of support X. A sampling scheme produces a sequence of samples $x_1, \ldots, x_N \in X$, such that for any (measurable) subset $I \subseteq X$,

$$\lim_{N \to \infty} \sum_{i=1}^{N} \frac{\mathbb{1}(x_i \in I)}{N} = \int_I p(x)dx, \text{ where } \mathbb{1}(\varphi) = \left\{ \begin{array}{ll} 1 & \text{if } \varphi \\ 0 & \text{otherwise} \end{array} \right. .$$

In other words, as we draw a large number of samples, the empirical sample distribution converges in the limit to the distribution p.

Suppose we were able to draw numerous samples according to the probability distribution Ω over $X_0 \times V$, defined as

$$\Omega(\vec{x}_0, \vec{v}) = \frac{1}{W} e^{-K \cdot R(\vec{x}_0, \vec{v}; \mathcal{S}, \varphi)},$$

wherein $K > 0$ is some chosen weighting factor and W is used to normalize the total mass of the distribution over $X_0 \times V$. Given the nature of the distribution, the probability of encountering inputs $\vec{x}_0, \vec{v}$ that yield negative robustness values (if such inputs exist) is exponentially larger than that of obtaining a positive robustness value. The precise ratio of these probabilities is controlled by K. Drawing samples according to Ω promises to be an effective way of searching for falsifications. However, there are two main problems: (a) Ω is not known in a closed form. To compute $\Omega(\vec{x}_0, \vec{v})$, we obtain $R(\vec{x}_0, \vec{v}; \mathcal{S}, \varphi)$ by simulating the system $\mathcal{S}$ over the inputs $(\vec{x}_0, \vec{v})$. However, the normalizing factor W is also unknown. (b) Techniques that attempt to sample inputs according to Ω often require a large number of simulations to converge [28].

An alternative approach is to start from a family of distributions $\mathcal{F}$ (eg., normal distributions) and attempt to find a distribution which is as close to Ω as possible. The tradeoff involved here is that we are sampling from a distribution family $\mathcal{F}$, which may not contain the distribution Ω. On the other hand, the distributions in $\mathcal{F}$ are chosen from known families such as normal or piecewise uniform families that are relatively easier to sample from. The cross-entropy method due to Rubinstein and Kroese attempts to solve this problem in a systematic manner [33, 32].

3. CROSS-ENTROPY METHOD

In this section, we present a brief overview of the cross entropy method which is a widely used rare-event simulation technique. Further details including a theoretical analysis of cross-entropy method are available elsewhere [32, 33, 6].

Our presentation will focus mostly on how cross-entropy method can be used to sample from a distribution Ω over the space of inputs $X_0 \times V$. As a first step, we fix a family of distributions p_θ, parameterized by a set of parameters $\theta \in P$.

- **Piecewise-Uniform Family:** The piecewise uniform family is useful when the input space $X_0 \times V$ is bounded. We partition the input space into a set of mutually disjoint measurable cells $C_1, \ldots, C_k$, wherein each C_i is bounded and has a finite volume. The family is parameterized by the individual cell sampling probabilities $\theta : (p_1, \ldots, p_k) \in [0, 1]^k$, such that, $\sum_{i=1}^{k} p_i = 1$. Here p_k denotes the probability that an input from the cell C_i is chosen. In order to sample from a given distribution p_θ in the family, we choose a cell according C_i with probability p_i. Next we choose input $(\vec{x}_0, u) \in C_i$, uniformly at random.

  The piecewise uniform family can be made to approximate any distribution with arbitrary precision by (a) increasing the number of partitions and (b) by choosing the probabilities of each partition appropriately.

- **Gaussian Distribution:** A multivariate Gaussian distribution $N_{\vec{\mu}, C}$ is parameterized by its mean $\vec{\mu}$ and its co-variance matrix C (a positive semi-definite matrix). These distributions (and other exponential distributions) are suitable when $X_0 \times V$ is unbounded. A simple extension to this model considers a mixture of Gaussian distributions, by averaging a fixed number of Gaussian distributions.

3.1 Overview of Cross-Entropy Method

Let Ω be a (complex) distribution over $I : X_0 \times V$ that we wish to sample from. We assume that $\Omega(\vec{x}, \vec{v}) \neq 0$ for all $(\vec{x}, \vec{v}) \in X_0 \times V$. In general, we may not know Ω as a closed form formula. However, for any two points $(\vec{x}_0, \vec{v}_0)$ and $(\vec{x}_1, \vec{v}_1)$ in the input space I, it is possible to compute the ratio $\frac{\Omega(\vec{x}_0, \vec{v}_0)}{\Omega(\vec{x}_1, \vec{v}_1)}$. Consequently, it is possible to compare the values of Ω at two or more points and rank these points according to the value of Ω.

Let p_θ be a family of distributions parameterized by $\theta \in P$. We assume that each p_θ has a set of support that contains $X_0 \times V$. In other words, $p_\theta(\vec{x}, \vec{v}) \neq 0$ for all $(\vec{x}, \vec{v}) \in X_0 \times V$. Our goal is to find a distribution p_θ from the family that is "as close" to Ω as possible. However, the notion of the "closeness" of two distributions needs to be formalized. We use the standard Kullback-Liebler (KL) divergence from information theory.

DEFINITION 3.1 (KULLBACK-LIEBLER DIVERGENCE). *Let us assume two distributions $p(\cdot)$ and $q(\cdot)$ over some set of support S, such that $\forall \vec{x} \in S, p(\vec{x}) \neq 0$, $q(\vec{x}) \neq 0$. The Kullback-Liebler (KL) divergence is defined as*

$$\mathcal{D}(p, q) = \int_S \log\left(\frac{p(x)}{q(x)}\right) p(x)dx = E_p\left[\log\left(\frac{p(x)}{q(x)}\right)\right],$$

wherein E_p denotes the expectation over the distribution p.

Note that the KL divergence is not a metric. In general, $\mathcal{D}(p, q) \neq \mathcal{D}(q, p)$. However, it can be shown that for all distributions p, q, $\mathcal{D}(p, q) \geq 0$. Furthermore, $\mathcal{D}(p, q) = 0$ iff $p = q$.

Our goal here is to choose a distribution p_θ from the chosen family that minimizes the KL divergence $\mathcal{D}(\Omega, p_\theta)$ [2]. Since Ω is not known in a closed form, it is not possible to evaluate $\mathcal{D}(\Omega, p_\theta)$ for a

---

[2] Note that this is not the same as minimizing $\mathcal{D}(p_\theta, \Omega)$. The choice of Ω as the first argument makes the minimization over samples possible without knowing Ω in a closed form.

given θ. The idea is to adaptively search for suitable parameter values θ by performing the optimization over finitely many data points obtained through sampling. Therefore, the cross-entropy method proceeds by approximating $\mathcal{D}(\Omega, p_\theta)$ empirically from samples and adaptively choosing values of θ. We start with some initial $\theta(0) \in P$ and iterate until some termination criterion.

(a) Draw a fixed number N_s according to p_θ using the current set of parameters $\theta = \theta(h)$.

(b) Let $\vec{x}^{(0)}, \ldots, \vec{x}^{(N_s)}$ be the samples sorted in descending order according to their Ω values.

(c) Choose the top m samples for some $m \ll N_s$.

(d) Obtain a new set of parameters $\theta(h + 1)$ by *tilting*. The new parameter set $\theta(h+1)$ minimizes the empirically estimated KL divergence $\mathcal{D}(\Omega, p_\theta)$ over the sample points $\vec{x}^{(0)}, \ldots, \vec{x}^{(m-1)}$, for all $\theta \in P$.

$$\theta(h + 1) = \operatorname*{argmin}_{\theta \in P} \left(-\frac{1}{m} \sum_{i=0}^{m-1} \left(\frac{\log(p_\theta(\vec{x}^{(i)}))\Omega(\vec{x}^{(i)})}{p_{\theta(h)}(\vec{x}^{(i)})} \right) \right).$$

The derivation of the formula above is shown elsewhere [32].

Termination is based upon some fixed convergence criterion. After termination, we sample extensively from the final distribution $\theta(h + 1)$ to search for a possible violation.

Tilting: Given the distribution $\theta(h) \in P$ for the current iteration and the sample points $\vec{x}^{(0)}, \ldots, \vec{x}^{(m-1)}$, we seek to minimize the empirical KL divergence over the sample points

$$\theta(h + 1) = \operatorname*{argmin}_{\theta \in P} \left(-\frac{1}{m} \sum_{i=0}^{m-1} \left(\frac{\log(p_\theta(\vec{x}^{(i)}))\Omega(\vec{x}^{(i)})}{p_{\theta(h)}(\vec{x}^{(i)})} \right) \right),$$

to obtain the parameters for the subsequent iteration. Writing $\gamma_i = \frac{\Omega(\vec{x}^{(i)})}{p_{\theta(h)}(\vec{x}^{(i)})}$, we note that γ_i can be evaluated for each sample up to some fixed but unknown positive scaling factor W. However, this suffices to carry out the optimization for tilting. Simplifying, we obtain

$$\theta(h + 1) = \operatorname*{argmax}_{\theta \in P} \left(\sum_{i=0}^{m-1} \gamma_i \log(p_\theta(\vec{x}^{(i)})) \right). \quad (1)$$

The result depends, in general, on the distribution family chosen. It is relatively straightforward to solve for the optima above by computing partial derivatives w.r.t θ to obtain a closed form for standard families such as piecewise uniform and exponential distributions [32]. This yields an *updating rule* Θ_p for family p:

$$\theta(h + 1) = \Theta_p(\theta(h), \vec{x}^{(0)}, \gamma_0, \ldots, \vec{x}^{(m-1)}, \gamma_{m-1}). \quad (2)$$

Updating Rules for Piecewise Uniform Distributions: Let us assume that the input space $X_0 \times V$ is partitioned into disjoint cells $C_1, \ldots, C_k$. Let $\vec{x}^{(1)}, \ldots, \vec{x}^{(m)}$ be the samples chosen for tilting. Our goal is to update the current values of the cell sampling probabilities $\vec{\theta}(h) : (\theta_{h,1}, \ldots, \theta_{h,k})$ to yield new set of parameters $\vec{\theta}(h + 1)$ according to Eq. (2). This can be performed by setting the partial derivatives with respect to each unknown parameter $\theta_{h+1,j}$ to zero. The resulting update formula is given by

$$\theta_{h+1,j} = \frac{\sum_{i=0}^{m-1} \mathbb{1}(\vec{x}^{(i)} \in C_j)\gamma_i}{\sum_{i=0}^{m-1} \gamma_i},$$

wherein $\mathbb{1}(a \in S) = \begin{cases} 1 & \text{if } a \in S \\ 0 & \text{otherwise} \end{cases}$ In practice, the tilting is always performed *gradually* using a discount factor λ, by updating

$$\theta(h + 1) = \lambda\theta(h) + (1 - \lambda)\theta'(h).$$

Updating rules for other families such as the Gaussian distributions and "natural exponential families" (NEF) are considered by Rubinstein and Kroese [32].

3.2 Illustrative Example

We now illustrate the operation of the cross-entropy method for finding an appropriate insulin infusion schedule for controlling the blood glucose level of a type II diabetic patient following the ingestion of a meal. The model and the parameters chosen have been inspired by the work of Fisher [19]. The dynamics of insulin and glucose in the patient are modeled by the ODE

$$\begin{aligned} \frac{dG}{dt} &= -p_1 G - X(G + G_b) + P(t) \\ \frac{dX}{dt} &= -p_2 X + p_3 I \\ \frac{dI}{dt} &= -n(I + I_b) + u(t)/V_I \end{aligned}$$

wherein state variable G refers to the level of glucose in the blood plasma above a fixed basal value G_b, I refers to the level of insulin above a fixed basal value I_b and X is a quantity that is proportional to the level of insulin that is effective in controlling blood glucose level. The function $P(t)$ refers to the addition of glucose in the blood after digestion. Following Fisher, we set $P(t) = ke^{-Bt}$ to model the characteristic peak and decay of the level of glucose added to the blood during the digestion process. The input $u(t)$ refers to the insulin infused directly by means of a direct infusion into the blood, wherein $0 \leq u(t) \leq 3$ for all $t \geq 0$.

Initial conditions are chosen from the intervals $G(0) \in [6, 10]$, $X(0) \in [0.05, 0.1]$ and $I(0) \in [-.1, .1]$. We wish to find an initial condition and a value of $u(t)$ that falsifies the MTL property

$$\varphi : \neg(\Box_{[0,20.0]}(G \in [-2, 10]) \ \wedge \ \Box_{[20,200.0]}(G \in [-1, 1])).$$

Informally, φ specifies that the value of glucose should *not* be in the range $[-2, 10]$ during the first 20 minutes, or *fail to* remain the range $[-1, 1]$ over the next 180 minutes.

We ran a cross-entropy sampling guided by trace robustness to search for a suitable input. Each signal $u(t)$ is represented by a spline with 4 control points. This yields 7 input parameters. The range of permissible values for each input parameter is subdivided into 10 equally spaced subintervals. Figure 3 shows the final results of applying the cross-entropy method for 25 iterations lasting roughly 570 seconds. The technique does not find a falsifying input, it finds an input schedule that comes quite close yielding a low robustness value of 0.3. Figure 3 plots the minimal robustness trace. The run of cross-entropy method is illustrated by showing the tilted probability distributions at iteration numbers $1, 5, \ldots, 25$.

4. FACTORED INPUT DISTRIBUTIONS

In this section, we present some basic ideas on how families of input distributions may be formed and represented for applying the cross-entropy method for falsifying temporal properties. In general, there are two conflicting concerns that affect the choice of a family of distributions: (a) the ability to represent arbitrary input distributions to a good degree of approximation and (b) keeping the number of parameters that describe the family small.

We focus on piecewise uniform distributions obtained by subdividing the input space into many disjoint cells $C_1, \ldots, C_K$. Let us represent the vector of inputs in $X_0 \times V \subseteq \mathbb{R}^k$ by $(z_1, \ldots, z_k) \in \mathbb{R}^k$. We have assumed that the set of legal input values form a

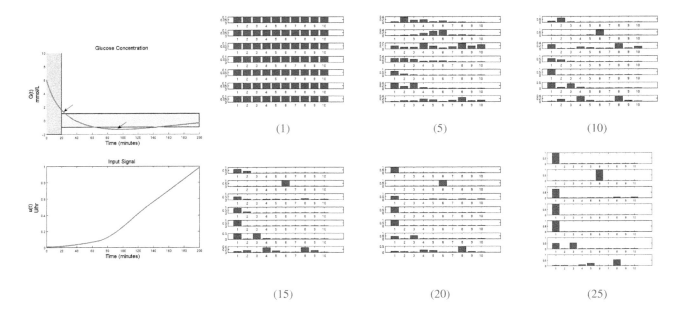

(1)   (5)   (10)

(15)   (20)   (25)

Figure 3: Results of cross-entropy method for the insulin glucose model. (Left) plot showing the least robust simulation result. (Right) Probability distributions over the various input subintervals at rounds $1, 5, \ldots, 25$.

bounded box $[a_1, b_1] \times [a_2, b_2] \times \cdots \times [a_k, b_k]$. We partition the set of possible values for each input variable $z_i \in [a_i, b_i]$ into a fixed number $n > 0$ different disjoint sub-intervals $U_{i,1}, \ldots, U_{i,n}$ [3]. This represents a partitioning of input space into n^k rectangular cells, wherein each cell $C_{j_1, \ldots, j_k}$ is a product of intervals $U_{1,j_1} \times U_{2,j_2} \times \cdots \times U_{k,j_k}$. As a result, representing the piecewise uniform distribution requires n^k parameters, which is exponential in the dimensionality of the input vector. Therefore, we consider tradeoffs in representing the family by means of factored distributions.

Fully Factored Distribution: A simple scheme for representing probability distributions over the cells is to associate a uniform probability value $P_{i,j}$ for each cell $U_{i,j}$ for input z_i and interval $U_{i,j}$, such that

$$\forall\, i \in [1, k] \sum_{j=1}^{n} P_{i,j} = 1 \, .$$

The family of fully factored distributions are parameterized by the values $P_{i,j}$ for $i \in [1, k]$ and $j \in [1, n]$. The probability of choosing a cell $C_{j_1, \ldots, j_k}$ is assumed to be given by the product

$$\mathsf{P}(C_{j_1, \ldots, j_k}) = \Pi_{i=1}^{k} P_{i,j_i} \, .$$

Once a cell is chosen using the discrete distribution defined above, a point in the cell is chosen uniformly at random. In other words, the choice of a cell is obtained by independently choosing intervals for each input z_i.

We will now derive the update rule for tilting using families of fully factored piecewise uniform distributions by solving the optimization involved in Equation (1). Let $\vec{x}^{(1)}, \ldots, \vec{x}^{(m)}$ be the m samples used to compute the tilting. Furthermore, for each sample, we obtain the value $\gamma_l = \frac{W \Omega(\vec{x}^{(l)})}{p_{\theta(h)}(\vec{x}^{(l)})}$. Our goal is to compute

[3]For simplicity, we assume that the number of subdivisions along each dimension is the same.

optimal parameters $\theta^* = (P_{1,1}, \ldots, P_{k,n})$ such that

$$\theta^* = \mathsf{argmax} \left(\sum_{l=0}^{m-1} \gamma_l \log(p_\theta(\vec{x}^{(l)})) \right) \tag{3}$$

We may write $\log(p_\theta(\vec{x}^{(l)}))$ as

$$\log(p_\theta(\vec{x}^{(l)})) = \sum_{i=1}^{k} \sum_{j=1}^{n} \log(P_{i,j}) \mathbb{1}(\vec{x}_i^{(l)} \in U_{i,j}) \, .$$

Lemma 4.1. *The optimal value of parameters $P_{i,j}$ that maximizes the objective in Equation (3) are given by*

$$P_{i,j} = \frac{\sum_{l=0}^{m-1} \gamma_l \mathbb{1}(\vec{x}_i^{(l)} \in U_{i,j})}{\sum_{l=1}^{m} \gamma_l} \, .$$

PROOF. This lemma is a special case of the more general Lemma 4.2 for graphical models that will be presented subsequently. $\square$

One of the key advantages of a fully factored form of the input distribution is that the number of parameters representing the family is simply $k \times n$ as opposed to n^k. However, the assumption of independent choice of intervals along each dimension diminishes the ability to represent arbitrary probability distributions.

Example 4.1. *Figure 4 shows a distribution over two inputs z_1, z_2 wherein there is a significant degree of correlation between the choices of particular intervals for z_1 and for z_2. A fully factored representation loses this information to produce a poor approximation of this distribution. This situation presents interesting parallels to the general problem of abstracting sets of states that is considered in techniques such as symbolic model checking and abstract interpretation of systems.*

Graphical Model Factoring: An alternative to a fully factored representation consists of maintaining correlations between some of the input variables. In the setting of this paper, two inputs are

130

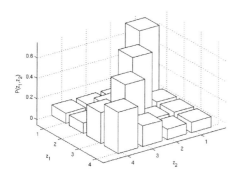

Figure 4: A distribution that cannot be factored.

Node	Cond. Table Type
z_1	$P(z_1 \in U_{1,i})$
z_2	$P(z_2 \in U_{2,i} \mid z_1 \in U_{1,i_1})$
z_3	$P\left(z_3 \in U_{3,i} \;\middle|\; \begin{array}{l} z_1 \in U_{1,i_1}, \\ z_2 \in U_{2,i_2} \end{array} \right)$
z_4	$P(z_4 \in U_{4,i})$

Figure 5: Example graphical model over 4 **variables** $z_1, \ldots, z_4$ **along with the types of tables associated with each node.**

correlated if, for the purposes of finding a falsifying input, the value chosen of one variable will affect the choice of a value for the other. Often, it is natural to consider correlations between certain classes of inputs during falsification. For instance, the value of a control input u at two adjacent time intervals can often be regarded as correlated. Depending on how input signals are parameterized, the choice of an input for the next time step may need to take the current choice of input into consideration.

In this section, we consider generic graphical models that can represent a factored probability distribution. Once again, we assume that the input space for input variable z_i has been partitioned into pairwise disjoint sub-intervals $U_{i,1}, \ldots, U_{i,n}$ for $i \in [1, k]$.

A graphical model G is a directed acyclic graph (DAG) with nodes $N = \{z_1, \ldots, z_k\}$, one node for each variable and a set of directed edges $E \subseteq N \times N$. A graphical model represents a factored distribution. For each node z_j, let $\{e_1 : z_{j_1} \to z_j, \ldots, z_{j_l} \to z_j\}$ represent the set of all incoming edges into z_j. We associate a conditional probability table $\mathbb{T}_j$ that has entries of the form

$$P(z_j \in U_{j,i} \mid z_{j_1} \in U_{j_1,i_1} \wedge \cdots \wedge z_{j_l} \in U_{j_l,i_l}), \\ \text{for } i, i_1, \ldots, i_l \in [1, n] \qquad (4)$$

Thus, each variable is associated with a table of conditional probabilities for the variable belonging to a sub-interval in its domain, given a combination of choices of sub-intervals for the predecessors of the variable in the graph. The overall distribution is written as a product of its factors:

$$\Pr \left(\begin{array}{l} z_1 \in U_{1,l_1} \\ \cdots \\ z_k \in U_{k,l_k} \end{array} \right) = \prod_{i=1}^{k} P \left(z_i \in U_{i,l_i} \;\middle|\; \bigwedge_{z_j \to z_i \in E} z_j \in U_{j,l_j} \right) .$$

A fully factored distribution is simply a graphical model G with the empty set of edges.

Example 4.2. *Figure 5 shows an example of a graphical model along with the type of conditional probability table for each node. The overall probability of drawing a sample from a cell in the input space is written out as a product of individual probabilities from each of the tables in the model according to Equation (4).*

As a result, each graphical model G represents a family of piecewise uniform distributions parameterized by the entries in the tables associated with each node in the graph. The number of such parameters is bounded by $O(kn^{\Delta+1})$ wherein Δ is the maximum in-degree of any node in the graph. Consider an entry in a table of the form shown in Eq. (4). The *event associated* with the entry is denoted by the predicate:

$$z_j \in U_{j,i} \;\wedge\; z_{j_1} \in U_{j_1,i_1} \wedge \cdots \wedge z_{j_l} \in U_{j_l,i_l} .$$

Once again, we consider update rules for factored distributions for solving the optimization involved in Equation 1. Let $\vec{x}^{(1)}, \ldots, \vec{x}^{(m)}$ be the m samples used to compute the tilting with associated weights $\gamma_1, \ldots, \gamma_m$. Our goal is to compute optimal parameters $\theta^* = (P_1, \ldots, P_N)$ where each entry P_i stands for some unknown table entry representing some conditional property in the graphical model. Our goal once again is to optimize

$$\theta^* = \mathsf{argmax} \left(\sum_{l=0}^{m-1} \gamma_l \log(p_\theta(\vec{x}^{(l)})) \right) \qquad (5)$$

The update rule for graphical models considers entries in a given table $\mathbb{T}_i$ associated with a node z_i, for $i \in [1, k]$. For parameter $P_{i,j}$, let $\varphi_{i,j}$ denote the associated event. Furthermore, let $\mathbb{1}(\vec{x}^{(l)} \models \varphi_{i,j})$ denote the condition that the lth sample satisfies the event associated with table entry $P_{i,j}$.

Lemma 4.2. *The optimal parameter value for parameter $P_{i,j}$ in table $\mathbb{T}_i$ that maximizes the objective in Equation (5) is given by*

$$P_{i,j} = \frac{\sum_{l=0}^{m-1} \gamma_l \mathbb{1}(\vec{x}^{(l)} \models \varphi_{i,j})}{\sum_{l=0}^{m-1} \sum_{r \in \mathsf{Entries}(\mathbb{T}_i)} \gamma_l \mathbb{1}(\vec{x}^{(l)} \models \varphi_{i,r})} .$$

PROOF. A proof of this theorem is given in the appendix. $\square$

The lemma above shows that the updating rule for factored distributions is quite simple given the samples $\vec{x}^{(l)}$ and weights γ_l.

We now briefly comment on the choice of an appropriate graphical model for factoring the input. Often, the fully factored representation is the easiest to implement. As mentioned earlier, this representation can be improved by tracking the joint distribution between the value of parameters that pertain to an input signal at the current time step to the input at the next time step. However, decisions on other inputs may need to be considered jointly for successful falsification, in practice.

Currently, it is unclear as to how such inputs may be identified. If, for instance, the function of the inputs to the system are well understood, it may sometimes be possible to classify sets as inputs as tightly coupled or otherwise. However, this requires detailed knowledge of the system's inner workings. In this regard, the problem of automatically identifying an ideal factoring of the input distribution for testing remains an open challenge.

5. IMPLEMENTATION & EXPERIMENTAL EVALUATION

We have implemented a prototype version of the techniques described thus far inside the S-Taliro framework for falsification of MTL properties. S-Taliro is implemented as a Matlab toolbox and supports the specification of a variety of system models including

Simulink/Stateflow diagrams, Matlab functions and C programs interfaced with Matlab. The latest version of the tool supports various core primitives such as the specification of MTL formulas through a simple, user-friendly interface, various utilities to simulate models and visualize trajectories, support for input parameterization, ranging from piecewise constant inputs to splines obtained by specifying control points, and support for robustness metrics over both continuous and hybrid traces. S-Taliro includes implementations of various search heuristics for optimization including UR: uniform random sampling and MC: Monte-Carlo sampling with simulated annealing. A detailed description of the framework is available elsewhere [3]. Furthermore, the latest version of the tool (along with the benchmarks used here) are available on-line as a open-source tool[4].

The implementation of the cross entropy method inside S-Taliro directly uses the key primitives implemented inside S-Taliro. Currently, our implementation supports piecewise uniform probability distributions in a fully factored form. Support for graphical models is currently being implemented.

Experimental Evaluation: Table 2 briefly describes the benchmarks used in our evaluation along with the properties checked for these benchmarks. These benchmarks along with a detailed explanation of the properties are available as part of the S-Taliro distribution. Furthermore, more detailed and up-to-date data comparing the various solvers on a larger set of benchmarks will be made available on our tool website.

Experimental Results: Table 3 shows the experimental comparisons over the set of benchmarks described in Table 2. We ran a fixed number of repetitions for each benchmark and property. Each run had a limit on the total number of tests (simulations) permitted as indicated in the table. The cross entropy method was applied for the maximum number of iterations that corresponds to 100 simulations per iteration. Each technique terminates upon encountering a falsification. Due to the sheer size and number of these experiments, we ran them on a cluster with many different machines of roughly similar specifications — Intel machines running 64 bit operating systems with $6 - 12$ cores and $6 - 32$ GB of RAM. To facilitate comparison, we run all instances of each benchmark on the same machine (different cores).

Table 3 reports for each benchmark instance, the number of repetitions that resulted in a falsification and the average, minimum and maximum times. We notice from this comparison that the cross entropy method performed quite well on the IG, Mod and Air benchmarks, resulting in the most amount of falsifications and was competitive on the remaining AT and PT benchmarks, wherein there were no clear winners between the three techniques compared. The cross entropy seems to outperform Monte Carlo simulations both in terms of time and number of falsifications on all but a few of the benchmarks, and is often competitive or better than uniform random testing which has negligible overhead.

6. RELATED WORK

It is well known that falsification of temporal logic properties for hybrid systems is a hard problem [1]. As a result, testing is a natural approach to the verification of continuous and hybrid systems [23]. The question of how to guide the choice of test cases better is an active area of research.

In this regard, Monte-Carlo techniques have been explored quite extensively. The use of Monte Carlo techniques for model checking was considered previously by Grosu and Smolka [21] in the

form of random walks over the state space of the system and by our previous work in the form of input sampling using Markov-Chain Monte-Carlo (MCMC) techniques [34, 28]. The techniques presented in the latter work were implemented as part of the S-Taliro framework [3]. The two approaches are quite distinct from each other. In practice, the rate convergence of random walks on the state space depends critically on the topology of the state transition graph. On the other hand, techniques that walk the state space can be extended readily to the case of systems with control inputs without requiring a finite parameterization of the control. The problem of integrating the two approaches remains a challenge.

In practice, the use of MCMC techniques has proven problematic for certain benchmarks due to the slow rate of convergence of MCMC techniques and their susceptibility to local minima in the search space. This has been instrumental in our quest for efficient stochastic search techniques that can exhibit faster convergence to the desired underlying distribution. We have also explored the use of other optimization techniques including ant-colony optimization (ACO) and genetic algorithms (GA) in conjunction with robustness metrics in the S-Taliro framework [2].

Other approaches to testing hybrid systems have focused on the use of state-space exploration techniques such as Rapidly exploring Random Trees (RRTs) [16, 4, 5, 27, 29] as well as notions of robustness over simulation trajectories [14, 20, 22, 25]. The work of Dang et al. attempts to bridge these approaches [13].

On the research front of falsification/verification of temporal logic properties through testing, the results are limited [30, 31, 17]. The work that is the closest to ours appears in [31]. The authors of that work develop a different notion of robustness for temporal logic specifications, which is also used as a fitness function for optimization problems. Besides the differences in the application domain, i.e., [31] focuses on parameter estimation for biological systems, whereas our paper deals with the falsification of hybrid systems. Furthermore, we have extended robustness metrics from purely continuous to hybrid trajectories, wherein we define robustness of trajectories using quasi-metrics instead of metrics [28].

Younes and Simmons, and more recently, Clarke et al. have proposed the technique of *Statistical Model Checking* (SMC) [36, 10], which generates uniform random inputs to a system subject to some constraints, thus converting a given system into a stochastic system. A probabilistic model checker can be used to prove assertions on the probability that the system satisfies a given temporal property φ within some given confidence interval. Statistical model checking, like our technique, requires a simulator to be available for the system but not a transition relation representation. In contrast to SMC, our approach is guided by a robustness metric towards less robust trajectories. On the other hand, the complex nature of the system and the robustness metrics imply that we cannot yet provide guarantees on the probability of satisfaction of the formula. Recent observations by Clarke and Zuliani have noted the need for importance sampling and rare-event simulation techniques for Statistical model checking [11]. Some of the ideas from this work on the use of factored input distributions and graphical models can also benefit statistical model checkers.

The work of Chockler et al. explores the use of the cross-entropy method for finding bugs in concurrent programs [7] and more recently for reconstructing concurrent executions for program replay [8]. Additionally, the use of cross-entropy method as a general combinatorial state-space search technique has been well-studied [5].

---

[4]https://sites.google.com/a/asu.edu/s-taliro

[5]Cf. Rubinstein et al. [32] and the web site http://www.cemethod.org for a description.

Table 2: Benchmark systems and properties used in our evaluation.

Name	Description	Model Type	Property Type	Tests
Mod1-3	Third order Delta-Sigma Modulator [12] with varying initial conditions	S/S diagram	$\Box a$	1000
IG1-3	Insulin Glucose control (Cf. Section 3.2) with varying initial conditions	ODE (matlab function)	$\Box_{[0,20.0]}p \wedge \Box_{[20,200.0]}q$	1000
AT1	Auto Transmission Simulink demo [37]	S/S diagram	$\neg(\Diamond p_1 \wedge \Diamond_{[0,10]}p_3)$	1000
AT2			$\neg(\Diamond(p_1 \wedge \Diamond_{[0,7.5]}p_3))$	1000
AT3-5	different predicates $q_{i,j}$		$\neg(\Diamond q_{1,i} \wedge \Diamond q_{2,i} \wedge \Diamond q_{3,i})$	1000
PT1	Power train model [9]	Checkmate model [35]	$\neg\Diamond(g_2 \wedge \Diamond(g_1 \wedge \Diamond g_2))$	1000
PT2			$\Box((\neg g_1 \wedge Xg_1) \Rightarrow \Box_{[0,2.5]}\neg g_2)$	1000
Air1	Aircraft model [26]	ODE (matlab function)	$\neg(\Box_{[.5,1.5]}a \wedge \Diamond_{[3,4]}b)$	500
Air2			$\neg(\Box_{[0,4]}a \wedge \Diamond_{[3.5,4]}d)$	1000
Air3			$\neg\Diamond_{[1,3]}e$	2000
Air4			$\neg\Box_{[0,.5]}h$	2500
Air5			$\neg\Box_{[2,2.5]}i$	2500

7. CONCLUSION

In conclusion, we have presented a framework for falsification of temporal logic properties using the Cross-Entropy method guided by a notion of robustness of trajectories w.r.t MTL formulae. We have also presented some ideas behind using factored probability distributions in the cross-entropy method and extended our notions to handle distributions factored using graphical models. Experimental results seem quite promising. In the future, we wish to run further experiments to quantify the effect of factoring on the overall performance. Furthermore, the problem of automatically identifying correlated input variables that can jointly influence the falsification remains to be investigated. Finally, we also wish to consider the application of our ideas to more general classes of distributions.

8. ACKNOWLEDGEMENTS

The authors would like to thank the anonymous reviewers for their detailed comments. This work was supported, in part, by NSF awards CNS-1016994, CPS-1035845 and CNS-1017074.

9. REFERENCES

[1] R. Alur, C. Courcoubetis, N. Halbwachs, T. A. Henzinger, P.-H. Ho, X. Nicollin, A. Olivero, J. Sifakis, and S. Yovine. The algorithmic analysis of hybrid systems. *Theoretical Computer Science*, 138(1):3–34, 1995.

[2] Y. S. R. Annapureddy and G. E. Fainekos. Ant colonies for temporal logic falsification of hybrid systems. In *Proc. IEEE Industrial Electronics*, pages 91 – 96, 2010.

[3] Y. S. R. Annapureddy, C. Liu, G. E. Fainekos, and S. Sankaranarayanan. S-taliro: A tool for temporal logic falsification for hybrid systems. In *TACAS*, volume 6605 of *LNCS*, pages 254–257. Springer, 2011.

[4] A. Bhatia and E. Frazzoli. Incremental search methods for reachability analysis of continuous and hybrid systems. In *HSCC*, volume 2993 of *LNCS*, pages 142–156. Springer, 2004.

[5] M. Branicky, M. Curtiss, J. Levine, and S. Morgan. Sampling-based planning, control and verification of hybrid systems. *IEE Proc.-Control Theory Appl.*, 153(5):575–590, 2006.

[6] J. A. Bucklew. *Introduction to Rare-Event Simulations.* Springer, 2004.

[7] H. Chockler, E. Farchi, B. Godlin, and S. Novikov. Cross-entropy based testing. In *FMCAD*, pages 101–108. IEEE Computer Society, 2007.

[8] H. Chockler, E. Farchi, B. Godlin, and S. Novikov. Cross-entropy-based replay of concurrent programs. In *Fundamental Approaches to Software Engineering*, volume 5503 of *LNCS*, pages 201–215. Springer, 2009.

[9] A. Chutinan and K. R. Butts. Dynamic analysis of hybrid system models for design validation. Technical report, Ford Motor Company, 2002.

[10] E. Clarke, A. Donze, and A. Legay. Statistical model checking of analog mixed-signal circuits with an application to a third order $\delta - \sigma$ modulator. In *Hardware and Software: Verification and Testing*, volume 5394/2009 of *LNCS*, pages 149–163, 2009.

[11] E. M. Clarke and P. Zuliani. Statistical model checking for cyber-physical systems. In *ATVA*, volume 6996 of *LNCS*, pages 1–12. Springer, 2011.

[12] T. Dang, A. Donzé, and O. Maler. Verification of analog and mixed-signal circuits using hybrid system techniques. In *ICFEM*, volume 3142 of *LNCS*, pages 97–109. Springer, 2004.

[13] T. Dang, A. Donze, O. Maler, and N. Shalev. Sensitive state-space exploration. In *Proc. of the 47th IEEE CDC*, pages 4049–4054, Dec. 2008.

[14] A. Donzé and O. Maler. Systematic simulation using sensitivity analysis. In *HSCC*, volume 4416 of *LNCS*, pages 174–189. Springer, 2007.

[15] M. Egerstedt and C. Martin. *Control Theoretic Splines: Optimal Control, Statistics, and Path Planning.* Princeton University Press, 2009.

[16] J. M. Esposito, J. Kim, and V. Kumar. Adaptive RRTs for validating hybrid robotic control systems. In *Proceedings of the International Workshop on the Algorithmic Foundations of Robotics*, 2004.

[17] G. Fainekos, A. Girard, and G. J. Pappas. Temporal logic verification using simulation. In *FORMATS*, volume 4202 of *LNCS*, pages 171–186. Springer, 2006.

[18] G. Fainekos and G. Pappas. Robustness of temporal logic specifications for continuous-time signals. *Theoretical Computer Science*, 410(42):4262–4291, 2009.

Table 3: Experimental comparison of the cross-entropy method with other optimization engines available in S-Taliro. Experiments were run on a variety of machines in a cluster. To enable comparison, each row is executed on different cores of the same machine. All timings are in seconds, rounded to the nearest integer. Note: MC run on PT2 did not finish after many days (`dnf`). Legend: #F: number of falsifying runs, av: average, lb: min, ub: max, #Rnds: number of iterations for CE.

Bench.	# Runs	Cross Entropy (CE)			Monte Carlo (MC)		Unif. Rand. (UR)	
		#F	Time (av,lb,ub)	#Rnds (lb,ub)	#F	Time (av,lb,ub)	#F	Time (av,lb,ub)
IG1	25	**25**	47,[3,91]	[1,4]	2	299,[3,443]	20	103,[1,275]
IG2	25	**25**	65,[20,124]	[1,6]	0	257,[209,317]	17	156,[25,279]
IG3	25	**25**	141,[81,286]	[3,7]	0	270,[184,324]	4	256,[33,298]
Mod1	100	**97**	15,[1,43]	[1,10]	84	11,[0,92]	81	19,[0,43]
Mod2	100	**87**	25,[1,43]	[1,10]	58	16,[0,94]	40	28,[0,38]
Mod3	100	13	41,[0,50]	[1,10]	**21**	61,[6,94]	1	37,[5,44]
AT1	100	36	102,[43,116]	[5,10]	**51**	61,[7,94]	0	94,[93,99]
AT2	100	0	111,[97,114]	[10,10]	0	93,[92,93]	0	93,[92,93]
AT3	100	**99**	34,[0,114]	[1,10]	93	24,[0,138]	86	56,[0,139]
AT4	100	97	53,[1,116]	[1,10]	94	25,[0,128]	55	81,[1,127]
AT5	100	0	111,[98,121]	[10,10]	0	115,[110,139]	0	111,[109,115]
PT1	25	25	170,[7,886]	[1,2]	23	754,[14,7630]	25	99,[14,329]
PT2	25	24	1013,[32,6381]	[1,10]	dnf	dnf	**25**	689,[21,2392]
Air1	100	**100**	**8,[0,29]**	[1,1]	100	43,[1,177]	100	10,[1,296]
Air2	100	100	134,[3,386]	[1,9]	**100**	**68,[6,244]**	69	345,[1,612]
Air3	100	**99**	316,[120,984]	[3,20]	78	511,[50,1290]	3	1030,[7,1244]
Air4	100	**100**	**2,[0,10]**	[1,1]	100	54,[0,233]	100	5,[0,77]
Air5	100	**100**	**10,[0,53]**	[1,1]	100	77,[0,256]	100	12,[0,57]

[19] M. E. Fisher. A semiclosed-loop algorithm for the control of blood glucose levels in diabetics. *IEEE transactions on bio-medical engineering*, 38(1):57–61, 1991.

[20] A. Girard and G. J. Pappas. Verification using simulation. In *HSCC*, volume 3927 of *LNCS*, pages 272 – 286. Springer, 2006.

[21] R. Grosu and S. Smolka. Monte carlo model checking. In *TACAS*, volume 3440 of *LNCS*, pages 271–286, 2005.

[22] A. A. Julius, G. E. Fainekos, M. Anand, I. Lee, and G. J. Pappas. Robust test generation and coverage for hybrid systems. In *HSCC*, number 4416 in LNCS, pages 329–342. Springer, 2007.

[23] J. Kapinski, B. H. Krogh, O. Maler, and O. Stursberg. On systematic simulation of open continuous systems. In *HSCC*, volume 2623 of *LNCS*, pages 283–297. Springer, 2003.

[24] R. Koymans. Specifying real-time properties with metric temporal logic. *Real-Time Systems*, 2(4):255–299, 1990.

[25] F. Lerda, J. Kapinski, E. M. Clarke, and B. H. Krogh. Verification of supervisory control software using state proximity and merging. In *HSCC*, volume 4981 of *LNCS*, pages 344–357. Springer, 2008.

[26] J. Lygeros. On reachability and minimum cost optimal control. *Automatica*, 40:917–927, 2004.

[27] T. Nahhal and T. Dang. Test coverage for continuous and hybrid systems. In *CAV*, volume 4590 of *LNCS*, pages 449–462. Springer, 2007.

[28] T. Nghiem, S. Sankaranarayanan, G. E. Fainekos, F. Ivančić, A. Gupta, and G. J. Pappas. Monte-carlo techniques for falsification of temporal properties of non-linear hybrid systems. In *HSCC*, pages 211–220. ACM Press, 2010.

[29] E. Plaku, L. E. Kavraki, and M. Y. Vardi. Hybrid systems: From verification to falsification. In *CAV*, volume 4590 of *LNCS*, pages 463–476. Springer, 2007.

[30] E. Plaku, L. E. Kavraki, and M. Y. Vardi. Falsification of LTL safety properties in hybrid systems. In *TACAS*, volume 5505 of *LNCS*, pages 368 – 382, 2009.

[31] A. Rizk, G. Batt, F. Fages, and S. Soliman. On a continuous degree of satisfaction of temporal logic formulae with applications to systems biology. In *6th International Conference on Computational Methods in Systems Biology*, number 5307 in LNCS, pages 251–268. Springer, 2008.

[32] R. Y. Rubinstein and D. P. Kroese. *The Cross-Entropy Method: An unified approach to combinatorial optimization, Monte-Carlo Simulation and Machine Learning*. Springer–Verlag, 2004.

[33] R. Y. Rubinstein and D. P. Kroese. *Simulation and the Monte Carlo Method*. Wiley Series in Probability and Mathematical Statistics, 2008.

[34] S. Sankaranarayanan, R. M. Chang, G. Jiang, and F. Ivančić. State space exploration using feedback constraint generation and Monte-Carlo sampling. In *ESEC/SIGSOFT FSE*, pages 321–330. ACM, 2007.

[35] B. I. Silva, K. Richeson, B. H. Krogh, and A. Chutinan. Modeling and verification of hybrid dynamical system using checkmate. In *ADPM 2000*, 2000.

[36] H. L. S. Younes and R. G. Simmons. Statistical probabilitistic model checking with a focus on time-bounded properties. *Information & Computation*, 204(9):1368–1409, 2006.

[37] Q. Zhao, B. H. Krogh, and P. Hubbard. Generating test inputs for embedded control systems. *IEEE Control Systems Magazine*, pages 49–57, August 2003.

Dynamically Stable Bipedal Robotic Walking with NAO via Human-Inspired Hybrid Zero Dynamics

Aaron D. Ames
Department of Mechanical
Engineering,
Texas A&M University,
College Station, TX 77843
aames@tamu.edu

Eric A. Cousineau
Department of Mechanical
Engineering,
Texas A&M University,
College Station, TX 77843
eacousineau@tamu.edu

Matthew J. Powell
Department of Mechanical
Engineering,
Texas A&M University,
College Station, TX 77843
mjpowell@tamu.edu

ABSTRACT

This paper demonstrates the process of utilizing human lo-comotion data to formally design controllers that yield prov-ably stable robotic walking and experimentally realizing these formal methods to achieve dynamically stable bipedal robotic walking on the NAO robot. Beginning with walking data, outputs—or functions of the kinematics—are determined that result in a low-dimensional representation of human lo-comotion. These same outputs can be considered on a robot, and *human-inspired control* is used to drive the outputs of the robot to the outputs of the human. An optimization problem is presented that determines the parameters of this controller that provide the best fit of the human data while simultaneously ensuring *partial hybrid zero dynamics*. The main formal result of this paper is a proof that these same parameters result in a stable hybrid periodic orbit with a fixed point that can be computed in closed form. Thus, starting with only human data we obtain a stable walking gait for the bipedal robot model. These formal results are validated through experimentation: implementing the stable walking found in simulation on NAO results in dynamically stable robotic walking that shows excellent agreement with the simulated behavior from which it was derived.

Categories and Subject Descriptors

G.1.0 [**Numerical Analysis**]: General—*Stability (and in-stability)*; G.1.6 [**Mathematics of Computing**]: Opti-mization—*Nonlinear programming*; I.6.8 [**Simulation and Modeling**]: Types of Simulation—*Continuous, Discrete event*

General Terms

Theory, Algorithms, Experimentation

Keywords

hybrid systems, bipedal robotic walking, nonlinear dynamics and control, human-data based optimization

1. INTRODUCTION

Aldebaran's commercially available NAO robot ships with a pre-packaged walking algorithm called the "Stable and Omnidirectional Walk"; this algorithm implements a pat-tern generation technique which utilizes the Zero-Moment Point (ZMP)[1, 11]. Indeed, the ZMP is a popular choice of controller in the robotic walking community [20]. Other interesting approaches to the bipedal robotic walking prob-lem have surfaced in the field's long history, including pas-sive walking and controlled symmetries [6, 18], capture point [14], geometric reduction [4, 8, 17] and hybrid nonlinear feed-back control [7, 22], to name a only a few. Of the current research in the field, the philosophy toward walking taken in this paper can be best related to the spring-loaded inverted pendulum [9], or SLIP model, due to its methodology of representing locomotion by a simple "virtual" system. Com-mon to these approaches is the application of control theory and understanding of dynamics to achieve and implement impressive walking algorithms and motion generators; how-ever, there exists a significant disparity between the walking achieved with these methods and the actual, dynamically stable walking displayed by humans.

This paper presents a distinctively different approach to the bipedal robotic walking control design problem: look to human walking data to motivate the *formal design* of con-trollers that achieve provably stable robotic walking. The main idea is that regardless of the complexity present in human walking—hundreds of degrees of freedom coupled with highly nonlinear dynam-ics and forcing due to the 57 muscles employed during hu-man walking [15]—the essen-tial information needed to un-derstand walking is encoded by a simple class of functions. In other words, taking the control theorist approach to understanding a complex and unknown system, we view the human walking system as a "black box," where the "in-put" to the system is a spe-cific walking behavior, and we seek "outputs" of this system

Figure 1: Experimental demonstration of NAO displaying dynamically stable walking.

that characterize these walking behaviors. These outputs

can then be utilized in the design of robotic controllers—the outputs of the robot can be driven to the outputs of the human, resulting in "human-like" robotic walking.

Given human walking as the motivation for achieving robotic walking, this paper begins by looking at human walking data, i.e., angles over time, achieved through motion capture of subjects walking on flat ground at a "natural" pace. Indeed, work with human data to construct low dimensional representations of human walking has been performed [19] by fitting human data with Bézier curves; however, the work presented here suggests insight beyond achieving "best fits" to data. By studying human data, we discover a collection of outputs that appear to characterize human walking—they are mutually exclusive, thus providing a low dimensional representation of the system's behavior. Moreover, we find that these *human outputs*, as computed from the data, appear to be described by a very simple function: the time solution to a linear spring-mass-damper system. We term this function the *canonical human walking function*, and verify that in fact this function describes the human data by showing that it can be fit to the human data with a remarkably high correlation coefficient. Utilizing the human outputs and their time-based representation given by the canonical walking functions, we construct a *human-inspired* controller that drives the outputs of the robot to the outputs of the human as represented by the canonical walking functions.

The main result of this paper is a formal method for determining the parameters of the human-inspired controller that provably results in stable robotic walking for a planar biped that is as "human-like" as possible. In particular, we introduce an optimization problem where the cost is the least squares fit of the outputs of the robot to the human output data subject to constraints that ensure *partial hybrid zero dynamics* [3], i.e., constraints that ensure that the zero dynamics surface associated with the relative degree 2 output functions is invariant through impact. This invariance allows us to characterize the behavior of the hybrid system modeling a bipedal robot (which is 10 dimensional for the model considered) through a 2-dimensional hybrid system. Utilizing this reduced dimensional representation, we are able to prove the main result of this paper: the parameters that solve the partial hybrid zero dynamics optimization problem imply the existence of an exponentially stable hybrid periodic orbit, i.e., the existence of a stable walking gait; moreover, the fixed point of the Poincaré map associated with this periodic orbit can be explicitly computed from these parameters. In other words, using only the human data, we are able to automatically generate parameters for the human inspired controller that imply the existence of a stable walking gait, and we can explicitly compute the initial condition to this walking gait from these parameters.

To supplement the main theoretical developments of this paper, we experimentally apply them to Aldebaran's NAO robot [1]. By considering the 2D hybrid system model of this robot, we use the main results of the paper to obtain stable robotic walking in simulation using only human data. The trajectories obtained through simulation are implemented on NAO, together with a simple online lateral stability feedback controller. The end result is dynamically stable walking on NAO that is markedly more human-like than pre-existing walking achieved with NAO (as evidenced by the walking itself and the comparison of this walking with the pre-existing NAO walking, both of which can be seen at [2]). Thus we

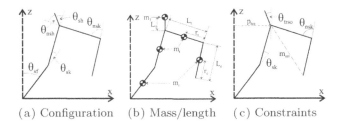

(a) Configuration (b) Mass/length (c) Constraints

Figure 2: The modeled robot's configuration, mass & length distribution, and virtual constraints (outputs).

have successfully utilized human data to formally achieve "human-like" robotic walking and demonstrated these results experimentally.

2. HUMAN WALKING DATA

As the ultimate goal of this work is to develop a control scheme which yields stable human-like robotic walking, we turn to the human locomotion data for insight in the design process. Examination of human walking data reveals that certain outputs of the human locomotion system can be represented as second order linear system responses. This section, therefore, introduces these outputs and shows that the human data for these outputs can be accurately fit by the time-solution to a linear mass-spring-damper system.

Human Walking Experiment. The goal of this experiment was to track the evolution of the spatial positions of specific points on the human body during walking on flat ground—this collection of position data forms the raw kinematic outputs of human walking. For each trial, LED sensors were fixed to a test subject in key locations, such as the joints, along the lower body—as the test subject walked forward, the spatial position of each LED sensors was measured at 480 Hz. A total of 11 trials per test subject and a total of 9 test subjects were considered. For purposes of this paper, the mean data from all 9 subjects are considered; see [5] for more information regarding the walking experiments.

Human Outputs. Common in the bipedal robotic walking literature is the employment of nonlinear feedback linearization [16, 22]. In this method, "virtual outputs" are specified which, upon successful application of feedback linearization control, constrain the motion of a controlled robot. These virtual outputs are functions of state, and thus are independent of the robot's actuator dynamics. Furthermore, the same outputs can be computed from human walking data — the result is a direct kinematic relationship between robot and human walking, despite the morphological and dynamical differences in the two systems. With this in mind, we consider the following virtual output functions (see Fig. 2):

1. The linearization of the x-position of the hip, p_{hip}, given by:

$$\delta p_{\text{hip}}(\theta) = L_c(-\theta_{sf}) + L_t(-\theta_{sf} - \theta_{sk}) \qquad (1)$$

with L_c and L_t the length of the calf and thigh.

2. The linearization of the slope of the non-stance leg m_{nsl}, (the tangent of the angle between the z-axis and the line on the non-stance leg connecting the ankle and

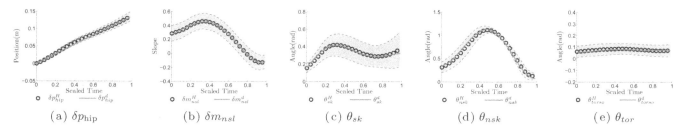

| (a) δp_{hip} | (b) δm_{nsl} | (c) θ_{sk} | (d) θ_{nsk} | (e) θ_{tor} |

Figure 3: The mean human output data for the nine subjects, computed with the parameters for NAO, with error bands showing one standard deviation from the mean, and the canonical walking function fits.

hip), given by:

$$\delta m_{nsl}(\theta) = -\theta_{sf} - \theta_{sk} - \theta_{sh} - \theta_{nsh} + \frac{L_c}{L_c + L_t}\theta_{nsk}. \quad (2)$$

3. The angle of the stance knee, θ_{sk},

4. The angle of the non-stance knee, θ_{nsk},

5. The angle of the torso from vertical,

$$\theta_{tor}(\theta) = \theta_{sf} + \theta_{sk} + \theta_{sh}. \quad (3)$$

These outputs, shown in Fig. 3, were computed from the experimental human walking data which was scaled to the robot by computing $\delta p_{\text{hip}}(\theta)$ and $\delta m_{nsl}(\theta)$ using the NAO's length distribution. This figure also shows the mean of each output computed from the data from nine subjects and error bands showing one standard deviation from this mean. Note that the motivation for considering the linearization of the position of the hip and the non-stance slope (rather than their original nonlinear formulations, as was considered in [3]) will be seen later in the paper—it allows for a simple representation of the partial hybrid zero dynamics.

Human Walking Functions. Visual inspection of the outputs as computed from the human data for the three subjects (see Fig. 3) shows that all of the human outputs appear to be described by two simple functions. In particular, the linearized position of the hip appears to be essentially a linear function of time:

$$\delta p_{\text{hip}}^d(t, v) = v_{hip}t. \quad (4)$$

The remaining human outputs, δm_{nsl}, θ_{sk}, θ_{nsk}, θ_{tor} appear to be described by the solution to a linear mass-spring-damper system. With this in mind, define the *canonical human walking function* as:

$$y_H(t, \alpha) = e^{-\alpha_4 t}(\alpha_1 \cos(\alpha_2 t) + \alpha_3 \sin(\alpha_2 t)) + \alpha_5. \quad (5)$$

This function can be related to the more standard form of the time solution of a mass-spring-damper system by noting that $\alpha_1 = c_0$, $\alpha_2 = \omega_d$, $\alpha_3 = c_1$, $\alpha_4 = \zeta\omega_n$ and $\alpha_5 = g$, where ζ is the damping ratio, ω_n is the natural frequency, $\omega_d = \omega_n\sqrt{1 - \zeta^2}$ is the damped natural frequency, c_0 and c_1 are determined by the initial conditions of the system, and g is a gravity related constant. In particular, with (5), for the 4 remaining human outputs, we write:

$$m_{nsl}^d(t, \alpha_{nsl}) = y_H(t, \alpha_{nsl}), \quad \theta_{tor}^d(t, \alpha_{nsl}) = y_H(t, \alpha_{tor}),$$

$$\theta_{sk}^d(t, \alpha_{sk}) = y_H(t, \alpha_{sk}), \quad \theta_{nsk}^d(t, \alpha_{nsk}) = y_H(t, \alpha_{nsk}),$$

$$(6)$$

where, e.g., $\alpha_{nsl} = (\alpha_{nsl,1}, \alpha_{nsl,2}, \alpha_{nsl,3}, \alpha_{nsl,4}, \alpha_{nsl,5})$ in (5). The parameters of all of the outputs can be combined to yield a single vector: $\alpha = (v_{\text{hip}}, \alpha_{nsl}, \alpha_{nsk}, \alpha_{sk}, \alpha_{tor}) \in \mathbb{R}^{21}$. If it can be verified that these functions accurately fit the mean human output data, then it can be concluded that humans appear to act like linear spring-mass-damper systems for the chosen outputs.

Human-Data-Based Cost Function. The goal is to show that the human walking functions accurately describe the human data. This will be achieved by simply fitting (5) to the human walking data to achieve a least squares fit. From the mean human walking data, we obtain discrete times, $t^H[k]$, and discrete values for the output functions: $\delta p_{\text{hip}}^H[k]$, $\delta m_{nsl}^H[k]$, $\theta_{sk}^H[k]$, $\theta_{nsk}^H[k]$, and $\theta_{tor}^H[k]$ where here $k \in \{1, \ldots, K\} \subset \mathbb{N}$ with K the number of data points. Represent the mean human output data by $y_i^H[k]$ and the canonical walking functions by $y_i^d(t, \alpha_i)$ for $i \in \text{Output} = \{hip, msl, sk, nsk, tor\}$; for example, $y_{msl}^H[k] = \delta m_{nsl}^H[k]$ and $y_{msl}^d(t, \alpha_{msl}) = \delta m_{nsl}^d(t, \alpha_{nsl})$. Define the following human-data-based cost function:

$$\text{Cost}_{\text{HD}}(\alpha) = \sum_{k=1}^{K} \sum_{i \in \text{Output}} \left(y_i^H[k] - y_i^d(t^H[k], \alpha_i)\right)^2 \quad (7)$$

which is simply the sum of squared residuals. To determine the parameters for the human walking functions, we need only solve the optimization problem:

$$\alpha^* = \underset{\alpha \in \mathbb{R}^{21}}{\text{argmin}} \ \text{Cost}_{\text{HD}}(\alpha) \quad (8)$$

which yields the least squares fit of the mean human output data with the canonical walking functions. The parameters given by solving this optimization problem are stated in Table 1. The correlations, as given in the same table, show that the fitted walking functions very closely model the human output data, i.e., the chosen human walking functions appear to be, in fact, canonical. Indeed, the coefficients of correlation are all very high, ranging from 0.8767 to 0.9997. The accuracy of the fits can be seen in Fig. 3.

3. BIPEDAL ROBOT MODEL (NAO)

Bipedal walking robots naturally display continuous and discrete behavior throughout the course of a step—the continuous behavior occurs when the leg swings forward and the discrete behavior occurs when the foot strikes the ground. It is, therefore, natural to model robots of this form by hybrid systems [5, 17] (also referred to as systems with impulsive effects or systems with impulse effects [7, 8]). This

$y_{H,2} = e^{-\alpha_4 t}(\alpha_1 \cos(\alpha_2 t) + \alpha_3 \sin(\alpha_2 t)) + \alpha_5$							
Fun.	v_{hip}	α_1	α_2	α_3	α_4	α_5	Cor.
δp_{hip}	0.2288	*	*	*	*	*	0.9984
δm_{nsl}	*	-0.0065	8.9157	0.1162	-2.2638	0.2750	0.9997
θ_{sk}	*	-0.1600	12.4473	0.0980	3.6061	0.3240	0.9751
θ_{nsk}	*	-0.3322	-10.2618	-0.1109	-0.9345	0.6772	0.9948
θ_{tor}	*	-0.0166	10.4416	-0.0033	3.2976	0.0729	0.8767

Table 1: Parameter values and correlation coefficients of the canonical human walking functions obtained from optimization about the mean human data and NAO robot model.

section introduces the basic formalisms of hybrid systems along with the specific hybrid model obtained for the robot that is considered in this paper: NAO, as shown in Fig. 1. It is important to note that the model of NAO used in this work is the 2D, planar model with point feet. Analysis of the 3D and finite foot models is a topic of future work.

Hybrid Systems. A (simple) *hybrid control system* is a tuple,

$$\mathscr{HC} = (\mathcal{D}, U, S, \Delta, f, g),$$

where $\mathcal{D}$ is the *domain* with $\mathcal{D} \subseteq \mathbb{R}^n$ a smooth submanifold of the state space $\mathbb{R}^n$, $U \subseteq \mathbb{R}^m$ is the set of admissible controls, $S \subset \mathcal{D}$ is a proper subset of $\mathcal{D}$ called the *guard* or *switching surface*, $\Delta : S \to \mathcal{D}$ is a smooth map called the *reset map*, and (f, g) is a *control system* on $\mathcal{D}$, i.e., in coordinates: $\dot{x} = f(x) + g(x)u$. A *hybrid system* is a hybrid control system with $U = \emptyset$, e.g., any applicable feedback controllers have been applied, making the system closed-loop. In this case,

$$\mathscr{H} = (\mathcal{D}, S, \Delta, f),$$

where f is a *dynamical system* on $\mathcal{D} \subseteq \mathbb{R}^n$, i.e., $\dot{x} = f(x)$.

Periodic Orbits. Stable bipedal robotic walking corresponds to stable periodic orbits in hybrid systems. For simplicity, we consider periodic orbits of hybrid systems with fixed points on the guard (for more general definitions, see [8, 21]). Let $\varphi(t, x_0)$ be the solution to $\dot{x} = f(x)$ with initial condition $x_0 \in \mathcal{D}$. For $x^* \in S$, we say that φ is *periodic* with period $T > 0$ if $\varphi(T, \Delta(x^*)) = x^*$. A set $\mathcal{O}$ is a *periodic orbit* with *fixed point* x^* if $\mathcal{O} = \{\varphi(t, \Delta(x^*)) : 0 \leq t \leq T\}$ for a periodic solution φ. Associated with a periodic orbit is a Poincaré map [21]; specifically, taking S to be the Poincaré section, one obtains the Poincaré map $P : S \to S$ which is a partial function:

$$P(x) = \varphi(T_I(x), \Delta(x)),$$

where T_I is the *time-to-impact function* [22]. As with smooth dynamical systems, the stability of the Poincaré map determines the stability of the periodic orbit $\mathcal{O}$. In particular, the Poincaré map is (locally) exponentially stable (as a discrete time system $x_{k+1} = P(x_k)$) at the fixed point x^* if and only if the periodic orbit $\mathcal{O}$ is (locally) exponentially stable [12]. Although it is not possible to analytically compute the Poincaré map, it is possible to numerically compute its Jacobian. Thus, if the eigenvalues of the Jacobian have magnitude less than one, the stability of the periodic orbit $\mathcal{O}$ has been numerically verified.

NAO Hybrid Model. Utilizing the mass and inertia properties of the NAO robot provided in the specifications sheet

[1], we can formally model this robot as a hybrid control system:

$$\mathscr{HC}_R = (\mathcal{D}_R, U_R, S_R, \Delta_R, f_R, g_R). \qquad (9)$$

The method used to construct the individual elements of this hybrid system will now be discussed.

Continuous Dynamics: The configuration space of the robot $\mathcal{Q}_R$ is given in coordinates by:

$$\theta = (\theta_{sf}, \theta_{sk}, \theta_{sh}, \theta_{nsh}, \theta_{nsk})^T,$$

where, as illustrated in Fig. 2, θ_{sf} is the angle of the stance foot, θ_{sk} is the angle of the stance knee, θ_{sh} is the angle of the torso with the stance thigh, θ_{nsh} is the angle of the non-stance thigh with the torso, and θ_{nsk} is the angle of the non-stance (or swing) knee. Calculating the mass and inertia properties of each link of the robot using the specifications of the robot allows for the construction of the Lagrangian:

$$\mathcal{L}_R(\theta, \dot{\theta}) = \frac{1}{2}\dot{\theta}^T D(\theta)\dot{\theta} - V(\theta). \qquad (10)$$

Explicitly, this is done symbolically through the method of exponential twists (see [13]). The Euler-Lagrange equations yield the equations of motion of the form:

$$D(\theta)\ddot{\theta} + H(\theta, \dot{\theta}) = B(\theta)u.$$

Converting the equations of motion to a first order ODE yields the affine control system (f_R, g_R):

$$f_R(\theta, \dot{\theta}) = \begin{bmatrix} \dot{\theta} \\ -D^{-1}(\theta)H(\theta, \dot{\theta}) \end{bmatrix}, \quad g_R(\theta) = \begin{bmatrix} \mathbf{0} \\ D^{-1}(\theta)B(\theta) \end{bmatrix},$$

with $U_R = \mathbb{R}^5$ and $B(\theta) \in \mathbb{R}^{5 \times 5}$.

Domain and Guard: The domain specifies the allowable configuration of the system as specified by a unilateral constraint function h_R; for the biped considered in this paper, this function specifies that the non-stance foot must be above the ground, i.e., h_R is the height of the non-stance foot. In particular, the domain $\mathcal{D}_R$ is given by:

$$\mathcal{D}_R = \left\{ (\theta, \dot{\theta}) \in T\mathcal{Q}_R : h_R(\theta) \geq 0 \right\}.$$

The guard is just the boundary of the domain with the additional assumption that the unilateral constraint is decreasing:

$$S_R = \left\{ (\theta, \dot{\theta}) \in T\mathcal{Q}_R : h_R(\theta) = 0 \text{ and } dh_R(\theta)\dot{\theta} < 0 \right\},$$

where $dh_R(\theta)$ is the Jacobian of h_R at θ.

Discrete Dynamics. The discrete dynamics of the robot determine how the velocities of the robot change when the foot impacts the ground, while simultaneously switching the "stance" and "non-stance" legs. In particular, the reset map Δ_R is given by:

$$\Delta_R : S_R \to \mathcal{D}_R, \qquad \Delta_R(\theta, \dot{\theta}) = \begin{bmatrix} \Delta_\theta \theta \\ \Delta_{\dot{\theta}}(\theta)\dot{\theta} \end{bmatrix}, \qquad (11)$$

where Δ_θ is the relabeling matrix which switches the stance and non-stance leg at impact (by appropriately changing the angles). Here, $\Delta_{\dot{\theta}}$ determines the change in velocity due to impact; we forgo the detailed discussion on its computation, but detailed descriptions can be found in [10], [8] and [3]. In particular, it is computed by considering extended coordinates that include the position of the stance foot and employing a perfectly plastic impact law that results in the pre-impact non-stance foot being fixed post-impact, wherein it becomes the stance foot.

4. HUMAN-INSPIRED CONTROL

In this section, we construct a human-inspired controller that drives the outputs of the robot to the outputs of the human (as represented by canonical walking functions). Moreover, we render this control law autonomous through a parameterization of time based upon the position of the hip. The end result is a feedback control that is used to obtain stable bipedal robotic walking.

Parameterization of Time. Attracted by the robustness of *autonomous* control, we introduce a state-based parameterization of time in our system; this is a common practice [23, 22], except that in this case we pick a parameterization as motivated by human data. Examination of human data reveals that the (linearized) forward position of the hip evolves in an approximately linear manner with respect to time, that is $\delta p_{hip}(t, v_{hip}) \approx v_{hip}t$, where p_{hip} denotes the forward position of the hip and v_{hip} denotes the forward velocity of the hip. Taking advantage of this observation, the following parameterization of time is formed:

$$\tau(\theta) = \frac{\delta p_{\text{hip}}^R(\theta) - \delta p_{\text{hip}}^R(\theta^+)}{v_{\text{hip}}}. \tag{12}$$

where $\delta p_{\text{hip}}^R(\theta^+)$ is the (linearized) forward position of the robot's hip at the beginning of the current step, and v_{hip} is the forward velocity of the hip (which is an element α).

Output Functions. Based upon the human outputs and their time-based representation given by the canonical walking functions, we define relative degree 1 and (vector) relative 2 outputs for the robot based upon our desire for the robot to have the same output behavior as the human. (Note that it will not be formally verified that these are, in fact relative degree 1 and 2 outputs until the decoupling matrix is introduced; see [16] for a formal definition.)

With the goal of controlling the velocity of the robot, we define the relative degree 1 output from the actual velocity of the hip and the desired velocity of the hip:

$$y_{a,1}(\theta, \dot{\theta}) = \delta \dot{p}_{\text{hip}}^R(\theta, \dot{\theta}) = d\delta p_{\text{hip}}^R(\theta)\dot{\theta}, \qquad y_{d,1} = v_{\text{hip}}. \tag{13}$$

where $\delta p_{\text{hip}}^R(\theta)$ is given in (1). Since $y_{a,1}$ is the output of a mechanical system that depends on both position and velocity, it is relative degree 1. Similarly, with the goal of the robot tracking the human outputs, we consider the following actual and desired outputs:

$$y_{a,2}(\theta) = \begin{bmatrix} \delta m_{nsl}^R(\theta) \\ \theta_{sk} \\ \theta_{nsk} \\ \theta_{tor}^R(\theta) \end{bmatrix}, \quad y_{d,2}(t) = \begin{bmatrix} m_{nsl}^d(t, \alpha_{nsl}) \\ \theta_{sk}^d(t, \alpha_{sk}) \\ \theta_{nsk}^d(t, \alpha_{nsk}) \\ \theta_{tor}^d(t, \alpha_{tor}) \end{bmatrix}, \tag{14}$$

where δm_{nsl}^R and θ_{tor}^R are the functions given in (2) and (3) computed with the parameters of the robot, and $y_{d,2}$ consists of the human walking functions given in (6). This is the first point in which it becomes apparent why we linearized the output functions describing the position of the hip and the non-stance leg slope; because of their linear form:

$$y_{a,2}(\theta) = H\theta \tag{15}$$

for $H \in \mathbb{R}^{4 \times 5}$ with full row rank.

The goal is to drive the outputs to the outputs of the human as represented by the canonical walking functions, which motivates the final form of the outputs to be used in feedback linearization:

$$y_1(\theta, \dot{\theta}) = y_{a,1}(\theta, \dot{\theta}) - v_{hip}, \tag{16}$$
$$y_2(\theta) = y_{a,2}(\theta) - y_{d,2}(\tau(\theta)) \tag{17}$$

These outputs can be grouped together to form a single vector of *human-inspired outputs*:

$$y(\theta, \dot{\theta}) = \begin{bmatrix} y_1(\theta, \dot{\theta}) \\ y_2(\theta) \end{bmatrix} \tag{18}$$

where y_1 and y_2 will be seen to be relative degree 1 and vector relative degree 2 outputs, respectively. These outputs yield a *human-inspired controller*:

$$u(\theta, \dot{\theta}) = -\mathcal{A}^{-1}(\theta, \dot{\theta}) \left(\begin{bmatrix} 0 \\ L_{f_R} L_{f_R} y_2(\theta) \end{bmatrix} \right. \tag{19}$$
$$\left. + \begin{bmatrix} L_{f_R} y_1(\theta, \dot{\theta}) \\ 2\varepsilon L_{f_R} y_2(\theta, \dot{\theta}) \end{bmatrix} + \begin{bmatrix} \varepsilon y_1(\theta, \dot{\theta}) \\ \varepsilon^2 y_2(\theta) \end{bmatrix} \right),$$

with control gain ε and decoupling matrix $\mathcal{A}(\theta)$ given by

$$\mathcal{A}(\theta, \dot{\theta}) = \begin{bmatrix} L_{g_R} y_1(\theta, \dot{\theta}) \\ L_{g_R} L_{f_R} y_2(\theta, \dot{\theta}) \end{bmatrix}$$

Note that the decoupling matrix is non-singular exactly because of the choice of output functions, i.e., as was discussed in Sect. 2, care was taken when defining the human outputs so that they were "mutually exclusive." It follows that for a control gain $\varepsilon > 0$, the control law u renders the output exponentially stable [16]. That is, the human-inspired output $y \to 0$ exponentially at a rate of ε; in other words, the outputs of the robot will converge to the canonical human walking functions exponentially.

Applying the feedback control law in (19) to the hybrid control system modeling the bipedal robot being considered, $\mathcal{HC}_R$ as given in (9), yields a hybrid system:

$$\mathcal{H}_R^{(\alpha,\varepsilon)} = (\mathcal{D}_R, S_R, \Delta_R, f_R^{(\alpha,\varepsilon)}), \tag{20}$$

where, $\mathcal{D}_R$, S_R, and Δ_R are defined as for $\mathcal{HC}_R$, and

$$f_R^{(\alpha,\varepsilon)}(\theta, \dot{\theta}) = f_R(\theta, \dot{\theta}) + g_R(\theta, \dot{\theta})u(\theta, \dot{\theta}),$$

where the dependence of $f_R^{(\alpha,\varepsilon)}$ on the vector of parameters, α, and the control gain for the human-inspired controller, ε, has been made explicit.

5. HUMAN-INSPIRED PARTIAL HYBRID ZERO DYNAMICS

This section presents the main result of this paper through a culmination of the concepts presented thus far. Specifically, we present a method of obtaining parameters of the human-inspired controller (19) which provides the best fit of the human data, by minimizing (7), subject to constraints that guarantee that the resulting hybrid control system (20) has a stable periodic orbit. Furthermore, it is proven that a fixed point for this stable periodic orbit can be computed in closed form in the limit as $\varepsilon \to \infty$.

Hybrid Zero Dynamics (HZD). The human-inspired control law (19) drives the human-inspired outputs $y(\theta, \dot{\theta}) \to 0$

exponentially at a rate of ε. In particular, for the *continuous* dynamics of the hybrid system $\mathscr{H}_R^{(\alpha,\varepsilon)}$, the controller renders the *zero dynamics surface*:

$$\mathbf{Z}_\alpha = \{(\theta,\dot{\theta}) \in T\mathcal{Q}_R : y(\theta,\dot{\theta}) = \mathbf{0}_5,\ L_{f_R}y_2(\theta,\dot{\theta}) = \mathbf{0}_4\} \quad (21)$$

exponentially stable. Note that here $\mathbf{0}_p \in \mathbb{R}^p$ is a vector of zeros, and we make the dependence of $\mathbf{Z}_\alpha$ on the set of parameters explicit. It is at this point that continuous systems and hybrid systems diverge: while this surface is invariant for the continuous dynamics, it is not necessarily invariant for the hybrid dynamics. In particular, the discrete impacts in the system cause the state to be "thrown" off of the zero dynamics surface. Therefore, a hybrid system has *hybrid zero dynamics* if the zero dynamics are invariant through impact: $\Delta_R(S_R \cap \mathbf{Z}_\alpha) \subset \mathbf{Z}_\alpha$.

Partial Hybrid Zero Dynamics (PHZD). While the realization of HZD is the "best case scenario," it is quite difficult in the case of bipedal robotic walking since it would force the hybrid system to evolve on a 1-dimensional manifold. Therefore, we seek to enforce zero dynamics only for the relative degree 2 outputs. We refer to this as the *partial zero dynamics surface*, given by:

$$\mathbf{PZ}_\alpha = \{(\theta,\dot{\theta}) \in T\mathcal{Q}_R : y_2(\theta) = \mathbf{0}_4,\ L_{f_R}y_2(\theta,\dot{\theta}) = \mathbf{0}_4\} \quad (22)$$

The motivation for considering this surface is that it allows some "freedom" in the movement of the system to account for differences between the robot and human models. Moreover, since the only output that is not included in the partial zero dynamics surface is the output that forces the forward hip velocity to be constant, enforcing partial hybrid zero dynamics simply means that we allow the velocity of the hip to compensate for the shocks in the system due to impact.

Problem Statement. The goal of *human-inspired PHZD* is to find parameters α^* that solve the following constrained optimization problem:

$$\alpha^* = \underset{\alpha \in \mathbb{R}^{21}}{\operatorname{argmin}}\ \mathrm{Cost}_{\mathrm{HD}}(\alpha) \quad (23)$$

$$\text{s.t}\quad \Delta_R(S_R \cap \mathbf{Z}_\alpha) \subset \mathbf{PZ}_\alpha \quad (\text{PHZD})$$

with $\mathrm{Cost}_{\mathrm{HD}}$ the cost given in (7). This is simply the optimization problem in (8) that was used to determine the parameters of the canonical human walking functions that gave the best fit of the human walking functions to the human output data, but subject to constraints that ensure PHZD. The formal goal of this section is to restate (PHZD) in such a way that it can be practically solved.

Partial Zero Dynamics. This section utilizes the fact that the human outputs were specifically chosen to be linear in order to explicitly construct the *partial hybrid zero dynamics*. In particular, we reformulate the constructions in [22] in such a way as to be applicable to full-actuation (which is assumed in this case) and reframe them in the context of canonical human walking functions. Because of the specific choice of y_a in (14), we begin by picking the following representation of the partial zero dynamics:

$$\xi_1 = \delta p_{\mathrm{hip}}^R(\theta) =: c\theta \quad (24)$$

$$\xi_2 = y_{a,1}(\theta,\dot{\theta}) = \delta\dot{p}_{\mathrm{hip}}^R(\theta,\dot{\theta}) =: c\dot{\theta}$$

where $c \in \mathbb{R}^{1\times5}$ is obtained from (1). Moreover, since ξ_1 is just the linearized position of the hip, which was used to

parameterize time (12), we can write $y_{d,2}(\tau(\theta)) = y_{d,2}(\xi_1)$. Picking the coordinates

$$\eta_1 = y_a(\theta) = H\theta \quad (25)$$

$$\eta_2 = L_{f_R}y_{a,2}(\theta,\dot{\theta}) = H\dot{\theta}$$

with H as in (15), and defining

$$\Phi(\xi_1) = \begin{bmatrix} c \\ H \end{bmatrix}^{-1} \begin{pmatrix} \xi_1 \\ y_{d,2}(\xi_1) \end{pmatrix}$$

$$\Psi(\xi_1) = \begin{bmatrix} c \\ H \end{bmatrix}^{-1} \begin{pmatrix} 1 \\ \frac{\partial y_{d,2}(\xi_1)}{\partial \xi_1} \end{pmatrix}$$

it follows that for $\theta = \Phi(\xi_1)$ and $\dot{\theta} = \Psi(\xi_1)\xi_2$, $(\theta,\dot{\theta}) \in \mathbf{PZ}_\alpha$.

As a result of the fact that we have full actuation and completely linearize the dynamics with (19), it follows that the relative degree 1 output evolves according to $\dot{y}_1 = -\varepsilon y_1$. Therefore, because of the definition of the partial zero dynamics, the partial hybrid zero dynamics evolve according to the linear ODE:

$$\dot{\xi}_1 = \xi_2 \quad (26)$$

$$\dot{\xi}_2 = -\varepsilon(\xi_2 - v_{\mathrm{hip}}).$$

The advantage of the partial zero dynamics representation introduced is that it allows for the existence and stability of a fixed point of the zero dynamics to be determined *without integrating the ODE*. Specifically, given a point on the guard $(\theta^-,\dot{\theta}^-) \in S_R$ with its post-impact state $(\theta^+,\dot{\theta}^+) = \Delta_R(\theta^-,\dot{\theta}^-)$, we can compute $\xi_1^- = \delta p_{\mathrm{hip}}^R(\theta^-)$ and $\xi_1^+ = \delta p_{\mathrm{hip}}^R(\theta^+)$. From this, if (PHZD) is satisfied, the change in ξ_1 and ξ_2 due to this impact can be determined through:

$$\xi_1^+ = \delta p_{\mathrm{hip}}^R(\Delta_\theta \theta^-) \quad (27)$$

$$\xi_2^+ = \Delta_{\mathbf{PZ}}(\theta^-)\xi_2^-$$

where θ^- is a point that is chosen *a priori* and

$$\Delta_{\mathbf{PZ}}(\theta^-) := c\Delta_{\dot{\theta}}(\theta^-)\Psi(\delta p_{\mathrm{hip}}^R(\theta^-)). \quad (28)$$

In essence, this defines a 2-dimensional hybrid system and therefore, when considering the existence and stability of a periodic orbit in the partial hybrid zero dynamics surface, one need only consider the restricted Poincaré map:

$$\rho : S_R \cap \mathbf{PZ}_\alpha \to S_R \cap \mathbf{PZ}_\alpha \quad (29)$$

where

$$S_R \cap \mathbf{PZ}_\alpha \cong \{(\xi_1,\xi_2) \in \mathbf{PZ}_\alpha : \xi_1 = \xi_1^-,\quad \xi_2 \in \mathbb{R}_{\geq 0}\}$$

In other words, the hyperplane $\xi_1 = \xi_1^-$ can be chosen as the Poincaré section. The Poincaré map for the partial hybrid zero dynamics is therefore a 1-dimensional (partial) map $\rho : S_R \cap \mathbf{PZ}_\alpha \to S_R \cap \mathbf{PZ}_\alpha$, and so ρ can be viewed as only a function of ξ_2 and therefore defines a discrete time dynamical system: $\xi_2[k+1] = \rho(\xi_2[k])$.

Inverse Kinematics. To achieve the goal of restating (23) in a way that is independent of state variables (position and velocity), we can use the outputs and guard functions to explicitly solve for the configuration of the system $\vartheta(\alpha) \in \mathcal{Q}_R$ on the guard ($h_R(\vartheta(\alpha)) = 0$) in terms of the parameters α. In particular, let

$$\vartheta(\alpha) = \theta \quad \text{s.t} \quad \begin{bmatrix} y_2(\Delta_\theta\theta) \\ h_R(\theta) \end{bmatrix} = \begin{bmatrix} \mathbf{0}_4 \\ 0 \end{bmatrix}, \quad (30)$$

where Δ_θ is the relabeling matrix (11). Note that $\vartheta(\alpha)$ exists because of the specific structure of the outputs $y_2(\Delta_\theta\theta)$ chosen. In fact, the reason for considering y_2 at the point $\Delta_\theta\theta$ is because this implies that the configuration at the beginning of the step is $\theta^+ = \Delta_\theta\theta$ and thus $\tau(\Delta_\theta\theta) = 0$ implying that: $y_2(\Delta_\theta\theta) = H\Delta_\theta\theta - y_{d,2}(0)$, or (30) has a solution because of the simple form that y_2 takes at $\Delta_\theta\theta$.

Using $\vartheta(\alpha)$, we can explicitly solve for a point $(\vartheta(\alpha), \dot{\vartheta}(\alpha)) \in \mathbf{Z}_\alpha \cap S_R$. In particular, let

$$Y(\theta) = \left[\begin{array}{c} d\delta p_{\mathrm{hip}}^R(\theta) \\ dy_2(\theta) \end{array} \right], \tag{31}$$

It follows from the definition of y_1 and y_2 that

$$\left[\begin{array}{c} y_1(\theta, \dot{\theta}) \\ L_{f_R}y_2(\theta, \dot{\theta}) \end{array} \right] = Y(\theta)\dot{\theta} - \left[\begin{array}{c} v_{\mathrm{hip}} \\ \mathbf{0}_4 \end{array} \right]. \tag{32}$$

Therefore, define

$$\dot{\vartheta}(\alpha) = Y^{-1}(\vartheta(\alpha)) \left[\begin{array}{c} v_{\mathrm{hip}} \\ \mathbf{0}_4 \end{array} \right], \tag{33}$$

where Y is invertible because of the choice of outputs.

Human-Inspired Optimization. With the notation of this section in hand, we define a *human-inspired optimization problem*; a proof of this theorem can be found in [3]. This constrained optimization uses the human data as a cost function (through the human-data-based cost (7)), but enforces constraints that, as is seen in the main result, ensure that the bipedal robot has a stable walking gait.

Theorem 1. The parameters α^* solving the constrained optimization problem:

$$\alpha^* = \underset{\alpha \in \mathbb{R}^{21}}{\mathrm{argmin}} \ \mathrm{Cost}_{\mathrm{HD}}(\alpha) \tag{34}$$

$$\text{s.t} \quad y_2(\vartheta(\alpha)) = \mathbf{0}_4 \tag{C1}$$

$$dy_2(\Delta_\theta\vartheta(\alpha))\Delta_{\dot{\theta}}(\vartheta(\alpha))\dot{\vartheta}(\alpha) = \mathbf{0}_4 \tag{C2}$$

$$dh_R(\vartheta(\alpha))\dot{\vartheta}(\alpha) < 0 \tag{C3}$$

yield partial hybrid zero dynamics: $\Delta_R(S_R \cap \mathbf{Z}_{\alpha^*}) \subset \mathbf{PZ}_{\alpha^*}$.

Main Result. The main result of this paper is that the point $(\vartheta(\alpha^*), \dot{\vartheta}(\alpha^*))$, determined through the inverse kinematics and utilizing the parameters obtained by solving the optimization problem in Theorem 1, is "essentially" the fixed point to a stable hybrid periodic orbit. Thus, the optimization problem in (34) not only ensures partial hybrid zero dynamics, but it automatically yields a fixed point to a stable walking gait that can be computed in closed form from the parameters of the human-inspired controller. Moreover, since the cost function (7) only depends on human walking data, we automatically generate a controller for a stable walking gait, its parameters, a stable hybrid periodic orbit and its fixed point using only human data.

Theorem 2. Let α^* be the parameters solving (34). If

$$\tau(\vartheta(\alpha^*)) = \frac{\delta p_{\mathrm{hip}}^R(\vartheta(\alpha^*)) - \delta p_{\mathrm{hip}}^R(\Delta_\theta\vartheta(\alpha^*))}{v_{\mathrm{hip}}^*} > 0$$

then there exists a constant $\bar{\varepsilon} > 0$ such that for all $\varepsilon > \bar{\varepsilon}$ the hybrid system $\mathscr{H}_R^{(\alpha^*, \varepsilon)}$ has an exponentially stable periodic orbit. Moreover, the fixed point of this periodic orbit, $(\theta_\varepsilon^*, \dot{\theta}_\varepsilon^*)$, is dependent on ε and satisfies the property that:

$$\lim_{\varepsilon \to \infty} (\theta_\varepsilon^*, \dot{\theta}_\varepsilon^*) = (\vartheta(\alpha^*), \dot{\vartheta}(\alpha^*)). \tag{35}$$

PROOF. From the proof of Theorem 1 in [3] it follows that $(\vartheta(\alpha^*), \dot{\vartheta}(\alpha^*)) \in \mathbf{Z}_\alpha \cap S_R$. Letting $\xi_1(\alpha^*)$ and $\xi_2(\alpha^*)$ be the representation of this point in the partial hybrid zero dynamics coordinates (24), the fact that $(\vartheta(\alpha^*), \dot{\vartheta}(\alpha^*)) \in \mathbf{Z}_\alpha$ implies that $\xi_2(\alpha^*) = v_{\mathrm{hip}}^*$. By picking $\theta^- = \vartheta(\alpha^*)$ in (27), it follows that $\xi_1^- = \xi_1(\alpha^*)$. Due to the fact that the zero dynamics evolve in a linear fashion according to (26), the Poincaré map (29) can be explicitly computed; for $\xi_2 \in S_R \cap \mathbf{PZ}_\alpha$, it is given by

$$\rho_\varepsilon(\xi_2) = v_{\mathrm{hip}}^* \left(1 + W \left(e^{-\varepsilon\tau(\vartheta(\alpha^*))} e^{\gamma(\xi_2)} \gamma(\xi_2) \right) \right)$$

where W is the Lambert W function (or product logarithm) and

$$\gamma(\xi_2) = \frac{\Delta_{\mathbf{PZ}}(\vartheta(\alpha^*))\xi_2 - v_{\mathrm{hip}}^*}{v_{\mathrm{hip}}^*}$$

determines the change in the (linearized) velocity of the hip relative to v_{hip}^*; or, in other words, the perturbation away from the zero dynamics surface $\mathbf{Z}_\alpha$. From the explicit form of the reduced Poincaré map ρ it follows that:

$$\lim_{\varepsilon \to \infty} \rho_\varepsilon(\xi_2) = v_{\mathrm{hip}}^* = \xi_2(\alpha^*) \tag{36}$$

since $W(0) = 0$ and $\tau(\vartheta(\alpha^*)) > 0$.

To prove the existence of a periodic orbit for the partial hybrid zero dynamics, we need only prove the existence of a fixed point for ρ_ε. Consider a ball of radius $\delta > 0$ around v_{hip}^*, i.e., for $\xi_2 \in B_\delta(v_{\mathrm{hip}}^*)$, $|\xi_2 - v_{\mathrm{hip}}^*| < \delta$. Then for this δ it follows by (36) that there exists a $\varepsilon_1 > 0$ such that for all $\varepsilon > \varepsilon_1$, $|\rho_\varepsilon(\xi_2) - v_{\mathrm{hip}}| < \delta$. Therefore, $\rho_\varepsilon : B_\delta(v_{\mathrm{hip}}^*) \to B_\delta(v_{\mathrm{hip}}^*)$. By the Brouwer fixed-point theorem, it follows that there exists a fixed point of ρ_ε, i.e., $\xi_2^*(\varepsilon)$, dependent on ε and satisfying $\rho_\varepsilon(\xi_2^*(\varepsilon)) = \xi_2^*(\varepsilon)$, and the hybrid partial zero dynamics has a periodic orbit. To prove the stability of this periodic orbit, we need only check the derivative of ρ_ε at $\xi_2^*(\varepsilon)$ and ensure that its magnitude is less than 1. The derivative ρ_ε can be explicitly computed as:

$$\rho_\varepsilon'(\xi_2^*(\varepsilon)) = \left\{ \begin{array}{ll} e^{-\varepsilon\tau(\vartheta(\alpha^*))}\Delta_{\mathbf{PZ}}(\vartheta(\alpha^*)) & \text{if} \quad \xi_2^*(\varepsilon) = v_{\mathrm{hip}}^* \\ \frac{\Delta_{\mathbf{PZ}}(\vartheta(\alpha^*))^2(\xi_2^*(\varepsilon) - v_{\mathrm{hip}}^*)}{\Delta_{\mathbf{PZ}}(\vartheta(\alpha^*))\xi_2^*(\varepsilon) - v_{\mathrm{hip}}^*} & \text{otherwise} \end{array} \right.$$

Since $\xi_2^*(\varepsilon) \to v_{\mathrm{hip}}^* = \xi_2(\alpha^*)$ as $\varepsilon \to \infty$, it follows that

$$\lim_{\varepsilon \to \infty} \rho_\varepsilon'(\xi_2^*(\varepsilon)) = 0.$$

Therefore, there exists an $\varepsilon_2 > 0$ such that for $\varepsilon > \varepsilon_2$, $|\rho_\varepsilon'(\xi_2^*(\varepsilon))| < 1$ establishing the stability of the periodic orbit for the partial hybrid zero dynamics.

Finally, by Theorem 4.5 of [22] (see also [12]) a stable fixed point for the restricted Poincaré map ρ_ε implies that:

$$(\theta_\varepsilon^*, \dot{\theta}_\varepsilon^*) = (\Phi(\xi_1(\alpha^*)), \Psi(\xi_1(\alpha^*))\xi_2^*(\varepsilon)) \tag{37}$$

is a stable fixed point of the Poincaré map P_ε for the hybrid system $\mathscr{H}_R^{(\alpha^*, \varepsilon)}$ for ε sufficiently large, i.e., for $\varepsilon > \varepsilon_3$. Since (37) clearly satisfies (35), picking $\bar{\varepsilon} = \max\{\varepsilon_1, \varepsilon_2, \varepsilon_3\}$ implies the desired result. $\square$

6. NAO IMPLEMENTATION

In this section, we show that the formal results of this paper can be used to achieve stable walking in a simulation of the NAO robot. Furthermore, by implementing the trajectories found in simulation, coupled with a lateral stability controller on the actual NAO robot (Fig. 4), we experimentally achieve dynamically stable bipedal robotic walking; since the main purpose of this paper is the formal results, the discussion of the experimental results will necessarily be brief. We acknowledge that, as the formal results presented in this paper consider only the 2D sagittal dynamics of NAO, while the experimental implementation presented here is a good indication of successful control for complete validation of the theory, the 3D model with feet is required; this is a topic reserved for future work.

6.1 NAO Walking Simulation

We begin by discussing how the main results of this paper, Theorem 1 and 2, can be used to achieve walking in simulation for the 2D hybrid system model of NAO. These simulation results will serve as the basis for the control of the actual NAO robot.

Stable Robotic Walking. Beginning with the mean human output data, computed from the experimental human walking data and normalized with the NAO parameters, we apply the optimization in Theorem 1. To achieve practical results, additional constraints were enforced in this optimization which limited the maximum joint velocity to 3 rad/s and ensured proper foot clearance. This results in the parameters α^* for the human-inspired controller. As a result of Theorem 2, we automatically know that the parameters α^* will result in stable robotic walking for sufficiently large control gain ε. Picking $\varepsilon = 25$ and simulating the hybrid system $\mathscr{H}_R^{(\alpha^*,\varepsilon)}$ from the initial condition $(\vartheta(\alpha), \dot{\vartheta}(\alpha))$ verifies that we do, in fact, have a walking gait, i.e., a periodic orbit (see Fig. 5 and Fig. 6). Moreover, we can verify the fact that the chosen ε results in a stable walking gait by checking the eigenvalues of the Poincaré map; we find that the magnitude of the maximum eigenvalue is $\lambda = 0.1059$, thus verifying the exponential stability guaranteed by Theorem 2. Furthermore, and as indicated in Fig. 5, the resulting walking exhibits partial hybrid zero dynamics. Finally, we computed the specific cost of transport (SCOT) for this walking to be 0.33 which, given the differences between NAO and a human, is reasonably close to the human value of 0.20 (see [6]). It is important to note that, since the simulated model only has point feet (which was used to approximate the fact that the feet are assumed to always be flat during the walking on the actual NAO robot), the walking obtained in simulation is necessarily dynamically stable.

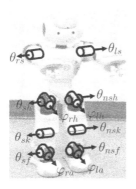

Figure 4: Angle conventions for NAO with right foot as stance foot.

Walking from Rest. In addition to stable, periodic walking, the robustness of the human-inspired control law allows for the robot to start from rest and converge to the walking periodic orbit corresponding to the walking gait. As shown in Fig. 5, trajectories of the system when started from rest converge to the stable limit periodic orbit predicted by Theorem 2. Convergence is also seen in a plot of the human

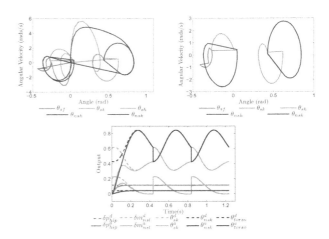

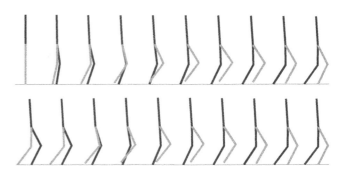

Figure 5: Periodic orbits for the simulated behavior of NAO starting from rest, i.e., a zero initial condition (top left) and the fixed point of the periodic orbit (top right). Starting from rest, the actual outputs of NAO converge to the desired outputs and display partial hybrid zero dynamics (bottom).

Figure 6: Snapshots of the walking gaits from the NAO simulation starting from zero initial conditions (top) and starting from the fixed point $(\vartheta(\alpha), \dot{\vartheta}(\alpha))$ (bottom).

inspired outputs; in Fig. 5 the convergence of the actual outputs of the robot to the desired outputs can be seen. Tiles of the first step of the walking, starting from rest, can be seen in Fig. 6. As discussed in the following section, the trajectories of the simulated NAO model, starting from rest, can be used to experimentally achieve walking in the real NAO robot.

6.2 NAO Walking Experiment

The end goal of the human-inspired walking control design process is the realization of stable walking on an actual robot. Aldebaran's NAO robot was chosen for implementation of the ideas presented in this paper; therefore, we use it as a testbed to show experimental validation of the formal results for the 2D model of the NAO presented in this paper and, more generally, the framework of human-inspired control.

Implementation. To implement the simulated walking behavior on NAO, we use trajectory tracking of the simulated behavior for the sagittal angles and design and implement a lateral stability controller to maintain lateral balance through the walking gait. Specifically, stance and swing joint

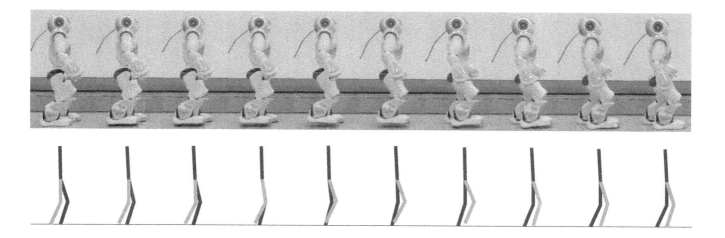

Figure 7: Comparison of the snapshots of the actual (top) and simulated (bottom) walking gaits over one step.

angle trajectories are taken from the simulated behavior of the robot. The control software then takes these individual steps and compiles them into joint trajectories for sagittal angles of the left and right legs (essentially "undoing" the simplifying assumption of a "stance" and "non-stance" leg used in the modeling of the robot). To help maintain lateral stability during walking, we implement a simple online feedback controller with the objective of driving the absolute vertical roll-angle of the NAO's chest to zero in order to decrease lateral instability. In particular, we measure the absolute angle of NAO's chest, φ_{chest}^a, through the onboard IMU. The desired lateral angles of NAO are then defined as $\varphi_{lh}^d = \varphi_{rh}^d = K_{hip}\varphi_{chest}^a$ and $\varphi_{la}^d = \varphi_{ra}^d = -K_{ankle}\varphi_{chest}^a$, with $K_{hip} = 0.7$ and $K_{ankle} = 0.77$, which NAO then tracks with the onboard joint angle controllers.

Results. Implementing the simulated trajectories of the human-inspired walking control on NAO results in dynamically stable walking on the *actual* NAO robot. Tiles of the walking gait achieved in experimentation can be seen in Fig. 7; in that figure, the experimental walking is compared against tiles of the simulated walking taken at the same time instances showing that, in fact, there is good agreement. To provide qualitative evidence of this, the simulated and experimentally observed figures are plotted in Fig. 8; this shows excellent agreement between simulation and experimentation. In this same figure, the effects of the lateral stability controller are shown; the lateral angles oscillate to provide stability in the lateral plane. To verify that the walking obtained on NAO is dynamically stable, we compute the position of the center of mass from the experimental data and check to ensure that it is not over the foot during the course of the walking. Due to the size of the feet on NAO, we find that the y-position of the center of mass is more revealing; as shown in Fig. 9, the center of mass is almost never over the feet during the walking gait. Thus we conclude that the robotic walking achieved is dynamically stable. Finally, the human-inspired walking that was obtained on NAO subjectively appears more human-like that other walking gaits that have been achieved for NAO. We invite readers to form their own opinions by watching the video of the human-inspired robotic walking, and its

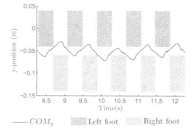

Figure 9: The y-position of the center of mass over multiple steps, with the width of the left and right foot indicated. Since the position of the center of mass is not over either the left or right foot, the experimental walking obtained is dynamically stable.

comparison with the pre-existing (ZMP) walking, which is available online [2].

7. CONCLUSIONS

This paper presents a formal, human-inspired approach to bipedal robotic walking, proving through Theorem 1 and 2 that, by using only human data, parameters to the human-inspired controller can be determined that simultaneously: provide the best fit of the human data, yield partial hybrid zero dynamics, imply the existence of a stable walking gait, and allow the fixed point for this stable walking gait to be explicitly computed. As a result, this method allows for the rapid generation of stable walking gaits during the controller development for bipedal robotic walking simulations and experiments, such as those performed on Aldebaran's NAO robot in this paper. Future work on this topic includes expansion of the formal results to the 3D model of NAO and examination of the accompanying constraints, such as ZMP and friction.

Acknowledgments

The work of A. D. Ames is supported by NSF grant CNS-0953823 and NHARP award 00512-0184-2009. The work of M. J. Powell is supported by NASA grant NNX11AN06H.

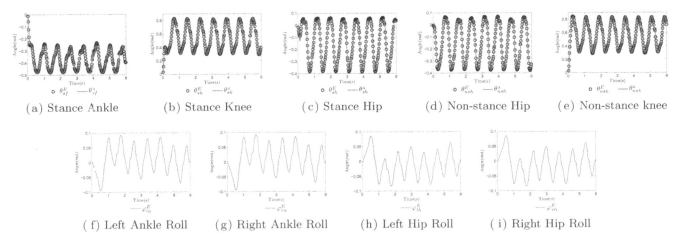

| (a) Stance Ankle | (b) Stance Knee | (c) Stance Hip | (d) Non-stance Hip | (e) Non-stance knee |

| (f) Left Ankle Roll | (g) Right Ankle Roll | (h) Left Hip Roll | (i) Right Hip Roll |

Figure 8: Simulated (desired) and experimental joint trajectories for the sagittal plane (a)-(e), and angles in the lateral plane controlled through the lateral stability controller (f)-(i) as seen in experimentation (see Fig. 4 for the angle conventions).

8. REFERENCES

[1] http://www.aldebaran-robotics.com/.

[2] http://www.youtube.com/watch?v=OBGHU-e1kc0/.

[3] A. D. Ames. First steps toward automatically generating bipedal robotic walking from human data. In *8th International Workshop on Robotic Motion and Control, RoMoCo'11*, Poland, June 2011.

[4] A. D. Ames and R. D. Gregg. Stably extending two-dimensional bipedal walking to three dimensions. In *26th American Control Conference*, New York, NY, 2007.

[5] A. D. Ames, R. Vasudevan, and R. Bajcsy. Human-data based cost of bipedal robotic walking. In *Hybrid Systems: Computation and Control*, Chicago, IL, 2011.

[6] S. Collins and A. Ruina. A bipedal walking robot with efficient and human-like gait. In *International Conference on Robotics and Automation*, Barcelona, Spain, 2005.

[7] J. W. Grizzle, G. Abba, and F. Plestan. Asymptotically stable walking for biped robots: Analysis via systems with impulse effects. *IEEE TAC*, 46(1):51–64, 2001.

[8] J. W. Grizzle, C. Chevallereau, A. D. Ames, and R. W. Sinnet. 3D bipedal robotic walking: models, feedback control, and open problems. In *IFAC Symposium on Nonlinear Control Systems*, Bologna, Italy, 2010.

[9] P. Holmes, R. Full, D. Koditschek, and J. Guckenheimer. The dynamics of legged locomotion: Models, analyses, and challenges. *SIAM Review*, 48:207–304, 2006.

[10] Y. Hürmüzlü and D. B. Marghitu. Rigid body collions of planar kinematic chains with multiple contact points. *Intl. J. of Robotics Research*, 13(1):82–92, 1994.

[11] S. Kajita, F. Kanehiro, K. Kaneko, K. Fujiwara, K. Harada, K. Yokoi, and H. Hirukawa. Biped walking pattern generator allowing auxiliary ZMP control. In *IEEE/RSJ Intl. Conf. on Intelligent Robots and Systems*, pages 2993–2999, Beijing, P.R. China, 2006.

[12] B. Morris and J. Grizzle. A restricted Poincaré map for determining exponentially stable periodic orbits in systems with impulse effects: Application to bipedal robots. In *IEEE Conf. on Decision and Control*, Seville, Spain, 2005.

[13] R. M. Murray, Z. Li, and S. S. Sastry. *A Mathematical Introduction to Robotic Manipulation*. CRC Press, Boca Raton, 1994.

[14] J. Pratt, J. Carff, and S. Drakunov. Capture point: A step toward humanoid push recovery. In *in 6th IEEE-RAS International Conference on Humanoid Robots*, Genoa, Italy, 2006.

[15] J. Rose and J. G. Gamble. *Human Walking*. Lippincott Williams & Wilkins, Philadelphia, 2005.

[16] S. S. Sastry. *Nonlinear Systems: Analysis, Stability and Control*. Springer, New York, 1999.

[17] R. W. Sinnet and A. D. Ames. 3D bipedal walking with knees and feet: A hybrid geometric approach. In *48th IEEE Conference on Decision and Control*, Shanghai, P.R. China, 2009.

[18] M. W. Spong and F. Bullo. Controlled symmetries and passive walking. *IEEE TAC*, 50(7):1025–1031, 2005.

[19] S. Srinivasan, I. A. Raptis, and E. R. Westervelt. Low-dimensional sagittal plane model of normal human walking. *ASME J. of Biomechanical Eng.*, 130(5), 2008.

[20] M. Vukobratović and B. Borovac. Zero-moment point—thirty-five years of its life. *Intl. J. of Humanoid Robotics*, 1(1):157–173, 2005.

[21] E. Wendel and A. D. Ames. Rank properties of Poincaré maps for hybrid systems with applications to bipedal walking. In *Hybrid Systems: Computation and Control*, Stockholm, Sweden, 2010.

[22] E. R. Westervelt, J. W. Grizzle, C. Chevallereau, J. H. Choi, and B. Morris. *Feedback Control of Dynamic Bipedal Robot Locomotion*. CRC Press, Boca Raton, 2007.

[23] E. R. Westervelt, J. W. Grizzle, and D. E. Koditschek. Hybrid zero dynamics of planar biped walkers. *IEEE TAC*, 48(1):42–56, 2003.

Efficient Algorithms for Collision Avoidance at Intersections

Alessandro Colombo
Massachusetts Institute of Technology
77 Massachusetts Avenue
Cambridge, MA, 02139
acolombo@mit.edu

Domitilla Del Vecchio
Massachusetts Institute of Technology
77 Massachusetts Avenue
Cambridge, MA, 02139
ddv@mit.edu

ABSTRACT

We consider the problem of synthesising the least restrictive controller for collision avoidance of multiple vehicles at an intersection. The largest set of states for which there exists a control that avoids collisions is known as the maximal controlled invariant set. Exploiting results from the scheduling literature we prove that, for a general model of vehicle dynamics at an intersection, the problem of checking membership in the maximal controlled invariant set is NP-hard. We then describe an algorithm that solves this problem approximately and with provable error bounds. The approximate solution is used to design a supervisor for collision avoidance whose complexity scales polynomially with the number of vehicles. The supervisor is based on a hybrid algorithm that employs a dynamic model of the vehicles and periodically solves a scheduling problem.

Categories and Subject Descriptors

I.2.8 [**Artificial Intelligence**]: Problem Solving, Control Methods, and Search—*Control theory, Scheduling* ; I.2.9 [**Artificial Intelligence**]: Robotics—*Autonomous vehicles*

General Terms

Algorithms, Theory

Keywords

Intelligent transportation system, collision, complexity, hybrid, safety, scheduling

1. INTRODUCTION

An intelligent transportation system is a set of tightly interacting physical, computational, and communication resources that collaborate to enhance the performance of a transportation network. Of the possible performance metrics safety is, for obvious reasons, considered of primary importance [24]. A number of solutions have been proposed

to improve vehicular safety, typically addressing the stability of the longitudinal or lateral dynamics of a vehicle, or reducing the risk of rear-end collisions [1–3]. A much harder problem, both from a technological and a computational point of view, is that of preventing collisions caused by drivers' mistakes when vehicles traverse an intersection. From a control perspective, this problem is ideally solved by determining the largest set of states for which there exists a control that avoids collisions, which is known as the *maximal controlled invariant set* [21]. The set of all controls that make this set invariant is the least restrictive among all control sets that enforce safety. A multi-objective control problem with safety as the primary objective and some other performance metric, for example fuel consumption, as secondary objective, can be solved hierarchically once this control set is determined, by optimizing within the control set. The problem of determining the maximal controlled invariant set for pairs of vehicles at an intersection is solved in [9, 10, 14, 15]. These results exploit the monotonicity of the vehicles' dynamics to derive a computationally efficient control law, but do not apply to more than two vehicles. An algorithm that addresses multi-vehicle collisions, based on abstraction, has been proposed in [5]. Here, the control problem is reduced to the control of a finite automaton, and the maximal controlled invariant set is approximated by a set of allowed states of the automaton. However, the size of the automaton scales exponentially with the size of the problem, thus limiting the applicability to a small number of vehicles. An algorithmic approach to safety enforcing based on time slot assignment, which can handle a larger number of vehicles, is found in [18]. It allows to design a safe control law, but it does not provide means to assess the performance of the result by any metric.

In the context of this paper, membership in the maximal controlled invariant set is determined by solving the following problem.

Problem A (Safety, informal statement) *Given the initial state of a set of n agents moving along n different paths crossing at an intersection, determine if there exists an input signal that leads all agents through the intersection avoiding collisions.*

Notice that we assume that agents move along different paths, and that all paths intersect at a common point, as in Fig. 1. Extensions to our results that allow to handle more complex cases, like multilane intersections with multiple agents on each lane, are currently under study. The approach we follow consists in mapping Problem A onto a

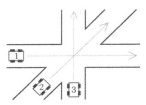

Figure 1: Example of intersection topology.

scheduling problem [22], where the intersection represents a machine, and the time spent by each agent in the intersection is the length of the job to be executed on the machine. We develop this analogy rigorously, proving that a formal restatement of the above problem is indeed equivalent, in a strong sense, to a modified version of a standard scheduling problem. Through this artifice, we can formally prove that Problem A, for a general class of vehicle dynamics, is NP-complete. This justifies the design of approximate algorithms to solve the problem. We revert again to the scheduling version of Problem A and we leverage results in the operations research literature to devise an approximate solution that has polynomial complexity and is within provable bounds from an optimal solution.

We use the exact solution of Problem A to design the least restrictive safety-enforcing controller, which solves the following problem.

Problem B (Supervisor, informal statement) *Given a set of agents as in Problem A, design a supervisor that, given a desired input, returns the desired input unless this will cause a collision at some future time, in which case it returns a safe input.*

The supervised system is hybrid: agents have continuous dynamics, while the allowed inputs are selected at discrete time instants through the solution of the scheduling version of Problem A. We then synthesise the above controller using the approximate solution of Problem A, obtaining an approximate solution of Problem B within provable bounds of the exact one. The resulting controller enforces safety as long as all agents behave according to the model.

Our solutions exploit algorithms that are well known in the scheduling literature. The proof that these algorithms can be used to solve Problem A, and their use as solution of a control problem, constitute the main contributions of this paper, and are new results to the best of our knowledge.

The paper is organised as follows. In the next section, we introduce some standard concepts of computational complexity theory and operations research which are used in the paper. In Section 3, we formalize Problem A and we reformulate it in terms of a scheduling problem. Then, in Section 4, we prove that the two formulations are equivalent, and we prove complexity results. Section 5 proposes the exact and approximate solution of Problem A. Both solutions are used in Section 6 to provide a solution to Problem B. Finally, in Section 7 we apply the proposed algorithms on a simple model of vehicle dynamics.

2. MATHEMATICAL FOUNDATIONS

As mentioned in the Introduction, the results of this paper revolve around the translation of Problem A into a scheduling problem. In order to carry out the proofs, we introduce

some standard machinery from the literature on scheduling and computational complexity theory.

Scheduling is the decision-making process of assigning to a number of jobs a *schedule*, that is, a set of execution times, to satisfy given requirements [22]. The standard formalism to describe a scheduling problem was introduced in [13]. It represents a problem by the string $\alpha|\beta|\gamma$, where the field α describes the machine environment (e.g. the number of machines), the field β defines the jobs characteristics (such as unequal release dates or constraints on duration), and the field γ defines the optimality criterion. This paper is concerned with two closely related scheduling problems: $1|\mathbf{r}_i|\text{Lmax}$, and $1|\mathbf{r}_i, \mathbf{p}_i = 1|\text{Lmax}$ introduced in the following definitions.

Definition 2.1 ($1|\mathbf{r}_i|\text{Lmax}$) *Given a set of n jobs to be run on a single machine, with release times $\mathbf{r}_i \in \mathbb{R}_+$, deadlines $\mathbf{d}_i \in \mathbb{R}_+$, and durations $\mathbf{p}_i \in \mathbb{R}_+$, find a schedule $\mathbf{T} = (\mathbf{T}_1, ..., \mathbf{T}_n) \in \mathbb{R}_+^n$ such that, for all $i \in \{1, ..., n\}$,*

$$\mathbf{T}_i \geq \mathbf{r}_i,$$

for all $i \neq j$,

$$\mathbf{T}_i \geq \mathbf{T}_j \Rightarrow \mathbf{T}_i \geq \mathbf{T}_j + \mathbf{p}_j,$$

and such that $\text{Lmax} := \max_i(\mathbf{T}_i + \mathbf{p}_i - \mathbf{d}_i)$ is minimized.

The second problem, $1|\mathbf{r}_i, \mathbf{p}_i = 1|\text{Lmax}$, is identical to the one above, except that $\mathbf{p}_i = 1$ for all jobs.

The above problems are *optimization problems*. Computational complexity theory focuses instead on *decision problems*, problems that have a binary answer in $\{yes, no\}$ [6]. When a problem P returns "*yes*" for an instance I we say that P accepts I, denoted $I \in P$. Any optimization problem can be cast into a decision problem by imposing a bound on the optimized quantity. Although the solution of a decision problem carries less information than that of the associated optimization problem, analysing the complexity of a decision algorithm is still relevant to the original optimization problem. Indeed, the computational complexity of a decision problem cannot be higher than that of the corresponding optimization problem, since an optimal solution is immediately mapped onto an answer to the decision problem.

We use the notation $DEC(\alpha|\beta|\gamma, \delta)$ to represent the decision problem "does $\alpha|\beta|\gamma$ have a solution with $\gamma \leq \delta$?" Thus, $DEC(1|\mathbf{r}_i|\text{Lmax}, 0)$ is stated as follows.

Definition 2.2 ($DEC(1|\mathbf{r}_i|\text{Lmax}, 0)$) *Given a set of n jobs to be run on a single machine, with release times $\mathbf{r}_i \in \mathbb{R}_+$, deadlines $\mathbf{d}_i \in \mathbb{R}_+$, and durations $\mathbf{p}_i \in \mathbb{R}_+$, determine if there exists a schedule $\mathbf{T} = (\mathbf{T}_1, ..., \mathbf{T}_n) \in \mathbb{R}_+^n$ such that, for all $i \in \{1, ..., n\}$,*

$$\mathbf{r}_i \leq \mathbf{T}_i \leq \mathbf{d}_i - \mathbf{p}_i,$$

and for all $i \neq j$,

$$\mathbf{T}_i \geq \mathbf{T}_j \Rightarrow \mathbf{T}_i \geq \mathbf{T}_j + \mathbf{p}_j.$$

The statement of $DEC(1|\mathbf{r}_i, \mathbf{p}_i = 1|\text{Lmax}, 0)$ is obtained by adding the constraint $\mathbf{p}_i = 1$ for all i.

The concepts of *reducibility* and *equivalence* [6, 19] are used when comparing the complexity of different problems.

Definition 2.3 *A problem P1 is reducible to a problem P2 if for every instance I of P1 an instance I' of P2 can be constructed in polynomial-bounded time, such that $I \in P1 \Leftrightarrow I' \in P2$. In this case, we write $P1 \propto P2$.*

Two problems $P1$ and $P2$ are equivalent, denoted $P1 \simeq P2$, if $P1 \propto P2$ and $P2 \propto P1$.

Problem $DEC(1|\mathbf{r}_i|\text{Lmax}, 0)$ has been shown to be NP-complete by reduction of Knapsack [19]. It can be solved by enumerative algorithms that systematically test all the possible permutations of jobs. Unlike $DEC(1|\mathbf{r}_i|\text{Lmax}, 0)$, $DEC(1|\mathbf{r}_i, \mathbf{p}_i = 1|\text{Lmax}, 0)$ has an exact $O(n^3)$-time solution, reported in [12] and implemented in Algorithm 1. The so-

---

Algorithm 1 Solution of $DEC(1|\mathbf{r}_i, \mathbf{p}_i = 1|\text{Lmax}, 0)$

1: **procedure** POLYNOMIALTIME($\mathbf{r}, \mathbf{d}$)
2:     **for all** $i \in \{1, \dots, n\}$ **do** $F_i \leftarrow \emptyset$, $c_i \leftarrow \emptyset$
3:     **end for**
4:     sort jobs in increasing $\mathbf{r}_i$ ($\mathbf{r}_1 \leq \mathbf{r}_2 \leq \mathbf{r}_3 \leq \dots$)
5:     **for** $i = n$ downto 1 **do**   ▷ Part I: forbidden regions
6:         **for all** $j \in \{1, \dots, n\}$ such that $\mathbf{d}_j \geq \mathbf{d}_i$ **do**
7:             **if** $c_j = \emptyset$ **then** $c_j \leftarrow \mathbf{d}_j - 1$
8:             **else** $c_j \leftarrow c_j - 1$
9:             **end if**
10:            **while** $c_j \in F_k$ for some F_k **do** $c_j \leftarrow \inf(F_k)$
11:            **end while**
12:         **end for**
13:         **if** $i = 1$ or $\mathbf{r}_{i-1} < \mathbf{r}_i$ **then** $c \leftarrow \min_i(c_i)$
14:             **if** $c < \mathbf{r}_i$ **then return** $\{\emptyset, no\}$
15:             **end if**
16:             **if** $c \in [\mathbf{r}_i, \mathbf{r}_i + 1]$ **then** $F_i \leftarrow [c - 1, \mathbf{r}_i]$
17:         **end if**
18:         **end if**
19:     **end for**
20:     $t \leftarrow 0$
21:     **for** $i = 1$ to n **do**   ▷ Part II: schedule
22:         $r_{min} \leftarrow \min\{\mathbf{r}_j : \text{job } j \text{ has not been scheduled}\}$
23:         $t \leftarrow \max\{t, r_{min}\}$
24:         **while** $t \in F_j$ for some j **do** $t \leftarrow \sup(F_j)$
25:         **end while**
26:         $j \leftarrow \{i : \text{job } i \text{ has least deadline among those ready at } t\}$
27:         $\mathsf{T}_j \leftarrow t$
28:         $t \leftarrow t + 1$
29:     **end for**
30:     **return** $\{\mathsf{T}, yes\}$
31: **end procedure**

---

lution of the decision problem only requires the binary answer, but Algorithm 1 returns a schedule T along with the binary answer. The information on the schedule is used in the following sections to design an approximate solution to Problem A. The algorithm starts by computing a set of *forbidden regions*, i.e., intervals $F_i \subset \mathbb{R}$ during which no job can be started. Then, it schedules jobs by increasing deadline order, ensuring no job is started during a forbidden region.

3. FORMALIZATION OF PROBLEM A

Consider the system

$$\dot{\mathbf{x}} = f(\mathbf{x}, \mathbf{u}), \quad \mathbf{y} = h(\mathbf{x}) \tag{1}$$

given by the parallel composition of the dynamics of n (possibly different) agents

$$\dot{x}_i = f_i(x_i, u_i), \quad y_i = h_i(x_i) \tag{2}$$

with $x_i \in X_i \subseteq \mathbb{R}^r$, $u_i \in U_i \subset \mathbb{R}^s$, $y_i \in Y_i \subseteq \mathbb{R}$, and $h_i(x_i)$ continuous in x_i. The functional space of the inputs signals $u_i(t)$, $t \in [0, \infty)$, is $\mathcal{U}_i$. The aggregate states, inputs and outputs of all agents are denoted $\mathbf{x}$, $\mathbf{u}$ and $\mathbf{y}$, respectively. The corresponding sets are $\mathcal{U}$, X, U, and Y, respectively. Assume that (1) has unique solutions. This is ensured, for example, if (1) is locally Lipschitz [17], while uniqueness conditions for piecewise smooth systems are reported in [11]. Assume that systems (2) are output-monotone [4] and that the positivity cone of the output y_i is $\mathbb{R}_+$. This means that there exist two convex cones $K_x^i \subset \mathbb{R}^r$ and $K_u^i \subset \mathbb{R}^s$, such that $x_i(0) - x_i'(0) \in K_x^i$ and $u_i(t) - u_i'(t) \in K_u^i$ for all $t \geq 0$ imply $y_i(t) - y_i'(t) \in \mathbb{R}_+$ for all $t \geq 0$. Assume also that the set U_i is compact and is a partially ordered set [8] with respect to its positivity cone, with a unique maximum, called $u_{i,max}$, and minimum, called $u_{i,min}$. Finally, assume that $\dot{y}_i$ is bounded to a strictly positive interval $[\dot{y}_{i,min}, \dot{y}_{i,max}]$ for all i. When the state of agent i at a specified time t_0 is $x_i(t_0)$, a trajectory starting at $x_i(t_0)$ or the corresponding output signal at time $t \geq t_0$, with input u_i in $[t_0, t]$, are denoted $x_i(t, u_i, x_i(t_0))$ and $y_i(t, u_i, x_i(t_0))$, respectively. For the sake of brevity, when $t_0 = 0$ we use the notation $x_i(t, u_i)$ and $y_i(t, u_i)$. When the particular input is not important, we write simply $x_i(t)$ and $y_i(t)$, and when time is not important we simply use the variable name without arguments.

We assign to each system i an open interval (a_i, b_i), and we say that two agents i and j *collide* if the outputs of the corresponding systems verify the condition $y_i(t) \in (a_i, b_i)$ and $y_j(t) \in (a_j, b_j)$ at the same time instant t. We say that a set of agents $\{i, j, ..\}$ collides if any pair of agents in the set collides. The subset of Y of collision points is called the *bad set*, denoted B_+:

$$B_+ := \{\mathbf{y} \in Y : y_i \in (a_i, b_i) \text{ and } y_j \in (a_j, b_j), \text{ for some } i \neq j\}.$$

We start by formalizing Problem A. Notice that it is a decision problem, in the sense introduced in Section 2. Then, we propose an alternative formulation in the form of another decision problem, that can be proved to be equivalent.

Problem A (Safety, formal statement) *Given initial conditions $\mathbf{x}(0)$, determine if there exists an input signal $\mathbf{u}(t)$ that guarantees that $\mathbf{y}(t, \mathbf{u}) \notin B_+$ for all $t \geq 0$.*

An instance of Problem A is described by the initial conditions $\mathbf{x}(0)$, and by the set

$$\Theta := \{f, h, X, U, \mathcal{U}, Y, a_1, \dots, a_n, b_1, \dots, b_n\}. \tag{3}$$

The instance $\{\mathbf{x}(0), \Theta\} \in$ Problem A if and only if $\mathbf{x}(0)$ belongs to the maximal controlled invariant set of system (1), with parameters Θ. In order to reformulate Problem A as a scheduling problem, we introduce three quantities: R_i, D_i, and P_i. These play a similar role to the release times, deadlines, and job durations of Section 2. Specifically, for each agent i, if $y_i(0) \leq a_i$ define

$$R_i := \inf_{u_i \in \mathcal{U}_i} \{t : y_i(t, u_i) = a_i\}, \quad D_i := \sup_{u_i \in \mathcal{U}_i} \{t : y_i(t, u_i) = a_i\},$$

and set $R_i = D_i = 0$ if $y_i(0) > a_i$. Since (2) is output-monotone we have that, if $y_i(0) \leq a_i$,

$$R_i = \{t : y_i(t, u_{i,max}) = a_i\}, \quad D_i = \{t : y_i(t, u_{i,min}) = a_i\}. \tag{4}$$

These two quantities are, respectively, the minimum and maximum time at which the output of system i can reach a_i. Notice that R_i and D_i are always well defined, since (1) has unique solutions and $\dot{y}_i \geq \dot{y}_{i,min} > 0$. For each agent i such that $y_i(0) \leq a_i$, given a real number T_i, define

$$P_i(T_i) := \inf_{u_i \in \mathcal{U}_i} \{t \geq 0 : y_i(t, u_i) = b_i\} \tag{5}$$

with constraint

$$y_i(t, u_i) \leq a_i \, \forall \, t < T_i. \tag{6}$$

If the constraint cannot be satisfied, set $P_i(T_i) := \infty$. If $y_i(0) \in (a_i, b_i)$ define $P_i(T_i) := \{t : y_i(t, u_{i,max}) = b_i\}$, and if $y_i(0) \geq b_i$ define $P_i(T_i) := 0$. $P_i(T_i)$ is the earliest time that i can reach b_i, if it does not pass a_i before T_i.

Recall that quantities R_i, D_i, and $P_i(T_i)$ defined above depend on the initial condition $x_i(0)$ through $y_i(t)$. Problem A is reformulated as follows.

Problem 1 (Scheduling) *Given initial conditions* $\mathbf{x}(0)$, *determine if there exists a schedule* $\mathbf{T} = (T_1, \ldots, T_n) \in \mathbb{R}^n$ *such that, for all* i,

$$R_i \leq T_i \leq D_i, \tag{7}$$

and for all $i \neq j$,

$$T_i \geq T_j \Rightarrow T_i \geq P_j(T_j). \tag{8}$$

As for Problem A, an instance of Problem 1 is described by the set $\{\mathbf{x}(0), \Theta\}$.

Notice that the quantity D_i in (7) plays a role that is formally similar to the quantity $\mathbf{d}_i - \mathbf{p}_i$ in the definition of $DEC(1|\mathbf{r}_i|\mathbf{L}_{max})$, that is, D_i is a deadline minus a job duration. This choice, as opposed to letting D_i be a deadline, allows to simplify the proofs in the following section.

Example 3.1 Consider system (1) with $f_i(x_i, u_i) = u_i$, $h_i(x_i) = x_i$, $x_i \in \mathbb{R}$, $u_i \in [1, 2]$, and $i \in \{1, 2, 3\}$. Let $(x_1(0), a_1, b_1) = (0, 2, 4)$, $(x_2(0), a_2, b_2) = (2, 4, 6)$, $(x_3(0), a_3, b_3) = (4, 6, 8)$. According to (4) we have $(R_1, D_1) = (1, 2)$, $(R_2, D_2) = (2, 4)$, $(R_3, D_3) = (3, 6)$, and according to (5), $P_i(T_i) = T_i + 1$, since $b_i - a_i = 2$ and $u_{i,max} = 2$ for all i. Therefore, any schedule $\mathbf{T}$ with $T_1 \in [1, 2]$, $T_2 \in [T_1 + 1, 4]$, $T_3 \in [T_2 + 1, 6]$, is feasible for Problem 1. Similarly, the schedule $\mathbf{T}$ with $T_1 \in [1, 2]$, $T_2 = 4$, $T_3 = 3$ is feasible.

4. PROBLEMS A AND 1 ARE EQUIVALENT AND NP-HARD

Theorem 4.1 *Problem A* $\simeq$ *Problem 1*.

PROOF. We must show that Problem A is reducible to Problem 1 and *vice versa*. Notice that for both Problems an instance is fully described by the set $\{\mathbf{x}(0), \Theta\}$, thus the mapping between instances of the two problems is the identity (which has obviously polynomially bounded running

time). Proving equivalence thus amounts to proving that for a given $\{\mathbf{x}(0), \Theta\}$,

$$\{\mathbf{x}(0), \Theta\} \in \text{Problem A} \Leftrightarrow \{\mathbf{x}(0), \Theta\} \in \text{Problem 1}.$$

$(\{\mathbf{x}(0), \Theta\} \in$ Problem A $\Rightarrow \{\mathbf{x}(0), \Theta\} \in$ Problem 1): Assume that $\tilde{\mathbf{y}}(t, \tilde{\mathbf{u}})$ satisfies the constraints of Problem A. The time instants at which $\tilde{\mathbf{y}}(t, \tilde{\mathbf{u}})$ crosses each of the planes $y_i = a_i$ define a vector $\mathbf{T}$ (notice that synchronous crossings are forbidden by $\tilde{\mathbf{y}} \notin B_+$), and we can set $T_i = 0$ if $y_i(0) > a_i$. This $\mathbf{T}$ satisfies (7) given the definition of R_i and D_i. Moreover, the time instants at which $\tilde{\mathbf{y}}(t, \tilde{\mathbf{u}})$ crosses the planes $y_i = b_i$ defines a vector $\tilde{\mathbf{P}} = (\tilde{P}_1, \ldots, \tilde{P}_n)$, and for all $T_i \geq T_j$, $T_i \geq \tilde{P}_j$, otherwise $\tilde{\mathbf{y}}(t, \tilde{\mathbf{u}}) \cap B_+ \neq \emptyset$. Since $P_i(T_i)$ is the minimum time at which agent i can exit the intersection, provided it enters no earlier than T_i, we have that $P_i(T_i) \leq \tilde{P}_i$. Therefore $\mathbf{T}$ also satisfies (8).

$(\{\mathbf{x}(0), \Theta\} \in$ Problem A $\Leftarrow \{\mathbf{x}(0), \Theta\} \in$ Problem 1): Assume that Problem 1 accepts the instance $\{\mathbf{x}(0), \Theta\}$. Assume that $y_i(0) \leq a_i$ for all i and, without loss of generality, that $T_n \geq T_i$ for all $i \in \{1, \ldots, n-1\}$. To satisfy condition (8), the schedule must be such that $P_i(T_i)$ is finite for all $i \in \{1, \ldots, n-1\}$. Thus by definition of $P_i(T_i)$, there exists an input such that $y_i(t) \leq a_i$ for all $t < T_i$, and $y_i(t) = b_i$ when $t = P_i(T_i)$. To satisfy (7) and (8), with this input each y_i enters the interval (a_i, b_i) no earlier than T_i, leaves the interval at $P_i(T_i)$, and the intervals $(T_i, P_i(T_i))$ do not intersect. Thus agents $1, \ldots, n-1$ do not collide. Then, setting $u_n = u_{n,min}$, we know that agent n reaches a_n at time $t_n = D_n$. By (7), $t_n \geq T_n$, and by (8) $T_n \geq P_i(T_i)$ for all $i \in \{1, \ldots, n-1\}$. Thus when $y_n \in (a_i, b_i)$, $y_i \geq b_i$ for all $i \in \{1, \ldots, n-1\}$, hence agents $1, \ldots, n$ do not collide.

If for some systems i we have $y_i(0) > a_i$, then $R_i = 0$ and $D_i = 0$. By (7) this implies $T_i = 0$. For agents with $y_i(0) > a_i$, by definition of P_i we have that $P_i(0) = 0$ if $y_i(0) \geq b_i$, and $P_i(0) > 0$ otherwise. Problem 1 accepts $\{\mathbf{x}(0), \Theta\}$ only if there exists at most one agent such that $a_i < y_i(0) < b_i$, otherwise we would have $T_i = T_j = 0$ and $P_i(T_i), P_j(T_j) > 0$ which contradicts (8). Assume, without loss of generality, that agents $1, \ldots, m-1$ have $y_i(0) \geq b_i$, and agent m has $y_m(0) \in (a_m, b_m)$. Agents $1, \ldots, m-1$ do not collide regardless of the input. Agent m has input such that $y_m(P_m(T_m)) = b_i$, and agents $m+1, \ldots, n$ reach a_i at $t \geq P_m(T_m)$ with a collision-free input, by the reasoning above. $\square$

Now let $\mathcal{PC}(U_i)$ be the set of piecewise constant functions $\mathbb{R} \to U_i$. To prove NP-hardness of Problems A and 1 we consider the particular set of instances obtained by fixing

$$\begin{aligned} f_i(x_i, u_i) = u_i, \quad h_i(x_i) = x_i, \quad X_i = \mathbb{R}, \quad Y_i = \mathbb{R} \\ U_i = [u_{i,min}, u_{i,max}] \subset \mathbb{R}, \quad \mathcal{U}_i = \mathcal{PC}(U_i), \end{aligned} \tag{9}$$

and show that $DEC(1|\mathbf{r}_i|\text{Lmax}, 0)$, which is NP-complete (see [19]), can be reduced to Problem 1.

Theorem 4.2 *Consider* $1|\mathbf{r}_i|\text{Lmax}$ *with* $n > 1$ *jobs, and Problem 1 with* n *agents. Then,*

$$DEC(1|\mathbf{r}_i|\text{Lmax}, 0) \propto \text{Problem 1}.$$

PROOF. Consider the set of instances of Problem 1 that satisfy (9). One such instance with n agents is described by n sets of numbers $(x_i(0), a_i, b_i, u_{i,min}, u_{i,max})$, while an instance of $DEC(1|\mathbf{r}_i|\text{Lmax}, 0)$ with n jobs is described by n sets of numbers $(\mathbf{r}_i, \mathbf{d}_i, \mathbf{p}_i)$. Let us call $\mathbf{x}(0), \mathbf{a}, \mathbf{b}, \mathbf{u}_{min}$,

$\mathbf{u}_{max}$, $\mathbf{r}$, $\mathbf{d}$, $\mathbf{p}$ the n-dimensional vector of the corresponding quantities. To prove the theorem, we must find a mapping $g : (\mathbf{r}, \mathbf{d}, \mathbf{p}) \mapsto (\mathbf{x}(0), \mathbf{a}, \mathbf{b}, \mathbf{u}_{min}, \mathbf{u}_{max})$, and prove that

$$(\mathbf{r}, \mathbf{d}, \mathbf{p}) \in DEC(1|\mathbf{r}_i|\text{Lmax}, 0) \Leftrightarrow g(\mathbf{r}, \mathbf{d}, \mathbf{p}) \in \text{Problem 1},$$

which is equivalent to

$$(\mathbf{r}, \mathbf{d}, \mathbf{p}) \in DEC(1|\mathbf{r}_i|\text{Lmax}, 0) \Rightarrow g(\mathbf{r}, \mathbf{d}, \mathbf{p}) \in \text{Problem 1}$$
$$\text{and}$$
$$(\mathbf{r}, \mathbf{d}, \mathbf{p}) \notin DEC(1|\mathbf{r}_i|\text{Lmax}, 0) \Rightarrow g(\mathbf{r}, \mathbf{d}, \mathbf{p}) \notin \text{Problem 1}.$$
$$(10)$$

We begin by assuming, without loss of generality, that $\mathbf{r}_i, \mathbf{d}_i > 0$ for all i. This can always be ensured by adding a constant to $\mathbf{r}$ and $\mathbf{d}$. To construct the mapping g, partition the set of instances $(\mathbf{r}, \mathbf{d}, \mathbf{p})$ in two groups: (i) instances such that, for some i, $\mathbf{d}_i - \mathbf{p}_i < \mathbf{r}_i$; (ii) all other instances.

For all instances in group (i), set the image of g to an arbitrary non-accepted instance of Problem 1, e.g. set $x_i(0) \in (a_i, b_i)$, $x_j(0) \in (a_j, b_j)$ for some $i \neq j$. This is possible since $n > 1$. Given that for all instances in group (i) $(\mathbf{r}, \mathbf{d}, \mathbf{p}) \notin DEC(1|\mathbf{r}_i|\text{Lmax}, 0)$, and that, by construction, $g(\mathbf{r}, \mathbf{d}, \mathbf{p}) \notin \text{Problem 1}$, mapping g restricted to instances of group (i) satisfies (10).

For the instances in group (ii), set $(\mathbf{r}_i, \mathbf{d}_i, \mathbf{p}_i) \mapsto (x_i(0), a_i, b_i, u_{i,min}, u_{i,max})$ with

$$x_i(0) = 0, \quad a_i = \mathbf{r}_i, \quad b_i = (\mathbf{p}_i + \mathbf{r}_i),$$
$$u_{i,min} = \mathbf{r}_i / (\mathbf{d}_i - \mathbf{p}_i), \quad u_{i,max} = 1. \quad (11)$$

The two above sets of equations transform every instance of $DEC(1|\mathbf{r}_i|\text{Lmax}, 0)$ in group (ii) into an instance of Problem 1. Writing (4) and (5) explicitly for a system that satisfies (9), we have

$$R_i = \frac{a_i - x_i(0)}{u_{i,max}}, \quad D_i = \frac{a_i - x_i(0)}{u_{i,min}}, \quad P_i(T_i) = \frac{b_i - a_i}{u_{i,max}} + T_i.$$

Rewriting the right-hand sides of these using (11) we obtain $R_i = \mathbf{r}_i$, $D_i = \mathbf{d}_i - \mathbf{p}_i$, $P_i(T_i) = \mathbf{p}_i + T_i$. The above equations formally transform the conditions on $(\mathbf{r}_i, \mathbf{d}_i, \mathbf{p}_i)$ of $DEC(1|\mathbf{r}_j|\text{Lmax}, 0)$ into the conditions on (R_i, D_i, P_i) in (7) and (8) of Problem 1, therefore g restricted to instances of group (ii) satisfies (10). This concludes the proof. $\square$

From the above theorem, and from the equivalence of Problems 1 and A, we obtain

Lemma 4.3 *Problems 1 and A are NP-hard*

PROOF. $DEC(1|\mathbf{r}_i|\text{Lmax}, 0)$ is reducible to Problem 1, and since the first is NP-complete, the second is NP-hard. Also, by Theorem 4.1, Problem A is NP-hard. $\square$

5. SOLUTION OF PROBLEM A

Consider the set $\mathcal{P}$ of all permutations of the index vector $(1, \ldots, n)$. Let π be a member of $\mathcal{P}$, and π_i be the i-th index of the permutation. Once the parameters of system (1) are specified, Problem 1 can be solved for an arbitrary set of initial conditions $\mathbf{x}(0)$ by Algorithm 2. Since Problems A and 1 are equivalent, the same algorithm solves Problem A. Algorithm 2 explores all the possible permutations in $\mathcal{P}$, and since the cardinality of the search space grows factorially in the number of agents n, so does the running time of the algorithm. As we have seen, Problem 1 is NP-hard, so unsurprisingly there is no known way to find a solution to all instances in polynomial time with respect to

---

Algorithm 2 Solution of Problem 1
```
1:  procedure EXACTSOLUTION(x(0))
2:      for all i ∈ {1, ..., n} do
3:          given x_i(0) calculate R_i, D_i
4:      end for
5:      for all π ∈ P do
6:          T_{π_1} ← R_{π_1}
7:          for i = 2 → n do
8:              T_{π_i} ← max(P_{π_{i-1}}(T_{π_{i-1}}), R_{π_i})
9:          end for
10:         if T_i ≤ D_i for all i ∈ {1, ..., n} then
11:             return {T, yes}
12:         end if
13:     end for
14:     return {∅, no}
15: end procedure
```

---

n. Moreover, since our ultimate goal is to use an algorithm that solves Problem A to construct the control law required by Problem B, and this must run in real time, even an algorithm with good average running time, but exponential worst-case time, would not be good enough. Using results from the scheduling literature, however, we can design algorithms that provide an approximate solution to Problem 1 in polynomial time. The approach that we propose consists in adding an additional constraint to Problem 1, so that it becomes solvable in polynomial time. Then we gauge the effect of this additional constraint on the solutions. We start by proving the following

Lemma 5.1 *Consider system (2) and R_i, D_i defined in (4), and assume that $\mathcal{U}_i$ is path connected, that solutions of (1) depend continuously on the input, and that h_i is continuous. If $y_i(0) < a_i$ then, for any $T_i \in [R_i, D_i]$ there exists a $u_i \in \mathcal{U}_i$ such that $y_i(T_i, u_i) = a_i$.*

PROOF. By assumption solutions of (1) depend continuously on the input, therefore by continuity of h_i, $y_i(t, u_i)$ depends continuously on u_i. Since $y_i(0) < a_i$, $\dot{y}_i \geq \dot{y}_{i,min} > 0$, and (1) has unique solutions, $\{t : y_i(t, u_i) = a_i\}$ defines a single-valued, continuous map $M : \mathcal{U}_i \to [R_i, D_i]$. Finally, since $\mathcal{U}_i$ is path connected, there is a continuous path in $\mathcal{U}_i$ connecting the inputs corresponding to R_i and D_i. The image of a continuous path under a continuous map is a continuous path, connecting points R_i and D_i, and therefore covers the whole interval $[R_i, D_i]$, that is, M is surjective. $\square$

Now define the quantity

$$\delta_{max} := \max_{i \in \{1, \ldots, n\}} \sup_{x_i(0) \in X_i : y_i(0) = a_i} \{t : y_i(t, u_{i,max}) = b_i\}.$$
$$(12)$$

This is the minimum worst-case time necessary for y_i to go from a_i to b_i. From here on we assume the hypotheses of Lemma 5.1. This implies that there exists an input $u_i \in \mathcal{U}_i$ such that $y_i(T_i, u_i) = a_i$, and using (12) that $y_i(T_i + \delta_{max}, u_i) \geq b_i$, so that by the definition of $P_i(T_i)$, $P_i(T_i) \leq T_i + \delta_{max}$. We modify Problem 1 as follows.

Problem 2 (Approximation) *Given initial conditions $\mathbf{x}(0)$, determine if there exists a schedule $\mathbf{T} = (T_1, \ldots, T_n) \in \mathbb{R}^n$ such that, for all i,*

$$R_i \leq T_i \leq D_i,$$

and for all $i \neq j$, if $T_j = 0$ then

$$T_i \geq T_j \Rightarrow T_i \geq P_j(T_j),$$

if $T_j > 0$ then

$$T_i \geq T_j \Rightarrow T_i \geq T_j + \delta_{max}.$$

Any schedule that satisfies Problem 2 also satisfies Problem 1, since $T_j + \delta_{max} \geq P_j(T_j)$. By solving Problem 2 however, we allocate the resource (the intersection) for more time that is strictly needed by each agent. We are thus trading maximum traffic flow with computational speed.

By (4) $R_i = 0 \Leftrightarrow D_i = 0$, and agents with $R_i = D_i = 0$ do not contribute to the combinatorial complexity of Problem 1 as T_i has a unique possible value. By normalizing the data of Problem 2 to make $\delta_{max} = 1$, and then setting $R_i = r_i$, $D_i = d_i - 1$, $T_i = T_i$, Problem 2 for agents with $R_i, D_i > 0$ becomes formally equivalent to $DEC(1|r_i, p_i = 1|Lmax, 0)$, which is solved in polynomial time by Algorithm 1. Algorithm 3 solves Problem 2 treating separately agents with $y_i(0) \geq a_i$, for which $R_i = D_i = 0$, and agents with $y_i(0) < a_i$. In the pseudocode of APPROXIMATESOLUTION, without loss of generality, we assume that $y_i(0) \geq a_i$ for $i = 1, \ldots, m$, and $y_i(0) < a_i$ for $i = m+1, \ldots, n$. Since Algorithm 3 provides

---

Algorithm 3 Solution of Problem 2

1: **procedure** APPROXIMATESOLUTION($\mathbf{x}(0)$)
2:     **for all** $i \in \{1, \ldots, n\}$ **do** given $x_i(0)$ calculate R_i, D_i
3:     **end for**
4:     **if** $y_i(0) \in [a_i, b_i)$ for two different $i \in \{1, \ldots, m\}$ **then**
5:         **return** $\{\emptyset, \text{no}\}$
6:     **end if**
7:     **for all** $i \in \{1, \ldots, m\}$ **do** $T_i \leftarrow 0$
8:     **end for**
9:     $R_{bound} \leftarrow \max\{P_1(0), \ldots, P_m(0)\}$
10:     **for all** $i \in \{m+1, \ldots, n\}$ **do** $R_i \leftarrow \max(R_i, R_{bound})$
11:     **end for**
12:     set δ_{max} as in (12)
13:     $\mathbf{r} = (R_{m+1}/\delta_{max}, \ldots, R_n/\delta_{max})$
14:     $\mathbf{d} = (D_{m+1}/\delta_{max} + 1, \ldots, D_n/\delta_{max} + 1)$
15:     $\{T_{m+1}, \ldots, T_n, \text{answer}\} = \text{POLYNOMIALTIME}(\mathbf{r}, \mathbf{d})$
16:     **for** $i = m+1 \rightarrow n$ **do** $T_i \leftarrow T_i \delta_{max}$
17:     **end for**
18:     **return** $\{\mathbf{T}, \text{answer}\}$
19: **end procedure**

---

an approximate solution to Problem 1, we need a measure of the quality of this solution. We perform this by providing an upper bound to the quantity $\sup_{\mathbf{u} \in \mathcal{U}} \inf_{t \geq 0, b \in B_+} \|\mathbf{y}(t, \mathbf{u}) - b\|_\infty$, calculated over all $\mathbf{x}(0)$ for which Algorithm 3 returns "no". This is the maximum over all possible inputs $\mathbf{u} \in \mathcal{U}$ of the distance of $\mathbf{y}(t, \mathbf{u})$ from the bad set B_+, and, as such, it gives a measure of how much Algorithm 3 "overestimates" B_+. To provide the upper bound we first introduce the following result.

Lemma 5.2 *For a given* $\mathbf{x}(0)$, *take an arbitrary* $\mathbf{u} \in \mathcal{U}$, *and define a schedule* $\mathbf{T}$ *as* $T_i = \{t : y_i(t, u_i) = a_i\}$ *for all* i *such that* $y_i(0) < a_i$, *and* $T_i = 0$ *for all other* i. *Assume that, for some* i *and* j, $y_i(0) < a_i$, $y_j(0) \leq a_j$, $T_i \geq T_j$, *and* $T_i - T_j \leq \delta_{max}$, *that is, two jobs are scheduled within* δ_{max}

---

of each other. Then

$$\inf_{t \geq 0, b \in B_+} \|\mathbf{y}(t, \mathbf{u}) - b\|_\infty \leq \max_{i \in \{1, \ldots, n\}} \dot{y}_{i,max} \left(\delta_{max} - \frac{b_i - a_i}{\dot{y}_{i,max}} \right),$$

PROOF. Since $\dot{y}_j \leq \dot{y}_{j,max}$, y_j remains in the interval (a_j, b_j) for a time interval greater or equal to $(b_j - a_j)/\dot{y}_{j,max}$, therefore $y_j(T_i, u_j) - b_j \leq \dot{y}_{j,max} \left(\delta_{max} - \frac{b_j - a_j}{\dot{y}_{j,max}} \right)$, while $y_i(T_i, u_i) = a_i$. The set of points in Y with $y_i = a_i$, $y_j = b_j$ is on the boundary of B_+, therefore

$$\inf_{b \in B_+} \|\mathbf{y}(T_i, \mathbf{u}) - b\|_\infty \leq y_j(T_i, u_j) - b_j \leq$$
$$\max_{i \in \{1, \ldots, n\}} \dot{y}_{i,max} \left(\delta_{max} - \frac{b_i - a_i}{\dot{y}_{i,max}} \right).$$

$\square$

Theorem 5.3 *If for a given* $\mathbf{x}(0)$ APPROXIMATESOLUTION *returns "no", then*

$$\sup_{\mathbf{u} \in \mathcal{U}} \inf_{t \geq 0, b \in B_+} \|\mathbf{y}(t, \mathbf{u}) - b\|_\infty \leq \\ \max_{i \in \{1, \ldots, n\}} \dot{y}_{i,max} \left(\delta_{max} - \frac{b_i - a_i}{\dot{y}_{i,max}} \right). \quad (13)$$

PROOF. APPROXIMATESOLUTION returns "no" if $y_i(0) \in [a_i, b_i)$ for two different i, or if POLYNOMIALTIME at line 15 returns "no". In the first case the left hand side of (13) is equal to 0, since $\mathbf{y}(0)$ is on the boundary of B_+, and (13) is verified. In the second case, if POLYNOMIALTIME returns "no" then, for any schedule $\mathbf{T}$ with $T_i \in [R_i, D_i]$ for all i, there exist i and j with $y_i(0) < a_i$, $y_j(0) < a_j$, $T_j \leq T_i$, such that $T_i - T_j < \delta_{max}$. This is a consequence of the fact that POLYNOMIALTIME solves $DEC(1|r_i, p_i = 1|Lmax, 0)$ exactly. By the reasoning above, for any $\mathbf{u} \in \mathcal{U}$, the schedule $\mathbf{T}$ defined by $T_i = \{t : y_i(t, u_i) = a_i\}$ if $y_i(0) < a_i$, $T_i = 0$ otherwise, has $T_i \in [R_i, D_i]$ for all i, and satisfies the hypotheses of Lemma 5.2. This completes the proof. $\square$

According to the above theorem, if APPROXIMATESOLUTION cannot find a feasible schedule for an initial condition $\mathbf{x}(0)$, then all outputs $\mathbf{y}(t, \mathbf{u})$ with $\mathbf{u} \in \mathcal{U}$ intersect the *extended bad set*

$$\hat{B}_+ := \\ \left\{ \mathbf{y} : \inf_{b \in B_+} \|\mathbf{y} - b\|_\infty \leq \max_{i \in \{1, \ldots, n\}} \dot{y}_{i,max} \left(\delta_{max} - \frac{b_i - a_i}{\dot{y}_{i,max}} \right) \right\}. \quad (14)$$

6. SOLUTION OF PROBLEM B

Problem B requires to design a supervisor that, given the current state of the system and a desired input, returns the desired input if this does not cause a collision at some future time, or a safe input otherwise. Thus, the input returned by the supervisor must keep the state of system (1) within the maximal controlled invariant set. As we have seen in the previous sections, membership in this set is determined by solving Problem A or its scheduling version, Problem 1. In Section 5 we have provided an exact and an approximate algorithm to solve these problems. We can exploit these algorithms in the solution of Problem B by designing the supervised system as a hybrid system. This is obtained from matching the continuous dynamics of (1) with a discrete-time control map. At the k-th iteration, the control map takes as arguments the current state $\mathbf{x}(k\tau)$ and desired (constant) value $\mathbf{v}_k \in U$ of the input for $t \in [k\tau, (k+1)\tau]$, and returns an input signal $\mathbf{u}_{out}$, with value in U, defined for $t \in [k\tau, (k+1)\tau]$. The choice of the returned input signal is based on the solution of Problem 1. The sought supervisor is the map $s : (\mathbf{x}(k\tau), \mathbf{v}_k) \mapsto \mathbf{u}_{out}$. To give a precise meaning to the statement of Problem B, we must formally define the conditions under which a desired input may cause a collision. Given $\mathbf{v}_k$, consider the two signals $\bar{\mathbf{u}}_k$ and $\bar{\mathbf{u}}_k^\infty$ defined as follows: the first is defined on the interval $[k\tau, (k+1)\tau]$ and identically equal to $\mathbf{v}_k$; the second is an element of $\mathcal{U}$ defined on $[k\tau, \infty)$, and such that $\bar{\mathbf{u}}_k^\infty(t) = \bar{\mathbf{u}}_k(t)$ when $t \in [k\tau, (k+1)\tau]$. Additionally, given $\mathbf{x}(k\tau)$, call $\mathbf{u}_{k,safe}^\infty(t) \in \mathcal{U}$ a control signal such that $\mathbf{y}(t, \mathbf{u}_{k,safe}^\infty, \mathbf{x}(k\tau)) \notin B_+$ for all $t \geq k\tau$ (if such control exists), and call $\mathbf{u}_{k,safe}$ the restriction of $\mathbf{u}_{k,safe}^\infty$ to the interval $[k\tau, (k+1)\tau]$. If $\mathbf{u}_{k,safe}^\infty$ does not exists, let $\mathbf{u}_{k,safe}^\infty, \mathbf{u}_{k,safe} = \emptyset$. Problem B is formally stated as follows

Problem B (Supervisor, formal statement) *Design the supervisor $s(\mathbf{x}(k\tau), \mathbf{v}_k)$ for system (1) such that*

$$s(\mathbf{x}(k\tau), \mathbf{v}_k) = \begin{cases} \bar{\mathbf{u}}_k & if \ \exists \, \bar{\mathbf{u}}_k^\infty(t) \in \mathcal{U} : \\ & \mathbf{y}(t, \bar{\mathbf{u}}_k^\infty, \mathbf{x}(k\tau)) \notin B_+ \forall t \geq k\tau \\ \mathbf{u}_{k,safe} & otherwise, \end{cases}$$

and so that it is non-blocking: if $\mathbf{u}_{out} = s(\mathbf{x}(k\tau), \mathbf{u}_k) \neq \emptyset$, then for any $\mathbf{v}_{k+1}$, $k \geq 0$, $s(\mathbf{x}((k+1)\tau, \mathbf{u}_{out}, \mathbf{x}(k\tau)), \mathbf{v}_{k+1}) \neq \emptyset$.

Given a system of the form (1) and the state $\mathbf{x}(k\tau)$ at some time $k\tau$, the procedure EXACTSOLUTION in Algorithm 2 returns a binary value (*yes/no*), and a schedule $\mathbf{T}$. We can use this information to design the supervisor in Problem B. To this end, introduce the operator $\sigma(x_i(0), T_i)$, associated to the function $P_i(T_i)$. For all agents with $y_i(0) \leq a_i$, let

$$\sigma(x_i(0), T_i) := \arg \inf_{u_i \in \mathcal{U}} \{t \geq 0 : y_i(t, u_i) = b_i\}, \qquad (15)$$

with constraint

$$y_i(t, u_i) \leq a_i \, \forall \, t < T_i, \qquad (16)$$

This is the input u_i that brings $y(t, u_i, x_i)$ at b_i at $t = P_i(T_i)$ (see (5)). If the constraint cannot be satisfied, set $\sigma(x_i(0), T_i) := \emptyset$. If $y_i(0) \in (a_i, b_i)$ define $\sigma(x_i(0), T_i) := u_{i,max}$, and if $y_i(0) \geq b_i$ define $\sigma(x_i(0), T_i) := 0$. If the input is not unique, let σ return one among the possible solutions. Call $\sigma(\mathbf{x}(0), \mathbf{T})$ the vector $(\sigma(x_1(0), T_1), \ldots, \sigma(x_n(0), T_n))$. Assume that, at $t = 0$, we have EXACTSOLUTION$(\mathbf{x}(0)) = \{\mathbf{T}_0, yes\}$, and define $\mathbf{u}_{0,safe}^\infty = \sigma(\mathbf{x}_0, \mathbf{T}_0)$ and $\mathbf{u}_{0,safe}$ as the restriction of $\mathbf{u}_{0,safe}^\infty$ to the time interval $[0, \tau]$. At each iteration $k = 0, 1, 2, \ldots$, the supervisor map $s(\mathbf{x}(k\tau), \mathbf{v}_k)$ is defined by Algorithm 4, using the current state $\mathbf{x}(k\tau)$, the desired input $\mathbf{v}_k$, and the value $\mathbf{u}_{k,safe}$ calculated at the previous iteration. The algorithm returns $\bar{\mathbf{u}}_k$ (the desired input), if the state reached with this input is within the maximal controlled invariant set; otherwise it returns $\mathbf{u}_{k,safe}$. To prove that Algorithm 4 correctly solves Problem B, we use the two following lemmas as intermediate results.

Lemma 6.1 *If* EXACTSOLUTION$(\mathbf{x}(k\tau)) = \{\mathbf{T}, yes\}$, *then* $\sigma(\mathbf{x}(k\tau), \mathbf{T}) \neq \emptyset$.

PROOF. The existence of an input $\sigma(\mathbf{x}(k\tau), \mathbf{T})$ corresponding to the schedule $\mathbf{T}$ is proved as in the proof of Theorem 4.1. $\square$

Algorithm 4 Implementation of the supervisor map

```
1: procedure s(x(kτ), v_k)
2:    ū_k(t) ← v_k ∀ t ∈ [kτ, (k+1)τ]
3:    {T, answer} ←
4:        EXACTSOLUTION(x((k+1)τ, ū_k, x(kτ)))
5:    if answer = yes then
6:        u^∞_{k+1,safe} ← σ(x((k+1)τ, ū_k, x(kτ)), T)
7:        u_{k+1,safe} ← u^∞_{k+1,safe} restricted to [kτ, (k+1)τ]
8:        return ū_k
9:    else
10:       {T, answer} ←
11:           EXACTSOLUTION(x((k+1)τ, u_{k,safe}, x(kτ)))
12:       u^∞_{k+1,safe} ← σ(x((k+1)τ, u_{k,safe}, x(kτ)), T)
13:       u_{k+1,safe} ← u^∞_{k+1,safe} restricted to [kτ, (k+1)τ]
14:       return u_{k,safe}
15:   end if
16: end procedure
```

Lemma 6.2 *If* EXACTSOLUTION$(\mathbf{x}(k\tau)) = \{\mathbf{T}, yes\}$, *defining* $\mathbf{u} := \sigma(\mathbf{x}(k\tau), \mathbf{T})$, EXACTSOLUTION$(\mathbf{x}((k+1)\tau, \mathbf{u}, \mathbf{x}(k\tau)))$ *returns "yes".*

PROOF. The input $\mathbf{u}$ is well defined by Lemma 6.1. Call $\mathbf{y}(t, \mathbf{u}, \mathbf{x}(k\tau))$ the corresponding output trajectory, defined from time $(k\tau)$, and let $\tilde{\mathbf{u}}$ be $\mathbf{u}$ restricted to the interval $[(k+1)\tau, \infty)$. Clearly if $\mathbf{y}(t, \mathbf{u}, \mathbf{x}(k\tau)) \cap B_+ = \emptyset$, then $\mathbf{y}(t, \tilde{\mathbf{u}}, \mathbf{x}((k+1)\tau, \mathbf{u}, \mathbf{x}(k\tau)) \cap B_+ = \emptyset$, therefore $\{\mathbf{x}((k+1)\tau, \mathbf{u}, \mathbf{x}(k\tau)), \Theta\} \in$ Problem A, with Θ defined by (3). Since Problem A $\simeq$ Problem 1, $\{\mathbf{x}((k+1)\tau, \mathbf{u}, \mathbf{x}(k\tau)), \Theta\} \in$ Problem 1. $\square$

Theorem 6.3 *Assume that $s(\mathbf{x}(0), \mathbf{v}_0) \neq \emptyset$. Then, the supervisor $s(\mathbf{x}(k\tau), \mathbf{v}_k)$ defined by Algorithm 4 solves Problem B.*

PROOF. To be a solution of Problem B, $s(\mathbf{x}(k\tau), \mathbf{v}_k)$ (i) must return $\bar{\mathbf{u}}_k$ unless all possible $\bar{\mathbf{u}}_k^\infty$ would eventually cause a collision and (ii) it must be nonblocking.

To prove (i), note that Algorithm 4 returns $\bar{\mathbf{u}}_k$ unless EXACTSOLUTION at line 4 returns "no". If 4 returns "no", then $\{\mathbf{x}((k+1)\tau, \bar{\mathbf{u}}, \mathbf{x}(k\tau)), \Theta\} \notin$ Problem 1, and by equivalence of Problems A and 1, $\{\mathbf{x}((k+1)\tau, \bar{\mathbf{u}}, \mathbf{x}(k\tau)), \Theta\} \notin$ Problem A. Thus by definition of Problem A and of $\bar{\mathbf{u}}_k^\infty$, for all $\bar{\mathbf{u}}_k^\infty$, $\mathbf{y}(t, \bar{\mathbf{u}}_k^\infty, \mathbf{x}(k\tau)) \cap B_+ \neq \emptyset$.

To prove (ii) we can proceed by induction: by assumption $s(\mathbf{x}(0), \mathbf{v}_0) \neq \emptyset$, and we must show that if $\mathbf{u}_{out} = s(\mathbf{x}(k\tau), \mathbf{v}_k) \neq \emptyset$, then $s(\mathbf{x}((k+1)\tau, \mathbf{u}_{out}, \mathbf{x}(k\tau)), \mathbf{v}_{k+1}) \neq \emptyset$. First notice that $s(\mathbf{x}((k+1)\tau, \mathbf{u}_{out}, \mathbf{x}(k\tau)), \mathbf{v}_{k+1}) \neq \emptyset$ as long as $\mathbf{u}_{k+1,safe} \neq \emptyset$, so all we have to do is to show that $\mathbf{u}_{k+1,safe} \neq \emptyset$. State $\mathbf{x}((k+1)\tau, \mathbf{u}_{out}, \mathbf{x}(k\tau))$ is reached either with an input $\mathbf{u}_{out} = \bar{\mathbf{u}}$ (lines 5-8 in Algorithm 4) or $\mathbf{u}_{out} = \mathbf{u}_{k,safe}$ (lines 9-14). In the first case, by Lemma 6.1 line 4 of Algorithm 4 ensures that σ at line 6 is nonempty. In the second case, by Lemma 6.2 the procedure EXACTSOLUTION at line 11 must return $\{\mathbf{T}, yes\}$, and by Lemma 6.1 this implies that σ at line 12 is nonempty. $\square$

Notice that, if the step τ is increased, the "restrictiveness" of Algorithm 4 is unaffected. Indeed, for any value of τ the algorithm returns the desired input if and only if this does not cause collisions. The size of τ is thus only a matter of engineering and design convenience.

Algorithm 4 is based on the procedure EXACTSOLUTION, whose running time scales factorially with the number of agents. Therefore, it can be applied only to relatively small problems. To achieve a control law that scales polynomially with the number of controlled agents, we proceed as follows. Define σ_{approx} as σ in (15) with constraint (16) replaced by $y_i(T_i, u_i) = a_i$. Notice that Lemma 5.1 ensures that an input satisfying this constraint exists if $y_i(0) \leq a_i$ and $T_i \in [R_i, D_i]$. Then, at lines 4 and 11 of Algorithm 4 substitute EXACTSOLUTION with APPROXIMATESOLUTION defined by Algorithm 3, and at lines 6 and 12 substitute σ with σ_{approx}.

Through the substitution, the supervisor retains the non-blocking property defined by Problem B, but it allows only a subset of all collision-free trajectories. More precisely we have the following result.

Theorem 6.4 *Consider the extended bad set $\hat{B}_+$ defined in (14). Call $\hat{s}(\mathbf{x}(k\tau), \mathbf{v}_k)$ the supervisor defined in Problem B substituting $\hat{B}_+$ to B_+, and call $s_{approx}(\mathbf{x}(k\tau), \mathbf{v}_k)$ the supervisor defined by Algorithm 4 modified as detailed above. Then $s_{approx}(\mathbf{x}(k\tau), \mathbf{v}_k)$ is no more restrictive than $\hat{s}(\mathbf{x}(k\tau), \mathbf{v}_k)$, that is, if $s_{approx}(\mathbf{x}(k\tau), \mathbf{v}_k) = \mathbf{u}_{k,safe}$ then $\hat{s}(\mathbf{x}(k\tau), \mathbf{v}_k) = \mathbf{u}_{k,safe}$. Moreover if $s_{approx}(\mathbf{x}(0), \mathbf{v}_0) \neq \emptyset$ then the supervisor is non-blocking in the sense defined in Problem B.*

To prove this result we use two intermediate lemmas.

Lemma 6.5 *If APPROXIMATESOLUTION$(\mathbf{x}(k\tau)) = \{\mathbf{T}, yes\}$, then $\sigma_{approx}(\mathbf{x}(k\tau), \mathbf{T}) \neq \emptyset$.*

PROOF. By the definition of Problems 1 and 2, APPROXIMATESOLUTION$(\mathbf{x}(k\tau)) = \{\mathbf{T}, yes\}$ implies that EXACTSOLUTION$(\mathbf{x}(k\tau)) = \{\mathbf{T}, yes\}$, the result follows from Lemma 6.1. $\square$

Lemma 6.6 *If APPROXIMATESOLUTION$(\mathbf{x}(k\tau)) = \{\mathbf{T}, yes\}$, defining $\mathbf{u} := \sigma_{approx}(\mathbf{x}(k\tau), \mathbf{T})$, APPROXIMATESOLUTION$(\mathbf{x}((k+1)\tau, \mathbf{u}, \mathbf{x}(k\tau))$ returns "yes".*

PROOF. Assume, without loss of generality, that $\mathbf{y}(k\tau)$ is such that $y_i(k\tau) \geq a_i$ for $i \in \{1, \dots, m\}$, while $y_i(k\tau) < a_i$ for all other agents. Also, assume that $\mathbf{y}((k+1)\tau, \mathbf{u}, \mathbf{x}(k\tau))$ is such that $y_i((k+1)\tau, u_i, x_i(k\tau)) \geq a_i$ for $i \in \{1, \dots, p\}$ with $p \geq m$, while $y_i((k+1)\tau, u_i, x_i(k\tau)) < a_i$ for all other agents. APPROXIMATESOLUTION$(\mathbf{x}((k+1)\tau, \mathbf{u}, \mathbf{x}(k\tau))$ returns a positive answer provided that (i) no more than one of the agents $1, \dots, p$ are in $[a_i, b_i]$ and (ii) POLYNOMIAL-TIME at line 15 finds a feasible schedule. (i) is ensured by condition APPROXIMATESOLUTION$(\mathbf{x}(k\tau)) = \{\mathbf{T}, yes\}$ and by having $\mathbf{u} := \sigma_{approx}(\mathbf{x}(k\tau), \mathbf{T})$. To have (ii) POLYNOMI-ALTIME must find a feasible schedule. According to Definition 2.2, this is a schedule $\mathbf{T}$ such that $\mathbf{T}_i \in [\mathbf{r}_i, \mathbf{d}_i]$, and such that $|\mathbf{T}_i - \mathbf{T}_j| \geq 1$ for all $i \neq j$. Since POLYNOMI-ALTIME solves $DEC(1|\mathbf{r}_i, \mathbf{p}_i = 1|\mathbf{Lmax}, 0)$ exactly, it always returns a positive answer if a feasible schedule exists. Since APPROXIMATESOLUTION$(\mathbf{x}(k\tau)) = \{\mathbf{T}, yes\}$, elements of $\mathbf{T}$ corresponding to agents $m+1, \dots, n$ satisfy $|T_i - T_j| \geq \delta_{max}$ for $i \neq j$. By the definition of σ_{approx}, $y_i(T_i + k\tau, u_i, x_i(k\tau)) = a_i$. Consider $\mathbf{x}((k+1)\tau) := \mathbf{x}((k+1)\tau, \mathbf{u}, \mathbf{x}(k\tau))$, and the input $\tilde{\mathbf{u}}$ equal to $\mathbf{u}$ restricted to the interval $[(k+1)\tau, \infty)$. For all $i \in \{p, \dots, n\}$, call $T_i' = \{t : y_i(t, \tilde{u}_i, x_i((k+1)\tau)\} = a_i$, and call R_i' and D_i' the quantities defined in (4) with respect to initial condition $x_i((k+1)\tau)$. For all such i, $T_i' = T_i - \tau$, therefore all T_i' are at least at distance δ_{max} from each

other. Moreover, $T_i' \in [R_i', D_i']$ by construction. The schedule $\mathbf{T} = (T_p'/\delta_{max}, \dots, T_n'/\delta_{max})$ is thus a feasible schedule for $DEC(1|\mathbf{r}_i, \mathbf{p}_i = 1|\mathbf{Lmax}, 0)$. $\square$

PROOF OF THEOREM 6.4. By Theorem 5.3 and by (14), the procedure APPROXIMATESOLUTION returns "yes" if there is an input that keeps the state outside of $\hat{B}_+$, thus $s_{approx}(\mathbf{x}(k\tau), \mathbf{v}_k)$ is no more restrictive than $\hat{s}(\mathbf{x}(k\tau), \mathbf{v}_k)$. To prove nonblockingness, one can proceed as in the proof of nonblockingness of Theorem 6.3, substituting Lemmas 6.5 and 6.6 and procedure APPROXIMATESOLUTION to Lemmas 6.1 and 6.2 and procedure EXACTSOLUTION. $\square$

7. EXAMPLES

To compute the quantities $P_i(T_i)$ and σ or σ_{approx} required by Algorithm 4, we must solve an optimization problem on the set of inputs $\mathcal{U}$. In general, such a problem may be solved numerically [7, 16]. For illustration purposes, here we discuss the case in which $f_i(x, u)$ in (2) is a double integrator with saturation on the input function:

$$f_i(x_i, u_i) = \begin{pmatrix} 0 & 1 \\ 0 & 0 \end{pmatrix} x_i + \begin{pmatrix} 0 \\ C \end{pmatrix} u, \quad h(x_i) = (1, 0) \cdot x_i,$$

$$(17)$$

with $x_i \in \mathbb{R}^2$ and $u_i \in \mathbb{R}$, where

$$C := \begin{cases} 1 \text{ if } (0,1) \cdot x_i \in (\dot{y}_{i,min}, \dot{y}_{i,max}) \text{ or} \\ \quad (0,1) \cdot x_i = \dot{y}_{i,max} \text{ and } u_i < 0 \text{ or} \\ \quad (0,1) \cdot x_i = \dot{y}_{i,min} \text{ and } u_i > 0 \\ 0 \text{ otherwise.} \end{cases}$$

The quantity $y_i = (1, 0) \cdot x_i$ is the position of agent i along its path, while $\dot{y}_i = (0, 1) \cdot x_i$ is the velocity. This is a simple model of longitudinal vehicle dynamics when friction is negligible, and it satisfies the assumptions of Section 3 and of Lemma 5.1. Notice that the presented algorithm can handle more general models, including linear and nonlinear friction terms, such as those discussed in [25].

In the case of equations (17), the optimization problem on $\mathcal{U}$ is solved analytically using standard variational calculus [16, 20]. When no feasible input allows to reach a_i at time T_i with $\dot{y}_i(T_i) = \dot{y}_{i,max}$, extremal solutions can be proved to have the signal u_i composed of three segments with values $u_{i,min}, 0, u_{i,max}$ (in this order), or two segments with values $u_{i,min}, u_{i,max}$ (in this order), or a single segment with value $u_{i,min}$ or $u_{i,max}$. In the case that $\dot{y}_{i,max}$ can be attained before reaching a_i, there exists a continuum of optimal solutions. Since σ and σ_{approx} are required to return a unique solution, in these cases we fix their image to the unique optimal solution obtained with input sequence $u_{i,min}, 0, u_{i,max}, 0$.

Using the optimal inputs defined above to construct σ and σ_{approx}, we have implemented the supervisor described by Algorithm 4, for a set of identical agents with dynamics described by (17), with $\dot{y}_{i,min} = 5Km/h$ ($1.39m/s$), $\dot{y}_{i,max} = 50Km/h$ ($13.9m/s$), $u_{i,min} = -2m/s^2$, $u_{i,max} = 1m/s^2$, and an interval (a_i, b_i) that is $10m$ wide for all agents. The supervisor runs at discrete time steps of length $\tau = 1/10s$. In all cases, we have assigned to each agent a fixed "desired speed", that the driver tries to maintain, by accelerating or braking if necessary, unless forced to a different input by the supervisor. For a 3-agent system, Figure 2 represents a "slice" in the space Y, for fixed velocities $\dot{\mathbf{y}}(0) = (9, 11, 13)$ m/s, of the complement of the maximal controlled invariant

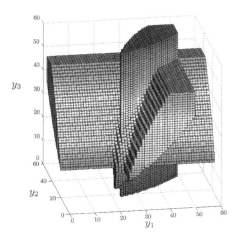

Figure 2: Complement of the maximal controlled invariant set, in the space Y for fixed velocities. Axes are in meters. For all agents, $(a_i, b_i) = (40, 50)$.

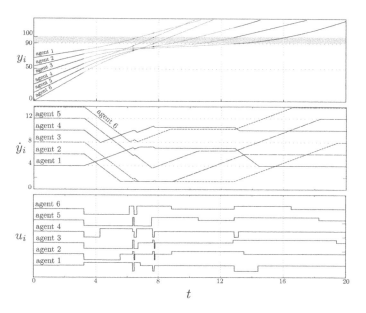

Figure 3: Positions (y_i), velocities $(\dot{y}_i)$, and input (u_i) of 6 agents controlled by the supervisor in Algorithm 4, using ExactSolution and σ. The interval $(a_i, b_i) = (90, 100)$ is represented in gray and equal for all agents. Position curves are in black when the supervisor accepts the agents' desired inputs, in red when the supervisor overrides the desired input.

set. Computing this set for systems with large state space is known to be a hard problem, and research has been focusing on calculating approximations [23]. The procedure EXACT-SOLUTION in Algorithm 2, exploiting the system's structure, provides a practical technique to determine if a state is inside this set for few agents (0.01 seconds for 6 agents on a modern laptop). Using the procedure APPROXIMATESOLUTION in Algorithm 3, the same test can be executed approximately, with error bound given by Theorem 5.3, on much larger problems. Figures 3 and 4 depict the trajectories of six agents controlled by the supervisor, using EXACTSOLUTION and σ, or APPROXIMATESOLUTION and σ_{approx}, respectively. The interval $(a_i, b_i) = (90, 100)$ (in gray) is equal for all agents. In these simulations, the initial positions and velocities were selected so that, in the absence of supervisor, all agents would enter the interval (a_i, b_i) at the same time. For the sake of simplicity, we let Algorithm 4 return an input (desired input, or override) for all agents, before and after the intersection. Agents past the intersection could apply an arbitrary input without affecting safety, but including this option would make the algorithm longer without adding significant insight.

Notice that, while in Figure 3 agents occupy the gray band in contiguous time intervals, in Figure 4 there is some idle time between the instant when an agent leaves the gray band and when following agent enters it. The maximum distance of the trajectory in Figure 4 from B_+ is bounded as proved in Theorem 5.3. For the parameters specified above, the bound is equal to $35.77m$. To prove that this bound is tight, we have repeated the simulation for 15 agents with the same parameters as above. The result is shown in Figure 5, where the trajectory reaches the bound exactly.

8. CONCLUSIONS

We have considered the problem of determining membership in the maximal controlled invariant set for a general class of systems describing vehicle dynamics at an intersection. Using results from the scheduling literature and computational complexity theory we have proved that the exact

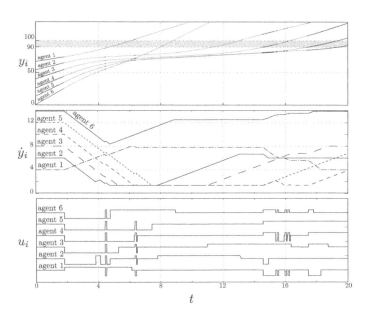

Figure 4: The same numerical experiment of Figure 3 is executed using the supervisor in Algorithm 4, using ApproximateSolution and σ_{approx}.

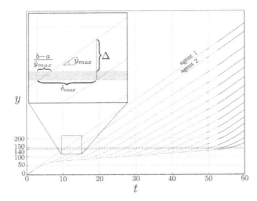

Figure 5: 15 agents supervised using Algorithm 4, with procedure ApproximateSolution. The bound given in Theorem 5.3, here denoted Δ, is reached exactly by the trajectory.

solution of this problem is NP-complete. We have proposed an approximate solution whose running time scales polynomially with the number of agents. Based on these results, we have designed the least restrictive supervisor (solving Problem B exactly), whose running time scales factorially with the number of controlled agents. The supervised system has a hybrid structure, where the continuous dynamics of the agents are controlled based on the result of a scheduling problem solved at regular time intervals. By modifying this supervisor, we have obtained an approximate solution with polynomial running time, and we have provided a tight bound on the approximation. The supervisor acts as a filter between a desired input, here assumed to be generated by the driver, and the physical system. This structure is easily coupled with other controllers, acting between the driver input and the supervisor, to pursue secondary performance objectives within the set of safe control actions allowed by the supervisor.

The results presented here assume that each agent moves along a different path and computes the exact or approximate supervisor through a centralised algorithm. We are currently working on relaxing both constraints, allowing multiple agents to move on the same path or along merging paths, and implementing the solution as a distributed algorithm, to further improve scalability.

9. REFERENCES

[1] Car 2 Car Communication Consortium. http://www.car-to-car.org.

[2] Cooperative Intersection Collision Avoidance Systems (CICAS). http://www.its.dot.gov/cicas.

[3] Vehicle Infrastructure Integration Consortium (VIIC). http://www.vehicle-infrastructure.org.

[4] D. Angeli and E. D. Sontag. Monotone control systems. *IEEE Trans. Autom. Control*, 48:1684–1698, 2003.

[5] A. Colombo and D. Del Vecchio. Supervisory control of differentially flat systems based on abstraction. In *50th IEEE Conference on Decision and Control*, 2011.

[6] T. H. Cormen, C. E. Leiserson, R. L. Rivest, and C. Stein. *Introduction to Algorithms*. MIT Press, 2009.

[7] B. Dacorogna. *Direct Methods in the Calculus of Variations*. Springer, 2008.

[8] B. A. Davey and H. A. Priestley. *Introduction to Lattices and Order*. Cambridge University Press, 2002.

[9] V. Desaraju, H. C. Ro, M. Yang, E. Tay, S. Roth, and D. Del Vecchio. Partial order techniques for vehicle collision avoidance: Application to an autonomous roundabout test-bed. In *ICRA '09. IEEE International Conference on Robotics and Automation*, 2009.

[10] J. Duperret, M. Hafner, and D. Del Vecchio. Formal design of a provably safe robotic roundabout system. In *Proc. of IEEE/RSJ International Conference on Intelligent Robots and Systems*, 2010.

[11] A. F. Filippov. *Differential Equations with Discontinuous Righthand Sides*. Kluwer Academic Publishers, Dordrecht, 1988.

[12] M. R. Garey, D. S. Johnson, B. B. Simons, and R. E. Tarjan. Scheduling unit-time tasks with arbitrary release times and deadlines. *SIAM J. Comput.*, 6:416–426, 1981.

[13] R. L. Graham, E. L. Lawler, J. K. Lenstra, and A. H. G Rinnooy Kan. Optimization and approximation in deterministic sequencing and scheduling: a survey. *Annals of discrete mathematics*, 4:287–326, 1979.

[14] M. R. Hafner, D. Cunningham, L. Caminiti, and D. Del Vecchio. Automated vehicle-to-vehicle collision avoidance at intersections. In *Proc. of ITS World Congress*, 2011.

[15] M. R. Hafner and D. Del Vecchio. Computational tools for the safety control of a class of piecewise continuous systems with imperfect information on a partial order. *SIAM J. Contr. Opt.*, To Appear.

[16] E. Bryson Jr. and Y. Ho. *Applied optimal control*. Ginn and Company, 1969.

[17] H. K. Khalil. *Nonlinear systems*. Prentice-Hall, 2002.

[18] H. Kowshik, D. Caveney, and P. R. Kumar. Provable systemwide safety in intelligent intersections. *IEEE Trans. Veh. Technol.*, 60:804–818, 2011.

[19] J. K. Lenstra, A. H. G. Rinnooy Kan, and P. Brucker. Complexity of machine scheduling problems. *Annals of discrete mathematics*, 1:343–362, 1977.

[20] D. G. Luenberger. *Optimization by vector space methods*. Wiley, 1969.

[21] J. Lygeros, C. Tomlin, and S. Sastry. Controllers for reachability specifications for hybrid systems. *Automatica*, 35:349–370, 1999.

[22] M. L. Pinedo. *Scheduling: Theory, Algorithms, and Systems*. Springer, 2008.

[23] C. J. Tomlin, I. Mitchell, A. M. Bayen, and M. Oishi. Computational techniques for the verification of hybrid systems. *Proc. IEEE*, 91:986–1001, 2003.

[24] U.S. Department of Transportation. ITS Strategic Research Plan 2010-2014. http://www.its.dot.gov/strategic_plan2010_2014/.

[25] R. Verma, D. Del Vecchio, and H. K. Fathy. Development of a scaled vehicle with longitudinal dynamics of an HMMWV for an ITS testbed. *IEEE/ASME Transactions on Mechatronics*, 13:1–12, 2008.

Parameter Estimation for Stochastic Hybrid Models of Biochemical Reaction Networks

Linar Mikeev, Verena Wolf

Computer Science Department
Saarland University
Saarbrücken, Germany
{mikeev,wolf}@cs.uni-saarland.de

ABSTRACT

The dynamics of biochemical reaction networks can be accurately described by stochastic hybrid models, where we assume that large chemical populations evolve deterministically and continuously over time while small populations change through random discrete reactions.

We propose an algorithm for estimating the parameters of a given biochemical reaction network based on a stochastic hybrid model. We assume that noisy time series measurements of the chemical populations are available and follow a maximum likelihood approach to calibrate the parameters. We numerically approximate the likelihood and its derivatives for concrete values of the parameters and show that, based on this approximation, the maximization of the likelihood can be done efficiently.

We substantiate the usefulness of our approach by applying it to several case studies from systems biology.

Categories and Subject Descriptors

G.3 [**Mathematics of Computing**]: PROBABILITY AND STATISTICS—*Markov Processes*; I.2 [**ARTIFICIAL INTELLIGENCE**]: Learning—*Parameter learning*

Keywords

biochemical reactions, stochastic hybrid model, parameter identification

1. INTRODUCTION

A popular dynamical model in systems biology is a system of ordinary differential equations (ODEs) that describes the time evolution of the concentrations of certain molecular species in a biological compartment. This macroscopic model is based on the theory of chemical kinetics and assumes that the concentrations in a well-stirred system change deterministically and continuously in time. It provides an appropriate description of a chemically reacting system as

long as the numbers of molecules of the chemical species are large. In living cells, however, the chemical populations can be low (e.g. a single DNA molecule, tens or a few hundreds of RNA or protein molecules). In this case the underlying assumptions of the ODE approach are violated and a more detailed model is necessary, which takes into account the inherently discrete and stochastic nature of chemical reactions.

The theory of stochastic chemical kinetics provides an appropriate description by means of a discrete-state Markov process, that is, a continuous-time Markov chain (CTMC) that represents the chemical populations as random variables [6]. In the thermodynamic limit (when the number of molecules and the volume of the system approach infinity) the Markov model and the macroscopic ODE description are equal [13]. Therefore, the ODE approach can be used to approximate the CTMC only if all populations are large. Moreover, it is possible to extend the ODE approach such that higher-order moments (e.g. the (co-)variances of the populations) are approximated as well [5, 10].

Discrete-state Markov models that describe chemical reactions, however, suffer from the largeness problem of the state space. This is particularly severe if, besides the small populations that make a discrete representation necessary, there are large populations involved. In such cases, stochastic hybrid models provide an appropriate description of the reaction network, since they use a discrete state space only for those parts where a discrete representation is necessary [19].

The estimation of kinetic constants is an essential part of the typical research cycle in systems biology. Usually, time series data is analyzed to learn the structure of a biochemical reaction network and to calibrate the reaction rate parameters. The direct measurement of parameters through wet-lab experiments is often difficult or even impracticable. There are extensive research efforts to estimate the reaction rate parameters of macroscopic models based on ODEs. The problem of finding parameters that minimize the difference between observed and predicted data is usually multimodal due to non-linear constraints and thus requires global optimization techniques. The estimated parameters, however, differ from those of the corresponding stochastic model since even the mean behavior of the stochastic model can largely deviate from the behavior of the deterministic model [15]. Therefore, if the reaction network involves small populations, then parameter estimation techniques for stochastic models are necessary to provide appropriate calibrations.

Here, we consider noisy time series measurements of the

system state as they are available from wet-lab experiments. Recent experimental imaging techniques such as high-resolution fluorescence microscopy can measure small molecule counts with measurement errors of less than one molecule [7]. We assume that the structure of the underlying reaction network is known but certain reaction rate constants of the network are unknown. Then we identify those constants that maximize the likelihood of the time series data. For this, we consider a stochastic hybrid model of the reaction network where small populations are represented by discrete random variables (modes of the hybrid model) and large populations evolve continuously and deterministically over time. In the resulting stochastic hybrid model changes of the small populations may induce changes of the continuous dynamics of large populations.

Our main contribution consists in devising an efficient algorithm for the numerical approximation of the likelihood and its derivatives w.r.t. the reaction rate constants. Previous techniques are often based on Monte-Carlo sampling because direct numerical solutions of stochastic hybrid systems require the solution of a system of partial differential equations. Thus, the continuous part of the state space has to be discretized and, if the discrete part of the state space is large, appropriate truncations have to developed. Here, we exploit that for the large populations, it is often sufficient to know the expected number of molecules conditioned on the mode of the system. Based on this, the mode probabilities can be integrated over time. This allows a fast and accurate approximation of the probability distribution of the model and can be used for the estimation of parameters based on the maximum likelihood method. We propose an iterative algorithm to approximate the likelihood of the given time series data. Moreover, we show how first and second order derivatives of the likelihood w.r.t. the parameters can be approximated as well. Then we use a global optimization technique to maximize the likelihood. Knowing first and second order derivatives, this maximization is efficient and provides good estimates even for complex reaction networks. Moreover, we can also approximate the standard deviations of the estimators.

After introducing the discrete-state stochastic model in Section 2, we discuss the stochastic hybrid model in Section 3. We introduce the maximum likelihood method in Section 4 and present our approximation method in Section 5. Finally, we report on experimental results for three reaction networks (Section 6) and discuss related work in Section 7.

2. PURELY DISCRETE MODEL

According to Gillespie's theory of stochastic chemical kinetics, a well-stirred mixture of n molecular species in a volume with fixed size and fixed temperature can be represented as a continuous-time Markov chain $\{\mathbf{X}(t), t \geq 0\}$ [6]. The random vector $\mathbf{X}(t) = (X_1(t), \ldots, X_n(t))$ describes the chemical populations at time t, i.e., $X_i(t)$ is the number of molecules of type $i \in \{1, \ldots, n\}$ at time t. Thus, the state space of $\mathbf{X}$ is $\mathbb{Z}_+^n = \{0, 1, \ldots\}^n$. The state changes of $\mathbf{X}$ are triggered by the occurrences of chemical reactions, which are of m different types. For $j \in \{1, \ldots, m\}$ let $\mathbf{v}_j \in \mathbb{Z}^n$ be the nonzero change vector of the j-th reaction type, that is, $\mathbf{v}_j = \mathbf{v}_j^- + \mathbf{v}_j^+$ where $\mathbf{v}_j^-$ contains only non-positive entries, which specify how many molecules of each species are consumed (reactants) if an instance of the reaction occurs.

Thus, a reaction of type j is only possible in state $\mathbf{x}$ if $\mathbf{x} + \mathbf{v}_j^-$ is non-negative, since only then there are enough reactant molecules present. The vector $\mathbf{v}_j^+$ contains only non-negative entries, which specify how many molecules of each species are produced (products). Thus, if $\mathbf{X}(t) = \mathbf{x}$ for some $\mathbf{x} \in \mathbb{Z}_+^n$ with $\mathbf{x} + \mathbf{v}_j^-$ being non-negative, then $\mathbf{X}(t + dt) = \mathbf{x} + \mathbf{v}_j$ is the state of the system after the occurrence of the j-th reaction within the infinitesimal time interval $[t, t + dt)$.

Each reaction type has an associated rate function, denoted by $\alpha_1, \ldots, \alpha_m$, which is such that $\alpha_j(\mathbf{x}) \cdot dt$ is the probability that, given $\mathbf{X}(t) = \mathbf{x}$, one instance of the j-th reaction occurs within $[t, t + dt)$. The value $\alpha_j(\mathbf{x})$ is proportional to the number of distinct reactant combinations in state $\mathbf{x}$. More precisely, if $\mathbf{x} = (x_1, \ldots, x_n)$ is a state for which $\mathbf{x} + \mathbf{v}_j^-$ is nonnegative then, for reactions with at most two reactants[1],

$$\alpha_j(\mathbf{x}) = \begin{cases} c_j & \text{if } \mathbf{v}_j^- = (0, \ldots, 0), \\ c_j \cdot x_i & \text{if } \mathbf{v}_j^- = -\mathbf{e}_i, \\ c_j \cdot x_i \cdot x_\ell & \text{if } \mathbf{v}_j^- = -\mathbf{e}_i - \mathbf{e}_\ell, \\ c_j \cdot \binom{x_i}{2} = c_j \cdot \frac{x_i \cdot (x_i - 1)}{2} & \text{if } \mathbf{v}_j^- = -2 \cdot \mathbf{e}_i, \end{cases} \quad (1)$$

where $i \neq \ell$, $c_j > 0$, and $\mathbf{e}_i$ is the vector with the i-th entry 1 and all other entries 0.

EXAMPLE 1. *We consider the Lotka-Volterra reaction network with three reactions that involve two different species X_1 and X_2. The reactions and change vectors are*

$$\begin{array}{lll} X_1 & \to & 2X_1 & \mathbf{v}_1 = (1, 0) \\ X_1 + X_2 & \to & 2X_2 & \mathbf{v}_2 = (-1, 1) \\ X_2 & \to & \emptyset & \mathbf{v}_3 = (0, 1) \end{array}$$

and the corresponding rate functions are $\alpha_1(x_1, x_2) = c_1 \cdot x_1$, $\alpha_2(x_1, x_2) = c_2 \cdot x_1 \cdot x_2$, and $\alpha_3(x_1, x_2) = c_3 \cdot x_2$.

The Chemical Master Equation. For $\mathbf{x} \in \mathbb{Z}_+^n$ and $t \geq 0$, let $p(\mathbf{x}, t)$ denote the probability $P(\mathbf{X}(t) = \mathbf{x})$ and let $\mathbf{p}(t)$ be the row vector with entries $p(\mathbf{x}, t)$ where we assume some fixed enumeration of all possible states $\mathbf{x}$.

Given $\mathbf{v}_1^-, \ldots, \mathbf{v}_m^-, \mathbf{v}_1^+, \ldots, \mathbf{v}_m^+, \alpha_1, \ldots, \alpha_m$, and some initial distribution $\mathbf{p}(0)$, the Markov chain $\mathbf{X}$ is uniquely specified and its evolution is given by the chemical master equation (CME)

$$\begin{aligned} \frac{d}{dt} p(\mathbf{x}, t) = &\sum_{j: \mathbf{x} - \mathbf{v}_j^+ \geq 0} \alpha_j(\mathbf{x} - \mathbf{v}_j) p(\mathbf{x} - \mathbf{v}_j, t) \\ &- \sum_{j: \mathbf{x} + \mathbf{v}_j^- \geq 0} \alpha_j(\mathbf{x}) p(\mathbf{x}, t). \end{aligned} \quad (2)$$

Later, we will use the matrix-vector form

$$\frac{d}{dt} \mathbf{p}(t) = \mathbf{p}(t) Q, \quad (3)$$

where Q is the infinitesimal generator matrix of $\mathbf{X}$, i.e., Q has entry $\alpha_j(\mathbf{x})$ for the pair $(\mathbf{x}, \mathbf{x} + \mathbf{v}_j)$ of states if $\mathbf{x} + \mathbf{v}_j^-$ is nonnegative and the diagonal entries are the negative sum of the off-diagonal elements of the corresponding row.

From (2) it is straightforward to derive the following system of ordinary differential equations (ODEs) for the expected populations:

$$\frac{d}{dt} E[\mathbf{X}(t)] = \sum_{j=1}^m \mathbf{v}_j E[\alpha_j(\mathbf{X}(t))] \quad (4)$$

---

[1]Here we consider only reactions with at most two reactants since more complex reactions can usually be decomposed into reactions with at most two reactants.

If the expected rates $E[\alpha_j(\mathbf{X}(t)]$ are approximated by $\alpha_j(E[\mathbf{X}(t)])$, we arrive at the so-called rate equations

$$\frac{d}{dt}\mathbf{z}(t) = \sum_{j=1}^{m} \mathbf{v}_j \alpha_j(\mathbf{z}(t)) \qquad (5)$$

where $\mathbf{z}(t) \approx E[\mathbf{X}(t)]$. This popular approximation is shown to be exact in the deterministic limit [13] where the Markov chains follows with probability one the deterministic trajectory of the rate equations. In order to derive the deterministic limit one can scale the Markov chain with the volume times Avogadro's number. The deterministic limit is reached when the volume and the molecule numbers tend to infinity (while the chemical concentrations remain constant) and (5) is derived by applying the law of large numbers which is exact in the limit. Therefore, (5) is an accurate approximation of the Markov chain when all molecular species are present in high numbers. Moreover, the probability distribution of the Markov chain can be accurately approximated by a multivariate normal distribution where the variance vanishes in the deterministic limit.

In many systems, however, one has to consider species with both large and small molecule numbers. In this case the approximation in (5) can become arbitrarily poor. If, on the other hand, we consider the original Markov chain then an efficient approximation of (2) is only possible if all populations remain small with high probability. One can dynamically truncate the (probably infinite) state space and restrict to a small number of significant states in each time interval of the numerical integration of (2) [16]. If not all populations remain small, then the main part of the probability mass distributes on a large number of states and such approximations become inefficient. If the probability distribution of the Markov chain can be accurately represented based on a small number of moments of $\mathbf{X}(t)$, then an efficient approximation of (2) can be achieved by a moment closure technique [10, 5] where besides (4) further ODEs are used to approximate higher order moments. Note that when moments of higher order are approximated then a more accurate estimation of the expected rate $E[\alpha_j(\mathbf{X}(t)]$ can be derived compared to the approximation $\alpha_j(E[\mathbf{X}(t)])$ which is used in (5).

3. STOCHASTIC HYBRID MODEL

In this section, we introduce a stochastic hybrid approach that is particularly well suited for systems with both large and small populations and a probability distribution that is difficult to represent based on the moments of $\mathbf{X}(t)$. For instance, the distribution of the Markov chain in Example 1 has a significant portion of probability mass on the line where $X_2 = 0$ (for $t \to \infty$ we have $P(X_2 = 0) = 1$) while the rest of the probability mass distributes on the remainder of the 2-dimensional state space. A moment-based representation cannot accurately describe the mass at $X_2 = 0$ even if many moments are included. Similar problems occur with multistable distributions (see also Example 2 below) and other systems where the discreteness of certain events is important.

In our hybrid approach, we split $\mathbf{X}(t)$ into small, discrete populations $\mathbf{M}(t)$ and large, continuous populations $\mathbf{Y}(t)$, i.e. $\mathbf{X}(t) = (\mathbf{M}(t), \mathbf{Y}(t))$. The idea is to use the rate equations in (5) for those parts of the Markov chain where the molecule numbers are high and to assume stochastic jumps where the molecule numbers are small. In the sequel, we will refer to the state $\mathbf{M}(t)$ of the small, discrete populations as

the *mode* of the system at time t. Let n^d be the dimension of $\mathbf{M}(t)$ and n^c the dimension of $\mathbf{Y}(t)$, i.e. $n = n^d + n^c$. We define $\mathbf{v}_j^d$ and $\mathbf{v}_j^c$ as the components of $\mathbf{v}_j$ that belong to $\mathbf{M}(t)$ and $\mathbf{Y}(t)$, respectively. Next, we assume that instead of the probability distribution of $\mathbf{Y}(t)$ conditioned on $\mathbf{M}(t) = \mathbf{m}$ we only have the conditional expectation

$$E[\mathbf{Y}(t) \mid \mathbf{M}(t) = \mathbf{m}] = \sum_{\mathbf{y}} \mathbf{y} \cdot P(\mathbf{Y}(t) = \mathbf{y} \mid \mathbf{M}(t) = \mathbf{m}).$$

Thus, in order to integrate the probabilities of $\mathbf{M}(t) = \mathbf{m}$ over time, we do not consider the complete probability distribution of the Markov chain, but only the distribution of $\mathbf{M}(t)$ and (an approximation of) the conditional expectations $E[\mathbf{Y}(t) \mid \mathbf{M}(t) = \mathbf{m}]$ for all $\mathbf{m}$. Moreover, we assume that the conditional expectations evolve deterministically according to the rate equations (see (5)) while the discrete part of the Markov chain performs stochastic jumps. Let us write $\mathbf{y_m}(t)$ for the approximation of $E[\mathbf{Y}(t) \mid \mathbf{M}(t) = \mathbf{m}]$ and let $\mathcal{R}^d \subseteq \{1, \ldots, m\}$ be the set of reaction indices j for which $\mathbf{v}_j^d$ is nonzero. Similarly, we define $\mathcal{R}^c \subseteq \{1, \ldots, m\}$ as the set of indices j such that $\mathbf{v}_j^c$ is nonzero. Under the assumptions described above, the CME (see (2)) then gives the following ODE for the evolution of the distribution of $\mathbf{M}(t)$:

$$\frac{d}{dt}P(\mathbf{M}(t) = \mathbf{m}) = \sum_{j \in \mathcal{R}^d} P(\mathbf{M}(t) = \mathbf{m} - \mathbf{v}_j^d)$$
$$\alpha_j(\mathbf{m} - \mathbf{v}_j^d, \mathbf{y}_{\mathbf{m} - \mathbf{v}_j^d}(t)) \qquad (6)$$
$$- \sum_j P(\mathbf{M}(t) = \mathbf{m}) \alpha_j(\mathbf{m}, \mathbf{y_m}(t)).$$

Let $\mathbf{m}$ be such that $P(\mathbf{M}(t) = \mathbf{m}) > 0$. For the evolution of $\mathbf{y_m}(t)$ we assume the following deterministic continuous dynamics (where we omit the argument t of $\mathbf{y_m}$ to improve readability)

$$\frac{d}{dt}\mathbf{y_m} = \sum_{j \in \mathcal{R}^d} P(\mathbf{M}(t) = \mathbf{m} - \mathbf{v}_j^d)$$
$$\alpha_j(\mathbf{m} - \mathbf{v}_j^d, \mathbf{y}_{\mathbf{m} - \mathbf{v}_j^d}) \mathbf{y}_{\mathbf{m} - \mathbf{v}_j^d} / P(\mathbf{M}(t) = \mathbf{m}) \qquad (7)$$
$$- \sum_{j \in \mathcal{R}^d} \alpha_j(\mathbf{m}, \mathbf{y_m}) \mathbf{y_m} + \sum_{j \in \mathcal{R}^c} \mathbf{v}_j^c \alpha_j(\mathbf{m}, \mathbf{y_m})$$

which can be derived by a Wentzel-Kramers-Brillouin approximation of the conditional probability distribution of the continuous populations combined with a multiscale expansion of the CME [17]. The intuition behind (7) is that the conditional expectations are integrated in each mode $\mathbf{m}$ according to the "local" rate equations (last term with summation over $j \in \mathcal{R}^c$) and propagated between states in the same way as probabilities (two terms with summation over $j \in \mathcal{R}^d$). Note that $P(\mathbf{M}(t) = \mathbf{m} - \mathbf{v}_j^d) \alpha_j(\mathbf{m} - \mathbf{v}_j^d, \mathbf{y}_{\mathbf{m} - \mathbf{v}_j^d})$ is the probability inflow to mode $\mathbf{m}$ w.r.t. reaction j. Thus, the conditional expectation of the predecessor mode $\mathbf{m} - \mathbf{v}_j^d$ is propagated to $\mathbf{m}$ relative to the inflow of probability from $\mathbf{m} - \mathbf{v}_j^d$ divided by the total inflow $P(\mathbf{M}(t) = \mathbf{m})$ to $\mathbf{m}$. Similarly, the second term represents the propagation of the conditional expectation from $\mathbf{m}$ to $\mathbf{m}$ (selfloop).

EXAMPLE 2. *We consider a gene regulatory network with two genes that have overlapping promoter sites on the DNA and express proteins P_1 and P_2, respectively. The expression of the gene product P_1 of the first gene is suppressed whenever a molecule of type P_2 binds to the promoter region and vice versa [15]. We illustrate the network in Figure 1.*

The state of the promoter corresponds to the state of the three discrete populations (DNA, DNA.P_1, DNA.P_2) which

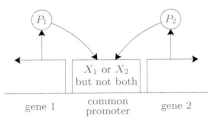

Figure 1: Illustration of the exclusive switch.

can only be zero or one, respectively. Thus, $\mathbf{M}(t) \in \{(1,0,0),$ $(0,1,0),(0,0,1)\}$ for all t. The number of P_1 and P_2 molecules is given by the continuous populations $Y_1(t)$ and $Y_2(t)$. In mode $\mathbf{m} = (1,0,0)$, two discrete jumps are possible at rates $b_1 Y_1(t)$ and $b_2 Y_2(t)$ (binding of P_1 or P_2 to the promoter) where $b_1, b_2 > 0$ are reaction rate constants (see Figure 2). In modes $(0,1,0)$ and $(0,0,1)$ unbinding of the corresponding protein occurs at rates u_1 and u_2, respectively. The local rate equations for $Y_1(t)$ and $Y_2(t)$ are listed in Figure 2 for each mode (boxes below the corresponding mode), where k_i is the rate at which proteins are produced by gene i and $d_i Y_i(t)$ is the rate at which proteins of type P_i degrade ($i \in \{1,2\}$). Note that discrete jumps that affect continuous populations are part of the local rate equations (e.g. the terms $-b_1 Y_1$ and $-b_2 Y_2$), because all changes of large populations are assumed to be deterministic and continuous. This is reasonable if we assume that stochastic effects originate from the discrete random changes of small populations while large populations evolve purely continuously. If we do not include these terms in the ODE but take the corresponding chemical reactions into account as discrete stochastic jumps, then the trajectories of the continuous species would contain discontinuities.

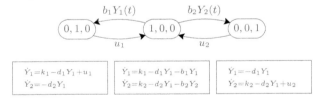

Figure 2: Transitions and local rate equations of the exclusive switch.

Without mode changes, the conditional expectations could be approximated by simply integrating the local rate equations. If mode changes occur, however, we must take into account the conditional expectations of other modes in order to compute the conditional expectations at a particular time t for a certain mode.

Note that this hybrid formulation differs from previous work [19, 11] in that no information about the conditional probabilities $P(\mathbf{Y}(t) \leq \mathbf{y} | \mathbf{M}(t) = \mathbf{m})$ or the corresponding densities is given. It is closer to a moment closure approach which is applied only to parts of the system. There is substantial experimental evidence for the accuracy of the above hybrid approach w.r.t. the original Markov chain [17, 9]. The main advantage of the approach is that the direct numerical simulation is computationally cheap compared to the simulation of the original Markov chain and also compared to other hybrid models. Moreover, it considers a moment-based representation only for those parts where such a representation is appropriate.

It is possible to improve the accuracy of the hybrid approach by adding information about higher moments. For this, we first consider a more accurate approximation of the first moments in (4) based on a moment closure technique[2] [5]:

$$\frac{d}{dt}\mu_i = \sum_{j=1}^{m} v_{ji}\left(\alpha_j(\mu) + 0.5 \sum_{k,l} H_{kl}(\alpha_j(\mu))C_{kl}\right) \quad (8)$$

where $\mu = (\mu_1, \ldots, \mu_n)$ is the vector of the first moments of the molecule numbers, v_{ji} is the i-th entry of the change vector $\mathbf{v}_j$, and $H(\cdot)$ is the Hessian matrix with entries $H_{kl}(\cdot)$. The covariance C_{kl} of the k-th and the l-th population are approximated as

$$\frac{d}{dt}C_{ih} = \sum_{j=1}^{m}\left(v_{ji}\sum_k \frac{\partial\alpha_j(\mu)}{\partial\mu_k}C_{kh} + v_{jh}\sum_l \frac{\partial\alpha_j(\mu)}{\partial\mu_l}C_{il}\right)$$
$$+ \sum_{j=1}^{m} v_{ji}v_{jh}\left(\alpha_j(\mu) + 0.5\sum_{k,l} H_{kl}(\alpha_j(\mu))C_{kl}\right). \quad (9)$$

Note that (8) is exact while (9) gives an approximation of the covariances. Obviously, we can use (8) and (9) to approximate conditional expectations and conditional variances. For this we simply replace the last term in (7) (which is equal to the local rate equations) by the right side of (8). Then, μ are the conditional expectations and C_{kl} are the conditional covariances. Thus, in each mode $\mathbf{m}$ we approximate the conditional expectation $\mathbf{y_m}$ by integrating (7) where the local rate equations are replaced by the right side of (8). In addition we approximate the conditional covariances for each pair of continuous populations by integrating an ODE similar to (7). More precisely, we treat the conditional covariances like additional deterministic variables and integrate them using (9). Adding the covariances in Example 2 means that instead of $3 \cdot (1 + 2) = 9$ equations, we would integrate $3 \cdot (1 + 2 + 3) = 18$ equations (in each mode there are three additional ODEs: two for the variances and one for the covariance between Y_1 and Y_2).

4. MAXIMUM LIKELIHOOD ESTIMATION

Assume that a network of chemical reactions is given but the reaction rate constants and initial conditions are unknown. Thus, we have given a parametric Markov chain $\mathbf{X}$ and our goal is to estimate "optimal" values for the parameters, i.e. parameters that maximize the probability of certain observations. We consider K noisy time-series measurements of molecular counts as they are available from wet-lab experiments e.g. using high-resolution fluorescence microscopy [7]. Let

$$\mathbf{O}^k(t_\ell) = \left(O_1^k(t_\ell), \ldots, O_n^k(t_\ell)\right)$$

be the vector of molecular counts corresponding to the k-th observation sequence, where $t_1, \ldots, t_R \in \mathbb{R}_{\geq 0}$ ($t_1 < \ldots < t_R$) are the time instances at which the measurements were made. In order to take measurement errors into account, we assume that

$$\mathbf{O}^k(t_\ell) = \mathbf{X}(t_\ell) + \xi(t_\ell)$$

where $\mathbf{X}(t_\ell)$ is the true state of the Markov chain at time t_ℓ and the error term vectors $\xi(t_\ell)$ are independent and identically normally distributed with mean $\mathbf{0}$ and covariance matrix Σ. We assume that the entries of Σ are parameters and that initially the chain starts with probability one an the

---

[2]Again, we omit the argument t to improve readability.

(unknown) initial state $\mathbf{x}_0$. Both Σ and $\mathbf{x}_0$ are estimated as well.

Let f denote the joint density of $\mathbf{O}^k(t_1), \ldots, \mathbf{O}^k(t_R)$ and let $\mathbf{c} = (c_1, \ldots, c_m)$ be the vector of the (unknown) stochastic reaction rate constants. Then the likelihood of the k-th observation sequence is

$$
\begin{aligned}
\mathcal{L}_k&(\mathbf{x}_0, \mathbf{c}, \Sigma) \\
&= f\left(\mathbf{O}^k(t_1), \ldots, \mathbf{O}^k(t_R)\right) \\
&= \sum_{\mathbf{x}_1} \cdots \sum_{\mathbf{x}_R} P(\mathbf{X}(t_1) = \mathbf{x}_1, \ldots, \mathbf{X}(t_R) = \mathbf{x}_R) \\
&\quad \cdot f(\mathbf{O}^k(t_1), \ldots, \mathbf{O}^k(t_R) | \mathbf{X}(t_1) = \mathbf{x}_1, \ldots, \mathbf{X}(t_R) = \mathbf{x}_R),
\end{aligned} \tag{10}
$$

that is, $\mathcal{L}_k$ is the probability to observe $\mathbf{O}^k(t_1), \ldots, \mathbf{O}^k(t_R)$. Note that $\mathcal{L}_k$ depends on the initial state $\mathbf{x}_0$ and the rate parameters $\mathbf{c}$ since the state sequence probability $P(\cdot)$ does. Furthermore, $\mathcal{L}_k$ depends on Σ since the conditional density f in the last row does so. The total likelihood equals the product of the likelihoods of all individual sequences

$$
\mathcal{L}(\mathbf{x}_0, \mathbf{c}, \Sigma) = \prod_{k=1}^K \mathcal{L}_k(\mathbf{x}_0, \mathbf{c}, \Sigma). \tag{11}
$$

In order to find values $\mathbf{x}_0^*, \mathbf{c}^*, \Sigma^*$ that maximize the likelihood, we have to solve the nonlinear optimization problem

$$
\max_{\mathbf{x}_0, \mathbf{c}, \Sigma} \mathcal{L}(\mathbf{x}_0, \mathbf{c}, \Sigma) \tag{12}
$$

or, equivalently, we minimize the negative logarithm of the likelihood. The main difficulty is the efficient approximation of $\mathcal{L}_k$ (or $-\log \mathcal{L}_k$) for given parameter values as well as the approximation of the derivatives of $\mathcal{L}_k$ w.r.t. the parameters. Note that since we assume independence between the measurement errors, the conditional density in (10) can be written as

$$
\begin{aligned}
f&\left(\mathbf{O}^k(t_1), \ldots, \mathbf{O}^k(t_R) \mid \mathbf{X}(t_1) = \mathbf{x}_1, \ldots, \mathbf{X}(t_R) = \mathbf{x}_R\right) \\
&= \prod_{\ell=1}^R f(\mathbf{O}^k(t_\ell) \mid \mathbf{X}(t_\ell) = \mathbf{x}_\ell)
\end{aligned}
$$

and $f(\mathbf{O}^k(t_\ell) \mid \mathbf{X}(t_\ell) = \mathbf{x}_\ell)$ equals the density of the normal distribution at $\mathbf{O}^k(t_\ell) - \mathbf{x}_\ell$ (called "weight" of state x_ℓ), i.e.,

$$
f(\mathbf{O}^k(t_\ell) \mid \mathbf{X}(t_\ell) = \mathbf{x}_\ell) = \phi_{\mathbf{0}, \Sigma}(\mathbf{O}^k(t_\ell) - \mathbf{x}_\ell),
$$

where $\mathbf{0}$ is the vector with all entries zero and $\phi_{\mu, \Sigma}$ is the density of the multivariate normal distribution with mean μ and covariance matrix Σ. The sums in (10), however, range over all states of the Markov chain and the probability $P(\mathbf{X}(t_1) = \mathbf{x}_1, \ldots, \mathbf{X}(t_R) = \mathbf{x}_R)$ requires a transient analysis, i.e., the solution of the CME. In the sequel, we focus on the approximation of $\mathcal{L}$ and its derivatives for given values of $\mathbf{x}_0, \mathbf{c}$, and Σ. For the optimization problem (12) we then use MATLAB's Global Search, an optimization method that uses a heuristic for the starting points in the parameter space and, for each chosen starting point, it follows the gradient until a local maximum is reached. For this, global search calls functions that, for given values $\mathbf{x}_0, \mathbf{c}$, and Σ, provides an approximation of $\mathcal{L}$ and its derivatives of first and second order. We use the hybrid approach proposed in (6) and (7) to provide such functions.

5. APPROXIMATION OF THE LIKELIHOOD AND ITS DERIVATIVES

In this section we first describe an algorithm that is based on a purely discrete model and use it as a basis for the approximation of the likelihood based on the hybrid approach in (6) and (7).

5.1 Purely discrete approach

Let I be the identity matrix and let W_ℓ^k be a diagonal matrix with diagonal entries $\phi_{\mathbf{0}, \Sigma}(\mathbf{O}^k(t_\ell) - \mathbf{x}_\ell)$ for each $\mathbf{x}_\ell$ (called weight matrix). Thus, the diagonal entries are equal to the weights of the k-th observation sequence at time point t_ℓ. Let $P(t)$ be the transition probability matrix of $\mathbf{X}$ for time step $t \geq 0$ i.e., the solution of the Kolmogorov forward and backward differential equations[3]

$$
\frac{d}{dt} P(t) = P(t)Q, \qquad \frac{d}{dt} P(t) = Q P(t),
$$

where $P(0) = I$. Here, Q is the generator matrix of the original Markov chain. Letting $P_\ell = P(t_\ell - t_{\ell-1})$, it has been shown that (10) can be written in a matrix-vector form as

$$
\mathcal{L}_k = \mathbf{p}(t_0) P_1 W_1^k P_2 W_2^k \cdots P_R W_R^k \mathbf{e}, \tag{13}
$$

where $t_1 \geq t_0 = 0$ and $\mathbf{e}$ is the column vector with all entries one (see [2, 18] for more details). Note that since the matrices W_ℓ^k contain one diagonal entry for each state, the summation over all states $\mathbf{x}$ in (10) is represented by a vector-matrix product in (13).

We now describe an iterative scheme to compute $\mathcal{L}_k$ based on (13), assuming that the state space is small. Afterwards we explain how to modify the approach if the state space is large (or infinite) but the expected population numbers are small. From here on we drop index k and assume $K = 1$ since for $K > 1$ we simply perform the computation for each observation sequence and multiply the corresponding values of $\mathcal{L}_k$ (see (11)). A recursive scheme for the computation of (13) is given by

$$
\mathbf{u}(t_\ell) = \mathbf{u}(t_{\ell-1}) P_\ell W_\ell, \tag{14}
$$

where $\mathbf{u}(t_0) = \mathbf{p}(t_0)$ and $\mathcal{L} = \mathbf{u}(t_R)\mathbf{e}$. Instead of computing P_ℓ in (14) explicitly, we solve the system of ODEs

$$
\frac{d}{dt} \mathbf{r}(t) = \mathbf{r}(t) Q \tag{15}
$$

for the time interval $[t_{\ell-1}, t_\ell]$ with initial condition $\mathbf{r}(t_{\ell-1}) = \mathbf{u}(t_{\ell-1})$. After that we calculate $\mathbf{u}(t_\ell) = \mathbf{r}(t_\ell) W_\ell$. Finally we obtain $\mathcal{L}_k = \mathbf{u}(t_R)\mathbf{e}$. Note that this is correct since from the Kolmogorov forward differential equation we know that for any vector $\mathbf{r}(t)$ the product $\mathbf{r}(t) P_\ell$ is given by integrating (15) for $t_\ell - t_{\ell-1}$ time units.

For the derivatives of $\mathcal{L}$ we get a similar iteration. Here, we only give details for $\mathbf{c}$ and refer to Appendix A for details about the derivatives w.r.t. $\mathbf{x}_0$ and Σ. From (14) we obtain

$$
\frac{\partial \mathbf{u}(t_\ell)}{\partial c_j} = \left(\frac{\partial \mathbf{u}(t_{\ell-1})}{\partial c_j} P_\ell + \mathbf{u}(t_{\ell-1}) \frac{\partial}{\partial c_j} P_\ell \right) W_\ell, \tag{16}
$$

where $\frac{\partial \mathbf{u}(t_0)}{\partial c_j} = \mathbf{0}$. For the computation of (16) we solve (simultaneously with (15))

$$
\frac{\partial}{\partial t} \mathbf{s}_j(t) = \mathbf{s}_j(t) Q + \mathbf{r}(t) \frac{\partial}{\partial c_j} Q, \tag{17}
$$

for the time interval $[t_{\ell-1}, t_\ell]$ with initial condition $\mathbf{s}_j(t_{\ell-1}) = \frac{\partial \mathbf{u}(t_{\ell-1})}{\partial c_j}$. After solving (17) we obtain

$$
\frac{\partial \mathbf{u}(t_\ell)}{\partial c_j} = \mathbf{s}_j(t_\ell) W_\ell.
$$

---

[3]Note that the solution $P(t)$ is guaranteed to exist if the Markov chain is regular [1], which is in practice always the case. E.g. it is sufficient that all rate functions $\alpha_j(\mathbf{x})$ are of the form (1).

and compute $\frac{\partial}{\partial c_j}\mathcal{L}_k$ as $\frac{\partial}{\partial c_j}\mathbf{u}(t_R)\mathbf{e}$. We also compute the second derivatives of the likelihood using similar schemes.

If the state space of the Markov chain is large (or even infinite), we still can efficiently approximate the above values by using inexact numerical integration as long as the expected molecule numbers remain small. The main idea is to work with a dynamical state space where during the numerical integration we consider only differential equations that correspond to states that contribute significantly to the likelihood (see [2] for more details), i.e., during the numerical integration we always consider a finite subset of states. States are added to or removed from this subset according to a small threshold. More precisely, in each step of the numerical integration we consider only those states where the corresponding entry in the vector $\mathbf{r}$ is greater than a certain threshold. If it is, however, likely that certain species occur in high numbers then the inexact numerical integration is inefficient or even infeasible since a large number of states contribute significantly to the likelihood. In such cases, a hybrid approach for the approximation of the likelihood is more appropriate.

5.2 Stochastic hybrid approach

If we again consider the splitting $\mathbf{X}(t) = (\mathbf{M}(t), \mathbf{Y}(t))$ as described in Section 3 and assume that $\mathbf{Y}(t)$ is continuous then $\mathcal{L}_k(\mathbf{x}_0, \mathbf{c}, \Sigma)$ equals

$$\sum_{\mathbf{m}_1} \cdots \sum_{\mathbf{m}_R} P(\mathbf{M}(t_1) = \mathbf{m}_1, \ldots, \mathbf{M}(t_R) = \mathbf{m}_R)$$
$$\int_{\mathbf{y}_1} \cdots \int_{\mathbf{y}_R} g(\mathbf{y}_1, \ldots, \mathbf{y}_R | \mathbf{M}(t_1) = \mathbf{m}_1, \ldots, \mathbf{M}(t_R) = \mathbf{m}_R) \quad (18)$$
$$\prod_{\ell=1}^{R} (\mathbf{O}(t_\ell) | \mathbf{M}(t_\ell) = \mathbf{m}_\ell, \mathbf{Y}(t_\ell) = \mathbf{y}_\ell),$$

where g is the conditional probability density of the continuous populations. To simplify the presentation, we drop the index k of the observation sequence and write $\mathbf{O}(t_\ell)$ instead of $\mathbf{O}^k(t_\ell)$, $\mathcal{L}$ instead of $\mathcal{L}_k$, etc. We propose an approximation of $\mathcal{L}$ based on (6) and (7) and use an iteration similar to (14) where in each step we approximate the joint distribution of $M(t)$ and $Y(t)$ as

$$P(\mathbf{M}(t) = \mathbf{m}, \mathbf{Y}(t) = \mathbf{y}) = \begin{cases} P(\mathbf{M}(t) = \mathbf{m}) \text{ if } \mathbf{y} = \\ \qquad E[\mathbf{Y}(t) \mid \mathbf{M}(t) = \mathbf{m}], \\ 0 \qquad\qquad \text{otherwise.} \end{cases}$$

Thus, the number of entries in the vector $\mathbf{u}(t_\ell)$ (see (14)) equals the number of possible modes. Moreover, the entry of mode $\mathbf{m}_\ell$ in the weight matrix W_ℓ is equal to

$$\phi_{0,\Sigma}\left((\mathbf{m}_\ell, \mathbf{y}_{\mathbf{m}_\ell}(t_\ell)) - \mathbf{O}(t_\ell)\right).$$

where $\mathbf{y}_{\mathbf{m}_\ell}(t_\ell) \approx E[\mathbf{Y}(t_\ell) \mid \mathbf{M}(t_\ell) = \mathbf{m}_\ell]$. Since the approximation of $E[\mathbf{Y}(t_\ell) \mid \mathbf{M}(t_\ell) = \mathbf{m}_\ell]$ is needed in the ℓ's step, we use the following iterative scheme to compute $\mathcal{L}_k$:

1. First, solve (6) and (7) until the final observation time point t_R is reached. Store the mode probabilities and the approximated conditional expectations $\mathbf{y}_{\mathbf{m}}(t)$.

2. Let $\mathbf{p}$ be the vector with entries $P(\mathbf{M}(t_1) = \mathbf{m})$ for all $\mathbf{m}$. Compute the weighted distribution $\mathbf{q}_1$ as $\mathbf{p}W_1$ where W_ℓ is a diagonal matrix such that the entry that corresponds to mode $\mathbf{m}$ is given by $\phi_{0,\Sigma}((\mathbf{m}, \mathbf{y}_{\mathbf{m}}(t_\ell)) - \mathbf{O}(t_\ell))$ for $\ell \in \{1, \ldots, R\}$.

3. Solve the following system of ODEs:
$$\frac{d}{dt}\mathbf{r}(t) = \mathbf{r}(t)Q(t)$$

for $t_2 - t_1$ time units with initial vector q_1. Here, $Q(t)$ is the generator matrix of the discrete part of the hybrid model, i.e., Q contains the transition rates at which the mode changes (see (6)). Note that in general $Q(t)$ may depend on t because the entries may depend on $\mathbf{y}_{\mathbf{m}}(t)$.

4. Multiply the vector that results from the integration in the previous step with W_2. Let $\mathbf{q}_2$ be the resulting vector. Proceed with q_ℓ for $\ell \geq 2$ as with q_1 in step 3 to reach the final observation time t_R. In each integration step multiply with the resulting vector with the corresponding weight matrix W_ℓ.

The derivatives of the likelihood are computed by simultaneously solving systems of ODEs similar to (17). Differentiating (6) w.r.t. some rate constant c_j gives further ODEs for the derivative of the mode probability which may involve the derivatives of the approximated conditional expectations $\mathbf{y}_{\mathbf{m}}$. Thus, in Step 1 of the algorithm described above, we simultaneously compute the derivatives of $P(\mathbf{M}(t) = \mathbf{m})$ and $\mathbf{y}_{\mathbf{m}}$ w.r.t. all parameters. Note that differentiating (7) w.r.t. c_j yields on ODE that may involve mode probabilities and their derivatives as well as conditional expectations and their derivatives. Then, in Step 2 we have to use the derivatives of $\mathbf{y}_{\mathbf{m}}$ to correctly weight the vectors $\frac{\partial}{\partial c_j}\mathbf{p}$. Note that differentiating (14) now gives

$$\frac{\partial \mathbf{u}(t_\ell)}{\partial c_j} = \left(\frac{\partial \mathbf{u}(t_{\ell-1})}{\partial c_j}P_\ell + \mathbf{u}(t_{\ell-1})\frac{\partial}{\partial c_j}P_\ell\right)W_\ell$$
$$+ \mathbf{u}(t_{\ell-1})P_\ell\frac{\partial}{\partial c_j}W_\ell,$$

since W_ℓ depends on c_j through $\mathbf{y}_{\mathbf{m}}$. The entries of $\frac{\partial}{\partial c_j}W_\ell$ are the derivatives of $\phi_{0,\Sigma}((\mathbf{m}, \mathbf{y}_{\mathbf{m}}(t_\ell)) - \mathbf{O}(t_\ell))$ w.r.t. c_j. In Step 3 we have additional ODEs for the (weighted) derivatives of the mode probabilities. All other parts of the algorithm remain the same. Note that if we want to compute second order derivatives or the derivative of the likelihood w.r.t. the initial conditions or Σ, the procedure is very similar (see also Appendix A).

It is clear that if higher moments of the conditional densities are needed to identify parameters, then the above approach has to be extended accordingly. Moreover, if we assume that there is no measurement error, then the weights become zero except if the deterministic trajectory of the conditional expectations are equal to the observations of the continuous variables. Since an exact match is unlikely for realistic applications, the likelihood will be zero. Therefore, it is advantageous to include information about higher moments. Here, we consider the case where information about the conditional covariances is added as described in Section 3. This changes the algorithm for approximating the likelihood as follows. In Step 1 we approximate the mode probabilities, the conditional expectations, the conditional covariances, and all derivatives. Assuming that Σ is a block diagonal matrix, i.e., measurement errors of discrete and continuous populations are not correlated, in Step 2 the weight of mode $\mathbf{m}$ is now given by

$$\phi_{0,\Sigma^d}\left(\mathbf{O}^d(t_\ell) - \mathbf{m}\right) \cdot \phi_{0,\Sigma^c+V}\left(\mathbf{O}^c(t_\ell) - \mathbf{y}_{\mathbf{m}}(t_\ell)\right),$$

where $\mathbf{O}(t_\ell) = (\mathbf{O}^d(t_\ell), \mathbf{O}^c(t_\ell))$, Σ^d and Σ^c are the diagonal blocks of Σ that correspond to the discrete and continuous populations, and V is the (approximated) covariance matrix

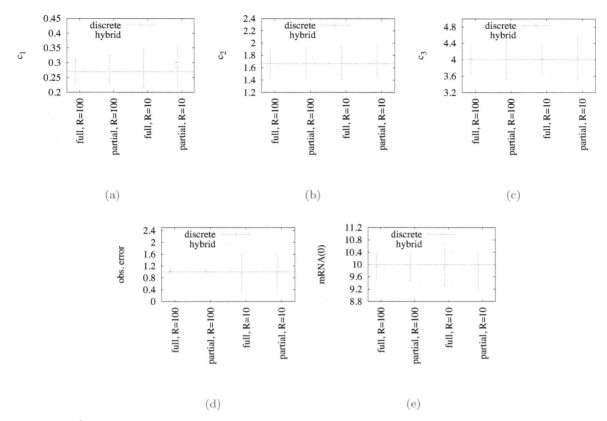

Figure 3: Parameter estimates with standard deviations for the gene expression example.

conditioned on mode $\mathbf{m}$ at time t_ℓ. The rationale behind this is that due to the independence of the measurement errors, we can split the multivariate density in two parts according to the splitting into discrete and a continuous populations. Moreover, given the conditional expectations $\mu = \mathbf{y_m}(t_\ell)$ and the covariances V, we assume that the conditional distribution follows a multivariate normal distribution with mean μ and covariance matrix V. Then we exploit that the convolution of two normal distributions, that we get in (18), is again a normal distribution (where the covariance matrix is the sum of the covariance matrices of the convoluted distributions). Thus, the steps outlined above remain the same, except that the weight matrices W_ℓ change, i.e., besides the conditional expectations they contain information about the conditional variances. Now, even if measurement errors are not taken into account, the weights are nonzero (as long as the conditional variances are so).

As for the purely discrete case, if $K > 0$ then we consider the product of the individual likelihoods of the different observation sequences.

6. EXPERIMENTAL RESULTS

In this section we present experimental results of our hybrid approach where we approximate the conditional expectations and also the conditional covariances. We generated time series data for three different examples from systems biology using Monte-Carlo simulation and added error terms $\xi(t_\ell)$ to the population vector at time t_ℓ. We considered

equidistant observation intervals but our algorithm works for the non-equidistant case as well. Besides the network described in Example 2 we consider the gene expression example from [3] where a single DNA molecule is used for the transcription of mRNA molecules. Moreover, we estimate parameters for a multi-attractor model related to cellular transdifferentiation.

We remark that for all examples, the rate equations (see (5)) give a very poor approximation of the average molecule numbers while the hybrid approach for a transient analysis (cf. (6) and (7)) is very accurate.

For the generation of time series data we fix the (true) constants $\mathbf{c}$ and the initial condition $\mathbf{x}_0$ and, for simplicity, we assume that Σ is a diagonal matrix with all diagonal entries equal to the (common) standard deviation σ^2 of the error terms. Note that this means that we assume that at each observation time point the measurement errors of the different species are independent of each other. We estimate $\mathbf{c}$, $\mathbf{x}_0$, and σ^2 such that the likelihood of the time series becomes maximal under these parameters. Since in practice only few observation sequences are available, we estimate the parameters based on $K = 5$ observation sequences.

Our algorithm for the approximation of the likelihood is implemented in C++ and we run it on an Intel Core i7 at 2.8 Ghz with 8 GB main memory. It is linked to MATLAB's optimization toolbox which we use to minimize the negative log-likelihood. Since we use a global optimization method (MATLAB's global search), the running time of our method depends on the tightness of the intervals that we use as constraints for the unknown parameters as well as on the number of starting points of the global search procedure. We chose intervals that correspond to the order of magnitude of the parameters, i.e., if $c_j \in O(10^n)$ for some $n \in \mathbb{Z}$ then we use the interval $[10^{n-1}, 10^{n+1}]$ as a constraint for c_j. E.g. if $c_j = 0.1$ then $n = -1$ and we use the interval $[10^{-2}, 10^0]$. For the examples that we considered, a single starting point (the midpoint of the interval) was sufficient to accurately estimate the parameters. In general, of course, one has to cover the search space as good as possible to ensure that the global optimum is found. For the simplest example (gene expression), we used 20 starting points while for the other two more complex examples we simply started from the midpoints of the intervals. Clearly, the running time increases linearly with the number of starting points.

Since the initial molecular counts may not become integers during the optimization procedure we approximate the initial probability distribution by a multivariate normal distribution with mean $\mathbf{x}_0$ and a small variance so that the neighboring integer points are covered. For our experimental results we chose a variance of 0.1.

6.1 Gene expression

In the gene expression model, the transcription of a gene is stopped at a certain (stochastic) rate. If the gene is blocked, then at a certain rate it may become active again. The model consists of three reactions that involve three different species X_1 (for activated DNA), X_2 (for deactivated DNA) and X_3 (for mRNA). The reactions and change vectors are

$$
\begin{aligned}
X_1 &\rightarrow X_2 & \mathbf{v}_1 &= (-1, 1, 0) \\
X_2 &\rightarrow X_1 & \mathbf{v}_2 &= (1, -1, 0) \\
X_1 &\rightarrow X_1 + X_3 & \mathbf{v}_3 &= (0, 0, 1)
\end{aligned}
$$

and the corresponding rate functions are $\alpha_1(x_1, x_2, x_3) = c_1 \cdot x_1$, $\alpha_2(x_1, x_2, x_3) = c_2 \cdot x_2$, and $\alpha_3(x_1, x_2, x_3) = c_3 \cdot x_1$. In the stochastic hybrid approach, the mode corresponds to the state of X_1 and X_2 while X_3 is a continuous population.

For the gene expression network described above we chose a time horizon of $t = 100$ and for the true rate constants c_1, c_2, c_3 we chose the same numbers as in [3] (on a ten times faster time scale). For the variance of the error term that represents the measurement error, we chose $\sigma^2 = 1.0$ for the X_3 population (mRNA). Since we consider only a single DNA molecule, we assume that $\sigma^2 = 0$ for both X_1 and X_2. As initial conditions we chose $\mathbf{x}_0 = (0, 1, 10)$, i.e., we start with one deactivated DNA molecule and ten mRNA molecules. We plot the true (dotted blue line) and the estimated parameters (error bars) in Figure 3 where in the results with label "full" we consider the case that all three populations can be observed[4]. Since it is unrealistic to assume that the state of the DNA (activated or not) can be measured in the wet-lab, in the rows with label "partial" we consider the case that only the mRNA population can be observed. Of course, this makes the estimation more difficult since less information is available to calibrate parameters. We considered two cases for the number of observation points, $R = 10$ and $R = 100$ (see labels on the x-axis of Figure 3), that is, for instance in the first case we have $t_1 = 10, t_2 = 20, \ldots, t_R = 100$. We compare our hybrid solution proposed in Section 5.2 with a solution based on a purely discrete model (see Section 5.1). In Figure 3, we plot

the results of the discrete and the hybrid approach using error bars in green for the hybrid approach and error bars in red for the purely discrete approach. Obviously, the discrete approach give a more accurate estimation of the likelihood and is therefore always more accurate than the hybrid estimation. On the other hand, the discrete approach is very time consuming or even infeasible for more complex models as we consider them in the sequel. We remark, however, that the hybrid approach is in most cases nearly as accurate as the discrete approach.

Since for this example the running times for the estimation of the parameters is short (less than one minute), we repeated the generation of batches of five observation sequences and the estimation of parameters 100 times to approximate the mean and the standard deviation of the estimators. The plots in Figure 3 therefore show the mean of 100 estimation procedures and the corresponding standard deviation. Since for real applications one cannot repeat the estimation, alternative ways for approximating the standard deviation of the estimators have to be considered. The most common approach is to approximate the standard deviations by considering the entries of the Fisher information matrix, which we can derive from the second order derivatives of the likelihood. For the gene expression example, this approximation is quite good. For instance, for the results of the discrete approach in Figure 3 (a) we get approximated standard deviations of 0.0378, 0.2363, 0.0272, 0.0711, and 0.3309 for the five parameters. For the hybrid approach, we get 0.0428, 0.2623, 0.3224, 0.1170, and 0.5265. The results for the remaining cases are similar and omitted here.

6.2 Exclusive switch

The exclusive switch (see Example 2) consists of the following ten reactions (to improve readability, we use explicit names for the five chemical species instead of $X_1, \ldots, X_5$):

$$
\begin{aligned}
Dna &\rightarrow Dna + P_1 & &\textit{production of } P_1 \\
Dna &\rightarrow Dna + P_2 & &\textit{production of } P_2 \\
P_1 &\rightarrow \emptyset & &\textit{degradation of } P_1 \\
P_2 &\rightarrow \emptyset & &\textit{degradation of } P_2 \\
Dna + P_1 &\rightarrow Dna.P_1; & &\textit{binding of } P_1 \\
Dna + P_2 &\rightarrow Dna.P_2 & &\textit{binding of } P_2 \\
Dna.P_1 &\rightarrow Dna + P_1 & &\textit{unbinding of } P_2 \\
Dna.P_2 &\rightarrow Dna + P_2 & &\textit{unbinding of } P_2 \\
Dna.P_1 &\rightarrow Dna.P_1 + P_1 & &\textit{production of } P_1 \\
Dna.P_2 &\rightarrow Dna.P_2 + P_2 & &\textit{production of } P_2
\end{aligned}
$$

For all reactions where proteins are produced we assume a common rate constant k. Similarly, the rate constant of degradation is d, binding to the promoter has rate constant b, and unbinding from the promoter occurs at rate u. With this simplification the running time is about 40 minutes while it takes up to three hours if all eight constants have to be estimated (note that the last two and the first two reactions always have the same rate constants). We chose a time horizon of $t = 100$, number of observation points $R = 10$, and true rate constants. We plot the results of our parameter estimation in Figure 4. For this example network, we did not compute the standard deviations of the estimators since this would require more than 30 hours. Instead, we used the entries of the Fisher information matrix to estimate the standard deviations, which is a widely-used way of approximating the standard deviations. For simplicity, we

---

[4]We remark that it is enough to observe either X_1 or X_2 since $X_1 + X_2 = 1$.

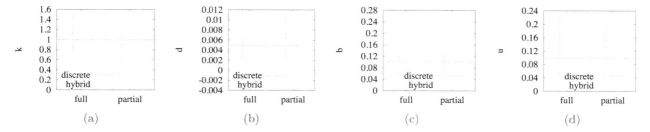

(a)   (b)   (c)   (d)

Figure 4: Parameter estimates with standard deviations for the exclusive switch example.

did not estimate the parameter σ^2 and the initial conditions (a single DNA molecule and no proteins) but assumed that these values are given. If we estimate these parameters as well then the running time increases polynomially, since the number of ODEs that have to be solved increases polynomially. For simplicity we chose a fixed variance of $\sigma^2 = 1.0$ for the measurement error of all populations. We consider time series data where all populations are observed (see labels "full" on the x-axis of Figure 4) and time series data where only the number of protein molecules is observed (see labels "partial"). The results show that the estimation of the hybrid approach is of similar accuracy as that of the purely discrete approach even though the hybrid model partially works with moment-based representation of the probability distributions. We remark that for the results in Figure 4 the discrete approach takes twice as long than the hybrid approach. This becomes worse if the observation time points are far away from each other and if the protein numbers are higher, since more and more states have to be considered during the numerical integration. Note that during the integration of the discrete model each time an observation time point is reached the multiplication with the weight matrix leads to a considerable truncation of the state space while between two observation time points the truncation is based only on the (weighted) probabilities.

For the partial observations, both the hybrid and the discrete approach give estimations that are less accurate compared to full observations. Note that for parameter $u = 0.1$ the discrete approach is worse than the hybrid approach because the likelihood becomes maximal for $u = 0.1512$. The more accurate value of the hybrid approach is due to the coarser approximation of the likelihood. For parameters k, d, b, however, the discrete approach is better, which conforms to our expectations.

6.3 Multi-Attractor model

Our final example is a part of the multi-attractor model considered by Zhou et al. [21]. It consists of the three genes MafA, Pax4, and δ-gene, which interact with each other as illustrated in Figure 6. The corresponding proteins bind to specific promoter regions on the DNA and (de-)activate the genes. The reaction network has 2^3 modes (since each gene can be on or off) and three continuous populations (the proteins of the three genes). The edges between the nodes in Figure 6 show whether the protein of a specific gene can bind to the promoter region of another gene. Moreover, edges with normal arrow heads correspond to binding without inhibition while the edges with line heads show inhibition.

We list all 24 reactions in Appendix B. We consider a

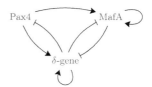

Figure 6: Interactions of the multi-attractor model.

time horizon of $t = 10$ and initial conditions where all genes are active and no proteins are present. To simplify the estimation procedure, we assume that there is a common rate constant for all protein production reactions (k), for all protein degradations (d), binding (b) and unbinding (u) reactions. We plot the chosen true constants and the estimations based on our hybrid approach in Figure 5. As for the exclusive switch, we consider time series data where all populations are observed and data where only the number of protein molecules observed (always with measurement errors represented by $\sigma^2 = 1.0$, not estimated). We estimate the standard deviations of the estimators using the Fisher information matrix. Note that for this example, it becomes infeasible to use a purely discrete approach if the observation points are far away from each other ($R = 10$) since the number of states that have to be considered becomes too large. For the hybrid approach, the running time was about five hours.

For the partial observations (see "partial" in Figure 5), the estimated values are not very accurate. This has several reasons. First, the observations are only five random trajectories of the Markov chain (we did not choose particularly favorable trajectories but simply generated them at random). Secondly, for the parameters u and b, partial observations do not seem to suffice for an accurate estimation even if we have $R = 100$ observation time points. The high standard deviations that we approximated based on the Fisher information matrix, however, show that more information is necessary to derive accurate estimations. As expected, the estimates for the full observations are more accurate. We remark that it is out of the scope of this paper to examine when there is enough information available to estimate certain parameters accurately.

7. RELATED WORK

Several approaches for the estimation of parameters of stochastic hybrid models of chemical reaction networks exist. Some of them are based on a Markov Chain Monte Carlo method [12, 8] while Reinker et al. use a maximum likelihood approach, but propose a numerical approximation of

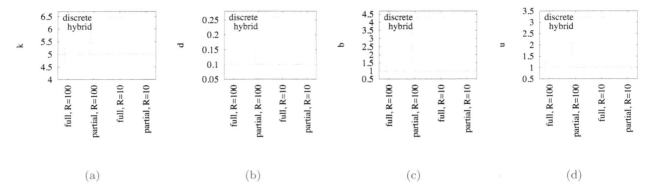

(a)   (b)   (c)   (d)

Figure 5: Parameter estimates with standard deviations for the multi-attractor example.

the likelihood for a discrete-state Markov model of biochemical reaction networks [18]. A similar approach is taken by Tian et al. as well as Angius and Horváth, where the likelihood function is evaluated by Monte Carlo simulation [20, 3]. As opposed to that, here, we use a stochastic hybrid model and a direct numerical approach to approximate the likelihood of the data. Cinquemani et al. use a similar model as ours, but minimize prediction errors [4] while we minimize the (negative) log-likelihood.

Our stochastic hybrid model has the advantage that it does not suffer from the largeness problem in discrete-state systems. Moreover, it relies on an explicit representation of mode probabilities while other models rely on a moment-based representation [10]. Compared to other estimation methods, the maximum likelihood approach that we use has desirable mathematical properties. Specifically, maximum likelihood estimators become minimum variance unbiased estimators and are asymptotically normal as the sample size increases. We remark that it is difficult to compare the accuracy and efficiency of different parameter estimation algorithms since currently implementations of such algorithms are not publicly available except for our own previously developed estimation method for purely discrete models [2], which we use for a comparison in Section 6.

8.   CONCLUSIONS

Parameter inference for purely discrete models of chemical reaction networks demands huge computational resources. Here, we use a stochastic hybrid model that relies on an accurate but computationally cheap approximation of the dynamics of large chemical populations. In this way we mitigate the largeness problem of state spaces of purely discrete models. We proposed an efficient numerical approximation method for the stochastic hybrid model to derive maximum likelihood estimators for a given set of noisy observations of the network.

As future work, we plan to integrate our parameter estimation technique into SHAVE [14], a tool for the analysis of stochastic hybrid models of chemical reactions, and to use it for the estimation of parameters in more complex networks. Moreover, we will apply our technique to other application domains of stochastic hybrid systems and consider more sophisticated optimization methods to improve the efficiency if many parameters have to be estimated.

9.   ACKNOWLEDGMENTS

This research has been partially funded by the German Research Council (DFG) as part of the Cluster of Excellence on Multimodal Computing and Interaction at Saarland University and the Transregional Collaborative Research Center "Automatic Verification and Analysis of Complex Systems" (SFB/TR 14 AVACS).

10.   REFERENCES

[1] W. Anderson. *Continuous-time Markov chains: An applications-oriented approach.* Springer, 1991.

[2] A. Andreychenko, L. Mikeev, D. Spieler, and V. Wolf. Parameter identification for Markov models of biochemical reactions. In *Proceedings of CAV'11*, Lecture Notes of Computer Science, 2011.

[3] A. Angius and A. Horváth. The Monte Carlo EM method for the parameter estimation of biological models. In *Proc. of Workshop on Practical Applications of Stochastic Modelling (PASM)*, ENTCS, 2011.

[4] E. Cinquemani, A. Milias, S. Summers, and J. Lygeros. Stochastic dynamics of genetic networks: modelling and parameter identification. *Bioinformatics*, 24(23):2748–2754, 2008.

[5] S. Engblom. Computing the moments of high dimensional solutions of the master equation. *Appl. Math. Comput.*, 180:498–515, 2006.

[6] D. T. Gillespie. *Markov Processes.* Academic Press., 1992.

[7] I. Golding, J. Paulsson, S. Zawilski, and E. Cox. Real-time kinetics of gene activity in individual bacteria. *Cell*, 123(6):1025–1036, December 2005.

[8] A. Golightly and D. Wilkinson. Bayesian inference for stochastic kinetic models using a diffusion approximation. *Biometrics*, (61):781–788, 2005.

[9] T. Henzinger, M. Mateescu, L. Mikeev, and V. Wolf. Hybrid numerical solution of the chemical master equation. In *Proc. of CMSB*, ACM International Conference Proceeding Series, pages 55–65, 2010.

[10] J. Hespanha. Moment closure for biochemical networks. In *Proc. of the Third Int. Symp. on Control, Communications and Signal Processing*, 2008.

[11] P. Kouretas, K. Koutroumpas, J. Lygeros, and Z. Lygerou. Stochastic hybrid modelling of

biochemical processes. In *C.G.Cassandras and J.Lygeros, editors, Stochastic Hybrid Systems, Automation and Control Engineering Series,* volume 24. Taylor & Francis Group/CRC Press, 2006.

[12] K. Koutroumpas, E. Cinquemani, P. Kouretas, and J. Lygeros. Parameter identification for stochastic hybrid systems using randomized optimization: A case study on subtilin production by bacillus subtilis. *Nonlinear Analysis: Hybrid Systems*, 2(3):786–802, 2008.

[13] T. G. Kurtz. The relationship between stochastic and deterministic models for chemical reactions. *J. Chem. Phys.*, 57(7):2976 –2978, 1972.

[14] M. Lapin, L. Mikeev, and V. Wolf. SHAVE – Stochastic hybrid analysis of Markov population models. In *Proc. of HSCC*, ACM International Conference Proceeding Series, 2011.

[15] A. Loinger, A. Lipshtat, N. Q. Balaban, and O. Biham. Stochastic simulations of genetic switch systems. *Physical Review E*, 75:021904, 2007.

[16] M. Mateescu, V. Wolf, F. Didier, and T. Henzinger. Fast adaptive uniformisation of the chemical master equation. *IET Systems Biology Journal*, 4(6), 2010.

[17] S. Menz, J. Latorre, C. Schütte, and W. Huisinga. Hybrid stochastic-deterministic solution of the chemical master equation. *SIAM Interdisciplinary Journal Multiscale Modeling and Simulation*, 2011. Under review.

[18] S. Reinker, R. Altman, and J. Timmer. Parameter estimation in stochastic biochemical reactions. *IEEE Proc. Syst. Biol*, 153:168–178, 2006.

[19] A. Singh and J. Hespanha. Stochastic hybrid systems for studying biochemical processes. *Phil. Trans. R. Soc. A*, 368(1930):4995–5011, Nov. 2010.

[20] T. Tian, S. Xu, J. Gao, and K. Burrage. Simulated maximum likelihood method for estimating kinetic rates in gene expression. *Bioinformatics*, (23):84–91, 2007.

[21] J. Zhou, L. Brusch, and S. Huang. Predicting pancreas cell fate decisions and reprogramming with a hierarchical multi-attractor model. *PLoS ONE*, 6(3):e14752+, 2011.

APPENDIX

A. DERIVATIVES OF THE LIKELIHOOD

Let $\mathbf{x}_0 = (x_1, \ldots, x_n)$ be the vector of initial molecule numbers and let $\Sigma_{i_1 i_2}$ be the entries of the matrix Σ, where $i_1, i_2 \in \{1, \ldots, n\}$. Since the initial molecular counts may not become integers during the optimization procedure we approximate the initial probability distribution by a multivariate normal distribution with mean $\mathbf{x}_0$ and a small variance so that the neighboring integer points are covered. For our experimental results we chose a variance of 0.1.

For $i \in \{1, \ldots, n\}$

$$\frac{\partial \mathbf{u}(t_\ell)}{\partial x_i} = \frac{\partial \mathbf{u}(t_{\ell-1})}{\partial x_i} P_\ell W_\ell, \tag{19}$$

$$\frac{\partial \mathbf{u}(t_\ell)}{\partial \Sigma_{i_1 i_2}} = \left(\frac{\partial \mathbf{u}(t_{\ell-1})}{\partial \Sigma_{i_1 i_2}} W_\ell + \mathbf{u}(t_{\ell-1}) \frac{\partial}{\partial \Sigma_{i_1 i_2}} W_\ell \right) P_\ell, \tag{20}$$

where $\frac{\partial \mathbf{u}(t_0)}{\partial \Sigma_{i_1 i_2}} = \mathbf{0}$ and $\frac{\partial \mathbf{u}(t_0)}{\partial x_i} = \frac{\partial \mathbf{p}(t_0)}{\partial x_i}$.

For the computation of (19) and (20) we simultaneously solve

$$\frac{d}{dt} \mathbf{v}_i(t) = \mathbf{v}_i(t) Q, \tag{21}$$

$$\frac{d}{dt} \mathbf{y}_{i_1 i_2}(t) = \mathbf{y}_{i_1 i_2}(t) Q \tag{22}$$

for the time interval $[t_{\ell-1}, t_\ell]$ with initial conditions $\mathbf{v}_i(t_{\ell-1}) = \frac{\partial \mathbf{u}(t_{\ell-1})}{\partial x_i}$ and $\mathbf{y}_{i_1 i_2}(t_{\ell-1}) = \frac{\partial \mathbf{u}(t_{\ell-1})}{\partial \Sigma_{i_1 i_2}}$. After solving (21) and (22) we obtain

$$\frac{\partial \mathbf{u}(t_\ell)}{\partial x_i} = \mathbf{v}_i(t_\ell) W_\ell,$$

$$\frac{\partial \mathbf{u}(t_\ell)}{\partial \Sigma_{i_1 i_2}} = \mathbf{y}_{i_1 i_2}(t_\ell) W_\ell + \mathbf{r}(t_\ell) \frac{\partial}{\partial \Sigma_{i_1 i_2}} W_\ell.$$

We compute $\frac{\partial}{\partial \lambda} \mathcal{L}_k$ as $\frac{\partial}{\partial \lambda} \mathbf{u}(t_R) \mathbf{e}$ where λ is either x_i or $\Sigma_{i_1 i_2}$. We also compute the second derivatives of the likelihood using similar schemes.

B. REACTIONS OF THE MULTI-ATTRACTOR MODEL

The multi-attractor model involves the three species MafAProt, DeltaProt, and PaxProt that represent the proteins of the three gene and it involves ten species that represent the state of the genes: MafADna, DeltaDna, PaxDna, MafADnaPaxProt, DeltaDnaMafAProt, PaxDnaDeltaProt, MafADnaDeltaProt, DeltaDnaPaxProt, PaxDnaMafAProt, MafADnaMafAProt, DeltaDnaDeltaProt. The chemical reactions are as follows:

$$
\begin{aligned}
\text{PaxDna} &\xrightarrow{k} \text{PaxDna} + \text{PaxProt} \\
\text{PaxProt} &\xrightarrow{d} \emptyset \\
\text{PaxDna} + \text{DeltaProt} &\xrightarrow{b} \text{PaxDnaDeltaProt} \\
\text{PaxDnaDeltaProt} &\xrightarrow{u} \text{PaxDna} + \text{DeltaProt} \\
\text{MafADNA} &\xrightarrow{k} \text{MafADna} + \text{MafAProt} \\
\text{MafAProt} &\xrightarrow{d} \emptyset \\
\text{MafADna} + \text{PaxProt} &\xrightarrow{b} \text{MafADnaPaxProt} \\
\text{MafADnaPaxProt} &\xrightarrow{u} \text{MafADna} + \text{PaxProt} \\
\text{MafADnaPaxProt} &\xrightarrow{k} \text{MafADnaPaxProt} + \text{MafAProt} \\
\text{MafADna} + \text{MafAProt} &\xrightarrow{b} \text{MafADnaMafAProt} \\
\text{MafADnaMafAProt} &\xrightarrow{u} \text{MafADna} + \text{MafAProt} \\
\text{MafADnaMafAProt} &\xrightarrow{k} \text{MafADnaMafAProt} + \text{MafAProt} \\
\text{MafADna} + \text{DeltaProt} &\xrightarrow{b} \text{MafADnaDeltaProt} \\
\text{MafADnaDeltaProt} &\xrightarrow{u} \text{MafADna} + \text{DeltaProt} \\
\text{DeltaDna} &\xrightarrow{k} \text{DeltaDna} + \text{DeltaProt} \\
\text{DeltaProt} &\xrightarrow{d} \emptyset \\
\text{DeltaDna} + \text{PaxProt} &\xrightarrow{b} \text{DeltaDnaPaxProt} \\
\text{DeltaDnaPaxProt} &\xrightarrow{u} \text{DeltaDna} + \text{PaxProt} \\
\text{DeltaDnaPaxProt} &\xrightarrow{k} \text{DeltaDnaPaxProt} + \text{DeltaProt} \\
\text{DeltaDna} + \text{MafAProt} &\xrightarrow{b} \text{DeltaDnaMafAProt} \\
\text{DeltaDnaMafAProt} &\xrightarrow{u} \text{DeltaDna} + \text{MafAProt} \\
\text{DeltaDna} + \text{DeltaProt} &\xrightarrow{b} \text{DeltaDnaDeltaProt} \\
\text{DeltaDnaDeltaProt} &\xrightarrow{u} \text{DeltaDna} + \text{DeltaProt} \\
\text{DeltaDnaDeltaProt} &\xrightarrow{k} \text{DeltaDnaDeltaProt} + \text{DeltaProt}
\end{aligned}
$$

From Hybrid Data-Flow Languages to Hybrid Automata: A Complete Translation [*]

Peter Schrammel
INRIA Grenoble – Rhône-Alpes
655 Avenue de l'Europe
38330 Montbonnot St-Martin, France
peter.schrammel@inria.fr

Bertrand Jeannet
INRIA Grenoble – Rhône-Alpes
655 Avenue de l'Europe
38330 Montbonnot St-Martin, France
bertrand.jeannet@inria.fr

ABSTRACT

Hybrid systems are used to model embedded computing systems interacting with their physical environment. There is a conceptual mismatch between high-level hybrid system languages like SIMULINK, which are used for simulation, and hybrid automata, the most suitable representation for safety verification. Indeed, in simulation languages the interaction between discrete and continuous execution steps is specified using the concept of zero-crossings, whereas hybrid automata exploit the notion of staying conditions. We describe a translation from a hybrid data-flow language to logiconumerical hybrid automata that points out this issue carefully. We expose various zero-crossing semantics, propose a sound translation, and discuss to which extent the original semantics is preserved.

Categories and Subject Descriptors

D.2.1 [**Software Engineering**]: Requirements/Specification—*Languages*; D.2.4 [**Software Engineering**]: Software / Program Verification—*Formal methods*; I.6.2 [**Computing Methodologies**]: Simulation and Modelling—*Simulation Languages*

General Terms

Languages, Verification

Keywords

Data-Flow Languages, Hybrid Systems, Hybrid Automata, Verification

1. INTRODUCTION

The motivation of this paper is the *verification of safety properties* of hybrid systems, like, for example, safety-critical controllers interacting with their physical environment as

found in modern transport systems. The verification of such properties amounts to checking whether the reachable state space stays within the invariant specified by the property.

Specifying hybrid systems. Languages like SIMULINK[1], MODELICA[2], and ZELUS [6] have been developed to support the modelling, implementation and simulation of hybrid systems. They offer features like modularity, hierarchy and a data-flow or equational syntax.

SIMULINK for example uses a data-flow-based description of the behavior of continuous- and discrete-time variables; STATEFLOW extends it with the ability of automata-based specifications of the discrete-time behavior. ZELUS extends the synchronous, data-flow programming language LUCID-SYNCHRONE [26] with differential equations. In these languages, discrete execution steps that interrupt the continuous-time evolution are triggered by the activation of *zero-crossings*.[3] Roughly speaking, a zero-crossing is an event occurring during the integration of an ordinary differential equation (ODE) $\dot{x}(t) = f(x(t), u(t))$, when some expression $z(x(t))$ changes sign from negative to positive. A zero-crossing may also be triggered by a discrete execution step as in SIMULINK. All these data-flow languages are primarily designed for simulation, hence their semantics is mostly deterministic.

On the other hand, the concept of *hybrid automata* [3, 19, 20] was developed for the verification of hybrid systems. They are lower-level representations of hybrid systems with a non-deterministic semantics by default, and in which continuous-time evolution is governed by staying conditions, usually referred to as *location invariants*.

Hence, there is a conceptual mismatch between high-level hybrid system languages and hybrid automata. The main differences between *simulation* and *verification* formalisms can be summarized as follows:
- equation-based versus automata-based
- continuous modes implicitly encoded in Boolean variables versus their explicit encoding with locations
- discrete transitions triggered by zero-crossings versus combinations of staying conditions and guards
- deterministic, open systems with inputs versus non-deterministic, closed systems.

Our primary goal is to formalize the translation from a hybrid data-flow formalism to hybrid automata, and in particular to focus on the translation of zero-crossings. How-

---

[*]This work was supported by the ANR project VEDECY and the INRIA large-scale initiative SYNCHRONICS.

---

[1]http://www.mathworks.com
[2]http://www.modelica.org
[3]STATEFLOW also allows to trigger discrete jumps by ordinary guards that are not interpreted as zero-crossings.

ever, a secondary aspect we have in mind is that we want to address hybrid systems specified as the composition of a discrete controller and its physical environment. This means that the discrete part of the system's state space might be complex, and defined by Boolean variables and numerical variables (counters, thresholds, etc. manipulated by the controller). The consequence is that we want to translate the data-flow input language to *logico-numerical* hybrid automata, that can manipulate symbolically discrete variables, in addition to continuous variables governed by differential equations. Such automata allow a compact representation by not requiring the enumeration of the discrete state space.

Verifying hybrid systems. There is a vast literature on hybrid system verification based on hybrid automata. Here, we cite only some selected methods, that can be classified as follows:

Bounded-time analysis methods analyze systems up to some time horizon. Systems with linear or non-linear dynamics require a time discretization: either a so-called flow-pipe (a set of convex sets over-approximating the possible trajectories) is constructed by set integration [10, 16, 17], or the discretized system is saturated by constraint propagation techniques [15, 27].

Unbounded-time methods are more challenging, because unbounded time raises a termination issue. [18] analyzes systems with *piecewise constant dynamics* with convex polyhedra and solves the termination issue by the use of *widening* [12]. [8] extends this approach, by considering the verification of hybrid systems with a large discrete state space and by combining symbolically properties on Boolean and numerical variables within the abstract interpretation framework. Recently a method exploiting max-strategy iteration on template polyhedra was proposed in [13].

Contributions. Our contributions can be summarized as follows:

1. We present the general principles behind the translation of a simple, yet complete *hybrid data-flow language* that serves as a low-level formalism for languages such as SIMULINK or ZELUS, to *logico-numerical hybrid automata*, *i.e.* an extension of classical hybrid automata by Boolean variables. This extension prepares us w.r.t. the verification of programs with a large Boolean state space.

2. We discuss the various *zero-crossing semantics* that appear in the source simulation language. We propose sound translations to hybrid automata, and we investigate the extent to which these translations preserve the original semantics.

Related work. Recent articles describe translations of hybrid system languages, like SIMULINK/STATEFLOW, to hybrid automata, but they only treat a subset of the ways in which discrete transitions may be activated. A translation of a subset of the SIMULINK/STATEFLOW language to hybrid automata is proposed in [2] for the purpose of verification. They handle STATEFLOW diagrams of which the translation is rather straightforward, but they do not handle proper zero-crossings. Another translation of a subset of the SIMULINK/STATEFLOW language to hybrid automata with the goal of improving simulation coverage is presented in [4], but they only consider deterministic models, and similarly they do not handle zero-crossings. The tool HyLINK [24], which performs a translation of SIMULINK/STATEFLOW

models to hybrid automata, targets the applications of verification and controller synthesis. It is restricted to more or less the same subset as [2]. They introduce blocks for specifying non-deterministic inputs as required by verification methods. A formal definition of the translation is ongoing work. The translation of discrete-time SIMULINK models with periodic triggers to LUSTRE is presented in [31]. The inverse of what we are doing, namely the embedding of hybrid automata in a hybrid system language (here SCICOS), is the goal of [25].

Organisation of the article. §§2 and 3 introduce the hybrid data-flow formalism and logico-numerical hybrid automata respectively. §§4 to 7 describe our contributions. After discussing the results in §8 we conclude in §9.

2. HYBRID DATA-FLOW MODEL

SIMULINK and ZELUS are full programming languages with constructs for modularity. In order to abstract from such constructs, we present here a lower-level data-flow formalism that will serve as the generic input language for the translation.

As this formalism is dedicated not only to simulation, but also serves as a specification language, we use the notion of *inputs* constrained by an *assertion* as in LUSTRE [9]. This allows us to give a semantics to the components of a more general system. Simulation can still be performed by connecting a component with inputs to an input generator, see for instance [28] for the simulation of discrete synchronous systems.

Notations. We will use the following notations:

$s = (b, x)$: state variable vector, with b discrete (Boolean and numerical) and x continuous numerical subvectors, *e.g.* $((b_1, b_2, n_1), x_1, x_2, x_3) \in (\mathbb{B}^2 \times \mathbb{Z}) \times \mathbb{R}^3$

i : input variable vector, *e.g.* $(\beta_1, \xi_1, \xi_2) \in \mathbb{B} \times \mathbb{R}^2$

$e(s, i)$: an arithmetic expression without test, *e.g.* $n + 2x + \xi$

$up(e(s, i))$: a zero-crossing, *e.g.* $up(x + \xi - n)$

$\varphi^Z(s, i)$: a logical combination of zero-crossings, *e.g.* $up(z_1) \wedge \neg up(z_2) \vee up(z_3)$

$\phi(b)$: a Boolean expression over discrete state variables

$\Phi(s, i)$: an arbitrary expression without zero-crossings

Program model. A hybrid data-flow program is defined by:

$$\left\{ \begin{array}{l} \mathcal{I}(s) \\ \mathcal{A}(s, i) \wedge \left\{ \begin{array}{l} \dot{x} = f^c(s, i) \\ s' = f^d(s, i) \end{array} \right. \end{array} \right.$$

where the predicate $\mathcal{I}(s)$ defines the initial states, the predicate $\mathcal{A}(s, i)$ is the global *assertion* constraining the inputs, the continous flow equations $\dot{x} = f^c(s, i)$ and the discrete transition functions $s' = f^d(s, i)$ are of the form:

$$\dot{x} = \left\{ \begin{array}{c} \cdots \\ e_\ell(s, i) \text{ if } \phi_\ell(b) \\ \cdots \end{array} \right. \qquad s' = \left\{ \begin{array}{c} \cdots \\ \Phi_j(s, i) \text{ if } \varphi^Z_j(s, i) \\ \cdots \end{array} \right.$$

We assume that the conditions ϕ_ℓ define a partition of the discrete state space, and that $\forall s \exists i : \mathcal{A}(s, i)$ (*i.e.* the assertion does not constrain the state-space).

Furthermore the zero-crossing formulas φ^Z_j must be exclusive in order to guarantee determinism, *i.e.* only a single φ^Z_j may be activated at the same instant. Real languages

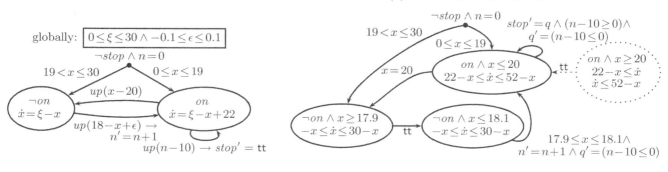

```
let node main xi eps = (n,x) where
  assert 0<=xi && xi<=30 &&
         -0.1<=eps && eps<=0.1 and
  der x = if on then xi-x+22 else xi-x
          init xi and
  on = (xi<=19) ->
          true every up(18-x+eps)
        | false every up(x-20) and
  n = 0 -> (last n)+1 every up(18-x+eps) and
  stop = false -> true every up(n-10)
```

(a) ZELUS thermostat

$$\mathcal{I}(on, stop, n, x) = \neg stop \wedge n = 0 \wedge 0 \leq x \leq 30 \wedge$$
$$(x \leq 19 \wedge on \vee x > 19 \wedge \neg on)$$

$$\mathcal{A}((on, stop, n, x), (\xi, \epsilon)) = 0 \leq \xi \leq 30 \wedge -0.1 \leq \epsilon \leq 0.1$$

$$\dot{x} = \begin{cases} \xi - x + 22 & \text{if } on \\ \xi - x & \text{if } \neg on \end{cases}$$

$$(on', stop', n', x') = \begin{cases} (\text{ff}, stop, n, x) & \text{if } up(x - 20) \\ (\text{tt}, stop, n + 1, x) & \text{if } up(18 - x + \epsilon) \\ (on, \text{tt}, n, x) & \text{if } up(n - 10) \end{cases}$$

(b) Intermediate data-flow model

(c) Partitioned data-flow model

(d) Resulting Hybrid Automaton, with q a state Boolean variable introduced by the translation

Figure 1: Translation of the Thermostat example described in Example 1

achieve this goal using *if-then-else* constructs or with the help of priorities, *e.g.* based on the order zero-crossings occur in the source code.

A second requirement is that $\forall j : \varphi_j^Z \Rightarrow \bigvee_m up(z_m)$, where $up(z_1), \ldots, up(z_M)$ are the zero-crossings occurring in the program; this condition prevents from taking a discrete transition when no zero-crossing is activated.

Although hybrid system languages often include explicit automata representations, for uniformity of presentation we assume that they have first been transformed into data-flow equations, see [11] for instance.

EXAMPLE 1. *Fig. 1a shows a variant of the classical thermostat example. The input xi represents the external temperature, the input eps models the inaccuracy of the temperature sensor[4], the continuous state variable x is the room temperature, the discrete Boolean state variable on indicates the state of the heating system, and the discrete integer state variable n counts the number of times the temperature goes from below to above 18 degrees (modulo the uncertainty). At last, the state variable stop becomes true when "n reaches 10 from below".*

Fig. 1b shows its translation to our intermediate formalism. Observe that this translation factorizes the evolution of discrete variables according to the zero-crossing conditions.

Semantics of zero-crossings. A *zero-crossing* is an expression of the form $up(z)$ that becomes true when the sign of $z(s, i)$, an arithmetic expression without tests, switches from negative to positive during an execution. Instead of just a valuation of variables of the form (s_k, i_k) zero-crossings

are interpreted on an execution fragment of the form $(s_{k-1}, i_{k-1}) \rightarrow (s_k, i_k)$, *i.e.* two consecutive configurations of an execution trace. We will use the notation $(s_{k-1}, i_{k-1}, s_k, i_k)$ for short. Several interpretations are possible which are discussed in §4. For now, we arbitrarily select the so-called "contact" semantics, formally defined as:

$$(s_{k-1}, i_{k-1}, s_k, i_k) \models up(z(s, i)) \text{ iff } \begin{cases} z(s_{k-1}, i_{k-1}) < 0 \\ z(s_k, i_k) \geq 0 \end{cases} \quad (1)$$

In other words, a zero-crossing $up(z)$ is activated (and taken into account for computing the next step $k+1$) if the expression z was strictly negative in the previous step $k-1$ and evaluates to some positive value or zero in the current step k.

A zero-crossing formula, *i.e.* a logical combination of zero-crossings, $\varphi^Z(s, i)$ is activated iff it evaluates to true when interpreting the zero-crossings $up(z_m)$ occurring in φ^Z using their corresponding constraints over a given $(s_{k-1}, i_{k-1}, s_k, i_k)$ as in (1).

Semantics. We define a trace semantics based on an ideal discretization of the continuous equations, following [6]. This semantics uses the theory of non-standard analysis [23, 29] to model the way typical simulators proceed, relying on a variable-step numerical integration solver (such as SUNDIALS CVODE [21]). Such solvers are given an initial state x_0, an ODE $\dot{x}(t) = f(x(t))$, and a finite set of zero-crossing expressions z_j. Then they integrate the ODE until at least one of the zero-crossings is activated. When this happens, the control is given back to the main simulation loop, which executes one or several discrete execution steps before continuing integration.

According to this approach, an execution of a hybrid data-flow program is a trace $(s_0, i_0) \rightarrow (s_1, i_1) \rightarrow (s_2, i_2) \rightarrow \ldots$ such that $\mathcal{I}(s_0)$, $\rightarrow = \rightarrow_c \cup \rightarrow_d$ and

---

[4]We do not use eps in the expression $up(x-20)$, in order to show an example of a deterministic zero-crossing.

$$(\boldsymbol{s}_k, \boldsymbol{i}_k) \rightarrow_c (\boldsymbol{s}_{k+1}, \boldsymbol{i}_{k+1}) \iff \mathcal{A}(\boldsymbol{s}_k, \boldsymbol{i}_k) \wedge$$

$$\exists l, \exists \partial > 0 : \begin{cases} \phi_\ell(\boldsymbol{b}_k) \wedge \forall j : \neg((\boldsymbol{s}_{k-1}, \boldsymbol{i}_{k-1}, \boldsymbol{s}_k, \boldsymbol{i}_k) \models \varphi_j^Z(\boldsymbol{s}, \boldsymbol{i})) \\ (\boldsymbol{b}_{k+1}, \boldsymbol{x}_{k+1}) = (\boldsymbol{b}_k, \boldsymbol{x}_k + \boldsymbol{e}_\ell(\boldsymbol{s}_k, \boldsymbol{i}_k) \cdot \partial) \end{cases}$$

$$(\boldsymbol{s}_k, \boldsymbol{i}_k) \rightarrow_d (\boldsymbol{s}_{k+1}, \boldsymbol{i}_{k+1}) \iff \mathcal{A}(\boldsymbol{s}_k, \boldsymbol{i}_k) \wedge$$

$$\exists j : \begin{cases} (\boldsymbol{s}_{k-1}, \boldsymbol{i}_{k-1}, \boldsymbol{s}_k, \boldsymbol{i}_k) \models \varphi_j^Z(\boldsymbol{s}, \boldsymbol{i}) \wedge \\ \quad \forall j' < j : \neg((\boldsymbol{s}_{k-1}, \boldsymbol{i}_{k-1}, \boldsymbol{s}_k, \boldsymbol{i}_k) \models \varphi_{j'}^Z(\boldsymbol{s}, \boldsymbol{i})) \\ \boldsymbol{s}_{k+1} = \Phi_j(\boldsymbol{s}_k, \boldsymbol{i}_k) \end{cases}$$

where ∂ is an infinitesimal (*c.f.* non-standard analysis).

A transition $\rightarrow_c$ corresponds to an infinitesimal continuous-time evolution, which is possible only if no zero-crossing condition φ_j^Z has been activated in the previous execution step. A transition $\rightarrow_d$ corresponds to a discrete transition triggered by the first enabled φ_j^Z.

We pinpoint some properties of this formalism:

(1) Discrete transitions are always guarded by zero-crossings, and continuous modes are always defined by a Boolean expression over discrete variables, which are piecewise constant in continuous time. This is to go sure that a mode change (change of dynamics) can only happen on discrete transitions.

(2) Furthermore, discrete transitions are *urgent*, *i.e.* they must be taken at the first point in time possible.

(3) Zero-crossings may not only be triggered by continuous evolution, but also by discrete transitions. This is the case in Example 1: if the zero-crossing $up(18 - x + \epsilon)$ occurs when $n = 9$, n is first incremented to 10, activating the zero-crossing $up(n - 10)$ which makes *stop* become true. This feature can cause infinite sequences of discrete zero-crossings. Such a behaviour can be avoided by forbidding circular dependencies between states variables through zero-crossings in the source program.

Partitioned representation. The hybrid data-flow model we have defined does not have any concept of control structure. However, for pedagogical purpose, one can partition the state space to generate an explicit automaton which may be easier to understand, see Fig. 1c. When doing this, partial evaluation may be used to simplify expressions and removing infeasible transitions. This has been done on Fig. 1c.

Standardization. As already mentioned the semantics of the hybrid data flow model is based on non-standard analysis, which allows to give an unambiguous meaning to hybrid systems even if they contain Zeno behavior for instance.

However, the semantics of the output formalism of our translation, *i.e.* hybrid automata, relies on standard analysis. Hence non-standard behaviors need to be mapped to standard behaviors. This is called *standardization*: since each standard system has a non-standard representation, a non-standard system is standardizable if it is a non-standard representation of a standard system.

In the following we give some intuitions about the relationships between non-standard and standard analysis; we refer to [23, 7] for further details.

The set $^*\mathbb{N}$ of non-standard positive integers is $\mathbb{N}$ augmented by infinitely large integers. The set $^*\mathbb{R}$ of non-standard reals contains $\mathbb{R}$, but also (positive and negative) infinitely large and infinitesimally small numbers, and non-standard infinitesimals ∂ are the inverse of infinite numbers. For each real number x, $^*\mathbb{R}$ contains non-standard real numbers that are only infinitesimally away from x. The standardization operator for converting non-standard reals

to standard reals $st : {}^*\mathbb{R} \to \mathbb{R}$ identifies these equivalence classes of non-standard reals: $\forall x \in \mathbb{R} : \forall \partial : st(x + \partial) = x$ where ∂ is an infinitesimal $\in {}^*\mathbb{R}$.

W.r.t. continuous evolution, we have the following property: A non-standard sequence consisting of infinitesimal continuous steps

$$(\boldsymbol{s}_0, \boldsymbol{i}_0) \to \ldots \to (\boldsymbol{s}_n, \boldsymbol{i}_n)$$

with $n \in {}^*\mathbb{N}$, $\boldsymbol{x}_0 \in \mathbb{R}^p$, $\boldsymbol{x}_n \in \mathbb{R}^p$, has the following standard meaning: assuming that the input sequence $\boldsymbol{i}_0 \to \ldots \to \boldsymbol{i}_n$ forms a continuous function $\boldsymbol{i} : [0, \delta] \to I$, the sequence $\boldsymbol{s}_0 \to \ldots \to \boldsymbol{s}_n$ corresponds to a continuous function $\boldsymbol{s} : [0, \delta] \to S$ with

$$\boldsymbol{x}(\delta') = \boldsymbol{x}_0 + \int_0^{\delta'} \boldsymbol{e}_\ell((\boldsymbol{b}_0, \boldsymbol{x}(t)), \boldsymbol{i}(t)) dt$$

for $\delta' \in [0, \delta]$, $\delta = st(n\partial) \in \mathbb{R}^{\geq 0}$, and I and S denote the input and state space respectively.

However, we can write programs that are not standardizable, *i.e.* non-standard and standard meaning differ: For example the program fragment $b' = (x > 0)$ if $up(x)$ with "crossing" semantics (see §4) gives us $b' = \mathsf{tt}$ in the non-standard interpretation, but $b' = \mathsf{ff}$ in the standard interpretation.

Naturally, we can only correctly translate standardizable programs.

3. LOGICO-NUMERICAL HYBRID AUTOMATA

Hybrid automata [3, 19, 20] are a well-established formalism for modelling hybrid systems. Our definition is more general in the sense that we allow also Boolean variables and tests in the expressions appearing in the automata. Fig. 1d depicts an example of a hybrid automaton.

DEFINITION 1. *A logico-numerical hybrid automaton (HA) is a directed graph defined by $\langle L, F, J, \Sigma^0 \rangle$ where*
- *L is the finite set of locations,*
- *$F : L \to \mathcal{V}$ is a function that returns for each location the flow relation $V(\boldsymbol{s}, \dot{\boldsymbol{x}}) \in \mathcal{V}$ relating the state variables $\boldsymbol{s}$ and the time-derivatives $\dot{\boldsymbol{x}}$ of the numerical state variables, and*
- *$J \subseteq L \times \mathcal{R} \times L$ defines a finite set of arcs between locations with the discrete transition relation $R(\boldsymbol{s}, \boldsymbol{s}') \in \mathcal{R}$ over the state variables $\boldsymbol{s}$.*
- *$\Sigma^0 : L \to \mathcal{S}$ is a function that returns for each location the set of initial states $S^0 \in \mathcal{S}$, which have to satisfy $\forall \ell : \forall \boldsymbol{s} : \Sigma^0(\ell)(\boldsymbol{s}) \Rightarrow \exists \dot{\boldsymbol{x}} : F(\ell)(\boldsymbol{s}, \dot{\boldsymbol{x}})$.*

Further notations:
- $C_\ell(\boldsymbol{s}) = \exists \dot{\boldsymbol{x}} : V(\boldsymbol{s}, \dot{\boldsymbol{x}})$ is the *staying condition* of the flow $V = F(\ell)$.
- $G_{\ell, \ell'}(\boldsymbol{s}) = \exists \boldsymbol{s}' : R(\boldsymbol{s}, \boldsymbol{s}')$ is the *guard* of the arc $(\ell, R, \ell') \in J$.

Semantics. We use the following definitions: Let $T_{[0, \delta]}$ be the set of differentiable trajectories $[0, \delta] \to \mathbb{R}^n$. The function $flow_V$ returns the set of end states of trajectories $\tau \in T$ starting in the given state and that obey the flow relation V:

$$flow_V(\boldsymbol{b}, \boldsymbol{x}) =$$

$$\left\{ (\boldsymbol{b}, \boldsymbol{x}') \;\middle|\; \begin{array}{l} \exists \delta > 0, \exists \tau \in T_{[0, \delta]} : \\ \tau(0) = \boldsymbol{x} \wedge \tau(\delta) = \boldsymbol{x}' \wedge \\ \forall \delta' \in [0, \delta] : C(\boldsymbol{b}, \tau(\delta')) \wedge \\ \forall \delta' \in (0, \delta) : V((\boldsymbol{b}, \tau(\delta')), \dot{\tau}(\delta')) \end{array} \right\}$$

170

We define the concrete semantics in terms of an *execution* of a hybrid automaton, which is a (possibly) infinite trace $(\ell_0, s_0) \rightarrow (\ell_1, s_1) \rightarrow (\ell_2, s_2) \rightarrow \ldots$ with $\rightarrow = \rightarrow_c \cup \rightarrow_d$ and

$$(\ell, s) \rightarrow_c (\ell', s') \quad \Leftrightarrow \quad \ell = \ell' \wedge V = F(\ell) \wedge s' \in flow_V(\{s\})$$
$$(\ell, s) \rightarrow_d (\ell', s') \quad \Leftrightarrow \quad \exists (\ell, R, \ell') \in J : R(s, s') \wedge C_{\ell'}(s')$$

If we eliminate all Boolean variables by enumerating their valuations and encoding them with locations, the semantics above will be equivalent to the semantics of standard hybrid automata that deal only with numerical variables.

The concrete semantics of hybrid automata exhibit three kinds of non-determinism:

- Non-determinism w.r.t. *flow* transitions, *i.e.* the choice between different continuous evolutions due to the differential inclusions defined by the vector field V.
- Non-determinism w.r.t. *flow and jump* transitions: The choice between flow and jump transitions due to an overlapping of staying condition and guards.
- Non-determinism w.r.t. *jump* transitions, which is the choice between several jump transitions.

4. SEMANTICS OF ZERO-CROSSINGS

The fundamental difference between the zero-crossing concept used in our input language and the combination of staying and jump conditions in our output language is that the activation of a zero-crossings depends on the history (*i.e.* a part of the past trajectory) whereas the truth value of staying and jump conditions depends only on the current state.

Continuous vs. discrete zero-crossings. As mentioned in §2, a zero-crossing can be activated in two ways:

- It can be triggered by a continuous time evolution, as $up(x-20)$ in Fig. 1c; in this case it is active during the second step of an execution fragment $s \xrightarrow{i}_c s' \xrightarrow{i'}_d s''$;
- It can be triggered by a discrete transition, as $up(n-10)$ in Fig. 1c; in this case it is active during the second step of an execution fragment $s \xrightarrow{i}_d s' \xrightarrow{i'}_d s''$;

Because a zero-crossing may depend on both discrete and continuous variables, the same zero-crossing $up(e)$ can be triggered in both ways in an execution. We will use the terms *continuous* (resp. *discrete*) *zero-crossing* for indicating its source of activation.

Three semantics for zero-crossings. We consider an execution fragment $\xrightarrow{i_{k-1}} s_{k-1} \xrightarrow{i_k} s_k$ and we define $z_k = z(s_k, i_k)$. There are three natural choices for the semantics of zero-crossings:

- "At-zero" semantics : $z_{k-1} \leq 0 \wedge z_k \geq 0$
- "Contact" semantics : $z_{k-1} < 0 \wedge z_k \geq 0$
- "Crossing" semantics : $z_{k-1} \leq 0 \wedge z_k > 0$

Figs. 3b, 3e and 3h illustrate the activation of continuous zero-crossings for some typical trajectories according to each semantics.

The last two semantics are used in simulators. The zero-crossing semantics of SIMULINK is the disjunction of these semantics. In MODELICA it is up to the programmer to choose between these two semantics.

We state the first option, because it fits better to the semantics of hybrid automata (as it does not involve strict inequalities).

Chattering behaviour. An issue specific to the "crossing" semantics is that it is possible to write programs that produce executions that contain periodic sequences of infinitesimal continuous evolutions with distinct dynamics. This happens for example when a trajectory *chatters* along a surface with opposed zero-crossings, like in the following example.

EXAMPLE 2. *(see Fig. 2)*

$$\mathcal{I} = (b \wedge x = -1 \wedge y = 0) \quad \text{tt} \rightarrow \begin{cases} b' = \begin{cases} \text{ff} & \text{if } up(x) \\ \text{tt} & \text{if } up(-x) \end{cases} \\ \dot{x} = 1 \\ \dot{y} = \begin{cases} 1 & \text{if } b \\ -1 & \text{if } \neg b \end{cases} \end{cases}$$

In some cases it is possible to standardize such systems by identifying the chattering behavior and replace it by a so-called *sliding mode* [14, 32, 1], *i.e.* a dynamics that defines the corresponding trajectory "in" this surface. However, this is not feasible in the general case (*i.e.* a specification which does not correspond necessarily to a physical model). Thus, we will translate such programs into hybrid automata that allow chattering in their concrete semantics.

(a) Chattering trajectory   (b) Equivalent sliding mode

Figure 2: Sliding modes

§5 focuses on the translation of continuous zero-crossings, whereas §6 will discuss the case of discrete zero-crossings, the translation of which is much less dependent on the choice of one of the three zero-crossing semantics. However, because of the limitations of the hybrid automata model, in all cases the translation will add behavior that is not present in the original program.

5. TRANSLATION OF CONTINUOUS ZERO-CROSSINGS

5.1 Simplest case: one zero-crossing, no inputs

We investigate here the translation of continuous zero-crossings of the form $up(z(x))$: for the sake of simplicity, we assume that there are neither inputs i nor discrete variables b in z. We consider the simple case of an origin location l_1 with a single discrete transition $s' = \Phi(s)$ if $up(z(x))$ going from l_1 to a location l_2, such that $\phi_1(b) \wedge (s' = \Phi(s)) \Rightarrow \phi_2(b')$, see Fig. 3a. As the satisfaction of a zero-crossing depends on the history, the principle of the translation is to add locations to record the history of the continuous evolution.

"At-zero" semantics. The translation of "at-zero" semantics ($z_{k-1} \leq 0 \wedge z_k \geq 0$) is depicted in Fig. 3c. The origin location is partitioned in two locations: there is a discrete transition from left to right, but not from right to left to force the urgency of the discrete transition when $z = 0$ is reached from below 0. The zero-crossing condition translates to $z = 0$.

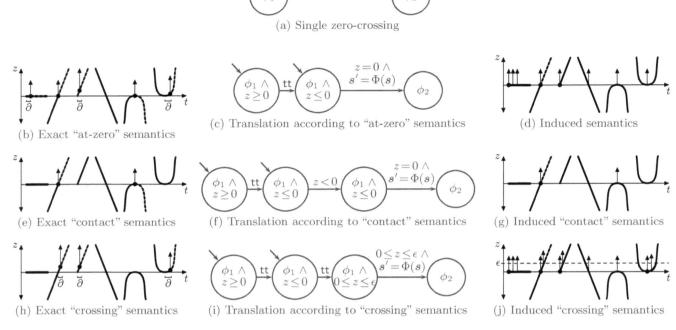

(a) Single zero-crossing

(b) Exact "at-zero" semantics

(c) Translation according to "at-zero" semantics

(d) Induced semantics

(e) Exact "contact" semantics

(f) Translation according to "contact" semantics

(g) Induced "contact" semantics

(h) Exact "crossing" semantics

(i) Translation according to "crossing" semantics

(j) Induced "crossing" semantics

Notes: (1) The arrows pointing upwards indicate on the left-hand side the points where zero-crossings are activated, and on the right-hand side the points where the jump transition may be taken non-deterministically. The dotted trajectories indicate that the preceding transition is urgent.
(2) When s does not appear in the jump condition of a HA, the equality $s' = s$ is implicit.
(3) The flow function $\dot{x} = f^c(s)$ in the first location in Fig. 3a, translates to the flow relation $V_1(\dot{x}, s) = (\phi_1(b) \wedge \dot{x} = f^c(s))$, not shown in the figures.

Figure 3: Zero-crossing semantics of the hybrid data-flow language and their translations. From left to right: typical trajectories in the original semantics, proposed translation to hybrid automata, and their typical trajectories.

The rationale for the condition $z = 0$ is based on the assumption of continuity of the function $z(t) = z(\boldsymbol{x}(t))$ and the urgency of the zero-crossing: $z(t_{k-1}) < 0 \wedge z(t_k) \geq 0$ with $t_{k-1} < t_k$ implies that there exists $t \in (t_{k-1}, t_k]$ such that $z(t) = 0$.

This translation induces two kinds of approximations in terms of executions:
- We lose urgency for all trajectories but the second one in Fig. 3d. In case of the first trajectory the zero-crossing may be triggered in a dense interval of time.
- We add a jump transition in the fourth trajectory because one is not able to distinguish whether the state $z = 0$ is reached from below or from above 0.

We will not consider any more the "at-zero" semantics in the sequel, as – to our knowledge – it is not used by any simulation tool.

"Contact" semantics. In order to translate the "contact" semantics defined as $z_{k-1} < 0 \wedge z_k \geq 0$, we split the original location into three locations as depicted on Fig. 3f. The two locations with the staying condition $z \leq 0$ are connected by a transition guarded by $z < 0$: this is in order to check that the trajectory was actually strictly below zero before touching zero. This prohibits the triggering of the jump transition in

the first, third and last trajectory in Fig. 3g. This induces the following approximation:
- The loss of urgency for the fifth trajectory that touches (possibly several times) the line $z = 0$ from below.

Observe, that the "at-zero" translation in Fig. 3c is actually a sound translation of the "contact" semantics, though with coarser approximations.

"Crossing" semantics. The "crossing" semantics ($z_{k-1} \leq 0 \wedge z_k > 0$) is more subtle to translate. By continuity of the function $z(t) = z(\boldsymbol{x}(t))$ we can deduce that $z(t) = 0$ is valid at the zero-crossing point in standard semantics: by standardizing $z(t) \leq 0 \wedge z(t+\partial) > 0$ we get $st(z(t)) = st(z(t+\partial)) = 0$.

However, we cannot simply reuse the "at-zero" translation in Fig. 3c, because it is not sound w.r.t. chattering behaviors: in Ex. 2 time cannot advance, because only discrete transitions can be taken. Since we do not rely on standardizing chattering behaviors we have to allow chattering in the standard semantics. For that reason we allow the trajectories to actually go beyond zero, but only up to a constant $\epsilon > 0$ (see Fig. 3i). As a consequence, we have the following approximation:
- Urgency is completely lost. In case of the second, third and last trajectories the zero-crossing may be triggered in

a bounded time interval with a dense interval of values for z (see Fig. 3j).

Observe, that this translation simulates the translations of the other two semantics.

REMARK 1 (CHOICE OF ϵ). *Any translation involving an ϵ close to zero is not really well-suited for verification: computations with arbitrary-precision rationals become indeed very expensive (e.g. least common denominators become huge).*

5.2 One zero-crossing with inputs

Now we investigate the translation of zero-crossings of the form $up(z(\boldsymbol{x},\boldsymbol{i}))$, where the inputs $\boldsymbol{i}$ have to satisfy an assertion $\mathcal{A}(\boldsymbol{s},\boldsymbol{i})$, see §2. We assume that in the discrete infinitesimal semantics of §2 inputs tend to continuous trajectories (between two discrete transitions). Inputs allow us to introduce non-determinism in a model, as illustrated by Fig. 1. The principle of the translation remains the same as in the previous section and depicted on Fig. 3, except that the computation of jump and flow transition relations involves an existential quantification of the inputs $\boldsymbol{i}$. The process is illustrated by Fig. 4.

We use the notation $\boxminus\psi = \overline{\neg\psi}$, where $\overline{}$ denotes the topological closure operator. We have for instance $\boxminus(z \leq 0) = z \geq 0$.

Considering the "contact" semantics and using the continuity of the function $z(\boldsymbol{x}(t),\boldsymbol{i}(t))$ during continuous evolution (see §2) the condition

$$\exists i_{k-1},i_k : z(\boldsymbol{x}_{k-1},i_{k-1}) < 0 \wedge \mathcal{A}(\boldsymbol{s}_{k-1},i_{k-1}) \wedge$$
$$z(\boldsymbol{x}_k,i_k) \geq 0 \qquad \wedge \mathcal{A}(\boldsymbol{s}_k,i_k) \wedge \boldsymbol{s}' = \Phi(\boldsymbol{s}_k,i_k)$$

is equivalent to

$$\exists i_{k-1},i_k : z(\boldsymbol{x}_{k-1},i_{k-1}) < 0 \wedge \mathcal{A}(\boldsymbol{s}_{k-1},i_{k-1}) \wedge$$
$$z(\boldsymbol{x}_k,i_k) = 0 \qquad \wedge \mathcal{A}(\boldsymbol{s}_k,i_k) \wedge \boldsymbol{s}' = \Phi(\boldsymbol{s}_k,i_k)$$

which in turn is equivalent to

$$\exists \boldsymbol{i} : z(\boldsymbol{x}_{k-1},\boldsymbol{i}) < 0 \wedge \mathcal{A}(\boldsymbol{s}_{k-1},\boldsymbol{i}) \wedge$$
$$\exists \boldsymbol{i} : z(\boldsymbol{x}_k,\boldsymbol{i}) = 0 \quad \wedge \mathcal{A}(\boldsymbol{s}_k,\boldsymbol{i}) \wedge \boldsymbol{s}' = \Phi(\boldsymbol{s}_k,\boldsymbol{i}) \qquad (2)$$

- The first line of Eqn. (2) defines the new guard of the transition between the second and third locations of Fig 3f:

$$\exists \boldsymbol{i} : \mathcal{A}(\boldsymbol{s},\boldsymbol{i}) \wedge z(\boldsymbol{x},\boldsymbol{i}) < 0$$

- The second line gives us the new transition relation between the third and fourth locations of Fig. 3f:

$$R(\boldsymbol{s},\boldsymbol{s}') = \exists \boldsymbol{i} : \mathcal{A}(\boldsymbol{s},\boldsymbol{i}) \wedge z(\boldsymbol{x},\boldsymbol{i}) = 0 \wedge \boldsymbol{s}' = \Phi(\boldsymbol{s},\boldsymbol{i})$$

- The new flow relation of the second and third locations is

$$\exists \boldsymbol{i} : \mathcal{A}(\boldsymbol{s},\boldsymbol{i}) \wedge z(\boldsymbol{x},\boldsymbol{i}) \leq 0 \wedge \phi_1(\boldsymbol{b}) \wedge \dot{\boldsymbol{x}} = e_1(\boldsymbol{s},\boldsymbol{i})$$

which induces the staying condition

$$\psi_{23}(\boldsymbol{s}) = \exists \boldsymbol{i} : \mathcal{A}(\boldsymbol{s},\boldsymbol{i}) \wedge z(\boldsymbol{x},\boldsymbol{i}) \leq 0)$$

- The new flow relation of the first location of Fig. 3f is

$$V_1(s,\dot{\boldsymbol{x}}) = \exists \boldsymbol{i} : \mathcal{A}(\boldsymbol{s},\boldsymbol{i}) \wedge z(\boldsymbol{x},\boldsymbol{i}) \geq 0 \wedge \phi_1(\boldsymbol{b}) \wedge \dot{\boldsymbol{x}} = e_1(\boldsymbol{s},\boldsymbol{i})$$

The result is illustrated by Fig. 4b. One can strengthen the flow relation V_1 by conjoining it with $\boxminus\psi_{23}$, so as to minimize the non-determinism between staying in the first location or jumping to the second location, as done in Fig. 4c.[5]

---

[5] We use the operator $\boxminus$ instead of $\neg$ in order to obtain a topologically closed flow relation.

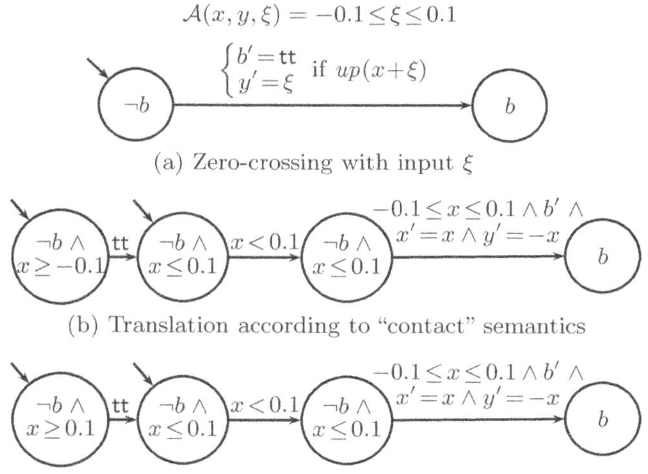

(a) Zero-crossing with input ξ

(b) Translation according to "contact" semantics

(c) Strengthening the staying condition of the first location

Figure 4: Translation of a continuous zero-crossing with inputs, described in Example 3

EXAMPLE 3. *Fig. 4b illustrates this translation on the original system of Fig. 4a, where b,x,y are state variables and ξ is a numerical input variable constrained by the assertion. The jump condition of the rightmost transition is obtained from* $\exists \xi : (-0.1 \leq \xi \leq 0.1 \wedge x+\xi = 0 \wedge b' = \mathsf{tt} \wedge x' = x \wedge y' = \xi)$
$$= \exists \xi : (-0.1 \leq \xi \leq 0.1 \wedge x = -\xi \wedge b' \wedge x' = x \wedge y' = -x)$$
$$= -0.1 \leq x \leq 0.1 \wedge b' \wedge x' = x \wedge y' = -x$$
Observe that we obtain the non-trivial relation $y = -x$ after the jump transition.

5.3 Logical combinations of zero-crossings

We consider here a discrete transition function of the form $\boldsymbol{s}' = \Phi(\boldsymbol{s},\boldsymbol{i})$ if $\varphi^Z(\boldsymbol{s},\boldsymbol{i})$ where φ^Z is a logical combination of zero-crossings $up(z_1),\dots,up(z_M)$ satisfying the assumption of §2.

Why do we need such logical combinations? Conjunctions and negations typically occur when combining two parallel equations $s_i' = \Phi_i$ if $up(z_i)$ for $i = 1,2$, which results in an equation

$$(s_1',s_2') = \begin{cases} (\Phi_1,\Phi_2) & \text{if } up(z_1) \wedge up(z_2) \\ (\Phi_1,s_2) & \text{if } up(z_1) \wedge \neg up(z_2) \\ (s_1,\Phi_2) & \text{if } up(z_2) \wedge \neg up(z_1) \end{cases}$$

A specification of the form $s' = \begin{cases} \Phi_1 & \text{if } up(z_1) \\ \Phi_2 & \text{else if } up(z_2) \end{cases}$

is similarly translated to $s' = \begin{cases} \Phi_1 & \text{if } up(z_1) \\ \Phi_2 & \text{if } \neg up(z_1) \wedge up(z_2) \end{cases}$

Disjunctions allow to express that the same transition may be triggered by different zero-crossings:

$$s' = \Phi \text{ if } up(z_1) \vee up(z_2)$$

Because successive graph refinements are cumbersome to describe, we reformulate the translation scheme of the previous sections by using additional discrete state variables to the system, rather than by introducing locations. This will make it easier to explain this generalization. We sketch this principle using the "contact" semantics (the translation for the general case will be presented in §7).

To encode locations, we add M discrete state variables $q_1 \ldots q_M$ of the enumerated type $\{\mathsf{above}, \mathsf{below}, \mathsf{ready}\}$ for each distinct zero-crossing $up(z_m)$ occuring in the zero-crossing formulas φ^Z.

– Their transition relations are defined as

$$R_m = \;\mathbf{match}\; q_m \;\mathbf{with}$$
$$\mathsf{above} \rightarrow q'_m \in \{\mathsf{above}, \mathsf{below}\}$$
$$\mathsf{below} \rightarrow z_m < 0 \wedge q'_m = \mathsf{ready} \qquad \vee \; q'_m = q_m$$
$$\mathsf{ready} \rightarrow z_m = 0 \wedge q'_m \in \{\mathsf{above}, \mathsf{below}\} \vee q'_m = q_m$$

– The staying condition defined by the zero-crossing $up(z_m)$ is:

$$C_m = \;\mathbf{match}\; q_m \;\mathbf{with}$$
$$\mathsf{above} \quad \rightarrow \quad z_m \geq 0$$
$$\mathsf{below} \quad \rightarrow \quad z_m \leq 0$$
$$\mathsf{ready} \quad \rightarrow \quad z_m \leq 0$$

– The activation condition G_m associated to the zero-crossing $up(z_m)$ is $G_m = (q_m = \mathsf{ready}) \wedge (z_m = 0)$

We can now build the global flow and discrete transition relations:

$$R((\boldsymbol{q}, \boldsymbol{s}), (\boldsymbol{q}', \boldsymbol{s}')) = \left(\bigwedge_m R_m \right) \wedge (\neg H \wedge \boldsymbol{s}' = \boldsymbol{s} \vee H \wedge \boldsymbol{s}' = \boldsymbol{\Phi})$$
$$V((\boldsymbol{q}, \boldsymbol{s}), \dot{\boldsymbol{x}}) \quad = \left(\bigwedge_m C_m \right) \wedge \left(\bigvee_\ell (\phi_\ell(\boldsymbol{b}) \wedge \dot{\boldsymbol{x}} = \dot{\boldsymbol{e}}_\ell(\boldsymbol{s})) \right) \tag{3}$$

with $H = \varphi^Z[\forall m : up(z_m) \leftarrow G_m]$ where $e[x \leftarrow y]$ means that x is substituted by y in expression e.

In order to obtain an explicit automaton one has to enumerate the valuations of the discrete state variables $\boldsymbol{q}$ and to encode them into explicit locations (see §8).

It is interesting to mention that this translation keeps enough information in order to preserve urgency in case of conjunctions like $\boldsymbol{s}' = \boldsymbol{\Phi}$ if $up(z_1) \wedge up(z_2)$ where the trajectory can move all around the intersection $z_1 = 0 \wedge z_2 = 0$ while not satisfying both zero-crossings at the same time. Fig. 5 gives an illustration of such a trajectory.

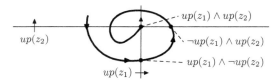

Figure 5: Conjunction of two zero-crossings

6. TRANSLATION OF DISCRETE ZERO-CROSSINGS

Discrete zero-crossings are activated by discrete transitions. Discrete zero-crossings occur in so-called *zero-crossing cascades*, which are sequences of zero-crossings of which the first one is triggered by continuous evolution, whereas the others are discrete zero-crossings. Example 1 contains such a zero-crossing cascade, which is commented in §2 point (3).

The translation explained in §5.1 is not sound for discrete zero-crossings because we have supposed that the zero-crossings are activated by continuous evolution.

Principle of translation. The translation that we propose applies the same principle as above to encode the history of the execution into locations (using discrete state variables).

We explain it using the "contact" semantics (again without inputs and logical combinations of zero-crossings). We consider $\boldsymbol{s}' = \boldsymbol{\Phi}$ if $up(z)$ and we introduce a Boolean variable q^d, which holds at each step k the value of $z < 0$ at step $k - 1$.

– The evolution of q^d is defined by the initial state $q^d = \mathsf{ff}$ and the relation $R^d = ((q^d)' = (z < 0))$;
– The condition $up(z_m)$ is translated to the activation condition $G^d = (q^d \wedge z \geq 0)$;
– The global transition relation R is generated as in Eqn. (3).

Interrupting continuous evolution. The transitions as translated above are not urgent, *i.e.* the continuous states can evolve on intermediate states of a cascade. We need to prohibit this evolution explicitly if one of the discrete zero-crossings is activated. This is done by strengthening the global flow relation $V(\boldsymbol{q}, \boldsymbol{s}, \dot{\boldsymbol{x}})$ with $V' = V \wedge \boxtimes G^d$.

In case of inputs, we have $G^d = (q^d \wedge z(\boldsymbol{s}, \boldsymbol{i}) \geq 0)$ and we take $V' = V \wedge \boxtimes(\forall \boldsymbol{i} : G^d)$: the idea is that in a state $(\boldsymbol{q}, \boldsymbol{s})$, if the discrete zero-crossing is activated for any input (*i.e.* $\forall \boldsymbol{i} : G^d$), then the continuous evolution is blocked. Otherwise, for some input, the discrete zero-crossing is not activated and the continuous evolution should be possible.

REMARK 2. *A zero-crossings can be both discrete and continuous, e.g. $up(x + n)$. In this case it is translated twice: once as a continuous zero-crossing and a second time as a discrete one.*

REMARK 3 (COMPRESSING CASCADES). *Zero-crossing cascades can be "compressed" into a single discrete transition triggered by a continuous zero-crossing by composing the discrete transitions forming the cascade. This is possible if there are no instantaneous cyclic dependencies between the variables. The advantage of this kind of preprocessing is that the translation does not have to deal with discrete zero-crossings. However, care must be taken w.r.t. safety verification, because this transformation does not preserve the set of reachable states (it removes intermediate states).*

7. THE COMPLETE TRANSLATION

We give here the formulas for the complete translation of a hybrid data-flow program

$$\mathcal{I}(\boldsymbol{s}) \quad , \quad \mathcal{A}(\boldsymbol{s}, \boldsymbol{i}) \wedge \begin{cases} \dot{\boldsymbol{x}} = \begin{cases} \cdots \\ \boldsymbol{e}_\ell(\boldsymbol{s}, \boldsymbol{i}) \text{ if } \phi_\ell(\boldsymbol{b}) \\ \cdots \end{cases} \\ \boldsymbol{s}' = \begin{cases} \cdots \\ \boldsymbol{\Phi}_j(\boldsymbol{s}, \boldsymbol{i}) \text{ if } \varphi^Z_j(\boldsymbol{s}, \boldsymbol{i}) \\ \cdots \end{cases} \end{cases}$$

as defined in §2 to a hybrid automaton by combining all the concepts presented in §5 and §6.

We use the notation ζ^σ_m to denote the constraints induced by a zero-crossing $up(z_m)$, *e.g.* $\zeta^{\cdot = 0}_m = (z_m = 0)$ or $\zeta^{0 < \cdot \leq \epsilon}_m = (0 < z_m \leq \epsilon)$.

Discrete zero-crossings. For each discrete zero-crossing $up(z_m)$ we introduce a Boolean state variable q^d_m.

$$R^d_m = (q'^d_m = \zeta^\sigma_m)$$
$$G^d_m = (q^d_j \wedge \zeta^{\overline{\sigma}}_m)$$

	σ	$\overline{\sigma}$
"contact"	$\cdot < 0$	$\cdot \geq 0$
"crossing"	$\cdot \leq 0$	$\cdot > 0$

Continuous zero-crossings. For each continuous zero-crossing $up(z_m)$ we introduce a state variable q^c_m.

– Their transition relations are defined as follows:

	θ	σ
"contact"	$\cdot < 0$	$\cdot = 0$
"crossing"	$\cdot = 0$	$0 \le \cdot \le \epsilon$

$$R_m^c = \textbf{match } q_m^c \textbf{ with}$$
$$\text{above} \to q'^c_m \in \{\text{above}, \text{below}\}$$
$$\text{below} \to ((q_m^c)' = q_m^c) \vee ((q_m^c)' = \text{ready}) \wedge \zeta_m^\theta$$
$$\text{ready} \to (q_m^c)' \in \{\text{above}, \text{below}\} \wedge \zeta_m^\sigma \vee (q_m^c)' = q_m^c$$

– The activation conditions G_m^c are defined as

$$G_m^c = (q_m^c = \text{ready}) \wedge \zeta_m^\sigma$$

	σ
"contact"	$\cdot = 0$
"crossing"	$0 \le \cdot \le \epsilon$

– Using $\psi = \bigvee_\ell (\phi_\ell(\boldsymbol{b}) \wedge \dot{\boldsymbol{x}} = \boldsymbol{e}_\ell(\boldsymbol{s}, \boldsymbol{i}))$ we define the partial flow relations (containing the staying conditions):

	σ
"contact"	$\cdot \le 0$
"crossing"	$0 \le \cdot \le \epsilon$

$$V_m = \textbf{match } q_m^c \textbf{ with}$$
$$\text{above} \to \left\{ \begin{array}{l} (\exists \boldsymbol{i} : \mathcal{A}(\boldsymbol{s}, \boldsymbol{i}) \wedge \zeta_m^{\ge 0} \wedge \psi) \wedge \\ (\boxdot \exists \boldsymbol{i} : \mathcal{A}(\boldsymbol{s}, \boldsymbol{i}) \wedge \zeta_m^{\le 0}) \end{array} \right.$$
$$\text{below} \to \exists \boldsymbol{i} : \mathcal{A}(\boldsymbol{s}, \boldsymbol{i}) \wedge \zeta_m^{\le 0} \wedge \psi$$
$$\text{ready} \to \exists \boldsymbol{i} : \mathcal{A}(\boldsymbol{s}, \boldsymbol{i}) \wedge \zeta_m^\sigma \wedge \psi$$

Transition relations. We define $G_m = G_m^c \vee G_m^d$ and $R_m = R_m^c \wedge R_m^d$. Now, we can finally put things together and define the jump and flow transition relations:

$$R((\boldsymbol{q}, \boldsymbol{s}), (\boldsymbol{q}', \boldsymbol{s}')) = \exists \boldsymbol{i} : \left\{ \begin{array}{l} \mathcal{A}(\boldsymbol{s}, \boldsymbol{i}) \wedge (\bigwedge_m R_m) \wedge \\ \left(\neg (\bigvee_j H_j) \wedge \boldsymbol{s}' = \boldsymbol{s} \vee \right. \\ \left. \bigvee_j (H_j \wedge \boldsymbol{s}' = \Phi_j) \right) \end{array} \right.$$

$$V((\boldsymbol{q}, \boldsymbol{s}), \dot{\boldsymbol{x}}) = \left\{ \begin{array}{l} \bigvee_m V_m((\boldsymbol{q}, \boldsymbol{s}), \dot{\boldsymbol{x}}) \wedge \\ \boxdot (\forall \boldsymbol{i} : \mathcal{A}(\boldsymbol{s}, \boldsymbol{i}) \wedge \bigvee_j H_j^d) \end{array} \right.$$

with $H_j = \varphi_j^Z [\forall m : up(z_m) \leftarrow G_m]$.

We obtain a hybrid automaton $\langle \{\ell_0\}, F, J, \Sigma^0 \rangle$ with
– $F(\ell_0) = V$,
– $J = \{(\ell_0, R, \ell_0)\}$, and
– $\Sigma^0(\ell_0) = \{(\boldsymbol{q}, \boldsymbol{s}) \mid \boldsymbol{q}^d = \textbf{ff} \wedge \bigwedge_m q_m^c \in \{\text{above}, \text{below}\} \wedge \mathcal{I}(\boldsymbol{s})\}$
For the proofs of the complete translation we refer to [30].

8. DISCUSSION

We have presented the complete translation of a hybrid data-flow specification to a hybrid automaton. However, further preprocessing steps are necessary to enable verification using classical hybrid analysis methods.

Explicit representation. As explained in §5.3 we have chosen to present our translation by encoding the locations of the HA with N additional finite-state variables $\boldsymbol{q}$. This results in a HA with a single location and a single self-loop jump transition. Of course, it is possible to expand this "compressed" representation into a more explicit one, such as shown in Figs. 3 and 4. This is done by enumerating the valuations of these finite-state variables and by partitioning the system into these $\mathcal{O}(2^N)$ states. As already mentioned in §2, partial evaluation may be used to simplify expressions and to remove infeasible jump transitions.

Convexification of staying conditions and guards. The induced staying conditions $C(\boldsymbol{s})$ and guards $G(\boldsymbol{s})$ of jump transitions might be non-convex w.r.t. numerical constraints. For verification it is necessary to transform these conditions into the form $\bigvee_k \Delta_k$ with $\Delta_k = \phi_k(\boldsymbol{b}) \wedge \varphi_k^C(\boldsymbol{s})$, where $\phi_k(\boldsymbol{b})$ is an arbitrary formula over Boolean variables

and $\varphi_k^C(\boldsymbol{s})$ is a conjunction of numerical constraints. For staying conditions, the system has to be partitioned according to these Δ_k; for guards, arcs are split w.r.t. the Δ_k.

EXAMPLE 4. *The non-convex flow transition V*

$$\begin{array}{l} (b_1 \vee \neg b_2) \wedge \overbrace{(x \le 0 \vee x \ge 5)}^{\text{non-convex numerical condition}} \wedge (\dot{x} = 1 - x) \vee \\ (\neg b_1 \wedge b_2) \wedge (0 \le x \le 5) \wedge (\dot{x} = 1) \end{array}$$

has to be transformed into

$$\begin{array}{l} (b_1 \vee \neg b_2) \wedge (x \le 0) \wedge (\dot{x} = 1 - x) \vee \\ (b_1 \vee \neg b_2) \wedge (x \ge 5) \wedge (\dot{x} = 1 - x) \vee \\ (\neg b_1 \wedge b_2) \wedge (0 \le x \le 5) \wedge (\dot{x} = 1) \end{array}$$

Then, the system is going to be partitioned into three locations, one for each line.

Approximations during analysis. In §5.1 we have explained that the translation to hybrid automata loses several properties, like determinism and urgency, which may result in an overapproximation in terms of reachable states. Moreover, hybrid reachability analysis methods further approximate the reachable states with (finite disjunctions of) convex sets, such as convex polyhedra.

The translation with "contact" semantics involves strict inequalities. Thus, the analysis may benefit from the ability of representing open sets. A suitable abstract domain might be in this case convex polyhedra with strict inequalities [5]. Otherwise, if the analysis can only handle closed sets, the translation with "contact" semantics (Fig. 3g) will behave like the one for "at-zero" semantics (Fig. 3d).

Preliminary experiments. We have implemented a prototype tool that makes use of the BDDAPRON library [22] to handle logico-numerical formulas represented as MTBDDs.

First experiments showed that – as expected – the major parameter affecting performance is the number of zero-crossings, which becomes apparent when making locations explicit as described at the beginning of this section. In the applications that we are targeting, *i.e.* synchronous controllers connected to their physical environment, zero-crossings are (1) those used for modeling the sampling of inputs and (2) those in the environment model. Since the number of (1) is usually small, the total number of zero-crossings inherently depends on the complexity of the environment model in practice.

9. CONCLUSION

We have presented a complete translation of a hybrid data-flow formalism to logico-numerical hybrid automata. In comparison to previously proposed translations, our translation handles zero-crossings.

To achieve this, we considered a simple yet expressive hybrid data-flow formalism to which large subsets of existing hybrid system languages can actually be reduced.

We discussed different choices of zero-crossing semantics and their possible translations to hybrid automata. Since hybrid automata are not as expressive as the source language, we can only provide sound over-approximations of the original semantics.

However, this is counterbalanced by the fact that existing hybrid verification tools such as HyTech [20], PHAVer

[16] and SPACEEX [17] are all based on the standard hybrid automata model.

Though, these tools require to encode Boolean variables explicitly in locations. As this enumeration results in an exponential blow-up of the hybrid automaton size, we assume that this is a major bottleneck in verifying controllers with complex discrete state spaces jointly with their physical environment. Therefore future work will comprise the development of methods and tools for combining classical hybrid system analysis with implicit handling of Boolean variables in order to counter state space explosion. Our translation to logico-numerical hybrid automata lays the basis for such an approach.

10. REFERENCES

[1] V. Acary and B. Brogliato. *Numerical Methods for Nonsmooth Dynamical Systems: Applications in Mechanics and Electronics*. 2008.

[2] A. Agrawal, G. Simon, and G. Karsai. Semantic translation of Simulink/Stateflow models to hybrid automata using graph transformations. *ENTCS*, 109, 2004.

[3] R. Alur, C. Courcoubetis, N. Halbwachs, T. Henzinger, P.-H. Ho, X. Nicollin, A. Olivero, J. Sifakis, and S. Yovine. The algorithmic analysis of hybrid systems. *Theoretical Computer Science*, 138, 1995.

[4] R. Alur, A. Kanade, S. Ramesh, and K. C. Shashidhar. Symbolic analysis for improving simulation coverage of Simulink/Stateflow models. In *Embedded Software*, 2008.

[5] R. Bagnara, P. M. Hill, and E. Zaffanella. Not necessarily closed convex polyhedra and the double description method. *Formal Aspects of Computing*, 17(2), 2005.

[6] A. Benveniste, T. Bourke, B. Caillaud, and M. Pouzet. Divide and recycle: types and compilation for a hybrid synchronous language. In *LCTES*, 2011.

[7] A. Benveniste, B. Caillaud, and M. Pouzet. The fundamentals of hyrid systems modelers. In *Conference on Decision and Control*, 2010.

[8] X. Briand and B. Jeannet. Combining control and data abstraction in the verification of hybrid systems. *Computer-Aided Design of Integrated Circuits and Systems*, 29(10), 2010.

[9] P. Caspi, D. Pilaud, N. Halbwachs, and J. A. Plaice. LUSTRE: a declarative language for real-time programming. In *POPL*, 1987.

[10] A. Chutinan and B. H. Krogh. Verification of polyhedral-invariant hybrid automata using polygonal flow pipe approximations. In *HSCC*, volume 1569 of *LNCS*, 1999.

[11] J.-L. Colaço, B. Pagano, and M. Pouzet. A conservative extension of synchronous data-flow with state machines. In *Int. Conf. On Embedded Software, EMSOFT'05*, 2005.

[12] P. Cousot and R. Cousot. Comparing the Galois connection and widening/narrowing approaches to abstract interpretation. In *PLILP'92*, volume 631 of *LNCS*, Jan. 1992.

[13] T. Dang and T. M. Gawlitza. Discretizing affine hybrid automata with uncertainty. In *Automated Technology for Verification and Analysis*, volume 6996 of *LNCS*, 2011.

[14] A. F. Filippov. Differential equations with discontinuous right-hand sides. *Mathematicheskii Sbornik*, 51(1), 1960.

[15] M. Fränzle and C. Herde. HySAT: An efficient proof engine for bounded model checking of hybrid systems. *Formal Methods in System Design*, 30(3), 2007.

[16] G. Frehse. PHAVer: Algorithmic verification of hybrid systems past HyTech. In *HSCC*, volume 3414 of *LNCS*, 2005.

[17] G. Frehse, C. L. Guernic, A. Donzé, R. Ray, O. Lebeltel, R. Ripado, A. Girard, T. Dang, and O. Maler. SpaceEx: Scalable verification of hybrid systems. In *Computer-Aided Verification*, volume 6806 of *LNCS*, 2011.

[18] N. Halbwachs, Y.-E. Proy, and P. Roumanoff. Verification of real-time systems using linear relation analysis. *Formal Methods in System Design*, 11(2), 1997.

[19] T. A. Henzinger. The theory of hybrid automata. In *Logic in Computer Science*, 1996.

[20] T. A. Henzinger, P.-H. Ho, and H. Wong-Toi. HyTech: A model checker for hybrid systems. *Journal on Software Tools for Technology Transfer*, 1(1-2), 1997.

[21] A. C. Hindmarsh, P. N. Brown, K. E. Grant, S. L. Lee, R. Serban, D. E. Shumaker, and C. S. Woodward. Sundials: Suite of nonlinear and differential/algebraic equation solvers. *ACM Trans. Math. Softw.*, 31(3), 2005.

[22] B. Jeannet. Bddapron: A logico-numerical abstract domain library. http://pop-art.inrialpes.fr/~bjeannet/bjeannet-forge/bddapron/, 2009.

[23] T. Lindstrøm. An invitation to nonstandard analysis. In N. Cutland, editor, *Nonstandard Analysis and its Applications*, pages 1–105. Cambridge University Press, 1988.

[24] K. Manamcheri, S. Mitra, S. Bak, and M. Caccamo. A step towards verification and synthesis from Simulink/Stateflow models. In *HSCC*, 2011.

[25] M. Najafi and R. Nikoukhah. Implementation of hybrid automata in Scicos. In *Control Applications*, 2007.

[26] M. Pouzet. *Lucid Synchrone, version 3. Tutorial and reference manual*. Université Paris-Sud, LRI, 2006.

[27] S. Ratschan and Z. She. Safety verification of hybrid systems by constraint propagation-based abstraction refinement. *Transactions on Embedded Computing Systems*, 6(1), 2007.

[28] P. Raymond, Y. Roux, and E. Jahier. Lutin: A language for specifying and executing reactive scenarios. *EURASIP J. on Embedded Systems*, 2008.

[29] A. Robinson. *Non-Standard Analysis*. 1996.

[30] P. Schrammel and B. Jeannet. From hybrid system data-flow to hybrid automata: A complete translation. Technical Report 7859, INRIA, Jan 2012.

[31] S. Tripakis, C. Sofronis, P. Caspi, and A. Curic. Translating discrete-time Simulink to Lustre. *Embedded Computing Systems*, 4(4), 2005.

[32] V. I. Utkin. *Sliding modes in Control and optimization*. 1992.

Efficient Computation of Generalized Input-to-State $\mathcal{L}_2$-Gains of Discrete-Time Switched Linear Systems

Vamsi Putta
School of Electrical and
Computer Engineering
Purdue University
West Lafayette, IN 47906
vputta@purdue.edu

Guangwei Zhu
School of Electrical and
Computer Engineering
Purdue University
West Lafayette, IN 47906
guangwei@purdue.edu

Jianghai Hu
School of Electrical and
Computer Engineering
Purdue University
West Lafayette, IN 47906
jianghai@purdue.edu

Jinglai Shen
Department of Mathematics
and Statistics
University of Maryland
Baltimore, MD 21250
shenj@umbc.edu

ABSTRACT

This paper proposes an efficient way to compute the $\mathcal{L}_2$-gain of discrete-time switched linear systems. Using the notion of generating functions, generalized versions of $\mathcal{L}_2$-gains under arbitrary switching are studied. An efficient numerical algorithm is formulated by which these generalized $\mathcal{L}_2$-gains can be estimated. The proposed method mitigates the problem of conservative bounds. Numerical examples are provided to illustrate the algorithm.

Categories and Subject Descriptors

F.2.0 [**Analysis of Algorithms and Problem Complexity**]: General; I.2.8 [**Artificial Intelligence**]: Problem Solving, Control Methods, and Search—*dynamic programming, control theory*

General Terms

Algorithms, performance, theory

Keywords

L2-gains, switched linear systems, input-to-state stability, generating functions

1. INTRODUCTION

Switched linear systems form an important class of hybrid systems and are being used to model a diverse range of engineering systems [11]. Stability aspects of switched linear systems have received a lot of attention in the past decade. The survey papers [15, 12] provide a review of the results on this subject.

Estimating the input-to-state (or output) gains for switched linear systems has long been recognized as an open problem [5, 6]. Recent research in this area has focused on obtaining bounds for the $\mathcal{L}_2$-gains of the switched linear systems under various switching conditions. The analysis of $\mathcal{L}_2$-gain under slow switching was reported in [4], while [16] used an average dwell time condition. Using common storage functions, it was proved in [7, 8] that the solutions to the $\mathcal{L}_2$-gain problem of continuous-time switched linear systems can be characterized using a finite parametrization. A multiple Lyapunov function approach was used to study $\mathcal{L}_2$-gains of general switched systems in [18]. The paper [13] addressed the $\mathcal{L}_2$-gain problem by characterizing the most destabilizing switching law, leading to a sufficient condition for bounding the $\mathcal{L}_2$-gain of first order SISO systems. More recently, the variation of $\mathcal{L}_2$-gain of discrete-time switched linear systems with dwell time was studied in [1, 2]. LMI based sufficiency conditions were proposed to bound the $\mathcal{L}_2$-gains under dwell time constraints (extensible to arbitrary switching). Less conservative LMI conditions are proposed in [10], though the worst case complexity increases rapidly with the number of subsystems.

The present paper focuses on estimating the $\mathcal{L}_2$-gain numerically using an efficient algorithm. Most of the existing results tend to be either conservative or computationally expensive to verify. Using the newly introduced notion of generating functions [14, 9], we can derive necessary and sufficient conditions to characterize the input-to-state $\mathcal{L}_2$-gains of discrete-time switched linear systems under arbitrary switching. Thus an efficient iterative algorithm (based on [17]) for computing the generating functions enables us to compute bounds on the input-to-state $\mathcal{L}_2$-gains. By having a necessary and sufficient condition, the input-to-state $\mathcal{L}_2$-gains can be estimated to a desired precision while avoiding conservative bounds. An added advantage of this approach is that it enables us to study a more general version of the $\mathcal{L}_2$-gain where the input and the state energy are weighted

HSCC '12, April 17–19, 2012, Beijing, China.
Copyright 2012 ACM 978-1-4503-1220-2/12/04 ...$10.00.

by an exponential discount factor. This allows us to characterize both the trajectory growth rates and energy amplification using a single metric.

The paper is organized as follows. We describe the problem under consideration and present some preliminary results in Section 2. The notion and properties of controlled generating functions are described briefly in Section 3. Section 4 contains the main results of this paper where we formulate an iterative algorithm for the computation of the generalized $\mathcal{L}_2$-gains. A relaxed version of the algorithm that enables faster computations at the cost of slight inaccuracy is also discussed. Some numerical examples are included in Section 5 for illustrating the algorithm. Finally concluding remarks are made in Section 6.

2. PRELIMINARIES

Throughout the paper we consider discrete-time controlled switched linear systems (SLSs) with dynamics given by

$$x(t+1) = A_{\sigma(t)}x(t) + B_{\sigma(t)}u(t), \quad t = 0, 1, \ldots. \quad (1)$$

Here $(A_i \in \mathbb{R}^{n \times n}, B_i \in \mathbb{R}^{n \times m})$ are the state and input matrices indexed by $i \in \mathcal{M} := \{1, \ldots, M\}$. $\sigma(t) \in \mathcal{M}$ represents the switching law that determines the unique dynamics observed at any time t. The state and the input control input are denoted by $x(t)$ and $u(t)$ respectively. For simplicity, we often use u to denote the control input sequence $\{u(t)\}_{t=0,1,\ldots}$, and σ the switching sequence $\{\sigma(t)\}_{t=0,1,\ldots}$. We also assume that at least one of the B_i is nonzero.

Denote by $x(t; \sigma, z, u)$ the state trajectory of the controlled SLS (1) starting from the initial state $x(0) = z$ under the switching sequence σ and the control input u. For a fixed σ, system (1) becomes a linear time-varying system, whose solution $x(t; \sigma, z, u)$ is jointly linear in z and u. The reachable set $\mathcal{R}$ is defined as the set of all states that can be reached within a finite time starting from a zero initial state under arbitrary control laws. In the present paper we assume that the reachable set of SLS (1) is a subspace over $\mathbb{R}^n$ which in general might not always be the case [3].

The dynamics of the corresponding autonomous SLS are given by

$$x(t+1) = A_{\sigma(t)}x(t), \quad t = 0, 1, \ldots. \quad (2)$$

Denote by $x(t; \sigma, z)$ the solution to (2) starting from $x(0) = z$ under the switching sequence σ. Then $x(t; \sigma, z)$ is exactly the solution $x(t; \sigma, z, u)$ to the controlled SLS (1) with $u = 0$.

2.1 Generalized $\mathcal{L}_2$-Gain

We are concerned with the estimation of the following generalized input-to-state gains (introduced in [14]).

$$[\kappa(\lambda)]^2 := \sup_{\sigma} \sup_{0 \neq u \in \mathcal{U}_c} \frac{\sum_{t=0}^{\infty} \lambda^t \|x(t+1; \sigma, 0, u)\|^2}{\sum_{t=0}^{\infty} \lambda^t \|u(t)\|^2}, \quad (3)$$

where $\lambda \in \mathbb{R}_+ := [0, \infty)$ is a discount factor, and $\mathcal{U}_c$ is the space of all u with finite duration (identically zero after a finite time). The classical definition of $\mathcal{L}_2$-gain (denoted by κ) is obtained by setting $\lambda = 1$ in (3).

The above definition of the generalized $\mathcal{L}_2$-gain captures both the worst-case energy amplification and the worst-case trajectory growth rates. A finite generalized $\mathcal{L}_2$-gain not only implies convergence of the state trajectories but also bounds their rate of decay. In this sense, the generalized

$\mathcal{L}_2$-gain can be used as a single metric representing information of two important factors in SLS stability. Furthermore the generalized $\mathcal{L}_2$-gain of a SLS can also be viewed as the classical $\mathcal{L}_2$-gain of a scaled version of the SLS. To see this consider the following SLS obtained by scaling (1):

$$\tilde{x}(k+1) = \tilde{A}_{\sigma(k)}\tilde{x}(k) + \tilde{B}_{\sigma(k)}\tilde{u}(k),$$

where $\tilde{A}_i = \sqrt{\lambda} \cdot A_i, \tilde{B}_i = \sqrt{\lambda} \cdot B_i$, with the same initial condition $\tilde{x}(0) = z$. Applying the transformed control input law $\tilde{u}(k) = \sqrt{\lambda^k} \cdot u(k)$ results in a transformed state trajectory $\tilde{x}(k) = \sqrt{\lambda^k} \cdot x(k)$. Writing the definition of the classical gain for the scaled SLS, we immediately obtain the generalized $\mathcal{L}_2$-gain of the original SLS.

2.2 Properties

We report some relevant properties of the generalized $\mathcal{L}_2$-gain. The proofs can be found in [14].

PROPOSITION 1. *The $\mathcal{L}_2$-gain $\kappa(\lambda)$ as a function of $\lambda \in \mathbb{R}_+$ has the following properties:*

1. *At $\lambda = 0$, $\kappa(0) = \max_{i \in \mathcal{M}} \sigma_{\max}(B_i)$, where $\sigma_{\max}(B_i)$ denotes the largest singular value of B_i;*

2. *$\kappa(\lambda)$ is a lower semi-continuous function in $\lambda \in \mathbb{R}_+$.*

3. *$\kappa(\lambda)$ is a non-decreasing function in λ.*

3. GENERATING FUNCTIONS

In [14], the concept of controlled generating functions is introduced and some of their useful properties are derived. For each $\lambda, \gamma \in \mathbb{R}_+$, the strong generating function $G_{\lambda,\gamma} : \mathbb{R}^n \to \mathbb{R}_+ \cup \{\infty\}$ of the SLS (1) is defined as

$$G_{\lambda,\gamma}(z)$$
$$:= \sup_{\sigma, u \in \mathcal{U}_c} \left[\sum_{t=0}^{\infty} \lambda^t \|x(t; \sigma, z, u)\|^2 - \gamma^2 \lambda \sum_{t=0}^{\infty} \lambda^t \|u(t)\|^2 \right] \quad (4)$$

$$= \|z\|^2 + \lambda \cdot \sup_{\sigma, u \in \mathcal{U}_c} \sum_{t=0}^{\infty} \lambda^t \left[\|x(t+1; \sigma, z, u)\|^2 - \gamma^2 \|u(t)\|^2 \right]$$

$$(5)$$

for $\lambda, \gamma \in \mathbb{R}_+$ and $z \in \mathbb{R}^n$. This definition allows the choice of the hybrid control law (σ, u) to excite the largest state energy with limited input energy. A finite horizon version can also be defined as follows,

$$G_{\lambda,\gamma,k}(z)$$
$$:= \sup_{\sigma, u \in \mathcal{U}_k} \left[\sum_{t=0}^{k} \lambda^t \|x(t; \sigma, z, u)\|^2 - \gamma^2 \lambda \sum_{t=0}^{k-1} \lambda^t \|u(t)\|^2 \right] \quad (6)$$

$$= \|z\|^2 + \lambda \cdot \sup_{\sigma, u \in \mathcal{U}_k} \sum_{t=0}^{k} \lambda^t \left[\|x(t+1; \sigma, z, u)\|^2 - \gamma^2 \|u(t)\|^2 \right].$$

$$(7)$$

The properties of strong generating functions have been investigated and reported in [14]. We present some relevant ones here without proofs.

PROPOSITION 2. *For any $\lambda, \gamma \in \mathbb{R}_+$, the strong generating function $G_{\lambda,\gamma}(\cdot)$ and its k-horizon version $G_{\lambda,\gamma,k}(\cdot)$ for any $k \in \mathbb{N}$ have the following properties*

1. **(Homogeneity)**: $G_{\lambda,\gamma}(\cdot)$ and $G_{\lambda,\gamma,k}(\cdot)$ are both homogeneous of degree two, i.e., for any nonzero $\alpha \in \mathbb{R}$, $G_{\lambda,\gamma}(\alpha z) = \alpha^2 G_{\lambda,\gamma}(z)$ and $G_{\lambda,\gamma,k}(\alpha z) = \alpha^2 G_{\lambda,\gamma,k}(z)$, $\forall z \in \mathbb{R}^n$. Thus, $G_{\lambda,\gamma}(0) \in \{0, \infty\}$.

2. **(Bellman Equation)**: For all $z \in \mathbb{R}^n$,

$$G_{\lambda,\gamma,k+1}(z) = \|z\|^2 + \lambda \cdot \sup_{i \in \mathcal{M}, v \in \mathbb{R}^m} \big[-\gamma^2 \|v\|^2 + G_{\lambda,\gamma,k}(A_i z + B_i v) \big],$$

$$G_{\lambda,\gamma}(z) = \|z\|^2 + \lambda \cdot \sup_{i \in \mathcal{M}, v \in \mathbb{R}^m} \big[-\gamma^2 \|v\|^2 + G_{\lambda,\gamma}(A_i z + B_i v) \big]. \quad (8)$$

3. **(Monotonicity)**: For any $z \in \mathbb{R}^n$, $G_{\lambda,\gamma}(z)$ and $G_{\lambda,\gamma,k}(z)$ are non-increasing in $\gamma \in \mathbb{R}_+$ (for fixed λ); and non-decreasing in $\lambda \in \mathbb{R}_+$ (for fixed γ).

4. **(Convergence)** $G_{\lambda,\gamma,k}(z) \uparrow G_{\lambda,\gamma}(z)$ as $k \to \infty$.

The idea of defining trajectory dependent power series called generating functions is adopted from [9], where exponential stability of autonomous SLS was characterized using autonomous generating functions $G_\lambda : \mathbb{R}^n \to \mathbb{R}_+ \cup \{\infty\}$ defined as

$$G_\lambda(z) := \sup_\sigma \sum_{t=0}^{\infty} \lambda^t \|x(t; \sigma, z)\|^2, \quad \forall z \in \mathbb{R}^n. \quad (9)$$

3.1 Radius of Convergence

The monotonicity of $G_{\lambda,\gamma}(z)$ enables us to define a radius of convergence for the generating function. For $\gamma \in \mathbb{R}_+$, the *radius of convergence* of the generating function $G_{\lambda,\gamma}(z)$ (on $\mathbb{R}^n$) is defined as

$$\lambda^*(\gamma) := \sup\{\lambda \,|\, G_{\lambda,\gamma}(z) < \infty, \; \forall z \in \mathbb{R}^n\}.$$

More generally, for the reachable subspace $\mathcal{R}$ of $\mathbb{R}^n$ the radius of convergence of $G_{\lambda,\gamma}(z)$ on $\mathcal{R}$ is defined as

$$\lambda^*_{\mathcal{R}}(\gamma) := \sup\{\lambda \,|\, G_{\lambda,\gamma}(z) < \infty, \; \forall z \in \mathcal{R}\}.$$

Note that $\mathcal{R}$ is always invariant under the subsystem dynamics and is assumed to be a subspace. This assumption on the reachable set is not too restrictive since reachability is a generic property—any randomly generated SLS is reachable with probability one.

PROPOSITION 3. *The radius of convergence $\lambda^*_{\mathcal{R}}(\gamma)$ of the generating function on the reachable subspace $\mathcal{R}$ as a function of $\gamma \in \mathbb{R}_+$ has the following properties.*

1. $\lambda^*_{\mathcal{R}}(\gamma) \equiv 0$ *for* $0 \leq \gamma < \max_{i \in \mathcal{M}} \sigma_{\max}(B_i)$;

2. $\lambda^*_{\mathcal{R}}(\gamma)$ *is a non-decreasing function of γ for* $\gamma \geq \max_{i \in \mathcal{M}} \sigma_{\max}(B_i)$;

We now show how the $\mathcal{L}_2$-gain can be characterized by the radius of convergence of $G_{\lambda,\gamma}(z)$ on $\mathcal{R}$. As we will observe, this result provides a necessary and sufficient condition for the $\mathcal{L}_2$-gain to lie below a given value based on the convergence of the generating function. Ultimately we can utilize this result for bounding the $\mathcal{L}_2$-gain provided the generating function can be efficiently tested for convergence. This result and its proof have been reported in [14].

PROPOSITION 4. *($\mathcal{L}_2$-gain characterization) For $\lambda > 0$ and $\gamma \in \mathbb{R}_+$, the following statements are equivalent:*

1. $\kappa(\lambda) \leq \gamma$, *where $\kappa(\lambda)$ is the generalized $\mathcal{L}_2$-gain defined in (3);*

2. $\lambda \leq \lambda^*_{\mathcal{R}}(\gamma)$, *where $\mathcal{R}$ is the reachable subspace of the SLS (1) from the origin.*

3. $G_{\lambda,\gamma}(\cdot) < \infty$

In other words, the generalized $\mathcal{L}_2$-gain $\kappa(\lambda)$ and the radius of convergence $\lambda^*_{\mathcal{R}}(\gamma)$ are (generalized) inverse functions of each other. This property implies that the strong generating function $G_{\lambda,\gamma}(\cdot)$ is finite if and only if the value of γ is greater than generalized $\mathcal{L}_2$-gain $\kappa(\lambda)$. Based on the convergence of the strong generating function, it is thus possible to bound $\kappa(\lambda)$ in terms of γ. Since the condition is both necessary and sufficient, one can use a bisection type algorithm to accurately estimate the $\kappa(\lambda)$.

For systems whose reachable set is not a subspace, it is still possible to define a (restricted) generating function and a corresponding radius of convergence by restricting the SLS to a subspace invariant under the subsystem dynamics. Such a subspace would always be contained within the reachable set. The generalized $\mathcal{L}_2$-gain of the restricted SLS would be the worst case weighted energy gain among all the state trajectories starting in the invariant subspace. Using (restricted) generating functions, it is possible to estimate the generalized $\mathcal{L}_2$-gain for the restricted system using similar principles as discussed above.

4. NUMERICAL COMPUTATION

In this section we present methods to compute the generating functions numerically. A numerical method to compute the generating function enables us to use Proposition 4 to estimate the generalized $\mathcal{L}_2$-gains. We first prove that any finite horizon generating functions can be represented by a piecewise quadratic function and utilize this structure to formulate an iterative algorithm for efficient computation.

We begin by observing that the generating function (or k-horizon generating function) can be thought of as an infinite (or finite) horizon performance index that needs to be maximized over all possible switching and control laws. Since the generating function has quadratic terms, this optimization is equivalent to the discrete-time switched linear quadratic regulator (DSLQR) problem. One obvious way of achieving the maximum is through Dynamic Programming (DP). The Bellman equation in Proposition 2 gives the value iteration procedure for computing the strong generating function through DP. However the lack of an analytic closed form for the generating function necessitates numerical methods for finding the supremum at each step. This introduces inaccuracies and limits the computational efficiency of this procedure. Thus a more efficient method for computing the strong generating function is needed.

It has been shown in [17] that the finite horizon value function of a DSLQR problem is piecewise quadratic and can be completely characterized by a finite number of positive semidefinite (p.s.d) matrices. An efficient algorithm for computing the value function based on this characterization was also discussed. We now restate the relevant results here in notation consistent with our framework.

Denote by $\mathcal{A}$ the set (convex cone) of all $n \times n$ symmetric positive definite matrices. For the SLS given in (1), the Riccatti Mapping $\rho_{\lambda,\gamma,i}(P) : \mathcal{A} \to \mathcal{A}$ of subsystem $i \in \mathcal{M}$, with $\lambda > 0$ and sufficiently large $\gamma > 0$, is defined as

$$\rho_{\lambda,\gamma,i}(P) := I + \lambda \cdot A_i^T P A_i$$
$$+ \lambda \cdot A_i^T P B_i \left(\gamma^2 I - B_i^T P B_i \right)^{-1} B_i^T P A_i. \quad (10)$$

For any subset $\mathcal{H}$ of $\mathcal{A}$, the Switched Riccatti Mapping $\rho_{\lambda,\gamma,\mathcal{M}}(\mathcal{H})$ is defined by

$$\rho_{\lambda,\gamma,\mathcal{M}}(\mathcal{H}) = \{ \rho_{\lambda,\gamma,i}(P) : \text{for some } i \in \mathcal{M} \text{ and } P \in \mathcal{H} \}.$$

Starting with the initial condition $\mathcal{H}_0 = \{I\}$, we generate a sequence of sets through the iteration $\mathcal{H}_{k+1} = \rho_{\lambda,\gamma,\mathcal{M}}(\mathcal{H}_k)$. These sets are called the Switched Riccatti Sets (SRSs) and have the property of completely characterizing $G_{\lambda,\gamma,k}(\cdot)$ as follows.

PROPOSITION 5. *For all $k \in \mathbb{N} \cup \{0\}$,*

$$G_{\lambda,\gamma,k}(z) = \max_{P \in \mathcal{H}_k} z^T P z. \quad (11)$$

PROOF. The proposition can be proved by induction. For $k = 0$ the statement (11) holds as

$$G_{\lambda,\gamma,0} = \|z\|^2 = \max_{P \in \{I\}} z^T P z.$$

If (11) holds for some $k \geq 0$, then from the Bellman's equation in Proposition 2,

$$G_{\lambda,\gamma,k+1}(z) = \|z\|^2 + \lambda \sup_{i \in \mathcal{M}, v \in \mathbb{R}^n} \left[-\gamma^2 \|v\|^2 + G_{\lambda,\gamma,k}(A_i z + B_i v) \right],$$

$$= z^T z + \lambda \sup_{i \in \mathcal{M}, v \in \mathbb{R}^n, P \in \mathcal{H}_k} \left[-\gamma^2 v^T v \right.$$
$$\left. + (A_i z + B_i v)^T P (A_i z + B_i v) \right],$$

$$= \sup_{i \in \mathcal{M}, P \in \mathcal{H}_k, v \in \mathbb{R}^n} \left[z^T \left(I + \lambda \cdot A_i^T P A_i \right) z \right.$$
$$+ \lambda \cdot v^T \left(-\gamma^2 I + B_i^T P B_i \right) v$$
$$\left. + 2\lambda \cdot v^T B_i^T P A_i z \right].$$

The expression inside the brackets is quadratic in v. The supremum can be found (provided γ is sufficiently large) as,

$$G_{\lambda,\gamma,k+1} = \sup_{i \in \mathcal{M}, P \in \mathcal{H}_k} z^T \left(I + \lambda \cdot A_i^T P A_i \right.$$
$$\left. + \lambda \cdot A_i^T P B_i \left[\gamma^2 I - B_i^T P B_i \right]^{-1} B_i^T P A_i \right) z,$$

$$= \max_{i \in \mathcal{M}, P \in \mathcal{H}_{k+1}} z^T P z,$$

$$= \max_{P \in \mathcal{H}_{k+1}} z^T P z.$$

This proves the theorem. $\square$

Remark 1. Proposition 5 states that the finite horizon generating functions can be exactly represented by a finite number of positive definite matrices thus removing the need for gridding the state space during computation. Also by Proposition 2, the strong generating function can be computed as a pointwise limit of piecewise quadratic functions.

Remark 2. Finite parametrization of a common storage function was derived in [8] for bounding the $\mathcal{L}_2$-gain of a continuous-time SLS. Our contribution is to explicitly derive the relation for discrete-time systems and (as we will demonstrate in the Section 4.1) generate an effective iterative algorithm to compute bounds on the $\mathcal{L}_2$-gain.

Estimating generalized $\mathcal{L}_2$-gains from the strong generating function involves checking the convergence of the generating functions. To do this, it might be essential to compute the finite horizon generating function $G_{\lambda,\gamma,k}$ over a large time horizon k. This might be impracticable as the number of matrices in $\mathcal{H}_k$ required to represent $G_{\lambda,\gamma,k}$ increases exponentially with k. Applying the Switched Riccati Mapping to this exponentially increasing family of matrices forms the major computational bottleneck in computing generating functions and thus $\mathcal{L}_2$-gains. A more efficient way of managing both memory requirements and computational time is to prune redundant matrices which do not lead to a supremum at each step, as detailed in [17]. This idea is introduced in the context of generating functions in the next section.

4.1 Algorithm for Computing $G_{\lambda,\gamma}(z)$

We now present an algorithm for computing the strong generating functions using the characterization presented in Proposition 5. The algorithm is a specialization of the general one in [17] to the strong generating functions with paralle development. The key idea of the algorithm is the removal of all those matrices which do not contribute to the maximum in (11) for any $z \in \mathbb{R}^n$. To this end we introduce the idea of algebraic redundant matrices in the present context.

Definition 1. A matrix $\hat{P} \in \mathcal{H} \subset \mathcal{A}$ is called redundant w.r.t H if for any $z \in \mathbb{R}^n$, there exists a matrix $P \in \mathcal{H}$ such that $P \neq \hat{P}$ and $z^T P z \geq z^T \hat{P} z$.

If a matrix $\hat{P}$ is redundant w.r.t a SRS $\mathcal{H}_k$, then the generating function $G_{\lambda,\gamma,k}$ can be represented exactly using the set $\mathcal{H}_k \setminus \{\hat{P}\}$. This implies $\hat{P}$ can be removed without causing any error. Hence to maintain ease of computation, we should remove as many redundant matrices as possible at each step of computing the SRSs. However, testing redundancy is in itself a challenging problem. From a geometric viewpoint, any matrix $\hat{P} \in \mathcal{H}_k \subset \mathcal{A}$ represents a unique ellipsoid $\{z \in \mathbb{R}^n : z^T \hat{P} z \leq 1\}$. A matrix $\hat{P}$ is redundant w.r.t $\mathcal{H}_k$ if and only if its corresponding ellipsoid completely covers the intersection of the ellipsoids for matrices in $\mathcal{H}_k \setminus \{\hat{P}\}$. This leads to an easily verifiable sufficient condition given in the following lemma.

LEMMA 1. $\hat{P} \in \mathcal{H}_k$ *is redundant w.r.t $\mathcal{H}_k$ if there exist non-negative constants $\{\alpha_i\}_{i=1}^{|\mathcal{H}_k|-1}$ such that $\sum_{i=1}^{|\mathcal{H}_k|-1} \alpha_i P_i \succeq \hat{P}$, where $\{P_i\}_{i=1}^{|\mathcal{H}_k|-1}$ is an enumeration of $\mathcal{H}_k \setminus \{\hat{P}\}$.*

PROOF. The proof follows from the fact that $\sum_{i=1}^{|\mathcal{H}_k|-1} \alpha_i P_i$ represents an ellipsoid containing the intersection of all the ellipsoids represented by matrices $\{P_i\}_{i=1}^{|\mathcal{H}_k|-1}$. $\square$

The condition stated in Lemma 1 can be tested using convex optimization techniques. Most redundant matrices can be eliminated this way leading to less computation time. Algorithm 1 summarizes the idea of pruning based on Lemma 1.

ALGORITHM 1. *1. Initialize $k := 0$, $\mathcal{H}_0 = \{I\}$;*

2. Initialize $H_{k+1} = \emptyset$

3. repeat for every $i \in \mathcal{M}$

   - repeat for all $\hat{P} \in \mathcal{H}_k$
   - Compute $P_i = \rho_{\lambda,\gamma,i}(\hat{P})$.
   - $\mathcal{H}_{k+1} = \mathcal{H}_{k+1} \cup P_i$.
   - end repeat

4. end repeat

5. If any $P \in \mathcal{H}_{k+1}$ satisfies the condition of Lemma 1 w.r.t $\mathcal{H}_{k+1}$, then $\mathcal{H}_{k+1} = \mathcal{H}_{k+1} \setminus \{P\}$;

6. Set $G_{\lambda,\gamma,k+1}(z) = \max_{P \in \mathcal{H}_{k+1}} z^T P z$;

7. $k := k+1$;

8. Iterate till $G_{\lambda,\gamma,k}(\cdot)$ converges within tolerance (or appears to diverge);

It is to be noted that the sets $\mathcal{H}_k$ returned in Algorithm 1 contain only the non-redundant matrices from the actual SRS generated by the Riccatti equation. However, they are functionally equivalent to the SRS as they both define the same generating function and hence we denote these sets by the same notation.

Algorithm 1 alleviates the computational burden incurred in applying the Switched Riccati Mapping for an exponentially growing number of matrices at the cost of introducing a Linear Matrix Inequality(LMI) computation(which has a complexity polynomial in the state space dimension) for redundancy check at each step. The algorithm proves most efficient for SLS comprising of a large number of subsystems with a small state-space dimension where the number of redundant matrices is typically large enough to offset the redundancy check complexity. Additionally, it is also possible to prune redundant matrices only when the Switched Riccati Set becomes large enough to warrant it, leading to more efficient computation.

The above idea of redundancy can be further relaxed to reduce computational complexity (number of matrices required to describe the generating function) at the expense of accuracy. We describe such an relaxation algorithm in the next section.

4.2 Relaxation Algorithm for Approximate Computations

We begin by modifying the definition of redundancy to allow for slight errors in characterizing the strong generating functions.

Definition 2. A matrix $\hat{P} \in \mathcal{H}_k$ is called ϵ-redundant with respect to $\mathcal{H}_k$ if $\forall z \in \mathbb{R}^n \exists P \in \mathcal{H}_k \setminus \hat{P}$ such that $z^T P z \geq z^T \hat{P} z - \epsilon \|z\|^2$.

By the same reasoning as in Lemma 1, a sufficient condition for ϵ-redundancy can be given as follows.

LEMMA 2. $\hat{P} \in \mathcal{H}_k$ is ϵ-redundant w.r.t $\mathcal{H}_k$ if there exist non-negative constants $\{\alpha_i\}_{i=1}^{|\mathcal{H}_k|-1}$ such that $\sum_{i=1}^{|\mathcal{H}_k|-1} \alpha_i P_i + \epsilon \cdot I \succeq \hat{P}$, where $\{P_i\}_{i=1}^{|\mathcal{H}_k|-1}$ is an enumeration of $\mathcal{H}_k \setminus \{\hat{P}\}$ and I is an Identity matrix of appropriate dimension.

If we denote by $\mathcal{H}^\epsilon$ the set formed by removing all the ϵ-redundant matrices from a set $\mathcal{H}$, the following relationship follows from definition 2.

$$\max_{P \in \mathcal{H}} z^T P z - \epsilon \|z\|^2 \leq \max_{P \in \mathcal{H}^\epsilon} z^T P z \leq \max_{P \in \mathcal{H}} z^T P z. \quad (12)$$

Hence pruning the ϵ-redundant matrices from a SRS $\mathcal{H}_k$ introduces an error of at most $\epsilon \|z\|^2$ in the representation of the generating function.

Lemma 2 can be incorporated into Algorithm 1 to compute relaxed subsets $\mathcal{H}_k^\epsilon$ of the SRS's $\mathcal{H}_k$ iteratively. The sets $\mathcal{H}_k^\epsilon$ can be used to define approximations of the strong generating functions as follows,

$$G_{\lambda,\gamma,k}^\epsilon(z) := \max_{P \in \mathcal{H}_k^\epsilon} z^T P z. \quad (13)$$

Here, $G_{\lambda,\gamma,k}^\epsilon$ is an under approximation of the finite horizon generating function $G_{\lambda,\gamma,k}$ (as $\mathcal{H}_k^\epsilon \subseteq \mathcal{H}_k$). Since errors will be introduced in the representation of the generating functions at each iteration, it is desired that the cumulative effects of these errors are bounded. This will ensure that the numerical value of the infinite horizon generating function will be close to the actual value. The following proposition gives a bound on the error incurred.

PROPOSITION 6. *For all $k \geq 0$ and $z \in \mathbb{R}^n$, the following condition holds:*

$$G_{\lambda,\gamma,k}^\epsilon(z) \geq G_{\lambda,\gamma,k}(z) - \epsilon \sum_{t=0}^{k} \lambda^t \|x(t; \sigma_{k,z}^*, z, u_{k,z}^*)\|^2, \quad (14)$$

where $u_{k,z}^* \in \mathcal{U}_k$ and $\left(\sigma_{k,z}^*, u_{k,z}^*\right)$ is the hybrid control law achieving the maximum in the definition of $G_{\lambda,\gamma,k}(z)$.

PROOF. The proof is by induction. For $k = 0$, $G_{\lambda,\gamma,k}^\epsilon(z) = G_{\lambda,\gamma,k}(z) = \|z\|^2$. Assume the statement is true for some $k \geq 0$. We shall show it is true for $k+1$ as well.

Define $\tilde{G}_{\lambda,\gamma,k+1}^\epsilon(z)$ as follows.

$$\tilde{G}_{\lambda,\gamma,k+1}^\epsilon(z) = \|z\|^2 + \lambda \max_{i,v} \left\{ -\gamma^2 \|v\|^2 + G_{\lambda,\gamma,k}^\epsilon(A_i z + B_i u) \right\}. \quad (15)$$

As in Theorem 5, it can be proved that $\tilde{G}_{\lambda,\gamma,k+1}^\epsilon(z) = \max_{P \in \rho_{\lambda,\gamma,M}(\mathcal{H}_k^\epsilon)} z^T P z$. It follows from (12) that

$$\tilde{G}_{\lambda,\gamma,k+1}^\epsilon(z) - \epsilon \|z\|^2 \leq G_{\lambda,\gamma,k+1}^\epsilon(z) \leq \tilde{G}_{\lambda,\gamma,k+1}^\epsilon(z). \quad (16)$$

From (15) and the induction hypothesis (14) we have,

$$\tilde{G}_{\lambda,\gamma,k+1}^\epsilon(z) \geq \|z\|^2 + \lambda \max_{i,v} \{ -\gamma^2 \|v\|^2 + G_{\lambda,\gamma,k}(A_i z + B_i v)$$
$$- \epsilon \sum_{t=0}^{k} \lambda^t \|x(t; \sigma_{k,A_i z + B_i v}^*, A_i z + B_i v, u_{k,A_i z + B_i v}^*)\|^2 \}. \quad (17)$$

Partition the optimal switching sequence $\sigma_{k+1,z}^* = (\sigma, \sigma')$ and $u_{k+1,z}^* = (u, u')$ with $u' \in \mathcal{U}_k$ and $\sigma \in \mathcal{M}$. Then $x(1; \sigma_{k+1,z}^*, z, u_{k+1,z}^*) = A_\sigma z + B_\sigma u$. Therefore, by the Bellman's principle the k-horizon trajectory starting from $A_\sigma z + B_\sigma u$ will coincide with the last k steps of the $k+1$-trajectory starting from z. This implies

$$\sigma' = \sigma_{k,A_\sigma z + B_\sigma u}^*, \quad u' = u_{k,A_\sigma z + B_\sigma u}^*, \quad \text{and}$$
$$x(t+1; \sigma_{k+1,z}^*, z, u_{k+1,z}^*) = x(t; \sigma', A_\sigma z + B_\sigma u, u').$$

Also, $G_{\lambda,\gamma,k+1}(z) = \|z\|^2 + \lambda\left\{-\gamma^2\|u\|^2 + G_{\lambda,\gamma,k}(A_\sigma z + B_\sigma u)\right\}$ from the optimality of the trajectory (Bellman's Equation). Choosing $i = \sigma$ and $v = u$, we have

$$\tilde{G}^\epsilon_{\lambda,\gamma,k+1}(z) \geq \|z\|^2 + \lambda\bigg\{-\gamma^2\|u\|^2 + G_{\lambda,\gamma,k}(A_\sigma z + B_\sigma u)$$

$$-\epsilon\sum_{t=0}^{k}\lambda^t\|x(t;\sigma', A_\sigma z + B_\sigma u, u')\|^2\bigg\},$$

$$\geq G_{\lambda,\gamma,k+1}(z) - \epsilon\sum_{t=1}^{k+1}\|x(t;\sigma^*_{k+1,z}, z, u^*_{k+1,z})\|^2.$$

Combining with (16), we have

$$G^\epsilon_{\lambda,\gamma,k+1}(z) \geq G_{\lambda,\gamma,k+1}(z) - \epsilon\sum_{t=0}^{k+1}\|x(t;\sigma^*_{k+1,z}, z, u^*_{k+1,z})\|^2.$$

Thus the statement holds for $k+1$ as well. $\square$

Thus the error from successive approximations is bounded by a fraction of the state energy of the SLS. If $G_{\lambda,\gamma}(z) < \infty$, then the state energy will also be bounded and hence relaxation can be used to compute the infinite horizon generating function to any desired accuracy by choosing a sufficiently small tolerance ϵ.

5. NUMERICAL EXAMPLES

Example 1. We consider the SLS with the following subsystems.

$$A_1 = \begin{bmatrix}\frac{1}{2} & \frac{2}{5} \\ \frac{1}{3} & \frac{1}{3}\end{bmatrix}, B_1 = \begin{bmatrix}1 \\ \frac{1}{1}\end{bmatrix}; \qquad A_2 = \begin{bmatrix}\frac{3}{5} & \frac{1}{3} \\ \frac{1}{2} & \frac{1}{4}\end{bmatrix}, B_2 = \begin{bmatrix}0 \\ 1\end{bmatrix};$$

$$A_3 = \begin{bmatrix}\frac{1}{3} & \frac{1}{2} \\ \frac{1}{3} & \frac{1}{4}\end{bmatrix}, B_3 = \begin{bmatrix}\frac{1}{2} \\ 1\end{bmatrix}; \qquad A_4 = \begin{bmatrix}\frac{1}{6} & \frac{1}{5} \\ \frac{1}{4} & \frac{1}{2}\end{bmatrix}, B_4 = \begin{bmatrix}1 \\ 1\end{bmatrix}.$$

The dynamics were selected randomly from a set of proper fractions to ensure stability under arbitrary switching and reachability. Algorithm 1 is used to compute the generating function $G_{\lambda,\gamma,k}(\cdot)$ for $\lambda = 1.1$ and $\gamma = 8$. The computations indicate that the matrices required to represent the generating function $G_{\lambda,\gamma,k}$ do not change significantly after $k = 50$ iterations. Hence convergence can be inferred. Also the number of matrices required to describe the generating function remains constant at 5 instead of growing exponentially. Due to the small number of matrices involved, no relaxation was required to manage complexity. The following 5 matrices were sufficient to characterize the generating function.

$$G_{\lambda\gamma,k} = \max\{z^T P_1 z, z^T P_2 z, z^T P_3 z, z^T P_4 z, z^T P_5 z\},$$

where

$$P_1 = \begin{bmatrix}5.6223 & 2.4604 \\ 2.4604 & 2.3101\end{bmatrix}, \quad P_2 = \begin{bmatrix}1.7701 & 1.2813 \\ 1.2813 & 3.1464\end{bmatrix},$$

$$P_3 = \begin{bmatrix}4.2323 & 2.7597 \\ 2.7597 & 3.3596\end{bmatrix}, \quad P_4 = \begin{bmatrix}5.7712 & 2.5317 \\ 2.5317 & 2.3610\end{bmatrix},$$

$$P_5 = \begin{bmatrix}2.7774 & 2.1657 \\ 2.1657 & 3.6759\end{bmatrix}.$$

Figure 1 depicts the level curves of $G_{\lambda,\gamma,k}(\cdot) = 1$ at various k. Convergence of $G_{\lambda,\gamma,k}(\cdot)$ as $k \to \infty$ is observed. By Proposition 4, we conclude that the strong generating function $G_{\lambda,\gamma}(\cdot)$ is finite everywhere for $\lambda = 1.1$ and $\gamma = 8$.

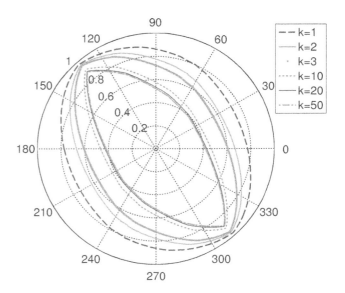

Figure 1: Level curves $G_{\lambda,\gamma,k}(\cdot) = 1$ on the unit circle for $\lambda = 1.1$, $\gamma = 8$ with k varying

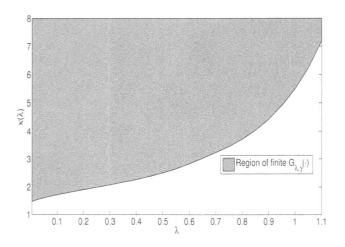

Figure 2: Plot of $\kappa(\lambda)$ vs λ for Example 1

By repeating the computations for different values of λ and γ, we can compute the generalized $\mathcal{L}_2$-gain $\kappa(\lambda)$ as a function of the discount factor λ. See Figure 2 for such a plot. The shaded region represents the region of convergence of the generating function $G_{\lambda,\gamma}(\cdot)$. From Proposition 4, the boundary curve represents the graphs of both the generalize $\mathcal{L}_2$ gain $\kappa(\lambda)$ as a function of λ, and the radius of convergence of the generating function $\lambda^*(\gamma)$ as a function of γ. At $\lambda = 1$, Figure 2 shows that the generalized $\mathcal{L}_2$-gain of the given SLS is less than 5.8. A finer estimate can be obtained using a bisection type algorithm.

Example 2. The following example illustrates the importance of having a necessary and sufficient condition in the computation of the $\mathcal{L}_2$-gain. For the 2-dimensional SLS defined by the following matrices

$$A_1 = \begin{bmatrix} 0.9 & 0 \\ 0 & 1 \end{bmatrix}, \qquad B_1 = \begin{bmatrix} 1 \\ 0 \end{bmatrix};$$

$$A_2 = \begin{bmatrix} 0.5 & 0.6 \\ -0.7 & -1.2 \end{bmatrix}, \qquad B_2 = \begin{bmatrix} 0 \\ 1 \end{bmatrix},$$

approaches based on sufficient conditions (such as the one in [2]) usually fail or give a conservative result in estimating the $\mathcal{L}_2$-gain. (The problem arises due to the lack of a common quadratic Lyapunov function ensuring asymptotic stability of the SLS in question). Using the convergence of the generating function however, we are able to estimate the (classical) $\mathcal{L}_2$-gain of the SLS as 13.6 ($G_{\lambda=1,\gamma=13.6}(\cdot) < \infty$). This bound can further be improved using a bisection approach.

To demonstrate the effectiveness of the algorithm, it was tested on randomly generated SLS's with 3 stable single input subsystems of in a three dimensional state space. Generating functions were computed upto the horizon of $k = 75$ with $\lambda = 0.75, \gamma = 15$. The computations were run till a significant number (250 in total) of SLS's were found that exhibited convergent behavior for the above parameters. Figure 3 depicts the number of matrices required to completely characterize the generating function. A maximum of 19 matrices were required to do so while a majority of the generating functions could be exactly represented using 6 matrices. It must be noted that these results represent only a fraction of the SLS's with three-dimensional state space as convergence for a given λ and γ is not guaranteed for a randomly generated SLS's. Studying a larger sample size is in general computationally prohibitive. Running on an Intel Core2Duo desktop and using SeDuMi for LMI programming, computation took 3-15 minutes for $k = 75$ iterations of the generating functions for a single randomly generated SLS. Convergence was usually inferred within 30 iterations though more (≈ 100) iterations were required when the value of λ is closer to the radius of convergence.

Example 3. We consider the following three-dimensional example:

$$A_1 = \begin{bmatrix} 0.5 & 0 & -0.7 \\ 0 & 0.3 & 0 \\ 0 & -0.4 & -0.6 \end{bmatrix}, B_1 = \begin{bmatrix} 0.4 \\ 0.9 \\ 0.1 \end{bmatrix};$$

$$A_2 = \begin{bmatrix} 0.5 & 0 & 0 \\ 0.4 & 0.2 & 0.3 \\ 0 & 0 & 0.3 \end{bmatrix}, B_2 = \begin{bmatrix} 0.4 \\ 0.8 \\ 0 \end{bmatrix};$$

$$A_3 = \begin{bmatrix} 0 & -1 & 0 \\ 0.9 & 0.2 & 0.3 \\ -0.2 & 0.3 & -0.5 \end{bmatrix}, B_3 = \begin{bmatrix} 0.1 \\ 0.2 \\ 0.1 \end{bmatrix}.$$

Using algorithm 1, we compute the generating function $G_{\lambda,\gamma,k}$ for $\lambda = 1.1, \gamma = 35$ and $k = 200$. The unit ball of the generating function is shown in figure 4. The generating function is completely characterized by 6-matrices instead of the theoretical 3^{200} matrices.

Example 4. To demonstrate the effect of relaxation, the following SLS is considered. This system was chosen from

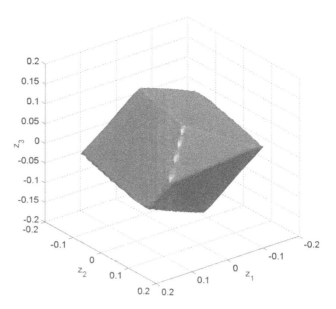

Figure 4: Unit ball of $G_{\lambda,\gamma,k}(z)$ for Example 3

the randomly generated systems used in studying the effectiveness of algorithm 1 mentioned earlier.

$$A_1 = \begin{bmatrix} 0.1515 & 0.2351 & 0.3763 \\ 0.2696 & 0.3257 & 0.1295 \\ 0.0822 & 0.2374 & 0.2100 \end{bmatrix}, B_1 = \begin{bmatrix} 0.9981 \\ 0.1132 \\ 0.3316 \end{bmatrix};$$

$$A_2 = \begin{bmatrix} 0.1719 & 0.1846 & 0.1186 \\ 0.2420 & 0.2792 & 0.3645 \\ 0.0066 & 0.3453 & 0.1936 \end{bmatrix}, B_2 = \begin{bmatrix} 0.6511 \\ 0.2015 \\ 0.7880 \end{bmatrix};$$

$$A_3 = \begin{bmatrix} 0.3249 & 0.0105 & 0.1955 \\ 0.0499 & 0.1833 & 0.3756 \\ 0.2664 & 0.0009 & 0.4905 \end{bmatrix}, B_3 = \begin{bmatrix} 0.2872 \\ 0.0415 \\ 0.6339 \end{bmatrix}.$$

For $\lambda = 0.75, \gamma = 15$ and time horizon $k = 75$, the generating functions were computed using algorithm 1 and its relaxed version. After $k = 75$ iterations, the generating function had exactly 19 non-redundant matrices. Figure 5 shows the unit ball $\{z : G_{\lambda=0.75,\gamma=15,k=75}(z) = 1\}$ obtained from the computation. Using a relaxation parameter of $\epsilon = 10^{-3}$ decreased the number of non-redundant matrices to 14, while using a $\epsilon = 10^{-2}$ cut the number of matrices to 9. In both the relaxed versions, the maximum error incurred due to the approximation was less than 10^{-3} for all initial conditions on the unit ball in $\mathbb{R}^3$. We infer that the computational savings can be significant in higher dimensional systems with a large number of subsystems. The variation of the generalized $\mathcal{L}_2$-gains as a function of the discount factor λ can be seen in Figure 6.

6. CONCLUSION

We were able to derive an efficient algorithm for the estimation of $\mathcal{L}_2$-gains for discrete-time switched linear systems through the computation of the corresponding generating functions. The proposed algorithm can be further relaxed to trade off accuracy with computational complexity. Future directions include deriving tighter bounds on the relaxation

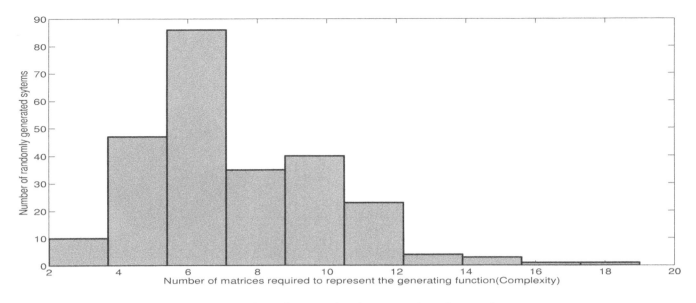

Figure 3: Distribution of non-redundant matrices for random systems

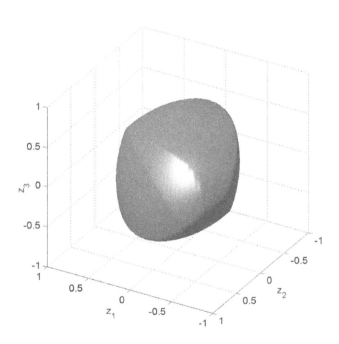

Figure 5: Unit ball of $G_{\lambda,\gamma,k}$ for Example 4

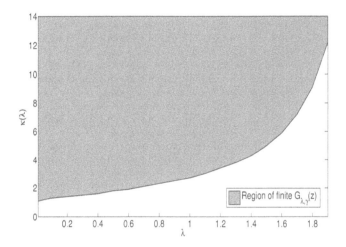

Figure 6: Plot of $\kappa(\lambda)$ vs λ for Example 4

error and investigating $\mathcal{L}_2$-gains under input and switching constraints.

7. ACKNOWLEDGMENTS

This work was supported in part by the National Science Foundation under Grants CNS-0643805 and ECCS-0900960.

8. REFERENCES

[1] P. Colaneri, P. Bolzern, and J. Geromel. Root mean square gain of discrete-time switched linear systems under dwell time constraints. *Automatica*, 47(8):1677 – 1684, 2011.

[2] P. Colaneri and J. Geromel. RMS gain with dwell time for discrete-time switched linear systems. In *Control and Automation, 2008 16th Mediterranean Conference on*, pages 107–112, june 2008.

[3] S. Ge, Z. Sun, and T. Lee. Reachability and controllability of switched linear discrete-time systems. *Automatic Control, IEEE Transactions on*, 46(9):1437–1441, 2002.

[4] J. Hespanha. Root-mean-square gains of switched linear systems. *Automatic Control, IEEE Transactions on*, 48(11):2040–2045, 2003.

[5] J. Hespanha. $\mathcal{L}_2$-induced gains of switched linear systems. In V. Blondel and A. Megretski, editors, *Unsolved problems in mathematical systems and*

control theory, pages 131–133. Princeton University Press, 2004.

[6] J. Hespanha and A. Morse. Input-output gains of switched linear systems. *Open problems in mathematical systems and control theory*, page 121, 1999.

[7] K. Hirata and J. P. Hespanha. $\mathcal{L}_2$-induced gain analysis for a class of switched systems. In *Proceedings of the 48th Conf. on Decision and Control*, Dec. 2009.

[8] K. Hirata and J. P. Hespanha. $\mathcal{L}_2$-induced gain analysis of switched linear systems via finitely parametrized storage functions. In *Proceedings of the 2010 American Control Conference*, June 2010.

[9] J. Hu, J. Shen, and W. Zhang. Generating functions of switched linear systems: analysis, computation, and stability applications. *Automatic Control, IEEE Transactions on*, 56(5):1059–1074, 2011.

[10] J. Lee and G. E. Dullerud. Optimal disturbance attenuation for Discrete-Time switched and markovian jump linear systems. *SIAM Journal on Control and Optimization*, 45:1329, 2006.

[11] D. Liberzon. *Switching in systems and control.* Springer, 2003.

[12] H. Lin and P. Antsaklis. Stability and stabilizability of switched linear systems: A survey of recent results. *Automatic Control, IEEE Transactions on*, 54(2):308–322, 2009.

[13] M. Margaliot and J. Hespanha. Root-mean-square gains of switched linear systems: A variational approach. *Automatica*, 44(9):2398–2402, 2008.

[14] V. Putta, G. Zhu, J. Shen, and J. Hu. A study of the generalized input-to-state $\mathcal{L}_2$-gain of discrete-time switched linear systems. In *50th Conf. on Decision and Control*, pages 435–440, Dec. 2011.

[15] R. Shorten, F. Wirth, O. Mason, K. Wulff, and C. King. Stability criteria for switched and hybrid systems. *SIAM review*, 49(4):545, 2007.

[16] G. Zhai, B. Hu, K. Yasuda, and A. Michel. Qualitative analysis of discrete-time switched systems. In *Proceedings of the 2002 American Control Conference*, volume 3, pages 1880 – 1885, 2002.

[17] W. Zhang, J. Hu, and A. Abate. On the value functions of the discrete-time switched LQR problem. *Automatic Control, IEEE Transactions on*, 54(11):2669–2674, 2009.

[18] J. Zhao and D. Hill. On stability, $\mathcal{L}_2$-gain and H_∞ control for switched systems. *Automatica*, 44(5):1220–1232, 2008.

Algebraic Analysis on Asymptotic Stability of Switched Hybrid Systems

Zhikun She, Bai Xue
SKLSDE, LMIB and School of Mathematics and Systems Science, Beihang University, China
zhikun.she@buaa.edu.cn, xuebai0402@163.com

ABSTRACT

In this paper we propose a mechanisable approach for discovering multiple Lyapunov functions for switched hybrid systems. We start with the classical definition on asymptotic stability, which can be assured by the existence of multiple Lyapunov functions. Then, we derive an algebraizable sufficient condition on multiple Lyapunov functions in quadratic form for asymptotic stability analysis. Since different modes are considered, in addition to real root classification, we further apply a projection operator step by step to under-approximate this sufficient condition and obtain a set of semi-algebraic sets which only involve the coefficients of the multiple Lyapunov function. Moreover, for each step, we use the information on modes to optimize our intermediate computation results. Finally, we compute a sample point in the resulting semi-algebraic sets for coefficients. We tested our approach on five examples using prototypical implementation. The computation and comparison results demonstrate the applicability and efficiency of our approach.

Categories and Subject Descriptors

I.1 [**Symbolic and algebraic manipulation**]: Applications, Algorithms; J.7 [**Computers in other systems**]: Real time

General Terms

Verification, Theory, Algorithms

Keywords

Multiple Lyapunov functions, real root classification, projection operator, semi-algebraic sets

1. INTRODUCTION

Asymptotic stability of switched hybrid systems has recently received growing attentions in the analysis and design of control systems. A sufficient condition for verifying

HSCC'12, April 17–19, 2012, Beijing, China.
Copyright 2012 ACM 978-1-4503-1220-2/12/04 ...$10.00.

asymptotic stability of switched hybrid system is the existence of common Lypunov functions or multiple Lypunov functions [12, 2]. Therefore, the computation of common or multiple Lyapunov functions has also become a very interesting topic in computer, control and system sciences.

When the differential equations in subsystems are polynomials, due to decidability of the theory of real-closed fields [32], one can verify the existence of common Lyapunov functions or multiple Lyapunov functions by quantifier elimination (QE) based method [14, 30, 4]. However, all the existing decision procedures (e.g., implemented in the software packages QEPCAD [3] or REDLOG [7]), while being able to solve impressively difficult examples, are not enough to be able to solve this problem in practice.

Another choice is to linearize the subsystems and then use linear matrix inequalities (LMI) based method for computing common or multiple Lyapunov functions [2, 15, 9]. Further, without linearization, one can use the sum of squares programming (SOS) based method [18, 19, 16] to compute common or multiple Lyapunov functions by relaxation to linear matrix inequalities. However, Hilbert has already pointed out that apart from three special cases, not all nonnegative polynomials can be formulated as sums of squares [22].

Recently, an automatable decompositional method has been proposed for the computation of Lyapunov functions [13] by using graph-based reasoning to decompose hybrid automata into subgraphs and then solving semi-definite optimization problems to obtain local Lyapunov functions.

In this paper, following the algebraic idea in [27], we propose a mechanisable technique for asymptotic stability analysis of switched hybrid systems whose subsystems have polynomial vector fields. Note that a direct extension of [27] only fits systems whose subsystems are all asymptotically stable.

We start with the classical definition on asymptotic stability of switched hybrid systems, which can be assured by the existence of multiple Lyapunov functions. Then, we construct an algebraizable sufficient condition on the existence of multiple Lyapunov functions in quadratic form, which is solvable due to the theory of real-closed fields [32]. Note that since different modes are considered, this sufficient condition is more complex than the one in [27]. Especially, we need to compute two non-collinear vectors in the corresponding state space of each mode.

For efficient computation, we first transform the constraints to equivalent ones and then under-approximate the equivalent ones step by step in a conservative way, arriving at semi-algebraic sets only involving the coefficients of the preassumed multiple Lyapunov function. Based on these resulting semi-algebraic sets, we can compute a sample point for the coefficients to obtain a multiple Lyapunov function. Again, since different modes are considered, our algorithms for under-approximation are also more complex than the ones in [27] although their structures are similar. First, in addition to real root classification, we further apply a projection operator to assure that eliminated variables do not appear in later steps. Second, we use the information on each mode to optimize our intermediate computation results at each step to obtain simpler ones.

We prototypically implemented our algorithms based on the semi-algebraic set solver DISCOVERER [33] with manual intervention and tested it on five examples. The computation results demonstrate the applicability of our approach.

Compared to LMI based method, our current approach can work on systems whose subsystems may be degenerate. Moreover, compared to SOS based method, our approach can work for cases where the non-negative polynomials can not be practically formulated as sums of squares.

Note that our approach can also be potentially useful for verifying other properties of hybrid systems (e.g., verifying safety by generating invariants [8]).

The structure of the paper is as follows: We start with the classical definition on asymptotic stability of switched hybrid systems in Section 2; In Section 3, we present an algebraizable sufficient condition on multiple Lyapunov functions for asymptotic stability analysis; In Section 4, we use a real root classification and projection operator based approach for computing multiple Lyapunov functions; We analyze the correctness of our approach in Section 5 and give a brief introduction to our implementation in Section 6; We provide some computation and comparison results in Section 7 and conclude the paper in Section 8.

2. PROBLEM DEFINITIONS

A switched hybrid system SHS is a system of form $\dot{\vec{x}} = f_i(\vec{x})$, where $i \in \mathcal{M}$, $\mathcal{M} = \{1, \cdots, N\}$ is the set of discrete modes, $\vec{x} \in \mathcal{X}_i$, $\mathcal{X}_i \subset \mathbb{R}^n$ is the continuous state space of mode i, and $f_i(\vec{x})$ is a vector field describing the dynamics of mode i. For two modes i and j, where $i \neq j$, a switch from mode i to mode j needs to occur if the evolution in mode i hits the switching condition defined by a constraint over $\vec{x}$. Moreover, a switch must occur before the evolution in mode i leaves its corresponding continuous state space $\mathcal{X}_i$ and there are only finite switches in finite time.

A trajectory of a SHS is a finite or an infinite sequence of flows $r_0(t), r_1(t), \cdots, r_p(t), \cdots$, associated with a time sequence $T_0, T_1, \cdots, T_p, \cdots$, such that

1. every flow $r_p(t)$ is associated with a mode i and evolves according to $\dot{r}_p(t) = f_i(r_p(t))$,

2. for each $p > 0$, $r_{p-1}(T_p)$ satisfies the switching constraints and $r_p(0) = r_{p-1}(T_p)$.

We denote a trajectory $r_0(t), \cdots, r_p(t), \cdots$ by $\vec{x}(t)$ satisfying

1. $\vec{x}(0) = r_0(0)$, for all $p \geq 0$, $\vec{x}(\sum_{i=0}^{p} T_i) = r_p(T_p) = r_{p+1}(0)$, and

2. for all $t \in (\sum_{i=0}^{p-1} T_i, \sum_{i=0}^{p} T_i)$, $\vec{x}(t) = r_p(t - \sum_{i=0}^{p-1} T_i)$.

DEFINITION 1 (ASYMPTOTICALLY STABLE). *A switched hybrid system is called stable if*

$$\forall \epsilon > 0 \exists \delta > 0 \forall t > 0 \left[\|\vec{x}(0)\| < \delta \Rightarrow \|\vec{x}(t)\| < \epsilon \right]$$

holds, and attractive if for all trajectories $\vec{x}(t)$,

$$\lim_{t \to +\infty} \vec{x}(t) = \vec{0},$$

where $\vec{0}$ is its equilibrium point. A switched hybrid system is called asymptotically stable if it is both stable and attractive.

Even if we have Lyapunov functions for each subsystem defined by $\dot{\vec{x}} = f_i(\vec{x})$ individually, we still need to impose restrictions on switching to guarantee stability, which can be easily seen from the following example.

EXAMPLE 1. *Consider $f_i(x)$, where*

$$f_1(\vec{x}) = \begin{pmatrix} -x_1 + 10x_2 \\ -100x_1 - x_2 \end{pmatrix} \text{ and } f_2(\vec{x}) = \begin{pmatrix} -x_1 + 100x_2 \\ -10x_1 - x_2 \end{pmatrix}.$$

Clearly, $\dot{\vec{x}} = f_i(\vec{x})$ is globally stable for $i = 1, 2$. But the switched system using $f_1(\vec{x})$ in the second and fourth quadrants and $f_2(\vec{x})$ in the first and third quadrants is unstable, which can be easily seen from Fig. 1.

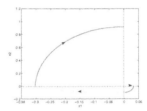

Fig. 1 A Trajectory of Example 1.

Moreover, even if we have at least one unstable subsystem, we can still guarantee stability after imposing certain restrictions on switching, which can be seen below.

EXAMPLE 2. *Consider $f_i(\vec{x})$, where*

$$f_1(\vec{x}) = \begin{pmatrix} -x_1 - 100x_2 \\ 10x_1 - x_2 \end{pmatrix} \text{ and } f_2(\vec{x}) = \begin{pmatrix} x_1 + 10x_2 \\ -100x_1 + x_2 \end{pmatrix}.$$

Clearly, $\dot{\vec{x}} = f_1(\vec{x})$ is globally stable and $\vec{x} = f_2(\vec{x})$ is unstable. However, if we define $\mathcal{X}_1 = \mathbb{R}^2$ and $\mathcal{X}_2 = \{\vec{x} : -10x_1 - x_2 \geq 0, 2x_1 - x_2 \geq 0\}$ and a switch from mode i to mode j need to occur if a trajectory in mode i hits the switching surface $g_{i,j}^T \vec{x} = 0$, where $i, j \in \{1, 2\}$, $i \neq j$, $g_{1,2} = (-10, -1)$ and $g_{2,1} = (2, -1)$, then the switched system is globally stable, which can be easily seen from Fig. 2.

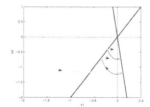

Fig. 2 A Trajectory of Example 2.

In general, stability verification is undecidable [1]. In this paper, we consider a switched hybrid system of form

$$\dot{\vec{x}} = f_i(\vec{x}), i \in \mathcal{M} = \{1, \cdots, N\}, \vec{x} \in \mathcal{X}_i \subset \mathbb{R}^n, \quad (1)$$

where f_i is a polynomial vector field satisfying $f_i(\vec{0}) = \vec{0}$, $\mathcal{X}_i$ is a union of polyhedral sets defined by form $\{\vec{x} | E_{i,j} \vec{x} \geq \vec{0}, E_{i,j}$ is an $n \times n$ matrix$\}$ such that $\mathcal{X}_i = \bigcup_{j=1}^{l_i} \{\vec{x} | E_{i,j} \vec{x} \geq$

$\vec{0}$, $E_{i,j}$ is an $n \times n$ matrix}, $\bigcup_{i \in \mathcal{M}} \mathcal{X}_i = \mathbb{R}^n$ and for two vectors $\vec{x}, \vec{y} \in \mathbb{R}^n$, $\vec{x} \geq \vec{y}$ means $x_1 \geq y_1, \ldots, x_n \geq y_n$. In addition, for a switch from mode i to mode j, where $i \neq j$, its switching constraint is given by $\vee_{r=1}^{l_{i,j}} [g_{i,j,r}^T \vec{x} = 0]$, where $g_{i,j,r} \in \mathbb{R}^{n \times 1}$ and $g_{i,j,r} \neq \vec{0}$. Letting $S_{i,j} = \cup_{r=1}^{l_{i,j}} \{\vec{x} : g_{i,j,r}^T \vec{x} = 0\}$, we assume that $S_{i,j} \cap S_{i,k} = \emptyset$ for all $j \neq k$. For simplicity, we denote such a system as PS.

Note that the assumption that $f_i(\vec{0}) = \vec{0}$ for all i has already been used in the literature [2, 16].

To prove asymptotic stability of a given system PS, it is sufficient to verify the existence of multiple Lyapunov functions, which will be discussed in Section 3.

3. AN EXISTENCE CONDITION FOR MULTIPLE LYAPUNOV FUNCTIONS

In this section, we will construct an algebraizable sufficient condition for asymptotic stability analysis of switched hybrid systems. To start with, we will introduce a classical theorem on multiple Lyapunov functions for switched hybrid systems as follows.

THEOREM 1. *[12] For a given system* PS, *if there exist a neighborhood* $\mathbb{U}$ *of the origin and continuously differentiable functions* $V_i(\vec{x}) : \mathcal{X}_i \to \mathbb{R}$, $i \in \mathcal{M}$, *such that*

1. *for each* $i \in \mathcal{M}$, $V_i(\vec{0}) = 0$ *and* $\frac{d}{dt} V_i(\vec{0}) = 0$;

2. *for each* $i \in \mathcal{M}$ *and each* $\vec{x} \in \mathcal{X}_i \cap \mathbb{U}$, *if* $\vec{x} \neq \vec{0}$, *then* $V_i(\vec{x}) > 0$;

3. *for each* $i \in \mathcal{M}$ *and each* $\vec{x} \in \mathcal{X}_i \cap \mathbb{U}$, *if* $\vec{x} \neq \vec{0}$, *then* $\frac{d}{dt} V_i(\vec{x}) = (\nabla V_i(\vec{x}))^T \circ f_i(\vec{x}) < 0$; *and,*

4. *if* $\vec{x} \in S_{i,j} \cap \mathbb{U}$, *then* $V_i(\vec{x}) \geq V_j(\vec{x})$,

then PS *is asymptotically stable. Here, the family* $\{V_i(\vec{x}) : i \in \mathcal{M}\}$ *is called as a multiple Lyapunov function (or, MLF).*

For each $i \in \mathcal{M}$, let $V_i = V_i(\vec{x})$ be a quadratic form and $\mathcal{X}_i$ be $\bigcup_{j=1}^{l_i} \{\vec{x} | E_{i,j} \vec{x} \geq \vec{0}, E_{i,j}$ is an $n \times n$ matrix}. In addition, represent $\dot{V}_i = \frac{d}{dt} V_i(\vec{x}) = (\nabla V_i(\vec{x}))^T \cdot f_i(x)$ as $\sum_{k=2}^{m_i} v_{i,k}(\vec{x})$, where m_i is the degree of $\dot{V}_i$ and $v_{i,k}(\vec{x})$ is the sum of all homogeneous polynomials of degree k in $\dot{V}_i$. For constructing an algebraizable sufficient condition for asymptotic stability analysis, we additionally need the following theorem.

THEOREM 2. *Let* $p = p(\vec{x})$ *be a polynomial of degree* $m \geq 2$. *If* $p(\vec{x})$ *is positive definite in* $\mathbb{W} = \{\vec{x} : E\vec{x} \geq \vec{0}, E \in \mathbb{R}^{n \times n}\}$, *then for every polynomial* $q(\vec{x})$ *of form* $\sum_{i=m+1}^{k} q_i(\vec{x})$, *where* $q_i(\vec{x})$ *is a homogeneous polynomial of degree* i, *there is a neighborhood* $\mathbb{U}$ *of* $\vec{x} = \vec{0}$ *such that the sum* $p(\vec{x}) + q(\vec{x})$ *is positive definite in* $\{\vec{x} : \vec{x} \in \mathbb{U} \cap \mathbb{W}\}$.

PROOF. First, we transform the Cartesian coordinates $(x_1, \cdots, x_n)$ to polar coordinates $(r, \theta_1, \cdots, \theta_{n-1})$. Letting

$$\begin{cases} x_1 = r\cos\theta_1 \\ x_2 = r\sin\theta_1\cos\theta_2 \\ \cdots \\ x_n = r\sin\theta_1\sin\theta_2 \cdots \sin\theta_{n-2}\sin\theta_{n-1} \end{cases}$$

where $0 \leq r < +\infty, 0 \leq \theta_1, \cdots, \theta_{n-2} \leq \pi, 0 \leq \theta_{n-1} \leq 2\pi$, we get $p(r, \vec{\theta}) = r^2 \phi_2(\vec{\theta}) + r^3 \phi_3(\vec{\theta}) + \cdots + r^m \phi_m(\vec{\theta})$, and $q(r, \vec{\theta}) = \sum_{i=m+1}^{k} r^i \phi_i(\vec{\theta})$.

Since $\mathbb{W}$ is defined to be $\{\vec{x} : E\vec{x} \geq \vec{0}, E \in \mathbb{R}^{n \times n}\}$, we can find $\theta_{1,1}$, $\theta_{1,2}$, $\cdots$, $\theta_{n-1,1}$ and $\theta_{n-1,2}$ such that $\mathbb{W}$ is equivalent to $\{(r, \vec{\theta}) : 0 \leq r < +\infty, \theta_{1,1} \leq \theta_1 \leq \theta_{1,2}, \cdots, \theta_{n-1,1} \leq \theta_{n-1} \leq \theta_{n-1,2}\}$, where $\vec{\theta} = (\theta_1, \cdots, \theta_{n-1})$.

Letting $\Omega_1 = \{\vec{\theta} : \theta_{1,1} \leq \theta_1 \leq \theta_{1,2}, \cdots, \theta_{n-1,1} \leq \theta_{n-1} \leq \theta_{n-1,2}\}$ and $f(r, \vec{\theta}) = p(r, \vec{\theta}) + q(r, \vec{\theta})$, for proving our theorem, it is sufficient to only prove that there is an $l > 0$ such that $f(r, \vec{\theta})$ is positive definite in $\{(r, \vec{\theta}) : 0 < r < l, \vec{\theta} \in \Omega_1\}$.

Since $p(r, \vec{\theta})$ is positive definite, then there is no $\vec{\theta} \in \Omega_1$ such that $\phi_2(\vec{\theta}) = 0$, $\cdots$, and $\phi_m(\vec{\theta}) = 0$. Let $\Omega_{i-1} = \{\vec{\theta} : \phi_2(\vec{\theta}) = 0, \cdots, \phi_{i-1}(\vec{\theta}) = 0\}$, where $3 \leq i \leq m - 1$.

Clearly, for every $2 \leq i \leq m - 1$, Ω_{i-1} is compact, $\Omega_{i-1} \subseteq \Omega_{i-2} \subseteq \cdots \subseteq \Omega_2 \subseteq \Omega$ and there is an $2 \leq I \leq m - 1$ such that if $\Omega_{I-1} \neq \emptyset$, then for all $\vec{\theta} \in \Omega_{I-1}$, $\phi_I(\vec{\theta}) \neq 0$.

We can get a subset ω' from the set $\omega = \{2, \cdots, I\}$ using the following strategy: (1) let $s := I - 1$ and $\omega' := \omega$; (2) if $s \geq 2$ and there exists a k such that $\Omega_s = \Omega_k$, where $1 \leq k < s$, then $\omega' := \omega' \setminus \{s\}$, $s := s - 1$ and return to (2). Denote ω' as $\{I_1, \cdots, I_j, I_{j+1}\}$, where $I_1 < \cdots < I_{j+1}$. Clearly, $I_1 = 1$, $I_{j+1} = I$ and for each $k = 2, \cdots, j + 1$ and for each s satisfying $I_{k-1} < s < I_k$, $\phi_s(\vec{\theta}) \equiv 0$ in $\Omega_{I_{k-1}}$.

For all $\vec{\theta} \in \Omega_{I_j}$, $p(r, \vec{\theta}) = r^I(\phi_I(\theta) + r\phi_{I+1}(\theta) + \cdots)$. According to the assumption that $p(r, \vec{\theta})$ is positive definite, for all $\vec{\theta} \in \Omega_{I_j}$, $\phi_I(\vec{\theta}) > 0$. Since Ω_{I_j} is compact, there exists a $\varepsilon_I > 0$ such that $\phi_I(\vec{\theta}) \geq \varepsilon_I$. Thus, there is an open set H_{I_j} such that $\Omega_{I_j} \subsetneq H_{I_j}$ and for all $\vec{\theta} \in H_{I_j}$, $\phi_I(\vec{\theta}) \geq \frac{\varepsilon_I}{2}$.

Due to the assumption that $p(r, \vec{\theta})$ is positive definite, $\phi_{I_j}(\vec{\theta}) \geq 0$ in $\Omega_{I_{j-1}}$. So, for all $\vec{\theta} \in H_{I_j} \cap \Omega_{I_{j-1}}$, $p(r, \vec{\theta}) = r^{I_j}(\phi_{I_j}(\theta) + r^{I_{j+1}-I_j}\phi_{I_{j+1}}(\theta) + \cdots) \geq r^{I_j}(\frac{\varepsilon_I}{2} + r\phi_{I+1}(\vec{\theta}) + \cdots)$. Thus, there exists $r_{I_{j+1}} > 0$ such that $f(r, \vec{\theta})$ is positive definite in $\{(r, \theta) : 0 < r < r_{I_{j+1}}, \theta \in H_{I_j} \cap \Omega_{I_{j-1}}\}$.

Let $\Omega'_{I_{j-1}} = \Omega_{I_{j-1}} \setminus H_{I_j}$. Then, $\phi_{I_j}(\vec{\theta}) \neq 0$ in $\Omega'_{I_{j-1}}$. Due to the assumption that $p(r, \vec{\theta})$ is positive definite, $\phi_{I_j}(\vec{\theta}) > 0$ in $\Omega'_{I_{j-1}}$. Since $\Omega'_{I_{j-1}}$ is also compact, there exists a $\varepsilon_{I_j} > 0$ such that $\phi_{I_j}(\vec{\theta}) \geq \varepsilon_{I_j}$. Thus, there is an open set $H_{I_{j-1}}$ such that $\Omega'_{I_{j-1}} \subsetneq H_{I_{j-1}}$ and for all $\vec{\theta} \in H_{I_{j-1}}$, $\phi_{I_j}(\vec{\theta}) \geq \frac{\varepsilon_{I_j}}{2}$.

Due to the assumption that $p(r, \vec{\theta})$ is positive definite, $\phi_{I_{j-1}}(\vec{\theta}) \geq 0$ in $\Omega_{I_{j-2}}$. So, for all $\vec{\theta} \in H_{I_{j-1}} \cap \Omega_{I_{j-2}}$, $p(r, \vec{\theta}) = r^{I_{j-1}}(\phi_{I_{j-1}}(\theta) + r^{I_j-I_{j-1}}\phi_{I_j}(\theta) + \cdots) \geq r^{I_j}(\frac{\varepsilon_{I_j}}{2} + r\phi_I(\vec{\theta}) + \cdots)$. Thus, there exists $r_{I_j} > 0$ such that $f(r, \vec{\theta})$ is positive definite in $\{(r, \vec{\theta}) : 0 < r < r_{I_j}, \theta \in H_{I_{j-1}} \cap \Omega_{I_{j-2}}\}$.

Due to the deductive method, we can prove that there exist an open set H_{I_i} and $r_{I_{i+1}} > 0$ such that $f(r, \vec{\theta})$ is positive definite in $\{(r, \theta) : 0 < r < r_{I_3}, \theta \in H_{I_i} \cap \Omega_{I_{i-1}}\}$, where $i = 2, \cdots, j - 1$.

According to the assumption that $p(r, \vec{\theta})$ is positive definite, $\phi_{I_2}(\vec{\theta}) > 0$ in $\Omega_1 \setminus \cup_{k=1}^{j-1}(\Omega_{I_k} \cap H_{I_{k+1}})$. Since $\Omega_1 \setminus \cup_{k=1}^{j-1}(\Omega_{I_k} \cap H_{I_{k+1}})$ is also compact, there exists a $\varepsilon_{I_2} > 0$ such that $\phi_{I_2}(\vec{\theta}) \geq \varepsilon_{I_2}$ for all $\vec{\theta} \in \Omega_1 \setminus \cup_{k=1}^{j-1}(\Omega_{I_k} \cap H_{I_{k+1}})$. Thus, there exists $r_{I_2} > 0$ such that $f(r, \vec{\theta})$ is positive definite in $\{(r, \vec{\theta}) : 0 < r < r_2, \vec{\theta} \in \Omega_1 \setminus \cup_{k=1}^{j-1}(\Omega_{I_k} \cap H_{I_{k+1}})\}$.

So, letting $r_0 = \min\{r_{I_2}, \cdots, r_{I_{j+1}}\}$, $f(r, \vec{\theta})$ is positive definite in $\{(r, \vec{\theta}) : 0 < r < r_0, \vec{\theta} \in \Omega_1\}$. $\square$

Now, based on Theorems 1 and 2, we can construct an algebraizable sufficient condition — which can then be used to compute multiple Lyapunov functions in quadratic form by a real root classification and projection operator based algebraic approach in Section 4 — as follows.

THEOREM 3. *For a given* PS, *if there exist functions* $V_i(\vec{x})$ *in quadratic form,* $i \in \mathcal{M}$, *such that*

1. *for each* $i \in \mathcal{M}$ *and each* $j \in \{1, \ldots, l_i\}$,

   (1a) $\forall \vec{x}[\vec{x} \in \mathcal{X}_i \wedge \vec{x} \neq \vec{0} \Rightarrow V_i(\vec{x}) \neq 0]$, *and*

   (1b) $\exists \vec{x}_{i,j_1}, \vec{x}_{i,j_2} \big[E_{i,j}\vec{x}_{i,j_1} \geq \vec{0} \wedge E_{i,j}\vec{x}_{i,j_2} \geq \vec{0} \wedge (\vec{x}_{i,j_1}, \vec{x}_{i,j_2})$
   $\neq \|\vec{x}_{i,j_1}\|\|\vec{x}_{i,j_2}\| \wedge V_i(\vec{x}_{i,j_1}) > 0 \wedge V_i(\vec{x}_{i,j_2}) > 0 \big]$,
   where $(\cdot, \cdot)$ *is the inner product of vectors,* [1]

2. *for each* $i \in \mathcal{M}$ *and each* $j \in \{1, \ldots, l_i\}$, *there exists a positive integer* $m_{i,c} \leq m_i$ *such that*

   (2a) $\forall \vec{x}[\vec{x} \in \mathcal{X}_i \wedge \vec{x} \neq \vec{0} \Rightarrow \sum_{k=2}^{m_{i,c}} v_{i,k}(\vec{x}) \neq 0]$, *and*

   (2b) $\exists \vec{x}_{i,j_1}, \vec{x}_{i,j_2} \big[E_{i,j}\vec{x}_{i,j_1} \geq \vec{0} \wedge E_{i,j}\vec{x}_{i,j_2} \geq \vec{0} \wedge (\vec{x}_{i,j_1},$
   $\vec{x}_{i,j_2}) \neq \|\vec{x}_{i,j_1}\|\|\vec{x}_{i,j_2}\| \wedge \sum_{k=2}^{m_{i,c}} v_{i,k}(\vec{x}_{i,j_1}) < 0 \wedge$
   $\sum_{k=2}^{m_{i,c}} v_{i,k}(\vec{x}_{i,j_2}) < 0 \big]$,

3. $\forall \vec{x}[[\vee_{r=1}^{l_{i,j}} g_{i,j,r}^T \vec{x} = 0] \Rightarrow V_i(\vec{x}) - V_j(\vec{x}) \geq 0]$,

then the family $\{V_i(\vec{x}) : i \in \mathcal{M}\}$ *is a multiple Lyapunov function, implying that* PS *is asymptotically stable.*

PROOF. For each $i \in \mathcal{M}$, since $V_i(\vec{x})$ is a polynomial in quadratic form, it is clear that $V_i(\vec{0}) = 0$ and $\frac{d}{dt}V_i(\vec{0}) = 0$.

Due to the condition (1a), for each $i \in \mathcal{M}$, $\vec{0}$ is the unique solution of $V_i(\vec{x}) = 0$ in $\mathcal{X}_i$. We want to prove that for each $i \in \mathcal{M}$ and each $\vec{x} \in \mathcal{X}_i$, if $\vec{x} \neq \vec{0}$, then $V_i(\vec{x}) > 0$. [2]

Suppose that for each $i \in \mathcal{M}$, there is a point $\vec{x}_{i,j_3} \in \mathcal{X}_i$ such that $\vec{x}_{i,j_3} \neq \vec{0}$ and $V_i(\vec{x}_{i,j_3}) < 0$. Thus, there is a $j \in \{1, \ldots, l_i\}$ such that $\vec{x}_{i,j_3} \in \{\vec{x}|E_{i,j}\vec{x} \geq \vec{0}\}$. For this j, according to the condition (1b), there are two points $\vec{x}_{i,j_1}$ and $\vec{x}_{i,j_2}$ such that $(\vec{x}_{i,j_1}, \vec{x}_{i,j_2}) \neq \|\vec{x}_{i,j_1}\|\|\vec{x}_{i,j_2}\|$, $E_{i,j}\vec{x}_{i,j_1} \geq \vec{0}$, $E_{i,j}\vec{x}_{i,j_2} \geq \vec{0}$, $V_i(\vec{x}_{i,j_1}) > 0$ and $V_i(\vec{x}_{i,j_2}) > 0$.

Letting $f(t) = \vec{x}_{i,j_3} + t(\vec{x}_{i,j_1} - \vec{x}_{i,j_3})$, where $f(0) = \vec{x}_{i,j_3}$ and $f(1) = \vec{x}_{i,j_1}$, we have $V_i(f(0)) < 0$ and $V_i(f(1)) > 0$. So there exists a $t' \in (0, 1)$ such that $V_i(f(t')) = 0$, implying that $\vec{x}_{i,j_3} + t'(\vec{x}_{i,j_1} - \vec{x}_{i,j_3}) = \vec{0}$ or $\vec{x}_{i,j_3} + t'(\vec{x}_{i,j_1} - \vec{x}_{i,j_3}) \notin \mathcal{X}_i$. Since the set $\{\vec{x}|E_{i,j}\vec{x} \geq \vec{0}\}$ is convex and connected, we have: $\vec{x}_{i,j_3} + t'(\vec{x}_{i,j_1} - \vec{x}_{i,j_3}) \in \{\vec{x}|E_{i,j}\vec{x} \geq \vec{0}\} \subset \mathcal{X}_i$. Thus, $\vec{x}_{i,j_3} + t'(\vec{x}_{i,j_1} - \vec{x}_{i,j_3}) = \vec{0}$.

Similarly, letting $g(t) = \vec{x}_{i,j_3} + t(\vec{x}_{i,j_2} - \vec{x}_{i,j_3})$, there is a $t'' \in (0, 1)$ such that $V_i(g(t'')) = 0$, implying that $\vec{x}_{i,j_3} + t''(\vec{x}_{i,j_2} - \vec{x}_{i,j_3}) = \vec{0}$ or $\vec{x}_{i,j_3} + t''(\vec{x}_{i,j_2} - \vec{x}_{i,j_3}) \notin \mathcal{X}_i$. Since the set $\{\vec{x}|E_{i,j}\vec{x} \geq \vec{0}\}$ is convex and connected, we have: $\vec{x}_{i,j_3} + t''(\vec{x}_{i,j_2} - \vec{x}_{i,j_3}) \in \mathcal{X}_i$. Thus, $\vec{x}_{i,j_3} + t''(\vec{x}_{i,j_2} - \vec{x}_{i,j_3}) = \vec{0}$.

Hence, $(\vec{x}_{i,j_1}, \vec{x}_{i,j_2}) = \|\vec{x}_{i,j_1}\|\|\vec{x}_{i,j_2}\|$, contradicting the assumption that $(\vec{x}_{i,j_1}, \vec{x}_{i,j_2}) \neq \|\vec{x}_{i,j_1}\|\|\vec{x}_{i,j_2}\|$. So, for all $\vec{x} \in \{\vec{x} \in \mathcal{X}_i | \vec{x} \neq \vec{0}\}$, $V_i(\vec{x}) > 0$.

[1] Note that when $E_{i,j} = (a)_{1 \times 1}$ and $a \neq 0$, the condition (1b) should be replaced by $\exists x[x \neq 0 \wedge ax \geq 0 \wedge V_i(x) > 0]$ and the condition (2b) should be replaced by $\exists x[x \neq 0 \wedge ax \geq 0 \wedge \sum_{k=2}^{m_{i,c}} v_{i,k}(x) < 0]$.

[2] Note that for the case that $E_{i,j} = (a)_{1 \times 1}$ and $a \neq 0$, according to the replaced condition, we can also prove that for each $i \in \mathcal{M}$ and each $\vec{x} \in \mathcal{X}_i$, if $\vec{x} \neq \vec{0}$, then $V_i(\vec{x}) > 0$. That is, if there is a point $y \neq 0$ such that $y \neq x$, $ay \geq 0$ and $V(y) < 0$, due to the zero point theorem, then there is a point $z \neq 0$ such that $az \geq 0$ and $V(z) = 0$, contradicting the condition (1a).

Similarly, according to the conditions (2a) and (2b), we can get $\sum_{j=2}^{m_c} v_{i,j}(\vec{x}) < 0$ for all $\vec{x} \in \{\vec{x}|\vec{x} \neq \vec{0} \wedge \mathcal{X}_i\}$. Since all terms in $\dot{V}(\vec{x}) - \sum_{k=2}^{m_c} v_{i,k}(\vec{x})$ have degree greater than m_c, from Theorem 2, there is a neighborhood $\mathbb{U}_i$ of the origin such that for all $\vec{x} \in \{\vec{x} \in \mathcal{X}_i \cap \mathbb{U}|\vec{x} \neq \vec{0}\}$, $\dot{V}_i(\vec{x}) < 0$.

Letting $\mathbb{U} = \cap_i \mathbb{U}_i$, from Theorem 1, the family $\{V_i(\vec{x}) : i \in \mathcal{M}\}$ is a multiple Lyapunov function of PS, implying that PS is asymptotically stable. $\square$

4. REAL ROOT CLASSIFICATION BASED APPROACH FOR COMPUTING MULTIPLE LYAPUNOV FUNCTIONS

In Section 3, for a given system PS, we have derived an algebraizable sufficient condition for asymptotic stability analysis, which is formulated as Theorem 3. However, there are still no efficient methods in the literature for directly finding such a multiple Lyapunov function. In this section, we will under-approximate the constraints in Theorem 3 respectively in the sense that every solution of the under-approximation is also a solution of the original condition, formulate these under-approximations as a semi-algebraic set, and then compute a sample point in the semi-algebraic set to form a multiple Lyapunov function.

For each $i \in \mathcal{M}$, we represent $V_i(\vec{x}) = \vec{x}^T P_i \vec{x}$ as $L_i(\vec{x}, \vec{p}_i)$ and $\sum_{k=2}^{m_{i,c}} v_{i,k}(\vec{x})$ as $\dot{L}_{i,m_{i,c}}(\vec{x}, \vec{p}_i)$, where $P_i = (p_{j,k})_{n \times n}$ is a symmetric matrix and $\vec{p}_i = (p_{1,1}, \ldots, p_{1,n}, p_{2,1}, \ldots, p_{n,n})$.

Let us start with solving the condition (3). Since for each i, j, r, $g_{i,j,r} \neq \vec{0}$, we can formulate $g_{i,j,r}^T \vec{x} = 0$ as $x_{h_r} = G_{i,j,r}^T \vec{z}$, where $1 \leq h_r \leq n, \vec{z} = (x_1, \cdots, x_{h_r-1}, x_{h_r+1}, \cdots, x_n)$ and $G_{i,j,r} \in \mathbb{R}^{n-1}$. Then, for all $\vec{x} \in \{\vec{x} : g_{i,j,r}^T \vec{x} = 0\}$, we can formulate $V_i(\vec{x}, \vec{p}_i) - V_j(\vec{x}, \vec{p}_j)$ as $V_{i,j}(\vec{z}, \vec{p}_i, \vec{p}_j, G_{i,j,r}) = \vec{z}^T Q_{ijr} \vec{z}$, where Q_{ijr} is a symmetric matrix depending on $\vec{p}_i, \vec{p}_j$ and $G_{i,j,r}$. Let $h(\lambda) = \lambda^n + c_{n-1}(\vec{p}_i, \vec{p}_j, G_{i,j,r})\lambda^{n-1} + \cdots + c_0(\vec{p}_i, \vec{p}_j, G_{i,j,r})$ be the characteristic polynomial of Q_{ijr}. To make $V_{i,j}(\vec{z}, \vec{p}_i, \vec{p}_j, G_{i,j,r}) = \vec{z}^T Q_{ijr} \vec{z} \geq 0$ for all $\vec{z} \in \mathbb{R}^{n-1}$, due to the Descartes rule [24], it is equivalent to finding $\vec{p}_i$ and $\vec{p}_j$ such that $\Lambda_{3,i,j,r}(\vec{p}_i, \vec{p}_j)$ holds, where

$$\Lambda_{3,i,j,r}(\vec{p}_i, \vec{p}_j) = \bigvee_{k=0}^{n-1} \Big[\big[\wedge_{l=0}^{k-1} c_l(\vec{p}_i, \vec{p}_j, G_{i,j,r}) = 0 \big]$$
$$\bigwedge \big[\wedge_{l=k}^{n-1} (-1)^{n-l} c_l(\vec{p}_i, \vec{p}_j, G_{i,j,r}) > 0 \big] \Big].$$

Then, letting $\Lambda_{3,i,j}(\vec{p}_i, \vec{p}_j) = \wedge_{r=1}^{l_{i,j}} \Lambda_{3,i,j,r}$, to make the condition (3) hold, it is enough to under-approximatively find $\vec{p}_i$ and $\vec{p}_j$ such that $\Lambda_{3,i,j}(\vec{p}_i, \vec{p}_j)$ holds.

Notice that the condition (1) and the condition (2) have similar formula and $V_i(\vec{x})$ in the condition (1) has degree of 2 and $\sum_{k=2}^{m_{i,c}} v_{i,k}(\vec{x})$ in the condition (2) has degree of at least 2. We can first consider under-approximating the conditions (2a) and (2b) and then apply the same approach for the conditions (1a) and (1b).

For under-approximating the condition (2a), for each i, we equivalently transform $\forall \vec{x}[[\vec{x} \in \mathcal{X}_i \wedge \vec{x} \neq \vec{0}] \Rightarrow \dot{L}_{i,m_{i,c}}(\vec{x}, \vec{p}_i) \neq 0]$ to $\bigwedge_{j=1}^{l_i} \phi_{i,j}(\vec{p}_i)$, where $\phi_{i,j}(\vec{p}_i) = [\forall \vec{x}[[E_{i,j}\vec{x} \geq \vec{0} \wedge \vec{x} \neq \vec{0}] \Rightarrow \dot{L}_{i,m_{i,c}}(\vec{x}, \vec{p}_i) \neq 0]]$. Further, for each $j \in \{1, \ldots, l_i\}$, $\phi_{i,j}(\vec{p}_i)$ is equivalently transformed to $\bigwedge_{k=1}^{n} \phi_{i,j,k}(\vec{p}_i)$, where $\phi_{i,j,k}(\vec{p}_i) = [\forall \vec{x}_k[[E_{i,j}\vec{x}_k \geq \vec{0} \wedge x_k \neq 0] \Rightarrow \dot{L}_{i,m_{i,c}}(\vec{x}_k, \vec{p}_i) \neq 0]]$ and $\vec{x}_k = (0, \cdots, 0, x_k, \cdots, x_n)$. Assume that, for each $\phi_{i,j,k}(\vec{p}_i)$, we have a real root classification and projection operator based method — which will be discussed later in this section — to get an under-approximative constraint $\Lambda_{1,i,j,k}^{m_{i,c}}(\vec{p}_i)$ that only involves $\vec{p}_i$. Thus, we can obtain a big conjunction $\bigwedge_{j=1}^{l_i} \bigwedge_{k=1}^{n} \Lambda_{1,i,j,k}^{m_{i,c}}(\vec{p}_i)$, denoted as $\Lambda_{1,i}^{m_{i,c}}(\vec{p}_i)$.

For solving the condition (2b), we first compute two points $\vec{y}$ and $\vec{z}$ [3] in the region defined by $E_{i,j}\vec{x} \geq \vec{0}$ as follows: if the rank of $E_{i,j}$ is less than n, let $\vec{y}$ be a nonzero solution of $E_{i,j}\vec{x} = \vec{0}$ and $\vec{z} = -\vec{y}$; otherwise, let $\vec{y}$ be the solution of $E_{i,j}\vec{x} = (1,0,\ldots,0)^T$ and $\vec{z}$ be the solution of $E_{i,j}\vec{x} = (0,1,\ldots,0)^T$. Then, we simply replace the condition (2b) by the constraint $[\dot{L}_{i,m_{i,c}}(\vec{y},\vec{p}_i) < 0 \wedge \dot{L}_{i,m_{i,c}}(\vec{z},\vec{p}_i) < 0]$, denoted as $\Lambda_{2,i,j}^{m_{i,c}}$. Note that such a replacement will not lose information, which will be analyzed in Section 5. Let $\Lambda_{2,i}^{m_{i,c}}(\vec{p}_i) = \bigwedge_{j=1}^{l_i} \Lambda_{2,i,j}^{m_{i,c}}$.

Similarly, for each $i \in \mathcal{M}$, we can under-approximate the condition (1a) and (1b) in Theorem 3 to get the constraints $\Lambda_{1,i}^{V_i}(\vec{p}_i)$ and $\Lambda_{2,i}^{V_i}(\vec{p}_i)$, respectively.

Combining all above discussions, we get a conjunction

$$\bigwedge_{i=1}^{N}\left[\Lambda_{1,i}^{V_i} \wedge \Lambda_{2,i}^{V_i} \wedge \Lambda_{1,i}^{m_{i,c}} \wedge \Lambda_{2,i}^{m_{i,c}} \wedge [\bigwedge_{j=1}^{N}\Lambda_{3,i,j}]\right],$$

which can be formulated as a set of semi-algebraic sets. Note that computation of a sample point in a semi-algebraic set by *SASsolver* will be described in Section 6. Thus, we have Algorithm 1 for computing quadratic MLFs as follows.

Algorithm 1 Computing MLFs in quadratic form

Input: A given switched hybrid system **PS**.
Output: Asymptotically stable or Unknown.
1: for each mode $i \in \mathcal{M}$, choose a quadratic form $V_i(\vec{x}, \vec{p}_i)$, where $\vec{p}_i$ is a parameter.
2: **for** $m_{1,c} = 2 : 1 : m_1$ **do**
3: $\quad\cdots$
4: $\quad$ **for** $m_{N,c} = 2 : 1 : m_N$ **do**
5: $\qquad$ compute the conjunction $\bigwedge_{i=1}^{N}\left[\Lambda_{1,i}^{V_i} \wedge \Lambda_{2,i}^{V_i} \wedge \Lambda_{1,i}^{m_{i,c}} \wedge \Lambda_{2,i}^{m_{i,c}} \wedge [\bigwedge_{j=1}^{N}\Lambda_{3,i,j}]\right]$.
6: $\qquad$ apply **SASsolver** to $\bigwedge_{i=1}^{N}\left[\Lambda_{1,i}^{V_i} \wedge \Lambda_{2,i}^{V_i} \wedge \Lambda_{1,i}^{m_{i,c}} \wedge \Lambda_{2,i}^{m_{i,c}} \wedge [\bigwedge_{j=1}^{N}\Lambda_{3,i,j}]\right]$.
7: $\qquad$ **if** SASsolver returns a sample point over $\vec{p}_1, \ldots \vec{p}_N$ **then**
8: $\qquad\quad$ put it into V_i and return $\{V_i(\vec{x}) : i \in \mathcal{M}\}$ as a MLF, associated with "Asymptotically Stable", and halt.
9: $\qquad$ **end if**
10: $\quad$ **end for**
11: $\quad\cdots$
12: **end for**
13: return Unknown.

Now the problem is how to use a real root classification and projection operator based technique to get our under-approximative constraint $\Lambda_{1,i,j,k}^{m_{i,c}}$ required in Algorithm 1.

We start with the following three preparations for solving $\forall x_k[E^k\vec{x}^k \geq \vec{0} \wedge x_{k'} \neq 0 \Rightarrow g(x_1,\cdots,x_k,\vec{p})\Delta 0]$, where E^k is a $k \times k$ matrix, $\vec{x}^k = (x_1,\cdots,x_k)$, $k' \in \{1,\cdots,k\}$, $g(x_1,\cdots,x_k,\vec{p})$ is a polynomial and $\Delta \in \{<,\leq,\neq\}$.

1. First, let E^{k-1} be a $(k-1) \times (k-1)$ matrix such that $\{\vec{x}^{k-1} : E^{k-1}\vec{x}^{k-1} \geq \vec{0}\}$ is the projection region of

$\{\vec{x}^k : E^k\vec{x}^k \geq \vec{0}\}$ in the space spanned by the axes $x_1, \cdots, x_{k-2}$ and x_{k-1}.

2. Second, if x_k appears in $g(x_1,\cdots,x_k,\vec{p})$, we use the real root classification in [33] to get a sufficient and necessary condition $\delta_{k,k',1}$, which can be an empty set, such that $\{g(x_1,\cdots,x_k,\vec{p}) = 0, E^k\vec{x}^k \geq \vec{0}, x_{k'} \neq 0\}$ has no solution about x_k. Thus, $\forall x_k[E^k\vec{x}^k \geq \vec{0} \wedge x_{k'} \neq 0 \Rightarrow g(x_1,\cdots,x_k,\vec{p}) \neq 0]$ holds if and only if $\delta_{k,k',1}$ holds. $\delta_{k,k',1}$ can be formulated as a disjunction of conjunctions (i.e., $\delta_{k,k',1} = \bigvee_{m=1}^{l_{k,k'}} \delta_{k,k',m,1}$), where for each conjunctions $\delta_{k,k',m,1}$, its conjuncts are of form $h_{k,k',m,s}(x_1,\cdots,x_{k-1},\vec{p})\Delta 0$, where $\Delta \in \{=,<,\leq,\neq\}$ and $s = 1,\cdots,l_{k,k',m}$. Denote $\delta_{k,k',1}$ as $\texttt{rrc}(k,k',g)$. Clearly, the variable x_k does not appear in $\texttt{rrc}(k,k',g)$. Note that this real root classification has been contained in the Maple package [4] and will be briefly discussed in Section 6.

3. Third, similar to the process for solving the condition (2b), we compute two points $\vec{y}^k$ and $\vec{z}^k$ in $\{\vec{x}^k \in \mathbb{R}^k : E^k\vec{x}^k \geq \vec{0}\}$ to get a conjunction $\delta_{k,k',2}$ [5] $= [g(\vec{y}^k,\vec{p}_i) < 0 \wedge g(\vec{z}^k,\vec{p}_i) < 0]$. Clearly, according to the proof of Theorem 3, $\forall x_k[E^k\vec{x}^k \geq \vec{0} \wedge x_{k'} \neq 0 \Rightarrow g(x_1,\cdots,x_k,\vec{p}) < 0]$ holds if and only if $\delta_{k,k',1} \wedge \delta_{k,k',2}$ holds, which will be assured by the proof of Lemma 2 in Section 5. Denote $\delta_{k,k',1} \wedge \delta_{k,k',2}$ as $\texttt{ve}(k,k',g(x_1,\cdots,x_k,\vec{p}))$. Note that since under-approximation is considered, in order to make $\forall x_k[E^k\vec{x}^k \geq \vec{0} \wedge x_{k'} \neq 0 \Rightarrow g(x_1,\cdots,x_k,\vec{p}) \leq 0]$ hold, it is enough to simply require $\forall x_k[E^k\vec{x}^k \geq \vec{0} \wedge x_{k'} \neq 0 \Rightarrow g(x_1,\cdots,x_k,\vec{p}) < 0]$ hold.

Based on the above three preparations, we can use Algorithm 2 to get an under-approximation $\forall \vec{x}^{k-1}[E^{k-1}\vec{x}^{k-1} \geq \vec{0} \wedge x_{k'} \neq 0 \Rightarrow \delta_{k,k'}]$ for $\forall \vec{x}^k[E^k\vec{x}^k \geq \vec{0} \wedge x_{k'} \neq 0 \Rightarrow \bigvee_{m=1}^{l} \bigwedge_{s=1}^{l_m} h_{m,s}(x_1,\cdots,x_k,\vec{p})\Delta 0]$, where $\Delta \in \{=,<,\leq,\neq\}$, which can be assured by Lemma 2 in Section 5.

Note that according to [27], $\forall \vec{x}^{k-1}[x_{k'} \neq 0 \Rightarrow \delta_{k,k'}]$ is also an under-approximation for $\forall \vec{x}^k[E^k\vec{x}^k \geq \vec{0} \wedge x_{k'} \neq 0 \Rightarrow \bigvee_{m=1}^{l} \bigwedge_{s=1}^{l_m} h_{m,s}(x_1,\cdots,x_k,\vec{p})\Delta 0]$. However, if we use this under-approximation for further computation, our approach only fits systems whose subsystems are all asymptotically stable since the information on the state space of each mode is ignored in this under-approximation.

Moreover, it is easily seen that the variable x_k does not appear in the under-approximation $\forall \vec{x}^{k-1}[E^{k-1}\vec{x}^{k-1} \geq \vec{0} \wedge x_{k'} \neq 0 \Rightarrow \delta_{k,k'}]$. This is because $E^k\vec{x}^k \geq \vec{0}$ is replaced with $E^{k-1}\vec{x}^{k-1} \geq \vec{0}$ by using the projection operator.

After obtaining $\delta_{k,k'}$ that do not contain x_k, we would like to optimize $\delta_{k,k'}$ based on $E^{k-1}\vec{x}^{k-1} \geq \vec{0}$ to get a simpler under-approximation $\delta'_{k,k'}$ such that

1. there is no polynomial of form $h(\vec{x}^{k-1})$ in $\delta'_{k,k'}$, and

2. $[E^{k-1}\vec{x}^{k-1} \geq \vec{0} \wedge x_{k'} \neq 0 \Rightarrow \delta'_{k,k'}]$ implies $[E^{k-1}\vec{x}^{k-1} \geq \vec{0} \wedge x_{k'} \neq 0 \Rightarrow \delta_{k,k'}]$.

Without loss of generality, for every conjunction $\delta_{k,k',m} = \bigwedge_{s=1}^{l'_m} h'_{m,s}(x_1,\cdots,x_{k-1},\vec{p})\Delta 0$, $m \in \{1,\ldots,l'\}$, assume that

---

[3] When $E_{i,j} = (a)_{1\times1}$, we can choose ± 1 as two points if $a = 0$ and $sgn(a)$ as a point if $a \neq 0$.

[4] http://www.maplesoft.com/products/Maple/index.aspx.
[5] When $E^k = (a)_{1\times1}$, $\delta_{k,k',2} = [g(1,\vec{p}) > 0 \wedge g(-1,\vec{p}_i) > 0]$ if $a = 0$ and $\delta_{k,k',2} = [g(sgn(a),\vec{p}_i) > 0]$ if $a \neq 0$.

Algorithm 2 Computing the under-approximation $\delta_{k,k'}$

Input: $\forall \vec{x}^k[[E^k\vec{x}^k \geq 0 \wedge x_{k'} \neq 0] \Rightarrow \bigvee_{m=1}^{l} \bigwedge_{s=1}^{l_m} h_{m,s}(x_1,\cdots,x_k,\vec{p})\Delta 0].$

Output: an under-approximation constraint $\delta_{k,k'}$.

1: **for** $m = 1 : 1 : l$ **do**
2:   **for** $s = 1 : 1 : l_m$ **do**
3:     **if** $x_{k'}$ does not appear in $h_{m,s}(x_1,\cdots,x_k,\vec{p})$ **then**
4:       let $\delta_{m,s} = [h_{m,s}\Delta 0]$;
5:     **else**
6:       **if** Δ in $h_{m,s}\Delta 0$ is "=" **then**
7:         formulate $h_{m,s}$ as $\sum_{c=0}^{d_{m,s}} h_{m,s,d}(x_1,\cdots,x_{k-1})x_k^d$ and let $\delta_{m,s} = [\bigwedge_{d=0}^{d_{m,s}} h_{m,s,d}(x_1,\cdots,x_{k-1}) = 0]$;
8:       **else**
9:         **if** $\Delta \in \{<,\leq\}$ **then**
10:           let $\delta_{m,s} = \mathtt{ve}(k,k',h_{m,s}(x_1,\cdots,x_k,\vec{p}))$;
11:         **else**
12:           let $\delta_{m,s} = \mathtt{rrc}(k,k',h_{m,s}(x_1,\cdots,x_k,\vec{p}))$;
13:         **end if**
14:       **end if**
15:     **end if**
16:   **end for**
17: **end for**
18: formulate $\bigvee_{m=1}^{l} \bigwedge_{s=1}^{l_m} \delta_{m,s}$ as $\delta_{k,k'}$ and return $\delta_{k,k'}$, where $\delta_{k,k'} = [\bigvee_{m=1}^{l'} \bigwedge_{s=1}^{l'_m} h'_{m,s}(x_1,\cdots,x_{k-1},\vec{p})\Delta 0]$.

Algorithm 3 Optimize $\delta_{k,k'}$

Input: $\delta_{k,k'}$ satisfying the above assumptions.
Output: a simpler under-approximation $\delta'_{k,k'}$.

1: $\phi := [false]$;
2: **for** $p = 1 : 1 : m'$ **do**
3:   $\Omega_p := \bigwedge_{s=1}^{n_p} h'_{p,s}(\vec{x}^{k-1})\Delta 0$;
4:   **for** $q = p + 1 : 1 : m'$ **do**
5:     $p' := q$ and $\Omega_p := \Omega_p \vee [\bigwedge_{s=1}^{n_{p'}} h'_{p',s}(\vec{x}^{k-1})\Delta 0]$;
6:     **while** $p' \leq m'$ **do**
7:       **if** $\{\vec{x}^{k-1}|\Omega_p \text{ holds}\} \not\supseteq \{\vec{x}^{k-1}|E^{k-1}\vec{x}^{k-1} \geq 0 \wedge x'_k \neq 0\}$ **then**
8:         $p' := p' + 1$;
9:         **if** $p' \leq m'$, **then** $\Omega_p := \Omega_p \vee [\bigwedge_{s=1}^{n_{p'}} h'_{p',s}(\vec{x}^{k-1})\Delta 0]$;
10:       **else**
11:         $\phi := \phi \vee [\bigwedge_{l=p}^{p'}[\bigwedge_{s=n_m+1}^{l'_m} h'_{m,s}(\vec{x}^{k-1},\vec{p})\Delta 0]]$;
12:         $p' := m' + 1$;
13:       **end if**
14:     **end while**
15:   **end for**
16: **end for**
17: formulate $\phi \vee [\bigvee_{m=m'+1}^{l'} [\bigwedge_{s=n_m+1}^{l'_m} h'_{m,s}(\vec{x}^{k-1},\vec{p})\Delta 0]]$ as $\bigvee_{m=1}^{l''} \bigwedge_{s=1}^{k''_m} h''_{m,s}(\vec{x}^{k-1},\vec{p})\Delta 0$, denoted by $\delta'_{k,k'}$.
18: return $\delta'_{k,k'}$.

---

its first n_m ($0 \leq n_m \leq l'_m$) conjuncts does not contain the parameter $\vec{p}$. Moreover, for $\delta_{k,k'} = \bigvee_{m=1}^{l'}\delta_{k,k',m}$, assume that its first m' ($0 \leq m' \leq l'$) disjuncts all satisfy

$$\{\vec{x}^{k-1}|E^{k-1}\vec{x}^{k-1} \geq \vec{0} \wedge x_{k'} \neq 0\} \not\subseteq \{\vec{x}^{k-1}| \bigwedge_{s=1}^{n_m} h'_{m,s}(\vec{x}^{k-1})\Delta 0\},$$

which can be easily verified by applying REDLOG to

$$\forall \vec{x}^{k-1} \left[[E^{k-1}\vec{x}^{k-1} \geq \vec{0} \wedge x_{k'} \neq 0] \Rightarrow \bigwedge_{s=1}^{n_m} h'_{m,s}(\vec{x}^{k-1})\Delta 0 \right].$$

Based on the above assumptions, we can design Algorithm 3 for optimizing $\delta_{k,k'}$.

Let $\mathtt{OPTIM}(\delta_{k,k'})$ be the output of Algorithm 3 with the input $\delta_{k,k'}$. If there exists $\vec{p}_0$ such that $\forall \vec{x}^{k-1}[E^{k-1}\vec{x}^{k-1} \geq \vec{0} \wedge x_{k'} \neq 0 \Rightarrow \mathtt{OPTIM}(\delta_{k,k'})|_{\vec{p}=\vec{p}_0}$ holds, then $\forall \vec{x}^{k-1}[E^{k-1}\vec{x}^{k-1} \geq \vec{0} \wedge x_{k'} \neq 0 \Rightarrow \delta_{k,k'}|_{\vec{p}=\vec{p}_0}$ holds, which can be assured by Lemma 3 in Section 5.

Based on Algorithms 2 and 3, for the conjunct $\phi_{1,1,1} = \forall \vec{x}[[E_{1,1}\vec{x} \geq \vec{0} \wedge x_1 \neq 0] \Rightarrow \dot{L}_{1,m_{1,c}}(\vec{x},\vec{p}_1) \neq 0]$, we can eliminate the variables $x_n,\cdots,x_1$ step by step, arriving at the under-approximation $\Lambda_{1,1,1,1}^{m_{1,c}}$ that only involves $\vec{p}_1$. This procedure can be formally formalized as Algorithm 4.

If there is a $\vec{p}_{1,0}$ such that $\Lambda_{1,1,1,1}^{m_{1,c}}$ holds, then

$$\forall \vec{x} \left[[E_{1,1}\vec{x} \geq \vec{0} \wedge x_1 \neq 0] \Rightarrow \dot{L}_{1,m_{1,c}}(\vec{x},\vec{p}_{1,0}) \neq 0 \right]$$

holds, which can be obtained from Lemma 4 in Section 5.

Similarly, for each conjunct $\phi_{i,j,k}$, we can get an under-approximative constraint $\Lambda_{1,i,j,k}^{m_{i,c}}$. Thus we can obtain the under-approximative constraint $\Lambda_{1,i}^{m_{i,c}} = \bigwedge_{j=1}^{l_i} \bigwedge_{k=1}^{n} \Lambda_{1,i,j,k}^{m_{i,c}}$ for the condition (2b), where $i = 1,\ldots,N$.

In a similar way, we can get the under-approximative constraint $\Lambda_{1,i}^{V_i}$ for the condition (1b), where $i = 1,\ldots,N$.

Algorithm 4 Computing the under-approximation $\Lambda_{1,1,1,1}^{m_{1,c}}$

Input: $\phi_{1,1,1} = \forall \vec{x}[[E_{1,1}\vec{x} \geq 0 \wedge x_1 \neq 0] \Rightarrow \dot{L}_{1,m_{1,c}}(\vec{x},\vec{p}_1) \neq 0]$.
Output: an under-approximation constraint $\Lambda_{1,1,1,1}$.

1: let $g_1(x_1,\cdots,x_n,\vec{p}_1) = \dot{L}_{1,m_{1,c}}(\vec{x},\vec{p}_1)$;
2: let $\delta_{n,1} = \mathtt{OPTIM}(\mathtt{rrc}(n,1,g_1(x_1,\cdots,x_n,\vec{p}_1)))$;
3: **for** $i = n - 1 : -1 : 1$ **do**
4:   use Algorithm 2 for the input $\forall x_i[E_{1,1}^i\vec{x}^i \geq \vec{0} \wedge x_1 \neq 0 \Rightarrow \delta_{1+i,1}]$ to get $\delta_{i,1}$;
5:   $\delta_{i,1} := \mathtt{OPTIM}(\delta_{i,1})$;
6: **end for**
7: Return $\Lambda_{1,1,1,1}^{m_{1,c}} = \delta_{1,1}$.

Thus, we finish explaining our algebraic approach.

REMARK 1. *In Algorithm 1, $m_{1,c},\cdots,m_{N,c}$ are required to increase with 1 each step instead of 2 used in [27] since $\dot{V}_i(\vec{x})$ is required to be negative definite in $\mathcal{X}_i$ instead of $\mathbb{R}^n$, where $i = 1,\cdots,N$.*

REMARK 2. *When we replace $\sum_{k=2}^{m_{i,c}}$ by $\sum_{k=1}^{m_{i,c}}$ in Theorem 3 and let $m_{1,c},\ldots,m_{N,c}$ start from 1 in Algorithm 1 instead of 2, our proposed algebraic approach is also applicable for systems that do not satisfy $f_i(\vec{0}) = \vec{0}$, e.g., switched affine systems [12]. Due to the space limit, we will not extend such an applicability in this paper.*

5. CORRECTNESS ANALYSIS

In this section, we will analyze the correctness of our under-approximations required in Algorithm 1.

First, we try to analyze that the simplification for solving the condition (2b) will not lose information. For this, let $\vec{y}$ and $\vec{z}$ be the two computed points satisfying $E\vec{x} \geq \vec{0}$ by using the strategy introduced in Section 6. Clearly, $\vec{y}$ and $\vec{z}$

satisfy $E\vec{y} \geq \vec{0}$, $E\vec{z} \geq \vec{0}$ and $(\vec{y}, \vec{z}) \neq \|\vec{y}\|\|\vec{z}\|$. Moreover, let
$\Omega_1 = \{\vec{p} : \forall \vec{x}[E\vec{x} \geq \vec{0} \wedge \vec{x} \neq \vec{0} \Rightarrow \dot{L}(\vec{x}, \vec{p}) \neq 0]\}$,
$\Omega_2 = \{\vec{p} : \exists \vec{x}_1, \vec{x}_2[[E\vec{x}_1 \geq \vec{0} \wedge E\vec{x}_2 \geq \vec{0}$
$\wedge (\vec{x}_1, \vec{x}_2) \neq \|\vec{x}_1\|\|\vec{x}_2\|] \Rightarrow \dot{L}(\vec{x}_1, \vec{p}) < 0 \wedge \dot{L}(\vec{x}_2, \vec{p}) < 0]\}$,
$\Omega_3 = \{\vec{p} : \vec{p} \in \Omega_1 \wedge \vec{p} \in \Omega_2\}$, and
$\Omega_4 = \{\vec{p} : \vec{p} \in \Omega_1 \wedge \dot{L}(\vec{y}, \vec{p}) < 0 \wedge \dot{L}(\vec{z}, \vec{p}) < 0\}$.

Then the correctness of this simplification can be assured by the following lemma.

LEMMA 1. $\Omega_3 = \Omega_4$.

PROOF. According to the proof of Theorem 3, if $\vec{p}_0 \in \Omega_3$, then $\forall \vec{x}[E\vec{x} \geq \vec{0} \wedge \vec{x} \neq \vec{0} \Rightarrow \dot{L}(\vec{x}, \vec{p}_0) < 0]$ holds. So, $\dot{L}(\vec{y}, \vec{p}_0) < 0$ and $\dot{L}(\vec{z}, \vec{p}_0) < 0$. Thus, $\vec{p}_0 \in \Omega_4$, implying that $\Omega_3 \subseteq \Omega_4$.

Similarly, if $\vec{p}_0 \in \Omega_4$, then $\forall \vec{x}[E\vec{x} \geq \vec{0} \wedge \vec{x} \neq \vec{0} \Rightarrow \dot{L}(\vec{x}, \vec{p}_0) < 0]$ holds, implying that $\vec{p}_0 \in \Omega_2$. Thus $\Omega_4 \subseteq \Omega_3$.

Hence, $\Omega_3 = \Omega_4$. $\square$

Second, we try to prove that for each $i \in \{1, \cdots, N\}$, $j \in \{1, \cdots, l_i\}$, $k \in \{1, \cdots, n\}$, the solution set of $\Lambda_{1,i,j,k}^{m_{i,c}}$ is a subset of the solution set of $\phi_{i,j,k}$.

We start with proving Lemma 2 and Lemma 3, which imply that our projection operator based method can result in under-approximation.

LEMMA 2. Assume that $\{\vec{x}^{k-1} : E^{k-1}\vec{x}^{k-1} \geq \vec{0}\}$ is the projection region of $\{\vec{x}^k : E^k\vec{x}^k \geq \vec{0}\}$ in the space spanned by the axes $x_1, \cdots, x_{k-2}$ and x_{k-1}. For each m and s, let each $h_{m,s}(x_1, \cdots, x_k, \vec{p}_i)$ be a polynomial and $\delta_{m,s} = \mathtt{rrc}(k, k', h_{m,s})$. For all $\vec{p}_0$ satisfying $\forall \vec{x}^{k-1}[E^{k-1}\vec{x}^{k-1} \geq \vec{0} \wedge x_{k'} \neq 0 \Rightarrow \vee_m \wedge_s [\delta_{m,s} \wedge h_{m,s}(\vec{y}^k, \vec{p}_0) < 0 \wedge h_{m,s}(\vec{z}^k, \vec{p}_0) < 0]]$, where $\vec{y}^k$ and $\vec{z}^k$ are the points satisfying $E^k\vec{y}^k \geq \vec{0}$, $E^k\vec{z}^k \geq \vec{0}$ and $(\vec{y}^k, \vec{z}^k) \neq \|\vec{y}^k\|\|\vec{z}^k\|$, $\forall \vec{x}^k[E^k\vec{x}^k \geq \vec{0} \wedge x_{k'} \neq 0 \Rightarrow \vee_m \wedge_s h_{m,s}(x_1, \cdots, x_k, \vec{p}_0)\Delta 0]$ holds, where $\Delta \in \{<, \leq\}$.

PROOF. Suppose that $\vec{p}_0$ makes $\forall \vec{x}^{k-1}[E^{k-1}\vec{x}^{k-1} \geq \vec{0} \wedge x_{k'} \neq 0 \Rightarrow \vee_m \wedge_s \delta_{m,s}|_{\vec{p}=\vec{p}_0} \wedge h_{m,s}(\vec{z}^k, \vec{p}_0) < 0 \wedge h_{m,s}(\vec{y}^k, \vec{p}_0) < 0]$ hold.

Let $S'_{m,s} = \{\vec{x}^{k-1} : [E^{k-1}\vec{x}^{k-1} \geq \vec{0} \wedge x_{k'} \neq 0] \wedge [\delta_{m,s}|_{\vec{p}=\vec{p}_0} \wedge h_{m,s}(\vec{z}^k, \vec{p}_0) < 0 \wedge h_{m,s}(\vec{y}^k, \vec{p}_0) < 0]]\}$ and $S'_m = \{\vec{x}^{k-1} : [E^{k-1}\vec{x}^{k-1} \geq \vec{0} \wedge x_{k'} \neq 0] \wedge [\wedge_s[\delta_{m,s}|_{\vec{p}=\vec{p}_0} \wedge h_{m,s}(\vec{y}^k, \vec{p}_0) < 0 \wedge h_{m,s}(\vec{z}^k, \vec{p}_0) < 0]]\}$. Then, $S'_m = \cap_s S'_{m,s}$ and $\cup_m S'_m = \{\vec{x}^{k-1} : E^{k-1}\vec{x}^{k-1} \geq \vec{0} \wedge x_{k'} \neq 0\}$.

Let $S''_{m,s} = \{\vec{x}^{k-1} : [E^k\vec{x}^k \geq \vec{0} \wedge x_{k'} \neq 0] \wedge [\forall x_k[E^k\vec{x}^k \geq \vec{0} \wedge x_{k'} \neq 0 \Rightarrow h_{m,s}(\vec{x}^k, \vec{p}_0) < 0]]\}$. For proving this lemma, it is sufficient to prove that $S'_{m,s} = S''_{m,s}$.

According to the assumptions that

1. $\delta_{m,s} = \mathtt{rrc}(k, k', h_{m,s})$ is a sufficient and necessary condition obtained by using real root classification such that $\forall x_k[E^k\vec{x}^k \geq \vec{0} \wedge x_{k'} \neq 0 \Rightarrow h_{m,s}(\vec{x}^k, \vec{p}_i) \neq 0]$ holds, and

2. $\{\vec{x}^{k-1} : E^{k-1}\vec{x}^{k-1} \geq \vec{0}\}$ is the projection region of $\{\vec{x}^k : E^k\vec{x}^k \geq \vec{0}\}$,

then $\{\vec{x}^{k-1} : [E^{k-1}\vec{x}^{k-1} \wedge x_{k'} \neq 0 \wedge \delta_{m,s}|_{\vec{p}=\vec{p}_0}]\}$ equals $\{\vec{x}^{k-1} : [E^k\vec{x}^k \geq \vec{0} \wedge x_{k'} \neq 0] \wedge [\forall x_k[E^k\vec{x}^k \geq \vec{0} \wedge x_{k'} \neq 0 \Rightarrow h_{m,s}(\vec{x}^k, \vec{p}_0) \neq 0]]\}$. Thus, $S'_{m,s} = \{\vec{x}^{k-1} : [E^k\vec{x} \geq \vec{0} \wedge x_{k'} \neq 0] \wedge [\forall x_k[E^k\vec{x}^k \geq \vec{0} \wedge x_{k'} \neq 0 \Rightarrow [h_{m,s}(\vec{x}^k, \vec{p}_0) \neq 0 \wedge h_{m,s}(\vec{y}^k, \vec{p}_0) < 0 \wedge h_{m,s}(\vec{z}^k, \vec{p}_0) < 0]]]\}$.

According to Theorem 3, $\{\vec{x}^{k-1} : \forall x_k[E^k\vec{x}^k \geq \vec{0} \wedge x_{k'} \neq 0 \Rightarrow [h_{m,s}(\vec{x}^k, \vec{p}_0) \neq 0 \wedge h_{m,s}(\vec{z}^k, \vec{p}_0) < 0 \wedge h_{m,s}(\vec{z}^k, \vec{p}_0) < 0]]\}$

equals $\{\vec{x}^{k-1} : \forall x_k[E^k\vec{x}^k \geq \vec{0} \wedge x_{k'} \neq 0 \Rightarrow h_{m,s}(\vec{x}^k, \vec{p}_0) < 0]\}$. So $S''_{m,s} = \{\vec{x}^{k-1} : [E^k\vec{x}^k \geq \vec{0} \wedge x_{k'} \neq 0] \wedge [\forall x_k[E^k\vec{x}^k \geq \vec{0} \wedge x_{k'} \neq 0 \Rightarrow [h_{m,s}(\vec{x}^k, \vec{p}_0) \neq 0 \wedge h_{m,s}(\vec{y}^k, \vec{p}_0) < 0 \wedge h_{m,s}(\vec{z}^k, \vec{p}_0) < 0]]]\}$.

Thus, $S'_{m,s} = S''_{m,s}$, implying that $\cup_m \cap_s S''_{m,s} = \cup_m \cap_s S'_{m,s} = \{\vec{x}^{k-1} | E^{k-1}\vec{x}^{k-1} \geq \vec{0} \wedge x_{k'} \neq 0\}$.

If $\vec{x}^k = (\vec{x}^{k-1}, x_k)$ satisfies $E^k\vec{x}^k \geq \vec{0} \wedge x_{k'} \neq 0$, then $\vec{x}^{k-1}$ satisfies $E^{k-1}\vec{x}^{k-1} \geq \vec{0} \wedge x_{k'} \neq 0$. Then, there is an m such that the constraint $\forall x_k[E^k\vec{x}^k \geq \vec{0} \wedge x_{k'} \neq 0 \Rightarrow \wedge_s h_{m,s}(\vec{x}^k, \vec{p}_0) < 0]$ holds. Since x_k satisfies $E^k\vec{x}^k \geq \vec{0} \wedge x_{k'} \neq 0$, then $\wedge_s h_{m,s}(\vec{x}^k, \vec{p}_0) < 0$ holds.

Thus, $\forall \vec{x}^k[E^k\vec{x}^k \geq \vec{0} \wedge x_{k'} \neq 0 \Rightarrow \vee_m \wedge_s h_{m,s}(\vec{x}^k, \vec{p}_0) < 0]$ holds. So, $\forall \vec{x}^k[E^k\vec{x}^k \geq \vec{0} \wedge x_{k'} \neq 0 \Rightarrow \vee_m \wedge_s h_{m,s}(\vec{x}^k, \vec{p}_0)\Delta 0)]$ holds, where $\Delta \in \{<, \leq\}$. $\square$

LEMMA 3. Let $\delta'_{k,k'} = \mathtt{OPTIM}(\delta_{k,k'})$. For all $\vec{p}_0$ such that $\forall \vec{x}^{k-1}[E^{k-1}\vec{x}^{k-1} \geq \vec{0} \wedge x_{k'} \neq 0 \Rightarrow \delta'_{k,k'}|_{\vec{p}=\vec{p}_0}]$ holds, the constraint $\forall \vec{x}^{k-1}[E^{k-1}\vec{x}^{k-1} \geq \vec{0} \wedge x_{k'} \neq 0 \Rightarrow \delta_{k,k'}|_{\vec{p}=\vec{p}_0}]$ holds.

PROOF. Let $\delta_{k,k'} = [\vee_{m=1}^{l'} \wedge_{s=1}^{l'_m} h'_{m,s}(\vec{x}^{k-1}, \vec{p})\Delta 0]$ and $\delta'_{k,k'} = \mathtt{OPTIM}(\delta_{k,k'}) = \phi \vee [\vee_{m=m'+1}^{l'}[\wedge_{s=1}^{l'_m} h'_{m,s}(\vec{x}^{k-1}, \vec{p})\Delta 0]]$, where ϕ is the intermediate result in Algorithm 3.

Moreover, suppose that $\vec{p}_0$ makes $\forall \vec{x}^{k-1}[E^{k-1}\vec{x}^{k-1} \geq \vec{0} \wedge x_{k'} \neq 0 \Rightarrow \delta'_{k,k'}|_{\vec{p}=\vec{p}_0}]$ hold.

Let $W = \{\vec{x}^{k-1} : E^{k-1}\vec{x}^{k-1} \geq \vec{0} \wedge x_{k'} \neq 0 \wedge \delta_{k,k'}|_{\vec{p}=\vec{p}_0}\}$ and $W' = \{\vec{x}^{k-1} : E^{k-1}\vec{x}^{k-1} \geq \vec{0} \wedge x_{k'} \neq 0 \wedge \delta'_{k,k'}|_{\vec{p}=\vec{p}_0}\}$. For proving this lemma, it is sufficient to prove that $W' \subseteq W$.

Let $\vec{x}_0^{k-1}$ be an arbitrary but fixed point in W'. We have the following two cases:

1. If $\vec{x}_0^{k-1}$ satisfies $\vee_{m=m'+1}^{l'} \wedge_{s=1}^{l'_m} h'_{m,s}(\vec{x}^{k-1}, \vec{p}_0)\Delta 0$, then $\vec{x}_0^{k-1} \in W$.

2. If $\vec{x}_0^{k-1}$ satisfies ϕ, by Algorithm 3, there exist $q_0 \in \{1, \cdots, m'\}$ and $q_0' \in \{q_0 + 1, \cdots, m'\}$ such that $\vec{x}_0^{k-1}$ satisfies $\wedge_{m=q_0}^{q_0'}[\wedge_{s=n_m+1}^{l'_m} h'_{m,s}(\vec{x}^{k-1}, \vec{p}_0)\Delta 0]$. Moreover, $\{\vec{x}^{k-1} : \vee_{m=q_0}^{q_0'}[\wedge_{s=1}^{n_m} h_{m,s}(\vec{x}^{k-1})\Delta 0]\} \supseteq \{\vec{x}^{k-1} : E^{k-1}\vec{x}^{k-1} \geq \vec{0} \wedge x_{k'} \neq 0\}$. So there exists $j \in \{q_0, \cdots, q_0'\}$ such that $\vec{x}_0^{k-1} \in \{\vec{x}^{k-1} : \wedge_{s=1}^{n_j} h_{j,s}(\vec{x}^{k-1})\Delta 0\}$. Hence, $\vec{x}_0^{k-1} \in \{\vec{x}^{k-1} : \wedge_{s=1}^{l_j} h_{j,s}(\vec{x}^{k-1}, \vec{p}_0)\Delta 0\}$ and then $\vec{x}_0^{k-1} \in \{\vec{x}^{k-1} : \vee_{m=1}^{l'} \wedge_{s=1}^{l_m} h_{m,s}(\vec{x}^{k-1}, \vec{p}_0)\Delta 0\}$, implying that $\vec{x}_0^{k-1} \in W$.

Thus, $W' \subseteq W$ and we finish the proof. $\square$

Based on Lemmas 2 and 3, we have the following lemma:

LEMMA 4. For all $\vec{p}_{10}$ such that $\Lambda_{1,1,1,1}^{m_{1,c}}$ holds, where $\Lambda_{1,1,1,1}^{m_{1,c}}$ is the output of Algorithm 4 with the input $\forall \vec{x}[E_{1,1}\vec{x} \neq \vec{0} \wedge x_1 \neq 0 \Rightarrow \dot{L}_{m_{1,c}}(\vec{x}, \vec{p}_1) \neq 0]$, $\forall \vec{x}[E_{1,1}\vec{x} \geq \vec{0} \wedge x_1 \neq 0 \Rightarrow \dot{L}_{m_{1,c}}(\vec{x}, \vec{p}_{10}) \neq 0]$ holds.

PROOF. In order to prove that $\forall \vec{x}[E_{1,1}\vec{x} \geq \vec{0} \wedge x_1 \neq 0 \Rightarrow \dot{L}_{m_{1,c}}(\vec{x}, \vec{p}_{10}) \neq 0]$ holds, it is sufficient to prove: if $\vec{x}$ satisfies $E_{1,1}\vec{x} \geq \vec{0} \wedge x_1 \neq 0$, then $\dot{L}_{m_{1,c}}(\vec{x}, \vec{p}_{10}) \neq 0$.

According to Algorithm 4, $\delta_{1,1}^{m_{1,c}} = \Lambda_{1,1,1,1}^{m_{1,c}}$. If $\vec{p}_{10}$ makes $\Lambda_{1,1,1,1}^{m_{1,c}}$ holds, from Lemmas 2 and 3, $\vec{p}_{10}$ makes $\forall x_1[E_{1,1}^1 x_1 \geq \vec{0} \wedge x_1 \neq 0 \Rightarrow \delta_{2,1}]$ hold.

Moveover, we can deductively prove: for all $i \in \{1, \cdots, n-1\}$, if $\vec{p}_{10}$ makes $\forall \vec{x}^{i-1}[E_{1,1}^{i-1}\vec{x}^{i-1} \geq \vec{0} \wedge x_1 \neq 0 \Rightarrow \delta_{i,1}]$ hold, then $\vec{p}_{10}$ makes $\forall \vec{x}^i[E_{1,1}^i\vec{x}^i \geq \vec{0} \wedge x_1 \neq 0 \Rightarrow \delta_{i+1,1}]$ hold, where $\{\vec{x}^{i-1} : E_{1,1}^{i-1}\vec{x}^{i-1} \geq \vec{0}\}$ is the projection region of $\{\vec{x}^i : E_{1,1}^i\vec{x}^i \geq \vec{0}\}$ in the space spanned by the axes $x_1, \ldots, x_{i-2}$ and x_{i-1}.

Thus, $\forall \vec{x}^{n-1}[E_{1,1}^{n-1}\vec{x}^{n-1} \geq \vec{0} \wedge x_1 \neq 0 \Rightarrow \delta_{n,1}]$ hold, where $\{\vec{x}^{n-1} : E_{1,1}^{n-1}\vec{x}^{n-1} \geq \vec{0}\}$ is the projection region of $\{\vec{x} : E_{1,1}\vec{x} \geq \vec{0}\}$ in the space spanned by the axes $x_1, \ldots, x_{n-1}$.

In addition, since $\delta_{n,1}$ is a sufficient and necessary condition obtained by using real root classification such that $\{E_{1,1}\vec{x} \geq \vec{0}, x_1 \neq 0, \dot{L}_{m_{1,c}}(\vec{x},\vec{p}_1) = 0\}$ has no solution about x_n, then $\delta_{n,1}$ holds if and only if $\forall x_n[E_{1,1}\vec{x} \geq \vec{0} \wedge x_1 \neq 0 \Rightarrow \dot{L}_{m_{1,c}}(\vec{x},\vec{p}_{10}) \neq 0]$ holds.

Clearly, if $\vec{x} = (\vec{x}^{n-1}, x_n)$ satisfies $E_{1,1}\vec{x} \geq \vec{0} \wedge x_1 \neq 0$, then $\vec{x}^{n-1}$ satisfies $E_{1,1}^{n-1}\vec{x}^{n-1} \geq \vec{0} \wedge x_1 \neq 0$, implying that $\delta_{n,1}$ holds. Thus, $\forall x_n[E_{1,1}\vec{x} \geq \vec{0} \wedge x_1 \neq 0 \Rightarrow \dot{L}_{m_{1,c}}(\vec{x},\vec{p}_{10}) \neq 0]$ also holds. Since x_n satisfies $E_{1,1}\vec{x} \geq \vec{0} \wedge x_1 \neq 0$, then $\dot{L}_{m_{1,c}}(\vec{x},\vec{p}_{10}) \neq 0$.

Hence, $\forall \vec{x}[E_{1,1}\vec{x} \geq \vec{0} \wedge x_1 \neq 0 \Rightarrow \dot{L}_{m_{1,c}}(\vec{x},\vec{p}_{10}) \neq \vec{0}]$ holds. $\square$

Similarly, we have the following lemma.

LEMMA 5. *For all $\vec{p}_{i0}$ such that $\Lambda_{1,i,j,k}^{m_{i,c}}$ holds, $\forall \vec{x}[E_{i,j}\vec{x}_k \geq \vec{0} \wedge x_k \neq 0 \Rightarrow \dot{L}_{m_{i,c}}(\vec{x}_k,\vec{p}_{i0}) \neq 0]$ holds, where $i \in \{1, \cdots, N\}$, $j \in \{1, \ldots, l_i\}$ and $k \in \{1, \cdots, n\}$.*

Thus, we finish proving that for each $i \in \{1, \cdots, N\}, j \in \{1, \cdots, l_i\}, k \in \{1, \cdots, n\}$, the solution set of $\Lambda_{1,i,j,k}^{m_{i,c}}$ is a subset of the solution set of $\phi_{i,j,k}$. .

Third, we try to prove that the computed sample point in the resulting algebraic set can form a multiple Lyapunov function, which is assured by the following theorem.

THEOREM 4. *For all $(\vec{p}_{10}, \cdots, \vec{p}_{N0})$ such that $\bigwedge_{i=1}^N[\Lambda_{1,i}^{V_i} \wedge \Lambda_{2,i}^{V_i} \wedge \Lambda_{1,i}^{m_{i,c}} \wedge \Lambda_{2,i}^{m_{i,c}} \wedge [\bigwedge_{j=1}^N \Lambda_{3,i,j}]]$ holds, the family $\{V_i(\vec{x},\vec{p}_{i0})\}$ is a multiple Lyapunov function.*

PROOF. Assume that $(\vec{p}_{10}, \cdots, \vec{p}_{N0})$ makes $\bigwedge_{i=1}^N[\Lambda_{1,i}^{V_i} \wedge \Lambda_{2,i}^{V_i} \wedge \Lambda_{1,i}^{m_{i,c}} \wedge \Lambda_{2,i}^{m_{i,c}} \wedge [\bigwedge_{j=1}^N \Lambda_{3,i,j}]]$ hold. Then,

1. according to Lemma 5, $\wedge_i \wedge_j \wedge_k \phi_{i,j,k}(\vec{p}_{i0})$ holds. For every $i \in \{1, \cdots, N\}$, since $\forall \vec{x}[\vec{x} \in \mathcal{X}_i \wedge \vec{x} \neq \vec{0} \Rightarrow \dot{L}_{m_{i,c}}(\vec{x},\vec{p}_{i0})]$ is equivalent to $\wedge_j \wedge_k \phi_{i,j,k}(\vec{p}_{i0})$, then $\forall \vec{x}[\vec{x} \in \mathcal{X}_i \wedge \vec{x} \neq \vec{0} \Rightarrow \dot{L}_{m_{i,c}}(\vec{x},\vec{p}_{i0}) \neq 0]$ holds.

2. for every $i \in \{1, \cdots, N\}$ and every $j \in \{1, \ldots, l_i\}$, there are two points $\vec{y}_{ij}$ and $\vec{z}_{ij}$ satisfying $E_{i,j}\vec{y}_{ij} \geq \vec{0}$, $E_{i,j}\vec{z}_{ij} \geq \vec{0}$ and $(\vec{y}_{ij}, \vec{z}_{ij}) \neq \|\vec{y}_{ij}\|\vec{z}_{ij}\|$ such that $[\dot{L}_{m_{i,c}}(\vec{y}_{ij},\vec{p}_{i0}) < 0 \wedge \dot{L}_{m_{i,c}}(\vec{z}_{ij},\vec{p}_{i0}) < 0]$ holds.

Hence, the condition (1) in Theorem 3 holds. Similarly, the condition (2) in Theorem 3 also holds.

Since $\Lambda_{3,i,j,r}$ is equivalent to $\forall \vec{x}[g_{i,j,r}^T\vec{x} = 0 \Rightarrow V_i(\vec{x},\vec{p}_{i0}) - V_j(\vec{x},\vec{p}_{j0}) \geq 0]$, the condition (3) in Theorem 3 holds.

Thus, from Theorem 3, the family $\{V_i(\vec{x},\vec{p}_{i0})\}$ is a multiple Lyapunov function. $\square$

6. IMPLEMENTATION

We implemented our algorithm based on DISCOVERER, which is a solver to a semi-algebraic set that is defined as a set of form $g(\vec{x},\vec{p})\Delta 0$, where $\vec{x} \in \mathbb{R}^n$ is a variable, $\vec{p} \in \mathbb{R}^d$ is a parameter, $g(\vec{x},\vec{p})$ is a polynomial and $\Delta \in \{=, >, \geq, \neq\}$.

Simply speaking, our implementation consists of the following three main steps:

1. The first main step is to use real root classification to get a sufficient and necessary condition over $x_1, \cdots, x_{i-1}$, $x_{i+1}, \cdots, x_n, \vec{p}$ such that $\{g(\vec{x},\vec{p}) = 0, E\vec{x} \geq \vec{0}, x_i \neq 0\}$, where $E \in \mathbb{R}^{n \times n}$, has no solution about the variable x_i, where $i \in \{1, \cdots, n\}$. Concretely, we orderly call the commands *tofind* and *Tofind*, which are implemented in DISCOVERER by using real root classification and can return a sufficient and necessary condition over $x_1, \cdots, x_{i-1}, x_{i+1}, \cdots, x_n$ and $\vec{p}$ such that $\{g(\vec{x},\vec{p}) = 0, E\vec{x} \geq \vec{0}, x_i \neq 0\}$ has exactly N distinct real solutions, where N is a non-negative integer.

2. The second main step is to compute two points satisfying $E\vec{x} \geq \vec{0}$, where E is a $n \times n$ matrix and $n \geq 2$, using the following strategy: if the rank of E is less than n, use Gauss elimination to compute a non-zero solution $\vec{x}$ of $E\vec{x} = \vec{0}$ and then $\pm\vec{x}$ are the required two points; otherwise, apply Gauss elimination to compute the solutions of $E\vec{x} = (1,0,\ldots,0)^T$ and $E\vec{x} = (0,1,\ldots,0)^T$, respectively.

3. The third main step is to solve the resulting conjunction using SASsolver [24]. Concretely, after getting the conjunction which only involves the parameters $\vec{p}$, we reformulate this conjunction as a set of semi-algebraic sets and then solve each semi-algebraic set one by one by using SASsolver, which is implemented using an adaptive partial cylindrical algebraic decomposition [5]. Here, for a semi-algebraic set, SASsolver returns a sample point (i.e., it is a solution) or an empty set (i.e., this semi-algebraic set has no solution).

7. COMPUTATIONS AND COMPARISONS

In this section, we test the prototypical implementation of Algorithm 1 on five examples and compare it with the LMI based method, the SOS based method and the generic quantifier elimination method, respectively.

EXAMPLE 3. *Consider the following switched system [9]:*

$$\dot{\vec{x}} = f_i(\vec{x}), i \in \mathcal{M} = \{1,2\}, \vec{x} \in \mathcal{X}_i \subset \mathbb{R}^n,$$

where $f_1 = \begin{pmatrix} -4x_1 + 3x_2 + 6x_1x_2 \\ -3x_1 - 2x_2 \end{pmatrix}$, $f_2 = \begin{pmatrix} -4x_1 + x_2 \\ -x_1 - 2x_2 + x_1^2 \end{pmatrix}$; $\mathcal{X}_1 = \bigcup_{j=1}^2\{\vec{x}|E_{1,j} \geq \vec{0}\}$, $\mathcal{X}_2 = \bigcup_{j=1}^2\{\vec{x}|E_{2,j}\vec{x} \geq \vec{0}\}$; $E_{1,1} = \begin{pmatrix} 3 & 4 \\ 4 & 3 \end{pmatrix}$, $E_{1,2} = \begin{pmatrix} -3 & -4 \\ -4 & -3 \end{pmatrix}$; $E_{2,1} = \begin{pmatrix} 3 & 4 \\ -4 & -3 \end{pmatrix}$, $E_{2,2} = \begin{pmatrix} -3 & -4 \\ 4 & 3 \end{pmatrix}$; $g_{1,2}^T = (3,4), g_{2,1}^T = (4,3)$.

In this system, each subsystem is asymptotically stable.
Suppose that $V_i(\vec{x}) = a_ix_1^2 + b_ix_1x_2 + c_ix_2^2$, $i = 1,2$. By Algorithm 1, we get $\{V_i(\vec{x}), i = 1,2\}$ as a MLF, where $V_1(\vec{x}) = x_1^2 + x_2^2$ and $V_2(\vec{x}) = -x_1^2 - \frac{21}{8}x_1x_2 + x_2^2$. $\square$

EXAMPLE 4. *Consider the following switched system [9]:*

$$\dot{\vec{x}} = f_i(\vec{x}), i \in \mathcal{M} = \{1,2\}, \vec{x} \in \mathcal{X}_i \subset \mathbb{R}^n,$$

where $f_1(\vec{x}) = \begin{pmatrix} -x_1 - 100x_2 \\ 10x_1 - x_2 \end{pmatrix}$, $f_2(\vec{x}) = \begin{pmatrix} x_1 + 10x_2 \\ -100x_1 + x_2 \end{pmatrix}$; $\mathcal{X}_1 = \{\vec{x}|E_1\vec{x} \geq \vec{0}\}$, $\mathcal{X}_2 = \{\vec{x}|E_2\vec{x} \geq \vec{0}\}$; $E_1 = \begin{pmatrix} 0 & 0 \\ 0 & 0 \end{pmatrix}$, $E_2 = \begin{pmatrix} -10 & -1 \\ 2 & -1 \end{pmatrix}$; $g_{1,2}^T = (-10,-1), g_{2,1}^T = (2,-1)$.

In this system, the first subsystem $\dot{\vec{x}} = f_1(\vec{x})$ is asymptotically stable and the second one $\dot{\vec{x}} = f_2(\vec{x})$ is unstable.

Suppose that $V_i(\vec{x}) = a_i x_1^2 + b_i x_1 x_2 + c_i x_2^2$, $i = 1, 2$. By Algorithm 1, we get $\{V_i(\vec{x}), i = 1, 2\}$ as a multiple Lyapunov function, where $V_1(\vec{x}) = \frac{21}{2} x_1^2 - x_1 x_2 + \frac{21}{16} x_2^2$ and $V_2(\vec{x}) = \frac{39}{256} x_1^2 + \frac{1}{64} x_1 x_2 + \frac{25}{16} x_2^2$. $\square$

EXAMPLE 5. *Consider the following switched system:*

$$\dot{\vec{x}} = f_i(\vec{x}), i \in \mathcal{M} = \{1, 2\}, \vec{x} \in \mathcal{X}_i \subset \mathbb{R}^n,$$

where $f_1 = \begin{pmatrix} -x_1^3 + x_1 x_2^2 \\ -x_2 - 2x_2 x_1^2 \end{pmatrix}$, $f_2 = \begin{pmatrix} \frac{1}{2} x_2 - x_1(1 - (x_1^2 + x_2^2)) \\ x_1 - \frac{1}{3} x_2(1 - (x_1^2 + x_2^2)) \end{pmatrix}$; $\mathcal{X}_1 = \bigcup_{j=1}^2 \{\vec{x} | E_{1,j} \vec{x} \geq \vec{0}\}$, $\mathcal{X}_2 = \bigcup_{j=1}^2 \{\vec{x} | E_{2,j} \vec{x} \geq \vec{0}\}$; $E_{1,1} = \begin{pmatrix} 1 & 0 \\ 0 & 1 \end{pmatrix}$, $E_{1,2} = \begin{pmatrix} -1 & 0 \\ 0 & -1 \end{pmatrix}$; $E_{2,1} = \begin{pmatrix} -1 & 0 \\ 0 & 1 \end{pmatrix}$, $E_{2,2} = \begin{pmatrix} 1 & 0 \\ 0 & -1 \end{pmatrix}$; $g_{1,2,1}^T = (0, 1)$, $g_{1,2,2}^T = (1, 0)$, $g_{2,1,1}^T = (0, 1)$, $g_{2,1,2}^T = (1, 0)$; $S_{1,2} = \cup_{r=1}^2 \{\vec{x} : g_{1,2,r}^T \vec{x} = 0\}$, $S_{2,1} = \cup_{r=1}^2 \{\vec{x} : g_{2,1,r}^T \vec{x} = 0\}$.

In this system, the first subsystem $\dot{\vec{x}} = f_1(\vec{x})$ is asymptotically stable and the second one $\dot{\vec{x}} = f_2(\vec{x})$ is unstable. Moreover, the linearization of the first subsystem has one eigenvalue equal to zero.

Suppose that $V_i(\vec{x}) = a_i x_1^2 + b_i x_1 x_2 + c_i x_2^2$, $i = 1, 2$. By Algorithm 1, we get $\{V_i(\vec{x}), i = 1, 2\}$ as a multiple Lyapunov function, where $V_1(\vec{x}) = \frac{5}{32} x_1^2 + x_2^2$ and $V_2(\vec{x}) = \frac{5}{32} x_1^2 - \frac{5}{16} x_1 x_2 + x_2^2$. $\square$

EXAMPLE 6. *Consider the following switched system:*

$$\dot{\vec{x}} = f_i(\vec{x}), i \in \mathcal{M} = \{1, 2\}, \vec{x} \in \mathcal{X}_i \subset \mathbb{R}^n,$$

where $f_1(\vec{x}) = \begin{pmatrix} -x_1 - 2x_1 x_2^2 \\ -x_2^3 + x_1^2 x_2 \end{pmatrix}$, $f_2(\vec{x}) = \begin{pmatrix} x_1 x_2^2 - x_1^3 \\ -x_2^3 x_2 - x_2^3 \end{pmatrix}$; $\mathcal{X}_1 = \bigcup_{j=1}^2 \{\vec{x} | E_{1,j} \vec{x} \geq \vec{0}\}$, $\mathcal{X}_2 = \bigcup_{j=1}^2 \{\vec{x} | E_{2,j} \vec{x} \geq \vec{0}\}$; $E_{1,1} = \begin{pmatrix} 1 & 10 \\ -1 & 2 \end{pmatrix}$, $E_{1,2} = \begin{pmatrix} -1 & -10 \\ 1 & -2 \end{pmatrix}$; $E_{2,1} = \begin{pmatrix} 1 & 10 \\ 1 & -2 \end{pmatrix}$, $E_{2,2} = \begin{pmatrix} -1 & -10 \\ -1 & 2 \end{pmatrix}$; $g_{1,2}^T = (1, 10), g_{2,1}^T = (-1, 2)$.

In this system, each subsystem is asymptotically stable. Moreover, the linearization of the subsystem $\dot{\vec{x}} = f_1(\vec{x})$ has one eigenvalue equal to zero and the linearization of the subsystem $\dot{\vec{x}} = f_2(\vec{x})$ has two eigenvalues both equal to zero.

Suppose that $V_i(\vec{x}) = a_i x_1^2 + b_i x_1 x_2 + c_i x_2^2$, $i = 1, 2$. By Algorithm 1 we get $\{V_i(\vec{x}), i = 1, 2\}$ as a multiple Lyapunov function, where $V_1(\vec{x}) = \frac{771}{512} x_1^2 - 8 x_1 x_2 + 10 x_2^2$ and $V_2(\vec{x}) = \frac{3}{100} x_1^2 - \frac{3}{200} x_1 x_2 - \frac{9}{200} x_2^2$. $\square$

EXAMPLE 7. *Consider the following switched system:*

$$\dot{\vec{x}} = f_i(\vec{x}), i \in \mathcal{M} = \{1, 2\}, \vec{x} \in \mathcal{X}_i \subset \mathbb{R}^n,$$

$f_1 = \begin{pmatrix} -x_1 - 3x_2 + 2x_3 + x_2 x_3 \\ 3x_1 - x_2 - x_3 + x_1 x_3 \\ -2x_1 + x_2 - x_3 + x_1 x_2 \end{pmatrix}$, $f_2 = \begin{pmatrix} x_2 - x_1^3 \\ -x_1 - x_2^3 + x_2 x_3^4 \\ -x_3 + x_2^3 x_3 \end{pmatrix}$; $\mathcal{X}_1 = \{\vec{x} | E_1 \vec{x} \geq \vec{0}\}$, $\mathcal{X}_2 = \{\vec{x} | E_2 \vec{x} \geq \vec{0}\}$, $E_1 = \begin{pmatrix} 1 & 1 & 1 \\ 0 & 0 & 0 \\ 0 & 0 & 0 \end{pmatrix}$, $E_2 = \begin{pmatrix} 0 & 0 & 0 \\ 0 & 0 & 0 \\ 0 & 0 & 0 \end{pmatrix}$, and $g_{1,2}^T = g_{2,1}^T = (1, 1, 1)$.

In this system, each subsystem is asymptotically stable. Moreover, the linearization of the subsystem $\dot{\vec{x}} = f_2(\vec{x})$ has two eigenvalues with real part equal to zero.

Suppose that $V_1(\vec{x}) = a_1 x_1^2 + b_1 x_2^2 + c_1 x_3^2 + d_1 x_1 x_2 + e_1 x_1 x_3$ and $V_2(\vec{x}) = a_2 x_1^2 + b_2 x_2^2 + c_2 x_3^2 + d_2 x_1 x_3$. By Algorithm 1, we get $\{V_i(\vec{x}), i = 1, 2\}$ as a multiple Lyapunov function, where $V_1(\vec{x}) = \frac{23}{11} x_1^2 + \frac{13}{11} x_2^2 + \frac{16}{11} x_3^2 + \frac{10}{11} x_1 x_3$ and $V_2(\vec{x}) = \frac{18}{11} x_1^2 + \frac{18}{11} x_2^2 + x_3^2$. $\square$

We have also used the LMI based method, the SOS based method and the generic QE based method, respectively, arriving at the following computation results:

1. The LMI based method can work for Examples 3 and 4 but not for Examples 5, 6 and 7 since for each example, there is at least one subsystem whose linearization has at least one eigenvalue with real part equal to zero.

2. According to the theory described in [16, 31] and the bilinear programming solver [10], pre-assuming all polynomials to be quadratic polynomials, the SOS based method returns "stopped by line search failure" for all examples except Example 7 and for Example 7, the program does not terminate within five hours. Moreover, for all examples listed above, we also used polynomials of degree $d > 2$ but the program still either returned failures or did not terminate within five hours.

3. After applying REDLOG (a generic QE tool) to check whether there is a solution of parameters in the same pre-assumed quadratic form $\{V_i(\vec{x})\}$ resulting in a multiple Lyapunov function, there is a positive answer for Examples 3 and 4, but the program does not terminate within five hours for Examples 5, 6 and 7.

Summing up all the above computation results, our current algebraic approach is to some extent more efficient than the LMI, SOS and generic QE based methods. The reasons may lie in the following facts: LMI is unpractical for degenerate systems; LMI and SOS use floating computation such that certain non-negative polynomials cannot be practically formulated as sums of squares; QE uses CAD whose computational complexity is doubly exponential in the number of total variables while DISCOVERER uses an adaptive CAD where some variables can be eliminated by Ritt-Wu's method due to the existence of equations.

8. CONCLUSIONS

In this paper, we proposed an algebraic approach for analyzing asymptotic stability of switched hybrid systems. That is, we used a real root classification and projection operator based algebraic approach to arrive at a semi-algebraic set which only involves the coefficients of the pre-assumed quadratic form and then solved the resulting semi-algebraic set for the coefficients. We prototypically implemented our algorithm based on DISCOVERER with manual intervention and tested it on five examples. The computation and comparison results demonstrated the applicability, efficiency and promise of our algebraic approach.

Our short-term goal is to further optimize our algorithm and make it fully automatic, associated with complexity analysis of the algorithm [24, 29, 25]. Our long-term goal is to verify the stability of general nonlinear hybrid systems [6] in the Lyapunov sense by computing multiple Lyapunov functions [2], or in the practical sense [11] by computing multiple Lyapunov-like functions [21, 26] or by computing transition systems [20, 17, 28, 23].

Acknowledgements

This work was supported by NSFC-61003021, Beijing Nova Program and SKLSDE-2011ZX-16. The authors are most grateful for the numerous inspiring discussions with Dr. Stefan Ratschan and Prof. T. John Koo. Moreover, the authors would like to thank the four anonymous reviewers for their favorable comments.

9. REFERENCES

[1] V. D. Blondel, O. Bournez, P. Koiran, J. N. Tsitsiklis. The Stability of saturated linear dynamical systems is undecidable. *Journal of Computer and System Sciences*, 62(3): 442–462, 2001.

[2] M. S. Branicky. Multiple Lyapunov functions and other analysis tools for switched and hybrid systems. *IEEE TAC*, 43(4): 475–482, 1998.

[3] C. W. Brown. QEPCAD B: a system for computing with semi-algebraic sets via cylindrical algebraic decomposition. *SIGSAM Bull*, 38(1): 23–24, 2004.

[4] G. E. Collins. Quantifier elimination for the elementary theory of real closed fields by cylindrical algebraic decomposition. *Leture Notes in Computer Science*, Vol. 33, pp. 134–183, 1975.

[5] G. E. Collins, H. Hong. Partial cylindrical algebraic decomposition for quantifier elimination. *Journal of Symbolic Computation*, 12: 299–328, 1991.

[6] R. A. Decarlo, M. S. Branicky, M.S., S. Pettersson. Perspective and results on the stability annd stabilizability of hybrid systems. *Proceedings of the IEEE*, 88(7): 1069–1081, 2000.

[7] A. Dolzmann, T. Sturm. REDLOG: computer algebra meets computer logic. *SIGSAM Bull*, 31(2): 2–9, 1997.

[8] S. Gulwani, A. Tiwari. Constraint-Based Approach for Analysis of Hybrid Systems. In *CAV 2008*, pp. 190–203.

[9] M. Johansson, A. Rantzer. Computation of piecewise quadratic Lyapunov functions for hybrid systems. *IEEE TAC*, 43(4): 555–559, 1998.

[10] M. Kočvara, M. Stingl. PENBMI User's Guide. Avaiable from http://www.penopt.com, 2005.

[11] V. Lakshmikantham, S. Leela, A. Martynyuk, Practical Stability of Nonlinear Systems, World Scientific, 1990.

[12] J. Lunze, F. Lamnabhi-Lagarrigue, editors. Handbook of Hybrid Systems Control: Theory, Tools, Applications. Cambridge University Press, 2009.

[13] J. Oehlerking, O. Theel. Decompositional construction of Lyapunov functions for hybrid system. In *HSCC 2009*, LNCS, Vol. 5469, pp. 276–290, 2009.

[14] T. V. Nguyen, T. Mori, Y. Mori. Existence conditions of a common quadratic Lyapunov function for a set of second-order systems. *Trans. of the SICE*, 42(3): 241–246, 2006.

[15] S. Pettersson, B. Lennartson. An LMI approach for stability analysis of nonlinear systems. In *Proc. of the 4th European Control Conference*, 1997.

[16] A. Papachristodoulou, S. Prajna. Robust Stability Analysis of Nonlinear Hybrid Systems. *IEEE TAC*, 54(5): 1035-1041, 2009.

[17] A. Podelski, S. Wagner. Model checking of hybrid systems: From reachability towards stability. In J. Hespanha and A. Tiwari, editors, *Hybrid Systems: Computation and Control, Lecture Notes in Computer Science*, Vol. 3927, pp. 507-521, 2006.

[18] S. Prajna, A. Papachristodoulou, P. Seiler, P.A. Parrilo. SOSTOOLS – Sum of Squares Optimization Toolbox for MATLAB. Available from http://www.cds.caltech.edu/sostools, 2004.

[19] S. Prajna, A. Papachristodoulou. Analysis of Switched and Hybrid Systems Beyond Piecewise Quadratic Methods. In *Proceedings of the American Control Conference*, pp. 2779–2784, 2003.

[20] S. Ratschan, Z. She. Safety verification of hybrid systems by constraint propagation-based abstraction refinement. *ACM Trans. on Embedded Computing Systems*, 6(1), Article No. 8, pp. 1–23, 2007.

[21] S. Ratschan, Z. She. Providing a basin of attraction to a target region of polynomial systems by computation of Lyapunov-like functions. *SIAM Journal on Control and Optimization*, 48(7): 4377-4394, 2010.

[22] B. Reznick. Some concrete aspects of Hilbert's 17th problem. *Contemporary Mathematics*, 253: 251–272, 2000.

[23] Z. She. Termination Analysis of Safety Verification for Non-linear Robust Hybrid Systems. In *Proceedings of the 8th International Conference on Informatics in Control, Automation and Robotics*, pp. 251-261, SciTePress, 2011.

[24] Z. She, B.Xia, R. Xiao, Z. Zheng. A semi-algebraic approach for asymptotic stability analysis. *Nonlinear Analysis: Hybrid system*, 3(4): 588–596, 2009.

[25] Z. She, B. Xia, Z. Zheng. Condition number based complexity estimate for solving polynomial systems, *Journal of Computational and Applied Mathematics*, 235(8): 2670-2678, 2011.

[26] Z. She, B. Xue. Computing a basin of attraction to a target region by solving bilinear semi-definite problems. In *Proceedings of the 13th International Conference on Computer Algebra in Scientific Computing, Lecture Notes in Computer Science*, Vol. 6885, pp. 333-344, Springer, 2011.

[27] Z. She, B. Xue, Z. Zheng. Algebraic Analysis on Asymptotic Stability of Continuous Dynamical Systems. In *Proceedings of the 36th International Symposium on Symbolic and Algebraic Computation*, pp. 313-320, 2011.

[28] Z. She, Z. Zheng. Tightened reachability constraints for the verification of linear hybrid systems. *Nonlinear Analysis: Hybrid Systems*, 2(4): 1222–1231, 2008.

[29] Z. She, Z. Zheng. Condition number based complexity estimate for solving local extrema, *Journal of Computational and Applied Mathematics*, 230(1): 233-242, 2009.

[30] H. Shinozaki, T. Mori, Y. Kuroe. Solving Common Lyapunov Function Problem. In *Proceedings of the Annual Conference of the Institute of Systems, Control and Information Engineers*, pp. 135–136, 2003.

[31] W. Tan, A. Packard. Stability region analysis using polynomial and composite polynomial Lyapunov functions and sum-of-squares programming. *IEEE TAC*, 53(2): 565–571, 2008.

[32] A. Tarski. A Decision Method for Elementary Algebra and Geometry, Univ. of California Press, 1951.

[33] L. Yang, B. Xia. Automated deduction in real geometry. In *Geometric Computation*, pp. 248–298, World Scientific, 2004.

Pre-orders for Reasoning about Stability

Pavithra Prabhakar [*]
California Institute of
Technology and IMDEA
Software Institute
1200 East California
Boulevard
Pasadena, CA 91125
pavithra@caltech.edu

Geir Dullerud
University of Illinois at
Urbana-Champaign
340 Mechanical Engineering
Building
1206 West Green Street
Urbana, IL 61801
dullerud@illinois.edu

Mahesh Viswanathan
University of Illinois at
Urbana-Champaign
Department of Computer
Science
201 N Goodwin Avenue
Urbana, IL 61801
vmahesh@illinois.edu

ABSTRACT

Pre-orders between processes, like simulation, have played a central role in the verification and analysis of discrete-state systems. Logical characterization of such pre-orders have allowed one to verify the correctness of a system by analyzing an abstraction of the system. In this paper, we investigate whether this approach can be feasibly applied to reason about stability properties of a system.

Stability is an important property of systems that have a continuous component in their state space; it stipulates that when a system is started somewhere close to its ideal starting state, its behavior is close to its ideal, desired behavior. In [6], it was shown that stability with respect to equilibrium states is not preserved by bisimulation and hence additional continuity constraints were imposed on the bisimulation relation to ensure preservation of Lyapunov stability. We first show that stability of trajectories is not invariant even under the notion of bisimulation with continuity conditions introduced in [6]. We then present the notion of uniformly continuous simulations — namely, simulation with some additional uniform continuity conditions on the relation — that can be used to reason about stability of trajectories. Finally, we show that uniformly continuous simulations are widely prevalent, by recasting many classical results on proving stability of dynamical and hybrid systems as establishing the existence of a simple, obviously stable system that simulates the desired system through uniformly continuous simulations.

Categories and Subject Descriptors

D.2.4 [**Software**]: Software Engineering—*Software/Program Verification*

---

[*]This work was done while the first author was a student at the University of Illinois at Urbana-Champaign.

General Terms

Theory, Verification

Keywords

Stability, Pre-orders, Bisimulations, Uniform Continuity, Verification

1. INTRODUCTION

Bisimulation [23] is the canonical congruence that is used to understand when two systems are intended to be equivalent. It is taken to be the finest behavioral congruence that one would like to impose, and correctness specifications are often invariant under bisimulation, i.e., if two systems are bisimilar then either both satisfy the specification or neither one does. Given the efficiency of computing bisimulation quotients, bisimulation is often the basis of minimizing transition systems [22]. Variants of bisimulation, such as simulation are often used to *abstract* a system, and construct a simpler system that ignores some of the details of the system that maybe irrelevant to the satisfaction of the specification. Simulation and abstraction form the basis of verifying infinite state systems [5, 1].

Stability is the most common fundamental requirement imposed on dynamical and hybrid systems. Hybrid systems [17] are those whose system states evolve continuously with real-time modelling physical processes, while making occasional discrete mode changes, to reflect steps taken by a discrete, digital controller, or operating environment. Such models arise particularly naturally when describing embedded and cyber-physical systems. In such systems, stability is not just a design goal, but is often the principal requirement, so much so that unstable systems are deemed "unusable". Intuitively, stability requires that when a system is started somewhere close to its ideal starting state, its subsequent behavior is close to its ideally desired behavior. For example, it would not be acceptable for the performance of a robot to crucially depend on its initial position being known to infinite accuracy; more precisely, given any ideal starting orientation there should be some (open) neighborhood of this orientation for which all trajectories that start in this neighborhood remain close, and furthermore, it should be possible to ensure that the trajectories are as close as desired by making the neighborhood sufficiently small.

However, stability is not bisimulation invariant. This was first observed by Cuijpers in [6]. The stability requirement suggests that continuity requirements must be imposed on the witnessing bisimulation (or simulation) relation. Cuijpers considered the problem of Lyapunov stability of an equilibrium state x_*, which informally requires that if the system is started close to x_* then it stays close to x_* at all times. He showed that if a system T_1 with equilibrium point x_* is simulated by T_2 with equilibrium point y_* by a relation R that relates x_* and y_*, is upper semi-continuous, and R^{-1} is lower semi-continuous [18], and if T_2 is Lyapunov stable near y_* then T_1 is Lyapunov stable near x_*.

Cuijpers' result, unfortunately, does not extend when one considers stronger notions of stability, like asymptotic stability, or the (Lyapunov or asymptotic) stability of trajectories [1]. To see this, consider a standard dynamical system[2] D_1 that has two state variables x, y taking values in $\mathbb{R}$, with the set of initial states being $\{(0, y) \mid y \in \mathbb{R}_{\geq 0}\}$. The execution map of D_1 is the function $f((x, y), t)$ which prescribes the state at time t provided the state at time 0 was (x, y); specifically, here $f((0, y), t) = (t, y)$. Observe that such a system is stable with respect to the trajectory $\tau = [t \mapsto (t, 0)]_{t \in \mathbb{R}_{\geq 0}}$, as executions that start close to $(0, 0)$ remain close to τ at all times. Let us consider another dynamical system D_2 that has the same state space, and same initial states, but whose execution map is $g((0, y), t) = (t, y(1 + t))$. Observe that this system is not stable with respect to its trajectory τ, because no matter how close an initial condition $(0, y_0)$ is to the origin, the resulting execution $g((0, y_0), t)$ will diverge from τ. On the other hand, the relation $R = \{((x_1, y_1), (x_2, y_2)) \mid x_2 = x_1 \text{ and } y_2 = y_1(1 + x_1)\}$ is a bisimulation between the systems D_1 and D_2. Observe that R is bi-continuous and hence R is the kind of bisimulation considered by Cuijpers.

In this paper, we identify congruences and pre-orders that allow one to reason about stability of trajectories. Our main observation is that in this case, *uniform* continuity conditions must be imposed on simulation and bisimulation relations. Thus, we introduce the notions of *uniformly continuous bisimulation* and *uniformly continuous simulation* and show that stability (Lyapunov or asymptotic) of trajectories is invariant under the new notion of bisimulation. Moreover we show that uniformly continuous simulations yield the right notion of abstraction for stability — if D_1 is uniformly simulated by D_2 and D_2 is stable then D_1 is also stable — yielding a mechanism for reasoning about stability.

Having established that uniformly continuous simulations and bisimulations define the right semantics for stability, we ask whether they arise naturally in practice. To substantiate the usefulness claim of the new relations, we investigate a number of classical results in control theory and hybrid systems, and show that the new pre-orders are widely prevalent and form the basis of stability proofs. The Hartman-Grobman theorem [14, 15, 16] is an important result that says that the behavior of any dynamical system near a hyperbolic equilibrium point is topologically the same as the behavior of a linear system near the same equilibrium point. We observe that, in fact, the Hartman-Grobman theorem establishes that there is a uniformly continuous bisimulation between the dynamical system and its linearization.

Next we look at various results for establishing stability of dynamical and hybrid systems. The most common method for establishing stability of dynamical systems is that of Lyapunov theory [20], which requires finding a (Lyapunov) function from the state space of the dynamical system to $\mathbb{R}$ that is positive definite, and decreases along every behavior of the dynamical system. We observe that a Lyapunov function constructs a dynamical system whose stability is simple to prove. Moreover, the properties of a Lyapunov function ensure that the system constructed by the Lyapunov function uniformly continuously simulates original dynamical system. Thus, the proof of Lyapunov's theorem can be seen as constructing a simpler system which uniformly continuously simulates the original system and proving the stability of this simpler system. We also consider a technique for establishing the stability of a hybrid system using multiple Lyapunov functions. Once again we demonstrate that the result can be recast as saying that the existence of multiple Lyapunov functions of certain kind imply that the dynamical system can be abstracted (via uniformly continuous simulations) into a system for which stability can be proved easily, and therefore conclude the stability of the original hybrid system.

Related Work.

Pre-orders and bisimulations have been widely used in the analysis of hybrid systems. Bisimulation relations have been widely used in safety verification of hybrid systems, and are the main technical tool in proving decidability of several subclasses of hybrid systems including timed and o-minimal systems [2, 21, 4]. The notion of approximate simulations and bisimulations have been introduced and used for simplifying the continuous dynamics and reducing the state space of standard dynamical and hybrid systems [10, 11, 12, 24] for safety verification.

Pre-orders and bisimulations to reason about stability were first considered by Cuijpers [6]. The notion of bi-continuous bisimulation was introduced as the semantic basis for reasoning about the Lyapunov stability of a single or set of equilibrium points. However, as argued in the introduction and in Section 4.1, this notion is not sufficient to reason about stronger stability notions like asymptotic stability or the stability of trajectories. We introduce uniformity conditions to reason about such stronger notions.

Finally, modal and temporal logics [8, 7, 9] have been extended with topological operators to reason about robustness of controllers. However, they are expressively inadequate to reason about the notions of stability considered here.

2. PRELIMINARIES

Notation.

Let $\mathbb{R}$ and $\mathbb{R}_{\geq 0}$ denote the set of reals and non-negative reals, respectively. Let $\mathbb{R}_\infty$ denote the set $\mathbb{R}_{\geq 0} \cup \{\infty\}$, where ∞ denotes the largest element of $\mathbb{R}_\infty$, that is, $x < \infty$ for all $x \in \mathbb{R}_{\geq 0}$. Also, for all $x \in \mathbb{R}_\infty$, $x + \infty = \infty$. Let $\mathbb{N}$ denote the set of all natural numbers $\{0, 1, 2, \cdots\}$, and let $[n]$ denote the first n natural numbers, that is, $[n] = \{0, 1, 2, \cdots, n-1\}$. Let *Int* denote the set of all closed intervals of the form $[0, T]$, where $T \in \mathbb{R}_{\geq 0}$, and the infinite interval $[0, \infty)$.

---

[1] Stability near an equilibrium point is the special case of stability of a trajectory, as the only trajectory from the equilibrium point stays at the equilibrium point.

[2] A standard dynamical system, in this paper, refers to a hybrid system without any discrete transitions.

Functions and Relations.

Given a function F, let $Dom(F)$ denote the domain of F. Given a function $F : A \to B$ and a set $A' \subseteq A$, $F(A')$ denotes the set $\{F(a) \,|\, a \in A'\}$. Given a binary relation $R \subseteq A \times B$, R^{-1} denotes the set $\{(x, y) \,|\, (y, x) \in R\}$. For a binary relation R, we will interchangeably use "$(x, y) \in R$" and "$R(x, y)$" to denote that $(x, y) \in R$.

Sequences.

A sequence σ is a function whose domain is either $[n]$ for some $n \in \mathbb{N}$ or the set of natural numbers $\mathbb{N}$. Length of a sequence σ, denoted $|\sigma|$, is n if $Dom(\sigma) = [n]$ or ∞ otherwise. Given a sequence $\sigma : \mathbb{N} \to \mathbb{R}$ and an element r of $\mathbb{R}_\infty$ we use $\sum_{i=0}^{\infty} \sigma(i) = r$ to denote the standard limit condition $\lim_{N \to \infty} \sum_{i=0}^{N} \sigma(i) = r$.

Extended Metric Space.

An *extended metric space* is a pair (M, d) where M is a set and $d : M \times M \to \mathbb{R}_\infty$ is a distance function such that for all m_1, m_2 and m_3,

1. (Identity of indiscernibles) $d(m_1, m_2) = 0$ if and only if $m_1 = m_2$.

2. (Symmetry) $d(m_1, m_2) = d(m_2, m_1)$.

3. (Triangle inequality) $d(m_1, m_3) \leq d(m_1, m_2) + d(m_2, m_3)$.

When the metric on M is clear we will simply refer to M as a metric space.

Let us fix an extended metric space (M, d) for the rest of this section. We define an open ball of radius ϵ around a point x to be the set of all points which are within a distance ϵ from x. Formally, an *open ball* is a set of the form $B_\epsilon(x) = \{y \in M \,|\, d(x, y) < \epsilon\}$. An *open set* is a subset of M which is a union of open balls. Given a set $X \subseteq M$, a *neighborhood* of X is an open set in M which contains X. Given a subset X of M, an ϵ-neighborhood of X is the set $B_\epsilon(X) = \bigcup_{x \in X} B_\epsilon(x)$. A subset X of M is *compact* if for every collection of open sets $\{U_\alpha\}_{\alpha \in A}$ such that $X \subseteq \bigcup_{\alpha \in A} U_\alpha$, there is a finite subset J of A such that $X \subseteq \bigcup_{i \in J} U_i$.

Set Valued Functions.

We consider set valued functions and define continuity of these functions. We choose not to treat set valued functions as single valued functions whose co-domain is a power set, since as argued in [18], it leads to strong notions of continuity, which are not satisfied by many functions. A *set valued function* $F : A \leadsto B$ is a function which maps every element of A to a set of elements in B. Given a set $A' \subseteq A$, $F(A')$ will denote the set $\bigcup_{a \in A'} F(a)$. Given a binary relation $R \subseteq A \times B$, we use R also to denote the set valued function $R : A \leadsto B$ given by $R(x) = \{y \,|\, (x, y) \in R\}$. Further, $F^{-1} : B \leadsto A$ will denote the set valued function which maps $b \in B$ to the set $\{a \in A \,|\, b \in F(a)\}$.

Continuity of Set Valued Functions.

Let $F : A \leadsto B$ be a set valued function, where A and B are extended metric spaces. We define upper semi-continuity of F which is a generalization of the "δ, ϵ - definition" of continuity for single valued functions [18]. The function $F : A \leadsto B$ is said to be *upper semi-continuous* at $a \in Dom(F)$

if and only if

$$\forall \epsilon > 0, \exists \delta > 0 \text{ such that } F(B_\delta(a)) \subseteq B_\epsilon(F(a)).$$

If F is upper semi-continuous at every $a \in Dom(F)$ we simply say that F is upper semi-continuous. Next we define a "uniform" version of the above definition, where, analogous to the case of single valued functions, corresponding to an ϵ, there exists a δ which works for every point in the domain.

Definition 1. A function $F : A \leadsto B$ is said to be *uniformly continuous* if and only if

$$\forall \epsilon > 0, \exists \delta > 0 \text{ such that } \forall a \in Dom(A), F(B_\delta(a)) \subseteq B_\epsilon(F(a)).$$

We refer to uniform upper semi-continuity as just uniform continuity, because it turns out that the two notions of upper and lower semi-continuity coincide with the addition of uniformity condition, i.e., uniform upper semi-continuity is equivalent to uniform lower semi-continuity.

Next, we state some properties about upper semi-continuous and uniformly continuous functions.

PROPOSITION 1. *Let $F : A \leadsto B$ be a set-valued upper semi-continuous function. Then:*

- F^{-1} *is also an upper semi-continuous function.*

- *If A is compact, then F is also uniformly continuous.*

3. HYBRID SYSTEMS

In this section, we present certain definitions related to hybrid systems. Hybrid systems are systems with mixed discrete-continuous behaviors, which are widely prevalent in various application domains including automotive, aeronautics, manufacturing and so on. There are many models for such systems, including the popular model of a hybrid automaton [17], which captures the discrete dynamics as a finite state automaton and the continuous dynamics as differential equations. In this exposition, we will not concern ourselves with any particular representation of these systems, but will use a generic semantic model with trajectories modeling continuous evolution and transitions modeling discrete transitions.

3.1 Hybrid Transition Systems

We begin by defining the two components of a hybrid transition system, namely, trajectories and transitions.

Given a set S, a *trajectory* over S is a function $\tau : D \to S$, where $D \in Int$ is an interval. Let $Traj(S)$ denote the set of all trajectories over S. A *transition* over a set S is a pair $\alpha = (s_1, s_2) \in S \times S$. Let $Trans(S)$ denote the set of all transitions over S.

Definition 2. A *hybrid transition system* (HTS) $\mathcal{H}$ is a tuple (S, Σ, Δ), where S is a set of states, $\Sigma \subseteq Trans(S)$ is a set of transitions and $\Delta \subseteq Traj(S)$ is a set of trajectories.

Notation We will denote the elements of a HTS using appropriate annotations, for example, the elements of $\mathcal{H}_i$ are $(S_i, \Sigma_i, \Delta_i)$, the elements of $\mathcal{H}'$ are (S', Σ', Δ') and so on.

Next, we define an execution of a hybrid transition system. We will need the notions of first and last elements of transitions and trajectories. For a trajectory τ, $First(\tau) = \tau(0)$, and $Last(\tau)$ is defined only if $Dom(\tau)$ is a finite interval, and $Last(\tau) = \tau(T)$ where $Dom(\tau) = [0, T]$. For a transition $\alpha = (s_1, s_2)$, $First(\alpha) = s_1$ and $Last(\alpha) = s_2$. An execution is a finite or infinite sequence of trajectories and transitions which have matching end-points.

Definition 3. An *execution* of $\mathcal{H}$ is a sequence $\sigma : D \to \Sigma \cup \Delta$, where $D = [n]$ for some $n \in \mathbb{N}$ or $D = \mathbb{N}$, such that for each $0 \leq i < |\sigma| - 1$, $Last(\sigma(i)) = First(\sigma(i+1))$. Let $Exec(\mathcal{H})$ denote the set of all executions of $\mathcal{H}$.

In particular, this implies that all trajectories in an execution, except possibly the last, have finite domain.

In order to define distance between executions, we interpret an execution as a set which we call the graph of the execution. A graph of an execution consists of triples (t, i, x) such that x is a state that is reached after time t has elapsed along the execution, and i is the number of discrete transitions that have taken place before time t. Let us first define a function $Size : Traj(S) \cup Trans(S) \to \mathbb{R}_{\geq 0}$ which assigns a size to the trajectories and transitions. For $\tau \in Traj(S)$, $Size(\tau) = T$ if $Dom(\tau) = [0, T]$ and $Size(\tau) = \infty$ if $Dom(\tau) = [0, \infty)$. For $\alpha \in Trans(S)$, $Size(\alpha) = 0$.

Definition 4. For an execution σ and $j \in Dom(\sigma)$, let $T_j = \sum_{k=0}^{j-1} Size(\sigma(k))$ and $K_j = |\{k \mid k < j, \ \sigma(k) \text{ is a transition}\}|$. The *graph* of an execution σ, denoted, $Gph(\sigma)$, is the set of all triples (i, t, x) such that there exists $j \in Dom(\sigma)$ satisfying the following:

- $t \in [T_j, T_j + Size(\sigma(j))]]$.

- If $\sigma(j)$ is a trajectory, then $i = K_j$ and $x = \sigma(j)(t - T_j)$.

- If $\sigma(j)$ is a transition, then either $i = K_j$ and $x = First(\sigma)$, or $i = K_j + 1$ and $x = Last(\sigma)$.

Given a set of executions $\mathcal{T}$, we denote by $First(\mathcal{T})$ the set of starting points of executions in $\mathcal{T}$, that is, $First(\mathcal{T}) = \{First(\sigma(0)) \mid \sigma \in \mathcal{T}\}$. We will denote the set of states appearing in an execution σ as $States(\sigma)$. For a transition α, $States(\alpha) = \{First(\alpha), Last(\alpha)\}$, for a trajectory $\tau \in \Delta$, $States(\tau) = \{\tau(t) \mid t \in Dom(\tau)\}$, and for an execution σ, $States(\sigma) = \bigcup_{i \in Dom(\sigma)} States(\sigma(i))$.

Let $\mathcal{H} = (S, \Sigma, \Delta)$ be a hybrid transition system and $g : S \rightsquigarrow S'$ be a set valued function whose domain is the state space of $\mathcal{H}$. We extend g to be a set valued function from $Traj(S)$ to $Traj(S')$ and from $Trans(S)$ to $Trans(S')$ as follows. Given a trajectory $\tau \in Traj(S)$, $g(\tau)$ is the set of trajectories τ' such that domain $Dom(\tau') = Dom(\tau)$ and $\tau'(t) \in g(\tau(t))$ for all $t \in Dom(\tau)$. Similarly, for a transition $\alpha = (s_1, s_2) \in Trans(S)$, $g(\alpha) = \{(s_1', s_2') \mid s_1' \in g(s_1), s_2' \in g(s_2)\}$. Also, for an execution σ of $\mathcal{H}$, $g(\sigma)$ is the set of all σ' such that $Dom(\sigma') = Dom(\sigma)$ and for each $i \in Dom(\sigma)$, $\sigma'(i) \in g(\sigma(i))$. If g is a single valued function, then we use $g(\tau)$, $g(\alpha)$ and $g(\sigma)$ to denote the unique element mapped by g. We define $g(\mathcal{H})$ to be the *HTS* obtained by applying g component-wise, that is, $g(\mathcal{H}) = (g(S), g(\Sigma), g(\Delta))$.

Metric Hybrid Transition Systems.
A metric hybrid transition system is a hybrid transition system whose set of states is equipped with a metric. A *metric hybrid transition system* (*MHS*) is a pair $(\mathcal{H}, d)$ where $\mathcal{H} = (S, \Sigma, \Delta)$ is a hybrid transition system, and (S, d) is an extended metric space. The metric d on the state space can

be lifted to executions, which will then be used to define stability. Before defining this extension, recall that given an extended metric space (M, d), the *Hausdorff distance* between $A, B \subseteq M$, also denoted $d(A, B)$, is given by the maximum of

$$\{\sup_{p \in A} \inf_{q \in B} d(p, q), \sup_{p \in B} \inf_{q \in A} d(p, q)\}.$$

Definition 5. Let $(\mathcal{H}, d)$ be a metric transition system with $\mathcal{H} = (S, \Sigma, \Delta)$. For $(t_1, i_1, x_1), (t_2, i_2, x_2) \in \mathbb{R}_{\geq 0} \times \mathbb{N} \times S$, let

$$d((t_1, i_1, x_1), (t_2, i_2, x_2)) = \max\{|t_1 - t_2|, |i_1 - i_2|, d(x_1, x_2)\}.$$

The *distance between executions* $\sigma_1, \sigma_2 \in Exec(\mathcal{H})$, denoted as $d(\sigma_1, \sigma_2)$, is defined as $d(Gph(\sigma_1), Gph(\sigma_2))$.

The above definition of distance between two hybrid executions is borrowed from [13].

Two executions are said to converge, if the distance between the two decreases as we consider smaller and smaller suffixes. Given a subset G of $\mathbb{R}_{\geq 0} \times \mathbb{N} \times S$ and a $T \in \mathbb{R}_{\geq 0}$, let us denote by $G|_T$ the set $\{(t, i, x) \in G \mid t \geq T\}$.

Definition 6. Two executions σ_1 and σ_2 are said to *converge* if for every real $\epsilon > 0$, there exists a time $T \in \mathbb{R}_{\geq 0}$ such that $d(Gph(\sigma_1)|_T, Gph(\sigma_2)|_T) < \epsilon$.

We will use the predicate $Conv(\sigma_1, \sigma_2)$ to denote the fact that σ_1 and σ_2 converge.

3.2 Simulations and Bisimulations

We define the notion of simulation and bisimulation between hybrid transition systems along the lines of [19].

Definition 7. Given two hybrid transition systems $\mathcal{H}_1 = (S_1, \Sigma_1, \Delta_1)$ and $\mathcal{H}_2 = (S_2, \Sigma_2, \Delta_2)$, a binary relation $R \subseteq S_1 \times S_2$ is said to be a *simulation relation* from $\mathcal{H}_1$ to $\mathcal{H}_2$, denoted $\mathcal{H}_1 \preceq_R \mathcal{H}_2$, if for every $(s_1, s_2) \in R$, the following conditions hold:

- for every state s_1' such that $(s_1, s_1') \in \Sigma_1$, there exists a state s_2' such that $(s_2, s_2') \in \Sigma_2$ and $(s_1', s_2') \in R$; and

- for every trajectory $\tau_1 \in \Delta_1$ such that $First(\tau_1) = s_1$, there exists a trajectory $\tau_2 \in \Delta_2$ such that $First(\tau_2) = s_2$, and $\tau_2 \in R(\tau_1)$.

Intuitively, if there exists a simulation relation from $\mathcal{H}_1$ to $\mathcal{H}_2$, then $\mathcal{H}_2$ has more behaviors than $\mathcal{H}_1$. $\mathcal{H}_2$ is also referred to as an abstraction of $\mathcal{H}_1$. Simulations preserve various discrete time properties, such as, safety properties, in that, if $\mathcal{H}_1 \preceq_R \mathcal{H}_2$ and $\mathcal{H}_2$ satisfies the property, then we can conclude that $\mathcal{H}_1$ satisfies the property as well.

Definition 8. A binary relation $R \subseteq S_1 \times S_2$ is a *bisimulation relation* between $\mathcal{H}_1$ and $\mathcal{H}_2$, if R is a simulation relation from $\mathcal{H}_1$ to $\mathcal{H}_2$ and R^{-1} is a simulation relation from $\mathcal{H}_2$ to $\mathcal{H}_1$.

We will use $\mathcal{H}_1 \sim_R \mathcal{H}_2$ to denote the fact that R is a bisimulation relation between $\mathcal{H}_1$ and $\mathcal{H}_2$. So a bisimulation relation preserves properties in both directions, in that, $\mathcal{H}_1$ satisfies a bisimulation invariant property iff $\mathcal{H}_2$ satisfies it.

3.3 Stability of Hybrid Transition Systems

In this section, we introduce various properties related to the stability of systems (a good introductory book is [20]). Intuitively, stability is a property that requires that a system when started close to the ideal starting state, behaves in a manner that is close to its ideal, desired behavior.

Lyapunov Stability.

We first define the notion of Lyapunov stability. Given a *HTS* $\mathcal{H}$ and a set of executions $\mathcal{T} \subseteq Exec(\mathcal{H})$, we say that $\mathcal{H}$ is *Lyapunov stable* (*LS*) with respect to $\mathcal{T}$, if for every $\epsilon > 0$ in $\mathbb{R}_{\geq 0}$, there exists a $\delta > 0$ in $\mathbb{R}_{\geq 0}$ such that the following condition holds:

$$\forall \sigma \in Exec(\mathcal{H}), d(First(\sigma(0)), First(\mathcal{T})) < \delta \implies$$

$$\exists \rho \in \mathcal{T}, d(\sigma, \rho) < \epsilon. \tag{1}$$

The above statement says that for every execution σ of the system $\mathcal{H}$ which starts with in a distance δ of some execution ρ' in $\mathcal{T}$, there exists an execution ρ in $\mathcal{T}$ which is with in distance ϵ from σ.

Asymptotic Stability.

Next we define a stronger notion of stability called asymptotic stability which in addition to Lyapunov stability requires that the executions starting close also converge as time goes to infinity. A *HTS* $\mathcal{H}$ is said to be *asymptotically stable* (*AS*) with respect to a set of execution $\mathcal{T} \subseteq Exec(\mathcal{H})$, if it is Lyapunov stable and there exists a $\delta > 0$ in $\mathbb{R}_{\geq 0}$ such that

$$\forall \sigma \in Exec(\mathcal{H}), d(First(\sigma(0)), First(\mathcal{T})) < \delta \implies$$

$$\exists \rho \in \mathcal{T}, Conv(\sigma, \rho). \tag{2}$$

So a system $\mathcal{H}$ is asymptotically stable with respect to a set of its executions $\mathcal{T}$ if $\mathcal{H}$ is Lyapunov stable with respect to $\mathcal{T}$ and every execution starting within a distance of δ from the starting point of some execution in $\mathcal{T}$ converges to some execution in $\mathcal{T}$.

Remark 1. The notions of stability with respect to an equilibrium point are a special case of the notion of stability with respect to trajectories, as an equilibrium point has the property that the only trajectory from the equilibrium point is one that stays there.

4. UNIFORMLY CONTINUOUS RELATIONS AND STABILITY PRESERVATION

The main focus of this paper is to examine the right preorders required to reason about stability properties. In the discrete setting, most interesting properties are known to be invariant under the classical notion of bisimulation. However, as shown in [6], stability is not invariant under bisimulation. That is, even with respect to a set of points (the trajectories in $\mathcal{T}$ essentially correspond to the trivial evolution of the equilibrium points), there are systems which are bisimilar, but such that only one of them is stable. Cuijpers [6] introduces bisimulations with additional continuity conditions and shows that they preserve stability with respect to a set of equilibrium points. More precisely, Cuijpers' result is as follows. Recall, a set of points X is stable if for every open neighborhood U of X, there exists a neighborhood V of X such that all trajectories starting from V remain with in U. It is shown that if R is a simulation with certain continuity conditions on R and R^{-1}, then stability with respect to a set of points is preserved (See Theorem 2 of [6]). We observe that the notion of continuous bisimulation introduced in [6] does not suffice when one considers

stability of trajectories. In fact, it does not even suffice to reason about asymptotic stability with respect to a set of points. Next, we discuss these observations; some of the details have been postponed to Appendix A.

4.1 Insufficiency of Continuity

Lyapunov Stability of Trajectories.

Let us consider the dynamical systems D_1 and D_2 from the introduction. Note that system D_1 is Lyapunov stable with respect to the trajectory $[t \mapsto (t, 0)]_{t \in \mathbb{R}_{\geq 0}}$, and the system D_2 is not Lyapunov stable with respect to the same trajectory. However, the relation R between the states of D_1 and D_2 is a bisimulation relation. Moreover, R is bicontinuous, that is, both R and R^{-1} (when interpreted as single valued functions) are continuous. This shows that bisimulation even with additional continuity restrictions, which subsume the continuity restrictions in [6], does not suffice to preserve Lyapunov stability.

Asymptotic Stability of Trajectories.

Next let us consider a dynamical system D_3 which is similar to D_2 except that $g((0, y), t) = ye^{-t}$. Note that D_3 is asymptotically stable. Then the relation R' between D_1 and D_3 given by $\{((x_1, y_1), (x_2, y_2)) \mid x_1 = x_2 \text{ and } y_2 = y_1 e^{-x_1}\}$ is a bi-continuous bisimulation between D_1 and D_3, however, D_3 is asymptotically stable, where as D_1 is not. So the continuity conditions in [6] on bisimulation relations, do not suffice to reason about asymptotic stability of trajectories. In fact, they do not suffice even to reason about asymptotic stability with respect to a set of points (see Appendix A for more details).

4.2 Uniformly Continuous Simulations and Bisimulations

In this section, we introduce the notion of uniformly continuous simulations which add certain uniformity conditions on the relation, and show that they suffice to preserve both Lyapunov and asymptotic stability of trajectories.

Definition 9. A *uniformly continuous simulation* from a *HTS* $\mathcal{H}_1$ to a *HTS* $\mathcal{H}_2$ is a binary relation $R \subseteq S_1 \times S_2$ such that R is a simulation from $\mathcal{H}_1$ to $\mathcal{H}_2$, and R and R^{-1} are uniformly continuous functions.

The main result of this section is that uniformly continuous simulations serve as the right foundation for abstractions when verifying stability properties. That is, we will show that if $\mathcal{H}_1$ is uniformly continuously simulated by $\mathcal{H}_2$ and $\mathcal{H}_2$ is stable with respect to $\mathcal{T}_2$ then $\mathcal{H}_1$ will be stable with respect to $\mathcal{T}_1$. However, for such an observation to hold, the simulation relation between H_1 and H_2 should also relate the executions $\mathcal{T}_1$ and $\mathcal{T}_2$. So before proving the main result of this section, we first formally define how the simulation relation should relate the sets $\mathcal{T}_1$ and $\mathcal{T}_2$.

Definition 10. Given *HTS*s $\mathcal{H}_1$ and $\mathcal{H}_2$, and sets of executions $\mathcal{T}_1 \subseteq Exec(\mathcal{H}_1)$ and $\mathcal{T}_2 \subseteq Exec(\mathcal{H}_2)$, a binary relation $R \subseteq S_1 \times S_2$ is said to be *semi-complete* with respect to $\mathcal{T}_1$ and $\mathcal{T}_2$ if the following hold:

- $R(First(\mathcal{T}_1)) = First(\mathcal{T}_2)$.

- For every $\rho_2 \in \mathcal{T}_2$, there is an execution in $\rho_1 \in \mathcal{T}_1$ such that $\rho_2 \in R(\rho_1)$.

- For every $x \in States(\mathcal{T}_2)$, $R^{-1}(x)$ is a singleton.

- There exists $\delta > 0$ such that for all $x \in B_\delta(First(\mathcal{T}_1))$, there exists a y such that $R(x, y)$.

R is *complete* with respect to $\mathcal{T}_1$ and $\mathcal{T}_2$ if R and R^{-1} are semi-complete with respect to $\mathcal{T}_1$ and $\mathcal{T}_2$.

The next theorem states that uniformly continuous simulations preserve Lyapunov and asymptotic stability.

THEOREM 1 (STABILITY PRESERVATION THEOREM). *Let $\mathcal{H}_1$ and $\mathcal{H}_2$ be two hybrid transition systems and $\mathcal{T}_1 \subseteq Exec(\mathcal{H}_1)$ and $\mathcal{T}_2 \subseteq Exec(\mathcal{H}_2)$ be two sets of execution. Let $R \subseteq S_1 \times S_2$ be a uniformly continuous simulation from $\mathcal{H}_1$ to $\mathcal{H}_2$, and let R be semi-complete with respect to $\mathcal{T}_1$ and $\mathcal{T}_2$. Then the following hold:*

1. *If $\mathcal{H}_2$ is Lyapunov stable with respect to $\mathcal{T}_2$ then $\mathcal{H}_1$ is Lyapunov stable with respect to $\mathcal{T}_1$.*

2. *If $\mathcal{H}_2$ is asymptotically stable with respect to $\mathcal{T}_2$ then $\mathcal{H}_1$ is asymptotically stable with respect to $\mathcal{T}_1$.*

PROOF. (Lyapunov stability preservation) Let $\mathcal{H}_2$ be Lyapunov stable with respect to $\mathcal{T}_2$. We will show that $\mathcal{H}_1$ is Lyapunov stable with respect to $\mathcal{T}_1$. Let us fix an $\epsilon > 0$. We need to show that there exists a $\delta > 0$ such that Equation (1) holds. The uniform continuity of R^{-1} gives us an element of $\mathbb{R}_{\geq 0}$ corresponding to the ϵ above. Let us call it ϵ'. We can assume that $\epsilon' < \epsilon$. Lyapunov stability of $\mathcal{T}_2$ gives us an element of $\mathbb{R}_{\geq 0}$ corresponding to the ϵ'. Let us call it δ'. Finally, uniform continuity of R gives us an element of $\mathbb{R}_{\geq 0}$ corresponding to δ', which we call δ. Let us assume without loss of generality that δ satisfies the last condition in the definition of semi-completeness of R with respect to $\mathcal{T}_1$ and $\mathcal{T}_2$.

Let $\sigma_1 \in Exec(\mathcal{H}_1)$ be such $d(First(\sigma_1(0)), First(\mathcal{T}_1)) < \delta$. We need to show that there exists a $\rho_1 \in \mathcal{T}_1$ such that $d(\sigma_1, \rho_1) < \epsilon$. $d(First(\sigma_1(0)), First(\mathcal{T}_1)) < \delta$ implies that for every $s \in R(First(\sigma_1(0)))$, there exists s' in $R(First(\mathcal{T}_1))$ such that $d(s, s') < \delta'$ (uniform continuity of R). Consider a σ_2 in $Exec(\mathcal{H}_2)$ which simulates σ_1, that is, $\sigma_2 \in R(\sigma_1)$. Then since $First(\sigma_2)$ is in $R(First(\sigma_1(0)))$ (definition of simulation), there exists $s' \in R(First(\mathcal{T}_1))$ such that $d(s, s') < \delta'$, that is, $d(First(\sigma_2), First(\mathcal{T}_2)) < \delta'$ (since due to semi-completeness $R(First(\mathcal{T}_1)) = First(\mathcal{T}_2)$). Then from the Lyapunov stability of $\mathcal{H}_2$, there exists a ρ_2 in $\mathcal{T}_2$ such that $d(\sigma_2, \rho_2) < \epsilon'$. Let ρ_1 be a trajectory in $\mathcal{T}_1$ such that $\rho_2 \in R(\rho_1)$ (ρ_1 exists due to the second condition in the definition of semi-completeness). We will show that $d(\sigma_1, \rho_1) < \epsilon$.

Let (t_1, i_1, x_1) be in $Gph(\sigma_1)$. Then (t_1, i_1, y_1) is in $Gph(\sigma_2)$ for some $y_1 \in R(x_1)$. (t_1, i_1, y_1) is with in distance ϵ' from some (t_2, i_2, y_2) in $Gph(\rho_2)$. In particular, $d(y_1, y_2) < \epsilon'$, $|t_1 - t_2| < \epsilon'$ and $|i - j| < \epsilon'$. Since $R^{-1}(y_2)$ is a singleton (from the third condition of the definition of semi-completeness), say x_2, every point in $R^{-1}(y_1)$ is with in distance ϵ from x_2. In particular, $d(x_1, x_2) < \epsilon$, and hence (t_1, i_1, x_1) is with in distance ϵ from (t_2, i_2, x_2) (since $\epsilon' < \epsilon$). The argument is similar when we fix a (t_2, i_2, x_2) in $Gph(\rho_1)$. Hence, $d(\sigma_1, \rho_1) < \epsilon$.

(Asymptotic stability preservation) Let $\mathcal{H}_2$ be asymptotically stable with respect to $\mathcal{T}_2$. We will show that $\mathcal{H}_1$ is asymptotically stable with respect to $\mathcal{T}_1$. Let $\delta' > 0$ be such that for every σ_2 starting with in a δ' ball of $First(\mathcal{T}_2)$,

there exists a ρ_2 in $\mathcal{T}_2$, such that $Conv(\sigma_2, \rho_2)$. Let δ be an element of $\mathbb{R}_{\geq 0}$ given by the uniform continuity of R. We will show that for every σ_1 starting with in a δ ball of $First(\mathcal{T}_1)$, there exists a ρ_1 in $\mathcal{T}_1$, such that $Conv(\sigma_1, \rho_1)$. (This is enough since the preservation of Lyapunov stability follows from the previous part). Let us fix such a σ_1. Then similar to an argument in the previous part, there exists a σ_2 which simulates σ_1 and $d(First(\sigma_2), First(\mathcal{T}_2)) < \delta'$. Then from the asymptotic stability of $\mathcal{H}_2$ there exists ρ_2 in $\mathcal{T}_2$ such that $Conv(\sigma_2, \rho_2)$. Let ρ_1 be a trajectory in $\mathcal{T}_1$ such that $\rho_2 \in R(\rho_1)$. We will show that $Conv(\sigma_1, \rho_1)$. Let us fix an $\epsilon > 0$. We need to show that there exist $T \in \mathbb{R}_{\geq 0}$ such that $d(Gph(\sigma_1)|_T, Gph(\rho_1)|_T) < \epsilon$. Let us choose ϵ' as before. There exist $T \in \mathbb{R}_{\geq 0}$ such that $d(Gph(\sigma_2)|_T, Gph(\rho_2)|_T) < \epsilon'$. We show that the same T works in $\mathcal{H}_1$ for the ϵ. The proof is similar to showing that $d(\sigma_1, \rho_2) < \epsilon$ in the previous part (replace $Gph(\sigma_i)$ by $Gph(\sigma_i)|_T$). □

The above theorem implies that the stability of a system $\mathcal{H}_1$ can be concluded by analysing a potentially simpler system $\mathcal{H}_2$ which uniformly continuously simulates $\mathcal{H}_1$.

Remark 2. Observe that the definition of stability crucially depends on the notion of distance between two executions. The definition used in this paper has been argued to be useful in [13] and accounts for all the discrete transitions in the execution. However, there might be situations where for stability purposes we might want to ignore the effects of these discrete transitions because these changes happen on a set of "measure 0" in the time domain. More precisely, let an execution σ be a function with domain $[0, \infty)$ obtained by first dropping all the (discrete) transitions and then concatenating all the trajectories in order. The distance between two executions is then the supremum of the pointwise distance between their corresponding functions. It can be easily observed that the above proof of Theorem 1 works even for this definition of distance between executions. Thus, stability preservation by our definition of simulation is not very tightly bound to the specific definition of distance between executions.

As a corollary of Theorem 1, we obtain that Lyapunov stability and asymptotic stability are invariant under uniformly continuous bisimulations.

Definition 11. A *uniformly continuous bisimulation* between two HTSs $\mathcal{H}_1$ and $\mathcal{H}_2$ is a binary relation $R \subseteq S_1 \times S_2$ such that R is a uniformly continuous simulation from $\mathcal{H}_1$ to $\mathcal{H}_2$ and R^{-1} is a uniformly continuous simulation from $\mathcal{H}_2$ to $\mathcal{H}_1$.

COROLLARY 1. *Let $\mathcal{H}_1$ and $\mathcal{H}_2$ be two hybrid transition systems and $\mathcal{T}_1 \subseteq Exec(\mathcal{H}_1)$ and $\mathcal{T}_2 \subseteq Exec(\mathcal{H}_2)$ be two sets of execution. Let $R \subseteq S_1 \times S_2$ be a uniformly continuous bisimulation between $\mathcal{H}_1$ and $\mathcal{H}_2$, and let R be complete with respect to $\mathcal{T}_1$ and $\mathcal{T}_2$. Then the following hold:*

1. *$\mathcal{H}_1$ is Lyapunov stable with respect to $\mathcal{T}_1$ if and only if $\mathcal{H}_2$ is Lyapunov stable with respect to $\mathcal{T}_2$.*

2. *$\mathcal{H}_1$ is asymptotically stable with respect to $\mathcal{T}_1$ if and only if $\mathcal{H}_2$ is asymptotically stable with respect to $\mathcal{T}_2$.*

5. APPLICATIONS OF THE STABILITY PRESERVATION THEOREM

In this section, we show that various methods used in proving Lyapunov and asymptotic stability of systems can be formulated as constructing a simpler system which uniformly continuously simulates the original system and showing that the simpler system is Lyapunov or asymptotically stable, respectively.

5.1 Lyapunov Functions

We will show that Lyapunov's direct method for proving stability of dynamical systems can be interpreted as first constructing a simpler system using a Lyapunov function which uniformly continuously simulates the original system, and then establishing the stability of the simpler system. Then Theorem 1 gives us the stability of the original system.

Consider the following time-invariant system,

$$\dot{x} = f(x), \qquad x \in \mathbb{R}^n, \tag{3}$$

where $f : \mathbb{R}^n \to \mathbb{R}$ and let $\bar{0}$ be an equilibrium point, that is, $f(\bar{0}) = \bar{0}$.

We can associate a hybrid transition system $\mathcal{H}_f = (S, \Sigma, \Delta)$ with the dynamical system in (3), where $S = \mathbb{R}^n$, $\Sigma = \emptyset$, Δ is the set of C^1 trajectories[3] $\tau : D \to \mathbb{R}^n$ (where $D \in Int$) such that $d\tau(t)/dt = f(\tau(t))$. Let the metric d be the Euclidean distance. Let $\mathcal{T}_{f,x}$ be the set of all trajectories $\tau \in \Delta$ corresponding to an equilibrium point x, that is, τ such that $\tau(t) = x$ for all $t \in Dom(\tau)$.

Next we state Lyapunov's theorem which provides a sufficient condition for the stability of a system.

THEOREM 2 (LYAPUNOV [20]). *Suppose that there exists a neighborhood Ω of $\bar{0}$ and a positive definite C^1 function $V : \mathbb{R}^n \to \mathbb{R}$ satisfying the algebraic condition:*

$$\dot{V}(x) \leq 0, \qquad \forall x \in \Omega, \tag{4}$$

where $\dot{V}(x) = \frac{\partial V}{\partial x} f(x)$. Then System (3) is Lyapunov stable. Furthermore, if $\dot{V}$ satisfies

$$\dot{V}(x) < 0, \qquad \forall x \in \Omega/\{0\}, \tag{5}$$

then System (3) is asymptotically stable.

A C^1 positive definite function satisfying inequality (4) is called a *weak Lyapunov function* for f over Ω and one satisfying (5) is called a *Lyapunov function*.

The following theorem formulates Lyapunov's first method as a stability preserving reduction to a simpler system using uniformly continuous simulations.

THEOREM 3. *Let $\dot{x} = f(x)$, $x \in \mathbb{R}^n$ be a dynamical system with an equilibrium point $\bar{0}$. Suppose that $V : \mathbb{R}^n \to \mathbb{R}$ is a (weak) Lyapunov function for the dynamical system. Then:*

- *$V(\mathcal{H}_f)$ is (Lyapunov) asymptotically stable.*

- *V restricted to a set containing a δ-neighborhood of $First(\mathcal{T}_{f,\bar{0}})$ is a uniformly continuous simulation which is semi-complete with respect to $\mathcal{T}_{f,\bar{0}}$ and $V(\mathcal{T}_{f,\bar{0}})$.*

Therefore, $\mathcal{H}_f$ is (Lyapunov) asymptotically stable.

---
[3] C^1 is the set of continuously differentiable functions.

So Lyapunov's theorem can be casted as reducing the original system to a simpler system by uniformly upper continuous simulations and proving the stability of the simpler system. The steps in the above theorem give an alternate proof of Lyapunov and asymptotic stability using Theorem 1.

5.2 Multiple Lyapunov Functions

We show that proving stability of switched systems using multiple Lyapunov functions can be recast into the framework of Theorem 1.

A *switched system* consists of a set of dynamical systems and a switching signal which specifies the times at which the system switches its dynamics. Let us fix the following switched system with N dynamical systems.

$$\dot{x} = f_i(x), \ i \in [N], \ x \in \mathbb{R}^n,$$

$$\alpha = (\{t_i\}_{i \in \mathbb{N}}, \{\omega_i\}_{i \in \mathbb{N}}), t_i \in \mathbb{R}_{\geq 0}, \omega_i \in [N]. \tag{6}$$

The *switching signal* $\alpha = (\{t_i\}_{i \in \mathbb{N}}, \{\omega_i\}_{i \in \mathbb{N}})$ is a monotonically increasing divergent sequence, that is, it satisfies $t_0 = 0$, $t_i < t_j$ for $j > i$ and for every $T \in \mathbb{R}_{\geq 0}$, there exists a k such that $t_k > T$.

The solution of this system is the set of functions $\sigma : [0, \infty) \to \mathbb{R}^n$ such that σ restricted to the interval between two switching times is a solution to the corresponding differential equation. Let $\sigma[a, b]$ denote the function from $[0, b-a]$ to $\mathbb{R}^n$ such that $\sigma[a, b](t) = \sigma(a + t)$. σ is a solution of (6) if for every $i \in \mathbb{N}$, $\sigma[t_i, t_{i+1}]$ is a solution of the differential equation $\dot{x} = f_{\omega_i}(x)$.

We can associate a HTS $\mathcal{H}_{f_1, \cdots, f_N, \alpha}$ with the switched system in (6) given by (S, Σ, Δ), where $S = \mathbb{N} \times \mathbb{R}^n$, $\Sigma = \{((i, x), (i + 1, x)) \mid i \in \mathbb{N}, x \in \mathbb{R}^n\}$, and Δ consists of trajectories $\tau : [0, t_{i+1} - t_i] \to \{i\} \times \mathbb{R}^n$ for some $i \in \mathbb{N}$ such that there exists a trajectory $\theta : [0, t_{i+1} - t_i] \to \mathbb{R}^n$ which is a solution of the differential equation $\dot{x} = f_{\omega_i}(x)$, and the value of $\tau(t)$ is $(i, \theta(t))$. We can associate a metric d over S, where $d((i, x), (j, y))$ is the Euclidean distance between x and y if $i = j$ and ∞ otherwise. Let $\mathcal{T}_{f_1, \cdots, f_N, \alpha, \bar{0}}$ be the set of all executions σ in $Exec(\mathcal{H}_{f_1, \cdots, f_N, \alpha})$ such that $States(\sigma) \subseteq [N] \times \{\bar{0}\}$.

Next we state a result on the multiple Lyapunov method for stability analysis. Given a switching sequence $\alpha = (\{t_i\}_{i \in \mathbb{N}}, \{\omega_i\}_{i \in \mathbb{N}})$, we say that t_i and t_j are *adjacent* if t_j is the first switching time after t_i such that $\omega_i = \omega_j$.

THEOREM 4 (MULTIPLE LYAPUNOV METHOD [3]). *Let us consider the switched system of (6). Suppose there exist N weak Lyapunov functions V_i for f_i over a neighborhood Ω of $\bar{0}$ such that for any pair of adjacent switching times t_i and t_j, $V_{\omega_i}(\sigma(t_j)) \leq V_{\omega_i}(\sigma(t_i))$ for every solution σ of the switched system. Then the switched system is Lyapunov stable.*

We call a vector of functions $\bar{V} = (V_1, \cdots, V_N)$ satisfying the hypothesis of Theorem 4, a *multiple Lyapunov function* for the switched system (6).

The above theorem can again be formulated as establishing a function from the HTS $\mathcal{H}_{f_1, \cdots, f_N, \alpha}$ to a simpler HTS using the functions $V_1, \cdots, V_N$ such that the simpler system is Lyapunov stable and the mapping is a uniformly continuous simulation, thereby proving the stability of the original system.

Given a vector of functions $\bar{V} = (V_1, \cdots, V_k)$, where $V_i : \mathbb{R}^m \to \mathbb{R}$ for $1 \le i \le k$, and a switching signal $\alpha = (\{t_i\}_{i \in \mathbb{N}}, \{\omega_i\}_{i \in \mathbb{N}})$, we define a function $\bar{V}[\alpha] : \mathbb{N} \times \mathbb{R}^m \to \mathbb{N} \times \mathbb{R}$, such that $\bar{V}[\alpha](i, x) = (i, V_{\omega_i}(x))$.

THEOREM 5. *Given the switched system in Equation (6), let $\bar{V}$ be a multiple Lyapunov function for the switched system. Then:*

- *$\bar{V}[\alpha](\mathcal{H}_{f_1, \cdots, f_N, \alpha})$ is Lyapunov stable.*

- *$\bar{V}[\alpha]$ when restricted to a set containing a δ-neighborhood of $First(\mathcal{T}_{f_1, \cdots, f_N, \alpha, \bar{0}})$ is a uniformly continuous simulation which is semi-complete with respect to the sets $\mathcal{T}_{f_1, \cdots, f_N, \alpha, \bar{0}}$ and $\bar{V}[\alpha](\mathcal{T}_{f_1, \cdots, f_N, \alpha, \bar{0}})$.*

Therefore, $\mathcal{H}_{f_1, \cdots, f_N, \alpha}$ is Lyapunov stable.

5.3 Hartman-Grobman Theorem

We consider a theorem due to Hartman-Grobman which constructs linear approximations of non-linear dynamics and establishes a homeomorphism between the two dynamics. We show that the homeomorphic mapping from the non-linear dynamics to the linear dynamics is a uniformly continuous bisimulation. And hence one can use these reductions from non-linear to linear dynamics to potentially establish stability properties of non-linear dynamics by proving stability of the simpler linear dynamics, and using Theorem 1 to deduce the stability of the non-linear dynamics.

THEOREM 6 (LOCAL HARTMAN-GROBMAN THEOREM). *Consider a system $\dot{x} = F(x)$, where $F : \Omega \to \mathbb{R}^n$ and $\Omega \subseteq \mathbb{R}^n$ is an open set. Suppose that $x_0 \in \Omega$ is a hyperbolic equilibrium point of the system, that is, $A = DF(x_0)$ is a hyperbolic matrix, where DF denotes the Jacobian of F. Let φ be the (local) flow generated by the system, that is, $\varphi : \mathbb{R}^n \times \mathbb{R}_{\ge 0} \to \mathbb{R}^n$ is a differentiable function such that $d\varphi(x, t)/dt = F(\varphi(x, t))$ for all $t \in \mathbb{R}_{\ge 0}$.*
Then there exists neighborhoods U and V of x_0 and a homeomorphism $h : U \to V$ such that $\varphi(h(x), t) = h(x_0 + e^{tA}(x - x_0))$ whenever $x \in U$ and $x_0 + e^{tA}(x - x_0) \in U$.

Let us call a function h satisfying the above condition, a *Hartman-Grobman* function associated with the dynamical system $\dot{x} = F(x)$. Given a HTS $\mathcal{H} = (S, \Sigma, \Delta)$, the restriction of $\mathcal{H}$ to a set $X \subseteq S$ is the HTS $(X, \Sigma \cap Trans(X), \Delta \cap Traj(S))$.

Remark 3. The terminologies referred to in the above theorem are standard. However, we define them in the Appendix for the sake of completeness.

THEOREM 7. *Let $\dot{x} = F(x)$ be a dynamical system, where $F : \Omega \to \mathbb{R}^n$ and $\Omega \subseteq \mathbb{R}^n$ is an open set, and let $x_0 \in \Omega$ be a hyperbolic equilibrium point. Let G be a function from $\mathbb{R}^n$ to $\mathbb{R}^n$ such that $G(x) = Ax$ where $A = DF(x_0)$. Let h be a Hartman-Grobman function associated with the above dynamical system. Then, there exists a set X containing a δ-neighborhood of $First(T_{G, x_0})$ such that h restricted to this set is a uniformly continuous bisimulation from $\mathcal{H}_G$ restricted to X to $\mathcal{H}_F$ restricted to $h(X)$ and is complete with respect to T_{G, x_0} and T_{F, x_0}.*

Again, we see that the reduction defined in Hartman-Grobman theorem from the non-linear dynamics to linear dynamics is a uniformly continuous bisimulation. We can use Theorem 7 along with Theorem 1 to deduce that $\mathcal{H}_F$ restricted to $h(X)$ is Lyapunov (asymptotically) stable iff $\mathcal{H}_G$ restricted to X is Lyapunov (asymptotically) stable.

6. CONCLUSIONS

In this paper, we investigated pre-orders for reasoning about stability properties of dynamical and hybrid systems. We showed that bisimulation relations with continuity conditions, introduced in [6], are inadequate when stronger notions of stability like asymptotic stability, or the stability of trajectories is considered. We, therefore, introduced uniformly continuous simulations and bisimulations and showed that they form the semantic basis to reason about stability. Using such notions, we showed that, classical reasoning principles in control theory can be recast in a more "computer-science-like light", wherein they can be seen as being founded on abstracting/simplifying a system and then relying on the reflection of certain logical properties by the abstraction relation.

As argued in [6], one by-product of investigating the continuity requirements on simulations and bisimulations needed to reason about stability, is that it allows one to conclude the inadequacy of the modal logic in [8] to express stability properties. What is the right logic to express properties like stability? That remains open. Just like Hennessy-Milner logic serves as the logical foundation for classical simulation and bisimulation, the right modal logic that can express stability might form the logical basis for the simulation and bisimulation relations introduced here.

Acknowledgements

We would like to thank the anonymous referees for pointing us to the work in [6] on bisimulations for preservation of stability with respect to sets of points.

7. REFERENCES

[1] R. Alur, T. Dang, and F. Ivancic. Counter-Example Guided Predicate Abstraction of Hybrid Systems. In *Tools and Algorithms for the Construction and Analysis of Systems*, pages 208–223, 2003.

[2] R. Alur and D. Dill. A theory of timed automata. *Theoretical Computer Science*, 126:183–235, 1994.

[3] M. S. Branicky. Stability of hybrid systems: state of the art. In *Conference on Decision and Control*, pages 120–125, 1997.

[4] T. Brihaye and C. Michaux. On the expressiveness and decidability of o-minimal hybrid systems. *Journal of Complexity*, 21(4):447–478, 2005.

[5] E. Clarke, O. Grumberg, S. Jha, Y. Lu, and H. Veith. Counterexample-Guided Abstraction Refinement. In *Computer Aided Verification*, pages 154–169, 2000.

[6] P. J. L. Cuijpers. On bicontinuous bisimulation and the preservation of stability. In *Proceedings of the International Conference on Hybrid Systems: Computation and Control*, pages 676–679, 2007.

[7] J. Davoren. Topological semantics and bisimulations for intuitionistic modal logics and their classical companion logics. In *Proceedings of the International Conference on Logical Foundations of Computer Science*, pages 162–180, 2007.

[8] J. Davoren and R. Goré. Bimodal logics for reasoning about continuous dynamics. In *Advances in Modal Logic*, volume 3, pages 91–110. 2002.

[9] G. Fainekos and G. Pappas. Robustness of temporal logic specifications. In *Proceedings of the International*

Conference on Formal Approaches to Testing and Runtime Verification, 2006.

[10] A. Girard, A. A. Julius, and G. J. Pappas. Approximate simulation relations for hybrid systems. *Discrete Event Dynamic Systems*, 18(2):163–179, 2008.

[11] A. Girard and G. J. Pappas. Approximate bisimulation relations for constrained linear systems. *Automatica*, 43(8):1307–1317, 2007.

[12] A. Girard, G. Pola, and P. Tabuada. Approximately bisimilar symbolic models for incrementally stable switched systems. In *Proceedings of the International Conference on Hybrid Systems: Computation and Control*, pages 201–214, 2008.

[13] R. Goebel, R. Sanfelice, and A. Teel. Hybrid dynamical systems. *IEEE Control Systems, Control Systems Magazine*, 29:28–93, 2009.

[14] D. Grobman. Homeomorphism of systems of differential equations. *Doklady Akad. Nauk SSSR*, 128:880–881, 1959.

[15] D. Grobman. Topological classification of neighborhoods of a singularity in *n*-space. *Mat. Sbornik*, 56(98):77–94, 1962.

[16] P. Hartman. A lemma in the theory of structural stability of differential equations. *Proceedings of the American Mathematical Society*, 11:610–620, 1960.

[17] T. A. Henzinger. The Theory of Hybrid Automata. In *Logic In Computer Science*, pages 278–292, 1996.

[18] H. F. Jean-Pierre Aubin. *Set-valued Analysis*. Boston : Birkhauser, 1990.

[19] D. K. Kaynar, N. A. Lynch, R. Segala, and F. W. Vaandrager. Timed I/O Automata: A Mathematical Framework for Modeling and Analyzing Real-Time Systems. In *Real-Time Systems Symposium*, pages 166–177. IEEE Computer Society, 2003.

[20] H. K. Khalil. *Nonlinear Systems*. Prentice-Hall, Upper Saddle River, NJ, 1996.

[21] G. Lafferriere, G. Pappas, and S. Sastry. O-minimal Hybrid Systems. *Mathematics of Control, Signals, and Systems*, 13(1):1–21, 2000.

[22] D. Lee and M. Yannakakis. Online Minimization of Transition Systems (Extended Abstract). In *Symposium on Theory Of Computing*, pages 264–274. ACM, 1992.

[23] R. Milner. *Communication and Concurrency*. Prentice-Hall, Inc, 1989.

[24] P. Prabhakar, V. Vladimerou, M. Viswanathan, and G. Dullerud. Verifying tolerant systems using polynomial approximations. In *Proceedings of the IEEE Real Time Systems Symposium*, 2009.

APPENDIX

A. COMPARISON WITH PREVIOUS DEFINITIONS

We begin by showing that the notion of simulation and bisimulation introduced in [6] are not sufficient to reason about stability of trajectories even with an additional constraint of continuity on the relation.

Lyapunov Stability of Trajectories.

Consider a hybrid transition system $\mathcal{H}_1 = (S_1, \Sigma_1, \Delta_1)$,

where

- the state space S_1 is the set $\mathbb{R}^2_{\geq 0}$, which is the positive quadrant of the two dimensional plane;

- the set of transitions Σ_1 is the empty set; and

- Δ_1 is the set $\{f_m \,|\, m \in \mathbb{R}_{\geq 0}\}$, where for a particular $m \in \mathbb{R}_{\geq 0}$, $f_m : [0, \infty) \to \mathbb{R}^2_{\geq 0}$ is the trajectory such that $f(t) = (t, m)$.

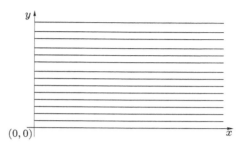

Figure 1: A *HTS* **which is Lyapunov stable**

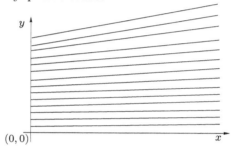

Figure 2:   An   unstable *HTS*

As shown in Figure 1, $\mathcal{H}_1$ consists of trajectories which start on the positive y-axis and evolve parallel to the positive x-axis. It is easy to see that $\mathcal{H}_1$ is Lyapunov stable with respect to the unique trajectory τ_1 which starts at the origin and moves along the x-axis.

Now let us consider another system $\mathcal{H}_2 = (S_2, \Sigma_2, \Delta_2)$, shown in Figure 2, which is similar to $\mathcal{H}_1$, that is, $S_2 = S_1$ and $\Sigma_2 = \Sigma_1$, except that $\Delta_2 = \{f_m : [0, \infty) \to \mathbb{R}_{\geq 0} \,|\, f_m(t) = (t, m(1 + t)), m \in \mathbb{R}_{\geq 0}\}$. The trajectories of $\mathcal{H}_2$ start on the positive y-axis and evolve along a straight line whose slope is given by the y intercept. So they form a diverging set of straight lines. Consider the trajectory τ_2 which starts at the origin and evolves along the x-axis. Note that $\mathcal{H}_2$ is not Lyapunov stable with respect to $\{\tau_2\}$.

However, $R = \{((x_1, y_1), (x_2, y_2)) \,|\, x_1 = x_2 \text{ and } y_2 = y_1(1 + x_1)\}$ is a bisimulation relation between $\mathcal{H}_1$ and $\mathcal{H}_2$, in fact, a bi-continuous bijection, that is, R and R^{-1} (when considered as single valued functions) are continuous. Thus, Lyapunov stability with respect to trajectories is not invariant under the bisimulations that are only continuous.

Asymptotic Stability of Trajectories.

We can show in a similar fashion that bi-continuous bisimulations do not preserve asymptotic stability. For example, consider a system $\mathcal{H}_3$ which is similar to $\mathcal{H}_2$ except that f_m

is defined as $f_m(i) = (t, me^{-t})$. Note that $\mathcal{H}_1$ is not asymptotically stable, where as $\mathcal{H}_3$ is. And there is a bi-continuous bisimulation relation given by $R = \{((x_1, y_1), (x_2, y_2)) \mid x_1 = x_2$ and $y_2 = y_1 e^{-x_1}\}$.

Insufficiency of the continuity conditions in [6] for asymptotic stability with respect to a set of points.

Consider a system $\mathcal{T}_1$ with statespace $\mathbb{R}$ and the equilibrium point 0. Let the trajectory x starting at any point $x(0) > 0$ in $\mathbb{R}$ be such that $x(t) > 0$ for all t, $x(t_1) > x(t_2)$ for all $t_1 < t_2$ and $x(t) \to 0$ as $t \to \infty$. Similarly, a trajectory x starting at any point $x(0) < 0$ in $\mathbb{R}$ be such that $x(t) < 0$ for all t, $x(t_1) < x(t_2)$ for all $t_1 < t_2$ and $x(t) \to 0$ as $t \to \infty$. Note that $\mathcal{T}_1$ is asymptotically stable with respect to the equilibrium 0.

Next consider a system $\mathcal{T}_2$ with statespace $\mathbb{R}$ such that every points is an equilibrium point. Note that $\mathcal{T}_2$ is stable with respect to 0, but not asymptotically stable.

Now, we define a relation R from $\mathcal{T}_1$ to $\mathcal{T}_2$ satisfying the hypothesis of Theorem 2 of [6]. $R = \{(x, y) \in \mathbb{R}^2 \mid y \geq x > 0$ or $0 < x \leq y\}$. Then R satisfies the following:

- R^{-1} is a simulation, that is, if x_1 can go to x_2 in time t in $\mathcal{T}_2$, then for every y_1 such that $(x_1, y_1) \in R^{-1}$, there exists a y_2 such that y_2 can be reached from y_1 in time t and $(x_2, y_2) \in R^{-1}$,

- R is upper semi-continuous, and

- R^{-1} is lower semi-continuous, that is for any open set X, $R(X) = \{y \mid \exists x \in X : (x, y) \in R\}$ is an open set.

It can be verified that R satisfies the above conditions and hence the hypothesis of Theorem 2 in [6]. However, the conclusion of the theorem does not hold for asymptotic stability because it would state that if $\mathcal{T}_1$ is asymptotically stable with respect to a closed set S, then $\mathcal{T}_2$ is asymptotically stable with respect to $R(S)$. Note however that $\mathcal{T}_1$ is asymptotically stable with respect to $\{0\}$, however $\mathcal{T}_2$ is not asymptotically stable with respect to $R(\{0\}) = \{0\}$.

B. PRELIMINARIES AND PROOFS OF THEOREMS

In this section, we recall certain standard definitions and provide proofs of theorems in Section 5.

B.1 Preliminaries

Consider a C^1 (i.e., continuously differentiable) function $V : \mathbb{R}^n \to \mathbb{R}$. It is called *positive definite* if $V(\bar{0}) = 0$ and $V(x) > 0$ for all $x \neq 0$. Let

$$\dot{V}(x) = \frac{\partial V}{\partial x} f(x),$$

and note that $\dot{V}$ is the time derivative of $V(x(t))$, where $x(t)$ is a solution of the Equation 3.

Below, we present the definitions of terminologies used in Theorem 6. A function $f : A \to B$, where $A, B \subseteq \mathbb{R}^n$ is a *homeomorphism* if f is a bijection and both f and f^{-1} are continuous. A function $F : \mathbb{R}^n \to \mathbb{R}^m$ is given by m-real valued component functions, $y_1(x), \cdots, y_m(x)$, where $x = (x_1, \cdots, x_n)$. The partial derivatives of all these functions (if they exist) can be organized in a $m \times n$ matrix called the *Jacobian* of F, denoted by $DF(x)$, where the entry in the i-th row and j-th column is $\partial y_i / \partial x_j$.

Given an n-vector $a = (a_1, \cdots, a_n) \in \mathbb{R}^n$, $DF(a)$ is the matrix obtained by substituting x_i in the terms of the matrix $DF(x_1, \cdots, x_n)$ by a_i. A square matrix A is *hyperbolic* if none of its eigen values are purely imaginary values (including 0).

B.2 Proof of Theorem 3

PROOF. (Sketch.) Proof of Part (1): Let $\mathcal{H}_f = (S_1, \Sigma_1, \Delta_1)$, and $V(\mathcal{H}_f) = (S_2, \Sigma_2, \Delta_2)$. We need to show that if V is a weak Lyapunov function, then $V(\mathcal{H}_f)$ is Lyapunov stable, and if V is a Lyapunov function, then $V(\mathcal{H}_f)$ is asymptotically stable.

Let Ω be an open subset around $\bar{0}$ as given by Lyapunov's theorem. Observe that if V is a weak Lyapunov function, then for every $\tau \in \Delta_2$ such that $\tau(0) \in V(\Omega)$, for any $t_1 < t_2$, $\tau(t_1) \geq \tau(t_2)$, since $\dot{V}(x) \leq 0$ for every $x \in \Omega$ and τ arises from a trajectory of $\mathcal{H}_f$. Hence the distance of $\tau(t)$ from 0 is non-increasing as time t progresses. Since for any $\tau^* \in V(\mathcal{T}_{f,\bar{0}})$, $\tau^*(t) = 0$ for any t, $d(\tau(t), \tau^*(t)) \leq d(\tau(0), \tau^*(0))$. So given any $\epsilon > 0$, choose a δ' which is less than δ and ϵ. Then $V(\mathcal{H}_f)$ is Lyapunov stable with respect to δ', that is, any τ starting with in δ'-neighborhood of $First(V(\mathcal{T}_{f,\bar{0}}))$ (which is same as $V(First(\mathcal{T}_{f,\bar{0}}))$ in this case) remains with in a distance of ϵ from some trajectory in $V(\mathcal{T}_{f,\bar{0}})$.

Next, if V is a Lyapunov function, we need to show that in addition to the above, there is a neighborhood of $First(V(\mathcal{T}_{f,\bar{0}}))$ such that trajectories starting from it converge to some trajectory in $V(\mathcal{T}_{f,\bar{0}})$. Let Ω be the set associated with the Lyapunov function f such that $\dot{V}(x) < 0$ for all $x \in \Omega$. We will show that $V(\Omega)$ is such a neighborhood. It suffices to show that for any trajectory $\tau : [0, \infty) \to S_2$ starting from a state $x \in V(\Omega)$, τ converges to 0. Since V is positive and decreasing along any solution τ, it has a limit $c \geq 0$ as $t \to \infty$. If $c = 0$, then we are done. Otherwise, the solution cannot enter the set $\{x : V(x) < c\}$. In this case, the solution evolves in a compact set that does not contain the origin. Let the compact set be C. Let $d = max_{x \in C} \dot{V}(x)$; this number is well defined due to compactness of C and negative due to 5. We have $\dot{V} \leq d$, and hence $V(t) \leq V(0) + dt$. But then V will eventually become smaller than c, which is a contradiction.

Proof of Part (2): V restricted to a set containing a δ-neighborhood of $First(\mathcal{T}_{f,\bar{0}})$ is a uniformly continuous simulation. First observe that V is a simulation relation from $\mathcal{H}_f$ to $V(\mathcal{H}_f)$ by definition, and V is an upper semi-continuous function (since it is continuous). Therefore its inverse V^{-1} is also upper semi-continuous. Further, Ω is an open set around $\bar{0}$, hence $V(\Omega)$ is an open set around $V(\bar{0}) = 0$. Let δ be such that a closed ball of radius δ around 0 is contained in $V(\Omega)$. Then V restricted to the compact set, closed ball of radius δ around 0, is a uniformly continuous function and hence so is V^{-1}. Note that V restricted to the compact set is also a simulation owing to V being a decreasing function. V is semi-complete, since the first three conditions are trivially true and the fourth condition is true because of the previous observation.

Conclusion: Let V restricted to the closed ball of radius δ be the function V'. Since V' is a uniformly continuous simulation between $\mathcal{H}_1 = \mathcal{H}_f$ and $\mathcal{H}_2 = V(\mathcal{H}_f)$ and is semi-complete with respect to $\mathcal{T}_1 = \mathcal{T}_{f,\bar{0}}$ and $\mathcal{T}_2 = V(\mathcal{T}_2)$; and $\mathcal{H}_2$ is (Lyapunov) asymptotically stable, it follows from Theorem 1 that $\mathcal{H}_f = \mathcal{H}_1$ is (Lyapunov) asymptotically stable. $\square$

Probabilistic Invariance of Mixed Deterministic-Stochastic Dynamical Systems *

Sadegh Esmaeil Zadeh Soudjani
Delft Center for Systems & Control
TU Delft - Delft University of Technology
Delft, The Netherlands
S.EsmaeilZadehSoudjani@tudelft.nl

Alessandro Abate
Delft Center for Systems & Control
TU Delft - Delft University of Technology
Delft, The Netherlands
A.Abate@tudelft.nl

ABSTRACT
This work is concerned with the computation of probabilistic invariance (or safety) over a finite horizon for mixed deterministic-stochastic, discrete-time processes over a continuous state space. The models of interest are made up of two sets of (possibly coupled) variables: the first set of variables has associated dynamics that are described by deterministic maps (vector fields), whereas the complement has dynamics that are characterized by a stochastic kernel. The contribution shows that the probabilistic invariance problem can be separated into two parts: a deterministic reachability analysis, and a probabilistic invariance problem that depends on the outcome of the first. This technique shows advantages over a fully probabilistic approach, and allows putting forward an approximation algorithm with explicit error bounds. The technique is tested on a case study modeling a chemical reaction network.

Categories and Subject Descriptors
G.3 [**Probability and Statistics**]: Markov processes, Stochastic processes; G.4 [**Mathematical Software**]: Algorithm design and analysis, Verification

General Terms
Algorithms, Verification

Keywords
Invariance and safety, Mixed deterministic-stochastic dynamics, Finite approximations, Chemical reaction networks

*This work is supported by the European Commission MoVeS project FP7-ICT-2009-5 257005, by the European Commission Marie Curie grant MANTRAS 249295, by the European Commission NoE HYCON2 FP7-ICT-2009-5 257462, and by the NWO VENI grant 016.103.020.

1. INTRODUCTION
Given a stochastic process evolving over a state space and a set of interest (known as invariance domain, or safe set) that is a subset of the state space, the probabilistic invariance problem is concerned with the computation of the probability that a realization of the process, started anywhere on the state space, remains within the invariance set over a given time horizon.

Probabilistic invariance (or its dual, reachability) has been investigated for various models and with multiple techniques. Classical results on models with discrete state spaces are recapitulated in [3], whereas recent work deals with hybrid models in continuous- [5, 11] and discrete-time [2], respectively.

In this contribution, we are interested in working with processes that evolve in discrete time over a continuous state space (we shall consider an Euclidean vector space for the sake of simplicity, however the results are susceptible of being extended to hybrid spaces). Furthermore, we deal with models with explicit mixed deterministic-stochastic dynamics. With regards to the probabilistic invariance problem, we shall focus on the finite horizon case.

Mixed deterministic-stochastic dynamics naturally arise in a number of situations or application domains. For instance, this feature is expected in models with variables that take values within ranges that are dimensionally different. Of interest to this study, one such case is represented by a chemically reacting network in an environment with both rare and abundant species [8]. Mixed deterministic-stochastic models are composed of two complementary sets of variables, possibly coupled between each other. The first set of variables has associated dynamics that depend on deterministic maps, namely vector fields. The complement set has dynamics characterized by a stochastic kernel.

A naïve approach to the probabilistic invariance problem for mixed deterministic-stochastic models would merely tackle it as a safety verification instance over degenerate systems (by degenerate systems we refer to probabilistic laws that are concentrated deterministically, i.e. whose support consists of a single point). This would not only be a computationally expensive solution, but also lead to the inability to leverage computational techniques that apply exclusively to non-degenerate systems [1].

The contribution originally shows that the probabilistic invariance problem can be separated into two parts: a deterministic reachability analysis, and a probabilistic invariance problem that depends on the outcome of the first. Deterministic reachability analysis is a rather mature field of research with ample software tool support, whereas the second problem can harvest recent developments [2, 5, 11]. We argue that this decomposition approach can lead to computational improvements – for instance, whenever the first deterministic problem yields a "false" outcome (i.e., no states are deterministically safe over the given time horizon), no further probabilistic invariance calculation is necessary. This advantage of the proposed approach also leads to an approximation algorithm to compute the quantity of interest with explicit error bounds.

The contribution is structured as follows. Section 2 introduces the model class and the problem statement. Section 3 focuses on the properties of the value functions that characterize probabilistic invariance. Section 4 puts forward an approximation scheme for the computation of the desired quantities based on the discretization of the state space, and explicitly characterizes its error. Section 6 presents a case study from Systems Biology.

2. PRELIMINARIES

2.1 Model

We consider a stochastic process over a continuous state-space $\mathcal{S}$. We assume that $\mathcal{S}$ is endowed with a metric and is Borel measurable. We denote by $\mathcal{B}(\mathcal{S})$ the associated sigma algebra. The process is Markovian and driven in discrete time by the following mixed deterministic-stochastic dynamics:

$$\begin{cases} x_1(k+1) = f_1(x_1(k), x_2(k), h(k)) \\ x_2(k+1) = f_2(x_1(k), x_2(k)). \end{cases} \quad (1)$$

In model (1),

- $h(\cdot)$ is an i.i.d. random sequence with known distribution;

- $x_1(k) \in \mathbb{R}^{n_1}$ is a vector-valued random sequence with dynamics that are directly affected by the random variable $h(\cdot)$ at a given time;

- $x_2(k) \in \mathbb{R}^{n_2}$ is a vector-valued random sequence with dynamics characterized by a given deterministic vector field f_2.

Denote by

$$x(k) = \begin{bmatrix} x_1(k) \\ x_2(k) \end{bmatrix} \in \mathbb{R}^n = \mathcal{S}, \quad n = n_1 + n_2,$$

the state variable of the whole model in (1). The knowledge of the distribution of random variable $h(\cdot)$ at a given time allows to characterize a conditional stochastic kernel $T_x(\cdot|x)$ that assigns to each point $x \in \mathcal{S}$ a probability measure $T_x(\cdot|x)$, so that for any set $A \in \mathcal{B}(\mathcal{S}), P_x(x(k+1) \in A) = \int_A T_x(d\bar{x}|x(k) = x)$, where P_x denotes the conditional probability $P(\cdot|x)$, and P is a probability measure defined over the canonical sample space (with associated σ-algebra) for the above stochastic process [4].

The special structure of model (1) allows expressing the density function of the stochastic kernel T_x as follows:

$$t_x(\bar{x}|x) = t_x(\bar{x}_1|x_1, x_2)\delta(\bar{x}_2 - f_2(x_1, x_2)), \quad (2)$$

for $x = (x_1, x_2)^T$ and where $\delta(x - a)$ is the continuous Dirac delta function shifted at point a. The first term $t_x(\bar{x}_1|x_1, x_2)$

depends on the stochastic part of the dynamical model, whereas the second term $\delta(\bar{x}_2 - f_2(x_1, x_2))$ hinges on the deterministic vector field.

2.2 Problem statement

Consider a compact Borel set $A \subset \mathcal{B}(\mathcal{S})$. We are interested to solve the following probabilistic invariance problem over a finite time horizon $[0, N]$: to characterize and compute the probability that an execution with an initial condition $x_0 \in \mathcal{S}$ remains within set A during the whole time horizon, namely

$$p_{x_0}(A) \doteq P\{x(k) \in A, \forall k \in [0, N]|x(0) = x_0\}. \quad (3)$$

A characterization of the problem in (3) is addressed in the following result [2].

PROPOSITION 1 (BELLMAN RECURSION). *Introduce functions $V_k : \mathcal{S} \to [0, 1], k \in [0, N]$, and define them backward-recursively as follows:*

$$V_k(x) = \mathbb{I}_A(x) \int_{\mathcal{S}} V_{k+1}(x_{k+1})T_x(dx_{k+1}|x), \quad (4)$$

where $V_N(x)$ is initialized as the indicator function of set A: $V_N(x) = \mathbb{I}_A(x)$. Then the solution of problem (3) is $p_{x_0}(A) = V_0(x_0)$, for any $x_0 \in \mathcal{S}$.

A solution of $p_{x_0}(A)$ is seldom analytic, which warrants the development of techniques and algorithms to compute an approximation of it. The work in [1] puts forward a discretization approach with proven error bounds, under continuity conditions of the stochastic kernel T_x. Such bounds are refined in [7], by leveraging an adaptive partitioning approach with improved (local) error computations.

The goal of this contribution is first to tailor problem (3) to the structure of model (1), then to provide a technique to compute the solution of (3) by a numerical scheme with associated errors.

3. PROPERTIES OF THE VALUE FUNCTIONS

3.1 On the support of the value functions

With focus on the recursion step in Equation (4), let us define the support of function V_k as:

$$supp(V_k) = \{x \in \mathcal{S}|V_k(x) \neq 0\}, \quad k \in [0, N-1],$$

and $supp(V_N) = A$. The support of the value functions V_k plays an important role in the problem definition, as elaborated in the following observations:

- since $\forall x \notin A, V_k(x) = 0$, then

$$\forall k \in [0, N], \quad supp(V_k) \subseteq A;$$

- by direct inductive argument, it can be shown that

$$\forall k \in [0, N-1], \forall x \in A, \quad 0 \leq V_k(x) \leq V_{k+1}(x),$$

which leads to conclude that

$$supp(V_k) \subseteq supp(V_{k+1}).$$

Notice that, because of the constant value of the cost function on the complement of the set A, the integral in (4) is effectively computed only over A (rather than on $\mathcal{S}$). Furthermore, the observations above suggest that it is possible to adapt the integration domain in (4) to the actual support of the value functions, as follows:

$$V_k(x) = V_k(x_1, x_2) = \qquad (5)$$

$$\int_{supp(V_{k+1})} V_{k+1}(\bar{x}_1, \bar{x}_2) t_x(\bar{x}_1 | x_1, x_2) \delta(\bar{x}_2 - f_2(x_1, x_2)) d\bar{x}_2 d\bar{x}_1,$$

where we have used the expression in (2). Characterizing the sets $supp(V_k), k \in [0, N-1)$, becomes thus critical for the optimization of the original recursion in (4). However, in general it is complicated to exactly determine the sets $supp(V_k)$, in particular due to the need to characterize $supp(t_x(\cdot | x))$ as a function of x.

To mitigate this complication, let us introduce two projection maps as follows:

$$\Pi_1 : \mathbb{R}^n \to \mathbb{R}^{n_1} \qquad \Pi_2 : \mathbb{R}^n \to \mathbb{R}^{n_2}$$
$$\Pi_1 \left(\begin{bmatrix} x_1 \\ x_2 \end{bmatrix} \right) = x_1, \qquad \Pi_2 \left(\begin{bmatrix} x_1 \\ x_2 \end{bmatrix} \right) = x_2.$$

We can determine an over-approximation of the sets $supp(V_k)$ as follows:

$$supp(V_k) \subseteq$$
$$\{(x_1, x_2) \in supp(V_{k+1}) | f_2(x_1, x_2) \in \Pi_2(supp(V_{k+1}))\}.$$

Notice that in general the above inclusion is strict. This suggests to over-approximate the sets $supp(V_k)$ by Γ_k, as defined by the following recursive procedure:

$$\begin{cases} \Gamma_N = A, \\ \Gamma_k = \{(x_1, x_2) \in \Gamma_{k+1} | f_2(x_1, x_2) \in \Pi_2(\Gamma_{k+1})\}. \end{cases} \qquad (6)$$

The sequence $\{\Gamma_k\}_{k=0}^N$ is endowed with the following facts:

- $supp(V_k) \subseteq \Gamma_k$, then $\forall x_0 \notin \Gamma_0, p_{x_0}(A) = 0$;

- $A = \Gamma_N \supseteq \Gamma_{N-1} \supseteq \Gamma_{N-2} \supseteq ... \supseteq \Gamma_0$;

- if there exists a positive integer $k_0 \leq N$ such that $\Gamma_{k_0} = \Gamma_{k_0+1}$, then for all $0 \leq k \leq k_0, \Gamma_k = \Gamma_{k_0+1}$;

- if there exists a positive integer $k_0 \leq N$ such that $\Pi_2(\Gamma_{k_0}) = \Pi_2(\Gamma_{k_0+1})$, then for all $0 \leq k \leq k_0, \Gamma_k = \Gamma_{k_0}$.

These properties highlight the dependence of the sets Γ_k (we will denote them simply as *support sets*) on the deterministic vector field f_2, particularly over the points that are mapped by f_2 outside of the support sets.

3.2 Simplifying the Bellman recursion

With focus on the support sets introduced in (6), define additionally the following quantities: for any $x_2 \in \Pi_2(\Gamma_k)$,

$$\Gamma_k^1(x_2) = \{x_1 \in \Pi_1(\Gamma_k) | (x_1, x_2) \in \Gamma_k\}.$$

Recall the recursive formula in (5) for V_k. By definition of Γ_k, we know that V_k is equal to zero outside of the set Γ_k. We can then simplify the recursive formula to the following:

$$V_k(x_1, x_2) = \int_{\Gamma_{k+1}^1(f_2(x_1, x_2))} V_{k+1}(\bar{x}_1, f_2(x_1, x_2)) t_x(\bar{x}_1 | x_1, x_2) d\bar{x}_1, \quad (7)$$

for any $(x_1, x_2) \in \Gamma_k$. This formulation characterizes the value functions V_k in terms of the sets Γ_k.

3.3 Continuity of the value functions

We are interested in establishing the continuity of the value functions over their support. To achieve this, the following set of assumptions is needed.

ASSUMPTION 1. *Suppose that the kernel T_x admits a density function t_x as in (2). Furthermore, suppose that the density function t_x, the vector field f_2, and the parametrized sets $\Gamma_k^1(x_2)$ satisfy the following conditions:*

1. $|t_x(\bar{x}_1 | x_1, x_2) - t_x(\bar{x}_1 | x_1', x_2')| \leq h_1 \| (x_1, x_2) - (x_1', x_2') \|$, *for any $\bar{x}_1 \in \Pi_1(A)$ and $(x_1, x_2), (x_1', x_2') \in A$;*

2. $\| f_2(x_1, x_2) - f_2(x_1', x_2') \| \leq h_2 \| (x_1, x_2) - (x_1', x_2') \|$, *for any $(x_1, x_2), (x_1', x_2') \in A$;*

3. $\mathcal{L}(\Gamma_k^1(x_2) \triangle \Gamma_k^1(x_2')) \leq \theta_k \| x_2 - x_2' \|$, *for any $x_2, x_2' \in \Pi_2(\Gamma_k), k \in [0, N]$,*

where h_1, h_2, θ_k are finite constants. Here $\mathcal{L}$ is the Lebesgue measure over $\mathbb{R}^{n_1}$, whereas $\triangle$ denotes the symmetric difference of two sets.

The first two are continuity assumptions on the density and on the vector field. The third assumption is a regularity requirement on the variation of the (projection along the x_1 variables of the) support sets, as a function of the x_2 coordinates. Intuitively, this last assumption depends on the actual shape of the support sets Γ_k and on f_2 – as such, it has to hold over the entire time horizon $[0, N]$.

THEOREM 1. *If Assumption 1 is valid, then the value functions V_k are Lipschitz continuous on Γ_k, namely $\forall (x_1, x_2), (x_1', x_2') \in \Gamma_k$,*

$$|V_k(x_1, x_2) - V_k(x_1', x_2')| \leq \lambda_k \| (x_1, x_2) - (x_1', x_2') \|,$$

where the finite Lipschitz constant λ_k satisfies the recursive formula:

$$\lambda_k = (h_1 L_{k+1} + M h_2 \theta_{k+1}) + h_2 M^\star \lambda_{k+1}, \quad 0 \leq k < N,$$

initialized with $\lambda_N = 0$, and where:

$$L_k = \mathcal{L}(\Pi_1(\Gamma_k)),$$
$$M = \sup \{t_x(\bar{x}_1 | x_1, x_2) | x_1, x_2 \in A, \bar{x}_1 \in \Pi_1(A)\},$$
$$M^\star = \sup_{(x_1, x_2) \in A} \int_{\Pi_1(A)} t_x(\bar{x}_1 | x_1, x_2) d\bar{x}_1.$$

PROOF. Since $V_N(x) = \mathbb{I}_A(x)$, it follows that $\lambda_N = 0$. Now suppose that the statement holds at step $k+1$: $\forall (x_1, x_2), (x_1', x_2') \in \Gamma_{k+1}$,

$$|V_{k+1}(x_1, x_2) - V_{k+1}(x_1', x_2')| \leq \lambda_{k+1} \| (x_1, x_2) - (x_1', x_2') \|.$$

Select any two states $(x_1, x_2), (x_1', x_2') \in \Gamma_k$ and express the inequality via (7) as:

$$|V_k(x_1, x_2) - V_k(x_1', x_2')| =$$

$$\left| \int_{\Gamma_{k+1}^1(f_2(x_1, x_2))} V_{k+1}(\bar{x}_1, f_2(x_1, x_2)) t_x(\bar{x}_1 | x_1, x_2) d\bar{x}_1 - \int_{\Gamma_{k+1}^1(f_2(x_1', x_2'))} V_{k+1}(\bar{x}_1, f_2(x_1', x_2')) t_x(\bar{x}_1 | x_1', x_2') d\bar{x}_1 \right|.$$

To ease the notational burden, let us introduce sets $A^\star \doteq \Gamma^1_{k+1}(f_2(x_1, x_2))$ and $B^\star \doteq \Gamma^1_{k+1}(f_2(x'_1, x'_2))$. Then:

$$|V_k(x_1, x_2) - V_k(x'_1, x'_2)| =$$

$$= \left| \int_{A^\star} V_{k+1}(\bar{x}_1, f_2(x_1, x_2)) t_x(\bar{x}_1 | x_1, x_2) d\bar{x}_1 \right.$$

$$\left. - \int_{B^\star} V_{k+1}(\bar{x}_1, f_2(x'_1, x'_2)) t_x(\bar{x}_1 | x'_1, x'_2) d\bar{x}_1 \right|$$

$$\leq \left| \int_{A^\star \cap B^\star} V_{k+1}(\bar{x}_1, f_2(x_1, x_2)) t_x(\bar{x}_1 | x_1, x_2) d\bar{x}_1 \right.$$

$$\left. - \int_{A^\star \cap B^\star} V_{k+1}(\bar{x}_1, f_2(x'_1, x'_2)) t_x(\bar{x}_1 | x'_1, x'_2) d\bar{x}_1 \right|$$

$$+ \left| \int_{A^\star \setminus B^\star} V_{k+1}(\bar{x}_1, f_2(x_1, x_2)) t_x(\bar{x}_1 | x_1, x_2) d\bar{x}_1 \right.$$

$$\left. - \int_{B^\star \setminus A^\star} V_{k+1}(\bar{x}_1, f_2(x'_1, x'_2)) t_x(\bar{x}_1 | x'_1, x'_2) d\bar{x}_1 \right|.$$

The above inequality is made up of two main terms, of which the first can be upper bounded as follows:

$$\left| \int_{A^\star \cap B^\star} V_{k+1}(\bar{x}_1, f_2(x_1, x_2)) t_x(\bar{x}_1 | x_1, x_2) d\bar{x}_1 \right.$$

$$\left. - \int_{A^\star \cap B^\star} V_{k+1}(\bar{x}_1, f_2(x'_1, x'_2)) t_x(\bar{x}_1 | x'_1, x'_2) d\bar{x}_1 \right|$$

$$\leq \left| \int_{A^\star \cap B^\star} V_{k+1}(\bar{x}_1, f_2(x_1, x_2)) \left[t_x(\bar{x}_1 | x_1, x_2) - t_x(\bar{x}_1 | x'_1, x'_2) \right] d\bar{x}_1 \right.$$

$$+ \int_{A^\star \cap B^\star} t_x(\bar{x}_1 | x'_1, x'_2) \cdot$$

$$\left. \left[V_{k+1}(\bar{x}_1, f_2(x_1, x_2)) - V_{k+1}(\bar{x}_1, f_2(x'_1, x'_2)) \right] d\bar{x}_1 \right|$$

$$\leq \int_{A^\star \cap B^\star} V_{k+1}(\bar{x}_1, f_2(x_1, x_2)) \left| t_x(\bar{x}_1 | x_1, x_2) - t_x(\bar{x}_1 | x'_1, x'_2) \right| d\bar{x}_1$$

$$+ \int_{A^\star \cap B^\star} t_x(\bar{x}_1 | x'_1, x'_2) \cdot$$

$$\left| V_{k+1}(\bar{x}_1, f_2(x_1, x_2)) - V_{k+1}(\bar{x}_1, f_2(x'_1, x'_2)) \right| d\bar{x}_1$$

$$\leq h_1 \| (x_1, x_2) - (x'_1, x'_2) \| \mathcal{L} \left(A^\star \cap B^\star \right)$$

$$+ \lambda_{k+1} \int_{A^\star \cap B^\star} \| (\bar{x}_1, f_2(x_1, x_2)) - (\bar{x}_1, f_2(x'_1, x'_2)) \| t_x(\bar{x}_1 | x'_1, x'_2) d\bar{x}_1$$

$$\leq h_1 \| (x_1, x_2) - (x'_1, x'_2) \| \mathcal{L} \left(\Pi_1(\Gamma_{k+1}) \right)$$

$$+ \lambda_{k+1} h_2 \| (x_1, x_2) - (x'_1, x'_2) \| \int_{A^\star \cap B^\star} t_x(\bar{x}_1 | x'_1, x'_2) d\bar{x}_1$$

$$\leq (h_1 L_{k+1} + h_2 M^\star \lambda_{k+1}) \| (x_1, x_2) - (x'_1, x'_2) \|.$$

Recalling that the value functions take values in the interval $[0, 1]$, the second term is upper bounded as follows:

$$\left| \int_{A^\star \setminus B^\star} V_{k+1}(\bar{x}_1, f_2(x_1, x_2)) t_x(\bar{x}_1 | x_1, x_2) d\bar{x}_1 \right.$$

$$\left. - \int_{B^\star \setminus A^\star} V_{k+1}(\bar{x}_1, f_2(x'_1, x'_2)) t_x(\bar{x}_1 | x'_1, x'_2) d\bar{x}_1 \right|$$

$$\leq \left| \int_{A^\star \setminus B^\star} V_{k+1}(\bar{x}_1, f_2(x_1, x_2)) t_x(\bar{x}_1 | x_1, x_2) d\bar{x}_1 \right.$$

$$+ \left| \int_{B^\star \setminus A^\star} V_{k+1}(\bar{x}_1, f_2(x'_1, x'_2)) t_x(\bar{x}_1 | x'_1, x'_2) d\bar{x}_1 \right|$$

$$\leq M \mathcal{L}(A^\star \setminus B^\star) + M \mathcal{L}(B^\star \setminus A^\star) = M \mathcal{L}(A^\star \triangle B^\star)$$

$$= M \mathcal{L} \left(\Gamma^1_{k+1}(f_2(x_1, x_2)) \triangle \Gamma^1_{k+1}(f_2(x'_1, x'_2)) \right)$$

$$\leq M \theta_{k+1} \| f_2(x_1, x_2) - f_2(x'_1, x'_2) \|$$

$$\leq M \theta_{k+1} h_2 \| (x_1, x_2) - (x'_1, x'_2) \|.$$

Collecting the two bounds, we obtain:

$$|V_k(x_1, x_2) - V_k(x'_1, x'_2)|$$

$$\leq (h_1 L_{k+1} + h_2 M^\star \lambda_{k+1}) \| (x_1, x_2) - (x'_1, x'_2) \|$$

$$+ M \theta_{k+1} h_2 \| (x_1, x_2) - (x^\star_1, x^\star_2) \|$$

$$= (h_1 L_{k+1} + h_2 M^\star \lambda_{k+1} + M \theta_{k+1} h_2) \| (x_1, x_2) - (x'_1, x'_2) \|$$

$$= \lambda_k \| (x_1, x_2) - (x'_1, x'_2) \|,$$

which completes the proof. $\square$

Notice that $0 \leq M^\star \leq 1$ and that the quantities M and M* (hence, the overall bound) can be further refined to functions of the time step k.

4. APPROXIMATION SCHEME AND QUANTIFICATION OF THE ERROR

In this section we propose an approximation scheme to perform the computations in (7), and furthermore explicitly quantify its error. To keep the notations light, in (7) we replace the generic integration domain $\Gamma^1_{k+1}(f_2(x_1, x_2))$ by $\Pi_1(A)$ – however, the procedure applies similarly to the general case.

4.1 Approximation scheme for computation

Select an arbitrary partition of the invariant set $A = \cup^p_{i=1} A_i$, $A_{i_1} \cap A_{i_2} = \emptyset$, $i_1, i_2 = 1, \ldots, p$, $i_1 \neq i_2$, where p represents the cardinality. The whole state space $\mathcal{S}$ can be also partitioned by adding the complement set $A_{p+1} = \mathcal{S} \setminus A$. Pick any point $x^i = (x^i_1, x^i_2) \in A_i, i = 1, \ldots, p+1$. Notice that $\Pi_1(A) = \Pi_1(\cup^p_{i=1} A_i) = \cup^p_{i=1} \Pi_1(A_i)$, however the sets $\Pi_1(A_i)$ produce a cover (in general not a partition) of the set $\Pi_1(A)$. To make up for this, we can additionally select an arbitrary partition $\Pi_1(A) = \cup^q_{j=1} X_j$ for the projection of the safe set along the first variable. This allows to express, $\forall (x_1, x_2) \in A$:

$$V_k(x_1, x_2) = \int_{\Pi_1(A)} V_{k+1}(\bar{x}_1, f_2(x_1, x_2)) t_x(\bar{x}_1 | x_1, x_2) d\bar{x}_1$$

$$= \sum^q_{j=1} \int_{X_j} V_{k+1}(\bar{x}_1, f_2(x_1, x_2)) t_x(\bar{x}_1 | x_1, x_2) d\bar{x}_1.$$

Let us now approximate the value functions V_k by piecewise constant ones $\bar{V}_k$, which are computed over the selected points $\{x^i \in A_i\}^{p+1}_{i=1}$, as follows:

$$\bar{V}_k(x_1, x_2) = \sum^{p+1}_{i=1} \bar{V}_k(x^i_1, x^i_2) \mathbb{I}_{A_i}(x_1, x_2),$$

$\forall (x_1, x_2) \in A$. Denote $V^i_k \doteq \bar{V}_k(x^i_1, x^i_2)$. These functions are initialized as $V^i_N = 1, i = 1, \ldots, p, V^{p+1}_N = 0$, and recursively computed as follows:

$$V^i_k = \sum^q_{j=1} \int_{X_j} \bar{V}_{k+1}(\bar{x}_1, f_2(x^i_1, x^i_2)) t_x(\bar{x}_1 | x^i_1, x^i_2) d\bar{x}_1.$$

In this formulation the values of $\bar{V}_{k+1}$ over the hyperplane $X_j \times \{f_2(x^i_1, x^i_2)\}$ are needed. In order to implement the procedure in a discrete manner, the function $\bar{V}_{k+1}$ should be constant over this hyperplane. This feature is achieved by raising the following assumption on the partition sets X_j of $\Pi_1(A)$:

$$\forall i, j \;\exists i' : \; X_j \times \{f_2(x_1^i, x_2^i)\} \subseteq A_{i'}.$$

Notice that this assumption does not depend on the step k, and is immediately satisfiable by selecting a partition for A uniformly along the first variable x_1, while considering non-redundant sets of $\Pi_1(A_i)$ as a partition for $\Pi_1(A)$.

Consider a map $i' = R(i, j)$, which assigns to each partition set X_j and value $f_2^i \doteq f_2(x_1^i, x_2^i)$ the corresponding partition set $A_{i'}$ containing $X_j \times f_2^i$. Having this map, we are able to formulate the discrete version of our continuous recursive procedure (7) as:

$$V_k^i = \sum_{j=1}^{q} V_{k+1}^{i'} \int_{X_j} t_x(\bar{x}_1 | x_1^i, x_2^i) d\bar{x}_1. \qquad (8)$$

To recapitulate, the following steps are required to implement the algorithm:

- Select a partition $\cup_i A_i$ of the invariant set A and the associated partition $\cup_j X_j$ of $\Pi_1(A)$;

- Compute the map $i' = R(i, j)$ based on the selected partitions;

- Compute the marginal matrix P with the entries: $P_{ij} = \int_{X_j} t_x(\bar{x}_1 | x_1^i, x_2^i) d\bar{x}_1$;

- Compute recursively: $V_k^i = \sum_{j=1}^{q} P_{ij} V_{k+1}^{i'}$ as in (8), initialized by $V_N^i = 1$;

- Use the support set Γ_k at step k to set the required entries equal to zero, namely $V_k^i = 0$ for all i such that $A_i \subset \mathcal{S} \backslash \Gamma_k$.

Note that in the above steps we allow for additional approximation error, since there exist partition sets that may cross the boundaries of the support sets, and which are not contained in neither Γ_k nor $\mathcal{S} \backslash \Gamma_k$. In order to avoid this error, we should further adapt the selected partition to the boundaries of support sets.

4.2 Bound on the approximation error

THEOREM 2. *Suppose we approximate the value functions V_k by the piecewise constant functions $\bar{V}_k$, as described in the previous section. Then the approximation error is upper bounded, $\forall (x_1, x_2) \in \Gamma_k$, by*

$$|V_k(x_1, x_2) - \bar{V}_k(x_1, x_2)| \leq E_k,$$

where

$$E_k = \lambda_k \delta + M^\star E_{k+1},$$

initialized by $E_N = 0$, and where δ is the partition size of $\cup_{i=1}^{p} A_i$ (namely, $\delta = \max_{i=1}^{p} \delta_i$, where δ_i is the diameter of A_i), λ_k is the Lipschitz constant of the value function V_k, and $M^\star$ is defined as in Theorem 1.

PROOF. We reason again by induction. The statement holds for $k = N$, since $V_N = \bar{V}_N = \mathbb{I}_A$. Suppose now that it is valid for step $k + 1$. Noting that $\forall (x_1, x_2) \in A, \exists i : (x_1, x_2) \in A_i$, then:

$$|V_k(x_1, x_2) - \bar{V}_k(x_1, x_2)| = |V_k(x_1, x_2) - \bar{V}_k(x_1^i, x_2^i)|$$

$$\leq |V_k(x_1, x_2) - V_k(x_1^i, x_2^i)| + |V_k(x_1^i, x_2^i) - \bar{V}_k(x_1^i, x_2^i)|$$

$$\leq \lambda_k \delta + \left| \sum_{j=1}^{p} \int_{X_j} V_{k+1}(\bar{x}_1, f_2(x_1^i, x_2^i)) t_x(\bar{x}_1 | x_1^i, x_2^i) d\bar{x}_1 \right.$$

$$\left. - \sum_{j=1}^{p} \int_{X_j} \bar{V}_{k+1}(\bar{x}_1, f_2(x_1^i, x_2^i)) t_x(\bar{x}_1 | x_1^i, x_2^i) d\bar{x}_1 \right|$$

$$\leq \lambda_k \delta + \sum_{j=1}^{p} \int_{X_j} \left| V_{k+1}(\bar{x}_1, f_2(x_1^i, x_2^i)) - \bar{V}_{k+1}(\bar{x}_1, f_2(x_1^i, x_2^i)) \right| \cdot$$

$$t_x(\bar{x}_1 | x_1^i, x_2^i) d\bar{x}_1$$

$$\leq \lambda_k \delta + \sum_{j=1}^{p} \int_{X_j} E_{k+1} t_x(\bar{x}_1 | x_1^i, x_2^i) d\bar{x}_1$$

$$\leq \lambda_k \delta + E_{k+1} \int_{\Pi_1(A)} t_x(\bar{x}_1 | x_1^i, x_2^i) d\bar{x}_1$$

$$\leq \lambda_k \delta + M^\star E_{k+1},$$

which equals to E_k. $\square$

Note that the constant $M^\star$ can be replaced by a decreasing finite sequence $\{M_k^\star\}_{k=N}^1$, which yields a lower abstraction error.

5. AFFINE DETERMINISTIC DYNAMICS ON POLYTOPIC INVARIANT SET

It is in general difficult to find an explicit and computable bound for Condition 3 in Assumption 1. Such a bound depends directly on the shape of the sets Γ_k. However, a bound can be derived for models with deterministic dynamics that are affine and when the invariant set is a convex polytope. Under these conditions, the following lemma gives an explicit representation for the invariant sets Γ_k.

LEMMA 1. *Suppose that the deterministic dynamics in (1) are characterized by affine functions, namely:*

$$f_2(x_1, x_2) = A_1 x_1 + A_2 x_2 + A_3,$$

where $A_1 \in \mathbb{R}^{n_2 \times n_1}, A_2 \in \mathbb{R}^{n_2 \times n_2}, A_3 \in \mathbb{R}^{n_2 \times 1}$. Furthermore, suppose that the invariant set A is a (bounded) convex polytope, characterized by the following set of linear inequalities:

$$A = \left\{ (x_1, x_2) \in \mathbb{R}^n | A_N^1 x_1 + A_N^2 x_2 \leq B_N \right\}.$$

Then the support sets $\Gamma_k, k = N - 1, \ldots, 0$, are also bounded convex polytopes.

PROOF. Based on Equation (6), we can compute the sets $\Gamma_k, k = 0, \ldots, N - 1$, as:

$$\Gamma_k = f_2^{-1}(\Pi_2(\Gamma_{k+1})) \cap \Gamma_{k+1}.$$

Suppose Γ_{k+1} is compact and convex then $\Pi_2(\Gamma_{k+1})$ is also a compact and convex set since the operator Π_2 is linear. Additionally, as the function f_2 is linear (and continuous), then $f_2^{-1}(\Pi_2(\Gamma_{k+1}))$ is also compact and convex.

Suppose now that set Γ_{k+1} is a polytope in $\mathbb{R}^n$, characterized by the following set of linear inequalities:

$$\Gamma_{k+1} = \left\{ (x_1, x_2) \in \mathbb{R}^n | A_{k+1}^1 x_1 + A_{k+1}^2 x_2 \leq B_{k+1} \right\}.$$

Then $\Pi_2(\Gamma_{k+1})$ is also a polytope in n_2 dimensions, characterized by:

$$\Pi_2(\Gamma_{k+1}) = \{x_2 \in \mathbb{R}^{n_2} | C_{k+1}x_2 \le D_{k+1}\}.$$

Techniques to perform a perpendicular projection of bounded polytopes allow to obtain $\Pi_2(\Gamma_{k+1})$ from Γ_{k+1}. [9] proved that the polyhedral projection is equivalent to the feasibility of a parametric linear programming problem. The MPT toolbox [12] constructs a vertex representation of Γ_{k+1}, having its half-space representation (vertex enumeration problem); it then projects these vertices based on the Π_2 operator; and finally it obtains a half-space representation of $\Pi_2(\Gamma_{k+1})$ from its vertex representation (facet enumeration problem).

Having obtained matrices C_{k+1}, D_{k+1} expressing $\Pi_2(\Gamma_{k+1})$, we can find Γ_k as follows:

$$
\begin{aligned}
\Gamma_k &= \{(x_1, x_2) \in \Gamma_{k+1} | f_2(x_1, x_2) \in \Pi_2(\Gamma_{k+1})\} \\
&= \{(x_1, x_2) \in \Gamma_{k+1} | C_{k+1}f_2(x_1, x_2) \le D_{k+1}\} \\
&= \{(x_1, x_2) \in \Gamma_{k+1} | C_{k+1}(A_1 x_1 + A_2 x_2 + A_3) \le D_{k+1}\} \\
&= \{(x_1, x_2) \in \Gamma_{k+1} | C_{k+1}A_1 x_1 + C_{k+1}A_2 x_2 \le \\
&\qquad\qquad (D_{k+1} - C_{k+1}A_3)\}.
\end{aligned}
$$

Then Γ_k is a convex and bounded polytope with the following half-space representation:

$$\Gamma_k = \{(x_1, x_2) \in \mathbb{R}^n | A_k^1 x_1 + A_k^2 x_2 \le B_k\}, \qquad (9)$$

where:

$$
A_k^1 = \begin{bmatrix} C_{k+1}A_1 \\ A_{k+1}^1 \end{bmatrix}, A_k^2 = \begin{bmatrix} C_{k+1}A_2 \\ A_{k+1}^2 \end{bmatrix},
$$
$$
B_k = \begin{bmatrix} D_{k+1} - C_{k+1}A_3 \\ B_{k+1} \end{bmatrix}.
$$

Note that this representation is not unique: it is possible to eliminate redundant half-spaces in the representation of Γ_k in each step. $\square$

The following theorem derives the bound for Condition 3 in Assumption 1.

THEOREM 3. *Suppose Γ_k is a bounded convex polytope with the representation in (9). Then the sets $\Gamma_k^1(x_2)$ are polytopes in $\mathbb{R}^{n_1}$, which satisfy the Condition 3 in Assumption 1 with the following constant:*

$$\theta_k = \sum_{i=1, A_k^1(i) \ne 0}^{m_k} s_k(i) \frac{\|A_k^2(i)\|}{\|A_k^1(i)\|}.$$

The vectors $A_k^1(i)$ and $A_k^2(i)$ represent the ith row of A_k^1 and A_k^2, respectively. The constant m_k accounts for the number of inequalities in the half-space representation of Γ_k, i.e. m_k is equal to the number of rows of A_k^1 (we do not account for the rows of A_k^1 that are equal to the zero vector). The constant $s_k(i)$ is computed as follows:

1. *if $n_1 = 1$ then $s_k(i) = 1$.*

2. *if $n_1 \ge 2$, project $\Pi_1(\Gamma_k)$ along the normal to the ith hyperplane, i.e. along vector $A_k^1(i)$. The result is a polytope in $\mathbb{R}^{n_1-1}$, namely $\Pi^\perp(\Pi_1(\Gamma_k))$. Then $s_k(i) = \mathcal{L}(\Pi^\perp(\Pi_1(\Gamma_k)))$ or any upper bound for this Lebesgue measure.*

PROOF. Recall the definition of $\Gamma_k^1(x_2)$: for any $x_2 \in \Pi_2(\Gamma_k)$

$$
\begin{aligned}
\Gamma_k^1(x_2) &= \{x_1 \in \Pi_1(\Gamma_k) | (x_1, x_2) \in \Gamma_k\} \\
&= \{x_1 \in \mathbb{R}^{n_1} | A_1^k x_1 \le B_k - A_k^2 x_2\}.
\end{aligned}
$$

For any fixed x_2 the set $\Gamma_k^1(x_2)$ is represented by a set of linear inequalities, which again characterizes a polytope. Each facet of the polytope is represented by one row of the above half-space representation:

$$A_1^k(i)x_1 \le B_k(i) - A_k^2(i)x_2, \quad i = 1, \ldots, m_k.$$

The normal vector to this hyperplane in $\mathbb{R}^{n_1}$ is independent of parameter x_2. Varying x_2 to x_2', we obtain two parallel hyperplanes in $\mathbb{R}^{n_1}$. The volume bounded within the two hyperplanes is proportional to their distance d:

$$
\begin{aligned}
d &= \frac{|(B_k(i) - A_k^2(i)x_2) - (B_k(i) - A_k^2(i)x_2')|}{\|A_k^1(i)\|} \\
&= \frac{|A_k^2(i)(x_2 - x_2')|}{\|A_k^1(i)\|}.
\end{aligned}
$$

Suppose the values of $s_k(i)$ are defined as in the statement. Then:

$$
\begin{aligned}
\mathcal{L}&(\Gamma_k^1(x_2) \triangle \Gamma_k^1(x_2')) \\
&\le \sum_{i=1}^{m_k} s_k(i) \frac{|A_2^k(i)(x_2 - x_2')|}{\|A_1^k(i)\|} \\
&= \sum_{i=1}^{m_k} s_k(i) \frac{\|A_2^k(i)\|}{\|A_1^k(i)\|} \|(x_2 - x_2')\| \\
&= \theta_k \|(x_2 - x_2')\|,
\end{aligned}
$$

which completes the proof. $\square$

For the sake of completeness, let us explicitly derive the Lipschitz constant required for Condition 2 in Assumption 1, given affine deterministic dynamics.

PROPOSITION 2. *The Lipschitz constant of the affine function $f_2(x_1, x_2) = A_1 x_1 + A_2 x_2 + A_3$ is equal to:*

$$h_2 = \|[A_1, A_2]\|_2.$$

PROOF.

$$
\begin{aligned}
\|f_2(x_1, x_2) - f_2(x_1', x_2')\| &= \|A_1(x_1 - x_1') + A_2(x_2 - x_2')\| \\
&= \|[A_1, A_2][x_1 - x_1', x_2 - x_2']^T\| \\
&\le \|[A_1, A_2]\|_2 \|(x_1, x_2) - (x_1', x_2')\|.
\end{aligned}
$$

$\square$

6. CASE STUDY

This section applies the probabilistic invariance problem and the results derived above to a chemical reaction network characterized by species with heterogeneous concentrations. The dynamics of chemically reacting environments can be described by the general Chemical Master Equation (CME) [8], which unfortunately has seldom an analytical solution and is usually quite hard to integrate. Alternatively, species dynamics in time are studied via the Stochastic Simulation Algorithm (SSA) [8], which is a computational scheme that has attracted much research. Among the various approaches to approximate and speed up the SSA, the work in [10] has

Table 1: Parameters for the case study, taken from [6], and expressed in $[s^{-1}]$.

investigated one that is based on the use of first- and second-order approximations: species that are abundant in the environment are associated with deterministic dynamics (ordinary differential equations), whereas species with negligible numbers are given probabilistic dynamics (stochastic differential equations).

The underlying stoichiometry, reaction and degradation rates are directly taken from [6] and summarized in Table 1. Let us introduce the following vector:

$$x = \begin{bmatrix} D & D^* & M & P \end{bmatrix}^T,$$

describing the (low) concentration of an inactive and active gene (D and D^* respectively), as well as the (relatively abundant) concentration of m-RNA (M) and of a protein (P). The continuous dynamics are described by the following stochastic differential equation:

$$dx = f(x)dt + \sigma(x)dW.$$

Time is discretized with sampling interval Δ, according to an Euler-Maruyama, first-order scheme, obtaining:

$$x(k+1) = x(k) + f(x(k))\Delta + \sigma(x(k))\sqrt{\Delta}W(k),$$

where $f(x) = Ax$ and

$$A = \begin{bmatrix} -k_a & k_d & 0 & 0 \\ k_a & -k_d & 0 & 0 \\ 0 & k_r & -\gamma_r & 0 \\ 0 & 0 & k_p & -\gamma_p \end{bmatrix},$$

and

$$\sigma(x) = \begin{bmatrix} -\sqrt{k_a D} & \sqrt{k_d D^*} \\ \sqrt{k_a D} & -\sqrt{k_d D^*} \\ 0 & 0 \\ 0 & 0 \end{bmatrix},$$

and finally $W(k) = [W_1(k), W_2(k)]^T$, and $W_i(k), i = 1, 2, k \in \mathbb{N} \cup \{0\}$, are independent standard Normal random variables, which are also independent of the initial condition of the process. The steady-state values for the dynamics are estimated as in [10]:

- $P_{ss} = 65\,[nM] \Rightarrow M_{ss} = \frac{\gamma_p}{k_p}P_{ss}$,

- $D_{ss} = D_{ss}^* = \frac{\gamma_r}{k_r}M_{ss} = \frac{\gamma_r}{k_r}\frac{\gamma_p}{k_p}P_{ss} = \frac{\gamma_p}{bk_r}P_{ss}$.

Since the dynamics of D and D^* are coupled, it is possible to eliminate the variable D, which leads to the following dynamical system:

$$x_1(k+1) = (1 - k_d\Delta - k_a\Delta)x_1(k) + 2k_a\Delta D_{ss}^*$$
$$+ \sqrt{2k_a\Delta D_{ss}^*}W(k)$$
$$x_2(k+1) = k_r\Delta x_1(k) + (1 - \gamma_r\Delta)x_2(k)$$
$$x_3(k+1) = k_p\Delta x_2(k) + (1 - \gamma_p\Delta)x_3(k),$$

where we have denoted

$$\begin{bmatrix} D^* & M & P \end{bmatrix}^T = \begin{bmatrix} x_1 & x_2 & x_3 \end{bmatrix}^T,$$

and $W(k), k \in \mathbb{N} \cup \{0\}$, are again independent standard Normal random variables. Notice that the model is mixed deterministic-stochastic: namely, deterministic over the dynamics of x_2 (M), x_3 (P), whereas stochastic for x_1 (D^*).

We select a hyper-box A around the steady state values defined above, and compute probabilistic invariance over this region, for a given time horizon. The hyper-box is characterized by the parameters r_1, r_2, and r_3 as:

$$\left|\frac{x_1 - D_{ss}^*}{D_{ss}^*}\right| \le r_1, \quad \left|\frac{x_2 - M_{ss}}{M_{ss}}\right| \le r_2, \quad \left|\frac{x_3 - P_{ss}}{P_{ss}}\right| \le r_3.$$

The kernel for the x_1 dynamics is Normal and admits a density $t_x(\bar{x}_1|x_1) \sim \mathcal{N}(\mu, \sigma)$, where the mean is an affine function of the conditional variable x_1 and the variance is constant:

$$\mu = (1 - k_d\Delta - k_a\Delta)x_1 + 2k_a\Delta D_{ss}^*, \quad \sigma = \sqrt{2k_a\Delta D_{ss}^*}.$$

The Lipschitz constant h_1 is computed based on the maximum norm of the partial derivative of the density function with respect to the conditional variable x_1:

$$h_1 = \max\left\{\left|\frac{\partial t_x}{\partial x_1}(\bar{x}_1|x_1)\right| \Big| x_1, \bar{x}_1 \in \Pi_1(A)\right\}$$
$$= (1 - k_d\Delta - k_a\Delta)\frac{\exp(-0.5)}{\sigma^2\sqrt{2\pi}}.$$

The constants M and M^* have been considered independent of the step k and take the following values:

$$M = \frac{1}{\sigma\sqrt{2\pi}},$$
$$M^* = 2\int_0^{\frac{r_1}{\sigma}D_{ss}^*} \frac{1}{\sqrt{2\pi}}\exp\left[-\frac{u^2}{2}\right]du = \text{erf}\left(\frac{r_1}{\sigma\sqrt{2}}D_{ss}^*\right),$$

where erf is the error function.

6.1 First Experiment (original parameters)

Suppose we select equal rates for the hyper-box that defines the invariance set: $r_i = r, i = 1, 2, 3$. It can be explicitly shown that in this case the invariance set does not shrink backwards, namely since

$$\forall(x_1, x_2, x_3) \in A, \qquad f_2(x_1, x_2, x_3) \in \Pi_2(A),$$

then the support sets are such that

$$\Gamma_{N-1} = A \Rightarrow \Gamma_k = A \quad \forall k \in \{0, 1, ..., N\}.$$

This fact also means that, with regards to Assumption 1,

$$\Gamma_k^1(x_2, x_3) = \Pi_1(A) = [(1 - r)D_{ss}^*, (1 + r)D_{ss}^*],$$

which leads to $\theta_k = 0$. The parameters L_k required for the error bounds are:

$$L = L_k = \mathcal{L}(\Pi_1(\Gamma_k)) = \mathcal{L}(\Pi_1(A))$$
$$= (1 + r)D_{ss}^* - (1 - r)D_{ss}^* = 2rD_{ss}^*.$$

We have selected a time horizon $N = 10$, a time discretization step $\Delta = 1$, and a parameter $r = 0.05$. Recall that $n_1 = 1, n_2 = 2$. This has lead to a variance $\sigma = 0.03$ and to constants

$$h_1 = 227.7, h_2 = 1.02, L = 0.05, M = 12.25, M^* = 0.58.$$

Finally, the abstraction error can be computed as $E_0 = 70.01\delta$. A partition size $\delta = 0.03$ has been selected for the experiment. Figure 1 shows the level set $V_8 = 0.12$ together with the invariant set (transparent bounding box).

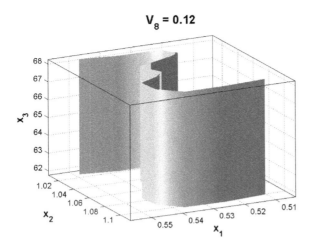

Figure 1: Representation of the level set $V_8 = 0.12$ for the value function of the first experiment.

6.2 Second Experiment (rescaled parameters)

It is easily seen that Γ_k are all equal by selecting the rates for the invariance hyper-box such that $r_1 \leq r_2 \leq r_3$. In order to show the efficiency of the proposed algorithm, the following rates have been thus selected:

$$r_1 = 0.20, \quad r_2 = 0.10, \quad r_3 = 0.05.$$

Furthermore, we have rescaled the constants $k_r, k_p, \gamma_r, \gamma_p$ by a factor of 100. The equilibrium point of the dynamics is not affected by this choice, and we obtain a variance $\sigma = 0.32$ and the following constants:

$$h_1 = 1.82, h_2 = 4.43, M = 12.25, M^* = 0.99.$$

The algorithm results in time varying support sets Γ_k, however it turns out that $\Pi_1(\Gamma_k) = \Pi_1(A)$ for any k. This leads to constants $L = L_k = \mathcal{L}(\Pi_1(A)) = 0.21$. We have selected again a time horizon $N = 10$, a time discretization step $\Delta = 1$, and a partition size $\delta = 0.03$.

Figure 2 displays the support sets Γ_N, Γ_{N-1}, and Γ_0. Notice that the sets shrink as time decreases.

Over the support sets Γ_k, the probabilistic invariance is computed. Figure 3 displays the level sets of $V_0(x) = p_x(A)$, for varying invariance levels: $0, 0.02, 0.04, 0.06, 0.08, 0.1$. Notice that the set of points $V_0 = 0$ cover a region that is the complement of in Γ_0 in A (cfr. the top left plot in Figure 3 with the bottom plot in Figure 2).

Figure 4 displays the level set $V_k(x) = 0.1$, for varying time instants $k = 2, 4, 6, 8$. Additionally, for $k = 0$ we obtain the last (bottom-right) plot of Figure 3.

7. CONCLUSIONS

This work has presented an approach to compute probabilistic invariance (or safety) over a finite horizon for mixed deterministic-stochastic, discrete time processes. The computational technique, based on state-space discretization, has been associated to an explicit error bound. On the theoretical side, the contribution has shown that the problem under study can be separated into a deterministic reachability problem, and a probabilistic invariance one that depends

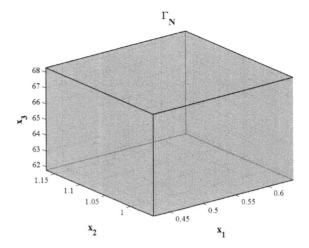

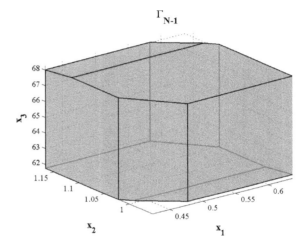

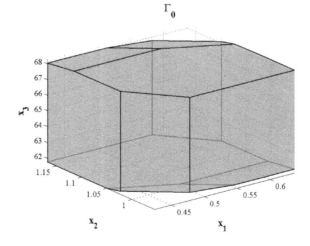

Figure 2: Representation of the support sets Γ_N, Γ_{N-1}, and Γ_0 for the second experiment.

214

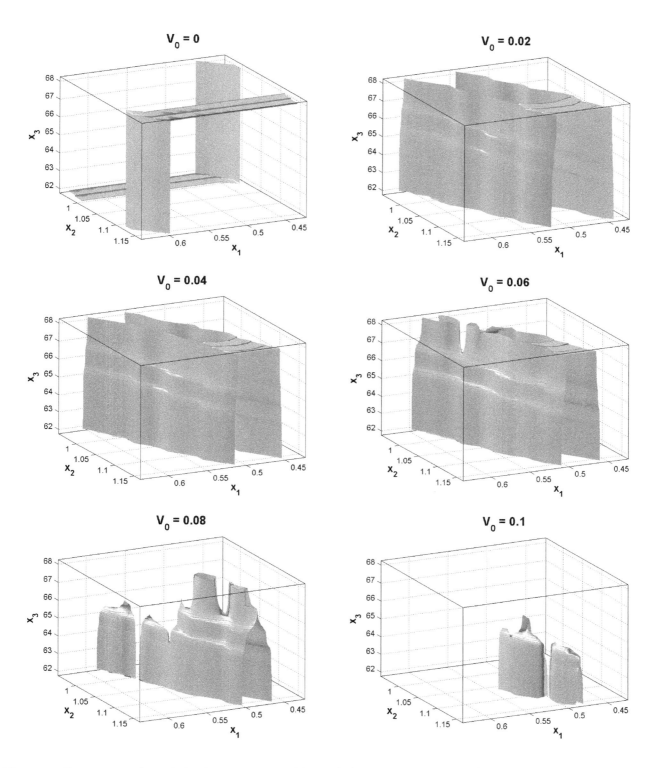

Figure 3: Representation of the level sets of $V_0(x) = p_x(A)$, for varying levels $(0, 0.02, 0.04, 0.06, 0.08, 0.1)$, for the second experiment.

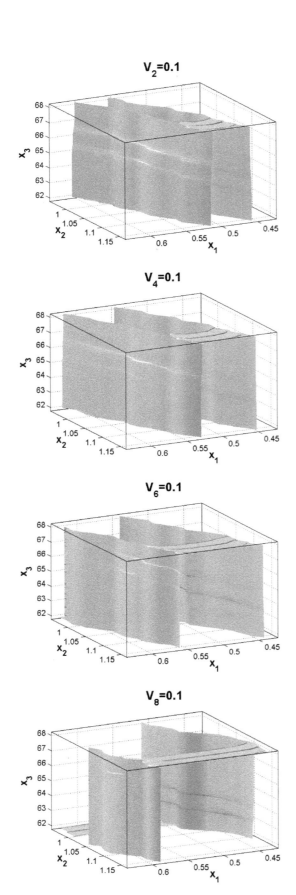

Figure 4: Representation of the level set $V_k(x) = 0.1$, for varying time instants $k = 2, 4, 6, 8$, for the second experiment.

on the outcome of the first. The technique has been tested on a case study modeling a chemical reaction network.

The authors are interested in extensions and further computational improvements of the proposed method.

Acknowledgments

Thanks to Andreas Milias-Argeitis for the discussions on the case study.

8. REFERENCES

[1] A. Abate, J.-P. Katoen, J. Lygeros, and M. Prandini. Approximate model checking of stochastic hybrid systems. *European Journal of Control*, (6):624–641, 2010.

[2] A. Abate, M. Prandini, J. Lygeros, and S. Sastry. Probabilistic reachability and safety for controlled discrete time stochastic hybrid systems. *Automatica*, 44(11):2724–2734, November 2008.

[3] C. Baier and J.-P. Katoen. *Principles of Model Checking*. MIT Press, 2008.

[4] D. P. Bertsekas and S. E. Shreve. *Stochastic Optimal Control: The Discrete-Time Case*. Athena Scientific, 1996.

[5] M. Bujorianu and J. Lygeros. Reachability questions in piecewise deterministic Markov processes. In O. Maler and A. Pnueli, editors, *Hybrid Systems: Computation and Control*, number 2623 in Lecture Notes in Computer Sciences, pages 126–140. Springer Verlag, Berlin Heidelberg, 2003.

[6] R. Bundschuh, F. Hayot, and C. Jayaprakash. The role of dimerization in noise reduction of simple genetic networks. *Journal of Theoretical Biology*, 220(2):261–269, 2003.

[7] S. Esmaeil Zadeh Soudjani and A. Abate. Adaptive gridding for abstraction and verification of stochastic hybrid systems. In *Proceedings of the 8th International Conference on Quantitative Evaluation of SysTems*, pages 59–69, Aachen, DE, September 2011.

[8] D. Gillespie. Exact stochastic simulation of coupled chemical reactions. *Physical Chemistry*, 81(25):2340–2361, 1977.

[9] C. Jones, E. Kerrigan, and J. Maciejowski. On polyhedral projection and parametric programming. *Journal of Optimization Theory and Applications*, 3(137), 2008.

[10] R. Khanin and D. Higham. Chemical Master Equation and Langevin regimes for a gene transcription model. In M. Calder and S. Gilmore, editors, *Computational Methods in Systems Biology*, volume 4695 of *Lecture Notes in Computer Science*, pages 1–14. Springer Berlin / Heidelberg, 2007.

[11] K. Koutsoukos and D. Riley. Computational methods for reachability analysis of stochastic hybrid systems. In J. Hespanha and A. Tiwari, editors, *Hybrid Systems: Computation and Control*, number 3927 in Lecture Notes in Computer Sciences, pages 377–391. Springer-Verlag, Berlin, 2006.

[12] M. Kvasnica, P. Grieder, and M. Baotić. Multi-parametric toolbox (MPT), 2004.

Rare-Event Verification for Stochastic Hybrid Systems

Paolo Zuliani
Computer Science
Department
Carnegie Mellon University
Pittsburgh, PA, USA
pzuliani@cs.cmu.edu

Christel Baier
Fakultät Informatik
TU Dresden
Dresden, Germany
baier@tcs.inf.tu-dresden.de

Edmund M. Clarke
Computer Science
Department
Carnegie Mellon University
Pittsburgh, PA, USA
emc@cs.cmu.edu

ABSTRACT

In this paper we address the problem of verifying in stochastic hybrid systems temporal logic properties whose probability of being true is very small — rare events. It is well known that sampling-based (Monte Carlo) techniques, such as statistical model checking, do not perform well for estimating rare-event probabilities. The problem is that the sample size required for good accuracy grows too large as the event probability tends to zero. However, several techniques have been developed to address this problem. We focus on importance sampling techniques, which bias the original system to compute highly accurate and efficient estimates. The main difficulty in importance sampling is to devise a good biasing density, that is, a density yielding a low-variance estimator. In this paper, we show how to use the cross-entropy method for generating approximately optimal biasing densities for statistical model checking. We apply the method with importance sampling and statistical model checking for estimating rare-event probabilities in stochastic hybrid systems coded as Stateflow/Simulink diagrams.

Categories and Subject Descriptors

C.3 [**Special-purpose and application-base systems**]: Real-time and embedded systems; D.2.4 [**Software Engineering**]: Software/Program Verification—*statistical methods, formal methods*

Keywords

Probabilistic model checking, hybrid systems, stochastic systems, rare events, statistical model checking

1. INTRODUCTION

Stochastic hybrid systems [2] are among the most difficult systems to verify. They combine discrete, continuous, and probabilistic behavior, thereby exacerbating the state explosion problem that afflicts many automated verification techniques (*e.g.*, model checking). In particular, temporal logic

verification for stochastic hybrid systems is currently outside the reach of formal verification methods. To deal with this problem, one can instead use *statistical* model checking. This technique blends randomized (*i.e.*, Monte Carlo) simulation, model checking, and statistical analysis, and it enjoys better scalability than other formal verification techniques [17, 16]. With statistical model checking one can compute approximations of the probability that a stochastic hybrid system satisfies a given temporal logic specification. The accuracy of the computed probability can be controlled by the user (the probability is usually given with a *confidence interval*, and the user can control *width* and *coverage* of the interval). Naturally, higher accuracy will require more simulations. Since the vast majority of the computational cost of statistical model checking is due to system simulation, it is important to keep the *sample size* — the number of simulations — as small as possible. In most cases, statistical model checking techniques can give accurate estimates with feasible sample sizes, *i.e.*, smaller than 10^4. However, it is well known that Monte Carlo techniques, such as statistical model checking, suffer from the *rare-event* problem [10]. An event is said rare when it occurs with very small probability. For example, the negation of a safety property can be thought as a rare event: it should be very unlikely that the system is unsafe. Now, the problem is that estimating accurately rare-event probabilities using standard Monte Carlo techniques requires very high sample sizes. Thus, these techniques quickly become unfeasible, as we next explain.

The Monte Carlo approach for estimating probabilities relies on the strong law of large numbers for its correctness, and on relative frequencies for computing estimates. The strong law of large numbers states that if $X_1, X_2, \ldots$ is a sequence of independent and identically distributed (iid) random variables with $\mathrm{E}[|X_1|] < \infty$, then

$$\mathrm{P}\left(\lim_{n \to \infty} \frac{S_n}{n} = \mu \right) = 1$$

where $S_n = \sum_{i=1}^{n} X_i$ and $\mu = \mathrm{E}[X_1]$. Therefore, we can approximate μ by taking the average of a *finite* number of realizations (samples) of X_1, since we know that the average will not converge to μ only for a negligible subset of realizations (a set of measure 0). It can be shown that the condition $\mathrm{E}[|X_1|] < \infty$ is necessary and sufficient for the average $\frac{S_n}{n}$ to converge to a finite limit (with probability 1). Also, the strong law of large numbers holds in the case that $\mu = \mathrm{E}[X_1]$ exists but it is not finite [14, Chapter 4].

Now, suppose we want to estimate $p = \mathrm{P}(X \in B)$, the probability that X belongs to a given Borel set B, where X is a random variable defined over a probability space $(\Omega, \mathcal{F}, P)$. First, we obtain a number of independent realizations of $I_B(X)$, the indicator function of B — $I_B(x)$ is 1 if $x \in B$ ("$X \in B$ has occurred"), 0 otherwise. Then, we compute their average and return that as the estimate of p. Note that the random variable $I_B(X)$ is a Bernoulli of success parameter p, that is, $P(I_B(X) = 1) = p$. Also, note that $p = E[I_B(X)]$. Therefore, given a finite sequence $X_1, \ldots, X_N$ of random variables iid as X, we define the *crude Monte Carlo estimator* as $\hat{p} = \frac{1}{N} \sum_{i=1}^{N} I_B(X_i)$. By the strong law of large numbers $\hat{p}$ converges to p as $N \to \infty$ (with probability 1). Also, $\hat{p}$ is *unbiased* (*i.e.*, $E[\hat{p}] = p$).

The speed of convergence of $\hat{p}$ depends on the variance of $I_B(X)$, which is finite (it is of course $p(1-p)$). In particular, from the central limit theorem it follows that for large N the distribution of $\hat{p}$ is approximately a normal distribution of mean p and variance $Var(I_B(X))/N$. From this we can compute approximate *confidence intervals* for p in the following way. Let z_γ denote the γ-quantile of the standard normal distribution, *i.e.*, the number such that $P(\mathcal{N} \leq z_\gamma) = \gamma$, where $\mathcal{N}$ is a normal random variable with mean 0 and variance 1. Then, for $\alpha < 1$ and large N the following holds:

$$P\left(|p - \hat{p}| \leq z_{1-\frac{\alpha}{2}} \frac{\mathcal{S}}{\sqrt{N}}\right) \approx 1 - \alpha$$

where $\mathcal{S}$ is the square root of *sample variance*

$$\mathcal{S}^2 \stackrel{\text{def}}{=} \frac{1}{N-1} \sum_{i=1}^{N} (I_B(X_i) - \hat{p})^2$$

which, again by the strong law of large numbers, converges to $Var(I_B(X))$ with probability 1. The term $2z_{1-\frac{\alpha}{2}} \frac{\mathcal{S}}{\sqrt{N}}$ is the *absolute width* of the $(1-\alpha)100\%$ confidence interval. In the rare event case ($p \ll 1$) it is very important to have confidence intervals of *relative* width, *i.e.*, we would like an estimate $\hat{p}$ such that

$$P(|p - \hat{p}| \leq \delta p) \approx 1 - \alpha$$

for some small $\delta > 0$. Clearly, a confidence interval of absolute width 0.01 would not make much sense if we wanted to estimate, say, $p = 10^{-10}$. For example, it can be shown that a 99% approximate confidence interval of relative width δ needs about $\frac{1-p}{p\delta^2}$ samples. To estimate $p = 10^{-8}$ with a relative width $\delta = 0.01$ we would thus need about $N \approx \frac{1}{p\delta^2} = 10^{12}$ samples — an unfeasible quantity. Furthermore, we see that if $p \to 0$ while δ is fixed, the sample size grows larger and larger.

Finally, an important quantity associated with the estimator $\hat{p}$ is its *relative error*:

$$RE(\hat{p}) \stackrel{\text{def}}{=} \frac{\sqrt{Var(\hat{p})}}{E[\hat{p}]}$$

and intuitively it is a "measure" of the accuracy of the estimator $\hat{p}$ with respect to its standard deviation. Since $\hat{p}$ is unbiased, the sample $X_1, \ldots, X_N$ is iid, and $p \ll 1$, it follows that

$$RE(\hat{p}) = \frac{\sqrt{Var(I_B(X))/N}}{p} = \frac{\sqrt{p(1-p)}}{p\sqrt{N}} \approx \sqrt{\frac{1}{Np}}.$$

It is easy to see that if N is kept constant and $p \to 0$, then $RE(\hat{p}) \to \infty$. Therefore, in order to keep the relative error low as $X \in B$ becomes rarer, we need to increase the sample

size. This means that the crude MC estimator is useless in the rare-event case.

A possible solution to this problem is to search for another estimator whose variance is smaller than $Var(\hat{p})$, for a given sample size. Importance sampling is a technique for devising estimators with reduced variance, and thus with low relative error. In particular, in importance sampling the original system is biased to increase the likelihood of the event of interest. The samples are then weighted in order to obtain unbiased estimates. The main difficulty in importance sampling is to devise a good biasing distribution, that is, one yielding a low-variance estimator. The cross-entropy method is a recent technique that can help in devising a biased distribution.

In this work we use statistical model checking with importance sampling and the cross-entropy method for estimating rare-event probabilities in stochastic hybrid systems. The paper is divided as follows. In Section 2 we briefly recapitulate temporal logic and statistical model checking; in Section 3 we define our semantic model for stochastic hybrid systems; in Sections 4 and 5 we introduce importance sampling and the cross-entropy method, respectively. Finally, in Section 6 we apply the techniques to an example of stochastic hybrid system modeled in Stateflow/Simulink.

2. STATISTICAL MODEL CHECKING

We give a short introduction to temporal logic and statistical model checking. In this paper, we use Bounded Linear Temporal Logic (BLTL) [7, 21, 6] as our specification language. BLTL restricts Linear Temporal Logic (LTL) [9] with time bounds on the temporal operators. For example, we can specify that "within 10 time units the system will shut down and the shutdown signal will be ON *until* then" as the BLTL formula

$$\texttt{shutdown\_ON} \; \mathbf{U}^{10} \; \texttt{sysdown}$$

where shutdown_ON and sysdown are predicates over the system's state space and time defined to be true iff the shutdown signal is ON and iff the system is down at that time, respectively. Again, a BLTL formula expressing the specification "it is not the case that in the *future* 25 time units the system is *globally* down for one time unit" is written as

$$\neg(\mathbf{F}^{25} \mathbf{G}^1 \; \texttt{sysdown})$$

where the $\mathbf{F}^{25}$ operator encodes "future 25 time units", and $\mathbf{G}^1$ expresses "globally for one time unit". Formally, the syntax of BLTL is given by:

$$\phi ::= y \sim v \mid (\phi_1 \vee \phi_2) \mid (\phi_1 \wedge \phi_2) \mid \neg\phi_1 \mid (\phi_1 \mathbf{U}^t \phi_2),$$

where $\sim \in \{\geq, \leq, =\}$, $y \in SV$ (the finite set of state variables), $v \in \mathbb{R}$, $t \in \mathbb{R}_{>0}$, and $\neg, \wedge, \vee$ are the usual Boolean connectives. Formulae of the type $y \sim v$ are also called atomic propositions (AP). The formula $\phi_1 \mathbf{U}^t \phi_2$ holds true if and only if, *within* time t, ϕ_2 will be true and ϕ_1 will hold *until* then. Note that the operators $\mathbf{F}^t$ and $\mathbf{G}^t$ referenced above can be easily defined in terms of the until $\mathbf{U}^t$ operator: $\mathbf{F}^t \phi = true \; \mathbf{U}^t \phi$ requires ϕ to hold true within time t (*true* is the atomic proposition identically true); $\mathbf{G}^t \phi = \neg \mathbf{F}^t \neg \phi$ requires ϕ to hold true up to time t.

The semantics of BLTL formulae [7, 21, 6] is defined with respect to system traces (or executions). A trace is a sequence $\sigma = (s_0, t_0), (s_1, t_1), \ldots$ where the s_i's are states and the t_i's represent time. The pair (s_i, t_i) expresses the fact that the system moved to state s_{i+1} after having spent t_i time units in state s_i. The trace suffix of σ starting at $k \in \mathbb{N}$ is denoted by σ^k, and σ^0 denotes the full trace σ.

Definition 1. The *semantics* of BLTL for a trace σ^k is:

- $\sigma^k \models AP$ iff   *AP holds true in state s_k;*
- $\sigma^k \models \phi_1 \vee \phi_2$ iff $\sigma^k \models \phi_1$ *or* $\sigma^k \models \phi_2$;
- $\sigma^k \models \phi_1 \wedge \phi_2$ iff $\sigma^k \models \phi_1$ *and* $\sigma^k \models \phi_2$;
- $\sigma^k \models \neg\phi_1$ iff $\sigma^k \models \phi_1$ *does not hold;*
- $\sigma^k \models \phi_1 \mathbf{U}^t \phi_2$ iff $\exists i \geq 0$ *such that*

   a) $\sum_{l=0}^{i-1} t_{k+l} \leq t$, and

   b) $\sigma^{k+i} \models \phi_2$, and

   c) $\forall\, 0 \leq j < i,\ \sigma^{k+j} \models \phi_1$.

If the trace σ satisfies the property ϕ we write $\sigma \models \phi$.

Statistical model checking [19, 18, 5, 13, 4] combines Monte Carlo simulation, model checking, and statistical analysis, for verifying stochastic systems. Its main assumption is the existence of a probability measure P over the set of system traces satisfying a given BLTL formula. In particular, for every BLTL formula ϕ, the probability $P\{\sigma \mid \sigma \models \phi\}$ must be well-defined. Given a stochastic process and probability measure over it, this requirement does not pose any problem in practice — see [20] for more details. In the next Section we define a model for stochastic hybrid systems and we show that it induces a well-defined stochastic process and a unique probability measure over the process' traces. This is clearly a crucial requirement for statistical model checking to make sense.

Suppose now that $p = P\{\sigma \mid \sigma \models \phi\}$ for a given formula ϕ. The verification problem is thus to compute (or approximate) p. Statistical model checking treats it as a statistical inference problem, and solves it through randomized sampling of the system traces. The traces are model checked to determine whether ϕ holds, and the number of satisfying traces is used to *estimate* p. Specifically, we seek to approximate probabilistically (*i.e.*, compute with high probability a value close to) p. Note that the system behavior with respect to ϕ can be characterized as a Bernoulli random variable under the measure P. Given a system trace σ we can define the Bernoulli random variable Z to be 1 if $\sigma \models \phi$, and 0 otherwise. Thus, $P(Z = 1) = p$ (and of course $P(Z = 0) = 1 - p$). In statistical model checking, one therefore aims at estimating the success parameter of Z. Statistical techniques are applied to independent samples of Z to estimate p. In particular, to obtain n samples of Z we first have to run n iid system simulations that yield the traces $\sigma_1, \ldots, \sigma_n$, and then we check property ϕ on each trace σ_i. To estimate p, one can then use fixed-sample size statistical techniques such as the Chernoff-Hoeffding bound [5], or sequential techniques such as Bayesian credibility intervals [21]. Another statistical model checking approach [19, 18] uses statistical hypothesis testing techniques aimed at deciding whether p is greater than a given threshold. However, such techniques suffer from the rare-event problem, too.

We have seen that in order to generate each sample of Z we need to check property ϕ on a trace. Because BLTL properties are time-bounded, it is possible to decide whether a trace σ satisfies a given property only by checking a finite prefix of σ [21]. That result assumes that the system un-

der verification does not exhibit Zeno behavior. In particular, for any system trace σ it must be $\sum_{i=0}^{\infty} t_i = \infty$, which means that the system cannot make an infinite number of transitions in a finite amount of time. This assumption is widely adopted and it is sufficient for ensuring termination of statistical model checking algorithms. (However, it is not always necessary. For example, for finite-state continuous-time Markov chains it can be shown that the set of traces exhibiting Zeno behavior has measure zero [1].)

3. STOCHASTIC HYBRID SYSTEMS

In this Section we present our semantic model for stochastic hybrid systems, and we prove that it induces a well-defined Markov process. The model is especially suited for capturing the behavior of simulation engines for hybrid systems, such as Stateflow/Simulink.

3.1 Preliminaries

We shall consider stochastic processes over Polish spaces. A Polish space is a separable topological space metrizable by a complete metric. A Borel set in a topological space is a set formed by countable union, intersection, or relative complement of open sets (equivalently, closed sets). Given a Polish space S, we denote its Borel σ-algebra by $\mathcal{B}(S)$.

Definition 2. A *stochastic kernel* on a measurable space $(S, \mathcal{B}(S))$ is a function $K: S \times \mathcal{B}(S) \to [0, 1]$ such that:

- for each $x \in S$, $K(x, \cdot)$ is a probability measure on $\mathcal{B}(S)$; and
- for each $B \in \mathcal{B}(S)$, $K(\cdot, B)$ is a (Borel) measurable function on S.

Since we consider discrete time systems, we define the sample space $\Omega = S^\omega$ and the product σ-algebra $\mathcal{F}$ of Ω. Given a stochastic kernel K on $(\Omega, \mathcal{F})$ and an initial state $x \in S$, then Kolmogorov's theorem shows [14, Section II.9] that there exists a unique probability measure P defined on $(\Omega, \mathcal{F})$ and a Markov process $\{X_t : t \in \mathbb{N}\}$ such that for all $B \in \mathcal{B}(S)$ and for all $x_i \in S$:

- $P(X_1 \in B) = \delta_B(x)$; and
- $P(X_{t+1} \in B \mid (x_1, \ldots, x_t)) = P(X_{t+1} \in B \mid x_t) = K(x_t, B)$

where δ_B is the usual Dirac measure.

Our aim is to introduce a hybrid automaton model and a "probabilistic simulation function" that will induce a stochastic kernel, in order to use Kolmogorov's theorem.

3.2 Hybrid Automata

We first define non-probabilistic hybrid automata.

Definition 3. A *discrete-time hybrid automaton* (DTHA) consists of:

- a continuous state space $\mathbb{R}^n$;
- a finite set Q of *locations*;
- an edge relation $E \subseteq Q \times Q$ (control switches);
- one initial state $(q_0, x_0) \in Q \times \mathbb{R}^n$;
- a *flow* function $\varphi : Q \times \mathbb{R}_{>0} \times \mathbb{R}^n \to \mathbb{R}^n$ representing the time evolution of the (continuous) state, in a specific location. For each $q \in Q$, the flow function

$$\varphi_q : \mathbb{R}_{>0} \times \mathbb{R}^n, \ (t,x) \mapsto \varphi(q,t,x),$$

is (Borel) measurable.

- a *jump* function $jump : E \times \mathbb{R}^n \to \mathbb{R}^n$, representing the (possibly) discontinuous change of state after switching location.

A DTHA may feature nondeterminism because of multiple outgoing edges from a location. We assume that the directed graph (Q, E) of locations does not have self-loops or terminal locations, i.e., $(q,q) \notin E$ for all $q \in Q$ and for each $q \in Q$ there is at least one edge $(q,q') \in E$. Also, note that continuous flow functions are automatically (Borel) measurable.

Notation:. If $e \in E$, we shall write $jump_e(x)$ for $jump(e,x)$. Similarly, if $q \in Q$ then φ_q denotes the function $(t,x) \mapsto \varphi(q,t,x)$.

Definition 4. The *semantics* of a DTHA is a transition system $\mathcal{T}$ with

- state space $S = Q \times \mathbb{R}^n$

- initial state $s_0 = (q_0, x_0) \in S$

- transition relation $\longrightarrow \subseteq S \times (E \cup \mathbb{R}_{>0}) \times S$ given by the following two rules:

$x' = \varphi_q(t,x)$	$e = (q,q') \in E, \quad x' = jump_e(x)$
$(q,x) \longrightarrow_t (q,x')$	$(q,x) \longrightarrow_e (q',x')$
continuous transition	discrete transition
(time passage)	(switching location)

Any nondeterminism in a DTHA is resolved by a *simulation function*. In particular, such function can capture the determinism necessary for simulating a DTHA. An example is the "12 o'clock" graphical rule in Stateflow diagrams. (It states that the first edge, in clockwise orientation from 12, that is enabled shall be selected.)

Definition 5. A *simulation function* for a DTHA is a map

$$\Delta : S \to E \cup \mathbb{R}_{>0}$$

A simulation function induces a subsystem of $\mathcal{T}$ where each state $s \in S$ has a unique successor state, namely the unique state s' such that $s \longrightarrow_\sigma s'$ where $\sigma = \Delta(s)$. In particular, Δ induces an infinite path in $\mathcal{T}$:

$$s_0\, s_1\, s_2\, s_3\, \ldots \quad \text{where} \quad s_i \longrightarrow_{\Delta(s_i)} s_{i+1} \quad \text{for } i = 0, 1, 2, \ldots$$

An alternative definition of a deterministic simulation function could be to take the absolute time as an additional parameter. That is,

$$\Delta : S \times \mathbb{R}_{\geqslant 0} \to E \cup \mathbb{R}_{>0}$$

which induces a timed path of $\mathcal{T}$:

$$path(\Delta) = (s_0, \theta_0)\,(s_1, \theta_1)\,(s_2, \theta_2)\,\ldots \in (S \times \mathbb{R}_{\geqslant 0}^n)^\omega$$

where s_0 is the initial state of $\mathcal{T}$, $\theta_0 = 0$ and for each $i \in \mathbb{N}$:

- if $\Delta(s_i, \theta_i) = e \in E$ then $\theta_{i+1} = \theta_i$ and s_{i+1} is the unique state in S such that $s_i \longrightarrow_e s_{i+1}$

- if $\Delta(s_i, \theta_i) = t \in \mathbb{R}_{>0}$ then $\theta_{i+1} = \theta_i + t$ and s_{i+1} is the unique state in S such that $s_i \longrightarrow_t s_{i+1}$

This is slightly more "powerful" since it allows to make different choices for the same state s when visiting s at different time instances. A corresponding time-dependent (or even history-dependent) definition of probabilistic simulation functions could be defined for the probabilistic case. In this paper we exclusively deal with Markovian systems, so we shall not pursue the more general case.

Now, Discrete Time Stochastic Hybrid Automata (DT-SHA) are obtained by replacing the (deterministic) simulation function Δ with a probabilistic version. The *probabilistic* simulation function decides for each state $s = (q,x) \in S$

- either to take some continuous transition; in which case the size of the time step will be "sampled" according to some probability distribution over the non-negative reals;

- or to take some discrete transition; in which case the choice of which edge $(q,q') \in E$ to take is resolved according to a probability distribution over

$$E(q) = \{ e \in E : e = (q,q') \text{ for some } q' \in Q \}.$$

Remember that we suppose $E(q) \neq \varnothing$ for all $q \in Q$.

We denote by $\mathbb{P}(\cdot)$ the set of probability measures over $(\cdot)$.

Definition 6. A *probabilistic simulation function* is a map

$$\lambda : S \to \mathbb{P}(\mathcal{B}(\mathbb{R}_{>0})) \cup \mathbb{P}(E)$$

satisfying the conditions (where we assume $s = (q,x) \in S$):

(P1) For each state $s \in S$ such that $\lambda(s) \in \mathbb{P}(E)$ and each edge $e \in E$ we have:

$$\text{if } e = (p,p') \text{ where } p \neq q \text{ then } \lambda(s)(e) = 0$$

This is equivalent to $\sum_{e \in E(q)} \lambda(s)(e) = 1$.

(P2) For each state $s \in S$ such that $\lambda(s) \in \mathbb{P}(\mathcal{B}(\mathbb{R}_{>0}))$, we define the function

$$\Pi_s : \mathcal{B}(S) \to [0,1], \quad \Pi_s(B) \stackrel{\text{def}}{=} \lambda(s)(time(s,B))$$

where $time(s,B)$ is the set of time points for which evolution (from state $s = (q,x) \in S$) of $\varphi_{q,x}(\cdot) = \varphi_q(\cdot, x)$ ends up in B. Formally,

$$time(s,B) \stackrel{\text{def}}{=} \{ t \in \mathbb{R}_{>0} : \varphi_q(t,x) \in B \} = \varphi_{q,x}^{-1}(B_q)$$

where

$$\varphi_{q,x} : \mathbb{R}_{>0} \to \mathbb{R}^n, \quad \varphi_{q,x}(t) = \varphi_q(t,x)$$
$$B_q \stackrel{\text{def}}{=} \{ y \in \mathbb{R}^n : (q,y) \in B \}.$$

(P3) The sets of states for which λ is a probability measure over reals and over E must be measurable. That is, the sets

$$S_c \stackrel{\text{def}}{=} \{ s \in S : \lambda(s) \in \mathbb{P}(\mathcal{B}(\mathbb{R}_{>0})) \}$$
$$S_d \stackrel{\text{def}}{=} \{ s \in S : \lambda(s) \in \mathbb{P}(E) \}$$

are measurable.

(P4) For each edge $e = (q,q') \in E$, the function $\psi_e : S_d \to [0,1]$, $s \mapsto \lambda(s)(e)$ is measurable over S_d.

(P5) For each Borel-set $B \subseteq \mathcal{B}(S)$, the function $\phi_B : S_c \to [0, 1]$, $s \mapsto \lambda(s)(time(s, B))$ is measurable over S_c.

Remark 1. In condition (P2) for fixed state $s = (q, x)$, the function $\varphi_{q,x}$ is measurable when we require that φ is measurable. If B is a measurable subset of $S = Q \times \mathbb{R}^n$ then $B_q = \{y \in \mathbb{R}^n : (q, y) \in B\}$ is a measurable subset of $\mathbb{R}^n$. Therefore, the pre-image $\varphi_{q,x}^{-1}(B_q)$ is a measurable subset of $\mathbb{R}_{>0}$.

As Q is finite, the measures over E are discrete. For measures over the non-negative reals if, for example, $\lambda(s)$ corresponds to an exponential distribution of parameter $\kappa(s) \in \mathbb{R}_{>0}$, then for all $T \in \mathcal{B}(\mathbb{R}_{>0})$

$$\lambda(s)(T) = \int_T \kappa(s) \cdot e^{-\kappa(s)t} dt .$$

We can now define the stochastic kernel induced by a probabilistic simulation function.

Definition 7. A probabilistic simulation function λ induces the stochastic kernel $\Pi : S \times \mathcal{B}(S) \to [0, 1]$ defined as follows:

$$\Pi(s, B) \stackrel{\text{def}}{=} \begin{cases} \Pi_s(B) & \text{if } s \in S_c \\ \Psi_s(B) & \text{if } s \in S_d \end{cases}$$

where Π_s is as per Definition 6 (condition P2), and Ψ_s is the map

$$\Psi_s(B) \stackrel{\text{def}}{=} \sum_{e \in Edges(s,B)} \psi_e(s) = \sum_{e \in Edges(s,B)} \lambda(s)(e)$$

where $Edges(s, B)$ is the set of edges for which a transition from state s results in a state in B. Formally (where $s = (q, x) \in S$):

$$Edges(s, B) \stackrel{\text{def}}{=} \{e = (q, q') \in E : (q', jump_e(x)) \in B\}.$$

PROPOSITION 1. *The function Π of Definition 7 is a stochastic kernel.*

PROOF. We start by showing that for each state $s \in S$, $\Pi(s, \cdot)$ is a probability measure over $\mathcal{B}(S)$. If $\lambda(s) \in \mathbb{P}(\mathcal{B}(\mathbb{R}_{>0}))$ then by condition (P2) in Definition 6

$$\Pi(s, B) = \Pi_s(B) = \lambda(s)\big(\varphi_{q,x}^{-1}(B_q)\big)$$

and this is indeed a probability measure. If $\lambda(s) \in \mathbb{P}(E)$, then

$$\Pi(s, B) = \Psi_s(B) = \sum_{(q,q') \in E} \lambda(s)(e) \cdot \delta_B(q', jump_e(x))$$

where δ_B is the Dirac measure over B. Condition (P1) and the assumption that $(q, q') \in E$ for at least one location $q' \in Q$ ensure that $\Pi(s, S) = 1$. Since E is finite, this is a probability measure too.

Next, we need to show that for each $B \in \mathcal{B}(S)$, the function $\Pi_B : S \to [0, 1]$, $s \mapsto \Pi(s, B)$ is measurable. We must thus show that for any $I \in \mathcal{B}([0, 1])$ the set $\Pi_B^{-1}(I)$ is measurable. Note that:

$$\Pi_B^{-1}(I) = \{s \in S : \Pi(s, B) \in I\}$$
$$= \{s \in S_c : \Pi_s(B) \in I\} \cup \{s \in S_d : \Psi_s(B) \in I\}$$
$$= \{s \in S_c : \phi_B(s) \in I\} \cup \{s \in S_d : \Psi_s(B) \in I\}$$
$$= \phi_B^{-1}(I) \cup \{s \in S_d : \sum_{e \in Edges(s,B)} \psi_s(e) \in I\}$$

Measurability of $\Pi_B^{-1}(I)$ follows thus directly from conditions (P4)-(P5) and $\cup$−closedness. $\square$

Proposition 1 enables us to show (see Section 3.1) the existence of the discrete-time Markov process and the probability measure over the product σ-algebra $\mathcal{F}$ for our stochastic hybrid systems model.

4. IMPORTANCE SAMPLING

Importance Sampling is a variance-reduction technique for the Monte Carlo method. Here we present a brief overview of the technique — the interested reader can find more details in [15], for example.

4.1 Basics

Consider the general case of estimating $c = \mathrm{E}[g(X)]$ for a random variable X and a measurable function $g : \mathbb{R} \to \mathbb{R}^{\geqslant 0}$, assuming $0 < c < \infty$. We also assume that the distribution of X is absolutely continuous with respect to the Lebesgue measure, and denote by f the corresponding density. Recall that in statistical model checking we are interested in determining the probability that a stochastic system satisfies a certain temporal logic formula ϕ. In this setting, the function g is just the model checker that verifies whether a trace satisfies ϕ. Therefore, given a random trace σ, the random variable $g(\sigma)$ is a Bernoulli — 1 if the trace σ satisfies ϕ, and 0 otherwise.

Let $X_1, \ldots, X_N$ be random variables iid as X. The *crude Monte Carlo* (MC) estimator is $\hat{c} \stackrel{\text{def}}{=} \frac{1}{N} \sum_{i=1}^N g(X_i)$. By the strong law of large numbers, $\hat{c}$ converges to c with probability 1. (Clearly, the sequence $g(X_1), \ldots, g(X_N)$ is iid with mean $\mathrm{E}[g(X)]$, so the law of large numbers applies.) Also, $\hat{c}$ is unbiased, and its variance is

$$\mathrm{Var}(\hat{c}) = \frac{1}{N}(\mathrm{E}[g^2(X)] - c^2) . \tag{1}$$

We now introduce Importance Sampling. Suppose we had another (absolutely continuous) distribution for X, with corresponding density f_*, such that the ratio f/f_* is well-defined. Importance sampling is based upon the following identity:

$$c = \mathrm{E}[g(X)]$$
$$= \int_{\mathbb{R}} g(x)f(x) \, dx$$
$$= \int_{\mathbb{R}} g(x)\frac{f(x)}{f_*(x)} f_*(x) \, dx$$
$$= \int_{\mathbb{R}} g(x)W(x) f_*(x) \, dx$$
$$= \mathrm{E}_*[g(X)W(X)] \tag{2}$$

where E_* denotes expectation with respect to the density f_*. The term $W(x) = \frac{f(x)}{f_*(x)}$ is the *likelihood ratio*. We require that for all x such that $g(x)f(x) > 0$, it must be $f_*(x) > 0$; the density f_* is known as the *biasing* (or *proposal*) density.

Definition 8. Let $X_1, \ldots, X_N$ be random variables iid with density f_*. The *Importance Sampling* (IS) estimator is

$$\hat{c}_{\mathrm{IS}} = \frac{1}{N} \sum_{i=1}^N g(X_i)W(X_i)$$

where $W(x) = f(x)/f_*(x)$ is the likelihood ratio.

Note that the samples X_i's are drawn from the proposal distribution. The IS estimator is unbiased by (2), and its variance is (see Appendix A):

$$\text{Var}(\hat{c}_{\text{IS}}) = \frac{1}{N}\left(\text{E}_*[g^2(X)W^2(X)] - c^2\right) . \tag{3}$$

The key problem in importance sampling is to find a proposal density such that the variance (3) of the IS estimator is smaller than the variance (1) of the crude MC estimator.

4.2 Optimal bias

It is not difficult to show that there exists a proposal density which can minimize the variance (3) of the IS estimator. In particular, if the function g is non-negative the following *optimal proposal* density results in a zero-variance estimator:

$$f_*(x) \stackrel{\text{def}}{=} \frac{g(x)f(x)}{c} . \tag{4}$$

When g is a real (non necessarily positive) function the variance can be minimized, although the minimum is non-zero — see Appendix A.

The claim that (4) gives a zero-variance estimator can be easily verified:

$$\hat{c}_{\text{IS}} = \frac{1}{N}\sum_{i=1}^{N} g(X_i)W(X_i) = \frac{1}{N}\sum_{i=1}^{N} g(X_i)\frac{f(X_i)}{f_*(X_i)}$$
$$= \frac{c}{N}\sum_{i=1}^{N} g(X_i)\frac{f(X_i)}{g(X_i)f(X_i)} = c .$$

Therefore, for any sample size (with at least one sample x for which $g(x) \neq 0$) the IS estimator is constant. But this does not help in practice, since f_* depends on $c = \text{E}[g(X)]$, the (unknown) quantity we are trying to estimate. Therefore, instead of trying to come up with the optimal density, it may be preferable to search in a parametrized family of densities for a biasing density "close" to the optimal one. This is exactly the approach taken by the cross-entropy method, as we show in the next Section.

5. THE CROSS-ENTROPY METHOD

The cross-entropy method was introduced in 1999 by Rubinstein [11]. It assumes that the original (or nominal) density f of X belongs to a parametric family $\{f(\cdot, u) \mid u \in \mathcal{U}\}$, and in particular $f(\cdot) = f(\cdot, v)$ for some fixed $v \in \mathcal{U}$. The method seeks the density in the family which minimizes the Kullback-Leibler divergence with the optimal proposal density. Basically, to estimate probabilities using importance sampling and the cross-entropy method, we perform two steps. First, we find a density with minimal Kullback-Leibler divergence with respect to the optimal proposal density. Second, we perform importance sampling with the proposal density computed in the previous step to estimate $\text{E}[g(X)]$. Both steps require sampling, and in practice the number of samples generated for the second step will be much larger than for the first.

Definition 9. The *Kullback-Leibler* divergence of two densities f, h is

$$\mathcal{D}(f, h) = \int_{\mathbb{R}} f(x) \ln \frac{f(x)}{h(x)} \, dx.$$

The Kullback-Leibler divergence is also known as the *cross-entropy* (CE). Formally, it is not a distance, since it is not symmetric, *i.e.*, $\mathcal{D}(f, h) \neq \mathcal{D}(h, f)$ in general. However, it can be shown (see Appendix B) that $\mathcal{D}$ is always non-negative, and that $\mathcal{D}(f, h) = 0$ iff $f = h$. Therefore, the CE can be useful in assessing how close two densities are.

Our task is to estimate $c = \text{E}[g(X)]$, where X is a random variable with density f and g is a non-negative, measurable function. Again, the idea of the CE method is to find a density in the parametric family such that the CE with the optimal proposal density f_* is minimal. Therefore, we need to solve the minimization problem:

$$u^* \stackrel{\text{def}}{=} \operatorname*{argmin}_{u \in \mathcal{U}} \mathcal{D}(f_*(\cdot), f(\cdot, u))$$

where $f_*(x) = g(x)f(x, v)/c$ is the optimal proposal density. It is easy to transform the minimization problem into a maximization problem:

$$\operatorname*{argmin}_{u \in \mathcal{U}} \mathcal{D}(f_*(\cdot), f(\cdot, u)) = \operatorname*{argmin}_{u \in \mathcal{U}} \text{E}_*\left[\ln \frac{f_*(X)}{f(X, u)}\right]$$
$$= \operatorname*{argmin}_{u \in \mathcal{U}} \int_{\mathbb{R}} f_*(x) \ln f_*(x) \, dx - \int_{\mathbb{R}} f_*(x) \ln f(x, u) \, dx$$
$$= \operatorname*{argmax}_{u \in \mathcal{U}} \int_{\mathbb{R}} f_*(x) \ln f(x, u) \, dx$$
$$= \operatorname*{argmax}_{u \in \mathcal{U}} \int_{\mathbb{R}} g(x)f(x, v) \ln f(x, u) \, dx$$
$$= \operatorname*{argmax}_{u \in \mathcal{U}} \text{E}[g(X) \ln f(X, u)]$$

where in the second step we used the fact is $\mathcal{D}$ is non-negative and that the first integral does not depend on u. It is worth to observe that in the maximization problem the dependency on f_* has disappeared, thus simplifying it. In fact, Rubinstein and Kroese [12] show that for certain families of densities the maximization problem can be solved *analytically*. Assume now that $\mathbf{X}$ is a random vector, *i.e.*, $\mathbf{X}{:}\Omega \to \mathbb{R}^n$ (of course g must be defined over $\mathbb{R}^n$). Note that this does not change what we obtained so far. The following Proposition gives the optimal parameter $\mathbf{u}^* \stackrel{\text{def}}{=} \operatorname*{argmax}_{u \in \mathcal{U}} \text{E}[g(\mathbf{X}) \ln f(\mathbf{X}, u)]$ when $\mathbf{X}$ is a vector of independent, one-dimensional exponential family of distributions.

PROPOSITION 2. *[12] Let $\mathbf{X}$ be a random vector of n independent one-dimensional exponential distributions parametrized by the mean; $g{:}\mathbb{R}^n \to \mathbb{R}^{\geqslant 0}$ be a measurable function. Then the optimal parameter $\mathbf{u}^* = (u_1^*, \ldots, u_n^*)$ is*

$$u_j^* = \frac{\text{E}[g(\mathbf{X})X_j]}{\text{E}[g(\mathbf{X})]}$$

where X_j is the j-th component of $\mathbf{X}$.

From the Proposition, we see that the optimal parameter depends on the quantity we are estimating, *i.e.*, $\text{E}[g(\mathbf{X})]$. Therefore, $\mathbf{u}^*$ needs itself to be estimated by Monte Carlo simulation. More specifically, the j-th component of $\mathbf{u}^*$ may be estimated from iid random variables $\mathbf{X}_1, \ldots, \mathbf{X}_N$ (as in the Proposition above) by

$$\hat{u}_j^* = \frac{\sum_{i=1}^{N} g(\mathbf{X}_i)X_{ij}}{\sum_{i=1}^{N} g(\mathbf{X}_i)} \tag{5}$$

where X_{ij} is the j-th component of $\mathbf{X}_i$. However, recall that in statistical model checking $g(\mathbf{X}_i)$ is either 1 or 0 — a sample trace either satisfies a given temporal logic property or it does not. Also, in the rare-event case it will be very unlikely to sample traces that satisfy the temporal logic property. This means that for reasonable sample sizes the estimator in (5) would most likely be $\frac{0}{0}$, thereby of little use.

This problem can be solved by noting that, for an arbitrary *tilting* parameter $w \in \mathcal{U}$, the following holds

$$u_j^* = \frac{\mathrm{E}[g(\mathbf{X})X_j]}{\mathrm{E}[g(\mathbf{X})]} = \frac{\mathrm{E}_w[g(\mathbf{X})W(\mathbf{X}, w)X_j]}{\mathrm{E}_w[g(\mathbf{X})W(\mathbf{X}, w)]}$$

where $W(x, w) = f(x)/f(x, w)$ and $f(x) = f(x, v)$ is the nominal density of $\mathbf{X}$. It is important to note that the expectation is computed with respect to the proposal density $f(\cdot, w)$. Now, we can use Monte Carlo simulation again to estimate u_j^* by

$$\hat{u}_j^* = \frac{\sum_{i=1}^N g(\mathbf{X}_i)W(\mathbf{X}_i, w)X_{ij}}{\sum_{i=1}^N g(\mathbf{X}_i)W(\mathbf{X}_i, w)} \qquad (6)$$

where the $\mathbf{X}_i$'s are sampled from $f(\cdot, w)$. In other terms, we use importance sampling with a proposal density given by the tilting parameter w. Naturally, w must be chosen in such a way to avoid the $\frac{0}{0}$ problem of the estimator (6). Therefore, w should increase the probability of the event $g(\mathbf{X}) = 1$, *i.e.*, we should sample more often traces satisfying the given temporal property. However, it is not required to "guess" a tilting parameter close to the optimal one: it is often sufficient that the chosen w increases the probability of the rare event in the range 0.01-0.1. This enables meaningful estimates of the optimal $\mathbf{u}^*$ using (6).

We point it out that the CE method does not guarantee that the computed proposal density minimizes the variance (3). This is because in general the optimal proposal density may not belong to the parametric family. However, the CE method has been shown to work very well in many applications [12]. As we show in the next Section, the CE method works well with statistical model checking, too.

Finally, Rubinstein [11] has presented a multi-level CE algorithm for estimating the probability of rare events of the form $\{g(X) \geqslant \gamma\}$, where g is a real function and γ a constant. The algorithm first gets N samples $X_1, \ldots X_N$ of the system under the nominal (unbiased) distribution. Then it computes the sample quantile of the $g(X_i)$'s, and it adaptively tunes γ to make the event of interest more frequent. Besides the more restricted class of events considered, this algorithm does not work in our case. In statistical model checking the function g is in fact the model checker that checks whether a simulation trace satisfies the given temporal logic formula. Function g thus returns either 0 or 1. When computing the sample quantile one has to order the values of the $g(X_i)$'s. But these would most likely all be 0, since the system is sampled with the original distribution, under which the event $\{g(X) \geqslant \gamma\}$ is rare. Therefore, this technique is not directly applicable in our case.

6. EXPERIMENTS

We have applied the cross-entropy method to an example of stochastic hybrid system modeled in Stateflow/Simulink. The model implements a fault-tolerant controller for an aircraft elevator system[1]. The model is part of a larger Simulink

[1] More information about the model is available at `http://mathworks.com/products/stateflow/demos.html?file=/products/demos/shipping/stateflow/sf_aircraft.html`

modeling of the HL-20 crew rescue vehicle developed by NASA [3]. Typically, the two horizontal tails on the sides of an aircraft fuselage are each governed by one elevator, and there are two independent hydraulic actuators per elevator — four in total. During normal operation, each elevator is positioned by its corresponding outer actuator, and an inner actuator can be used in case of malfunctioning. The two outer actuators are driven by two separate hydraulic circuits, while the two inner actuators are both connected to a third hydraulic circuit. The outer actuators operates during normal use, and in case of failure the inner actuators can be operated. The system should ensure that at any given time only one set of actuators (*i.e.*, either outer or inner) position the elevators. If a fault arises in the outer actuators or in their corresponding hydraulic circuits, the system will activate the inner actuators; the outer actuators will be switched off and eventually isolated if the fault persists. Failures in the hydraulic circuits may be temporary, and a failed circuit can always placed back online if the fault condition terminates. The control logic of the system is implemented as a Stateflow diagram, while the hydraulic actuators and the elevators are modeled using Simulink. More details about the model can be found in [8].

We have modified the Stateflow/Simulink model by adding random failures in the three hydraulic circuits only. A failure is modeled as an out-of-bounds reading of the circuit pressure. We model failure injection as three independent Poisson processes. When a failure in a hydraulic circuit occurs, the circuit will stay in faulty condition for one second, after which the pressure reading returns to its normal value, and the fail condition terminates. The nominal fault rates for the three circuits were all set to 1/3600. In our experiments we estimated the probability of BLTL formula ϕ:

$$\phi = \mathbf{F}^{25}\mathbf{G}^1((\mathrm{H1}_{fail} \vee \mathrm{H3}_{fail}) \wedge \mathrm{H2}_{fail})$$

where H1 and H3 denote the hydraulic circuits driving the outer actuators, and H2 denotes the circuit driving the inner actuators. Informally, we want to estimate the probability that, within 25 seconds, the horizontal tails do not respond to the control inputs for a duration of one second. Since the fault rates of the three hydraulic circuits are low (1/3600), we expect ϕ to be a rare event.

We have performed three experiments, depending on the number of samples used to compute the optimal CE rates and in importance sampling (the higher numbers are always used for importance sampling). The proposal density is implemented by changing the fault rates of the three Poisson processes modeling the fault injection. The initial fault rates (tilting rates) for the computation of the optimal bias were 1/10, except for the first experiment (100/1,000 samples) where we used 1/8. This because during the computation of the CE rates the proportion of satisfying traces was too low. All our experiments have been performed on a 3.2GHz Intel Xeon computer running Matlab R2010a.

In Table 1 we report the estimate for the probability that ϕ holds, the (approximate) relative error, the total computation time (*i.e.*, simulation, model checking, and cross-entropy calculations), and the (approximately) optimal rates computed by the CE method. These were the actual rates used in importance sampling. The relative error is computed as the ratio between the estimated standard deviation of the estimate and the estimate itself. (We recall that the standard deviation can be estimated by the square root

Samples	Estimate	RE	Time	Rates
100 1,000	1.58×10^{-14}	0.58	0.23	1/1.00 1/2.00 1/1.00
1,000 10,000	8.54×10^{-14}	0.24	2.45	1/0.98 1/2.01 1/1.02
10,000 100,000	8.11×10^{-14}	0.17	23.9	1/0.52 1/2.01 1/1.48

Table 1: Cross-Entropy and Importance Sampling. Samples used for CE rates computation and importance sampling; probability estimate; relative error; total computation time (hours); computed cross-entropy rates.

of the sample variance $\frac{1}{N-1}\sum_{i=1}^{N}(g(X_i)W(X_i) - \hat{c})^2$, where $X_1, \ldots, X_N$ are iid as the proposal distribution, and $\hat{c}$ is the probability estimated by importance sampling on the same sample $X_1, \ldots, X_N$.)

The table shows that statistical model checking with importance sampling and cross-entropy can efficiently estimate rare-event probabilities. In particular, with a feasible sample size of 10^4 it is possible to estimate probabilities in the order of 10^{-14} with reasonable accuracy (RE = 0.24). Clearly, standard statistical model checking and crude Monte Carlo would need an unfeasible number of samples to provide similar levels of accuracy. Also, we see that by increasing the sample size the relative error decreases — as one would expect — thereby yielding more accurate estimates.

Finally, since each sample can be generated independently from the others, Monte Carlo methods can readily take advantage of parallel/multi-core systems. That further contributes in making statistical model checking an effective technique.

7. CONCLUSIONS

In this paper we have addressed the verification of rare events for stochastic hybrid systems via statistical model checking. We have proposed a semantic model for stochastic hybrid systems that is tailored for simulation environments. We have shown that the model induces a Markov process and a well-defined probability measure, and it is thus usable with statistical model checking. Previous works have shown that statistical model checking can efficiently verify large, "difficult" systems. However, this verification technique suffers from the rare-event problem: if the property to verify is true with an extremely small probability, then statistical model checking becomes inefficient. In particular, a large number of simulations is required to obtain an accurate estimate of the probability. The problem can be tackled by combining importance sampling and the cross-entropy method with statistical model checking, as we have proposed. Our initial findings indicate that this combination can efficiently address the verification of rare events for stochastic hybrid systems.

8. ACKNOWLEDGMENTS

This research was sponsored by the GSRC under contract no. 1041377 (Princeton University), the National Science Foundation under contracts no. CNS0926181 and no. CNS0931985, the Semiconductor Research Corporation under contract no. 2005TJ1366, General Motors under contract no. GMCMUCRLNV301, the Office of Naval Research under award no. N000141010188, the DFG-project QuaOS, and the Collaborative Research Center HAEC (SFB 912) funded by the DFG.

9. REFERENCES

[1] C. Baier, B. R. Haverkort, H. Hermanns, and J.-P. Katoen. Model-checking algorithms for continuous-time Markov chains. *IEEE Trans. Software Eng.*, 29(6):524–541, 2003.

[2] H. A. P. Blom and J. Lygeros, editors. *Stochastic Hybrid Systems*, volume 337 of *Lecture Notes in Control and Information Sciences*. Springer, 2006.

[3] S. Gage. NASA HL-20 lifting body airframe modeled with Simulink and the aerospace blockset. *MATLAB Digest*, 10(4), 2002.

[4] R. Grosu and S. A. Smolka. Monte Carlo Model Checking. In *TACAS*, volume 3440 of *LNCS*, pages 271–286, 2005.

[5] T. Hérault, R. Lassaigne, F. Magniette, and S. Peyronnet. Approximate probabilistic model checking. In *VMCAI*, volume 2937 of *LNCS*, pages 73–84, 2004.

[6] S. K. Jha, E. M. Clarke, C. J. Langmead, A. Legay, A. Platzer, and P. Zuliani. A Bayesian approach to Model Checking biological systems. In *CMSB*, volume 5688 of *LNCS*, pages 218–234, 2009.

[7] O. Maler and D. Nickovic. Monitoring temporal properties of continuous signals. In *FORMATS*, volume 3253 of *LNCS*, pages 152–166, 2004.

[8] P. J. Mosterman and J. Ghidella. Model reuse for the training of fault scenarios in aerospace. In *Proceedings of the AIAA Modeling and Simulation Technologies Conference*, 2004.

[9] A. Pnueli. The temporal logic of programs. In *FOCS*, pages 46–57. IEEE, 1977.

[10] G. Rubino and B. Tuffin, editors. *Rare Event Simulation using Monte Carlo Methods*. Wiley, 2009.

[11] R. Y. Rubinstein. The cross-entropy method for combinatorial and continuous optimization. *Methodology and Computing in Applied Probability*, 1:127–190, 1999.

[12] R. Y. Rubinstein and D. P. Kroese. *The Cross-Entropy Method*. Springer, 2004.

[13] K. Sen, M. Viswanathan, and G. Agha. Statistical model checking of black-box probabilistic systems. In *CAV*, volume 3114 of *LNCS*, pages 202–215, 2004.

[14] A. N. Shiryaev. *Probability*. Springer, 1995.

[15] R. Srinivasan. *Importance Sampling*. Springer, 2002.

[16] H. L. S. Younes, E. M. Clarke, and P. Zuliani. Statistical verification of probabilistic properties with unbounded until. In *SBMF*, volume 6527 of *LNCS*, pages 144–160, 2010.

[17] H. L. S. Younes, M. Z. Kwiatkowska, G. Norman, and D. Parker. Numerical vs. statistical probabilistic model checking. *STTT*, 8(3):216–228, 2006.

[18] H. L. S. Younes and D. J. Musliner. Probabilistic plan verification through acceptance sampling. In *AIPS*

Workshop on Planning via Model Checking, pages 81–88, 2002.

[19] H. L. S. Younes and R. G. Simmons. Probabilistic verification of discrete event systems using acceptance sampling. In *CAV*, volume 2404 of *LNCS*, pages 223–235, 2002.

[20] H. L. S. Younes and R. G. Simmons. Statistical probabilistic model checking with a focus on time-bounded properties. *Inf. Comput.*, 204(9):1368–1409, 2006.

[21] P. Zuliani, A. Platzer, and E. M. Clarke. Bayesian statistical model checking with application to Stateflow/Simulink verification. In *HSCC*, pages 243–252, 2010.

APPENDIX

For completeness, we report some standard results about importance sampling [15] and the cross-entropy [12].

A. IMPORTANCE SAMPLING

We calculate the variance of the IS estimator of Definition 8. In the following, Var_* denotes variance taken with respect to the biasing density f_*. The variance of the IS estimator is

$$\mathrm{Var}(\hat{c}_{\mathrm{IS}}) = \mathrm{Var}_* \left(\frac{1}{N} \sum_{i=1}^{N} g(X_i) W(X_i) \right)$$

$$= \frac{1}{N^2} \sum_{i=1}^{N} \mathrm{Var}_*(g(X_i) W(X_i))$$

$$= \frac{1}{N} \mathrm{Var}_*(g(X) W(X))$$

$$= \frac{1}{N} (\mathrm{E}_*[g^2(X) W^2(X)] - \mathrm{E}_*^2[g(X) W(X)])$$

$$= \frac{1}{N} (\mathrm{E}_*[g^2(X) W^2(X)] - c^2) \tag{7}$$

where by (2) it is $c = \mathrm{E}_*[g(X) W(X)] = \mathrm{E}[g(X)]$. Also, the variance can be expressed in a slightly different form. Continuing from (7) we have

$$\mathrm{Var}(\hat{c}_{\mathrm{IS}}) = \frac{1}{N} \left(\int_{\mathbb{R}} g^2(x) \frac{f^2(x)}{f_*^2(x)} f_*(x) \, dx - c^2 \right)$$

$$= \frac{1}{N} \left(\int_{\mathbb{R}} g^2(x) \frac{f(x)}{f_*(x)} f(x) \, dx - c^2 \right)$$

$$= \frac{1}{N} (\mathrm{E}[g^2(X) W(X)] - c^2)$$

We now calculate the optimal biasing density. Since the variance is always non-negative, we need to minimize the expectation term in (7). By Jensen's inequality we get

$$E_*[g^2(X) W^2(X)] \geqslant E_*^2[|g(X)| W(X)] \tag{8}$$

$$= E_*^2 [|g(X)| \frac{f(X)}{f_*(X)}]$$

$$= \left(\int |g(x)| \frac{f(x)}{f_*(x)} f_*(x) \, dx \right)^2$$

$$= E^2[|g(X)|] \tag{9}$$

and, since the square function is strictly convex, equality holds in (8) iff the random variable $|g(X)| W(X)$ is constant, *i.e.*,

$$|g(X)| W(X) = k$$

for some constant k and $X \sim f_*$ (because in (8) the expectation is computed with respect to f_*). But $W(x) = \frac{f(x)}{f_*(x)}$, so we deduce that

$$f_*(x) = \frac{1}{k} |g(x)| f(x) \tag{10}$$

is the *optimal* biasing density, *i.e.*, the density which minimizes the variance (7) by attaining the lower bound in (9). It remains to calculate k: when $|g(X)| W(X) = k$, we have immediately from (9) that $k = \mathrm{E}[|g(X)|]$. Therefore, from (7) the variance of the IS estimator is

$$\mathrm{Var}_*(\hat{c}_{\mathrm{IS}}) = \frac{1}{N} (k^2 - c^2)$$

which in general may be non-zero, but will of course tend to zero as $N \to \infty$. Note that when g is non-negative, then $k = \mathrm{E}[|g(X)|] = \mathrm{E}[g(X)] = c$ and therefore $\mathrm{Var}_*(\hat{c}_{\mathrm{IS}}) = 0$.

B. CROSS-ENTROPY

We show that the cross-entropy (or Kullback-Leibler divergence) of two densities f ang g is always non-negative. Recall its definition

$$\mathcal{D}(f, g) = \int_{\mathbb{R}} f(x) \ln \frac{f(x)}{g(x)} \, dx = \mathrm{E} \left[\ln \frac{f(X)}{g(X)} \right]$$

where X is a random variable with density f. The proof is a simple application of Jensen's inequality (note that $- \ln$ is a convex function):

$$\mathrm{E} \left[\ln \frac{f(X)}{g(X)} \right] = \mathrm{E} \left[-\ln \frac{g(X)}{f(X)} \right] \geqslant$$

$$- \ln \mathrm{E} \left[\frac{g(X)}{f(X)} \right] = - \ln \int_{\mathbb{R}} g(x) \, dx = 0$$

where the last equality holds because g is a probability density. Also, it follows that $\mathcal{D}(f, g) = 0$ iff $f = g$.

Regularization of Bellman Equations for Infinite-horizon Probabilistic Properties[*]

Ilya Tkachev
Delft Center for Systems & Control
TU Delft - Delft University of Technology
Delft, The Netherlands
I.Tkachev@tudelft.nl

Alessandro Abate
Delft Center for Systems & Control
TU Delft - Delft University of Technology
Delft, The Netherlands
A.Abate@tudelft.nl

ABSTRACT

This work studies Bellman integral equations arising in infinite-horizon probabilistic verification problems for discrete time homogeneous Markov processes over general state spaces. The problems of interest are expressed via specifications such as probabilistic reachability, invariance, reach-avoid and mean exit time. The contribution shows that the uniqueness of the solutions of the corresponding Bellman equations depends on the presence of absorbing sets within the state space. Furthermore, the work puts forward methods to modify the integral equations to obtain unique solutions for them, techniques to compute such solutions with explicit bounds on the approximation error, and conditions to characterize the possible presence of absorbing sets over the state space.

Categories and Subject Descriptors

G.3 [**Probability and Statistics**]: Markov processes; Stochastic processes

Keywords

Markov processes, probabilistic properties, Bellman equations, absorbing sets.

1. INTRODUCTION

Bellman recursions and related Bellman fixpoint equations play a prominent role in various problems in optimal control, verification, operations research and economics.

In the context of probabilistic verification, Bellman recursions are used to express properties formulated in PCTL, a modal logic that accommodates for probabilistic requirements [3] that can be efficiently computed via model checkers [7, 9]. Verification

[*]This work is supported by the European Commission MoVeS project FP7-ICT-2009-5 257005, by the European Commission Marie Curie grant MANTRAS 249295, by the European Commission NoE HYCON2 FP7-ICT-2009-5 257462, and by the NWO VENI grant 016.103.020.

of PCTL specifications has been widely studied over stochastic processes with countable spaces, but only in part addressed for processes on continuous (uncountable) spaces [1]. In the latter case, and with regards to finite time horizon specifications, [1] has provided explicit bounds on the error of computation via Bellman recursions using a state space discretization approach. On the other hand, such results are missing for the important instance of infinite time horizon properties. In this challenging case, specifications are shown to be characterized in two possible ways: either as limits of Bellman recursions, or as solution of Bellman integral equations. From the second perspective, [11] has provided necessary conditions for Bellman equation to have a unique solution. However, due to the conservatism of these conditions, a large class of processes is left uncovered.

The focus of this paper is on understanding when the solution of a given Bellman equation is unique, and on how to compute it with explicit convergence rates or with explicit bounds on the approximation error. The contribution shows that the uniqueness of the solution of the considered class of integral equations depends on the presence of absorbing sets within the state space. In particular, the absence of absorbing sets allows us not only to establish uniqueness, but also to put forward techniques to compute these solutions. On the other hand, in the presence of absorbing sets this work proposes explicit modifications of the Bellman equations, which allow for unique solutions and for approximations methods with explicit error bounds and convergence rates. To the best of authors' knowledge, there exist no general methods to compute infinite time horizon probabilistic properties with explicit bounds on the error. Hence, the goal of the paper is to develop such methods, while leaving computational improvements and scalability issues to later work.

Given the central role played by absorbing sets for this class of problems, this paper also investigates in what instances or under what conditions it is possible to ensure the absence of such sets, or conversely to either characterize them or to approximately compute them.

The contribution is structured as follows. Section 2 introduces the notations and explains the problem under investigation. As reference properties, the contribution looks at probabilistic reachability, invariance, reach-avoid and mean exit time (see Section 2.3). Section 2.2 introduces a case study, employed to clarify and give examples for the discussed notions and presented results. Section 3 deals with uniqueness issues, regularizations, and computations of a number of different properties. Furthermore, Section 4 studies the characterization of absorbing sets.

2. PRELIMINARIES

2.1 Notations and basic concepts

We consider a homogeneous Markov process X in discrete time. The state space $\mathscr{X}$ is a Borel space and its Borel σ-algebra is denoted as $\mathscr{B}(\mathscr{X})$[6]. The process X is characterized by its transition kernel $T(A|x)$, which is such that $x \mapsto T(A|x)$ is a measurable function for any $A \in \mathscr{B}(\mathscr{X})$, and such that $T(\cdot|x)$ is a probability measure on $(\mathscr{X}, \mathscr{B}(\mathscr{X}))$, for all $x \in \mathscr{X}$.

The sample space is a space of trajectories $\Omega = \mathscr{X}^{\mathbb{N}_0}$ endowed with a product σ-algebra $\mathscr{F}$, where $\mathbb{N}_0 = \mathbb{N} \cup \{0\}$. X_k is the value of X at the time k. With P_x we denote the probability measure induced by T, such that $\mathsf{P}_x\{X_0 = x\} = 1$, and with E_x the corresponding expectation.

We say that a random variable τ is a stopping time if for all $n \geq 0$ it holds that $\{\tau \leq n\} \in \mathscr{F}_n$. For a set $B \in \mathscr{B}(\mathscr{X})$ we define the first hitting time $\tau_B = \inf\{n \geq 0 : X_n \in B\}$ and the first exit time $\varsigma_B = \tau_{B^c}$, both of which are clearly stopping times.

The space $\mathbb{B}(\mathscr{X})$ of all measurable functions $f : \mathscr{X} \to \mathbb{R}$ that are bounded on $\mathscr{X}$ is a Banach space with a norm $\|f\| = \sup_{x \in \mathscr{X}} |f(x)|$ [5]. For any $B \in \mathscr{B}(\mathscr{X})$ its indicator function $1_B(x)$ is in $\mathbb{B}(\mathscr{X})$ with $\|1_B\| = 1$.

If $\mathscr{J}$ is an operator acting on $\mathbb{B}(\mathscr{X})$, then we define the norm of $\mathscr{J}$ as follows:

$$\|\mathscr{J}\| = \sup_{f \in \mathbb{B}(\mathscr{X})} \frac{\|\mathscr{J}f\|}{\|f\|}.$$

If for an operator $\mathscr{J}$ it holds that $\|\mathscr{J}f_1 - \mathscr{J}f_2\| \leq \alpha\|f_1 - f_2\|$ for all $f_1, f_2 \in \mathbb{B}(\mathscr{X})$ and some $\alpha < 1$, then we say that $\mathscr{J}$ is a contraction (with rate α). In addition, with $\mathscr{C}(B)$ we denote the class of real-valued functions defined on $\mathbb{B}(\mathscr{X})$ that are continuous on $B \in \mathscr{B}(\mathscr{X})$ and we put $\mathbb{L}(\mathscr{X})$ to be the space of all measurable functions $f : \mathscr{X} \to (-\infty, \infty]$.

Since $\mathscr{X}$ is a subset of a Polish space, it is metrizable. We select a generic metric and denote it by ρ. Finally, for any subset $A \subseteq \mathscr{X}$ we define by $\bar{A}$ the closure of A, by A° the interior of A, and by ∂A the boundary of A. For any $a, b \in \mathbb{R}$ we put $a \wedge b = \min\{a, b\}$.

In this work we are focused on transition kernels T that admit a Lipschitz continuous density.

ASSUMPTION 1. *Assume that there exists a σ-finite Borel measure μ on $(\mathscr{X}, \mathscr{B}(\mathscr{X}))$ such that $\mu(B) < \infty$ for any compact set B. In addition, let there exist a Lipschitz continuous function $\xi : \mathscr{X} \times \mathscr{X} \to \mathbb{R}_{\geq 0}$ for any $A \in \mathscr{B}(\mathscr{X})$, satisfying*

$$T(A|x) = \int_A \xi(x, y)\mu(dy). \tag{2.1}$$

Function ξ is the density of the transition kernel T with respect to the measure μ. By $\beta \in (0, \infty)$ we denote the Lipschitz constant of ξ. Note that a large class of processes admits Assumption 1, for instance Markov Chains [10] and dtSHS [1].

REMARK 1 (ON ASSUMPTION 1). *By [6, Example C.6, p. 176] Assumption 1 is sufficient for X to admit the strong Feller property [6, Appendix C, p. 174] hence the results of [14] are applicable.*

2.2 Case study

In order to illustrate the results of this work, we use a Markov process X as a benchmark to do verification of its infinite-horizon properties. The state space of X is hybrid, namely given by

$\mathscr{X} = \bigcup_{i=1}^4 \{l_i\} \times [0, 1]$, see Figure 1. $L = \{l_i\}_{i=1}^4$ is a set of discrete locations, each of which is associated to the continuous interval $[0, 1]$. For any $x \in \mathscr{X}$ we write $x = (l_x, c_x)$, where $l_x \in L$ and $c_x \in [0, 1]$. The metric on $\mathscr{X}$ is given as

$$\rho(l_x, c_x, l_y, c_y) = \begin{cases} 1, & \text{if } l_x \neq l_y; \\ |c_x - c_y|, & \text{if } l_x = l_y. \end{cases}$$

Such a metric endows $\mathscr{X}$ with the Borel σ-algebra $\mathscr{B}(\mathscr{X})$. Clearly, any $A \in \mathscr{B}(\mathscr{X})$ admits a unique representation $A = \bigcup_{i=1}^4 \{l_i\} \times A^i$ where $A^i \in \mathscr{B}([0, 1])$ for $1 \leq i \leq 4$. The measure μ on $(\mathscr{X}, \mathscr{B}(\mathscr{X}))$ is such that $\mu(A) = \sum_{i=1}^4 \lambda(A^i)$, where λ is the Lebesgue measure over $[0, 1]$.

In the following, the probability density function of the normal distribution is denoted by

$$f_{\mathscr{N}}(x, y, \sigma) = \frac{1}{\sqrt{2\pi}\sigma}e^{-\frac{(y-x)^2}{2\sigma^2}},$$

and we also define $\Phi(x, y, \sigma) = \int_0^y f_{\mathscr{N}}(x, s, \sigma)\,ds$.

At each time step the process X moves according to the following rule: first, it selects a discrete location according to a discrete distribution that depends on the current state; then, it resets over the continuous domain $[0, 1]$ according to a continuous probabilistic law that depends also on the new location. These semantics can be precisely characterized by the transition kernel T as:

$$\xi(l_x, c_x, l_y, c_y) = \sum_{i,j=1}^4 \delta_{ij}(l_x, l_y)p_{ij}(c_x)\xi_{ij}(c_x, c_y).$$

Here $\delta_{ij}(l_x, l_y) = 1$ only if $l_x = i, l_y = j$, and zero otherwise. The functions p_{ij} and ξ_{ij} are location-dependent and different from zero only if (see Figure 1)

$$(i, j) \in \{(1, 1), (2, 3), (2, 4), (3, 3), (3, 4), (4, 2), (4, 4)\}.$$

The quantity $p_{11} \equiv 1$, since from location l_1 jumps to other locations are not allowed. The corresponding continuous density is a truncated normal with $\xi_{11}(c_x, c_y) = \frac{f_{\mathscr{N}}(c_x, c_y, 0.3)}{\Phi(c_x, 1, 0.3)}$.

From location l_2 discrete jumps are allowed to any other, except l_3. The discrete jump distribution is given by functions $p_{21}(c_x) = \frac{c_x^2}{2}, p_{24}(c_x) = \frac{c_x}{2}$ and $p_{22}(c_x) = 1 - \frac{1}{2}(c_x + c_x^2)$. The continuous reset distribution over the new locations is simply uniform: $\xi_{21} = \xi_{24} \equiv 1$, and is truncated normal if the location does not change: $\xi_{22}(c_x, c_y) = \frac{f_{\mathscr{N}}(c_x, c_y, 0.4)}{\Phi(c_x, 1, 0.4)}$.

For the last two locations we have $p_{33}(c_x) = c_x^2, p_{44}(c_x) = c_x$ and $p_{34}(c_x) = 1 - c_x^2, p_{42}(c_x) = 1 - c_x$. Finally,

$$\xi_{33}(c_x, c_y) = \xi_{44}(c_x, c_y) = \frac{f_{\mathscr{N}}(c_x, c_y, 0.5)}{\Phi(c_x, 1, 0.5)}$$

and

$$\xi_{34}(c_x, c_y) = \xi_{42}(c_x, c_y) \equiv 1.$$

2.3 Specifications and related operators

This work is focused on operators and corresponding fixpoint equations arising in the theory of discrete-time Markov processes. As in [4] we are especially interested in the study of properties

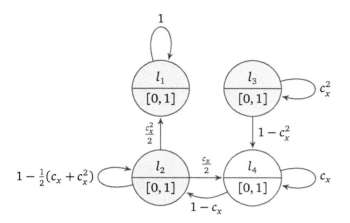

Figure 1: Case study: gray nodes denote the safe set.

related to the first exit time from some set $A \in \mathscr{B}(\mathscr{X})$. Most of them can be expressed through the distribution of ς_A.

Denote $p_n(x;A) = \mathsf{P}_x\{\varsigma_A = n\}$ and $p(x;A) = \mathsf{P}_x\{\varsigma_A = \infty\}$. The *reachability* value function is the cumulative distribution function for ς_A and is given by $v_n(x;A^c) = \mathsf{P}_x\{\varsigma_A \le n\}$.

The *invariance* value function is the tail probability for ς_A, i.e. $u_n(x;A) = \mathsf{P}_x\{\varsigma_A > n\} = 1 - v_n(x;A^c)$. It is worth mentioning that for the infinite-horizon invariance $u(x;A) := \lim_{n\to\infty} u_n(x;A) = p(x;A)$ and clearly, $u(x;A) = 1 - v(x;A^c)$.

Besides the distribution of ς_A, one important characteristic is its mean $t(x;A) = \mathsf{E}_x[\varsigma_A]$: we will show how the properties of this function depend on the invariance value function $u(x;A)$.

Finally, we consider the reach-avoid value function denoted as $w_n(x;A,B) = \mathsf{P}_x\{\tau_B < \varsigma_A \wedge n\}$ for any $A, B \in \mathscr{B}(\mathscr{X}), n \ge 0$, and the infinite-horizon version $w(x;A,B) = \mathsf{P}_x\{\tau_B < \varsigma_A \wedge \infty\} = \lim_{n\to\infty} w_n(x;A,B)$[13].

To compute the value of these functions an operator approach is used. Two basic operators, namely the linear *transition* $\mathscr{P}$ and the *invariance* $\mathscr{I}_A$, are defined as follows:

$$\mathscr{P}f(x) = \mathsf{E}_x[f(X_1)] = \int_{\mathscr{X}} f(y)T(dy|x).$$

$$\mathscr{I}_A f(x) = 1_A(x)\mathscr{P}f(x).$$

Clearly, it holds that $\|\mathscr{P}\| = 1$ and that in general $\|\mathscr{I}_A\| \le 1$. By *Bellman equation* we refer to an equation of the form

$$f(x) = g(x) + \mathscr{I}_A f(x), \tag{2.2}$$

with $A \in \mathscr{B}(\mathscr{X})$ and $g \in \mathbb{B}(\mathscr{X})$. The choice of g determines the related problem of probabilistic verification, namely

$$f(x) = \mathscr{I}_A f(x) \tag{2.3}$$

for the invariance problem and

$$f(x) = 1_B(x) + \mathscr{I}_{A\setminus B} f(x) \tag{2.4}$$

for the reach-avoid one. Let us introduce the shorthand

$$\mathscr{R}_{A,B}f(x) := 1_B(x) + \mathscr{I}_{A\setminus B}f(x).$$

A solution for equations (2.3) or (2.4) always exists in $\mathbb{B}(\mathscr{X})$ and is given by the value functions $u(x;A)$ and $w(x;A,B)$ respectively, which are constructed as follows:

$$\begin{cases} u_{n+1}(x;A) &= \mathscr{I}_A u_n(x;A) \\ u_0(x;A) &= 1_A(x); \end{cases}$$

and

$$\begin{cases} w_{n+1}(x;A,B) &= \mathscr{R}_{A,B}w_n(x;A,B) \\ w_0(x;A,B) &= 1_B(x), \end{cases}$$

with $u(x;A) = \lim_{n\to\infty} u_n(x;A)$ and $w(x;A,B) = \lim_{n\to\infty} w_n(x;A,B)$ pointwise and monotonically [11, 14].

For the mean exit time we have $g(x) = 1_A(x)$, thus the Bellman equation is given by

$$f(x) = 1_A(x) + \mathscr{I}_A f(x) \tag{2.5}$$

as in [10], and the solution exists in $\mathbb{L}(\mathscr{X})$ but may not exist in $\mathbb{B}(\mathscr{X})$. Such a solution is given by the value function

$$t(x;A) = \sum_{n=1}^{\infty} np_n(x;A) + p(x;A) \cdot \infty \tag{2.6}$$

where $p(x;A) \cdot \infty = \infty$ if $p(x;A) > 0$, and is equal to 0 otherwise.

Finally, we introduce the operator $\mathscr{H}_A$ defined for any function $f \in \mathbb{B}(\mathscr{X})$ and set $A \in \mathscr{B}(\mathscr{X})$ by

$$\mathscr{H}_A f(x) = \mathscr{P} 1_A(x) f(x),$$

which is to be used throughout the work.

3. UNIQUE SOLUTIONS OF BELLMAN EQUATIONS

3.1 Simple and absorbing sets

The Bellman equation in (2.2) is a linear equation, so whenever it is solved on $\mathbb{B}(\mathscr{X})$ the uniqueness of its solution holds if and only if the solution is unique for its homogeneous version (2.3), which happens to be the equation for the invariance value function. Due to this reason we first study the properties of equation (2.3).

PROPOSITION 1. *For any $n \ge 0$ it holds that $u_n(x;A) \in \mathscr{C}(A)$.*

PROOF. The proof immediately follows from Remark 1. □

LEMMA 1. *Equation (2.3) has a unique solution if and only if $u(x;A) = 0$ for all $x \in \mathscr{X}$.*

PROOF. Equation (2.3) is linear and homogeneous, so if it has a unique solution then it is the zero solution. The other direction was proved in [11, Proposition 9]. □

Based on the results above, we have to verify the triviality of the invariance problem: namely, if its value function is equal to zero everywhere which is clearly equivalent to being equal to zero just on A. This instance can be characterized by the presence of absorbing sets, which are defined in the following.

DEFINITION 1 (ABSORBING AND SIMPLE SETS). *A non-empty set $A' \in \mathscr{B}(\mathscr{X})$ is called absorbing if for all $x \in A'$ it holds that*

$$T(A'|x) = 1.$$

Given a set $A \in \mathscr{B}(\mathscr{X})$, the set A' is the largest absorbing subset of A if for any absorbing set $A'' \subseteq A$ it holds that $A'' \subseteq A'$. A set $A \in \mathscr{B}(\mathscr{X})$ is called simple if it does not contain any absorbing set.

3.2 Simplicity and uniqueness of solution of Bellman equations

LEMMA 2. *[14, Theorem 3] Let A be a compact set, then it is simple if and only if $u(x;A) = 0$ for all $x \in \mathscr{X}$.*

If A is compact, then it is simple if and only if equation (2.3) has a unique (zero) solution. This fact leads to the following questions:

1. how to verify if a given compact set A is simple?

2. how to solve equation (2.3) if the compact set A is not simple?

The rest of this Section provides an answer to these questions. Given a set $A \in \mathscr{B}(\mathscr{X})$ define for any $n \geq 0$

$$A_n = \{x \in A : u_n(x;A) = 1\}, \qquad A_0 = A.$$

LEMMA 3. *[14, Lemma 1] For all $n \geq 0$ it holds that $A_{n+1} \subseteq A_n$ and*

$$A_{n+1} = \{x : T(A_n|x) = 1\}. \tag{3.1}$$

Since $A_{n+1} \subseteq A_n$ is a non-increasing sequence of sets, the limit $A_\infty := \bigcap_{n=0}^{\infty} A_n$ always exists, though it may be empty. Moreover, by [14, Theorem 3] if A is not simple, then A_∞ is its largest absorbing subset.

REMARK 2. *The sequence A_n can be effectively used to verify the simplicity of a set A as well as to overapproximate its largest absorbing subset.*

Let us introduce the quantity

$$m(A) = \inf\{m \geq 0 : \sup_{x \in \mathscr{X}} u_m(x, A) < 1\}$$

and $\alpha(A) = \sup_{x \in \mathscr{X}} u_{m(A)}(x, A)$.

LEMMA 4. *A compact set A is simple if and only if $m(A) < \infty$.*

PROOF. If $m(A) < \infty$, then by [14, Theorem 2] the solution of the invariance problem is trivial: $u(x;A) = 0$ for all $x \in \mathscr{X}$. Thus A is simple. Let us suppose now that A is simple but $m(A) = \infty$. Consider a function $u_n(x;A), n \geq 0$. Since by Proposition 1 it is a continuous function on a compact set A with $\sup_{x \in \mathscr{X}} u_n(x, A) = 1$, it holds that A_n is a non-empty compact set. Thus, A_∞ is also non-empty, which contradicts the simplicity of A. $\square$

THEOREM 1. *A compact set A is simple if and only if $\mathscr{I}_A^m$ is a contraction for some $m > 0$. In this case for any $g \in \mathscr{B}(\mathscr{X})$ Equation (2.2) admits a solution $f(x) \in \mathscr{B}(\mathscr{X})$, which is unique in $\mathbb{B}(\mathscr{X})$ and given by $f(x) = \lim_{n \to \infty} f_n(x)$ with any $f_0 \in \mathbb{B}(\mathscr{X})$ and such that*

$$f_{n+1}(x) = \mathscr{J}^{m(A)+1} f_n(x).$$

Here $\mathscr{J}$ is given as $\mathscr{J}h(x) = g(x) + \mathscr{I}_A h(x)$ for any $h \in \mathbb{B}(\mathscr{X})$. Moreover, the following bound holds for all $n \geq 0$

$$\|f - f_n\| \leq \frac{\alpha^n(A)}{1 - \alpha(A)} \|\mathscr{J}^{m(A)+1} f_0 - f_0\|.$$

PROOF. If $\mathscr{I}_A^m$ is a contraction, then the solution of (2.3) is unique, hence A is simple. On the other hand, if A is simple then $m(A) < \infty$ and

$$\mathscr{I}_A^{m(A)+1} f(x) \leq \mathscr{I}_A^{m(A)} \|f\| 1_A(x) \leq \alpha(A) \|f\|,$$

which proves that $\mathscr{I}_A^{m(A)+1}$ is contractive with rate $\alpha(A)$. This fact implies that for any $g \in \mathscr{B}(\mathscr{X})$ the operator $\mathscr{J}^{m(A)+1}$ is a contraction on $\mathbb{B}(\mathscr{X})$ with rate $\alpha(A)$, and the rest of the proof immediately follows from the Contraction Mapping Theorem [8]. $\square$

REMARK 3. *The finite horizon value function f_n can be computed with explicit bounds on the error, for example with the space discretization algorithm in [1].*
The paper [11] showed a special instance of this theorem, namely that $m(A) = 1$ implies contractivity and uniqueness.

Below we also need the following corollary.

COROLLARY 1. *If A is compact and simple then $\mathscr{H}_A^{m(A)+1}$ is a contraction on $\mathbb{B}(\mathscr{X})$.*

PROOF. For all $x \in A$ it holds that $(\mathscr{H}_A^n 1)(x) = u_n(x;A)$ so $\sup_{x \in A}(\mathscr{H}_A^{m(A)} 1)(x) = \alpha(A) < 1$. Now, for an arbitrary $f \in \mathbb{B}(\mathscr{X})$:

$$\left\| \mathscr{H}_A^{m(A)+1} f \right\| \leq \int_A \left\| \mathscr{H}_A^{m(A)} f(x) \right\| \xi(x, y) \mu(dy)$$

$$\leq \int_A \alpha(A) \|f\| \xi(x, y) \mu(dy) \leq \alpha(A) \|f\|.$$

$\square$

3.3 Modified Bellman equations over sets that are not simple

We employ Theorem 1 to provide an answer to the second question above: how to solve (2.3) if the compact set A is not simple. We put forward a modification of the original Bellman equation that has a unique solution given by the function $u(x;A) = \mathsf{P}_x\{\varsigma_A = \infty\}$.
We start by discussing some additional facts about simplicity and absorbance.

LEMMA 5. *Let A and A' be respectively simple and absorbing sets, then for any $C \in \mathscr{B}(\mathscr{X})$ such that $\mu(C) = 0$ it holds that $A \cup C$ is simple and $A' \setminus C$ is absorbing. In particular, $\mu(A') > 0$.*

PROOF. Consider an arbitrary set $C \in \mathscr{B}(\mathscr{X})$ of zero measure. If A' is absorbing then for any $x \in A' \setminus C$ it holds that

$$T(A' \setminus C|x) = \int_{A' \setminus C} \xi(x, y) \mu(dy) = \int_{A'} \xi(x, y) \mu(dy) = T(A'|x) = 1,$$

so the absorbance of $A' \setminus C$ is proved. Now let the set A be simple. Suppose that $A \cup C$ is not simple, so there is an absorbing set $A' \subseteq A \cup C$. This means that $A' \setminus C \subseteq A$ is an absorbing set, which contradicts the simplicity of A. $\square$

LEMMA 6. *If $\mu(A) < \infty$ then $u(x;A)$ is Lipschitz on A.*

PROOF. Recall that $u(x;A)$ is a solution of (2.3). Now, for any $x', x'' \in A$ we have

$$|u(x';A) - u(x'';A)| \leq \int_A |\xi(x', y) - \xi(x'', y)| \mu(dy)$$

$$\leq \beta \mu(A) \rho(x', x'').$$

$\square$

Note that if A is compact and hence of finite measure, the sequence of continuous functions $u_n(x;A)$ converges pointwise and monotonically to a continuous function $u(x;A)$, thus by Dini's theorem [12] the convergence is uniform on A.

THEOREM 2 (MODIFIED BELLMAN EQUATION). *Let $A \in \mathcal{B}(\mathcal{X})$ be compact, $A' \subset A$ be the largest absorbing subset of A, and $\mu(\partial A') = 0$. Then $u(x;A)$ is the unique solution of the equation*

$$u(x;A) = 1_A(x) + \mathcal{I}_{A \setminus A'} u(x;A). \tag{3.2}$$

PROOF. Let us start from the original Bellman equation (2.3) and raise trivial restrictions on its solution:

$$u(x;A) = \begin{cases} 1, & \text{if } x \in A', \\ 0, & \text{if } x \in A^c. \end{cases}$$

Using this information, we obtain from (2.3):

$$u(x;A) = 1_A(x)T(A'|x) + 1_A(x) \int_{A \setminus A'} u(y;A)\xi(x,y)\mu(dy).$$

If $x \in A'$, then $\int_{A \setminus A'} u(y;A)\xi(x,y)\mu(dy) = 0$, hence

$$u(x;A) = 1_A(x)T(A'|x) + 1_{A \setminus A'}(x) \int_{A \setminus A'} u(y;A)\xi(x,y)\mu(dy),$$

or equivalently $u(x;A) = 1_{A'}(x) + \mathcal{I}_{A \setminus A'} u(x;A)$. We are left to show that (3.2) has a unique solution. First, $A \setminus A'$ is simple and since $\mu(\partial A') = 0$ the set $A^* = \overline{A \setminus A'}$ is simple by Lemma 5. Moreover, it is a closed subset of a compact set A, so A^* is compact. By Theorem 1 there exists a finite $m < \infty$ such that $\mathcal{I}_{A^*}^m$ is a contraction, so the same holds for $\mathcal{I}_{A \setminus A'}^m$. This implies that (3.2) has a unique solution in $\mathbb{B}(\mathcal{X})$. $\square$

REMARK 4. *The condition $\mu(\partial A') = 0$ is used to avoid some degenerate cases – for instance, when A' is a Smith-Volterra-Cantor set in $\mathbb{R}$, which has a boundary of finite Lebesgue measure.*
A computational note: since $\mathcal{I}_{A \setminus A'}$ in (3.2) is a contraction on $\mathbb{B}(\mathcal{X})$, the invariance value function can be found by the iterative procedure – with associated bounds – given in Theorem 1.

For the reach-avoid problem a similar result easily follows.

COROLLARY 2. *Let $A, B \in \mathcal{B}(\mathcal{X})$ be such that $\mu(A \setminus B) < \infty$, then $w(x;A,B) \in \text{Lip}(A \setminus B)$. If in addition $A \setminus B$ is compact and A' is the largest absorbing subset of $A \setminus B$ and is such that $\mu(\partial A') = 0$, then*

$$w(x;A,B) = w(x;A^*,B) \tag{3.3}$$

where $A^* = A \setminus (A')^\circ$.

3.4 Approximate solution of modified Bellman equations

To derive the modified Bellman equations we have explicitly assumed to have knowledge of the largest absorbing subset A' of a set A. Here we relax this assumption and employ only an over- and under-approximation of the set A': let us consider sets C, D, such that $C \subseteq A' \subseteq D$ and so that D is open. Based on the proof of Theorem 2 it is clear that for any set A it holds that

$$u(x;A) = 1_A(x)T(A'|x) + 1_A(x) \int_{A \setminus A'} u(y;A)\xi(x,y)\mu(dy). \tag{3.4}$$

Let us introduce an approximation $\tilde{u}$ of u, as the solution of the following integral equation:

$$\tilde{u}(x) = 1_A(x)T(D|x) + 1_A(x) \int_{A \setminus D} \tilde{u}(y)\xi(x,y)\mu(dy). \tag{3.5}$$

Next we show that $\|\tilde{u} - u\| \leq M\mu(D \setminus C)$, for a finite constant M, and then provide a method to calculate $\tilde{u}$ with any desired accuracy.

THEOREM 3. *Let A be a compact set. The following bound holds:*

$$\|\tilde{u} - u\| \leq \frac{\xi_2(\xi_1^{m+1} - 1)}{(\xi_1 - 1)(1 - \alpha)} \mu(D \setminus C), \tag{3.6}$$

where $m = m(A \setminus D), \alpha = \alpha(A \setminus D)$. Here ξ_1, ξ_2 are given by $\xi_1 = \sup\{\xi(x,y) | x \in A \setminus C, y \in A \setminus D\}$, $\xi_2 = \sup\{\xi(x,y) | x \in A \setminus C, y \in D \setminus C\}$.

PROOF. Let us define a function $h(x) = \tilde{u}(x) - u(x;A)$. Since $h(x) = 0, \forall x \in A^c$, let us focus on the case $x \in A$. From (3.4) and (3.5) it follows that

$$h(x) = g(x) + \mathcal{H}_{A \setminus D} h(x), \tag{3.7}$$

where $g(x) = \int_{D \setminus A'} (1 - u(y;A))\xi(x,y)\mu(dy)$.

From Corollary 1 we have that $\|\mathcal{H}_{A \setminus D}^{m+1} f\| \leq \alpha\|f\|$ for any $f \in \mathbb{B}(\mathcal{X})$. Now, (3.7) is equivalent to

$$h(x) = \sum_{k=0}^{m} \mathcal{H}_{A \setminus D}^k g(x) + \mathcal{H}_{A \setminus D}^{m+1} h(x),$$

hence $(1 - \alpha)\|h(x)\| \leq \sum_{k=0}^{m} \|\mathcal{H}_{A \setminus D}^k g(x)\|$. Since $\|\mathcal{H}_{A \setminus D}^k g(x)\| \leq \xi_1^k \xi_2 \mu(D \setminus C)$, we obtain (3.6). $\square$

Having derived bounds on $\|\tilde{u} - u\|$, we need a procedure to calculate $\tilde{u}(x)$ for all $x \in A$. To do this we define the following sequence: $\tilde{u}_0(x) = 1_A(x)T(D|x)$ and

$$\tilde{u}_{n+1}(x) = 1_A(x)T(D|x) + 1_A(x)\mathcal{H}_{A \setminus D}\tilde{u}_n(x).$$

PROPOSITION 2. *Given $m = m(A \setminus D)$ and $\alpha = \alpha(A \setminus D)$, for all $n > 0$ the following bound holds:*

$$\|\tilde{u} - \tilde{u}_n\| \leq \frac{m+2}{1-\alpha} \alpha^{\lfloor \frac{n}{m+2} \rfloor}.$$

PROOF. Define a function $\Delta_n(x) = \tilde{u}_{n+1}(x) - \tilde{u}_n(x)$, then

$$\Delta_n(x) = 1_A(x)\mathcal{H}_{A \setminus D}\Delta_{n-1}(x)$$

and $\Delta_0(x) = 1_A(x)\mathcal{H}_{A \setminus D}T(D|x)$. Since $\mathcal{H}_{A \setminus D}^{m+1}$ is a contraction on $\mathbb{B}(\mathcal{X})$ we have that

$$\|\Delta_{k(m+2)}(x)\| \leq \alpha^k$$

for all $k \geq 0$. The desired inequality follows from

$$\|\tilde{u}(x) - \tilde{u}_n(x)\| \leq \sum_{k=n}^{\infty} \|\Delta_k(x)\|.$$

$\square$

3.5 Probabilistic invariance: an example

Let us refer to the case study of Section 2.2 to elucidate the application of the methods we have developed for the study of the infinite-horizon probabilistic invariance. Let the invariant set $A = \bigcup_{i=1}^{3} \{l_i\} \times [0,1]$ – in Figure 1, this is labeled with gray nodes. Let us start by finding the largest absorbing subset A' of A. To do it we calculate the sets A_n as suggested in Lemma 3:

$$A_0 = A$$
$$A_1 = (\{l_1\} \times [0,1]) \cup (\{l_2\} \times \{0\})$$
$$A_2 = A_3 = \{l_1\} \times [0,1],$$

which leads to conclude that $A' = A_\infty = \{l_1\} \times [0,1]$. Let us denote $u^i(c_x) = u(l_i, c_x; A)$. It is clear that $u^4(c_x) = 0$ and $u^1(c_x) = 1$, for any $c_x \in [0,1]$. Let us now consider the other two locations. If $l_x = l_3$ then $T(A'|x) = 0$ and $T(\{l_2\} \times [0,1]|x) = 0$ so the modified Bellman equation (3.2) reduces to

$$
u^3(c_x) = \int_0^1 u^3(c_y) p_{33}(c_x) \xi_{33}(c_x, c_y) \lambda(dc_y)
$$

$$
= \int_0^1 u^3(c_y) c_x^2 \frac{f_{\mathcal{N}}(c_x, c_y, 0.5)}{\Phi(c_x, 1, 0.5)} \lambda(dc_y),
$$

which has a unique zero solution. Let us now focus on $l_x = l_2$, where $T(A'|x) = \frac{c_x}{2}$, so we obtain

$$
u^2(c_x) = \frac{c_x}{2} + \int_0^1 u^2(c_y)\left(1 - \frac{1}{2}(c_x + c_x^2)\right)\frac{f_{\mathcal{N}}(c_x, c_y, 0.4)}{\Phi(c_x, 1, 0.4)}\lambda(dc_y),
$$

which is a Fredholm equation of the second kind, and has a unique solution that can be computed by applying well-developed numerical methods [2]. The overall results are summarized in Figure 3.5, which displays the value functions $u^i(c_x), c_x \in [0,1], i \in L$.

3.6 Distribution and mean of first exit time

In the current section we focus on the mean value of the first exit time ς_A, for a compact set A. Recall that $p_n(x;A) = \mathsf{P}_x\{\varsigma_A = n\}$ and $p(x;A) = \mathsf{P}_x\{\varsigma_A = \infty\}$. From this definition it is clear that

$$
\begin{cases}
p_0(x;A) &= 1_{A^c}(x) \\
p_n(x;A) &= u_{n-1}(x;A) - u_n(x;A), \quad n \in \mathbb{N} \\
p(x;A) &= u(x;A),
\end{cases} \tag{3.8}
$$

thus $p_{n+1}(x;A) = \mathscr{I}_A p_n(x;A)$, for all $n \geq 0$. Since A is compact and $\xi \in \mathrm{Lip}(\mathscr{X})$, one can apply a space discretization procedure [1] to compute an approximate value of p_n, with an arbitrarily small bound on the error.

The problem of the mean value for the exit time $t(x;A) = \mathsf{E}_x[\varsigma_A]$ is slightly different from what we considered above, since in general $t \in \mathbb{L}(\mathscr{X})$ (rather than in $\mathbb{B}(\mathscr{X})$). Recall that from (2.6) and from the equality $p(x;A) = u(x;A)$ we know that $t(x;A) = \infty$ if $x \in A^+$, where

$$
A^+ := \{x \in A : u(x;A) > 0\}. \tag{3.9}
$$

We now show that if A is compact, then this set contains the only points where $t(x;A)$ takes an infinite value.

THEOREM 4. *Let A be compact and A^+ is defined by (3.9). Then*

$$
t(x;A) = \begin{cases}
\infty, & \text{for } x \in A^+ \\
h(x), & \text{for } x \in A \setminus A^+ \\
0, & \text{for } x \in A^c,
\end{cases} \tag{3.10}
$$

where $h(x)$ is the unique solution of the following equation:

$$
h(x) = 1_{A \setminus A^+}(x) + \mathscr{I}_{A \setminus A^+} h(x). \tag{3.11}
$$

In particular, if A is simple then $t(x;A)$ is bounded and the unique solution of (2.5).

PROOF. We have already proved that $t(x;A) = \infty$ for $x \in A^+$ and $t(x;A) = 0$ for $x \in A^c$. We use this information to rewrite (2.5) as:

$$
t(x;A) = 1_A(x) + 1_A(x)\left(\int_{A \setminus A^+} t(y;A)\xi(x,y)\mu(dy) + T(A^+|x)\cdot\infty\right).
$$

Note now that if $x \in A \setminus A^+$, then $T(A^+|x) = 0$. Indeed,

$$
0 = u(x;A) = \int_A u(y;A)\xi(x,y)\mu(dy),
$$

and since the integrand is non-negative, it is equal to 0 μ-a.e. From this it follows that

$$
t(x;A) = 1 + \int_{A \setminus A^+} t(y;A)\xi(x,y)\mu(dy),
$$

for all $x \in A \setminus A^+$. So

$$
t(x;A) = 1_{A^+}(x)\cdot\infty + 1_{A \setminus A^+}(x)h(x),
$$

where $h(x) = 1 + \mathscr{H}_{A \setminus A^+}h(x)$ for all $x \in A \setminus A^+$.

Let us prove now that $A \setminus A^+$ is compact and simple. First of all, since A is compact, $u(x;A) \in \mathscr{C}(A)$ from Lemma 6. This means that A^+ is open in A and hence $A \setminus A^+$ is compact. Next, for the largest absorbing subset $A' \subseteq A$ it clearly holds that $A' \subseteq A^+$.

From Corollary 1 we conclude that $\mathscr{H}^m$ is a contraction on $\mathbb{B}(\mathscr{X})$ with rate $\alpha = \alpha(A \setminus A^+)$, where $m = m(A \setminus A^+) + 1$. This leads to the uniqueness of h, which now can be found with any bound on the error as in Theorem 1, so (3.10) is proved.

Finally, if the set A is simple, $A^+ = \emptyset$, so the last assertion of the theorem immediately follows from (3.10). $\square$

3.7 Mean of first exit time: an example

We illustrate obtained results by providing an example, where we characterize the value function $t(x;A)$ for the Markov process of the case study in Section 2.2 and the set $A = \bigcup_{i=1}^3 \{l_i\} \times [0,1]$ as in Section 3.5.

From the solution of the infinite-horizon probabilistic invariance problem, we can determine the set $A^+ = \bigcup_{i=1,2} \{l_i\} \times [0,1]$. Thus $A \setminus A^+ = \{l_3\} \times [0,1]$. From Theorem 4 we conclude that

$$
t(x;A) = \begin{cases}
\infty, & \text{for } l_x \in \{l_1, l_2\} \\
h(x), & \text{for } l_x = l_3 \\
0, & \text{for } l_x = l_4,
\end{cases}
$$

where $h(x)$ is a unique solution of (3.11). Since we are only interested in its values for $l_x = l_3$ we denote (similar as before) $t^3(c_x) := t(l_3, c_x)$ then $t^3(c_x)$ is the unique solution of the following Fredholm equation of the second kind:

$$
t^3(c_x) = 1 + \int_0^1 t^3(c_y) p_{33}(c_x) \xi_{33}(c_x, c_y) \lambda(dc_y)
$$

$$
= \int_0^1 t^3(c_y) c_x^2 \frac{f_{\mathcal{N}}(c_x, c_y, 0.5)}{\Phi(c_x, 1, 0.5)} \lambda(dc_y).
$$

The solution is computed according to [2], and represented in Figure 3.7. Note that for the point $x = (l_3, 0)$ the value function $t(x;A) = 1$. Indeed, for this point it holds that $T(A^c|x) = 1$,

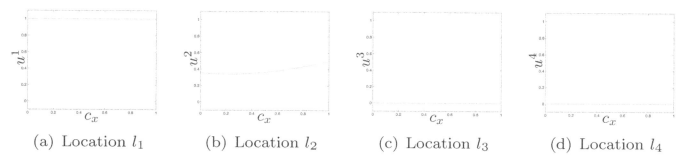

(a) Location l_1 (b) Location l_2 (c) Location l_3 (d) Location l_4

Figure 2: Solution of the infinite-horizon probabilistic invariance problem discussed in Section 3.5.

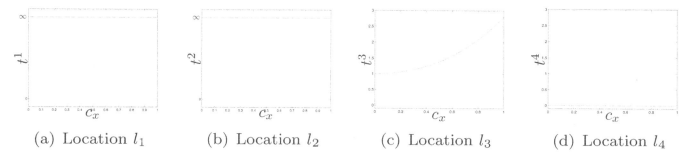

(a) Location l_1 (b) Location l_2 (c) Location l_3 (d) Location l_4

Figure 3: Solution of the mean of first exit time problem discussed in Section 3.7.

hence starting from this point the process will leave the set A almost surely in one step.

4. COMPUTATION OF ABSORBING SETS

4.1 Characterization of absorbing sets

In the previous chapters we have emphasized the role that absorbing sets play in the computation of the value function of infinite-horizon specifications of Markov processes. This leads to the need to characterize the largest absorbing set A' of a given compact set A, or alternatively to establish the simplicity of A. These are in general difficult goals: this section focuses on approximation techniques to tackle this class of problems, and focuses on models that allow the verification of simplicity of A or to find its largest absorbing subset A'.

A general procedure to characterize the largest absorbing set is suggested in Lemma 3: it computes the sequence $(A_n)_{n\geq0}$. This sequence is such that if $A_m = A_{m+1}$ for some $m \geq 0$, then $A_\infty = A_m$. Note that in this case either A_∞ is empty – hence A is simple – or non-empty, which leads to $A' = A_\infty$. We have explicitly applied this procedure in the example of Section 3.5, which has resulted in an analytical characterization of the sets A_n.

This general approach presents two issues. The first arises when the sets A_n can be only over-approximated numerically – also, due to over-approximation errors, it may be hard to check the set equality $A_m = A_{m+1}$ for some m. Secondly, even if sets A_n can be computed analytically, it may be hard to characterize the limit $A_\infty = \lim_{n\to\infty} A_n$. To mitigate these limitations, we have proposed to use an open neighborhood (over-approximation) of A_n as a candidate for the set D in Theorem 3.

Absorbing sets can be found analytically when a Markov process X is expressed by a recursive formula, such as

$$X_{n+1} = F(X_n, \eta_n),$$

where η_n are iid random variables. This happens for instance in the case of stochastic difference equations with linear drift and diffusion terms, which admit the origin as a absorbing point. However, experience has shown that for many such models admitting analytical characterization of an absorbing set, finding a measure μ, such that T is absolutely continuous with respect to μ and its density is Lipshitz continuous, is often problematic. We do not further pursue this characterization in the present contribution.

Finally, there are instances when both the verification of simplicity of A and the computation of A' up to admissible precision are decidable procedures. The simplest one is represented by Markov Chains but this case can be generalized to a larger class of Markov processes. We focus on such processes in Section 4.2 – before, we give a characterization of absorbing sets that we later use to find such procedures.

Let $s(x) = \{y \in \mathcal{X} : \xi(x, y) > 0\}$, so clearly $s(x) \in \mathcal{B}(\mathcal{X})$. The following proposition gives a characterization of an absorbing set in terms of sets $s(x)$.

PROPOSITION 3. *Let $A' \in \mathcal{B}(\mathcal{X})$, then A' is absorbing if and only if $\mu(s(x) \setminus A') = 0$ for all $x \in A'$.*

PROOF. Notice that A' is absorbing if and only if $\int_{A'} \xi(x, y)\mu(dy) = 1$ for any $x \in A'$, and further that $\int_{A \cap s^c(x)} \xi(x, y)\mu(dy) = 0$ for any $A \in \mathcal{B}(\mathcal{X})$. Thus $\int_A \xi(x, y)\mu(dy) = \int_{A \cap s(x)} \xi(x, y)\mu(dy)$ and hence

$$\int_{s(x)} \xi(x, y)\mu(dy) = 1$$

233

for all $x \in \mathcal{X}$. If $x \in A'$ then

$$0 = \int_{s(x)} \xi(x,y)\mu(dy) - \int_{A'} \xi(x,y)\mu(dy)$$

$$= \int_{s(x)} \xi(x,y)\mu(dy) - \int_{A' \cap s(x)} \xi(x,y)\mu(dy),$$

so $\int_{s(x)\backslash A'} \xi(x,y)\mu(dy) = 0$ and hence $\mu(s(x)\backslash A') = 0$ since $\xi \geq 0$.

For the opposite direction, assuming that $\mu(s(x) \setminus A') = 0$ for all $x \in A'$, we have:

$$\int_{A'} \xi(x,y)\mu(dy) = \int_{s(x) \cap A'} \xi(x,y)\mu(dy)$$

$$= 1 - \int_{s(x)\backslash A'} \xi(x,y)\mu(dy) = 1,$$

then A' is absorbing. $\square$

4.2 Densities with a hybrid structure

We describe a class of processes for which the characterization of absorbing subsets is a solvable problem. We show how to find the largest absorbing subset A' of a given set A up to a set of a measure zero, which is sufficient for the modified Bellman equations introduced in Section 3 and thus allow applying the developed theory to solve infinite-horizon problems.

Consider densities with a hybrid structure, namely made up of a discrete part – similar to Markov Chains – and a continuous part. More precisely, we suppose that there exists a disjoint collection of sets (cells) $\mathfrak{Q} = (q_i)_{i=1}^N$ such that

1. q_i is open, $\mu(q_i) > 0$ and $\mu(\partial q_i) = 0$ for all $1 \leq i \leq N$,

2. $\overline{Q} = \mathcal{X}$ where $Q = \bigcup_{i=1}^N q_i$,

3. for any $1 \leq i, j \leq N$

   - either $\xi(x,y) > 0$ for all $x \in q_i$ and $y \in q_j$ (we write then $i \rightarrow j$),
   - or $\xi(x,y) = 0$ for all $x \in q_i$ and $y \in q_j$.

Some comments on these assumptions are in order:

- the described structure is a generalization of a finite-state Markov Chain, since for the finite state space $\mathcal{X}$ one can select $q_i = x_i$ and all assumptions are satisfied;

- another instance of this model is given by discrete-time Stochastic Hybrid Systems [1], where $\mathfrak{Q}$ can be derived from the set of locations (modes) and each set q_i corresponds to the associated continuous domain. The assumptions above indicate that whenever there is a positive transition probability between locations $l \rightarrow l'$, then the corresponding stochastic kernel has a full support. For instance, for the process described in Section 2.2, we can select $q_i = l_i \times (0,1)$, for all $1 \leq i \leq 4$;

- furthermore, these assumptions are satisfied for the case when $\mathcal{X} = \mathbb{R}^n$ and the support of ξ is made up of a finite union of hypercubes in $\mathbb{R}^n \times \mathbb{R}^n$ aligned with the coordinate axes.

Let us introduce an adjacency matrix $\mathbb{Q}$ of dimension $N \times N$, with the entry on the i-th row and j-th column equal to 1 if $i \rightarrow j$ and equal to 0 otherwise. $\mathbb{Q}$ plays a role in solving the problem of verification of simplicity, as well as in finding the largest absorbing subset of a given set. To formally describe both procedures we first introduce the following concepts, denoting

- for $x \in Q$ a *discrete closure* as $\lceil x \rceil = \{j : x \in q_j\}$ and for $A \subseteq \mathcal{X}$

$$\lceil A \rceil = \bigcup_{x \in A \cap Q} \lceil x \rceil;$$

- for $x \in Q^c$ a *discrete neighborhood* as $\mathfrak{n}(x) = \{j : x \in \overline{q_j}\}$;

- for $A \subset \mathcal{X}$ a *discrete interior* as

$$\lfloor A \rfloor = \{j : \mu(q_j \setminus A) = 0\}$$

and put

$$Q_A = \bigcup_{i \in \lfloor A \rfloor} \overline{q_i}; \tag{4.1}$$

- for $x \in Q$ a *discrete support* as $\mathfrak{s}(x) = \{j : \lceil x \rceil \rightarrow j\}$ and for $A \subseteq \mathcal{X}$

$$\mathfrak{s}(A) = \bigcup_{x \in A \cap Q} \mathfrak{s}(x);$$

- if $B \subseteq \mathcal{X}$ admits representation $B = \bigcup_{i \in \lceil B \rceil} q_i$ then we call it a *multicell*.

For all $x \in Q$, the unique cell that point x belongs to is given by $q_{\lceil x \rceil}$, so $\lceil A \rceil$ is the set of indexes of the cells that set A overlaps with. $\mathfrak{n}(x)$ denotes the set of indexes of the cells that the boundary $x \in Q^c$ belongs to. A cell q_i is a subset of A – with the possible exception of a set of measure zero – if and only if $i \in \lfloor A \rfloor$. Finally, given a point $x \in Q$, $T(q_i|x) > 0$ if and only if $i \in \mathfrak{s}(x)$. Clearly, $\mathfrak{s}(x)$ is not empty for any $x \in Q$ and $\mathfrak{n}(x)$ is not empty for any $x \in Q^c$. Also, $\mathfrak{s}(x)$ depends only on $\lceil x \rceil$ for $x \in Q$.

EXAMPLE 1. *Let us consider the process described in Section 2.2, define $q_i = \{l_i\} \times (0,1), 1 \leq i \leq 4$, and select point $x = (l_2, \frac{1}{2})$. For this point, $\lceil x \rceil = \{2\}$ since $x \in l_2$, and $\mathfrak{s}(x) = \{1, 2, 4\}$ since x admits a non-zero probability to transition to locations l_1, l_2, and l_4. A second point $y = (l_1, 1)$ is such that $y \notin Q$ and $\mathfrak{n}(y) = q_1$.*

Additionally, the set $B = \bigcup_{i=1}^3 q_i = \bigcup_{i=1}^3 \{l_1\} \times (0,1)$ is a multicell.

Note that the invariant set $A = \bigcup_{i=1}^3 \{l_1\} \times [0,1] = \overline{B}$, which is the closure of the multicell B and which is not a multicell. For set A it can be seen that $\lceil A \rceil = \{1, 2, 3\}$, that $\lfloor A \rfloor = \{1, 2, 3\}$, and that the discrete interior will not change if we eliminate any single point from A, e.g. $\lfloor A \setminus \{(l_1, \frac{1}{2})\} \rfloor = \{1, 2, 3\}$. Finally, given two sets A and q_2, their discrete support are $\mathfrak{s}(A) = \{1, 2, 3, 4\}$ and $\mathfrak{s}(q_2) = \{1, 2, 4\}$ respectively.

The plan is to tackle the verification of simplicity first for multicells, then to extend the procedure to arbitrary sets. In order to employ the absorbance characterization provided in Proposition 3, it is important to establish a connection between sets $s(x)$ and $\mathfrak{s}(x)$. (We indeed show in the following that for an absorbing set its discrete support is a subset of the discrete interior.)

LEMMA 7. *For any $x \in Q$, $q_i \subset s(x)$ if $i \in \mathfrak{s}(x)$, and*

$$\bigcup_{i \in \mathfrak{s}(x)} \overline{q_i} = \overline{s(x)}.$$

If $x \in Q^c$ then $\overline{s(x)} \subseteq \overline{s(x')}$ for any $x' \in q_i$ and $i \in \mathfrak{n}(x)$.

PROOF. For $x \in Q$ if $i \in \mathfrak{s}(x)$ and $y \in q_i$ then $\xi(x, y) > 0$. Hence, $q_i \in s(x)$ for $i \in \mathfrak{s}(x)$. Suppose now that $y \in \overline{s(x)}$. Then in each neighborhood of y there exists $y' \in Q$ such that $\xi(x, y') > 0$, so there exists $i \in \mathfrak{s}(x)$ such that $y \in \overline{q_i}$. Note that $\overline{s(x)}$ for $x \in Q$ depends now only on $\lceil x \rceil$.

Suppose now that $x \in Q^c$ and for some $y \in \mathcal{X}$ we have $\xi(x, y) > 0$. Due to continuity of ξ, for any $i \in \mathfrak{n}(x)$ there exists $x' \in q_i$ such that $\xi(x', y) > 0$, so $s(x) \subseteq s(x')$. Since $\overline{s(x')}$ depends only on $\lceil x' \rceil = i$, we have proven the last statement of the proposition. $\square$

LEMMA 8. *If A' is an absorbing set then $\mathfrak{s}(A') \subseteq \lfloor A' \rfloor$. In particular, $\lfloor A' \rfloor \neq \emptyset$. Any set A such that $\lfloor A \rfloor = \emptyset$ is simple.*

PROOF. Note that $A' \cap Q$ is non-empty since $\mu(A') > 0$. Take $x \in A' \cap Q$ then

$$0 = \mu(s(x) \setminus A') = \mu\left(\bigcup_{i \in \mathfrak{s}(x)} \overline{q_i} \setminus A'\right) \geq \max_{i \in \mathfrak{s}(x)} \mu(q_i \setminus A'),$$

so $\mathfrak{s}(x) \in \lfloor A' \rfloor$ for all $x \in A' \cap Q$ and $\mathfrak{s}(A') \subseteq \lfloor A' \rfloor$. Since for all $x \in Q$ it holds that $\mathfrak{s}(x) \neq \emptyset$ then $\lfloor A' \rfloor$ contains at least one element. Finally, if $\lfloor A \rfloor = \emptyset$ then any subset of A has an empty discrete interior, so A is simple. $\square$

EXAMPLE 2. *For the process in Section 2.2 consider the set $A' = \{l_1\} \times [0, 1]$. It holds that $\mathfrak{s}(A') = \{1\} = \lfloor A' \rfloor$. The preceding lemma confirms that it is absorbing, as we already showed in Section 3.5.*

The next proposition provides the solution to the problem of verification of simplicity for a multicell B, and is based on operations over the adjacency matrix $\mathbb{Q}$.

PROPOSITION 4. *Let $C \subset \lceil B \rceil$ be the largest index set such that if $i \in C$ and $i \to j$, then $j \in C$. If C is empty then B is simple. If C is not empty then the multicell*

$$C' := \bigcup_{i \in C} q_i$$

is an absorbing subset of B and $\mu(B' \setminus C') = 0$, where B' is the largest absorbing subset of B.

PROOF. First, since B is a multicell, $C' \subseteq B$. Next, if $x \in C'$ then $x \in Q$ and $\lceil x \rceil \in C$. By construction of C it follows that $\mathfrak{s}(x) \subset C$ for all $x \in C'$, so $\mu(s(x) \setminus C') = 0$ for all $x \in C'$ and this set is absorbing.

Consider now $x \in B'$. Clearly, $q_{\lceil x \rceil} \subseteq B'$ since $\mathfrak{s}(x) = \mathfrak{s}(x')$ for all $x' \in q_{\lceil x \rceil}$, thus $\mu(s(x) \setminus B') = 0$ implies $\mu(s(x') \setminus B') = 0$. As a consequence, $\lceil B' \rceil = \lfloor B' \rfloor$.

If for some $i \in \lceil B' \rceil$ exists j such that $i \to j$ but $j \notin \lceil B' \rceil$ then for $x \in q_i \subseteq B$ we have $\mu(s(x) \setminus B') \geq \mu(q_j) > 0$, so for all $i \in \lceil B' \rceil$ and j such that $i \to j$ it holds that $j \in \lceil B' \rceil$. Hence, $\lceil B' \rceil \subseteq C$ which means that $\mu(C' \setminus B') = 0$. $\square$

Set C' can be computed with a standard procedure over $\mathbb{Q}$ in $\mathcal{O}(N^2)$ [3]. We have shown how to verify the simplicity of a multicell, now we extend the result to an arbitrary set.

PROPOSITION 5. *Let $A \in \mathcal{B}(\mathcal{X})$, then A is not simple if and only if there exists a multicell B such that $A \cap B$ is absorbing and $\lceil B \rceil \subseteq \lfloor A \rfloor$. Moreover, $\mathfrak{s}(A') \subseteq \lfloor A \rfloor$.*

PROOF. Obviously, if there exists such a set B then A has an absorbing subset $A \cap B$ and hence it is not simple. Suppose now that A is not simple and A' is the largest absorbing subset of A. Consider a multicell

$$B = \bigcup_{i \in \mathfrak{s}(A')} q_i.$$

Since A' is absorbing, for all $x \in A'$ it holds that $\mu(s(x) \setminus A') = 0$ hence for any $i \in \mathfrak{s}(A')$ we obtain that $\mu(q_i \setminus A') = 0$ and $A' \cap q_i \neq \emptyset$, which leads to $\mathfrak{s}(q_i) \subseteq \mathfrak{s}(A')$ and $\mathfrak{s}(B) \subseteq \mathfrak{s}(A')$.

On the other hand, if $x \in B$ then

$$s(x) \subseteq \bigcup_{i \in \mathfrak{s}(x)} \overline{q_i} \subseteq \bigcup_{i \in \mathfrak{s}(B)} \overline{q_i}$$

and that

$$\mu(s(x) \setminus B) \leq \mu\left(\bigcup_{i \in \mathfrak{s}(B)} \overline{q_i} \setminus \bigcup_{i \in \mathfrak{s}(A')} q_i\right) \leq \mu\left(\bigcup_{i \in \mathfrak{s}(B)} \partial q_i\right) = 0,$$

which proves that B is absorbing.

Note that $\lceil B \rceil = \mathfrak{s}(A')$ from the construction of B. We showed that $\mu(q_i \setminus A') = 0$ for any $i \in \mathfrak{s}(A')$, so $\lceil B \rceil \subseteq \lfloor A \rfloor$. $\square$

Note that we have reduced the simplicity verification problem to that for multicells, which we know how to solve. The final step is to find the relation between the largest absorbing sets of A and Q_A. This leads us to an algorithm for finding such a set for an arbitrary A.

PROPOSITION 6. *If A' is the largest absorbing subset of A then $Q' = A' \cap Q_A$ is the largest absorbing subset of Q_A. Moreover, for $x \in A \cap Q$ condition $\mathfrak{s}(x) \subseteq \lceil Q' \rceil$ is satisfied if and only if $x \in A'$.*

PROOF. For $x \in Q' \cap Q$ then $x \in A' \cap Q$ and hence

$$\mu(s(x) \setminus Q') = \mu\left(s(x) \setminus (A' \cap Q_A)\right)$$
$$\leq \mu(s(x) \setminus A') + \mu\left(s(x) \setminus Q_A\right) = 0.$$

For $x \in Q' \setminus Q$ by Lemma 7 there exists $x' \in Q' \cap Q$ such that $\overline{s(x)} \subseteq \overline{s(x')}$ and hence $\mu(s(x) \setminus Q') = 0$ for all $x \in Q'$, so Q is absorbing.

If $Q'' \subseteq Q_A$ is absorbing then $Q'' \cup A'$ is absorbing and hence $Q'' \subseteq A'$, so $Q'' \subseteq Q'$, which proves the statement of the proposition.

Note that we proved that for any $x \in A' \cap Q$ it holds that $\mu(s(x) \setminus Q') = 0$. Suppose that there exists $x \in A' \cap Q$ and $i \in \mathfrak{s}(x) \setminus \lceil Q' \rceil$, then

$$\mu(s(x) \setminus Q') \geq \mu\left(\bigcup_{j \in \mathfrak{s}(x)} \overline{q_i} \setminus \bigcup_{j \in \lceil Q' \rceil} \overline{q_i}\right) \geq \mu(\overline{q_i}) > 0,$$

hence for all $x \in A' \cap Q$ it holds that $\mathfrak{s}(x) \subseteq \lceil Q' \rceil$. On the other hand, if for $x \in A \cap Q$ it holds that $\mathfrak{s}(x) \subseteq \lceil Q' \rceil$, then by Lemma 7 $\mu(s(x) \setminus Q') = 0$ and $x \in Q' \subseteq A'$. $\square$

The construction of the largest absorbing subset of A, up to a set of measure zero, develops along the following two steps:

1. given a set A, find the largest absorbing subset Q' of Q_A, up to a set of measure zero, by applying Proposition 4. To find Q' one should find the largest absorbing set of Q_A° with

the method given in Proposition 4. This set differs from Q' only up to set of measure zero. If Q_A is simple, then A is simple by Proposition 5;

2. consider $x \in A \cap Q$. By Proposition 6 one can have $x \in A'$ if and only if $\mathfrak{s}(x) \subseteq \lceil Q' \rceil$. On the other hand, if $x \in A'$ then $x' \in A'$ for all $x' \in q_{\lceil x \rceil} \cap A$ since $\mathfrak{s}(x) = \mathfrak{s}(x')$. This means that it is sufficient to consider just one representative point x_i from each set $q_i \cap A$ where $i \in \lceil A \rceil$ and $q_i \cap A \subseteq A'$ if and only if $\mathfrak{s}(x_i) \subseteq \lceil Q' \rceil$. Now the only points which may still be left out are in Q^c, however $\mu(Q^c) = 0$.

EXAMPLE 3. *Consider the Markov process given in Section 2.2 and let us apply the developed algorithm. Recall that we set $q_i = \{l_i\} \times (0,1)$, so the adjacency matrix has the form*

$$\mathbb{Q} = \begin{pmatrix} 1 & 0 & 0 & 0 \\ 1 & 1 & 0 & 1 \\ 0 & 0 & 1 & 1 \\ 0 & 1 & 0 & 1 \end{pmatrix}.$$

For the safe set A we know that $Q_A = \bigcup_{i=1}^{3} \overline{q}_i$, so according to the algorithm we first look for the largest absorbing subset Q' of Q_A. This is done according to Proposition 4, which finds the largest index set $C \subseteq \lceil Q_A \rceil$ such that $i \in C$ and $i \to j$ implies $j \in C$.

Recall that $\lceil Q_A \rceil = \{1,2,3\}$. Let us find C: if $2 \in C$ or $3 \in C$ then it is necessary that $4 \in C$ because $2 \to 4$ and $3 \to 4$. Due to this fact it is only possible to have $1 \in C$. Since $1 \to 1$ only, we conclude that $C = \{1\}$ and $C' = q_1$.

To build A' we start off with C'. We consider $i \in \lceil A \rceil = \{1,2,3\}$ and add $q_i \cap A$ to A' if for all $x_i \in q_i$ it holds that $\mathfrak{s}(x_i) \subseteq \lceil Q' \rceil$. Clearly this holds only for $i = 1$, hence $q_1 \subseteq A'$, $\mu(A' \setminus q_1) = 0$. Note that this outcome corresponds with the $A' = \{l_1\} \times [0,1]$ that was found in Section 3.5.

5. CONCLUSIONS AND FUTURE WORK

This work has discussed issues related to the solution of integral Bellman equations and has showed that absorbing sets play a prominent role both in the analysis of such problems and in the computation of a solution with explicit bounds on the error. The contribution has shown that, in the case of compact simple sets, the solution is unique and can be found in a finite number of steps with any precision. On the other hand, in the presence of a set that is not simple, the knowledge of its largest absorbing set is again crucial for finding the solution of Bellman equation. The work has also highlighted the differences in the solution of invariance, reach-avoid, and mean exit time problems.

Both the verification of simplicity and the characterization of the largest absorbing subset of a given set are difficult problems in general, though in some cases they admit solvable procedures, as it was shown in Section 4. The authors are interested in generalizing these solvable procedures. Furthermore, the authors are also interested in extensions to other infinite time horizon properties, as well as to the continuous time case.

6. REFERENCES

[1] A. Abate, J.-P. Katoen, J. Lygeros, and M. Prandini. Approximate model checking of stochastic hybrid systems. *European Journal of Control*, 16:624–641, December 2010.

[2] K.E. Atkinson. *The numerical solution of integral equations of the second kind*, volume 4. Cambridge University Press, 1997.

[3] C. Baier and J.-P. Katoen. *Principles of model checking*. The MIT Press, 2008.

[4] D. Chatterjee, E. Cinquemani, and J. Lygeros. Maximizing the probability of attaining a target prior to extinction. *Nonlinear Analysis: Hybrid Systems*, 5(2):367 – 381, 2011.

[5] E.B. Dynkin. *Markov processes*, volume 1,2. Springer-Verlag, 1965.

[6] O. Hernández-Lerma and J. B. Lasserre. *Discrete-time Markov control processes*, volume 30 of *Applications of Mathematics (New York)*. Springer-Verlag, New York, 1996.

[7] A. Hinton, M. Kwiatkowska, G. Norman, and D. Parker. PRISM: A tool for automatic verification of probabilistic systems. In H. Hermanns and J. Palsberg, editors, *Tools and Algorithms for the Construction and Analysis of Systems*, volume 3920 of *Lecture Notes in Computer Science*, pages 441–444. Springer Verlag, Berlin Heidelberg, 2006.

[8] J.K. Hunter and B. Nachtergaele. *Applied analysis*. World Scientific Pub Co Inc, 2001.

[9] J.-P. Katoen, M. Khattri, and I. S. Zapreev. A Markov reward model checker. In *IEEE Proceedings of the International Conference on Quantitative Evaluation of Systems*, pages 243–244, 2005.

[10] J.R. Norris. *Markov chains. Cambridge series in statistical and probabilistic mathematics*. Cambridge University Press, 1998.

[11] F. Ramponi, D. Chatterjee, S. Summers, and J. Lygeros. On the connections between PCTL and dynamic programming. In *Proceedings of the 13th ACM international conference on Hybrid Systems: Computation and Control*, pages 253–262, 2010.

[12] W. Rudin. *Principles of mathematical analysis*, volume 275. McGraw-Hill New York, 1976.

[13] S. Summers and J. Lygeros. Verification of discrete time stochastic hybrid systems: A stochastic reach-avoid decision problem. *Automatica*, 46(12):1951–1961, 2010.

[14] I. Tkachev and A. Abate. On infinite-horizon probabilistic properties and stochastic bisimulation functions. In *Proceedings of the 50th IEEE Conference on Decision and Control and European Control Conference*, pages 526–531, Orlando, FL, December 2011.

Passivity and Stability of Switched Systems Under Quantization

Feng Zhu
Department of Electrical
Engineering
University of Notre Dame
Notre Dame, IN, 46556
fzhu1@nd.edu

Han Yu
Department of Electrical
Engineering
University of Notre Dame
Notre Dame, IN, 46556
hyu@nd.edu

Michael J. McCourt
Department of Electrical
Engineering
University of Notre Dame
Notre Dame, IN, 46556
mmccour1@nd.edu

Panos J. Antsaklis
Department of Electrical
Engineering
University of Notre Dame
Notre Dame, IN, 46556
antsaklis.1@nd.edu

ABSTRACT

Passivity theory is a well-established tool for analysis and synthesis of dynamical systems. Recently, this work has been extended to switched and hybrid systems where passivity and stability results of single systems as well as interconnected systems are derived. However, the results may no longer hold when quantization is present as is the case with digital controllers or communication channels. The contribution in this paper is to introduce a control framework under which passivity for switched and non-switched systems can be maintained. This framework centers on the use of an input-output coordinate transformation to recover the passivity property. In order to present these results, background material is provided on passive quantization and output strict passivity for switched and non-switched systems. The proposed framework is first presented for non-switched systems and then generalized to switched systems.

Categories and Subject Descriptors

J.2 [**Physical Sciences and Engineering**]: Engineering

General Terms

Theory

Keywords

Passivity, Switched Systems, Quantization

1. INTRODUCTION

The notion of passivity, which originated in electrical network theory, is a characterization of system input/output behavior based on a generalized notion of energy. Along with Lyapunov function techniques, passivity theory is widely used in analysis and control of nonlinear systems [24, 10, 11, 13]. It is well known that passive systems are stable. Additionally, the parallel interconnection and the negative feedback interconnection of two passive systems is still a passive system. These results provide open-loop conditions to guarantee closed-loop stability. These well known results are summarized along with some recent results in [7]. These results have been extended to switched systems in [14, 15, 16, 17, 22, 29].

Although traditional passivity theory has been applied successfully in various classical nonlinear systems, this property is vulnerable to discretization, quantization and other factors introduced by digital controllers or communication channels in modern control systems. In digital control system design, a continuous-time system is first discretized into a sampled-data system. However, it is pointed out in [21, 3, 23, 19, 5] that passivity is not preserved under discretization, which means the discretized system may not be passive even if the original continuous-time system is passive. Exactly how much passivity is lost under standard discretization has been quantified in [21]. The passivity degradation under the standard discretization can be characterized in terms of passivity indices and sampling time. In [19, 23], a novel average passivity for discrete-time systems was proposed in order to preserve the passivity property losslessly under any sampling time. Besides preserving passivity in discrete-time, stability and stabilization of discrete-time passive systems were also considered in recent work [1, 20]. The problem of finding the maximum sampling time preserving passivity for linear discrete-time systems was considered in [1]. It was shown that the feedback system is exponentially stable if the time-varying asynchronous sampling times embedded in feedback connection are bounded by the maximum sampling time. Two passivity-based control strategies for the problem of stabilizing sampled-data systems were presented in [20].

In addition to discretization, the effect of quantization also needs to be considered when digital controllers interact with the environment by means of analog-to-digital converters or digital-to-analog converters that have a finite resolution. Moreover, quantization is necessary when the information between plants and controllers is transmitted through communication networks. In fact, the problem of control using quantized feedback has been an active research area for a long time. Most of the work [8, 12, 4, 6, 18] concentrates on understanding and mitigating the effects of quantization for feedback stability and stabilization. The existing results on passivity and quantization effects mainly focus on certain specific problems, depending on what kind of systems are considered. In signal processing systems [25], passivity analysis and passification of LTI systems with quantization was treated as an uncertainty described by integral quadratic constraints. In networked control systems, conditions were derived [9] under which the closed-loop networked control system is passive in the presence of sensor quantization and network induced delay. The problem of closed-loop stability for input-affine passive systems with quantized output feedback was investigated in [2]. Recent results [26, 27] used passivity to achieve $\mathcal{L}_2$ stability in the presence of communication delays and signal quantization for networked control systems. To the authors' best knowledge, there is no published results on either preserving passivity under quantization in general or stability conditions for switched systems under quantization.

In this paper, the main contributions are the derivation of conditions under which the passive structure of an output strictly passive (OSP) system can be preserved under quantization and its application in stability for passive switched systems with passive quantizers. The passivity preservation relies on an input/output transformation on the quantized input and output. The result shows that one can find such transformation so that the same passivity index of the original OSP system, with respect to the transformed input and output, will be recovered. The result is relatively general since we only require the system to be OSP and the quantizers to be passive, which characterize many practical quantizers. Although the passivity preserving condition is initially derived for non-switched systems, it can be extended to passive switched systems where the input/output transformation can switch between different transformations according to the current active subsystem. Therefore, passivity of passive switched systems under quantization can be guaranteed and the stability conditions in [15, 16] can be applied.

The rest of the paper is as follows. In Section 2, background material on discrete-time passive systems and passive switched systems is covered. The notion of passive quantizers is introduced. The conditions on preserving passivity under quantization for OSP systems are given in Section 3. Section 4 extends the passivity-preserving conditions for non-switched systems to passive switched systems and then the stability conditions on passive switched systems are obtained. An example is provided in Section 5 to demonstrate the methods used in this paper. Some conclusions are provided in Section 6.

2. BACKGROUND MATERIAL

2.1 Passivity for Discrete-Time Systems

The work in this paper is based on passivity for discrete-

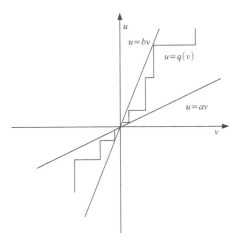

Figure 1: A general quantizer bounded by a cone

time non-switched systems with time index $k \in \mathbb{Z}^+$. A system has input $u(k) \in \mathbb{R}^m$, output $y(k) \in \mathbb{R}^m$, and internal state $x(k) \in \mathbb{R}^n$ and can be modeled as

$$\begin{aligned} x(k+1) &= f(x(k), u(k)) \\ y(k) &= h(x(k), u(k)). \end{aligned} \quad (1)$$

A discrete-time system is passive if it stores and dissipates energy supplied to the system without generating its own energy. The passivity property is typically demonstrated by finding a positive energy storage function and showing that the energy stored in the system at any time step is bounded by the energy supplied to the system.

Definition 1. *A discrete-time system (1) is passive if there exists a positive energy storage function $V(x)$ ($V(x) > 0, \forall x \neq 0$) such that the following inequality holds for all $k \geq k_0$*

$$\Delta V(x(k)) := V(x(k+1)) - V(x(k)) \leq u^T(k)y(k) - \rho y^T(k)y(k) \quad (2)$$

for $\rho \geq 0$. When $\rho > 0$ this system is called output strictly passive.

2.2 Passive Quantizers

Consider a quantizer $q(\cdot)$ with an input v and an output u, where $v \in \mathbb{R}$ and $u \in \mathcal{U}$. $\mathcal{U} \subset \mathbb{R}$ is a quantized set whose elements are distinct quantized levels.

Definition 2. *[26] A quantizer is called a passive quantizer if its input v and output u satisfy*

$$av^2 \leq uv \leq bv^2 \quad (3)$$

where $u = q(v)$ and $0 \leq a \leq b < \infty$.

The notion of a passive quantizer [26] is based on conic systems theory [28]. A passive quantizer is a special case of a memoryless conic system. This can be seen in Fig. 1, where a quantizer satisfying (3) has its input and output mapping bounded in a cone characterized by two lines with slope a and b. The quantizer is called "passive" since the condition $uv \geq 0$ holds for all inputs v. This is the general condition for a memoryless nonlinearity to be passive [13]. The notion of passivity for quantizers can capture many quantizers

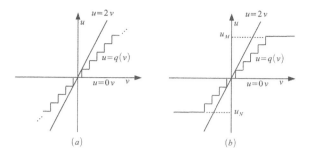

Figure 2: (a) A uniform quantizer with infinite quantization levels (b) A uniform quantizer with finite quantization levels

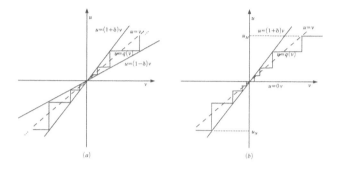

Figure 3: (a) A logarithmic quantizer with infinite quantization levels (b) A logarithmic quantizer with finite quantization levels

used in practice, such as the uniform mid-tread quantizer (Fig. 2), the logarithmic quantizer (Fig. 3) and many non-standard quantizers (Fig. 1).

We can find the values of a and b from a quantizer's input and output mapping. For example, we can show that $a = 0$, $b = 2$ for a uniform mid-tread quantizer with infinite/finite quantization levels; $a = 0$, $b = 1 + \delta$ for a logarithmic quantizer with finite quantization levels; and $a = 1 - \delta$, $b = 1 + \delta$ for a logarithmic quantizer with infinite quantization levels, where $1 > \delta > 0$ is a constant quantization gain.

It is worth pointing out that a quantized system in Fig. 4 is not necessarily a passive system even if the quantizers Q_c and Q_p are passive quantizers. This leads us to resort input-output transformations introduced in Section III to preserve passivity.

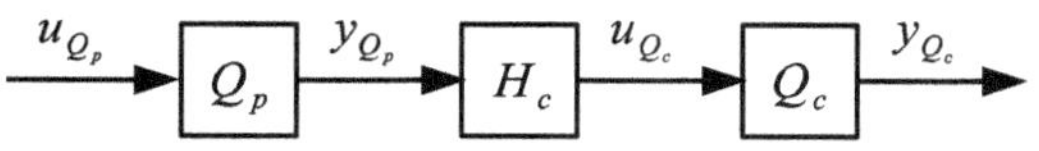

$$u_{Q_p} \longrightarrow \boxed{Q_p} \xrightarrow{y_{Q_p}} \boxed{H_c} \xrightarrow{u_{Q_c}} \boxed{Q_c} \xrightarrow{y_{Q_c}}$$

Figure 4: A general system with input and output quantization

2.3 Passivity for Switched Systems

A nonlinear switched system consists of a finite set of subsystems with nonlinear dynamics. The finite number of subsystems can be enumerated, $\{1, 2, ..., P\}$. At any point in time, a single subsystem i is active and the dynamics are nonlinear and time-invariant. The time-varying nature

of these systems comes from the switching behavior. The switching signal $\sigma(k)$ is a function that maps the time to the index of the active subsystem, $\sigma : \mathbb{Z}^+ \to \{1, ..., P\}$. This function is piecewise constant and only changes at switching instants. The model with the switching signal is given by

$$\begin{aligned} x(k+1) &= f_{\sigma(k)}(x(k), u(k)) \\ y(k) &= h_{\sigma(k)}(x(k), u(k)). \end{aligned} \tag{4}$$

The switching instants can be listed in order k_1, k_2, etc. Alternatively, the notation k_{i_p} will be used to denote the pth time that subsystem i becomes active. For example, the first subsystem ($i = 1$) becomes active for the first time ($p = 1$) at time k_0 ($k_0 = k_{1_1}$). The second subsystem $i = 2$ becomes active at time k_1 ($k_1 = k_{2_1}$) and so forth. By using these two notations in conjunction, it is possible to list completely the times that a system becomes active as well as the times it becomes inactive. Subsystem i becomes active the pth time at time k_{i_p} and then inactive at time $k_{(i_p+1)}$. That same subsystem becomes active again at time $k_{i_{(p+1)}}$.

An indicator set will be defined to signify regions where a particular subsystem is active. Consider subsystem i that is active from k_{i_1} to $k_{(i_1+1)}$, k_{i_2} to $k_{(i_2+1)}$, etc. The set of times I_i can be defined to indicate those time intervals where subsystem i is active,

$$I_i = \bigcup_{p=1}^{K_i} \{k_{i_p}, ..., k_{(i_p+1)}\}. \tag{5}$$

This notation will be used to draw a distinction between the active and inactive time intervals of a system.

The notion of passivity for switched systems used in this paper is based on previous work on decomposable dissipativity for switched systems. This approach has been used in continuous-time [29, 22] and in discrete-time [14]. The concept of decomposable dissipativity is based on the fact that systems typically store energy differently when they are active compared to when they are inactive. The solution is to decompose the supply rate into an active portion and an inactive portion. When a subsystem is inactive, it may have a different supply rate depending on which other subsystem is active. The definition given here is a special case of [14]. While that work presented a very general definition, the authors didn't consider stability of interconnected systems. Traditionally, stability of feedback interconnections is one of the main benefits of dissipativity theory.

In decomposable dissipativity, the multiple energy storage function approach is taken. This allows for each subsystem i to have a unique notion of energy captured by the storage function $V_i(x)$. This notion of energy is positive, i.e. for all i, $V_i(x) > 0$ for all $x \neq 0$. The notion of supplied energy for a subsystem i while it is inactive may be unique for each active subsystem $j \neq i$. This results in several inactive energy supply rates for each i and j. These rates may be a function of input, output, state, and time and will be denoted as $\omega_i^j(u, y, x, k)$. When each subsystem is inactive, the following inequality holds for each active subsystem j at an appropriate time $t \in I_j$ ($\forall i$)

Passivity for discrete-time switched systems is given in the following definition. Recall that a function $\alpha : \mathbb{R}^+ \to \mathbb{R}^+$ is class K_∞ if $\alpha(0) = 0$, α is non-decreasing, and α is radially unbounded.

Definition 3. *Consider a discrete-time switched system (4). This system is passive if there exists a positive storage* function $V_i(x)$, for each subsystem i, with the property that for some K_∞ functions $\underline{\alpha_i}$ and $\overline{\alpha_i}$,

$$\underline{\alpha_i}(||x||) \leq V_i(x) \leq \overline{\alpha_i}(||x||),$$

such that the following conditions hold for all i.

1. During the active time period $k \in I_i$ of each subsystem i, the system is passive ($\rho_i \geq 0$)

$$V_i(x(k+1)) - V_i(x(k)) \leq u^T y - \rho_i y^T y. \quad (6)$$

2. When each subsystem i is inactive, it is dissipative with respect to a cross supply rate that may be specific to the active subsystem j. For $k \in I_j$

$$V_i(x(k+1)) - V_i(x(k)) \leq \omega_i^j(u, y, x, k). \quad (7)$$

3. The cross supply rates are absolutely summable for all switching sequences $\forall i$ and $\forall j \neq i$,

$$\sum_{k=k_0}^{\infty} |\omega_i^j(u, y, x, k)| < L, \quad (8)$$

where L is an arbitrarily large finite constant.

When $\rho_i > 0$ for all i, the switched system is called output strictly passive.

This definition is a natural extension of passivity for non-switched systems. Consider the case when there exists a common storage function for the switched system such that equation (6) holds for all i. In this case, passivity for switched systems reduces to the traditional notion of passivity for non-switched systems.

3. PRESERVING PASSIVITY UNDER QUANTIZATION

3.1 Proposed Passification Scheme

The main problem addressed in this paper is the problem of preserving passivity with signal quantization at the system input, the system output, or both (Fig. 4). As mentioned previously, the quantizers of interest Q_c and Q_p are passive and memoryless with

$$Q_c : a_c u_{Q_c}^2 \leq u_{Q_c} y_{Q_c} \leq b_c y_{Q_c}^2, \text{ with } 0 \leq a_c < b_c < \infty;$$
$$Q_p : a_p u_{Q_p}^2 \leq u_{Q_p} y_{Q_p} \leq b_p y_{Q_p}^2, \text{ with } 0 \leq a_p < b_p < \infty; \quad (9)$$

where u_{Q_c} represents the input of the quantizer Q_c and y_{Q_c} is the output of Q_c. The same holds for Q_p. If the input to the quantizer is vector, the quantization function acts component-wise on the input vector. One can verify

$$\left\|y_{Q_c}\right\|_2^2 \leq b_c^2 \left\|u_{Q_c}\right\|_2^2 \text{ and } \left\|y_{Q_p}\right\|_2^2 \leq b_p^2 \left\|u_{Q_p}\right\|_2^2. \quad (10)$$

The passification scheme proposed in this paper is shown in Fig. 5. As mentioned, H_c is a discrete-time output strictly passive system such that

$$\Delta V_c(k) = V_c(k+1) - V_c(k) \leq u_c^T(k)y_c(k) - \rho_c y_c^T(k)y_c(k), \quad (11)$$

where $u_c, y_c \in \mathbb{R}^m$, $0 < \rho_c < \infty$, $V_c \in \mathbb{R}^+$ is the storage function of H_c.

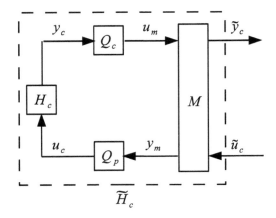

Figure 5: Proposed scheme to preserve passivity under quantization

The block M shown in Fig. 5 is an input/output coordinate transformation such that

$$\begin{bmatrix} u_m \\ y_m \end{bmatrix} = M \begin{bmatrix} \tilde{y}_c \\ \tilde{u}_c \end{bmatrix} = \begin{bmatrix} m_{11}I_m & m_{12}I_m \\ m_{21}I_m & m_{22}I_m \end{bmatrix} \begin{bmatrix} \tilde{y}_c \\ \tilde{u}_c \end{bmatrix}, \quad (12)$$

where $m_{ij} \in \mathbb{R}$, $u_m, y_m \in \mathbb{R}^m$ and $\tilde{u}_c, \tilde{y}_c \in \mathbb{R}^m$. An appropriate transformation will be found in order to maintain the passivity property of H_C.

3.2 Main Results on Preserving Passivity

In this section, we apply the proposed set-up in Fig. 5 to show how passivity of the system H_c is preserved under quantization. Similar set-up to recover passivity of the original system over communication networks under network induced delays and signal quantization have been reported in [26, 27]. The result is stated in Theorem 1.

THEOREM 1. *Consider an OSP system H_C in the proposed scheme shown in Fig. 5 with passive quantizers Q_c and Q_p. If a transformation M is chosen such that*

$$m_{21} = 0, \quad m_{11}^2 = 2b_c^2$$
$$m_{11}m_{12} = \frac{-b_c^2}{\rho_c}, \quad m_{12}^2 = \frac{b_c^2 b_p^2}{\rho_c^2} m_{22}^2, \quad (13)$$

then the subsystem $\tilde{H}_c : \tilde{u}_c \to \tilde{y}_c$ is output strictly passive such that

$$\Delta V_c(k) = V_c(k+1) - V_c(k) \leq \tilde{u}_c^T(k)\tilde{y}_c(k) - \rho_c \tilde{y}_c^T(k)\tilde{y}_c(k).$$

PROOF. The system H_c being output strictly passive implies the following

$$\Delta V_c(k) = V_c(k+1) - V_c(k) \leq u_c^T(k)y_c(k) - \rho_c y_c^T(k)y_c(k)$$
$$= -\frac{1}{2\rho_c} \left[u_c(k) - \rho_c y_c(k)\right]^T \left[u_c(k) - \rho_c y_c(k)\right]$$
$$+ \frac{1}{2\rho_c} u_c^T(k)u_c(k) - \frac{\rho_c}{2} y_c^T(k)y_c^T(k)$$
$$\leq \frac{1}{2\rho_c} \left\|u_c(k)\right\|_2^2 - \frac{\rho_c}{2} \left\|y_c(k)\right\|_2^2.$$
$$\quad (14)$$

Since the quantizers function component-wise on the input vectors, in view of (9), one can verify that

$$\left\|u_m\right\|_2^2 = \sum_{i=1}^m u_{mi}^2 \leq \sum_{i=1}^m b_c^2 y_{ci}^2 = b_c^2 \left\|y_c\right\|_2^2 \quad (15)$$

where u_{m_i} is the component of vector u_m and y_{c_i} is the component of vector y_c. We can rewrite this as

$$-\|y_c\|_2 \leq -\frac{1}{b_c^2}\|u_m\|_2^2. \qquad (16)$$

Similarly, we can find

$$\|u_c\|_2^2 \leq b_p^2\|y_m\|_2^2. \qquad (17)$$

Substituting (16) and (17) into (14), gives

$$\Delta V_c(k) \leq \frac{b_p^2}{2\rho_c}\|y_m(k)\|_2^2 - \frac{\rho_c}{2b_c^2}\|u_m(k)\|_2^2. \qquad (18)$$

Considering the transformation M,

$$\begin{cases} u_m(k) = m_{11}\tilde{y}_c(k) + m_{12}\tilde{u}_c(k) \\ y_m(k) = m_{21}\tilde{y}_c(k) + m_{22}\tilde{u}_c(k), \end{cases} \qquad (19)$$

equation (18) can be written as

$$\begin{aligned} \Delta V_c(k) \leq \; &\frac{b_p^2}{2\rho_c}\|m_{21}\tilde{y}_c(k) + m_{22}\tilde{u}_c(k)\|_2^2 \\ &- \frac{\rho_c}{2b_c^2}\|m_{11}\tilde{y}_c(k) + m_{12}\tilde{u}_c(k)\|_2^2 \end{aligned} \qquad (20)$$

thus

$$\begin{aligned} \Delta V_c(k) \leq \; &\left(\frac{b_p^2}{\rho_c}m_{21}m_{22} - \frac{\rho_c}{b_c^2}m_{11}m_{12}\right)\tilde{u}_c^T(k)\tilde{y}_c(k) \\ &- \left(\frac{\rho_c}{2b_c^2}m_{11}^2 - \frac{b_p^2}{2\rho_c}m_{21}^2\right)\|\tilde{y}_c(k)\|_2^2 \\ &- \left(\frac{\rho_c}{2b_c^2}m_{12}^2 - \frac{b_p^2}{2\rho_c}m_{22}^2\right)\|\tilde{u}_c(k)\|_2^2. \end{aligned} \qquad (21)$$

With the parameters of M as chosen in (13), one can verify that

$$\Delta V_c(k) \leq \tilde{u}_c^T(k)\tilde{y}_c(k) - \rho_c\tilde{y}_c^T(k)\tilde{y}_c(k), \qquad (22)$$

which shows that $\tilde{H}_C$ is OSP. $\square$

The implementation of the transformation M chosen in Theorem 1 is illustrated in Fig. 6. The transformation chosen is a specific one that preserves passivity. In fact, the choice of transformation M is not unique. One can find a different transformation from (13), which gives designers freedom to choose from various transformation candidates according to different specifications. In general, any M is allowable as long as it is invertible and satisfies the result (22).

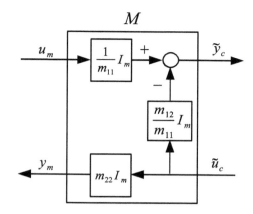

Figure 6: Implementation of M in Theorem 1

Remark 1. *Although Theorem 1 is derived based on discrete-time OSP systems, the result remains valid for continuous-time OSP systems and the same transformation can be applied to preserve passivity.*

Remark 2. *For the case where only one of the quantizers is needed, one can choose $b_c = 1$ when only input quantizer Q_p is present or $b_p = 1$ when only output quantizer Q_c is present.*

Remark 3. *Since $\tilde{H}_c$ is an OSP system, the negative feedback interconnection of $\tilde{H}_c$ with another OSP system H_p, as shown in Fig. 7, is also passive and thus the stability condition can be derived from traditional passive systems theory. The same idea is extended to switched systems in Section IV.*

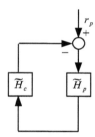

Figure 7: Negative feedback interconnection of two OSP systems

4. STABILITY OF PASSIVE SWITCHED SYSTEMS WITH QUANTIZATION

4.1 Stability of Passive Switched Systems

Passive systems form an important class of dynamical systems. For one, these systems are common in practice. Additionally, passivity can be used to simplify analysis. Passivity is a property that implies stability and the property is preserved when systems are combined in feedback. Combining these two results gives open-loop conditions for closed-loop stability. Additionally, large scale systems can be shown to be stable if each component is passive and the components are sequentially combined in feedback or in parallel. The following results are discrete-time extensions of the work presented in [15]. They will appear in [17]. The first result concerns stability of a single passive switched system.

THEOREM 2. *A passive discrete-time switched system is stable for zero input ($u(k) = 0, \forall k$).*

The passivity property can be used when considering interconnections of systems. The following result shows stability of the feedback interconnection of two passive systems.

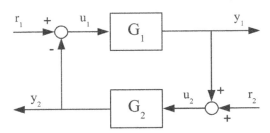

Figure 8: The negative feedback interconnection of two systems.

THEOREM 3. *The feedback interconnection (Fig. 8) of two passive switched systems G_1 and G_2 forms a passive switched system.*

As in the non-switched case, these results can be used to verify closed loop stability by showing that the two systems in feedback are passive. This result can also be used from a design perspective. When controlling a passive switched system, any passive controller is stabilizing without additional conditions. This allows for a large class of controllers to be applied directly including traditional PI controllers.

4.2 Passification of Quantized Switched Systems

The work presented in Section 3 can be extended to switched systems. The structure of the passification scheme remains the same (Fig. 5) with the system H_C being modeled as a switched system according to the dynamics (4). Now that the system dynamics are time-varying, the transformation M must also be time-varying

$$M(k) = \begin{bmatrix} m_{11}(k)I_m & m_{12}(k)I_m \\ m_{21}(k)I_m & m_{22}(k)I_m \end{bmatrix}. \qquad (23)$$

The matrix $M(k)$ will be piecewise constant, belonging to a finite set of constant matrices. There will be at most one constant matrix for each subsystem of the given switched system.

The transformation M can switch as H_C switches. In order for this to be allowable, the switching signal of H_C must be known or measurable in real time. From the perspective of this paper, the system H_C is a designed controller so it should be possible to measure the switching signal. Additionally, the set of ρ_i that define the OSP switched system should be known. A function $\rho(k)$ can be defined such that

$$\rho(k) = \rho_i \quad \text{for active subsystem } i. \qquad (24)$$

This function is piecewise constant and changes as the switching signal changes. This function is used to demonstrate passivity in the following theorem.

THEOREM 4. *Consider an output strictly passive discrete-time switched system H_C (4). This system is placed in the structure (Fig. 5) with passive quantizers defined by the constants a_c, b_c, a_p, and b_p. This control structure preserves the output strict passivity property of system H_C if the transformation $M(k)$ is chosen according to the following time-varying equations*

$$m_{21}(k) = 0, \quad m_{11}^2(k) = 2b_c^2 \qquad (25)$$

$$m_{11}m_{12}(k) = \frac{-b_c^2}{\rho(k)}, \quad m_{12}^2(k)(t) = \frac{b_c^2 b_p^2}{\rho^2(k)}m_{22}^2(k), \qquad (26)$$

PROOF. Since H_C is OSP, for each subsystem i there exists a V_i to satisfy the passive inequality with $\rho_i > 0$ for $i \in \{1, ..., P\}$,

$$V_i(x(k+1)) \le V_i(x(k)) + u_c^T(k)y_c(k) - \rho_i y_c(k)^T y_c(k). \qquad (27)$$

The quantizers satisfy the following inequalities,

$$||u_m||_2 \le b_c ||y_c||_2 \text{ and } ||u_c||_2 \le b_p ||y_m||_2.$$

Applying Theorem 1, the OSP structure of each active subsystem is preserved at each time step by the transformation $M(k)$. The storage functions V_i are also preserved with the structure.

Now the inactive behavior can be analyzed. For each inactive subsystem i and for all active subsystems $j \ne i$, there exists a cross supply rate ω_i^j. For each one, a modified supply rate can be introduced such that

$$\tilde{\omega}_i^j(\tilde{u}_c, \tilde{y}_c, x, k) = \omega_i^j(u_c, y_c, x, k), \forall i, j. \qquad (28)$$

These new cross supply rates imply

$$V_i(x(k+1)) \le V_i(x(k)) + \tilde{\omega}_i^j(\tilde{u}_c, \tilde{y}_c, x, k) \qquad (29)$$

and

$$\sum_{k=k_0}^{\infty} |\tilde{\omega}_i^j(\tilde{u}_c, \tilde{y}_c, x, k)| < L, \qquad (30)$$

where L is an arbitrarily large finite constant given by (8). Since these hold for all i and j, the inactive behavior is dissipative and the supply rates are still absolutely summable. All the conditions for the switched system to be passive are satisfied. The proposed scheme maintains passivity of the switched systems. $\square$

As mentioned earlier, this choice of transformation $M(k)$ is not unique. The conditions listed in the theorem are sufficient to preserve passivity after the quantization effect but there is an entire class of transformations that will also preserve passivity.

This result can be used to preserve passivity of a single system. This can be used with previous results to show stability of feedback interconnections (Fig. 8). When this system is combined in negative feedback with another passive switched system, the overall interconnection is a passive switched system so is stable using Theorem 2 and 3. An example is provided in the following section to demonstrate how this result can be used.

5. EXAMPLE

The work presented in this paper is a method of maintaining passivity for discrete-time switched systems with quantization. The following example illustrates how this method can be applied to a practical system. A linear example was chosen, however, the results are valid for nonlinear switched systems. The switched system H_C chosen is a switched system with two subsystems.

The first subsystem of H_C is modeled by the following dynamics

$$x(k+1) = \begin{bmatrix} -0.060 & 0.173 \\ 0.125 & 0 \end{bmatrix} x(k) + \begin{bmatrix} 1 \\ 0 \end{bmatrix} u(k) \quad (31)$$

$$y(k) = \begin{bmatrix} -0.74 & 0.346 \end{bmatrix} x(k) + 2u(k). \quad (32)$$

The second subsystem of H_C is

$$x(k+1) = \begin{bmatrix} -0.179 & 0.169 \\ 0.125 & 0 \end{bmatrix} x(k) + \begin{bmatrix} 1 \\ 0 \end{bmatrix} u(k) \quad (33)$$

$$y(k) = \begin{bmatrix} -0.667 & 0.158 \end{bmatrix} x(k) + 0.94u(k). \quad (34)$$

This system can be shown to be a passive switched system using the definition given in this paper. The storage functions to show passivity (6) are

$$V_1(x) = x^T(k) \begin{bmatrix} 0.761 & -0.016 \\ -0.016 & 0.96 \end{bmatrix} x(k) \quad (35)$$

$$V_2(x) = x^T(k) \begin{bmatrix} 0.671 & -0.019 \\ -0.019 & 0.989 \end{bmatrix} x(k) \quad (36)$$

with cross supply rates

$$\omega_2^1(u, y, x, k) = u^T(k)y(k) + \frac{1}{10}(x_1^2 + x_2^2) \quad (37)$$

$$\omega_1^2(u, y, x, k) = u^T(k)y(k) + \frac{2}{5}x_1^2. \quad (38)$$

These rates satisfy (7-8). The system is OSP with $\rho_1 = 0.202$ and $\rho_2 = 0.295$.

Both input and output quantization are applied to the controller. The quantizers are uniform with quantization interval 0.1. It can be shown that these are passive quantizers with $a = 0$ and $b = 2$.

The transformation $M(k)$ can take on values in the set $\{M_1, M_2\}$ where

$$M_1 = \begin{bmatrix} 2.83 & -7.00 \\ 0 & 0.354 \end{bmatrix} \quad (39)$$

$$M_2 = \begin{bmatrix} 2.83 & -4.79 \\ 0 & 0.354 \end{bmatrix}, \quad (40)$$

given by (25-26). Transformation $M(k) = M_1$ when subsystem $i = 1$ is active and $M(k) = M_2$ when subsystem $i = 2$ is active.

The switched controller with quantization and transformation $M(k)$ was simulated in feedback with a passive plant. The plant has the following dynamics

$$x(k+1) = \begin{bmatrix} -0.020 & 0.865 \\ 1 & 0 \end{bmatrix} x(k) + \begin{bmatrix} 2 \\ 0 \end{bmatrix} u(k) \quad (41)$$

$$y(k) = \begin{bmatrix} -0.330 & 0.865 \end{bmatrix} x(k) + 2u(k). \quad (42)$$

The feedback interconnection of these two systems forms a passive switched system. When simulated, both the state of the plant and the controller converge to a set near the origin for arbitrary switching. The convergence of the plant state and output are as shown in Fig. 9 with switching signal Fig. 10.

This example demonstrates the methods introduced in this paper. The example chosen was straightforward, being a linear switched system with two subsystems. However,

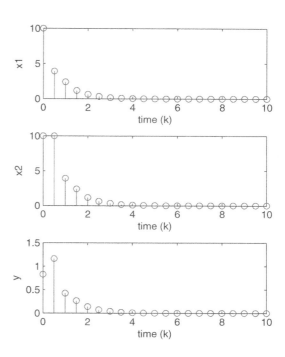

Figure 9: The first two panels show stability of the plant state x_1 and x_2. The third panel shows the system output y.

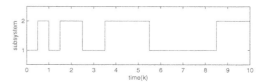

Figure 10: The switching signal of controller H_c that switches between subsystems 1 and 2 is shown.

these methods apply to nonlinear switched systems with any arbitrary finite number of subsystems.

6. CONCLUSION

In this paper, we introduced a scheme to preserve the output strict passivity property of a system with passive input and output quantization by using an input-output coordinate transformation. Then we showed that the same scheme can be applied to switched systems and thus the stability of interconnected passive switched systems can be guaranteed from the results. The example demonstrated how these methods can be applied to a practical quantized switched system.

ACKNOWLEDGMENTS

The support of the National Science Foundation under Grant No. CNS-1035655 is gratefully acknowledged.

7. REFERENCES

[1] C. Canudas De Wit and J. Ramos Cueli. Passivity of interconnected asynchronous discrete-time systems. In *17th IFAC World Congress*, 2008.

[2] F. Ceragioli and C. De Persis. Discontinuous stabilization of nonlinear systems: Quantized and switching controls. In *IEEE Conference on Decision and Control*, pages 783 –788, 2006.

[3] R. Costa-Castelló and E. Fossas. On preserving passivity in sampled-data linear systems. In *American Control Conference*, pages 4373–4378, 2006.

[4] R. E. Curry. *Estimation and Control with Quantized Measurements*. MIT Press, Cambridge, MA, 1970.

[5] M. De la Sen. Preserving positive realness through discretization. In *American Control Conference*, volume 2, pages 1144 –1148, 2000.

[6] D. F. Delchamps. Stabilizing a linear system with quantized state feedback. *IEEE Transactions on Automatic Control*, 35(8):916–924, 1990.

[7] C. Ebenbauer, T. Raff, and F. Allgöwer. Dissipation inequalities in systems theory: An introduction and recent results. In R. Jeltsch and G. Wanner, editors, *Invited Lectures of the International Congress on Industrial and Applied Mathematics 2007*, pages 23–42. European Mathematical Society Publishing House, 2009.

[8] M. Fu and L. Xie. The sector bound approach to quantized feedback control. *IEEE Transactions on Automatic Control*, 50(11):1698–1710, 2005.

[9] H. Gao, T. Chen, and T. Chai. Passivity and passification for networked control systems. *SIAM Journal on Control and Optimization*, 46(4):1299 – 1322, 2007.

[10] D. J. Hill and P. J. Moylan. The stability of nonlinear dissipative systems. *IEEE Transactions on Automatic Control*, 21(5):708–711, 1976.

[11] A. Isidori. *Nonlinear Control Systems, 3rd edition*. Springer, 1995.

[12] R. E. Kalman. Nonlinear aspects of sampled-data control systems. In *Proc. Symp. Nonlinear Circuit Theory*, volume VII, 1956.

[13] H. K. Khalil. *Nonlinear Systems, 3rd edition*. Prentice Hall, 2002.

[14] B. Liu and D. J. Hill. Decomposable dissipativity and related stability for discrete-time switched systems. *IEEE Transactions on Automatic Control*, 56(7):1666–1671, 2011.

[15] M. J. McCourt and P. J. Antsaklis. Control design for switched systems using passivity indices. In *American Control Conference*, pages 2499–2504, 2010.

[16] M. J. McCourt and P. J. Antsaklis. Stability of networked passive switched systems. In *IEEE Conference on Decision and Control (CDC)*, pages 1263–1268, 2010.

[17] M. J. McCourt and P. J. Antsaklis. Stability of interconnected switched wystems using QSR dissipativity with multiple supply rates. In *American Control Conference (Submitted)*, 2012.

[18] R. K. Miller, A. N. Michel, and J. A. Farrel. Quantizer effects on steady state error specifications of digital control systems. *IEEE Transactions on Automatic Control*, 34(6):916–924, 1989.

[19] S. Monaco, D. Normand-Cyrot, and F. Tiefensee. From passivity under sampling to a new discrete-time passivity concept. In *IEEE Conference on Decision and Control*, pages 3157 –3162, 2008.

[20] S. Monaco, D. Normand-Cyrot, and F. Tiefensee. Sampled-data stabilization; a pbc approach. *IEEE Transactions on Automatic Control*, 56(4):907 –912, 2011.

[21] Y. Oishi. Passivity degradation under the discretization with the zero-order hold and the ideal sampler. In *IEEE Conference on Decision and Control (CDC)*, pages 7613 –7617, 2010.

[22] A. R. Teel. Asymptotic stability for hybrid systems via decomposition, dissipativity, and detectability. In *Conference on Decision and Control*, pages 7419–7424, 2010.

[23] F. Tiefensee, S. Monaco, and D. Normand-Cyrot. Average passivity for discrete-time and sampled-data linear systems. In *IEEE Conference on Decision and Control*, pages 7594 –7599, 2010.

[24] J. C. Willems. Dissipative dynamical systems, part i: General theory. *Archive for Rational Mechanics and Analysis*, 45(5):321–351, 1972.

[25] L. Xie, M. Fu, and H. Li. Passivity analysis and passification for uncertain signal processing systems. *IEEE Transactions on Signal Processing*, 46(9):2394 –2403, 1998.

[26] H. Yu and P. J. Antsaklis. Event-triggered output feedback control for networked control systems using passivity: Achieving l2 stability in the presence of communication delays and signal quantization. *Automatica (Submitted)*, 2011.

[27] H. Yu and P. J. Antsaklis. Event-triggered output feedback control for networked control systems using passivity: Time-varying network induced delays (accepted). In *IEEE Conference on Decision and Control (CDC)*, 2011.

[28] G. Zames. On the input-output stability of time-varying nonlinear feedback systems–Part I: Conditions derived using concepts of loop gain, conicity, and positivity. *IEEE Transactions on Automatic Control*, 11(2):228–238, 1966.

[29] J. Zhao and D. J. Hill. Dissipativity Theory for Switched Systems. *IEEE Transactions on Automatic Control*, 53(4):941–953, 2008.

Stabilizing Bit-Rates in Quantized Event Triggered Control Systems

Lichun Li
Dept. of Electrical Eng.
University of Notre Dame
Notre Dame, IN 46556, USA
lli3@nd.edu

Xiaofeng Wang
Dept. of Mech. Science/Eng.
University of Illinois
Urbana, IL 61801, USA
wangx@illinois.edu

Michael Lemmon
Dept. of Electrical Eng.
University of Notre Dame
Notre Dame, IN 46556, USA
lemmon@nd.edu

ABSTRACT

Event triggered systems are feedback systems that sample the state when the novelty in that state exceeds a threshold. Prior work has demonstrated that event-triggered feedback may have inter-sampling intervals that are, on average, greater than the sampling periods found in comparably performing periodic sampled data systems. This fact has been used to justify the claim that event-triggered systems are more efficient in their use of communication or computational resources than periodic sampled data systems. If, however, one accounts for quantization effects and maximum acceptable delays, then it is quite possible that the actual bit-rates generated by event triggered systems may be greater than that of periodically triggered systems. This paper examines the bit-rates required to asymptotically stabilize nonlinear event triggered systems. An increasing upper bound on the stabilizing bit-rate with respect to the norm of the state is derived. This increasing upper bound on the stabilizing bit-rate reveals the efficient attentiveness property of event triggered systems, i.e. the farther the state is away from the origin, the higher the stabilizing bit-rate will be. Moreover, this paper presents the conditions under which the stabilizing bit-rates asymptotically go to 0.

Categories and Subject Descriptors

I.2.8 [**Problem Solving, Control Methods, and Search**]: Control theory; C.3 [**Special-Purpose And Application-Based Systems**]: Real-time and embedded systems

Keywords

event triggered control, quantization, sampled-data systems

1. INTRODUCTION

State-dependent event triggered control systems are systems that transmit the system state over the feedback channel when the difference between the current state and last sampled-state exceeds a state-dependent threshold. These

systems were originally viewed as embedded computational systems [11]. In this case, one was interested in reducing how often the system state was sampled, as a means of reducing processor utilization. The concept of event triggering can be easily extended to networked control systems [6] and wireless sensor-actuator networks [1], in which case the sampled state is *transmitted* over a communication channel.

Early interest in event triggered control was driven by experimental results suggesting that these systems could have longer inter-sampling intervals than comparably performing periodic sampled-data systems [9, 10, 13]. In extending this idea to networked control systems, one might suppose that event triggering can also reduce the system's usage of the communication channel since it might reduce the frequency at which feedback states are transported across the channel. This extension, however, is complicated by the fact that the communication channel is discrete in nature. Sampled states must first be quantized into a finite number of bits before being transmitted across the channel. Moreover, the transmitted bits must be delivered with a delay that does not de-stabilize the system. So an accurate measure of channel usage is the bit-rate as defined by the number of bits per sampled state divided by the acceptable delay in message delivery. It means that the system's *stabilizing bit-rate* (i.e., the bit-rate assuring closed-loop stability) rather than the inter-transmission interval (i.e. the time between consecutive transmissions of the sampled state) provides a more realistic measure of channel usage in event triggered networked control systems.

Prior work in state-dependent event triggered control has used two different techniques to bound the inter-transmission times and acceptable delays. The method used in [10] bounds the minimum inter-transmission delay as a function of the open-loop system's Lipschitz constant. This work goes on to show that system stability is preserved for sufficiently small delays. More accurate measures of inter-transmission intervals were obtained in [3] using scaling properties of homogeneous systems. Quantitative bounds on both the inter-transmission time and maximum acceptable delay were obtained for self-triggered $\mathcal{L}_2$ systems in [14] and networked control systems [16]. The results in [14, 16] are significant because they show how the delay and inter-transmission time scale as a function of the last sampled state. These scaling properties led to the characterization [15] of event triggered systems whose inter-transmission times exhibited *efficient attentiveness* (i.e. the inter-transmission intervals asymptotically approach infinity as the state approaches its equilibrium point). The approach used in this paper builds upon the techniques used in [15] to characterize how stabilizing bit-rates scale as the system state approaches the equilibrium point.

This paper's bound on stabilizing bit-rate is reminiscent of earlier work on dynamic quantization. Prior work showed that static quantization maps required an infinite number of bits to achieve asymptotic stability [5]. With a finite number of bits, the best one can achieve is ultimate boundedness [17] when using static maps. This led to the development of dynamic quantization maps [4] in which the quantization map is dynamically varied to track state uncertainty. For linear systems, one was able to obtain bounds on the bit-rates that were necessary and sufficient for stability, assuming a single sample period delay [12]. In the case of nonlinear systems, lower bounds on the quantization rates were obtained in [8]. The quantization maps developed in this paper are dynamic maps, similar to those used in [8]. This paper shows that the bit-rate sufficient for stabilizing a nonlinear system are bounded from above by an increasing function with respect to the norm of the state. So, the farther the state is away from the origin, the higher bit-rate is needed to stabilize the event triggered system. This increasing upper bound on the stabilizing bit-rate reflects the efficient attentiveness property of the event triggered system. we also find that, as the state approaches its equilibrium, the stabilizing bit-rate converges to a finite constant. Moreover, in some cases, the stabilizing bit-rate goes to 0 as the state approaches the origin.

The remainder of this paper is organized as follows. The notational conventions used throughout the paper are described in section 2. Section 3 describes the system model. Results on the asymptotic stability of quantized event triggered systems will be found in section 4. The paper's main results characterizing the increasing upper bound on the stabilizing bit-rate and the asymptotic behavior of the stabilizing bit-rate will be found in section 5. Section 6 describes simulation results supporting the paper's main findings. Future work is stated in section 7.

2. MATHEMATICAL PRELIMINARIES

Throughout this paper the linear space of real n-vectors will be denoted as $\mathbb{R}^n$ and the set of non-negative reals will be denoted as $\mathbb{R}^+$. The infinity norm of a vector $x \in \mathbb{R}^n$ will be denoted as $\|x\|$. Given the real-valued function $x(\cdot) : \mathbb{R}^+ \to \mathbb{R}^n$, we let $x(t)$ denote the value x takes at time $t \in \mathbb{R}^+$. The $\mathcal{L}$ infinity norm of a function $x(\cdot) : \mathbb{R}^+ \to \mathbb{R}^n$ is defined as $\|x\|_{\mathcal{L}_\infty} = \text{ess sup}_{t \geq 0} \|x(t)\|$. This function is said to be essentially bounded if $\|x\|_{\mathcal{L}_\infty} = M < \infty$ and the linear space of all essentially bounded real-valued functions will be denoted as $\mathcal{L}_\infty$. A subset $\Omega \subset \mathbb{R}^n$ is said to be compact if it is closed and bounded.

We say function g has *non-negative* order, if $\lim_{s \to 0} g(s) < \infty$. With this definition, we have the following two lemmas.

LEMMA 2.1. *Let $g : [0, \nu] \to \mathbb{R}^+$ be a continuous, positive definite function with non-negative order for some $\nu \geq 0$. There must exist continuous, positive definite, increasing functions $\underline{h}$ and $\overline{h}$ defined on $[0, \nu]$ such that*

$$\underline{h}(s) \leq g(s) \leq \overline{h}(s), \forall s \in [0, \nu],$$
$$\lim_{s \to 0} g(s) = \lim_{s \to 0} \underline{h}(s) = \lim_{s \to 0} \overline{h}(s).$$

PROOF. See Lemma 4.3 in [7]. □

LEMMA 2.2. *Let $g_i : [0, \nu] \to \mathbb{R}^+$ be a continuous, positive definite, and strictly increasing function with $g_i(0) = 0$ for $i = 1, 2, 3$. If $g_1(s) < s$, and $\frac{g_2(s)}{g_3(s)}$ has non-negative order, i.e. $\lim_{s \to 0} \frac{g_2(s)}{g_3(s)} \leq c_1 < \infty$, then*

$$\lim_{s \to 0} \frac{g_2(s)}{g_3(|s - g_1(s)|)} \leq c_2 < \infty. \qquad (1)$$

Moreover, if $c_1 = 0$, then $c_2 = 0$.

PROOF. Since $g_1(s) < s$, there exists a constant $\epsilon \in (0, 1)$ such that $g_1(s) \leq \epsilon s$ for all $s \in [0, \nu]$.

$$\lim_{s \to 0} \frac{g_2(s)}{g_3(s - g_1(s))} \leq \lim_{s \to 0} \frac{g_2(s)/g_3(s)}{g_3((1 - \epsilon)s)/g_3(s)}$$
$$\leq c_2 < \infty.$$

If $c_1 = 0$, then $c_2 = 0$. □

A given real valued function $V(\cdot) : \mathbb{R}^n \to \mathbb{R}$ is positive definite if $V(x) > 0$ for all $x \neq 0$. The function V is said to be radially unbounded if $V(x) \to \infty$ as $\|x\| \to \infty$. A function $\alpha(\cdot) : \mathbb{R}^+ \to \mathbb{R}^+$ is class $\mathcal{K}$ if it is continuous, strictly increasing and $\alpha(0) = 0$. A function $\beta : \mathbb{R}^+ \times \mathbb{R}^+ \to \mathbb{R}^+$ is class $\mathcal{KL}$ if $\beta(\cdot, t)$ is class $\mathcal{K}$ for each fixed $t \geq 0$ and $\beta(r, t)$ decreases to 0 as $t \to \infty$ for each fixed $r \geq 0$.

Let Ω be a compact subset of $\mathbb{R}^n$. We say $f(\cdot) : \Omega \to \mathbb{R}^n$ is Lipschitz on Ω if for any $x, y \in \Omega$, we know there exists a constant $L \geq 0$ such that

$$\|f(x) - f(y)\| \leq L\|x - y\|.$$

Consider a system whose state trajectory $x(\cdot) : \mathbb{R}^+ \to \mathbb{R}^n$ satisfies the initial value problem,

$$\dot{x}(t) = f(x(t)), \quad x(0) = x_0$$

A point $\overline{x} \in \mathbb{R}^n$ is an *equilibrium point* of f if $f(\overline{x}) = 0$. We say that the equilibrium point is *stable* if for all $\epsilon > 0$ there exists $\delta > 0$ such that $\|x_0 - \overline{x}\| < \delta$ implies $\|x(t) - \overline{x}\| < \epsilon$ for all $t \geq 0$. We say the equilibrium point is *asymptotically stable* if it is stable and $x(t) \to 0$ as $t \to \infty$.

Consider a system whose state trajectory $x(\cdot) : \mathbb{R}^+ \to \mathbb{R}^n$ satisfies the initial value problem,

$$\dot{x}(t) = f(x(t), w(t)), \quad x(0) = x_0 \qquad (2)$$

where $w(\cdot) : [0, \infty) \to \mathbb{R}^m$ is an essentially bounded real function.

Let $x = 0$ be an equilibrium point for (2) with $w(t) = 0$ and $\Upsilon \subset \mathbb{R}^n$ be a domain containing $x = 0$. Let $V : \Upsilon \to \mathbb{R}$ be a continuously differentiable function such that

$$\underline{\alpha}(\|x\|) \leq V \leq \overline{\alpha}(\|x\|), \qquad (3)$$
$$\frac{\partial V}{\partial x} f(x, w) \leq -\alpha(\|x\|) + \gamma(\|w\|), \qquad (4)$$

for all $(x, w) \in \Upsilon \times \mathbb{R}^m$, where $\underline{\alpha}, \overline{\alpha}$ are class $\mathcal{K}_\infty$ functions, and α, γ are class $\mathcal{K}$ functions, then the system (2) is input-to-state stable (ISS). The function V is called *ISS-Lyapunov function*.

3. PROBLEM STATEMENT

The system under study is a networked event triggered control system with quantization. Figure 1 is a block diagram showing the components of this system.

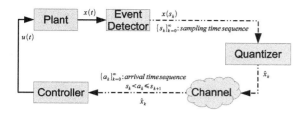

Figure 1: Networked event triggered System with Quantization

The *plant*'s state trajectory $x(\cdot) : \mathbb{R}^+ \to \mathbb{R}^n$ is an absolutely continuous function satisfying the initial value problem,

$$\dot{x}(t) = f(x(t), u(t)), \quad x(0) = x_0 \tag{5}$$

where $f : \mathbb{R}^n \times \mathbb{R}^m \to \mathbb{R}^n$ is locally Lipschitz and satisfies $f(0,0) = 0$. The control signal $u(\cdot) : \mathbb{R}^+ \to \mathbb{R}^m$ is generated by the *controller* in figure 1. The vector $x_0 \in \mathbb{R}^n$ is the plant's initial condition.

The system state, $x(t)$, at time t is measured by the *event detector*. The event detector decides when to hand over the system state to the *quantizer*. The sequence of *sampling times* is denoted as $\{s_k\}_{k=0}^{\infty}$. For notational convenience, the kth consecutively sampled state $x(s_k)$ will be denoted as x_k. The kth *inter-sampling* interval is defined as $T_k = s_{k+1} - s_k$.

Upon receiving the sampled state, $x_k \in \mathbb{R}^n$, the *quantizer* converts this real vector into a finite bit representation. This quantized state is denoted as $\hat{x}_k \in \mathbb{R}^n$. The finite nature of the representation is modeled as a *quantization error*

$$\bar{e}_q(\|x_k\|) \ge \|x_k - \hat{x}_k\| \tag{6}$$

where $\bar{e}_q(\cdot) : \mathbb{R}^+ \to \mathbb{R}^+$ is actually a class $\mathcal{K}$ function of the norm of the last sampled state. By representing the quantization error in this manner, we obtain a dynamic quantizer similar to that used in previous papers on dynamic quantization [12, 8].

We define the *gap* between the current state and quantized state as $e_k(t) = x(t) - \hat{x}_k$. We assume that quantization is done instantaneously and that the quantizer transmits the quantized sampled state, $\hat{x}_k$, across the *channel*. The transmission times are therefore equivalent to the sampling times generated by the event trigger. The rest of the paper uses the terms transmission and sampling in an interchangeable way. The sampling times $\{s_k\}$ are generated by the event trigger so that the gap is always less than a state-dependent threshold function

$$\|e_k(t)\| \le \theta(\|\hat{x}_k\|) \tag{7}$$

for all $t \in [s_k, s_{k+1}]$ where $k = 0, 1, \ldots, \infty$. The function $\theta(\cdot) : \mathbb{R}^+ \to \mathbb{R}^+$ is a class $\mathcal{K}$ function called the *threshold function*.

We assume that the quantized state, $\hat{x}_k$, is always successfully delivered to the controller. The channel, however, is assumed to introduce a finite delay into the delivery time. In particular, the arrival time of the kth sampled state $\hat{x}_k$ at the controller is denoted as $a_k \in \mathbb{R}^+$. This time is strictly greater than s_k. The delay of the kth message is $D_k = a_k - s_k$. We need to assume some orderliness to the transmission and delivery of such messages. In particular, we require that the transmission times, s_k, and arrival times, a_k, satisfy the

following order $s_k < a_k \le s_{k+1}$ for $k = 0, 1, \ldots, \infty$. Such a sequence of transmissions and arrivals will be said to be *admissible*.

Upon the arrival of the kth quantized state, $\hat{x}_k$, at the controller, a control input is computed and then held until the next quantized state is received. In other words, the control signal takes the form

$$u(t) = u_k = K(\hat{x}_k) \tag{8}$$

for $t \in [a_k, a_{k+1})$. The function $K(\cdot) : \mathbb{R}^n \to \mathbb{R}^m$ satisfying $K(0) = 0$. As has been done in previous papers [10], this paper assumes that K is chosen so the system

$$\dot{x}(t) = f(x(t), K(x(t) - e(t))) \tag{9}$$

is input-to-state stable with respect to the signal $e \in \mathcal{L}_\infty$. This means, of course, that there exists a function $V(\cdot) : \mathbb{R}^+ \to \mathbb{R}^+$ satisfying the conditions in equations (3-4) for all $x \in \Upsilon$ where $\Upsilon \subseteq \mathbb{R}^n$. Note that this can be a very restrictive assumption since such K may not always exist [2].

4. ASYMPTOTIC STABILITY

This section characterizes a threshold function eq. (7), a quantization error function eq. (6) and a maximum delay sequence $\{\Delta_k\}_{k=0}^{\infty}$ such that the event triggered system described in section 3 is asymptotically stable.

To analyze the asymptotic stability of the event triggered system, let's first look at equation (9) and see how $\|e_k\|$ should be to assure the asymptotic stability. Since our controller is based on the quantized state $\hat{x}_k$ for all $t \in [a_k, a_{k+1})$, it is easy to see that $e(t)$ in (9) takes the form of

$$e(t) = e_k(t), \forall t \in [a_k, a_{k+1}), \forall k = 0, 1, \cdots, \infty,$$

and the Lyapunov function V must satisfy (3) and

$$\frac{\partial V}{\partial x} f(x, e) \le -\alpha(\|x\|) + \gamma(\|e_k\|), \forall t \in [a_k, a_{k+1}), \tag{10}$$

for all $k = 0, 1, \cdots, \infty$ and all $x \in \Upsilon$. Let's define a function $\xi : \mathbb{R}^+ \to \mathbb{R}^+$ as

$$\xi(\|x\|) = \gamma^{-1}(\upsilon\alpha(\|x\|)), \text{for some } \upsilon \in (0, 1). \tag{11}$$

From equation (10), it's easy to have the following lemma.

LEMMA 4.1. *If $\|e_k(t)\| \le \xi(\|x(t)\|)$ for all $t \in [a_k, a_{k+1})$ and all $k = 0, 1, \cdots, \infty$, then the event triggered system described in section 3 is asymptotically stable, i.e. there must exist a class $\mathcal{KL}$ function β such that*

$$\|x(t)\| \le \beta(\|x_0\|, t), \forall t \ge 0.$$

PROOF. First of all, we know that the Lyapunov function V satisfies (3).

Secondly, if we apply ξ (equation (11)) to equation (10), we have

$$\frac{\partial V}{\partial x} f(x, e) \le -(1 - \upsilon)\alpha(\|x\|), \text{for some } \upsilon \in (0, 1).$$

Therefore, the event triggered system is asymptotically stable. $\square$

With Lemma 4.1, it is natural to consider a threshold function satisfying $\theta(\|\hat{x}_k\|) < \xi(\|x(t)\|)$. But we notice that θ and ξ have different variables. So, the next step is to find a lower bound on $\xi(\|x(t)\|)$ such that this lower bound depends on quantized state $\hat{x}_k$ instead of the real time state $x(t)$. To do so, we define $\underline{\xi} : \mathbb{R}^+ \to \mathbb{R}^+$ as

$$\underline{\xi}(s) = \sup\{\epsilon : \epsilon \leq \min\{\xi(s - \epsilon), s\}, \forall s \in [0, \eta]\}, \quad (12)$$

where $\eta = 2\beta(\|x_0\|, 0)$. With $\underline{\xi}$ defined in (12), we have the following corollary.

COROLLARY 4.2. *If* $\|e_k(t)\| \leq \underline{\xi}(\|\hat{x}_k\|)$ *for all* $t \in [a_k, a_{k+1})$ *and all* $k = 0, 1, \cdots, \infty$, *then the event triggered system described in section 3 is asymptotically stable.*

PROOF. If we show that $\underline{\xi}(\|\hat{x}_k\|) \leq \xi(\|x(t)\|)$ for all $t \in [a_k, a_{k+1})$ and all $k = 0, 1, \cdots, \infty$, with Lemma 4.1, this corollary is true.

From the definition of $\underline{\xi}(\|\hat{x}_k\|)$ (equation (12)), we have

$$\underline{\xi}(\|\hat{x}_k\|) \leq \xi(\|\hat{x}_k\| - \underline{\xi}(\|\hat{x}_k\|)).$$

Since $\|e_k(t)\| \leq \underline{\xi}(\|\hat{x}_k\|)$, it is easy to see that

$$\underline{\xi}(\|\hat{x}_k\|) \leq \xi(\|\hat{x}_k\| - \|e_k(t)\|) \leq \xi(\|x(t)\|).$$

$\square$

With Corollary 4.2, if we choose a threshold function satisfying $\theta(\|\hat{x}_k\|) < \underline{\xi}(\|\hat{x}_k\|)$, then we guarantee that $\|e_k(t)\| \leq \underline{\xi}(\|\hat{x}_k\|)$ for all $t \in [a_k, s_{k+1}]$ and all $k = 0, 1, \cdots, \infty$. To assure asymptotic stability, we still need to make sure that

$$\|e_k(t)\| \leq \underline{\xi}(\|\hat{x}_k\|), \forall t \in [s_{k+1}, a_{k+1}), k = 0, 1, \cdots, \infty. \quad (13)$$

This is done by bounding the delay D_{k+1} from above by a state dependent function Δ_{k+1}. On one hand, the upper bound Δ_{k+1} makes sure that equation (13) holds. On the other hand, Δ_{k+1} also assures that the time sequences $\{s_k\}_{k=0}^{\infty}$ and $\{a_k\}_{k=0}^{\infty}$ are admissible. To define this Δ_{k+1}, we first define $\underline{T}_{k+1}$ to be the minimum inter-sampling interval and $\overline{D}_{k+1}$ to be the maximum delay under the assumption of admissibility such that equation (13) holds. Δ_{k+1}, then, is defined as

$$\Delta_{k+1} = \min\{\underline{T}_{k+1}, \overline{D}_{k+1}\}. \quad (14)$$

We easily see that if $D_{k+1} \leq \Delta_{k+1}$, then equation (13) and admissibility are both guaranteed. Now, let's analyze the explicit forms of $\underline{T}_{k+1}$ and $\overline{D}_{k+1}$.

For the convenience of the analysis, some conventions are introduced first. We assume that the plant is locally Lipschitz on *compacts*. In particular, this means if we let Ω_k be a compact set containing $\hat{x}_k$ and all possible trajectories of $x(t)$ for any $t \in [a_k, a_{k+1})$, then

$$\|f(x, K(\hat{x}_k))\| \leq \psi(\hat{x}_k, K(\hat{x}_k)) + L_{\Omega_k}\|e_k\| \quad (15)$$

where $\psi_k(\hat{x}_k, K(\hat{x}_k)) = \|f(\hat{x}_k, K(\hat{x}_k))\|$. L_{Ω_k} is the Lipschitz constants with respect to x over compact set Ω_k. Besides, we also define two ball sets B_1 and B_2 in the forms of

$$B_1 = \{x \in \mathbb{R}^n : \|x\| \leq \beta(\|x_0\|, 0)\},$$
$$B_2 = \{x \in \mathbb{R}^n : \|x\| \leq 2\beta(\|x_0\|, 0)\}.$$

PROPOSITION 4.3. *For all* $x_k \in B_1$ *and* $\hat{x}_k \in B_2$, *assume the following inequality*

$$\bar{e}_q(\|x_k\|) < \min\{\theta(\|\hat{x}_k\|), \|x_k\|\} \quad (16)$$

holds. The inter-sampling interval T_k *is always bounded from below by* $\underline{T}_k$, *i.e.* $T_k \geq \underline{T}_k$, *where* $\underline{T}_k$ *takes the form of*

$$\underline{T}_k = \frac{1}{L_{\Omega_k}}\left(\ln\left(1 + \frac{L_{\Omega_k}\theta(\|\hat{x}_k\|)}{\Psi_{k,k-1}(\hat{x}_k, \hat{x}_{k-1})}\right) \right.$$
$$\left. - \ln\left(1 + \frac{L_{\Omega_k}\bar{e}_q(\|x_k\|)}{\Psi_{k,k-1}(\hat{x}_k, \hat{x}_{k-1})}\right) \right), \quad (17)$$

$\Psi_{k,k-1}$ *takes the form of*

$$\Psi_{k,k-1}(\hat{x}_k, \hat{x}_{k-1}) = |\psi(\hat{x}_k, K(\hat{x}_k)) - \psi(\hat{x}_k, K(\hat{x}_{k-1}))|$$
$$+ \psi(\hat{x}_k, K(\hat{x}_{k-1})),$$

and Ω_k *takes the form of*

$$\Omega_k = \{x \in \mathbb{R}^n : \|x\| \leq \|\hat{x}_k\| + \underline{\xi}(\|\hat{x}_k\|)\}. \quad (18)$$

PROOF. To get the explicit form of $\underline{T}_k$, we need to analyze the dynamic behavior of $\|e_k(t)\|$ during the intervals $[s_k, a_k)$ and $[a_k, s_{k+1}]$.

For interval $[s_k, a_k)$, from (5) and (15), the derivative of $\|e_k(t)\|$ satisfies

$$\frac{d\|e_k(t)\|}{dt} \leq \|\dot{e}_k(t)\| \leq \psi(\hat{x}_k, K(\hat{x}_{k-1})) + L_{\Omega_k}\|e_k(t)\|.$$

According to the comparison principle, we have

$$\|e_k(a_k)\| \leq \frac{\psi(\hat{x}_k, K(\hat{x}_{k-1}))}{L_{\Omega_k}}(e^{L_{\Omega_k}D_k} - 1)$$
$$+ \bar{e}_q(\|x_k\|)e^{L_{\Omega_k}D_k}.$$

For interval $[a_k, s_{k+1}]$, from (5) and (15), the derivative of $\|e_k(t)\|$ satisfies

$$\frac{d\|e_k(t)\|}{dt} \leq \|\dot{e}_k(t)\| \leq \psi(\hat{x}_k, K(\hat{x}_k)) + L_{\Omega_k}\|e_k(t)\|. \quad (19)$$

With $\|e_k(a_k)\|$ as the initial condition, we have

$$\|e_k(s_{k+1})\| \leq \frac{\Psi_{k,k-1}(\hat{x}_k, \hat{x}_{k-1})}{L_{\Omega_k}}(e^{L_{\Omega_k}T_k} - 1)$$
$$+ \bar{e}_q(\|x_k\|)e^{L_{\Omega_k}T_k}.$$

Since $\|e_k(s_{k+1})\| = \theta(\|\hat{x}_k\|)$, it can be derived that $T_k \geq \underline{T}_k$ where $\underline{T}_k$ takes the form of (17). $\square$

REMARK 4.4. *The assumption (16) assures that* $\underline{T}_k$ *is always positive, and hence prevent the Zeno behavior (infinite fast sampling).*

By now, we have had the explicit form of $\underline{T}_k$. The same technique is used to derive the explicit form of $\overline{D}_k$.

PROPOSITION 4.5. *For all* $x_k \in B_1$ *and* $\hat{x}_k \in B_2$, *assume equation (16) and the following inequality*

$$\theta(\|\hat{x}_k\|) < \underline{\xi}(\|\hat{x}_k\|) \quad (20)$$

hold. Equation (13) is true, if

$$D_{k+1} \leq \Delta_{k+1} = \min\{\underline{T}_{k+1}, \overline{D}_{k+1}\}, \quad (21)$$

where $\underline{T}_{k+1}$ *is defined in (17) and* $\overline{D}_{k+1}$ *is defined as*

$$\overline{D}_{k+1} = \frac{1}{L_{\Omega_k}}\left(\ln\left(1 + L_{\Omega_k}\frac{\underline{\xi}(\|\hat{x}_k\|)}{\psi(\hat{x}_k, K(\hat{x}_k))}\right) \right.$$
$$\left. - \ln\left(1 + L_{\Omega_k}\frac{\theta(\|\hat{x}_k\|)}{\psi(\hat{x}_k, K(\hat{x}_k))}\right) \right), \quad (22)$$

where Ω_k *takes the form of (18).*

PROOF. Since $D_k \leq \Delta_k \leq \underline{T}_k$, we know that the sequence of transmissions and arrivals are admissible. So, equation (19) still holds for interval $[s_{k+1}, a_{k+1})$. With $\|e_k(s_{k+1})\| = \theta(\|\hat{x}_k\|)$, we can derive that

$$\|e_k(a_{k+1})\| \leq \frac{\psi(\hat{x}_k, K(\hat{x}_k))}{L_{\Omega_k}}(e^{L_{\Omega_k} D_{k+1}} - 1) + \theta(\|\hat{x}_k\|)e^{L_{\Omega_k} D_{k+1}}. \tag{23}$$

We notice that the right hand side of (23) is an increasing function with respect to D_{k+1}. So, to make sure that equation (13) holds, we let the right hand side of (23) be less than or equal to $\underline{\xi}(\|\hat{x}_k\|)$, and hence get that $D_{k+1} \leq \overline{D}_{k+1}$ where $\overline{D}_{k+1}$ is defined as in (22). $\square$

REMARK 4.6. *Assumption (20) assures that $\overline{D}_{k+1}$ is always positive, and hence, together with assumption (16), guarantees that the maximum acceptable delay is always positive.*

We notice that Proposition 4.3 and 4.5 are based on the fact that L_{Ω_k} is finite, i.e. Ω_k is closed and bounded. So, to make our proof strict, we show, in the next lemma, that with assumptions (16), (20) and (21), x_k is bounded. It implies that $\hat{x}_k$ is bounded, and so is Ω_k.

LEMMA 4.7. *If assumptions (16), (20) and (21) hold, x_k lies in the ball set B_1, i.e. $\|x_k\| \leq \beta(x_0, 0)$.*

PROOF. Let's assume that there exists a positive integer k' such that

$$\|x_k\| \leq \beta(\|x_0\|, s_k), \forall k = 0, 1, \cdots, k', \tag{24}$$
$$\|x_{k'+1}\| > \beta(\|x_0\|, s_{k'+1}). \tag{25}$$

We will show that equation (24) implies that $\|e_k(t)\| \leq \underline{\xi}(\|\hat{x}_k\|)$ for all $t \in [a_k, a_{k+1})$ and all $k = 0, 1, \cdots, k'$. This indicates that the state trajectory satisfies $\|x(t)\| \leq \beta(x_0, t)$ for all $t \in [0, a_{k+1})$ according to Corollary 4.2. The assertion ($\|x(t)\| \leq \beta(x_0, t)$ for all $t \in [0, a_{k+1})$) contradicts our assumption in (25), and this lemma is shown to be true.

For intervals $[a_k, s_{k+1}]$ where $k = 0, 1, \cdots, k'$, since both $\|e_k(t)\| \leq \theta(\|\hat{x}_k\|)$ and (20) hold, $\|e_k(t)\| \leq \underline{\xi}(\|\hat{x}_k\|)$ for all $t \in [a_k, s_{k+1}]$ and all $k = 0, 1, \cdots, k'$..

Now, let's consider intervals $[s_{k+1}, a_{k+1})$ where $k = 0, 1, \cdots, k'$. Since x_k is bounded for $k = 0, 1, \cdots, k'$, $\hat{x}_k$ must be bounded and so is Ω_k. So, we have finite L_{Ω_k} for $k = 0, 1, \cdots, k'$ and positive maximum acceptable delay Δ_k for $k = 0, 1, \cdots, k' + 1$. Since assumption (16), (20) and (21) hold, according to Proposition 4.5, we have $\|e_k(t)\| \leq \underline{\xi}(\|\hat{x}_k\|)$ for all $t \in [s_{k+1}, a_{k+1})$ and all $k = 0, 1, \cdots, k'$.

Therefore, $\|e_k(t)\| \leq \underline{\xi}(\|\hat{x}_k\|)$ for all $t \in [a_k, a_{k+1})$ and all $k = 0, 1, \cdots, k'$. With the analysis above, this lemma is true. $\square$

From Corollary 4.2, Proposition 4.5 and Lemma 4.7, we conclude this section in the following theorem.

THEOREM 4.8. *If assumptions (16), (20) and (21) hold, then the event triggered system described in section 3 is asymptotically stable.*

As mentioned in our introduction, a more realistic measure of stabilizing bit-rate is the ratio of bits per sampled state to the maximum acceptable delay. So, the maximum acceptable delay Δ_k provided by Theorem 4.8 is very important in the analysis of stabilizing bit-rate in the next section.

5. STABILIZING BIT-RATE

Stabilizing bit-rate is the bit-rate which is sufficient to guarantee the asymptotic stability of the system. We first show, in subsection 5.1, that under some conditions, the stabilizing bit-rate is always bounded from above by a continuous increasing function with respect to (w.r.t.) the norm of the state. Then, in subsection 5.2, it is found that under the same conditions, the stabilizing bit-rate asymptotically converges to a finite number as the state approaches 0. In some cases, the stabilizing bit-rate goes to 0 as state x approaches 0. These results indicate that under some conditions, the event triggered system is efficient attentive, i.e. the stabilizing bit-rate monotonically decreases as the system converges to its equilibrium point.

Before talking about the stabilizing bit-rate, we first give a quantization map for the system given quantization error $\overline{e}_q(\|x_k\|)$. Since at sampling time s_k, both sensor and controller understand that $\|e_{k-1}(s_k)\| = \theta(\|\hat{x}_{k-1}\|)$, we only need to quantize the surface of the box $\{e_{k-1} : \|e_{k-1}\| \leq \theta(\|\hat{x}_{k-1}\|)\}$. First, we use $\lceil \log_2 2n \rceil$ bits to identify which side e_{k-1} lies on, and then we cut this side uniformly into $\left\lceil \frac{\theta(\|\hat{x}_{k-1}\|)}{\overline{e}_q(\|x_k\|)} \right\rceil^{n-1}$ parts. If $e_{k-1}(s_k)$ lies on one of the small parts, then $e_{k-1}(s_k)$ will be quantized as the center of this part, and $\hat{x}_k$ can be calculated to be the sum of $\hat{x}_{k-1}$ and the quantized $e_{k-1}(s_k)$. In all, the number of bits used at the kth sampling is

$$N_k = \lceil \log_2 2n \rceil + (n-1) \left\lceil \log_2 \left\lceil \frac{\theta(\|\hat{x}_{k-1}\|)}{\overline{e}_q(\|x_k\|)} \right\rceil \right\rceil \tag{26}$$

We should notice that the number of bits transmitted at each time can be different, since we fix the quantization error instead of the number of bits.

Now, let's define the stabilizing bit-rate as

$$\underline{r}_k = \frac{N_k}{\Delta_k}. \tag{27}$$

For convenience of the rest of this paper, we define $\phi_c(\|\hat{x}_k\|)$ as a class $\mathcal{K}$ function satisfying

$$\psi(\hat{x}_k, K(\hat{x}_k)) \leq \phi_c(\|\hat{x}_k\|), \forall \hat{x}_k \in B_2 \tag{28}$$

and $\phi_u(\|\hat{x}_k\|)$ as a class $\mathcal{K}$ function satisfying

$$u_k = \|K(\hat{x}_k)\| \leq \phi_u(\|\hat{x}_k\|), \forall \hat{x}_k \in B_2. \tag{29}$$

With these preliminaries, we show that the stabilizing bit-rate is bounded from above by a continuous increasing function w.r.t. the norm of the state. This is done by bounding N_k from above by a continuous increasing function and bounding Δ_k from below by a continuous decreasing function.

5.1 Increasing Upper Bound on Stabilizing Bit-Rate

5.1.1 *Increasing upper bound on N_k w.r.t. $\|\hat{x}_{k-1}\|$*

THEOREM 5.1. *If all the conditions in theorem 4.8 hold, and*

$$\lim_{s \to 0} \frac{\theta(s)}{\overline{e}_q(s)} < \infty, \tag{30}$$

then there exists a continuous increasing function $\overline{N}_k(\|\hat{x}_{k-1}\|)$ such that

$$N_k \leq \overline{N}_k(\|\hat{x}_{k-1}\|).$$

PROOF. From equation (27), we see that the key point in the proof is that there exists a continuous increasing function $h_1(s)$ such that

$$\frac{\theta(\|\hat{x}_{k-1}\|)}{\overline{e}_q(\|x_k\|)} \leq h_1(\|\hat{x}_{k-1}\|).$$

First, we notice that $\|x_k\| \geq |\|\hat{x}_{k-1}\| - \theta(\|\hat{x}_{k-1}\|)|$. So, we have

$$\frac{\theta(\|\hat{x}_{k-1}\|)}{\overline{e}_q(\|x_k\|)} \leq \frac{\theta(\|\hat{x}_{k-1}\|)}{\overline{e}_q(|\|\hat{x}_{k-1}\| - \theta(\|\hat{x}_{k-1}\|)|)}.$$

Second, from equation (20) and (12), we know that $\theta(s) < s$. Together with the fact that $\frac{\theta(s)}{\overline{e}_q(s)}$ has non-negative order (equation (30)), Lemma 2.2 tells us that the right hand side of the above inequality has *non-negative* order. According to Lemma 2.1, there must exist a continuous increasing function $h_1(s)$ such that

$$\frac{\theta(s)}{\overline{e}_q(|s - \theta(s)|)} \leq h_1(s), \tag{31}$$

$$\lim_{s \to 0} \frac{\theta(s)}{\overline{e}_q(|s - \theta(s)|)} = \lim_{s \to 0} h_1(s). \tag{32}$$

Therefore, we can conclude that there exists a continuous increasing function $\overline{N}_k(\|\hat{x}_{k-1}\|)$ which takes the form of

$$\overline{N}_k(s) = \lceil \log_2 2n \rceil + (n-1)\lceil \log_2 \lceil h_1(s) \rceil \rceil, \tag{33}$$

such that

$$N_k \leq \overline{N}_k(\|\hat{x}_{k-1}\|).$$

□

Next, we show that the maximum acceptable delay Δ_k has a continuous decreasing lower bound w.r.t the norm of the state.

5.1.2 *Decreasing lower bound on Δ_k w.r.t. $\|\hat{x}_{k-1}\|$*

To find a decreasing lower bound on $\Delta_k = \min\{\overline{D}_k, \underline{T}_k\}$, we first find a decreasing lower bound on $\overline{D}_k$ indicated by $\overline{D}'_k$, and then a decreasing lower bound on $\underline{T}_k$ indicated by $\underline{T}'_k$. It is easy to see that the decreasing lower bound on Δ_k is the minimum of $\overline{D}'_k$ and $\underline{T}'_k$.

LEMMA 5.2. *If all the conditions in theorem 4.8 hold and there exists a finite constant ρ_1 such that*

$$\lim_{s \to 0} \frac{\phi_c(s)}{\theta(s)} = \rho_1 < \infty, \tag{34}$$

then there exists a continuous decreasing function $\overline{D}'_k(\|\hat{x}_{k-1}\|)$ such that

$$\overline{D}_k \geq \overline{D}'_k(\|\hat{x}_{k-1}\|).$$

PROOF. First, let's define a constant $c_1 \in (0,1)$ satisfying

$$\frac{\theta(s)}{\xi(s)} \leq c_1, \forall s \in B_2, \tag{35}$$

From equation (28), we have

$$\overline{D}_k \geq \frac{1}{L_{\Omega_{k-1}}} \ln\left(1 + L_{\Omega_{k-1}} \frac{1 - c_1}{\frac{\phi_c(\|\hat{x}_{k-1}\|)}{\xi(\|\hat{x}_{k-1}\|)} + L_{\Omega_{k-1}} c_1}\right).$$

We see that the key point in this proof is to find a continuous increasing function h_2 such that

$$\frac{\phi_c(s)}{\xi(s)} \leq h_2(s). \tag{36}$$

From equation (20) and (34), we know that $\frac{\phi_c(\|\hat{x}_{k-1}\|)}{\xi(\|\hat{x}_{k-1}\|)}$ has non-negative order. Together with the fact that $\frac{\phi_c(\|\hat{x}_{k-1}\|)}{\xi(\|\hat{x}_{k-1}\|)}$ is continuous and positive definite, according to Lemma 2.1, we prove the existence of h_2. Moreover, $h_2(s)$ also satisfies

$$\lim_{s \to 0} \frac{\phi_c(s)}{\xi(s)} = \lim_{s \to 0} h_2(s). \tag{37}$$

Therefore, we show that there exists a continuous decreasing function $\overline{D}'_k(\|\hat{x}_{k-1}\|)$ in the form of

$$\overline{D}'_k(s) = \frac{1}{L_{\Omega_{k-1}}} \ln\left(1 + L_{\Omega_{k-1}} \frac{1 - c_1}{h_2(s) + L_{\Omega_{k-1}} c_1}\right), \tag{38}$$

such that

$$\overline{D}_k \geq \overline{D}'_k(\|\hat{x}_{k-1}\|).$$

□

Next, we show that there exists a continuous decreasing lower bound on $\underline{T}_k$ w.r.t. $\|\hat{x}_{k-1}\|$. For the convenience of the rest of this paper, we derive an upper bound and a lower bound on $\|\hat{x}_k\|$ w.r.t. $\hat{x}_{k-1}$.

LEMMA 5.3. *Let $\varsigma(s) = s + \theta(s) + \overline{e}_q(s + \theta(s))$. $\|\hat{x}_k\|$ is bounded from above by $\varsigma(\|\hat{x}_{k-1}\|)$, i.e.*

$$\|\hat{x}_k\| \leq \varsigma(\|\hat{x}_{k-1}\|).$$

PROOF. From equation (6), we have

$$\|\hat{x}_k\| \leq \|x_k\| + \overline{e}_q(\|x_k\|).$$

Moreover, equation (7) implies that $\|x_k\| \leq \|\hat{x}_{k-1}\| + \theta(\|\hat{x}_{k-1}\|)$, and we have

$$\|\hat{x}_k\| \leq \|\hat{x}_{k-1}\| + \theta(\|\hat{x}_{k-1}\|) + \overline{e}_q(\|\hat{x}_{k-1}\| + \theta(\|\hat{x}_{k-1}\|))$$
$$= \varsigma(\|\hat{x}_{k-1}\|).$$

□

LEMMA 5.4. *There exists a continuous increasing function $\underline{h}(s)$ satisfying*

$$|s - \overline{e}_q(s)| \geq \underline{h}(s), \tag{39}$$

$$\lim_{s \to 0} |s - \overline{e}_q(s)| = \lim_{s \to 0} \underline{h}(s), \tag{40}$$

such that

$$\|\hat{x}_k\| \geq \underline{h}(|\|\hat{x}_{k-1}\| - \theta(\|\hat{x}_{k-1}\|)|).$$

PROOF. From equation (6), we have

$$\|\hat{x}_k\| \geq |\|x_k\| - \overline{e}_q(\|x_k\|)|.$$

From equation (16), we know that the right hand side of the above inequality is continuous, positive definite and with non-negative order. According to Lemma 2.1, there must exist a continuous, positive definite, increasing function $\underline{h}$ satisfying equation (39) and (40). So, we have

$$\|\hat{x}_k\| \geq \underline{h}(\|x_k\|) \geq \underline{h}(\|\hat{x}_{k-1}\| - \theta(\|\hat{x}_{k-1}\|)).$$

The last inequality is derived from equation (7). □

Now, let's state the lemma about the decreasing lower bound on the minimum interval.

LEMMA 5.5. *If all the conditions in theorem 4.8 and equation (34) are satisfied, and there exists a finite constant ρ_2 such that*

$$\lim_{s \to 0} \frac{\phi_u(s)}{\theta(s)} = \rho_2 < \infty, \qquad (41)$$

then there exists a continuous decreasing function $\underline{T}'_k(\|\hat{x}_{k-1}\|)$ such that

$$\underline{T}_k \geq \underline{T}'_k(\|\hat{x}_{k-1}\|).$$

PROOF. Let $c_2 \in (0, 1)$ be a constant satisfying

$$\frac{\bar{e}_q(\|x_k\|)}{\theta(\|\hat{x}_k\|)} \leq c_2, \forall x_k \in B_1, \qquad (42)$$

From equation(28), we have

$$\underline{T}_k \geq \frac{1}{L_{\Omega_k}} \ln\left(1 + L_{\Omega_k}\frac{1 - c_2}{h'(\|\hat{x}_k\|, \|\hat{x}_{k-1}\|) + L_{\Omega_k}c_2}\right), \quad (43)$$

where

$$h'(\|\hat{x}_k\|, \|\hat{x}_{k-1}\|) = 3\frac{\phi_c(\|\hat{x}_k\|)}{\theta(\|\hat{x}_k\|)} + 2L_{\Omega_k}\frac{\phi_u(\|\hat{x}_k\|)}{\theta(\|\hat{x}_k\|)} + 2L_{\Omega_k}\frac{\phi_u(\|\hat{x}_{k-1}\|)}{\theta(\|\hat{x}_k\|)}.$$

The key point in this proof is to find continuous increasing functions h_i for $i = 3, 4, 5$ such that

$$\frac{\phi_c(\|\hat{x}_k\|)}{\theta(\|\hat{x}_k\|)} \leq h_3(\|\hat{x}_k\|), \qquad (44)$$

$$\frac{\phi_u(\|\hat{x}_k\|)}{\theta(\|\hat{x}_k\|)} \leq h_4(\|\hat{x}_k\|), \qquad (45)$$

$$\frac{\phi_u(\|\hat{x}_{k-1}\|)}{\theta(\|\hat{x}_k\|)} \leq h_5(\|\hat{x}_{k-1}\|). \qquad (46)$$

For equation (44), we know that $\frac{\phi_c(\|\hat{x}_k\|)}{\theta(\|\hat{x}_k\|)}$ is continuous, positive definite and with non-negative order. According to Lemma 2.1, there exists a continuous increasing function h_3 satisfying (44). Moreover, h_3 also satisfies

$$\lim_{s \to 0} \frac{\phi_c(s)}{\theta(s)} = \lim_{s \to 0} h_3(s). \qquad (47)$$

With the same technique of showing equation (44), we show the existence of h_4 such that equation (45) holds. In addition, h_4 also satisfies

$$\lim_{s \to 0} \frac{\phi_u(s)}{\theta(s)} = \lim_{s \to 0} h_4(s). \qquad (48)$$

For equation (46), according to Lemma 5.4, we have

$$\frac{\phi_u(\|\hat{x}_{k-1}\|)}{\theta(\|\hat{x}_k\|)} \leq \frac{\phi_u(\|\hat{x}_{k-1}\|)}{\theta(\underline{h}(\|\hat{x}_{k-1}\| - \theta(\|\hat{x}_{k-1}\|)))}.$$

According to Lemma 2.2, we show that the right hand side of the above inequality has non-negative order. Together

with the fact that it is also continuous and positive definite, according to Lemma 2.1, we proof the existence of a continuous increasing function $h_5(s)$ satisfying the following inequalities

$$\frac{\phi_u(s)}{\theta(\underline{h}(|s - \theta(s)|))} \leq h_5(s), \qquad (49)$$

$$\lim_{s \to 0} \frac{\phi_u(s)}{\theta(\underline{h}(|s - \theta(s)|))} = \lim_{s \to 0} h_5(s). \qquad (50)$$

So, equation(46) is shown.

By now, we have shown that

$$\underline{T}_k \geq \frac{1}{L_{\Omega_k}} \ln\left(1 + L_{\Omega_k}\frac{1 - c_2}{h'(\|\hat{x}_k\|, \|\hat{x}_{k-1}\|) + L_{\Omega_k}c_2}\right)$$

$$\geq \frac{1}{L_{\Omega_k}} \ln\left(1 + L_{\Omega_k}\frac{1 - c_2}{\tilde{h}(\|\hat{x}_k\|, \|\hat{x}_{k-1}\|) + L_{\Omega_k}c_2}\right)$$

where

$$\tilde{h}(\|\hat{x}_k\|, \|\hat{x}_{k-1}\|) = 3h_3(\|\hat{x}_k\|) + 2L_{\Omega_k}h_4(\|\hat{x}_k\|) + 2L_{\Omega_k}h_5(\|\hat{x}_{k-1}\|).$$

Since we prefer the lower bound on $\underline{T}_k$ depends solely on $\|\hat{x}_{k-1}\|$ to keep the variable of $\underline{T}'$ consistent with the variable of $\overline{N}$ and $\overline{D}'$, by taking advantage of Lemma 5.4, we show that $\underline{T}_k \geq \underline{T}'_k(\|\hat{x}_{k-1}\|)$ where $\underline{T}'_k(s)$ takes the form of

$$\underline{T}'_k(s) = \frac{1}{L_{\Omega'_k}} \ln\left(1 + L_{\Omega'_k}\frac{1 - c_2}{h(s) + L_{\Omega'_k}c_2}\right), \qquad (51)$$

where $h(s) = 3h_3(\varsigma(s)) + 2L_{\Omega'_k}(h_4(\varsigma(s)) + h_5(s))$, and

$$\Omega'_k = \{x : \|x\| \leq \varsigma(\|\hat{x}_{k-1}\|) + \underline{\xi}(\varsigma(\|\hat{x}_{k-1}\|))\}.$$

□

With Lemma 5.2 and 5.5, we get a decreasing lower bound on the maximum acceptable delay Δ_k.

THEOREM 5.6. *If all the condition in theorem 4.8 hold, and equation (34) and (41) are satisfied, then there exists a continuous decreasing function $\underline{\Delta}_k(\|\hat{x}_{k-1}\|)$ which bounds Δ_k from below, i.e. $\Delta_k \geq \underline{\Delta}_k(\|\hat{x}_{k-1}\|)$, where*

$$\underline{\Delta}_k(\|\hat{x}_{k-1}\|) = \min\{\underline{D}'_k(\|\hat{x}_{k-1}\|), \underline{T}'_k(\|\hat{x}_{k-1}\|)\}, \qquad (52)$$

and $\underline{D}_k(\|\hat{x}_{k-1}\|)$ and $\underline{T}_k(\|\hat{x}_{k-1}\|)$ are defined in Lemma 5.2 and 5.5, respectively.

5.1.3 Increasing upper bound on $\underline{r}_k$ w.r.t. $\|\hat{x}_{k-1}\|$

With Theorem 5.1 and 5.6, it is easy to find an upper bound on $\underline{r}_k$ which is increasing w.r.t. $\|\hat{x}_{k-1}\|$.

THEOREM 5.7. *If all the condition in theorem 4.8 hold, and equation (30), (34) and (41) are satisfied, then there exists a continuous, positive definite, increasing function $\overline{r}_k(\|\hat{x}_{k-1}\|)$ which bounds $\underline{r}_k$ from above, i.e. $\underline{r}_k \leq \overline{r}_k(\|\hat{x}_{k-1}\|)$, where*

$$\overline{r}_k(\|\hat{x}_{k-1}\|) = \frac{\overline{N}_k(\|\hat{x}_{k-1}\|)}{\underline{\Delta}_k(\|\hat{x}_{k-1}\|)}, \qquad (53)$$

$\overline{N}_k(\|\hat{x}_{k-1}\|)$ *and $\underline{\Delta}_k(\|\hat{x}_{k-1}\|)$ are defined in Theorem 5.1 and 5.6, respectively.*

REMARK 5.8. *Theorem 5.7 indicates that the farther the state is away from the origin, the higher the stabilizing bit-rate will be.*

REMARK 5.9. *Theorem 5.7 provides a guide on how to assign communication resources to event triggered control systems ahead of time. Theorem 5.7 tells us that the stabilizing bit-rate is bounded from above by an increasing function w.r.t. $\|\hat{x}_{k-1}\|$. Moreover, since the event triggered system is asymptotically stable, $\|\hat{x}_{k-1}\|$ is bounded from above by a class $\mathcal{KL}$ function $\beta(\|x_0\|, t)$. Therefore, we know, ahead of time, an upper bound on the stabilizing bit-rate which relies on the initial state and time, and hence can decide the sufficient communication resources to stabilize the event triggered system.*

5.2 Asymptotic Behavior of Stabilizing Bit-Rates as State Approaches the Origin

Last subsection provides an increasing upper bound on the stabilizing bit-rate w.r.t. $\|\hat{x}_{k-1}\|$. Since the event triggered system is asymptotically stable, $\hat{x}_k$ gradually goes to the origin, and the stabilizing bit-rate converges to a steady point. This subsection studies the asymptotic behavior of the stabilizing bit-rate as the state approaches the origin. It is shown that under some conditions, the stabilizing bit-rate converges to 0 as the state approaches the origin.

The next theorem states and proves that under the same conditions as Theorem 5.7, the stabilizing bit-rate converges to a finite number as the system approaches its equilibrium.

THEOREM 5.10. *If all the conditions in Theorem 5.7 hold, then the stabilizing bit-rate converges to a finite number, i.e.*

$$\lim_{x \to 0} \underline{r}_k < \infty.$$

PROOF. Theorem 5.10 is true if we show that the upper bound on $\underline{r}_k$, $\overline{r}_k$, converges to a finite number, i.e.

$$\lim_{x \to 0} \overline{r}_k < \infty. \tag{54}$$

According to the definition of $\overline{r}_k$ (equation (53)), we see that the following inequalities indicate equation (54).

$$\lim_{x \to 0} \overline{N}_k < \infty \tag{55}$$

$$\lim_{x \to 0} \overline{D}'_k > 0 \tag{56}$$

$$\lim_{x \to 0} \underline{T}'_k > 0 \tag{57}$$

According to equation (33), the key point to assure equation (55) is that $\lim_{s \to 0} h_1(s) < \infty$. From equation (32), we have

$$\lim_{s \to 0} h_1(s) = \lim_{s \to 0} \frac{\theta(s)}{\bar{e}_q(|s - \theta(s)|)}.$$

According to Lemma 2.2, since $\theta(s) < s$ (from equation (20) and (12)) and condition (30) is satisfied,

$$\lim_{s \to 0} h_1(s) = \lim_{s \to 0} \frac{\theta(s)}{\bar{e}_q(|s - \theta(s)|)} < \infty,$$

and hence equation (55) is true.

From equation (52), we see that to assure equation (56), $h_2(s)$ needs to converge to a finite number as s approaches 0, i.e $\lim_{s \to 0} h_2(s) < \infty$. From equation (37), we have

$$\lim_{s \to 0} h_2(s) = \lim_{s \to 0} \frac{\phi_c(s)}{\xi(s)}.$$

Since conditions (20) and (34) are satisfied, we conclude that

$$\lim_{s \to 0} h_2(s) < \lim_{s \to 0} \frac{\phi_c(s)}{\theta(s)} < \infty.$$

Equation (57) is indicated by the facts that $\lim_{s \to 0} h_i(s) < \infty$ for any $i = 3, 4, 5$ (see equation (51)). From equation (47) and (48), since conditions (34) and (41) are satisfied, we know that $\lim_{s \to 0} h_i(s) < \infty$ where $i = 3, 4$. For $h_5(s)$, from equation (50) and (40), we have

$$\lim_{s \to 0} h_5(s) = \lim_{s \to 0} \frac{\phi_u(s)}{\theta(s - \theta(s) - \bar{e}_q(s - \theta(s)))}. \tag{58}$$

From equation (20) and (12), we see that

$$\theta(s) < s, \forall s \in B_2.$$

So, there must exist a constant $\epsilon_1 \in (0, 1)$ such that

$$\theta(s) < \epsilon_1 s, \forall s \in B_2.$$

With the same technique, we also know that there exists a constant $\epsilon_2 \in (0, 1)$ such that

$$\bar{e}_q(s) < \epsilon_2 s, \forall s \in B_1.$$

Together with equation (58), we have

$$\lim_{s \to 0} h_5(s) < \lim_{s \to 0} \frac{\phi_u(s)}{\theta(s)} \frac{\theta(s)}{\theta((1 - \epsilon_2)(1 - \epsilon_1)s)} < \infty$$

The last inequality is derived from equation (41). $\square$

Theorem 5.10 says that generally speaking, the stabilizing bit-rate converges to a finite number when the state approaches the origin. In a special case when the Lipschitz constant L_{Ω_k} converges to 0 as the state approaches the origin, we expect not only finite but also 0 stabilizing bit-rate. The next theorem states the conditions under which the stabilizing bit-rate goes to 0 as the state approaches the origin.

THEOREM 5.11. *If all the conditions in Theorem 5.7 hold with $\rho_1 = \rho_2 = 0$ and the Lipschitz constant L_{Ω_k} satisfies*

$$\lim_{x \to 0} L_{\Omega_k} = 0,$$

then the stabilizing bit-rate converges to 0 as the state approaches the origin, i.e.

$$\lim_{x \to 0} \underline{r}_k = 0.$$

PROOF. With the same technique of showing Theorem 5.10, Theorem 5.11 is proven. $\square$

6. SIMULATION RESULTS

This section uses a nonlinear system to demonstrate our main results in section 4 and 5. Besides, we also compare the performance and the stabilizing bit-rate of event triggered quantized system with the performance and the stabilizing bit-rate of periodic quantization system.

Now, let's consider a nonlinear system

$$\dot{x}_1 = x_1^3 + x_2^3 + u_1$$
$$\dot{x}_2 = -x_1^3 + x_2^3 + u_2$$

with $u_1 = -3\hat{x}_1^3$, $u_2 = -3\hat{x}_2^3$, and $x_0 = [1; 1]$. It's easy to see that $\phi_c(s) = 3s^3$, $\phi_u(s) = 3s^3$ and $L = 14\|x\|$. We give the ISS-Lyapunov function as $V = x_1^4 + x_2^4$. It can be

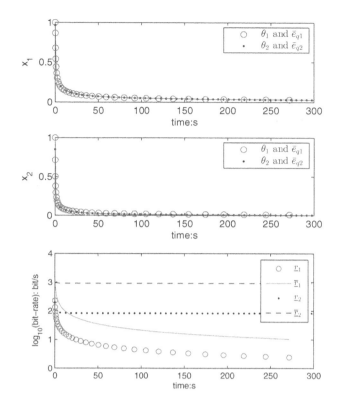

Figure 2: Comparison of two different pairs of threshold functions and quantization error functions

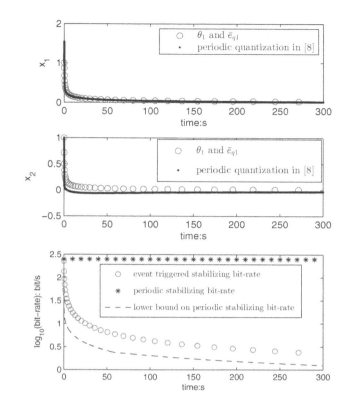

Figure 3: Comparison of event triggered quantization and periodic quantization

shown that (4) is satisfied with $\Upsilon = \{x : \|x\| \leq 1\}$, if we set $\xi(s) = \left(\frac{0.4s^6}{1216}\right)^{0.25}$. From (12), we have $\underline{\xi}(s) = 0.2s^{1.5}$. From (20) and (16), we choose two pairs of threshold functions and quantization errors. The first pair is $\theta_1(s) = 0.075s^{1.5}$ and $\bar{e}_{q1}(s) = 0.025s^{1.5}$. The second pair is $\theta_2(s) = 0.15s^3$ and $\bar{e}_{q2}(s) = 0.05s^3$. The first pair satisfies $\lim_{s \to 0} \frac{\phi_c(s)}{\theta_1(s)} = \lim_{s \to 0} \frac{\phi_u(s)}{\theta_1(s)} = 0$, and according to Theorem 5.11, the stabilizing bit-rate should converge to 0. The stabilizing bit-rate of the second pair converges to a finite number other than 0.

We ran the system for 300 seconds to see whether there are differences between the stabilizing bit-rates of the two pairs of threshold functions and quantization errors. The delay in the communication network is set to be Δ_k. The system trajectories and stabilizing bit-rates are shown in figure 2. The top two plots in this figure give the state trajectories of the two pairs of threshold functions and quantization errors (expressed by circles and dots, respectively) with x-axes indicating time and y-axes indicating state. We can see that they are all asymptotically stable. The bottom plot shows the stabilizing bit-rates of the two pairs of threshold functions and quantization errors with x-axis indicating time and y-axis indicating $\log_{10} r_k$. The stabilizing bit-rate of the first pair $\underline{r}_1$ and its upper bound $\overline{r}_1$ are indicated by circles and solid line, respectively. We see that $\overline{r}_1$ is always above $\underline{r}_1$, and is about 5 times greater than $\underline{r}_1$ in the worst case. Moreover, as x goes to the origin, both $\underline{r}_1$ and $\overline{r}_1$ converges to 0, which is as expected. The upper bound on the stabilizing bit-rate $\overline{r}_2$ given by the second pair (dashed line) is always

above the stabilizing bit-rate $\underline{r}_2$ (dots). Each of them converges to a constant in less than 10 seconds. The constant that $\overline{r}_2$ converges to is about 10 times as the constant that $\underline{r}_2$ converges to.

Moreover, we are interested in comparing our results with Liberzon's work in [8]. To make these two works comparable, we first find the longest period to stabilize the system using periodic quantization (uniform quantization), and then we set the delay of each transmission to be one period. The longest period we found to stabilize the system is $T = 0.015s$, and the least number of bits of each transmission is $N = 2\log_2(\lceil e^{L\Omega_k T} \rceil)$ if $\lceil e^{L\Omega_k T} \rceil$ is odd. Otherwise, $N = 2\log_2(\lceil e^{L\Omega_k T} \rceil + 1)$(In [8], N is required to be odd). In this experiment, we still use $L_{\Omega_k} = 14\|\hat{x}_k\|$.

The state trajectory (dots) of periodic quantization is shown in the top two plots of Figure 3. We see that it is asymptotically stable, but x_1 (shown in the top plot of Figure 3) has very big overshoot in the transient process. In periodic quantization, x_1 starts from 1, goes up to 1.5, and then decreases gradually to 0. Compared with the performance incurred by the periodic quantization, the trajectory of event triggered quantization (circles) has smoother transient process, and almost the same convergence rate. Now, let's look at the stabilizing bit-rate using the periodic quantization. The lower bound on the stabilizing bit-rate using periodic transmission is indicated by dashed line. When we look at the actual stabilizing bit-rate (stars) calculated from simulation, we find that it is more than 100 times higher than the theoretical minimum stabilizing bit-rate in the worst case, though we use the longest period and the least number of bits. That's because when we calculate N, we first compute $e^{L_{\Omega_k} T}$ which is always only a little bit above 1, and then take the ceil function of it which becomes 2, finally since it is not odd, we add 1 to it to make it odd. So we start from $e^{L_{\Omega_k} T}$ which is only a little bit above 1, and end with 3. Hence, the number of bits transmitted is always much greater than the theoretical one, which results in higher stabilizing bit-rate than the theoretical lower bound on stabilizing bit-rate. This is especially true when L_{Ω_k} and T are small. If we compared the stabilizing bit-rate using periodic transmission (stars) with the stabilizing bit-rate using event triggered quantization (circles), we can see that our stabilizing bit-rate is always less than the stabilizing bit-rate using periodic transmission. Moreover, our stabilizing bit-rate, in the best case, is about 2 times of the the theoretical lower bound on the stabilizing bit-rate presented in [8]. In all, we conclude that event triggered quantization achieves better performance than the periodic quantization while using lower bit-rate than the periodic one.

7. FUTURE WORK

The results in this paper can be used as a foundation to study the scheduling problem in networked control systems. This paper provides the maximum delay Δ_k and the stabilizing bit-rate $\underline{r}_k$. With this information, communication channel can assign the communication resource to different control systems. Interesting topics includes the necessary and/or sufficient bandwidth to stabilize all control systems in the network, and the scheduling policy to achieve the necessary and/or sufficient bandwidth.

8. ACKNOWLEDGEMENT

The authors acknowledge the partial financial support of the National Science Foundation NSF-CNS-0931195 and NSF-ECCS-0925229.

9. REFERENCES

[1] I. Akyildiz and I. Kasimoglu. Wireless sensor and actor networks: research challenges. *Ad hoc networks*, 2(4):351–367, 2004.

[2] D. Angeli, E. Sontag, and Y. Wang. A characterization of integral input-to-state stability. *IEEE Transactions on Automatic Control*, 45(6):1082–1097, 2000.

[3] A. Anta and P. Tabuada. Isochronous manifolds in self-triggered control. In *Decision and Control, 2009 held jointly with the 2009 28th Chinese Control Conference. CDC/CCC 2009. Proceedings of the 48th IEEE Conference on*, pages 3194–3199. IEEE, 2009.

[4] R. Brockett and D. Liberzon. Quantized feedback stabilization of linear systems. *Automatic Control, IEEE Transactions on*, 45(7):1279–1289, 2000.

[5] D. Delchamps. Stabilizing a linear system with quantized state feedback. *Automatic Control, IEEE Transactions on*, 35(8):916–924, 1990.

[6] J. Hespanha, P. Naghshtabrizi, and Y. Xu. A survey of recent results in networked control systems. *Proceedings of the IEEE*, 95(1):138–162, 2007.

[7] H. Khalil and J. Grizzle. *Nonlinear systems*, volume 3. Prentice hall, 1992.

[8] D. Liberzon and J. Hespanha. Stabilization of nonlinear systems with limited information feedback.

[9] *Automatic Control, IEEE Transactions on*, 50(6):910–915, 2005.

[9] J. Sandee, W. Heemels, and P. van den Bosch. Case studies in event-driven control. In *Hybrid Systems: computation and control*, pages 762–765. Springer, 2007.

[10] P. Tabuada. Event-triggered real-time scheduling of stabilizing control tasks. In *Automatic Control, IEEE Transactions on*, volume 52, pages 1680–1685. IEEE, 2007.

[11] P. Tabuada and X. Wang. Preliminary results on state-trigered scheduling of stabilizing control tasks. In *Decision and Control, 2006 45th IEEE Conference on*, pages 282–287. IEEE, 2006.

[12] S. Tatikonda and S. Mitter. Control under communication constraints. *Automatic Control, IEEE Transactions on*, 49(7):1056–1068, 2004.

[13] X. Wang and M. Lemmon. Finite-gain l2 stability in distributed event-triggered networked control systems with data dropouts. In *the European Control Conference*, 2009.

[14] X. Wang and M. Lemmon. Self-Triggered Feedback Control Systems With Finite-Gain L_2 Stability. In *Automatic Control, IEEE Transactions on*, volume 54, pages 452–467. IEEE, 2009.

[15] X. Wang and M. Lemmon. Attentively efficient controllers for event-triggered feedback systems. In *IEEE Conference on Decsion and Control*, 2011.

[16] X. Wang and M. Lemmon. Event-triggering in distributed networked control systems. *Automatic Control, IEEE Transactions on*, 56(3):586 –601, march 2011.

[17] W. Wong and R. Brockett. Systems with finite communication bandwidth constraints. ii. stabilization with limited information feedback. *Automatic Control, IEEE Transactions on*, 44(5):1049–1053, 1999.

A Symbolic Approach to the Design of Nonlinear Networked Control Systems*

Alessandro Borri   Giordano Pola   Maria D. Di Benedetto

Department of Electrical and Information Engineering
Center of Excellence for Research DEWS
University of L'Aquila - 67100 L'Aquila, Italy
{alessandro.borri,giordano.pola,mariadomenica.dibenedetto}@univaq.it

ABSTRACT

Networked control systems (NCS) are spatially distributed systems where communication among plants, sensors, actuators and controllers occurs in a shared communication network. NCS have been studied for the last ten years and important research results have been obtained. These results are in the area of stability and stabilizability. However, while important, these results must be complemented in different areas to be able to design effective NCS. In this paper we approach the control design of NCS using symbolic (finite) models. Symbolic models are abstract descriptions of continuous systems where one symbol corresponds to an "aggregate" of continuous states. We consider a fairly general multiple-loop network architecture where plants communicate with digital controllers through a shared, non-ideal, communication network characterized by variable sampling and transmission intervals, variable communication delays, quantization errors, packet losses and limited bandwidth. We first derive a procedure to obtain symbolic models that are proven to approximate NCS in the sense of alternating approximate bisimulation. We then use these symbolic models to design symbolic controllers that realize specifications expressed in terms of automata on infinite strings. An example is provided where we address the control design of a pair of nonlinear control systems sharing a common communication network. The closed-loop NCS obtained is validated through the OMNeT++ network simulation framework.

Categories and Subject Descriptors

I.2.8 [**Artificial Intelligence**]: Problem Solving, Control Methods, and Search—*Control theory*

*The research leading to these results has been partially supported by the Center of Excellence DEWS and received funding from the European Union Seventh Framework Programme [FP7/2007-2013] under grant agreement n. 257462 HYCON2 Network of excellence.

Keywords

Networked control systems, symbolic models, symbolic control, alternating approximate bisimulation

1. INTRODUCTION

In the last decade, the integration of physical processes with networked computing units led to a new generation of control systems, termed Networked Control Systems (NCS). NCS are complex, heterogeneous, spatially distributed systems where physical processes interact with distributed computing units through non–ideal communication networks. While the process is often described by continuous dynamics, algorithms implemented on microprocessors in the computing units are generally modeled by finite state machines or other models of computation. In addition, communication network properties depend on the features of the communication channel and of the protocol selected, e.g. sharing rules and wired versus wireless network. In the last few years NCS have been the object of great interest in the research community and important research results have been obtained with respect to stability and stabilizability problems, see e.g. [9, 7, 8]. However, these results must be complemented to meet more general and complex specifications when controlling a NCS. In this paper, we propose to approach the control design of NCS by using symbolic (finite) models (see e.g. [2, 18] and the references therein), which are typically used to address control problems where software and hardware interact with the physical world.

This paper presents two connected results. The first is a novel approach to NCS modeling, where a wide class of non-idealities in the communication network are considered such as variable sampling/transmission intervals, variable communication delays, quantization errors, packet dropouts and limited bandwidth. By using this general approach to modeling a NCS, we can derive symbolic models that approximate incrementally stable [3] nonlinear NCS in the sense of alternating approximate bisimulation [16] with arbitrarily good accuracy. This result is strong since the existence of an alternating approximate bisimulation guarantees that (i) control strategies synthesized on the symbolic models can be applied to the original NCS, independently of the particular realization of the non–idealities in the communication network; (ii) if a solution does not exist for the given control problem (with desired accuracy) for the symbolic model, no control strategy exists for the original NCS. The second result is about the design of a NCS where the control specifications are expressed in terms of automata on infinite strings. Given a NCS and a specification, we explicitly derive a symbolic controller such that the controlled system meets the specification *in the presence of the considered non-idealities in the communication network*. To illustrate the use of our results, we apply the methodology to derive a controller for a pair of nonlinear systems sharing a common communication network. To validate the controller, the closed–loop NCS is simulated in the OMNeT++ network simulation framework [19]. The results of this paper follow the approach on construction of symbolic models for nonlinear control systems reported in [14, 16, 15, 13, 20].

The paper is organized as follows. Section 2 introduces the notation employed in the sequel. In Section 3 we present the class of networked control systems that we consider in the paper. Section 4 reports some preliminary definitions of the notions of systems, approximate bisimulation and approximate parallel composition. Section 5 proposes symbolic models that approximate incrementally stable NCS in the sense of alternating approximately bisimulation. In Section 6 we address the symbolic control design of NCS. A realistic implementation of the symbolic control of a NCS on OMNeT++ is included in Section 7. Section 8 offers concluding remarks.

2. NOTATION

The identity map on a set A is denoted by 1_A. Given two sets A and B, if A is a subset of B we denote by $1_A : A \hookrightarrow B$ or simply by $\imath$ the natural inclusion map taking any $a \in A$ to $\imath(a) = a \in B$. Given a set A we denote $A^2 = A \times A$ and $A^{n+1} = A \times A^n$ for any $n \in \mathbb{N}$. Given a pair of sets A and B and a function $f : A \to B$ we denote by $f^{-1} : B \to A$ the inverse function of f such that $f^{-1}(b) = a$ if and only if $f(a) = b$ for any $a \in A$. Given a pair of sets A and B and a relation $\mathcal{R} \subseteq A \times B$, the symbol $\mathcal{R}^{-1}$ denotes the inverse relation of $\mathcal{R}$, i.e. $\mathcal{R}^{-1} := \{(b, a) \in B \times A : (a, b) \in \mathcal{R}\}$. The symbols $\mathbb{N}$, $\mathbb{N}_0$, $\mathbb{Z}$, $\mathbb{R}$, $\mathbb{R}^+$ and $\mathbb{R}_0^+$ denote the set of natural, nonnegative integer, integer, real, positive real, and nonnegative real numbers, respectively. Given an interval $[a, b] \subseteq \mathbb{R}$ with $a \leq b$ we denote by $[a; b]$ the set $[a, b] \cap \mathbb{N}$. We denote by $\lfloor x \rfloor := \max\{n \in \mathbb{Z} | n \leq x\}$ the floor and by $\lceil x \rceil := \min\{n \in \mathbb{Z} | n \geq x\}$ the ceiling of a real number x. Given a vector $x \in \mathbb{R}^n$ we denote by $\|x\|$ the infinity norm and by $\|x\|_2$ the Euclidean norm of x. A continuous function $\gamma : \mathbb{R}_0^+ \to \mathbb{R}_0^+$ is said to belong to class $\mathcal{K}$ if it is strictly increasing and $\gamma(0) = 0$; a function γ is said to belong to class $\mathcal{K}_\infty$ if $\gamma \in \mathcal{K}$ and $\gamma(r) \to \infty$ as $r \to \infty$. A continuous function $\beta : \mathbb{R}_0^+ \times \mathbb{R}_0^+ \to \mathbb{R}_0^+$ is said to belong to class $\mathcal{KL}$ if for each fixed s the map $\beta(r, s)$ belongs to class $\mathcal{K}_\infty$ with respect to r and for each fixed r the map $\beta(r, s)$ is decreasing with respect to s and $\beta(r, s) \to 0$ as $s \to \infty$. Given $\mu \in \mathbb{R}^+$ and $A \subseteq \mathbb{R}^n$, we set $[A]_\mu = \mu \mathbb{Z}^n \cap A$; if $B = \bigcup_{i \in [1;N]} A^i$ then $[B]_\mu = \bigcup_{i \in [1;N]}([A]_\mu)^i$. Consider a bounded set $A \subseteq \mathbb{R}^n$ with interior. Let $H = [a_1, b_1] \times [a_2, b_2] \times \cdots \times [a_n, b_n]$ be the smallest hyperrectangle containing A and set $\hat{\mu}_A = \min_{i=1,2,\ldots,n}(b_i - a_i)$. It is readily seen that for any $\mu \leq \hat{\mu}_A$ and any $a \in A$ there always exists $b \in [A]_\mu$ such that $\|a - b\| \leq \mu$. Given $a \in A \subseteq \mathbb{R}^n$ and a precision $\mu \in \mathbb{R}^+$, the symbol $[a]_\mu$ denotes a vector in $\mu \mathbb{Z}^n$ such that $\|a - [a]_\mu\| \leq \mu/2$. Any vector $[c]_\mu$ with $a \in A$ can be encoded by a finite binary word of length $\lceil \log_2 |[A]_\mu| \rceil$.

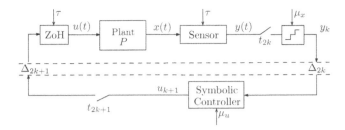

Figure 1: Networked control system.

3. NETWORKED CONTROL SYSTEMS

The class of Network Control Systems (NCS) that we consider in this paper has been inspired by the models reviewed in [7] and is depicted in Figure 1. The sub–systems composing the NCS are described hereafter.

Plant. The plant P of the NCS is a nonlinear control system in the form of:

$$\begin{cases} \dot{x}(t) = f(x(t), u(t)), \\ x \in X \subseteq \mathbb{R}^n, \\ x(0) \in X_0 \subseteq X, \\ u(\cdot) \in \mathcal{U}, \end{cases} \quad (1)$$

where $x(t)$ and $u(t)$ are the state and the control input at time $t \in \mathbb{R}_0^+$, X is the state space, X_0 is the set of initial states and $\mathcal{U}$ is the set of control inputs that are supposed to be piecewise–constant functions of time from intervals of the form $]a, b[\subseteq \mathbb{R}$ to $U \subseteq \mathbb{R}^m$. The set U is assumed to be compact, convex with the origin as an interior point. The function $f : X \times U \to X$ is such that $f(0, 0) = 0$ and assumed to be Lipschitz on compact sets. In the sequel we denote by $\mathbf{x}(t, x_0, u)$ the state reached by (1) at time t under the control input u from the initial state x_0; this point is uniquely determined, since the assumptions on f ensure existence and uniqueness of trajectories. We assume that the control system P is forward complete, namely that every trajectory is defined on an interval of the form $]a, \infty[$. Sufficient and necessary conditions for a control system to be forward complete can be found in [4].

Holder and Sensor. A Zero-order-Holder (ZoH) and a (ideal) sensor are placed before and after the plant P, respectively. We assume that:

(A.1) The ZoH and the sensor are synchronized and update their output values at times that are integer multiples of the same interval $\tau \in \mathbb{R}^+$, i.e.

$$u(s\tau + t) = u(s\tau), \quad y(s\tau + t) = y(s\tau) = x(s\tau),$$

for $t \in [0, \tau[$ and $s \in \mathbb{N}_0$, where s is the index of the sampling interval (starting from 0).

Symbolic controller. A symbolic controller is a function:

$$C : [X]_{\mu_x} \to [U]_{\mu_u},$$

with $\mu_x, \mu_u \in \mathbb{R}^+$. In the sequel we suppose that $\mu_x \leq \hat{\mu}_X$ and $\mu_u \leq \hat{\mu}_U$ so that the domain and co–domain of C are non–empty. If X is bounded, the quantization on X implies that the amount of information associated with any function C so defined is finite. We assume that:

(A.2) There is a time-varying computation time

$$\Delta_k^{\text{ctrl}} \in [\Delta_{\min}^{\text{ctrl}}, \Delta_{\max}^{\text{ctrl}}], \ k \in \mathbb{N},$$

for the symbolic controller to return its output value.

Limited bandwidth. Let $B_{\max} \in \mathbb{R}^+$ be the maximum capacity of the digital communication channel (expressed in bits per second (bps)). Such a constraint imposes a minimum positive 'time-to-send', in order to send finite-length information through the communication channel. This requires, in turn, state and input to be quantized before being sent through the network. The minimum sending intervals in the two branches of the network on the feedback loop are given by:

$$\Delta_{\text{send}}^{\text{sc}} = \frac{\lceil \log_2 |[X]_{\mu_x}| \rceil}{B_{\max}}, \quad \Delta_{\text{send}}^{\text{ca}} = \frac{\lceil \log_2 |[U]_{\mu_u}| \rceil}{B_{\max}},$$

where 'sc' refers to the sensor-to-controller branch and 'ca' to the controller-to-actuator branch of the network.

Time-varying unknown bounded delays. The actual time occurring for the data to cross the network is larger than the minimum sending time given by the bandwidth requirements. We define the sequence $\{\bar{\Delta}_k^{\text{delay}}\}_{k \in \mathbb{N}_0}$ that takes into account time-varying network delays including e.g. congestion, other accesses to the communication channel and any kind of scheduling protocol. The delays induced by the two branches of the network on the feedback loop are:

$$\Delta_{2k} = \Delta_{\text{send}}^{\text{sc}} + \bar{\Delta}_{2k}^{\text{delay}}, \quad \Delta_{2k+1} = \Delta_{\text{send}}^{\text{ca}} + \bar{\Delta}_{2k+1}^{\text{delay}}.$$

Furthermore we consider a sequence $\{\Delta_k^{\text{req}}\}_{k \in \mathbb{N}_0}$ of network *waiting times* that model the delay between the network request and the network access. In the proposed NCS, any scheduling protocol can be considered, provided that it satisfies:

(A.3) The sequence of network communication delays is bounded, i.e.

$$\bar{\Delta}_k^{\text{delay}} \in [\Delta_{\min}^{\text{delay}}, \bar{\Delta}_{\max}^{\text{delay}}],$$

for all $k \in \mathbb{N}_0$.

(A.4) The sequence of network waiting times is bounded, i.e.

$$\Delta_k^{\text{req}} \in [0, \Delta_{\max}^{\text{req}}],$$

for all $k \in \mathbb{N}_0$.

Packet dropout. Assume that one or more messages can be lost during the transmission through the network. Because of the bounded delays introduced by the network (see Assumptions (A.2), (A.3), (A.4)), if a node does not receive new information within a time less than

$$\Delta_{\text{send}}^{\text{sc}} + \Delta_{\max}^{\text{ctrl}} + \Delta_{\text{send}}^{\text{ca}} + 2\Delta_{\max}^{\text{req}} + 2\bar{\Delta}_{\max}^{\text{delay}},$$

a message is lost. By following the *emulation approach*, see e.g. [7], in dealing with dropout we assume that:

(A.5) The maximum number of subsequent dropouts over the network is bounded.

The previous assumption allows us to manage packet loss by considering an increased *equivalent delay* $\Delta_{\max}^{\text{delay}}$ introduced by the network, instead of the original $\bar{\Delta}_{\max}^{\text{delay}}$.

We now describe recursively the evolution of the NCS, starting from the initial time $t = 0$. Consider the k-th iteration in the feedback loop. The sensor requests access to the network and after a waiting time Δ_{2k}^{req}, it sends at time t_{2k} the latest available sample $y_k = [y(t_{2k})]_{\mu_x}$ where μ_x is the precision of the quantizer that follows the sensor in the NCS scheme (see Figure 1).

The *sensor-to-controller (sc)* link of the network introduces a delay Δ_{2k}, after which the sample reaches the controller that computes in Δ_k^{ctrl} time units the value $u_{k+1} = C(y_k)$. The controller requests access to the network and sends the control sample u_{k+1} at time t_{2k+1} (after a bounded waiting time $\Delta_{2k+1}^{\text{req}}$).

The *controller-to-actuator (ca)* link of the network introduces a delay Δ_{2k+1}, after which the sample reaches the ZoH. At time $t = A_{k+1}\tau$ the ZoH is refreshed to the control value u_{k+1} where $A_{k+1} := \lceil (t_{2k+1} + \Delta_k^{\text{ca}})/\tau \rceil$. The next iteration starts and the sensor requests access to the network again.

Consider now the sequence of control values $\{u_k\}_{k \in \mathbb{N}_0}$. Each value is held up for $N_k := A_{k+1} - A_k$ sampling intervals. Due to the bounded delays, one gets:

$$N_k \in [N_{\min}; N_{\max}],$$

with:

$$N_{\min} = \lceil \Delta_{\min}/\tau \rceil, \tag{2}$$
$$N_{\max} = \lceil \Delta_{\max}/\tau \rceil, \tag{3}$$

where we set:

$$\Delta_{\min} := \Delta_{\text{send}}^{\text{sc}} + \Delta_{\min}^{\text{ctrl}} + \Delta_{\text{send}}^{\text{ca}} + 2\Delta_{\min}^{\text{delay}}, \tag{4}$$
$$\Delta_{\max} := \Delta_{\text{send}}^{\text{sc}} + \Delta_{\max}^{\text{ctrl}} + \Delta_{\text{send}}^{\text{ca}} + 2\Delta_{\max}^{\text{req}} + 2\Delta_{\max}^{\text{delay}}. \tag{5}$$

For later purposes we collect the computation and communication parameters appearing in the previous description in the following vector:

$$\mathcal{C}_{\text{NCS}} = (\tau, \mu_x, \mu_u, B_{\max}, \Delta_{\min}, \Delta_{\max}). \tag{6}$$

In the sequel we refer to the described NCS by Σ. The collection of trajectories of the plant P in the NCS Σ is denoted by $\text{Traj}(\Sigma)$. Moreover we refer to a trajectory of Σ with initial state x_0 and control input u by $\mathbf{x}(., x_0, u)$.

4. SYSTEMS, APPROXIMATE EQUIVALENCE AND COMPOSITION

We will use the notion of systems as a unified mathematical framework to describe networked control systems as well as their symbolic models.

DEFINITION 4.1. *[18] A system S is a sextuple:*

$$S = (X, X_0, U, \longrightarrow, Y, H), \tag{7}$$

consisting of:

- *a set of states X;*

- *a set of initial states $X_0 \subseteq X$;*

- *a set of inputs U;*

- *a transition relation $\longrightarrow \subseteq X \times U \times X$;*

- *a set of outputs Y;*

- an output function $H : X \to Y$.

A transition $(x, u. x') \in \longrightarrow$ is denoted by $x \xrightarrow{u} x'$. For such a transition, state x' is called a u-successor, or simply a successor, of state x. The set of u-successors of a state x is denoted by $\text{Post}_u(x)$.

A state run of S is a (possibly infinite) sequence of transitions:

$$x_0 \xrightarrow{u_1} x_1 \xrightarrow{u_2} \dots \tag{8}$$

with $x_0 \in X_0$. An output run is a (possibly infinite) sequence $\{y_i\}_{i \in \mathbb{N}_0}$ such that there exists a state run of the form (8) with $y_i = H(x_i)$, $i \in \mathbb{N}_0$. System S is said to be:

- *countable*, if X and U are countable sets;

- *symbolic*, if X and U are finite sets;

- *metric*, if the output set Y is equipped with a metric $d : Y \times Y \to \mathbb{R}_0^+$;

- *deterministic*, if for any $x \in X$ and $u \in U$ there exists at most one state $x' \in X$ such that $x \xrightarrow{u} x'$;

- *non-blocking*, if for any $x \in X$ there exists at least one state $x' \in X$ such that $x \xrightarrow{u} x'$ for some $u \in U$.

DEFINITION 4.2. *Given two systems $S_i = (X_i, X_{0,i}, U_i, \xrightarrow{i}, Y_i, H_i)$ $(i = 1, 2)$, S_1 is a sub-system of S_2, denoted $S_1 \sqsubseteq S_2$, if $X_1 \subseteq X_2$, $X_{0,1} \subseteq X_{0,2}$, $U_1 \subseteq U_2$, $\xrightarrow{1} \subseteq \xrightarrow{2}$, $Y_1 \subseteq Y_2$, $H_1(x) = H_2(x)$ for any $x \in X_1$.*

In the sequel we consider bisimulation relations [11, 12] to relate properties of networked control systems and symbolic models. Intuitively, a bisimulation relation between a pair of systems S_1 and S_2 is a relation between the corresponding state sets explaining how a state run r_1 of S_1 can be transformed into a state run r_2 of S_2 and vice versa. While typical bisimulation relations require that r_1 and r_2 share the same output run, the notion of approximate bisimulation, introduced in [6], relaxes this condition by requiring the outputs of r_1 and r_2 to simply be close, where closeness is measured with respect to the metric on the output set.

DEFINITION 4.3. *[6] Let $S_i = (X_i, X_{0,i}, U_i, \xrightarrow{i}, Y_i, H_i)$ $(i = 1, 2)$ be metric systems with the same output sets $Y_1 = Y_2$ and metric d and consider a precision $\varepsilon \in \mathbb{R}_0^+$. A relation $\mathcal{R} \subseteq X_1 \times X_2$ is an ε-approximate simulation relation from S_1 to S_2 if the following conditions are satisfied:*

(i) *for every $x_1 \in X_{0,1}$ there exists $x_2 \in X_{0,2}$ such that $(x_1, x_2) \in \mathcal{R}$;*

(ii) *for every $(x_1, x_2) \in \mathcal{R}$ we have $d(H_1(x_1), H_2(x_2)) \le \varepsilon$;*

(iii) *for every $(x_1, x_2) \in \mathcal{R}$ the existence of $x_1 \xrightarrow{u_1} x_1'$ in S_1 implies the existence of $x_2 \xrightarrow{u_2} x_2'$ in S_2 satisfying $(x_1', x_2') \in \mathcal{R}$.*

System S_1 is ε-simulated by S_2 or S_2 ε-simulates S_1, denoted $S_1 \preceq_\varepsilon S_2$, if there exists an ε-approximate simulation relation from S_1 to S_2. The relation $\mathcal{R}$ is an ε-approximate bisimulation relation between S_1 and S_2 if $\mathcal{R}$ is an ε-approximate

simulation relation from S_1 to S_2 and $\mathcal{R}^{-1}$ is an ε-approximate simulation relation from S_2 to S_1. Furthermore, systems S_1 and S_2 are ε-bisimilar, denoted $S_1 \cong_\varepsilon S_2$, if there exists an ε-approximate bisimulation relation $\mathcal{R}$ between S_1 and S_2. When $\varepsilon = 0$ systems S_1 and S_2 are said to be exactly bisimilar.

In this work we also consider a generalization of approximate bisimulation, called alternating approximate bisimulation, that has been introduced in [16] to relate properties of control systems affected by non-determinism and their symbolic models.

DEFINITION 4.4. *[16, 18] Let $S_i = (X_i, X_{0,i}, U_i, \xrightarrow{i}, Y_i, H_i)$ $(i = 1, 2)$ be metric systems with the same output sets $Y_1 = Y_2$ and metric d and consider a precision $\varepsilon \in \mathbb{R}_0^+$. A relation $\mathcal{R} \subseteq X_1 \times X_2$ is an alternating ε-approximate (AεA) simulation relation from S_1 to S_2 if the following conditions are satisfied:*

(i) *for every $x_1 \in X_{0,1}$ there exists $x_2 \in X_{0,2}$ such that $(x_1, x_2) \in \mathcal{R}$;*

(ii) *for every $(x_1, x_2) \in \mathcal{R}$ we have $d(H_1(x_1), H_2(x_2)) \le \varepsilon$;*

(iii) *for every $(x_1, x_2) \in \mathcal{R}$ and for every $u_1 \in U_1$ there exists $u_2 \in U_2$ such that for every $x_2' \in \text{Post}_{u_2}(x_2)$ there exists $x_1' \in \text{Post}_{u_1}(x_1)$ satisfying $(x_1', x_2') \in \mathcal{R}$.*

System S_1 is alternating ε-simulated by S_2 or S_2 alternating ε-simulates S_1, denoted $S_1 \preceq_\varepsilon^{\text{alt}} S_2$, if there exists an A$\varepsilon$A simulation relation from S_1 to S_2. Relation $\mathcal{R}$ is an AεA bisimulation relation between S_1 and S_2 if $\mathcal{R}$ is an AεA simulation relation from S_1 to S_2 and $\mathcal{R}^{-1}$ is an AεA simulation relation from S_2 to S_1. Furthermore, systems S_1 and S_2 are AεA–bisimilar, denoted $S_1 \cong_\varepsilon^{\text{alt}} S_2$, if there exists an A$\varepsilon$A bisimulation relation $\mathcal{R}$ between S_1 and S_2.

When $\varepsilon = 0$, the above notion can be viewed as the two-player version of the notion of alternating bisimulation [1]. We conclude this section by introducing the notion of approximate parallel composition proposed in [17] that is employed in the sequel to capture (feedback) interaction between systems and symbolic controllers.

DEFINITION 4.5. *[17] Consider a pair of metric systems $S_i = (X_i, X_{0,i}, U_i, \xrightarrow{i}, Y_i, H_i)$ $(i = 1, 2)$ with the same output sets $Y_1 = Y_2$ and metric d, and a parameter $\theta \in \mathbb{R}_0^+$. The θ-approximate parallel composition of S_1 and S_2 is the system*

$$S_1 \|_\theta S_2 = (X, X_0, U, \longrightarrow, Y, H),$$

where:

- $X = \{(x_1, x_2) \in X_1 \times X_2 \mid d(H_1(x_1), H_2(x_2)) \le \theta\}$;

- $X_0 = X \cap (X_{0,1} \times X_{0,2})$;

- $U = U_1 \times U_2$;

- $(x_1, x_2) \xrightarrow{(u_1, u_2)} (x_1', x_2')$ if $x_1 \xrightarrow{u_1}_1 x_1'$ and $x_2 \xrightarrow{u_2}_2 x_2'$;

- $Y = Y_1$;

- $H(x_1, x_2) = H_1(x_1)$ for any $(x_1, x_2) \in X$.

The interested reader is referred to [17, 18] for a detailed description of the notion of approximate parallel composition and of its properties.

5. SYMBOLIC MODELS FOR NCS

In this section we propose symbolic models that approximate NCS in the sense of alternating approximate bisimulation. For notational simplicity we denote by u any constant control input $\tilde{u} \in \mathcal{U}$ s.t. $\tilde{u}(t) = u$ for all times $t \in \mathbb{R}^+$. Set

$$X_e = \bigcup_{N \in [N_{\min}; N_{\max}]} X^N.$$

Given the NCS Σ and the vector $\mathcal{C}_{\mathrm{NCS}}$ of parameters in (6), consider the following system:

$$S(\Sigma) := (X_\tau, X_{0,\tau}, U_\tau, \underset{\tau}{\longrightarrow}, Y_\tau, H_\tau),$$

where:

- X_τ is the subset of $X_0 \cup X_e$ such that for any $x = (x_1, x_2, ..., x_N) \in X_\tau$, with $N \in [N_{\min}; N_{\max}]$, the following conditions hold:

$$x_{i+1} = \mathbf{x}(\tau, x_i, u^-), \qquad i \in [1; N-2]; \quad (9)$$
$$x_N = \mathbf{x}(\tau, x_{N-1}, u^+); \quad (10)$$

for some constant functions $u^-, u^+ \in [U]_{\mu_u}$.

- $X_{0,\tau} = X_0$;

- $U_\tau = [U]_{\mu_u}$;

- $x^1 \xrightarrow[\tau]{u} x^2$, where:

$$\begin{cases} x_{i+1}^1 = \mathbf{x}(\tau, x_i^1, u_1^-), & i \in [1; N_1 - 2]; \\ x_{N_1}^1 = \mathbf{x}(\tau, x_{N_1-1}^1, u_1^+); \end{cases}$$

$$\begin{cases} x_{i+1}^2 = \mathbf{x}(\tau, x_i^2, u_2^-), & i \in [1; N_2 - 2]; \\ x_{N_2}^2 = \mathbf{x}(\tau, x_{N_2-1}^2, u_2^+); \end{cases}$$

$$\begin{cases} u_2^- = u_1^+; \\ u_2^+ = u; \\ x_1^2 = \mathbf{x}(\tau, x_{N_1}^1, u_2^-); \end{cases}$$

for some $N_1, N_2 \in [N_{\min}; N_{\max}]$;

- $Y_\tau = X_\tau$;

- $H_\tau = 1_{X_\tau}$.

Note that $S(\Sigma)$ is non-deterministic because, depending on the values of N_2, more than one u–successor of x^1 may exist. The construction of the set of states of $S(\Sigma)$ is based on an extended-state-space approach, and has been inspired by known approaches in the analysis of discrete–time time–varying delay systems, see e.g. [10]. Since the state vectors of $S(\Sigma)$ are built from trajectories of Σ sampled every τ time units, $S(\Sigma)$ collects all the information of the NCS Σ available at the sensor (see Figure 1) as formally stated in the following result.

THEOREM 5.1. *Given the NCS Σ and the system $S(\Sigma)$ the following properties hold:*

- *for any trajectory $\mathbf{x}(., x_0, u) \in Traj(\Sigma)$ of Σ, there exists a state run*

$$x^0 \xrightarrow{u_1} x^1 \xrightarrow{u_2} ..., \quad (11)$$

of $S(\Sigma)$ with $x^i = (x_1^i, x_2^i, ..., x_{N_i}^i)$ such that $x^0 = x_0$ and the sequence of states

$$x^0 \quad , \quad \underbrace{x_1^1, ..., x_{N_0+1}^1}_{x^1} \quad , \quad \underbrace{x_1^2, ..., x_{N_1}^2}_{x^2} \quad , \quad ... \quad (12)$$

obtained by concatenating each component of the vectors x^i, coincides with the sequence of sensor measurements

$$y(0), y(\tau), ..., y((N_0 + 1)\tau), y((N_0 + 2)\tau), ..., \\ y((N_0 + N_1 + 1)\tau), ... \quad (13)$$

in the NCS Σ;

- *for any state run (11) of $S(\Sigma)$, there exists a trajectory $\mathbf{x}(., x_0, u) \in Traj(\Sigma)$ of Σ such that the sequence of states in (12) coincides with the sequence (13) of sensor measurements in the NCS Σ.*

The proof of the above result is a direct consequence of the definition of $S(\Sigma)$ and is therefore omitted. System $S(\Sigma)$ can be regarded as a metric system with the metric d_{Y_τ} on Y_τ naturally induced by the metric $d_X(x_1, x_2) = \|x_1 - x_2\|$ on X, as follows. Given any $x^i = (x_1^i, x_2^i, ..., x_{N_i}^i)$, $i = 1, 2$, we set:

$$d_{Y_\tau}(x^1, x^2) := \begin{cases} \max_{i \in [1; N]} \|x_i^1 - x_i^2\|, & \text{if } N_1 = N_2 = N. \\ +\infty, & \text{otherwise.} \end{cases} \quad (14)$$

Although system $S(\Sigma)$ contains all the information of the NCS Σ available at the sensor, it is not a finite model. We now propose a system which approximates $S(\Sigma)$ and is symbolic. Define the following system:

$$S_*(\Sigma) := (X_*, U_*, \underset{*}{\longrightarrow}, Y_*, H_*), \quad (15)$$

where:

- X_* is the subset of $[X_0 \cup X_e]_{\mu_x}$ such that for any $x^* = (x_1^*, x_2^*, ..., x_N^*) \in X_*$, with $N \in [N_{\min}; N_{\max}]$, the following condition holds:

$$x_{i+1}^* = [\mathbf{x}(\tau, x_i^*, u_*^-)]_{\mu_x}, \qquad i \in [1; N-2]; \quad (16)$$
$$x_N^* = [\mathbf{x}(\tau, x_{N-1}^*, u_*^+)]_{\mu_x}; \quad (17)$$

for some constant functions $u_*^-, u_*^+ \in [U]_{\mu_u}$.

- $X_{0,*} = [X_0]_{\mu_x}$;

- $U_* = [U]_{\mu_u}$;

- $x^1 \xrightarrow[*]{u_*} x^2$, where:

$$\begin{cases} x_{i+1}^1 = [\mathbf{x}(\tau, x_i^1, u_1^-)]_{\mu_x}, & i \in [1; N_1 - 2]; \\ x_{N_1}^1 = [\mathbf{x}(\tau, x_{N_1-1}^1, u_1^+)]_{\mu_x}; \end{cases}$$

$$\begin{cases} x_{i+1}^2 = [\mathbf{x}(\tau, x_i^2, u_2^-)]_{\mu_x}, & i \in [1; N_2 - 2]; \\ x_{N_2}^2 = [\mathbf{x}(\tau, x_{N_2-1}^2, u_2^+)]_{\mu_x}; \end{cases}$$

$$\begin{cases} u_2^- = u_1^+; \\ u_2^+ = u_*; \\ x_1^2 = [\mathbf{x}(\tau, x_{N_1}^1, u_2^-)]_{\mu_x}; \end{cases}$$

for some $N_1, N_2 \in [N_{\min}; N_{\max}]$;

- $Y_* = X_\tau$;

- $H_* = \imath : X^* \hookrightarrow Y_*$.

System $S_*(\Sigma)$ is metric when we regard the set of outputs Y_* as being equipped with the metric in (14).

REMARK 5.2. *System $S_*(\Sigma)$ is countable and becomes symbolic when the set of states X is bounded. This model can be constructed in a finite number of steps, as inferable from its definition. Space complexity in storing data of $S_*(\Sigma)$ is generally rather large, because of the large size of the set of states X_e. This choice in the definition of X_e makes it easier to compare the NCS and $S_*(\Sigma)$ in terms of alternating approximate bisimulation as we will see in the forthcoming developments (see Theorem 5.8). However, for computational purposes it is possible to give a more concise representation of X_e as follows: any state $(x_1, x_2, \ldots, x_N)$ in X_e can be equivalently represented by the tuple (x_1, u^-, u^+, N) where u^- and u^+ are the control inputs in Eqns. (9)–(10).*

REMARK 5.3. *While the semantics of the NCS Σ is described in closed–loop, the symbolic models in (15) approximate the NCS in open–loop. Indeed, the symbolic models proposed approximate the plant P and the communication network, i.e. all entities in the NCS feedback loop except for the symbolic controller C (see Figure 1). This choice allows us to view the closed–loop NCS as the parallel composition [5] of two symbolic systems and therefore to adapt standard results in computer science for the control design of NCS, as shown in Section 6.*

A key ingredient of our results is the notion of incremental global asymptotic stability that we report hereafter.

DEFINITION 5.4. *[3] Control system (1) is incrementally globally asymptotically stable (δ–GAS) if it is forward complete and there exist a $\mathcal{KL}$ function β and a $\mathcal{K}_\infty$ function γ such that for any $t \in \mathbb{R}_0^+$, any $x_1, x_2 \in X$ and any $u \in \mathcal{U}$, the following condition is satisfied:*

$$\|\mathbf{x}(t, x_1, u) - \mathbf{x}(t, x_2, u)\| \leq \beta(\|x_1 - x_2\|, t).$$

The above incremental stability notion can be characterized in terms of dissipation inequalities, as follows.

DEFINITION 5.5. *[3] A smooth function $V : X \times X \to \mathbb{R}$ is called a δ–GAS Lyapunov function for the control system (1) if there exist $\lambda \in \mathbb{R}^+$ and $\mathcal{K}_\infty$ functions $\underline{\alpha}$ and $\overline{\alpha}$ such that, for any $x_1, x_2 \in X$ and any $u \in U$, the following conditions hold true:*

(i) $\underline{\alpha}(\|x_1 - x_2\|) \leq V(x_1, x_2) \leq \overline{\alpha}(\|x_1 - x_2\|)$,

(ii) $\frac{\partial V}{\partial x_1} f(x_1, u) + \frac{\partial V}{\partial x_2} f(x_2, u) \leq -\lambda V(x_1, x_2)$.

The following result adapted from [3] completely characterizes δ–GAS in terms of existence of δ–GAS Lyapunov functions.

THEOREM 5.6. *Control system (1) is δ–GAS if and only if it admits a δ–GAS Lyapunov function.*

REMARK 5.7. *In this paper we assume that the nonlinear control system P is δ–GAS. Backstepping techniques for the incremental stabilization of nonlinear control systems have been recently proposed in [21].*

We now have all the ingredients to present the main result of this section.

THEOREM 5.8. *Consider the NCS Σ and suppose that the control system P enjoys the following properties:*

(H1) There exists a δ–GAS Lyapunov function satisfying the inequality (ii) in Definition 5.5 for some $\lambda \in \mathbb{R}^+$;

(H2) There exists a $\mathcal{K}_\infty$ function γ such that[1]:

$$V(x, x') - V(x, x'') \leq \gamma(\|x' - x''\|),$$

for every $x, x', x'' \in X$.

For any desired precision $\varepsilon \in \mathbb{R}^+$, sampling time $\tau \in \mathbb{R}^+$ and state quantization $\mu_x \in \mathbb{R}^+$ satisfying the following inequality:

$$\mu_x \leq \min \left\{ \gamma^{-1}\left(\left(1 - e^{-\lambda\tau}\right) \underline{\alpha}(\varepsilon) \right), \overline{\alpha}^{-1}(\underline{\alpha}(\varepsilon)), \hat{\mu}_X \right\}, \quad (18)$$

systems $S(\Sigma)$ and $S_*(\Sigma)$ are $A\varepsilon A$–bisimilar.

PROOF. Consider the relation $\mathcal{R} \subseteq X_\tau \times X_*$ defined by $(x, x^*) \in \mathcal{R}$ if and only if:

- $x = (x_1, x_2, \ldots, x_N)$, $x^* = (x_1^*, x_2^*, \ldots, x_N^*)$, for some $N \in [N_{\min}; N_{\max}]$;

- $V(x_i, x_i^*) \leq \underline{\alpha}(\varepsilon)$ for $i \in [1; N]$;

- Eqns. (9), (10), (16), (17) hold for some $u^- = u_*^-$ and $u^+ = u_*^+$.

In the following we prove that $S(\Sigma) \preceq_\varepsilon^{\text{alt}} S_*(\Sigma)$, according to Definition 4.4. We first prove condition (i) of Definition 4.4. For any $x \in X_{0,\tau}$, choose $x^* \in X_{0,*}$ such that $x^* = [x]_{\mu_x}$, which implies that $\|x^* - x\| \leq \mu_x$. Hence, from condition (i) in Definition 5.5 and the inequality in (18) one gets:

$$V(x, x^*) \leq \overline{\alpha}(\mu_x) \leq \overline{\alpha}(\overline{\alpha}^{-1}(\underline{\alpha}(\varepsilon))) = \underline{\alpha}(\varepsilon), \quad (19)$$

which concludes the proof of condition (i). We now consider condition (ii) of Definition 4.4. For any $(x, x^*) \in \mathcal{R}$, from the definition of the metric given in (14), the definition of $\mathcal{R}$ and condition (i) in Definition 5.5, one can write:

$$d_{Y_\tau}(x, x^*) = \max_i \|x_i - x_i^*\| \leq \max_i \underline{\alpha}^{-1}(V(x_i, x_i^*))$$

$$\leq \underline{\alpha}^{-1}(\underline{\alpha}(\varepsilon)) = \varepsilon.$$

Next we show that condition (iii) in Definition 4.4 holds. Consider any $(x, x^*) \in \mathcal{R}$, with $x = (x_1, x_2, \ldots, x_N)$, $x^* = (x_1^*, x_2^*, \ldots, x_N^*)$, for some $N \in [N_{\min}; N_{\max}]$, and any $u \in U_\tau$; then pick $u_* = u \in U_*$. Now consider any $\bar{x}^* = (\bar{x}_1^*, \bar{x}_2^*, \ldots, \bar{x}_{\bar{N}}^*) \in \text{Post}_{u_*}(x^*) \subseteq X_*$ with $\bar{x}_{\bar{N}}^* = [\mathbf{x}(\tau, \bar{x}_{\bar{N}-1}^*, u_*)]_{\mu_x}$, for some $\bar{N} \in [N_{\min}; N_{\max}]$. Pick $\bar{x} = (\bar{x}_1, \bar{x}_2, \ldots, \bar{x}_{\bar{N}}) \in \text{Post}_u(x) \subseteq X_\tau$ with $\bar{x}_{\bar{N}} = \mathbf{x}(\tau, \bar{x}_{\bar{N}-1}, u)$ and define the state $\tilde{x}_1^* := \mathbf{x}(\tau, x_N^*, u_*^+)$. By Assumption (H1), condition (ii) in Definition 5.5 writes:

$$\frac{\partial V}{\partial x_N} f(x_N, u^+) + \frac{\partial V}{\partial x_N^*} f(x_N^*, u_*^+) \leq -\lambda V(x_N, x_N^*). \quad (20)$$

By considering Assumption (H2), the definitions of $\mathcal{R}$, $S(\Sigma)$ and $S_*(\Sigma)$, and by integrating the previous inequality, the following holds:

$$\begin{aligned} V(\bar{x}_1, \bar{x}_1^*) &\leq V(\bar{x}_1, \tilde{x}_1^*) + \gamma(\|\tilde{x}_1^* - \bar{x}_1^*\|) \\ &\leq e^{-\lambda\tau} V(x_N, x_N^*) + \gamma(\|\tilde{x}_1^* - \bar{x}_1^*\|) \quad (21) \\ &\leq e^{-\lambda\tau} \underline{\alpha}(\varepsilon) + \gamma(\mu_x) \leq \underline{\alpha}(\varepsilon), \end{aligned}$$

---

[1]Note that since V is smooth, if the state space X is bounded, which is the case in many concrete applications, one can always choose $\gamma(\|w - z\|) = \left(\sup_{x,y \in X} \|\frac{\partial V}{\partial y}(x, y)\| \right) \|w - z\|$.

where condition (18) has been used in the last step. By similar computations, it is possible to prove by induction that $V(\bar{x}_i, \bar{x}_i^*) \leq \underline{\alpha}(\varepsilon)$ implies $V(\bar{x}_{i+1}, \bar{x}_{i+1}^*) \leq \underline{\alpha}(\varepsilon)$, for any $i \in [1; \bar{N}-2]$. The last step $i = \bar{N}-1$ requires the use of the input $u = u_*$ instead of $u^+ = u_*^+$. By Assumption (H1) and defining $\tilde{x}_{\bar{N}}^* := \mathbf{x}(\tau, \bar{x}_{\bar{N}-1}^*, u_*)$, condition (ii) in Definition 5.5 writes:

$$\frac{\partial V}{\partial \bar{x}_{\bar{N}}} f(\bar{x}_{\bar{N}}, u) + \frac{\partial V}{\partial \bar{x}_{\bar{N}}^*} f(\bar{x}_{\bar{N}}^*, u_*) \leq -\lambda V(\bar{x}_{\bar{N}}, \bar{x}_{\bar{N}}^*). \quad (22)$$

By considering Assumption (H2), the definitions of $\mathcal{R}$, $S(\Sigma)$ and $S_*(\Sigma)$, and by integrating the previous inequality, the following holds:

$$\begin{aligned} V(\bar{x}_{\bar{N}}, \bar{x}_{\bar{N}}^*) &\leq V(\bar{x}_{\bar{N}}, \tilde{x}_{\bar{N}}^*) + \gamma(\|\tilde{x}_{\bar{N}}^* - \bar{x}_{\bar{N}}^*\|) \\ &\leq e^{-\lambda\tau} V(\bar{x}_{\bar{N}-1}, \bar{x}_{\bar{N}-1}^*) + \gamma(\|\tilde{x}_{\bar{N}}^* - \bar{x}_{\bar{N}}^*\|) \\ &\leq e^{-\lambda\tau} \underline{\alpha}(\varepsilon) + \gamma(\mu_x) \leq \underline{\alpha}(\varepsilon). \end{aligned} \quad (23)$$

Hence the inequality $V(\bar{x}_i, \bar{x}_i^*) \leq \underline{\alpha}(\varepsilon)$ has been proven for any $i \in [1; \bar{N}]$, implying $(\bar{x}, \bar{x}^*) \in \mathcal{R}$, which concludes the proof of condition (iii) of Definition 4.4.

We now consider the relation $\mathcal{R}^{-1}$ and we complete the prove by showing that $S_*(\Sigma) \preceq_\varepsilon^{\mathrm{alt}} S(\Sigma)$, according to Definition 4.4; we first prove condition (i) of Definition 4.4. For any $x^* \in X_{0,*}$, choose $x = x^* \in X_{0,\tau}$, which implies that $\|x^* - x\| = 0 \leq \mu_x$. Hence the inequality in (19) holds, which concludes the proof of condition (i). The proof of condition (ii) of Definition 4.4 for the relation $\mathcal{R}^{-1}$ is the same as the one for the relation $\mathcal{R}$ and is not reported. Next we show that condition (iii) in Definition 4.4 holds. Consider any $(x^*, x) \in \mathcal{R}^{-1}$, with $x^* = (x_1^*, x_2^*, ..., x_N^*)$, $x = (x_1, x_2, ..., x_N)$, for some $N \in [N_{\min}; N_{\max}]$, and any $u_* \in U_*$; then pick $u = u_* \in U_\tau$. Now consider any $\bar{x} = (\bar{x}_1, \bar{x}_2, ..., \bar{x}_{\bar{N}}) \in \mathrm{Post}_u(x) \subseteq X_\tau$ with $\bar{x}_{\bar{N}} = \mathbf{x}(\tau, \bar{x}_{\bar{N}-1}, u)$, for some $\bar{N} \in [N_{\min}; N_{\max}]$. Pick $\bar{x}^* = (\bar{x}_1^*, \bar{x}_2^*, ..., \bar{x}_{\bar{N}}^*) \in \mathrm{Post}_{u_*}(x^*) \subseteq X_*$ with $\bar{x}_{\bar{N}}^* = [\mathbf{x}(\tau, \bar{x}_{\bar{N}-1}^*, u_*)]_{\mu_x}$ and define the state $\tilde{x}_1^* := \mathbf{x}(\tau, x_N^*, u^+)$. After that, it is possible to rewrite exactly the same steps as in the proof of condition (iii) for $\mathcal{R}$, in particular Eqns. (20)–(23), implying that $V(\bar{x}_i, \bar{x}_i^*) \leq \underline{\alpha}(\varepsilon)$ for any $i \in [1; \bar{N}]$; as a consequence $(\bar{x}, \bar{x}^*) \in \mathcal{R}$, hence one gets $(\bar{x}^*, \bar{x}) \in \mathcal{R}^{-1}$, concluding the proof. $\square$

REMARK 5.9. *The symbolic models proposed in this section follow the work in [14, 16, 15, 13, 20]. In particular, the results of [15] deal with symbolic models for nonlinear time–delay systems. We note that such results are not of help in the construction of symbolic models for NCS because they do not consider time–varying delays in the control input signals, which is one of the key features in NCS.*

6. SYMBOLIC CONTROL DESIGN

We consider a control design problem where the NCS Σ has to satisfy a given specification robustly with respect to the non–idealities of the communication network. The class of specifications that we consider is expressed by the (non–deterministic) transition system [5]:

$$\mathcal{Q} = (X_q, X_q^0, \xrightarrow[q]{}), \quad (24)$$

where X_q is a finite subset of $\mathbb{R}^n$, $X_q^0 \subseteq X_q$ is the set of initial states and $\xrightarrow[q]{} \subseteq X_q \times X_q$ is the transition relation. We suppose that $\mathcal{Q}$ is accessible, i.e. for any state $x \in X_q$ there exists a finite path from an initial condition $x_0 \in X_q^0$ to x, i.e.

$$x_0 \xrightarrow[q]{} x_1 \xrightarrow[q]{} x_2 \xrightarrow[q]{} ... \xrightarrow[q]{} x.$$

Moreover we suppose that $\mathcal{Q}$ is non–blocking, i.e. for any $x \in X_q$ there exists $x' \in X_q$ such that $x \xrightarrow[q]{} x'$. For the subsequent developments we now reformulate the specification $\mathcal{Q}$ in the form of a system as in (7), as follows:

$$Q^e = (X_q^e, X_q^{e,0}, U_q, \xrightarrow[e,q]{}, Y_q^e, H_q^e), \quad (25)$$

defined as follows:

- X_q^e is the subset of $X_q^0 \cup \left(\bigcup_{N \in [N_{\min}; N_{\max}]} X_q^N \right)$ such that for any $x = (x_1, x_2, ..., x_N) \in X_q^e$, with $N \in [N_{\min}; N_{\max}]$, for any $i \in [1; N-1]$, the transition $x_i \xrightarrow[q]{} x_{i+1}$ is in $\mathcal{Q}$;

- $X_q^{e,0} = X_q^0$;

- $U_q = \{\bar{u}_q\}$, where $\bar{u}_q$ is a *dummy* symbol;

- $x^1 \xrightarrow[e,q]{\bar{u}_q} x^2$, where:

$$\begin{cases} x^1 = (x_1^1, x_2^1, ..., x_{N_1}^1), & N_1 \in [N_{\min}; N_{\max}]; \\ x^2 = (x_1^2, x_2^2, ..., x_{N_1}^2), & N_2 \in [N_{\min}; N_{\max}], \end{cases}$$

and the transition $x_{N_1}^1 \xrightarrow[q]{} x_1^2$ is in $\mathcal{Q}$;

- $Y_q^e = X_q^e$;

- $H_q^e = 1_{X_q^e}$,

where $N_{\min}$ and $N_{\max}$ are as in (2) and (3). In order to cope with non-determinism in the communication network, symbolic controllers need to be robust in the sense of the following definition.

DEFINITION 6.1. *Given a system*

$$S = (X_S, X_{S,0}, U_S, \xrightarrow[S]{}, Y_S, H_S),$$

a symbolic controller

$$C = (X_C, X_{C,0}, U_C, \xrightarrow[C]{}, Y_C, H_C),$$

is said to be robust *with respect to S with composition parameter $\theta \in \mathbb{R}^+$ if for any $u_s \in U_S$ and for each pair of transitions $x_s \xrightarrow[S]{u_s} x_s'$ and $x_s \xrightarrow[S]{u_s} x_s''$ in S, with $x_s' \neq x_s''$, the existence of a transition $(x_s, x_c) \xrightarrow{(u_s, u_c)} (x_s', x_c')$ in $S\|C$, for some $x_c, x_c' \in X_C$, implies the existence of a transition $(x_s, x_c) \xrightarrow{(u_s, u_c)} (x_s'', x_c'')$ in $S\|_\theta C$ for some $x_c'' \in X_C$.*

We are now ready to state the control problem that we address in this section.

PROBLEM 6.2. *Consider the NCS Σ, the specification Q^e in (25) and a desired precision $\varepsilon \in \mathbb{R}^+$. Find a parameter $\theta \in \mathbb{R}^+$ and a symbolic controller C such that:*

(1) C is robust with respect to $S(\Sigma)$ with composition parameter θ;

(2) $S(\Sigma)\|_\theta C \preceq_\varepsilon Q^e$;

(3) $S(\Sigma)\|_\theta C$ is non-blocking.

Condition (1) of Problem 6.2 is posed to cope with the non-determinism of $S(\Sigma)$. The approximate similarity inclusion in (2) requires the state trajectories of the NCS to be close to the ones of specification Q^e up to the accuracy ε. The non-blocking condition (3) prevents deadlocks in the interaction between the plant and the controller.

In the following definition, we provide the controller C^* that will be shown to solve Problem 6.2.

DEFINITION 6.3. *The symbolic controller C^* is the maximal sub-system² C of $S_*(\Sigma)\|_{\mu_x}Q^e$ that satisfies the following properties:*

- *C is non-blocking;*

- *for any $u_* \in U_*$ and for each pair of transitions $x \xrightarrow{u_*}_* x'$ and $x \xrightarrow{u_*}_* x''$ in $S_*(\Sigma)$, with $x' \neq x''$, the existence of a transition $(x,x_q) \xrightarrow{(u_*,\bar{u}_q)} (x',x_q')$ in C, for some x_q, x_q', implies the existence of a transition $(x,x_q) \xrightarrow{(u_*,\bar{u}_q)} (x'',x_q'')$ in C, for some x_q''.*

The following technical result will be useful in the sequel.

LEMMA 6.4. *Let $S_i = (X_i, X_{0,i}, U_i, \xrightarrow{}_i, Y_i, H_i)$ ($i = 1, 2, 3$) be metric systems with the same output sets $Y_1 = Y_2 = Y_3$ and metric d. Then the following statements hold:*

(i) [6] for any $\varepsilon_1 \leq \varepsilon_2$, $S_1 \preceq_{\varepsilon_1} S_2$ implies $S_1 \preceq_{\varepsilon_2} S_2$;

(ii) [6] if $S_1 \preceq_{\varepsilon_{12}} S_2$ and $S_2 \preceq_{\varepsilon_{23}} S_3$ then $S_1 \preceq_{\varepsilon_{12}+\varepsilon_{23}} S_3$;

(iii) [13] for any $\theta \in \mathbb{R}_0^+$, $S_1\|_{\theta}S_2 \preceq_{\theta} S_2$.

We are now ready to show that the controller C^* solves Problem 6.2.

THEOREM 6.5. *Consider the NCS Σ and the specification Q^e. Suppose that the control system P in Σ enjoys Assumptions (H1) and (H2) in Theorem 5.8. Then for any desired precision $\varepsilon \in \mathbb{R}^+$ and for any $\theta, \mu_x \in \mathbb{R}^+$ such that:*

$$\mu_x + \theta \leq \varepsilon, \tag{26}$$

$$\mu_x \leq \min\left\{\gamma^{-1}\left(\left(1 - e^{-\lambda\tau}\right)\underline{\alpha}(\theta)\right), \overline{\alpha}^{-1}(\underline{\alpha}(\theta)), \hat{\mu}_X\right\}, \tag{27}$$

the symbolic controller C^* solves Problem 6.2.

PROOF. First we prove condition (1) of Problem 6.2. Consider any $u \in U_\tau$, any state $x \in X_\tau$, and any pair of transitions $x \xrightarrow{u}_\tau x'$ and $x \xrightarrow{u}_\tau x''$ in $S(\Sigma)$, with $x' \neq x''$. Consider any transition $(x,x_c) \xrightarrow{(u,u_c)} (x',x_c')$ in $S(\Sigma)\|_{\theta}C^*$, where $x_c = (x_*,x_q)$, $x_c' = (x_*',x_q')$, $u_c = (u_*,\bar{u}_q)$, since $C^* \sqsubseteq S_*(\Sigma)\|_{\mu_x}Q^e$. Note that the transition $x_c \xrightarrow{u_c} x_c'$ (equivalently $(x_*,x_q) \xrightarrow{(u_*,\bar{u}_q)} (x_*',x_q')$) is in C^* by Definition 4.5. By definition of $S(\Sigma)$ and $S_*(\Sigma)$ and in view of condition (27) and Assumptions (H1)-(H2) in Theorem 5.8, ensuring that $S(\Sigma) \cong_{\theta}^{\mathrm{alt}} S_*(\Sigma)$, the existence of a transition $x \xrightarrow{u}_\tau x''$ in $S(\Sigma)$ implies the existence of a transition $x_* \xrightarrow{u_*}_* x_*''$ in

---

²Here maximality is defined with respect to the preorder induced by the notion of sub-system.

$S_*(\Sigma)$ s.t. $d_{Y_\tau}(x'', x_*'') \leq \theta$, with $x_*'' \neq x_*'$, in general. Furthermore, by Definition 6.3, the existence of the transitions $x_* \xrightarrow{u_*}_* x_*'$ and $x_* \xrightarrow{u_*}_* x_*''$ in $S_*(\Sigma)$ and of the transition $(x_*,x_q) \xrightarrow{(u_*,\bar{u}_q)} (x_*',x_q')$ in C^* implies the existence of a transition $(x_*,x_q) \xrightarrow{(u_*,\bar{u}_q)} (x_*'',x_q'')$ in C^* for some x_q''. Since $d_{Y_\tau}(x'', x_*'') \leq \theta$, the transition $(x,x_c) \xrightarrow{(u,u_c)} (x'', x_c'')$, with $x_c'' = (x_*'', x_q'')$, is in $S(\Sigma)\|_{\theta}C^*$, which concludes the proof of condition (1) of Problem 6.2.

We now show that condition (2) of Problem 6.2 is fulfilled. By Lemma 6.4 (iii), $S(\Sigma)\|_{\theta}C^* \preceq_{\theta} C^*$ and $S_*(\Sigma)\|_{\mu_x}Q^e \preceq_{\mu_x} Q^e$. Since C^* is a sub-system of $S_*(\Sigma)\|_{\mu_x}Q^e$ then $C^* \preceq_0 S_*(\Sigma)\|_{\mu_x}Q^e$. By Lemma 6.4 (i)-(ii), and from (26), $\mu_x + \theta \leq \varepsilon$, the above approximate similarity inclusions imply $S(\Sigma)\|_{\theta}C^* \preceq_{\varepsilon} Q^e$, which concludes the proof of condition (2) of Problem 6.2.

We finally show that also condition (3) holds. Consider any state (x,x_*,x_q) of $S(\Sigma)\|_{\theta}C^*$. Since C^* is non-blocking, for the state (x_*,x_q) of C^* there exists a state (x_*',x_q') of C^* such that $(x_*,x_q) \xrightarrow{(u_*,\bar{u}_q)} (x_*',x_q')$ is a transition of C^* for some $(u_*,\bar{u}_q)$. Since by the inequality in (27) and Theorem 5.8, $S(\Sigma)$ and $S_*(\Sigma)$ are $A\theta A$-bisimilar, for the transition $x_* \xrightarrow{u_*}_* x_*'$ in $S_*(\Sigma)$ there exists a transition $x \xrightarrow{u} x'$ in $S(\Sigma)$ such that $d_{Y_\tau}(x',x_*') \leq \theta$. This implies from Definition 4.5 that (x',x_*',x_q') is a state of $S(\Sigma)\|_{\theta}C^*$ and therefore that $(x,x_*,x_q) \xrightarrow{(u,u_*,\bar{u}_q)} (x',x_*',x_q')$ is a transition of $S(\Sigma)\|_{\theta}C^*$, which concludes the proof.

$\square$

7. AN ILLUSTRATIVE EXAMPLE

We consider a pair of nonlinear control systems P_a and P_b described by the following differential equations:

$$\dot{x} = \begin{bmatrix} \dot{x}_1 \\ \dot{x}_2 \end{bmatrix} = f(x,u) = \begin{bmatrix} x_2 \\ -5\sin(x_1) - 4x_2 + u \end{bmatrix}, \tag{28}$$

$$\dot{z} = \begin{bmatrix} \dot{z}_1 \\ \dot{z}_2 \end{bmatrix} = g(z,v) = \begin{bmatrix} -2.5z_1 + z_2^2 \\ 2z_1 - 6e^{z_2} + v + 6 \end{bmatrix}, \tag{29}$$

where $x \in X = X_0 = \left[-\frac{\pi}{3}, \frac{\pi}{3}\right[\times [-1,1[$, $u \in U = [-5,5]$, $z \in Z = Z_0 = [-1,1[\times[-1,1[$ and $v \in V = [-5,5]$. The two plants that are denoted by Σ_a and Σ_b, form a pair of NCS loops as the one depicted in Figure 1. The two controllers are supposed to run on a shared CPU that is able to control both processes. The shared network/computation parameters are $B_{\max} = 1\,\mathrm{kbit}/s$, $\tau = 0.2s$, $\Delta_{\min}^{\mathrm{ctrl}} = 0.001s$, $\Delta_{\max}^{\mathrm{ctrl}} = 0.01s$ and $\Delta_{\max}^{\mathrm{req}} = 0.1s$. The output quantization is chosen to be equal to $\mu_x = 2 \cdot 10^{-4}$ for both the NCS, while we set a different input quantization: $\mu_u = 0.0024$ for Σ_a and $\mu_u = 2 \cdot 10^{-4}$ for Σ_b. We assume that P_b is farther away than P_a (in terms of hops in the network topology) from the shared CPU, resulting in larger delays; in particular, we set $\Delta_{\min}^{\mathrm{delay},a} = 0.05s$, $\Delta_{\max}^{\mathrm{delay},a} = 0.12s$ for Σ_a and $\Delta_{\min}^{\mathrm{delay},b} = 0.1s$, $\Delta_{\max}^{\mathrm{delay},b} = 0.24s$ for Σ_b. As from Eqns. (2)-(5), this results in $N_{\min}^a = 1$, $N_{\max}^a = 3$ for Σ_a, and $N_{\min}^b = 2$, $N_{\max}^b = 4$ for Σ_b. We consider the following common quadratic Lyapunov function:

$$V(y,y') = \frac{1}{2}\|y - y'\|_2^2,$$

satisfying condition (i) of Definition 5.5 with $\underline{\alpha}(r) = 0.5\,r^2$ and $\overline{\alpha}(r) = r^2$, $r \in \mathbb{R}_0^+$. Furthermore, for the first control system P_a, one can write:

$$\frac{\partial V}{\partial x}f(x,u) + \frac{\partial V}{\partial x'}f(x',u) = (x - x')^T(f(x,u) - f(x',u)) =$$
$$\leq -0.75V(x,x').$$

Condition (ii) of Definition 5.5 is therefore fulfilled for P_a with $\lambda_a = 0.75$. Analogous computation for P_b leads to $\lambda_b = 0.2$. Hence, by Theorem 5.6, control systems (28) and (29) are δ–GAS. In order to construct symbolic models for Σ_a and Σ_b, we apply Theorem 5.8. Assumption (H1) holds by the incremental stability property proven above. Assumption (H2) of Theorem 5.6 holds with $\gamma(r) = 2.09r$ for P_a and $\gamma(r) = 2r$ for P_b. Finally, for a precision $\varepsilon_a = \pi/20$ and $\varepsilon_b = 0.2$ for Σ_a and Σ_b, respectively, the inequality in (18) holds. Hence, we can construct symbolic models for $S_*(\Sigma_a)$ and $S_*(\Sigma_b)$ that are $A\varepsilon_a A$ bisimilar and $A\varepsilon_b A$ bisimilar to $S(\Sigma_a)$ and $S(\Sigma_b)$. For $S_*(\Sigma_a)$, the resulting number of states is $1.8 \cdot 10^{22}$ and the number of control inputs is $2,049$; $S_*(\Sigma_b)$ instead contains $3.91 \cdot 10^{29}$ states and $16,385$ control inputs. Due to the large size of the symbolic models obtained, further details are not included here. We now use the results in Section 6 to solve trajectory tracking problems (on a finite time horizon), expressed in the form of Problem 6.2. We consider specifications expressed in the form of transition systems $\mathcal{Q}_a$ and $\mathcal{Q}_b$, as in (24). The specification $\mathcal{Q}_a$ is given by the following trajectory on the first state variable:

$$0.5 \longrightarrow 0.4 \longrightarrow 0.3 \longrightarrow 0.2 \longrightarrow 0.1 \longrightarrow$$
$$0 \longrightarrow -0.2 \longrightarrow -0.35 \longrightarrow -0.5 \longrightarrow$$
$$-0.6 \longrightarrow -0.7 \longrightarrow -0.8 \longrightarrow -0.8 \longrightarrow$$
$$-0.75 \longrightarrow -0.7,$$

while the specification $\mathcal{Q}_b$ is given by the following trajectory:

$$(0.5, 0.5) \longrightarrow (0.4, 0.3) \longrightarrow (0.3, 0.2) \longrightarrow (0.2, 0.1) \longrightarrow$$
$$(0.1, -0.1) \longrightarrow (0, -0.25) \longrightarrow (-0.1, -0.3) \longrightarrow$$
$$(-0.1, -0.4) \longrightarrow (-0.15, -0.4) \longrightarrow (-0.15, -0.4) \longrightarrow$$
$$(0.1, -0.3) \longrightarrow (0.2, -0.2) \longrightarrow (0.2, -0.1) \longrightarrow$$
$$(0.2, -0.1) \longrightarrow (0.2, -0.05).$$

For the choice of the interconnection parameter $\theta_a = 0.9\varepsilon_a$ and $\theta_b = 0.9\varepsilon_b$, for the two NCS loops, Theorem 6.5 holds and a controller C^* as from Definition (6.3) solves the control problem. Since the symbolic models of Σ_a and Σ_b have large size, a straightforward application of the results reported in the previous section for the design of the requested symbolic controllers would exhibit a large space and time computational complexity. For this reason in this example we adapt to NCS the algorithms proposed in [13] concerning the integrated symbolic control design of nonlinear control systems. More precisely, instead of first computing the symbolic models of the plants to then derive the symbolic controllers, we integrate the design of the symbolic controllers with the construction of the symbolic models. By using this approach we designed the requested symbolic controllers in $2,039s$ with a total memory occupation of $25,239$ integers; this computation has been performed on the Matlab suite through an Intel Core 2 Duo T5500 1.66GHz laptop with 4 GB RAM. The synthesized controllers has been validated through the OMNeT++ network simulation framework [19]. Communication delays are managed in OMNeT++ by means of a variable number of hops for each message and random delays over each network hop. We set a delay over the single

hop variable between $0.0125s$ and $0.02s$, and a number of network hops between 4 and 6 for Σ_a and between 8 and 12 for Σ_b. Figure 2 shows the OMNeT++ implementation of the two-loop network scheme with shared CPU. In Figures 3 and 4, we show the simulation results for the tracking problems considered, for a particular realization of the network uncertainties: it is easy to see that the specifications are indeed met.

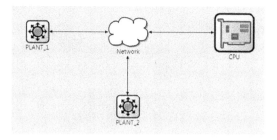

Figure 2: OMNeT++ implementation of Networked Control Systems with Symbolic Controller.

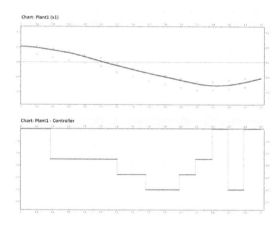

Figure 3: State trajectory and control input for the NCS Σ_a.

8. CONCLUSIONS

In this paper we proposed a symbolic approach to the control design of nonlinear NCS. Under the assumption of δ–GAS, symbolic models were proposed, which approximate NCS in the sense of alternating approximate bisimulation. These symbolic models were used to solve symbolic control problems on NCS where specifications are expressed in terms of automata on infinite strings. The assumption of δ–GAS in the plant control system of the NCS is a key ingredient in our results because if a digital controller is found which enforces the desired specification on the symbolic model, the notion of alternating approximate bisimulation guarantees that the specification is fulfilled on the NCS within a given accuracy that can be chosen as small as desired. Conversely if a control strategy solving the control problem does not exist, the notion of alternating approximate bisimulation guarantees that such a solution does not exist on the original NCS.

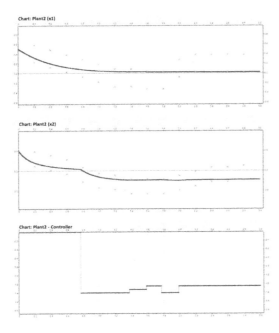

Figure 4: State trajectory and control input for the NCS Σ_b.

If compared with existing results on NCS, the main drawback of the proposed results is in the assumption of incremental stability on the plant control systems. One way to overcome this crucial assumption is to leverage the results reported in [20], which propose symbolic models approximating (possibly) unstable nonlinear control systems in the sense of alternating approximate simulation. This point is under investigation.

Acknowledgments

We are grateful to Pierdomenico Pepe for fruitful discussions on the topics of this paper and to Daniele De Gregorio and Quirino Lo Russo for the implementation of the example proposed in Section 7 in the OMNeT++ network simulation framework.

9. REFERENCES

[1] R. Alur, T. Henzinger, O. Kupferman, and M. Vardi. Alternating refinement relations. In *Proceedings of the 8th International Conference on Concurrency Theory*, number 1466 in Lecture Notes in Computer Science, pages 163–178. Springer, 1998.

[2] R. Alur, T. A. Henzinger, G. Lafferriere, and G. J. Pappas. Discrete abstractions of hybrid systems. *Proceedings of the IEEE*, 88:971–984, 2000.

[3] D. Angeli. A Lyapunov approach to incremental stability properties. *IEEE Transactions on Automatic Control*, 47(3):410–421, 2002.

[4] D. Angeli and E. Sontag. Forward completeness, unboundedness observability, and their Lyapunov characterizations. *Systems and Control Letters*, 38:209–217, 1999.

[5] E. Clarke, O. Grumberg, and D. Peled. *Model Checking*. MIT Press, 1999.

[6] A. Girard and G. Pappas. Approximation metrics for discrete and continuous systems. *IEEE Transactions on Automatic Control*, 52(5):782–798, 2007.

[7] W. Heemels and N. van de Wouw. Stability and stabilization of networked control systems. In A. Bemporad, M. Heemels, and M. Johansson, editors, *Networked Control Systems*, volume 406 of *Lecture notes in control and information sciences*, pages 203–253. Springer Verlag, London, 2011.

[8] W. Heemels, N. van de Wouw, R. Gielen, M. Donkers, L. Hetel, S. Olaru, M. Lazar, J. Daafouz, and S. Niculescu. Comparison of overapproximation methods for stability analysis of networked control systems. In K. Johansson and W. Yi, editors, *Hybrid Systems: Computation and Control*, volume 6174 of *Lecture Notes in Computer Science*, pages 181–191. Springer Verlag, Berlin, 2010.

[9] J. Hespanha, P. Naghshtabrizi, and X. Yonggang. A survey of recent results in networked control systems. *Proceedings of the IEEE*, 95(1):138–162, January 2007.

[10] M. Mahmoud. *Robust control and filtering for time-delay systems*. Vol. 5 of Control engineering. Marcel Dekker, 2000.

[11] R. Milner. *Communication and Concurrency*. Prentice Hall, 1989.

[12] D. Park. Concurrency and automata on infinite sequences. volume 104 of *Lecture Notes in Computer Science*, pages 167–183, 1981.

[13] G. Pola, A. Borri, and M. D. Di Benedetto. Integrated design of symbolic controllers for nonlinear systems. *IEEE Transactions on Automatic Control*, 57(2):534 –539, feb. 2012.

[14] G. Pola, A. Girard, and P. Tabuada. Approximately bisimilar symbolic models for nonlinear control systems. *Automatica*, 44:2508–2516, October 2008.

[15] G. Pola, P. Pepe, M. Di Benedetto, and P. Tabuada. Symbolic models for nonlinear time-delay systems using approximate bisimulations. *Systems and Control Letters*, 59:365–373, 2010.

[16] G. Pola and P. Tabuada. Symbolic models for nonlinear control systems: Alternating approximate bisimulations. *SIAM Journal on Control and Optimization*, 48(2):719–733, 2009.

[17] P. Tabuada. An approximate simulation approach to symbolic control. *IEEE Transactions on Automatic Control*, 53(6):1406–1418, 2008.

[18] P. Tabuada. *Verification and Control of Hybrid Systems: A Symbolic Approach*. Springer, 2009.

[19] A. Varga and R. Hornig. In *Simutools '08: Proceedings of the 1st international conference on Simulation tools and techniques for communications, networks and systems and workshops*, pages 1–10, ICST, Brussels, Belgium.

[20] M. Zamani, M. Mazo, G. Pola, and P. Tabuada. Symbolic models for nonlinear control systems without stability assumptions. *IEEE Transactions of Automatic Control*, 2012. In press, DOI: 10.1109/TAC.2011.2176409.

[21] M. Zamani and P. Tabuada. Backstepping design for incremental stability. *IEEE Transactions on Automatic Control*, 56(9):2184 –2189, sept. 2011.

Verification of Linear Duration Properties over Continuous Time Markov Chains[*]

Taolue Chen
Department of Computer Science
University of Oxford, UK

Marco Diciolla
Department of Computer Science
University of Oxford, UK

Marta Kwiatkowska
Department of Computer Science
University of Oxford, UK

Alexandru Mereacre
Department of Computer Science
University of Oxford, UK

ABSTRACT

Stochastic modeling and algorithmic verification techniques have been proved useful in analyzing and detecting unusual trends in performance and energy usage of systems such as power management controllers and wireless sensor devices. Many important properties are dependent on the cumulated time that the device spends in certain states, possibly intermittently. We study the problem of verifying *continuous-time Markov chains* (CTMCs) against *linear duration properties* (LDP), i.e. properties stated as conjunctions of linear constraints over the total duration of time spent in states that satisfy a given property. We identify two classes of LDP properties, eventuality duration properties (EDP) and invariance duration properties (IDP), respectively referring to the reachability of a set of goal states, within a time bound; and the continuous satisfaction of a duration property over an execution path. The central question that we address is how to compute the probability of the set of infinite timed paths of the CTMC that satisfy a given LDP. We present algorithms to approximate these probabilities up to a given precision, stating their complexity and error bounds. The algorithms mainly employ an adaptation of uniformization and the computation of volumes of multi-dimensional integrals under systems of linear constraints, together with different mechanisms to bound the errors.

Categories and Subject Descriptors

G.3 [**Probability and Statistics**]: Markov processes

General Terms

Verification

---

[*]This work is supported by the ERC Advanced Grant VERI-WARE.

Keywords

continuous-time Markov chains, linear duration logic, verification

1. INTRODUCTION

Stochastic modeling and verification [23] have become established as a means to analyze properties of system execution paths, for example dependability, performance and energy usage. Tools such as the probabilistic model checker PRISM [24] have been applied to model and verify many systems, ranging from embedded controllers and nanotechnology designs to wireless sensor devices and cloud computing, in some cases identifying flaws or unusual quantitative trends in system performance. The verification proceeds by subjecting a system model to algorithmic analysis against properties, typically expressed in probabilistic temporal logic, such as the probability of the vehicle hitting an obstacle is less than 10^{-4}, or the probability of an alarm bell ringing within 10 seconds is at least 95%. Many important properties, however, are dependent on the cumulated time that the system spends in certain states, possibly intermittently. Such *duration* properties, following the terminology of Duration Calculus (DC) [33], have been studied in the context of timed automata [1, 6, 22], but are not currently supported by existing probabilistic model checking tools. They can express, e.g., that the probability of an alarm bell ringing whenever the button has been pressed, possibly intermittently, for at least 2 seconds in total is at least 95%.

In this paper, we consider *Continuous-Time Markov Chain* (CTMC) models and study algorithmic verification for *linear duration properties* (LDP), i.e. properties involving linear constraints over cumulated residence time in certain states. CTMCs are widely used for performance and dependability analysis. CTMCs allow the modelling of real-time passage in conjunction with stochastic evolution governed by exponential distributions. They can be thought of as state transition systems, in which the system resides in a state on average for $1/r$ time units, where r is the exit rate, and transitions between the states are determined by a discrete probability distribution. As a concrete example of a system and property studied here, consider the dynamic power management system (DPMS) from [30], analysed in [29] against properties such as average power consumption. The DPMS includes a queue of requests, which have an exponentially distributed inter-arrival time, a power management controller and a service provider. The power management controller issues commands to the service provider depending on the power management policy, which involves switching between different power-saving modes. Fig. 1 depicts a CTMC model of the service provider for a Fujitsu disk drive. It consists of four states: *Busy, Idle, Standby* and *Sleep*. In this paper we are interested in computing the probability of, for instance, that *in 10 hours, the energy spent in Standby state is less than the energy spent in the Sleep state and the energy spent in the Idle state is less than one third of the energy spent in the Busy state*. We remark that the restriction to exponential distributions is not critical, since one can approximate any distribution by phase-type distributions, resulting in series-parallel combinations of exponential distributions [27].

The focus of CTMC model checking has primarily been on algorithms for specifications expressed in stochastic temporal logics, including *branching-time* variants, such as CSL [3], as well as *linear-time* temporal logic (LTL), whose verification reduces to the same problem for *embedded* discrete-time Markov chains (DTMCs). Model checking *deterministic* TA properties can be achieved by a reduction to computing the reachability probability in a *piecewise-deterministic Markov process* (PDP, [13]), based on the product construction between the CTMC and the DTA [10, 11, 4]. In [8], *time-bounded* verification of properties expressed by MTL or general TAs, which allow *nondeterminism*, is formulated. Approximation algorithms are proposed, based on path exploration of the CTMC, constraints generation and reduction to volume computation. There, "time-bounded" refers to the fact that only timed paths over a time interval of fixed, bounded length are considered, e.g. the probability of an alarm bell ringing whenever the button has been pressed for at least 2 seconds continuously. However, as pointed out in [1], the expressiveness of (D)TA/MTL is limited and *cannot* express *duration-bounded* causality properties which constrain the accumulated satisfaction times of state predicates along an execution path, visited possibly intermittently.

Contributions. We consider *linear duration formulas* (LDF) expressed as finite conjunctions of linear constraints on the cumulated time spent in certain states of the CTMC, see Eq. (1) for the precise formulation. Since we work with CTMCs, we interpret these formulas over finite and infinite *timed* paths. We distinguish two classes of linear duration properties. The difference lies in how to interpret LDF over *infinite* timed paths.

- *Eventuality Duration Property (EDP).* Similarly to [1, 22], given a set of goal states G, an infinite path is said to satisfy LDF if its prefix until G is reached satisfies EDP. We identify two variants, the timed-bounded case ($T < \infty$) and unbounded case ($T = \infty$).

- *Invariance Duration Property (IDP).* Similarly to [6], we require that *each* prefix of the infinite path satisfies LDF, again distinguishing the timed-bounded case ($T < \infty$) and the unbounded case ($T = \infty$). We remark that, in duration calculus, a stronger requirement is imposed, i.e., any fragment (not only the prefix, but also starting from an arbitrary state) of the infinite path must satisfy LDF. We do not adopt this view, as we work in the traditional setting of temporal logics, rather than an interval temporal logic.

The central questions we consider is how to compute the

probability of the set of timed paths of the CTMC which satisfy linear-time properties expressed as LDF. To the best of our knowledge, this is the first paper that considers duration properties for CTMCs. We now give a brief account of the techniques introduced in this paper.

We propose two approaches to verify the timed-bounded variant of EDP. First, we define a system of partial differential equations (PDEs) and a system of integral equations whose solutions capture the probability that an EDP is satisfied on a given CTMC. Second, we leverage the uniformization method [21], which reduces the problem to computing the probability of a set of finite timed paths under a system of linear constraints. This can be solved through the computation of volumes of convex polytopes in the general case, while, in the case that the LDF only involves one conjunct, it can be reduced to the computation of order statistics, which is more efficient. In the unbounded case, by exploiting Markov inequality, we show how to approximate the probability by choosing a sufficiently large time-bound. This is of independent interest, and can be used to improve our previous results [11, 8]. To verify an IDP, in the unbounded case we perform a graph analysis of the CTMC according to the LDF, and thus obtain a variant of EDP, which can be solved by extending the approaches developed in the previous case. In the time-bounded case, transient analysis of the CTMC is needed.

We remark that linear duration properties are closely related to *Markovian Reward Models* (MRM, [2]), which are CTMCs augmented with multiple reward structures assigning real-valued rewards to each state in the model. Properties of MRMs can be expressed in continuous stochastic reward logic (CSRL, [2]). CSRL model checking for MRMs [17, 12] involves timed-bounded and/or reward-bounded reachability problems, which can be formulated in terms of model checking of LDP, over CTMCs, by treating the rewards in MRM as coefficients of linear duration formulas. (This will be made clearer in Sect. 2.3.) We emphasise that, in contrast to [12], as the coefficients in LDF might be negative, we can deal with CSRL in MRMs with arbitrary rewards. The link to MRM (with arbitrary rewards) is beneficial, as energy constraints [7] studied in TA can be naturally adapted to stochastic models (like CTMCs), and can be solved by approaches presented in the current paper.

Related Work. Algorithmic verification of duration properties has primarily been studied in the setting of TA, for instance [1, 6, 22]. Similarly to our setting, TA also admit the unfolding of the system into timed execution paths, except that we have to calculate the probability of the set of paths satisfying a given property, rather than quantifying over their existence. The "duration bounded reachability" problem of [1] can be viewed as a subclass of EDP, in view of the requirement that all coefficients appearing in the linear constraints are nonnegative. Reachability for *integral graphs* [22] can be reduced to verification of EDP for TA, which is solved by mixed linear-integer programming. [6] extended branching real-time logic TCTL with duration constraints and studied response/persistence properties. For DC, which is based on interval temporal logic that differs from our setting, the focus has been on so called *linear durational invariants* (LDI, [34]). Again, TA (and their subclasses or extensions) are considered, and different techniques are proposed, for instance, reduction to linear programming or CTL, dis-

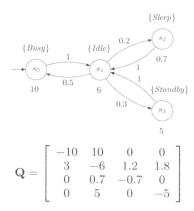

$$\mathbf{Q} = \begin{bmatrix} -10 & 10 & 0 & 0 \\ 3 & -6 & 1.2 & 1.8 \\ 0 & 0.7 & -0.7 & 0 \\ 0 & 5 & 0 & -5 \end{bmatrix}$$

Figure 1: An example CTMC

cretization, etc. We mention, e.g., [26, 31, 32], which are specific to TA and cannot be adapted to CTMCs.

There is only scant work addressing probabilistic/stochastic extensions of DC. Simple Probabilistic Duration Calculus, interpreted over (finite-state) continuous semi-Markov processes, is introduced in [20], together with the associated axiomatic system, and applied to QoS contracts in [16]. However, algorithmic verification is not addressed. [19] studied verification problems of (subclasses of) LDI in the setting of probabilistic TA which only involves discrete probabilities. The technique is an adaption of discretization for TA.

We also mention [5], which considers CTL and LTL extended with prefix-accumulation assertions for a quantitative extension of Kripke structure. (Un)decidability results are obtained. The prefix-accumulation assertions are similar to our linear constraints modulo the difference between models under consideration (CTMCs are a continuous model with randomization, whereas Kripke structures are a discrete model without randomization.) For further discussion, we refer the reader to the full version of the paper [9].

2. PRELIMINARIES

2.1 Continuous-time Markov chains

Given a set $\mathcal{H}$, let $\mathrm{Pr} \colon \mathcal{F}(\mathcal{H}) \to [0, 1]$ be a *probability measure* on the measurable space $(\mathcal{H}, \mathcal{F}(\mathcal{H}))$, where $\mathcal{F}(\mathcal{H})$ is a σ-algebra over $\mathcal{H}$.

Definition 1 *[CTMC] A (labeled) continuous-time Markov chain (CTMC) is a tuple $\mathcal{C} = (S, \mathrm{AP}, L, \alpha, \mathbf{P}, E)$ where: S is a finite set of states; AP is a finite set of atomic propositions; $L \colon S \to 2^{\mathrm{AP}}$ is the labeling function; α is the initial distribution over S; $\mathbf{P} \colon S \times S \to [0, 1]$ is a stochastic matrix; and $E \colon S \to \mathbb{R}_{\geq 0}$ is the exit rate function.*

Example 1 *An example CTMC is illustrated in Fig. 1, where $\mathrm{AP} = \{Busy, Idle, Sleep, Standby\}$ and $\alpha(s_0) = 1$ is the initial distribution. The exit rates are indicated at the states, whereas the transition probabilities are attached to the transitions. The CTMC is a model of the service provider of the DPMS system described in Sect. 1.*

In a CTMC $\mathcal{C}$, state residence times are *exponentially* distributed. More precisely, the residence time of the state $s \in S$ is a random variable governed by an exponential

distribution with parameter $E(s)$. Hence, the probability to exit state s in t time units (t.u. for short) is given by $\int_0^t E(s) \cdot e^{-E(s)\tau} d\tau$; and the probability to take the transition from s to s' in t t.u. equals $\mathbf{P}(s, s') \cdot \int_0^t E(s) \cdot e^{-E(s)\tau} d\tau$. A state s is *absorbing* if $\mathbf{P}(s, s') = 1$. We also define the *infinitesimal generator* $\mathbf{Q}$ of $\mathcal{C}$ as $\mathbf{Q} = \mathbf{E} \cdot \mathbf{P} - \mathbf{E}$, where $\mathbf{E}$ is the diagonal matrix with exit rates on diagonal. Occasionally we use $X(t)$ to denote the underlying *stochastic process* of $\mathcal{C}$. We write $\pi(t)$ for the *transient probability distribution*, where, for each $s \in S$, $\pi_s(t) = \mathrm{Pr}\{X(t) = s\}$ is the probability to be in state s at time t. It is well-known that $\pi(t)$ completely depends on the initial distribution α and the infinitesimal generator $\mathbf{Q}$, i.e., it is the solution of the Chapman-Komogorov equation $\frac{d\pi(t)}{dt} = \pi(t)\mathbf{Q}$ and $\pi(0) = \alpha$. Note that efficient algorithms (e.g. uniformization approach, cf. Sect. 3.1.2, Eq. (3)) exist to compute $\pi(t)$.

An *infinite timed* path in $\mathcal{C}$ is an infinite sequence $\rho = s_0 \xrightarrow{t_0} s_1 \xrightarrow{t_1} s_2 \cdots \xrightarrow{t_{n-1}} s_n \ldots$; and a *finite timed* path is a finite sequence $\sigma = s_0 \xrightarrow{t_0} \cdots \xrightarrow{t_{n-1}} s_n$. In both cases we assume that $t_i \in \mathbb{R}_{>0}$ for each $i \geq 0$; moreover, we write $\rho[0..n]$ for σ. Below we usually follow the convention to let ρ (resp. σ) range over infinite (resp. finite) timed paths, unless otherwise stated. We define $|\sigma| := n$ to be the length of a finite timed path σ. For a finite or infinite path θ, $\theta[n] := s_n$ is the $(n+1)$-th state of θ and $\theta\langle n \rangle := t_n$ is the time spent in state s_n; let $\theta@t$ be the state occupied in θ at time $t \in \mathbb{R}_{\geq 0}$, i.e. $\theta@t := \theta[n]$, where n is the smallest index such that $\sum_{i=0}^{n} \theta\langle i \rangle \geq t$. Let $Paths^{\mathcal{C}}$ denote the set of infinite timed paths in $\mathcal{C}$, with abbreviation $Paths$ when $\mathcal{C}$ is clear from the context. Intuitively, a timed path ρ suggests that the CTMC $\mathcal{C}$ starts in state s_0 and stays in this state for t_0 t.u., and then jumps to state s_1, staying there for t_1 t.u., and then jumps to s_2 and so on. An example timed path is $\rho = s_0 \xrightarrow{3} s_1 \xrightarrow{2} s_0 \xrightarrow{1.5} s_1 \xrightarrow{3.4} s_2 \ldots$ with $\rho[2] = s_0$ and $\rho@4 = \rho[1] = s_1$.

Sometimes we refer to *discrete time Markov chains* (DTMCs), denoted $\mathcal{D} = (S, \mathrm{AP}, \alpha, L, \mathbf{P})$, where the components of the tuple have the same meaning as those of CTMCs defined in Def. 1. In particular, we say such $\mathcal{D}$ is the *embedded DTMC* of the CTMC $\mathcal{C}$. Similarly, a (finite) *discrete* path $\varsigma = s_0 \to s_1 \to \ldots$ is a (finite) sequence of states; $\varsigma[n]$ denotes the state s_i, $\varsigma[0..n]$ denotes the prefix of length n of ς, and $|\varsigma|$ denotes the length of ς (in case that ς is finite). We also define $Paths^{\mathcal{D}}$ to be the set of all infinite paths of the DTMC $\mathcal{D}$. Given a finite discrete path $\varsigma = s_0 \to \cdots \to s_n$ of length n and $x_0, \ldots, x_{n-1} \in \mathbb{R}_{>0}$, we define $\varsigma[x_0, \ldots, x_{n-1}]$ to be the finite *timed* path σ such that $\sigma[i] := s_i$ and $\sigma\langle i \rangle := x_i$ for each $0 \leq i < n$. Let $\Gamma \subseteq \mathbb{R}_{>0}^n$, then $\varsigma[\Gamma] = \{\varsigma[x_0, \ldots, x_{n-1}] \mid (x_0, \ldots, x_{n-1}) \in \Gamma\}$.

The definition of a *Borel space* on timed paths of CTMCs follows [3]. A CTMC $\mathcal{C}$ yields a probability measure $\mathrm{Pr}^{\mathcal{C}}_\alpha$ on $Paths^{\mathcal{C}}$ as follows. Let $s_0, \ldots, s_k \in S$ with $\mathbf{P}(s_i, s_{i+1}) > 0$ for $0 \leq i < k$ and $I_0, \ldots, I_{k-1}$ be nonempty intervals in $\mathbb{R}_{\geq 0}$. Let $C(s_0, I_0, \ldots, I_{k-1}, s_k)$ denote the *cylinder set* consisting of all $\rho \in Paths$ such that $\rho[i] = s_i$ ($0 \leq i \leq k$) and $\rho\langle i \rangle \in I_i$ ($0 \leq i < k$). $\mathcal{F}(Paths)$ is the smallest σ-algebra on $Paths$ which contains all sets $C(s_0, I_0, \ldots, I_{k-1}, s_k)$ for all state sequences $(s_0, \ldots, s_k) \in S^{k+1}$ with $\mathbf{P}(s_i, s_{i+1}) > 0$ for $(0 \leq i < k)$ and $I_0, \ldots, I_{k-1}$ ranging over all sequences of nonempty intervals in $\mathbb{R}_{\geq 0}$. The *probability measure* $\mathrm{Pr}^{\mathcal{C}}_\alpha$

on $\mathcal{F}(Paths)$ is the unique measure defined by induction on k by $\mathrm{Pr}_\alpha^\mathcal{C}(C(s_0)) = \alpha(s_0)$ and for $k > 0$:

$$\mathrm{Pr}_\alpha^\mathcal{C}(C(s_0, I_0, \ldots, I_{k-1}, s_k)) = \mathrm{Pr}_\alpha^\mathcal{C}(C(s_0, I_0, \ldots, I_{k-2}, s_{k-1}))$$
$$\times \int_{I_{k-1}} \mathbf{P}(s_{k-1}, s_k) E(s_{k-1}) \cdot e^{-E(s_{k-1})\tau} d\tau.$$

Sometimes we write Pr instead of $\mathrm{Pr}_\alpha^\mathcal{C}$ when $\mathcal{C}$ and α are clear from the context. Elements of the σ-algebra denote events in the probability space. We now define two such events that will be needed later.

Definition 2 *Given a CTMC $\mathcal{C}$ and $B \subseteq S$, we define:*

- $\diamondsuit^{\leq T} B = \{\rho \in Paths^C \mid \exists n.\rho[n] \in B \text{ and } \sum_{i=0}^{n} \rho\langle i\rangle \leq T\}$, *i.e.,* $\diamondsuit^{\leq T} B$ *denotes the set of timed paths which reach B in time interval $[0, T]$. Note that $\mathrm{Pr}^\mathcal{C}(\diamondsuit^{\leq T} B)$ can be computed by a reduction to the computation of the transient probability distribution; see [3].*

- $\diamondsuit B = \{\rho \in Paths^C \mid \exists n.\rho[n] \in B\}$, *i.e.,* $\diamondsuit B$ *denotes the set of timed paths which reach B. (It is the unbounded variant of $\diamondsuit^{\leq T} B$.) Note that $\mathrm{Pr}^\mathcal{C}(\diamondsuit B)$ is essentially the reachability probability of B in the embedded DTMC of $\mathcal{C}$; see [3]. Moreover, we write $\mathrm{Prob}(s, \diamondsuit B)$ for the reachability probability of B when starting from the state s.*

2.2 Duration Properties

We first introduce a language which includes the propositional calculus augmented with the *duration function* $\int$ and linear inequalities. In the remainder of this section, we assume a CTMC $\mathcal{C} = (S, \mathrm{AP}, L, \alpha, \mathbf{P}, E)$.

State formulas, defined in the usual way over the propositions in AP and the boolean operators, can be evaluated over single states of CTMCs using the interpretation assigned to them by the labeling function L (see Def. 1). The *duration function* $\int$ is interpreted over a *finite* timed path. Let ap be a state formula and $\sigma = s_0 \xrightarrow{t_0} \ldots \xrightarrow{t_{n-1}} s_n$. The value of $\int ap$ for σ, denoted $[\![ap]\!]_\sigma$, is defined as $\sum_{0 \leq i < n, \sigma[i] \models ap} t_i$.
That is, the value of $\int ap$ equals the sum of durations spent in states satisfying ap.

A *linear duration formula* (LDF) is of the form

$$\varphi = \bigwedge_{j \in J}\left(\sum_{k \in K_j} c_{jk} \int ap_{jk} \leq M_j\right), \tag{1}$$

where $c_{jk}, M_j \in \mathbb{R}$, ap_{jk} are state formulas, and J, K_j for $j \in J$ are finite index sets. Below we usually assume that $J = \{0, \cdots, m\}$.

Remark 1 *We did not introduce the disjunction or (more general) boolean operators in Eq. (1) for simplicity. All our results can be generalized to these cases by the exclusion-inclusion principle [28], paying the price of higher complexity.*

Definition 3 *Given a finite timed path $\sigma = s_0 \xrightarrow{t_0} s_1 \xrightarrow{t_1} \ldots \xrightarrow{t_{n-1}} s_n$ and an LDF φ of the form defined in Eq. (1), we write $\sigma \models \varphi$ if for each $j \in J$, $\sum_{k \in K_j} c_{jk} \cdot [\![ap_{jk}]\!]_\sigma \leq M_j$.*

Example 2 *For the CTMC in Fig. 1, the LDF $\varphi = \int Idle - \frac{1}{3} \int Busy \leq 0$ expresses the constraint that during the evolution of the CTMC the accumulated time spent in the Idle state must be less than or equal to one third of the accumulated time spent in the Busy state.*

Inspired by the notation of [34], we shall also work on a slight extension of LDF, i.e., formulas of the form:[1]

$$\Phi := \int 1 \leq T \to \varphi,$$

where $T \in \mathbb{R}_{\geq 0} \cup \{\infty\}$. According to Def. 3, $\int 1$ denotes the total time spent on a finite timed path σ. Hence $\sigma \models \Phi$ if φ holds whenever the total time of σ is less or equal than T. Note that, if $T = \infty$, Φ simply degenerates to φ.

In general, given a CTMC and a duration property specified by an LDF, we are interested in computing the probability of *infinite timed* paths satisfying the LDF. We now generalize the satisfaction relation on finite paths, as defined in Def. 3, to *infinite* paths. Here we have two options, i.e., the *finitary* and *infinitary* conditions. The former is motivated by standard automata theory, while the latter is natural when one thinks of "globally" (e.g., the $\square$ operator in LTL).

Definition 4 *Let $\rho = s_0 \xrightarrow{t_0} s_1 \xrightarrow{t_1} \ldots$ be an infinite timed path and φ (or Φ) be an LDF.*

1. *Finitary satisfaction condition. Given a set of goal states $G \subseteq S$, we write $\rho \models^G \varphi$ if there exists the first $i \in \mathbb{N}$ such that (1) $\rho[i] \in G$, and (2) $\rho[0..i] \models \varphi$ (cf. Def. 3). Furthermore, we write $\rho \models_T^G \varphi$ for a given $T \in \mathbb{R}_{\geq 0}$, and if, in addition to (1) and (2), $\sum_{j=0}^{i-1} \rho\langle j\rangle \leq T$ holds.*

2. *Infinitary satisfaction condition. We write $\rho \models^\star \varphi$ if for any $n \geq 0$, $\rho[0..n] \models \varphi$ (cf. Def. 3).*

Problem Statements. Corresponding to Def. 4, we focus on algorithmic verification problems for two classes of LDP, i.e., *Eventuality Duration Property* (EDP) and *Invariance Duration Property* (IDP), as follows.

- **Verification of EDP.** Formally, given a CTMC $\mathcal{C}$, a set of *goal* states $G \subseteq S$, and an LDF $\Phi = \int 1 \leq T \to \varphi$, compute the probability of the set of infinite timed paths of $\mathcal{C}$ satisfying Φ under the *finitary satisfaction condition*. Depending on T, we distinguish two cases:

  - Time-bounded case: $T < \infty$, for which we denote the desired probability by $\boxed{\mathrm{Prob}(\mathcal{C} \models^G \Phi)}$.

  - Unbounded case: $T = \infty$, for which we denote the desired probability by $\boxed{\mathrm{Prob}(\mathcal{C} \models^G \varphi)}$. Note that this is valid as, in this case, Φ is simply equivalent to φ.

The algorithms for these two cases are given in Sect. 3.1 and Sect. 3.2, respectively.

---

[1]Note that 1 denotes "true", $\to$ denotes "imply" and $\int 1 \leq T \to \varphi$ is a single formula.

- **Verification of IDP.** Formally, given a CTMC $\mathcal{C}$ and an LDF $\Phi = \int 1 \leq T \to \varphi$, compute the probability of the set of infinite timed paths of $\mathcal{C}$ satisfying Φ under the *infinitary satisfaction condition*. We also have two cases, i.e., the time-bounded case and unbounded case, which we denote by $\boxed{\text{Prob}(\mathcal{C} \models^{\star} \Phi)}$ and $\boxed{\text{Prob}(\mathcal{C} \models^{\star} \varphi)}$, respectively. The algorithms for these two cases are given in Sect. 4.2 and Sect. 4.1, respectively.

2.3 Relationship to MRMs

Definition 5 *[MRM] A (labeled) MRM $\mathcal{M}$ is a pair $(\mathcal{C}, \mathbf{r})$ where $\mathcal{C}$ is CTMC, and $\mathbf{r} : S \to \mathbb{R}^d$ is a reward structure which assigns to each state $s \in S$ a vector of rewards $(r_1(s), \cdots, r_d(s))$.*

Remark 2 *The MRM defined in Def. 5 is more general than the one in [2], in the sense that we have multiple reward structures, and, more importantly, we allow arbitrary (instead of nonnegative) rewards associated with the states.*

For a CTMC $\mathcal{C}$ and LDF φ, we show how to construct an MRM $\mathcal{C}[\varphi]$. For every state $s_i \in S$, we define $r_{ji} = \sum_{t \in K_j, s_i \models ap_{jt}} c_{jt}$ for all $j \in J$. This yields a multiple reward structure $\mathbf{r}$ with $\mathbf{r}(s_i) = (r_{0i}, \cdots, r_{(|J|-1)i})$. Hence $\mathcal{C}[\varphi] = (\mathcal{C}, \mathbf{r})$. It is straightforward to see that the constraint expressed by LDF can be alternatively formulated as the "reward-bounded" constraint for MRMs, since $\sum_{k \in K_j} c_{jk} \int ap_{jk}$ essentially denotes the accumulated rewards along a finite timed path, and hence M_j can be regarded as the bound of the reward.

On the other hand, given an MRM and a vector of reward bounds M_j for each reward structure, we construct an LDF φ as $\bigwedge_{j \in J} \sum_{s \in S} r_j(s) \int @s \leq M_j$, where $@s$ is an atomic proposition which holds exactly at state s. Hence, the reward-bounded verification problem for MRMs can be encoded into verification of linear duration properties in CTMCs.

It is easy to see that this correspondence, stated in the unbounded case, can be adapted to the time-bounded case without any difficulties.

3. VERIFICATION OF EDP

Throughout this section, we fix a CTMC $\mathcal{C} = (S, AP, L, \alpha, \mathbf{P}, E)$ and an LDF $\Phi = \int 1 \leq T \to \bigwedge_{j \in J} (\sum_{k \in K_j} c_{jk} \int ap_{jk} \leq M_j)$.

3.1 Time-bounded Verification of EDP

Our task is to compute $\text{Prob}(\mathcal{C} \models^G \Phi)$. First observe that

Proposition 1 *Given a CTMC $\mathcal{C}$ and an LDF Φ, we have:*

$$\text{Prob}(\mathcal{C} \models^G \Phi) = \Pr(\Diamond G) - \Pr(\Diamond^{\leq T} G) + \text{Prob}(\mathcal{C} \models_T^G \varphi).$$

Recall that $\Pr(\Diamond G)$ and $\Pr(\Diamond^{\leq T} G)$ can be easily computed (cf. Def. 2). Hence, the remaining of this section is devoted to computing $\text{Prob}(\mathcal{C} \models_T^G \varphi) := \Pr(\{\rho \mid \rho \models_T^G \varphi\})$, i.e. the probability of the set of paths of the CTMC $\mathcal{C}$, which reach G in time interval $[0, T]$ and satisfy the LDF φ before that happens; see Def. 4(1).

3.1.1 PDE and Integral Formulations

In order to compute $\text{Prob}(\mathcal{C} \models_T^G \varphi)$, we shall use the link to MRMs established in Sect. 2.3. Recall that $\mathcal{C}[\varphi]$ is the MRM obtained from $\mathcal{C}$ and φ. We need an extra transformation over $\mathcal{C}[\varphi]$, namely, making each state $s \in G$ absorbing, and set $\mathbf{r}(s) = (0, \cdots, 0)$ (i.e., the rewards associated with s are all 0). We denote the resulting MRM by $\mathcal{C}[\varphi, G]$. Recall that $X(t)$ is the underlying stochastic process of the CTMC $\mathcal{C}$. We denote by $\mathbf{Y}(T)$ the vector of accumulated rewards in the MRM $\mathcal{C}[\varphi]$ (see Sect. 2.3) up to time T, i.e. $\mathbf{Y}(T) = (Y_0(T), \ldots, Y_{|J|-1}(T))$ and each $Y_j(T)$ $(j \in J)$ corresponds to a reward structure in CTMC $\mathcal{C}$. The vector of stochastic processes $\mathbf{Y}(T)$ is fully determined by $X(T)$ and the vector of reward structures of the state s is $\mathbf{r}(s_i) = (r_{0i}, \ldots, r_{(|J|-1)i})$, because $\mathbf{Y}(t) = \int_0^t \mathbf{r}(X(\tau)) d\tau$.

Define $\mathbf{F}(T, \mathbf{y})$ to be the matrix of the joint probability distribution of state and rewards with entries $\mathbf{F}(T, \mathbf{y})[s, s'] = F_s^{s'}(T, \mathbf{y})$ for $s, s' \in S$ and

$$F_s^{s'}(T, \mathbf{y}) = \Pr\left\{ X(T) = s', \bigwedge_{j \in J} Y_j(T) \leq y_j \mid X(0) = s \right\},$$

where $\mathbf{y} = (y_0, \cdots, y_{|J|-1})$. Note that, we define $\mathbf{F}(T, \mathbf{y})$ over the induced MRM $\mathcal{C}[\varphi, G]$.

Theorem 1 *Given a CTMC $\mathcal{C}$, an LDP formula φ, a vector $\mathbf{M} = (M_0, \ldots, M_{|J|-1})$, where M_j's are defined as in φ (cf. Eq. (1)) and a set of goal states G, we obtain the induced MRM $\mathcal{C}[\varphi, G]$, and we have:*

$$\text{Prob}(\mathcal{C} \models_T^G \varphi) = \sum_{s \in S} \sum_{s' \in G} \alpha(s) F_s^{s'}(T, \mathbf{M}).$$

Thm. 1 suggests a reduction to $\mathbf{F}(t, \mathbf{y})$, which we now characterize in terms of a system of PDEs.

Theorem 2 *For an MRM $\mathcal{C}[\varphi, G]$, the function $\mathbf{F}(t, \mathbf{y})$ is given by the following system of PDEs:*

$$\frac{\partial \mathbf{F}(t, \mathbf{y})}{\partial t} + \sum_{j \in J} \mathbf{D}_j \cdot \frac{\partial \mathbf{F}(t, \mathbf{y})}{\partial y_j} = \mathbf{Q} \cdot \mathbf{F}(t, \mathbf{y}), \qquad (2)$$

where $\mathbf{D}_j$ is a diagonal matrix such that $\mathbf{D}_j(s, s) = r_j(s)$.

The system of PDEs from Theorem 2 is a special case of the system of PDEs derived from Petri net specifications [18] and PDP models [13].

Example 3 *For the CTMC depicted in Fig.1, with $r(s_0) = 1$ and $r(s_1) = -1$, we can derive the following system of PDEs:*

$$\frac{\partial F_{s_0}^{s_1}(t, y)}{\partial t} + \frac{\partial F_{s_0}^{s_1}(t, y)}{\partial y} = 10 F_{s_1}^{s_1}(t, y) - 10 F_{s_0}^{s_1}(t, y),$$

$$\frac{\partial F_{s_1}^{s_0}(t, y)}{\partial t} - \frac{\partial F_{s_1}^{s_0}(t, y)}{\partial y} = -6 F_{s_1}^{s_0}(t, y) + 3 F_{s_0}^{s_0}(t, y),$$

$$+ 1.2 F_{s_2}^{s_0}(t, y) + 1.8 F_{s_3}^{s_0}(t, y).$$

We next provide an alternative characterization in terms of a system of integral equations, as follows.

Theorem 3 *The solution of the system of PDEs in Eq. (2) is the least fixpoint of the following system of integral equations:*

$$F_s^{s'}(t, \mathbf{y}) = e^{\mathbf{Q}(s,s)t} F_s^{s'}(0, \mathbf{y} - \mathbf{r}(s)t) +$$
$$\int_0^t \sum_{z \neq s} e^{\mathbf{Q}(s,s)x} \mathbf{Q}(s,z) F_z^{s'}(t-x, \mathbf{y} - \mathbf{r}(s)x) dx.$$

Thm. 2 and Thm. 3 imply that, to solve the bounded-time EDP verification problem, we need to solve (first-order) PDEs or integral equations. However, this is usually costly and numerically unstable [15]. We present solutions in the next section, based on uniformization.

3.1.2 Uniformization algorithm

In this section we present a uniformization algorithm to compute $F_s^{s'}(t, \mathbf{y})$. The *uniformization* method [21] consists in transforming the CTMC $\mathcal{C}$ into a behaviorally equivalent DTMC $\mathcal{D}$. (NB. this is *not* the embedded DTMC of $\mathcal{C}$.) The state space and initial distribution of $\mathcal{D}$ are the same as for $\mathcal{C}$. The probability matrix $\widehat{\mathbf{P}}$ of $\mathcal{D}$ is constructed by $\widehat{\mathbf{P}} = \mathbf{I} - \frac{\mathbf{Q}}{\Lambda}$, where Λ is the maximal exit rate of $\mathcal{C}$. We obtain

$$\pi(t) = e^{(\widehat{\mathbf{P}} - \mathbf{I})\Lambda t} = \sum_{n=0}^{\infty} \widehat{\mathbf{P}}^n \frac{(\Lambda t)^n}{n!} e^{-\Lambda t}. \tag{3}$$

We can apply the uniformization technique to efficiently compute $F_s^{s'}(t, \mathbf{y})$. First, we note that the infinite sum in Eq. (3) represents the probability $\frac{(\Lambda t)^n}{n!} e^{-\Lambda t}$ that exactly n Poisson arrivals occur in an interval of time $[0, t)$ multiplied with the probability $\widehat{\mathbf{P}}^n$ to take the state transitions corresponding to the arrivals. Then using Eq. (3) we obtain

$$F_s^{s'}(t, \mathbf{y}) = \sum_{n=0}^{\infty} e^{-\Lambda t} \frac{(\Lambda t)^n}{n!} \cdot \left(\sum_{\substack{\varsigma \in Paths^{\mathcal{D}} \\ |\varsigma| = n}} \Pr\{\varsigma \mid X(0) = s\} \cdot \right.$$
$$\left. \Pr\{X(n) = s', \mathbf{Y}(t) \leq \mathbf{y} \mid \varsigma\} \right),$$

where, for a given path $\varsigma = s \to s_1 \to \cdots \to s_{n-1} \to s'$, $\Pr\{\varsigma \mid X(0) = s\} = \widehat{\mathbf{P}}(s, s_1) \times \cdots \times \widehat{\mathbf{P}}(s_{n-1}, s')$ and $\Pr\{X(n) = s', \mathbf{Y}(t) \leq \mathbf{y} \mid \varsigma\}$ denotes the conditional probability that given the path ς at step n the state is s' and the total accumulated reward until time t is less than $\mathbf{y}$. The above equation can also be written as

$$F_s^{s'}(t, \mathbf{y}) = \sum_{n=0}^{\infty} e^{-\Lambda t} \frac{(\Lambda t)^n}{n!} \sum_{\substack{\varsigma \in Paths^{\mathcal{D}} \\ |\varsigma| = n \\ \varsigma[0] = s \\ \varsigma[n] = s'}} \text{Prob}(\varsigma) \cdot \Pr\{\mathbf{Y}(t) \leq \mathbf{y} \mid \varsigma\}. \tag{4}$$

Now the task is to compute $\Pr\{\mathbf{Y}(t) \leq \mathbf{y} \mid \varsigma\}$. We first present a general approach based on linear constraints.

Approach based on linear constraints.
We can calculate $\Pr\{\mathbf{Y}(t) \leq \mathbf{y} \mid \varsigma\}$ by reducing it to the computation of the volume of a convex polytope. The basic idea is to generate timed constraints over variables determining the residence time of each state along ς to make $\mathbf{Y}(t) \leq \mathbf{y}$ hold (which is equivalent to the LDF φ). The desired probability can thus be formulated as a multidimensional integral,

which can be computed by the efficient algorithm given in [25].

Given a *discrete* finite path ς of length k, an LDF φ, and a time-bound T, we define the set of linear constraints $\mathcal{S}$ generated in Alg. 1. In Alg. 1 line 3 generates the set of

---

Algorithm 1 Generate a set of linear constraints $\mathcal{S}$ induced by φ, ς and T

Require: LDF φ, a path ς of length k and a time-bound T
Ensure: $\mathcal{S} = $ set of linear constraints
1: $\mathcal{S} = \{\varnothing\}$
2: **for** $j \in J$ **do**
3: $\quad \mathcal{S} = \mathcal{S} \bigcup \left\{ \sum\limits_{i \in K_j} c_{ji} \cdot \sum\limits_{\substack{0 \leq \ell < k \\ \varsigma[\ell] \models ap_{ji}}} x_\ell \leq M_j \right\}$
4: **end for**
5: $\mathcal{S} = \mathcal{S} \bigcup \left\{ \sum\limits_{i=0}^{k-1} x_i \leq T \right\}$
6: $\mathcal{S} = \mathcal{S} \bigcup \{x_i > 0\}$ for all x_i
7: **return** $\mathcal{S}$

---

constraints from each conjunct in formula φ. In line 5 we add one more constraint to ensure that in the interval of time $[0, T]$ we will reach the last state of ς.

Example 4 *Let $\varphi = \int Idle - \frac{1}{3} \int Busy \leq 0 \wedge \int Idle - \frac{1}{4} \int Sleep \leq 0$ be an LDF, $\varsigma = s_0 \to s_1 \to s_2 \to s_1 \to s_3$ and the time-bound $t = 6$. The set of linear constraints $\mathcal{S}$ induced by ς, φ and t is:*

$$\mathcal{S} = \begin{cases} -\frac{1}{3} \cdot x_0 + x_1 + 0 \cdot x_2 + x_3 \leq 0 \\ 0 \cdot x_0 + x_1 - \frac{1}{4} \cdot x_2 + x_3 \leq 0 \\ x_0 + x_1 + x_2 + x_3 < 6 \\ x_0, x_1, x_2, x_3 > 0 \end{cases}$$

Lemma 1 *Let ς be a finite path of the CTMC $\mathcal{C}$, φ be an LDF and T a time-bound. Moreover, let $\mathcal{S}$ be the set of linear constraints obtained by Alg. 1. Then*

$$\varsigma[x_0, \ldots, x_{n-1}] \models \varphi \wedge \int 1 \leq T \quad \text{iff} \quad (x_0, \ldots, x_{n-1}) \in \mathcal{S}.$$

We define $\text{Prob}(\varsigma[\mathcal{S}]) := \Pr^{\mathcal{C}}(\{\rho \in Paths^{\mathcal{C}} \mid \exists (x_0, \ldots, x_{n-1}) \in \mathcal{S}. \rho[0..n] \in \varsigma[x_0, \ldots, x_{n-1}] \wedge \rho[0..n] \models \varphi\})$.

Theorem 4 *Let ς be a discrete path of the CTMC $\mathcal{C}$, $\mathcal{C}[\varphi, G]$ be the MRM induced by $\mathcal{C}$ and LDF φ, and $\mathcal{S}$ the set of linear constraints generated by ς, φ and time-bound t. Then*

$$\Pr^{\mathcal{C}[\varphi, G]}\{\mathbf{Y}(t) \leq \mathbf{y} \mid \varsigma\} = \text{Prob}(\varsigma[\mathcal{S}]).$$

For future use, declare the function $Volume\_int(\varsigma, \mathcal{S})$ which, given a finite discrete path $\varsigma = s_0 \to \cdots \to s_k$ of length k and a set of linear constraints $\mathcal{S}$ over $x_0, \cdots, x_{k-1}$, returns

$$\prod_{i=0}^{k-1} E(s_i) \cdot P(s_i, s_{i+1}) \cdot \underbrace{\int \cdots \int}_{k} \prod_{\mathcal{S}}^{k-1} e^{-E(s_i)\tau_i} dx_i. \tag{5}$$

$\text{Prob}(\varsigma[\mathcal{S}])$ equals $Volume\_int(\varsigma, \mathcal{S})$ when $\mathcal{S}$ is generated from Alg. 1.

Approach based on order statistics.

The problem of computing $\Pr\{Y(t) \leq y \mid \varsigma\}$ is reduced to the computation of the distribution of a linear combination of order statistics uniformly distributed in $[0, 1]$ in case $|J| = 1$, i.e., we have a single conjuct in LDF φ. This distribution is calculated through the numerically stable method described in [14]. The state rewards of the CTMC will become the coefficients of the order statistics.

Let $[0, t]$ be an interval of time, and n be the number of transitions in $[0, t]$. Given n transitions, we can divide the interval $[0, t]$ to $n+1$ intervals $I_1, \ldots, I_{n+1}$, and we assign an index i to each interval. Thus, if we stay in state s_1 in the first interval I_1 and state s_1 has reward r_1, we assign index 1 to the first interval. We can divide the CTMC into ℓ distinct reward classes. Without loss of generality, the reward classes are ordered such that $r_1 > \ldots > r_\ell$. We declare a vector $\mathbf{k} = (k_1, \ldots, k_\ell)$, where k_i records the number of times a state with reward r_i has been visited (when index i is not used, $k_i = 0$). Let U_i be the sum of the lengths of intervals of index i defined as follows:

$$
\begin{aligned}
U_1 &= I_1 + \cdots + I_{k_1}, \\
U_2 &= I_{k_1+1} + \cdots + I_{k_1+k_2}, \\
&\quad \vdots \\
U_\ell &= I_{k_1+\cdots+k_{\ell-1}+1} + \cdots + I_{k_1+\cdots+k_\ell}.
\end{aligned}
$$

Note that $\sum_{i=1}^{\ell} k_i = n + 1$. Then, for n transitions, the total accumulated reward yields: $Y(t) = \sum_{i=1}^{\ell} r_i U_i$.

Now the task is to find the probability $\Pr\{Y(t) \leq y \mid \varsigma\}$. We introduce a renumbering that enables us to disregard all indices that have not been used. Let z_1 be the index of the first nonzero k_i, z_2 be the index of the second nonzero k_i, and so on. Let M be the total number of nonzero k_i's. Then we get $Y(t) = \sum_{i=1}^{M} r_{z_i} U_{z_i}$. Let V_j be the j-th order statistic of a set of n independent and identically distributed random variables uniform on $[0, t]$. Note that defining $V_\ell = I_1 + \cdots + I_\ell$ we can re-express each U_i in terms of V_j. More specifically $U_1 = V_{k_1}, U_2 = V_{k_1+k_2} - V_{k_1}, \ldots, U_\ell = t - V_{k_1+\cdots+k_{\ell-1}}$. Rearranging the terms and defining $n_j = \sum_{i=1}^{j} k_i$ for $j = 1, \ldots, \ell-1$, we obtain $Y(t) = \sum_{j=1}^{\ell-1} (r_j - r_{j+1}) V_{n_j} + r_\ell t$. Finally, we get

$$
\Pr\{Y(t) \leq y \mid \varsigma\} = \Pr\left\{ \sum_{j=1}^{l-1} (r_j - r_{j+1}) V_{n_j} \leq y - r_\ell t \right\}.
$$

We can use the algorithm described in [14] to compute the distribution of order statistics uniformly distributed on $[0, 1]$, by normalizing with respect to t.

Example 5 *Let $\mathcal{C}$ be the CTMC in Fig. 1 with reward structure $\mathbf{r} = (1, -1, 0, 0)$ corresponding to the LDP formula $\varphi = \int Busy - \int Idle \leq 0$ and ς be the discrete path $\varsigma = s_0 \to s_1 \to s_0 \to s_1 \to s_3$. In order to calculate $\Pr\{Y(t) \leq 0 \mid \varsigma\}$ we define I_i as the time spent in $\varsigma[i]$ for $i \in \{1, \ldots, 5\}$. Let $Y(t)$ be the accumulated reward at time t. The task is to compute $\Pr\{Y(t) \leq 0 \mid \varsigma\}$. The accumulated reward is given by $Y(t) = -1 \cdot (I_2 + I_4) + 0 \cdot I_5 + 1 \cdot (I_1 + I_3)$. For every $i \in \{1, \ldots, 5\}$ we introduce a new variable I'_i such*

that $I'_1 = I_2$, $I'_2 = I_4$, $I'_3 = I_5$, $I'_4 = I_1$ and $I'_5 = I_3$. We obtain a decreasing order for vector $\mathbf{r}$ as follows: $1 > 0 > -1$. It is clear that we get three reward classes, i.e. $\ell = 3$. We define the vector $\mathbf{r}' = (-1, 0, 1)$, which is the vector of the reward classes. Let the vector $\mathbf{k} = (2, 1, 2)$ record the number of times a state with reward class r'_i ($i \in \{1, 2, 3\}$) is visited. Let $V_j = \sum_{k=1}^{j} I'_k$ for $1 \leq j \leq 5$. Each V_j is an uniformly distributed variable in $[0, t]$. We can express the accumulated reward in terms of order statistics as follows: $Y(t) = r'_3 \cdot V_2 + r'_2 \cdot (V_3 - V_2) + r'_1 \cdot (V_5 - V_3)$.

3.1.3 Algorithm

In order to compute $F_s^{s'}(t, \mathbf{y})$ we must pick a finite set $\mathcal{P}$ of paths from $Paths^{\mathcal{D}}$. Following [12], we introduce a threshold $w \in (0, 1)$ such that if $\mathrm{Prob}(\varsigma) > w$ then $\varsigma \in \mathcal{P}$. We also fix a maximum length N for the paths in $\mathcal{P}$. Now we define $\mathcal{P}(s, s', w, n) := \{\varsigma \in Paths^{\mathcal{D}} \mid |\varsigma| = n, \varsigma[0] = s, \varsigma[n] = s', \mathrm{Prob}(\varsigma) > w\}$. We can approximate $F_s^{s'}(t, \mathbf{y})$ as

$$
\widetilde{F_N}_s^{w\,s'}(t, \mathbf{y}) = \sum_{n=0}^{N} e^{-\Lambda t} \frac{(\Lambda t)^n}{n!} \sum_{\varsigma \in \mathcal{P}(s, s', w, n)} \mathrm{Prob}(\varsigma)\, \Pr\{\mathbf{Y}(t) \leq \mathbf{y} \mid \varsigma\},
$$

where w and N must be chosen as stated in Thm 5.

The approximation algorithm to compute $Prob = F_s^{s'}(t, \mathbf{y})$ is given in Alg. 2.

Algorithm 2 Compute $\widetilde{F_N}_s^{w\,s'}(t, \mathbf{y})$

1: $Prob = 0$
2: $Paths = \{s\}$
3: **while** $Paths \neq \varnothing$ **do**
4:     choose $\varsigma \in Paths$
5:     $Paths = Paths \setminus \{\varsigma\}$
6:     **if** $\mathrm{Prob}(\varsigma) > w$ and $|\varsigma| \leq N$ **then**
7:         **if** $\varsigma[|\varsigma|] = s'$ **then**
8:             $Prob\!+\!= e^{-\Lambda t} \frac{(\Lambda t)^{|\varsigma|}}{|\varsigma|!} \mathrm{Prob}(\varsigma) \Pr\{\mathbf{Y}(t) \leq \mathbf{y} \mid \varsigma\}$
9:         **end if**
10:         **for all** $s'' \in S$ **do**
11:             insert $(\varsigma \circ s'')$ into $Paths$
12:         **end for**
13:     **end if**
14: **end while**
15: **return** $Prob$

Note that $\circ$ represents the concatenation operator; $\varsigma[|\varsigma|]$ is the last state of ς.

Error Bound.

We give a bound for the truncation of the infinite sum to a finite one, considering only the discrete paths whose probability is greater than w.

Theorem 5 *Given $\varepsilon > 0$, for $N > \Lambda t e^2 + \ln\left(\frac{1}{\varepsilon}\right)$, and $w < \dfrac{\varepsilon}{\sum_{n=0}^{N} e^{-\Lambda t} \frac{(\Lambda t)^n}{n!}}$, we have $\left| F_s^{s'}(t, \mathbf{y}) - \widetilde{F_N}_s^{w\,s'}(t, \mathbf{y}) \right| \leq 2\varepsilon$.*

Complexity.

We analyze the complexity of Alg. 2. Recall that $|S|$ the number of states of $\mathcal{C}$. Alg. 2 is composed of two main steps:

(1) find all paths of length at most N; and (2) for each of those paths ς, compute $\Pr\{\mathbf{Y}(t) \leq \mathbf{y} \mid \varsigma\}$.

Theorem 6 *The complexity of Alg. 2 is $\mathcal{O}(|S|^N \cdot N^{|J|-1})$ using the linear constraint based approach, and $\mathcal{O}(|S|^N \cdot N^2)$ using the order statistics based approach.*

3.2 Unbounded Verification of EDP

In this section we show how to compute $\text{Prob}(\mathcal{C} \models^G \varphi)$. The main idea is that we approximate $\text{Prob}(\mathcal{C} \models^G \varphi)$ by $\text{Prob}(\mathcal{C} \models^G_T \varphi)$ for a sufficiently large $T \in \mathbb{R}_{\geq 0}$. Hence, we reduce the problem to time-bounded verification of EDP, which has been solved in Sect. 3.1. We shall exploit the celebrated Markov inequality. Hence, we first show how to compute the expected time to reach G in $\mathcal{C}$.

Definition 6 *We define a random variable $T_G : \text{Paths}^{\mathcal{C}} \to \mathbb{R}_{\geq 0}$ that will denote the first entrance time in a state $s \in G$. More specifically, given a path ρ:*

$$T_G(\rho) = \begin{cases} 0 & \forall j \in \mathbb{N}.\ \rho[j] \notin G \\ \sum_{j=0}^{k-1} \rho\langle j \rangle & o/w,\ \text{where}\ k = \min\{l \mid \rho[l] \in G\}. \end{cases}$$

Lemma 2 *The expected first entrance time $\mathbb{E}_s[T_G]$ from any state $s \in G$ to reach G can be characterized by the following system of linear equations: $\mathbb{E}_s[T_G] = \frac{\text{Prob}(s, \Diamond G)}{E(s)} + \sum_{s' \in S} \mathbf{P}(s, s')\mathbb{E}_{s'}[T_G]$ if $s \notin G$, 0 otherwise, where $\text{Prob}(s, \Diamond G)$ is defined in Def. 2.*

Now we can state the main result of this section.

Theorem 7 $\text{Prob}(\mathcal{C} \models^G \varphi) - \text{Prob}(\mathcal{C} \models^G_T \varphi) \leq \sum_{s \in S} \alpha(s)\frac{\mathbb{E}_s[T_G]}{T}$.

Thanks to this theorem, given an error bound ε and a set of goal states G, we can pick a time bound T such that $T \geq \sum_{s \in S} \alpha(s)\frac{\mathbb{E}_s[T_G]}{\varepsilon}$ and compute $\text{Prob}(\mathcal{C} \models^G_T \varphi)$.

Remark 3 *Here we use Markov inequality. Alternatively one could use the Chebyshev's inequality, which would sharpen Thm. 7 and hence allow a relatively smaller T, at a cost of computing the variance of T_G (instead of the expectation). We choose the current formulation for simplicity.*

4. VERIFICATION OF IDP

In this section, we tackle IDP w.r.t. $\Phi = \int 1 \leq T \to \bigwedge_{j \in J}(\sum_{k \in K_j} c_{jk} \int ap_{jk} \leq M_j)$. As highlighted in Sect. 2, we shall distinguish two cases according to whether T is finite or infinite. First, we give some definitions and algorithms that are common to both cases.

Given an LDF φ, a *discrete* finite path ς of length k and a time-bound T, we define the set of linear constraints $\mathcal{S}$ as in Alg. 3. Note that here $\mathcal{S}$ is different from the one obtained from Alg. 1.

Lemma 3 *Let ς be a finite path of the CTMC $\mathcal{C}$, φ be an LDF and t a time-bound. Moreover, let $\mathcal{S}$ be the set of linear constraints obtained by Alg. 3. Then*

$$\varsigma[x_0, \ldots, x_{n-1}] \models^\star \varphi \wedge \int 1 \leq T \quad \text{iff} \quad (x_0, \ldots, x_{n-1}) \in \mathcal{S}.$$

Algorithm 3 Generate a set of linear constraints $\mathcal{S}$ induced by φ, ς and T

Require: LDF φ, a path ς of length k and a time-bound T
Ensure: $\mathcal{S} =$ set of linear constraints
1: $\mathcal{S} = \{\varnothing\}$
2: **for** $z = 0;\ z < k;\ z{+}{+}$ **do**
3:    **for** $j \in J$ **do**
4:      $\mathcal{S} = \mathcal{S} \bigcup \left\{ \sum_{i \in K_j} c_{ji} \cdot \sum_{\substack{0 \leq \ell \leq z \\ \varsigma[\ell] \models ap_{ji}}} x_\ell \leq M_j \right\}$
5:    **end for**
6: **end for**
7: $\mathcal{S} = \mathcal{S} \bigcup \left\{ \sum_{i=0}^{k-1} x_i \leq T \right\}$
8: $\mathcal{S} = \mathcal{S} \bigcup \{x_i > 0\}$ for all x_i
9: **return** $\mathcal{S}$

We define $\text{Prob}^\star(\varsigma[\mathcal{S}]) := \Pr^{\mathcal{C}}(\{\rho \in \text{Paths}^{\mathcal{C}} \mid \exists\ (x_0, \ldots, x_{n-1}) \in \mathcal{S}.\ \rho[0..n] \in \varsigma[x_0, \ldots, x_{n-1}] \wedge \rho[0..n] \models^\star \varphi\})$, which can be computed by the function $Volume\_int(\varsigma, \mathcal{S})$ (cf. Eq. (5)), where $\mathcal{S}$ is the set of constraints generated from Alg. 3.

Given an infinite timed path ρ, we write $\rho \models^\star_{G,T} \varphi$ if there is some $n \in \mathbb{N}$ such that (1) $\rho[n] \in G$ and $\sum_{i=0}^n \rho\langle i \rangle \leq T$, and (2) for each $0 \leq i \leq n$, $\sum_{j=0}^i \rho\langle j \rangle \leq T$, $\rho[0..i] \models \varphi$. Our task now is to approximate the probability $\boxed{\text{Prob}(\mathcal{C} \models^\star_{G,T} \varphi)}$. For this purpose, we define Alg. 4 that computes an approximation $\widetilde{\text{Prob}}_N(\mathcal{C} \models^\star_{G,T} \varphi)$ of $\text{Prob}(\mathcal{C} \models^\star_{G,T} \varphi)$.

Algorithm 4 Compute $\widetilde{\text{Prob}}_N(\mathcal{C} \models^\star_{G,T} \varphi)$

Require: A CTMC $\mathcal{C}$, an LDF formula φ, set of goal states G, time-bound T, and N
1: **for all** $\varsigma \in \text{Paths}^{\mathcal{D}}$ s.t. $\exists i.\varsigma[i] \in G$ and $|\varsigma| \leq N$ **do**
2:    Generate $\mathcal{S}$ from φ, ς, and T, by Alg. 3
3:    Prob$+ = Volume\_int(\varsigma, \mathcal{S})$
4: **end for**
5: **return** Prob

4.1 Unbounded Verification of IDP

We are interested in computing $\text{Prob}(\mathcal{C} \models^\star \varphi)$.

Definition 7 *[BSCC] Assume a CTMC $\mathcal{C}$. A set of states $B \subseteq S$ is a strongly connected component (SCC) of $\mathcal{C}$ if, for any two states $s, s' \in B$, there exists a path $\varsigma = s_0 \to s_1 \to \ldots \to s_n$ such that $s_i \in B$ for $0 \leq i \leq n$, $s_0 = s$ and $s_n = s'$. An SCC B is a bottom strongly connected component (BSCC) if no state outside B is reachable from any state in B.*

Definition 8 *Given a BSCC B of the CTMC $\mathcal{C}$ and an LDF φ, we say B is bad w.r.t. j-th conjunct in φ, φ_j, if $\exists s \in B.\ \exists i \in K_j.\ ap_{ji} \in L(s) \wedge c_{ji} > 0$; otherwise B is good. We say B is good w.r.t. φ (written $B \models \varphi$) if B is good for each conjunct of φ; otherwise B is bad (written $B \not\models \varphi$).*

Lemma 4 *Given a CTMC $\mathcal{C} = (S, \text{AP}, L, \alpha, \mathbf{P}, E)$, an LDF φ and a BSCC B we have that, if B is good, then $\Pr^{\mathcal{C}}\{\{\rho \mid \rho \models^\star \varphi\} \mid \Diamond B\} = 1$; and, if B is bad, then $\Pr^{\mathcal{C}}\{\{\rho \mid \rho \models^\star \varphi\} \mid \Diamond B\} = 0$.*

Definition 9 *Given a CTMC $\mathcal{C} = (S, \mathrm{AP}, L, \alpha, \mathbf{P}, E)$ and an LDF φ, we define a new CTMC $\mathcal{C}^a = (S, \mathrm{AP}^a, L^a, \alpha, \mathbf{P}^a, E)$ as follows: $\mathrm{AP}^a = \mathrm{AP} \cup \{\bot\}$, where $\bot$ is fresh; for every good BSCC $B \subseteq S$ and $s \in B$ make s absorbing and let $L^a(s) = L(s) \cup \{\bot\}$; for all other states $s \in S \backslash B$ and $s' \in S$, $\mathbf{P}^a(s, s') = \mathbf{P}(s, s')$, $L^a(s) = L(s)$.*

Example 6 *As an example consider the CTMC $\mathcal{C}$ from Fig. 2 (left), in which there are two BSCCs $B_1 = \{s_4, s_5\}$ and $B_2 = \{s_1, s_2, s_3\}$. Moreover, assume that $B_1 \not\models \varphi$ and $B_2 \models \varphi$ for a given LDF φ. After applying Def. 9 to $\mathcal{C}$ we get $\mathcal{C}^a$ shown on the right, where the labels of the states s_1, s_2 and s_3 are augmented with the label $\{\bot\}$ and all the other labels are left unchanged.*

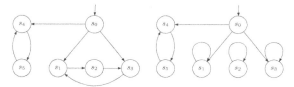

Figure 2: Example BSCC.

We write $\rho \models^\star_G \varphi$ if there exists some $n \in \mathbb{N}$ such that (1) $\rho[n] \in G$, and (2) for each $0 \le i \le n$, $\rho[0..i] \models \varphi$.

Proposition 2 *Given a CTMC $\mathcal{C} = (S, \mathrm{AP}, L, \alpha, \mathbf{P}, E)$ and an LDF φ, we have that $\mathrm{Prob}(\mathcal{C} \models^\star \varphi) = \mathrm{Pr}^{\mathcal{C}^a}(\{\rho \mid \rho \models^\star_G \varphi\})$, where $G = \{s \in S \mid \bot \in L(s)\}$.*

4.1.1 Algorithm

Algorithm 5 Compute $\widetilde{\mathrm{Prob}}(\mathcal{C} \models^\star \varphi)$

Require: A CTMC $\mathcal{C}$, an LDF formula φ, ε_1 and ε_2
1: Identify all BSCCs B in $\mathcal{C}$
2: $G = \{\varnothing\}$
3: $\mathrm{Prob} = 0$
4: **for each** BSCC B **do**
5:   **if** $B \models \varphi$ **then**
6:     Make every state in B absorbing
7:     $G = G \cup B$
8:   **end if**
9: **end for**
10: Compute $\sum_{s \in S} \alpha(s) \mathbb{E}_s[T_G]$
11: Choose $T > \sum_{s \in S} \alpha(s) \frac{\mathbb{E}_s[T_G]}{\varepsilon_1}$ and $N \ge \Lambda T e^2 + \ln(\frac{1}{\varepsilon_2})$
12: $\mathrm{Prob} = \widetilde{\mathrm{Prob}}_N(\mathcal{C} \models^\star_{G,T} \varphi)$
13: **return** Prob

Alg. 5 computes $\widetilde{\mathrm{Prob}}(\mathcal{C} \models^\star \varphi)$ which is an approximation of $\mathrm{Prob}(\mathcal{C} \models^\star \varphi)$. Lines 4-9 obtain $\mathcal{C}^a$ and the goal states G, according to Def. 9, then the algorithm calls the function $\widetilde{\mathrm{Prob}}_N(\mathcal{C} \models^\star_{G,T} \varphi)$, by choosing T and N, according to the specified error bounds ε_1 and ε_2 respectively.

Error Bound.

Intuitively, there are two factors that contribute to the error introduced by Alg. 5:

- the error introduced by approximating $\mathrm{Pr}^{\mathcal{C}^a}(\{\rho \mid \rho \models^\star_G \varphi\})$ by $\mathrm{Prob}(\mathcal{C}^a \models^\star_{G,T} \varphi)$, which can be obtained in a similar way to Thm. 7. We denote it by ε_1;

- the error introduced through approximating $\mathrm{Prob}(\mathcal{C}^a \models^\star_{G,T} \varphi)$ by $\widetilde{\mathrm{Prob}}_N(\mathcal{C}^a \models^\star_{G,T} \varphi)$. We denote it by ε_2.

Theorem 8 *Given ε_1 and ε_2, we have that*

$$\mathrm{Prob}(\mathcal{C} \models^\star \varphi) - \widetilde{\mathrm{Prob}}(\mathcal{C} \models^\star \varphi) \le \varepsilon_1 + \varepsilon_2.$$

where $\widetilde{\mathrm{Prob}}(\mathcal{C} \models^\star \varphi)$ is given in Alg. 5.

Remark 4 *Given ε a priori, one practical way is to let $\varepsilon_1 = \varepsilon_2 = \frac{\varepsilon}{2}$, and hence $T = 2 \sum_{s \in S} \alpha(s) \frac{\mathbb{E}_s[T_G]}{\varepsilon}$ and $N = 2 \sum_{s \in S} \alpha(s) \mathbb{E}_s[T_G] \frac{\Lambda e^2}{\varepsilon} + \ln(\frac{4}{\varepsilon})$ suffice.*

4.2 Time-bounded Verification of IDP

In this section we show how to deal with the time-bounded variant of IDP. Given an infinite timed path ρ, we write $\rho \models^{\star, G}_T \varphi$ if $\rho \models^\star \varphi$ and $\rho@T \in G$. The following theorem plays a pivotal role.

Theorem 9 *Given a CTMC $\mathcal{C}$ and an LDF Φ we have*

$$\mathrm{Prob}(\mathcal{C} \models^\star \Phi) = \sum_{s \in S} \mathrm{Prob}(\mathcal{C} \models^{\star, \{s\}}_T \varphi).$$

The solution boils down to the computation of $\mathrm{Prob}(\mathcal{C} \models^{\star, \{s\}}_T \varphi)$ for each state s. It follows that we compute the approximation $\widetilde{\mathrm{Prob}}(\mathcal{C} \models^\star \Phi)$ by bounding the lenghts of the paths, as shown in Alg. 6. We have the following error bound.

Algorithm 6 Compute $\widetilde{\mathrm{Prob}}(\mathcal{C} \models^\star \Phi)$

Require: A CTMC $\mathcal{C}$, an LDF Φ and ε
1: $\mathrm{Prob} = 0$
2: Chose $N \ge \Lambda T e^2 + \ln(\frac{|S|}{\varepsilon})$
3: **for all** $s \in S$ **do**
4:   **for all** $\varsigma \in Paths^{\mathcal{D}}$ s.t. $\exists n.\varsigma[n] = s$ and $|\varsigma| \le N$ **do**
5:     $\mathcal{S} = \{\varnothing\}$
6:     **for** $z = 0;\ z < |\varsigma|;\ z{+}{+}$ **do**
7:       **for** $j \in J$ **do**
8:         $\mathcal{S} = \mathcal{S} \bigcup \left\{ \sum_{i \in K_j} c_{ji} \cdot \sum_{\substack{0 \le \ell \le z \\ \varsigma[\ell] \models ap_{ji}}} x_\ell \le M_j \right\}$
9:       **end for**
10:   **end for**
11:     $\mathcal{S} = \mathcal{S} \bigcup \left\{ \sum_{i=0}^n x_i = T \right\}$
12:     $\mathcal{S} = \mathcal{S} \bigcup \{x_i > 0\}$ for all x_i
13:     $\mathrm{Prob}{+}{=} Volume\_int(\varsigma, \mathcal{S})$
14:   **end for**
15: **end for**
16: **return** Prob

Theorem 10 *Given ε and $N \in \mathbb{N}$, it holds that:*

$$\mathrm{Prob}(\mathcal{C} \models^\star \Phi) - \widetilde{\mathrm{Prob}}(\mathcal{C} \models^\star \Phi) < \varepsilon.$$

5. CONCLUSION

We have studied the problem of verifying CTMCs against linear durational properties. We focused on two classes of

LDPs, namely, eventuality duration properties and invariance duration properties. The central question we solved is, what is the probability of the set of infinite timed paths of the CTMC which satisfy the given LDP? We presented different algorithms to approximate these probabilities up to a given precision, stating their complexity and error bounds. The implementation of algorithms presented in this paper in PRISM is in progress.

As future work, we plan to study algorithmic verification of more complex duration properties, for instance *response* and *persistence*, as in [6]. It is also interesting to study specifications combining duration properties and temporal properties (in traditional real-time logics, e.g., MTL). The verification of these specifications would be challenging. Extending the current work to CTMDPs is another possible direction.

6. REFERENCES

[1] R. Alur, C. Courcoubetis, and T. A. Henzinger. Computing accumulated delays in real-time systems. In *Formal Methods in System Design*, 11(2):137–155, 1997.

[2] C. Baier, B. R. Haverkort, H. Hermanns, and J.-P. Katoen. On the logical characterisation of performability properties. In *ICALP'00*, LNCS 1853, pp. 780–792. Springer, 2000.

[3] C. Baier, B. R. Haverkort, H. Hermanns, and J.-P. Katoen. Model-checking algorithms for continuous-time Markov chains. In *IEEE Trans. Software Eng.*, 29(6):524–541, 2003.

[4] B. Barbot, T. Chen, T. Han, J.-P. Katoen, and A. Mereacre. Efficient CTMC model checking of linear real-time objectives. In *TACAS'11*, LNCS 6605, pp. 128–142. Springer, 2011.

[5] U. Boker, K. Chatterjee, T. A. Henzinger, and O. Kupferman. Temporal specifications with accumulative values. In *LICS'11*, pp. 43–52. IEEE, 2011.

[6] A. Bouajjani, R. Echahed, and J. Sifakis. On model checking for real-time properties with durations. In *LICS'93*, pp. 147–159. IEEE, 1993.

[7] P. Bouyer, U. Fahrenberg, K. G. Larsen, and N. Markey. Timed automata with observers under energy constraints. In *HSCC'10*, pp. 61–70. ACM, 2010.

[8] T. Chen, M. Diciolla, M. Z. Kwiatkowska, and A. Mereacre. Time-bounded verification of CTMCs against real-time specifications. In *FORMATS'11*, LNCS 6919, pp. 26–42. Springer, 2011.

[9] T. Chen, M. Diciolla, M. Kwiatkowska, and A. Mereacre. *Verification of linear duration properties over conitnuous time Markov chains*. Technical report RR-12-02, Department of Computer Science, University of Oxford, 2012.

[10] T. Chen, T. Han, J.-P. Katoen, and A. Mereacre. Quantitative model checking of continuous-time Markov chains against timed automata specifications. In *LICS'09*, pp. 309–318. IEEE, 2009.

[11] T. Chen, T. Han, J.-P. Katoen, and A. Mereacre. Model checking of continuous-time Markov chains against timed automata specifications. In *Logical Methods in Computer Science*, 7(1–2):1–34, 2011.

[12] L. Cloth. *Model Checking Algorithms for Markov Reward Models*. PhD thesis, University of Twente, The Netherlands, 2006.

[13] M. H. A. Davis. *Markov Models and Optimization*. Chapman and Hall, 1993.

[14] M. C. Diniz, E. de Souza e Silva, and H. R. Gail. Calculating the distribution of a linear combination of uniform order statistics. In *INFORMS Journal on Computing*, 14(2):124–131, 2002.

[15] M. Gribaudo. *Hybrid Formalism for Performance Evaluation: Theory and Applications*. PhD thesis, Università di Torino, 2002.

[16] D. P. Guelev and D. V. Hung. Reasoning about QoS contracts in the probabilistic duration calculus. In *Electr. Notes Theor. Comput. Sci.*, 238(6):41–62, 2010.

[17] B. R. Haverkort, L. Cloth, H. Hermanns, J.-P. Katoen, and C. Baier. Model checking performability properties. In *DSN'02*, pp. 103–112. IEEE, 2002.

[18] G. Horton, V. G. Kulkarni, D. M. Nicol, and K. S. Trivedi. Fluid Stochastic Petri Nets: Theory, Applications, and Solution Techniques. In *European Journal of Operational Research*, 105(1):184–201, 1998.

[19] D. V. Hung and M. Zhang. On verification of probabilistic timed automata against probabilistic duration properties. In *RTCSA'07*, pp. 165–172. IEEE, 2007.

[20] D. V. Hung and C. Zhou. Probabilistic duration calculus for continuous time. In *Formal Asp. Comput.*, 11(1):21–44, 1999.

[21] A. Jensen. Markoff chains as an aid in the study of Markoff processes. In *Skand. Aktuarietidskrift*, 36:87–91, 1953.

[22] Y. Kesten, A. Pnueli, J. Sifakis, and S. Yovine. Decidable integration graphs. In *Inf. Comput.*, 150(2):209–243, 1999.

[23] M. Kwiatkowska, G. Norman, and D. Parker. Stochastic model checking. In *SFM'07*, LNCS 4486, pp. 220–270. Springer, 2007.

[24] M. Kwiatkowska, G. Norman, and D. Parker. PRISM 4.0: Verification of probabilistic real-time systems. In *CAV'11*, LNCS 6806, pp. 585–591. Springer, 2011.

[25] J. B. Lasserre and E. S. Zeron. A Laplace transform algorithm for the volume of a convex polytope. In *J. ACM*, 48(6):1126–1140, 2001.

[26] X. Li, D. V. Hung, and T. Zheng. Checking hybrid automata for linear duration invariants. In *ASIAN'97*, LNCS 1345, pp. 166–180. Springer, 1997.

[27] M. Neuts. *Matrix-Geometric solutions in stochastic models: An algorithimic approach*. John Hopkins University Press, 1981.

[28] Y. Nievergelt. *Foundations of logic and mathematics: applications to computer science and cryptography*. Springer, 2002.

[29] G. Norman, D. Parker, M. Kwiatkowska, S. Shukla, and R. Gupta. Using probabilistic model checking for dynamic power management. In *Formal Aspects of Computing*, 17(2):160–176, 2005.

[30] Q. Qiu, Q. Qu, and M. Pedram. Stochastic modeling of a power-managed system-construction and optimization. In *IEEE Transactions on Computer-Aided Design of Integrated Circuits and Systems*, 20(10):1200 –1217, 2001.

[31] P. H. Thai and D. V. Hung. Verifying linear duration constraints of timed automata. In *ICTAC'04*, LNCS 3407, pp. 295–309. Springer, 2004.

[32] M. Zhang, D. V. Hung, and Z. Liu. Verification of linear duration invariants by model checking CTL properties. In *ICTAC'08*, LNCS 5160, pp. 395–409. Springer, 2008.

[33] C. Zhou, C. A. R. Hoare, and A. P. Ravn. A calculus of durations. In *Inf. Process. Lett.*, 40(5):269–276, 1991.

[34] C. Zhou, J. Zhang, L. Yang, and X. Li. Linear duration invariants. In *FTRTFT'94*, LNCS 863, pp. 86–109. Springer, 1994.

Robust PCTL Model Checking *

Alessandro D'Innocenzo

Department of Electrical and
Information Engineering,
Center of Excellence DEWS
University of L'Aquila, Italy

alessandro.dinnocenzo@
univaq.it

Alessandro Abate

Delft Center for Systems and
Control
TU Delft – Delft University of
Technology, The Netherlands

a.abate@tudelft.nl

Joost-Pieter Katoen

Software Modeling and
Verification Group
RWTH Aachen University,
Germany

katoen@cs.rwth-
aachen.de

ABSTRACT

This paper deals with the notion of approximate probabilistic bisimulation (APB) relation for discrete-time labeled Markov Chains (LMC). In order to provide a quantified upper bound on a metric over probabilistic realizations for LMC, we exploit the structure and properties of the APB and leverage the mathematical framework of Markov set-Chains. Based on this bound, the article proves that the existence of an APB implies the preservation of robust PCTL formulae, which are formulae that allow being properly relaxed or strengthened, according to the underlying APB. This leads to a notion of robustness for probabilistic model checking.

Categories and Subject Descriptors

G.3, G.4 [**Mathematics of Computing**]: Probability and Statistics; Mathematical Software.

General Terms

Markov processes; Stochastic processes; Verification.

1. INTRODUCTION

For complex probabilistic systems with large state space dimension, automatic verification of probabilistic properties can be computationally prohibitive. An approach that is successfully used to cope with the issue of computational complexity and scalability that arise in formal verification of complex models is that of abstraction: a system – equivalent in some sense to the original system – with smaller state space or simpler dynamics is sought. The abstraction is usually an aggregated or lumped version of the concrete model.

*This work is supported by the European Commission MoVeS project FP7-ICT-2009-5 257005, by the European Commission Marie Curie grant MANTRAS 249295, by the European Commission NoE HYCON2 FP7-ICT-2009-5 257462, and by the NWO VENI grant 016.103.020.

Equivalence is usually introduced with reference to the notion of bisimulation [26, 27], which is an equivalence relation induced on the state space of the original system. System equivalence implies that certain properties of the original (complex) system are preserved by the (simpler) abstraction. Thus a specific property of interest can be checked more efficiently (that is, with a lower computational complexity) on the abstraction [21].

Often though, the exact notion of equivalence appears to be quite conservative, because it requires an exact match between trajectories of the concrete and of the abstract systems. In practice, severe problems may occur with the computation of exact bisimulation due to numerical errors, in particular for models with large state spaces [29]. This issue is even more taxing for probabilistic models: if an abstract system is verified on a model obtained with quantization/discretization errors in the transition probabilities, the effect of a small perturbation can invalidate the outcome of the procedure.

These issues have led to the introduction of an *approximate* notion of equivalence, which for deterministic systems was introduced in [15] via the notion of approximate bisimulation – a notion based on metrics over the distance between trajectories of concrete and abstract models.

In the context of non-deterministic models, the notion of approximate bisimulation has been used to perform model reduction while preserving properties expressed by temporal logics, e.g. TCTL [19]. Such properties are subsequently verified by the use of model checking procedures. In [8], a quantitative version of transition systems is considered, and different versions of trace and bisimulation distance are defined.

For probabilistic systems, the concept of (strong) probabilistic bisimulation has been introduced in [25] over discrete-time, finite-state Markov Chains. Bisimulation corresponds to what is also known as lumping. The use of approximate notions is advocated in [14] and motivated by the robustness issues mentioned above. Of course approximate notions are also likely to result in coarser bisimulations than those obtained with the exact notion. The work in [12] discusses approximate notions of bisimulations for discrete-time labeled Markov processes.

The reference model framework in this paper is that of discrete time labeled Markov Chains (LMC). We tailor the definition of approximate probabilistic bisimulation (APB) in [12] to LMC. As a first result of this paper, we provide a quantitative upper bound for a probabilistic realization metric in time (both over a finite and an infinite horizon) with an expression that depends on the approximation level of the APB. We provide these bounds first by exploiting the structure of the APB, then by employing the theory of Markov set-Chains (MSC) [18]. Since the APB notion induces a coarser bisimulation than the corresponding exact notion, it cannot be used to prove that all PCTL properties of the original system are preserved by an approximately bisimilar abstraction. As the main result of the paper, we prove that an APB with precision ε implies the preservation of ε-robust PCTL properties over the original system. PCTL [2, 22] is a discrete-time probabilistic temporal logic that allows modeling probabilistic specifications, to be then verified by probabilistic model checking using tools such as PRISM [23, 24] or MRMC [20].

The results obtained in this paper for finite LMC represent the first step towards robustness analysis for model checking of infinite state space systems as general as Stochastic Hybrid Systems (SHS). Indeed we aim to leverage the abstraction procedure we developed in [1], where we show how to derive a finite LMC abstraction of a SHS characterized by a finite precision, to subsequently verify properties of SHS by using classical PCTL model checking algorithms over the abstraction. In order to guarantee that the model checking result obtained over the abstraction also holds for the SHS, the accuracy of the abstraction needs to satisfy the constraints discussed in this paper.

The paper is structured as follows. In Section 2, we define LMC and introduce the notions of APB. In Section 3 we state quantified relations between the APB and a probabilistic realization metric both by exploiting the structure and properties of the APB (Section 3.1) and leveraging the mathematical framework of Markov set-Chains (Section 3.3). In Section 4 we recall basic notions of PCTL model checking (Section 4.1), and prove that the presence of an APB with precision ε implies the preservation of ε-robust PCTL formulae (Section 4.2). A case study is developed throughout the paper, to apply and clarify the presented notions and results.

2. APPROXIMATE BISIMULATION

Let AP be a finite, fixed set of atomic propositions.

DEFINITION 1. *[Discrete-time labeled Markov Chain] We define a discrete-time labeled Markov Chain (LMC) as a tuple (Q, P, L) consisting of:*

- *Q, a non-empty set of states of finite cardinality $n \in \mathbb{N}$;*

- *$P : Q \times Q \to [0, 1]$, a stochastic matrix that associates to each pair $(q_1, q_2) \in Q \times Q$ the transition probability from state q_1 to state q_2;*

- *$L : Q \to 2^{AP}$, a labeling function that associates to each state $q \in Q$ the set $L(q)$ of atomic propositions that are valid in q.*

A LMC can be related to a DTMC, as in [3], and is a subclass of the labeled Markov process (LMP) model as in [12].

Consider a LMC $M = (Q, P, L)$ and $k \in \mathbb{N}$. We define by $P^k(q, q')$ the probability that state q' is reached in k steps by an execution of M starting from state q. Given a set $A \in 2^Q$, we define by $P^k(q, A) = \sum_{q' \in A} P^k(q, q')$ the probability that the set of states A is reached in k steps starting from state q.

Given a LMC M, a relation $\Gamma \subseteq Q \times Q$ and a set $A \in 2^Q$, we introduce the set

$$\Gamma(A) = \{q \in Q \mid \exists q' \in A, (q, q') \in \Gamma\},$$

and say that A is Γ-closed if $\Gamma(A) \subseteq A$. The following definition is inspired by [10, 25].

DEFINITION 2. *[Probabilistic bisimulation] Given a LMC $M = (Q, P, L)$, a probabilistic bisimulation is an equivalence relation $\Gamma \subseteq Q \times Q$ such that for any $(q_1, q_2) \in \Gamma$ then $L(q_1) = L(q_2)$, and for any Γ-closed set $A \in 2^Q$,*

$$P(q_1, A) = P(q_2, A).$$

States $q_1, q_2 \in Q$ are probabilistic bisimilar, which is denoted by $q_1 \equiv q_2$, if there exists a probabilistic bisimulation Γ with $(q_1, q_2) \in \Gamma$.

The condition $P(q_1, A) = P(q_2, A)$ in the above definition is equivalent to the condition $P(q_1, \Gamma(A)) = P(q_2, \Gamma(A))$, since for an equivalence Γ we have $A = \Gamma(A)$. Any probabilistic bisimulation relation induces a partition of the state space, where the equivalence classes are made up of bisimilar states [3]. In particular, the equivalence classes are given by the Γ-closed sets $\{A_1, \ldots, A_m\}$. In the following, we will denote by m the number of Γ-closed sets that form a partition of the state space. A recursive algorithm to compute the maximal (coarsest) bisimulation of a LMC with time complexity $\mathcal{O}(|Q|^2 \log |Q|)$ has been proposed in [9]. Note that Definition 2 hinges on rather strong conditions on the transition probabilities, marginalized over the equivalence classes.

EXAMPLE 1. *Craps is a dice game where the players bet on the outcome of dice rolls. An LMC (Q, P, L) characterizes the dynamics (the possible outcomes) of the game – its transition probability matrix P is reported in Figure 1 [3, Section 10]. Given a set $AP = \{start, mid, won, lost\}$, the Markov Chain states*

$$Q = \{start, 4, 10, 5, 9, 6, 8, won, lost\}$$

are associated to the following labels:

$$L(start) = start, \quad L(i) = mid, i \in \{4, 10, 5, 9, 6, 8\},$$
$$L(won) = won, \quad L(lost) = lost.$$

The Markov Chain admits an (exact) probabilistic bisimu-

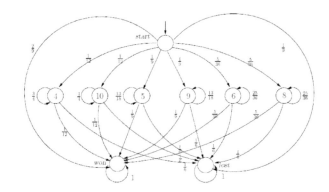

Figure 1: Concrete Markov Chain of the craps game.

lation, depicted in Figure 2, with the following collection of

6 equivalence classes:

$$\{start\}, \{4, 10\}, \{5, 9\}, \{6, 8\}, \{won\}, \{lost\}.$$

Each pair of vertices within an equivalence class denotes probabilistically bisimilar states.

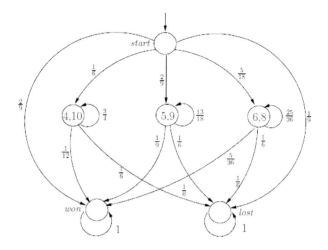

Figure 2: Bisimilar LMC for craps game.

Notice how even small perturbations on the transition probabilities or possible numerical approximations in matrix P would invalidate the exact probabilistic bisimulation relation of the above example. The concept of approximate probabilistic bisimulation has been introduced in [12] to overcome the above limitations. The definition in [12, Definition 10] has been introduced for LMP, and can be shown to directly tailor to the one given here for LMC.

DEFINITION 3. [Approximate probabilistic bisimulation] Given a LMC $M = (Q, P, L)$, an approximate probabilistic bisimulation with precision $0 \leq \varepsilon \leq 1$ (APB with precision ε) is a reflexive and symmetric relation $\Gamma_\varepsilon \subseteq Q \times Q$ such that for any $(q_1, q_2) \in \Gamma_\varepsilon$, then $L(q_1) = L(q_2)$ and for any Γ_ε-closed set $A \in 2^Q$,

$$|P(q_1, \Gamma_\varepsilon(A)) - P(q_2, \Gamma_\varepsilon(A))| \leq \varepsilon,$$

States $q_1, q_2 \in Q$ are probabilistic approximately bisimilar with precision ε, which is denoted by $q_1 \equiv_\varepsilon q_2$, if there exists an APB Γ_ε with precision ε, such that $(q_1, q_2) \in \Gamma_\varepsilon$.

It is easy to see that an APB with precision $\varepsilon = 0$ is an exact probabilistic bisimulation in the sense of Definition 2. For any given LMC with state space Q and approximation parameter $\varepsilon \in [0, 1]$, techniques to compute the largest APB with precision ε in time $\mathcal{O}(|Q|^7)$ are introduced in [12].

EXAMPLE 2. Let us consider a perturbed LMC $(Q, \tilde{P}, L)$ of (Q, P, L) in Example 1, which is defined as follows:

$$\tilde{P} = P + E,$$

where $E(i, j) = \varepsilon_{i,j}, |\varepsilon_{i,j}| \leq \min\{P(i, j), 1 - P(i, j)\}$, and $\sum_{j \in Q} \varepsilon_{i,j} = 0$. As an example, consider

$$\tilde{P}(start, i) = P(start, i) + \varepsilon_{start,i}, \quad \sum_{i \in Q} \varepsilon_{start,i} = 0.$$

Notice that $\tilde{P}$ is again a stochastic matrix. The LMC $(Q, \tilde{P}, L)$ admits an APB with precision $\varepsilon = 4\|E\|_\infty$. (The presence of the multiplicative factor is elucidated in the following set of inequalities.) In this example, the APB Γ_ε induces a collection of classes of ε-bisimilar pairs of states, which is equivalent to the partition of Q as described in Figure 2. This partition also corresponds to the collection of Γ_ε-closed sets. Let us consider the Γ_ε-closed set $A = \{start, won, lost\}$: since $\{5\} \equiv_\varepsilon \{9\}$, we obtain

$$|P(5, A) - P(9, A)|$$
$$= \left| \left(0 + \frac{1}{9} + \varepsilon_{5,won} + \frac{1}{6} + \varepsilon_{5,lost} \right) \right.$$
$$\left. - \left(0 + \frac{1}{9} + \varepsilon_{9,won} + \frac{1}{6} + \varepsilon_{9,lost} \right) \right|$$
$$\leq |\varepsilon_{5,won} - \varepsilon_{9,won}| + |\varepsilon_{5,lost} - \varepsilon_{9,lost}| \leq 2 \cdot 2\|E\|_\infty.$$

The precision bound $\varepsilon = 4\|E\|_\infty$ can be shown to hold regardless of the choice of ε-bisimilar pairs $q_1 \equiv_\varepsilon q_2$ and Γ_ε-closed set A.

Let us now introduce the quantity $\tilde{\varepsilon} := \frac{5}{36} - \frac{1}{9} = \frac{1}{9} - \frac{1}{12}$. If $\|E\|_\infty < \frac{\tilde{\varepsilon}}{2}$, then there exists a coarser APB that consists of 5 classes (instead of 6 as before) of ε-bisimilar states

$$\{start\}, \{4, 10, 5, 9\}, \{5, 9, 6, 8\}, \{won\}, \{lost\}.$$

The new APB is associated to a precision $\varepsilon = 4\tilde{\varepsilon}$, which can be checked as done above and imposing the bound on $\|E\|_\infty$. Note that the obtained APB with precision ε does not generate a partition of Q: this fact will be further discussed shortly. The collection of Γ_ε-closed sets is then

$$\{start\}, \{4, 10, 5, 9, 6, 8\}, \{won\}, \{lost\}.$$

As it is also evident in the above example, let us remark that an APB with precision ε does not usually induce a partition of the state space by equivalence classes that consist of ε-bisimilar states. This is due to the fact that APB with precision ε is not an equivalence relation, since in general it does not satisfy the transitive property. This entails that any two states belonging to the same Γ_ε-closed set are not necessarily ε-bisimilar: we show instead that they are $l\varepsilon$-bisimilar, with l a finite positive integer smaller than the diameter of the Γ_ε-closed set. To clarify and formalize this fact, we provide some connections between the concept of APB and graph theory [17].

DEFINITION 4. [APB graph] Given a LMC $M = (Q, P, L)$ and an APB Γ_ε, we define the associated APB graph $\mathcal{G} = (V, E)$ as $V = Q$ and $E = \Gamma_\varepsilon$. Since Γ_ε is symmetric, then $\mathcal{G}$ is an undirected graph.

The set $\{A_1, \ldots, A_m\}$ of all non-intersecting Γ_ε-closed sets forms a partition of the set Q. Moreover, the following straightforward result holds.

PROPOSITION 1. Given a LMC $M = (Q, P, L)$ and an APB Γ_ε, then the associated APB graph $\mathcal{G}$ has m connected components $\{\mathcal{G}_i = (V_i, E_i)\}_{i=1}^m$, and $\forall i \in \{1, \ldots, m\}$, $V_i = A_i$.

DEFINITION 5. [Central vertex, radius, and diameter of APB graph] Given a LMC $M = (Q, P, L)$, an APB Γ_ε and the associated APB graph $\mathcal{G}$, we select for each Γ_ε-closed set A_i any element $\bar{a}_i \in A_i$ as a central vertex of $\mathcal{G}_i$, and define the radius r_i and the diameter d_i associated to A_i as the radius and diameter of $\mathcal{G}_i$.

The radius of a graph is the minimum eccentricity of any of its vertices. The eccentricity of a vertex is its greatest possible distance from any other vertex in the graph. Thus a radius of a graph (and its central vertex) can be computed by first running the all-pairs-shortest-path algorithm, then maximizing the computed distance for any vertex, and finally minimizing the obtained value over the vertices of the graph. This can be done over un-weighted, un-directed graphs in polynomial time, at worst in $\mathcal{O}(n^3)$ [4]. Analogous considerations hold for the concept of graph diameter.

Figure 3 provides an example of APB and associated APB graph. The dashed ellipses denote Γ_ε-bisimilar states in Q. The Γ_ε-closed sets are $A_1 = \{1, 2, 4, 5, 8\}$, $A_2 = \{3, 6\}$, $A_3 = \{7, 10\}$, $A_4 = \{9, 11, 12\}$. The central vertex a_1 of $\mathcal{G}_1$ can be indifferently state 4 or state 5. The radius and the diameter of $\mathcal{G}_1$ are respectively $r_1 = 2$ and $d_1 = 3$.

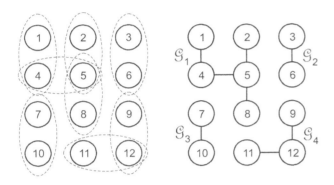

Figure 3: Left: APB - dashed ellipses define the Γ_ε relation. Right: associated APB graph $\mathcal{G} = \mathcal{G}_1 \cup \mathcal{G}_2 \cup \mathcal{G}_3 \cup \mathcal{G}_4$.

EXAMPLE 3. *With reference to the last instance of APB Γ_ε in Example 2, which is characterized by the following sets of Γ_ε bisimilar states*

$$\{start\}, \{4, 10, 5, 9\}, \{5, 9, 6, 8\}, \{won, lost\},$$

we obtain the following Γ_ε-closed sets:

$$A_1 = \{start\}, \ A_2 = \{4, 10, 5, 9, 6, 8\}, \ A_3 = \{won, lost\},$$

with radii $r_1 = 0, r_2 = 1, r_3 = 1$ and diameters $d_1 = 0, d_2 = 5, d_3 = 1$ The central vertices of the Γ_ε-closed sets are respectively start for $\mathcal{G}_1$, either 5 or 9 for $\mathcal{G}_2$, and either won or lost for $\mathcal{G}_3$. The APB graph is represented in Figure 4.

3. BISIMULATION BOUNDS ON REALIZATION DISTANCE

In this section we draw a connection between the notion of probabilistic realization distance over a LMC and that of APB. More precisely, we are interested in defining a metric on the distance in time between realizations of trajectories starting from two different initial conditions. We focus on initial conditions that are related by the notion of APB, and compute metrics over sets that are closed over this relation. We show explicit upper bounds in time for this distance.

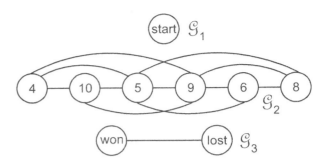

Figure 4: APB graph of Example 3.

DEFINITION 6. *[Probabilistic realization distance induced by Γ_ε] Given $M = (Q, P, L)$ and an APB $\Gamma_\varepsilon \subseteq Q \times Q$, we define a distance $d^k_{\Gamma_\varepsilon}(q_1, q_2)$ induced by Γ_ε at time $k \geq 1$ as follows:*

$$d^k_{\Gamma_\varepsilon}(q_1, q_2) = \max_{\forall A \ \Gamma_\varepsilon - closed} \left| P^k(q_1, \Gamma_\varepsilon(A)) - P^k(q_2, \Gamma_\varepsilon(A)) \right|.$$

We define $d^\infty_{\Gamma_\varepsilon}(q_1, q_2) = \lim_{k \to \infty} d^k_{\Gamma_\varepsilon}(q_1, q_2)$, if such limit exists.

Note that the probabilistic realization distance at time k induced by an APB Γ_ε between two LMC is the 1-norm distance at time k between the probability distributions, marginalized over the Γ_ε-closed sets.

Given $M = (Q, P, L)$ and an APB Γ_ε, let us introduce the quantity

$$d^k_\varepsilon(M) = \max_{(q_1, q_2) \in \Gamma_\varepsilon} d^k_{\Gamma_\varepsilon}(q_1, q_2). \tag{1}$$

3.1 Bound on finite-time realization distance

The next result draws an explicit bound on the finite-horizon realization distance. The bound depends on the existence of an APB Γ_ε, in particular on its precision ε and on the properties of the associated APB graph.

THEOREM 1. *Given a LMC $M = (Q, P, L)$ and an APB Γ_ε, then for any $(q_1, q_2) \in \Gamma_\varepsilon$ and for any $k \in \mathbb{N}$ the following holds:*

$$d^k_{\Gamma_\varepsilon}(q_1, q_2) \leq \varepsilon \left(m + \varepsilon \sum_{i=1}^{m} r_i \right)^{k-1}.$$

PROOF. Recall that $|Q| = n$ and that the m-dimensional ($m \leq n$) collection $\{A_i\}_{i=1}^m$ of Γ_ε-closed sets results in a partition of Q. Each set A_i, $i \in \{1, \ldots, m\}$ is associated to a central vertex $\bar{a}_i$ and a radius r_i (cfr. Def. 5). Consider any two states $q_1, q_2 \in Q : q_1 \equiv_\varepsilon q_2$. By Definition 3, for any Γ_ε-closed set A:

$$|P(q_1, A) - P(q_2, A)| \leq \varepsilon,$$

thus $d^1_{\Gamma_\varepsilon}(q_1, q_2) \leq \varepsilon$. As a next step, consider:

$$\left| P^2(q_1, A) - P^2(q_2, A) \right| = \left| \sum_{j=1}^{n} (P(q_1, q_j) - P(q_2, q_j)) P(q_j, A) \right|.$$

Notice that $\cup_{j=1}^{n}\{q_j\} = \cup_{i=1}^{m} A_i$. Consider a set $A_i \in \{A_i\}_{i=1}^m$, a generic state $q \in A_i$ and its central vertex $\bar{a}_i$, and the connected component $\mathcal{G}_i$ of the APB graph $\mathcal{G}$. By construction, there exists a finite-discrete path

$$\{q = s_0, s_1, \ldots, s_k, s_{k+1}, \ldots, \bar{a}_i\}$$

of cardinality at most r_i, which connects q with $\bar{a}_i$. Therefore, $\forall q \in A_i$, it holds that

$$P(q, A) \leq |P(q, A) - P(s_1, A)|$$
$$+ |P(s_1, A) - \ldots - P(s_k, A)| + |P(s_k, A) - P(s_{k+1}, A)|$$
$$+ |P(s_{k+1}, A) - \ldots - P(\bar{a}_i, A)| + P(\bar{a}_i, A).$$

Since $(s_k, s_{k+1}) \in \Gamma_\varepsilon$ for all $0 \leq k \leq r_i - 1$ by definition of $\mathcal{G}_i$, then $\forall A, A \Gamma_\varepsilon$-closed, it holds that

$$\forall k, |P(s_k, A) - P(s_{k+1}, A)| \leq \varepsilon.$$

We then obtain that

$$\forall q \in A_i, P(q, A) \leq P(\bar{a}_i, A) + r_i\varepsilon,$$

which leads to

$$\left| P^2(q_1, A) - P^2(q_2, A) \right| \leq$$
$$\left| \sum_{i=1}^m (P(q_1, A_i) - P(q_2, A_i)) (P(\bar{a}_i, A) + r_i\varepsilon) \right| \leq$$
$$\sum_{i=1}^m |P(q_1, A_i) - P(q_2, A_i)| (P(\bar{a}_i, A) + r_i\varepsilon) \leq$$
$$\left| \sum_{i=1}^m \varepsilon (P(\bar{a}_i, A) + r_i\varepsilon) \right| \leq \varepsilon \left(m + \varepsilon \sum_{i=1}^m r_i \right). \quad (2)$$

Inductively, we obtain

$$\left| P^k(q_1, A) - P^k(q_2, A) \right| \leq \varepsilon \left(m + \varepsilon \sum_{i=1}^m r_i \right)^{k-1},$$

which leads to the bound in the statement. $\square$

Notice that the derived bound can be practically conservative, in particular due to the inequality in (2), and can thus be substituted by a tighter lower-approximant, as the following example displays.

EXAMPLE 4. *Let us consider the first instance of APB discussed in Example 2. Note that the radii related to the Γ_ε-closed sets are equal either to 0 (for classes start, won, lost) or to 1 (for classes $(4, 10), (5, 9), (6, 8)$).*

At step k, the derived bound results in the quantity $\varepsilon(6 + 3\varepsilon)^{k-1}$, however this worst-case bound can be actually refined. For instance, consider the two states 4 and 10, which are ε-bisimilar, and the Γ_ε-closed set $A = \{$won$\}$. Then, the inequality in (2) can be refined as follows (refer to the incoming edges into set $\{$won$\}$ in Figure 2):

$$\left| P^k(4, A) - P^k(10, A) \right|$$
$$\leq \varepsilon \left(\frac{2}{9} + 0\varepsilon + \frac{1}{12} + 1\varepsilon + \frac{1}{9} + 1\varepsilon + \frac{5}{36} + 1\varepsilon + 0 + 0\varepsilon \right)^{k-1}$$
$$= \varepsilon \left(\frac{5}{9} + 3\varepsilon \right)^{k-1}.$$

Notice that the new bound is not only lower than $\varepsilon(6 + 3\varepsilon)^{k-1}$, but is also decreasing in time if $\varepsilon < \frac{4}{27}$.

Theorem 1 provides a bound that in general increases quickly with k if the argument of the exponent is larger than the unity. In order to try to generalize this bound to hold over an infinite horizon (cfr. Section 3.3), we introduce next the formalism and theory of Markov set-Chains.

3.2 Markov Set-Chains

The results illustrated in this section are from [18] and are also summarized in [1].

DEFINITION 7. *[18, Definition 2.5, Transition Set] Let $P, Q \in \mathbb{R}^{n \times n}$ be nonnegative matrices (not necessarily stochastic) with $P \leq Q$, where $\leq$ is element-wise. We define a transition set as $[\Pi] = [P, Q] = \{T \in \mathbb{R}^{n \times n} : T$ is a stochastic matrix and $P \leq T \leq Q\}$.*

In this paper, we assume that the set $[P, Q] \neq \emptyset$. A (discrete-time) Markov set-Chain can be formally introduced as follows.

DEFINITION 8. *[18, Definition 2.5, Markov set-Chain] Let $[\Pi]$ be a transition set, i.e. a compact set of $n \times n$ stochastic matrices. Consider the set of all inhomogeneous Markov Chains having their transition matrices in $[\Pi]$. We call the sequence $[\Pi], [\Pi]^2, \ldots$ a Markov set-Chain (MSC), where $[\Pi]^k$ is defined by induction as the set of all possible products $T_1 T_2 \cdots T_k$, such that $\forall i = 1, \ldots, k, T_i \in [\Pi]$.*

DEFINITION 9. *[18, Definition 1.2, Coefficient of Ergodicity of a Stochastic Matrix] For a stochastic matrix T, its coefficient of ergodicity is defined as follows:*

$$\mathcal{T}(T) = \frac{1}{2} \max_{i,j} ||a_i - a_j||,$$

where a_i, a_j are the i-th, j-th rows of T, and $|| \cdot ||$ is the standard 1-norm over row vectors: $||x|| = \sum_k |x_k|$.

It can be shown that the condition $\mathcal{T}(T) < 1$, along with the condition of irreducibility of the chain, implies the existence of a unique limiting and invariant distribution for the associated Markov Chain [18, 13]. The previous definition can be directly extended to MSC.

DEFINITION 10. *[18, Definition 3.1, Coefficient of Ergodicity of a Transition Set] For any transition set $[\Pi]$, its coefficient of ergodicity is defined over the stochastic matrices that define $[\Pi]$ as follows: $\mathcal{T}([\Pi]) = \max_{T \in [\Pi]} \mathcal{T}(T)$.*

Since $\mathcal{T}(\cdot)$ is a continuous function and $[\Pi]$ a compact set, the corresponding maximum argument exists.

THEOREM 2. *[18, Theorem 3.1] Let $[\Pi]$ be the interval $[P, Q]$ and $T \in [\Pi]$, then $|\mathcal{T}([\Pi]) - \mathcal{T}(T)| \leq ||Q - P||$.*

The used matrix norm is the induced 1-norm over row-vectors: $||T|| = \max_{x \neq 0} \frac{||xT||}{||x||}$. Let us define the diameter of a transition set:

$$\Delta([\Pi]) = \max_{T, T' \in [\Pi]} ||T - T'||.$$

The following result provides an upper bound for the diameter of the transition set $[\Pi]^k, k > 0$.

THEOREM 3. *[18, Theorems 3.4, 3.11] Given a MSC with transition set $[\Pi] = [P, Q]$, then*

$$\Delta([\Pi]^k) \leq \mathcal{T}([\Pi])^k + (\mathcal{T}([\Pi])^{k-1} + \ldots + 1)\Delta([\Pi]).$$

In particular, if $\mathcal{T}([\Pi]) < 1$, given any initial distribution set $[\pi_0]$, there exists a unique set $[\pi_\infty]$ that is invariant, i.e. such that $[\pi_\infty][\Pi] = [\pi_\infty]$, and moreover such that

$$\lim_{k \to \infty} [\pi_k] = \lim_{k \to \infty} [\pi_0][\Pi]^k = [\pi_\infty].$$

Furthermore, the following holds:

$$\Delta([\pi_\infty]) \leq \frac{\Delta([\Pi])}{1 - \mathcal{T}([\Pi])} \leq \frac{||Q - P||}{1 - \mathcal{T}([\Pi])}.$$

The notion of limit of a vector interval hinges on the Hausdorff distance [18], which is a distance between sets. The derived bounds are not necessarily tight, however they are sufficient for the objectives of the study (finiteness of bounds), and as such they will be used below. Tighter results can be obtained with more sophistication (cfr. the Hi-Lo method and the notion of scrambling coefficient in [18]).

3.3 Bound on infinite-time realization distance

On the basis of the MSC theory illustrated in the previous section, we provide a new bound for the probabilistic realization distance induced by an APB Γ_ε.

THEOREM 4. *Given a LMC $M = (Q, P, L)$ and an APB Γ_ε, then for any $(q_1, q_2) \in \Gamma_\varepsilon$ and $k \in \mathbb{N} \cup \{\infty\}$ the following holds:*

$$d_{\Gamma_\varepsilon}^k(q_1, q_2) \leq \tau^k + \varepsilon\lambda m \sum_{l=0}^{k-1} \tau^l,$$

where $\tau = \mathcal{T}(M) + \varepsilon\lambda m$, and $\lambda = \max_{i=1,\ldots,m} d_i$ is the maximum diameter among the connected components of the APB graph.

PROOF. Consider the APB Γ_ε on M. We define a MSC over the state space $Q_{[M]} = \{A_1, \ldots, A_m\}$ of Γ_ε-closed sets, and characterized by the following transition set $P_{[M]}$: for each $A_1, A_2 \in Q_{[M]}$, define

$$P_{[M]}(A_1, A_2) = [\min_{q \in A_1} \{P(q, A_2)\}, \max_{q \in A_1} \{P(q, A_2)\}].$$

Since the cardinality of the MSC $[M]$ is given by $m = |Q_{[M]}| \leq |Q| = n$, and since by Definition 3

$$\left| \min_{q \in A_1} \{P(q, A_2)\} - \max_{q \in A_1} \{P(q, A_2)\} \right| \leq \varepsilon d_1,$$

then $\Delta([M]) = \varepsilon\lambda m$: in fact (cfr. Section 3.2), $\Delta([M]) = \max_{i=1,\ldots,m} \sum_{j=1}^m \varepsilon d_i = \max_{i=1,\ldots,m} \varepsilon d_i m$. The coefficient of ergodicity $\mathcal{T}([M])$, according to Theorem 2, satisfies the inequality $\mathcal{T}(M) \leq \mathcal{T}([M]) \leq \mathcal{T}(M) + \varepsilon\lambda m = \tau$.

Given any $A_1, A_2 \in Q_{[M]}$ and any $q, q' \in A_1$, it follows that

$$P(q, A_2) \in P_{[M]}(A_1, A_2), \quad P(q', A_2) \in P_{[M]}(A_1, A_2).$$

Using the above set of inclusions, we can derive the following bound for any Γ_ε-closed set $A_2 \in Q_{[M]}$:

$$\left| P(q, A_2) - P(q', A_2) \right| \leq \Delta([M]),$$

Directly leveraging Theorem 3 this yields, $\forall k > 0$,

$$\left| P^k(q, A_2) - P^k(q', A_2) \right| \leq \Delta([M]^k) \leq \tau^k + \varepsilon\lambda m \sum_{l=0}^{k-1} \tau^l.$$

Thus, the following holds for all $(q_1, q_2) \in \Gamma_\varepsilon$:

$$d_{\Gamma_\varepsilon}^k(q_1, q_2) = \max_{\forall A \ \Gamma_\varepsilon - closed} \left| P^k(q_1, A) - P^k(q_2, A) \right|$$

$$\leq \tau^k + \varepsilon\lambda m \sum_{l=0}^{k-1} \tau^l,$$

which proves the statement. $\square$

The bound provided above is finite for any $k > 0$ if $\tau < 1$. Therefore, if the MSC $[M]$ is sufficiently ergodic (namely its coefficient of ergodicity is less then $1 - \varepsilon\lambda m$), then Theorem 4 also holds for $k \to \infty$ since the bound $d_\varepsilon^k(q_1, q_2)$ is finite in time for all $(q_1, q_2) \in \Gamma_\varepsilon$. In this instance, the result is stronger than the bound obtained in Theorem 1. Furthermore, a positive aspect of the above bound is that, under the ergodicity assumption, it does not accumulate in time, unlike other metrics [11, 28] that have to rely on discounting over time [12].

4. ROBUSTNESS OF PCTL FORMULAE

Robustness issue have been the main driver that has lead to an approximate concept of probabilistic bisimulation. In this section we go further along this research path by "robustifying" PCTL model checking.

4.1 Probabilistic Computation Tree Logic

Let $M = (Q, P, L)$ be a LMC, where $L = 2^{AP}$ and AP is a finite set of atomic propositions. We recall now syntax, semantics and model checking for PCTL.

DEFINITION 11. *[PCTL syntax, [16]] The syntax of PCTL is as follows:*

$$\Phi = \mathbf{true} \mid a \mid \neg\Phi \mid \Phi \wedge \Phi \mid \mathbb{P}_{\sim p}[\phi]$$

$$\phi = X\Phi \mid \Phi U^{\leq k}\Phi$$

where a is an atomic proposition, $\sim \in \{<, \leq, \geq, >\}$, $p \in [0, 1]$ and $k \in \mathbb{N} \cup \{\infty\}$.

PCTL formulae are interpreted over the states of a LMC. For the presentation of the syntax we distinguish between state formulae Φ and path formulae ϕ, which are evaluated over states and paths, respectively. A path $\mathbf{q}$ is an infinite sequence of states in the LMC $q_1 q_2 q_3 \ldots$, such that $P(q_i, q_{i+1}) > 0$. Let $\mathbf{q}(i)$ denote the i-th state in $\mathbf{q}$, i.e., $\mathbf{q}(i) = q_i$. For a state q and a PCTL formula Φ, we write $q \models \Phi$ to indicate that q satisfies Φ. Similarly, for a path $\mathbf{q}$ satisfying the path formula ϕ, we write $\mathbf{q} \models \phi$.

DEFINITION 12. *[PCTL semantics, [16]] The semantics of PCTL over LMC is defined as follows:*

$$
\begin{aligned}
q &\models \mathbf{true} & &\forall q \in Q \\
q &\models a & \Leftrightarrow \ & a \in L(q) \\
q &\models \neg\Phi & \Leftrightarrow \ & q \not\models \Phi \\
q &\models \Phi \wedge \Psi & \Leftrightarrow \ & q \models \Phi \wedge q \models \Psi \\
q &\models \mathbb{P}_{\sim p}[\phi] & \Leftrightarrow \ & Prob(\{\mathbf{q} : \mathbf{q}(0) = q : \mathbf{q} \models \phi\}) \sim p \\
\mathbf{q} &\models X\Phi & \Leftrightarrow \ & \mathbf{q}(1) \models \Phi \\
\mathbf{q} &\models \Phi U^{\leq k}\Psi & \Leftrightarrow \ & \exists i \in \mathbb{N} : (i \leq k \ \wedge \ \mathbf{q}(i) \models \Psi \ \wedge \\
& & & \forall j < i, (\mathbf{q}(j) \models \Phi)).
\end{aligned}
$$

where $Prob(\{\mathbf{q} : \mathbf{q}(0) = q : \mathbf{q} \models \phi\})$ is the probability that q generates a path $\mathbf{q}$ satisfying formula ϕ. We now summarize a model checking algorithm for PCTL over LMC [6, 7, 16]. The inputs to the algorithm are a LMC $M = (Q, P, L)$ and a PCTL formula Φ. The output is the set of states $Sat(\Phi) = \{q \in Q : q \models \Phi\}$, i.e. the set containing all the states of the model which satisfy Φ. The overall structure of the algorithm is identical to the model checking algorithm for CTL [5] (the non-probabilistic temporal logic which PCTL is based on) and can be summarized as follows:

$$Sat(\texttt{true}) = Q$$
$$Sat(a) = \{q \in Q : a \in L(q)\}$$
$$Sat(\neg \Phi) = Q \setminus Sat(\Phi)$$
$$Sat(\Phi \wedge \Psi) = Sat(\Phi) \cap Sat(\Psi)$$
$$Sat(\mathbb{P}_{\sim p}[\phi]) = \{q \in Q : Prob^M(q, \phi) \sim p\},$$

where $Prob^M(q, \phi)$ is the probability that q generates a path satisfying formula ϕ. Model checking for the majority of these formulae is trivial to implement and is, in fact, the same as for the non-probabilistic logic CTL. The exception is made up of formulae with the form $\mathbb{P}_{\sim p}[\phi]$. For these formulae, we have to calculate for all states q of the LMC, the probability $Prob^M(q, \phi)$, then compare these values to the bound $\sim p$ in the formula. We now describe how to compute these values for the two cases: $\mathbb{P}_{\sim p}[X\Phi]$ and $\mathbb{P}_{\sim p}[\Phi U^{\leq k}\Psi]$. Because of the recursive nature of the PCTL model checking algorithm, we can assume that the relevant sets $Sat(\Phi)$ and $Sat(\Psi)$ are already known.

$\mathbb{P}_{\sim p}[X\Phi]$ **formulae.** In this case, we need to compute the probability $Prob^M(q, X\Phi)$ for each $q \in Q$. This requires the probabilities of the immediate transitions from q:

$$Prob^M(q, X\Phi) = P(q, Sat(\Phi)). \qquad (3)$$

$\mathbb{P}_{\sim p}[\Phi U^{\leq k}\Psi], k \in \mathbb{N} \cup \{\infty\}$ **formulae.** For such formulae we need to determine the probabilities $Prob^M(q, \Phi U^{\leq k}\Psi)$ for all states q, where $k \in \mathbb{N} \cup \{\infty\}$. To this aim, we need the following definition:

DEFINITION 13. *[Formula-dependent LMC, [16]] Given a LMC $M = (Q, P, L)$ and a PCTL formula Φ, let $M[\Phi] = (Q, P[\Phi], L)$, where if $q \not\models \Phi$, then $P[\Phi](q, q') = P(q, q')$ for all $q' \in Q$, and if $q \models \Phi$, then $P[\Phi](q, q) = 1$ and $P[\Phi](q, q') = 0$ for all $q' \neq q$.*

Using this transformation we characterize $Prob^M(q, \Phi U^{\leq k}\Psi)$ as follows.

PROPOSITION 2. *[16] For any LMC $M = (Q, P, L)$, state $q \in Q$, PCTL formulae Φ and Ψ, and $k \in \mathbb{N}$:*

$$Prob^M(q, \Phi U^{\leq k}\Psi) = P^k_{M[\neg\Phi\vee\Psi]}(q, Sat(\Psi)). \qquad (4)$$

Model checking can be performed directly on $M[\neg\Phi \vee \Psi]$. For the unbounded until case, we obtain:

$$Prob^M(q, \Phi U^{\leq \infty}\Psi) = \lim_{k\to\infty} P^k_{M[\neg\Phi\vee\Psi]}(q, Sat(\Psi)).$$

We remark that $\lim_{k\to\infty} P^k_{M[\neg\Phi\vee\Psi]}(q, Sat(\Psi))$ always exists and is unique. This can be shown using the theory of labeled Markov Chains, and is also implied by the existence and uniqueness of a solution to unbounded until formulae [16, 22].

4.2 Robust PCTL

Given a PCTL formula Φ, a LMC M and a APB Γ_ε over M, we propose in the following definition an iterative recipe to construct a strengthened formula $S_\varepsilon(\Phi)$ and a relaxed formula $R_\varepsilon(\Phi)$. This definition will be used in the following to define the set of formulae that are preserved by an APB with precision ε.

DEFINITION 14. *[Strengthened and Relaxed PCTL formulae] Given a LMC M, a PCTL formula Φ and a non-negative real $\varepsilon > 0$, we define the ε-strengthened PCTL formula $S_\varepsilon(\Phi)$ and the ε-relaxed PCTL formula $R_\varepsilon(\Phi)$ by structural induction as follows:*

1. $S_\varepsilon(\texttt{true}) = \texttt{true}$,
   $R_\varepsilon(\texttt{true}) = \texttt{true}$.

2. $S_\varepsilon(a) = a$,
   $R_\varepsilon(a) = a$.

3. $S_\varepsilon(\neg\Phi) = \neg R_\varepsilon(\Phi)$,
   $R_\varepsilon(\neg\Phi) = \neg S_\varepsilon(\Phi)$.

4. $S_\varepsilon(\Phi \wedge \Psi) = S_\varepsilon(\Phi) \wedge S_\varepsilon(\Psi)$,
   $R_\varepsilon(\Phi \wedge \Psi) = R_\varepsilon(\Phi) \wedge R_\varepsilon(\Psi)$.

5. $S_\varepsilon(\mathbb{P}_{\sim p}[X\Phi]) = \mathbb{P}_{\sim p'}[X S_\varepsilon(\Phi)]$, *where:*

   $$p' = \begin{cases} p - \varepsilon & \text{if } \sim \in \{<, \leq\} \\ p + \varepsilon & \text{if } \sim \in \{>, \geq\}, \end{cases}$$

   $R_\varepsilon(\mathbb{P}_{\sim p}[X\Phi]) = \mathbb{P}_{\sim p'}[X R_\varepsilon(\Phi)]$, *where:*

   $$p' = \begin{cases} p + \varepsilon & \text{if } \sim \in \{<, \leq\} \\ p - \varepsilon & \text{if } \sim \in \{>, \geq\}. \end{cases}$$

6. $S_\varepsilon(\mathbb{P}_{\sim p}[\Phi U^{\leq k}\Psi]) = \mathbb{P}_{\sim p'}[S_\varepsilon(\Phi) U^{\leq k} S_\varepsilon(\Psi)]$, *where $k \in \mathbb{N} \cup \{\infty\}$ and:*

   $$p' = \begin{cases} p - d_\varepsilon^k(M) & \text{if } \sim \in \{<, \leq\} \\ p + d_\varepsilon^k(M) & \text{if } \sim \in \{>, \geq\}, \end{cases}$$

   $R_\varepsilon(\mathbb{P}_{\sim p}[\Phi U^{\leq k}\Psi]) = \mathbb{P}_{\sim p'}[R_\varepsilon(\Phi) U^{\leq k} R_\varepsilon(\Psi)]$, *where $k \in \mathbb{N} \cup \{\infty\}$ and:*

   $$p' = \begin{cases} p + d_\varepsilon^k(M) & \text{if } \sim \in \{<, \leq\} \\ p - d_\varepsilon^k(M) & \text{if } \sim \in \{>, \geq\}. \end{cases}$$

We say that a strengthened or relaxed formula $S_\varepsilon(\Phi)$ or $R_\varepsilon(\Phi)$ is *consistent* if in each step of the recursive substitution above $p' \in [0, 1]$. Note that *inconsistent* strengthened or relaxed formulae are either identically true (e.g. $\mathbb{P}_{\leq 1.1}[\cdot]$, $\mathbb{P}_{\geq -0.1}[\cdot]$) or identically false (e.g. $\mathbb{P}_{\geq 1.1}[\cdot]$, $\mathbb{P}_{\leq -0.1}[\cdot]$).

EXAMPLE 5. *Consider the first perturbed LMC $(Q, \tilde{P}, L)$ introduced in Example 2 and the formula*

$$\Phi = \mathbb{P}_{\geq\gamma}[start\, U^{\leq k}\, won].$$

Let us first compute the distance $d_\varepsilon^k(Q, \tilde{P}, L) := d_\varepsilon^k$ in (1), employing the finite-time bounds derived in Theorem 1, which we tailor to the case study at hand as discussed in Example 4. A few cases need to be considered. Select $A = \{won\}$. Notice that if $(i, j) \in \{(4, 10), (5, 9), (6, 8)\}$, then

$$\left| P^k(\{i\}, A) - P^k(\{j\}, A) \right| \leq \varepsilon \left(\frac{5}{9} + 3\varepsilon \right)^{k-1}.$$

If $A = \{\text{lost}\}$, then

$$\left| P^k(\{i\}, A) - P^k(\{j\}, A) \right| \leq \varepsilon \left(\frac{11}{18} + 3\varepsilon \right)^{k-1}.$$

If $A = \{(4, 10)\}$ or $A = \{(5, 9)\}$ or $A = \{(6, 8)\}$, then

$$\left| P^k(\{i\}, A) - P^k(\{j\}, A) \right| \leq \varepsilon \left(\frac{5}{6} + 3\varepsilon \right)^{k-1}.$$

The instance $A = \{\text{start}\}$ yields a trivial bound. In conclusion, we derive that $d_\varepsilon^k = \varepsilon \left(\frac{5}{6} + 3\varepsilon \right)^{k-1}$. It follows that

$$S_\varepsilon(\Phi) = \mathbb{P}_{\geq \gamma + d_\varepsilon^k}[\text{start}\, U^{\leq k}\, \text{won}],$$

whereas

$$R_\varepsilon(\Phi) = \mathbb{P}_{\geq \gamma - d_\varepsilon^k}[\text{start}\, U^{\leq k}\, \text{won}].$$

Notice that assuming $\varepsilon \leq 1/18$, the distance bound is decreasing with time k. Furthermore, $S_0(\Phi) = R_0(\Phi) = \Phi$.

DEFINITION 15. [ε-robustness of a PCTL formula] Given a LMC M, a PCTL formula Φ and a non-negative real $\varepsilon > 0$, we say that Φ is ε-robust with respect to M if, for any $q \in Q$ and for any sub-formula Ψ of Φ, either $q \in Sat(S_\varepsilon(\Psi))$ or $q \notin Sat(R_\varepsilon(\Psi))$.

The above definition requires that the case $q \models R_\varepsilon(\Psi) \land \neg S_\varepsilon(\Psi)$ can not occur. The following Theorem establishes the main result of this paper.

THEOREM 5. Given a LMC M, an APB Γ_ε and a PCTL formula Φ, let Φ be ε-robust with respect to M. Then for each $q_1, q_2 \in Q$ such that $q_1 \equiv_\varepsilon q_2$ the following holds:

$$q_1 \in Sat(\Phi) \Leftrightarrow q_2 \in Sat(\Phi).$$

PROOF. (By induction on formula depth).
According to [6, 7, 16], model checking is performed over the parse tree of Φ where the root node is labeled with Φ itself, and leaves of the tree are labeled with either true or an atomic proposition a.

We prove the theorem by structural induction on Φ. For the base case, $\Phi = a$ for an atomic proposition a. Since $q_1 \equiv_\varepsilon q_2$, it follows that $L(q_1) = L(q_2)$, hence $q_1 \in Sat(a)$ iff $q_2 \in Sat(a)$. Then, we prove the induction step for the negation, next and until (bounded and unbounded) operators. The induction step for the other formulae is trivial.

$\neg \Phi$ formulae (negation):
Let $q_1 \in Sat(\neg \Phi)$, then $q_1 \notin Sat(\Phi)$. The induction hypothesis implies that $\forall q_1, q_2$ such that $q_1 \equiv_\varepsilon q_2$ then

$$q_1 \in Sat(\Phi) \Leftrightarrow q_2 \in Sat(\Phi),$$

which implies that

$$q_1 \notin Sat(\Phi) \Leftrightarrow q_2 \notin Sat(\Phi).$$

The above statement directly implies that

$$q_1 \in Sat(\neg \Phi) \Leftrightarrow q_2 \in Sat(\neg \Phi).$$

$\mathbb{P}_{\sim p}[X\Phi]$ formulae (next operator):
Let $q_1 \in Sat(\mathbb{P}_{\sim p}[X\Phi])$, then equation (3) implies that:

$$P(q_1, Sat(\Phi)) \sim p.$$

The induction hypothesis implies that $\forall q_1', q_2'$ such that $q_1' \equiv_\varepsilon q_2'$ the following holds:

$$q_1' \in Sat(\Phi) \Leftrightarrow q_2' \in Sat(\Phi). \tag{5}$$

Therefore $Sat(\Phi)$ is a Γ_ε-closed set. Given any $q_2 \in Q$ such that $q_1 \equiv_\varepsilon q_2$, Definition 3 implies that:

$$|P(q_1, Sat(\Phi)) - P(q_2, Sat(\Phi))| \leq \varepsilon. \tag{6}$$

It follows that, if $\sim \in \{<, \leq\}$, then:

$$P(q_2, Sat(\Phi)) \sim P(q_1, Sat(\Phi)) + \varepsilon.$$

Since $q_1 \in Sat(\mathbb{P}_{\sim p}[X\Phi])$, the robustness assumption implies that $q_1 \in Sat(S_\varepsilon(\mathbb{P}_{\sim p}[X\Phi]))$, thus:

$$P(q_1, Sat(\Phi)) + \varepsilon \sim p - \varepsilon + \varepsilon = p.$$

Analogously, if $\sim \in \{>, \geq\}$, then:

$$P(q_2, Sat(\Phi)) \sim p + \varepsilon - \varepsilon = p.$$

The above reasoning implies that

$$q_1 \in Sat(\mathbb{P}_{\sim p}[X\Phi]) \Rightarrow q_2 \in Sat(\mathbb{P}_{\sim p}[X\Phi]).$$

To complete the induction step, we need to prove that

$$q_1 \notin Sat(\mathbb{P}_{\sim p}[X\Phi]) \Rightarrow q_2 \notin Sat(\mathbb{P}_{\sim p}[X\Phi]).$$

The proof is analogous and is thus omitted.
$\mathbb{P}_{\sim p}[\Phi U^{\leq k}\Psi], k \in \mathbb{N} \cup \{\infty\}$ formulae (bounded and unbounded until operators):
Let $q \in Sat(\mathbb{P}_{\sim p}[\Phi U^{\leq k}\Psi])$, $k \in \mathbb{N} \cup \{\infty\}$, then equation (4) implies that:

$$P_{M[\neg \Phi \lor \Psi]}^k(q, Sat(\Psi)) \sim p.$$

The induction hypothesis implies that $\forall q_1', q_2'$ such that $q_1' \equiv_\varepsilon q_2'$ the following hold:

$$q_1' \in Sat(\neg \Phi) \Leftrightarrow q_2' \in Sat(\neg \Phi),$$
$$q_1' \in Sat(\Psi) \Leftrightarrow q_2' \in Sat(\Psi).$$

Therefore $Sat(\neg \Phi)$ and $Sat(\Psi)$ are Γ_ε-closed sets, and the following holds:

$$\forall (q_1, q_2) \in \Gamma_\varepsilon,\ q_1' \in Sat(\neg \Phi \lor \Psi)$$
$$\Leftrightarrow q_1' \in Sat(\neg \Phi) \lor q_1' \in Sat(\Psi)$$
$$\Leftrightarrow q_2' \in Sat(\neg \Phi) \lor q_2' \in Sat(\Psi)$$
$$\Leftrightarrow q_2' \in Sat(\neg \Phi \lor \Psi).$$

Therefore $Sat(\neg \Phi \lor \Psi)$ is a Γ_ε-closed set, and the following property holds for the LMC $M[\neg \Phi \lor \Psi]$:

$$\forall (q_1, q_2) \in \Gamma_\varepsilon,\ \text{either } q_1, q_2 \in Sat(\neg \Phi \lor \Psi)$$
$$\text{or } q_1, q_2 \notin Sat(\neg \Phi \lor \Psi).$$

We prove now that Γ_ε is an APB over the LMC $M[\neg \Phi \lor \Psi]$. Pick any $(q_1, q_2) \in \Gamma_\varepsilon$. If $q_1, q_2 \in Sat(\neg \Phi \lor \Psi)$, then by Definition 13:

$$P[\neg \Phi \lor \Psi](q_1, q_1) = P[\neg \Phi \lor \Psi](q_2, q_2) = 1,$$
$$\forall q' \neq q_1,\ P[\neg \Phi \lor \Psi](q_1, q') = 0,$$
$$\forall q' \neq q_2,\ P[\neg \Phi \lor \Psi](q_2, q') = 0.$$

Therefore, for any Γ_ε-closed set $A \neq Sat(\neg \Phi \lor \Psi)$,

$$|P[\neg \Phi \lor \Psi](q_1, A) - P[\neg \Phi \lor \Psi](q_2, A)| = 0 - 0 \leq \varepsilon,$$

and

$$|P[\neg \Phi \lor \Psi](q_1, Sat(\neg \Phi \lor \Psi)) - P[\neg \Phi \lor \Psi](q_2, Sat(\neg \Phi \lor \Psi))|$$
$$= 1 - 1 \leq \varepsilon.$$

If $q_1, q_2 \notin Sat(\neg\Phi \vee \Psi)$, then by Definition 13:

$$\forall q' \in Q, \; P[\neg\Phi \vee \Psi](q_1, q') = P(q_1, q') \text{ and}$$
$$P[\neg\Phi \vee \Psi](q_2, q') = P(q_2, q').$$

Therefore, for any Γ_ε-closed set A

$$|P[\neg\Phi \vee \Psi](q_1, A) - P[\neg\Phi \vee \Psi](q_2, A)|$$
$$= |P(q_1, A) - P(q_2, A)| \leq \varepsilon.$$

Since the condition of Definition 3 is satisfied, then Γ_ε is an APB over the LMC $M[\neg\Phi \vee \Psi]$. Therefore, Theorem 4 implies that for any Γ_ε-closed set A the following holds, for each $k \in \mathbb{N} \cup \{\infty\}$:

$$\left| P^k_{M[\neg\Phi \vee \Psi]}(q_1, A) - P^k_{M[\neg\Phi \vee \Psi]}(q_2, A) \right| \leq d^k_\varepsilon(M[\neg\Phi \vee \Psi]), \tag{7}$$

where $P^k_{M[\neg\Phi \vee \Psi]}(q, A)$ is the probability that the set A is reached in k steps by an execution of $M[\neg\Phi \vee \Psi]$ starting from state q. If $\sim \in \{<, \leq\}$ then using the robustness assumption and by applying Equation (7) with $A = Sat(\Psi)$, it follows that:

$$P^k_{M[\neg\Phi \vee \Psi]}(q_2, Sat(\Psi)) \sim P^k_{M[\neg\Phi \vee \Psi]}(q_1, Sat(\Psi)) + d^k_\varepsilon(M)$$
$$\sim p - d^k_\varepsilon(M) + d^k_\varepsilon(M) = p.$$

Analogously, if $\sim \in \{>, \geq\}$, then:

$$P^k_{M[\neg\Phi \vee \Psi]}(q_2, Sat(\Psi)) \sim p + d^k_\varepsilon(M) - d^k_\varepsilon(M) = p.$$

The above reasoning implies that

$$q_1 \in Sat(\mathbb{P}_{\sim p}[\Phi U^{\leq k} \Psi]) \Rightarrow q_2 \in Sat(\mathbb{P}_{\sim p}[\Phi U^{\leq k} \Psi]).$$

To complete the induction step, we need to prove that

$$q_1 \notin Sat(\mathbb{P}_{\sim p}[\Phi U^{\leq k} \Psi]) \Rightarrow q_2 \notin Sat(\mathbb{P}_{\sim p}[\Phi U^{\leq k} \Psi]).$$

The proof is analogous and is thus omitted.

The above steps imply that $q_1 \in Sat(\Phi) \Leftrightarrow q_2 \in Sat(\Phi)$, and this completes the proof. $\square$

The above result allows the verification of a PCTL formula Φ over a numerical model M_ε obtained from a concrete model M, where the transition probabilities of M_ε are obtained by approximation with precision ε. If Φ is ε robust over M_ε, then the PCTL model checking results over M_ε can be exported over M. Otherwise, it is necessary to use a more refined numerical model. Characterizing the existence of a strictly positive precision $\varepsilon' > 0$ that allows PCTL model checking of Φ over $M_{\varepsilon'}$ is an interesting question for future work.

EXAMPLE 6. *Consider the LMC* $(Q, \tilde{P}, L)$ *discussed in Example 5, which is a perturbed version of* (Q, P, L) *in Example 1. As suggested in [10], the definitions of (probabilistic bisimulation and of) APB can be extended to relate two different LMC: this is achieved by considering an APB over the cross product of the two LMC. We are here interested in verifying properties of* (Q, P, L) *over* $(Q, \tilde{P}, L)$*. Suppose that* $\tilde{P}$ *is obtained by quantization of* P*. This example argues that an increase in the quantization precision allows verifying on* $(Q, \tilde{P}, L)$ *a larger set of PCTL properties for* (Q, P, L)*.*

Assume that the quantization is obtained by truncating the elements of P *within its third decimal digit: for instance* $5/36 = 0.13\overline{8}$ *is approximated by 0.139, whereas* $1/9 = 0.\overline{1}$

is approximated by 0.111. It is easy to realize that $\tilde{P}$ *can be related to an error bound* $\|E\|_\infty = 5 \cdot 10^{-4}$ *and thus to an APB with approximation precision* $\varepsilon = 2 \cdot 10^{-3}$*. Similarly, if* $\tilde{P}$ *is obtained by truncating the elements of* P *within its* i^{th} *decimal digit, then* $\varepsilon = 2 \cdot 10^{-i}$*. Recall that in Example 5 we have established that* $d^k_\varepsilon = \varepsilon \left(\frac{5}{6} + 3\varepsilon\right)^{k-1}$*. The bounded until formula*

$$\Phi = \mathbb{P}_{\geq \gamma}[start\, U^{\leq k}\, won]$$

is robust if $d^k_\varepsilon \leq \gamma \leq 1 - d^k_\varepsilon$*: this can be established by application of Definition 15 over any* $q \in Q$*. Figure 5 plots this upper bound on* γ*, over different approximation digits and time horizons. Select* $\gamma = 0.7$*, and assume that the approximation digit is strictly greater than one. If* Φ *is true on* $(Q, \tilde{P}, L)$ *for any* $k > 1$*, being* Φ *robust then* Φ *is also true on* (Q, P, L) *for any* $k > 1$*. If instead the approximation digit is one then regardless of the value of* Φ *on* $(Q, \tilde{P}, L)$ *for any* $k > 1$*, since* Φ *not robust, we cannot draw any conclusion on the validity of* Φ *over* (Q, P, L)*.*

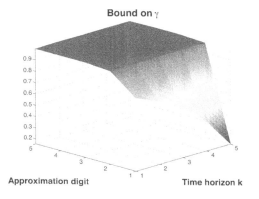

Bound on γ

Approximation digit

Time horizon k

Figure 5: Robustness bounds on γ for formula $\Phi = \mathbb{P}_{\geq \gamma}[\text{start}\, U^{\leq k}\, \text{won}]$.

Consider now the formula $\Phi = \mathbb{P}_{\leq \gamma}[X\, lost]$*. Then* $S_\varepsilon(\Phi) = \mathbb{P}_{\leq \gamma - \varepsilon}[X\, lost]$ *and* $R_\varepsilon(\Phi) = \mathbb{P}_{\leq \gamma + \varepsilon}[X\, lost]$*. Robustness can again be studied via Definition 15, applied on any* $q \in Q$*. The allowed interval for* ε *is* $[0, 5/12]$*. In particular, if* $0 \leq \varepsilon < 1/36$*, then*

$$\gamma \in [\varepsilon, 1/9] \cup [1/9 + \varepsilon, 1/6 - \varepsilon] \cup [1/6 + \varepsilon, 1 - \varepsilon],$$

whereas if $1/36 \leq \varepsilon < 1/18$*, then*

$$\gamma \in [\varepsilon, 1/9 - \varepsilon] \cup [1/6 + \varepsilon, 1 - \varepsilon],$$

and if $1/18 \leq \varepsilon \leq 5/12$*, then*

$$\gamma \in [1/6 + \varepsilon, 1 - \varepsilon].$$

With focus on the approximated LMC $(Q, \tilde{P}, L)$*, again as the approximation increases to* i *digits,* Φ *grows in robustness. Given a particular approximation digit, if* Φ *is robust then we can safely claim that checking* $j \models \Phi$ *and* $k \models \Phi$ *is equivalent for any* $j, k \in \{4, 10, 5, 9, 6, 8\}$*.*

5. CONCLUSIONS

With focus on labeled Markov Chains (LMC) in discrete-time, this work has utilized the notion of approximate probabilistic bisimulation (APB) to introduce bounds on probabilistic realization metrics in time between approximately bisimilar states. As the main contribution of the paper, we have shown that the presence of an APB implies the preservation of (properly defined) robust PCTL formulae. This result allows the verification of a PCTL formula executed over an abstract model obtained as an approximation of a concrete model, e.g. over a numerical model where the transition probabilities are obtained by finite-precision approximation.

As for future work, it is of interest to understand what model properties (ergodicity, presence of absorbing classes) yield APB resulting in finite bounds for the probabilistic realization metrics. Furthermore, as discussed in Section 1, we aim to leverage on the abstraction procedure we developed in [1] and on the results developed in this paper to verify properties of continuous models as general as Stochastic Hybrid Systems by using classical PCTL model checking algorithms over a finite LMC abstraction which satisfies some accuracy constraints.

6. REFERENCES

[1] A. Abate, A. D'Innocenzo, and M.D. Di Benedetto. Approximate abstractions of stochastic hybrid systems. *IEEE Transactions on Automatic Control*, 56(11):2688–2694, November 2011.

[2] A. Aziz, K. Sanwal, V. Singhal, and R. Brayton. Model-checking continuous time Markov chains. *ACM Transactions on Computational Logic*, 1(1):162–170, 2000.

[3] C. Baier and J.-P. Katoen. *Principles of Model Checking*. The MIT Press, Cambridge, MA, 2008.

[4] T.M. Chan. All-pairs shortest paths for unweighted undirected graphs in o(mn) time. In *Proceedings of the seventeenth annual ACM-SIAM Symposium on Discrete Algorithm (SODA '06)*, pages 514–523, 2006.

[5] E. Clarke, E. Emerson, and A. Sistla. Automatic verification of finite-state concurrent systems using temporal logics. *ACM Transactions on Programming Languages and Systems*, 8(2):244–263, 1968.

[6] C. Courcoubetis and M. Yannakakis. Verifying temporal properties of finite state probabilistic programs. In *Proceedings of the 29th Annual Symposium on Foundations of Computer Science (FOCS '88)*, pages 338–345, December 1988.

[7] C. Courcoubetis and M. Yannakakis. The complexity of probabilistic verification. *Journal of the ACM*, 42(4):857–907, 1995.

[8] L. de Alfaro, M. Faella, and M. Stoelinga. Linear and branching system metrics. *IEEE Transactions on Software Engineering*, 35(2):258–273, 2009.

[9] S. Derisavi, H. Hermanns, and W.H. Sanders. Optimal state-space lumping in Markov chains. *Information Processing Letters*, 87(6):309–315, September 2003.

[10] J. Desharnais, A. Edalat, and P. Panangaden. Bisimulation for labeled Markov processes. *Information and Computation*, 179(2):163–193, December 2002.

[11] J. Desharnais, V. Gupta, R. Jagadeesan, and P. Panangaden. Metrics for labeled Markov processes. *Theoretical Computer Science*, 318(3):323–354, 2004.

[12] J. Desharnais, F. Laviolette, and M. Tracol. Approximate analysis of probabilistic processes: logic, simulation and games. In *Proceedings of the International Conference on Quantitative Evaluation of SysTems (QEST '08)*, pages 264–273, Sept. 2008.

[13] R. Durrett. *Probability: Theory and Examples - Third Edition*. Duxbury Press, 2004.

[14] A. Giacalone, C.-C. Jou, and S.A. Smolka. Algebraic reasoning for probabilistic concurrent systems. In *Proceedings of the IFIP TC2 Working Conference on Programming Concepts and Methods*, pages 443–458, 1990.

[15] A. Girard and G.J. Pappas. Approximation metrics for discrete and continuous systems. *IEEE Transactions on Automatic Control*, 52(5):782–798, 2007.

[16] H. Hansson and B. Jonsson. A logic for reasoning about time and reliability. *Formal Aspects of Computing*, 6(5):512–535, 1994.

[17] F. Harary. *Graph Theory*. Addison-Wesley, 1994.

[18] H.J. Hartfiel. *Markov set-Chains*, volume 1695 of *Lecture Notes in Mathematics*. Springer-Verlag Berlin Heidelberg, 1998.

[19] T. A. Henzinger, R. Majumdar, and V. Prabhu. Quantifying similarities between timed systems. In *Proceedings of the Third International Conference on Formal Modeling and Analysis of Timed Systems (FORMATS '05)*, volume 3829 of *Lecture Notes in Computer Science*, pages 226–241. Springer, 2005.

[20] J.-P. Katoen, E.M. Hahn, H. Hermanns, D.N. Jansen, and I. Zapreev. The ins and outs of the probabilistic model checker MRMC. In *Proceedings of the International Conference on Quantitative Evaluation of SysTems (QEST '09)*, pages 167–176, 2009.

[21] J.-P. Katoen, T. Kemna, I.S. Zapreev, and D.N. Jansen. Bisimulation minimisation mostly speeds up probabilistic model checking. In Orna Grumberg and Michael Huth, editors, *Proceedings of Tools and Algorithms for the Construction and Analysis of Systems (TACAS '07)*, volume 4424 of *LNCS*, pages 87–101. Springer, 2007.

[22] M. Kwiatkowska, G. Norman, and D. Parker. Stochastic model checking. In M. Bernardo and J. Hillston, editors, *Formal Methods for the Design of Computer, Communication and Software Systems: Performance Evaluation (SFM '07)*, volume 4486 of *Lecture Notes in Computer Science*, pages 220–270. Springer Verlag, 2007.

[23] M. Kwiatkowska, G. Norman, and D. Parker. PRISM: Probabilistic model checking for performance and reliability analysis. *ACM SIGMETRICS Performance Evaluation Review*, 2009.

[24] M. Kwiatkowska, G. Norman, and D. Parker. PRISM 4.0: Verification of probabilistic real-time systems. In *Proc. 23rd International Conference on Computer Aided Verification (CAV'11)*, volume 6806 of *LNCS*, pages 585–591. Springer, 2011.

[25] K.G. Larsen and A. Skou. Bisimulation through probabilistic testing. *Information and Computation*, 94:1–28, 1991.

[26] R. Milner. *A Calculus of Communicating Systems*. Springer-Verlag New York, Inc., Secaucus, NJ, 1982.

[27] D. Park. Concurrency and automata on infinite sequences. In *Proceedings of the 5th GI-Conference on Theoretical Computer Science*, pages 167–183, 1981.

[28] F. van Breugel and J. Worrell. Approximating and computing behavioural distances in probabilistic transition systems. *Theoretical Computer Science*, 360(1-3):373–385, 2006.

[29] R. Wimmer and B. Becker. Correctness issues of symbolic bisimulation computation for Markov chains. In *Proceedings of MMB-DFT, LNCS vol. 5987*, pages 287–301, 2010.

NCSWT: An Integrated Modeling and Simulation Tool for Networked Control Systems

Emeka Eyisi*, Jia Bai*, Derek Riley**, Jiannian Weng*, Yan Wei*, Yuan Xue*,
Xenofon Koutsoukos* and Janos Szipanovits*

*Institute for Software Integrated Systems
EECS Department
Vanderbilt University
Nashville, TN, USA

**Department of Computer Science
University of Wisconsin-Parkside
Kenosha, WI, USA

ABSTRACT

This paper presents the Networked Control Systems Windtunnel (NCSWT), an integrated modeling and simulation tool for the evaluation of networked control systems (NCS). NCSWT integrates Matlab/Simulink and ns-2 using the High Level Architecture (HLA). Our implementation of the NCSWT based on HLA guarantees accurate time synchronization and data communication in heterogenous simulations. NCSWT uses the Model Integrated Computing (MIC) techniques to define HLA-based model constructs such as federates representing the simulators and interactions between the simulators. NCSWT also uses MIC techniques to define models representing the control system and network dynamics for the rapid synthesis of simulations.

Categories and Subject Descriptors

I.6.7 [**SIMULATION AND MODELING**]: Simulation Support Systems—*Environments*

General Terms

Design, Experimentation

Keywords

Modeling, Simulation, Networked Control Systems, HLA

1. INTRODUCTION

Networked control systems (NCS) have gained increasing attention in recent years due to their cost effective and flexible applications [6]. NCS are often employed in critical settings, therefore the assurance of properties such as stability, performance, safety and security are essential. Currently, many NCS are designed without considering the effects of the network operating environment (e.g time-varying delays and packet losses). Such limitations in the system design phase can lead to catastrophic consequences when the actual systems are deployed as the overall system behavior depends on network dynamics and uncertainties.

As NCS become increasingly complex, it becomes more challenging to formally analyze their performance, stability, safety and security properties. As a result, there is a pressing need to evaluate both the control and network components of NCS together for a rapidly growing number of applications, such as unmanned aerial vehicles (UAVs) and industrial control systems. Simulation is a powerful technique for evaluation and can be used at various design stages, but it requires the support of appropriate tools during both the design-time and run-time stages in order for the process to be efficient and less prone to errors.

Currently, several simulators have been used for NCS but have limited capabilites. For example, Matlab/Simulink is a popular tool for the evaluation control systems [3]. Although network simulation is provided in Matlab/Simulink using toolboxes such as True-Time [7], the accuracy of the simulation depends on the level of abstraction of the network protocol models. Specifically, TrueTime only supports link layer protocols but not higher level protocols such as TCP or UDP protocols, which are essential for simulating the communication network of a NCS. Packet-level network simulators such as ns-2 [2], provide a detailed implementation of the network stack for packet level data transmission. Yet, using only ns-2 for NCS evaluation requires the control algorithm to be fully implmented in a high-level language such as C++. This becomes very difficult as the complexity of the NCS increases. In order to develop a realistic and accurate simulation of NCS, we need a modeling and simulation environment that can integrate existing tools for the simulation of the control dynamics as well as the networking system of a NCS.

The integration of existing tools for the simulation of NCS, although very beneficial, faces several challenges. The first challenge is the design-time scalability of modeling NCS. This involves the ability to rapidly design and model NCS of various complexity and size. The second challenge is time synchronization of the heterogenous simulation components during execution. Given that the simulators operate in potentially different time scales using disparate time models, time synchronization between the simulators is critical to preserve the correctness of the simulation. The third challenge involves the data communication between the simulators to ensure consistent data semantics during the simulation. Finally, the fourth challenge involves the run-time scalability which is the ability of the simulation environment to handle the simulation of large and complex NCS.

In order to address these challenges, we present an integrated modeling and simulation tool for NCS, called the Networked Control Systems Wind Tunnel (NCSWT) [1], which combines the network simulation capabilities of ns-2 with the control design and simulation capabilities of Matlab/Simulink. NCSWT addresses the challenge of design-time scalability of modeling NCS by adopting the Model Integrated Computing (MIC) techniques [12]. MIC is an approach for the development of complex software systems, applicable in all phases of system design and maintenance. The key idea in MIC is to create Domain-Specific Modeling Languages (DSMLs) using a meta-modeling framework, and then, describe objects in terms of the domain-specific models. We present three DSMLs which abstract a NCS simulation from three design views at two levels: at the low level are the simulation models for the control subsystem and the networking subsystem of a NCS, defined by the the Control Design Modeling Language (CDML) and the Network Design Modeling Language (NDML) respectively; at the high level is the NCS integration model, based on the High Level Architecture (HLA) standards, defined by the NCSWT model integration language (NCSWT MIL). The DSMLs, developed using the Generic Modeling Environment (GME) [15], facilitate the rapid design and modeling of NCS. The DSMLs are designed to ensure the consistency of data semantics among the simulators used in the simulation of a NCS.

NCSWT addresses the challenges involving time synchronization and data communication by adopting the High Level Architecture (HLA) for the implementation of the run-time simulation environment [14]. HLA is a standard for simulation interoperability that allows independently developed simulations, each designed for a particular problem domain, to be combined into a larger and more complex simulation. In HLA, the independent simulators are known as federates and the larger simulation formed by the interconnection of the federates is known as the federation. The HLA standard provides a set of services to accurately handle time management and data distribution among the independent simulators. NCSWT utilizes the time management services provided by the HLA to ensure that the time model in the control system simulated in Matlab/Simulink and the time model in the networking system simulated in ns-2 are synchronized. NCSWT also utilizes the data distribution services to ensure the correct exchange of data between the simulations of the control dynamics and communication network of a NCS.

Finally, we demonstrate the NCSWT tool through an evaluation in Section 4. We list the required software packages for NCSWT tool and discuss the design-time efficiency and run-time efficiency for a specific NCS case study.

2. RELATED WORK

Several efforts have been made towards integrating multiple simulators in order to effectively simulate NCS. A tool chain Picc-SIM was developed in [13], that allows the integration of Matlab/Simulink models with ns-2. PiccSIM also provides a graphical user interface for the design of networked control systems and the automatic code generation of ns-2 and Matlab/Simulink models. In [9], a special simulator coupling, implemented in C/C++ is used to integrate the simulators, ModelSim, Matlab/Simulink and ns-2 to establish the communication between the simulators. Other tool integration projects also targeted for NCS include [10] [5] [8] and references therein.

NCSWT differs from these other simulation tools for NCS in multiple aspects. First, our integration of Matlab/Simulink and ns-2 for the simulation of NCS is based on the HLA standard, and hence, ensures a correct and valid NCS simulation. Secondly, our model-based approach provides a clear model of NCS architecture that tightly integrates the control design and communication network in NCS providing a well-defined abstraction of the information exchange between the two subsystems. Such a design-time modeling environment that supports NCS integration is not available with existing tools. As a result, the interactions between the control system and networking components are described in an ad-hoc manner, resulting in possibly error-prone designs. Finally, the design-time efficiency and automatic code generation based on DSMLS is a strong feature of our tool.

In [16], we presented a preliminary version of NCSWT which is substantially different from the current version. First, the early work in [16] is a pure run-time simulation environment while the current version presents an integrated modeling and simulation tool suite. Second, the current version has a new run-time environment implementation based on only Linux compared with the Linux-Windows-based implementation presented in [16]. This revision eliminates the need of using TCP sockets to perform a proprietary communication protocol between the two simulators and significantly improves the run-time efficiency.

3. NCSWT

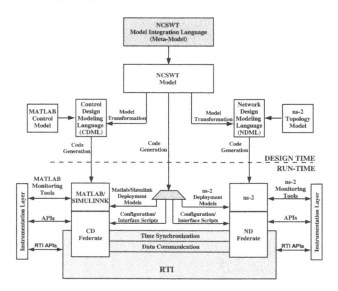

Figure 1: Overview of NCSWT

Figure. 1 shows an overview of the NCSWT tool architecture. The architecture is composed of two main parts, the design-time models and the run-time components. We provide a brief description of NCSWT, a more detailed description of the tool along with extensive experimental validations and results from case studies are provided in [1].

3.1 Design-Time Models

In Figure. 1, the design-time models are used to define the NCS and its components in order to facilitate the simulation of a NCS at run-time. The design-time models are defined by three DSMLs.

3.1.1 NCSWT Model Integration Language (NCSWT MIL)

The NCSWT MIL specifies the NCS in terms of HLA-based constructs, such as federates representing the simulators for each of the components of the NCS and interactions representing the communication between the simulators. A model created using NCSWT MIL is refered to as the base architecture of the NCS. From the base architecture model, the executables for configuring the run-time environment for a specific NCS are generated. The NCSWT MIL is an extension of the work in [11] which introduces a DSML for HLA-based simulations. The NCSWT MIL describes the tight coupling between the control design and the networking subsystems of the NCS by defining how the two subsystems interact. Two types of federates can be modeled in the NCSWT MIL, the *CDFederate* and the *NDFederate*. The *CDFederate* models an instance of the Matlab/Simulink simulator for each corresponding control design component of NCS while the *NDFederate* models an instance of the ns-2 simulator for simulating the communication network of NCS.

Three type of interactions can be modeled in the NCSWT MIL to represent information exchange in NCS, *NetworkInteraction*, *CrossLayerInteraction* and *ControlDesignInteraction*. The *NetworkInteraction* models the exchange of packets over the communication network. The *CrossLayerInteraction* models the information exchange between the network and application layers of a network protocol stack and the *ControlDesignInteraction* models the information exchanged between components of the control system that are transmitted or received, by other means other than the communication network.

3.1.2 Control Design Modeling Language (CDML)

The CDML defines the modeling concepts for specifying the dynamic behavior of the control design components. These include the dynamics of the plant (system to be controlled) and the digital controller. A model created by CDML is a refinement of the base architecture model of a NCS, created in the NCSWT MIL, with the details regarding the dynamics of the control system added. In order to maintain consistency with the base architecture model defined in the NCSWT MIL, a model transformation is used to transform the base architecture model to a model in CDML. Then the control design concepts in CDML are used to specify the dynamics of the components in the NCS. In CDML, using a set of modeling primitives such as T_s (Sampling Time), ModelName, ModelLibraryName etc., a user can specify the model and parameters that define the dynamic behavior of a control system component. Using the defined parameters in CDML, executable Matlab/Simulink code can be generated for implementing the control system.

3.1.3 Network Design Modeling Language (NDML)

The NDML defines the modeling concepts for specifying the dynamics of the communication network. This includes the capacity, loss rate models, routing and other additional properties to realize a communication network. Similar to CDML, a model transformation is used to transform the base architecture model to a model in NDML. Then the concepts defined in NDML are used to specify the network properties for the NCS. A user can specify the transport agent, loss model of network links and other various network properties to simulate the network dynamics. Run-time network configuration and model scripts can then be generated based on the defined parameters for deployment on ns-2.

3.2 Run-Time Components

In Figure. 1, the run-time components represent the main software components and interfaces for the actual realization of a simulation using the HLA framework. These components include the Run-Time infrastructure (RTI), the federates, and all the necessary configuration and glue code for the interfaces as well as monitoring tools for visualizing and evaluating the results.

3.2.1 Run-Time Infrastructure (RTI) and Federates

The RTI, an implmentation of the HLA standard, manages the coordination of time and data passed between federates. Using interactions, federates communicate between each other through the RTI. A number of commercial and academic RTI implementations are available. Currently, we use Portico 1.0.2, an open source cross-platform HLA implementation which supports both C++ and Java clients [4].

Each federate represents a single instance of the corresponding simulator's interface to the RTI. For example, the *NDFederate* is a software component that interfaces the ns-2 simulator with the RTI.

We briefly describe the NCSWT run-time services provided by the RTI.

(a) Time Synchronization: In a HLA-based federation, each federate has its own logical time. The RTI preserves the causality of the federation by ensuring that no simulation receives an event that occured in the past relative to its own. The RTI ensures the accurate progression of time through the use of a time advance grant request (TAR) and time advance grant (TAG) mechanism [16]. For ns-2, this mechanism is integrated into the ns-2 scheduler while in Matlab/Simulink, the mechanism is integrated as part of the interface code to the Matlab federate.

(b) Data Communication: The RTI uses a publish-and subscribe mechanism for passing messages through the federation in order to ensure the consistent data communication and coordination between the federates [16]. The type of messages exchanged between the federates are defined by the interactions modeled in the NCSWT MIL during the design-time and is integrated in the generated code deployed during the run-time simulation.

4. EVALUATION

The simulation of a NCS using the NCSWT tool requires two major steps. The first step involves the modeling of NCS using the three DSMLs discussed in Section 3.1, followed by the generation of all the necessary models, configurations and glue code for the simulation of the NCS. This step is performed on a computer running a Windows operating system. The second step involves the deployment of the generated models, configurations, and glue code followed by the execution of the simulation. This step is performed on a computer running a Linux operating system.

The NCSWT tool requires the software packages as shown in Table 1. Matlab/Simulink and ns-2 are used for the simulation of the control design and networking subsystems of the NCS respectively. Portico 1.0.2 is the RTI implementation of the HLA used for running the federation. GME is the graphical environment used for the modeling and generation of all the necessary components for the simulation of the NCS. UDM is utilized in the model transformations from NCSWT MIL to CDML and NDML. Microsoft Visual Studio is used for the execution of the code generators and model transformations from the three DSMLs. Eclipse is used for the compilation of the run-time components required for the simulation. We have evaluated the NCSWT tool using various NCS case

Table 1: Required Software Packages

1. Matlab/Simulink, www.mathworks.com
2. ns-2, http://isi.edu/nsnam/ns
3. Portico 1.0.2, www.porticoproject.org
4. Generic Modeling Environment (GME), www.isis.vanderbilt.edu/Projects/gme
4. Universal Data Model (UDM), www.isis.vanderbilt.edu/tools/UDM
5. Microsoft Visual Studio 2008 or later, www.microsoft.com/visualstudio
6. Eclipse, www.eclipse.org

studies some of which include a NCS composed of a single plant and controller and a NCS composed of multiple plants and multiple controllers with asynchronous sampling times [16].

We present some results for a single linear continuous-time plant and single linear discrete-time controller NCS. This NCS involves the digital control of an unmanned aerial vehicle (UAV), representing the plant, over a 802.11b wireless network to track a desired trajectory. In order to provide insights about the efficiency of using the NCSWT tool, we present the design-time efficiency and the run-time efficiency. For the design-time efficiency, we consider the amount of code that is automatically generated for simulating the NCS. Table 2 provides a summary of the size of code and models that are automatically generated from the design-time models. For the run-time efficiency, we consider the actual time it takes to

Table 2: Generated Code for NCS Example

Files	Size
1. Matlab models	100 Kilobytes
2. Matlab glue code	132 Kilobytes
3. ns-2 model and topology scripts	20 Kilobytes
4. ns-2 glue code	160 Kilobytes
5. Federation startup script	4 Kilobytes

simulate the NCS. Table 3 shows the time durations for simulating the NCS in various multi-hop network topologies and in the presence of network uncertainties such as packet loss and time varying delays. The time durations shown in the table are the actual times required to run 100 seconds of logical simulation time.

Table 3: Time Efficiency for NCS Example

Scenarios		Actual Duration (in minutes)
Nominal		5.5
Packet Losses	20%	8.4
	30%	11.4
	40%	13.5
Multi-hop Network	3 hops	17.4
	4 hops	22.2
	5 hops	26.2

5. CONCLUSION

We presented the integration tool, NCSWT for the modeling and simulation of networked control systems. We described the HLA-based approach guiding the tool's implementation as well as the MIC techniques for the rapid synthesis of components required for the simulation of a NCS. Additionally, we provided an evaluation of tool.

6. ACKNOWLEDGEMENT

This work is supported in part by the U.S. Army Research Office (ARO W911NF-10-1-0005), the National Science Foundation (CNS-1035655, CCF-0820088) and Lockheed Martin. The views and conclusions contained herein are those of the authors and should not be interpreted as necessarily representing the official policies or endorsements, either expressed or implied, of the U.S. Government.

7. REFERENCES

[1] NCSWT: An Integrated Modeling and Simulation Tool for Networked Control Systems. http://vanets.vuse.vanderbilt.edu/dokuwiki/doku.php?id=research:cps.

[2] The Network Simulator ns-2. http://isi.edu/nsnam/ns/, 2004.

[3] MATLAB, The Language of Technical Computing. http://www.mathworks.com, 2008.

[4] Portico RTI. http://www.porticoproject.org, 2010.

[5] A. Al-Hammouri, M. Branicky, and V. Liberatore. Co-simulation Tools for Networked Control Systems. *Hybrid Systems Computation and Control, Lecture Notes in Computer Science*, 4981:16–29, 2008.

[6] P. Antsaklis and J. Baillieul. Special Issue on Technology of Networked Control Systems. *Proc. of the IEEE*, 95(1):5–8, Jan. 2007.

[7] A. Cervin, M. Ohlin, and D. Henriksson. Simulation of Networked Control Systems Using TrueTime. *In Proc. 3rd Int. Wkshp. on Networked Control Systems: Tolerant to Faults*, 2007.

[8] M. Hasan, H. Yu, A. Carrington, and T. Yang. Co-simulation of wireless networked control systems over mobile ad hoc network using SIMULINK and OPNET. *IET Comm.*, 3(8):1297–1310, Aug. 2009.

[9] U. Hatnik and S. Altmann. Using ModelSim, Matlab/Simulink and NS for Simulation of Distributed Systems. *Int. Conf. on Parallel Computing in Electrical Engineering*, 0:114–119, 2004.

[10] O. Heimlich, R. Sailer, and L. Budzisz. NMLab: A Co-simulation Framework for Matlab and NS-2. In *2010 Second Int. Conf. on Advances in System Simulation (SIMUL)*, pages 152–157, Aug. 2010.

[11] G. Hemingway, H. Neema, H. Nine, J. Sztipanovits, and G. Karsai. Rapid synthesis of high-level architecture-based heterogeneous simulation: a model-based integration approach. *SIMULATION*, 2011.

[12] G. Karsai, J. Sztipanovits, A. Ledeczi, and T. Bapty. Model-Integrated Development of Embedded Software. *Proc. of the IEEE*, 91(1):145–164, Jan 2003.

[13] T. Kohtamaki, M. Pohjola, J. Brand, and L. Eriksson. PiccSim Toolchain - Design, Simulation, and Automatic Implementation of Wireless Networked Control Systems. In *IEEE Conf. on Networking, Sensing, and Control*, 2009.

[14] F. Kuhl, J. Dahmann, and R. Weatherly. *Creating Computer Simulation Systems: An Introduction to the High Level Architecture*. Prentice Hall PTR, 1999.

[15] A. Ledeczi, M. Maroti, A. Bakay, G. Karsai, J. Garrett, C. Thomason, G. Nordstrom, J. Sprinkle, and P. Volgyesi. The Generic Modeling Environment. *Wkshp. on Intelligent Sig. Proc.*, May 2001.

[16] D. Riley, E. Eyisi, J. Bai, Y. Xue, X. Koutsoukos, and J. Sztipanovits. Networked Control System Wind Tunnel (NCSWT)- An evaluation tool for networked multi-agent systems. In *4th Int. ICST Conf. on Simulation Tools and Techniques (SIMUTools 2011)*,, March 2011.

Computing Bounded Reach Sets from Sampled Simulation Traces *

Zhenqi Huang
University of Illinois at Urbana-Champaign
247 CSL
1308 W. Main Street
Urbana, Illinois, 61801
zhuang25@illinois.edu

Sayan Mitra
University of Illinois at Urbana-Champaign
266 CSL (Mail Code: 228)
1308 W. Main Street
Urbana, Illinois, 61801
mitras@illinois.edu

ABSTRACT

This paper presents an algorithm which uses simulation traces and formal models for computing overapproximations of reach sets of deterministic hybrid systems. The implementation of the algorithm in a tool, *ybrid race Veri er   V* , uses Mathwork's Simulink/Stateflow (SLSF) environment for generating simulation traces and for obtaining formal models. Computation of the overapproximation relies on computing error bounds in the dynamics obtained from the formal model. Verification results from three case studies, namely, a version of the navigation benchmark, an engine control system, and a satellite system suggest that this combined formal analysis and simulation based approach may scale to larger problems.

Categories and Subject Descriptors

D.2.5 [**Software Engineering**]: Testing and Debugging—*ymbolic execution*

Keywords

verification, hybrid automata

1. INTRODUCTION

For a deterministic hybrid automaton, an initial state and a time-bound uniquely determines an execution. Denote $\alpha(x_0, t)$, α for short, as an execution starts at x_0 and evolves for T time. For the purposes of safety verification, we would like to compute the set of states that are reached by this execution α. Exact computation of this set is intractable, and for several special classes of automata approximation algorithms have been proposed (see, for example, [2, 4, 10]). On the other hand, simulation tools, such as Mathwork's Simulink/Stateflow (SLSF), effectively compute simulation

---

*This research is supported by a research grant from John Deere Company and NSF (Contract No CNS-1016791).

traces from the models. In this paper, we explore how such simulation traces can aid verification.

Our main contribution is an algorithm for computing an overapproximation of the reach set of a specific execution from simulation traces. For the purposes of discussion, let us fix an execution α and a particular simulation trace $x_0, x_1, \ldots, x_l$. In using the simulation engine, Matlab's ODE solvers for example, the user can set an *absolute tolerance*. For a given absolute tolerance of $c > 0$, the simulation engine guarantees that if a simulation trace point x_k is on α, then the following simulation point x_{k+1} is within c distance of α. This does not, however, provide any guarantees about the overall accumulated error nor about the error between successive simulation points. In this paper, we show how these errors can be bounded using information from a formal model of the system. In particular, we use continuity and the Lipschitz constants of the functions describing the differential equations and resets. The algorithm is implemented in a tool called *ybrid race Veri er   V* . HTV translates SLSF models to hybrid automata using HyLink [12] and uses the simulation traces in conjunction with the automaton for analysis. We applied **HTV** to three examples: (1) a navigation benchmark, (2) an autonomous satellite system, and (3) an engine control system with upto 4 continuous state variables and 9 locations. For these relatively small examples HTV successfully generates overapproximations for both linear and non-linear systems and verifies safety properties in seconds. This leads us to contemplate that this method may scale to larger systems.

Related Work. SLSF models are now widely used in model-based real-time system design. Several recent papers address the problem of formally verifying SLSF models from the simulation traces generated by the models. The verification approach presented in [8] generates a symbolic trace from a given simulation trace by carefully instrumenting the model. The symbolic traces are then used to compute a set of initial states that from which all traces visit the same sequence of locations. In this work we do not instrument the model and we do not assume that the trace generated by the simulation engine is arbitrarily accurate. The approach presented in [1] and [5] searches for counterexamples to Metric Temporal Logic (MTL) properties for (possibly non-linear) hybrid systems through minimization of a robustness metric. The global minimization is carried out using Monte-Carlo techniques. In contrast, our analysis approach is deterministic and currently targets only safety properties. In our previous work, we developed HyLink [11, 12] which is a tool for translating SLSF models to hybrid automata. Guaranteed ODE solvers have been developed to compute error bounds on the solutions of differential equations. For example, the C++ library in [3] solves an initial value problem and computes a discrete sequence of error terms which upper bound the distances to the true solution at each sampled point. Our tool on the other hand is integrated with the modeling environment and computes a tube containing the true execution explicitly. Furthermore, our approach handles hybrid models directly.

2. PRELIMINARIES

In this paper, we discuss a class of deterministic hybrid automata; see [9, 13] for a detailed exposition. Let V as a set of variables. Each variable $v \in V$ is associated with a type, $type(v)$, which defines the set of values v can take. A valuation $\mathbf{v}$ maps each $v \in V$ to a value in $type(v)$. By $\mathbf{v}.x$ and $\mathbf{v}.loc$ we refer to the values of the variables x and loc at $\mathbf{v}$. We denote $val(V)$ as the set of all valuations of V. For a set of variables V a trajectory τ is a function $\tau : [0, t] \mapsto val(V)$, where t is a non-negative real. We define $\tau.fstate = \tau(0), \tau.lstate = \tau(t), \tau.dur = t$. By vector or matrix norm $|| \cdot ||$ we refer to infinity norm.

Definition 1. *A hybrid Automaton $\mathcal{A}$ is a tuple $(V, \mathcal{L}, Q, q_0, Grd, Inv, \mathcal{T})$ where*

- *$V = X \cup \{loc\}$ is a set of variables, where loc is a discrete variable of finite type $\mathcal{L}$ called the set of locations, and each $x \in X$ is a continuous real-valued variable. $Q \subseteq val(V)$ is a set of states.*

- *$Grd : \mathcal{L} \times \mathcal{L} \to 2^{val(X)}$, is a function that maps each pair $i, j \in \mathcal{L}$ to a set in $val(X)$. A transition $\mathbf{v} \to \mathbf{v}'$ can occur iff $\mathbf{v}.X \in Grd(\mathbf{v}.loc, \mathbf{v}'.loc)$ and $\mathbf{v}.X = \mathbf{v}'.X$, and we write this transition as $\mathbf{v} \to \mathbf{v}'$. That is, the transitions do not change the continuous state.*

- *$Inv : \mathcal{L} \mapsto 2^{val(X)}$ is a function that maps each location to a set of states, called invariant set.*

- *$\mathcal{T}$ is a set of trajectories for V such that along each $\tau \in \mathcal{T}$ i) loc remains constant and ii) the continuous variables X evolve according to a differential equation $\dot{X} = f_{\tau(0).loc}(X)$.*

Semantics. An execution captures a particular run of the hybrid automaton. In this paper, we consider hybrid automata that are *deterministic*. That is, from any state there is at most one transition or a unique trajectory of non-zero duration. Formally, an *execution* starting from a state $\mathbf{v}_0$ is a finite sequence of trajectories $\tau_0 \tau_1 \cdots \tau_n$, where for each i, $\tau_i.lstate \to \tau_{i+1}.fstate$ and $\tau(0) = \mathbf{v}_0$. We define the duration of an execution as $\sum_i \tau_i.dur$. For an execution of duration at least t starting from $\mathbf{v}_0$, we denote the valuation of the variables at time t by $\alpha(\mathbf{v}_0, t)$. A state $\mathbf{v} \in Q$ is said to be reachable from $\mathbf{v}_0$ if there exists t such that $\alpha(\mathbf{v}_0, t) = \mathbf{v}$.

We will make the following additional assumptions throughout this paper.

Assumption 1 (Dwell time). *There exists a minimum dwell time $\Delta > 0$ such that along any execution, no two discrete transitions occur within Δ time of each other.*

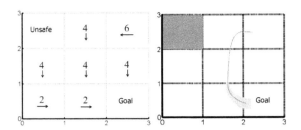

Figure 1: Overapproximation of reach set for the navigation system.

Assumption 2 (Lipschitz). *For each location $i \in \mathcal{L}$, the function f_i the right hand side of the differential equation is Lipschitz with a Lipschitz constant $L_i > 0$.*

Assumption 3 (Bounded derivative difference). *For $i, j \in \mathcal{L}$, there exists an upper bound $D_{i,j}$ such that for all $y \in Grd(i, j)$, $||f_i(y) - f_j(y)|| \leq D_{i,j}$.*

Assumption 1 is satisfied by most well-designed systems that do not have Zeno executions. This ensures that along any execution, at a given time there is a unique valuation of the variables. Assumption 2 is satisfied if f_i has a bounded derivative over $Inv(i)$. If the guards are compact then Assumption 2 implies Assumption 3.

Example 1 We consider a version of the 3×3 navigation benchmark [7]. This is a deterministic hybrid automaton $\mathcal{A}$ with 4 continuous variables $X = (x, y, vx, vy)$ and 9 locations $\mathcal{L} = \{(i, j) | i, j \in \{1, 2, 3\}\}$. The system evolves according to differential equation $\dot{X} = AX - Bu(i, j)$, where

$$A = \begin{bmatrix} 0 & 0 & 1 & 0 \\ 0 & 0 & 0 & 1 \\ 0 & 0 & -1.2 & 0.1 \\ 0 & 0 & 0.1 & -1.2 \end{bmatrix} \text{ and } B = \begin{bmatrix} 0 & 0 \\ 0 & 0 \\ -1.2 & 0.1 \\ 0.1 & -1.2 \end{bmatrix}.$$

The input u is assigned to be a constant in each modes $u(i, j) = [\sin((\pi c(i, j))/4), \cos((\pi c(i, j))/4)]^T$, where $c(i, j) \in \{0, 1, \cdots, 7\}$ determines a direction vector of location (i, j).

The different regions and an execution is visualized in Figure 1. In this example, the Lipschitz constants of all the locations equal $L_i = ||A|| = 1.3$. For two locations the difference in the derivatives is bounded by $D = 2||B||$.

Next, we define c-sampled traces which are related to the simulation traces we can get from SLSF models.

Definition 2. *For a hybrid automaton $\mathcal{A}$, a start state $\mathbf{v}_0$, a step error constant $c > 0$, and a time-bound $t_l > 0$, a c-sampled trace β is a finite (V, T)-sequence $\beta = (\mathbf{v}_0, t_0), (\mathbf{v}_1, t_1), \cdots, (\mathbf{v}_l, t_l)$, for each $k \in \{0, \cdots, l-1\}$,*

$$||\alpha(\mathbf{v}_k, t_{k+1} - t_k).X - \mathbf{v}_{k+1}.X|| \leq c.$$

That is, the $(k+1)^{st}$ sample point in the trace is at most c distance away from the execution starting from the sampled trace at k.

3. OVERAPPROXIMATION OF REACH SET

From a given c-sampled trace β we want to compute the set of all the states that are reachable by any execution that can generate β. Our approach involves two steps: first, we find the accumulated simulation error corresponding to every step, and then we propagate a tube around each sampled point in β that is guaranteed to contain all executions that may have generated β.

3.1 Estimating Accumulated Error

We discuss how fast the error possibly diverges from the real trace given a c-sampled trace. For the remainder of the paper, we fix the initial state $\mathbf{v}_0$ and the sampled trace β of length $l + 1$. Let $\{\epsilon_k\}_0^l$ be a collection of error bounds for β that satisfy the following: for $k \in \{0, \ldots, l\}$, $||\alpha(\mathbf{v}_0, t_k).X - \mathbf{v}_k.X|| \leq \epsilon_k$. That is, the true state of the execution starting from $\mathbf{v}_0$ at time t_k is within ϵ_k distance of the kth sampled point $\mathbf{v}_k.X$. Using the following lemma, $\{\epsilon_k\}$ are computed iteratively (starting from a given ϵ_0) provided transitions do not occur in any of the $[t_k, t_{k+1}]$ intervals.

Lemma 1. *If $\forall t \in [t_k, t_{k+1}]$, $\alpha(\mathbf{v}_0, t).loc = i$ for some $i \in \mathcal{L}$, then*

$$\epsilon_{k+1} \leq \epsilon_k e^{L_i(t_{k+1} - t_k)} + c.$$

In the special case of a linear autonomous hybrid system we have the following corollary.

Corollary 1. *If $\forall t \in [t_k, t_{k+1}]$, $\alpha(, \mathbf{v}_0, t).loc = i$ and the continuous states evolve follo s $\dot{X} = A_i X + B_i$, hen*

$$\epsilon_{k+1} \leq \epsilon_k ||e^{A_i(t_{k+1} - t_k)}|| + c.$$

On the other hand, if a transition occurs in the interval $[t_k, t_{k+1}]$, the following error bound holds.

Lemma 2. *If there exists $\eta \in [t_k, t_{k+1}]$ such that a single transition from location i to j occurs in $\alpha(\mathbf{v}_0)$ at time η, then there exists a constant $M > 0$ such that*

$$\epsilon_{k+1} \leq (\epsilon_k + M/L_j)e^{L(t_{k+1} - t_k)} - M/L_j + c,$$

here $L = max\{L_i, L_j\}$.

Setting $M = \sup_{x \in Inv(i) \cup Inv(j)} ||f_i(x) - f_j(x)||$ satisfies the above condition, but a smaller range for x based on reachability analysis from i can provide tighter bounds.

Lemmas 1 and 2 provides a sequence of error bounds $\{\epsilon_k\}$ such that $\forall\ k \in \{0, \cdots, l\}$, $||\alpha(\mathbf{v}_0, t_k).X - \mathbf{v}_k.X|| \leq \epsilon_k$. We define the sequence γ from β by attaching these error bounds. $\gamma = (v_0, t_0, \epsilon_0)(v_1, t_1, \epsilon_1) \cdots (v_l, t_l, \epsilon_l)$.

3.2 Reach Set Between Sampled Points

With a given sampled trace with error bounds (γ) we compute a tube containing all reachable states any execution that may generate the sampled trace β. This tube is the union of all tube segments between every two consecutive sample points. To build the tube containing the real execution, we execute Algorithm 1.

In this algorithm, the kth tube segment is overapproximated by a ball B' centered at $\mathbf{v}_k.X$ with the radius ϵ'. The initial estimate of ϵ' is ϵ_k and in each iteration this estimate is bloated by a constant factor $b > 1$ until the terminating condition holds. The terminating condition requires that ϵ' is less than the original error estimate ϵ_i added to the maximum possible increase in the error ($m(t_{i+1} - t_i)$). Assumption 2 guarantees that if the sample period satisfies $L(t_{k+1} - t_k) < 1$ then this loop is going to terminate. The union of all B's, the set R, contains the real execution and is returned by the algorithm.

```
R ← ∅ ;
for i ← 0 to l − 1 do
    ϵ′ ← ϵ_i;
    do
        ϵ′ ← b * ϵ′;
        B′ ← B(v_i.X, ϵ′);
        m ← sup ||f(x)||;
            x∈B′
    while  ϵ′ < m * (t_{i+1} − t_i) + ϵ_i;
    R ← R ∪ B′;
end
return R;
```

Algorithm 1: Overestimation of Reach Set

4. IMPLEMENTATION AND EXPERIMENTAL EVALUATION

We developed a tool, *ybrid race Veri er HTV* , that implements the above algorithms for over-approximating the reach set based on a sampled trace. First, from a SLSF model a sampled trace is generated. In addition, a hybrid automaton translation representing the SLSF model is obtained using the HyLink tool [12]. HTV can handle both linear and non-linear hybrid automata. We applied HTV to verify safety properties of the navigation benchmark [6], a satellites system, and an engine control system. Performance of the tool is shown in Table 1; discussions of these results appear below.

An instance of navigation benchmark is given earlier in Example 1. The reach set computed by HTV for this instance of the navigation benchmark is shown in Figure 1. The top left region is unsafe, the real execution is shown by the dark line, and the gray region shown the overapproximation of the reach set.

Our second example is a hybrid system model of two satellites—one active and the other passive. The active satellite changes its orbit and the passive satellite remains on the same orbit. The unsafe set corresponds to the set of positions in which the two satellites are too close. The continuous state of the system $X = (\nu_1, \nu_2)$ captures the angular position of the two satellites. The discrete state $\mathcal{L} = \{1, 2\}$ captures the two possible orbits of the active satellite. The guards model the relative angular positions at which the orbital transition must occur. The differential equation for the passive satellite is $\dot{\nu}_1 = \frac{1.0077}{(1 + 0.3 \cos(\nu_1))^2}$. The differential equations for the the active satellite is $\dot{\nu}_2 = \frac{0.9933}{1 + 0.3 \cos(\nu_2)^2}$ in orbit 1 and $\dot{\nu}_2 = \frac{1.0446}{(1 + 0.25 \cos(\nu_2 - 0.44))^2}$ in orbit 2.

The computed reach set is shown in Figure 2. The figure on the left is the reach set in Cartesian coordinate. The darker area contains the execution of passive satellite and the lighter area contains the execution of active satellite. The figure on the right is the phase portrait. The darker tiny rectangle denotes the unsafe region near the intersection of the two orbits. We observe that in the absence of discrete transitions the error bound increases according to Lemma 1. A non-zero initial error bound will expand exponentially. After a transition at step i, according to Lemma 2, an $O(\delta)$ term adds to ϵ_i which increases the growth rate of the error bound. The passive satellite does not have transitions and therefore its overapproximation for the reach set is tighter than that of the active satellite. Nevertheless, the

Table 1: Tool performance

Benchmark	#variables,locations	Real time	#sample points	Sim time	Reach time	#transitions	max error
Navigation I	4,4	2s	8030	8s	15s	2	2.0e-3
Navigation II	4,9	4s	16036	15s	35s	4	0.275
Satellites	2,2	6.5s	52046	15s	30s	1	0.3475
Engine control	4,2	5s	2026	5s	10s	2	13.27

overapproximation of the combined reach set does not intersect with the unsafe states in this example and safety is verified.

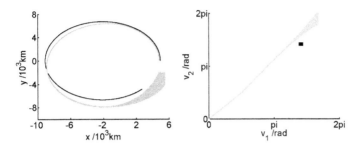

Figure 2: Overapproximation of reach set for the satellite system.

Our final example is a hybrid model of a linear engine control system with 4 continuous variables $X = (n_f, n_c, x_1, x_2)$ and 2 locations $\{1, 2\}$. The dynamics in each location is $\dot{X} = A_i X + u_i$, $i \in \{1, 2\}$. Where,

$$A_1 = \begin{bmatrix} -3.961 & 0.7344 & 672.7 & 0 \\ -3.704 & -1.774 & 1437 & 0 \\ -0.004285 & 0 & 0 & 0 \\ -0.01497 & 0.007887 & 5.543 & -5.425 \end{bmatrix}, u_1 = \begin{bmatrix} 1973 \\ 4257 \\ 2.354 \\ 11.92 \end{bmatrix}$$

$$A_2 = \begin{bmatrix} -2.145 & 0.4919 & 0 & 672.7 \\ 0.1758 & -4.394 & 0 & 1437 \\ -0.0301 & -0.02322 & -12.74 & 12.74 \\ 0 & -0.002217 & 0 & 0 \end{bmatrix}, u_2 = \begin{bmatrix} 699 \\ 1493 \\ -22.14 \\ 1.264 \end{bmatrix}$$

The invariants of locations are $Inv(1) : w \leq 0$, $Inv(2) : w > 0$. Where $w = -0.0027n_f + 0.001823n_c + x1 - x2 + 1.0468$. The required safety property is that n_c remains below a threshold.

In this case the A_i matrices are Hurwitz. In each location, different executions converge to each other. According to Corollary 1, the error bound shrinks when $\epsilon_k > \frac{c}{1 - ||e^{A(t_{k+1} - t_k)}||}$.

The overall performance of **HTV** is shown in Table 1. The second column gives the number of continuous variables and locations. The following columns give the duration of simulation trace (Real time), the number of sampled points (l), the actual time taken for the generation of the simulation trace (Sim time), the run time of **HTV** for computing the overapproximation of reach set (Reach time), the number of transitions, and the maximum error in $\{\epsilon_k\}$'s. We observe that **HTV** 's running time reduces with (1) smaller Lipschitz constants, (2) fewer transitions, and (3) for stable systems. Furthermore, the memory requirement for **HTV** grows only linearly with the number of sample points and the dimension of the system. This is because **HTV** stores the sampled trace and the polyhedral overapproximation of the reach set between a pair of consecutive sample points. These observations suggest that this combined formal analysis and simulation based approach may scale to larger problems.

5. REFERENCES

[1] Y. Annapureddy, C. Liu, G. Fainekos, and S. Sankaranarayanan. S-taliro: A tool for temporal logic falsification for hybrid systems. In *A A*, 2011.

[2] E. Asarin, O. Bournez, T. Dang, and O. Maler. Approximate reachability analysis of piecewise-linear dynamical systems. In , volume 1790, pages 20–31, 2000.

[3] O. Bouissou and M. Martel. Grklib: a guaranteed runge kutta library. In *I A* , 2006.

[4] T. Dang and O. Maler. Reachability analysis via face lifting. In . Springer-Verlag, 1998.

[5] G. E. Fainekos and G. J. Pappas. Robustness of temporal logic specifications for continuous-time signals. , 410:4262–4291, September 2009.

[6] A. Fehnker and F. Ivancic. Benchmarks for hybrid systems verification. In R. Alur and G. J. Pappas, editors, , volume 2993 of *L* , pages 326–341. Springer, 2004.

[7] A. A. Julius, G. E. Fainekos, M. Anand, I. Lee, and G. J. Pappas. Robust test generation and coverage for hybrid systems. In A. Bemporad, A. Bichi, and G. Buttazzo, editors, , volume 4416 of *L* , pages 329–342. Springer, 2007.

[8] A. Kanade, R. Alur, F. Ivancic, S. Ramesh, S. Sankaranarayanan, and K. Shashidhar. Generating and analyzing symbolic traces of simulink/stateflow models. In *AV*, 2009.

[9] D. K. Kaynar, N. Lynch, R. Segala, and F. Vaandrager. *he heory of imed I/ Automata*. Synthesis Lectures on Computer Science. Morgan Claypool, November 2005. Also available as Technical Report MIT-LCS-TR-917.

[10] K.-D. Kim, S. Mitra, and P. R. Kumar. Bounded epsilon-reachability of linear hybrid automata with a deterministic and transversal discrete transition condition. In , 2010.

[11] K. Manamcheri. Translation of simulink/stateflow models to hybrid automata. Master's thesis, University of Illinois at Urbana-Champaign, 2011.

[12] K. Manamcheri, S. Mitra, S. Bak, and M. Caccamo. A step towards verification and synthesis from simulink/stateflow models. In , 2011.

[13] S. Mitra. *A Veri cation rame or for ybrid ystems*. PhD thesis, Massachusetts Institute of Technology, Cambridge, MA 02139, September 2007.

Author Index